TOEFL® 5 lb. Book of Practice Problems

TOEFL® 5 lb. Book of Practice Problems, First Edition

10-digit International Standard Book Number: 1-5062-1871-7
13-digit International Standard Book Number: 978-1-5062-1871-7
eISBN: 978-1-5062-1872-4

Note: TOEFL, Test of English as a Foreign Language, Educational Testing Service, and
ETS are all registered trademarks of the Educational Testing Service (ETS), which
neither sponsors nor is affiliated in any way with this product.

Layout Design: Dan Frey and Mike Wolff
Production Editor: Matthew Callan
Cover Design: Frank Callaghan
Illustration and Graphics: Derek Frankhouser

TABLE OF CONTENTS

Section 1: Introduction

Section 2: Practice

Appendices

Dear Student,

Thank you for picking up a copy of the TOEFL® 5 lb. Book of Practice Problems. I hope this book provides the guidance you need to get the most out of your studies.

Before writing this book, we asked a bunch of TOEFL students what they wanted. They said, "Give us a lot of good practice." So that's what we've tried to do.

Please tell us what *you* want, too. If you have any questions or comments in general, please email our Student Services team at toefl@manhattanprep.com.

Or give us a shout at 212-721-7400 (or 800-576-4628 in the U.S. or Canada).

We try to keep all our books free of errors. But if you think we've goofed, please visit manhattanprep.com/toefl/errata.

I look forward to hearing from you. Thanks again, and best of luck preparing for the TOEFL!

Sincerely,

Chris Ryan
Vice President of Academics
Manhattan Prep

HOW TO ACCESS YOUR ONLINE RESOURCES

IF YOU PURCHASED A PRINT VERSION OF THIS BOOK

1. Create an account with Manhattan Prep at this website:
manhattanprep.com/toefl/register

2. Follow the instructions on the screen. Your one year of online access be-gins on the day that you register your book at the above URL. You only need to register your product *once* at the above URL. To use your online resources any time *after* you have completed the registration process, log in at the following URL:
manhattanprep.com/toefl/studentcenter

Please note that online access is nontransferable. This means that only *new* and *unregistered* copies of the book will grant you online access. Previously used books will *not* provide any online resources.

IF YOU PURCHASED AN EBOOK VERSION OF THIS BOOK

1. Create an account with Manhattan Prep at this website:
manhattanprep.com/toefl/register

2. Email a copy of your purchase receipt to **toefl@manhattanprep.com** to activate your resources. Please be sure to use the same email address to create an account that you used to purchase the eBook.

Email **toefl@manhattanprep.com** or call 800-576-4628 with any questions.

Introduction

Chapter 1

How to Use This Book

Read Me

Welcome! This introduction will help you get the most out of the five pounds of questions that you just bought.

What the TOEFL Tests

The TOEFL (the Test of English as a Foreign Language) tests the English-language skills of people who would like to study at a university or college that teaches in English.

The TOEFL measures your ability to read and understand passages written in general academic English. It also measures your ability to understand spoken lectures on academic topics, as well as conversations about common situations that might occur on university campuses.

Finally, the TOEFL measures your ability to *produce* functional English in response to general questions and to specific short readings, lectures, and conversations. You'll speak some responses and write others.

Like any standardized test, the TOEFL can feel a little artificial. But remember, you're planning to attend an English-speaking college or university. The better you get at TOEFL English, the better you'll be at college English.

Your preparation for the TOEFL isn't just preparation for the TOEFL. It can help you succeed in your future academic program.

What the TOEFL Is

The TOEFL consists of four separate sections. Each section focuses on a different set of English skills: reading, listening, speaking, or writing. The whole test takes between three and four hours.

Section 1: Reading

You will have 60 to 80 minutes to read three or four academic passages. You will answer between 12 and 14 questions per passage. The topics are drawn from science and the humanities. Most of the questions will be multiple-choice.

Section 2: Listening

You will have 60 to 90 minutes to respond to questions about some lectures and some conversations. You will listen to four to six different lectures and answer six questions about each lecture. You will also listen to two or three conversations and answer five questions about each conversation. Most of the questions will be multiple choice.

Break. There is a 10-minute break between Sections 2 and 3.

Section 3: Speaking

You will have 20 minutes to complete six different speaking tasks. You will listen to or read some information and then have between 15 and 30 seconds to prepare your response. You will then speak aloud for between 45 and 60 seconds.

Section 4: Writing

You will have 50 minutes to write two essays. You will be given topics for each essay.

Go to *www.ets.org/toefl* for more details and logistics. At the TOEFL's official site, you can sign up for the test, get the latest information directly from the test-makers, and find even more practice questions. The book *The Official Guide to the TOEFL Test* is another great source of both information and practice.

What's in This Book

Before you take the real exam, you will want to **exercise your skills on a lot of good TOEFL-style questions.** That's why this book exists.

This book, together with its online-only chapters, contains **over 1,500 questions** that mirror the content and format of the TOEFL. The proportions of various question types, topics, and difficulties roughly reflect the proportions of the exam. That said, we've added an extra dose of Reading passages and Listening lectures, because academic material is good for you.

The printed book contains 1,048 questions. We couldn't fit any more and stay even close to five pounds! You'll find hundreds of additional questions in the online-only chapters. Be sure to take advantage of these additional problems. They're part of the book.

Chapter 2 contains a short diagnostic test, with 28 questions across six different prompts. With this test, you can figure out how to prioritize your studies.

Chapters 3 through 6 contain 516 Reading questions across 38 academic passages. The first three chapters are organized by topic (Humanities, Social Science, and Natural Science), so that you can concentrate on the topics you need to practice most. The final chapter offers mixed practice. Each chapter is followed by an answer key and a full set of explanations (this is the case throughout the book).

MANHATTAN PREP

Chapters 7 through 12 contain 360 Listening questions across 60 academic lectures. These six chapters are again organized by topic. Spend more time on the topics that are more challenging for you. For Listening questions, you'll access the audio tracks online.

Chapters 13 and 14 contain 80 Listening questions across 16 campus conversations. These chapters are mixed by conversation type. Again, you'll access the audio tracks online.

Chapters 15 through 20 contain 48 Speaking questions. These six chapters correspond to the six different types of speaking tasks. You will need to record yourself speaking your answers to these questions. Some tasks also have audio tracks for you to listen to.

Chapters 21 and 22 contain 16 Writing questions. These two chapters correspond to the two types of writing tasks. You will need to type an essay in response to these questions. Some tasks also have audio tracks.

The Appendices provide optional skill-building support. The appendices include advice about how to learn vocabulary, how to practice reading at a university level, and how to write complex sentences. The appendices also provide guidance about maximizing your score on test day.

Finally, the online-only chapters (23 through 36) contain 456 more practice questions of every type. Chapters 23 and 24 contain 218 Reading questions across 16 passages of mixed topics. Chapters 25 and 26 contain 102 Listening questions across 17 lectures of mixed topics, while Chapters 27 and 28 contain 75 Listening questions across 15 conversations of various types. Chapters 29 through 34 contain 46 Speaking questions, representing all six types. Chapters 35 and 36 contain 15 Writing questions, representing both types.

4 Ways to Use This Book

1. Practice and Prioritize

Now that you've opened the book, put pen to paper. Do some questions! **Get started with the Diagnostic chapter.**

Use your results to help you decide which sections of the test you want to address first. **Start with a weaker area**—but don't start with your *weakest* area. Give yourself an opportunity to improve something. This will help motivate you to keep going. And, as your overall skills improve, you will make more progress on your weakest area.

Study consistently—every day, if you can. Often, people think that if they don't have time to study for two or three hours, they shouldn't bother to study today. That's not true! Even 20 or 30 minutes can make a big difference—if you do it every day.

2. Practice in Various Ways

Here are a few ideas.

Do some questions untimed and do others timed. By doing some questions without timing yourself, you give your brain a chance to wrestle with the issues in a less stressed way. That can be good for learning. But you should also do some questions under time pressure. After all, the real test will put you on the clock. Ultimately, you should practice as you play: mimic real test conditions most of the time, especially as you get closer to test day.

Here are some timing guidelines:

Reading: 20 minutes per passage (and accompanying questions). Spend a couple of minutes scanning the passage to get the main ideas, then dive into the questions. Fortunately, the questions follow the general order of the passage, so you don't have to jump around.

Listening: 10 minutes per lecture or conversation (and accompanying questions). After you listen to the audio, you will have approximately 6 to 7 minutes left to answer the questions.

Speaking: Train yourself to use all but 5 to 10 seconds of the given time for that task. For instance, if you are given 60 seconds to respond, aim to respond in 50 to 55 seconds. This will help you to make sure you give a complete response in the given time.

Writing: Spend about two minutes brainstorming and organizing your essay. Then start writing. Leave yourself about three minutes at the end to re-read your essay and fix any errors or typos. (It's okay if you still have some errors! That is expected.)

Do some questions individually and do others in sets. At first, stop after each question and check your answer. See what you can learn from that question before you try another. As you progress, though, shift more and more of your work to sets of questions. You don't have to do a huge number of questions at once. But doing a full passage, or doing one of each of the six Speaking tasks in a row, is a more realistic workout.

Do some sets of questions and/or passages by topic or type and do other sets that are mixed. The traditional way to develop a skill is to drill it: Do the same kind of question/passage, or nearly the same kind, repeatedly. This approach works up to a point. On the real test, you will have to jump around among topics. So practice "mixed" sets, in which you do passages, lectures, or conversations that are not so closely related to each other. Doing mixed sets forces you to become better at switching gears and distinguishing cases—just like the real test will force you to do.

3. Practice, Review, and Redo

You will probably want to **do some of these questions more than once**. So don't write in this book. Instead, do your work in a separate notebook. Then you can come back later and redo passages and questions under time pressure. That way, you can be sure that you can tackle similar material on the real exam. You have lots of questions available to you, but you don't always want to do new material. Going back over the same ground again—really forcing yourself to redo the work—may be the most valuable part of your preparation.

4. Put This Book Down

Seriously! Now go get a *different* book: *The Official Guide to the TOEFL Test* or one of the volumes of *Official TOEFL iBT Tests*. These books are from **ETS**, the makers of the TOEFL.

Why on earth would we recommend that you use a different book from this one? The reason is that every third-party TOEFL preparation book—every book written by people like us who are *not* the test-makers—must fall a little short. Only the *Official Guide* (or materials that you get from *www.ets.org/toefl*) can provide *actual* questions retired from the TOEFL.

At a couple of points along the way, especially toward the end of your preparation, **do a timed practice test using real TOEFL questions.** Make sure that you apply test-room conditions as best you can—turn off your cell phone, close the door, make sure your spell-check and grammar-check are turned off when you write your essay, etc. Then score your results.

Such practice tests give you the most authentic measure of what you might get on the real exam that day. No practice test is perfect, even one with retired TOEFL questions in it, but you want to be able to trust your practice test score as much as possible. That score is not destiny—far from it! A practice test is not a crystal ball. But you need to **know your current level as accurately as you can**, so that you can figure out what you need to practice in order to get even better.

A great one-two punch for the TOEFL is **this five-pound book for your workouts, plus** *The Official Guide to the TOEFL Test* **for practice exams.**

4 Tips for Test Week—And Test Day

1. Do less new—redo old. The week before the test, your goal is to review what you already know. Avoid doing too many new questions. In fact, it's totally fine just to redo questions you've already seen. You need to rehearse what you know and feel good about it. You don't want to try to learn too much, tire yourself out, and crash on test day.

2. Sleep enough. There is no substitute for sleep. Your brain absolutely needs it. Prioritize the TOEFL over other commitments the week before the test. Stick to a consistent sleep schedule—go to bed at the same time every night and get up at the same time every morning. If you are nervous the night before and don't get enough sleep, you will still be okay if you got enough sleep for the week before.

3. Take a shot and move on. During the test, avoid getting bogged down on any one question. Take your best guess or make your best attempt. Then forget about that question and proceed to the next one. You won't feel great about every single answer—that's okay. You can still get a good score even if you mess up a few questions.

4. During the break, get up and drink a little sugar (a certain kind of sugar). The exam is a physical marathon as much as it is a psychic ordeal. By getting up and walking around, you re-energize your body, which is what your brain rides around in. On long tests that tax you physically and mentally, use your break to get back some of your mental energy.

Did you know your brain runs on glucose, a simple sugar? Quick delivery of glucose to your brain has been shown to counteract *decision fatigue*—the stupefied mental state you get into after you've made a whole bunch of decisions. Decision fatigue can easily strike when you're taking a long test.

Drink a little pure fruit juice or fresh coconut water. Do *not* chug a giant soda or some weird energy drink. Also stay away from caffeine. (You need to recover mental energy, not physical energy. Also, you don't want to have to go to the bathroom in 15 minutes!)

Get rid of that decision fatigue, and you'll start the next section in a much stronger and readier state of mind.

* * *

That's it—you're ready! Head for the Diagnostic Test. Good luck!

Diagnostic Test

The following diagnostic is a miniature version of the TOEFL. End to end, it will take you 70 to 75 minutes. The purpose of this short diagnostic is to expose you to the material and help you focus your studies, not to predict how you will do on the TOEFL. Do the best you can, of course. But interpret the results as guidance for your work, not as destiny.

Here is the format of the diagnostic:

Section	Questions	Time
1. Reading	One passage + 14 questions	20 minutes
2. Listening	One lecture + 6 questions One conversation + 5 questions	20 minutes
3. Speaking	One "Personal Choice" speaking task (type 2) One "Academic General/Specific" speaking task (type 4)	5–10 minutes
4. Writing	One "Integrated" writing task (type 1)	25 minutes

Set a timer for each section and do just that section. For Sections 1 and 2, write your answers down on a separate piece of paper. For Section 3, record your spoken response for later review (a smartphone is good for this purpose). For Section 4, type your response into a word processing program. Turn off spell-check and grammar-check features.

When you are ready, set a timer to count down 20 minutes. Turn to Section 1 and begin working.

Section 1: Reading

One passage + 14 questions.

20 minutes total.

2.1 Ice on the Antarctic Peninsula

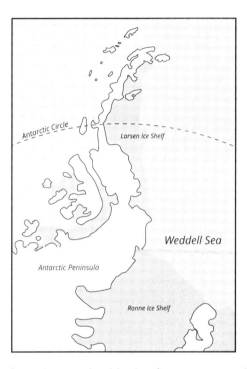

The Antarctic Peninsula juts out from the mainland body of Antarctica, and includes the northernmost point on the continent. Over 800 miles (about 1,290 kilometers) in length, the peninsula extends more than three degrees latitude beyond the Antarctic Circle and comes within 620 miles (about 995 kilometers) of the southernmost tip of South America. This mountainous peninsula carries a vast amount of land ice and borders several of the largest ice shelves[1] in the world. The problem is, it's melting.

ice shelf[1]: a large sheet of ice floating in the ocean that is permanently attached to a coastline

Most of Antarctica currently has a climate below freezing for the entire year. As a result, the scant precipitation it does receive in the form of snow stays frozen year-round and simply accumulates, very slowly, over time. The Antarctic Peninsula, however, has a slightly milder climate, and thus, snow and ice on it can and do melt every year. The west coast of the peninsula is milder than the east coast, so there are fewer ice shelves along the west coast.

One of the largest of the west coast ice shelves is the Wilkins Ice Shelf. This shelf has seen rapid deterioration over the past decade due to climate warming. As recently as 2007, the Wilkins Ice Shelf was about 5,400 square miles (14,000 square kilometers) in size, or roughly the size of the state of Connecticut. In 2008 alone, over 900 square miles (2,400 square kilometers) of the ice shelf collapsed. Researchers believe that the entire ice shelf could disintegrate at any time now.

Perhaps even more alarming and less anticipated is the fact that larger ice shelves along the east coast of the peninsula are also melting. The Larsen Ice Shelf, which spans much of the length of the eastern edge of the northern part of the Antarctic Peninsula, is historically divided by scientists into three sections: Larsen A, Larsen B, and Larsen C. Larsen A, the northernmost and smallest section, completely disintegrated in 1995. Larsen B experienced a rapid and near-complete deterioration in all but the southernmost portion in 2012. Within the span of months, it shrank from 4,445 square miles (about 11,500 square kilometers) in size to less than 1,400 square miles (about 3,625 square kilometers). The remnants of Larsen B are now less than half that size and are expected to disappear completely by 2020.

Larsen C, the southernmost section of the Larsen Ice Shelf, and by far the largest at about 19,300 square miles (50,000 square kilometers), is also now menaced by warming temperatures. As recently as 2004, scientists believed that Larsen C was completely stable. However, new reports indicate that a wide crack has developed in the northeast portion of the ice shelf; this crack is now 80 miles (about 130 kilometers) long and growing at a rate of more than 1 mile (1.6 kilometers) each month.

When ice shelves collapse or break away from the coastline they are connected to, sea levels do not directly rise, since the ice shelves were already floating in the ocean. A shelf is similar to an ice cube in a glass of water—the melting of the ice cube does not increase the level of water in the glass. However, the ice shelves act as a protective barrier that prevents ice and snow from the land masses they are connected to from falling into the ocean. Land ice (usually in the form of glaciers, which are massive, very slowly moving bodies of ice) along the coastline becomes liable to accelerate, break apart, and fall into the ocean after the ice shelf bracing it from below has disappeared. When this land ice falls into the ocean, the effect is comparable to adding more ice cubes to the glass of water—the level of water in the glass rises immediately. Since the near-complete collapse of Larsen B in 2002, scientists have calculated that the glaciers along the coast where Larsen B was located have accelerated. By some estimates, they have experienced an eight-fold increase in speed, which is much faster than scientists had predicted. As a result, this land ice may drop into the ocean much faster than anyone had previously thought.

Now answer the questions.

Paragraph 1

S1 The Antarctic Peninsula juts out from the mainland body of Antarctica, and includes the northernmost point on the continent.

2   Over 800 miles (about 1,290 kilometers) in length, the peninsula extends more than three degrees latitude beyond the Antarctic Circle and comes within 620 miles (about 995 kilometers) of the southernmost tip of South America.

3   This mountainous peninsula carries a vast amount of land ice and borders several of the largest ice shelves in the world.

4   The problem is, it's melting.

Paragraph 2

S1 Most of Antarctica currently has a climate below freezing for the entire year.

2   As a result, the scant precipitation it does receive in the form of snow stays frozen year-round and simply accumulates, very slowly, over time.

3   The Antarctic Peninsula, however, has a slightly milder climate, and thus, snow and ice on it can and do melt every year.

4   The west coast of the peninsula is milder than the east coast, so there are fewer ice shelves along the west coast.

1. Which of the sentences below best expresses the essential information in the highlighted sentence in paragraph 1? Incorrect choices change the meaning in important ways or leave out essential information.

    (A) Over 800 miles (about 1,290 kilometers) in length, within 620 miles (about 995 kilometers) of the Antarctic Circle, the peninsula extends more than three degrees latitude beyond the southernmost tip of South America.

    (B) Over 800 miles (about 1,290 kilometers) in length, the peninsula's southernmost tip extends more than three degrees latitude along the Antarctic Circle and comes within 620 miles (about 995 kilometers) of South America.

    (C) The peninsula is over 800 miles (about 1,290 kilometers) long and extends more than three degrees latitude north of the Antarctic Circle, coming within 620 miles (about 995 kilometers) of South America.

    (D) The peninsula is over 620 miles (about 995 kilometers) in length and extends more than three degrees latitude, coming within 800 miles (about 1,290 kilometers) of South America.

2. The word "scant" in the passage is closest in meaning to

(A) solid

(B) scarce

(C) wintry

(D) ample

3. According to paragraphs 1 and 2, which of the following is true of the Antarctic Peninsula?

(A) It receives scant precipitation.

(B) Most of its ice shelves are located along its west coast.

(C) All of it lies within the Antarctic Circle.

(D) Some of its snow and ice melt annually.

Paragraph 3

S1   One of the largest of the west coast ice shelves is the Wilkins Ice Shelf.

2   This shelf has seen rapid deterioration over the past decade due to climate warming.

3   As recently as 2007, the Wilkins Ice Shelf was about 5,400 square miles (14,000 square kilometers) in size, or roughly the size of the state of Connecticut.

4   In 2008 alone, over 900 square miles (2,400 square kilometers) of the ice shelf collapsed.

5   Researchers believe that the entire ice shelf could disintegrate at any time now.

4. In paragraph 3, the author's primary purpose is to

(A) downplay the potential for the Wilkins Ice Shelf to disappear entirely

(B) explain why ice shelf changes on the west coast are more important than such changes on the east coast

(C) compare the size of the Wilkins Ice Shelf to that of Connecticut

(D) outline how quickly a particular ice shelf is deteriorating on the west coast

Paragraph 4

S1   Perhaps even more alarming and less anticipated is the fact that larger ice shelves along the east coast of the peninsula are also melting.

2   The Larsen Ice Shelf, which spans much of the length of the eastern edge of the northern part of the Antarctic Peninsula, is historically divided by scientists into three sections: Larsen A, Larsen B, and Larsen C.

3   Larsen A, the northernmost and smallest section, completely disintegrated in 1995.

4   Larsen B experienced a rapid and near-complete deterioration in all but the southernmost portion in 2012.

5   Within the span of months, it shrank from 4,445 square miles (about 11,500 square kilometers) in size to less than 1,400 square miles (about 3,625 square kilometers).

6   The remnants of Larsen B are now less than half that size and are expected to disappear completely by 2020.

5. Which of the following can be inferred from paragraph 4 about the Larsen ice shelves on the east coast of the Antarctic Peninsula?

   (A) Larsen ice shelves A, B, and C were named according to their relative size.

   (B) The total collapse of Larsen A has likely quickened the partial disintegration of Larsen B.

   (C) The east coast ice shelves had been considered more stable than the west coast ice shelves.

   (D) The rate of disintegration of the Larsen ice shelves will continue to increase.

6. Which of the following is true about the Larsen ice shelves, according to paragraph 4?

   (A) More of Larsen B was lost in 2012 than has been lost since.

   (B) Smaller ice shelves along the east coast are not disintegrating as fast as larger ice shelves are.

   (C) The northern parts of the Larsen Ice Shelf have remained the most intact.

   (D) Losses of these ice shelves have tended to occur smoothly.

7. The word "remnants" in the passage is closest in meaning to

   (A) losses

   (B) seeds

   (C) vestiges

   (D) neighbors

Paragraph 5

S1   Larsen C, the southernmost section of the Larsen Ice Shelf, and by far the largest at about 19,300 square miles (50,000 square kilometers), is also now menaced by warming temperatures.

2   As recently as 2004, scientists believed that Larsen C was completely stable.

3   However, new reports indicate that a wide crack has developed in the northeast portion of the ice shelf; this crack is now 80 miles (about 130 kilometers) long and growing at a rate of more than 1 mile (1.6 kilometers) each month.

8. What does the development of the crack in the northeast portion of the Larsen C ice shelf demonstrate?

   (A) Larsen C is more stable than many had previously thought.

   (B) Scientists' beliefs about the stability of Larsen C may be wrong.

   (C) Larsen C is likely to disintegrate in the near future.

   (D) Scientists are unable to prevent the crack from spreading.

9. The word "menaced" in the passage is closest in meaning to

   (A) damaged

   (B) threatened

   (C) frightened

   (D) condemned

Paragraph 6

S1   When ice shelves collapse or break away from the coastline they are connected to, sea levels do not directly rise, since the ice shelves were already floating in the ocean.

2   A shelf is similar to an ice cube in a glass of water—the melting of the ice cube does not increase the level of water in the glass.

3   However, the ice shelves act as a protective barrier that prevents ice and snow from the land masses they are connected to from falling into the ocean.

4   Land ice (usually in the form of glaciers, which are massive, very slowly moving bodies of ice) along the coastline becomes liable to accelerate, break apart, and fall into the ocean after the ice shelf bracing it from below has disappeared.

5   When this land ice falls into the ocean, the effect is comparable to adding more ice cubes to the glass of water—the level of water in the glass rises immediately.

6   Since the near-complete collapse of Larsen B in 2002, scientists have calculated that the glaciers along the coast where Larsen B was located have accelerated.

7   By some estimates, they have experienced an eight-fold increase in speed, which is much faster than scientists had predicted.

8   As a result, this land ice may drop into the ocean much faster than anyone had previously thought.

10. According to paragraph 6, all of the following statements about Antarctic ice that melts or falls into the ocean are true EXCEPT:

   (A) The collapse of floating ice shelves is unlikely to raise sea levels either directly or indirectly.

   (B) When floating ice shelves disintegrate, the level of the ocean is not immediately affected.

   (C) The structural failure of floating ice shelves tends to facilitate the descent of land ice into the ocean.

   (D) Glaciers that are no longer obstructed by floating ice shelves are likely to speed up or fall apart.

11. The word "liable" in the passage is closest in meaning to

   (A) apt

   (B) eager

   (C) obliged

   (D) unlikely

12. In paragraph 6, the author's primary purpose is to

    Ⓐ forecast that the Larsen ice shelves will soon disintegrate completely

    Ⓑ minimize the dangers of ice shelf collapse in comparison with those of glacier movement

    Ⓒ clarify the parallels between ice cubes in a glass and ice shelves

    Ⓓ explain the influence of ice shelf and land ice activity on sea level rise

Paragraph 4

S1–2 Perhaps even more alarming is the fact that larger ice shelves along the east coast of the peninsula are also melting. The Larsen Ice Shelf, which spans much of the length of the eastern edge of the northern part of the Antarctic Peninsula, is historically divided by scientists into three sections: Larsen A, Larsen B, and Larsen C.

3–4   **A** Larsen A, the northernmost and smallest section, completely disintegrated in 1995. Larsen B experienced a rapid and near-complete deterioration in all but the southernmost portion in 2012.

5   **B** Within the span of months, it shrank from 4,445 square miles (about 11,500 square kilometers) in size to less than 1,400 square miles (about 3,625 square kilometers).

6   **C** The remnants of Larsen B are now less than half that size and are expected to completely disappear by 2020.

End   **D**

> Look at the part of the passage that is displayed above. The letters [A], [B], [C], and [D] indicate where the following sentence could be added.

13. **While scientists had anticipated the near collapse of this ice shelf for some time, the rate at which it took place took everyone by surprise.**

    Where would the sentence best fit?

    Ⓐ Choice A

    Ⓑ Choice B

    Ⓒ Choice C

    Ⓓ Choice D

An introductory sentence for a brief summary of the passage is provided below. Complete the summary by selecting the THREE answer choices that express the most important ideas in the passage. Some sentences do not belong in the summary because they express ideas that are not presented in the passage or are minor ideas in the passage. This question is worth 2 points.

14. **Several large ice shelves bordering the Antarctic Peninsula are melting, with potentially dire consequences.**

   A   Ice shelves on both the west coast and the east coast of the peninsula have begun disintegrating at an alarming rate.

   B   The crack in the Larsen C ice shelf is growing at rate of a more than 1 mile (1.6 kilometers) each month.

   C   The destruction of floating ice shelves indirectly contributes to sea level rise by freeing trapped land ice, which can then slip into the ocean.

   D   Most of Antarctica currently has a climate below freezing for the entire year, with very little annual precipitation.

   E   The collapse of ice shelves along the east coast has in fact accelerated the progress of land ice toward the sea, at a rate even higher than expected.

   F   The only perfectly stable major ice shelf along either the east coast or the west coast of the peninsula is Larsen C.

Section 2: Listening

One lecture + 6 questions.

Listen once, and then answer the questions in order. That's how the TOEFL works. Don't go back. When you are instructed to listen to an additional audio track, do so.

One conversation + 5 questions.

Again, listen once, and then answer the questions in order.

20 minutes total.

2.2 Lecture for Diagnostic

 Listen to Track 1.

Now answer the questions.

1. What is the main purpose of this lecture?
   - (A) To illustrate the constancy of Orwell's political affiliations throughout his life and career
   - (B) To provide background information to help students evaluate an essay by Orwell
   - (C) To describe Orwell's position on health care
   - (D) To show how Orwell was fooled by Marxism

2. What is Orwell's primary criticism of society in the assigned essay, "How the Poor Die"?
   - (A) That capitalism is a callous and hypocritical system
   - (B) That the British government treated indigenous populations badly
   - (C) That dishwashing is an unhealthy occupation
   - (D) That the poor are treated with inhuman callousness

3. How did Orwell feel about Burma?
   - (A) He supported its colonial status.
   - (B) He championed its quest for independence.
   - (C) He was unexpectedly sympathetic to the native population there.
   - (D) He did not find it of professional interest.

4. What point does the professor make when he mentions that Orwell presented himself as a beggar and tramp?

   (A) The point is evidence of Orwell's communist sympathies.

   (B) The point is evidence of Orwell's impoverished upbringing.

   (C) The point is evidence of Orwell's dedication to his research.

   (D) The point is given as the cause of Orwell's poor health.

5. What does the professor imply about himself when he says that Orwell's humanity deserves respect? *Choose 2 answers.*

   A He holds communist sympathies.

   B He respects commitment to principles.

   C He believes humanity is the most important character trait.

   D He believes that humanity is a worthy principle.

 Listen to Track 2.

Now answer the question.

6. (A) To highlight the primitive nature of the war in Spain

   (B) To explain why *Homage to Catalonia* is not better known today

   (C) To excuse Stalinist excesses occurring during the period in question

   (D) To indicate that the Communist Party may have been viewed differently at that time

2.3 Conversation for Diagnostic

 Listen to Track 3.

Now answer the questions.

1. Why does the student go to see the professor?

   (A) To give the professor her short story assignment

   (B) To talk about her interest in writing short stories

   (C) To get suggestions for improving her short story

   (D) To ask whether she should include a character's background information in her story

2. What does the professor suggest the student do to improve her story? *Choose 2 answers.*

    A Make the story longer

    B Make the story more exciting

    C Add more information about the main character

    D Spend less time describing what her characters look like

3. What does the professor mention about the background of the character in the student's story?

    A That she has a daughter

    B That she grew up in another country

    C Where she went to school

    D Her name

4. What does the professor imply about the popularity of short stories?

    A Short stories are not usually popular.

    B Short stories about mysteries are more likely to be popular.

    C More people will read a short story if the characters are similar to them.

    D More people will read a short story if they understand and have sympathy for the main character.

5. Why does the professor mention another short story that he wrote?

    A To refocus the discussion on his own work

    B To help the student have a surprising new insight

    C To illustrate a point he is making

    D To warn the student not to follow his example

Section 3: Speaking

One "Personal Choice" speaking task (type 2).

One "Academic General/Specific" speaking task (type 4).

Follow the strict time limits given within each task.

5–10 minutes total.

2.4 Speaking Type 2 for Diagnostic

> You will now be asked to give your opinion about a familiar topic. Give yourself
> 15 seconds to prepare your response. Then record yourself speaking for 45 seconds.

 Listen to Track 4.

Some people prefer to socialize with friends in their spare time. Others prefer to do something by themselves, such as reading or exercising. Which do you prefer and why?

Preparation Time: 15 seconds

Response Time: 45 seconds

2.5 Speaking Type 4 for Diagnostic

> You will now read a short passage and listen to a lecture on the same topic. You will then
> be asked a question about them. After you hear the question, give yourself 30 seconds to
> prepare your response. Then record yourself speaking for 60 seconds.
>
> Listen to Track 5.
>
> Now read a passage about multitasking. You have 45 seconds to read the passage. Begin
> reading now.
>
> **Reading Time: 45 seconds**

Multitasking

Multitasking, or performing multiple tasks simultaneously, is sometimes believed to increase productivity. However, studies on attention and focus have shown that the human brain is strikingly inefficient at multitasking. Most people are unable to pay attention to multiple sources of information simultaneously, even if they think that they are able to do so. Most people who believe that they are multitasking are actually switching their attention among the multiple tasks rapidly, rather than paying attention to all of them at once. This switching of attention causes a substantial decrease in performance.

 Listen to Track 6.

Using the concept of multitasking, explain how supertaskers are different from most people.

Preparation Time: 30 seconds

Response Time: 60 seconds

Section 4: Writing

One "Integrated" writing task (type 1).

25 minutes.

2.6 Writing Type 1 for Diagnostic

Give yourself 3 minutes to read the passage.

Reading Time: 3 minutes

MOOCs, or "massive open online courses," represent a type of learning that is closely tied to modern technology. In a typical MOOC, any student is free to enroll and complete assignments. Learning is conducted entirely via the internet and typically involves watching recorded lectures and discussing class topics via online message boards. Although MOOCs are a significant achievement from a technological perspective, they have turned out to be detrimental to students.

Studies have shown that only a tiny percentage of students complete any given online course. While thousands of students might enroll, no more than 10% of the students typically complete the final exam. This suggests that students in this environment are not motivated to learn and to complete the coursework. This is likely related to the fact that students in a MOOC do not have a personal relationship with the professor. Without an instructor with whom they can interact, students are likely to feel as if their questions aren't being answered. Because students in a MOOC are largely anonymous to the professor and to each other, they may feel less motivated to complete the classwork. Compare a traditional course, in which it might be obvious to the professor and the other students that a student hasn't prepared for the class session, to a MOOC, in which it's likely that nobody will notice an unprepared student.

The MOOC environment also limits access to education for many students. Because a consistent Internet connection is required in order to use course materials, some students may not be able to consistently follow the course. Other students, in areas where the internet is less widely available, may not be able to enroll at all. This is supported by statistics on enrollment, which suggest that the majority of MOOC students come from well-off countries with widespread internet access.

 Listen to Track 7.

You have 20 minutes to plan and write your response. Your response will be judged on the basis of the quality of your writing and on how well your response presents the points in the lecture and their relationship to the reading passage. Typically, an effective response will be 150 to 225 words.

Response Time: 20 minutes

Summarize the points made in the lecture, being sure to explain how they cast doubt on the specific points made in the reading passage.

Answer Key—2.1 Ice on the Antarctic Peninsula

Question	Correct Answer	Right/ Wrong	Category
1	C		Simplify Sentence
2	B		Vocabulary
3	D		Fact
4	D		Purpose
5	C		Inference
6	A		Fact
7	C		Vocabulary
8	B		Fact
9	B		Vocabulary
10	A		Negative Fact
11	A		Vocabulary
12	D		Purpose
13	B		Insert Text
14	A, C, E		Summary

Answer Key—2.2 Lecture for Diagnostic

Question	Correct Answer	Right/ Wrong	Category
1	B		Gist-content
2	D		Detail
3	C		Detail
4	C		Function of What Is Said
5	B, D		Speaker's Attitude
6	D		Inference

Answer Key—2.3 Conversation for Diagnostic

Question	Correct Answer	Right/ Wrong	Category
1	C		Gist-purpose
2	B, C		Detail
3	A		Detail
4	D		Inference
5	C		Function of What Is Said

Answers and Explanations— 2.1 Ice on the Antarctic Peninsula

Paragraph 1	**Comments**
S1	The Antarctic Peninsula juts out from the mainland body of Antarctica, and includes the northernmost point on the continent.	What & where the Antarctic Peninsula is.
2	Over 800 miles (about 1,290 kilometers) in length, the peninsula extends more than three degrees latitude beyond the Antarctic Circle and comes within 620 miles (about 995 kilometers) of the southernmost tip of South America.	
3	This mountainous peninsula carries a vast amount of land ice and borders several of the largest ice shelves in the world.	It has lots of land ice and borders big ice shelves.
4	The problem is, it's melting.	But it's melting.

Paragraph 2	**Comments**
S1	Most of Antarctica currently has a climate below freezing for the entire year.	Most of Antarctica is below freezing.
2	As a result, the scant precipitation it does receive in the form of snow stays frozen year-round and simply accumulates, very slowly, over time.	So precipitation freezes and accumulates.
3	The Antarctic Peninsula, however, has a slightly milder climate, and thus, snow and ice on it can and do melt every year.	But the Antarctic Peninsula is a little warmer, so ice melts every year.
4	The west coast of the peninsula is milder than the east coast, so there are fewer ice shelves along the west coast.	Warmer on west coast, fewer ice shelves there.

2

1. Which of the sentences below best expresses the essential information in the highlighted sentence in paragraph 1? Incorrect choices change the meaning in important ways or leave out essential information.

SIMPLIFY SENTENCE. The first part of S2 provides the length of the peninsula. The second part describes how far north it extends. The third part states how close it comes to South America. This sentence is filled with technical facts, so it can't be simplified greatly. But the wrong answers will mix up the facts.

✗ (A) Over 800 miles (about 1,290 kilometers) in length, within 620 miles (about 995 kilometers) of the Antarctic Circle, the peninsula extends more than three degrees latitude beyond the southernmost tip of South America.

This version transposes "Antarctic Circle" (which should be the piece that the peninsula extends three degrees beyond) and "southernmost tip of South America" (which should be the piece the peninsula comes within 620 miles of).

✗ (B) Over 800 miles (about 1,290 kilometers) in length, the peninsula's southernmost tip extends more than three degrees latitude along the Antarctic Circle and comes within 620 miles (about 995 kilometers) of South America.

It's actually the northernmost tip of the peninsula that extends more than three degrees beyond the Antarctic Circle, not the southernmost tip. Also, this tip extends beyond the Antarctic Circle, not along it.

✓ (C) The peninsula is over 800 miles (about 1,290 kilometers) long and extends more than three degrees latitude north of the Antarctic Circle, coming within 620 miles (about 995 kilometers) of South America.

CORRECT. This choice reorders parts 1 and 2 of the sentence and removes "southernmost tip of" South America. But this omission is fixed with the mention that the peninsula extends north past the Antarctic Circle.

✗ (D) The peninsula is over 620 miles (about 995 kilometers) in length and extends more than three degrees latitude, coming within 800 miles (about 1,290 kilometers) of South America.

This sentence incorrectly transposes 620 miles with 800 miles. It also eliminates "the Antarctic Circle" entirely, changing the meaning of "extends more than three degrees latitude."

2. The word "scant" in the passage is closest in meaning to

VOCABULARY. "Scant" = small or limited (in amount), slight, negligible.

✗ (A) solid

Unrelated. "Solid" = hard or rock-like.

✓ (B) scarce

CORRECT. "The scant precipitation it does receive in the form of snow" = the scarce, limited precipitation it receives in the form of snow.

✗ (C) wintry

Unrelated. "Wintry" might come to mind because the sentence is talking about snow. The sentence is trying to say that there is not very much precipitation.

✗ (D) ample

Opposite.

28

3.   According to paragraphs 1 and 2, which of the following is true of the Antarctic Peninsula?   **FACT.** Both paragraphs are devoted to discussing the Antarctic Peninsula, so the right answer could be anywhere.

✗   (A) It receives scant precipitation.   P2 S1–2 mention that "most of Antarctica" receives scant precipitation. But these sentences contrast with S3, which focuses on the Antarctic Peninsula. So you can't be sure that the peninsula also receives scant precipitation.

✗   (B) Most of its ice shelves are located along its west coast.   P2 S4: "The west coast of the peninsula is milder than the east coast, so there are fewer ice shelves along the west coast."

✗   (C) All of it lies within the Antarctic Circle.   P1 S2: "The peninsula extends more than three degrees latitude beyond the Antarctic Circle."

✓   (D) Some of its snow and ice melt annually.   **CORRECT.** P2 S3: "The Antarctic Peninsula, however, has a slightly milder climate, and thus, snow and ice on it can and do melt every year."

Paragraph 3	**Comments**
S1 One of the largest of the west coast ice shelves is the Wilkins Ice Shelf.	Wilkins Ice Shelf in west.
2 This shelf has seen rapid deterioration over the past decade due to climate warming.	Has rapidly deteriorated.
3 As recently as 2007, the Wilkins Ice Shelf was about 5,400 square miles (14,000 square kilometers) in size, or roughly the size of the state of Connecticut.	
4 In 2008 alone, over 900 square miles (2,400 square kilometers) of the ice shelf collapsed.	
5 Researchers believe that the entire ice shelf could disintegrate at any time now.	Whole thing could collapse at any time.

4.   In paragraph 3, the author's primary purpose is to

   ✗   (A) downplay the potential for the Wilkins Ice Shelf to disappear entirely

   ✗   (B) explain why ice shelf changes on the west coast are more important than such changes on the east coast

   ✗   (C) compare the size of the Wilkins Ice Shelf to that of Connecticut

   ✓   (D) outline how quickly a particular ice shelf is deteriorating on the west coast

PURPOSE. P3 describes the Wilkins Ice Shelf on the west coast of the Antarctic Peninsula, its size, and its rate of deterioration.

If anything, the author's tone in describing the melting of the Wilkins Ice Shelf is one of sober realism. The purpose is not to downplay any changes that are occurring.

P3 does not compare the west coast of the peninsula to the east coast of the peninsula in any way. In fact, the east coast is not mentioned at all.

S3 mentions that these two objects are about the same size. But the point of this comparison is to illustrate for the reader how large the ice shelf is, roughly. This is not the primary purpose of the whole paragraph.

CORRECT. P3 explores the case of the Wilkins Ice Shelf, emphasizing how fast it has deteriorated and pointing out that it could finally disintegrate at any time.

	Paragraph 4	Comments
S1	Perhaps even more alarming and less anticipated is the fact that larger ice shelves along the east coast of the peninsula are also melting.	Even worse: large shelves in east are also melting.
2	The Larsen Ice Shelf, which spans much of the length of the eastern edge of the northern part of the Antarctic Peninsula, is historically divided by scientists into three sections: Larsen A, Larsen B, and Larsen C.	Larsen Ice Shelf.
3	Larsen A, the northernmost and smallest section, completely disintegrated in 1995.	Larsen A is gone.
4	Larsen B experienced a rapid and near-complete deterioration in all but the southernmost portion in 2012.	Larsen B is almost gone.
5	Within the span of months, it shrank from 4,445 square miles (about 11,500 square kilometers) in size to less than 1,400 square miles (about 3,625 square kilometers).	
6	The **remnants** of Larsen B are now less than half that size and are expected to disappear completely by 2020.	

5. Which of the following can be inferred from paragraph 4 about the Larsen ice shelves on the east coast of the Antarctic Peninsula?

INFERENCE. Most of P4 discusses the Larsen ice shelves. The correct answer must be clearly supported in the text.

✗ (A) Larsen ice shelves A, B, and C were named according to their relative size.

Larsen A was the smallest shelf, and Larsen C is the largest (not stated in paragraph 4). But nothing in the paragraph indicates why the Larsen ice shelves were named as they were.

✗ (B) The total collapse of Larsen A has likely quickened the partial disintegration of Larsen B.

This idea may be plausible. But the paragraph draws no causal link between the two events.

✓ (C) The east coast ice shelves had been considered more stable than the west coast ice shelves.

CORRECT. S1: "Perhaps *even more alarming and less anticipated* is the fact that larger ice shelves along the east coast of the peninsula are also melting." This phrasing (particularly the words "less anticipated") indicates that the melting of the east coast ice shelves was not considered as likely as the melting of the west coast ice shelves.

✗ (D) The rate of disintegration of the Larsen ice shelves will continue to increase.

Nothing can be properly inferred from the paragraph about what *will* happen. Any supportable predictions would need to be hedged with phrases such as "probably," "expected to," and the like.

6. Which of the following is true about the Larsen ice shelves, according to paragraph 4?

FACT. Most of P4 discusses the Larsen ice shelves. The correct answer must be clearly stated or supported in the text.

✓ (A) More of Larsen B was lost in 2012 than has been lost since.

CORRECT. S5 states that Larsen B "shrank from 4,445 square miles (about 11,500 square kilometers) in size to less than 1,400 square miles (about 3,625 square kilometers)." That is, more than two-thirds of the ice shelf was lost in 2012 alone. That's more than half of the shelf. So more must have been lost in 2012 than can have been lost since.

✗ (B) Smaller ice shelves along the east coast are not disintegrating as fast as larger ice shelves are.

S1 discusses what is happening to the larger ice shelves on the east coast. The rest of the paragraph discusses Larsen A and Larsen B (two sections of a larger ice shelf). But smaller ice shelves on the east coast (if such exist) are never mentioned.

✗ (C) The northern parts of the Larsen Ice Shelf have remained the most intact.

Actually, the southern parts appear to be more intact. The northernmost section (Larsen A) collapsed first (S3). Likewise, what remains of Larsen B is its southernmost part (S4).

✗ (D) Losses of these ice shelves have tended to occur smoothly.

Nothing in the paragraph indicates that the losses have occurred smoothly, even in general. In fact, it seems that the losses have not been smooth, but rather punctuated by quick periods of destruction.

7.   The word "remnants" in the passage is closest in meaning to

     ✗   (A) losses

     ✗   (B) seeds

     ✓   (C) vestiges

     ✗   (D) neighbors

VOCABULARY. "Remnant" = remainder, trace, what is left over.

Opposite. Remnants are what is *not* lost.

Opposite in another sense. Seeds are beginnings that give rise to larger things. Remnants are endings, what's left when larger things disintegrate.

CORRECT. "The remnants of Larsen B" = the vestiges or remains of Larsen B.

"Neighbors" would refer to *other* ice shelves, not the remains of Larsen B.

Paragraph 5	Comments
S1 Larsen C, the southernmost section of the Larsen Ice Shelf, and by far the largest at about 19,300 square miles (50,000 square kilometers), is also now menaced by warming temperatures.	Larsen C is also menaced.
2 As recently as 2004, scientists believed that Larsen C was completely stable.	Used to be considered stable.
3 However, new reports indicate that a wide crack has developed in the northeast portion of the ice shelf; this crack is now 80 miles (about 130 kilometers) long and growing at a rate of more than 1 mile (1.6 kilometers) each month.	But it has a growing crack.

2

8. What does the development of the crack in the northeast portion of the Larsen C ice shelf demonstrate?

FACT. S3 discusses this crack, including its size and rate of growth. The "however" indicates that S3 contrasts with the previous sentence.

✗ (A) Larsen C is more stable than many had previously thought.

If anything, the development of this crack indicates that the ice shelf is *less* stable than previously thought, not more so.

✓ (B) Scientists' beliefs about the stability of Larsen C may be wrong.

CORRECT. S2: "As recently as 2004, scientists believed that Larsen C was completely stable." S3 goes on to contradict this notion by pointing out the development of this large and growing crack in the ice shelf.

✗ (C) Larsen C is likely to disintegrate in the near future.

S3 indicates that Larsen C may be less stable than scientists had thought. But that does not necessarily mean the ice shelf is about to disintegrate.

✗ (D) Scientists are unable to prevent the crack from spreading.

This may seem true in the real world. But the development of the crack, as described in S3, does not itself signal that scientists are unable to prevent the crack from spreading. Perhaps they can do so indirectly, through advocacy to slow down or reverse some of the possible causes of climate change.

9. The word "menaced" in the passage is closest in meaning to

VOCABULARY. "Menace" = threaten, put in danger or jeopardy.

✗ (A) damaged

Not quite. Something can be menaced or threatened without being damaged. And something can be damaged without being subject to further danger.

✓ (B) threatened

CORRECT. "Larsen C ... is also now menaced by warming temperatures" = it is threatened by warming temperatures.

✗ (C) frightened

You can only frighten something that can feel fear. "Frightened" can be a synonym for "menaced" for a living thing. But the Larsen C ice shelf cannot feel fear, so it cannot be frightened.

✗ (D) condemned

Not quite. This is too extreme. "Condemned" = sentenced or doomed (to something like destruction). But the warming temperatures might not actually destroy Larsen C.

Paragraph 6	**Comments**
S1	When ice shelves collapse or break away from the coastline they are connected to, sea levels do not directly rise, since the ice shelves were already floating in the ocean.	What happens when ice shelves collapse. Sea levels don't directly rise.
2	A shelf is similar to an ice cube in a glass of water—the melting of the ice cube does not increase the level of water in the glass.	Like floating ice cubes that melt. They don't raise the water level.
3	However, the ice shelves act as a protective barrier that prevents ice and snow from the land masses they are connected to from falling into the ocean.	But ice shelves prevent land ice from sliding into the ocean.
4	Land ice (usually in the form of glaciers, which are massive, very slowly moving bodies of ice) along the coastline becomes liable to accelerate, break apart, and fall into the ocean after the ice shelf bracing it from below has disappeared.	Glaciers accelerate into the water.
5	When this land ice falls into the ocean, the effect is comparable to adding more ice cubes to the glass of water—the level of water in the glass rises immediately.	Adding land ice = adding ice cubes = raising the water level.
6	Since the near-complete collapse of Larsen B in 2002, scientists have calculated that the glaciers along the coast where Larsen B was located have accelerated.	Glaciers near Larsen B have accelerated.
7	By some estimates, they have experienced an eight-fold increase in speed, which is much faster than scientists had predicted.	
8	As a result, this land ice may drop into the ocean much faster than anyone had previously thought.	

2

MANHATTAN PREP

10. According to paragraph 6, all of the following statements about Antarctic ice that melts or falls into the ocean are true EXCEPT:

NEGATIVE FACT. The entire paragraph discusses ice in different forms, either melting or falling into the ocean, and the impact that these processes have on sea levels and other bodies of ice. Three answer choices will be supported by text in P4. One answer choice will not be.

✓ (A) The collapse of floating ice shelves is unlikely to raise sea levels either directly or indirectly.

CORRECT. S1 points out that the floating ice shelves do not directly contribute to a rise in sea levels. But they act as a protective barrier preventing land ice from falling into the ocean (S3). When the shelves collapse, the land ice can fall into the ocean (S4). This does increase sea levels (S5).

✗ (B) When floating ice shelves disintegrate, the level of the ocean is not immediately affected.

S1: "When ice shelves collapse or break away from the coastline they are connected to, sea levels do not directly rise."

✗ (C) The structural failure of floating ice shelves tends to facilitate the descent of land ice into the ocean.

S3–4: "The ice shelves act as a protective barrier that prevents ice and snow from the land masses they are connected to from falling into the ocean. Land ice ... along the coastline becomes liable to ... fall into the ocean."

✗ (D) Glaciers that are no longer obstructed by floating ice shelves are likely to speed up or fall apart.

S4: "Land ice (usually in the form of glaciers, which are massive, very slowly moving bodies of ice) along the coastline becomes liable to accelerate, break apart, and fall into the ocean."

11. The word "liable" in the passage is closest in meaning to

VOCABULARY. "Liable" to do something = likely or predisposed to do it. Note that another common definition of the word "liable" is to be responsible for or accountable for something. That meaning doesn't make sense here though.

✓ (A) apt

CORRECT. "Land ice ... along the coastline becomes liable to accelerate" = it becomes apt to accelerate, or likely to accelerate.

✗ (B) eager

Not quite. Only something (or someone) that can feel enthusiasm or excitement can be eager.

✗ (C) obliged

Unrelated. "Obliged" = thankful, grateful, in someone's debt. Might be tempting because of the alternate definition of "liable."

✗ (D) unlikely

Opposite. "Unlikely" = doubtful or improbable.

12. In paragraph 6, the author's primary purpose is to

PURPOSE. P6 discusses the process by which ice falls into the sea—both land ice and ice shelves—and explains what types of events lead to ocean level rise and what types do not. P6 also explains how ice shelves slow down or prevent the flow of land ice into the ocean.

✗ (A) forecast that the Larsen ice shelves will soon disintegrate completely

The collapse of the Larsen ice shelves is discussed in previous paragraphs. The only mention of these ice shelves in this paragraph is the acceleration of land ice headed to the ocean in Larsen B after parts of it had collapsed. Even this mention is not the primary purpose of the paragraph.

✗ (B) minimize the dangers of ice shelf collapse in comparison with those of glacier movement

The dangers aren't really being evaluated in a comparative way, as if one phenomenon were less dangerous than the other. Rather, the author is explaining how ice shelf collapse can raise sea levels *indirectly,* by enabling glacier movement into the ocean. In other words, the dangers of ice shelf collapse are the *result* of the dangers of glacier movement. The author is not minimizing the dangers of ice shelf collapse.

✗ (C) clarify the parallels between ice cubes in a glass and ice shelves

The analogy comparing ice shelves and land ice to ice cubes in a glass of water is used to illustrate why one form of ice can directly cause sea level rise (land ice), while the other cannot (floating ice shelves). But laying out this analogy is not the primary purpose of the paragraph.

✓ (D) explain the influence of ice shelf and land ice activity on sea level rise

CORRECT. The paragraph makes it clear that floating ice shelves melting or collapsing into the ocean do not directly cause sea level rise, but land ice falling into the ocean does. Furthermore, the paragraph describes how floating ice shelves help slow or prevent land ice from reaching the ocean.

Paragraph 4	**Comments**

S1–2   Perhaps even more alarming is the fact that larger ice shelves along the east coast of the peninsula are also melting. The Larsen Ice Shelf, which spans much of the length of the eastern edge of the northern part of the Antarctic Peninsula, is historically divided by scientists into three sections: Larsen A, Larsen B, and Larsen C.

3–4   **A** Larsen A, the northernmost and smallest section, completely disintegrated in 1995. Larsen B experienced a rapid and near-complete deterioration in all but the southernmost portion in 2012.

> The new sentence refers to the near collapse of an ice shelf. But such a near collapse has not yet been described.

5   **B** Within the span of months, it shrank from 4,445 square miles (about 11,500 square kilometers) in size to less than 1,400 square miles (about 3,625 square kilometers).

> **CORRECT.** The new phrase "the near collapse of this ice shelf" refers to the "near-complete deterioration" of Larsen B in S4.

6   **C** The remnants of Larsen B are now less than half that size and are expected to completely disappear by 2020.

> Placing the new sentence here interrupts the direct connection between S5 and S6. The words "that size" in S6 need to refer back in a clear way to the second size in S5.

End   **D**

> Placing the new sentence here would imply that "the near collapse of this ice shelf" refers to the remnants of Larsen B. That reference is incorrect. Also, the "surprise" element of the new sentence is more logically placed earlier in the paragraph.

13.   **While scientists had anticipated the near collapse of this ice shelf for some time, the rate at which it took place took everyone by surprise.**

> **INSERT TEXT.** The phrase "the near collapse of this ice shelf" needs to make sense. So the prior sentence should discuss this near collapse, making clear which ice shelf was involved. Also, the insertion of this new sentence should not interrupt the logical connection between existing sentences.

   Where would the sentence best fit?

   ✗   (A) Choice A

   ✓   (B) Choice B   **CORRECT.**

   ✗   (C) Choice C

   ✗   (D) Choice D

	Whole Passage	**Comments**
P1	The Antarctic Peninsula juts out from the mainland body of Antarctica, and includes the northernmost point on the continent …	What & where the Antarctic Peninsula is. It has lots of land ice and borders big ice shelves. But it's melting.
P2	Most of Antarctica currently has a climate below freezing for the entire year …	Most of Antarctica is below freezing. So precipitation freezes and accumulates. But the Antarctic Peninsula is a little warmer, so ice melts every year. Warmer on west coast, fewer ice shelves there.
P3	One of the largest of the west coast ice shelves is the Wilkins Ice Shelf …	Wilkins Ice Shelf in west. Has rapidly deteriorated. Whole thing could collapse at any time.
P4	Perhaps even more alarming and less anticipated is the fact that larger ice shelves along the east coast of the peninsula are also melting …	Even worse: large shelves in east are also melting. Larsen Ice Shelf. Larsen A is gone. Larsen B is almost gone.
P5	Larsen C, the southernmost section of the Larsen Ice Shelf, and by far the largest at about 19,300 square miles (50,000 square kilometers), is also now menaced by warming temperatures …	Larsen C is also menaced. Used to be considered stable. But it has a growing crack.
P6	When ice shelves collapse or break away from the coastline they are connected to, sea levels do not directly rise, since the ice shelves were already floating in the ocean …	What happens when ice shelves collapse. Sea levels don't directly rise. Like floating ice cubes that melt. They don't raise the water level. But ice shelves prevent land ice from sliding into the ocean. Glaciers accelerate into the water. Adding land ice = adding ice cubes = raising the water level. Glaciers near Larsen B have accelerated.

14.

Several large ice shelves bordering the Antarctic Peninsula are melting, with potentially dire consequences.

SUMMARY. Correct answers must be clearly expressed in the passage. They must also be among the major points of the passage. They should tie as directly as possible to the summary given.

✓ [A] Ice shelves on both the west coast and the east coast of the peninsula have begun disintegrating at an alarming rate.

CORRECT. P3–5 discuss the Wilkins Ice Shelf and Larsen ice shelves in detail, describing how these important shelves are collapsing.

✗ [B] The crack in the Larsen C ice shelf is growing at rate of a more than 1 mile (1.6 kilometers) each month.

P5 mentions this fact. But it is a relatively particular detail about how this one shelf is threatened.

✓ [C] The destruction of floating ice shelves indirectly contributes to sea level rise by freeing trapped land ice, which can then slip into the ocean.

CORRECT. P6 discusses this crucial mechanism in detail, pointing out that the way ice shelves prevent sea level rise is by hindering land ice from reaching the ocean.

✗ [D] Most of Antarctica currently has a climate below freezing for the entire year, with very little annual precipitation.

This point is mentioned in P2. But in the context of a passage about the Antarctic Peninsula, this detail plays a small supporting role.

✓ [E] The collapse of ice shelves along the east coast has in fact accelerated the progress of land ice toward the sea, at a rate even higher than expected.

CORRECT. This is the closing point of P6. It is not elaborated upon in great detail, but it is the culmination of P6 (about how ice shelf collapse affects sea levels) and of the whole passage.

✗ [F] The only perfectly stable major ice shelf along either the east coast or the west coast of the peninsula is Larsen C.

In fact, scientists had thought that Larsen C was stable. But the ice shelf has developed a long and rapidly growing crack. Larsen C is the most stable of the three Larsen sections, but it is not exactly stable.

2

Answers and Explanations—2.2 Lecture for Diagnostic

George Orwell—Track 1

NARRATOR: Listen to part of a lecture in a literature class.

PROFESSOR: Okay, many of you might already be familiar with the work of Eric Arthur Blair. No? I forgot to mention that he wrote under the name of George Orwell. That seems to ring more bells… Most people remember him for his later works, such as *1984*. Tonight you'll read one of his earlier essays, "How the Poor Die." This work, along with his book, *Down and Out in London and Paris*, highlight themes that concerned him as a young man…thus, I thought that if we discussed those issues today, it might enrich your experience—as certainly, his concerns are relevant in today's world.

So…Orwell came from a family you might call gentry, or part of the privileged class, but not particularly wealthy. You know, if you've read any Dickens, *David Copperfield* or something, you know the, um… archetype. He finished university after the First World War and then, largely out of financial necessity, served as a government official in Myanmar, which was called Burma then. In fact, his first writing was about Asia and is far more, ah, empathetic…to the indigenous culture than you'd expect from an Englishman of his times. Check out his book *Burmese Days*, for example.

Anyway…after five years, Orwell returned to England and began writing. Although this was before the Great Depression, there was a great deal of hardship, unemployment, and homelessness. As you'll see in tonight's reading, this is the subject Orwell embraced. He really threw himself into this work documenting the suffering and degradations of poverty. You probably don't know that he researched his articles and books by going forth as a homeless beggar and a tramp himself…for weeks at a time. In 1928, while living in a working class neighborhood in Paris—working as a dishwasher for part of that time—Orwell became very sick and was bedridden in a public hospital. That experience in the common ward led to "How the Poor Die."

So what was Orwell's point? As you read it, you'll note that Orwell's concern goes beyond the horrific conditions. Indeed, his primary complaint is the dehumanization that the poor endure. Describing and decrying such treatment—and the smug moral superiority with which society dispensed it—is the constant theme of his work at this time. Yes, as you might have guessed, Orwell considered himself a man of the left—a socialist, in fact. He even attended Communist Party meetings. This may affront some of you. But it is best to note that Orwell was really a humanist. That is, his political stance stemmed far more from an advocacy of human decency and individual freedom than a, um…any loyalty to Marxist tenets. His enemies were callousness and hypocrisy rather than democracy or capitalism per se.

I would argue that Orwell's humanity in this sense should earn your respect, regardless of your political leanings. For his allegiance to that banner never wavered. How many people do you know who live by their principles? Please keep that in mind as you read tonight's assignment. And I say this based on his actions and work in the remainder of his life.

You see, in 1936, a civil war broke out in Spain between the duly elected Democratic Socialist government and the essentially fascist force led by General Franco. Nazi Germany and Mussolini's Italy aided the fascists. On the other hand, progressive young men from across Europe and even America flocked to Spain to fight for the Loyalists. Many of them joined the communist-organized International Brigades. Orwell planned to do so as well. However, for several reasons, he ended up joining a more anarchist-centered militia. So…consequently, he was in Barcelona when the majority communists launched a bloody purge against Orwell's cadre on false charges of disloyalty. Orwell saw it for the naked power play that it was. And that the communists were undermining the common goal of defeating the fascists in favor of exterminating those that had strayed from Stalinist ideology. And, once again, he was repulsed by both the hypocrisy and the vicious tyranny of the Stalinists.

Not too long thereafter, Orwell was wounded in combat and went back to England. He then wrote *Homage to Catalonia*, which detailed the treachery of the orthodox Communist Party. This won Orwell many enemies. Remember, this was 1938, and many viewed the Communist Party as the noble defender of the common man against the established elite, who seemingly were not suffering from the Great Depression as the masses were. Orwell stood firmly on the side of humanism. He severed his connections with leftist organizations. From this point on, his works attacked Stalinism as the greatest threat to freedom. And thus came about the works of his that you may have already read, such as *1984* and *Animal Farm*.

1.	What is the main purpose of this lecture?	**GIST-CONTENT.** The lecture discusses the primary concerns of Orwell's earlier works and his convictions.
✗	(A) To illustrate the constancy of Orwell's political affiliations throughout his life and career	The professor notes that Orwell remained true to his convictions. However, the last part of the lecture discusses a change in his political affiliations—specifically, his repudiation of the Communist Party.
✓	(B) To provide background information to help students evaluate an essay by Orwell	**CORRECT.** The first part of the lecture states that this is the professor's goal.
✗	(C) To describe Orwell's position on health care	"How the Poor Die" is described as an example of Orwell's concern for the mistreatment of the poor in general, not specifically about health concerns.
✗	(D) To show how Orwell was fooled by Marxism	The professor mentions that Orwell became disillusioned with Stalinism but does not indicate that Orwell was fooled in any way.

2

2.   What is Orwell's primary criticism of society in the assigned essay, "How the Poor Die"?

DETAIL. The professor says that the dehumanization of the poor was Orwell's main point.

✗   (A) That capitalism is a callous and hypocritical system

The professor notes that Orwell was not an enemy of democracy or capitalism *per se.*

✗   (B) That the British government treated indigenous populations badly

The professor says that Orwell was more sympathetic than many. But this point is not related to the essay in question.

✗   (C) That dishwashing is an unhealthy occupation

"How the Poor Die" is described as an example of Orwell's concern for the mistreatment of the poor in general, rather than an essay about the treatment he received specifically.

✓   (D) That the poor are treated with inhuman callousness

CORRECT. In the middle of the lecture, the professor says that the dehumanization of the poor was Orwell's main point in this essay.

3.   How did Orwell feel about Burma?

DETAIL. The professor discusses Orwell's feelings about Burma early in the lecture.

✗   (A) He supported its colonial status.

The professor notes only that Orwell went there out of financial necessity.

✗   (B) He championed its quest for independence.

This idea is not mentioned in the lecture.

✓   (C) He was unexpectedly sympathetic to the native population there.

CORRECT. Early in the lecture, the professor says that "his first writing was about Asia and is far more, ah…empathetic to the indigenous culture than you'd expect from an Englishman of his times."

✗   (D) He did not find it of professional interest.

The professor mentions that Orwell wrote a book about it, *Burmese Days,* which indicates interest.

4. What point does the professor make when he mentions that Orwell presented himself as a beggar and a tramp?

FUNCTION OF WHAT IS SAID. The professor mentions this point as evidence of Orwell's dedication to his research and his interest in humanism.

✗ (A) The point is evidence of Orwell's communist sympathies.

This information comes before any discussion of Orwell's dressing up as a beggar or tramp.

✗ (B) The point is evidence of Orwell's impoverished upbringing.

This period occurred during his adulthood and was a professional activity. Besides, the professor notes that Orwell was born into a reasonably wealthy family.

✓ (C) The point is evidence of Orwell's dedication to his research.

CORRECT. The professor states that "... this is the subject Orwell embraced. He really threw himself into this work documenting the suffering and degradations of poverty. You probably don't know that he researched his articles and books by going forth as a homeless beggar and a tramp himself."

✗ (D) The point is given as the cause of Orwell's poor health.

The professor only states that he became ill in Paris, and does not imply that going forth as a beggar and a tramp, in and of itself, had anything to do with his becoming ill.

5. What does the professor imply about himself when he says that Orwell's humanity deserves respect? *Choose 2 answers.*

SPEAKER'S ATTITUDE. The professor makes this statement in the middle of the lecture. Shortly thereafter he asks, "How many people do you know who live by their principles?"

✗ [A] He holds communist sympathies.

The professor believes that respect for Orwell should be given regardless of any political affiliations.

✓ [B] He respects commitment to principles.

CORRECT. The professor makes it clear that he respects people who live by their principles.

✗ [C] He believes humanity is the most important character trait.

The professor does not indicate that he believes humanity to be the most important character trait. He merely states that it merits respect.

✓ [D] He believes that humanity is a worthy principle.

CORRECT. This is a trait that the professor cites as worthy of respect.

Track 2

NARRATOR: Listen again to part of the lecture. Then answer the question.

PROFESSOR: He then wrote *Homage to Catalonia*, which detailed the treachery of the orthodox Communist Party. This won Orwell many enemies. Remember, this was 1938, and many viewed the Communist Party as the noble defender of the common man against the established elite, who seemingly were not suffering from the Great Depression as the masses were.

NARRATOR: Why does the professor say this?

PROFESSOR: Remember, this was 1938…

6.   **INFERENCE.** In this quote, the professor gives a caveat, or caution, about what time period he is referring to. He gives this caveat in order to clarify that the Communist Party was looked at differently at that time than it may be viewed by his students today.

✗   (A) To highlight the primitive nature of the war in Spain

The level of sophistication of the war in Spain is not discussed in the lecture.

✗   (B) To explain why *Homage to Catalonia* is not better known today

The fame of the book is not discussed.

✗   (C) To excuse Stalinist excesses occurring during the period in question

Neither the professor nor Orwell excuses Stalin.

✓   (D) To indicate that the Communist Party may have been viewed differently at that time

CORRECT. Immediately thereafter, the professor says that the Party was viewed as "defender of the common man against the established elite," implying that at that time, the Party may have had a different reputation from the one the professor's students might imagine.

2

MANHATTAN PREP

Answers and Explanations—
2.3 Conversation for Diagnostic

Draft Short Story—Track 3

NARRATOR: Listen to a conversation between a student and her professor.

STUDENT: Hi Professor Stevens. Is it ok if I sit down?

PROFESSOR: Yes, of course, please have a seat.

STUDENT: Ok, thanks.

PROFESSOR: So, um, what did you want to talk about today?

STUDENT: Well…I want to ask you about my short story, about the draft I sent to you last week. Did you have a chance to read it?

PROFESSOR: Oh, yes, I did. I just read it this morning. I…uh, I think this is a very good start and that you can make this a really interesting story. There are a few things I would suggest to make it even better.

STUDENT: Ok, great.

PROFESSOR: So first, um, I think you could add some more details about what your characters look like. That…that can help people who read your story imagine your characters—if you describe what they look like. For example, um, is this man tall? Is this woman old or young, things like that. And also, I think… you can add a tense or scary scene to your story. Something that will—something to make it exciting and make someone who reads it worry about your character.

STUDENT: Yeah, ok.

PROFESSOR: Another thing you can do is, uh…tell us more about the history of your character, her background…

STUDENT: Like where she grew up?

PROFESSOR: …sure, or about her relationship with her family. Something like that. Um…what I want to suggest is that you tell us more information about your main character's background so she is more likeable. That way when someone reads it they will care about her and want to know what will happen to her.

STUDENT: Do I need to do that?

PROFESSOR: Well…I think it is very important. Right now we don't know very much—well, nothing really, about your main character. All you have in the story is her name, but, uh…we don't know where she grew up, or who her family is, or…what she cares about. So it is not so interesting to someone who reads it. Do you understand?

STUDENT: Sure…but, is it ok to write extra information about the character's background? I was afraid it might be boring.

PROFESSOR: I remember when…when we talked about our ideas for the stories in class, you said that your character has a daughter, is that, uh, is that right?

STUDENT: Yes, that's…

PROFESSOR: Ok, so if you write that in your story…that your character has a daughter, and tell us about her daughter, then it might help us to worry about her more when she is in danger.

STUDENT: Oh, I see…I just worried that it might not be interesting to the reader.

PROFESSOR: No, no…um, one time I wrote a story about a character at work. But I, uh…I also included background information about where the character went to school, and that helped the reader to understand him, to, uh, understand who he was and to feel sympathy for him. The story was very popular. So I suggest you think about something that like that, something that will help us to know your character better.

STUDENT: Yeah, ok.

PROFESSOR: You can think about this for a few days—think about…well, what is the best information to include.

STUDENT: Got it.

1. Why does the student go to see the professor?

   ✗ (A) To give the professor her short story assignment

   ✗ (B) To talk about her interest in writing short stories

   ✓ (C) To get suggestions for improving her short story

   ✗ (D) To ask whether she should include a character's background information in her story

GIST-PURPOSE. What does the student ask the professor about?

The student and the professor discuss her short story. But she had already given it to him before this meeting.

The student's interest in writing short stories is not really part of the conversation. The professor and the student are talking about her specific short story.

CORRECT. The student begins the conversation by asking the professor if he has read her draft short story. Then they discuss his suggestions for improving it.

The student and the professor discuss this issue, and the student does ask questions about it. But it is not the main reason she goes to see the professor. She only asks questions about this issue after the professor suggests it.

2. What does the professor suggest the student do to improve her story? *Choose 2 answers.*

✗ [A] Make the story longer

✓ [B] Make the story more exciting

✓ [C] Add more information about the main character

✗ [D] Spend less time describing what her characters look like

DETAIL. What does the professor recommend to the student?

The professor suggests several additions to the story that might make it longer when the student revises it. However, he does not actually suggest that she make the story longer.

CORRECT. The professor suggests that the student add a tense or scary scene to make the story more exciting.

CORRECT. The professor and the student discuss the professor's suggestion that she include character background in her story.

This is the opposite of what the professor suggests. He recommends that the student add information about what her characters look like.

3. What does the professor mention about the background of the character in the student's story?

✓ (A) That she has a daughter

✗ (B) That she grew up in another country

✗ (C) Where she went to school

✗ (D) Her name

DETAIL. The professor and the student discuss including information about the main character in the student's story. What specific piece of information does the professor mention?

CORRECT. The professor suggests adding information about the character's background, such as her family or where she grew up. He then asks the student about the character having a daughter.

The professor mentions that the student might include information about where the character grew up, but he doesn't make any specific suggestions.

The professor mentions that he included information about where a character in his *own* story went to school. This was not mentioned about the character in the student's story.

The name of the character in the student's story is never mentioned.

4.   What does the professor imply about the popularity of short stories?

  ✗   (A) Short stories are not usually popular.

  ✗   (B) Short stories about mysteries are more likely to be popular.

  ✗   (C) More people will read a short story if the characters are similar to them.

  ✓   (D) More people will read a short story if they understand and have sympathy for the main character.

INFERENCE. Near the end of the conversation, the professor talks about his own short story and how popular it was.

The professor does not say this. In fact, he mentions that his own short story was popular.

The professor does not mention short stories about mysteries.

The professor does imply that more people will read a short story, and therefore it will be popular, under certain circumstances. But he does not mention, or imply, anything about whether the characters in the story are similar to the readers.

CORRECT. The professor gives the example of his own short story. He says that readers were able to understand and sympathize with his main character, and that the story was very popular. He implies that more people will read a story if they understand and sympathize with the main character.

5.   Why does the professor mention another short story that he wrote?

  ✗   (A) To refocus the discussion on his own work

  ✗   (B) To help the student have a surprising new insight

  ✓   (C) To illustrate a point he is making

  ✗   (D) To warn the student not to follow his example

FUNCTION OF WHAT IS SAID. What is the professor trying to tell the student by mentioning this story that he wrote?

The professor is not simply changing the subject. He is telling something about his own experience in order to show something about the student's short story.

The professor is only trying to make the student feel more comfortable about what he is suggesting by sharing his own experience. There is no "surprising new insight" involved.

CORRECT. The student is worried that readers will not be interested in background information about her main character. The professor illustrates his point, that readers will be interested, by telling a story about his own experience.

The professor is providing an example of something he did that was successful. He is encouraging the student to follow his example.

2

Answers and Explanations—
2.4 Speaking Type 2 for Diagnostic

Sample Spoken Response—Track 8

In my spare time I prefer to do things alone generally, such as, go to the movies alone, or read alone, or do some writing alone. And that's because, um, during my work, uh, I spend time with, uh, you know, groups of people all day long and I'm interacting with people constantly. And I…because I ride the subway at night I'm, you know, seeing a lot of people…interacting with people. And I live with a roommate and we tend to hang out quite a lot, uh, at our apartment. So when I have time that's truly my own or truly free, I do tend to like to spend that time alone to recharge and refresh myself, uh, so that I can be good for the next day.

Comments

> This is a strong response. The student states her opinion at the beginning of her response and offers several reasons to support that opinion. She finishes by summarizing her overall point. She could perhaps improve her response by saying "uh" less frequently, but it is okay to say this a few times.

Answers and Explanations—
2.5 Speaking Type 4 for Diagnostic

Multitasking—Track 6

NARRATOR: Now listen to part of a lecture on this topic in a psychology class.

PROFESSOR: Now, there are a small number of people who we call "supertaskers." Usually, when you do a study where you have people try to do two things at once…they do both of them poorly. For instance, you'll get people in the lab and you'll have them try to fly an airplane in a flight simulator, and then you'll also have them try to answer math problems at the same time. They'll do a much worse job with both of them than they would if they were doing them separately. But there are a few people, maybe two percent of the population, who don't seem to have the same problem. If you have them try to do math problems while they're doing the flight simulator, they'll do almost as well as they would just doing them on their own.

It seems like these people, the supertaskers, are somehow able to pay attention to multiple things at once. What you end up finding, is, it's not that they have unusually high brain activity. Actually, if you study what their brains are doing while they're multitasking, they're not working very hard. It seems like they don't use as many neurons to pay attention to something. Their brains stay "relaxed." That means they can actually pay attention to more than one thing at the same time, without getting overwhelmed.

NARRATOR: Using the concept of multitasking, explain how supertaskers are different from most people.

Sample Spoken Response—Track 9

Supertaskers are different from most people because most people can't multitask very well, because the brain can't actually focus on more than one thing at once, uh…and do it well. Most people think they're multitasking…aren't really focusing on multiple things at once. They're focusing on different things separately…very quickly and switching back and forth between them and doing a poor job, uh, overall of, you know, doing that work. Uh, but, supertaskers are only about two percent of the population, and they're different. They really can multitask, they really can pay attention to, uh, different things at once, or more than one thing at once, um, because their brains do something different. Their brains are very relaxed, um, and not overwhelmed to take this information, rather than, uh, to jump around between things.

Comments

The student provides a concise summary of the topic and clearly addresses the question that was asked. She uses the full response time to provide a detailed description. She might be able to improve her response by pausing very briefly to signal the end of a sentence. She tends to keep talking and adding to the sentence rather than finishing one sentence and then starting another.

Answers and Explanations— 2.6 Writing Type 1 for Diagnostic

MOOCs—Track 7

NARRATOR: Now listen to part of a lecture on the topic you just read about.

PROFESSOR: A lot of the reasons that people complain about MOOCs, well, normal classes have the same problems. In any class, there are students who are highly motivated, and students who don't care. They'd be unmotivated in the classroom, just like they'd be unmotivated in an online class. The problem just looks bigger in MOOCs, because of the way enrollment works. Remember that anybody can sign up for a MOOC. Some students are college students, or people who need to take the course for some reason or another, but a lot of people will just be folks who saw the course description and thought…that looks neat. They aren't paying anything, so it doesn't matter if they lose interest. They weren't really taking it seriously in the first place.

Another issue is communication—but there's actually been a lot of progress on that, technologically. Don't underestimate the power of technology to solve these problems! Some online classes will have office hours, where you can ask questions. A lot of them will assign a teaching assistant to each group of students, and you'll talk to them regularly. Plus, because of the message board format, you have more opportunities to ask your fellow students questions. It's a more distributed format—you might not always have access to the professor, but there are more people who you can talk to, and you have instant access to them.

Overall, MOOCs have done a lot of good for the educational system already. Look at the enrollment in these classes. You'll get classes taught by MIT professors, but the people attending them come from all over the world. They've actually made these professors, these classes, more accessible than they would have been otherwise. Without the MOOC, the only people who could've taken that class would be people who could afford to go to MIT.

Sample Written Response

The lecturer disagrees with the passage, which says that MOOCs are not helpful to learning and that modern technology is making traditional education less effective. The main points the lecturer makes are that 1) motivation and over-enrollment are skewing the perception of the efficacy of MOOCs, and 2) the technology that is part of a MOOC actually enhances the course.

While the passage claims that MOOCs are ineffective because only 10% of students pass the final exam, the lecturer points out that motivation and over-enrollment are probably the real cause of this. For instance, many more students join MOOCs because they are free and open to the public. Most of those students have no real stake in the course, such as college credit, so they are do no often finish it.

And the lecturer also disagrees with the claim in the passage that MOOCs are not engaging because there is not an instuctor to build a relationship with. According to the lecturuer, there are other advantages provided by the technology. For instance, while it may be impossible to talk to a university instructor byu attendiong office hours, students in a MOOC are able to discuss class topics on message boards with TAs and other student, so many more channels of communication are open. Students might even have more access to the instructor than students in a traditional classroom.

The lecturer is not convinced that traditional classroom settings are better than a MOOC and actually sees many advantages to a MOOC.

Comments

The student does quite a good job of summarizing the points made by the lecturer. He also illustrates how these points cast doubt on the claims made in the passage. He does have several typographical errors in the second and third paragraphs. But these errors are minor enough that they do not prevent the reader from understanding the essay.

Scoring

Using the answer keys, count up the number you got right on the Reading and Listening tasks.

Reading Passage: _____ correct out of 14 = _____ **% correct.**

Lecture: _____ correct out of 6.

Conversation: _____ correct out of 5.

Listening (Lecture + Conversation): _____ correct out of 11 = _____ **% correct.**

Study the sample responses for the Speaking tasks by listening to the audio tracks and reading the transcripts. Compare your responses to the samples. Give yourself points on each dimension of your response as follows:

A. Delivery = Clear pronunciation + Good pace.

B. Use of language = Clear sentence meanings + Correct grammar + Appropriate vocabulary.

C. Development of ideas = Appropriate content + Coherent structure, with a main point supported by examples.

4 points = Good, similar to the sample.

3 points = Fair, close to the sample but definitely below it.

2 points = Limited.

1 points = Poor.

Speaking Type 2

A. Delivery: _____ out of 4.

B. Use of language: _____ out of 4.

C. Development of ideas: _____ out of 4.

Speaking Type 2 (total): _____ out of 12.

Speaking Type 4

A. Delivery: _____ out of 4.

B. Use of language: _____ out of 4.

C. Development of ideas: _____ out of 4.

Speaking Type 4 (total): _____ out of 12.

Speaking (Type 2 + Type 4): _____ out of 24 = _____ **% of possible points.**

Study the sample response for the Writing task. Compare your responses to the sample. Give yourself points on each dimension of your response as follows:

A. Use of language = Clear sentence meanings + Correct grammar + Appropriate vocabulary.

B. Development of ideas = Appropriate content from both lecture and reading + Coherent structure that organizes and connects that content.

5 points = Good, similar to the sample.

4 points = Good but with significant flaws.

3 points = Fair.

2 points = Limited.

1 points = Poor.

Writing Type 1

A. Use of language: _____ out of 5.

B. Development of ideas: _____ out of 5.

Writing (total): _____ out of 10 = _____ **% of possible points.**

Summary

Write in the level you've achieved: **Fundamentals** (0-49%), **Fixes** (50-75%), or **Tweaks** (76-100%).

Reading: _____ % = _____.

Listening: _____ % = _____.

Speaking: _____ % = _____.

Writing: _____ % = _____.

These levels have little to do with the score you'll eventually achieve on the TOEFL. Rather, they are meant to help you focus your efforts. Plan to spend the most time and energy on the Fundamentals, a moderate amount on the Fixes, and the least on the Tweaks.

1. Fundamentals (0-49%)

You have a solid amount of work ahead of you in this area. You may need to work on your fundamental skills. Or you may need to apply those skills more effectively in the context of the TOEFL. If you're like most people, you'll need to do some of both.

Good news: you have this book. You have lots and lots of practice opportunities. Reread Chapter 1 to get ideas about how to plan your workouts.

Keep your chin up. Focus on this area. Commit to making improvements, and over time, you'll make them.

2. Fixes (50-75%)

You have the basics down, and you can rack up points in this area. But you have fixes to make. Maybe certain types of questions or topics threw you. Maybe your test-taking process has some holes in it, so you had to rush.

Again, good news: you have this book. You can make your fixes by working out with the practice problems and tasks in the following chapters.

3. Tweaks (76-100%)

Nice job! At most, you got just a few wrong or missed a few points. To progress further, you just need to make some small tweaks on a particular type of question or an aspect of your test-taking process.

Here is some really great news: you can spend most of your time elsewhere. Don't completely ignore this area, of course. Do a little work here and there. This will confirm your mastery and make you feel good about this whole TOEFL business.

Practice

Chapter 3
Reading A: Humanities

Reading passages and questions test your ability to comprehend and analyze academic information. Most questions are multiple-choice with four options (select one from A, B, C, or D). Some questions may ask you to select more than one option or to fill in a table.

Reading passages test your understanding of main ideas and details, as well as the organization of the passage or of specific parts of the passage. They also test your understanding of the relationship between different ideas and your ability to make inferences (messages implied by the passage).

How should you use this chapter? Here are some recommendations, according to the level you've reached in TOEFL Reading:

1. **Fundamentals**. Start with a topic-focused chapter, such as this one. Start with a topic that is a "medium weakness"—not your worst area but not your best either. At first, work untimed and check the answer after each question. Review the solutions closely, think carefully about the principles at work, and articulate what you've learned. Redo questions as necessary. As you improve, time yourself and do all of the questions for a passage at once, without stopping.

2. **Fixes**. Do one passage and set of questions untimed, examine the results, and learn your lessons. Next, test yourself with timed sets. When doing timed sets, don't check your answers until you're done with the whole set.

3. **Tweaks**. Confirm your mastery by doing a passage and question set under timed conditions. Concentrate on your weaker topic areas. Aim to improve the speed and ease of your process. As soon as you're ready, move to mixed-topic practice.

Good luck on Reading!

3.1 Realism and Modernism in Literary Fiction

Virginia Woolf, modernist author

While today we tend to think of realism—the attempt to portray real life as accurately as possible—as one of the major goals of literary fiction, this mode of representation was a revolutionary idea in the middle of the nineteenth century. With the goal of accurate presentation of real life in mind, nineteenth-century novelists embraced new subject matter for their work: the mundane details of everyday, usually middle- and lower-class lives.

This new subject matter and the desire to represent it accurately placed constraints on these authors. Realist novelists believed that we can all know and describe an objective reality, and this impacted both the structure and style of their novels. Writers in Russia, France, the United Kingdom, and the United States confronted these limitations in similar ways, in spite of their different backgrounds. Because these writers limited themselves to the world they could observe, and not one they could only imagine, realist novels tend to follow certain conventions, so that they remain faithful to real experiences. For example, most realist novels have linear plots and omniscient, or all-knowing, narrators. Plots that move both backward and forward in time, for example, are unusual because they differ from the perception of how our lives naturally unfold. However, the circumstances of human lives vary widely across time and place; that is why reading Tolstoy's *War and Peace* is a very different experience from reading George Eliot's *Middlemarch*. What varies is not so much the structure of the novel and the perspective of the narrator but the texture of the places and lives it describes. The details of everyday experience are thus limiting factors for the realist novelist.

MANHATTAN PREP

One might assume that the same constraints would hold for the next generation of novelists, the modernists. Modernists, however, made very different assumptions about how best to represent human life. Modernist novelists no longer assumed that the best representation of reality is also the most literal one, as the realists did. Virginia Woolf, for example, strove to describe the way our conscious mind works by focusing more on memory and reflection than on actual experience. Other authors further experimented with unusual language, shifts in time, and fractured sentences, among other devices, to depict the workings of consciousness. These authors were still trying to describe human experience, but they no longer took for granted that we all experience the world the same way. For example, William Faulkner, in his novel *The Sound and the Fury*, uses several different narrators who speak with different voices. He does this to portray the same characters and events from different perspectives. In other words, he is trying to represent human experience as subjective and varied, rather than as a universally knowable truth. He uses a number of literary devices, including unusual language and shifts in time, to capture variations in how different people think, focusing more on the nature of individual consciousness than on how people live (as the realists did).

Even though realism again became a dominant trend in fiction later in the twentieth century, the innovations of the modernists and the way they thought about the purpose of fiction have remained part of the contemporary novel. While later generations of novelists have continued to portray the details of everyday lives as the realists did, they also recognize that the ways different people experience life are shaped by the internal workings of their minds. Thus, these novelists incorporate both realistic description and innovative style and structure into their work.

> Now answer the questions.

3

Paragraph 1

S1   While today we tend to think of realism—the attempt to portray real life as accurately as possible—as one of the major goals of literary fiction, this mode of **representation** was a revolutionary idea in the middle of the nineteenth century.

2   With the goal of accurate presentation of real life in mind, nineteenth-century novelists embraced new subject matter for their work: the **mundane** details of everyday, usually middle- and lower-class lives.

1.   The word "**representation**" in the passage is closest in meaning to

   (A) election

   (B) metaphor

   (C) portrayal

   (D) study

2. Which of the following questions about literary realism is NOT answered in paragraph 1?

(A) When did literary realism first develop?

(B) What was the goal of literary realism?

(C) What subject matter did literary realists draw on?

(D) How did realism change the style and structure of authors' writings?

3. The word "mundane" in the passage is closest in meaning to

(A) extraordinary

(B) routine

(C) sophisticated

(D) weary

Paragraph 2

S1 This new subject matter and the desire to represent it accurately placed constraints on these authors.

2 Realist novelists believed that we can all know and describe an **objective** reality, and this impacted both the structure and style of their novels.

3 Writers in Russia, France, the United Kingdom, and the United States confronted these limitations in similar ways, in spite of their different backgrounds.

4 Because these writers limited themselves to the world they could observe, and not one they could only imagine, realist novels tend to follow certain conventions, so that they remain faithful to real experiences.

5 For example, most realist novels have linear plots and omniscient, or all-knowing, narrators.

6 Plots that move both backward and forward in time, for example, are unusual because they differ from the perception of how our lives naturally unfold.

7 However, the circumstances of human lives vary widely across time and place; that is why reading Tolstoy's *War and Peace* is a very different experience from reading George Eliot's *Middlemarch*.

8 What varies is not so much the structure of the novel and the perspective of the narrator but the texture of the places and lives it describes.

9 The details of everyday experience are thus limiting factors for the realist novelist.

4. Why does the author mention Russia and the United States in paragraph 2?

   (A) To demonstrate that art can reconcile opposing viewpoints

   (B) To describe the migration of realist ideas from one country to another

   (C) To illustrate that realism developed in similar ways in different societies

   (D) To introduce an analysis of the novel during times of tension between countries

5. The word "objective" in the passage is closest in meaning to

   (A) personal

   (B) unfeeling

   (C) ambiguous

   (D) factual

6. According to paragraph 2, which of the following characteristics varies in realist novels written in different countries?

   (A) Narrative perspective in the novels

   (B) The structure of the novels

   (C) Descriptions of particular details of everyday lives

   (D) The way the plot moves through time

7. Paragraph 2 suggests that which of the following is true of most narrators of realist novels?

   (A) They are fully aware of the events described.

   (B) Their perspective varies by country.

   (C) They are usually from the working class.

   (D) They typically use the third person.

8. According to paragraph 2, all of the following are characteristics of realist novels EXCEPT:

   (A) These novels include both forward and backward movements in time.

   (B) These novels attempt to describe the world as it really is.

   (C) Realist novels based in different societies display features that are alike.

   (D) These novels are narrated by all-knowing figures.

Paragraph 3

S1	One might assume that the same constraints would hold for the next generation of novelists, the modernists.
2	Modernists, however, made very different assumptions about how best to represent human life.
3	Modernist novelists no longer assumed that the best representation of reality was also the most literal one, as the realists did.
4	Virginia Woolf, for example, strove to describe the way our conscious mind works by focusing more on memory and reflection than on actual experience.
5	Other authors further experimented with unusual language, shifts in time, and fractured sentences, among other devices, to depict the workings of consciousness.
6	These authors were still trying to describe human experience, but they no longer took for granted that we all experience the world the same way.
7	For example, William Faulkner, in his novel *The Sound and the Fury*, uses several different narrators who speak with different voices.
8	He does this to portray the same characters and events from different perspectives.
9	In other words, he is trying to represent human experience as subjective and varied, rather than as a universally knowable truth.
10	He uses a number of literary devices, including unusual language and shifts in time, to capture variations in how different people think, focusing more on the nature of individual consciousness than on how people live (as the realists did).

9. The phrase "the most literal" in the passage is closest in meaning to

   (A) the most exact

   (B) the most dramatic

   (C) the most enhanced

   (D) the simplest

10. According to paragraph 3, which of the following is an important topic in Virginia Woolf's work?

   (A) Actual experience

   (B) Memory

   (C) Voice

   (D) Time shifts

11. The word "fractured" in the passage is closest in meaning to

   (A) polished

   (B) distorted

   (C) reinforced

   (D) splintered

12. According to paragraph 3, which of the following distinguishes William Faulkner's work from that of the realists?

   (A) He did not write about middle- and lower-class lives.

   (B) He did not believe that every person perceives his or her reality in a similar way.

   (C) He desired to capture variations in how people think by using linear plots.

   (D) He preferred to use a single, unreliable narrator who is not all-knowing.

Paragraph 3

P3 S10   He uses a number of literary devices, including unusual language and shifts in time, to capture variations in how different people think, focusing more on the nature of individual consciousness than on how people live (as the realists did).

Paragraph 4

P4 S1   **A** Even though realism again became a dominant trend in fiction later in the twentieth century, the innovations of the modernists and the way they thought about the purpose of fiction have remained part of the contemporary novel.

2   **B** While later generations of novelists have continued to portray the details of everyday lives as the realists did, they also recognize that the ways different people experience life are shaped by the internal workings of their minds.

3   **C** Thus, these novelists incorporate both realistic description and innovative style and structure into their work.

End   **D**

Look at the part of the passage that is displayed above. The letters [A], [B], [C], and [D] indicate where the following sentence could be added.

13. **To capture those interior mental operations, modern-day authors tend to make use of modernist devices, from shifts in time and narrative perspective to stream-of-consciousness narration.**

Where would the sentence best fit?

Ⓐ Choice A

Ⓑ Choice B

Ⓒ Choice C

Ⓓ Choice D

> An introductory sentence for a brief summary of the passage is provided below. Complete the summary by selecting the THREE answer choices that express the most important ideas in the passage. Some sentences do not belong in the summary because they express ideas that are not presented in the passage or are minor ideas in the passage. This question is worth 2 points.

14. **Realism, a mode of representing real life accurately in literary fiction, was actually revolutionary in the mid-nineteenth century.**

Ⓐ Believing that the world can be accurately represented, realist authors strove to depict the details of everyday lives.

Ⓑ Focused on the unique experiences of individual minds, modernist authors used unusual techniques to capture the nature of conscious thought.

Ⓒ William Faulkner, a leading modernist, wrote from a variety of perspectives in his novel *The Sound and the Fury*.

Ⓓ Contemporary authors often blend traditions, combining modernist methods and realist focus on representing daily lives authentically.

Ⓔ Realist Russian novels and realist American novels vary in the details of the lives they describe.

Ⓕ Before the nineteenth century, novelists primarily wrote about the lives of the wealthy.

3.2 Modern Schools of Acting

The eminent Russian theatre director Konstantin Stanislavski brought his Moscow Art Theatre to New York City in 1922. The piercing, psychological truths portrayed by actors trained in his technique surprised and captivated the American theatrical community, since this realism was largely unknown in the mannered, external style then current in the United States. The Stanislavski technique soon became the new standard. Its rise was spearheaded by a handful of young professional actors in New York; these disciples would form The Group Theatre, which dedicated itself to training and performing in that mode. This technique would begin to dominate theatre acting. Later it would spread to film in the United States, then throughout the Western world. However, a philosophical schism split The Group Theatre, and three dominant sects emerged, each led by a former original member. While all won success and respect, each became more convinced in the superiority of his or her approach.

Lee Strasberg and The Actors' Studio. Undoubtedly, Lee Strasberg (1901–82) garnered the greatest share of fame and fortune. His school, The Actors' Studio, at which a mere handful of the thousand annual applicants were accepted, won world renown as the epicenter of theatrical craft without commercial constraints. This was not surprising, as Strasberg had already basked in the limelight as co-founder and acknowledged leader of The Group Theatre—itself known for both its acting and intensive summer retreats devoted to training in virtually an athletic sense—during its groundbreaking successes in the 1930s. Furthermore, Strasberg codified Stanislavski's approach into a famous educational system of actor training known as "The Method." Strasberg's training revolved around "affective memory," infusing the emotional memories from the actor's own life into that of the character.

Public recognition of Strasberg as the guru of the art form was bolstered by the notable list of stars who had studied with him. In addition, while he rarely worked as an actor, one such performance earned him an Academy Award nomination for Best Supporting Actor. Today, decades after his death, The Actors' Studio remains an acclaimed institution, although belief in its superiority is now more prevalent in the general public than in the professional community.

Sanford Meisner and The Neighborhood Playhouse. Sanford Meisner (1905–97) was Strasberg's junior by four years. The younger man became a founding member of The Group Theatre and scored several artistic triumphs, including directing a production of *Waiting for Lefty,* which won acclaim both artistically and for its condemnation of the suffering of the working class during the Great Depression. Eventually, however, Meisner disagreed with Strasberg over the effectiveness of "affective memory." After it became known that Stanislavski himself had abandoned this technique, this disagreement became an artistic breach between the two men.

Meisner then headed the acting program at The Neighborhood Playhouse School of the Theatre. In that capacity, he transformed the school into a prestigious institution that exists to this day and developed his own acting curriculum, in which the actor prepared by channeling emotional imagination rather than delving into past experiences. While Meisner also trained an abundance of stars, he remained less widely known than Strasberg. Professionally, however, the Meisner technique is now the preferred and predominant technique in modern actor training. Sadly, the friendship between these two men did not survive their artistic divorce. While they both largely remained in Manhattan, they rarely spoke in the decades before Strasberg's death.

Stella Adler and the Stella Adler Studio of Acting. Stella Adler (1901–92), another original member of The Group Theatre, also broke with Strasberg over "affective memory" and developed her own version of actor training in the studio that she created. Unlike the men, who were the children of tradesmen, Stella Adler was part of a legendary acting family of the Yiddish theatre in New York. While she had a more extensive acting career, she too became most admired as an acting coach. Some of the great stars, including Marlon Brando, publicly credited their success to Adler's coaching. Although the studio she founded continues, her version of actor training has been less impactful, probably because the two men had a stronger institutional base and because the force of her singular personality was an immensely important component of her teaching.

> Now answer the questions.

Paragraph 1

S1   The eminent Russian theatre director Konstantin Stanislavski brought his Moscow Art Theatre to New York City in 1922.

2   The piercing, psychological truths portrayed by actors trained in his technique surprised and captivated the American theatrical community, since this realism was largely unknown in the mannered, external style then current in the United States.

3   The Stanislavski technique soon became the new standard.

4   Its rise was spearheaded by a handful of young professional actors in New York; these disciples would form The Group Theatre, which dedicated itself to training and performing in that mode.

5   This technique would begin to dominate theatre acting.

6   Later it would spread to film in the United States, then throughout the Western world.

7   However, a philosophical schism split The Group Theatre, and three dominant sects emerged, each led by a former original member.

8   While all won success and respect, each became more convinced in the superiority of his or her approach.

1. According to paragraph 1, what most interested actors and theatergoers in the United States about the Stanislavski technique initially?

   (A) The arrival of Russian artists

   (B) The revelation of psychological truths

   (C) The use of this technique in film

   (D) The conflict among the three Group Theatre members

2. According to paragraph 1, the Stanislavski technique was considered groundbreaking in the United States because

   (A) it portrayed realism

   (B) it originated in Russia

   (C) it produced mannered, artificial performances

   (D) it was also applicable to film acting

Paragraph 2

S1	**Lee Strasberg and The Actors' Studio.**
2	Undoubtedly, Lee Strasberg (1901–82) garnered the greatest share of fame and fortune.
3	His school, The Actors' Studio, at which a mere handful of the thousand annual applicants were accepted, won world renown as the epicenter of theatrical craft without commercial constraints.
4	This was not surprising, as Strasberg had already basked in the limelight as a co-founder and acknowledged leader of The Group Theatre—itself known for both its acting and its intensive summer retreats devoted to training in virtually an athletic sense—during its groundbreaking successes in the 1930s.
5	Furthermore, Strasberg codified Stanislavski's approach into a famous educational system of actor training known as "The Method."
6	Strasberg's training revolved around "affective memory," infusing the emotional memories from the actor's own life into that of the character.

3. According to paragraph 2, as part of their educational development, Strasberg trained actors to

   (A) apply for admission to the Actors' Studio

   (B) portray athletes on stage

   (C) draw on their personal experiences while acting

   (D) find alternatives to Stanislavski's techniques

4. Which of the sentences below best expresses the essential information in the highlighted sentence in paragraph 2? Incorrect choices change the meaning in important ways or leave out essential information.

   (A) Additionally, Strasberg and Stanislavski worked together to write a training manual called "The Method."

   (B) In addition, Strasberg created a covert code called "The Method" so that actors could study acting privately.

   (C) Moreover, Stanislavski approved of "The Method," Strasberg's training system for actors.

   (D) Strasberg also organized Stanislavski's techniques into the well-known training system, "The Method."

Paragraph 3

S1 Public recognition of Strasberg as the guru of the art form was **bolstered** by the notable list of stars who studied with him.

2 In addition, while he rarely worked as an actor, one such performance earned him an Academy Award nomination for Best Supporting Actor.

3 Today, decades after his death, The Actors' Studio remains an acclaimed institution, although belief in its superiority is now more prevalent in the general public than in the professional community.

5. The word "**bolstered**" in the passage is closest in meaning to

   (A) supported

   (B) celebrated

   (C) undermined

   (D) tainted

6. According to paragraphs 2 and 3, all of the following are mentioned as Strasberg's achievements EXCEPT:

   (A) He founded a successful school.

   (B) He helped start a professional theatre.

   (C) He won several Academy Awards.

   (D) He taught many successful film stars.

Paragraph 4

S1 **Sanford Meisner and The Neighborhood Playhouse.**

2 Sanford Meisner (1905–97) was Strasberg's junior by four years.

3 The younger man became a founding member of The Group Theatre and scored several artistic triumphs, including directing a production of *Waiting for Lefty,* which won acclaim both artistically and for its **condemnation** of the suffering of the working class during the Great Depression.

4 Eventually, however, Meisner disagreed with Strasberg over the effectiveness of "affective memory."

5 After it became known that Stanislavski himself had abandoned this technique, this disagreement became an artistic breach between the two men.

MANHATTAN PREP

7. The word "condemnation" in the passage is closest in meaning to

(A) example

(B) promotion

(C) criticism

(D) exploitation

8. According to paragraph 4, all of the following are true statements about Sanford Meisner EXCEPT:

(A) He was younger than Strasberg.

(B) He acted in *Waiting for Lefty*.

(C) He disagreed with Strasberg.

(D) He was artistically successful.

Paragraph 5

S1	Meisner then headed the acting program at The Neighborhood Playhouse School of the Theatre.
2	In that capacity, he transformed the school into a prestigious institution that exists to this day and developed his own acting curriculum, in which the actor prepared by channeling emotional imagination rather than delving into past experiences.
3	While Meisner also trained an abundance of stars, he remained less widely known than Strasberg.
4	Professionally, however, the Meisner technique is now the preferred and predominant technique in modern actor training.
5	Sadly, the friendship between these two men did not survive their artistic divorce.
6	While they both largely remained in Manhattan, they rarely spoke in the decades before Strasberg's death.

9. According to paragraph 5, which of the following is true of Meisner and his career?

(A) His technique made use of imagination rather than memory.

(B) His technique was shunned by professionals.

(C) His methods relied on accurate portrayals of physical mannerisms.

(D) He taught in the neighborhood where he lived.

10. The phrase "delving into" in the passage is closest in meaning to

(A) fantasizing about

(B) closely examining

(C) largely ignoring

(D) disagreeing with

Paragraph 6

S1   **Stella Adler and the Stella Adler Studio of Acting.**

2   Stella Adler (1901–92), another original member of The Group Theatre, also broke with Strasberg over "affective memory" and developed her own version of actor training in the studio that she created.

3   Unlike the men, who were the children of tradesmen, Stella Adler was part of a legendary acting family of the Yiddish theatre in New York.

4   While she had a more extensive acting career, she too became most admired as an acting coach.

5   Some of great stars, including Marlon Brando, publicly credited their success to Adler's coaching.

6   Although the studio she founded continues, her version of actor training has been less impactful, probably because the two men had a stronger institutional base and because the force of her singular personality was an immensely important component of her teaching.

11. The word "singular" in the passage is closest in meaning to

(A) abrasive

(B) pleasant

(C) ordinary

(D) striking

12. What is the author's purpose in presenting the information in paragraph 6?

(A) To demonstrate that Adler was the most successful of the three

(B) To illustrate the importance of the Yiddish theatre

(C) To contrast Stella Adler's career with those of her two former colleagues

(D) To offer a feminist critique of New York theatre in the 1930s

Paragraph 6

S1–2   **Stella Adler and the Stella Adler Studio of Acting.** Stella Adler (1901–92), another original member of The Group Theatre, also broke with Strasberg over "affective memory" and developed her own version of actor training in the studio that she created.

3   **A** Unlike the men, who were the children of tradesmen, Stella Adler was part of a legendary acting family of the Yiddish theatre in New York.

4–5   **B** While she had a more extensive acting career, she too became most admired as an acting coach. Some of great stars, including Marlon Brando, publicly credited their success to Adler's coaching.

6   **C** Although the studio she founded continues, her version of actor training has been less impactful, probably because the two men had a stronger institutional base and because the force of her singular personality was an immensely important component of her teaching.

End   **D**

Look at the part of the passage that is displayed above. The letters [A], [B], [C], and [D] indicate where the following sentence could be added.

13. **Thus, a history of the Stanislavski technique in the United States in the twentieth century would arguably state that there were two lasting versions of his technique but three great acting coaches.**

Where would the sentence best fit?

- (A) Choice A
- (B) Choice B
- (C) Choice C
- (D) Choice D

An introductory sentence for a brief summary of the passage is provided below. Complete the summary by selecting the THREE answer choices that express the most important ideas in the passage. Some sentences do not belong in the summary because they express ideas that are not presented in the passage or are minor ideas in the passage. This question is worth 2 points.

14. **In 1922, the Stanislavski technique came to New York and irrevocably changed how actors trained and performed.**

A   Today Stanislavski's approach remains the basis of several variations of actor training, but the dominant one was developed by a less known personage.

B   One of the leading practitioners of Stanislavski's method acting infused it with the culture of the Yiddish theatre.

C   The three major disciples of Stanislavski in the United States created prominent schools of acting with long lists of alumni.

D   Acting according to Stanislavski's approach proved to be more influential in film acting than in theatre acting.

E   The dispute that led to major variations of Stanislavski's techniques involved how to infuse realistic emotions into acting portrayals.

F   The innovation of modern acting training destroyed a friendship.

3.3 Habitats of the Blues

Ecologists long ago determined that environmental factors significantly affect the evolution of species. Determinants imposed by nature have caused once uniform animal populations to differentiate into separate races and then species. Now, similar patterns of differentiation have been noted in human cultural phenomena. The effect of environmental influences on a specific form of art can be seen in the evolution of blues music in the United States.

Musicologists have agreed that blues music—defined by specific chord progressions and lyrical structures—was created by African-American musicians in the rural areas of the southern United States in the late nineteenth century, particularly in the Mississippi River delta, located in Louisiana. As it is related to African music embedded in spirituals, the influence of environmental factors on this art form is already evident. Aside from its distinct scales and beat, rural blues music was characterized by the interplay of vocals and acoustic guitars. Lyrically, early blues expressed the hopes and fears of impoverished farmers, often voicing stories about droughts and floods, as well as poverty, oppression, and relationship woes.

In the early twentieth century, socioeconomic factors caused a migration of rural southern African Americans to northern urban centers. The change in locale soon led to modifications in the blues music that the migrants brought with them. Instead of being played in fields and road houses, blues now became the music of city bars and dance halls. By about 1950, urban blues became an art form distinct from the country blues that had engendered it. While this urban blues itself had variants in different cities, the dominant strain developed in Chicago; "Chicago Blues" became a brand in its own right.

The urban atmosphere changed the blues both instrumentally and lyrically. The faster, even frenetic, scrabble of city life undoubtedly led to the replacement of the acoustic guitar and banjo with the electric guitar and harmonica—called a "blues harp" by some—soon accompanied by drums and electric bass guitars as well. While relationship laments remained common, blues lyrics now reflected the types of hard times common to city life. Chicago bluesman Kevin Moore noted, "You have to put some new life into it, new blood, new perspectives. You can't keep talking about mules, workin' on the levee."

Chicago Blues soon received national exposure, and Chicago Blues musicians now commanded payments beyond the wildest dreams of their country predecessors, although admittedly far less than the sums given to rock-and-roll stars. Also, blues extended its reach geographically. Muddy Waters, originally from the Mississippi Delta, migrated to Chicago and then toured Great Britain and Europe, to much fanfare. This led to the growth of "British Blues," another recognizable strain influenced by a habitat even further removed from the cotton fields than Chicago was.

There are also other, lesser-known "habitats" that eventually transformed a branch of the blues into musical genres that few today would call blues. At the beginning of the 20th century, rural Caucasian musicians also played blues music. However, with the advent of the recording industry, marketing executives promoted their work as country music or folk music for a Caucasian audience while marketing music played by African Americans for African Americans as blues. Today, most country music bears little resemblance to country blues, let alone to Chicago Blues, and is widely considered a separate genre of music.

Now answer the questions.

3

Paragraph 1

S1   Ecologists long ago determined that environmental factors significantly affect the evolution of species.

2   Determinants imposed by nature have caused once uniform animal populations to differentiate into separate races and then species.

3   Now, similar patterns of differentiation have been noted in human cultural phenomena.

4   The effect of environmental influences on a specific form of art can be seen in the evolution of blues music in the United States.

1. Which of the following can be inferred about blues music in the United States from paragraph 1?
    (A) It reflected the ecological forces of animals.
    (B) It was produced by several races.
    (C) It developed distinct variants at some point.
    (D) It has been studied closely by ecologists.

2. Which of the sentences below best expresses the essential information in the highlighted sentence in paragraph 1? Incorrect choices change the meaning in important ways or leave out essential information.

(A) Species variation causes changes in cultural outcomes.

(B) Human cultural phenomena also appear to evolve and split over time.

(C) Environmental factors do not influence cultural evolution.

(D) All cultural phenomena are the same in humans and animals.

Paragraph 2

S1   Musicologists have agreed that blues music—defined by specific chord progressions and lyrical structures—was created by African-American musicians in the rural areas of the southern United States in the late nineteenth century, particularly in the Mississippi River delta, located in Louisiana.

2   As it is related to African music embedded in spirituals, the influence of environmental factors on this art form is already evident.

3   Aside from its distinct scales and beat, rural blues music was characterized by the interplay of vocals and acoustic guitars.

4   Lyrically, early blues expressed the hopes and fears of impoverished farmers, often voicing stories about droughts and floods, as well as poverty, oppression, and relationship woes.

3. The word "embedded" in the passage is closest in meaning to

(A) lacking

(B) sanctified

(C) mandated

(D) ingrained

4. All of the following are mentioned in paragraph 2 as characteristics of blues music EXCEPT:

(A) its commonalities with African music

(B) its particular musical structures

(C) its themes of farming hardships

(D) its origin as a response to slavery

Paragraph 3

S1   In the early twentieth century, socioeconomic factors caused a migration of rural southern African Americans to northern urban centers.

2   The change in locale soon led to modifications in the blues music that the migrants brought with them.

3   Instead of being played in fields and road houses, blues now became the music of city bars and dance halls.

4   By about 1950, urban blues became an art form distinct from the country blues that had engendered it.

5   While this urban blues itself had variants in different cities, the dominant strain developed in Chicago; "Chicago Blues" became a brand in its own right.

5. The word "modifications" in the passage is closest in meaning to

(A) alterations

(B) improvements

(C) combinations

(D) deteriorations

6. The word "engendered" in the passage is closest in meaning to

(A) preceded

(B) typified

(C) inspired

(D) distinguished

Paragraph 4

S1   The urban atmosphere changed the blues both instrumentally and lyrically.

2   The faster, even frenetic, scrabble of city life undoubtedly led to the replacement of the acoustic guitar and banjo with the electric guitar and harmonica—called a "blues harp" by some—soon accompanied by drums and electric bass guitars as well.

3   While relationship laments remained common, blues lyrics now reflected the types of hard times common to city life.

4   Chicago bluesman Kevin Moore noted, "You have to put some new life into it, new blood, new perspectives.

5   You can't keep talking about mules, workin' on the levee."

7. In paragraph 4, the author includes the quotation from Kevin Moore in order to

    (A) support the idea that urban blues lyrics evolved as a result of a new environment

    (B) emphasize the fact that Chicago did not suffer from droughts similar to those in the South

    (C) argue that hard times were less relevant to urban life than they were to rural life

    (D) explain why urban blues employed electric guitars, harmonicas, and drums

8. The author identifies the "faster, even frenetic, scrabble of city life" as a factor that

    (A) encouraged new kinds of lyrics such as relationship laments

    (B) supported the use of electric instruments in blues music

    (C) increased the appeal of blues music to Caucasian audiences

    (D) discouraged lyrics about such subjects as mules and levees

Paragraph 5

S1 Chicago Blues soon received national exposure, and Chicago Blues musicians now commanded payments beyond the wildest dreams of their country predecessors, although admittedly far less than the sums given to rock-and-roll stars.

2   Also, blues extended its reach geographically.

3   Muddy Waters, originally from the Mississippi Delta, migrated to Chicago and then toured Great Britain and elsewhere in Europe, to much fanfare.

4   This led to the growth of "British Blues," another recognizable strain influenced by a habitat even further removed from the cotton fields than Chicago was.

9. Which of the following statements about Chicago Blues is best supported by paragraph 5?

    (A) Chicago Blues musicians earned as much as rock-n-roll stars.

    (B) Chicago and Great Britain are equally removed from the cotton fields where blues was born.

    (C) The earnings of Chicago Blues musicians dwarfed those of country blues musicians.

    (D) Muddy Waters developed the musical variant known as "British Blues."

Paragraph 6

S1	There are also other, lesser-known "habitats" that eventually transformed a branch of the blues into musical genres that few today would call blues.
2	At the beginning of the twentieth century, rural Caucasian musicians also played blues music.
3	However, with the advent of the recording industry, marketing executives promoted **their** work as country music or folk music for a Caucasian audience while marketing music played by African Americans for African Americans as blues.
4	Today, most country music bears little resemblance to country blues, let alone to Chicago Blues, and is widely considered a separate genre of music.

10. The word "their" in the passage refers to

   (A) rural Caucasian musicians

   (B) marketing executives

   (C) the recording industry

   (D) African-American musicians

Paragraph 3

S1	In the early twentieth century, socioeconomic factors caused a migration of rural southern African Americans to northern urban centers.
2	[A] The change in locale soon led to modifications in the blues music that the migrants brought with them.
3	[B] Instead of being played in fields and road houses, blues now became the music of city bars and dance halls.
4–5	[C] By about 1950, urban blues became an art form distinct from the country blues that had engendered it. While this urban blues itself had variants in different cities, the dominant strain developed in Chicago; "Chicago Blues" became a brand in its own right.
End	[D]

Look at the part of the passage that is displayed above. The letters [A], [B], [C], and [D] indicate where the following sentence could be added.

11. **The association of the city of Chicago with the blues remains to this day.**

Where would the sentence best fit?

(A) Choice A

(B) Choice B

(C) Choice C

(D) Choice D

Select from the six choices below TWO that characterize rural or country blues only, THREE that characterize urban blues only, and ONE that characterizes both styles of music. This question is worth 2 points.

Rural or Country Blues Only	Urban Blues Only	Both Styles
•	•	•
•	•	
	•	

12. [A] International exposure and increased financial compensation

[B] Laments sung to accompaniment by an acoustic guitar

[C] The use of a blues harp

[D] Evolution influenced by environmental factors in the direction of differentiation

[E] Often performed in fields and road houses

[F] Development into a distinct art form around 1950

3.4 Photography

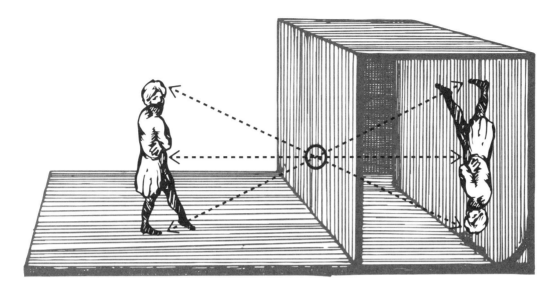

Photography is the art and science of still-image creation. It is accomplished through the recording of light or other electromagnetic radiation—indeed, the word "photography" comes from the Greek "photos," meaning "light," and "graphe," meaning "drawing or writing." Together, these words can be interpreted as "drawing with light." The nineteenth-century scientist and photographer John Herschel is typically credited with coining the term in the 1830s. However, some have claimed that others were independently using the term around the same period; a French painter used the term in his correspondence and a German astronomer spoke of the term in a newspaper article.

Photography began with the discovery of the *camera obscura*, or the "dark room." *Camera obscura* is the phenomenon by which a pinhole in the wall of a dark room will project an image, lit from outside the room, onto an inner wall of the enclosed dark room. The image is reversed and inverted, or flipped upside down. This is the same mechanism by which the human eye sees images, with the pupil as the pinhole (the brain simply flips the image back so that it is observed as normal). Since the sixteenth century, artists have used a device referred to as the "camera obscura" (named along with the natural phenomenon it captures) in order to assist in drawing. Scientists have also used it to observe solar eclipses, which are generally unsafe to view directly.

It is well-established that certain substances, such as particular salts, change color when exposed to sunlight. In 1727, German scientist Johann Heinrich Schulze discovered that certain salts darkened when exposed to sunlight, not because of heat or air, but as a response solely to the light itself. It was not until the early nineteenth century, however, that this chemical reaction was incorporated into what would become the photography that we know today. When the *camera obscura* process of projecting an image through the pinhole was applied to paper that had been chemically treated to be light-sensitive, modern photography was born. The pinhole camera became the first photographic camera.

Over the next number of decades, the camera underwent steady improvements. After the pinhole camera, the "daguerreotype" was invented, which involved not one but two boxes—an inner box and an outer box—which allowed the photographer to sharpen, or focus, the image. For years, photographers controlled the length of exposure time by manually removing the cap from the camera lens, the part of the camera

that captures the light from the subject and brings it into focus. The photographer then counted the required amount of time in seconds or minutes before returning the cap to cover the lens. Eventually, the "shutter," or mechanism that opens and closes the camera lens, was invented, freeing the photographer from this task in taking a photo. In 1885, American entrepreneur George Eastman began manufacturing the first photographic film—paper on which photographs could be taken. Starting in 1888, it was sold in a simple camera preloaded with the film. This camera was called the Kodak.

Today, most photography is conducted using digital cameras. In digital photography, an "image sensor" has replaced the traditional photographic film. This sensor is still a light-sensitive surface, but the image is stored as digital memory rather than etched directly onto a physical surface, as with photographic film. Some contemporary photographers, however, such as Cuban photographer Abelardo Morell, have chosen to work predominantly with early models of photography. A photography professor, he turned his classroom into a dark room in order to teach his students the optics behind the *camera obscura* technique. Morell is known for the images he takes using a "camera obscura," which range from panoramas of New York City to Italian landscapes. He flips his images right side up with an old-fashioned prism, though he does use a digital sensor instead of film to cut their exposure time. Morell even carries around a portable "camera obscura" with which he can project images onto the ground.

Now answer the questions.

Paragraph 1

S1   Photography is the art and science of still-image creation.

2   It is accomplished through the recording of light or other electromagnetic radiation—indeed, the word "photography" comes from the Greek "photos," meaning "light," and "graphe," meaning "drawing or writing."

3   Together, these words can be interpreted as "drawing with light."

4   The nineteenth-century scientist and photographer John Herschel is typically credited with coining the term in the 1830s.

5   However, some have claimed that others were independently using the term around the same period; a French painter used the term in his **correspondence**, and a German astronomer spoke of the term in a newspaper article.

1.   The word "correspondence" in the passage is closest in meaning to

    (A) communications

    (B) association

    (C) research

    (D) portfolio

2. According to paragraph 1, the origin of the term "photography" is

A defined as the craft of creating still images

B not attributed to scientist John Herschel

C both French and German

D two Greek words

Paragraph 2

S1	Photography began with the discovery of the *camera obscura*, or the "dark room."
2	*Camera obscura* is the phenomenon by which a pinhole in the wall of a dark room will project an image, lit from outside the room, onto an inner wall of the enclosed dark room.
3	The image is reversed and inverted, or flipped upside down.
4	This is the same mechanism by which the human eye sees images, with the pupil as the pinhole (the brain simply flips the image back so that it is observed as normal).
5	Since the sixteenth century, artists have used a device referred to as the "camera obscura" (named along with the natural phenomenon it captures) in order to assist in drawing.
6	Scientists have also used it to observe solar eclipses, which are generally unsafe to view directly.

3. The word "enclosed" in the passage is closest in meaning to

A attached

B trapped

C sealed

D exposed

4. Which of the sentences below best expresses the essential information in the highlighted portion of the passage? Incorrect choices change the meaning in important ways or leave out essential information.

A The image produced by the pupil (acting as the pinhole) is flipped back to normal by the brain through the *camera obscura* mechanism.

B In its role as a pinhole, the pupil flips back to normal the image seen by the human eye and brain by means of the *camera obscura* mechanism.

C Via the *camera obscura* mechanism, the "pinhole" pupil of the human eye produces a flipped image, which the brain then flips back to normal.

D Using the *camera obscura* mechanism to see images, the human eye flips the image observed by the brain back to normal through the pupil's pinhole.

5. All of the following are mentioned about the phenomenon of *camera obscura* in paragraph 2 EXCEPT:

   (A) It makes use of a pinhole in a wall.

   (B) It is not safe for use with solar eclipses.

   (C) It is a natural occurrence involving light.

   (D) A device that captures it is called by the same name.

Paragraph 3

S1	It is well-established that certain substances, such as particular salts, change color when exposed to sunlight.
2	In 1727, German scientist Johann Heinrich Schulze discovered that certain salts darkened when exposed to sunlight, not because of heat or air, but as a response solely to the light itself.
3	It was not until the early nineteenth century, however, that this chemical reaction was incorporated into what would become the photography that we know today.
4	When the *camera obscura* process of projecting an image through the pinhole was applied to paper that had been chemically treated to be light-sensitive, modern photography was born.
5	The pinhole camera became the first photographic camera.

6. The phrase "incorporated into" in the passage is closest in meaning to

   (A) included in

   (B) isolated from

   (C) established by

   (D) incarnated by

7. According to paragraph 3, under what specific conditions do certain salts studied by Johann Schulze darken?

   (A) When they are exposed to the light of the sun.

   (B) When they are heated but not lit by the sun.

   (C) When they are exposed to open air in darkness.

   (D) When they are exposed to both open air and the heat, but not the light of the sun.

8. The word "treated" in the passage is closest in meaning to

   (A) dissolved

   (B) contained

   (C) neglected

   (D) doctored

Paragraph 4

S1   Over the next number of decades, the camera underwent steady improvements.

2   After the pinhole camera, the "daguerreotype" was invented, which involved not one but two boxes—an inner box and an outer box—which allowed the photographer to sharpen, or focus, the image.

3   For years, photographers controlled the length of exposure time by manually removing the cap from the camera lens, the part of the camera that captures the light from the subject and that brings it into focus.

4   The photographer then counted the required amount of time in seconds or minutes before returning the cap to cover the lens.

5   Eventually, the "shutter," or mechanism that opens and closes the camera lens, was invented, freeing the photographer from this task in taking a photo.

6   In 1885, American entrepreneur George Eastman began manufacturing the first photographic film—paper on which photographs could be taken.

7   Starting in 1888, it was sold in a simple camera preloaded with the film.

8   This camera was called the Kodak.

9. Which of the following is mentioned in paragraph 4 about photographic film?

(A) It did not exist until it was built into the first Kodak camera.

(B) Cameras preloaded with it were sold starting in 1888.

(C) It was a critical part of the "shutter" mechanism.

(D) It improved upon the prior development of the shutter.

10. It can be inferred from paragraph 4 that the newly invented camera shutter

(A) took away from the photographer's freedom to determine the length of exposure time

(B) involved the same amount of work to operate as did manually opening and shutting the camera lens

(C) allowed the photographer to focus on other aspects of taking the photograph

(D) gave George Eastman the idea to create a camera with preloaded film

Paragraph 5

S1	Today, most photography is conducted using digital cameras.
2	In digital photography, an "image sensor" has replaced the traditional photographic film.
3	This sensor is still a light-sensitive surface, but the image is stored as digital memory rather than etched directly onto a physical surface, as with photographic film.
4	Some contemporary photographers, however, such as Cuban photographer Abelardo Morell, have chosen to work predominantly with early models of photography.
5	A photography professor, he turned his classroom into a dark room in order to teach his students the optics behind the *camera obscura* technique.
6	Morell is known for the images he takes using a "camera obscura," which range from panoramas of New York City to Italian landscapes.
7	He flips his images right side up with an old-fashioned prism, though he does use a digital sensor instead of film to cut their exposure time.
8	Morell even carries around a portable "camera obscura" with which he can project images onto the ground.

11. In paragraph 5, the author discusses Abelardo Morell's use of early photographic techniques in order to

   (A) argue that the most authentic methods of photography are the early ones

   (B) illustrate that not all contemporary photographers strictly use contemporary techniques

   (C) underline the importance of keeping early techniques alive and relevant

   (D) explain why modern photographic techniques are more efficient and effective than older ones

12. The word "their" in the passage refers to

   (A) camera

   (B) sensor

   (C) prism

   (D) images

Paragraph 3

S1   It is well-established that certain substances, such as particular salts, change color when exposed to sunlight.

2   **A** In 1727, German scientist Johann Heinrich Schulze discovered that certain salts darkened when exposed to sunlight, not because of heat or air, but as a response solely to the light itself.

3   **B** It was not until the early nineteenth century, however, that this chemical reaction was incorporated into what would become the photography that we know today.

4–5   **C** When the *camera obscura* process of projecting an image through the pinhole was applied to paper that had been chemically treated to be light-sensitive, modern photography was born. The pinhole camera became the first photographic camera.

End   **D**

> Look at the part of the passage that is displayed above. The letters [A], [B], [C], and [D] indicate where the following sentence could be added.

13. **This camera is especially interesting because, with no lens, its depth of field is very deep, so everything that appears in the frame is in focus.**

    Where would the sentence best fit?

    (A) Choice A

    (B) Choice B

    (C) Choice C

    (D) Choice D

An introductory sentence for a brief summary of the passage is provided below. Complete the summary by selecting the THREE answer choices that express the most important ideas in the passage. Some sentences do not belong in the summary because they express ideas that are not presented in the passage or are minor ideas in the passage. This question is worth 2 points.

14. **The history of photography as an art form dates back to its invention in the early 1800s.**

  A Cuban photographer Abelardo Morell is also a well-regarded professor of photography.

  B The *camera obscura* phenomenon was fundamental in the creation of the first photographic camera.

  C Cameras used by photographers have undergone changes in the years since photography was invented, from the film they use to the mechanisms by which they work.

  D The human brain works the same way as photographic cameras.

  E Scientists have used the *camera obscura* to observe solar eclipses.

  F Light-sensitive paper with certain chemical treatments allowed the *camera obscura* to become an actual photographic camera.

3.5 Stream of Consciousness

At the dawn of the twentieth century, European painting, which was then a far more influential art form than it is now, underwent a vast aesthetic revolution, shattering conventions that predated the Renaissance. Cubism, an innovative movement that would influence artists throughout the century, rejected the previous norm of realistic portrayals in favor of an abstract approach combining multiple perspectives. This radical departure, commonly thought to have been led by Pablo Picasso and Georges Braque, captivated the art world. It also inspired writers and musicians to infuse the same abstract quality into their works.

James Joyce and John Dos Passos were two renowned authors whose major works employed this nonlinear framework derived from Cubism, the writers applying words to paper in the same fractured manner that artists used when applying paint to canvas. Scholars have termed this literary style "stream-of-consciousness" writing. This technique constructs an inner monologue that creates a whole from dissociated parts and theoretically portrays the nonlinear patterns inherent in human thoughts.

Like Picasso and Braque, Joyce and Dos Passos enjoyed great artistic success, and their stylistic explorations profoundly influenced the generations of writers that followed them. Both men were interested in smashing established boundaries in the service of accurately displaying the emotional truth of human thoughts and feelings. James Joyce (1882–1941) was reared in a downwardly mobile Irish middle-class family but received a relatively elite education because of his intellect and talents. He resided in Europe for almost all of his adult life and eked out a living through various short-lived ventures, his art, and the generosity of patrons. His literary work largely remained anchored to his native Dublin. John Dos Passos (1896–1970) was the illegitimate son of John Randolph Dos Passos, who refused to accept his son until he was nearly an adult. However, his father's wealth allowed him to obtain a privileged education and undertake an educational tour of Europe. He then volunteered with an ambulance corps during the First World War, an experience that profoundly impacted him, as it did many of his generation. During his literary prime, Dos Passos was also an outspoken political progressive, but in the final third of his life he embraced very conservative causes.

Joyce's most renowned work, *Ulysses*, was published in 1922; however, in the United States, it was banned under an obscenity statute for more than 10 years. In this seminal work, Joyce transplants the plot and characters of Homer's Greek epic *The Odyssey* to early twentieth-century Dublin and condenses the timeline to a single day. In service of the stream-of-consciousness aesthetic, each chapter employs a different literary style, although all reject linear conventions, much as Cubist painting did. Furthermore, each chapter has a thematic association unrelated to the plot or source material. Because of its difficult vocabulary, its assumption that the reader is familiar with a vast array of historical and literary references, and its complex, metaphorical prose, *Ulysses* is not widely read. However, its fame and place in the literary canon far exceed its sales, as scholarly opinion considers it the fountainhead of literary modernism.

By contrast, John Dos Passos's work, also considered unique and innovative, proved far more accessible and popular, but it is now thought to be less important than *Ulysses*. His opus was a trilogy entitled *U.S.A.*, completed in 1938. This work chronicles the evolution of the United States from an agrarian, isolationist nation as the twentieth century began to the urban world power it became within a few decades. Dos Passos sought to reflect the feelings and consciousness of those times by employing what critics have called a "collage technique": newspaper clippings are inserted sporadically, and his disparate characters and plots intersect at seemingly random intervals.

The literary influence of Joyce, Dos Passos, and their peers remains pervasive to this day. In that sense, it can be argued that the movement that they spearheaded in the literary world was more momentous in the long run than the parallel revolution in the artistic world. While Cubism predated the stream-of-consciousness movement, it is now seen as more of a period in art than a guiding light, whereas the stream-of-consciousness style remains current in literature.

> Now answer the questions.

3

Paragraph 1

S1   At the dawn of the twentieth century, European painting, which was then a far more influential art form than it is now, underwent a vast aesthetic revolution, shattering conventions that predated the Renaissance.

2   Cubism, an innovative movement that would influence artists throughout the century, rejected the previous norm of realistic portrayals in favor of an abstract approach combining multiple perspectives.

3   This radical departure, commonly thought to have been led by Pablo Picasso and Georges Braque, captivated the art world.

4   It also inspired writers and musicians to infuse the same abstract quality into their works.

1. What can be inferred about European art from paragraph 1?

    (A) European painting was more influential in the early twentieth century than during the Renaissance.

    (B) Picasso was more captivating to the art world than Braque was.

    (C) Realistic portrayals were likely one of the conventions that predated the Renaissance.

    (D) The aesthetic revolution in European painting was probably inspired by writers using similar abstractions.

2. According to paragraph 1, all of the following are true statements about Cubism EXCEPT:

    (A) It employed multiple perspectives.

    (B) It influenced writers and musicians.

    (C) Its influence lasted for many decades.

    (D) It had less appeal to the public outside the art world.

Paragraph 2

S1 James Joyce and John Dos Passos were two renowned authors whose major works employed this nonlinear framework derived from Cubism, the writers applying words to paper in the same fractured manner that artists used when applying paint to canvas.

2   Scholars have termed this literary style "stream-of-consciousness" writing.

3   This technique constructs an inner monologue that creates a whole from **dissociated** parts and theoretically portrays the nonlinear patterns inherent in human thoughts.

3. The word "**dissociated**" in the passage is closest in meaning to

    (A) fragmented

    (B) reserved

    (C) aligned

    (D) unspoken

4. Which of the sentences below best expresses the essential information in the highlighted sentence in paragraph 2? Incorrect choices change the meaning in important ways or leave out essential information.

(A) In their major works, James Joyce and John Dos Passos applied nonlinear writing techniques derived from Cubism.

(B) Applying words to paper in the same fractured way, James Joyce and John Dos Passos derived the nonlinear framework of Cubism.

(C) James Joyce and John Dos Passos became renowned authors by using a nonlinear style that they derived from Cubism.

(D) Renowned authors James Joyce and John Dos Passos applied paint to canvas in a fractured, Cubist manner to write their major works.

Paragraph 3

S1   Like Picasso and Braque, Joyce and Dos Passos enjoyed great artistic success, and their stylistic explorations profoundly influenced the generations of writers that followed them.

2   Both men were interested in smashing established boundaries in the service of accurately displaying the emotional truth of human thoughts and feelings.

3   James Joyce (1882–1941) was reared in a downwardly mobile Irish middle-class family but received a relatively elite education because of his intellect and talents.

4   He resided in Europe for almost all of his adult life and eked out a living through various short-lived ventures, his art, and the generosity of patrons.

5   His literary work largely remained anchored to his native Dublin.

6   John Dos Passos (1896–1970) was the illegitimate son of John Randolph Dos Passos, who refused to accept his son until he was nearly an adult.

7   However, his father's wealth allowed him to obtain a privileged education and undertake an educational tour of Europe.

8   He then volunteered with an ambulance corps during the First World War, an experience that profoundly impacted him, as it did many of his generation.

9   During his literary prime, Dos Passos was also an outspoken political progressive, but in the final third of his life he embraced very conservative causes.

5. The phrase "eked out" in the passage is closest in meaning to

(A) enjoyed

(B) scratched out

(C) gave up

(D) provided

6. According to paragraph 3, which of the following is true about both Joyce and Dos Passos?

    (A) Both served in the ambulance corps in the First World War.

    (B) Both resided in Europe for the majority of their adulthoods.

    (C) Both were raised in middle-class families.

    (D) Both received educations reserved for just a few.

7. The phrase "an outspoken" in the passage is closest in meaning to

    (A) a disclosed

    (B) a fainthearted

    (C) a diplomatic

    (D) a forthright

Paragraph 4

S1 Joyce's most renowned work, *Ulysses*, was published in 1922; however, in the United States, it was banned under an obscenity statute for more than 10 years.

2   In this seminal work, Joyce transplants the plot and characters of Homer's Greek epic *The Odyssey* to early twentieth-century Dublin and condenses the timeline to a single day.

3   In service of the stream-of-consciousness aesthetic, each chapter employs a different literary style, although all reject linear conventions, much as Cubist painting did.

4   Furthermore, each chapter has a thematic association unrelated to the plot or source material.

5   Because of its difficult vocabulary, its assumption that the reader is familiar with a vast array of historical and literary references, and its complex, metaphorical prose, *Ulysses* is not widely read.

6   However, its fame and place in the literary canon far exceed its sales, as scholarly opinion considers it the fountainhead of literary modernism.

8. According to paragraph 4, *Ulysses* was not widely read in part because

    (A) it was banned for obscenity

    (B) it was inspired by Homer's epic *The Odyssey*

    (C) its vocabulary is obscure

    (D) it is the fountainhead of literary modernism

9. In paragraph 4, why does the author mention that each chapter has a unique literary style?

    (A) To demonstrate that *Ulysses* is the primary example of nonlinear writing in the twentieth century

    (B) To reject the effectiveness of linear conventions as typically used in literature

    (C) To show how the book tries to reflect stream-of-consciousness principles

    (D) To document why *Ulysses* was banned in the United States for obscenity

Paragraph 5

S1   By contrast, John Dos Passos's work, also considered unique and innovative, proved far more accessible and popular, but it is now thought to be less important than *Ulysses*.

2   His opus was a trilogy entitled *U.S.A.*, completed in 1938.

3   This work chronicles the evolution of the United States from an agrarian, isolationist nation as the twentieth century began to the urban world power it became within a few decades.

4   Dos Passos sought to reflect the feelings and consciousness of those times by employing what critics have called a "collage technique": newspaper clippings are inserted sporadically, and his disparate characters and plots intersect at seemingly random intervals.

10. The word "sporadically" in the passage is closest in meaning to

(A) prevalently

(B) irregularly

(C) steadily

(D) habitually

11. Paragraph 5 mentions which of the following as an aspect of a collage technique?

(A) The intersection of apparently unrelated people and circumstances

(B) An accessible and popular style

(C) An agrarian, isolationist perspective

(D) The sporadic insertion of clippings from private governmental reports

Paragraph 6

S1   The literary influence of Joyce, Dos Passos, and their peers remains pervasive to this day.

2   In that sense, it can be argued that the movement that they spearheaded in the literary world was more momentous in the long run than the parallel revolution in the artistic world.

3   While Cubism predated the stream-of-consciousness movement, it is now seen as more of a period in art than a guiding light, whereas the stream-of-consciousness style remains current in literature.

12. According to paragraph 6, which of the following is true about Cubism?

(A) It is currently as influential in art as the stream-of-consciousness style is in literature.

(B) It had more impact on art made early in the twentieth century than it does on art made today.

(C) It was predated by the stream-of-consciousness movement.

(D) It is considered as much a guiding light for current artists as an epoch in the history of art.

Paragraph 5

P5 S4   Dos Passos sought to reflect the feelings and consciousness of those times by employing what critics have called a "collage technique": newspaper clippings are inserted sporadically, and his disparate characters and plots intersect at seemingly random intervals.

Paragraph 6

P6 S1   [A] The literary influence of Joyce, Dos Passos, and their peers remains pervasive to this day.

2   [B] In that sense, it can be argued that the movement that they spearheaded in the literary world was more momentous than the parallel revolution in the artistic world.

3   [C] While Cubism predated the stream-of-consciousness movement, it is now seen as more of a period in art than a guiding light, whereas the stream-of-consciousness style remains current in literature.

End   [D]

Look at the part of the passage that is displayed above. The letters [A], [B], [C], and [D] indicate where the following sentence could be added.

---

13. **Where do these revolutions in literature and in art stand today, in the twenty-first century?**

Where would the sentence (a question) best fit?

(A) Choice A

(B) Choice B

(C) Choice C

(D) Choice D

An introductory sentence for a brief summary of the passage is provided below. Complete the summary by selecting the THREE answer choices that express the most important ideas in the passage. Some sentences do not belong in the summary because they express ideas that are not presented in the passage or are minor ideas in the passage. This question is worth 2 points.

14. **Cubism, an early twentieth-century revolution in art, also influenced the course of literature by inspiring prominent authors to infuse its principles into their works.**

A   Stream-of-consciousness writing was not popular with the public because of its difficult vocabulary.

B   Dos Passos was more progressive politically than Joyce because of his experience in the First World War.

C   The influence of stream-of-consciousness writing proved more lasting in the literary world than that of Cubism did in the art world.

D   In the early twentieth century, an artistic upheaval in European painting upended conventions and infused an abstract perspective into various art forms.

E   The fragmented, nonlinear techniques employed by Joyce and Dos Passos aimed to portray human thoughts authentically.

F   In their elite educations and European travels, Joyce and Dos Passos were representative of great writers of the period.

3

3.6 Henri Cartier-Bresson

The French photographer Henri Cartier-Bresson (1908–2004) was a pioneer of modern street photography and is regarded as the "father of photojournalism." Celebrated for the candid shots he took of everyday life in Paris, as well as for his photo-reporting around the world, he remains one of the most respected photographers of the twentieth century. His early life as an artist was not devoted to photography, however. When he was 19 years old, Cartier-Bresson began studying at the studio of Cubist painter and sculptor André Lhote. There, he learned to be a painter. He was educated in art theory and composition, and he discovered an interest in both modern and Renaissance art.

Meanwhile, throughout the 1920s, photography continued to develop as an art form, and in 1930, Cartier-Bresson became inspired by a photograph taken by Hungarian photographer Martin Munkacsi. In the photograph, titled "Three Boys at Lake Tanganyika," three young boys play in Lake Tanganyika, an expansive, freshwater lake that touches four countries on the African continent: Tanzania, the Democratic Republic of the Congo, Burundi, and Zambia. In the photo, the boys splash in the surf. The image features their silhouettes against the lake's foaming waves. It is a joyful scene. Cartier-Bresson credited the photograph with leading him to turn away from painting in order to focus on photography. He said of the picture, "I suddenly understood that photography can fix eternity in a moment."

Cartier-Bresson then acquired a German camera with a 50-millimeter (50-mm) lens—relatively small compared to the lenses used by professional photographers today. Despite having many opportunities to use a larger, more complex lens over the course of his career, Cartier-Bresson preferred his 50-mm lens for

several reasons. The most important of these was that with this lens, he was able to shoot without being conspicuous, which he resisted for fear of being seen as showing off. It allowed him to capture moments he might not have captured otherwise, as people often did not notice him shooting.

He also had a strong preference for shooting in black and white, believing that the myriad printing options available when shooting with color distorted the image he was seeing with his eyes. For this reason, he only shot in color when obliged to. In general, he bemoaned photography's trend toward focusing on ever-advancing processing techniques, believing that the fetishizing[1] of these techniques distracted people from what the art was truly about: seeing and capturing.

Images à la Sauvette (*The Decisive Moment* in the English edition), a book featuring over 100 of Cartier-Bresson's photographs, was published in 1952 with a cover drawn specifically for the book by renowned French painter Henri Matisse. The book quickly became a classic in the canon of literature on photography. Alongside the portfolio of his images in the book, Cartier-Bresson authored a 4,500-word introduction on his photographic philosophy. This introduction to the book is often referenced today in treatises and essays on the art and history of the photograph—in particular, the portions in which he elaborates on the book's title. To Cartier-Bresson, photography was about capturing in "a fraction of a second…the significance of an event." In a 1971 interview, Cartier-Bresson described the art as an act of affirmation. He rejected many similar titles in favor of *The Decisive Moment*, including *A pas de Loup*, which means "tiptoeing," a reference to how he, as a photographer, approached his subjects.

When Cartier-Bresson died in 2004, he had established a global reputation as one of the greatest photographers of all time. Yet, despite this fame, he was extremely timid and often shunned publicity. Thus, while he is revered for the photos he captured of faces around the world, he himself was rarely recognized.

Now answer the questions.

Paragraph 1

S1   The French photographer Henri Cartier-Bresson (1908–2004) was a pioneer of modern street photography and is regarded as the "father of photojournalism."

2   Celebrated for the candid shots he took of everyday life in Paris, as well as for his photo-reporting around the world, he remains one of the most respected photographers of the twentieth century.

3   His early life as an artist was not devoted to photography, however.

4   When he was 19 years old, Cartier-Bresson began studying at the studio of Cubist painter and sculptor André Lhote.

5   There, he learned to be a painter.

6   He was educated in art theory and composition, and he discovered an interest in both modern and Renaissance art.

fetishizing[1]: being overly committed to or obsessed about something, often in an irrational way

1. The word "candid" in the passage is closest in meaning to

   (A) theatrical

   (B) natural

   (C) simulated

   (D) intense

2. Paragraph 1 implies that prior to the 1920s,

   (A) most artists in France studied painting rather than other media

   (B) paintings were less abstract than they generally are today

   (C) modern street photography was likely not a well-established art form

   (D) Henri Cartier-Bresson was already emerging as a talented photojournalist

3. All of the following are mentioned about Henri Cartier-Bresson in paragraph 1 EXCEPT:

   (A) He was a legendary photojournalist.

   (B) He was first trained as a painter.

   (C) He was interested in both Renaissance and modern art.

   (D) His portrait photographs were widely celebrated.

Paragraph 2

S1   Meanwhile, throughout the 1920s, photography continued to develop as an art form, and in 1930, Cartier-Bresson became inspired by a photograph taken by Hungarian photographer Martin Munkacsi.

2   In the photograph, titled "Three Boys at Lake Tanganyika," three young boys play in Lake Tanganyika, an expansive, freshwater lake that touches four countries on the African continent: Tanzania, the Democratic Republic of the Congo, Burundi, and Zambia.

3   In the photo, the boys splash in the surf.

4   The image features their silhouettes against the lake's foaming waves.

5   It is a joyful scene.

6   Cartier-Bresson credited the photograph with leading him to turn away from painting in order to focus on photography.

7   He said of the picture, "I suddenly understood that photography can fix eternity in a moment."

4. The word "features" in the passage is closest in meaning to

(A) highlights

(B) hides

(C) smears

(D) shatters

5. According to paragraph 2, why did Cartier-Bresson switch from being a painter to being a photographer?

(A) He wanted to represent human silhouettes against natural backgrounds.

(B) He was inspired by the way a particular photograph captured a moment.

(C) He sought to introduce the world to the daily lives of African people.

(D) He hoped to establish an international career in Africa.

6. The author describes the image as "a joyful scene" in order to

(A) offer a reason why Cartier-Bresson considered photography superior to painting

(B) suggest that a less joyful photo would not have inspired Cartier-Bresson

(C) convey the spirit of the photograph that inspired Cartier-Bresson

(D) illustrate the highest purpose of photojournalism

Paragraph 3

S1 Cartier-Bresson then acquired a German camera with a 50-millimeter (50-mm) lens—relatively small compared to the lenses used by professional photographers today.

2 Despite having many opportunities to use a larger, more complex lens over the course of his career, Cartier-Bresson preferred his 50-mm lens for several reasons.

3 The most important of these was that with this lens, he was able to shoot without being conspicuous, which he resisted for fear of being seen as showing off.

4 It allowed him to capture moments he might not have captured otherwise, as people often did not notice him shooting.

7. The word "it" in the passage refers to

(A) fear

(B) a large, complex lens

(C) the reason for his preference

(D) his 50-mm lens

8. According to paragraph 3, what was the primary reason that Cartier-Bresson preferred to shoot with a 50-mm lens rather than with a larger lens?

  (A) To take his photographs in an unobtrusive way

  (B) To capture moments that he could have captured otherwise, but not as easily

  (C) To show off without being embarrassed as he shot

  (D) To maintain opportunities to use both kinds of lenses during his career

Paragraph 4

S1   He also had a strong preference for shooting in black and white, believing that the myriad printing options available when shooting with color distorted the image he was seeing with his eyes.

2   For this reason, he only shot in color when obliged to.

3   In general, he bemoaned photography's **trend** toward focusing on ever-advancing processing techniques, believing that the fetishizing of these techniques distracted people from what the art was truly about: seeing and capturing.

9. The word "**trend**" in the passage is closest in meaning to

  (A) contribution

  (B) hostility

  (C) movement

  (D) responsibility

Paragraph 5

S1   *Images à la Sauvette* (*The Decisive Moment* in the English edition), a book featuring over 100 of Cartier-Bresson's photographs, was published in 1952 with a cover drawn specifically for the book by renowned French painter Henri Matisse.

2   The book quickly became a classic in the canon of literature on photography.

3   Alongside the portfolio of his images in the book, Cartier-Bresson authored a 4,500-word introduction on his photographic philosophy.

4   This introduction to the book is often referenced today in treatises and essays on the art and history of the photograph—in particular, the portions in which he **elaborates on** the book's title.

5   To Cartier-Bresson, photography was about capturing in "a fraction of a second…the significance of an event."

6   In a 1971 interview, Cartier-Bresson described the art as an act of affirmation.

7   He rejected many similar titles in favor of *The Decisive Moment*, including *A pas de Loup*, which means "tiptoeing," a reference to how he, as a photographer, approached his subjects.

10. According to paragraph 5, which of the following statements about the book *The Decisive Moment* is true?

    (A) It contained both writing and photography by Cartier-Bresson.

    (B) It contained only Cartier-Bresson's most significant photographs.

    (C) Its cover was a photograph of Henri Matisse.

    (D) It is seldom referenced today in essays on the art and history of photography.

11. The phrase "elaborates on" in the passage is closest in meaning to

    (A) overemphasizes

    (B) writes more about

    (C) understates

    (D) simplifies

Paragraph 6

S1   When Cartier-Bresson died in 2004, he had established a global reputation as one of the greatest photographers of all time.

2   Yet, despite this fame, he was extremely timid and often shunned publicity.

3   Thus, while he is revered for the photos he captured of faces around the world, he himself was rarely recognized.

12. According to paragraph 6, what was the difference between Cartier-Bresson's reputation and his physical image?

    (A) His physical appearance was much more commonly known than his work.

    (B) He shunned publicity but was extremely timid and shy.

    (C) He established a global reputation on the basis of a locally known image.

    (D) He was recognized far and wide by name but not so often by sight.

Paragraph 5

S1   *Images à la Sauvette* (*The Decisive Moment* in the English edition), a book featuring over 100 of Cartier-Bresson's photographs, was published in 1952 with a cover drawn specifically for the book by renowned French painter Henri Matisse.

2–4   **A** The book quickly became a classic in the canon of literature on photography. Alongside the portfolio of his images in the book, Cartier-Bresson authored a 4,500-word introduction on his photographic philosophy. This introduction to the book is often referenced today in treatises and essays on the art and history of the photograph—in particular, the portions in which he elaborates on the book's title.

5–6   **B** To Cartier-Bresson, photography was about capturing in "a fraction of a second…the significance of an event." In a 1971 interview, Cartier-Bresson described the art as an act of affirmation.

7   **C** He rejected many similar titles in favor of *The Decisive Moment*, including *A pas de Loup*, which means "tiptoeing," a reference to how he, as a photographer, approached his subjects.

End   **D**

Look at the part of the passage that is displayed above. The letters [A], [B], [C], and [D] indicate where the following sentence could be added.

---

13. **Ultimately, in the title he chose to describe the photograph being sought rather than the seeking photographer.**

Where would the sentence best fit?

(A) Choice A

(B) Choice B

(C) Choice C

(D) Choice D

An introductory sentence for a brief summary of the passage is provided below. Complete the summary by selecting the THREE answer choices that express the most important ideas in the passage. Some sentences do not belong in the summary because they express ideas that are not presented in the passage or are minor ideas in the passage. This question is worth 2 points.

14. **Henri Cartier-Bresson was a groundbreaking photographer of the twentieth century.**

   A   Cartier-Bresson placed greater value on the scene captured in a photograph than on the techniques used to process the photograph.

   B   Cartier-Bresson started studying painting at the age of 19.

   C   The reason Cartier-Bresson used a 50-mm lens remains a vexing mystery.

   D   Cartier-Bresson's influential book *The Decisive Moment* showcases the photographer's work.

   E   An alternative title for *The Decisive Moment*, one that was ultimately discarded, was *Tiptoeing*.

   F   Inspired by a particular photograph of children playing in a lake, Cartier-Bresson decided to focus on photography over painting.

3.7 History of the Recording Industry

No invention was more fundamental to the development of the recording industry than the phonograph. Created in 1877 by Thomas Edison, the phonograph featured a conspicuous flaring horn about 12 inches (30 centimeters) tall, through which sound was projected. The original device played phonographic cylinders, which were soon replaced by records. A record is a disc etched with physical grooves representing the sounds to be replicated. When the disc was rotated at a certain speed, it caused vibrations in a stylus, or needle, that tracked the grooves. These vibrations were then picked up and amplified by a diaphragm, which transmitted sound to the flaring horn. Later versions of the phonograph, beginning in the 1920s, featured an electronic system for translating stylus vibration into sound (these electronic devices became known as "record players" or "turntables"). However, the basic mechanisms for recording sound on a rotating disc and reading it with a stylus have remained essentially unchanged from the original invention.

The phonograph was originally marketed as a business and legal services device. Edison's sales strategies targeted businesspeople, attorneys, and anyone else who might use shorthand or dictation as a means of recording ideas or spoken testimony. However, the phonograph eventually found its primary market elsewhere: the recording of sound for entertainment purposes. This market started with "phonograph parlors," the first of which appeared in 1889 in San Francisco. Customers would go to parlors and order a selection to be played for a nickel. This system was the precursor of the modern-day jukebox. Within a decade, nearly every major city in the United States had at least one phonograph parlor.

During the period 1890–1940, the recording industry was dominated by three companies: Victor, Columbia, and His Master's Voice, or HMV. By 1900, the industry was selling over 3 million records per year in the United States. The next two decades saw great prosperity in the industry, which attracted competition from a host of smaller producers. The competitors began undercutting each other's prices, while the phonograph itself was facing stiff competition from a new technology: radio. Radio programs offered special programming not available on records and featured a seemingly endless variety of available music. This caused many customers to stop purchasing records and to listen to the radio instead. During

the 1920s, revenue from the sale of recorded music fell by 50 percent as a result of these developments, which were followed by the onset of the Great Depression in late 1929. Many producers went out of business. It was not until the late 1930s, with the rising popularity of the combination radio-phonograph, the growing use of recorded sound in "talking" movies, and the recovery of the economy, that the recording industry began to recuperate.

The industry then experienced a boon in the 1940s. During World War II, the demand for recorded music for use in the United States armed services skyrocketed, leading to a temporary surge in the sales of recorded music despite rationing among consumers back home. At the same time, several lawsuits were brought forth by musicians against radio companies, who paid a royalty to the copyright owner (usually the studio) whenever recorded material was played. No royalty was paid to the musicians themselves. This led to a musicians' strike that lasted over two years, causing difficulties for the recording studios in the short term. However, the studios rebounded quickly when the strike ended, and radio broadcasters, the chief competitors to recording studios, now faced having to pay royalties to songwriters for every song they played.

The late 1940s also saw the introduction of an important new technology: "high fidelity" recording, which enabled sound recording over the complete range of audible frequencies with very little distortion. This technology allowed for the recording of sound that was much more authentic with respect to the original musical performance than was previously feasible. High fidelity, or "hi-fi," also enabled entire albums to be recorded on a single disc, rather than just one or two songs. Unfortunately, this development led to some exploitation by recording studios. If a song was discovered to be a success, either due to frequent purchases or due to radio popularity, the studio sometimes decided not to release the song as a single, which cost a fraction of a complete album. This forced consumers interested in buying the music to purchase the entire album at a much higher price.

Now answer the questions.

Paragraph 1

S1 No invention was more fundamental to the development of the recording industry than the phonograph.

2   Created in 1877 by Thomas Edison, the phonograph featured a conspicuous flaring horn about 12 inches (30 centimeters) tall, through which sound was projected.

3   The original device played phonographic cylinders, which were soon replaced by records.

4   A record is a disc etched with physical grooves representing the sounds to be replicated.

5   When the disc was rotated at a certain speed, it caused vibrations in a stylus, or needle, that tracked the grooves.

6   These vibrations were then picked up and amplified by a diaphragm, which transmitted sound to the flaring horn.

7   Later versions of the phonograph, beginning in the 1920s, featured an electronic system for translating stylus vibration into sound (these electronic devices became known as "record players" or "turntables").

8   However, the basic mechanisms for recording sound on a rotating disc and reading it with a stylus have remained essentially unchanged from the original invention.

1. The phrase "fundamental to" in the passage is closest in meaning to

   (A) crucial for

   (B) irrelevant to

   (C) typical of

   (D) welcoming toward

2. According to paragraph 1, which of the following is true of the phonograph?

   (A) It is a disc etched with physical grooves representing the sounds to be replicated.

   (B) Many of its original design features are similar to those of record players today.

   (C) The stylus of a phonograph projects sound directly through the flaring horn.

   (D) The original phonograph used electronics to translate stylus vibration into sound.

Paragraph 2

S1   The phonograph was originally marketed as a business and legal services device.

2   Edison's sales strategies targeted businesspeople, attorneys, and anyone else who might use shorthand or dictation as a means of recording ideas or spoken testimony.

3   However, the phonograph eventually found its primary market elsewhere: the recording of sound for entertainment purposes.

4   This market started with "phonograph parlors," the first of which appeared in 1889 in San Francisco.

5   Customers would go to parlors and order a selection to be played for a nickel.

6   This system was the **precursor** of the modern-day jukebox.

7   Within a decade, nearly every major city in the United States had at least one phonograph parlor.

3. The phrase "**precursor**" in the passage is closest in meaning to
    (A) descendant
    (B) inventor
    (C) antithesis
    (D) forerunner

4. Which of the following can be inferred about Edison's sales strategies from paragraph 2?
    (A) Edison eventually stopped targeting businesspeople and attorneys entirely.
    (B) Edison failed to seize sales opportunities in San Francisco.
    (C) Edison was initially wrong about the primary market for recording technology.
    (D) Edison preferred businesspeople and attorneys over other types of customers.

Paragraph 3

S1   During the period 1890–1940, the recording industry was dominated by three companies: Victor, Columbia, and His Master's Voice, or HMV.

2   By 1900, the industry was selling over 3 million records per year in the United States.

3   The next two decades saw great prosperity in the industry, which attracted competition from a host of smaller producers.

4   The competitors began undercutting each other's prices, while the phonograph itself was facing stiff competition from a new technology: radio.

5   Radio programs offered special programming not available on records and featured a seemingly endless variety of available music.

6   This caused many customers to stop purchasing records and to listen to the radio instead.

7   During the 1920s, revenue from the sale of recorded music fell by 50 percent as a result of these developments, which were followed by the onset of the Great Depression in late 1929.

8   Many producers went out of business.

9   It was not until the late 1930s, with the rising popularity of the combination radio-phonograph, the growing use of recorded sound in "talking" movies, and the recovery of the economy, that the recording industry began to recuperate.

5. According to paragraph 3, which of the following helped the major recording studios recuperate in the late 1930s?

   (A) The advent of so-called "talking" movies

   (B) A reduction in competitive pressure from smaller studios

   (C) Government restrictions on radio broadcasts of copyrighted material

   (D) Special programming that featured a nearly endless variety of music

6. Which of the following can be inferred from the author's claim in paragraph 3 that prosperity in the recording industry attracted competition from smaller producers?

   (A) The prosperity was caused by competition among the major recording studios.

   (B) The smaller producers were the driving force behind the rise of radio.

   (C) None of the smaller producers were positioned to become as dominant as the three major studios.

   (D) The prosperity eventually helped undermine itself through increased competition that lowered prices.

Paragraph 4

S1   The industry then experienced a boon in the 1940s.

2   During World War II, the demand for recorded music for use in the United States armed services skyrocketed, leading to a temporary surge in the sales of recorded music despite rationing among consumers back home.

3   At the same time, several lawsuits were brought forth by musicians against radio companies, who paid a royalty to the copyright owner (usually the studio) whenever recorded material was played.

4   No royalty was paid to the musicians themselves.

5   This led to a musicians' strike that lasted over two years, causing difficulties for the recording studios in the short term.

6   However, the studios rebounded quickly when the strike ended, and radio broadcasters, the chief competitors to recording studios, now faced having to pay royalties to songwriters for every song they played.

7.   The word "skyrocketed" in the passage is closest in meaning to

  (A) nosedived

  (B) mushroomed

  (C) plummeted

  (D) hovered

8.   According to paragraph 4, why did musicians go on strike?

  (A) To create financial difficulty for the recording studios

  (B) To pressure radio companies to pay them royalties

  (C) To enable musicians to initiate lawsuits against the radio companies

  (D) To become sole copyright owners of the music they created

Paragraph 5

S1   The late 1940s also saw the introduction of an important new technology: "high fidelity" recording, which enabled sound recording over the complete range of audible frequencies with very little distortion.

2   This technology allowed for the recording of sound that was much more **authentic** with respect to the original musical performance than was previously feasible.

3   High fidelity, or "hi-fi," also enabled entire albums to be recorded on a single disc, rather than just one or two songs.

4   Unfortunately, this development led to some exploitation by recording studios.

5   If a song was discovered to be a success, either due to frequent purchases or due to radio popularity, the studio sometimes decided not to release the song as a single, which cost a fraction of a complete album.

6   This forced consumers interested in buying the music to purchase the entire album at a much higher price.

9.   Which of the sentences below best expresses the essential information in the highlighted sentence in paragraph 5? Incorrect choices change the meaning in important ways or leave out essential information.

   (A) Sometimes the studio decided not to release a more expensive, complete album of songs discovered to be popular via purchase or radio play.

   (B) If songs were successful on the radio or at the point of purchase, the studio decided at times to release them as singles costing much less than complete albums.

   (C) Popular songs were often only released as part of a complete album, which cost more than a single.

   (D) At times, successful songs were either frequently purchased by customers or discovered by the studio to be popular on the radio.

10. The word "**authentic**" in the passage is closest in meaning to
   (A) artificial
   (B) old-fashioned
   (C) accurate
   (D) innovative

Paragraph 5

S1   The late 1940s also saw the introduction of an important new technology: "high fidelity" recording, which enabled sound recording over the complete range of audible frequencies with very little distortion.

2-3   **A** This technology allowed for the recording of sound that was much more authentic with respect to the original musical performance than was previously feasible. High fidelity, or "hi-fi," also enabled entire albums to be recorded on a single disc, rather than just one or two songs.

4-5   **B** Unfortunately, this development led to some exploitation by major recording studios. If a song was discovered to be a success, either due to frequent purchases or due to radio popularity, the studio sometimes decided not to release the song as a single, which cost a fraction of a complete album.

6   **C** This forced consumers interested in buying the music to purchase the entire album at a much higher price.

End   **D**

Look at the part of the passage that is displayed above. The letters [A], [B], [C], and [D] indicate where the following sentence could be added.

11. **As a result, many customers stopped purchasing music produced by major recording studios and shifted their spending toward recordings produced by smaller labels.**

Where would the sentence best fit?

(A) Choice A

(B) Choice B

(C) Choice C

(D) Choice D

12. This passage is developed primarily by

(A) chronicling important technological and business developments of an industry

(B) contrasting multiple interpretations of historical events

(C) evaluating the merits and drawbacks of the practices of the major recording studios

(D) describing the development of recording technology and its application across industries

Select from the six choices below TWO that characterize recorded music, TWO that characterize radio, and TWO that characterize both. This question is worth 2 points.

Recorded Music	Radio	Both
•	•	•
•	•	•

13. [A] Offered special programming and a wide variety of available music

[B] Began with the invention of the phonograph

[C] Suffered because of the musicians' strike in the 1940s

[D] Suffered greatly during the Great Depression

[E] Enabled sound to be heard for entertainment purposes

[F] Forced by lawsuits to pay royalties to musicians

3.8 Paleolithic Cave Art

The Paleolithic era is the period of history commonly known as "the Stone Age." It begins with the appearance of stone tools around 2.5 million years ago and ends approximately 12,000 years ago. It is quite late during the Paleolithic period—only around 40,000 years ago—that cave art first appears in the archaeological record. Found in various locations across the globe, sometimes deep in the inner chambers of caves and sometimes closer to their openings, this art reveals a modern human species that had evolved sufficiently to comprehend and appreciate symbolism.

Cave art is often divided into two categories: figurative (depicting animals and humans) and non-figurative (shapes that aren't animals or humans). Within both of these categories, the prevailing hypothesis is that the purpose of much of the art was to serve the spiritual practices of early humans. This is particularly likely in cases in which the art has been found deep within distant caverns, in locations that took great effort to reach and that required long, dark treks that might have featured many perilous obstacles, from bears to floods to falling rocks.

Among the oldest cave paintings found to date are those in Indonesia in the Pettakere Cave. Here, paintings of hands, in the form of 26 handprints, date somewhere between 35,000 and 40,000 years ago. The handprints, which are the same color as the cave wall, are outlined in red at the cave's entrance. It is believed that they were created by using the hand as a stencil and then spitting or blowing onto the wall a red dye obtained from certain foliage. Because the handprints appear at the entrance to the cave, it has been suggested that they were created to ward off evil spirits, preventing them from entering. Interestingly, the ritual of marking one's home with a handprint persists among the present-day local population near Pettakere, which has used the cave and others around it for many years. Among contemporary locals, when a new home is erected, both the new owner of a home and a priest will place handprints created with rice flour onto the first new beam of the house.

In Spain's Cantabria province in Europe, there are similar handprint paintings created by using the hand as a stencil and blowing pigment onto the cave wall. The oldest of these has been dated at more than 40,000 years old. The process used to make that determination is called "uranium-thorium dating," in which a sample of calcite that has accumulated on the surface of the paint is removed and analyzed for trace amounts of uranium and thorium to determine the sample's age. Scientists can conclude that whatever lies beneath must be at least as old as the calcite itself, but no upper bound can be placed on the age of the underlying paint. This implies that the paintings in Spain could actually be much more than 40,000 years old, potentially placing them very close to the time when modern humans, *Homo sapiens*, first appeared on the European continent.

Prior to that time, Neanderthals dominated Europe. Dating cave art back this far in history, therefore, could have major implications for our understanding of Neanderthals. If cave art were discovered that dates to the period and location in which the Neanderthals reigned, before the presence of modern humans, it would raise the question about who authored the paintings and whether they were indeed created by *Homo sapiens* at all.

Another important site is in the Chauvet cave in the Ardeche region of southern France. The paintings were found in this cave by a team of French cavers in 1994 and have been dated at around 30,000 years old. While the Chauvet paintings are not the earliest cave art discovered in Europe, they are the earliest figurative cave paintings yet discovered there. The Chauvet paintings are also notable for their breadth. They consist of hundreds of paintings of animals from over a dozen distinct species, including lions, panthers, and bears—predatory animals that do not frequently appear in other cave paintings from the Paleolithic era. Furthermore, deep inside the Chauvet cave are the cave's only human figures, including an intriguing figure that is half man and half bison, and another that is female.

Now answer the questions.

3

Paragraph 1

S1   The Paleolithic era is the period of history commonly known as "the Stone Age."

2   It begins with the appearance of stone tools around 2.5 million years ago and ends approximately 12,000 years ago.

3   It is quite late during the Paleolithic period—only around 40,000 years ago—that cave art first appears in the archaeological record.

4   Found in various locations across the globe, sometimes deep in the inner chambers of caves and sometimes closer to their openings, this art reveals a modern human species that had evolved sufficiently to comprehend and appreciate symbolism.

1. The word "reveals" in the passage is closest in meaning to

   (A) decorates

   (B) inspires

   (C) conceals

   (D) exposes

2. According to paragraph 1, the discovery of cave art first made 40,000 years ago was significant in that it established which of the following?

  Ⓐ An archaeological mystery was solved.

  Ⓑ Much of the art was found deep within caves.

  Ⓒ Those who created it understood symbolism.

  Ⓓ Little other cave art was created after about 40,000 years ago.

Paragraph 2

S1 Cave art is often divided into two categories: figurative (depicting animals and humans) and non-figurative (shapes that aren't animals or humans).

2   Within both of these categories, the prevailing hypothesis is that the purpose of much of the art was to serve the spiritual practices of early humans.

3   This is particularly likely in cases in which the art has been found deep within distant caverns, in locations that took great effort to reach and that required long, dark treks that might have featured many perilous obstacles, from bears to floods to falling rocks.

3. The word "hypothesis" in the passage is closest in meaning to

  Ⓐ approximation

  Ⓑ theory

  Ⓒ conclusion

  Ⓓ analysis

4. Paragraph 2 indicates that in locations deep within caverns, cave art was

  Ⓐ difficult and likely dangerous to access

  Ⓑ impossible to reach without artificial light

  Ⓒ particularly unlikely to have served spiritual needs

  Ⓓ more rarely created than art near cavern openings

5. Which of the following can be inferred from information given in paragraph 2?

  Ⓐ Not all art was necessarily used to serve the spiritual practices of early humans.

  Ⓑ Figurative cave art was more likely to serve spiritual practices of early humans than non-figurative cave art.

  Ⓒ Figurative and non-figurative cave art have been found in similar proportions deep within caverns.

  Ⓓ Perils encountered on the journey deep into caves were represented in the cave art found in such locations.

Paragraph 3

S1   Among the oldest cave paintings found to date are those in Indonesia in the Pettakere Cave.

2   Here, paintings of hands, in the form of 26 handprints, date somewhere between 35,000 and 40,000 years ago.

3   The handprints, which are the same color as the cave wall, are outlined in red at the cave's entrance.

4   It is believed that they were created by using the hand as a stencil and then spitting or blowing onto the wall a red dye obtained from certain foliage.

5   Because the handprints appear at the entrance to the cave, it has been suggested that they were created to ward off evil spirits, preventing them from entering.

6   Interestingly, the ritual of marking one's home with a handprint persists among the present-day local population near Pettakere, which has used the cave and others around it for many years.

7   Among contemporary locals, when a new home is erected, both the new owner of a home and a priest will place handprints created with rice flour onto the first new beam of the house.

6.   The word "obtained" in the passage is closest in meaning to

   (A) rebuffed

   (B) dismissed

   (C) assumed

   (D) extracted

7.   The word "persists" in the passage is closest in meaning to

   (A) fades

   (B) struggles

   (C) endures

   (D) resides

Paragraph 4

P4 S1   In Spain's Cantabria province in Europe, there are similar handprint paintings created by using the hand as a stencil and blowing pigment onto the cave wall.

2   The oldest of these has been dated at more than 40,000 years old.

3   The process used to make that determination is called "uranium-thorium dating," in which a sample of calcite that has accumulated on the surface of the paint is removed and analyzed for trace amounts of uranium and thorium to determine the sample's age.

4   Scientists can conclude that whatever lies beneath must be at least as old as the calcite itself, but no upper bound can be placed on the age of the underlying paint.

5   This **implies** that the paintings in Spain could actually be much more than 40,000 years old, potentially placing them very close to the time when modern humans, *Homo sapiens,* first appeared on the European continent.

Paragraph 5

P5 S1   Prior to that time, Neanderthals dominated Europe.

2   Dating cave art back this far in history, therefore, could have major implications for our understanding of Neanderthals.

3   If cave art were discovered that dates to the period and location in which the Neanderthals reigned, before the presence of modern humans, it would raise questions about who authored the paintings and whether they were indeed created by *Homo sapiens* at all.

8. The word "**implies**" in the passage is closest in meaning to

   (A) assures

   (B) suggests

   (C) disproves

   (D) affirms

9. In paragraphs 4 and 5, what evidence supports the claim that dating European cave art to much earlier than 40,000 years ago raises the question of who created the art?

   (A) When the art was created, it was created with dyes that modern humans did not have access to.

   (B) Prior to 40,000 years ago, Europe was dominated by Neanderthals, not modern humans.

   (C) Neanderthals seem to have been more capable of making figurative cave art than modern humans.

   (D) No upper bound can be placed on the age of the paintings by the uranium-thorium dating technique.

10. It can be inferred from paragraphs 4 and 5 that calcite that has accumulated on cave paintings must

  Ⓐ significantly obscure the painted images underneath

  Ⓑ have preserved the paint from wear and tear, allowing it to survive

  Ⓒ be removed carefully to avoid damage to the art

  Ⓓ be no older than the paintings themselves

Paragraph 6

S1 Another important site is in the Chauvet cave in the Ardeche region of southern France.

2 The paintings were found in this cave by a team of French cavers in 1994 and have been dated at around 30,000 years old.

3 While the Chauvet paintings are not the earliest cave art discovered in Europe, they are the earliest figurative cave paintings yet discovered there.

4 The Chauvet paintings are also notable for their breadth.

5 They consist of hundreds of paintings of animals from over a dozen distinct species, including lions, panthers, and bears—predatory animals that do not frequently appear in other cave paintings from the Paleolithic era.

6 Furthermore, deep inside the Chauvet cave are the cave's only human figures, including an intriguing figure that is half man and half bison, and another that is female.

11. In paragraph 6, the author mentions the figurative paintings discovered in the Chauvet cave in order to

  Ⓐ reinforce why the Chauvet cave paintings are considered remarkable

  Ⓑ point out that older non-figurative cave paintings have been discovered elsewhere in Europe

  Ⓒ underscore the fact that cave paintings can only be approximately dated

  Ⓓ assert the unique representations of certain predatory animals in these paintings

12. In paragraph 6, which of the following is NOT offered as a reason for which the Chauvet cave is regarded as significant?

  Ⓐ In 1994, a team of French cavers discovered the paintings, with colors still vibrant after 30,000 years.

  Ⓑ The cave contains the earliest figurative cave paintings yet discovered in Europe.

  Ⓒ At least one of the human figures represented deep within the cave is thought to be interesting.

  Ⓓ A broad range of animals are depicted, including predators rarely thus shown.

Paragraph 1

S1   The Paleolithic era is the period of history commonly known as "the Stone Age."

2   [A] It begins with the appearance of stone tools around 2.5 million years ago and ends approximately 12,000 years ago.

3   [B] It is quite late during the Paleolithic period—only around 40,000 years ago—that cave art first appears in the archaeological record.

4   [C] Found in various locations across the globe, sometimes deep in the inner chambers of caves and sometimes closer to their openings, this art reveals a modern human species that had evolved sufficiently to comprehend and appreciate symbolism.

End   [D]

Look at the part of the passage that is displayed above. The letters [A], [B], [C], and [D] indicate where the following sentence could be added.

13. **This cave art from the Paleolithic era consists of symbolic representations created by humans.**

Where would the sentence best fit?

(A) Choice A

(B) Choice B

(C) Choice C

(D) Choice D

An introductory sentence for a brief summary of the passage is provided below. Complete the summary by selecting the THREE answer choices that express the most important ideas in the passage. Some sentences do not belong in the summary because they express ideas that are not presented in the passage or are minor ideas in the passage. This question is worth 2 points.

14. **Paleolithic cave art reveals much about early humans.**

   A Some cave paintings have been dated via analysis of uranium and thorium within calcite that formed on top of the paintings.

   B The cave art created by early humans shows that they were capable of symbolic representation.

   C Human beings have evolved in a variety of ways since the days of the early humans who created cave art tens of thousands of years ago.

   D Paleolithic cave art provides a telling example of the underlying similarity between Neanderthals and early *Homo sapiens*.

   E Art deep within caves most likely had spiritual purposes, but art near cave entrances, such as handprints, may have also been part of ritual practice.

   F Methods that date cave paintings to 40,000 years ago or more raise questions about the painters, including their exact species.

3.9 Synesthesia

Does the sound of music have a color to you? Can you taste the sight of a particular shade of blue? Few people can. For most of us, the five primary senses—sight, hearing, taste, smell, and touch—are distinct categories; our brains process these sensory experiences as separate from one another and fundamentally unique. But for certain people known as "synesthetes," things are not so straightforward. For these people, the stimulation of one sense may trigger the activation of one or more other senses.

Just how prevalent synesthesia is remains unknown. Estimates range from 1 in 20 people to 1 in 25,000 people. The most common type of synesthesia is called "grapheme-color synesthesia," or seeing different letters as different colors. Still, there are many people who experience other forms of overlapping senses. One such person was the American composer Leonard Bernstein, who reported that when he listened to music, the timbre[1] of various sounds appeared to him visually as varied colors.

Other synesthetes may even have multiple forms of the condition at once. Twentieth-century Russian journalist Solomon Shereshevsky, for example, is reputed to have had a spectacular memory—he could memorize a speech word for word after hearing it only once, and could remember a complicated math formula within a strikingly short time frame. The method by which he did so was synesthesia, which for him existed among all five senses.

How does synesthesia work? In recent decades, scientists have been able to uncover the neurological basis for some kinds of synesthesia. Grapheme-color synesthetes, for example, display uncharacteristic neural

---

timbre[1]: the particular quality or tenor of sound or music, distinguishing, say, violins from trumpets playing the same note

activity in the color-based region of the visual cortex of their brains while reading, while people who are not grapheme-color synesthetes do not.

The genetic basis of synesthesia, however, remains somewhat of a mystery. In the early days of genetic research into the phenomenon, scientists hypothesized that the gene that brought about synesthesia was a dominant one located on the X chromosome. This was believed in part because the phenomenon appeared to be more common among women than men.

This belief has changed, however, as new research has challenged it. While there does appear to be a genetic basis of some sort, as revealed by the unusual brain activity associated with the condition, several developments have undermined the hypothesis that a dominant gene on the X chromosome is the precise genetic mechanism. One such development is that while early studies showed that more women than men are synesthetes, more recent and rigorous studies have suggested a more even distribution between the sexes. Furthermore, synesthesia can skip a generation, which means that if there is a gene for synesthesia, it cannot be a dominant gene, because dominant genes are not able to skip generations.

A study of a pair of identical female twins, one of whom is synesthetic and one of whom is not, raised further questions about the genetic basis of the phenomenon. Identical twins have the same genetic code—all of their genes are identical. For one to be synesthetic and the other not to be, therefore, is peculiar. The study raised the possibility of whether synesthesia can be environmentally triggered or suppressed. At the very least, it suggested there might be some explanation beyond the simple inheritance or non-inheritance of a synesthesia-causing gene.

But there is little evidence that synesthesia can be manipulated by one's environment. Efforts to "train" people to be synesthetes have been unsuccessful compared to actual synesthetes. While people can "teach" their brains to correlate certain letters with certain colors, for instance, the neural activity in their brains remains distinct from that of people who are naturally synesthetic.

A likely possibility is that the genetic basis for synesthesia does indeed lie on the X chromosome, as predicted by early researchers, and that the twin study can be explained by a phenomenon called "X-inactivation." X-inactivation is the process by which one of a female's two X chromosomes is rendered essentially inactive by the other X chromosome. X-inactivation occurs randomly and at the cellular level during the earliest stages of development of the female. In other words, one X chromosome may be active in one cell (while the other one is silenced), but in the neighboring cell, the situation is reversed. This genetic phenomenon could explain the twin study, because it leads to a different expression of the same genes in two female twins, which is precisely what was observed.

Now answer the questions.

Paragraph 1

S1   Does the sound of music have a color to you?

2   Can you taste the sight of a particular shade of blue?

3   Few people can.

4   For most of us, the five primary senses—sight, hearing, taste, smell, and touch—are distinct categories; our brains process these sensory experiences as separate from one another and fundamentally unique.

5   But for certain people known as "synesthetes," things are not so straightforward.

6   For these people, the stimulation of one sense may trigger the activation of one or more other senses.

1. The word "shade" in the passage is closest in meaning to

    (A) hue

    (B) glimpse

    (C) shadow

    (D) light

2. Which of the following can be inferred from paragraph 1?

    (A) The purpose of sensory perception is to separate sensory experiences into separate categories.

    (B) Generally, synesthetes process sensory experiences as unique and independent.

    (C) Sensory perception is substantially more difficult for synesthetes than for others.

    (D) Synesthetes do not always perceive different sensory experiences as separate and unique.

Paragraph 2

S1   Just how prevalent synesthesia is remains unknown.

2   Estimates range from 1 in 20 people to 1 in 25,000 people.

3   The most common type of synesthesia is called "grapheme-color synesthesia," or seeing different letters as different colors.

4   Still, there are many people who experience other forms of overlapping senses.

5   One such person was the American composer Leonard Bernstein, who reported that when he listened to music, the timbre of various sounds appeared to him visually as varied colors.

3. The word "prevalent" in the passage is closest in meaning to

    (A) successful

    (B) common

    (C) influential

    (D) unfavorable

4. According to paragraph 2, what kind of synesthesia did Leonard Bernstein experience?

    (A) When the colors in his field of vision changed, he heard different sounds.

    (B) Different qualities of sounds appeared to him as various colors.

    (C) The louder the music he heard was, the more colorful his vision became.

    (D) It was impossible for him to hear music without seeing letters.

Paragraph 3

P3 S1   Other synesthetes may even have multiple forms of the condition at once.

2   Twentieth-century Russian journalist Solomon Shereshevsky, for example, is reputed to have had a spectacular memory—he could memorize a speech word for word after hearing it only once, and could remember a complicated math formula within a strikingly short time frame.

3   The method by which he did so was synesthesia, which for him existed among all five senses.

Paragraph 4

P4 S1   How does synesthesia work?

2   In recent decades, scientists have been able to uncover the neurological basis for some kinds of synesthesia.

3   Grapheme-color synesthetes, for example, display uncharacteristic neural activity in the color-based region of the visual cortex of their brains while reading, while people who are not grapheme-color synesthetes do not.

5. According to paragraph 3, Solomon Shereshevsky had a remarkable memory because of which of the following?

    (A) He could quickly recall complex math formulas.

    (B) He primarily used vivid colors to remember.

    (C) His memories involved several senses at once.

    (D) He worked as a Russian journalist in the twentieth century.

6. Which of the sentences below best expresses the essential information in the highlighted portion of the passage? Incorrect choices change the meaning in important ways or leave out essential information.

   (A) When grapheme-color synesthetcs read, a region of their brains related to perceiving color are unusually active.

   (B) Grapheme-color synesthetes read when their brains display unusual activity in a color-based region of the visual cortex.

   (C) While reading text in various colors, grapheme-color synesthetes show unusual activity in the visual cortex of their brains.

   (D) The brains of grapheme-color synesthetes are unusually active in the color-based region of the visual cortex.

Paragraph 5

P5 S1 The genetic basis of synesthesia, however, remains somewhat of a mystery.

   2 In the early days of genetic research into the phenomenon, scientists hypothesized that the gene that brought about synesthesia was a dominant one located on the X chromosome.

   3 This was believed in part because the phenomenon appeared to be more common among women than men.

Paragraph 6

P6 S1 This belief has changed, however, as new research has challenged it.

   2 While there does appear to be a genetic basis of some sort, as revealed by the unusual brain activity associated with the condition, several developments have undermined the hypothesis that a dominant gene on the X chromosome is the precise genetic mechanism.

   3 One such development is that while early studies showed that more women than men are synesthetes, more recent and rigorous studies have suggested a more even distribution between the sexes.

   4 Furthermore, synesthesia can skip a generation, which means that if there is a gene for synesthesia, it cannot be a dominant gene, because dominant genes are not able to skip generations.

7. Which of the following can be inferred from paragraphs 5 and 6 about the studies showing synesthesia to be more common among women than men?

   (A) They have undermined an early hypothesis about the genetic basis of synesthesia.

   (B) They were correct at the time, but recent population changes have made them irrelevant.

   (C) They seem to have not been as accurate as later studies investigating the same issue.

   (D) They superseded earlier studies showing synesthesia to be evenly distributed between the sexes.

8. According to paragraph 5, synesthesia was once believed by researchers to be caused by

    (A) a gene situated on the non-dominant X chromosome

    (B) a non-dominant gene present only in women's chromosomes

    (C) a dominant gene that was situated on the X chromosome

    (D) a dominant gene not located on the X chromosome

9. According to paragraph 6, which of the following is true in general of genes that are dominant?

    (A) They are not located on the X chromosome.

    (B) They form the genetic basis of conditions such as synesthesia.

    (C) They are more evenly distributed between the sexes than previously thought.

    (D) They do not skip generations.

Paragraph 7

S1 A study of a pair of identical female twins, one of whom is synesthetic and one of whom is not, raised further questions about the genetic basis of the phenomenon.

2 Identical twins have the same genetic code—all of their genes are identical.

3 For one to be synesthetic and the other not to be, therefore, is peculiar.

4 The study raised the possibility of whether synesthesia can be environmentally triggered or suppressed.

5 At the very least, it suggested there might be some explanation beyond the simple inheritance or non-inheritance of a synesthesia-causing gene.

10. According to paragraph 7, the study of the two identical twins provided reason to believe which of the following?

    (A) Environmental factors may be able to cause or at least trigger synesthesia.

    (B) It is unlikely that synesthesia is influenced by genetic conditions.

    (C) The non-synesthetic twin lacked the gene for synesthesia that the other twin had.

    (D) Claims of synesthetic experiences by just one twin were probably mistaken.

Paragraph 8

S1 But there is little evidence that synesthesia can be manipulated by one's environment.

2 Efforts to "train" people to be synesthetes have been unsuccessful compared to actual synesthetes.

3 While people can "teach" their brains to correlate certain letters with certain colors, for instance, the neural activity in their brains remains distinct from that of people who are naturally synesthetic.

  MANHATTAN PREP

11. The word "correlate" in the passage is closest in meaning to

   (A) present

   (B) provide

   (C) repress

   (D) associate

Paragraph 9

S1 A likely possibility is that the genetic basis for synesthesia does indeed lie on the X chromosome, as predicted by early researchers, and that the twin study can be explained by a phenomenon called "X-inactivation."

2 [A] X-inactivation is the process by which one of a female's two X chromosomes is rendered essentially inactive by the other X chromosome.

3–4 [B] X-inactivation occurs randomly and at the cellular level during the earliest stages of development of the female. In other words, one X chromosome may be active in one cell (while the other one is silenced), but in the neighboring cell, the situation is reversed.

5 [C] This genetic phenomenon could explain the twin study, because it leads to a different expression of the same genes in two female twins, which is precisely what was observed.

End [D]

> Look at the part of the passage that is displayed above. The letters [A], [B], [C], and [D] indicate where the following sentence could be added.

12. **In contrast, X-inactivation is not experienced by males, who have only one X chromosome.**

   Where would the sentence best fit?
   (A) Choice A

   (B) Choice B

   (C) Choice C

   (D) Choice D

13. Which of the following best describes the author's presentation of information in the passage?

   (A) A number of studies are presented to support the assertion that synesthesia is primarily an environmental phenomenon.

   (B) The author uses logic to show that doubt about the causes of synesthesia is unwarranted.

   (C) The author introduces the condition of synesthesia and explores possible causes.

   (D) Two opposing points of view about synesthesia are described; the author concludes by advocating for further research.

An introductory sentence for a brief summary of the passage is provided below. Complete the summary by selecting the THREE answer choices that express the most important ideas in the passage. Some sentences do not belong in the summary because they express ideas that are not presented in the passage or are minor ideas in the passage. This question is worth 2 points.

14. **Synesthesia is a neurological phenomenon by which a small percentage of people have blended sensory experiences.**

   A   Great musicians and geniuses are often synesthetes, perceiving their medium in ways non-synesthetes cannot.

   B   Synesthesia manifests itself in various forms and can involve two or more senses at once.

   C   The true prevalence of synesthesia is likely to continue to be unknown.

   D   Research suggests that synesthesia may be linked to a gene located on the X chromosome.

   E   The neurological activity of synesthetes is unusual, in a way that cannot be simulated, it seems.

   F   As inherited genetic material, dominant genes are unable to skip generations.

3.10 Communication through Gesture

"Choking"

Throughout the world, people communicate using body language. Communicating through nonverbal, or physical, "language" occurs within and across cultures. Research has shown that gesture plays numerous roles in the effectiveness of our communication. Speech accompanied by gesture has been found to be much more engaging to the listener, and therefore greatly improves comprehension. Gesture during speech has been correlated with speakers who rise as leaders in society. Gesturing can also be beneficial to the speaker: one study found that children who were forced to gesture while talking through math problems learned better than children who were forced not to gesture. The gesturing children later scored higher on tests of similar problems.

The act of gesturing during speech is as universal as speech itself, and in fact, both vocalizing and gesturing physically involve the same area of the brain, leading scientists to surmise that they are evolutionarily linked. Even blind people gesture when speaking to other blind people. Helen Keller, the author and activist, and the first deafblind person to earn a bachelor of arts degree, had learned by the age of seven to communicate with her parents by hand gestures. Soon after, she learned a manual alphabet through finger spelling.

With regard to specific physical gestures, some are universal, while others vary across cultures. Some anthropologists and psychologists believe the smile to be a universal gesture for happiness or contentment. Another gesture believed to be universal is the act of a child stroking his or her own cheek, often with the back of the palm, to call for his or her mother. It has been reported that this gesture occurs spontaneously among children across cultures who have not been taught it. Additionally, some believe that clutching at one's throat is a universal sign for choking, and that displaying one's hands raised high above one's head is a universal display of triumph.

There is far more variation in gesturing across cultures than commonality, however. A gesture that varies by culture is holding up two fingers, the first and second fingers, in a skyward V-shape. In the United States, this is a gesture for "peace." In Australia, New Zealand, and the United Kingdom, however, it is used to signify contempt for authority. Accordingly, it is regarded as hostile and potentially rude. Similarly, an upward thumb ("thumbs up" in American English) is used to express approval in the United States, Australia, Canada, the United Kingdom, and Russia. But in Latin America, West Africa, Iran, Iraq, and Afghanistan, it is an insult. And wagging the index finger to beckon "come here" in the United States is, in the Philippines, considered insulting when directed toward another person; there, it is restricted to beckoning dogs. Therefore, to use it toward a person indicates that you see that person as inferior. Finally, in Japan, it is polite to give an object to another person using two hands, but not with only one—a behavior that is viewed as acceptable and harmless in other places.

A multicultural, transnational community that makes regular and systematic use of gesture to communicate is the deaf community. Unlike the casual gestures used sporadically within a culture to express opinion and emotion, including exaggerated gestures for effect (such as pantomime), within the deaf community there exist fully developed sign languages that correspond to spoken language. There is, however, no universal sign language used across cultures. For example, Denmark, Germany, France, and Turkey all have distinct sign languages. In the United States and the English-speaking parts of Canada, the primary sign language used in deaf communities is American Sign Language (ASL). ASL is closely related to French Sign Language (FSL), and ASL dialects are also used in other countries around the world, including in West Africa and parts of Southeast Asia.

Now answer the questions.

Paragraph 1

S1   Throughout the world, people communicate using body language.

2   Communicating through nonverbal, or physical, "language" occurs within and across cultures.

3   Research has shown that gesture plays numerous roles in the effectiveness of our communication.

4   Speech accompanied by gesture has been found to be much more engaging to the listener, and therefore greatly improves comprehension.

5   Gesture during speech has been correlated with speakers who rise as leaders in society.

6   Gesturing can also be beneficial to the speaker: one study found that children who were forced to gesture while talking through math problems learned better than children who were forced not to gesture.

7   The gesturing children later scored higher on tests of similar problems.

1.   The phrase "accompanied by" in the passage is closest in meaning to

  (A) studied with

  (B) betrayed by

  (C) unlinked to

  (D) paired with

2.   According to paragraph 1, there is evidence that gesturing helps children to

  (A) study math more effectively between tests

  (B) help each other grasp quantitative concepts

  (C) do math in a more concrete, informal way using their hands

  (D) be more successful at learning math

Paragraph 2

S1   The act of gesturing during speech is as universal as speech itself, and in fact, both vocalizing and gesturing physically involve the same area of the brain, leading scientists to surmise that they are evolutionarily linked.

2   Even blind people gesture when speaking to other blind people.

3   Helen Keller, the author and activist, and the first deafblind person to earn a bachelor of arts degree, had learned by the age of seven to communicate with her parents by hand gestures.

4   Soon after, she learned a manual alphabet through finger spelling.

3. The word "surmise" in the passage is closest in meaning to

   (A) speculate

   (B) doubt

   (C) confirm

   (D) deny

4. All of the following are mentioned about gesturing in paragraph 2 EXCEPT:

   (A) It involves the same part of the brain as speaking.

   (B) It was used by Helen Keller to communicate with her parents.

   (C) Its occurrence during speech is as universal as speech itself.

   (D) It is more suited to communicating subtle ideas than speech.

5. According to paragraph 2, how was Helen Keller able to use an alphabet composed of gestures?

   (A) She learned it.

   (B) She discovered it independently.

   (C) She developed it while earning her degree.

   (D) It was taught to her by her parents.

Paragraph 3

S1	With regard to specific physical gestures, some are universal, while others vary across cultures.
2	Some anthropologists and psychologists believe the smile to be a universal gesture for happiness or contentment.
3	Another gesture believed to be universal is the act of a child stroking his or her own cheek, often with the back of the palm, to call for his or her mother.
4	It has been reported that this gesture occurs spontaneously among children across cultures who have not been taught it.
5	Additionally, some believe that clutching at one's throat is a universal sign for choking, and that displaying one's hands raised high above one's head is a universal display of triumph.

6. The word "reported" in the passage is closest in meaning to

   (A) verified

   (B) alleged

   (C) concealed

   (D) flaunted

7. According to paragraph 3, what do some people believe about the gesture used by a child to call for his or her mother?

   (A) It can also mean triumph.

   (B) It typically involves the front of the palm.

   (C) It is shared universally.

   (D) It represents a stroke on the cheek that a mother might give.

8. How is paragraph 3 related to other aspects of the discussion of gesture in the passage?

   (A) It describes a dispute between two schools of thought about gestures.

   (B) It challenges earlier claims about gestures and presents a compromise.

   (C) It applies general concepts discussed earlier to specific examples of gestures.

   (D) It outlines a process through which gestures achieve qualities previously discussed.

Paragraph 4

S1	There is far more variation in gesturing across cultures than commonality, however.
2	A gesture that varies by culture is holding up two fingers, the first and second fingers, in a skyward V-shape.
3	In the United States, this is a gesture for "peace."
4	In Australia, New Zealand, and the United Kingdom, however, it is used to signify contempt for authority.
5	Accordingly, it is regarded as hostile and potentially rude.
6	Similarly, an upward thumb ("thumbs up" in American English) is used to express approval in the United States, Australia, Canada, the United Kingdom, and Russia.
7	But in Latin America, West Africa, Iran, Iraq, and Afghanistan, it is an insult.
8	And wagging the index finger to beckon "come here" in the United States is, in the Philippines, considered insulting when directed toward another person; there, it is **restricted to** beckoning dogs.
9	Therefore, to use it toward a person indicates that you see that person as inferior.
10	Finally, in Japan, it is polite to give an object to another person using two hands, but not with only one—a behavior that is viewed as acceptable and harmless in other places.

9. It can be inferred from paragraph 4 that

    (A) in the Philippines, one may find it offensive to be addressed with a gesture typically used for dogs

    (B) in Iraq, wagging the index finger is unacceptable

    (C) in the United States, a "thumbs up" is not always a positive gesture

    (D) in Japan, it is polite to use a single hand to pass an object to another person

10. The phrase "restricted to" in the passage is closest in meaning to

    (A) provided to

    (B) banned from

    (C) compressed into

    (D) limited to

Paragraph 5

S1   A multicultural, transnational community that makes regular and systematic use of gesture to communicate is the deaf community.

2   Unlike the casual gestures used sporadically within a culture to express opinion and emotion, including exaggerated gestures for effect (such as pantomime), within the deaf community there exist fully developed sign languages that correspond to spoken language.

3   There is, however, no universal sign language used across cultures.

4   For example, Denmark, Germany, France, and Turkey all have distinct sign languages.

5   In the United States and the English-speaking parts of Canada, the primary sign language used in deaf communities is American Sign Language (ASL).

6   ASL is closely related to French Sign Language (FSL), and ASL dialects are also used in other countries around the world, including in West Africa and parts of Southeast Asia.

11. Which of the sentences below best expresses the essential information in the highlighted portion of the passage? Incorrect choices change the meaning in important ways or leave out essential information.

    (A) Cultures in general tend to use gesture to convey more casual emotion and opinion than is expressed through fully developed sign languages by the deaf community.

    (B) The deaf community makes use of sign languages that are fully developed, unlike casual, expressive gestures used at random by general populations.

    (C) The deaf community uses casual gestures sporadically to express emotion and fully developed sign languages to correspond to spoken language.

    (D) The sporadic, exaggerated use of casual gestures to express emotion and opinion is not limited to the deaf community, which also has developed fully formed sign languages.

12. According to paragraph 5, American Sign Language (ASL) is used as a primary language by deaf communities in at least part of which of the following countries?

   (A) Denmark

   (B) Canada

   (C) France

   (D) Germany

Paragraph 3

S1	With regard to specific physical gestures, some are universal, while others vary across cultures.
2–3	[A] Some anthropologists and psychologists believe the smile to be a universal gesture for happiness or contentment. Another gesture believed to be universal is the act of a child stroking his or her own cheek, often with the back of the palm, to call for his or her mother.
4	[B] It has been reported that this gesture occurs spontaneously among children across cultures who have not been taught it.
5	[C] Additionally, some believe that clutching at one's throat is a universal sign for choking, and that displaying one's hands raised high above one's head is a universal display of triumph.
End	[D]

> Look at the part of the passage that is displayed above. The letters [A], [B], [C], and [D] indicate where the following sentence could be added.

13. **It should be noted, however, that spontaneous usage in an observed number of subjects does not necessarily mean that a gesture is universal.**

Where would the sentence best fit?

   (A) Choice A

   (B) Choice B

   (C) Choice C

   (D) Choice D

An introductory sentence for a brief summary of the passage is provided below. Complete the summary by selecting the THREE answer choices that express the most important ideas in the passage. Some sentences do not belong in the summary because they express ideas that are not presented in the passage or are minor ideas in the passage. This question is worth 2 points.

14. **People in all cultures across the world communicate through gesture.**

A   While communicating through gesture is a universal practice, the meaning of specific gestures tends to vary across cultures.

B   A gesture used commonly to call someone in one culture could be considered demeaning in another culture.

C   Gestural communication systems, as fully developed as spoken languages, are used by deaf communities around the world.

D   How well people learn a new concept can depend on whether gesture was involved.

E   Evidence suggests that the use of gesture during speech has many benefits, from helping children learn to improving the effectiveness of communication.

F   American Sign Language (ASL) is not used as a primary language outside of the United States.

Answer Key—3.1 Realism and Modernism in Literary Fiction

Question	Correct Answer	Right/Wrong	Category
1	C		Vocabulary
2	D		Negative Fact
3	B		Vocabulary
4	C		Purpose
5	D		Vocabulary
6	C		Fact
7	A		Inference
8	A		Negative Fact
9	A		Vocabulary
10	B		Fact
11	D		Vocabulary
12	B		Fact
13	C		Insert Text
14	A, B, D		Summary

Answer Key—3.2 Modern Schools of Acting

Question	Correct Answer	Right/Wrong	Category
1	B		Fact
2	A		Fact
3	C		Fact
4	D		Simplify Sentence
5	A		Vocabulary
6	C		Negative Fact
7	C		Vocabulary
8	B		Negative Fact
9	A		Fact
10	B		Vocabulary
11	D		Vocabulary
12	C		Purpose
13	D		Insert Text
14	A, C, E		Summary

MANHATTAN PREP

Answer Key—3.3 Habitats of the Blues

Question	Correct Answer	Right/Wrong	Category
1	C		Inference
2	B		Simplify Sentence
3	D		Vocabulary
4	D		Negative Fact
5	A		Vocabulary
6	C		Vocabulary
7	A		Purpose
8	B		Fact
9	C		Fact
10	A		Reference
11	D		Insert Text
12	Rural: B, E. Urban: A, C, F. Both: D.		Table

Answer Key—3.4 Photography

Question	Correct Answer	Right/Wrong	Category
1	A		Vocabulary
2	D		Fact
3	C		Vocabulary
4	C		Simplify Sentence
5	B		Negative Fact
6	A		Vocabulary
7	A		Fact
8	D		Vocabulary
9	B		Fact
10	C		Inference
11	B		Purpose
12	D		Reference
13	D		Insert Text
14	B, C, F		Summary

3

Answer Key—3.5 Stream of Consciousness

Question	Correct Answer	Right/Wrong	Category
1	C		Inference
2	D		Negative Fact
3	A		Vocabulary
4	A		Simplify Sentence
5	B		Vocabulary
6	D		Fact
7	D		Vocabulary
8	C		Fact
9	C		Purpose
10	B		Vocabulary
11	A		Fact
12	B		Fact
13	A		Insert Text
14	C, D, E		Summary

Answer Key—3.6 Henri Cartier-Bresson

Question	Correct Answer	Right/Wrong	Category
1	B		Vocabulary
2	C		Inference
3	D		Negative Fact
4	A		Vocabulary
5	B		Fact
6	C		Purpose
7	D		Reference
8	A		Fact
9	C		Vocabulary
10	A		Fact
11	B		Vocabulary
12	D		Fact
13	D		Insert Text
14	A, D, F		Summary

Answer Key—3.7 History of the Recording Industry

Question	Correct Answer	Right/Wrong	Category
1	A		Vocabulary
2	B		Fact
3	D		Vocabulary
4	C		Inference
5	A		Fact
6	D		Inference
7	B		Vocabulary
8	B		Fact
9	C		Simplify Sentence
10	C		Vocabulary
11	D		Insert Text
12	A		Purpose
13	Recorded: B, D. Radio: A, F. Both: C, E.		Table

Answer Key—3.8 Paleolithic Cave Art

Question	Correct Answer	Right/Wrong	Category
1	D		Vocabulary
2	C		Fact
3	B		Vocabulary
4	A		Fact
5	A		Inference
6	D		Vocabulary
7	C		Vocabulary
8	B		Vocabulary
9	B		Fact
10	D		Inference
11	A		Purpose
12	A		Negative Fact
13	C		Insert Text
14	B, E, F		Summary

Answer Key—3.9 Synesthesia

Question	Correct Answer	Right/Wrong	Category
1	A		Vocabulary
2	D		Inference
3	B		Vocabulary
4	B		Fact
5	C		Fact
6	A		Simplify Sentence
7	C		Inference
8	C		Fact
9	D		Fact
10	A		Fact
11	D		Vocabulary
12	B		Insert Text
13	C		Purpose
14	B, D, E		Summary

Answer Key—3.10 Communication through Gesture

Question	Correct Answer	Right/Wrong	Category
1	D		Vocabulary
2	D		Fact
3	A		Vocabulary
4	D		Negative Fact
5	A		Fact
6	B		Vocabulary
7	C		Fact
8	C		Purpose
9	A		Inference
10	D		Vocabulary
11	B		Simplify Sentence
12	B		Fact
13	C		Insert Text
14	A, C, E		Summary

Answers and Explanations—
3.1 Realism and Modernism in Literary Fiction

Paragraph 1	Comments
S1 While today we tend to think of realism—the attempt to portray real life as accurately as possible—as one of the major goals of literary fiction, this mode of representation was a revolutionary idea in the middle of the nineteenth century.	Realism is a major goal in fiction today. But it was once an innovation.
2 With the goal of accurate presentation of real life in mind, nineteenth-century novelists embraced new subject matter for their work: the mundane details of everyday, usually middle- and lower-class lives.	Realists chose new subject matter (everyday lives).

1.   The word "representation" in the passage is closest in meaning to

    ✗   (A) election

    ✗   (B) metaphor

    ✓   (C) portrayal

    ✗   (D) study

VOCABULARY. In this context, "representation" = picture, illustration, demonstration, description.

Unrelated. This wasn't a mode (way or approach) of election.

A metaphor compares two things to hint at a deeper meaning: the moon is a pie. Novelists might sometimes use metaphor to illustrate a point. But in general, "representation" means a more general way to show or illustrate things.

CORRECT. "This mode of representation was a revolutionary idea" = this kind of portrayal, or way of portraying or showing, was revolutionary.

Unrelated. This wasn't a mode (way) of studying.

2.   Which of the following questions about literary realism is NOT answered in paragraph 1?

    ✗   (A) When did literary realism first develop?

    ✗   (B) What was the goal of literary realism?

    ✗   (C) What subject matter did literary realists draw on?

    ✓   (D) How did realism change the style and structure of authors' writings?

NEGATIVE FACT. Three answer choices contain questions that are answered somewhere in P1. One answer choice contains a question that isn't answered in P1.

S1 states that literary realism was "revolutionary ... in the middle of the nineteenth century." So that's when this mode of fiction first developed, according to P1.

S2 notes that the goal was the "accurate presentation of real life."

S2 states that the "new subject matter"of the realists was "the mundane details of everyday ... lives."

CORRECT. This question isn't addressed or answered until the second paragraph.

3. The word "**mundane**" in the passage is closest in meaning to

    ✗ (A) extraordinary

    ✓ (B) routine

    ✗ (C) sophisticated

    ✗ (D) weary

VOCABULARY. "Mundane" = ordinary, everyday, commonplace.

Opposite. "Extraordinary" = remarkable, amazing, very great.

CORRECT. "The mundane details of everyday … lives" = the routine, ordinary details of these lives.

"Sophisticated" = "worldly" in the sense of "experienced, wise in the ways of the world." The word "mundane" can also mean "worldly" in the sense of "having to do with this world" (rather than heaven or other worlds). But mundane and sophisticated are not synonyms.

Unrelated. "Weary" = tired or exhausted.

Paragraph 2	**Comments**
S1 This new subject matter and the desire to represent it accurately placed constraints on these authors.	New subject matter constrained these authors.
2 Realist novelists believed that we can all know and describe an objective reality, and this impacted both the structure and style of their novels.	They believed we can describe an objective reality. This shaped style, structure of novels.
3 Writers in Russia, France, the United Kingdom, and the United States confronted these limitations in similar ways, in spite of their different backgrounds.	Similar problems faced by writers around the world.
4 Because these writers limited themselves to the world they could observe, and not one they could only imagine, realist novels tend to follow certain conventions, so that they remain faithful to real experiences.	Similar conventions in realist novels.
5 For example, most realist novels have linear plots and omniscient, or all-knowing, narrators.	Examples.
6 Plots that move both backward and forward in time, for example, are unusual because they differ from the perception of how our lives naturally unfold.	
7 However, the circumstances of human lives vary widely across time and place; that is why reading Tolstoy's *War and Peace* is a very different experience from reading George Eliot's *Middlemarch*.	But human circumstances vary.
8 What varies is not so much the structure of the novel and the perspective of the narrator but the texture of the places and lives it describes.	So texture & details in these novels vary.
9 The details of everyday experience are thus limiting factors for the realist novelist.	

4. Why does the author mention Russia and the United States in paragraph 2?

PURPOSE. S3: "Writers in Russia ... and the United States confronted these limitations in similar ways, in spite of their different backgrounds." Specific countries are mentioned as illustrations of "different backgrounds," supporting the main point of the sentence (that writers of different backgrounds confronted the issues in similar ways).

✗ (A) To demonstrate that art can reconcile opposing viewpoints

P2 doesn't mention this possible purpose of art.

✗ (B) To describe the migration of realist ideas from one country to another

The author mentions that realism occurred in several countries, but doesn't describe how it moved from place to place.

✓ (C) To illustrate that realism developed in similar ways in different societies

CORRECT. S3 mentions that authors in these different countries faced the challenges of realism "in similar ways."

✗ (D) To introduce an analysis of the novel during times of tension between countries

Times of tension between countries are not mentioned.

5. The word "objective" in the passage is closest in meaning to

VOCABULARY. "Objective" = unbiased, based on facts, observable by everyone in the same way.

✗ (A) personal

Opposite. "Personal" reality would be very subjective, the opposite of objective.

✗ (B) unfeeling

Not quite. "Unfeeling" would describe a person who is cruel and unsympathetic. That's not the same as "objective."

✗ (C) ambiguous

Also opposite. An "ambiguous" reality would have different truths for different people. It would not be observable by everyone in the same way.

✓ (D) factual

CORRECT. S2: "Realist novelists believed that we can all know and describe an objective reality" = they believed we can all describe a factual reality, based in the same set of facts for everyone.

6. According to paragraph 2, which of the following characteristics varies in realist novels written in different countries?

    FACT. S7: "The circumstances of human lives vary widely across time and place." S8: "What varies is not so much the structure of the novel and the perspective of the narrator but the texture of the places and lives it describes." So the answer should be "the texture of the places and lives" or an equivalent expression.

    ✗ (A) Narrative perspective in the novels

    S8: "What varies is not so much … the perspective of the narrator."

    ✗ (B) The structure of the novels

    S8: "What varies is not so much the structure of the novel."

    ✓ (C) Descriptions of particular details of everyday lives

    CORRECT. S8: "What varies is … the texture of the places and lives it describes." In other words, the particular details of everyday lives are different in novels written by realist authors from different countries.

    ✗ (D) The way the plot moves through time

    S5: "most realist novels have linear plots," or plots that move forward through time. S6 states that plots that move backwards and forwards in time are not common in realist novels.

7. Paragraph 2 suggests that which of the following is true of most narrators of realist novels?

    INFERENCE. S5: "most realist novels have … omniscient, or all-knowing, narrators."

    ✓ (A) They are fully aware of the events described.

    CORRECT. S5: most realist narrators are "omniscient, or all-knowing." So you can infer that they are fully aware of the events and other matters described in the novel.

    ✗ (B) Their perspective varies by country.

    S8 notes that the perspective of the narrator doesn't vary so much by country or society.

    ✗ (C) They are usually from the working class.

    P1 mentions that working-class lives often provide material for realist novels. But the paragraph makes no assertion about the class of the narrators.

    ✗ (D) They typically use the third person.

    P2 makes no claim about the person (such as third) that these narrators use, typically or not.

8. According to paragraph 2, all of the following are characteristics of realist novels EXCEPT:

    NEGATIVE FACT. Three answer choices are listed in P2 as characteristics of realist novels. One answer choice contains something else. This answer could be directly contradicted by the passage or just unmentioned as a characteristic of realist novels.

    ✓ (A) These novels include both forward and backward movements in time.

    CORRECT. The passage asserts the opposite. S6: "Plots that move both backward and forward in time … are unusual" (in realist novels).

    ✗ (B) These novels attempt to describe the world as it really is.

    S4 notes that these novels "remain faithful to real experiences." That is, they try to describe the world as it really is.

    ✗ (C) Realist novels based in different societies display features that are alike.

    S3–5 mention that writers in different countries "confronted these limitations in similar ways," and the novels "tend to follow certain conventions," such as "linear plots."

    ✗ (D) These novels are narrated by all-knowing figures.

    The passage states that "most realist novels have … omniscient, or all-knowing, narrators."

Paragraph 3	Comments
S1 One might assume that the same constraints would hold for the next generation of novelists, the modernists.	Modernists were the next generation.
2 Modernists, however, made very different assumptions about how best to represent human life.	Very different from realists.
3 Modernist novelists no longer assumed that the best representation of reality was also the most literal one, as the realists did.	Not as literal in describing reality.
4 Virginia Woolf, for example, strove to describe the way our conscious mind works by focusing more on memory and reflection than on actual experience.	Woolf: more on memory & reflection.
5 Other authors further experimented with unusual language, shifts in time, and fractured sentences, among other devices, to depict the workings of consciousness.	Others experimented with various devices.
6 These authors were still trying to describe human experience, but they no longer took for granted that we all experience the world the same way.	Still focused on human experience. But for modernists, humans experience in different ways.
7 For example, William Faulkner, in his novel *The Sound and the Fury*, uses several different narrators who speak with different voices.	Faulkner: several different narrators.
8 He does this to portray the same characters and events from different perspectives.	
9 In other words, he is trying to represent human experience as subjective and varied, rather than as a universally knowable truth.	Represented human experience as subjective.
10 He uses a number of literary devices, including unusual language and shifts in time, to capture variations in how different people think, focusing more on the nature of individual consciousness than on how people live (as the realists did).	

3

9. The phrase "the most literal" in the passage is closest in meaning to

VOCABULARY. "Literal" = exact, precise, accurate, as if letter by letter, without interpretation.

✓ (A) the most exact

CORRECT. S3: "Modernist novelists no longer assumed that the best representation of reality was also the most literal one" = they no longer assumed that the best representation was the most exact or precise one.

✗ (B) the most dramatic

In informal speech, people sometimes use "literally" to dramatize their statements ("I was literally going to die from embarrassment"). This is far from a literal use of the word "literal."

✗ (C) the most enhanced

Somewhat opposite. The enhancements in an "enhanced" (= improved) representation would not be literal. Computer images are sometimes "enhanced" to improve clarity, and so in that particular field, "enhanced" might actually imply a more exact representation. But in typical usage, "enhanced" means "changed for the better" *away* from the original reality.

✗ (D) the simplest

The "simplest" representation might not be the most exact. It could be oversimplified or made too simple.

10. According to paragraph 3, which of the following is an important topic in Virginia Woolf's work?

FACT. S4 is the only sentence that describes Woolf's work directly.

✗ (A) Actual experience

S4 implies the opposite: "focusing more on ... than on actual experience."

✓ (B) Memory

CORRECT. S4 notes that Woolf "strove to describe the way our conscious mind works by focusing more on memory and reflection than on actual experience."

✗ (C) Voice

Voice is not mentioned in S4.

✗ (D) Time shifts

Time shifts are not mentioned in S4.

11. The word "fractured" in the passage is closest in meaning to

VOCABULARY. "Fractured" = cracked or broken.

✗ (A) polished

In a way, the opposite. "Polished" sentences would be accomplished, masterful, or even expertly written.

✗ (B) distorted

Close but not quite. Something can be "distorted" (= twisted, warped) but not broken or cracked.

✗ (C) reinforced

Opposite. "Reinforced" = stronger, enhanced, improved.

✓ (D) splintered

CORRECT. "Fractured" sentences = splintered or broken sentences.

12. According to paragraph 3, which of the following distinguishes William Faulkner's work from that of the realists?

FACT. S7–10 describes Faulkner's work in detail. The author uses Faulkner as an example of how modernists differ from realists, which is the purpose of P3 as a whole. Comparisons of Faulkner to the realists are sometimes explicit, as in S10 ("as the realists did"), or implicit, as in S7 ("rather than as a universally knowable truth").

✗ (A) He did not write about middle- and lower-class lives.

Realists wrote about middle- and lower-class lives, according to earlier paragraphs. But P3 does not state what kinds of lives Faulkner wrote about, with regard to class.

✓ (B) He did not believe that every person perceives his or her reality in a similar way.

CORRECT. S9: "He is trying to represent human experience as subjective and varied, rather than as a universally knowable truth" (as the realists thought).

✗ (C) He desired to capture variations in how people think by using linear plots.

S10: "He uses a number of literary devices, including ... shifts in time, to capture variations in how people think." That is, he did not use the linear plots of the realists to accomplish his goal.

✗ (D) He preferred to use a single, unreliable narrator who is not all-knowing.

S7: "Faulkner ... uses several different narrators who speak with different voices."

3

Paragraph 3	Comments
P3 S10 He uses a number of literary devices, including unusual language and shifts in time, to capture variations in how different people think, focusing more on the nature of individual consciousness than on how people live (as the realists did).	

Paragraph 4	Comments
P4 S1 [A] Even though realism again became a dominant trend in fiction later in the twentieth century, the innovations of the modernists and the way they thought about the purpose of fiction have remained part of the contemporary novel.	You could argue that the "variations in how people think" in P3 S10 matches up to "interior mental operations" in the inserted sentence. But the previous sentence was about Faulkner, whereas the inserted sentence is about "modern-day authors." The transition is jarring. S1 serves as a much better introduction to P4, which focuses on how today's authors make use of both realism and modernism.
2 [B] While later generations of novelists have continued to portray the details of everyday lives as the realists did, they also recognize that the ways different people experience life are shaped by the internal workings of their minds.	S1 doesn't contain anything like "interior mental operations" for the inserted sentence to connect to.
3 [C] Thus, these novelists incorporate both realistic description and innovative style and structure into their work.	**CORRECT.** "Capture those interior mental operations" follows logically from "shaped by the internal workings of their minds." The inserted sentence flows nicely from S2, which states that modern-day authors recognize the underlying idea of modernism. The inserted sentence provides the result: therefore, these authors use modernist devices. Finally, S3 completes the picture: modern-day authors use both realism and modernism ("innovative style and structure").
End [D]	Like S1, S3 lacks anything like "interior mental operations" for the inserted sentence to connect to.

13.   **To capture those interior mental operations, modern-day authors tend to make use of modernist devices, from shifts in time and narrative perspective to stream-of-consciousness narration.**

Where would the sentence best fit?

INSERT TEXT. The inserted sentence begins with "those interior mental operations." So the previous sentence should refer to "interior mental operations," or an equivalent expression. Also, the sentence should not interrupt the existing logical flow of the sentences in P4. Instead, it should add to that flow.

✗ (A) Choice A

✗ (B) Choice B

✓ (C) Choice C   **CORRECT.**

✗ (D) Choice D

	Whole Passage	**Comments**
P1	While today we tend to think of realism …	Realism is a major goal in fiction today. But it was once an innovation. Realists chose new subject matter (everyday lives).
P2	This new subject matter and the desire to represent it accurately placed constraints …	New subject matter constrained these authors. They believed we can describe an objective reality. This shaped style, structure of novels. Similar problems faced by writers around the world. Similar conventions in realist novels. Examples. But human circumstances vary. So texture & details in these novels vary.
P3	One might assume that the same constraints would hold …	Modernists were the next generation. Very different from realists. Not as literal in describing reality. Woolf: more on memory & reflection. Others experimented with various devices. Still focused on human experience. But for modernists, humans experience in different ways. Faulkner: several different narrators. Represented human experience as subjective.
P4	Even though realism again became a dominant trend …	Realism became a dominant trend again. But contemporary authors draw on both traditions.

3

14. **Realism, a mode of representing real life accurately in literary fiction, was actually revolutionary in the mid-nineteenth century.**

SUMMARY. Correct answers must be clearly expressed in the passage. They must also be among the major points of the passage. They should tie as directly as possible to the summary given.

✓ A Believing that the world can be accurately represented, realist authors strove to depict the details of everyday lives.

CORRECT. Corresponds to much of P1 and P2, which summarize what realism is.

✓ B Focused on the unique experiences of individual minds, modernist authors used unusual techniques to capture the nature of conscious thought.

CORRECT. Corresponds to P3, which summarizes what modernism is.

✗ C William Faulkner, a leading modernist, wrote from a variety of perspectives in his novel *The Sound and the Fury*.

True, but only a minor detail in the passage as a whole.

✓ D Contemporary authors often blend traditions, combining modernist methods and realist focus on representing daily lives authentically.

CORRECT. Corresponds to P4, which describes how realism and modernism come together for contemporary authors.

✗ E Realist Russian novels and realist American novels vary in the details of the lives they describe.

True, but only a minor detail in the passage as a whole.

✗ F Before the nineteenth century, novelists primarily wrote about the lives of the wealthy.

At best, this point is only implied (the "new subject matter" in P1 is around middle- and lower-class lives). No discussion occurs around this point.

Answers and Explanations—
3.2 Modern Schools of Acting

Paragraph 1		Comments
S1	The eminent Russian theatre director Konstantin Stanislavski brought his Moscow Art Theatre to New York City in 1922.	A Russian director introduced a new acting approach to New York City.
2	The piercing, psychological truths portrayed by actors trained in his technique surprised and captivated the American theatrical community, since this realism was largely unknown in the mannered, external style then current in the United States.	
3	The Stanislavski technique soon became the new standard.	The approach was embraced by theatre professionals and the public.
4	Its rise was spearheaded by a handful of young professional actors in New York; these disciples would form The Group Theatre, which dedicated itself to training and performing in that mode.	
5	This technique would begin to dominate theatre acting.	
6	Later it would spread to film in the United States, then throughout the Western world.	
7	However, a philosophical schism split The Group Theatre, and three dominant sects emerged, each led by a former original member.	But three different interpretations emerged.
8	While all won success and respect, each became more convinced in the superiority of his or her approach.	

1. According to paragraph 1, what most interested actors and theatergoers in the United States about the Stanislavski technique initially?

FACT. The interest in Stanislavski in the United States is discussed in the first three sentences.

✗ (A) The arrival of Russian artists

The passage never states or suggests that the nationality of Stanislavski or his colleagues caused the interest in his work.

✓ (B) The revelation of psychological truths

CORRECT. S2: "The piercing psychological truths portrayed by actors trained in his technique surprised and captivated the American theatrical community. . ." In particular, the word "captivated" indicates intense interest.

✗ (C) The use of this technique in film

S6 indicates that its use in film came later, after the initial wave of interest.

✗ (D) The conflict among the three Group Theatre members

S7–8 describe this conflict, but it is not given as a reason for interest in Stanislavski's techniques.

2. According to paragraph 1, the Stanislavski technique was considered groundbreaking in the United States because

FACT. "Groundbreaking" = innovative or pioneering. In other words, how did the Stanislavski technique break new ground in the United States?

✓ (A) it portrayed realism

CORRECT. S2: "this realism was largely unknown in the mannered, external style then current in the United States." The realism was "largely unknown" before Stanislavski arrived, so this aspect of the technique was groundbreaking.

✗ (B) it originated in Russia

S1 states that Stanislavski was Russian, but this fact is unrelated to the impact of his technique.

✗ (C) it produced mannered, artificial performances

S2 says the opposite: "this realism was largely unknown in the mannered, external style then current in the United States." The word "mannered" means "artificial, unnatural, stilted."

✗ (D) it was also applicable to film acting

Not mentioned. S6 states that the technique was eventually used in film, but this is not given as evidence that it was groundbreaking.

Paragraph 2	**Comments**
S1 **Lee Strasberg and The Actors' Studio.**	
2 Undoubtedly, Lee Strasberg (1901–82) garnered the greatest share of fame and fortune.	Strasberg is most famous of the three.
3 His school, The Actors' Studio, at which a mere handful of the thousand annual applicants were accepted, won world renown as the epicenter of theatrical craft without commercial constraints.	Actors' Studio = center of theatrical craft.
4 This was not surprising, as Strasberg had already basked in the limelight as a co-founder and acknowledged leader of The Group Theatre—itself known for both its acting and its intensive summer retreats devoted to training in virtually an athletic sense—during its groundbreaking successes in the 1930s.	
5 Furthermore, Strasberg codified Stanislavski's approach into a famous educational system of actor training known as "The Method."	"The Method" training system.
6 Strasberg's training revolved around "affective memory," infusing the emotional memories from the actor's own life into that of the character.	Personal experiences go into acting.

3.   According to paragraph 2, as part of their educational development, Strasberg trained actors to

FACT. S5–6 discuss Strasberg's training system.

✗   (A) apply for admission to the Actors' Studio

S3 mentions that few applicants were accepted to Strasberg's school, but his training came later.

✗   (B) portray athletcs on stage

S4 describes "intensive summer retreats" that were "devoted to training in virtually an athletic sense." But this does not mean that the actors were being literally trained to perform as athletes. Here, "in virtually an athletic sense" means that the training was as difficult and intense as it would be for high-level athletes.

✓   (C) draw on their personal experiences while acting

CORRECT. S6: "Strasberg's training revolved around 'affective memory,' infusing the emotional memories from the actor's own life into that of the character."

✗   (D) find alternatives to Stanislavski's techniques

The training was to teach actors how to use Stanislavski's techniques, not look for alternatives.

4.   Which of the sentences below best expresses the essential information in the highlighted sentence in paragraph 2? Incorrect choices change the meaning in important ways or leave out essential information.

SIMPLIFY SENTENCE. "Codify" means to systematize or organize. S5 (highlighted) therefore indicates that Strasberg "codified" Stanislavski's approach, or turned it into a formal system for training actors. This famous system was called "The Method."

✗   (A) Additionally, Strasberg and Stanislavski worked together to write a training manual called "The Method."

This sentence discusses Strasberg creating a training based on Stanislavski's techniques. There is no mention of the two working together or of writing an actual manual.

✗   (B) In addition, Strasberg created a covert code called "The Method" so that actors could study acting privately.

"Codified" means "systematize" and is not related to secret or "covert" codes. Moreover, there is no discussion of doing any of this privately.

✗   (C) Moreover, Stanislavski approved of "The Method," Strasberg's training system for actors.

There is no mention in this sentence of Stanislavski's approval.

✓   (D) Strasberg also organized Stanislavski's techniques into the well-known training system, "The Method."

CORRECT. This version captures the key ideas of the original sentence: Strasberg took Stanislavski's approach and turned it into a famous educational system for actors.

Paragraph 3	Comments
S1 Public recognition of Strasberg as the guru of the art form was **bolstered** by the notable list of stars who studied with him.	Other achievements of Strasberg contributed to his fame.
2 In addition, while he rarely worked as an actor, one such performance earned him an Academy Award nomination for Best Supporting Actor.	
3 Today, decades after his death, The Actors' Studio remains an acclaimed institution, although belief in its superiority is now more prevalent in the general public than in the professional community.	

5.   The word "**bolstered**" in the passage is closest in meaning to

   ✓ (A) supported

   ✗ (B) celebrated

   ✗ (C) undermined

   ✗ (D) tainted

VOCABULARY. "Bolstered" = strengthened or supported.

CORRECT. "Public recognition ... was bolstered by the notable list of stars" = it was supported by that list of stars.

Something that is "celebrated" is greatly admired or honored.

Opposite. To "undermine" is to damage or weaken.

Opposite. Something that is "tainted" is undesirable or disgraced.

6.   According to paragraphs 2 and 3, all of the following are mentioned as Strasberg's achievements EXCEPT:

   ✗ (A) He founded a successful school.

   ✗ (B) He helped start a professional theatre.

   ✓ (C) He won several Academy Awards.

   ✗ (D) He taught many successful film stars.

NEGATIVE FACT. Three answers are true and supported by the passage. One answer is false or unsupported. Facts on Strasberg's achievements could be found anywhere in P2 or P3.

P2 S3: "His school, The Actors' Studio ... won world renown as the epicenter of theatrical craft ... "

P2 S4: "Strasberg had already basked in the limelight as a co-founder ... of The Group Theatre."

CORRECT. The passage only states that he was nominated for a single award, not several and not that he won. P3 S2: "one such performance earned him an Academy Award nomination for Best Supporting Actor."

P3 S1: "Public recognition of Strasberg as the guru of the art form was bolstered by the notable list of stars who had studied with him."

Paragraph 4	Comments
S1 **Sanford Meisner and The Neighborhood Playhouse.**	
2 Sanford Meisner (1905–97) was Strasberg's junior by four years.	
3 The younger man became a founding member of The Group Theatre and scored several artistic triumphs, including directing a production of *Waiting for Lefty*, which won acclaim both artistically and for its **condemnation** of the suffering of the working class during the Great Depression.	Meisner had artistic success.
4 Eventually, however, Meisner disagreed with Strasberg over the effectiveness of "affective memory."	But he disagreed with Strasberg.
5 After it became known that Stanislavski himself had abandoned this technique, this disagreement became an artistic breach between the two men.	

7. The word "**condemnation**" in the passage is closest in meaning to

   VOCABULARY. "Condemnation" = a strong statement of disapproval.

✗   (A) example

   The strong negative meaning of "condemnation" is not reflected here.

✗   (B) promotion

   Opposite. "Promotion" might indicate encouragement or support.

✓   (C) criticism

   CORRECT. The production of a play was known "for its condemnation of the suffering of the working class" = the production criticized this suffering.

✗   (D) exploitation

   "Exploitation" (taking advantage or using) can have a negative meaning but it is not related to condemnation.

8. According to paragraph 4, all of the following are true statements about Sanford Meisner EXCEPT:

   NEGATIVE FACT. Three answers are true and supported by the passage. One answer is false or unsupported. Facts on Meisner could be anywhere in P4.

✗   (A) He was younger than Strasberg.

   S2: "Strasberg's junior by four years."

✓   (B) He acted in *Waiting for Lefty*.

   CORRECT. S3: Meisner directed a production of *Waiting for Lefty*, but it is not mentioned whether he performed in the production.

✗   (C) He disagreed with Strasberg.

   S4: "Eventually, however, Meisner disagreed with Strasberg."

✗   (D) He was artistically successful.

   S3: Meisner directed a production of *Waiting for Lefty*, which won artistic acclaim.

Paragraph 5	Comments
S1 Meisner then headed the acting program at The Neighborhood Playhouse School of the Theatre.	Meisner's school.
2 In that capacity, he transformed the school into a prestigious institution that exists to this day and developed his own acting curriculum, in which the actor prepared by channeling emotional imagination rather than delving into past experiences.	Meisner's technique of emotional imagination.
3 While Meisner also trained an abundance of stars, he remained less widely known than Strasberg.	Less famous.
4 Professionally, however, the Meisner technique is now the preferred and predominant technique in modern actor training.	But dominant technique today.
5 Sadly, the friendship between these two men did not survive their artistic divorce.	Artistic "divorce" between Meisner and Strasberg.
6 While they both largely remained in Manhattan, they rarely spoke in the decades before Strasberg's death.	

9. According to paragraph 5, which of the following is true of Meisner and his career?

FACT. The entire paragraph is relevant.

✓ (A) His technique made use of imagination rather than memory.

CORRECT. S2: "He … developed his own acting curriculum, in which the actor prepared by channeling emotional imagination rather than delving into past experiences."

✗ (B) His technique was shunned by professionals.

S4 says the opposite: "the Meisner technique is now the preferred and predominant technique in modern actor training."

✗ (C) His methods relied on accurate portrayals of physical mannerisms.

Not mentioned in the passage.

✗ (D) He taught in the neighborhood where he lived.

Not mentioned. The Neighborhood Playhouse is merely the name of the school at which he taught.

10.   The phrase "delving into" in the passage is closest in meaning to

VOCABULARY. "Delve into" = dig into deeply, study in great detail.

✗ (A) fantasizing about

"Fantasizing" isn't the same as "delving," which is anchored in reality.

✓ (B) closely examining

CORRECT. "Delving into past experiences" = digging into them and examining them closely.

✗ (C) largely ignoring

Opposite.

✗ (D) disagreeing with

Because an actor digs more deeply into something does not mean that he or she will no longer agree with it.

Paragraph 6	**Comments**
S1 **Stella Adler and the Stella Adler Studio of Acting.**	
2 Stella Adler (1901–92), another original member of The Group Theatre, also broke with Strasberg over "affective memory" and developed her own version of actor training in the studio that she created.	Adler also broke with Strasberg.
3 Unlike the men, who were the children of tradesmen, Stella Adler was part of a legendary acting family of the Yiddish theatre in New York.	Part of an acting family.
4 While she had a more extensive acting career, she too became most admired as an acting coach.	Most admired as a coach.
5 Some of great stars, including Marlon Brando, publicly credited their success to Adler's coaching.	
6 Although the studio she founded continues, her version of actor training has been less impactful, probably because the two men had a stronger institutional base and because the force of her **singular** personality was an immensely important component of her teaching.	Less impactful version of training. Less institutional, more her personality.

11.   The word "singular" in the passage is closest in meaning to

VOCABULARY. "Singular" can mean "unique, unusual, out of the ordinary." Often this has a positive meaning, in that the thing is remarkable or exceptionally good.

✗ (A) abrasive

A "singular personality" is not necessarily abrasive (= rubbing the wrong way) or pleasant.

✗ (B) pleasant

This is not strong enough to support the meaning of "singular."

✗ (C) ordinary

Opposite. "Ordinary" is to have no special or distinctive features.

✓ (D) striking

CORRECT. "The force of her singular personality" = the impact of her striking (impressive or noticeable) personality and unique character.

12.   What is the author's purpose in presenting the information in paragraph 6?

   ✗ Ⓐ To demonstrate that Adler was the most successful of the three

   ✗ Ⓑ To illustrate the importance of the Yiddish theatre

   ✓ Ⓒ To contrast Stella Adler's career with those of her two former colleagues

   ✗ Ⓓ To offer a feminist critique of New York theatre in the 1930s

PURPOSE. Paragraph 6 discusses Stella Adler's career and contrasts it to those of Strasberg and Meisner.

This paragraph does not claim that one or another of the three leaders was the most successful. If anything, S6 states that Adler's training system has been less impactful.

The text mentions the Yiddish theatre to note that her background was different. But this sentence is just an aside to deepen the portrayal of Adler.

CORRECT. S2, S4, and S5 describe Adler's professional achievements. S3 and S6 compare her career to the careers of Strasberg and Meisner.

The paragraph does not attribute Adler's relative standing to her gender or otherwise draw on feminist theory.

Paragraph 6	**Comments**
S1–2 **Stella Adler and the Stella Adler Studio of Acting.** Stella Adler (1901–92), another original member of The Group Theatre, also broke with Strasberg over "affective memory" and developed her own version of actor training in the studio that she created.	
3 Ⓐ Unlike the men, who were the children of tradesmen, Stella Adler was part of a legendary acting family of the Yiddish theatre in New York.	The prior text doesn't directly lead to the idea that all three were great coaches but that only two of the schools were lasting.
4–5 Ⓑ While she had a more extensive acting career, she too became most admired as an acting coach. Some of great stars, including Marlon Brando, publicly credited their success to Adler's coaching.	The prior text doesn't directly lead to the idea that all three were great coaches but that only two of the schools were lasting.
6 Ⓒ Although the studio she founded continues, her version of actor training has been less impactful, probably because the two men had a stronger institutional base and because the force of her singular personality was an immensely important component of her teaching.	The prior text does discuss Adler's greatness as a coach, but it does not set up the idea that her school didn't have as much impact.
End Ⓓ	**CORRECT.** The previous sentence indicates that Adler's training system has been less impactful. The sentence presents the big idea that Stanislavski gave rise to two schools but three great coaches. This idea appropriately concludes the passage.

13.   **Thus, a history of the Stanislavski technique in the United States in the twentieth century would arguably state that there were two lasting versions of his technique but three great acting coaches.**

Where would the sentence best fit?

INSERT TEXT. The sentence begins with "Thus," indicating that the sentence is the logical result of or conclusion from the previous sentence or sentences. The subject of the sentence is "a history of the Stanislavski technique in the United States in the twentieth century." This subject is very broad, so the sentence is likely to come at or very near the end. The rest of the sentence discusses "two lasting versions of his technique but three great acting coaches." The "two lasting versions" are Strasberg's and Meisner's; the "three great acting coaches" are Strasberg, Meisner, and Adler. The previous sentence describes why Adler did not create a lasting version of Stanislavski's technique but was still considered one of the three great coaches. There isn't much that can follow the inserted sentence. It works very well as a summation of the entire passage.

✗ (A) Choice A

✗ (B) Choice B

✗ (C) Choice C

✓ (D) Choice D   **CORRECT.**

Whole Passage	**Comments**
P1 The eminent Russian theatre director Konstantin Stanislavski brought his Moscow Art Theatre to New York in 1922 …	A Russian director introduced a new acting approach to New York City. The approach was embraced by theatre professionals and the public. But three different interpretations emerged.
P2 Undoubtedly, Lee Strasberg (1901–82) garnered the greatest share of fame and fortune. His school …	Strasberg is most famous. Actors' Studio = center of theatrical craft. "The Method" training system. Personal experiences go into acting.
P3 Public recognition of Strasberg as the guru of the art form …	Other achievements of Strasberg contributed to his fame.
P4 Sanford Meisner (1905–97) was Strasberg's junior by four years …	Meisner had artistic success. But he disagreed with Strasberg.
P5 Meisner then headed the acting program at The Neighborhood Playhouse School …	Meisner's school. Meisner's technique of emotional imagination. Less famous. But dominant technique today. Artistic "divorce" between Meisner and Strasberg.
P6 Stella Adler (1901–92), another original member of The Group Theatre, also broke with Strasberg …	Adler also broke with Strasberg. Part of an acting family. Most admired as a coach. Less impactful version of training. Less institutional, more her personality.

14. **In 1922, the Stanislavski technique came to New York and irrevocably changed how actors trained and performed.**

SUMMARY. Correct answers must be clearly expressed in the passage. They must also be among the major points of the passage. They should tie as directly as possible to the summary given.

✓ **A** Today Stanislavski's approach remains the basis of several variations of actor training, but the dominant one was developed by a less known personage.

CORRECT. Corresponds to P5 S3–4 (Meisner is less known, but his version of Stanislavski is dominant).

✗ **B** One of the leading practitioners of Stanislavski's method acting infused it with the culture of the Yiddish theatre.

The passage mentions the Yiddish theatre as part of Stella Adler's background but never implies that that culture was part of Stanislavski's method.

✓ **C** The three major disciples of Stanislavski in the United States created prominent schools of acting with long lists of alumni.

CORRECT. The three disciples are Strasberg, Meisner, and Adler. P2–6 describe their schools and their influence on the acting profession.

✗ **D** Acting according to Stanislavski's approach proved to be more influential in film acting than in theatre acting.

P1 barely mentions the use of Stanislavski in film. Later references to film actors only indicate the quality of the coaching, not the form that the training was most suited to.

✓ **E** The dispute that led to major variations of Stanislavski's techniques involved how to infuse realistic emotions into acting portrayals.

CORRECT. P1: Stanislavski brought realism to United States theatre. His disciples argued over exactly how to train actors to tap into realistic emotions (e.g., the "affective memory" of Strasberg versus the emotional imagination of Meisner). These arguments are discussed in P2 S6, P4 S4–5, P5 S2 and P6 S2.

✗ **F** The innovation of modern acting training destroyed a friendship.

While the end of P5 mentions the demise of the friendship between Strasberg and Meisner, this fact is only a minor biographical detail, unconnected to the passage's purpose.

Answers and Explanations—3.3 Habitats of the Blues

	Paragraph 1	Comments
S1	Ecologists long ago determined that environmental factors significantly affect the evolution of species.	Environment affects evolution of species.
2	Determinants imposed by nature have caused once uniform animal populations to differentiate into separate races and then species.	Uniform populations differentiate (split apart).
3	Now, similar patterns of differentiation have been noted in human cultural phenomena.	Similar differentiation happens in human culture.
4	The effect of environmental influences on a specific form of art can be seen in the evolution of blues music in the United States.	Example: evolution of blues music.

1. Which of the following can be inferred about blues music in the United States from paragraph 1?

INFERENCE. P1 proposes that species in nature and phenomena (things that happen) of human culture follow similar patterns of evolution. That is, they differentiate or split into different varieties over time. S4 introduces blues music as an example of a cultural phenomenon that follows this pattern.

  ✗ (A) It reflected the ecological forces of animals.

This distorts the point. The evolutionary pattern of blues music is similar to the evolutionary pattern of animals. The paragraph doesn't argue that the music is actually related to animals or reflects their ecological forces (whatever that may mean).

  ✗ (B) It was produced by several races.

S2 states that animals evolved into different races. But this sentence does not discuss music.

  ✓ (C) It developed distinct variants at some point.

CORRECT. S1–2 state that environmental factors cause species to differentiate. S4 states that blues music followed the same pattern, so it must have "developed distinct variants" or different varieties at some point.

  ✗ (D) It has been studied closely by ecologists.

S1 only discusses ecologists' study of biological species, not of music.

2. Which of the sentences below best expresses the essential information in the highlighted sentence in paragraph 1? Incorrect choices change the meaning in important ways or leave out essential information.

SIMPLIFY SENTENCE. S3 asserts that human cultural phenomena evolve in a pattern similar to the way animal species (mentioned in S2) evolve. Namely, both cultural phenomena and animal species become differentiated over time, splitting into different varieties

✗ (A) Species variation causes changes in cultural outcomes.

No causal relationship is mentioned.

✓ (B) Human cultural phenomena also appear to evolve and split over time.

CORRECT. This choice successfully rephrases the main point of S3. The two patterns are properly compared here.

✗ (C) Environmental factors do not influence cultural evolution.

This is the opposite of what is said.

✗ (D) All cultural phenomena are the same in humans and animals.

The pattern of evolution and differentiation are similar. This is not to say that the phenomena themselves are the same.

Paragraph 2	Comments
S1 Musicologists have agreed that blues music—defined by specific chord progressions and lyrical structures—was created by African-American musicians in the rural areas of the southern United States in the late nineteenth century, particularly in the Mississippi River delta, located in Louisiana.	Blues music was created in the rural South by African-American musicians.
2 As it is related to African music embedded in spirituals, the influence of environmental factors on this art form is already evident.	Related to African music within spirituals. Influence of environmental factors.
3 Aside from its distinct scales and beat, rural blues music was characterized by the interplay of vocals and acoustic guitars.	Characteristics.
4 Lyrically, early blues expressed the hopes and fears of impoverished farmers, often voicing stories about droughts and floods, as well as poverty, oppression, and relationship woes.	Blues expressed hopes and fears of farmers.

3. The word "embedded" in the passage is closest in meaning to

VOCABULARY. "Embedded" = firmly and deeply fixed, ingrained or lodged.

✗ (A) lacking

Opposite. "Lacking" = absent of or missing.

✗ (B) sanctified

"Sanctify" = declare holy.

✗ (C) mandated

"Mandated" = approved or even ordered.

✓ (D) ingrained

CORRECT. "Ingrained" = firmly fixed or established, deeply embedded. "African music embedded in" = African music that has been filled with or deeply ingrained in spirituals.

4. All of the following are mentioned in paragraph 2 as characteristics of blues music EXCEPT:

NEGATIVE FACT. Three of the choices are mentioned in the paragraph as characteristics of blues music. One choice is not.

✗ (A) its commonalities with African music

S2: "related to African music embedded in spirituals."

✗ (B) its particular musical structures

S1: "defined by specific chord progressions and lyrical structures."

✗ (C) its themes of farming hardships

S4: "lyrically, early blues expressed the hopes and fears of impoverished farmers, often voicing stories about droughts and floods."

✓ (D) its origin as a response to slavery

CORRECT. Slavery is not mentioned in the paragraph.

Paragraph 3	Comments
S1 In the early twentieth century, socioeconomic factors caused a migration of rural southern African Americans to northern urban centers.	African Americans migrated from rural South to urban North.
2 The change in locale soon led to **modifications** in the blues music that the migrants brought with them.	This led to changes in blues music.
3 Instead of being played in fields and road houses, blues now became the music of city bars and dance halls.	
4 By about 1950, urban blues became an art form distinct from the country blues that had **engendered** it.	Urban blues became distinct from country blues.
5 While this urban blues itself had variants in different cities, the dominant strain developed in Chicago; "Chicago Blues" became a brand in its own right.	Chicago Blues was the dominant strain.

5.   The word "modifications" in the passage is closest in meaning to

✓ (A) alterations

✗ (B) improvements

✗ (C) combinations

✗ (D) deteriorations

VOCABULARY. "Modification" = change, adjustment, alteration.

CORRECT. "The change in locale soon led to modifications in the blues music" = the change in location led to alterations or changes in the music itself.

Too specific. The modifications or alterations may be improvements, making the music better, but they may not be.

Too specific.

"Deterioration" = a worsening or lessening. This negative meaning is not present in the sentence.

6.   The word "engendered" in the passage is closest in meaning to

✗ (A) preceded

✗ (B) typified

✓ (C) inspired

✗ (D) distinguished

VOCABULARY. "Engender" = cause, form, give birth to, inspire.

Not quite. Something can precede (= come before) something else but not engender or cause it.

"Typify" = to symbolize or be a representative example of something. These words are unrelated.

CORRECT. "Urban blues became ... distinct from the country blues that had engendered it" = urban blues became different from the country blues that had inspired it or caused it to happen.

To "distinguish" is to identify something as distinctive or different. These words are unrelated.

Paragraph 4	Comments
S1 The urban atmosphere changed the blues both instrumentally and lyrically.	The city changed the blues' instruments and lyrics.
2 The faster, even frenetic, scrabble of city life undoubtedly led to the replacement of the acoustic guitar and banjo with the electric guitar and harmonica—called a "blues harp" by some—soon accompanied by drums and electric bass guitars as well.	Faster city life led to new instruments.
3 While relationship laments remained common, blues lyrics now reflected the types of hard times common to city life.	Lyrics now reflected city life.
4 Chicago bluesman Kevin Moore noted, "You have to put some new life into it, new blood, new perspectives.	
5 You can't keep talking about mules, workin' on the levee."	

7. In paragraph 4, the author includes the quotation from Kevin Moore in order to

PURPOSE. The quotation in S4–5 describes how urban blues had to change: "You have to put new life into it ... You can't keep talking about mules ... "

✓ (A) support the idea that urban blues lyrics evolved as a result of a new environment

CORRECT. The quotation elaborates on the point made in S3 that urban blues lyrics changed to reflect city life.

✗ (B) emphasize the fact that Chicago did not suffer from droughts similar to those in the South

The change reflected different social conditions, not different weather.

✗ (C) argue that hard times were less relevant to urban life than they were to rural life

S3, which the quote supports, says that "lyrics now reflected the types of hard times common to city life." That is, hard times in the city were different, not irrelevant.

✗ (D) explain why urban blues employed electric guitars, harmonicas, and drums

The quote addresses changes in lyrics (in S3), not changes in instrumentation (in S2).

8. The author identifies the "faster, even frenetic, scrabble of city life" as a factor that

FACT. S2 goes on to describe the new instruments used in urban blues. According to S2, this new instrumentation was a result of the faster pace of city life.

✗ (A) encouraged new kinds of lyrics such as relationship laments

S3 notes that such lyrics "remained common" in urban blues. So they had been common in country blues. They were not new kinds of lyrics.

✓ (B) supported the use of electric instruments in blues music

CORRECT. S2: "undoubtedly led to the replacement of the acoustic guitar and banjo with the electric guitar and ... electric bass guitars."

✗ (C) increased the appeal of blues music to Caucasian audiences

The race or ethnicity of the audiences is not discussed in this paragraph.

✗ (D) discouraged lyrics about such subjects as mules and levees

S2 discusses *instrumental* changes to blues music. It may be true that the "faster, even frenetic, scrabble of city life" also led to the lyrical changes discussed in S3–5. But the author does not specifically say so.

	Paragraph 5	**Comments**
S1	Chicago Blues soon received national exposure, and Chicago Blues musicians now commanded payments beyond the wildest dreams of their country predecessors, although admittedly far less than the sums given to rock-and-roll stars.	Chicago Blues became popular. More money for the musicians.
2	Also, blues extended its reach geographically.	Blues music spread.
3	Muddy Waters, originally from the Mississippi Delta, migrated to Chicago and then toured Great Britain and elsewhere in Europe, to much fanfare.	
4	This led to the growth of "British Blues," another recognizable strain influenced by a habitat even further removed from the cotton fields than Chicago was.	Another variety was born: British Blues.

9. Which of the following statements about Chicago Blues is best supported by paragraph 5?

FACT. This paragraph discusses the spread of Chicago Blues to national and international stages.

✗ (A) Chicago Blues musicians earned as much as rock-n-roll stars.

S1: Chicago Blues musicians earned "far less than the sums given to rock-and-roll stars."

✗ (B) Chicago and Great Britain are equally removed from the cotton fields where blues was born.

S4: "a habitat [Great Britain] even further removed from the cotton fields than Chicago was."

✓ (C) The earnings of Chicago Blues musicians dwarfed those of country blues musicians.

CORRECT. S1: Chicago Blues players "commanded payments beyond the wildest dreams of their country predecessors."

✗ (D) Muddy Waters developed the musical variant known as "British Blues."

S3–4 only state that Muddy Waters toured Europe and thus inspired the development of "British Blues." It's not clear whether he developed this strand of music himself.

	Paragraph 6	**Comments**
S1	There are also other, lesser-known "habitats" that eventually transformed a branch of the blues into musical genres that few today would call blues.	Other habitats created new types of music out of blues.
2	At the beginning of the twentieth century, rural Caucasian musicians also played blues music.	
3	However, with the advent of the recording industry, marketing executives promoted **their** work as country music or folk music for a Caucasian audience while marketing music played by African Americans for African Americans as blues.	Blues music played by rural Caucasian musicians became country or folk music through separate marketing.
4	Today, most country music bears little resemblance to country blues, let alone to Chicago Blues, and is widely considered a separate genre of music.	Most country music today is very different from country blues.

10. The word "their" in the passage refers to

REFERENCE. S3: "marketing executives promoted their work as country music or folk music." Logically speaking, whose work was promoted as country music?

✓ (A) rural Caucasian musicians

CORRECT. S2 notes that "rural Caucasian musicians also played blues music." S3 states that marketing executives promoted the music of those Caucasian performers as country rather than blues. Logically, "their" refers back to "rural Caucasian musicians" in S2. With this reference, the two sentences make the most sense. These musicians also played blues, but the marketing executives promoted their (= the musicians') music as country.

✗ (B) marketing executives

In some contexts, "marketing executives promoted their work" could mean that they promoted their *own* work. However, the rest of the paragraph makes it clear whose work is meant. The "work" in question is the music produced by the rural Caucasian musicians mentioned in S2, not by the executives.

✗ (C) the recording industry

For one thing, "industry" is singular, but "their" is plural. So there's a grammatical mismatch. Also, the rural Caucasian musicians are the ones whose music or work is being promoted.

✗ (D) African-American musicians

Aside from the logical issues mentioned already, there's a structural problem here: African-American musicians are not mentioned earlier than "their" in this paragraph. Occasionally, a pronoun can refer to a later noun, but that noun should be the subject of the sentence, and the pronoun should come just before it (for instance, "Although *he* is a nice guy, *my friend Joe* sometimes acts mean").

	Paragraph 3	**Comments**
S1	In the early twentieth century, socioeconomic factors caused a migration of rural southern African Americans to northern urban centers.	
2	**A** The change in locale soon led to modifications in the blues music that the migrants brought with them.	Chicago is not specifically mentioned in S1.
3	**B** Instead of being played in fields and road houses, blues now became the music of city bars and dance halls.	Chicago is not specifically mentioned in S2.
4–5	**C** By about 1950, urban blues became an art form distinct from the country blues that had engendered it. While this urban blues itself had variants in different cities, the dominant strain developed in Chicago; "Chicago Blues" became a brand in its own right.	Chicago is not specifically mentioned in S3.
End	**D**	**CORRECT.** In this position, the new sentence logically follows S5, which discusses Chicago and its association with the blues.

11.   **The association of the city of Chicago with the blues remains to this day.**

Where would the sentence best fit?

INSERT TEXT. The prior sentence should mention Chicago and its association with the blues, because the point of the new sentence is that this association "remains to this day" (today).

✗ (A) Choice A

✗ (B) Choice B

✗ (C) Choice C

✓ (D) Choice D   **CORRECT.**

	Whole Passage	**Comments**
P1	Ecologists long ago determined that environmental factors significantly affect the evolution of species …	Environment affects evolution of species. Uniform populations differentiate (split apart). Similar differentiation happens in human culture. Example: evolution of blues music.
P2	Musicologists have agreed that blues music …	Blues music was created in the rural South by African American musicians. Related to African music within spirituals. Influence of environmental factors. Characteristics. Blues expressed hopes and fears of farmers.
P3	In the early twentieth century, socioeconomic factors caused a migration of rural southern African Americans …	African Americans migrated from rural South to urban North. This led to changes in blues music. Urban blues became distinct from country blues. Chicago Blues was the dominant strain.
P4	The urban atmosphere changed the blues both instrumentally and lyrically …	The city changed the blues' instruments and lyrics. Faster city life led to new instruments. Lyrics now reflected city life.
P5	Chicago Blues soon received national exposure, and Chicago Blues musicians …	Chicago Blues became popular. More money for the musicians. Blues music spread. Another variety was born: British Blues.
P6	There are also other, lesser-known "habitats" that eventually transformed a branch of the blues …	Other habitats created new types of music out of blues. Blues music played by rural Caucasian musicians became country or folk music through separate marketing. Most country music today is very different from country blues.

3

12.   Select from the six choices below TWO that characterize rural or country blues only, THREE that characterize urban blues only, and ONE that characterizes both styles of music.

TABLE. Correct answers do not have to convey a main idea. They just have to be justified by the passage. Characteristics of the two variations of blues music (rural/country and urban) are described throughout the passage.

A   International exposure and increased financial compensation

URBAN BLUES. P5 explains that Chicago Blues musicians toured Europe and received relatively rich compensation. This is contrasted to the lesser situation of country blues musicians.

B   Laments sung to accompaniment by an acoustic guitar

RURAL BLUES. P2 S3–4: "rural blues music was characterized by the interplay of vocals and acoustic guitars. Lyrically, early blues expressed the hopes and fears of impoverished farmers, often voicing stories about droughts and floods, as well as poverty, oppression, and relationship woes."

C   The use of a blues harp

URBAN BLUES. P4 explicitly mentions the blues harp as an aspect of urban blues.

D   Evolution influenced by environmental factors in the direction of differentiation

BOTH STYLES. P1 states that this pattern of evolution applies to blues music in general. In fact, the pattern is said to apply to human cultural phenomena in general.

E   Often performed in fields and road houses

RURAL BLUES. P3 lists this as a characteristic of rural blues.

F   Development into a distinct art form around 1950

URBAN BLUES. P3 S4: "By about 1950, urban blues became an art form distinct from the country blues that had engendered it."

Answers and Explanations—3.4 Photography

	Paragraph 1	**Comments**
S1	Photography is the art and science of still-image creation.	Photography is the creation of still images with light.
2	It is accomplished through the recording of light or other electromagnetic radiation—indeed, the word "photography" comes from the Greek "photos," meaning "light," and "graphe," meaning "drawing or writing."	
3	Together, these words can be interpreted as "drawing with light."	The word means "drawing with light."
4	The nineteenth-century scientist and photographer John Herschel is typically credited with coining the term in the 1830s.	History of the term.
5	However, some have claimed that others were independently using the term around the same period; a French painter used the term in his **correspondence**, and a German astronomer spoke of the term in a newspaper article.	

1.	The word "**correspondence**" in the passage is closest in meaning to	**VOCABULARY.** In this context, "correspondence" = communications, messages, letters.
✓	(A) communications	**CORRECT.** "A French painter used the term in his correspondence" = he used the term in written communications, such as letters.
✗	(B) association	"Correspondence" can mean "agreement, consistency, similarity," or possibly even "association" in other contexts. But as a concrete noun in the context of writing, "correspondence" means "communication(s)."
✗	(C) research	Unrelated. Using the terms in letters or other communications is not the same as using it in actual research.
✗	(D) portfolio	Unrelated. "Portfolio" = samples or examples of his artwork.

2. According to paragraph 1, the origin of the term "photography" is

FACT. S2–3 discuss the origin of the term linguistically: how the word itself derives from Greek. S4–5 discuss the origin of the word historically: who is said to have coined it and who actually used it first.

✗ Ⓐ defined as the craft of creating still images

Photography itself is "the art and science of still-image creation" (S1). But that is not the *origin* of the *term* "photography."

✗ Ⓑ not attributed to scientist John Herschel

S4: "The nineteenth-century scientist … John Herschel is typically credited with coining the term." S5 describes other's uses of the term, but that doesn't contradict the first part of the sentence.

✗ Ⓒ both French and German

S5 mentions a French painter and a German astronomer who used the word in correspondence in the 1830s. But that does not mean that the origin is French and German.

✓ Ⓓ two Greek words

CORRECT. S2 lists the two Greek words: "photos" (= light) and "graphe" (= drawing or writing).

Paragraph 2	Comments
S1 Photography began with the discovery of the *camera obscura,* or the "dark room."	Camera obscura = "dark room."
2 *Camera obscura* is the phenomenon by which a pinhole in the wall of a dark room will project an image, lit from outside the room, onto an inner wall of the enclosed dark room.	= Projection of image through a pinhole into a dark room.
3 The image is reversed and inverted, or flipped upside down.	
4 This is the same mechanism by which the human eye sees images, with the pupil as the pinhole (the brain simply flips the image back so that it is observed as normal).	Human eye works this way, too.
5 Since the sixteenth century, artists have used a device referred to as the "camera obscura" (named along with the natural phenomenon it captures) in order to assist in drawing.	Artists have used camera obscura device since 16th century.
6 Scientists have also used it to observe solar eclipses, which are generally unsafe to view directly.	Scientists have also used it.

3. The word "enclosed" in the passage is closest in meaning to

VOCABULARY. "Enclosed" = closed or sealed off. An open area can be "enclosed" by fences or walls, leaving an opening to the sky. But an enclosed *room* would be sealed more completely.

✗ (A) attached

Being closed or sealed off does not indicate whether the space is attached to something else.

✗ (B) trapped

The room is not "trapped," as if it were caught in a trap.

✓ (C) sealed

CORRECT. "A pinhole ... will project an image ... onto an inner wall of the enclosed dark room" = the pinhole will project the image onto an inner wall of the sealed, closed dark room.

✗ (D) exposed

Something exposed would be uncovered or made visible. In this context, the room is sealed and closed off. This is, in some ways, the opposite.

4. Which of the sentences below best expresses the essential information in the highlighted portion of the passage? Incorrect choices change the meaning in important ways or leave out essential information.

SIMPLIFY SENTENCE. S4 starts with "This is the same mechanism." The word "This" must refer back to *camera obscura*, the phenomenon described in S2–3 (the pinhole projection of a flipped image inside a dark room). S4 points out a direct correspondence between the pupil (of the human eye) and the pinhole described in *camera obscura*. Finally, S4 mentions in parentheses the fact that the brain flips the image back to make it appear normal.

✗ (A) The image produced by the pupil (acting as the pinhole) is flipped back to normal by the brain through the *camera obscura* mechanism.

The brain doesn't use *camera obscura* to flip the image back to normal. *Camera obscura* is how the flipped image was produced in the eye in the first place.

✗ (B) In its role as a pinhole, the pupil flips back to normal the image seen by the human eye and brain by means of the *camera obscura* mechanism.

The pupil doesn't flip the image back to normal. It flips the image in the first place. This choice doesn't clarify the different roles of the eye and the brain.

✓ (C) Via the *camera obscura* mechanism, the "pinhole" pupil of the human eye produces a flipped image, which the brain then flips back to normal.

CORRECT. This version reflects the central meaning of the original sentence: the *camera obscura* mechanism works in human sight. The pupil acts as the pinhole. A flipped image is produced in the eye. Finally, the brain flips it back to normal.

✗ (D) Using the *camera obscura* mechanism to see images, the human eye flips the image observed by the brain back to normal through the pupil's pinhole.

The eye doesn't flip the image back to normal through the pupil.

5. All of the following are mentioned about the phenomenon of *camera obscura* in paragraph 2 EXCEPT:

    ✗ (A) It makes use of a pinhole in a wall.

    ✓ (B) It is not safe for use with solar eclipses.

    ✗ (C) It is a natural occurrence involving light.

    ✗ (D) A device that captures it is called by the same name.

NEGATIVE FACT. Three of the answers will describe facts about *camera obscura* found in P2. Since the paragraph is all about *camera obscura*, these facts could be anywhere. One answer choice will not be found in P2. It will either be contradicted or just not present.

S2 describes how a pinhole in a wall is used in *camera obscura*.

CORRECT. S6: "Scientists have also used it to observe solar eclipses, which are generally unsafe to view directly." So *camera obscura* (as both the device and the underlying phenomenon) is in fact safe for use with solar eclipses.

S2 describes how light is involved in *camera obscura* ("lit from outside the room"). S5 calls the phenomenon natural.

S5: "artists have used a device referred to as the 'camera obscura' (named along with the natural phenomenon it captures)."

Paragraph 3	Comments
S1 It is well established that certain substances, such as particular salts, change color when exposed to sunlight.	Light makes certain substances change color.
2 In 1727, German scientist Johann Heinrich Schulze discovered that certain salts darkened when exposed to sunlight, not because of heat or air, but as a response solely to the light itself.	
3 It was not until the early nineteenth century, however, that this chemical reaction was **incorporated into** what would become the photography that we know today.	Incorporated into photography in the 19th century.
4 When the *camera obscura* process of projecting an image through the pinhole was applied to paper that had been chemically treated to be light-sensitive, modern photography was born.	*Camera obscura* + light-sensitive paper = photography.
5 The pinhole camera became the first photographic camera.	

6. The phrase "incorporated into" in the passage is closest in meaning to

VOCABULARY. "Incorporate into" = include, integrate, or assimilate into, combine with.

✓ (A) included in

CORRECT. S3: "this chemical reaction was incorporated into … the photography that we know today" = this reaction was included in, or integrated into, modern photography.

✗ (B) isolated from

Opposite.

✗ (C) established by

This is not related.

✗ (D) incarnated by

Not quite. "Incarnate" = give physical, real form to something, or be the tangible (= touchable) form of that thing. But this chemical reaction already existed in physical, real form, as described in S1–2. Photography did not "incarnate" the reaction; photography did not give form to it or become its tangible form.

7. According to paragraph 3, under what specific conditions do certain salts studied by Johann Schulze darken?

FACT. S2 describes Schulze's study of these salts. He discovered what specifically made them darken.

✓ (A) When they are exposed to the light of the sun.

CORRECT. S2: "Schulze discovered that certain salts darkened when exposed to sunlight, not because of heat or air, but as a response solely to the light itself."

✗ (B) When they are heated but not lit by the sun.

The salts do not darken in response to heat without light.

✗ (C) When they are exposed to open air in darkness.

The salts do not darken in the open air, if there is no light.

✗ (D) When they are exposed to both open air and the heat, but not the light of the sun.

The salts do not darken without exposure to light.

8. The word "treated" in the passage is closest in meaning to

VOCABULARY. In the context of chemistry, something that is "treated" has had a process applied to it. Often some kind of chemical has been added or painted on. A chemical treatment is an alteration in this fashion.

✗ (A) dissolved

You don't know what kind of alteration is described by "treated." But "dissolved" is not only too specific, it's too destructive. Paper that has been dissolved is no longer there.

✗ (B) contained

"Contain" = to hold within or consist of. This is not related.

✗ (C) neglected

"Neglect" = to fail to care for properly. This is not related.

✓ (D) doctored

CORRECT. "Paper that had been chemically treated to be light-sensitive" = paper that had been chemically doctored or altered to be light-sensitive. To "doctor" often means to "alter with an intent to deceive," but not always.

	Paragraph 4	Comments
S1	Over the next number of decades, the camera underwent steady improvements.	Steady improvements followed.
2	After the pinhole camera, the "daguerreotype" was invented, which involved not one but two boxes—an inner box and an outer box—which allowed the photographer to sharpen, or focus, the image.	Daguerreotype = 2 boxes.
3	For years, photographers controlled the length of exposure time by manually removing the cap from the camera lens, the part of the camera that captures the light from the subject and that brings it into focus.	
4	The photographer then counted the required amount of time in seconds or minutes before returning the cap to cover the lens.	
5	Eventually, the "shutter," or mechanism that opens and closes the camera lens, was invented, freeing the photographer from this task in taking a photo.	Shutter to control exposure time was invented.
6	In 1885, American entrepreneur George Eastman began manufacturing the first photographic film—paper on which photographs could be taken.	Photographic film.
7	Starting in 1888, it was sold in a simple camera preloaded with the film.	
8	This camera was called the Kodak.	Kodak camera.

9. Which of the following is mentioned in paragraph 4 about photographic film?

FACT. S6–7 mention photographic film explicitly.

✗ (A) It did not exist until it was built into the first Kodak camera.

S6 notes that the film existed in 1885. S7–8 states that the first Kodak camera (with preloaded film) was sold three years later, in 1888.

✓ (B) Cameras preloaded with it were sold starting in 1888.

CORRECT. S7–8 notes that the Kodak camera was sold in 1888, with photographic film preloaded.

✗ (C) It was a critical part of the "shutter" mechanism.

The "shutter" is mentioned in S5, but the manufacturing of the photographic film mentioned in S6 is not related.

✗ (D) It improved upon the prior development of the shutter.

Not supported in the passage.

10.   It can be inferred from paragraph 4 that the newly invented camera shutter

INFERENCE. S5 focuses on the invention of the camera shutter. This invention improved on the situation described in S3–4, in which the photographer used to take the lens cap off and put it back on manually, counting off the seconds required for the right exposure. The shutter essentially took over this task.

✗ (A) took away from the photographer's freedom to determine the length of exposure time

Unsupported in the passage.

✗ (B) involved the same amount of work to operate as did manually opening and shutting the camera lens

You are not told how much work it was to operate the shutter, relative to how much work the manual process had taken.

✓ (C) allowed the photographer to focus on other aspects of taking the photograph

CORRECT. The shutter replaced the need for the photographer to open and shut the lens manually, and that the invention of the shutter freed up the photographer from this task. Therefore, without this task to worry about, the photographer would be able to focus on other aspects of taking a photo.

✗ (D) gave George Eastman the idea to create a camera with pre-loaded film

S6 (which introduces Eastman) follows directly after S5 (which discusses the shutter). You might think, then, that S5 led to S6 and then to S7–8 (the preloaded camera). But there is no evidence to suggest this is the case. They are all just examples of the "steady improvements" mentioned in S1.

3

	Paragraph 5	Comments
S1	Today, most photography is conducted using digital cameras.	Most cameras are now digital.
2	In digital photography, an "image sensor" has replaced the traditional photographic film.	Image sensor, instead of film.
3	This sensor is still a light-sensitive surface, but the image is stored as digital memory rather than etched directly onto a physical surface, as with photographic film.	
4	Some contemporary photographers, however, such as Cuban photographer Abelardo Morell, have chosen to work predominantly with early models of photography.	But some modern photographers still use early methods. Example: Morell.
5	A photography professor, he turned his classroom into a dark room in order to teach his students the optics behind the *camera obscura* technique.	
6	Morell is known for the images he takes using a "camera obscura," which range from panoramas of New York City to Italian landscapes.	
7	He flips his images right side up with an old-fashioned prism, though he does use a digital sensor instead of film to cut their exposure time.	
8	Morell even carries around a portable "camera obscura" with which he can project images onto the ground.	

11.	In paragraph 5, the author discusses Abelardo Morell's use of early photographic techniques in order to	**PURPOSE.** S4–8 discuss Morell and his use of early techniques. This example serves as a contrast to S1, which declares that digital photography is dominant today.
✗ (A)	argue that the most authentic methods of photography are the early ones	The author does not pass judgment either way on early or modern photographic methods.
✓ (B)	illustrate that not all contemporary photographers strictly use contemporary techniques	**CORRECT.** S4: "Some contemporary photographers, however, such as Cuban photographer Abelardo Morell, have chosen to work predominantly with early models of photography." Notice that the "however" indicates the contrast with what has been previously stated: "Today, most photography is conducted using digital cameras" (S1).
✗ (C)	underline the importance of keeping early techniques alive and relevant	The author never states or hints at this opinion.
✗ (D)	explain why modern photographic techniques are more efficient and effective than older ones	The author never states or hints at this opinion.

12.   The word "their" in the passage refers to

REFERENCE. S7: "He flips his images right side up with an old-fashioned prism, though he does use a digital sensor instead of film to cut their exposure time." The exposure time of what?

✗   (A) camera

The camera, itself, would not need exposure time.

✗   (B) sensor

In theory, you could say "the exposure time of the sensors" (= the time during which the sensors are exposed). But in the sentence, "sensor" is given as singular, whereas "their" is plural. So "their" cannot refer to "sensors."

✗   (C) prism

The prism just flips the image. It does not need a certain amount of exposure time.

✓   (D) images

CORRECT. S7: "he does use a digital sensor instead of film to cut their exposure time" = he uses a sensor to cut the exposure time of his images. These images are referred to at the beginning of S7.

Paragraph 3	**Comments**
S1 It is well-established that certain substances, such as particular salts, change color when exposed to sunlight.	
2 [A] In 1727, German scientist Johann Heinrich Schulze discovered that certain salts darkened when exposed to sunlight, not because of heat or air, but as a response solely to the light itself.	S1 does not refer to a camera; the new sentence would not make sense here.
3 [B] It was not until the early nineteenth century, however, that this chemical reaction was incorporated into what would become the photography that we know today.	S2 does not refer to a camera; the new sentence would not make sense here.
4–5 [C] When the *camera obscura* process of projecting an image through the pinhole was applied to paper that had been chemically treated to be light-sensitive, modern photography was born. The pinhole camera became the first photographic camera.	S3 refers to "photography," but not to a specific camera.
End [D]	**CORRECT.** S5 describes the pinhole camera as the "first photographic camera." The inserted sentence provides additional relevant information about the pinhole camera (namely, that everything shown is in focus).

3

13. **This camera is especially interesting because, with no lens, its depth of field is very deep, so everything that appears in the frame is in focus.**

INSERT TEXT. "This" camera means that in the previous sentence, the same camera must have been discussed. So the correct placement of the new sentence should be right after a sentence discussing a camera, and it should make sense for the new information to apply to that camera.

Where would the sentence best fit?

✗ (A) Choice A

✗ (B) Choice B

✗ (C) Choice C

✓ (D) Choice D   **CORRECT.**

Whole Passage	**Comments**
P1 Photography is the art and science of still-image creation …	Photography is the creation of still images with light. The word means "drawing with light." History of the term.
P2 Photography began with the discovery of the *camera obscura*, or the "dark room" …	Camera obscura = "dark room" = projection of image through a pinhole into a dark room. Human eye works this way, too. Artists have used camera obscura device since 16th century. Scientists have also used it.
P3 It is well-established that certain substances, such as particular salts, change color when exposed to sunlight …	Light makes certain substances change color. Incorporated into photography in the 19th century. *Camera obscura* + light-sensitive paper = photography.
P4 Over the next number of decades, the camera underwent steady improvements …	Steady improvements followed. Daguerreotype = 2 boxes. Shutter to control exposure time was invented. Photographic film. Kodak camera.
P5 Today, most photography is conducted using digital cameras …	Most cameras are now digital. Image sensor, instead of film. But some modern photographers still use early methods. Example: Morell.

14. **The history of photography as an art form dates back to its invention in the early 1800s.**

SUMMARY. Correct answers must be clearly expressed in the passage. They must also be among the major points of the passage. They should tie as directly as possible to the summary given.

✗ ☐A☐ Cuban photographer Abelardo Morell is also a well-regarded professor of photography.

It is true that Morell is a photography professor (P5 S5). But you don't know whether he is well-regarded. More importantly, this detail is minor within the big picture of the passage.

✓ ☐B☐ The *camera obscura* phenomenon was fundamental in the creation of the first photographic camera.

CORRECT. P2 focuses on the phenomenon of *camera obscura*. P3 describes its marriage to light-sensitive paper, producing the first photographic camera. These are core ideas in the passage.

✓ ☐C☐ Cameras used by photographers have undergone changes in the years since photography was invented, from the film they use to the mechanisms by which they work.

CORRECT. P4 and P5 highlight and describe some of these developments in the history of photography.

✗ ☐D☐ The human brain works the same way as photographic cameras.

This is not supported by the passage. P2 S4 mentions that the human brain "flips the image back" to normal, after the miniature *camera obscura* of the eye produces an inverted image. But this does not mean that the brain works the same way as photographic cameras. Moreover, the mention of the human brain is just an aside within this passage.

✗ ☐E☐ Scientists have used the *camera obscura* to observe solar eclipses.

Mentioned in P2 S6. But this is a minor detail that is never elaborated upon.

✓ ☐F☐ Light-sensitive paper with certain chemical treatments allowed the *camera obscura* to become an actual photographic camera.

CORRECT. P3 describes the development of this kind of paper, which enabled the creation of the first modern photographic cameras out of the *camera obscura*.

3

Answers and Explanations—3.5 Stream of Consciousness

	Paragraph 1	Comments
S1	At the dawn of the twentieth century, European painting, which was then a far more influential art form than it is now, underwent a vast aesthetic revolution, shattering conventions that predated the Renaissance.	~1900: revolution in European painting.
2	Cubism, an innovative movement that would influence artists throughout the century, rejected the previous norm of realistic portrayals in favor of an abstract approach combining multiple perspectives.	Cubism: abstract, multiple perspectives.
3	This radical departure, commonly thought to have been led by Pablo Picasso and Georges Braque, captivated the art world.	Captivated art world.
4	It also inspired writers and musicians to infuse the same abstract quality into their works.	Also inspired writers and musicians.

1.   What can be inferred about European art from paragraph 1?

INFERENCE. P1 discusses the "vast aesthetic revolution" that European painting experienced with the rise of Cubism.

✗ (A) European painting was more influential in the early twentieth century than during the Renaissance.

S1: "At the dawn of the twentieth century, European painting ... was then a far more influential art form than it is now." The sentence mentions the Renaissance only in connection with the revolution that would be "shattering conventions that predated the Renaissance."

✗ (B) Picasso was more captivating to the art world than Braque was.

The text never compares the two painters. S4 only says that Cubism was "commonly thought to have been led by Pablo Picasso and Georges Braque."

✓ (C) Realistic portrayals were likely one of the conventions that predated the Renaissance.

CORRECT. S1: "underwent a vast aesthetic revolution, shattering conventions that predated the Renaissance." S2: "Cubism ... rejected the previous norm of realistic portrayals." So realistic portrayals were likely to have been one of the conventions that predated the Renaissance. You can't be sure, but you can infer that this is likely.

✗ (D) The aesthetic revolution in European painting was probably inspired by writers using similar abstractions.

Reversed. S4 states that writers were inspired by the revolution in painting, not that they inspired it.

2. According to paragraph 1, all of the following are true statements about Cubism EXCEPT:

NEGATIVE FACT. Three answers are true and supported by the passage. One answer is false or just unsupported. Cubism is introduced in S2, but since it actually is part of the "vast aesthetic revolution" described in S1, everywhere in P1 is fair game.

✗ (A) It employed multiple perspectives.

S2: "an abstract approach combining multiple perspectives."

✗ (B) It influenced writers and musicians.

S4: "It also inspired writers and musicians to infuse the same abstract quality into their works."

✗ (C) Its influence lasted for many decades.

S2: "would influence artists throughout the century."

✓ (D) It had less appeal to the public outside the art world.

CORRECT. The paragraph does not mention the general public and only states that it "captivated the art world" (S3).

Paragraph 2	Comments
S1 James Joyce and John Dos Passos were two renowned authors whose major works employed this nonlinear framework derived from Cubism, the writers applying words to paper in the same fractured manner that artists used when applying paint to canvas.	Joyce and Dos Passos = two writers who applied nonlinear Cubist principles.
2 Scholars have termed this literary style "stream-of-consciousness" writing.	"Stream-of-consciousness" writing.
3 This technique constructs an inner monologue that creates a whole from **dissociated** parts and theoretically portrays the nonlinear patterns inherent in human thoughts.	Inner monologue: nonlinear, separate parts.

3

3. The word "dissociated" in the passage is closest in meaning to

✓ (A) fragmented

✗ (B) reserved

✗ (C) aligned

✗ (D) unspoken

VOCABULARY. "Dissociated" = separated, disconnected, detached.

CORRECT. "an inner monologue ... creates a whole from dissociated parts" = it creates a whole out of fragmented, disconnected parts.

Unrelated. "Reserved" = slow to reveal emotions (shy or withdrawn), or holding something aside for a particular person or purpose (a reserved seat).

Opposite. "Aligned" = arranged or orderly.

Unrelated. "Unspoken" = not expressed in speech.

4. Which of the sentences below best expresses the essential information in the highlighted sentence in paragraph 2? Incorrect choices change the meaning in important ways or leave out essential information.

✓ (A) In their major works, James Joyce and John Dos Passos applied nonlinear writing techniques derived from Cubism.

✗ (B) Applying words to paper in the same fractured way, James Joyce and John Dos Passos derived the nonlinear framework of Cubism.

✗ (C) James Joyce and John Dos Passos became renowned authors by using a nonlinear style that they derived from Cubism.

✗ (D) Renowned authors James Joyce and John Dos Passos applied paint to canvas in a fractured, Cubist manner to write their major works.

SIMPLIFY SENTENCE. S1 introduces two important writers who borrowed Cubist principles from the art world and applied them to their work.

CORRECT. S1: "major works employed this nonlinear framework derived from Cubism, the writers applying words to paper in the same fractured manner that artists used when applying paint to canvas." The rephrased version captures this core meaning. It omits that Joyce and Dos Passos were renowned, but this omission is acceptable.

S1 does not say that the two writers themselves derived (= extracted, proved, or discovered) the nonlinear framework of Cubism itself. Rather, the framework the writers used was derived *from* Cubism.

S1 only mentions that they were renowned authors. It does not mention the source of their fame (whether it was from their use of Cubist methods or not).

S1 says that the two writers applied "words to paper in the same fractured manner that artists used when applying paint to canvas." You are not told that they literally applied paint to canvas.

MANHATTAN PREP

Paragraph 3	**Comments**
S1 Like Picasso and Braque, Joyce and Dos Passos enjoyed great artistic success, and their stylistic explorations profoundly influenced the generations of writers that followed them.	Both Joyce and Dos Passos were successful and influential.
2 Both men were interested in smashing established boundaries in the service of accurately displaying the emotional truth of human thoughts and feelings.	
3 James Joyce (1882–1941) was reared in a downwardly-mobile Irish middle-class family but received a relatively elite education because of his intellect and talents.	Joyce's life and career.
4 He resided in Europe for almost all of his adult life and eked out a living through various short-lived ventures, his art, and the generosity of patrons.	
5 His literary work largely remained anchored to his native Dublin.	
6 John Dos Passos (1896–1970) was the illegitimate son of John Randolph Dos Passos, who refused to accept his son until he was nearly an adult.	Dos Passos's life and career.
7 However, his father's wealth allowed him to obtain a privileged education and undertake an educational tour of Europe.	
8 He then volunteered with an ambulance corps during the First World War, an experience that profoundly impacted him, as it did many of his generation.	
9 During his literary prime, Dos Passos was also an outspoken political progressive, but in the final third of his life he embraced very conservative causes.	

5.   The phrase "eked out" in the passage is closest in meaning to

VOCABULARY. "Eke out" = scratch out, get a small amount of something by great effort. Often this is used in terms of supporting oneself or only "making a living" through great effort or difficulty. However, it might also mean to use something sparingly or to make a small amount of something last a long amount of time by using or consuming it carefully.

✗   (A) enjoyed

"Enjoy" would mean that he earned a lot through little effort. "Eke out" indicates that the reverse was true: he earned just a little through a lot of effort.

✓   (B) scratched out

CORRECT. "He ... eked out a living through various short-lived ventures" = he scratched out a living this way, he worked hard to earn small amounts of money.

✗   (C) gave up

This is, in many ways, the opposite. To "eke out" a living is to work quite hard at trying to support oneself. To give up would be to put forth none of the effort.

✗   (D) provided

The phrasing is wrong. A profession (or an employer) provides a living to or for someone. Moreover, "provide" lacks the key idea of "eke out": a lot of effort for a bare reward.

6.   According to paragraph 3, which of the following is true about both Joyce and Dos Passos?

FACT. S1–2 discuss both writers. S3–5 cover only Joyce, while the remaining sentences cover only Dos Passos.

✗   (A) Both served in the ambulance corps in the First World War.

S8 only mentions Dos Passos: "He then volunteered with an ambulance corps during the First World War."

✗   (B) Both resided in Europe for the majority of their adulthoods.

Only Joyce did so, as described in S4. As for Dos Passos, the passage only notes an educational tour in S7 and wartime service in S8.

✗   (C) Both were raised in middle-class families.

While Joyce was middle-class, Dos Passos was not. S7 mentions "his [Dos Passos'] father's wealth."

✓   (D) Both received educations reserved for just a few.

CORRECT. S3: "[Joyce] received a relatively elite education because of his intellect and talents." S7 describes the education Dos Passos received as "privileged." The words "elite" and "privileged" mean that these educations were reserved for just a few (people).

7.   The phrase "an outspoken" in the passage is closest in meaning to

VOCABULARY. "Outspoken" = frank, forthright, blunt, candid, and fearless in speech.

✗   (A) a disclosed

"Disclosed" = public, revealed, out in the open. This would mean that Dos Passos was public about being a political progressive, but it would not necessarily mean that he was frank and fearless in his statements.

✗   (B) a fainthearted

Opposite. A "fainthearted" person is cowardly and not so fearless in speech.

✗   (C) a diplomatic

Opposite in another way. A "diplomatic" person is tactful and not so frank or blunt.

✓   (D) a forthright

CORRECT. "Dos Passos was also an outspoken political progressive" = he was also a forthright political progressive, he was candid and fearless in expressing these political views.

	Paragraph 4	Comments
S1	Joyce's most renowned work, *Ulysses*, was published in 1922; however, in the United States, it was banned under an obscenity statute for more than 10 years.	Joyce's masterpiece, *Ulysses*.
2	In this seminal work, Joyce transplants the plot and characters of Homer's Greek epic *The Odyssey* to early twentieth-century Dublin and condenses the timeline to a single day.	
3	In service of the stream-of-consciousness aesthetic, each chapter employs a different literary style, although all reject linear conventions, much as Cubist painting did.	It exhibits a stream-of-consciousness aesthetic.
4	Furthermore, each chapter has a thematic association unrelated to the plot or source material.	
5	Because of its difficult vocabulary, its assumption that the reader is familiar with a vast array of historical and literary references, and its complex, metaphorical prose, *Ulysses* is not widely read.	*Ulysses* is difficult, complex, expects knowledge of reader = Not widely read.
6	However, its fame and place in the literary canon far exceed its sales, as scholarly opinion considers it the fountainhead of literary modernism.	But famous and influential.

8. According to paragraph 4, *Ulysses* was not widely read in part because

   ✗ (A) it was banned for obscenity

   ✗ (B) it was inspired by Homer's epic *The Odyssey*

   ✓ (C) its vocabulary is obscure

   ✗ (D) it is the fountainhead of literary modernism

FACT. S5 lists reasons why *Ulysses* is not widely read.

Ulysses was indeed banned for obscenity, according to S1. But this is not given as a reason for its lack of readership.

S2 mentions this fact, but only to describe the book, not to analyze its appeal.

CORRECT. S5: "Because of its difficult vocabulary ... *Ulysses* is not widely read."

S6 mentions this fact to explain the book's reputation and fame, not its readership.

9. In paragraph 4, why does the author mention that each chapter has a unique literary style?

   ✗ (A) To demonstrate that *Ulysses* is the primary example of nonlinear writing in the twentieth century

   ✗ (B) To reject the effectiveness of linear conventions as typically used in literature

   ✓ (C) To show how the book tries to reflect stream-of-consciousness principles

   ✗ (D) To document why *Ulysses* was banned in the United States for obscenity

PURPOSE. S3 states that each chapter has a different literary style. S3 also suggests why.

S3 only asserts that each chapter has its own style "in service of the stream-of-consciousness aesthetic." That doesn't necessarily mean that *Ulysses* is the *primary* example of nonlinear writing. P4 does call the book "seminal" (S2) and "the fountainhead for literary modernism" (S6). So *Ulysses* is probably a pretty good example of nonlinear writing. Even so, the passage is not arguing that *Ulysses* is the primary example.

S3 states that "all [the chapters] reject linear conventions." But the author is not therefore claiming that linear conventions are ineffective throughout literature.

CORRECT. S3: "In service of the stream-of-consciousness aesthetic, each chapter employs a different literary style." The phrase "in service of" indicates the goal of the different styles.

S1 provides this information solely as background. It is not related to the discussion of the book's literary style.

Paragraph 5	**Comments**
S1 By contrast, John Dos Passos's work, also considered unique and innovative, proved far more accessible and popular, but it is now thought to be less important than *Ulysses*.	Dos Passos's work: more popular but less important.
2 His opus was a trilogy entitled *U.S.A.*, completed in 1938.	*U.S.A.* trilogy.
3 This work chronicles the evolution of the United States from an agrarian, isolationist nation as the twentieth century began to the urban world power it became within a few decades.	
4 Dos Passos sought to reflect the feelings and consciousness of those times by employing what critics have called a "collage technique": newspaper clippings are inserted **sporadically**, and his disparate characters and plots intersect at seemingly random intervals.	Collage technique.

10.   The word "**sporadically**" in the passage is closest in meaning to

    ✗   (A) prevalently

    ✓   (B) irregularly

    ✗   (C) steadily

    ✗   (D) habitually

VOCABULARY. "Sporadically" = irregularly, intermittently, occurring at random intervals. The word also implies "infrequently," much as the word "occasionally" means both "at random" and "relatively rarely."

Opposite. "Prevalently" = everywhere or almost everywhere throughout.

CORRECT. "Newspaper clippings are inserted sporadically" = they are inserted irregularly, at random intervals.

Opposite in another sense. "Steadily" = regularly.

Also opposite. "Habitually" = frequently, regularly, routinely.

11.   Paragraph 5 mentions which of the following as an aspect of a collage technique?

    ✓   (A) The intersection of apparently unrelated people and circumstances

    ✗   (B) An accessible and popular style

    ✗   (C) An agrarian, isolationist perspective

    ✗   (D) The sporadic insertion of clippings from private governmental reports

FACT. S4 introduces and characterizes this literary device.

CORRECT. S4: "his disparate characters and plots intersect at seemingly random intervals." This is part of the description of the collage technique (after the colon). "Disparate" (= extremely different, even incompatible) can be rephrased as "apparently unrelated."

S1 mentions this as a general description of Dos Passos's work, but not as part of the collage technique.

S3 uses this phrase to describe the United States in 1900, not the collage technique.

S4 states that the collage technique includes the sporadic insertion of clippings from *newspapers*, not private governmental reports.

Paragraph 6	Comments
S1 The literary influence of Joyce, Dos Passos, and their peers remains pervasive to this day.	Influence of Joyce, Dos Passos etc. remains pervasive (= everywhere).
2 In that sense, it can be argued that the movement that they spearheaded in the literary world was more momentous in the long run than the parallel revolution in the artistic world.	Literary movement may have been more momentous than the artistic one.
3 While Cubism predated the stream-of-consciousness movement, it is now seen as more of a period in art than a guiding light, whereas the stream-of-consciousness style remains current in literature.	Cubism = historical phase, but stream of consciousness = still current.

12. According to paragraph 6, which of the following is true about Cubism?

FACT. Cubism's influence is described in S2 (the "parallel revolution") and in S3.

✗ (A) It is currently as influential in art as the stream-of-consciousness style is in literature.

It is not as influential. S3: "While Cubism predated the stream-of-consciousness movement, it is now seen as more of a period in art than a guiding light, whereas the stream-of-consciousness style remains current in literature."

✓ (B) It had more impact on art made early in the twentieth century than it does on art made today.

CORRECT. S3: "While Cubism predated the stream-of-consciousness movement, it is now seen as more of a period in art than a guiding light ... " That is, it is not now as much a guiding light as it once was (as described earlier in the passage).

✗ (C) It was predated by the stream-of-consciousness movement.

Opposite. S3 states that "Cubism predated the stream-of-consciousness movement," not the other way around.

✗ (D) It is considered as much a guiding light for current artists as an epoch in the history of art.

S3 notes that Cubism "is now seen as more of a period in art than a guiding light." That is, Cubism is not as much a guiding light as it is short-lived period in art.

Paragraph 5	Comments
P5 S4 Dos Passos sought to reflect the feelings and consciousness of those times by employing what critics have called a "collage technique": newspaper clippings are inserted sporadically, and his disparate characters and plots intersect at seemingly random intervals.	

Paragraph 6	Comments
P6 S1 **A** The literary influence of Joyce, Dos Passos, and their peers remains pervasive to this day.	**CORRECT.** Inserted here, the question sets up P6 well. Every sentence in the current version of the paragraph provides part of the answer.
2 **B** In that sense, it can be argued that the movement that they spearheaded in the literary world was more momentous than the parallel revolution in the artistic world.	Placing the question in the middle doesn't work, because the question is too general. S1 is already providing the answer.
3 **C** While Cubism predated the stream-of-consciousness movement, it is now seen as more of a period in art than a guiding light, whereas the stream-of-consciousness style remains current in literature.	Placing the question in the middle doesn't work, because the question is too general. S1–2 are already providing the answer.
End **D**	Placing the question here would leave it hanging. It is not meant as a question for the reader to go off and ponder after reading the passage. At this point, the author has already given a complete answer.

13. **Where do these revolutions in literature and in art stand today, in the twenty-first century?**

Where would the sentence (a question) best fit?

✓ (A) Choice A

✗ (B) Choice B

✗ (C) Choice C

✗ (D) Choice D

INSERT TEXT. This very general question about the current status of these literary and artistic revolutions demands an answer in the text. The question should come early, in order to "set the table" for the author's assessment of the current impact of the movements (stream of consciousness in literature and Cubism in art).

CORRECT.

	Whole Passage	**Comments**
P1	At the dawn of the twentieth century, European painting, which was then a far more influential art form than it is now, underwent a vast aesthetic revolution …	~1900: revolution in European painting. Cubism: abstract, multiple perspectives. Captivated art world. Also inspired writers and musicians.
P2	James Joyce and John Dos Passos were two renowned authors whose major works employed this nonlinear framework derived from Cubism …	Joyce and Dos Passos = two writers who applied nonlinear Cubist principles. "Stream-of-consciousness" writing. Inner monologue: nonlinear, separate parts.
P3	Like Picasso and Braque, Joyce and Dos Passos enjoyed great artistic success …	Both Joyce and Dos Passos were successful and influential. Joyce's life and career. Dos Passos's life and career.
P4	Joyce's most renowned work, *Ulysses*, was published in 1922; however, in the United States, it was banned …	Joyce's masterpiece, *Ulysses*. It exhibits a stream-of-consciousness aesthetic. *Ulysses* is difficult, complex, expects knowledge of reader = not widely read. But famous and influential.
P5	By contrast, John Dos Passos's work, also considered unique and innovative, proved far more accessible and popular …	Dos Passos's work: more popular but less important. *U.S.A.* trilogy. Collage technique.
P6	The literary influence of Joyce, Dos Passos, and their peers remains pervasive to this day …	Influence of Joyce, Dos Passos etc., remains pervasive (= everywhere). Literary movement may have been more momentous than the artistic one. Cubism = historical phase, but stream of consciousness = still current.

14.	**Cubism, an early twentieth-century revolution in art, also influenced the course of literature by inspiring prominent authors to infuse its principles into their works.**

SUMMARY. Correct answers must be clearly expressed in the passage. They must also be among the major points of the passage. They should tie as directly as possible to the summary given.

✗ A Stream-of-consciousness writing was not popular with the public because of its difficult vocabulary.

In P4, *Ulysses* is described this way. But this description is not applied to all stream-of-consciousness writing. In fact, P5 S1 states that Dos Passos's work "proved far more accessible and popular."

✗ B Dos Passos was more progressive politically than Joyce because of his experience in the First World War.

The passage never discusses Joyce's political leanings or his activities during the war.

✓ C The influence of stream-of-consciousness writing proved more lasting in the literary world than that of Cubism did in the art world.

CORRECT. This is the major point of P6.

✓ D In the early twentieth century, an artistic upheaval in European painting upended conventions and infused an abstract perspective into various art forms.

CORRECT. This is the major point of P1. It overlaps somewhat with the summary statement, in fact.

✓ E The fragmented, nonlinear techniques employed by Joyce and Dos Passos aimed to portray human thoughts authentically.

CORRECT. This corresponds to key parts of P2 and P3. These "fragmented, nonlinear techniques" are in fact stream of consciousness, the topic of the passage.

✗ F In their elite educations and European travels, Joyce and Dos Passos were representative of great writers of the period.

The passage only addresses the literary work of these two writers. It does not address whether they, or their life experiences, were representative of their peer group.

Answers and Explanations—3.6 Henri Cartier-Bresson

	Paragraph 1	**Comments**
S1	The French photographer Henri Cartier-Bresson (1908–2004) was a pioneer of modern street photography and is regarded as the "father of photojournalism."	Cartier-Bresson = pioneer of photojournalism.
2	Celebrated for the candid shots he took of everyday life in Paris, as well as for his photo-reporting around the world, he remains one of the most respected photographers of the twentieth century.	
3	His early life as an artist was not devoted to photography, however.	Early life as artist.
4	When he was 19 years old, Cartier-Bresson began studying at the studio of Cubist painter and sculptor André Lhote.	
5	There, he learned to be a painter.	He actually studied painting.
6	He was educated in art theory and composition, and he discovered an interest in both modern and Renaissance art.	

1. The word "candid" in the passage is closest in meaning to

    VOCABULARY. "Candid" = honest, truthful. In the context of photography, "candid" = unposed or natural rather than posed and artificial.

    ✗ (A) theatrical

    Opposite. "Theatrical" can mean "exaggerated emotionally."

    ✓ (B) natural

    CORRECT. "Celebrated for the candid shots he took of everyday life" = celebrated for the natural, unposed shots he took of everyday life

    ✗ (C) simulated

    Opposite. "Simulated" = artificial, posed, pretend.

    ✗ (D) intense

    Someone who says "candid" things (honest and truthful) might be perceived as intense, but this word is unrelated.

2.   Paragraph 1 implies that prior to the 1920s,

INFERENCE. This question is tricky, because there is no direct reference to the 1920s in the text. However, there are dates and years that provide anchor points for inferences.

✗ (A) most artists in France studied painting rather than other media

Nothing in the text implies that most artists in France studied painting preferentially at any time. Cartier-Bresson's personal experience of studying painting first can't be generalized to any other artists, let alone most other artists in France.

✗ (B) paintings were less abstract than they generally are today

The paragraph does not discuss at all any rise of abstraction in paintings.

✓ (C) modern street photography was likely not a well-established art form

CORRECT. S1: Cartier-Bresson was born in 1908. S4: he began studying painting 19 years later, which would be in 1927. According to S1, Cartier-Bresson was a "pioneer" of modern street photography. That is, he was one of the first photographers to engage in this practice. So it is unlikely that modern street photography was well-established before the 1920s.

✗ (D) henri Cartier-Bresson was already emerging as a talented photojournalist

In 1920, Cartier-Bresson was 11–12 years old (since you are told he was born in 1908). According to S3–4, he didn't begin studying art until he was 19 years old, so it is highly unlikely that he was emerging as a talented photojournalist!

3.   All of the following are mentioned about Henri Cartier-Bresson in paragraph 1 EXCEPT:

NEGATIVE FACT. Three answer choices are facts about Cartier-Bresson found in P1. They could be anywhere, because the whole paragraph is about him. One answer is not supported in P1. It could be false or simply not mentioned.

✗ (A) He was a legendary photojournalist.

S1 notes that he is considered to be the "father of photojournalism." This description certainly includes being a "legendary photojournalist."

✗ (B) He was first trained as a painter.

S5: "he learned to be a painter." This happens in his "early life as an artist" (S3) before he turned to photography.

✗ (C) He was interested in both Renaissance and modern art.

S6: "an interest in both modern and Renaissance art."

✓ (D) His portrait photographs were widely celebrated.

CORRECT. Portraits (whether paintings or photographs) are typically still-life representations focusing on a person's face, or the faces of a small group. Portraits are not mentioned in P1.

	Paragraph 2	**Comments**
S1	Meanwhile, throughout the 1920s, photography continued to develop as an art form, and in 1930, Cartier-Bresson became inspired by a photograph taken by Hungarian photographer Martin Munkacsi.	1930: a particular photograph inspired Cartier-Bresson.
2	In the photograph, titled "Three Boys at Lake Tanganyika," three young boys play in Lake Tanganyika, an expansive, freshwater lake that touches four countries on the African continent: Tanzania, the Democratic Republic of the Congo, Burundi, and Zambia.	
3	In the photo, the boys splash in the surf.	
4	The image features their silhouettes against the lake's foaming waves.	
5	It is a joyful scene.	
6	Cartier-Bresson credited the photograph with leading him to turn away from painting in order to focus on photography.	It led Cartier-Bresson to turn from painting to photography.
7	He said of the picture, "I suddenly understood that photography can fix eternity in a moment."	

4. The word "**features**" in the passage is closest in meaning to

  ✓   (A) highlights

  ✗   (B) hides

  ✗   (C) smears

  ✗   (D) shatters

VOCABULARY. In this context, "feature" = present, highlight, show clearly and distinctly.

CORRECT. "The image features their silhouettes against the lake's foaming waves" = the image highlights or clearly shows the silhouettes against the waves.

Opposite.

Opposite in a slightly different way. "Smear" = smudge, blur, make indistinct, whereas "feature" = show clearly.

Unrelated. "Shatter" can mean to break, but it can also mean to damage or destroy something abstract, such as a feeling or belief.

5. According to paragraph 2, why did Cartier-Bresson switch from being a painter to being a photographer?

FACT. The whole paragraph describes the catalyst for this switch: a specific photograph.

✗ (A) He wanted to represent human silhouettes against natural backgrounds.

The particular photograph that inspired Cartier-Bresson did represent human silhouettes against a natural background (S4). But there is nothing to suggest that these specific features of the photograph were what inspired Cartier-Bresson to change artistic directions, or that he wished to reproduce these exact characteristics in his own photographs.

✓ (B) He was inspired by the way a particular photograph captured a moment.

CORRECT. S1 states that Cartier-Bresson "became inspired by a photograph." S6 indicates that the photograph turned Cartier-Bresson from painting to photography. S7 provides a striking quote that captures the impact on the photographer: the photograph was able to "fix [= capture permanently] eternity in a moment."

✗ (C) He sought to introduce the world to the daily lives of African people.

The photograph that inspired Cartier-Bresson was taken in Africa, but the desire to share these specific takes of daily life with the world is never mentioned.

✗ (D) He hoped to establish an international career in Africa.

The crucial photograph happens to have been taken in Africa. But nothing in the text indicates that Cartier-Bresson was inspired to change careers because of the specific location of that image.

6. The author describes the image as "a joyful scene" in order to

PURPOSE. A short, simple sentence, S5 provides this assessment of the scene's emotion in the context of the broader description of the photograph in S2–5.

✗ (A) offer a reason why Cartier-Bresson considered photography superior to painting

It's not clear that Cartier-Bresson considered photography "superior" to painting in general, just that he saw photography as his own calling. Also, the joy in the scene is not presented as a specific reason for Cartier-Bresson's switch.

✗ (B) suggest that a less joyful photo would not have inspired Cartier-Bresson

This is extreme. Mentioning that the scene is joyful is not the same as suggesting that a scene with less joy would not have been inspiring to Cartier-Bresson.

✓ (C) convey the spirit of the photograph that inspired Cartier-Bresson

CORRECT. This is the only choice that the text can support. Calling the scene joyful, the author just conveys the spirit of the photograph. In fact, without S5, the emotion of the scene would not be entirely clear from the sensory descriptions in S2–4.

✗ (D) illustrate the highest purpose of photojournalism

Nothing in S5 or in nearby sentences suggests that the joy in this scene is necessarily representative of "the highest purpose of photojournalism," whatever that might be. S7 asserts the closest thing to what Cartier-Bresson might have believed the purpose to be: to "fix eternity in a moment." But you can't be sure that this idea corresponds to capturing the joy of a scene, or any other emotion. Perhaps emotionless moments would work just as well to have eternity "fixed" in them.

Paragraph 3	Comments
S1 Cartier-Bresson then acquired a German camera with a 50-millimeter (50-mm) lens—relatively small compared to the lenses used by professional photographers today.	Cartier-Bresson got a camera with a small 50-mm lens.
2 Despite having many opportunities to use a larger, more complex lens over the course of his career, Cartier-Bresson preferred his 50-mm lens for several reasons.	He preferred this lens.
3 The most important of these was that with this lens, he was able to shoot without being conspicuous, which he resisted for fear of being seen as showing off.	With it, he wasn't conspicuous (= wasn't very noticeable, attracting attention).
4 It allowed him to capture moments he might not have captured otherwise, as people often did not notice him shooting.	

7. The word "it" in the passage refers to

REFERENCE. S4 begins with "it," which is the subject of the sentence. What allowed Cartier-Bresson to capture moments he might not have captured otherwise?

✗ (A) fear

This is the closest noun in the previous sentence, but it does not make sense as the subject of S4.

✗ (B) a large, complex lens

S2 notes that Cartier-Bresson had the opportunity to use a larger, more complex lens, but he preferred a different lens.

✗ (C) the reason for his preference

The "reason for his preference" did not itself allow him to capture the moments he wanted to capture. Rather, the lens that he preferred did so.

✓ (D) his 50-mm lens

CORRECT. S2: "Cartier-Bresson preferred his 50-mm lens." S3: "with this lens, he could shoot without being conspicuous." S4: "It allowed him ..." = this 50-mm lens allowed him to capture moments he might not have captured otherwise.

8.   According to paragraph 3, what was the primary reason that Cartier-Bresson preferred to shoot with a 50-mm lens rather than with a larger lens?

FACT. S2: "Cartier-Bresson preferred his 50-mm lens for several reasons." S3–4 describe the most important of these reasons.

✓   (A) To take his photographs in an unobtrusive way

CORRECT. S3: "he was able to shoot without being conspicuous" = he could do so in an unobtrusive (= inconspicuous, not very noticeable) way.

✗   (B) To capture moments that he could have captured otherwise, but not as easily

Not quite. S4 notes that the lens "allowed him to capture moments he might *not* have captured otherwise." Those moments would have been impossible to capture, not harder but still possible.

✗   (C) To show off without being embarrassed as he shot

Opposite. S3 states that he specifically did not want to show off by shooting in a noticeable way.

✗   (D) To maintain opportunities to use both kinds of lenses during his career

This is a distortion of language from S2, which states that Cartier-Bresson had many opportunities to use a larger lens over the course of his career.

Paragraph 4	**Comments**
S1 He also had a strong preference for shooting in black and white, believing that the myriad printing options available when shooting with color distorted the image he was seeing with his eyes.	He preferred black-and-white photography.
2 For this reason, he only shot in color when obliged to.	
3 In general, he bemoaned photography's **trend** toward focusing on ever-advancing processing techniques, believing that the fetishizing of these techniques distracted people from what the art was truly about: seeing and capturing.	He disliked how photography focused on ever-advancing techniques.

3

9. The word "trend" in the passage is closest in meaning to

VOCABULARY. "Trend" = tendency, drift, inclination, movement.

  ✗ (A) contribution

Not quite. "Photography's *contribution* toward focusing on ever-advancing techniques" would mean that photography as a field was contributing to a broader focus (out in the world) on these techniques. But "trend" means that photography itself was moving that way on its own, without reference to any other field.

  ✗ (B) hostility

In some ways, the opposite. A "trend" is a movement toward something, presumably because of people's desire for it. "Hostility" would imply negative or angry feelings about the ever-advancing techniques.

  ✓ (C) movement

CORRECT. "He bemoaned photography's trend toward focusing on ever-advancing techniques" = he bemoaned (= mourned, lamented) photography's movement toward focusing on these techniques.

  ✗ (D) responsibility

He was unhappy about the move, in photography, toward advanced techniques. He was not unhappy about a belief that photography had some sort of responsibility to focus on those techniques.

Paragraph 5	**Comments**
S1 *Images à la Sauvette* (*The Decisive Moment* in the English edition), a book featuring over 100 of Cartier-Bresson's photographs, was published in 1952 with a cover drawn specifically for the book by renowned French painter Henri Matisse.	Cartier-Bresson's book, *The Decisive Moment*.
2 The book quickly became a classic in the canon of literature on photography.	Instant classic.
3 Alongside the portfolio of his images in the book, Cartier-Bresson authored a 4,500-word introduction on his photographic philosophy.	Introduction: his photographic philosophy.
4 This introduction to the book is often referenced today in treatises and essays on the art and history of the photograph—in particular, the portions in which he elaborates on the book's title.	
5 To Cartier-Bresson, photography was about capturing in "a fraction of a second…the significance of an event."	
6 In a 1971 interview, Cartier-Bresson described the art as an act of affirmation.	Photography = act of affirmation.
7 He rejected many similar titles in favor of *The Decisive Moment*, including *A pas de Loup*, which means "tiptoeing," a reference to how he, as a photographer, approached his subjects.	

10. According to paragraph 5, which of the following statements about the book *The Decisive Moment* is true?

FACT. S1–5 and S7 are directly about the book (and S6 seems to be indirectly so).

✓ (A) It contained both writing and photography by Cartier-Bresson.

CORRECT. S1 states the book contains "over 100 of Cartier-Bresson's photographs." S3: "Cartier-Bresson authored a 4,500-word introduction on his photographic philosophy."

✗ (B) It contained only Cartier-Bresson's most significant photographs.

S2 states that the book became a classic. It is very likely that the photographs Cartier-Bresson chose for the book are significant. But you are never told that these are his *most* significant photographs or that *only* those were included.

✗ (C) Its cover was a photograph of Henri Matisse.

S1 states the cover was "*drawn* ... by ... Henri Matisse." It was not a photograph of him.

✗ (D) It is seldom referenced today in essays on the art and history of photography.

Opposite. S4 notes that it is "often referenced today in treatises and essays on the art and history of the photograph." "Seldom" = rarely, the opposite of often.

11. The phrase "elaborates on" in the passage is closest in meaning to

VOCABULARY. "Elaborate on" = say more about, expand upon, go into more detail.

✗ (A) overemphasizes

When "overemphasizing" (placing excessive emphasis on) something, the speaker might elaborate on details. However, the meaning of overemphasize implies that the speaker isn't just telling you more, but also exaggerating the importance to some degree. This goes beyond the meaning of "elaborate."

✓ (B) writes more about

CORRECT. "He elaborates on the book's title" = he writes more about it, he goes into more detail or explanation about it.

✗ (C) understates

Opposite in some ways. To "understate" something is to describe it as smaller or lesser in importance than it actually is.

✗ (D) simplifies

To elaborate on or provide more details about something might make it more clear, but it doesn't necessarily simplify it (make it easier to understand).

3

Paragraph 6	Comments
S1 When Cartier-Bresson died in 2004, he had established a global reputation as one of the greatest photographers of all time.	Reputation as one of the greatest photographers ever.
2 Yet, despite this fame, he was extremely timid and often shunned publicity.	But he was shy.
3 Thus, while he is revered for the photos he captured of faces around the world, he himself was rarely recognized.	Was himself rarely recognized.

12. According to paragraph 6, what was the difference between Cartier-Bresson's reputation and his physical image?	**FACT.** S2 points out the contrast between Cartier-Bresson's fame and his personal behavior (he shunned publicity). S3 indicates the result.
✗ (A) His physical appearance was much more commonly known than his work.	Opposite, according to S3.
✗ (B) He shunned publicity but was extremely timid and shy.	"But" doesn't make sense: these two points are aligned. Neither one explains his fame. They both explain his near invisibility in public (S3).
✗ (C) He established a global reputation on the basis of a locally known image.	The first part of this choice is true (S1). But he didn't establish that global reputation "on the basis of a locally known image," as if it were *because* of his little-known image, known just "locally," that he was able to become globally famous. He became famous, not because of his public shyness, but because of his incredible photographs.
✓ (D) He was recognized far and wide by name but not so often by sight.	**CORRECT.** S3 states that he was "revered" (= highly respected, famous for good reasons) but "rarely recognized" in person. People on the street usually didn't know who he was.

Paragraph 5   **Comments**

S1   *Images à la Sauvette* (*The Decisive Moment* in the English edition), a book featuring over 100 of Cartier-Bresson's photographs, was published in 1952 with a cover drawn specifically for the book by renowned French painter Henri Matisse.

2–4   **A** The book quickly became a classic in the canon of literature on photography. Alongside the portfolio of his images in the book, Cartier-Bresson authored a 4,500-word introduction on his photographic philosophy. This introduction to the book is often referenced today in treatises and essays on the art and history of the photograph—in particular, the portions in which he elaborates on the book's title.

Placing the sentence here would make the pronoun "he" refer incorrectly to Matisse. Moreover, the previous sentence makes no mention of the process of choosing the title of the book.

5–6   **B** To Cartier-Bresson, photography was about capturing in "a fraction of a second…the significance of an event." In a 1971 interview, Cartier-Bresson described the art as an act of affirmation.

The prior sentence does end with "he elaborates on the book's title." But this is not a very specific reference to the decision process that Cartier-Bresson went through. Placing the new sentence here would leave mysterious what is meant by "the seeking photographer." And this placement would disrupt the logical flow between S4 and S5.

7   **C** He rejected many similar titles in favor of *The Decisive Moment*, including *A pas de Loup*, which means "tiptoeing," a reference to how he, as a photographer, approached his subjects.

The previous sentence does not refer to a decision among titles of the book.

End   **D**

CORRECT. The new sentence makes sense here. He chose to describe the "photograph being sought" with his title *The Decisive Moment.* He chose not to describe "the seeking photographer" with an alternative title that meant "Tiptoeing." The previous sentence describes this title-selection process in the most detail.

3

13.   **Ultimately, in the title he chose to describe the photograph being sought rather than the seeking photographer.**

Where would the sentence best fit?

✗   (A) Choice A

✗   (B) Choice B

✗   (C) Choice C

✓   (D) Choice D   **CORRECT.**

INSERT TEXT. The words "Ultimately" and "he chose" indicate that this new sentence describes the end of a decision process. The phrase "in the title" signals that the decision was about the title of the book (the subject of the paragraph). So the new sentence should be inserted right after (or just as) Cartier-Bresson chooses the title of his book, wherever that is described in the paragraph.

	Whole Passage	**Comments**
P1	The French photographer Henri Cartier-Bresson (1908–2004) was a pioneer of modern street photography …	Cartier-Bresson = pioneer of photojournalism. Early life as artist. He actually studied painting.
P2	Meanwhile, throughout the 1920s, photography continued to develop as an art form …	1930: a particular photograph inspired Cartier-Bresson. It led him to turn from painting to photography.
P3	Cartier-Bresson then acquired a German camera with a 50-millimeter (50-mm) lens …	Cartier-Bresson got a camera with a small 50-mm lens. He preferred this lens. With it, he wasn't conspicuous (= very noticeable, attracting attention).
P4	He also had a strong preference for shooting in black and white …	He preferred black-and-white photography. He disliked how photography focused on ever-advancing techniques.
P5	*Images à la Sauvette* (*The Decisive Moment* in the English edition), a book featuring over 100 of Cartier-Bresson's photographs …	Cartier-Bresson's book *The Decisive Moment*. Instant classic. Introduction: his photographic philosophy. Photography = act of affirmation.
P6	When Cartier-Bresson died in 2004, he had established a global reputation …	Reputation as one of the greatest photographers ever. But he was shy. Was himself rarely recognized.

14.   **Henri Cartier-Bresson was a groundbreaking photographer of the twentieth century.**

SUMMARY. Correct answers must be clearly expressed in the passage. They must also be among the major points of the passage. They should tie as directly as possible to the summary given.

✓ [A] Cartier-Bresson placed greater value on the scene captured in a photograph than on the techniques used to process the photograph.

CORRECT. This comparison is the key point of P4. Also, the great value Cartier-Bresson placed on the captured scene itself is echoed elsewhere.

✗ [B] Cartier-Bresson started studying painting at the age of 19.

While this fact is true (P1 S4), it is not a central idea in the passage. It's a minor detail that fills out the picture of Cartier-Bresson's early career in painting. More broadly, the passage does not dwell on his training in painting or draw connections between this art form and his later work in photography. Another passage might have done so, but not this one. Rather, this passage emphasizes the transition, the moment of clarity at which Cartier-Bresson knew he should drop painting for photography.

✗ [C] The reason Cartier-Bresson used a 50-mm lens remains a vexing mystery.

The passage does not say or suggest that the reason is a mystery. P3 in fact provides a key reason for Cartier-Bresson's use of this lens.

✓ [D] Cartier-Bresson's influential book *The Decisive Moment* showcases the photographer's work.

CORRECT. This is the subject of P5, a long and weighty paragraph in the passage.

✗ [E] An alternative title for *The Decisive Moment*, one that was ultimately discarded, was *Tiptoeing*.

This point is true (P5 S7). But it is too narrow of a point in the passage to be a central idea.

✓ [F] Inspired by a particular photograph of children playing in a lake, Cartier-Bresson decided to focus on photography over painting.

CORRECT. This moment of clarity and inspiration is the focus of P2.

3

Answers and Explanations— 3.7 History of the Recording Industry

	Paragraph 1	Comments
S1	No invention was more **fundamental to** the development of the recording industry than the phonograph.	Phonograph: crucial invention for recording industry.
2	Created in 1877 by Thomas Edison, the phonograph featured a conspicuous flaring horn about 12 inches (30 centimeters) tall, through which sound was projected.	How it worked: projecting sound through a horn.
3	The original device played phonographic cylinders, which were soon replaced by records.	
4	A record is a disc etched with physical grooves representing the sounds to be replicated.	
5	When the disc was rotated at a certain speed, it caused vibrations in a stylus, or needle, that tracked the grooves.	Rotating record (disc with grooves) vibrated a stylus.
6	These vibrations were then picked up and amplified by a diaphragm, which transmitted sound to the flaring horn.	Vibrations went to diaphragm, which passed sound to the horn.
7	Later versions of the phonograph, beginning in the 1920s, featured an electronic system for translating stylus vibration into sound (these electronic devices became known as "record players" or "turntables").	Later versions added electronics.
8	However, the basic mechanisms for recording sound on a rotating disc and reading it with a stylus have remained essentially unchanged from the original invention.	But basic mechanisms are still essentially unchanged.

1. The phrase "fundamental to" in the passage is closest in meaning to

    ✓ (A) crucial for

    ✗ (B) irrelevant to

    ✗ (C) typical of

    ✗ (D) welcoming toward

VOCABULARY. "Fundamental to" = essential, vital, basic to or for.

CORRECT. "No invention was more fundamental to the development of the recording industry than the phonograph" = no invention was more crucial for, or essential to, the industry's development than the phonograph.

Opposite.

"Typical of" would mean that the invention represented the industry well, or that it was an appropriate symbol of the industry. But that's not the same as being fundamental or necessary.

"Welcoming" (inviting) is unrelated to the essential nature of "fundamental."

2. According to paragraph 1, which of the following is true of the phonograph?

    ✗ (A) It is a disc etched with physical grooves representing the sounds to be replicated.

    ✓ (B) Many of its original design features are similar to those of record players today.

    ✗ (C) The stylus of a phonograph projects sound directly through the flaring horn.

    ✗ (D) The original phonograph used electronics to translate stylus vibration into sound.

FACT. All of P1 is devoted to the phonograph. The correct answer could be anywhere, but it must be supported in the text.

This is true of the records played on a phonograph, not of phonographs themselves. S4: "A record is a disc etched with physical grooves representing the sounds to be replicated." Even if you are not completely clear on whether the record is to be considered part of the phonograph, the phonograph has other parts (such as the flaring horn, the diaphragm, and the stylus).

CORRECT. S8: "the basic mechanisms for recording sound on a rotating disc and reading it with a stylus have remained essentially unchanged from the original invention." The rotating disc and stylus are design features of a phonograph. The term "record player" is given in S7.

S5–6 explain that the stylus picks up vibrations from the grooves in a record, which are *only then* translated into sound by the diaphragm, not by the stylus itself. The diaphragm is what projects the sound to the horn.

S7: "Later versions of the phonograph, beginning in the 1920s, featured an electronic system for translating stylus vibration into sound."

	Paragraph 2	**Comments**
S1	The phonograph was originally marketed as a business and legal services device.	Originally marketed for business and law.
2	Edison's sales strategies targeted businesspeople, attorneys, and anyone else who might use shorthand or dictation as a means of recording ideas or spoken testimony.	
3	However, the phonograph eventually found its primary market elsewhere: the recording of sound for entertainment purposes.	But it eventually found its primary market: entertainment.
4	This market started with "phonograph parlors," the first of which appeared in 1889 in San Francisco.	Phonograph parlors.
5	Customers would go to parlors and order a selection to be played for a nickel.	
6	This system was the **precursor** of the modern-day jukebox.	
7	Within a decade, nearly every major city in the United States had at least one phonograph parlor.	

3. The phrase "precursor" in the passage is closest in meaning to

VOCABULARY. "Precursor" = ancestor, predecessor, something that (or someone who) came before.

✗ (A) descendant

Opposite.

✗ (B) inventor

As an inanimate object, the phonograph parlor didn't "invent" the modern-day jukebox. People had to have invented the jukebox.

✗ (C) antithesis

"Antithesis" = direct opposite.

✓ (D) forerunner

CORRECT. "This system was the precursor of the modern-day jukebox" = the system was the forerunner or ancestor of the modern jukebox.

4.   Which of the following can be inferred about Edison's sales strategies from paragraph 2?

INFERENCE. S2: "Edison's sales strategies targeted business-people, attorneys, and anyone else who might use shorthand or dictation as a means of recording ideas or spoken testimony." However, S3 points out that "the phonograph eventually found its primary market elsewhere: the recording of sound for entertainment purposes." This suggests that Edison was initially wrong about the likely users and uses of phonographs.

✗ (A) Edison eventually stopped targeting businesspeople and attorneys entirely.

Too extreme. S2–3 make it clear that businesspeople and attorneys did not wind up being the primary market for recording technology. But this does not mean that Edison entirely stopped trying to sell to them.

✗ (B) Edison failed to seize sales opportunities in San Francisco.

S4 notes that the first phonograph parlor "appeared in 1889 in San Francisco." The paragraph goes on to explain that these parlors were for entertainment purposes. However, you can't infer that Edison failed to seize, or did not take advantage of, sales opportunities in San Francisco.

✓ (C) Edison was initially wrong about the primary market for recording technology.

CORRECT. S3 makes it clear that Edison's initial sales strategies failed to target the primary market that eventually emerged: entertainment.

✗ (D) Edison preferred business-people and attorneys over other types of customers.

Nothing in S2 indicates that Edison preferred some types of customer (businesspeople and attorneys) over other types ("anyone else who might use shorthand or dictation as a means of recording ideas or spoken testimony").

3

	Paragraph 3	**Comments**
S1	During the period 1890–1940, the recording industry was dominated by three companies: Victor, Columbia, and His Master's Voice, or HMV.	1890–1940: 3 companies dominated.
2	By 1900, the industry was selling over 3 million records per year in the United States.	
3	The next two decades saw great prosperity in the industry, which attracted competition from a host of smaller producers.	1900–1920: great prosperity.
4	The competitors began undercutting each other's prices, while the phonograph itself was facing stiff competition from a new technology: radio.	Then competition from smaller producers and from radio.
5	Radio programs offered special programming not available on records and featured a seemingly endless variety of available music.	
6	This caused many customers to stop purchasing records and to listen to the radio instead.	
7	During the 1920s, revenue from the sale of recorded music fell by 50 percent as a result of these developments, which were followed by the onset of the Great Depression in late 1929.	1920s: revenue fell, then Great Depression.
8	Many producers went out of business.	
9	It was not until the late 1930s, with the rising popularity of the combination radio-phonograph, the growing use of recorded sound in "talking" movies, and the recovery of the economy, that the recording industry began to recuperate.	Industry only recovered in the late 1930s (various reasons).

3

MANHATTAN PREP

5. According to paragraph 3, which of the following helped the major recording studios recuperate in the late 1930s?

FACT. S9 describes factors that helped the recording studios recuperate (= come back, recover) in the late 1930s.

✓ (A) the advent of so-called "talking" movies

CORRECT. S9: "It was not until the late 1930s, with … the growing use of recorded sound in 'talking' movies … that the recording industry began to recuperate."

✗ (B) a reduction in competitive pressure from smaller studios

S3–4 point out that the success of the recording industry prompted small studios to enter the business. This led to competitive pressure. Although S8 says that "many producers went out of business," there's no indication that the competitive pressure relaxed. In fact, this possible factor is not mentioned in S9 as one that contributed to the recovery of the industry.

✗ (C) government restrictions on radio broadcasts of copyrighted material

Nothing in the paragraph discusses government restrictions of any kind.

✗ (D) special programming that featured a nearly endless variety of music

S5 mentions this kind of special programming as a characteristic of radio programs, not of major recording studios that sold phonographic records.

6.　Which of the following can be inferred from the author's claim in paragraph 3 that prosperity in the recording industry attracted competition from smaller producers?

INFERENCE. S3: "The next two decades saw great prosperity in the industry, which attracted competition from a host of smaller producers." Those decades were from 1900 to 1920. The sentences before and after S3 provide more context for the claim. Any inference from this claim should be defensible.

✗　(A) The prosperity was caused by competition among the major recording studios.

The paragraph never reveals what exactly caused the prosperity. According to S3, the prosperity led to competition from smaller producers, which in turn undercut that prosperity.

✗　(B) The smaller producers were the driving force behind the rise of radio.

S4 mentions heightened competition in the recording industry from both small producers and a new technology: radio. However, nothing in the passage suggests that the smaller producers themselves had anything to do with the rise of radio.

✗　(C) None of the smaller producers were positioned to become as dominant as the three major studios.

Too extreme. There's no way to infer that none of the smaller producers could have become as dominant as the three major studios. Competition increased and prices fell, but still, maybe one of the smaller producers could have become a major if circumstances had worked out in that producer's favor (e.g., if it had exclusive contracts with performers that became exceptionally popular).

✓　(D) The prosperity eventually helped undermine itself through increased competition that lowered prices.

CORRECT. S4: "The competitors began undercutting each other's prices." The rest of S4 through S6 describe the rise of radio. S7: "During the 1920s, revenue from the sale of recorded music fell by 50 percent as a result of these developments" (= the rise of radio and the increased competition). You can properly infer that the prosperity referred to in S3 helped undermine (= weaken) itself, because it increased competition and lowered prices that the studios could charge.

3

Paragraph 4	Comments
S1 The industry then experienced a boon in the 1940s.	1940s: a boon (= unexpected benefit).
2 During World War II, the demand for recorded music for use in the United States armed services skyrocketed, leading to a temporary surge in the sales of recorded music despite rationing among consumers back home.	Armed forces had high demand for recorded music.
3 At the same time, several lawsuits were brought forth by musicians against radio companies, who paid a royalty to the copyright owner (usually the studio) whenever recorded material was played.	Also, musicians sued radio companies.
4 No royalty was paid to the musicians themselves.	
5 This led to a musicians' strike that lasted over two years, causing difficulties for the recording studios in the short term.	Lack of royalties led to musicians' strike.
6 However, the studios rebounded quickly when the strike ended, and radio broadcasters, the chief competitors to recording studios, now faced having to pay royalties to songwriters for every song they played.	Consequences for studios and radio broadcasters.

7. The word "skyrocketed" in the passage is closest in meaning to

   VOCABULARY. "Skyrocket" = increase dramatically, shoot up very quickly, like a rocket.

✗ (A) nosedived

   Opposite.

✓ (B) mushroomed

   CORRECT. "The demand for recorded music ... skyrocketed" = the demand mushroomed (= grew very quickly, like mushrooms).

✗ (C) plummeted

   Opposite.

✗ (D) hovered

   "Hover" = float nearby, without rising or falling quickly.

8.   According to paragraph 4, why did musicians go on strike?

FACT. S5: "This led to a musicians' strike." S3–4 describe the cause.

✗ (A) To create financial difficulty for the recording studios

S5 adds that the strike caused "difficulties for the recording studios in the short term." But this is mentioned as a side effect, not as the purpose of the strike.

✓ (B) To pressure radio companies to pay them royalties

CORRECT. S3 describes the lawsuits that musicians brought against radio companies, who paid royalties to the copyright owner of music that was played. But according to S4, "no royalty was paid to the musicians themselves." S5 states that this is what led to the strike. That is, the musicians wanted the radio companies to pay them royalties.

✗ (C) To enable musicians to initiate lawsuits against the radio companies

S3 and S5 make it clear that the lawsuits began *before* the musicians' strike. So the strike could not have enabled musicians to initiate the lawsuits.

✗ (D) To become sole copyright owners of the music they created

S3–4 mention that royalties were paid to copyright owners, which were usually the recording studios, not the musicians themselves. However, it is not clear that the purpose of the strike was to obtain copyright ownership of the recorded material—it was to obtain royalty payments. Furthermore, nothing in the passage suggests that the musicians wanted to be the *sole* owners of any copyright.

	Paragraph 5	Comments
S1	The late 1940s also saw the introduction of an important new technology: "high fidelity" recording, which enabled sound recording over the complete range of audible frequencies with very little distortion.	New: "High fidelity" recording, better than before.
2	This technology allowed for the recording of sound that was much more **authentic** with respect to the original musical performance than was previously feasible.	More authentic recording.
3	High fidelity, or "hi-fi," also enabled entire albums to be recorded on a single disc, rather than just one or two songs.	Also, an entire album could now fit on a disc.
4	Unfortunately, this development led to some exploitation by recording studios.	But this allowed exploitation.
5	If a song was discovered to be a success, either due to frequent purchases or due to radio popularity, the studio sometimes decided not to release the song as a single, which cost a fraction of a complete album.	
6	This forced consumers interested in buying the music to purchase the entire album at a much higher price.	Studios could release a popular song, not as a single, but only as part of a more expensive album.

9. Which of the sentences below best expresses the essential information in the highlighted sentence in paragraph 5? Incorrect choices change the meaning in important ways or leave out essential information.

SIMPLIFY SENTENCE. The first part of S5 describes a scenario: a song was discovered to be a success. The second part states that in some cases, the studio decided not to release that song as a single costing much less than a complete album.

✗ (A) Sometimes the studio decided not to release a more expensive, complete album of songs discovered to be popular via purchase or radio play.

Sometimes the studio decided not to release a *single* of a popular song. S5 says nothing about how studios decided whether to release full albums of popular songs.

✗ (B) If songs were successful on the radio or at the point of purchase, the studio decided at times to release them as singles costing much less than complete albums.

The studio sometimes decided *not* to release popular songs as singles.

✓ (C) Popular songs were often only released as part of a complete album, which cost more than a single.

CORRECT. This version captures the essence of S5. It does leave out the way in which a song's popularity was revealed (via radio play or direct sales). But that point is less important than the decision sometimes made by the studio not to release such songs as singles.

✗ (D) At times, successful songs were either frequently purchased by customers or discovered by the studio to be popular on the radio.

This version leaves out the core point of S5: what the studio sometimes decided to do (or not to do) with popular, successful songs. Namely, sometimes the studio didn't release them as cheaper singles.

10. The word "authentic" in the passage is closest in meaning to

VOCABULARY. "Authentic" = true, genuine, real.

✗ (A) artificial

Opposite.

✗ (B) old-fashioned

"Old-fashioned" = out-of-date, in an old style. That doesn't necessarily mean more authentic or true, as a recording.

✓ (C) accurate

CORRECT. "The recording of sound ... was much more authentic with respect to the original musical performance" = the recording was much more accurate with respect to the original performance. The recording reflected that performance more accurately and truly, in a more genuine and faithful way.

✗ (D) innovative

"Innovative" = advanced, original, or using new techniques.

	Paragraph 5	**Comments**
S1	The late 1940s also saw the introduction of an important new technology: "high fidelity" recording, which enabled sound recording over the complete range of audible frequencies with very little distortion.	
2–3	**A** This technology allowed for the recording of sound that was much more authentic with respect to the original musical performance than was previously feasible. High fidelity, or "hi-fi," also enabled entire albums to be recorded on a single disc, rather than just one or two songs.	The major studios did nothing wrong in S1. In fact, the experience of the music was improved for customers. So the new sentence doesn't belong here.
4–5	**B** Unfortunately, this development led to some exploitation by major recording studios. If a song was discovered to be a success, either due to frequent purchases or due to radio popularity, the studio sometimes decided not to release the song as a single, which cost a fraction of a complete album.	Placing the new sentence here doesn't work. Again, the major studios still did nothing wrong in S2–3, which describe how hi-fi was so much better than prior technology.
6	**C** This forced consumers interested in buying the music to purchase the entire album at a much higher price.	This placement is better, because S4–5 at least partially describe the "crime" the studios committed. But the bad effects on consumers still haven't been fully described. Moreover, the "This" in S6 no longer works. S6 can't be separated from S5, because "This" refers to the studio's decision (in S5) not to release a popular song as a single. With the new sentence inserted here, "This" incorrectly refers to the consumers' decisions to shift their purchases to smaller studios.
End	**D**	**CORRECT.** With this placement, "As a result … " correctly transitions from "This forced consumers … to purchase the entire album at a much higher price." The crime of the studios has been fully described at this point, so the new sentence can clearly describe the reactions of many customers.

3

11. **As a result, many customers stopped purchasing music produced by major recording studios and shifted their spending toward recordings produced by smaller labels.**

INSERT TEXT. The transition phrase "As a result" indicates that this sentence is the result of what came before. The result that this sentence describes is important: many customers actually stopped buying from the major recording studios. That unfortunate result (from the point of view of those studios) should be inserted after the "crime"—whatever the major studios did to upset customers.

Where would the sentence best fit?

✗ (A) Choice A

✗ (B) Choice B

✗ (C) Choice C

✓ (D) Choice D   **CORRECT.**

Whole Passage	Comments
P1 No invention was more fundamental to the development of the recording industry than the phonograph …	Phonograph: crucial invention for recording industry. How it worked: projecting sound through a horn. Rotating record (disc with grooves) vibrated a stylus. Vibrations went to diaphragm, which passed sound to the horn. Later versions added electronics. But basic mechanisms are still essentially unchanged.
P2 The phonograph was originally marketed as a business and legal services device …	Originally marketed for business and law. But it eventually found its primary market: entertainment. Phonograph parlors.
P3 During the period 1890–1940, the recording industry was dominated by three companies …	1890–1940: 3 companies dominated. 1900–1920: great prosperity. Then competition from smaller producers and from radio. 1920s: revenue fell, then Great Depression. Industry only recovered in the late 1930s (various reasons).
P4 The industry then experienced a boon in the 1940s …	1940s: a boon (= unexpected benefit). Armed forces had high demand for recorded music. Also, musicians sued radio companies. Lack of royalties led to musicians' strike. Consequences for studios and radio broadcasters.
P5 The late 1940s also saw the introduction of an important new technology: "high fidelity" recording …	New: "High fidelity" recording, better than before. More authentic recording. Also, an entire album could now fit on a disc. But this allowed exploitation. Studios could release a popular song, not as a single, but only as part of a more expensive album.

12.   This passage is developed primarily by

PURPOSE. The passage provides a chronological overview of the development of the recording industry from 1877 through the 1940s. It discusses major inventions, events, and business situations that shaped the industry and its products.

✓ (A) chronicling important technological and business developments of an industry

CORRECT. The passage is organized from earliest to latest developments in recorded sound, with detailed discussions of various technology improvements and business events in that industry.

✗ (B) contrasting multiple interpretations of historical events

Multiple interpretations of historical events would be something like this: "Historian X says that this event means Y, but historian Z says that it means W." No such "multiple interpretations" are presented, let alone contrasted.

✗ (C) evaluating the merits and drawbacks of the practices of the major recording studios

A major studio practice is called into question in P5. But evaluating the practices of the major studios is not the primary focus or development of the passage.

✗ (D) describing the development of recording technology and its application across industries

Some advances in recording technology are described, but their "application across industries" is not. The passage is squarely focused on the history of one industry, as the title says.

13.   Select from the six choices below TWO that characterize recorded music, TWO that characterize radio, and TWO that characterize both.

TABLE. Correct answers do not have to convey a main idea. They just have to be justified by the passage. Characteristics of recorded music are described throughout the passage. Characteristics of radio are more narrowly presented, as radio isn't introduced until the middle of P3.

| A | Offered special programming and a wide variety of available music |

RADIO. P3 S5: "Radio programs offered special programming not available on records and featured a seemingly endless variety of available music."

| B | Began with the invention of the phonograph |

RECORDED MUSIC. P2 S3: "However, the phonograph eventually found its primary market elsewhere: the recording of sound for entertainment purposes," the vast majority of which was recorded music.

| C | Suffered because of the musicians' strike in the 1940s |

BOTH. P4 S5–6: "a musicians' strike that lasted over two years, causing difficulties for the recording studios in the short term ... [Meanwhile] radio broadcasters ... now faced having to pay royalties to songwriters for every song they played."

| D | Suffered greatly during the Great Depression |

RECORDED MUSIC. P3 S7–8: "revenue from the sale of recorded music fell by 50 percent ... [and was] followed by the onset of the Great Depression in late 1929. Many [recorded music] producers went out of business." Radio did exist during the Great Depression. But it is not described as having suffered during that time.

| E | Enabled sound to be heard for entertainment purposes |

BOTH. Mentioned for recorded music in P2. Mentioned for radio in P3.

| F | Forced by lawsuits to pay royalties to musicians |

RADIO. Mentioned in P4 S6. Recording studios also make royalty payments to songwriters. But this fact is not mentioned in the passage, and these payments are not because of lawsuits.

3

Answers and Explanations—3.8 Paleolithic Cave Art

	Paragraph 1	Comments
S1	The Paleolithic era is the period of history commonly known as "the Stone Age."	Paleolithic = Stone Age.
2	It begins with the appearance of stone tools around 2.5 million years ago and ends approximately 12,000 years ago.	
3	It is quite late during the Paleolithic period—only around 40,000 years ago—that cave art first appears in the archaeological record.	Cave art appears late in period.
4	Found in various locations across the globe, sometimes deep in the inner chambers of caves and sometimes closer to their openings, this art reveals a modern human species that had evolved sufficiently to comprehend and appreciate symbolism.	Reveals modern humans who could appreciate symbolism.

1. The word "reveals" in the passage is closest in meaning to:

     VOCABULARY. "Reveal" = expose, uncover, show or portray something hidden.

  ✗ (A) decorates

     The art might have "decorated" the walls if it was meant to make them more attractive, but that is not mentioned here, neither is that related to "reveal."

  ✗ (B) inspires

     To "inspire" is to motivate someone to try or do something. This is unrelated here.

  ✗ (C) conceals

     Opposite.

  ✓ (D) exposes

     CORRECT. "This art reveals a modern human species" = this art exposes or shows a modern human species (which might not have been obvious beforehand).

2. According to paragraph 1, the discovery of cave art first made 40,000 years ago was significant in that it established which of the following?

     FACT. S3 mentions the discovery of cave art. S4 discusses implications.

  ✗ (A) An archaeological mystery was solved.

     A mystery is not mentioned at this point.

  ✗ (B) Much of the art was found deep within caves.

     While this is true (S4), it is not the reason why the discovery of the art was significant.

  ✓ (C) Those who created it understood symbolism.

     CORRECT. S4: "this art reveals a modern human species that had evolved sufficiently to comprehend and appreciate symbolism."

  ✗ (D) Little other cave art was created after about 40,000 years ago.

     This point is not made in the paragraph.

	Paragraph 2	**Comments**
S1	Cave art is often divided into two categories: figurative (depicting animals and humans) and non-figurative (shapes that aren't animals or humans).	Figurative and non-figurative cave art.
2	Within both of these categories, the prevailing **hypothesis** is that the purpose of much of the art was to serve the spiritual practices of early humans.	Both are believed to be for spiritual purposes.
3	This is particularly likely in cases in which the art has been found deep within distant caverns, in locations that took great effort to reach and that required long, dark treks that might have featured many perilous obstacles, from bears to floods to falling rocks.	Especially true for art deep within caves.

3. The word "hypothesis" in the passage is closest in meaning to

VOCABULARY. "Hypothesis" = initial theory or explanation used as a starting point for further investigation.

✗ (A) approximation

Not quite. "Approximation" = rough calculation or estimation. It's not the same thing as a preliminary explanation or theory.

✓ (B) theory

CORRECT. "The prevailing hypothesis is that the purpose of much of the art was to serve the spiritual practices of early humans" = the prevailing theory, or currently popular (but provisional) explanation is that the purpose of the art was to serve these spiritual practices.

✗ (C) conclusion

"Conclusion" indicates a much more final judgment than "hypothesis" does.

✗ (D) analysis

"Analysis" = investigation, inquiry and/or extraction of meaningful results from data. This is not the same as a hypothesis.

4. Paragraph 2 indicates that in locations deep within caverns, cave art was

FACT. S3 discusses cave art in such locations.

✓ (A) difficult and likely dangerous to access

CORRECT. S3 describes these locations as ones "that took great effort to reach and that required long, dark treks that might have featured many perilous obstacles, from bears to floods to falling rocks."

✗ (B) impossible to reach without artificial light

"Impossible" is too extreme, and artificial light is not discussed.

✗ (C) particularly unlikely to have served spiritual needs

Opposite. S2 indicates that cave art is thought to have served spiritual practices primarily. S3: "this is particularly likely" for art deep within caves.

✗ (D) more rarely created than art near cavern openings

This seems plausible. But the passage never states this point.

5. Which of the following can be inferred from information given in paragraph 2?

INFERENCE. No particular guidance is given, but the right answer must be clearly supported in the text of P2.

✓ (A) Not all art was necessarily used to serve the spiritual practices of early humans.

CORRECT. S2: "the prevailing hypothesis is that the purpose of *much* of the art was to serve the spiritual practices of early humans." This allows for the idea that some art might *not* serve a spiritual purpose.

✗ (B) Figurative cave art was more likely to serve spiritual practices of early humans than non-figurative cave art.

These two categories of cave art are defined and distinguished in S1. But S2–3, which put forth the claim about the spiritual role of cave art, make no distinction between these two types of art.

✗ (C) Figurative and non-figurative cave art have been found in similar proportions deep within caverns

The paragraph does not say anything about how much of each of these two categories of cave art has been found deep within caves (or near openings, for that matter).

✗ (D) Perils encountered on the journey deep into caves were represented in the cave art found in such locations.

Such perils (= dangers) are described at the end of S3. But the paragraph does not claim that these perils found their way into the art itself.

Paragraph 3	**Comments**
S1 Among the oldest cave paintings found to date are those in Indonesia in the Pettakere Cave.	Pettakere Cave: among oldest.
2 Here, paintings of hands, in the form of 26 handprints, date somewhere between 35,000 and 40,000 years ago.	Ancient handprints.
3 The handprints, which are the same color as the cave wall, are outlined in red at the cave's entrance.	Outlined in red at entrance.
4 It is believed that they were created by using the hand as a stencil and then spitting or blowing onto the wall a red dye obtained from certain foliage.	Created by spitting red dye over one's hand.
5 Because the handprints appear at the entrance to the cave, it has been suggested that they were created to ward off evil spirits, preventing them from entering.	Maybe to ward off evil spirits.
6 Interestingly, the ritual of marking one's home with a handprint persists among the present-day local population near Pettakere, which has used the cave and others around it for many years.	Ritual still happens today nearby.
7 Among contemporary locals, when a new home is erected, both the new owner of a home and a priest will place handprints created with rice flour onto the first new beam of the house.	Example: new home.

6.   The word "obtained" in the passage is closest in meaning to

VOCABULARY. "Obtain" = get, take, acquire, collect.

✗ (A) rebuffed

Unrelated. "Rebuff" = reject abruptly or thoughtlessly.

✗ (B) dismissed

In some ways, the opposite. To "dismiss" is to send away or force to leave.

✗ (C) assumed

Unrelated. "Assume" = believe without proof.

✓ (D) extracted

CORRECT. "A red dye obtained from certain foliage" = a red dye extracted or gotten in some way from this foliage (= leaves).

7.   The word "persists" in the passage is closest in meaning to

VOCABULARY. "Persist" = continue, endure, stick or hang around (perhaps in the face of contrary expectations).

✗ (A) fades

Opposite.

✗ (B) struggles

By itself, "struggle" often implies a negative outlook. If a custom "struggles" among a population, then that custom may not survive very long.

✓ (C) endures

CORRECT. "The ritual of marking one's home with a handprint persists among the present-day local population" = this ritual endures among the present-day population.

✗ (D) resides

Not quite. "Reside" = live, dwell. This does not convey the sense that the ritual has continued for a long time, maybe against expectations.

3

Paragraph 4	**Comments**
P4 S1 In Spain's Cantabria province in Europe, there are similar handprint paintings created by using the hand as a stencil and blowing pigment onto the cave wall.	Similar handprints in Spain.
2 The oldest of these has been dated at more than 40,000 years old.	Oldest > 40,000 yrs old.
3 The process used to make that determination is called "uranium-thorium dating," in which a sample of calcite that has accumulated on the surface of the paint is removed and analyzed for trace amounts of uranium and thorium to determine the sample's age.	Dating process.
4 Scientists can conclude that whatever lies beneath must be at least as old as the calcite itself, but no upper bound can be placed on the age of the underlying paint.	No upper bound on age.
5 This **implies** that the paintings in Spain could actually be much more than 40,000 years old, potentially placing them very close to the time when modern humans, *Homo sapiens*, first appeared on the European continent.	Implication: paintings could be much older than 40,000 years old. Could be when modern humans appeared in Europe.

Paragraph 5	**Comments**
P5 S1 Prior to that time, Neanderthals dominated Europe.	Before that, Neanderthals dominated.
2 Dating cave art back this far in history, therefore, could have major implications for our understanding of Neanderthals.	
3 If cave art were discovered that dates to the period and location in which the Neanderthals reigned, before the presence of modern humans, it would raise questions about who authored the paintings and whether they were indeed created by *Homo sapiens* at all.	If cave art is found from time of Neanderthals, have to rethink who made paintings.

8. The word "implies" in the passage is closest in meaning to

VOCABULARY. "Imply" = suggest, hint at indirectly.

✗ (A) assures

Too extreme. "Assure" = dispel any doubts or make sure of something. Assure also needs a personal object (you assure *someone* that something is true, or you assure *someone of* something).

✓ (B) suggests

CORRECT. "This implies … " = this (the point in the previous sentence) suggests something.

✗ (C) disproves

"Disprove" = prove false. You might *imply* that something is false, but it would lack the proof.

✗ (D) affirms

Also too extreme. "Affirm" = to state as a fact or defend.

 MANHATTAN PREP

9. In paragraphs 4 and 5, what evidence supports the claim that dating European cave art to much earlier than 40,000 years ago raises the question of who created the art?

FACT. P4 S5 points out that the paintings could be significantly older than 40,000 years old. The rest of that sentence, as well as P5, explores the implications. P5 S3 discusses the question that might arise about who created the art.

✗ (A) When the art was created, it was created with dyes that modern humans did not have access to.

This point is not made in the passage.

✓ (B) Prior to 40,000 years ago, Europe was dominated by Neanderthals, not modern humans.

CORRECT. The reason why dating the art prior to 40,000 years ago raises the question of authorship is that modern humans (*Homo sapiens*) are less likely to be the creators of the cave art. P4 S5 and P5 S1: "potentially placing them [the paintings] very close to the time when modern humans, *Homo sapiens*, first appeared on the European continent. Prior to that time, Neanderthals dominated Europe." So it might have been the Neanderthals who made the art.

✗ (C) Neanderthals seem to have been more capable of making figurative cave art than modern humans.

This point is not made in the passage.

✗ (D) No upper bound can be placed on the age of the paintings by the uranium-thorium dating technique.

This is true (P4 S4). But this just confirms the point that the paintings could be older than 40,000 years old. It's not evidence that supports raising any question about the authorship of the art.

10. It can be inferred from paragraphs 4 and 5 that calcite that has accumulated on cave paintings must

INFERENCE. P4 S3–4 discuss the calcite on cave paintings.

✗ (A) significantly obscure the painted images underneath

This may or may not be true in the real world. But the passage never mentions anything about how the calcite may or may not obscure (= hide) the artwork.

✗ (B) have preserved the paint from wear and tear, allowing it to survive

Likewise, this may or may not be true in the real world. But the passage makes no hint in this direction.

✗ (C) be removed carefully to avoid damage to the art

Once again, this may or may not be true in the real world. But the passage makes no hint in this direction.

✓ (D) be no older than the paintings themselves

CORRECT. P4 S4: "Scientists can conclude that whatever lies beneath must be at least as old as the calcite itself." So the calcite cannot be older than the paintings.

Paragraph 6	Comments
S1 Another important site is in the Chauvet cave in the Ardeche region of southern France.	Chauvet cave in France.
2 The paintings were found in this cave by a team of French cavers in 1994 and have been dated at around 30,000 years old.	
3 While the Chauvet paintings are not the earliest cave art discovered in Europe, they are the earliest figurative cave paintings yet discovered there.	Earliest figurative cave paintings.
4 The Chauvet paintings are also notable for their breadth.	
5 They consist of hundreds of paintings of animals from over a dozen distinct species, including lions, panthers, and bears—predatory animals that do not frequently appear in other cave paintings from the Paleolithic era.	Many paintings of different kinds of animals.
6 Furthermore, deep inside the Chauvet cave are the cave's only human figures, including an intriguing figure that is half man and half bison, and another that is female.	Human figures.

11.   In paragraph 6, the author mentions the figurative paintings discovered in the Chauvet cave in order to

PURPOSE. S3 mentions these figurative paintings. Later sentences go into more depth.

✓ (A) reinforce why the Chauvet cave paintings are considered remarkable

CORRECT. S1 introduces the Chauvet cave as "another important site." The whole paragraph is about the Chauvet cave and how "notable" (S4) it is. So S3 mentions the figurative paintings as "the earliest figurative cave paintings yet discovered there [in Europe]." The reason is to emphasize how important or remarkable the Chauvet cave paintings are.

✗ (B) point out that older non-figurative cave paintings have been discovered elsewhere in Europe

S3 presents this fact as a concession: "*While* the Chauvet paintings are not the earliest cave art discovered in Europe." So the author's intent is not to emphasize this point.

✗ (C) underscore the fact that cave paintings can only be approximately dated

This is never mentioned in the passage.

✗ (D) assert the unique representations of certain predatory animals in these paintings

Too extreme. S5 does not claim that these predatory animals are unique, but just that they "do not frequently appear in other cave paintings."

12.   In paragraph 6, which of the following is NOT offered as a reason for which the Chauvet cave is regarded as significant?

NEGATIVE FACT. Three answers will be found in the paragraph as reasons for the significance of the Chauvet cave. The correct answer will not be presented this way: it may even be true but not a reason for the significance of the cave.

✓   (A) In 1994, a team of French cavers discovered the paintings, with colors still vibrant after 30,000 years.

CORRECT. The discovery is mentioned in S2, but who discovered the paintings when is not a reason for their significance. Moreover, nothing is mentioned about the colors of the paintings still being vibrant.

✗   (B) The cave contains the earliest figurative cave paintings yet discovered in Europe.

Mentioned in S3.

✗   (C) At least one of the human figures represented deep within the cave is thought to be interesting.

S6: "deep inside the Chauvet cave are the cave's only human figures, including an intriguing figure that is half man and half bison."

✗   (D) A broad range of animals are depicted, including predators rarely thus shown.

S4: "notable for their breadth." S5: "hundreds of paintings of animals from over a dozen distinct species, including ... predatory animals that do not frequently appear in other cave paintings"

Paragraph 1	**Comments**

P1 S1   The Paleolithic era is the period of history commonly known as "the Stone Age."

2   **A** It begins with the appearance of stone tools around 2.5 million years ago and ends approximately 12,000 years ago.

Here at the beginning of the paragraph, cave art has not yet been introduced. The new sentence does not fit.

3   **B** It is quite late during the Paleolithic period—only around 40,000 years ago—that cave art first appears in the archaeological record.

S2 has still not introduced the term "cave art," so the new sentence doesn't work here.

4   **C** Found in various locations across the globe, sometimes deep in the inner chambers of caves and sometimes closer to their openings, this art reveals a modern human species that had evolved sufficiently to comprehend and appreciate symbolism.

CORRECT. S3 introduces the term "cave art." The new sentence gives a short definition. S4 expands upon that definition, offering more detail and elaborating on cave art's significance (what it reveals about its creators, namely, that they comprehended and appreciated symbolism).

End   **D**

The prior sentence (S4) certainly discusses cave art. But the point it makes about symbolism is more significant and profound than the simple definition in the new sentence. So the new sentence should come before S4, not after it.

13. **This cave art from the Paleo-lithic era consists of symbolic representations created by humans.**

Where would the sentence best fit?

✗ (A) Choice A

✗ (B) Choice B

✓ (C) Choice C

✗ (D) Choice D

INSERT TEXT. The new sentence begins with "This cave art." So the prior sentence must refer to cave art in a clear, direct way. The new sentence also provides a short definition of cave art, stating what it consists of. Thus, the insertion point should be very soon after the introduction of the term "cave art."

CORRECT.

	Passage	Comments
P1	The Paleolithic era is the period of history commonly known as "the Stone Age" …	Paleolithic = Stone Age. Cave art appears late in period. Reveals modern humans who could appreciate symbolism.
P2	Cave art is often divided into two categories: figurative (depicting animals and humans) and non-figurative …	Figurative and non-figurative cave art. Both are believed to be for spiritual purposes. Especially true for art deep within caves.
P3	Among the oldest cave paintings found to date are those in Indonesia in the Pettakere Cave …	Pettakere Cave: among oldest. Ancient handprints. Outlined in red at entrance. Created by spitting red dye over one's hand. Maybe to ward off evil spirits. Ritual still happens today nearby. Example: new home.
P4	In Spain's Cantabria province in Europe, there are similar handprint paintings …	Similar handprints in Spain. Oldest > 40,000 years old. Dating process. No upper bound on age. Implication: paintings could be much older than 40,000 years old. Could be when modern humans appeared in Europe.
P5	Prior to that time, Neanderthals dominated Europe …	Before that, Neanderthals dominated. If cave art is found from time of Neanderthals, have to rethink who made paintings.
P6	Another important site is in the Chauvet cave in the Ardeche region of southern France …	Chauvet cave in France. Earliest figurative cave paintings. Many paintings of different kinds of animals. Interesting human figures.

14.   **Paleolithic cave art reveals much about early humans.**

SUMMARY. Correct answers must be clearly expressed in the passage. They must also be among the major points of the passage. They should tie as directly as possible to the summary given.

✗   [A]   Some cave paintings have been dated via analysis of uranium and thorium within calcite that formed on top of the paintings.

This fact is given in P4 S3. But it is too specific a detail to count as a main idea. The passage does not focus on the science behind the dating process.

✓   [B]   The cave art created by early humans shows that they were capable of symbolic representation.

CORRECT. This key idea, probably the most important one of the passage, is outlined at the end of P1. It is then demonstrated through various examples in later paragraphs.

✗   [C]   Human beings have evolved in a variety of ways since the days of the early humans who created cave art tens of thousands of years ago.

This is certainly true based on our real-world knowledge, but this point is never mentioned in the passage.

✗   [D]   Paleolithic cave art provides a telling example of the underlying similarity between Neanderthals and early *Homo sapiens*.

The passage does not say this. It never compares Neanderthals and modern humans, except with respect to when they each were dominant in Europe.

✓   [E]   Art deep within caves most likely had spiritual purposes, but art near cave entrances, such as handprints, may have also been part of ritual practice.

CORRECT. P2 S2 states the accepted theory about the purpose of cave art: "to serve the spiritual practices of early humans." This point is an important refinement of the "symbolism" idea. P2 emphasizes the spiritual purpose of art deep within caves, while P3 explores the handprint example.

✓   [F]   Methods that date cave paintings to 40,000 years ago or more raise questions about the painters, including their exact species.

CORRECT. P4 and P5 explain these dating methods and their implications: namely, maybe Neanderthals and not modern humans made the cave paintings.

Answers and Explanations—3.9 Synesthesia

	Paragraph 1	Comments
S1	Does the sound of music have a color to you?	
2	Can you taste the sight of a particular shade of blue?	
3	Few people can.	
4	For most of us, the five primary senses—sight, hearing, taste, smell, and touch—are distinct categories; our brains process these sensory experiences as separate from one another and fundamentally unique.	For most people, the five senses are distinct.
5	But for certain people known as "synesthetes," things are not so straightforward.	Synesthetes.
6	For these people, the stimulation of one sense may trigger the activation of one or more other senses.	Synesthetes = one sense can trigger others.

1. The word "shade" in the passage is closest in meaning to

    VOCABULARY. In the context of colors, "shade" = particular tint, hue, or tonal variation in color.

    ✓ (A) hue

    CORRECT. "A particular shade of blue" = a particular hue or variation of the color blue.

    ✗ (B) glimpse

    Not quite. "Glimpse" = a quick sight of something. It's not a synonym for "shade."

    ✗ (C) shadow

    In other contexts, "shade" = shadow or darkness. "A particular shadow of blue" is not idiomatic English.

    ✗ (D) light

    "A particular light of blue" is not idiomatic English either. As a countable noun (one light, two lights), "a light" most often means a light fixture, a lamp or lantern. That doesn't make sense here.

2.   Which of the following can be inferred from paragraph 1?

INFERENCE. You must be able to prove the correct answer, using only the words in this paragraph.

✗   (A) The purpose of sensory perception is to separate sensory experiences into separate categories.

P1 does not discuss the purposes of sensory perception.

✗   (B) Generally, synesthetes process sensory experiences as unique and independent.

Opposite. S5 introduces synesthetes by way of contrast to "most of us," who process sensory experiences as separate and unique (S4).

✗   (C) Sensory perception is substantially more difficult for synesthetes than for others.

S5–6 discuss how "things are not so straightforward" for synesthetes, for whom an experience of one sense can trigger the experience of another. This may *seem* to make sensory perception substantially more difficult for synesthetes. But from the text you're given in P1, you can't properly draw that conclusion. All you know from P1 is that by being mixed in some way, sensory experiences are different for synesthetes.

✓   (D) Synesthetes do not always perceive different sensory experiences as separate and unique.

CORRECT. S6: "For these people [synesthetes], the stimulation of one sense may trigger the activation of one or more other senses." Synesthetes are contrasted to "most of us" (S4), who perceive sensory experiences as separate.

Paragraph 2	**Comments**
S1 Just how **prevalent** synesthesia is remains unknown.	No one knows how prevalent synesthesia is.
2 Estimates range from 1 in 20 people to 1 in 25,000 people.	
3 The most common type of synesthesia is called "grapheme-color synesthesia," or seeing different letters as different colors.	Most common type: see letters with colors.
4 Still, there are many people who experience other forms of overlapping senses.	But there are other types.
5 One such person was the American composer Leonard Bernstein, who reported that when he listened to music, the timbre of various sounds appeared to him visually as varied colors.	

3.   The word "prevalent" in the passage is closest in meaning to

    ✗ (A) successful

    ✓ (B) common

    ✗ (C) influential

    ✗ (D) unfavorable

VOCABULARY. "Prevalent" = common, frequent, widespread.

Not quite. The use of "successful" in this context would not be clear. Would it mean "successful at establishing itself in humans" (like a disease or other condition), or "successful in allowing synesthetes to interpret sensory information," or something else entirely?

CORRECT. "Just how prevalent synesthesia is remains unknown" = it is still not known how common or widespread synesthesia is.

These words *might* be related but aren't necessarily. Something that is influential (having great influence on someone or something) might also be prevalent, but it might be extremely rare as well.

These words are unrelated. Something unfavorable has a lack of support or approval. It has no bearing on how common or uncommon it is.

4.   According to paragraph 2, what kind of synesthesia did Leonard Bernstein experience?

    ✗ (A) When the colors in his field of vision changed, he heard different sounds.

    ✓ (B) Different qualities of sounds appeared to him as various colors.

    ✗ (C) The louder the music he heard was, the more colorful his vision became.

    ✗ (D) It was impossible for him to hear music without seeing letters.

FACT. S5 mentions Leonard Bernstein as an example of a synesthete.

S5 describes the opposite experience: different sounds in the world produced different colors in Bernstein's mind, not the other way around.

CORRECT. S5: "when he listened to music, the timbre of various sounds appeared to him visually as varied colors." That is, as the sounds Bernstein heard changed in quality, he saw different things.

The volume, or loudness, of the music is not discussed in S5.

S5 states that Bernstein saw colors, not letters, when he listened to music.

MANHATTAN PREP

Paragraph 3	Comments
P3 S1 Other synesthetes may even have multiple forms of the condition at once.	Can even have multiple forms of synesthesia.
2 Twentieth-century Russian journalist Solomon Shereshevsky, for example, is reputed to have had a spectacular memory—he could memorize a speech word for word after hearing it only once, and could remember a complicated math formula within a strikingly short time frame.	Example.
3 The method by which he did so was synesthesia, which for him existed among all five senses.	Amazing memory because his synesthesia involved all 5 senses.

Paragraph 4	Comments
P4 S1 How does synesthesia work?	How it works.
2 In recent decades, scientists have been able to uncover the neurological basis for some kinds of synesthesia.	Neurological basis.
3 Grapheme-color synesthetes, for example, display uncharacteristic neural activity in the color-based region of the visual cortex of their brains while reading, while people who are not grapheme-color synesthetes do not.	Example.

5. According to paragraph 3, Solomon Shereshevsky had a remarkable memory because of which of the following?

    FACT. S2–3 describe Shereshevsky's memory and the reason for it.

✗ (A) He could quickly recall complex math formulas.

    This is an example of Shereshevsky's remarkable memory, not the reason for it.

✗ (B) He primarily used vivid colors to remember.

    Not supported.

✓ (C) His memories involved several senses at once.

    CORRECT. S3: "The method by which he did so was synesthesia, which for him existed among all five senses." That is, his sensory experiences and his memories of those experiences involved several of his senses at the same time. Synesthesia is defined earlier, but it is the topic of the passage. What it means should be familiar by now.

✗ (D) He worked as a Russian journalist in the twentieth century.

    Shereshevsky is identified as a "twentieth-century Russian journalist" (S2). But this is not given as the reason for his spectacular memory.

6. Which of the sentences below best expresses the essential information in the highlighted portion of the passage? Incorrect choices change the meaning in important ways or leave out essential information.

SIMPLIFY SENTENCE. S3 gives an example of the "neurological basis" that scientists have found for some kinds of synesthesia.

✓ (A) When grapheme-color synesthetes read, a region of their brains related to perceiving color are unusually active.

CORRECT. Using fewer words, this version captures the meaning of the original. "Unusually" is enough to convey both "uncharacteristic" and the whole clause beginning with "while," which is unnecessary.

✗ (B) Grapheme-color synesthetes read when their brains display unusual activity in a color-based region of the visual cortex.

This reverses the causality in the original sentence. The unusual brain activity doesn't cause these synesthetes to read. Rather, the reading causes the unusual brain activity.

✗ (C) While reading text in various colors, grapheme-color synesthetes show unusual activity in the visual cortex of their brains.

The original does not mention reading text "in various colors." This is important, because these synesthetes experience colors that are not objectively there.

✗ (D) The brains of grapheme-color synesthetes are unusually active in the color-based region of the visual cortex.

This is true, but it leaves out an essential piece of information: namely, that this unusual activity happens when the synesthetes are reading.

Paragraph 5	Comments
P5 S1 The genetic basis of synesthesia, however, remains somewhat of a mystery.	But genetic basis is still a mystery.
2 In the early days of genetic research into the phenomenon, scientists hypothesized that the gene that brought about synesthesia was a dominant one located on the X chromosome.	Early hypothesis: dominant gene on X chromosome.
3 This was believed in part because the phenomenon appeared to be more common among women than men.	Reason.

Paragraph 6	Comments
P6 S1 This belief has changed, however, as new research has challenged it.	But new research has challenged.
2 While there does appear to be a genetic basis of some sort, as revealed by the unusual brain activity associated with the condition, several developments have undermined the hypothesis that a dominant gene on the X chromosome is the precise genetic mechanism.	Still a genetic basis, it seems, based on unusual brain activity. But some developments have weakened the early hypothesis.
3 One such development is that while early studies showed that more women than men are synesthetes, more recent and rigorous studies have suggested a more even distribution between the sexes.	Developments 1 & 2.
4 Furthermore, synesthesia can skip a generation, which means that if there is a gene for synesthesia, it cannot be a dominant gene, because dominant genes are not able to skip generations.	

7. Which of the following can be inferred from paragraphs 5 and 6 about the studies showing synesthesia to be more common among women than men?

INFERENCE. P5 S3 says that some studies showed synesthesia "appeared to be more common among women than men." P6 S3 notes that "more recent and rigorous [accurate] studies have suggested a more even distribution." The correct answer will be a valid inference you can make about the first set of studies.

✗ (A) They have undermined an early hypothesis about the genetic basis of synesthesia.

This is true of the later studies that suggested a more even distribution between the sexes (P6 S2–3).

✗ (B) They were correct at the time, but recent population changes have made them irrelevant.

The early studies have been contradicted by more recent studies. But the passage does not suggest that population changes are the reason why the early studies are now considered inaccurate.

✓ (C) They seem to have not been as accurate as later studies investigating the same issue.

CORRECT. P6 S3: "more recent and rigorous studies have suggested a more even distribution between the sexes." These newer studies are called "more rigorous" (the "more" carries across) and so can be trusted more. By implication, the earlier studies were not as rigorous. They reached a different conclusion because they were not as accurate, it seems.

✗ (D) They superseded earlier studies showing synesthesia to be evenly distributed between the sexes.

The timeline given in the passage is reversed.

8. According to paragraph 5, synesthesia was once believed by researchers to be caused by

FACT. P5 S2 describes what researchers once believed about the genetic cause of synesthesia.

✗ (A) a gene situated on the non-dominant X chromosome

This choice incorrectly changes "dominant" to "non-dominant" and applies the adjective to the noun "X chromosome," rather than to the noun "gene."

✗ (B) a non-dominant gene present only in women's chromosomes

The gene was thought to be dominant, not non-dominant. Also, S2 does not claim that it was only present in women's chromosomes. It was thought to be on the X chromosome, which apparently shows up more in women (since S3 indicates that the hypothesis was supported at the time by research showing synesthesia to be more present in women). But that doesn't mean that the gene was completely absent from men's chromosomes.

✓ (C) a dominant gene that was situated on the X chromosome

CORRECT. P5 S2: "scientists hypothesized that the gene that brought about synesthesia was a dominant one located on the X chromosome."

✗ (D) a dominant gene not located on the X chromosome

S2 indicates that the gene was thought to be located on the X chromosome.

9.   According to paragraph 6, which of the following is true in general of genes that are dominant?

FACT. P6 S2 mentions dominant genes. P6 S4 mentions a fact about dominant genes in general: they cannot skip a generation.

✗   (A) They are not located on the X chromosome.

Recent research has called into question the hypothesis that a dominant gene on the X chromosome is the precise genetic mechanism. That doesn't mean that no dominant genes are located on the X chromosome.

✗   (B) They form the genetic basis of conditions such as synesthesia.

The passage never discusses the role of dominant genes in other conditions than synesthesia.

✗   (C) They are more evenly distributed between the sexes than previously thought.

This is true of synesthesia (P6 S3), not of dominant genes.

✓   (D) They do not skip generations.

CORRECT. P6 S4: "dominant genes are not able to skip generations."

Paragraph 7	**Comments**
S1 A study of a pair of identical female twins, one of whom is synesthetic and one of whom is not, raised further questions about the genetic basis of the phenomenon.	Study of twins raised further questions. One has synesthesia, other doesn't.
2 Identical twins have the same genetic code—all of their genes are identical.	But twins have identical genes.
3 For one to be synesthetic and the other not to be, therefore, is peculiar.	
4 The study raised the possibility of whether synesthesia can be environmentally triggered or suppressed.	Can synesthesia be environmentally triggered or suppressed?
5 At the very least, it suggested there might be some explanation beyond the simple inheritance or non-inheritance of a synesthesia-causing gene.	Not a simple genetic explanation.

3

10. According to paragraph 7, the study of the two identical twins provided reason to believe which of the following?

FACT. S4–5 outline implications of the twin study.

✓ (A) Environmental factors may be able to cause or at least trigger synesthesia.

CORRECT. S4: "The study raised the possibility of whether synesthesia can be environmentally triggered or suppressed."

✗ (B) It is unlikely that synesthesia is influenced by genetic conditions.

Neither S4 nor S5 suggest that synesthesia is unlikely to be even *influenced* by genetic conditions. These sentences just suggest that something *in addition to* simple genetics seems to be at work.

✗ (C) The non-synesthetic twin lacked the gene for synesthesia that the other twin had.

S2: "identical twins have the same genetic code—all of their genes are identical." So it's not possible for one twin to lack a gene that the other one had.

✗ (D) Claims of synesthetic experiences by just one twin were probably mistaken.

Nothing in the paragraph indicates that the research should itself be doubted in any way.

Paragraph 8		**Comments**
S1	But there is little evidence that synesthesia can be manipulated by one's environment.	But you can't environmentally manipulate synesthesia, it seems.
2	Efforts to "train" people to be synesthetes have been unsuccessful compared to actual synesthetes.	Training is unsuccessful.
3	While people can "teach" their brains to **correlate** certain letters with certain colors, for instance, the neural activity in their brains remains distinct from that of people who are naturally synesthetic.	Brains can be taught to do associations, but neural activity is not the same.

11. The word "**correlate**" in the passage is closest in meaning to

VOCABULARY. "Correlate" = associate, relate to one another, gather in order to compare.

✗ (A) present

Unrelated. "Present" as a verb = to give formally or ceremonially (to present someone with an award).

✗ (B) provide

Unrelated. "Provide" = make available or supply.

✗ (C) repress

Unrelated. "Repress" = suppress, restrain, or prevent.

✓ (D) associate

CORRECT. "People can 'teach' their brains to correlate certain letters with certain colors" = people can teach their brains to associate certain letters with certain colors, or to relate them to one another.

Paragraph 9	Comments
S1 A likely possibility is that the genetic basis for synesthesia does indeed lie on the X chromosome, as predicted by early researchers, and that the twin study can be explained by a phenomenon called "X-inactivation."	
2 **A** X-inactivation is the process by which one of a female's two X chromosomes is rendered essentially inactive by the other X chromosome.	The inserted sentence does not make sense here, because X-inactivation has not yet been discussed.
3–4 **B** X-inactivation occurs randomly and at the cellular level during the earliest stages of development of the female. In other words, one X chromosome may be active in one cell (while the other one is silenced), but in the neighboring cell, the situation is reversed.	**CORRECT.** S2, the prior sentence, introduces the concept of X-inactivation. It also indicates that the phenomenon is experienced by females ("one of a female's two X chromosomes").
5 **C** This genetic phenomenon could explain the twin study, because it leads to a different expression of the same genes in two female twins, which is precisely what was observed.	This location for the sentence does not work well. First, the prior sentence (S4) does not specifically mention female experience of X-inactivation (although S3 does so). The contrast between male and female experience of the phenomenon is not drawn as sharply as it could be. Even more importantly, placing the new sentence here interrupts the flow of logic from the cellular operation of X-inactivation (S4) to how this explains the twin study (S5). So it weakens the force of the conclusion in S5.
End **D**	Placement of the new sentence here undermines the necessary contrast between female and male experience of X-inactivation. Moreover, it kills the impact of the conclusion in S5, which links back to earlier paragraphs. It should be left at the very end, in order to tie up both the paragraph and the passage.

12. **In contrast, X-inactivation is not experienced by males, who have only one X chromosome.**

Where would the sentence best fit?

✗ (A) Choice A

✓ (B) Choice B

✗ (C) Choice C

✗ (D) Choice D

INSERT TEXT. The transition phrase "In contrast" indicates that this inserted sentence should contrast with the previous sentence. The insertion states that X-inactivation is not experienced by males. So the brand-new concept of X-inactivation should be introduced before the insertion, and what is said about this concept just before the insertion should somehow indicate that X-inactivation is experienced by females.

CORRECT.

	Whole Passage	**Comments**
P1	Does the sound of music have a color to you? …	For most people, the five senses are distinct. But for synesthetes, one sense can trigger another.
2	Just how prevalent synesthesia is remains unknown …	No one knows how prevalent synesthesia is. Most common type: see letters with colors. But there are other types.
3	Other synesthetes may even have multiple forms of the condition at once …	Can even have multiple forms of synesthesia. Example. Amazing memory because his synesthesia involved all 5 senses.
4	How does synesthesia work? …	How it works. Neurological basis. Example.
5	The genetic basis of synesthesia, however, remains somewhat of a mystery …	But genetic basis is still a mystery. Early hypothesis: dominant gene on X chromosome. Reason.
6	This belief has changed, however, as new research has challenged it …	But new research has challenged. Still a genetic basis, it seems. But some developments have weakened the early hypothesis. Developments 1 & 2.
7	A study of a pair of identical female twins, one of whom is synesthetic and one of whom is not …	Study of twins raised further questions. One has synesthesia, other doesn't. But twins have identical genes. Can synesthesia be environmentally triggered? Not a simple genetic explanation.
8	But there is little evidence that synesthesia can be manipulated by one's environment …	But you can't environmentally manipulate synesthesia, it seems. Training is unsuccessful. Brains can be taught to do associations, but neural activity is not the same.
9	A likely possibility is that the genetic basis for synesthesia does indeed lie on the X chromosome …	Possibility: yes, gene on X chromosome. "X-inactivation" in females = inactivation of one X at random. Can explain twin study.

13. Which of the following best describes the author's presentation of information in the passage?

PURPOSE. The passage first introduces synesthesia (P1–3). The rest of the passage explores the question of what causes synesthesia, which "remains somewhat of a mystery" (P5 S1), although there is a "likely possibility" (P9 S1) for the genetic basis of the condition.

✗ (A) A number of studies are presented to support the assertion that synesthesia is primarily an environmental phenomenon.

The passage leans the other way, offering a "likely possibility" (P9) for the genetic basis of synesthesia.

✗ (B) The author uses logic to show that doubt about the causes of synesthesia is unwarranted.

P5 S1: "The genetic basis of synesthesia ... remains somewhat of a mystery." Doubt remains about the causes of the condition.

✓ (C) The author introduces the condition of synesthesia and explores possible causes.

CORRECT. The introduction in P1–3 is followed by an exploration of possible causes.

✗ (D) Two opposing points of view about synesthesia are described; the author concludes by advocating for further research.

Opposing points of view are described (genetic vs. environmental basis for synesthesia). The author acknowledges the ongoing mystery of what causes the condition. But the author does not call for further research at the end of the passage.

3

14. **Synesthesia is a neurological phenomenon by which a small percentage of people have blended sensory experiences.**

SUMMARY. Correct answers must be clearly expressed in the passage. They must also be among the major points of the passage. They should tie as directly as possible to the summary given.

✗ [A] Great musicians and geniuses are often synesthetes, perceiving their medium in ways non-synesthetes cannot.

The passage gives two personal examples of synesthetes. One of them happens to be a great musician (Leonard Bernstein in P2), and the other might be classified as a genius (Solomon Shereshevsky in P3). But these examples are never generalized to any statement about "great musicians and geniuses" in relation to synesthesia.

✓ [B] Synesthesia manifests itself in various forms and can involve two or more senses at once.

CORRECT. These basic descriptions of the condition are outlined in P2–3.

✗ [C] The true prevalence of synesthesia is likely to continue to be unknown.

P2 mentions that the prevalence of synesthesia is unknown. But the passage does not claim that the true prevalence will remain unknown or is likely to remain unknown.

✓ [D] Research suggests that synesthesia may be linked to a gene located on the X chromosome.

CORRECT. More than one paragraph explores this possibility. Although early research is challenged, the passage concludes by stating it is likely that the gene for synesthesia is in fact located on the X chromosome, but that the phenomenon of X-inactivation prevents the expression of the gene from following typical genetic patterns.

✓ [E] The neurological activity of synesthetes is unusual, in a way that cannot be simulated, it seems.

CORRECT. P4 introduces discussion of the neurological basis of synesthesia by pointing out the "uncharacteristic neural activity" of certain synesthetes. P6 echoes the point, highlighting the importance of this unusual brain activity in supporting a genetic explanation. P8 reiterates the unusual neural activity of synesthetes and indicates that synesthesia cannot be trained or faked. The unusual brain activity associated with synesthesia is a key aspect of the condition, supporting a likely biological explanation for it.

✗ [F] As inherited genetic material, dominant genes are unable to skip generations.

This point is true and mentioned at the end of P6. But this fact is brought up only to support one of two challenges to the initial hypothesis about the genetic basis of synesthesia. No further elaboration is given. The point does not qualify as a main idea of this passage.

Answers and Explanations—
3.10 Communication through Gesture

	Paragraph 1	**Comments**
S1	Throughout the world, people communicate using body language.	People everywhere use body language.
2	Communicating through nonverbal, or physical, "language" occurs within and across cultures.	
3	Research has shown that gesture plays numerous roles in the effectiveness of our communication.	Gesture makes our communication more effective.
4	Speech **accompanied by** gesture has been found to be much more engaging to the listener, and therefore greatly improves comprehension.	
5	Gesture during speech has been correlated with speakers who rise as leaders in society.	
6	Gesturing can also be beneficial to the speaker: one study found that children who were forced to gesture while talking through math problems learned better than children who were forced not to gesture.	Also benefits the speaker: better learning.
7	The gesturing children later scored higher on tests of similar problems.	

1. The phrase "accompanied by" in the passage is closest in meaning to

   VOCABULARY. "Accompany" = go together with, be a companion to.

   ✗ (A) studied with

   Unrelated. Speech is not being studied with gestures, rather it is being used or combined with gestures.

   ✗ (B) betrayed by

   Unrelated. Although "betrayed" often takes on the negative definition of being revealed through trickery or treachery, in language or communication it typically means to unintentionally reveal. For example, "Although she said she wanted to stay longer, her yawn betrayed her exhaustion."

   ✗ (C) unlinked to

   Opposite.

   ✓ (D) paired with

   CORRECT. "Speech accompanied by gesture" = speech paired with gesture, speech that has gesture happening at the same time.

2. According to paragraph 1, there is evidence that gesturing helps children to

   ✗ (A) study math more effectively between tests

   ✗ (B) help each other grasp quantitative concepts

   ✗ (C) do math in a more concrete, informal way using their hands

   ✓ (D) be more successful at learning math

FACT. S6–7 describe research that focused on children's use of gestures and how that was "beneficial."

The passage never mentions studying between tests.

The passage does not describe group work or collaborative learning done by the students.

Exactly how the gesturing helped the students to do better is never described.

CORRECT. S6–7: "children who were forced to gesture while talking through math problems learned better than children who were forced not to gesture. The gesturing children later scored higher on tests of similar problems." This evidence supports the claim that gesturing helps children learn math better (although it never specifies how).

Paragraph 2	**Comments**
S1 The act of gesturing during speech is as universal as speech itself, and in fact, both vocalizing and gesturing physically involve the same area of the brain, leading scientists to **surmise** that they are evolutionarily linked.	Gesturing during speech is universal. Both use the same brain parts and may be linked through evolution.
2 Even blind people gesture when speaking to other blind people.	Blind people gesture to other blind people.
3 Helen Keller, the author and activist, and the first deafblind person to earn a bachelor of arts degree, had learned by the age of seven to communicate with her parents by hand gestures.	Example: Helen Keller.
4 Soon after, she learned a manual alphabet through finger spelling.	

3. The word "**surmise**" in the passage is closest in meaning to

   ✓ (A) speculate

   ✗ (B) doubt

   ✗ (C) confirm

   ✗ (D) deny

VOCABULARY. "Surmise" = guess, hypothesize, speculate on the basis of limited evidence.

CORRECT. "Both vocalizing and gesturing ... involve the same area of the brain, leading scientists to surmise that they are evolutionarily linked" = these behaviors involve the same part of the brain, leading scientists to speculate or guess that they're linked through evolution.

Opposite.

Too strong. "Confirm" = prove, claim with 100% certainty.

Opposite (and too strong).

4. All of the following are mentioned about gesturing in paragraph 2 EXCEPT:

NEGATIVE FACT. Gesturing is discussed throughout P2, so the three wrong answers could be anywhere. One answer is not mentioned in P2.

✗ (A) It involves the same part of the brain as speaking.

S1: "vocalizing and gesturing physically involve the same area of the brain."

✗ (B) It was used by Helen Keller to communicate with her parents.

S3: "Helen Keller ... had learned by the age of seven to communicate with her parents by hand gestures."

✗ (C) Its occurrence during speech is as universal as speech itself.

S1: "The act of gesturing during speech is as universal as speech itself."

✓ (D) It is more suited to communicating subtle ideas than speech.

CORRECT. This idea is never expressed in P2.

5. According to paragraph 2, how was Helen Keller able to use an alphabet composed of gestures?

FACT. S4 discusses the "manual alphabet" that Keller learned.

✓ (A) She learned it.

CORRECT. S4: "she learned a manual alphabet through finger spelling."

✗ (B) She discovered it independently.

Not supported in the text.

✗ (C) She developed it while earning her degree.

Not supported in the text.

✗ (D) It was taught to her by her parents.

S4 does not say whether Keller learned the manual alphabet from her parents.

Paragraph 3	Comments
S1 With regard to specific physical gestures, some are universal, while others vary across cultures.	Some gestures are universal, while others vary.
2 Some anthropologists and psychologists believe the smile to be a universal gesture for happiness or contentment.	Universal (according to some): smile.
3 Another gesture believed to be universal is the act of a child stroking his or her own cheek, often with the back of the palm, to call for his or her mother.	Other examples that might be universal.
4 It has been reported that this gesture occurs spontaneously among children across cultures who have not been taught it.	
5 Additionally, some believe that clutching at one's throat is a universal sign for choking, and that displaying one's hands raised high above one's head is a universal display of triumph.	

6. The word "reported" in the passage is closest in meaning to

  ✗ (A) verified

  ✓ (B) alleged

  ✗ (C) concealed

  ✗ (D) flaunted

VOCABULARY. "Report" = say, claim, or allege.

Too strong. "Verify" = prove or confirm.

CORRECT. "It has been reported that this gesture occurs" = someone has alleged or said that this gesture occurs.

Opposite. "Conceal" = keep secret or hidden.

Too specific, and oddly so. "Flaunt" = show off, display in a boastful way.

7. According to paragraph 3, what do some people believe about the gesture used by a child to call for his or her mother?

  ✗ (A) It can also mean triumph.

  ✗ (B) It typically involves the front of the palm.

  ✓ (C) It is shared universally.

  ✗ (D) It represents a stroke on the cheek that a mother might give.

FACT. S3 describes this gesture and what some people believe about it.

A different gesture means triumph (S5).

S3: "often with the back of the palm."

CORRECT. S3: "believed to be universal."

This may be plausible. But S3 doesn't indicate what the gesture might represent or mean symbolically.

8. How is paragraph 3 related to other aspects of the discussion of gesture in the passage?

  ✗ (A) It describes a dispute between two schools of thought about gestures.

  ✗ (B) It challenges earlier claims about gestures and presents a compromise.

  ✓ (C) It applies general concepts discussed earlier to specific examples of gestures.

  ✗ (D) It outlines a process through which gestures achieve qualities previously discussed.

PURPOSE. P3 goes right away to specific examples: "With regard to specific physical gestures, some are universal, while others vary across cultures." The rest of the paragraph describes various examples.

No dispute is described.

No challenge is given.

CORRECT. P1–2 discuss gesturing in general and argue that it is universal. P3 applies the concept of universality (discussed earlier) to specific examples of gestures.

The "qualities previously discussed" could include universality. But P3 never discusses how gestures *become* universal or achieve universality. No process of development is described.

Paragraph 4	Comments
S1 There is far more variation in gesturing across cultures than commonality, however.	But there's more difference across cultures.
2 A gesture that varies by culture is holding up two fingers, the first and second fingers, in a skyward V-shape.	Various examples.
3 In the United States, this is a gesture for "peace."	
4 In Australia, New Zealand, and the United Kingdom, however, it is used to signify contempt for authority.	
5 Accordingly, it is regarded as hostile and potentially rude.	
6 Similarly, an upward thumb ("thumbs up" in American English) is used to express approval in the United States, Australia, Canada, the United Kingdom, and Russia.	
7 But in Latin America, West Africa, Iran, Iraq, and Afghanistan, it is an insult.	
8 And wagging the index finger to beckon "come here" in the United States is, in the Philippines, considered insulting when directed toward another person; there, it is **restricted** to beckoning dogs.	
9 Therefore, to use it toward a person indicates that you see that person as inferior.	
10 Finally, in Japan, it is polite to give an object to another person using two hands, but not with only one—a behavior that is viewed as acceptable and harmless in other places.	

3

9. It can be inferred from paragraph 4 that

INFERENCE. You are not told where to look specifically in P4. But the right answer must be clearly supported in the text of P4.

✓ (A) in the Philippines, one may find it offensive to be addressed with a gesture typically used for dogs

CORRECT. S8: "wagging the index finger to beckon 'come here' in the United States is, in the Philippines, considered insulting when directed toward another person; there, it is restricted to beckoning dogs."

✗ (B) in Iraq, wagging the index finger is unacceptable

S8–9 relate that this gesture is considered offensive in the Philippines. Iraq is not mentioned.

✗ (C) in the United States, a "thumbs up" is not always a positive gesture

The passage only describes the positive meaning of this gesture in the United States (S6).

✗ (D) in Japan, it is polite to use a single hand to pass an object to another person

Opposite. In Japan, unlike many other places, this would be seen as rude. Instead, polite behavior would have someone give an object to someone else using both hands.

10. The phrase "restricted to" in the passage is closest in meaning to

   ✗   (A) provided to

   ✗   (B) banned from

   ✗   (C) compressed into

   ✓   (D) limited to

VOCABULARY. "Restricted to" = limited to, confined to, constrained to.

Unrelated. "Provided to" (given to) doesn't share the meaning that the use is *only* for that purpose.

Opposite. This would mean that the gesture could *not* be used to beckon dogs. The original meaning is that the gesture is *only* used (or should only be used) to beckon dogs.

The physical sense of "restriction" is not meant here.

CORRECT. "There, it is restricted to beckoning dogs" = there, the gesture is limited to beckoning dogs, it is only used for this purpose.

Paragraph 5	Comments
S1 A multicultural, transnational community that makes regular and systematic use of gesture to communicate is the deaf community.	The deaf community worldwide uses gesture in systematic ways.
2 Unlike the casual gestures used sporadically within a culture to express opinion and emotion, including exaggerated gestures for effect (such as pantomime), within the deaf community there exist fully developed sign languages that correspond to spoken language.	Fully developed sign languages.
3 There is, however, no universal sign language used across cultures.	But no universal sign language.
4 For example, Denmark, Germany, France, and Turkey all have distinct sign languages.	Examples.
5 In the United States and the English-speaking parts of Canada, the primary sign language used in deaf communities is American Sign Language (ASL).	
6 ASL is closely related to French Sign Language (FSL), and ASL dialects are also used in other countries around the world, including in West Africa and parts of Southeast Asia.	

11.   Which of the sentences below best expresses the essential information in the highlighted portion of the passage? Incorrect choices change the meaning in important ways or leave out essential information.

SIMPLIFY SENTENCE. S2 is complicated. The core idea is that the deaf community uses fully developed sign languages, as developed as spoken languages. These sign languages are contrasted to the casual, sporadic gestures that are used more widely for expression.

✗   (A) Cultures in general tend to use gesture to convey more casual emotion and opinion than is expressed through fully developed sign languages by the deaf community.

The original sentence never claims that the fully developed sign languages do not express casual emotion and opinion. What is contrasted is the casual, sporadic use of gestures by the general population with the fully developed use of sign languages by the deaf community.

✓   (B) The deaf community makes use of sign languages that are fully developed, unlike casual, expressive gestures used at random by general populations.

CORRECT. This rephrasing captures the key ideas in the original sentence.

✗   (C) The deaf community uses casual gestures sporadically to express emotion and fully developed sign languages to correspond to spoken language.

This version fails to mention the broader populations within a culture. The original sentence attributes the casual use of gestures to those broader populations, not to the deaf community.

✗   (D) The sporadic, exaggerated use of casual gestures to express emotion and opinion is not limited to the deaf community, which also has developed fully formed sign languages.

This version also fails to mention the broader populations that make casual use of gestures.

3

12. According to paragraph 5, American Sign Language (ASL) is used as a primary language by deaf communities in at least part of which of the following countries?

FACT. S5–6 mention countries and regions where ASL is used.

✗ (A) Denmark

Mentioned as having a distinct sign language.

✓ (B) Canada

CORRECT. S5: "In the United States and the English-speaking parts of Canada, the primary sign language used in deaf communities is American Sign Language (ASL)."

✗ (C) France

While ASL is close to FSL (French Sign Language) according to S6, the passage does not state that ASL is used in France as a primary language.

✗ (D) Germany

Mentioned as having a distinct sign language.

Paragraph 3	**Comments**

S1 With regard to specific physical gestures, some are universal, while others vary across cultures.

2–3 **A** Some anthropologists and psychologists believe the smile to be a universal gesture for happiness or contentment. Another gesture believed to be universal is the act of a child stroking his or her own cheek, often with the back of the palm, to call for his or her mother.

The concept of "universal" gestures has been introduced but not "spontaneous usage." The contrasting "note" does not make sense here.

4 **B** It has been reported that this gesture occurs spontaneously among children across cultures who have not been taught it.

The concept of "universal" gestures has been introduced but not "spontaneous usage." The contrasting "note" does not make sense here.

5 **C** Additionally, some believe that clutching at one's throat is a universal sign for choking, and that displaying one's hands raised high above one's head is a universal display of triumph.

CORRECT. The passage has now talked about a gesture that is thought to be universal (a child stroking his or her own cheek …) and supports that point with the notion that it occurs spontaneously. The contrasting "note" makes sense here.

End **D**

Although this is safely after any discussion of "universal" and "spontaneous," it is too remote. The conversation has already moved on to other examples, neither of which are mentioned as being "spontaneously" used.

13. **It should be noted, however, that spontaneous usage in an observed number of subjects does not necessarily mean that a gesture is universal.**

Where would the sentence best fit?

✗ (A) Choice A

✗ (B) Choice B

✓ (C) Choice C

✗ (D) Choice D

INSERT TEXT. This sentence discusses the connection between "spontaneous usage" and whether the gesture is "universal." Note that this sentence indicates that the connection might *not* always be valid. Finally, the sentence begins with "It should be noted, however," an indication that this sentence is additional information that contrasts with what came before. Therefore this sentence should come after information that claims "spontaneous usage" as a basis for calling a gesture "universal."

CORRECT.

	Whole Passage	Comments
P1	Throughout the world, people communicate using body language …	People everywhere use body language. Gesture makes our communication more effective. Also benefits the speaker: better learning.
P2	The act of gesturing during speech is as universal as speech itself …	Gesturing during speech is universal. Both use the same brain parts and may be linked through evolution. Blind people gesture to other blind people. Example: Helen Keller.
P3	With regard to specific physical gestures, some are universal, while others vary across cultures …	Some gestures are universal, while others vary. Universal (according to some): smile. Other examples that might be universal.
P4	There is far more variation in gesturing across cultures than commonality, however …	But there's more difference across cultures. Various examples.
P5	A multicultural, transnational community that makes regular and systematic use of gesture to communicate is the deaf community …	The deaf community worldwide uses gesture in systematic ways. Fully developed sign languages. But no universal sign language. Examples.

14.   **People in all cultures across the world communicate through gesture.**

SUMMARY. Correct answers must be clearly expressed in the passage. They must also be among the major points of the passage. They should tie as directly as possible to the summary given.

✓ ☐A While communicating through gesture is a universal practice, the meaning of specific gestures tends to vary across cultures.

CORRECT. P3–4 make this point.

✗ ☐B A gesture used commonly to call someone in one culture could be considered demeaning in another culture.

This example is given in P4. But it is just one of many examples of how the meaning of gestures can vary. This detail is too minor to be a main idea.

✓ ☐C Gestural communication systems, as fully developed as spoken languages, are used by deaf communities around the world.

CORRECT. P5 focuses on these sign languages used by deaf communities.

✗ ☐D How well people learn a new concept can depend on whether gesture was involved.

This point was mentioned in one example of children learning math (P1). But it is not a central idea of the passage.

✓ ☐E Evidence suggests that the use of gesture during speech has many benefits, from helping children learn to improving the effectiveness of communication.

CORRECT. Much of the focus of P1 is on these benefits.

✗ ☐F American Sign Language (ASL) is not used as a primary language outside of the United States.

This is not true: ASL is used as a primary language in parts of Canada, according to P5. More to the point, this would be a minor detail.

3

Chapter 4
Reading B: Social Science

Reading passages and questions test your ability to comprehend and analyze academic information. Most questions are multiple-choice with four options (select one from A, B, C, or D). Some questions may ask you to select more than one option or to fill in a table.

Reading passages test your understanding of main ideas and details, as well as the organization of the passage or of specific parts of the passage. They also test your understanding of the relationship between different ideas and your ability to make inferences (messages implied by the passage).

How should you use this chapter? Here are some recommendations, according to the level you've reached in TOEFL Reading:

1. **Fundamentals.** Start with a topic-focused chapter, such as this one. Start with a topic that is a "medium weakness"—not your worst area but not your best either. At first, work untimed and check the answer after each question. Review the solutions closely, think carefully about the principles at work, and articulate what you've learned. Redo questions as necessary. As you improve, time yourself and do all of the questions for a passage at once, without stopping.

2. **Fixes.** Do one passage and set of questions untimed, examine the results, and learn your lessons. Next, test yourself with timed sets. When doing timed sets, don't check your answers until you're done with the whole set.

3. **Tweaks.** Confirm your mastery by doing a passage and question set under timed conditions. Concentrate on your weaker topic areas. Aim to improve the speed and ease of your process. As soon as you're ready, move to mixed-topic practice.

Good luck on Reading!

4.1 Cupule Rock Art

Parietal art is the archaeological term for human-made artwork—etchings, carvings, paintings, and drawings—typically done on cave walls or large blocks of stone. Also called "cave art" or "rock art," parietal art is found in many culturally diverse regions of the world and has been produced in many contexts throughout human history. The oldest known rock art dates from the Upper Paleolithic period and has been found in Europe, Australia, Asia, and Africa. The purpose of these remains of the Paleolithic period (as well as many other periods of prehistoric art) is not known. In the mid-1900s, however, researchers began to theorize that rock art was used as more than simple decoration. Archaeologists currently studying these artworks believe it likely that this art had religious and ritualistic significance.

When discussing rock art, researchers delineate individual pieces into one of three forms: 1) petroglyphs, which are carved into the rock surface; 2) pictographs, which are painted onto the surface; and 3) earth figures, formed on the ground. Petroglyphs are considered the earliest known parietal art, and the most prolific petroglyphs are thought to be cup stones, also known as "cupules." Cupules have been found on every continent except Antarctica and were produced during all three eras of the Stone Age (Paleolithic, Mesolithic, and Neolithic). In fact, many tribal cultures continue to create cupules to this day.

The actual term "cupule" was introduced in the early 1990s by Australian archaeologist Robert G. Bednarik. According to Bednarik and his colleagues, a cupule is a hemispherical[1] petroglyph created by hammering the rock surface with another hard object, in a process called percussion. In order to be defined as a cupule, the indentation in the rock must be man-made, intentional, percussion-produced, and primarily symbolic or non-utilitarian in nature, although there may be secondary utilitarian functions present.

Cupules are typically found in large groups and often number in the hundreds (or even thousands) in a single location. A recent series of research experiments conducted by the Indian archaeologist Giriraj Kumar has sought to understand the difficulty with which these large groupings of cupules were created. Over the course of five experiments, Kumar's team attempted to replicate cupules found at Daraki-Chattan, India. For each replicated cupule, the team collected a variety of data, such as specific descriptions of the hammer-stones used, the time needed to create the cupule, and the number of percussion strikes required. The research found that the pounding of a single cupule out of hard rock required a colossal expenditure of energy: some cupules required upwards of 20,000 blows, an effort that would take several hours to complete. Given that the Daraki-Chattan site includes over 500 cupules, creating such large formations would have required a great deal of time and dedication. Since cupules were chiefly symbolic, not practical, in nature, the immensity of the effort required to create them indicates the value these prehistoric cultures attached to certain non-utilitarian activities.

Experts have not yet agreed on a unified explanation of the cultural or artistic meaning of cupules. However, a theory by archaeologist Charles P. Mountford in the early 1940s proposed that the creation of cupules might be associated with fertility rites. To investigate this, Mountford studied an Aboriginal tribe who continued to create cupules. Mountford witnessed the tribe hammering cupules as part of a fertility ritual for the pink cockatoo. The Aborigines pounded the cupules into a rock thought to contain the life essence of this bird. As the cupules were pounded out, the mineral dust that arose was thought to increase the female cockatoo's production of eggs, which were a valuable food source for the Aborigines.

The earliest known examples of cupule art, dating back to between 290,000 and 700,000 B.C., were found in central India. It can be difficult for archaeologists to estimate the exact date of creation for many cupules, however, because some appear to have been reworked by later artists, sometimes thousands of years later. For instance, one cupule at Moda Bhata, India, created around 7,000 B.C., was re-pounded around A.D. 200. Some researchers were initially surprised that all of the oldest known cupules appear on highly weatherproof and extremely hard rock, given the great physical effort clearly needed to create such formations. These same researchers questioned why easier, softer rocks were not chosen. However, it is entirely possible that this pattern is the result of survivorship bias: cupules formed on hard and more weatherproof rock are more likely to survive to the present day. It is probable that archaeologists may one day discover even older cupules in weather-protected soft rock.

---

hemispherical[1]: relating to one half of a sphere (e.g., the top half of the Earth is known as the Northern Hemisphere)

  MANHATTAN PREP

> Now answer the questions.

Paragraph 1

S1   Parietal art is the archaeological term for human-made artwork—etchings, carvings, paintings, and drawings—typically done on cave walls or large blocks of stone.

2   Also called "cave art" or "rock art," parietal art is found in many culturally diverse regions of the world and has been produced in many contexts throughout human history.

3   The oldest known rock art dates from the Upper Paleolithic period and has been found in Europe, Australia, Asia, and Africa.

4   The purpose of these remains of the Paleolithic period (as well as many other periods of prehistoric art) is not known.

5   In the mid-1900s, however, researchers began to theorize that rock art was used as more than simple decoration.

6   Archaeologists currently studying these artworks believe it likely that this art had religious and ritualistic significance.

1. According to paragraph 1, recent archaeologists believe that rock art was
    (A) used primarily for decorative purposes
    (B) found only in areas where the culture has remained constant over long periods of time
    (C) probably an important aspect of a culture's religion or rituals
    (D) more likely to be an etching or carving than a painting or drawing

Paragraph 2

S1   When discussing rock art, researchers delineate individual pieces into one of three forms: 1) petroglyphs, which are carved into the rock surface; 2) pictographs, which are painted onto the surface; and 3) earth figures, formed on the ground.

2   Petroglyphs are considered the earliest known parietal art, and the most **prolific** petroglyphs are thought to be cup stones, also known as "cupules."

3   Cupules have been found on every continent except Antarctica and were produced during all three eras of the Stone Age (Paleolithic, Mesolithic, and Neolithic).

4   In fact, many tribal cultures continue to create cupules to this day.

2. In paragraph 2, why does the author mention the three eras of the Stone Age?

   (A) To support the claim that cupules are the most prolific petroglyphs

   (B) To argue that cupules are a modern form of parietal art

   (C) To show that the creation of cupules occured only during a very short time in history

   (D) To suggest further research into the reason prehistoric cultures created cupules

3. The word "**prolific**" in the passage is closest in meaning to

   (A) valuable

   (B) abnormal

   (C) abundant

   (D) excessive

4. According to paragraph 2, the primary categorization of rock art is influenced by

   (A) the continent on which the art was produced

   (B) whether the art is a cup stone or other type of petroglyph

   (C) the era of the Stone Age that the art dates from

   (D) the surface used and the process by which the art was created

4

Paragraph 3

S1 The actual term "cupule" was introduced in the early 1990s by Australian archaeologist Robert G. Bednarik.

2   According to Bednarik and his colleagues, a cupule is a hemispherical petroglyph created by hammering the rock surface with another hard object, in a process called percussion.

3   In order to be defined as a cupule, the indentation in the rock must be man-made, intentional, percussion-produced, and primarily symbolic or non-utilitarian in nature, although there may be secondary utilitarian functions present.

5. Each of the following corresponds to a requirement in the definition of cupules by Bednarik and his colleagues EXCEPT:

   (A) If created accidentally, an indentation is not considered a cupule.

   (B) The half-sphere indentation must have been created by hammering.

   (C) To be classified as a cupule, the rock art cannot have any useful function.

   (D) Cupules cannot be created by non-human forces such as erosion.

Paragraph 4

S1	Cupules are typically found in large groups and often number in the hundreds (or even thousands) in a single location.
2	A recent series of research experiments conducted by the Indian archaeologist Giriraj Kumar has sought to understand the difficulty with which these large groupings of cupules were created.
3	Over the course of five experiments, Kumar's team attempted to replicate cupules found at Daraki-Chattan, India.
4	For each replicated cupule, the team collected a variety of data, such as specific descriptions of the hammer-stones used, the time needed to create the cupule, and the number of percussion strikes required.
5	The research found that the pounding of a single cupule out of hard rock required a colossal expenditure of energy: some cupules required upwards of 20,000 blows, an effort that would take several hours to complete.
6	Given that the Daraki-Chattan site includes over 500 cupules, creating such large formations would have required a great deal of time and dedication.
7	Since cupules were chiefly symbolic, not practical, in nature, the immensity of the effort required to create them indicates the value these prehistoric cultures attached to certain non-utilitarian activities.

4

6. According to paragraph 4, which of the following is thought to be true of the importance of cupules to prehistoric cultures?

    (A) The hammering of cupule formations was a critical part of most prehistoric rituals.

    (B) Cupules were an early form of symbolic communication, allowing different prehistoric communities to signal their presence in an area.

    (C) Prehistoric cultures viewed cupules as primarily artistic and thus trivial in nature.

    (D) Because they were so challenging to make, cupules signify the value of symbolic activities for prehistoric cultures.

7. The word "immensity" in the passage is closest in meaning to

    (A) magnitude

    (B) harshness

    (C) insignificance

    (D) enjoyment

8. In paragraph 4, why does the author introduce Kumar's research?

 (A) To provide support for the importance of cupules to prehistoric cultures

 (B) To compare the various techniques used to create cupules

 (C) To demonstrate the effectiveness of researchers in replicating cupule production

 (D) To explain why cupules were useful in a significant way to prehistoric cultures

Paragraph 5

S1 Experts have not yet agreed on a **unified** explanation of the cultural or artistic meaning of cupules.

2 However, a theory by archaeologist Charles P. Mountford in the early 1940s proposed that the creation of cupules might be associated with fertility rites.

3 To investigate this, Mountford studied an Aboriginal tribe who continued to create cupules.

4 Mountford witnessed the tribe hammering cupules as part of a fertility ritual for the pink cockatoo.

5 The Aborigines pounded the cupules into a rock thought to contain the life essence of this bird.

6 As the cupules were pounded out, the mineral dust that arose was thought to increase the female cockatoo's production of eggs, which were a valuable food source for the Aborigines.

9. What did Mountford hope to evaluate with his research?

 (A) Whether the effort expended in creating cupules indicates their importance to prehistoric cultures

 (B) Whether the creation of cupules was associated with fertility rites

 (C) Whether the mineral dust created when cupules are pounded out has ritual purposes

 (D) Whether the date of a cupule can be determined through experimentation

10. The word "unified" in the passage is closest in meaning to

 (A) popular

 (B) simple

 (C) thorough

 (D) consolidated

Paragraph 6

S1   The earliest known examples of cupule art, dating back to between 290,000 and 700,000 B.C., were found in central India.

2   It can be difficult for archaeologists to estimate the exact date of creation for many cupules, however, because some appear to have been reworked by later artists, sometimes thousands of years later.

3   For instance, one cupule at Moda Bhata, India, created around 7,000 B.C., was re-pounded around A.D. 200.

4   Some researchers were initially surprised that all of the oldest known cupules appear on highly weatherproof and extremely hard rock, given the great physical effort clearly needed to create such formations.

5   These same researchers questioned why easier, softer rocks were not chosen.

6   However, it is entirely possible that this pattern is the result of survivorship bias: cupules formed on hard and more weatherproof rock are more likely to survive to the present day.

7   It is probable that archaeologists may one day discover even older cupules in weather-protected soft rock.

11. According to paragraph 6, the knowledge that some cupules were re-pounded suggests what difficulty for cupule research?

   (A) It makes it tough to determine the purpose of the cupule.

   (B) It complicates efforts to estimate when cupules were created.

   (C) It undermines the belief that cupules are more difficult to create in hard rock.

   (D) It indicates that survivorship bias had tainted the archaeological record.

12. Which of the sentences below best expresses the essential information in the highlighted sentence in paragraph 6? Incorrect choices change the meaning in important ways or leave out essential information.

   (A) Despite their initial surprise, several researchers confirmed that cupule formations are more difficult to create in hard rock, using the oldest known cupules.

   (B) Finding the oldest cupules in extremely hard rock, which would have required immense labor to shape, was unexpected to some scientists.

   (C) Researchers were surprised that the cupules that were most likely to survive the longest would be found in very hard, weatherproof rock, given the creation effort required.

   (D) Because cupules were extremely hard to make, scientists were astounded by the age of the oldest known cupules in weatherproof rock.

Paragraph 5

P5 S6   As the cupules were pounded out, the mineral dust that arose was thought to increase the female cockatoo's production of eggs, which were a valuable food source for the Aborigines.

Paragraph 6

P6
S1–2   **A** The earliest known examples of cupule art, dating back to between 290,000 and 700,000 B.C., were found in central India. It can be difficult for archaeologists to estimate the exact date of creation for many cupules, however, because some appear to have been reworked by later artists, sometimes thousands of years later.

3–5   **B** For instance, one cupule at Moda Bhata, India, created around 7,000 B.C., was re-pounded around A.D. 200. Some researchers were initially surprised that all of the oldest known cupules appear on highly weatherproof and extremely hard rock, given the great physical effort clearly needed to create such formations. These same researchers questioned why easier, softer rocks were not chosen.

6–7   **C** However, it is entirely possible that this pattern is the result of survivorship bias: cupules formed on hard and more weatherproof rock are more likely to survive to the present day. It is probable that archaeologists may one day discover even older cupules in weather-protected soft rock.

End   **D**

> Look at the part of the passage that is displayed above. The letters [A], [B], [C], and [D] indicate where the following sentence could be added.

13. **This doubt arises from the expectation that as cultures advanced in history, their tools advanced as well, suggesting that the tools used to hammer early cupules were more rudimentary and would be less successful when used on hard rock.**

Where would the sentence best fit?

(A) Choice A

(B) Choice B

(C) Choice C

(D) Choice D

An introductory sentence for a brief summary of the passage is provided below. Complete the summary by selecting the THREE answer choices that express the most important ideas in the passage. Some sentences do not belong in the summary because they express ideas that are not presented in the passage or are minor ideas in the passage. This question is worth 2 points.

14. **Throughout history and around the globe, humans have created artwork known as rock art.**

   A | Cupules, the oldest and most prevalent form of rock art, are defined as serving a predominantly symbolic purpose.

   B | The effort to create cupules was often made easier by soft rock and therefore supports their purely decorative purpose.

   C | Cupules have been successfully used to better understand the utilitarian purpose of parietal art.

   D | The effort to create the collections of cupules already discovered speaks to the importance that prehistoric cultures placed on symbolic activities.

   E | Archaeologists continue to investigate the age of cupules and their potential symbolic significance to prehistoric and present-day cultures.

   F | Recently, researchers and archaeologists have been able to come to an agreement on the specific meaning of cupules.

4.2 The Beaver Wars

The harsh aspects of globalization (international economic intertwining), including loss of livelihood and social disruption, have been the current focus of many pundits. Some condemn the suffering these dislocations have caused while others shrug off the human costs as an acceptable consequence in the service of progress, profit, and/or free-market principles. Unnoticed in this outcry is the general implicit agreement that the stresses of globalization are a modern, if not unique, crisis. However, the historical record proves that assumption to be utterly false. Perhaps the only unique aspect is that technology has multiplied the rapidity with which these disruptions evolve; still, for hundreds of years, economic changes on one continent have dramatically altered societies on another continent—societies that were far more isolated from each other than groups at a similar geographic distance are today. One notable historical example of this pattern would be the Beaver Wars.

In the seventeenth century, fur pelts were much in demand in Europe for making both hats and garments; this burgeoning demand caused Dutch, French, and English traders to exploit the vast resources of the North American continent despite the many additional costs. Many of these costs stemmed from the presence of the Iroquois Confederacy, a sophisticated political and social organization of tribes of Native Americans whose territory was centered in what is now much of New York State. By 1610, this territory bordered French trading outposts to the north and Dutch and English trading posts to the south and east. While the the French allied themselves with other largely Algonquin-speaking tribes of Native Americans, the Dutch and English supported their Iroquois trading partners. The ensuing competition for resources inflamed an already hostile relationship between the Algonquian and Iroquoian tribes into a full-blown war. Both sides launched raids that destroyed entire settlements, razing the structures, burning the crops, and killing or capturing all the inhabitants.

Beyond the direct stresses of war, the Iroquois Confederacy was profoundly changed by the economics of this European fashion trend. The introduction of European goods altered the way Iroquois tribes performed basic tasks; some of these goods soon became essentials. By 1640, the beaver population in traditional Iroquois lands had been exhausted. To maintain their revenue flow, the Iroquois were forced to attempt to annex the territories of their Native American neighbors. Unlike the French, the Dutch traders were willing to exchange firearms for furs. Thus, the Iroquois had an advantage in weaponry over other tribes that led to their dominance over other tribes in the region.

While the fortunes of this decades-long war ebbed and flowed, partly because of the intrigues of the European powers, by late in the seventeenth century the Iroquois had moved far beyond their original Hudson River lands. They depopulated the entire Ohio Valley and Lower Peninsula of Michigan, defeating the Algonquin-speaking tribes, including the Shawnee, Miami, and Potawatomi, whose surviving members fled to the west. In fact, this Iroquois offensive also drove the Lakota Sioux to the Dakotas, where they became nomadic mounted warriors, prominent in the United States frontier wars of the nineteenth century. To the north, the French effected a stalemate with the Iroquois only by committing a regiment of regulars, the Carignan-Salières regiment, to the fray in the 1660s.

Fighting nonetheless continued for the rest of the seventeenth century, spurred both by economic concerns and the ongoing political rivalry between France and England, as the Dutch eventually ceded their North American interests to the English. Horrific massacres, much like those of the ancient Greeks chronicled in the *Iliad*, were perpetrated by both the allegedly civilized Europeans and the Iroquois. Four to five generations of Iroquois lived their entire lives in an era of constant warfare. Finally, in 1701, despite English efforts to prolong a war that burdened France, the French and Iroquois signed the Great Peace of Montreal. This peace lasted for more than 20 years and allowed the dispossessed Algonquin tribes to slowly repopulate the Ohio Valley territory. Meanwhile, the Iroquois Confederacy was able to further advance its economic and technological position, as well as wield influence over their European rivals.

In sum, international trade and globalization hundreds of years ago caused profound and unforeseen economic consequences for peoples far removed from the initial catalyst. Much like today, some prospered, some failed, and some died. Furthermore, these same disruptive forces proved far more powerful than the will or policies of any of the entities involved. Global economic currents arguably cut as wide a swath across societies in the seventeenth century as they do today.

| Now answer the questions. |

Paragraph 1

S1   The harsh aspects of globalization (international economic intertwining), including loss of livelihood and social disruption, have been the current focus of many pundits.

2   Some condemn the suffering these dislocations have caused while others shrug off the human costs as an acceptable consequence in the service of progress, profit, and/or free-market principles.

3   Unnoticed in this outcry is the general implicit agreement that the stresses of globalization are a modern, if not unique, crisis.

4   However, the historical record proves that assumption to be utterly false.

5   Perhaps the only unique aspect is that technology has multiplied the rapidity with which these disruptions evolve; still, for hundreds of years, economic changes on one continent have dramatically altered societies on another continent—societies that were far more isolated from each other than groups at a similar geographic distance are today.

6   One notable historical example of this pattern would be the Beaver Wars.

1. The word "utterly" in the passage is closest in meaning to

    (A) mistakenly

    (B) partially

    (C) expressly

    (D) completely

2. According to paragraph 1, globalization today likely differs from earlier manifestations in what regard?

    (A) Its effects are felt across greater distances than they previously were.

    (B) It is now conducted for profit, progress, and/or in support of free-market principles.

    (C) Its effects are more negative than they previously were.

    (D) Its effects occur more rapidly than they previously had.

Paragraph 2

S1   In the seventeenth century, fur pelts were much in demand in Europe for making both hats and garments; this burgeoning demand caused Dutch, French, and English traders to exploit the vast resources of the North American continent despite the many additional costs.

2   Many of these costs stemmed from the presence of the Iroquois Confederacy, a sophisticated political and social organization of tribes of Native Americans whose territory was centered in what is now much of New York State.

3   By 1610, this territory bordered French trading outposts to the north and Dutch and English trading posts to the south and east.

4   While the the French allied themselves with other largely Algonquin-speaking tribes of Native Americans, the Dutch and English supported their Iroquois trading partners.

5   The ensuing competition for resources inflamed an already hostile relationship between the Algonquian and Iroquoian tribes into a full-blown war.

6   Both sides launched raids that destroyed entire settlements, razing the structures, burning the crops, and killing or capturing all the inhabitants.

3. According to paragraph 2, which of the following best characterizes the Iroquois Confederacy's relationship with the French traders?

   (A) It devolved into a war over the fur trade.

   (B) They eventually became allies in pursuit of profits from fur trading.

   (C) They were exclusive trading partners, monopolizing the fur trade.

   (D) They learned how to create a sophisticated society from the French.

4. The word "stemmed" in the passage is closest in meaning to

   (A) detached

   (B) derived

   (C) departed

   (D) dispersed

Paragraph 3

S1   Beyond the direct stresses of war, the Iroquois Confederacy was profoundly changed by the economics of this European fashion trend.

2   The introduction of European goods altered the way Iroquois tribes performed basic tasks; some of these goods soon became essentials.

3   By 1640, the beaver population in traditional Iroquois lands had been exhausted.

4   To maintain their revenue flow, the Iroquois were forced to attempt to **annex** the territories of their Native American neighbors.

5   Unlike the French, **the Dutch traders were willing to exchange firearms for furs.**

6   Thus, the Iroquois had an advantage in weaponry over other tribes that led to their dominance over other tribes in the region.

5. In paragraph 3, why does the author mention that "the Dutch traders were willing to exchange firearms for furs"?

    (A) To indicate the advantage that the Iroquois acquired over beavers and other game

    (B) To emphasize how the Iroquois gained superiority in their battles with the French

    (C) To explain a primary reason for the Iroquois's military success against neighboring tribes

    (D) To provide an example of how basic tasks in the daily life of the Iroquois were changed by outside economic forces

6. The word "annex" in the passage is closest in meaning to

    (A) conquer

    (B) destroy

    (C) surrender

    (D) exploit

Paragraph 4

S1   While the fortunes of this decades-long war ebbed and flowed, partly because of the intrigues of the European powers, by late in the seventeenth century the Iroquois had moved far beyond their original Hudson River lands.

2   They depopulated the entire Ohio Valley and Lower Peninsula of Michigan, defeating the Algonquin-speaking tribes, including the Shawnee, Miami, and Potawatomi, whose surviving members fled to the west.

3   In fact, this Iroquois offensive also drove the Lakota Sioux to the Dakotas, where they became nomadic mounted warriors, prominent in the United States frontier wars of the nineteenth century.

4   To the north, the French effected a stalemate with the Iroquois only by committing a regiment of regulars, the Carignan-Salières regiment, to the fray in the 1660s.

7.   It can be inferred from paragraph 4 that forcing the Lakota Sioux to the Dakotas was primarily significant from the author's perspective because

(A) the action forced the French to commit a regiment of regulars

(B) as a result, the Lakota Sioux did not live in one place for long

(C) the Lakota Sioux played an important role in nineteenth-century frontier wars of the United States

(D) the Lakota Sioux learned how to create a partially urbanized society from the Iroquois

8.   Which of the following best describes the organization of paragraph 4?

(A) A dubious claim is examined but rejected.

(B) A statement of fact is followed by supporting details.

(C) A previously unknown historical fact is documented.

(D) A statement of fact is followed by the citation of parallel cases.

Paragraph 5

S1   Fighting nonetheless continued for the rest of the seventeenth century, spurred both by economic concerns and the ongoing political rivalry between France and England, as the Dutch eventually ceded their North American interests to the English.

2   Horrific massacres, much like those of the ancient Greeks chronicled in the *Iliad*, were perpetrated by both the allegedly civilized Europeans and the Iroquois.

3   Four to five generations of Iroquois lived their entire lives in an era of constant warfare.

4   Finally, in 1701, despite English efforts to prolong a war that burdened France, the French and Iroquois signed the Great Peace of Montreal.

5   This peace lasted for more than 20 years and allowed the dispossessed Algonquin tribes to slowly repopulate the Ohio Valley territory.

6   Meanwhile, the Iroquois Confederacy was able to further advance its economic and technological position, as well as wield influence over their European rivals.

9. Which of the sentences below best expresses the essential information in the highlighted sentence in paragraph 5? Incorrect choices change the meaning in important ways or leave out essential information.

   (A) In the wars between the supposedly civilized Europeans and the Iroquois, the Greeks were guilty of horrible massacres, comparable to those in the *Iliad*.

   (B) The Europeans, who were alleged to be civilized, committed more atrocities like those recorded in the *Iliad* than the Iroquois did in the course of their wars.

   (C) In the wars between the Iroquois and the Europeans (who were supposedly civilized), both sides committed terrible atrocities, like those reported in the *Iliad*.

   (D) During the wars between the allegedly civilized Europeans and the Iroquois, dreadful massacres chronicled in the *Iliad* were committed by both sides.

10. The word "wield" in the passage is closest in meaning to

   (A) retain

   (B) exert

   (C) squander

   (D) gain

11. All of the following are mentioned in paragraph 5 as occurring before the Great Peace EXCEPT:

(A) Generations of Iroquois lived their entire lives at war.

(B) The Iroquois committed horrific massacres.

(C) The Dutch territories became English.

(D) Algonquin-speaking tribes repopulated the Ohio Valley.

Paragraph 6

S1 In sum, international trade and globalization hundreds of years ago caused profound and unforeseen economic consequences for peoples far removed from the initial catalyst.

2 [A] Much like today, some prospered, some failed, and some died.

3 [B] Furthermore, these same disruptive forces proved far more powerful than the will or policies of any of the entities involved.

4 [C] Global economic currents arguably cut as wide a swath across societies in the seventeenth century as they do today.

End [D]

Look at the part of the passage that is displayed above. The letters [A], [B], [C], and [D] indicate where the following sentence could be added.

12. **And along with economic gains and losses, these forces, as always, had powerful personal impacts on the people involved.**

Where would the sentence best fit?

(A) Choice A

(B) Choice B

(C) Choice C

(D) Choice D

Select from the seven phrases below TWO that correctly characterize the Dutch during the Beaver Wars and THREE that correctly characterize the Iroquois, as described in the passage. Two of the phrases will NOT be used. This question is worth 2 points.

The Dutch	**The Iroquois**
•	•
•	•
	•

13. A Became nomadic mounted warriors

 B Conquered neighboring territories

 C Waged and suffered through war for decades

 D Provided firearms in exchange for furs

 E Allied with Algonquin-speaking tribes

 F Had a sophisticated political organization

 G Relinquished North American territories

4.3 The Flynn Effect

Since 1930, scores measuring intelligence quotients (IQs) have been increasing steadily across the globe. James Flynn first discovered this phenomenon in the 1980s in the United States. Ensuing analysis found that it was occurring in virtually every country where such data was collected. This trend is referred to as "the Flynn Effect," a sustained increase in intelligence test scores worldwide with each passing year. Researchers have devoted a significant amount of study to the effect not only because of its geographic scope, but also because, mysteriously, the annual rise has occurred every year in more or less linear fashion over the past century.

Does this mean we are getting smarter? The definition of "intelligence" is hotly debated, but generally speaking, IQ tests are designed to measure both **fluid intelligence** and **crystallized intelligence**. Fluid intelligence refers to problem-solving abilities, such as looking for patterns, and using visual cues to solve problems. Crystallized intelligence refers to learned skills, such as math and vocabulary. When IQ tests are administered, the convention is to set the average of the test results to 100, with a standard deviation of 15 to 16 points. The test score distribution is restandardized with every new batch of test-takers, such that the number 100 consistently represents the average score of that year's test-takers. When younger subjects take older tests, their average score is higher than the previous group's average: the Flynn Effect. The Flynn Effect is driven more by gains in fluid intelligence than in crystallized intelligence.

While the cause of the Flynn Effect remains a mystery, scientists have been able to rule out some possible causes. The time frame in which these increases have occurred, along with their geographic scope, seem to preclude the cause being genetic (genetic evolution takes a long time to take effect, as it occurs over many generations via reproduction). The Flynn Effect, by contrast, refers to steady increases in measured intelligence over much shorter time frames. Further, the population groups among whom it is occurring,

often separated by great distances, do not interact extensively enough for reproduction to lead to shared genetic traits across the groups.

Researchers attempting to identify the cause of the Flynn Effect have therefore been left with what seems to be the only alternative: a changing global culture. Research over the past 30 years has focused on identifying possible causes rooted in culture. These have included improvements in nutrition, education, testing methods, and so forth. Further hypotheses have included increased complexity of social environments, changes in childrearing, advances in technology, and improved test-taking abilities.

A problem that researchers have faced in analyzing possible cultural factors is that the universality of the Flynn Effect seems in contradiction to the nature of culture itself, which by definition varies across time and space. In other words, different characteristics of places and population groups are what create divergence across cultures, and this diversity is a fundamental feature of the human population at large. Culture is different in Brazil than it is in Israel or Australia or Canada. But for cultural factors to be responsible for the Flynn Effect, they must essentially affect people across countries nearly identically. This would seem to be unlikely.

Further, factors such as improved nutrition would seem to affect nutritionally impoverished regions more dramatically than regions where nutritional resources have been stable for decades. In other words, if better nutrition is driving improved fluid intelligence, areas that have seen the most improvement in nutrition should see the largest increase in IQ scores, while in areas where nutritional resources have been widely available for a long time, IQ scores should be leveling off. But this is not the case. Regions with poor nutritional resources and regions with high nutritional resources have both shown steady gains over time, regardless of how nutritional resources have changed.

The mystery of how culture could be causing the Flynn Effect was further complicated by the research of Richard Lynn. Lynn devised a method of investigating just how early the increases in intelligence occurred in the lifetime of children by examining the IQs of newborn infants. He found that infant IQs have also been rising steadily. This would seem to further limit the impact of culture, given that newborns have not yet been subjected to cultural influences.

> Now answer the questions.

Paragraph 1

S1 Since 1930, scores measuring intelligence quotients (IQs) have been increasing steadily across the globe.

2 James Flynn first discovered this phenomenon in the 1980s in the United States.

3 Ensuing analysis found that it was occurring in virtually every country where such data was collected.

4 This trend is referred to as "the Flynn Effect," a sustained increase in intelligence test scores worldwide with each passing year.

5 Researchers have devoted a significant amount of study to the effect not only because of its geographic scope, but also because, mysteriously, the annual rise has occurred every year in more or less linear fashion over the past century.

1. The word "ensuing" in the passage is closest in meaning to

    (A) confirmatory

    (B) later

    (C) broader

    (D) rigorous

2. According to paragraph 1, which of the following is true about the Flynn Effect?

    (A) It is taking place all over the planet.

    (B) It is unique to the United States.

    (C) It is occurring at a lesser rate than previously.

    (D) Researchers have been studying this phenomenon since 1930.

Paragraph 2

S1   Does this mean we are getting smarter?

2   The definition of "intelligence" is hotly debated, but generally speaking, IQ tests are designed to measure both **fluid intelligence** and **crystallized intelligence**.

3   Fluid intelligence refers to problem-solving abilities, such as looking for patterns, and using visual cues to solve problems.

4   Crystallized intelligence refers to learned skills, such as math and vocabulary.

5   When IQ tests are administered, the convention is to set the average of the test results to 100, with a standard deviation of 15 to 16 points.

6   The test score distribution is restandardized with every new batch of test-takers, such that the number 100 consistently represents the average score of that year's test-takers.

7   When younger subjects take older tests, their average score is higher than the previous group's average: the Flynn Effect.

8   The Flynn Effect is driven more by gains in fluid intelligence than in crystallized intelligence.

3. The word "batch" in the passage is closest in meaning to

    (A) school

    (B) society

    (C) country

    (D) group

4. Which of the following can be inferred about crystallized intelligence from paragraph 2?

    (A) Crystallized intelligence is less likely to be improved through teaching than fluid intelligence.

    (B) Crystallized intelligence is more difficult to assess than fluid intelligence.

    (C) Higher crystallized intelligence scores demonstrate superior skills that have been taught to the test-taker.

    (D) Worse performance on assessments of crystallized intelligence indicates greater fragility or fragmentation of thinking.

Paragraph 3

S1 While the cause of the Flynn Effect remains a mystery, scientists have been able to rule out some possible causes.

2   The time frame in which these increases have occurred, along with their geographic scope, seem to preclude the cause being genetic (genetic evolution takes a long time to take effect, as it occurs over many generations via reproduction).

3   The Flynn Effect, by contrast, refers to steady increases in measured intelligence over much shorter time frames.

4   Further, the population groups among whom it is occurring, often separated by great distances, do not interact extensively enough for reproduction to lead to shared genetic traits across the groups.

5. According to paragraph 3, what factors have led researchers to rule out genetics as a cause of the Flynn Effect?

    (A) The extended distance and time over which the effect has occurred.

    (B) The restriction of the effect to narrow geographic regions.

    (C) The geographic scope of the effect, as well as its short time frame.

    (D) The fact that the effect has occurred in one defined population group, but not in other groups.

6. Which of the following can be inferred from paragraph 3 about the Flynn Effect?

    (A) Despite ruling out possible factors, researchers still do not know what causes the effect.

    (B) Despite efforts to identify a single cause, multiple causes of the effect seem to be at work.

    (C) Despite some criticism, it appears that cultural factors may be driving the effect.

    (D) Despite some findings to the contrary, it is likely that the effect does not actually exist.

	Paragraph 4
S1	Researchers attempting to identify the cause of the Flynn Effect have therefore been left with what seems to be the only alternative: a changing global culture.
2	Research over the past 30 years has focused on identifying possible causes rooted in culture.
3	These have included improvements in nutrition, education, testing methods, and so forth.
4	Further hypotheses have included increased complexity of social environments, changes in childrearing, advances in technology, and improved test-taking abilities.

7. Which one of the sentences below best expresses the essential information in the highlighted sentence of the passage? Incorrect choices change the meaning in important ways or leave out essential information.

   (A) Researchers are not certain that a changing global culture is responsible for the Flynn Effect.

   (B) Unable to definitively identify alternative causes, researchers seem to believe that a changing global culture might be responsible for the Flynn Effect.

   (C) Researchers have stopped looking for the cause of the Flynn Effect because a changing global culture is confusing the issue.

   (D) In their attempts to understand the Flynn Effect, a changing global culture has left researchers without an alternative.

8. The phrase "rooted in" in the passage is closest in meaning to

   (A) arising from

   (B) grown into

   (C) dug out of

   (D) distinct from

9. According to paragraph 4, why have researchers focused on improvements in nutrition, education, testing methods, and so forth?

   (A) These factors drive health and overall well-being globally.

   (B) These improvements are the reasons why the Flynn Effect exists.

   (C) These cultural factors are believed by researchers to vary by region.

   (D) These are cultural factors that could be causes of the Flynn Effect.

Paragraph 5

S1	A problem that researchers have faced in analyzing possible cultural factors is that the universality of the Flynn Effect seems in contradiction to the nature of culture itself, which by definition varies across time and space.
2	In other words, different characteristics of places and population groups are what create divergence across cultures, and this diversity is a fundamental feature of the human population at large.
3	Culture is different in Brazil than it is in Israel or Australia or Canada.
4	But for cultural factors to be responsible for the Flynn Effect, they must essentially affect people across countries nearly identically.
5	This would seem to be unlikely.

10. The word "divergence" in the passage is closest in meaning to

   (A) opposition

   (B) movement

   (C) alignment

   (D) variation

Paragraph 5

P5 S4–5	But for cultural factors to be responsible for the Flynn Effect, they must essentially affect people across countries nearly identically. This would seem to be unlikely.

Paragraph 6

P6 S1–2	[A] Further, factors such as improved nutrition would seem to affect nutritionally impoverished regions more dramatically than regions where nutritional resources have been stable for decades. In other words, if better nutrition is driving improved fluid intelligence, areas that have seen the most improvement in nutrition should see the largest increase in IQ scores, while in areas where nutritional resources have been widely available for a long time, IQ scores should be leveling off.
3	[B] But this is not the case.
4	[C] Regions with poor nutritional resources and regions with high nutritional resources have both shown steady gains over time, regardless of how nutritional resources have changed.
End	[D]

> Look at the part of the passage that is displayed above. The letters [A], [B], [C], and [D] indicate where the following sentence could be added.

  **MANHATTAN** PREP

11. **For example, the Netherlands (a developed nation with high levels of nutrition generally) would not see as dramatic a rise in IQ scores as would, say, The Gambia or another developing nation.**

Where would the sentence best fit?

(A) Choice A

(B) Choice B

(C) Choice C

(D) Choice D

12. This passage is developed primarily by

(A) outlining reasons to support one theory of an observed pattern

(B) arguing for a particular cause of a global phenomenon

(C) examining possible causes of a mysterious phenomenon

(D) discussing multiple problems with a single theory of an effect

Complete the table below by selecting THREE answer choices that are skills that would be representative of fluid intelligence and TWO that are skills that would be representative of crystallized intelligence.

Fluid Intelligence	Crystallized Intelligence
•	•
•	•
•	

13. [A] Solving a jigsaw puzzle by examining and putting together the pieces

[B] Doing an algebra problem

[C] Winning a spelling bee

[D] Matching shapes in a set of visual patterns

[E] Watching traffic to find a shortcut

4.4 Operation Barbarossa and Napoleon

On June 22, 1941, one year to the day after the signing of an armistice following his successful invasion of France, Adolf Hitler launched Operation Barbarossa, the code name for Nazi Germany's invasion of Russia (then the dominant part of the Soviet Union). Hitler had amassed an invading army of over 3 million soldiers, still the largest invading force in world history. What followed paralleled, in many ways, another failed invasion of Russia more than 100 years earlier by another tyrant: Napoleon Bonaparte, ruler of France. For both leaders, invading Russia would be the turning point in a war they had previously dominated, and would lead to their final defeat elsewhere in Europe.

Operation Barbarossa involved an invasion along three fronts. Army Group North was to conquer the Baltic countries and ultimately Leningrad. Army Group Center was to invade the heartland of present-day Russia and proceed to Moscow, the Soviet capital. Army Group South had orders to invade and conquer Ukraine and various southern cities in Russia to capture key economic resources, such as grain and oil. The conquest was one of annihilation: Nazi Germany viewed Soviet communism ("Bolshevism") as the mortal enemy of the Nazi's "National Socialist" political doctrine. Furthermore, National Socialism viewed Slavic and Jewish people—both predominant in Russia—as inferior to Germans. Therefore, the war was about conquest of land at all costs, and many civilians were targeted for forced labor or assassination.

By contrast, Napoleon's invasion was based on a trade disagreement. The real enemy of Napoleon was Britain, with whom France was at war, and his invasion of Russia was intended to force the Russian nobility to stop trading with Britain. His goal was to use his *grande armée* (French for "great army") to swiftly defeat the inferior Russian defending forces, march to Moscow, and force Tsar Alexander I to sign an agreement ceasing all trade with Britain. This would culminate in Britain's inability to continue to wage war with France, Napoleon reasoned. Britain would have to seek peace, thereby ending the decade-long Napoleonic Wars. Supposedly thus "fighting for an end to fighting," Napoleon's forces began the invasion on June 24, 1812, crossing the Neman River into Russia.

For each leader, the invasion had substantial initial success but ultimately met disaster. Russia is an enormous country geographically, and the distance to Moscow dwarfed that covered by any other invasion that either leader had successfully completed before. Supply lines for both invading armies quickly became stretched thin; troops and equipment were faced with exhaustion. To make matters worse, Russians engaged in scorched-earth tactics: as they retreated from the invading army, they burned or otherwise destroyed everything of value, so that no invading forces could use it. This dashed any hopes of living off the land. In addition, the Russian winter is exceptionally cold, and both leaders failed to make appropriate provisions for winter warfare, as both thought their invasion could be successfully completed before winter set in. Finally, while Russian armed resistance was light at first, it dramatically intensified as the invaders approached Moscow. By the end, invading troops met fierce Russian opposition while also combating hunger, privation, and extremely cold temperatures.

Unlike Hitler, Napoleon did successfully reach Moscow, only to find it ablaze and vacated. He waited with his army, trying to force the Russian tsar, now in exile, to sign a treaty. Meanwhile his army continued to starve, and the weather turned sharply colder. Napoleon was thus forced to leave Moscow to find provisions and shelter for his army, and this departure turned into an all-out retreat as appropriate provisions and shelter could not be found. As it attempted to flee Russia, Napoleon's army was massacred by hunger and temperatures of −25° Celsius much more than by Russian troops.

Hitler's invasion took a somewhat different path to disaster. While Army Groups North and South succeeded in fulfilling their objectives, Hitler's Army Group Center was stopped about 15 miles short of

Moscow by a Soviet counteroffensive. Army Group Center successfully fended off the Soviets and survived the cold Russian winter, but had suffered heavy losses. In 1942, German strategic objectives changed, and much of the strength of the invading force was redirected to southern Russia. The German advance to Moscow was thereby halted, and resounding defeats at the Battles of Stalingrad and Kursk permanently crippled the German war machine. It was only a matter of time before Soviet forces from the East and other Allied troops from the West could overwhelm and defeat Nazi Germany.

> Now answer the questions.

Paragraph 1

S1 On June 22, 1941, one year to the day after the signing of an armistice following his successful invasion of France, Adolf Hitler launched Operation Barbarossa, the code name for Nazi Germany's invasion of Russia (then the dominant part of the Soviet Union).

2 Hitler had amassed an invading army of over 3 million soldiers, still the largest invading force in world history.

3 What followed paralleled, in many ways, another failed invasion of Russia more than 100 years earlier by another tyrant: Napoleon Bonaparte, ruler of France.

4 For both leaders, invading Russia would be the turning point in a war they had previously dominated, and would lead to their final defeat elsewhere in Europe.

1. The author uses the phrase "What followed paralleled, in many ways, another failed invasion of Russia more than 100 years earlier" for which of the following reasons?

    (A) To point out that Napoleon's invasion and Hitler's invasion occurred in different centuries

    (B) To initiate a comparison between Operation Barbarossa and Napoleon's invasion of Russia

    (C) To introduce a broad category of military actions consisting of failed invasions of Russia

    (D) To compare the size of Hitler's army with that of Napoleon's army

2. According to paragraph 1, which of the following was true of both Operation Barbarossa and Napoleon's invasion of Russia?

    (A) Both Hitler and Napoleon were considered tyrants.

    (B) Both invasions failed because of inadequate planning.

    (C) Both invasions followed military victories in France.

    (D) Both invasions precipitated events that eventually led to defeat.

Paragraph 2

S1	Operation Barbarossa involved an invasion along three fronts.
2	Army Group North was to conquer the Baltic countries and ultimately Leningrad.
3	Army Group Center was to invade the heartland of present-day Russia and proceed to Moscow, the Soviet capital.
4	Army Group South had orders to invade and conquer Ukraine and various southern cities in Russia to capture key economic resources, such as grain and oil.
5	The conquest was one of annihilation: Nazi Germany viewed Soviet communism ("Bolshevism") as the mortal enemy of the Nazi's "National Socialist" political doctrine.
6	Furthermore, National Socialism viewed Slavic and Jewish people—both predominant in Russia—as inferior to Germans.
7	Therefore, the war was about conquest of land at all costs, and many civilians were targeted for forced labor or assassination.

3. The word "annihilation" in the passage is closest in meaning to

   (A) eradication

   (B) dismissal

   (C) introduction

   (D) victory

4. All of the following are mentioned in paragraph 2 as places targeted by Operation Barbarossa EXCEPT:

   (A) France

   (B) Ukraine

   (C) cities in southern Russia

   (D) Leningrad

Paragraph 3

S1   By contrast, Napoleon's invasion was based on a trade disagreement.

2   The real enemy of Napoleon was Britain, with whom France was at war, and his invasion of Russia was intended to force the Russian nobility to stop trading with Britain.

3   His goal was to use his *grande armée* (French for "great army") to swiftly defeat the inferior Russian defending forces, march to Moscow, and force Tsar Alexander I to sign an agreement ceasing all trade with Britain.

4   This would culminate in Britain's inability to continue to wage war with France, Napoleon reasoned.

5   Britain would have to seek peace, thereby ending the decade-long Napoleonic Wars.

6   Supposedly thus "fighting for an end to fighting," Napoleon's forces began the invasion on June 24, 1812, crossing the Neman River into Russia.

5. The word "inferior" in the passage is closest in meaning to

   (A) exceptional

   (B) high-handed

   (C) substandard

   (D) derivative

6. According to the paragraph, why did Napoleon believe that a successful invasion of Russia would lead Britain to "seek peace, thereby ending the decade-long Napoleonic Wars"?

   (A) Britain was supplying Russia with the means necessary to wage war against France.

   (B) Napoleon thought that Russia would be defeated if it were forced to sign a trade agreement ceasing all trade with Britain.

   (C) Both countries were trading with other countries in Europe, leading to the Napoleonic Wars.

   (D) Conquering Russia would force Russia to stop providing Britain with supplies for war against France.

4

	Paragraph 4
S1	For each leader, the invasion had substantial initial success but ultimately met disaster.
2	Russia is an enormous country geographically, and the distance to Moscow dwarfed that covered by any other invasion that either leader had successfully completed before.
3	Supply lines for both invading armies quickly became stretched thin; troops and equipment were faced with exhaustion.
4	To make matters worse, Russians engaged in scorched-earth tactics: as they retreated from the invading army, they burned or otherwise destroyed everything of value, so that no invading forces could use it.
5	This dashed any hopes of living off the land.
6	In addition, the Russian winter is exceptionally cold, and both leaders failed to make appropriate provisions for winter warfare, as both thought their invasion could be successfully completed before winter set in.
7	Finally, while Russian armed resistance was light at first, it dramatically intensified as the invaders approached Moscow.
8	By the end, invading troops met fierce Russian opposition while also combating hunger, **privation**, and extremely cold temperatures.

4

7. The word "**privation**" in the passage is closest in meaning to

   (A) expansion

   (B) hardship

   (C) bounty

   (D) restlessness

8. Which of the following does the author conclude was an important factor in the failure of Napoleon's invasion of Russia?

   (A) Napoleon's decision to begin his invasion in the middle of winter

   (B) The relatively slight distances that invading troops were to cover

   (C) The scorched-earth response of the retreating defenders

   (D) Intense military resistance at the beginning of the invasion

Paragraph 5

S1	Unlike Hitler, Napoleon did successfully reach Moscow, only to find it ablaze and vacated.
2	He waited with his army, trying to force the Russian tsar, now in exile, to sign a treaty.
3	Meanwhile his army continued to starve, and the weather turned sharply colder.
4	Napoleon was thus forced to leave Moscow to find provisions and shelter for his army, and this departure turned into an all-out retreat as appropriate provisions and shelter could not be found.
5	As it attempted to flee Russia, Napoleon's army was massacred by hunger and temperatures of −25° Celsius much more than by Russian troops.

9. The word "ablaze" in the passage is closest in meaning to

   (A) burning

   (B) embattled

   (C) deserted

   (D) trashed

Paragraph 6

S1	Hitler's invasion took a somewhat different path to disaster.
2	While Army Groups North and South succeeded in fulfilling their objectives, Hitler's Army Group Center was stopped about 15 miles short of Moscow by a Soviet counteroffensive.
3	Army Group Center successfully fended off the Soviets and survived the cold Russian winter, but had suffered heavy losses.
4	In 1942, German strategic objectives changed, and much of the strength of the invading force was redirected to southern Russia.
5	The German advance to Moscow was thereby halted, and resounding defeats at the Battles of Stalingrad and Kursk permanently crippled the German war machine.
6	It was only a matter of time before Soviet forces from the East and other Allied troops from the West could overwhelm and defeat Nazi Germany.

10. The word "crippled" in the passage is closest in meaning to

   (A) surrendered

   (B) empowered

   (C) incapacitated

   (D) extinguished

Paragraph 3

S1   By contrast, Napoleon's invasion was based on a trade disagreement.

2   [A] The real enemy of Napoleon was Britain, with whom France was at war, and his invasion of Russia was intended to force the Russian nobility to stop trading with Britain.

3   [B] His goal was to use his *grande armée* (French for "great army") to swiftly defeat the inferior Russian defending forces, march to Moscow, and force Tsar Alexander I to sign an agreement ceasing all trade with Britain.

4–5   [C] This would culminate in Britain's inability to continue to wage war with France, Napoleon reasoned. Britain would have to seek peace, thereby ending the decade-long Napoleonic Wars.

6   [D] Supposedly thus "fighting for an end to fighting," Napoleon's forces began the invasion on June 24, 1812, crossing the Neman River into Russia.

Look at the part of the passage that is displayed above. The letters [A], [B], [C], and [D] indicate where the following sentence could be added.

---

11. **Napoleon correctly believed that the goods Russia was sending to Britain were helping Britain to wage war against France, and he felt it was imperative to stop these shipments.**

Where would the sentence best fit?

(A) Choice A

(B) Choice B

(C) Choice C

(D) Choice D

> Select from the eight phrases below TWO that characterize Operation Barbarossa (Hitler's invasion) only, TWO that characterize Napoleon's invasion only, and THREE that characterize BOTH invasions. One of the phrases will NOT be used. This question is worth 2 points.

Operation Barbarossa Only	Napoleon's Invasion Only	Both Invasions
•	•	•
•	•	•
		•

12. A   Succeeded in reaching Moscow

B   Attempted to invade and conquer Ukraine

C   Supply lines for the invading army became stretched thin

D   Met fierce Russian opposition

E   Army was destroyed in Moscow

F   Goal of invasion was annihilation

G   Invasion was based on a trade disagreement

H   Failed to make appropriate provisions for winter warfare

4.5 The Kennewick Man

In 1996, while competing in a boating race in Columbia Park along the Columbia River near Kennewick, Washington, in the United States, Will Thomas stepped on something that felt like a large, round rock in the river bed. Upon inspection, this "rock" had teeth: Thomas had discovered a human skull. The bones of a nearly complete human skeleton were later unearthed at the site. This accidental discovery of "The Kennewick Man" may shed new light on the development of the first human societies in North America.

Scientists have argued that the first humans came to North America during the last glacial period, or ice age, via "Beringia," commonly known as the Bering land bridge. As in any glacial period, sea water levels were much lower than at other, more normal times; as a result, the waters of the present-day Bering Strait did not exist. Instead, present-day eastern Siberia in Russia and Alaska in North America were one continuous landmass. Thus, possible human migration from Asia across this land bridge was unimpeded for thousands of years. It is known that at least several thousand humans migrated from Eastern Siberia to North America via Beringia during this time. The standard hypothesis has been that these migrators constituted a single group of people with a common ancestral background, and that they were the first humans to inhabit North America. Indeed, evidence from many archaeological sites, including the original discovery in 1929 of ancient culture remains near Clovis, New Mexico, support this "Clovis First" hypothesis.

New theories have emerged that the Beringia migration was not the only source of human migration to North America during the prehistoric period, and perhaps not even the first. Advances in DNA testing have allowed scientists to group the discovered remains of Paleoamericans, or ancient Native Americans,

according to five haplogroups[1], labeled A, B, C, D, and X. Among people in Northeast Asia and among Native Americans, haplogroups A, B, C, and D are all commonplace, supporting the theory of a single-migration model via Beringia. However, haplogroup X is different. It is found in only select locations in North America, and virtually does not exist in Siberia. Furthermore, genetic mutations among this haplogroup suggest that people in haplogroup X may have settled thousands of years earlier than populations from the other haplogroups. This discovery gives weight to the possibility of earlier migrations to North America, possibly via coastal routes along the Pacific Ocean or even from Europe via the North Atlantic.

The Kennewick Man may help resolve these competing theories. Anthropological[2] analysis and carbon-dating techniques show that the skeleton is approximately 9,000 years old, but that the skeleton is distinctly different from most other Paleoamerican remains. The Kennewick Man had a relatively small face with a long, narrow skull. In contrast, Paleoamericans and modern Native Americans tend to have larger faces with shorter, broader skulls and prominent cheekbones. Also, resin models of other important bones indicate key differences in size and structure from those of other Paleoamericans. Indeed, of all current peoples, the Kennewick Man possessed physical attributes most similar to Polynesians. Present-day Polynesians, in turn, are most likely descended from the ancient Jōmon, the original inhabitants of the Japanese islands, who may have come into existence well over 15,000 years ago.

The Jōmon culture is known to have been dependent upon the oceans for survival, building primitive boats out of wood and using them for deep-sea fishing and exploration. If new theories are correct, the Jōmon may have sailed along the coastline of Beringia, from Asia to Alaska, with plenty of natural resources available to support the journey. This ocean-based journey could have occurred before the migration across the Bering land bridge, with small Jōmon civilizations developing along the Pacific coast. Later, when the land-based migrators made their crossing, the resulting populations could have overwhelmed the established Jōmon population, eventually resulting in the societies that constitute the ancestors of modern Native Americans.

> Now answer the questions.

Paragraph 1

S1   In 1996, while competing in a boating race in Columbia Park along the Columbia River near Kennewick, Washington, in the United States, Will Thomas stepped on something that felt like a large, round rock in the river bed.

2   Upon inspection, this "rock" had teeth: Thomas had discovered a human skull.

3   The bones of a nearly complete human skeleton were later unearthed at the site.

4   This accidental discovery of "The Kennewick Man" may shed new light on the development of the first human societies in North America.

---

haplogroups[1]: a group of people who share a common genetic lineage on either the male or female side

anthropological[2]: relating to anthropology, the study of human beings and various aspects of human societies

  MANHATTAN PREP

1. According to paragraph 1, which of the following is true about the discovery of
    "The Kennewick Man"?

    (A) Its skeleton was discovered before the skull was found.

    (B) It helped the first societies in North America to develop.

    (C) It was discovered after a purposeful search by an archaeologist.

    (D) At first, the finder thought he had stepped on a round rock.

2. The word "inspection" in the passage is closest in meaning to

    (A) removal

    (B) scrutiny

    (C) concealment

    (D) deliberation

Paragraph 2

S1 Scientists have argued that the first humans came to North America during the last glacial
    period, or ice age, via "Beringia," commonly known as the Bering land bridge.

2   As in any glacial period, sea water levels were much lower than at other, more normal times; as a
    result, the waters of the present-day Bering Strait did not exist.

3   Instead, present-day eastern Siberia in Russia and Alaska in North America were one
    continuous landmass.

4   Thus, possible human migration from Asia across this land bridge was unimpeded for
    thousands of years.

5   It is known that at least several thousand humans migrated from Eastern Siberia to North
    America via Beringia during this time.

6   The standard hypothesis has been that these migrators constituted a single group of people with a
    common ancestral background, and that they were the first humans to inhabit North America.

7   Indeed, evidence from many archaeological sites, including the original discovery in 1929 of
    ancient culture remains near Clovis, New Mexico, supports this "Clovis First" hypothesis.

3. In paragraph 2, what does the author imply about the "Clovis First" hypothesis?

    (A) It is synonymous with the standard hypothesis regarding migration to North America.

    (B) It suggests that most of the migrators to North America settled near present-day Clovis,
        New Mexico.

    (C) It suggests that some of the earliest settlers in North America migrated there in a manner other
        than by using Beringia.

    (D) It proposes that the first migration to North America likely consisted of people with multiple
        ancestral backgrounds.

4. According to paragraph 2, all of the following statements about the Bering land bridge migration are true EXCEPT:

(A) The land bridge only existed because an ice age was occurring at the time of the migrations.

(B) The standard hypothesis states that this migration constituted the first arrival of human inhabitants in North America.

(C) According to the standard hypothesis, the migration consisted of thousands of people over thousands of years in various groups.

(D) It was made possible by the fact that Siberia and Alaska were, at the time, one single landmass.

5. Which of the sentences below best expresses the essential information in the highlighted sentence in paragraph 2? Incorrect choices change the meaning in important ways or leave out essential information.

(A) As in any glacial period, sea water levels were much lower than those of the Bering Strait normally at the time.

(B) As in any glacial period, the waters of the present-day Bering Strait did not exist, leading to much lower sea water levels than normal at the time.

(C) The waters of the Bering Strait did not exist at that time because during any glacial period sea water levels are much lower than normal.

(D) Sea water levels were much lower than during other, more normal glacial periods, so the waters of the present-day Bering Strait did not exist.

Paragraph 3

S1   New theories have emerged that the Beringia migration was not the only source of human migration to North America during the prehistoric period, and perhaps not even the first.

2   Advances in DNA testing have allowed scientists to group the discovered remains of Paleoamericans, or ancient Native Americans, according to five haplogroups, labeled A, B, C, D, and X.

3   Among people in Northeast Asia and among Native Americans, haplogroups A, B, C, and D are all commonplace, supporting the theory of a single-migration model via Beringia.

4   However, haplogroup X is different.

5   It is found in only select locations in North America, and virtually does not exist in Siberia.

6   Furthermore, genetic mutations among this haplogroup suggest that people in haplogroup X may have settled thousands of years earlier than populations from the other haplogroups.

7   This discovery gives weight to the possibility of earlier migrations to North America, possibly via coastal routes along the Pacific Ocean or even from Europe via the North Atlantic.

6. The word "**commonplace**" in the passage is closest in meaning to

    (A) unexceptional

    (B) reciprocal

    (C) parochial

    (D) extraordinary

7. Why does the author use the phrase "**haplogroup X is different**"?

    (A) To predict that new haplogroups will be discovered elsewhere in North America

    (B) To show that haplogroup X does not exist in Paleoamericans

    (C) To indicate that haplogroup X does not support the single-migration model

    (D) To suggest that haplogroup X exhibits a greater rate of genetic mutations than other haplogroups

8. The word "**mutations**" in the passage is closest in meaning to

    (A) defections

    (B) regulations

    (C) inhibitions

    (D) transformations

Paragraph 4

4

S1	The Kennewick Man may help resolve these competing theories.
2	Anthropological analysis and carbon-dating techniques show that the skeleton is approximately 9,000 years old, but that the skeleton is distinctly different from most other Paleoamerican remains.
3	The Kennewick Man had a relatively small face with a long, narrow skull.
4	In contrast, Paleoamericans and modern Native Americans tend to have larger faces with shorter, broader skulls and **prominent** cheekbones.
5	Also, resin models of other important bones indicate key differences in size and structure from those of other Paleoamericans.
6	Indeed, of all current peoples, the Kennewick Man possessed physical attributes most similar to Polynesians.
7	Present-day Polynesians, in turn, are most likely descended from the ancient Jōmon, the original inhabitants of the Japanese islands, who may have come into existence well over 15,000 years ago.

9. The word "**prominent**" in the passage is closest in meaning to

    (A) pronounced

    (B) flat

    (C) unfamiliar

    (D) unassuming

10. Which of the following can be inferred from paragraph 4 about the relationship between the Kennewick Man and the Jōmon people?

   (A) His physical features suggest that the Kennewick Man likely descended, not from the Jōmon, but from Polynesians.

   (B) Physical attributes of the Kennewick Man suggest that he may be a descendant of the Jōmon.

   (C) The 6,000-year gap between the birth of the Jōmon and the Kennewick Man indicates little connection between the two.

   (D) Key differences in size and structure differentiate the Kennewick Man from his ancestral Jōmon people.

Paragraph 5

S1   The Jōmon culture is known to have been dependent upon the oceans for survival, building primitive boats out of wood and using them for deep-sea fishing and exploration.

2   If new theories are correct, the Jōmon may have sailed along the coastline of Beringia, from Asia to Alaska, with plenty of natural resources available to support the journey.

3   This ocean-based journey could have occurred before the migration across the Bering land bridge, with small Jōmon civilizations developing along the Pacific coast.

4   Later, when the land-based migrators made their crossing, the resulting populations could have **overwhelmed** the established Jōmon population, eventually resulting in the societies that constitute the ancestors of modern Native Americans.

11. The word "**overwhelmed**" in the passage is closest in meaning to

   (A) undermined

   (B) overpowered

   (C) resisted

   (D) captivated

12. According to paragraph 5, which of the following statements is true of Jōmon people?

   (A) They were native to the Pacific coast of North America.

   (B) They probably migrated to North America by crossing over the Bering land bridge.

   (C) If they sailed along the coastline of Beringia, they likely encountered a dearth of resources along the way.

   (D) They built wooden boats for fishing and exploration of the open seas.

Paragraph 4

S1–2   The Kennewick Man may help resolve these competing theories. Anthropological analysis and carbon dating techniques show that the skeleton is approximately 9,000 years old, but that the skeleton is distinctly different from most other Paleoamerican remains.

3–4   The Kennewick Man had a relatively small face with a long, narrow skull. In contrast, Paleoamericans and modern Native Americans tend to have larger faces with shorter, broader skulls and prominent cheekbones.

5–6   **B** Also, resin models of other important bones indicate key differences in size and structure from those of other Paleoamericans. Indeed, of all current peoples, the Kennewick Man possessed physical attributes most similar to Polynesians.

7   **C** Present-day Polynesians, in turn, are most likely descended from the ancient Jōmon, the original inhabitants of the Japanese islands, who may have come into existence well over 15,000 years ago.

End   **D**

> Look at the part of the passage that is displayed above. The letters [A], [B], [C], and [D] indicate where the following sentence could be added.

13. **This lends credence to the claim that the Kennewick Man may provide the first concrete evidence that members of the Jōmon people migrated to North America.**

Where would the sentence best fit?

(A) Choice A

(B) Choice B

(C) Choice C

(D) Choice D

An introductory sentence for a brief summary of the passage is provided below. Complete the summary by selecting the THREE answer choices that express the most important ideas in the passage. Some sentences do not belong in the summary because they express ideas that are not presented in the passage or are minor ideas in the passage. This question is worth 2 points.

14. **The discovery of the Kennewick Man has called into question long-standing theories about the migration patterns of the first human inhabitants of North America.**

A   The Kennewick Man was recently discovered by accident in the river bed of the Columbia River near Kennewick, Washington.

B   The standard hypothesis has held that the first inhabitants of North America migrated there during the last ice age via a landmass located where the Bering Strait now lies.

C   New DNA analysis techniques have shown that while some genetic markers can be found in both Northeast Asia and Native American tribes, haplogroup X follows a different pattern.

D   The Kennewick Man's skeleton reveals physical features that are similar to those of Polynesians, who likely descended from the Jōmon people.

E   The Jōmon culture is known by anthropologists to have made use of wooden boats for both fishing and exploration.

F   The Kennewick Man had a larger face and a shorter, broader skull with more prominent cheekbones than most Paleoamericans.

4.6 Harriet Tubman

In April 2016, the United States Treasury Department announced that Harriet Tubman (1822–1913) would replace Andrew Jackson on the front of the $20 bill. This made her the first woman in over 100 years, and the first African American ever, to appear on paper currency issued by the United States. This move was controversial, but Treasury Secretary Jacob Lew steadfastly supported the change, making it clear that he felt Tubman's life and accomplishments deserved to be celebrated. Indeed, while Tubman was a well-known anti-slavery activist, few people outside of the academic world are aware of the extent of her efforts and suffering to help bring about the abolition of slavery. Perhaps this lack of modern-day awareness is best exemplified by the shortage of common knowledge about her efforts as a scout and spy supporting the Combahee River Raid during the American Civil War.

Harriet Tubman was born into slavery in southeastern Maryland. Like most slave children, she was subject to violent punishment by her owners—even if no wrongdoing had been committed. She suffered a severe head injury at age 12 when a metal object was thrown by an owner at a slave he was attempting to punish. The object struck Tubman instead. She suffered greatly for the rest of her life as a result of this injury, with frequent severe headaches, vertigo[1], seizures, and extreme drowsiness.

---

vertigo[1]: unsteadiness, dizziness, and/or a perception of spinning, often brought on by changing the position of one's head

Tubman escaped enslavement in 1849, fleeing to Philadelphia about 150 miles to the north, where slavery was banned. Her freedom secured, she quickly made it her life's mission to support the abolitionist movement in any way she could. She started by returning to Maryland to free her own family. Later, she continued this work, helping relatives, friends, and eventually any slave she could to flee to the North. After passage of the Fugitive Slave Act of 1850, assisting slaves who were attempting to escape custody became a serious criminal offense throughout the United States. This made Tubman's difficult work even more perilous. However, she continued it successfully—now, she would have to help escaped slaves flee all the way to Canada, all the while risking being arrested herself.

In the late 1850s, she became more deeply involved with radical abolition efforts, helping John Brown plan his failed attack on the federal arsenal at Harpers Ferry in 1859. When the American Civil War broke out in 1861, Tubman immediately joined the Union army, as she felt that Union victory would almost certainly end slavery. At first, she worked as a cook and field nurse, but later became involved in scouting and intelligence gathering. In January 1863, President Abraham Lincoln issued his Emancipation Proclamation, a wartime measure that freed slaves from bondage. Despite this, many African Americans remained in captivity in the South, as the slave owners there continued to rebel against Lincoln and the North. Because of her widespread reputation for anti-slavery work, Tubman was able to learn critical information from slaves still in bondage in exchange for helping them to freedom. The success of the Combahee River Raid in South Carolina in June 1863 is largely due to her effectiveness in gaining knowledge about the location of Confederate defensive positions. Tubman was able to help the Union gunboats avoid ambushes as they navigated the river, simultaneously guiding the ships to locations along the riverbank where runaway slaves awaited rescue. In total, over 700 slaves were rescued by the boats, and the military objective was achieved: numerous plantations owned by prominent secessionists were raided and destroyed, with the newly rescued slaves assisting the Union soldiers.

After the war ended in 1865, slavery had been completely abolished in the United States. Tubman retired to her property in upstate New York and tended to her family and personal affairs for several decades. Later in life, she would continue her humanitarian work in different arenas. She became involved with the women's suffrage movement, fighting for women's right to vote, and she worked with the African Methodist church to provide assistance to elderly, poverty-stricken African Americans.

Now answer the questions.

Paragraph 1

P1 S1   In April 2016, the United States Treasury Department announced that Harriet Tubman (1822–1913) would replace Andrew Jackson on the front of the $20 bill.

2   This made her the first woman in over 100 years, and the first African American ever, to appear on paper currency issued by the United States.

3   This move was controversial, but Treasury Secretary Jacob Lew steadfastly supported the change, making it clear that he felt Tubman's life and accomplishments deserved to be celebrated.

4   Indeed, while Tubman was a well-known anti-slavery activist, few people outside of the academic world are aware of the extent of her efforts and suffering to help bring about the abolition of slavery.

5   Perhaps this lack of modern-day awareness is best exemplified by the shortage of common knowledge about her efforts as a scout and spy supporting the Combahee River Raid during the American Civil War.

Paragraph 2

P2 S1   Harriet Tubman was born into slavery in southeastern Maryland.

2   Like most slave children, she was subject to violent punishment by her owners—even if no wrongdoing had been committed.

3   She suffered a severe head injury at age 12 when a metal object was thrown by an owner at a slave he was attempting to punish.

4   The object struck Tubman instead.

5   She suffered greatly for the rest of her life as a result of this injury, with frequent severe headaches, vertigo, seizures, and extreme drowsiness.

1. Which of the sentences below best expresses the essential information in the highlighted sentence in paragraph 1? Incorrect choices change the meaning in important ways or leave out essential information.

   (A) Feeling that Tubman's accomplishments deserved celebration, Secretary Lew supported the controversy over putting Tubman on the $20 bill.

   (B) Despite claims that Tubman's accomplishments deserved to be celebrated, Secretary Lew called the move to put Tubman on the $20 bill controversial.

   (C) Secretary Lew maintained his support for the controversial move to put Tubman on the $20 bill, which he felt celebrated her accomplishments deservedly.

   (D) Secretary Lew's support for putting Tubman on the $20 bill was made clear by the controversy around the move, but he felt her accomplishments deserved celebration.

2. It can be inferred from paragraph 1 that between 1916 and 2016

   (A) an African-American person appeared on United States paper currency

   (B) several women appeared on United States paper currency

   (C) no African-American woman appeared on United States paper currency

   (D) no bills other than the $20 bill were updated

3. Which of the following best describes the relation of paragraph 1 to paragraph 2?

   (A) Paragraph 2 explains why the historical figure introduced in paragraph 1 deserves to be honored at a national level.

   (B) Paragraph 2 outlines the life and accomplishments of the historical figure who is introduced and celebrated in paragraph 1.

   (C) Paragraph 2 discusses reasons for a decision made about the historical figure who is introduced in paragraph 1.

   (D) Paragraph 2 initiates a biography of the historical figure introduced in modern, general terms in paragraph 1.

4. The word "exemplified" in the passage is closest in meaning to

   (A) broadcast

   (B) excused

   (C) illustrated

   (D) disguised

4

Paragraph 3

S1 Tubman escaped enslavement in 1849, fleeing to Philadelphia about 150 miles to the north, where slavery was banned.

2   Her freedom secured, she quickly made it her life's mission to support the abolitionist movement in any way she could.

3   She started by returning to Maryland to free her own family.

4   Later, she continued this work, helping relatives, friends, and eventually any slave she could to flee to the North.

5   After passage of the Fugitive Slave Act of 1850, assisting slaves who were attempting to escape custody became a serious criminal offense throughout the United States.

6   This made Tubman's difficult work even more perilous.

7   However, she continued it successfully—now, she would have to help escaped slaves flee all the way to Canada, all the while risking being arrested herself.

5. The word "custody" in the passage is closest in meaning to

(A) liberty

(B) authority

(C) encirclement

(D) captivity

6. According to paragraph 3, the Fugitive Slave Act of 1850 made Tubman's work more dangerous because

(A) it made aiding slaves attempting to escape a criminal offense

(B) if she were caught, Tubman could be forced back into slavery

(C) slavery had not yet been banned in Philadelphia

(D) it made it more difficult to return to Maryland to free her family and relatives

Paragraph 4

S1	In the late 1850s, she became more deeply involved with radical abolition efforts, helping John Brown plan his failed attack on the federal arsenal at Harpers Ferry in 1859.
2	When the American Civil War broke out in 1861, Tubman immediately joined the Union army, as she felt that Union victory would almost certainly end slavery.
3	At first, she worked as a cook and field nurse, but later became involved in scouting and intelligence gathering.
4	In January 1863, President Abraham Lincoln issued his Emancipation Proclamation, a wartime measure that freed slaves from bondage.
5	Despite this, many African Americans remained in captivity in the South, as the slave owners there continued to rebel against Lincoln and the North.
6	Because of her widespread reputation for anti-slavery work, Tubman was able to learn critical information from slaves still in bondage in exchange for helping them to freedom.
7	The success of the Combahee River Raid in South Carolina in June 1863 is largely due to her effectiveness in gaining knowledge about the location of Confederate defensive positions.
8	Tubman was able to help the Union gunboats avoid ambushes as they navigated the river, simultaneously guiding the ships to locations along the riverbank where runaway slaves awaited rescue.
9	In total, over 700 slaves were rescued by the boats, and the military objective was achieved: numerous plantations owned by prominent secessionists were raided and destroyed, with the newly rescued slaves assisting the Union soldiers.

7. According to paragraph 4, all of the following statements about Harriet Tubman's involvement with the Union Army are true EXCEPT:

    (A) She questioned plantation owners to learn Confederate defenses.

    (B) She helped slaves escape from bondage in the South.

    (C) At first, she worked as a cook, but then became a scout.

    (D) She helped Union troops avoid potentially deadly traps.

8. In paragraph 4, the author mentions Harriet Tubman's "widespread reputation for anti-slavery work" in order to

    (A) predict that some people would oppose her efforts

    (B) clarify that strangers knew of her and were willing to help her

    (C) demonstrate that not every Southern slave owner was her adversary

    (D) explore the reasons many slaves remained in bondage

9. The phrase "intelligence gathering" in the passage is closest in meaning to

    (A) conducting reconnaissance

    (B) attaining wisdom

    (C) finding artifacts

    (D) recruiting collaborators

10. According to paragraph 4, which of the following was true of many slaves in the South after the Emancipation Proclamation?

    (A) They inadvertently helped defeat the Union army during the Combahee River Raid.

    (B) They were willingly set free by their owners in response to the Emancipation Proclamation.

    (C) They were skeptical about sharing information that could pose risks to their personal safety.

    (D) They helped destroy a number of prominent plantations during the Combahee River Raid.

Paragraph 5

S1   After the war ended in 1865, slavery had been completely abolished in the United States.

2   Tubman retired to her property in upstate New York and tended to her family and personal affairs for several decades.

3   Later in life, she would continue her humanitarian work in different arenas.

4   She became involved with the women's suffrage movement, fighting for women's right to vote, and she worked with the African Methodist church to provide assistance to elderly, poverty-stricken African Americans.

11. The word "humanitarian" in the passage is closest in meaning to

   (A) revolutionary

   (B) charitable

   (C) anthropological

   (D) clandestine

12. According to paragraph 5, which of the following statements was true of Harriet Tubman after the war?

   (A) She continued to help slaves escape from bondage.

   (B) She became a politician in upstate New York.

   (C) She fought for women to gain the right to vote.

   (D) She immediately began doing other kinds of socially oriented work.

Paragraph 5

S1   After the war ended in 1865, slavery had been completely abolished in the United States.

2   [A] Tubman retired to her property in upstate New York and tended to her family and personal affairs for several decades.

3   [B] Later in life, she would continue her humanitarian work in different arenas.

4   [C] She became involved with the women's suffrage movement, fighting for women's right to vote, and she worked with the African Methodist church to provide assistance to elderly, poverty-stricken African Americans.

End   [D]

Look at the part of the passage that is displayed above. The letters [A], [B], [C], and [D] indicate where the following sentence could be added.

13. **During this time in retreat, Tubman was much less active in public efforts of a political or benevolent nature.**

   Where would the sentence best fit?

   (A) Choice A

   (B) Choice B

   (C) Choice C

   (D) Choice D

> An introductory sentence for a brief summary of the passage is provided below. Complete the summary by selecting the THREE answer choices that express the most important ideas in the passage. Some sentences do not belong in the summary because they express ideas that are not presented in the passage or are minor ideas in the passage. This question is worth 2 points.

14. **The decision to celebrate Harriet Tubman by putting her on the United States $20 bill honors her not only for her well-known efforts to free slaves but also for her less well-known efforts in the Union army to end slavery.**

    A   Born into slavery, Tubman overcame considerable adversity to free herself and later to help others do the same.

    B   Tubman worked as a scout during the American Civil War, gathering critical information for the Union army.

    C   Tubman is the first African American to appear on United States paper currency, but she is not the first woman.

    D   Upon joining the Union army, Tubman first worked as a cook and as a field nurse during the Civil War.

    E   The Fugitive Slave Act, which criminalized assistance offered to slaves attempting to free themselves, was passed in 1850.

    F   Tubman played a pivotal role in the successful Combahee River Raid, uncovering hidden defenses and rescuing hundreds of slaves.

4

4.7 The Sphinx

The Sphinx, a mythical creature with a lion's body and human head, has become inextricably linked with ancient Egyptian culture, undoubtedly because of the fame of the Great Sphinx of Giza in Egypt. However, in reality, sphinx-like creatures were prominent in many ancient cultures worldwide. The sphinx's ubiquity and the relative constancy of its meaning and legend in many cultures points to a human commonality whose spread extends far beyond Giza and the Sahara Desert.

The Egyptian sphinx sported a male human head and was apparently considered a benevolent god, although one that possessed great strength. As in many other cultures, sphinxes often guarded temple entrances. The famous Great Sphinx is generally not thought to be the oldest such Egyptian statue; many, but not all, scholars believe that one depicting Queen Hetepheres II, built in approximately 2600 BCE, is probably the oldest in Egypt. However, further north in present-day Turkey, Neolithic sphinx-like figures dating to 9500 BCE have been found.

Like its Egyptian cousin, the Greek sphinx guarded temple entrances and had the body of a lion. However, Greek sphinxes had a female head and often wings. Furthermore, Greek sphinxes were far more malevolent. A prominent Greek myth tells of the Sphinx guarding Thebes; it would pose a riddle to passersby: "What walks on four feet in the morning, two in the afternoon, and three at night?" It then killed the hapless travelers, who all failed to solve it. Finally, according to the myth, Oedipus, immortalized in Sophocles's ancient Greek play *Oedipus Rex*, solved the riddle: "Man. As an infant, he crawls on all fours; as an adult, he walks on two legs and in old age, he uses a 'walking' stick." The Sphinx then killed itself. This myth of this Sphinx still resonates in modern cultures; the French playwright Jean Cocteau reworked *Oedipus Rex* as *The Infernal Machine* in the twentieth century.

Sphinxes as gods are far from limited to Greece and the Middle East. On the contrary, such figures have been depicted in myths and legends across the breadth of Asia. Creatures with human heads and the haunches of lions have particular names in the Sanskrit, Tamil, Pali, and Thai languages. They are known and respected throughout the Indian subcontinent, as well as in Myanmar, Sri Lanka, and Thailand. To this day, in parts of India, sphinxes guard temples and are worshiped in rituals. Even farther afield, there is

MANHATTAN PREP

a similar creature in the Philippines that is part man and part eagle. Interestingly enough, local lore has it that this sphinx also asks travelers a riddle and kills those who cannot answer it, much as in Thebes.

India is not the only place where interest in sphinxes survived antiquity. In Europe, an artistic fascination with sphinxes began around 1500 and continued into the 1700s. In Freemasonry, a guild organization that began in medieval times and still exists today, sphinxes as guardians of secrecy are often sculpted in front of temples and adorn several Masonic badges.

While it is thus indisputable that the sphinx has had symbolic importance from prehistory to the present, uncertainty has arisen concerning the age of the most famous sphinx of all, the Great Sphinx of Giza in Egypt. Most scholars still subscribe to the conventional view that the Great Sphinx was built by the pharaoh Khafra around 2500 BCE. However, some point to stylistic features to argue that it must be one to two hundred years older. More radically, one theory suggests that the Great Sphinx is several thousand years older than generally thought. This hypothesis claims that the weathering pattern of the Great Sphinx indicates that extensive rainfall was the agent. As it is accepted that such rainfall ceased to be part of the Egyptian climate around 4000 BCE, this would mean that the Great Sphinx existed at least hundreds of years before that. While the majority opinion, with some scientific justification, argues that the damage to the stone could have been caused by wind erosion and that no other evidence of ancient Egyptians undertaking such constructions before 5000 BCE has surfaced, the rival theories have had enough credence to introduce uncertainty into the discussion. To this day, the exact age of the Great Sphinx remains a secret that it guards.

> Now answer the questions.

4

Paragraph 1

S1   The Sphinx, a mythical creature with a lion's body and human head, has become inextricably linked with ancient Egyptian culture, undoubtedly because of the fame of the Great Sphinx of Giza in Egypt.

2   However, in reality, sphinx-like creatures were prominent in many ancient cultures worldwide.

3   The sphinx's ubiquity and the relative constancy of its meaning and legend in many cultures points to a human commonality whose spread extends far beyond Giza and the Sahara Desert.

1. According to paragraph 1, all of the following were true about sphinxes EXCEPT:

    (A) Sphinxes had characteristics of both humans and other animals.

    (B) In ancient times, sphinxes played a not insignificant role in cultures outside of Egypt.

    (C) The Great Sphinx of Giza in Egypt is the first known example of its kind.

    (D) The symbolic meaning of sphinxes was roughly similar in several cultures.

Paragraph 2

S1 The Egyptian sphinx sported a male human head and was apparently considered a benevolent god, although one that possessed great strength.

2   As in many other cultures, sphinxes often guarded temple entrances.

3   The famous Great Sphinx is generally not thought to be the oldest such Egyptian statue; many, but not all, scholars believe that one depicting Queen Hetepheres II, built in approximately 2600 BCE, is probably the oldest in Egypt.

4   However, further north in present-day Turkey, Neolithic sphinx-like figures dating to 9500 BCE have been found.

2. The author mentions present-day Turkey in paragraph 2 in order to

    (A) indicate why the Great Sphinx is the oldest such Egyptian statue

    (B) highlight the fact that there are even older sphinxes in the world than Egyptian ones

    (C) emphasize the broad geographic spread of sphinxes in the ancient world

    (D) point out the difference between sphinx-like figures and true sphinxes

3. Which of the sentences below best expresses the essential information in the highlighted sentence in paragraph 2? Incorrect choices change the meaning in important ways or leave out essential information.

    (A) The Great Sphinx is generally thought to be older than the one depicting Queen Hetepheres II, built in 2600 BCE.

    (B) Many scholars believe that the Egyptian sphinx depicting a queen in 2600 BCE is likely to be about as old as the Great Sphinx.

    (C) The oldest sphinx in Egypt is probably not the Great Sphinx but another made in 2600 BCE to depict a queen.

    (D) There is no Egyptian sphinx older than the one depicting Queen Hetepheres II, built in 2600 BCE, except for the Great Sphinx.

4. The word "benevolent" in the passage is closest in meaning to

    (A) sacred

    (B) kindhearted

    (C) powerful

    (D) vengeful

	Paragraph 3
S1	Like its Egyptian cousin, the Greek sphinx guarded temple entrances and had the body of a lion.
2	However, Greek sphinxes had a female head and often wings.
3	Furthermore, Greek sphinxes were far more malevolent.
4	A prominent Greek myth tells of the Sphinx guarding Thebes; it would pose a riddle to passersby: "What walks on four feet in the morning, two in the afternoon, and three at night?"
5	It then killed the hapless travelers, who all failed to solve it.
6	Finally, according to the myth, Oedipus, immortalized in Sophocles's ancient Greek play *Oedipus Rex*, solved the riddle: "Man.
7	As an infant, he crawls on all fours; as an adult, he walks on two legs and in old age, he uses a 'walking' stick."
8	The Sphinx then killed itself.
9	This myth of this Sphinx still resonates in modern cultures; the French playwright Jean Cocteau reworked *Oedipus Rex* as *The Infernal Machine* in the twentieth century.

5. The word "**pose**" in the passage is closest in meaning to

   (A) pretend

   (B) shout

   (C) present

   (D) answer

6. According to paragraph 3, how did Greek sphinxes differ from Egyptian sphinxes?

   (A) They had the body of a lion.

   (B) They were able to fly.

   (C) They confronted passersby with riddles.

   (D) They were more vicious or spiteful.

7. According to paragraph 3, which of the following is true about Oedipus?

   (A) He was famously portrayed in a Greek play.

   (B) He was killed by the Sphinx of Thebes.

   (C) He was acquainted with Jean Cocteau.

   (D) Upon solving the riddle, he slew the Sphinx of Thebes.

Paragraph 4

S1	Sphinxes as gods are far from limited to Greece and the Middle East.
2	On the contrary, such figures have been depicted in myths and legends across the breadth of Asia.
3	Creatures with human heads and the haunches of lions have particular names in the Sanskrit, Tamil, Pali, and Thai languages.
4	They are known and respected throughout the Indian subcontinent, as well as in Myanmar, Sri Lanka, and Thailand.
5	To this day, in parts of India, sphinxes guard temples and are worshiped in rituals.
6	Even farther afield, there is a similar creature in the Philippines that is part man and part eagle.
7	Interestingly enough, local lore has it that this sphinx also asks travelers a riddle and kills those who cannot answer it, much as in Thebes.

8. Which of the following is named in paragraph 4 as a place in which a sphinx acts like the one in Thebes did?

   (A) Myanmar

   (B) Thailand

   (C) India

   (D) the Philippines

9. The word "They" in the passage refers to

   (A) human heads

   (B) creatures

   (C) lions

   (D) languages

Paragraph 5

S1	India is not the only place where interest in sphinxes survived antiquity.
2	In Europe, an artistic fascination with sphinxes began around 1500 and continued into the 1700s.
3	In Freemasonry, a guild organization that began in medieval times and still exists today, sphinxes as guardians of secrecy are often sculpted in front of temples and adorn several Masonic badges.

10. The word "**adorn**" in the passage is closest in meaning to

(A) decorate

(B) entitle

(C) shape

(D) represent

Paragraph 6

S1   While it is thus indisputable that the sphinx has had symbolic importance from prehistory to the present, uncertainty has arisen concerning the age of the most famous sphinx of all, the Great Sphinx of Giza in Egypt.

2   Most scholars still subscribe to the conventional view that the Great Sphinx was built by the pharaoh Khafra around 2500 BCE.

3   However, some point to stylistic features to argue that it must be one to two hundred years older.

4   More radically, one theory suggests that the Great Sphinx is several thousand years older than generally thought.

5   This hypothesis claims that the weathering pattern of the Great Sphinx indicates that extensive rainfall was the agent.

6   As it is accepted that such rainfall ceased to be part of the Egyptian climate around 4000 BCE, this would mean that the Great Sphinx existed at least hundreds of years before that.

7   While the majority opinion, with some scientific justification, argues that the damage to the stone could have been caused by wind erosion and that no other evidence of ancient Egyptians undertaking such constructions before 5000 BCE has surfaced, the rival theories have had enough credence to introduce uncertainty to the discussion.

8   To this day, the exact age of the Great Sphinx remains a secret that it guards.

11. According to paragraph 6, which of the following is evidence for the theory that the Great Sphinx was built closer to 5000 BCE?

(A) A pattern of erosion seemingly caused by heavy rains

(B) Certain stylistic aspects possibly indicating an older age

(C) The lack of evidence of similar constructions in Egypt dating to that time

(D) Accounts of the reign of the pharaoh Khafra

Paragraph 6

S1 While it is thus indisputable that the sphinx has had symbolic importance from prehistory to the present, uncertainty has arisen concerning the age of the most famous sphinx of all, the Great Sphinx of Giza in Egypt.

2 [A] Most scholars still subscribe to the conventional view that the Great Sphinx was built by the pharaoh Khafra around 2500 BCE.

3–6 [B] However, some point to stylistic features to argue that it must be one to two hundred years older. More radically, one theory suggests that the Great Sphinx is several thousand years older than generally thought. This hypothesis claims that the weathering pattern of the Great Sphinx indicates that extensive rainfall was the agent. As it is accepted that such rainfall ceased to be part of the Egyptian climate around 4000 BCE, this would mean that the Great Sphinx existed at least hundreds of years before that.

7–8 [C] While the majority opinion, with some scientific justification, argues that the damage to the stone could have been caused by wind erosion and that no other evidence of ancient Egyptians undertaking such constructions before 5000 BCE has surfaced, the rival theories have had enough credence to introduce uncertainty to the discussion. To this day, the exact age of the Great Sphinx remains a secret that it guards.

End [D]

Look at the part of the passage that is displayed above. The letters [A], [B], [C], and [D] indicate where the following sentence could be added.

12. **However, advances in laser technology and aerial surveying give hope that the Great Sphinx's secret may yet be discovered.**

   Where would the sentence best fit?

   (A) Choice A

   (B) Choice B

   (C) Choice C

   (D) Choice D

An introductory sentence for a brief summary of the passage is provided below. Complete the summary by selecting the THREE answer choices that express the most important ideas in the passage. Some sentences do not belong in the summary because they express ideas that are not presented in the passage or are minor ideas in the passage. This question is worth 2 points.

13. **The mythical sphinx, while inevitably imagined as the Great Sphinx of Giza in Egypt, is a worldwide phenomenon of lasting importance.**

   A   Both Greek and Thai sphinxes posed riddles.

   B   Sphinxes had a place in world cultures only until the 1700s.

   C   Not limited to Egypt or Greece, sphinxes figure in legends throughout Asia.

   D   There are older sphinxes than the one thought to depict Queen Hetepheres II.

   E   The emblematic Great Sphinx of Giza in Egypt cannot be dated with absolute certainty.

   F   Egyptian and Greek sphinxes served certain similar functions, but differed in temperament.

4.8 The Man Who Would Not Be King

Edward Albert Christian George Andrew Patrick David, known to his friends as David and, eventually, to the larger world as Edward VIII, was born in 1894. He was the great-grandson of the legendary Queen Victoria, and both his grandfather, Edward VII, and his father, George V, preceded him to the throne. Unlike his immediate predecessors, he reigned for less than a year. However, because he was the only British monarch to voluntarily abdicate the throne, and because of the racy circumstances of his abdication—it revolved around an American divorcée—he commanded the world stage in 1936 and nearly caused a constitutional crisis in the United Kingdom.

Like many royal heirs of that time, Edward had a haphazard education from private tutors. As a young man, aside from holding a military commission, he was confined to performing the ceremonial duties of his station as a prince. During the First World War, his request to serve in combat was denied, since his death or capture was considered too serious a mishap to be chanced. After the war, he resumed a life of representing the monarchy on international and domestic tours. While his status and dashing appearance made him quite successful in this capacity, as well as a darling of high society, he grew weary of the pointlessness of his role as the heir to the throne. Consequently, he devoted much of his energy to partying and affairs with several married women. His behavior disconcerted both the British politicians and his father, George V, who in fact accurately predicted that, as king, he would ruin himself within 12 months.

Edward began a passionate affair with Wallis Simpson, who at the time was estranged from her second husband, in 1934. Many accounts suggest that the relationship continued because she was the dominant figure and that he was utterly infatuated with her. In any case, this affair greatly disturbed George V, who refused to formally receive a divorcée, and his ministers. King George V then died in January 1936, and Edward ascended to the throne.

By summer, Edward decided to marry Wallis Simpson, but he faced staunch opposition from the Church of England, the Prime Minister, and the leaders of the Commonwealth nations. Edward had three choices: abdicate the throne, renounce Wallis Simpson, or marry her despite the opposition of his ministers, who would

resign and thus create a constitutional crisis. Edward eventually chose abdication, granting the throne to his brother George, as the combined power of church and state surpassed that of the king. For the moment, though, Edward triumphed in the court of public opinion, as he won worldwide sympathy from a radio broadcast during which he famously said, "I have found it impossible to carry the heavy burden of responsibility and to discharge my duties as king as I would wish to do without the help and support of the woman I love."

In the following years, the couple's fairy-tale romance took an unfortunate turn, as it was tarnished by conflict and suspicion stemming from both personal and political sources. Edward and Wallis moved to the European continent following his abdication and, especially after a publicized visit with Adolf Hitler, were accused of being Nazi sympathizers and worse. While no concrete evidence ever surfaced, a cloud of suspicion about their ultimate loyalties remained over their heads: during the Second World War, Edward, now the Duke of Windsor, was made Governor of the (distant) Bahamas, largely to isolate him.

This estrangement only increased Edward's animosity towards his family; in the decades to come, he only saw members of his family on a handful of occasions. After the war, Edward and Wallis lived in France and were prominent in high society. Such a lifestyle strained their financial means, and various speculative dealings caused some critics to deem them parasites, echoing past accusations of immorality and fascism. Following several years of health problems, Edward died in Paris in 1972; Wallis Simpson lived there for another 14 years. In spite of all the family conflict, Edward and Wallis were accepted by the royal family in death, and the two were interred together in the Royal Burial Ground.

> Now answer the questions.

4

Paragraph 1

S1   Edward Albert Christian George Andrew Patrick David, known to his friends as David and, eventually, to the larger world as Edward VIII, was born in 1894.

2   He was the great-grandson of the legendary Queen Victoria, and both his grandfather, Edward VII, and his father, George V, preceded him to the throne.

3   Unlike his immediate predecessors, he reigned for less than a year.

4   However, because he was the only British monarch to voluntarily abdicate the throne, and because of the racy circumstances of his abdication—it revolved around an American divorcée—he commanded the world stage in 1936 and nearly caused a constitutional crisis in the United Kingdom.

1. The word "racy" in the passage is closest in meaning to

   (A) bizarre

   (B) risqué

   (C) official

   (D) political

2. According to paragraph 1, the reign of Edward VIII was especially distinctive for which of the following reasons?

   (A) He was the great-grandson of Queen Victoria.

   (B) Both his father and grandfather were kings.

   (C) He abdicated the British throne voluntarily.

   (D) His reign was shorter than his father's.

Paragraph 2

S1	Like many royal heirs of that time, Edward had a haphazard education from private tutors.
2	As a young man, aside from holding a military commission, he was confined to performing the ceremonial duties of his station as a prince.
3	During the First World War, his request to serve in combat was denied, since his death or capture was considered too serious a mishap to be chanced.
4	After the war, he resumed a life of representing the monarchy on international and domestic tours.
5	While his status and dashing appearance made him quite successful in this capacity, as well as a darling of high society, he grew weary of the pointlessness of his role as the heir to the throne.
6	Consequently, he devoted much of his energy to partying and affairs with several married women.
7	His behavior disconcerted both the British politicians and his father, George V, who in fact accurately predicted that, as king, he would ruin himself within 12 months.

3. The author mentions "status and dashing appearance" in support of which of the following?

   (A) Edward's success as an emissary of the British Crown

   (B) The denial of Edward's request to serve in combat

   (C) Edward's activities as a partier and womanizer

   (D) The concern that British politicians had about Edward's behavior

4. According to paragraph 2, Edward did not serve in combat in the First World War because

   (A) the consequences of Edward becoming a casualty were too dire

   (B) Edward was occupied with his ceremonial duties

   (C) Edward's military training was haphazard

   (D) Edward was unwilling to chance death or capture

Paragraph 3

S1   Edward began a passionate affair with Wallis Simpson, who at the time was estranged from her second husband, in 1934.

2   Many accounts suggest that the relationship continued because she was the dominant figure and that he was utterly infatuated with her.

3   In any case, this affair greatly disturbed George V, who refused to formally receive a divorcée, and his ministers.

4   King George V then died in January 1936, and Edward ascended to the throne.

5.   According to paragraph 3, the affair between Edward and Wallis Simpson may have lasted because

   (A) it greatly upset his father, George V

   (B) he finally managed to ascend to the throne

   (C) Edward was deeply smitten with Wallis

   (D) she was estranged from her second husband

6.   The phrase "estranged from" in the passage is closest in meaning to

   (A) different from

   (B) alienated from

   (C) confused by

   (D) infuriated by

Paragraph 4

S1   By summer, Edward decided to marry Wallis Simpson, but he faced staunch opposition from the Church of England, the Prime Minister, and the leaders of the Commonwealth nations.

2   Edward had three choices: abdicate the throne, renounce Wallis Simpson, or marry her despite the opposition of his ministers, who would resign and thus create a constitutional crisis.

3   Edward eventually chose abdication, granting the throne to his brother George, as the combined power of church and state surpassed that of the king.

4   For the moment, though, Edward triumphed in the court of public opinion, as he won worldwide sympathy from a radio broadcast during which he famously said, "I have found it impossible to carry the heavy burden of responsibility and to discharge my duties as king as I would wish to do without the help and support of the woman I love."

7. According to paragraph 4, at the time of his abdication, the general public viewed Edward's actions with

   (A) indifference

   (B) disappointment

   (C) sympathy

   (D) alarm

8. The word "staunch" in the passage is closest in meaning to

   (A) hesitant

   (B) surly

   (C) honorable

   (D) stalwart

9. Which of the following can be inferred from paragraph 4 about the political power of the British monarchy at the time of Edward VIII?

   (A) It was constitutionally absolute.

   (B) It was amplified in the court of public opinion.

   (C) It was greater than that of Edward VIII's ministers.

   (D) It was less than that of church and state together.

4

Paragraph 5

S1 In the following years, the couple's fairy-tale romance took an unfortunate turn, as it was tarnished by conflict and suspicion stemming from both personal and political sources.

2   Edward and Wallis moved to the European continent following his abdication and, especially after a publicized visit with Adolf Hitler, were accused of being Nazi sympathizers and worse.

3   While no concrete evidence ever surfaced, a cloud of suspicion about their ultimate loyalties remained over their heads: during the Second World War, Edward, now the Duke of Windsor, was made Governor of the (distant) Bahamas, largely to isolate him.

10. According to paragraph 5, life for Edward and Wallis after the abdication included all of the following EXCEPT:

    (A) accusations of Nazi sympathies

    (B) suspicions of infidelity

    (C) residence outside of the United Kingdom in Europe

    (D) formal leadership in the Bahamas

11. Which of the sentences below best expresses the essential information in the highlighted sentence in paragraph 5? Incorrect choices change the meaning in important ways or leave out essential information.

(A) Edward's wartime governorship of the Bahamas isolated him from the cloud of suspicions remaining over him.

(B) No evidence ever arose to confirm the isolated suspicions that sent Edward to govern the remote Bahamas in wartime exile.

(C) In the face of unproven suspicions, Edward was named Duke of Windsor and Governor of the Bahamas during the war.

(D) Edward was posted to the distant Bahamas during the war because of unresolved suspicions about his loyalties.

Paragraph 6

S1   This estrangement only increased Edward's animosity towards his family; in the decades to come, he only saw members of his family on a handful of occasions.

2   **A** After the war, Edward and Wallis lived in France and were prominent in high society.

3   **B** Such a lifestyle strained their financial means, and various speculative dealings caused some critics to deem them parasites, echoing past accusations of immorality and fascism.

4   **C** Following several years of health problems, Edward died in Paris in 1972; Wallis Simpson lived there for another 14 years.

5   **D** In spite of all the family conflict, Edward and Wallis were accepted by the royal family in death, and the two were interred together in the Royal Burial Ground.

> Look at the part of the passage that is displayed above. The letters [A], [B], [C], and [D] indicate where the following sentence could be added.

12. **As Edward stood by Wallis through those years, he must have resented perceived slights by his brother, George VI, and by other relatives.**

Where would the sentence best fit?

(A) Choice A

(B) Choice B

(C) Choice C

(D) Choice D

An introductory sentence for a brief summary of the passage is provided below. Complete the summary by selecting the THREE answer choices that express the most important ideas in the passage. Some sentences do not belong in the summary because they express ideas that are not presented in the passage or are minor ideas in the passage. This question is worth 2 points.

13. **Edward VIII, a twentieth-century British king, occupies a unique place in the annals of the United Kingdom's monarchy.**

- [A] As heir apparent, Edward successfully represented the monarchy, but many worried about his fitness for kingship.

- [B] Edward's position allowed him to avoid combat duty in the First World War.

- [C] After his abdication, Edward visited Adolf Hitler and secretly espoused Nazism.

- [D] Wallis Simpson was considered an inappropriate spouse because she was an American.

- [E] Edward's short reign caused much political unrest because of his personal choices.

- [F] After abdicating, Edward lived the life he desired, but he was beset with personal, financial, and political difficulties.

4.9 Classroom Noise

It should come as no surprise to any teacher or parent that noise in a classroom environment is distracting and may impact a student's ability to learn. But what types of noise are most distracting? At what volume level does background noise begin to impact learning? How severe is the problem? Recent research can shed light on these important questions, and some of the results are surprising.

Perhaps the most consistent finding of the new research is the degree to which even low levels of noise can have a substantial impact on student performance. Noise levels are gauged in terms of a decibel scale—every increase of 10 decibels corresponds to a doubling of perceived loudness. Adult conversation at a distance of 3 feet is roughly in the range of 55 to 65 decibels. Ninety decibels is roughly the loudness achieved by a train whistle at a distance of 500 feet (about 152 meters) or a lawn mower at a distance of 25 feet (8 meters). Both of these are certainly jarring enough to catch most people's attention. In fact, 90 decibels is the level at which hearing loss can begin, if people are exposed to it on a sustained basis. Children are even more sensitive to loud sounds than adults. As a result, United States federal regulations mandate that all ambient classroom sounds above 90 decibels must be dampened; federal grants are made available for school districts to improve acoustics and soundproofing when these levels are exceeded.

New research, however, indicates that learning issues begin at a much lower noise level. Even barely detectable noise, such as whispering behind a student, noise from a neighboring classroom, or the turning on and off of electric equipment such as a heater, can be problematic. These noises, while barely perceptible—at levels as low as 30 or 35 decibels—cause the cortisol level in many students to increase. Cortisol is a hormone released in response to low blood sugar levels, waking up, and most importantly, stress. The increase of this "stress hormone" produces difficulties with focus, can lead to physical exhaustion, and can impair the ability of a person to convert new information into long-term memory. A 2013 study published in the *Journal of Urban Health* demonstrated that, after controlling for various other

socioeconomic[1] factors, among eight- and nine-year-old students a 10-decibel increase in background noise resulted in a predicted drop in test scores in both French and mathematics of about 5.5 percent. Many other studies conducted since 1980 have had similar findings: noisier classroom environments lead to decreases in reading aptitude, cognitive thinking skills, language acquisition, and even physical coordination.

Another interesting finding is that different types and levels of noise can have varying effects on different groups of children. In a study conducted at the University of Southampton, England, differing levels of "white noise," which sounds roughly like running water or hissing, were introduced into multiple classrooms. The study found that students with a higher ability to focus were most affected by the white noise at any volume, while students with attention difficulties actually performed better with low to moderate levels of white noise. Researchers speculate that this is true because the noise forced the students with attention difficulties to exert more effort to overcome the background noise, thereby temporarily improving their level of focus.

Finally, increased noise can place undue burden on teachers. In order for a teacher to keep the attention of his or her students, they must speak about 15 to 20 decibels more loudly than any competing noise. In addition, for every doubling of distance, the perceived loudness drops by about 6 decibels. Thus, a student sitting 24 feet (about 8 meters) from a teacher will perceive reduced volume of about 12 decibels relative to a student sitting 6 feet (2 meters) away. In a typical classroom, the teacher must speak as much as 30 decibels more loudly than any background noise. If that background noise is high, teachers are forced to practically shout to be heard by students in the back of the classroom. Such a loud level of speaking for hours per day can lead to significant physical strain, high blood pressure, and, eventually, vocal-cord scarring.

4

> Now answer the questions.

Paragraph 1

S1   It should come as no surprise to any teacher or parent that noise in a classroom environment is distracting and may impact a student's ability to learn.

2   But what types of noise are most distracting?

3   At what volume level does background noise begin to impact learning?

4   How severe is the problem?

5   Recent research can shed light on these important questions, and some of the results are surprising.

1. The phrase "shed light on" in the passage is closest in meaning to
    - (A) enflame
    - (B) clarify
    - (C) decide
    - (D) obscure

socioeconomic[1]: related to both social and economic factors in some combination, such as social status, income level, occupation, etc.

  MANHATTAN PREP

Paragraph 2

S1   Perhaps the most consistent finding of the new research is the degree to which even low levels of noise can have a substantial impact on student performance.

2   Noise levels are gauged in terms of a decibel scale—every increase of 10 decibels corresponds to a doubling of perceived loudness.

3   Adult conversation at a distance of 3 feet is roughly in the range of 55 to 65 decibels.

4   Ninety decibels is roughly the loudness achieved by a train whistle at a distance of 500 feet (about 152 meters) or a lawn mower at a distance of 25 feet (8 meters).

5   Both of these are certainly jarring enough to catch most people's attention.

6   In fact, 90 decibels is the level at which hearing loss can begin, if people are exposed to it on a sustained basis.

7   Children are even more sensitive to loud sounds than adults.

8   As a result, United States federal regulations mandate that all **ambient** classroom sounds above 90 decibels must be dampened; federal grants are made available for school districts to improve acoustics and soundproofing when these levels are exceeded.

2. Which of the sentences below best expresses the essential information in the highlighted sentence in paragraph 2? Incorrect choices change the meaning in important ways or leave out essential information.

    (A) A consistent finding of the new research is that low levels of noise can affect student performance more than loud noise.

    (B) Research on student performance strongly suggests that high levels of noise have the most substantial impact.

    (C) Even low levels of noise can seriously affect student performance, new research shows.

    (D) Much new research claims that consistent levels of noise have a substantial impact on student performance.

3. It can be inferred from paragraph 2 that

    (A) operating a lawn mower without hearing protection can lead to hearing loss

    (B) federal regulations controlling excessive classroom noise eliminate declines in student performance

    (C) adults are not generally capable of speaking at a loudness of 90 decibels

    (D) children are unlikely to suffer permanent damage caused by excessive classroom noise

4. The word "ambient" in the passage is closest in meaning to

    (A) remote

    (B) surrounding

    (C) dissonant

    (D) constant

Paragraph 3

S1 New research, however, indicates that learning issues begin at a much lower noise level.

2 Even barely detectable noise, such as whispering behind a student, noise from a neighboring classroom, or the turning on and off of electric equipment such as a heater, can be problematic.

3 These noises, while barely perceptible—at levels as low as 30 or 35 decibels   cause the cortisol level in many students to increase.

4 Cortisol is a hormone released in response to low blood sugar levels, waking up, and most importantly, stress.

5 The increase of this "stress hormone" produces difficulties with focus, can lead to physical exhaustion, and can impair the ability of a person to convert new information into long-term memory.

6 A 2013 study published in the *Journal of Urban Health* demonstrated that, after controlling for various other socioeconomic factors, among eight- and nine-year-old students a 10-decibel increase in background noise resulted in a predicted drop in test scores in both French and mathematics of about 5.5 percent.

7 Many other studies conducted since 1980 have had similar findings: noisier classroom environments lead to decreases in reading aptitude, cognitive thinking skills, language acquisition, and even physical coordination.

5. The word "problematic" in the passage is closest in meaning to

    (A) simplistic

    (B) deceptive

    (C) quizzical

    (D) troublesome

6. According to paragraph 3, what is the relationship between cortisol and noise in the classroom?

    (A) Cortisol is a hormone produced upon waking and in times of stress.

    (B) Cortisol can make classroom noises seem louder than they actually are.

    (C) Even soft classroom noises can increase the production of cortisol.

    (D) Elevated levels of cortisol can impair memory and lead to exhaustion.

7. Why does the author mention "decreases in reading aptitude, cognitive thinking skills, language acquisition, and even physical coordination"?

    (A) To restrict the known problems associated with excessive classroom noise to a specified list

    (B) To assert that these problems are not so important within the context of broader issues facing many students

    (C) To encourage teachers to take action to limit the extent of classroom noise

    (D) To illustrate the breadth of problems that studies have associated with noisy classrooms

Paragraph 4

S1   Another interesting finding is that different types and levels of noise can have varying effects on different groups of children.

2   In a study conducted at the University of Southampton, England, differing levels of "white noise," which sounds roughly like running water or hissing, were introduced into multiple classrooms.

3   The study found that students with a higher ability to focus were most affected by the white noise at any volume, while students with attention difficulties actually performed better with low to moderate levels of white noise.

4   Researchers speculate that this is true because the noise forced the students with attention difficulties to exert more effort to overcome the background noise, thereby temporarily improving their level of focus.

8. The word "this" in the passage refers to

    (A) what the study found

    (B) the study itself

    (C) the white noise

    (D) how students with attention difficulties performed

9. According to paragraph 4, an interesting finding from a research study conducted at the University of Southampton is that

    (A) white noise had no impact on students in the class who could focus their attention well

    (B) some students improved their performance with moderate levels of white noise

    (C) students in the class were affected roughly equally by different levels of white noise

    (D) students were more negatively affected by low levels of white noise than by higher levels

Paragraph 5

S1   Finally, increased noise can place undue burden on teachers.

2   In order for a teacher to keep the attention of his or her students, they must speak about 15 to 20 decibels more loudly than any competing noise.

3   In addition, for every doubling of distance, the perceived loudness drops by about 6 decibels.

4   Thus, a student sitting 24 feet (about 8 meters) from a teacher will perceive reduced volume of about 12 decibels relative to a student sitting 6 feet (2 meters) away.

5   In a typical classroom, the teacher must speak as much as 30 decibels more loudly than any background noise.

6   If that background noise is high, teachers are forced to practically shout to be heard by students in the back of the classroom.

7   Such a loud level of speaking for hours per day can lead to significant physical strain, high blood pressure, and, eventually, vocal-cord scarring.

10. The word "undue" in the passage is closest in meaning to

    (A) invisible

    (B) excessive

    (C) moderate

    (D) uncompensated

11. It can be inferred from paragraph 5 that if the distance between a noise and a person is halved, the perceived loudness will

    (A) decrease by about 12 decibels

    (B) decrease by about 6 decibels

    (C) increase by about 6 decibels

    (D) increase by about 12 decibels

12. According to paragraph 5, why does background noise in the classroom increase the burden on teachers? To receive credit, you must select TWO answer choices.

A   They must speak more loudly than any competing noise.

B   Talking loudly tends to scar a teacher's vocal cords immediately.

C   Classroom noise gives uninterested students an excuse for not paying attention.

D   Teachers must project their voices even more to reach the back of the room.

Paragraph 2

S1   Perhaps the most consistent finding of the new research is the degree to which even low levels of noise can have a substantial impact on student performance.

2–4   A Noise levels are gauged in terms of a decibel scale—every increase of 10 decibels corresponds to a doubling of perceived loudness. Adult conversation at a distance of 3 feet is roughly in the range of 55 to 65 decibels. Ninety decibels is roughly the loudness achieved by a train whistle at a distance of 500 feet (about 152 meters) or a lawn mower at a distance of 25 feet (8 meters).

5–6   B Both of these are certainly jarring enough to catch most people's attention. In fact, 90 decibels is the level at which hearing loss can begin, if people are exposed to it on a sustained basis.

7   C Children are even more sensitive to loud sounds than adults.

8   D As a result, United States federal regulations mandate that all ambient classroom sounds above 90 decibels must be dampened; federal grants are made available for school districts to improve acoustics and soundproofing when these levels are exceeded.

> Look at the part of the passage that is displayed above. The letters [A], [B], [C], and [D] indicate where the following sentence could be added.

13. **In recent years, these facts have caught the attention of the United States government.**

Where would the sentence best fit?

(A) Choice A

(B) Choice B

(C) Choice C

(D) Choice D

> An introductory sentence for a brief summary of the passage is provided below. Complete the summary by selecting the THREE answer choices that express the most important ideas in the passage. Some sentences do not belong in the summary because they express ideas that are not presented in the passage or are minor ideas in the passage. This question is worth 2 points.

14. **That classroom noise is undesirable may seem to be uncontroversial, but recent research has illuminated aspects of the issue that may be surprising.**

   A   United States law prevents background noise in classrooms from exceeding 90 decibels, but learning problems can begin at lower sound levels.

   B   Only a small number of students are affected by low or moderate levels of background noise.

   C   For every doubling of distance from a sound source, the perceived loudness drops by about 6 decibels.

   D   Even low levels of noise in a classroom can lead to difficulties in such areas as reading, thinking, and coordinated movement.

   E   Ninety decibels, the level at which hearing loss can begin, is roughly equal to the loudness of a lawn mower at a distance of 25 feet.

   F   To overcome classroom noise, teachers must speak much more loudly, potentially resulting in serious health consequences.

4.10 Urban Decay and Renewal

Urban decay is the process by which established cities, or parts of them, atrophy under the weight of any of several possible societal changes, falling into a state of dilapidation. Perhaps the most common reason for this process to begin is the loss of jobs due to a company closing or moving to another location. For example, if a manufacturer in a particular city experiences financial hardship and closes down, thousands of jobs could be lost. People that work at the factory would no longer commute to it; small businesses such as restaurants and shopping centers near the factory may suffer a decline in business and close, and so on. Soon, many residences and businesses near the factory may be abandoned, triggering an exodus from that neighborhood to other locations where the economy is more vibrant. This further depletes the economic activity in that area, with the ultimate result being that large zones of the city now exhibit urban blight, or the ugly, neglected landscape of abandoned buildings that can attract gangs or criminals. These factors can be prohibitive for new residents and businesses to consider re-entering the area. Additionally, this process depletes the city of tax revenue, which can lead to a cut in services provided by the city, further incentivizing remaining residents to leave.

Other factors may be the primary cause of urban decay. One such phenomenon in the United States is "white flight," which began shortly after World War II. White flight refers to the mass migration of European Americans away from urban centers to more homogeneous, sometimes newer suburban or exurban communities. This migration was facilitated by the development of the Interstate Highway System, which was funded by the Federal Aid Highway Act of 1956. The highway system made commuting longer distances to employment within urban centers much more practical. At the same time, the Second Great

Migration, which describes a wave of over 5 million African Americans from Southern states migrating to urban centers in the North, Midwest, and Western United States, contributed to population pressures in urban centers. This likely accelerated the trend of white flight.

Another factor arguably contributing to urban decay is rent control, wherein tenants are guaranteed a relatively affordable price for renting apartments within a city. Rent control can lead to an imbalance between the supply and demand for housing units. By keeping rents artificially low, the construction of new housing units is discouraged, and property owners may be forced to reduce expenditures on maintenance of existing homes. This can contribute to the deterioration of buildings within a neighborhood.

How can the process of urban decay be prevented or reversed? There are several potential mechanisms. One is gentrification, which is effectively the process of urban decay in reverse. With gentrification, wealthier outsiders become attracted to an urban area and move into it. This attracts investment and increases property values; new, lucrative businesses may emerge, and property owners have an incentive to invest in improvements. Tax revenues increase as the new residents with higher income populate the neighborhood. However, gentrification has its drawbacks. Pricing pressures created by the influx of new residents and businesses may render current residents unable to afford the neighborhood; existing businesses may experience hardship in the face of increased competition from new businesses. This displacement may create conflict between the "old guard" and the new residents of the neighborhood.

Another common mechanism for urban renewal is government-sponsored redevelopment projects. Large sections of a city may be acquired by the government, with existing structures refurbished or, more likely, demolished and replaced with new construction. This may include the development of commercial buildings, residential buildings, sporting venues, parks, bridges, or highways.

Many urban renewal projects have failed due to unintended consequences. For example, a highway or bridge construction project may leave an entire section of the city divided in half. Residents displaced by the project may relocate to another neighborhood entirely, further exacerbating the population decline that the project was intended to reverse. Traffic patterns may change, resulting in new opportunities for some businesses while severely impairing businesses that may now be bypassed because of the change in traffic flow. These kinds of possible consequences subject many urban renewal projects to scrutiny by (and political pressure from) residents, existing business owners, and advocacy groups.

> Now answer the questions.

Paragraph 1

S1   Urban decay is the process by which established cities, or parts of them, **atrophy** under the weight of any of several possible societal changes, falling into a state of dilapidation.

2   Perhaps the most common reason for this process to begin is the loss of jobs due to a company closing or moving to another location.

3   For example, if a manufacturer in a particular city experiences financial hardship and closes down, thousands of jobs could be lost.

4   People that work at the factory would no longer commute to it; small businesses such as restaurants and shopping centers near the factory may suffer a decline in business and close, and so on.

5   Soon, many residences and businesses near the factory may be abandoned, triggering an exodus from that neighborhood to other locations where the economy is more vibrant.

6   This further depletes the economic activity in that area, with the ultimate result being that large zones of the city now exhibit urban blight, or the ugly, neglected landscape of abandoned buildings that can attract gangs or criminals.

7   These factors can be prohibitive for new residents and businesses to consider re-entering the area.

8   Additionally, this process depletes the city of tax revenue, which can lead to a cut in services provided by the city, further incentivizing remaining residents to leave.

1. The word "atrophy" in the passage is closest in meaning to

    (A) flourish

    (B) proliferate

    (C) revolt

    (D) wither

2. Which of the following statements about urban decay can be inferred from paragraph 1?

    (A) Events other than the closing or relocation of a company can cause urban decay.

    (B) Employees at an urban factory live far away from the factory itself.

    (C) Gangs and criminals do not pay taxes.

    (D) New residents and businesses re-entering the area would compel gangs and criminals to leave.

3. In paragraph 1, why does the author mention small businesses closing after a factory has closed?

   (A) To contrast small businesses with large companies in terms of their ability to survive economic hardship

   (B) To suggest that factory employees are to blame for changing their spending habits after the factory closes

   (C) To underscore that the factory closing is merely the first step in a process that can lead to urban decay

   (D) To provide an example of an event that could interrupt the process of urban decay that might otherwise occur

Paragraph 2

P2 S1 Other factors may be the primary cause of urban decay.

2 One such phenomenon in the United States is "white flight," which began shortly after World War II.

3 White flight refers to the mass migration of European Americans away from urban centers to more homogeneous, sometimes newer suburban or exurban communities.

4 This migration was facilitated by the development of the Interstate Highway System, which was funded by the Federal Aid Highway Act of 1956.

5 The highway system made commuting longer distances to employment within urban centers much more practical.

6 At the same time, the Second Great Migration, which describes a wave of over 5 million African Americans from Southern states migrating to urban centers in the North, Midwest, and Western United States, contributed to population pressures in urban centers.

7 This likely accelerated the trend of white flight.

Paragraph 3

P3 S1 Another factor arguably contributing to urban decay is rent control, wherein tenants are guaranteed a relatively affordable price for renting apartments within a city.

2 Rent control can lead to an imbalance between the supply and demand for housing units.

3 By keeping rents artificially low, the construction of new housing units is discouraged, and property owners may be forced to reduce expenditures on maintenance of existing homes.

4 This can contribute to the deterioration of buildings within a neighborhood.

4. According to paragraph 2, which of the following is true of the Second Great Migration?

- Ⓐ It probably played a contributory role in white flight.

- Ⓑ It started to occur well before white flight began in earnest.

- Ⓒ It was facilitated by the Federal Aid Highway Act of 1956.

- Ⓓ It caused a population shortage and related problems in the Southern United States.

5. The word "accelerated" in the passage is closest in meaning to

- Ⓐ targeted

- Ⓑ hastened

- Ⓒ stressed

- Ⓓ impeded

6. Paragraphs 2 and 3 mention all of the following as possible contributors to urban decay EXCEPT:

- Ⓐ the development of the Interstate Highway System

- Ⓑ rent control

- Ⓒ the Second Great Migration

- Ⓓ the founding of exurban communities before World War II

4

Paragraph 4

S1	How can the process of urban decay be prevented or reversed?
2	There are several potential mechanisms.
3	One is gentrification, which is effectively the process of urban decay in reverse.
4	With gentrification, wealthier outsiders become attracted to an urban area and move into it.
5	This attracts investment and increases property values; new, lucrative businesses may emerge, and property owners have an incentive to invest in improvements.
6	Tax revenues increase as the new residents with higher income populate the neighborhood.
7	However, gentrification has its drawbacks.
8	Pricing pressures created by the influx of new residents and businesses may render current residents unable to afford the neighborhood; existing businesses may experience hardship in the face of increased competition from new businesses.
9	This displacement may create conflict between the "old guard" and the new residents of the neighborhood.

7. The word "lucrative" in the passage is closest in meaning to

    (A) competitive

    (B) growing

    (C) profitable

    (D) unsuccessful

8. According to paragraph 4, which of the following statements about gentrification is true?

    (A) It creates conditions that discourage additional investment in the area.

    (B) It can lead to displacements in a neighborhood, creating clashes among residents.

    (C) It tends to be the result of promotion or facilitation by government agencies.

    (D) It can lead to declines in property prices in the face of increased competition.

Paragraph 5

S1   Another common mechanism for urban renewal is government-sponsored redevelopment projects.

2   Large sections of a city may be acquired by the government, with existing structures refurbished or, more likely, demolished and replaced with new construction.

3   This may include the development of commercial buildings, residential buildings, sporting venues, parks, bridges, or highways.

4

9. According to paragraph 5, government-sponsored redevelopment projects

    (A) often meet with unexpected problems

    (B) usually involve renovating existing buildings or infrastructure

    (C) require substantial investment from private entities

    (D) may include the construction of sports facilities

Paragraph 6

S1   Many urban renewal projects have failed due to unintended consequences.

2   For example, a highway or bridge construction project may leave an entire section of the city divided in half.

3   Residents displaced by the project may relocate to another neighborhood entirely, further exacerbating the population decline that the project was intended to reverse.

4   Traffic patterns may change, resulting in new opportunities for some businesses while severely impairing businesses that may now be bypassed because of the change in traffic flow.

5   These kinds of possible consequences subject many urban renewal projects to scrutiny by (and political pressure from) residents, existing business owners, and advocacy groups.

10. The word "exacerbating" in the passage is closest in meaning to

(A) intensifying

(B) hindering

(C) alleviating

(D) signaling

11. Paragraph 6 supports which of the following statements about the unintended consequences of urban renewal projects?

(A) They typically result from serious mistakes in the planning process.

(B) They generally involve either subtle or dramatic changes in traffic patterns.

(C) Residents and activists often pay close attention to urban renewal projects in order to avoid these consequences.

(D) Government projects are more likely to experience unintended consequences than privately planned development projects.

Paragraph 5

P5 S1   Another common mechanism for urban renewal is government-sponsored redevelopment projects.

2-3   **A** Large sections of a city may be acquired by the government, with existing structures refurbished or, more likely, demolished and replaced with new construction. This may include the development of commercial buildings, residential buildings, sporting venues, parks, bridges, or highways.

End   **B**

Paragraph 6

P6 S1   Many urban renewal projects have failed due to unintended consequences.

2-4   **C** For example, a highway or bridge construction project may leave an entire section of the city divided in half. Residents displaced by the project may relocate to another neighborhood entirely, further exacerbating the population decline that the project was intended to reverse. Traffic patterns may change, resulting in new opportunities for some businesses while severely impairing businesses that may now be bypassed because of the change in traffic flow.

5   **D** These kinds of possible consequences subject many urban renewal projects to scrutiny by (and political pressure from) residents, existing business owners, and advocacy groups.

> Look at the part of the passage that is displayed above. The letters [A], [B], [C], and [D] indicate where the following sentence could be added.

12. **Many such large-scale construction projects were undertaken in the United States after passage of the Fair Housing Act of 1949, which provided for federal funds to help cities pay for them.**

Where would the sentence best fit?

(A) Choice A

(B) Choice B

(C) Choice C

(D) Choice D

> Select from the seven phrases below THREE that contribute to urban decay and TWO that contribute to urban renewal. Two of the phrases will NOT be used. This question is worth 2 points.

Urban Decay	Urban Renewal
•	•
•	•
•	

13. [A] White flight

[B] An increase in tax rates

[C] Rent control

[D] Gentrification

[E] The presence of small businesses such as restaurants

[F] Loss of manufacturing facilities

[G] Government-sponsored construction

4

Answer Key—4.1 Cupule Rock Art

Question	Correct Answer	Right/Wrong	Category
1	C		Fact
2	A		Purpose
3	C		Vocabulary
4	D		Fact
5	C		Negative Fact
6	D		Fact
7	A		Vocabulary
8	A		Purpose
9	B		Fact
10	D		Vocabulary
11	B		Fact
12	B		Simplify Sentence
13	C		Insert Text
14	A, D, E		Summary

Answer Key—4.2 The Beaver Wars

Question	Correct Answer	Right/Wrong	Category
1	D		Vocabulary
2	D		Fact
3	A		Fact
4	B		Vocabulary
5	C		Purpose
6	A		Vocabulary
7	C		Inference
8	B		Purpose
9	C		Simplify Sentence
10	B		Vocabulary
11	D		Negative Fact
12	A		Insert Text
13	Dutch: D, G. Iroquois: B, C, F. Neither: A, E.		Table

Answer Key—4.3 The Flynn Effect

Question	Correct Answer	Right/Wrong	Category
1	B		Vocabulary
2	A		Fact
3	D		Vocabulary
4	C		Inference
5	C		Fact
6	A		Inference
7	B		Simplify Sentence
8	A		Vocabulary
9	D		Fact
10	D		Vocabulary
11	B		Insert Text
12	C		Purpose
13	Fluid: A, D, E. Crystallized: B, C.		Table

Answer Key—4.4 Operation Barbarossa and Napoleon

Question	Correct Answer	Right/Wrong	Category
1	B		Purpose
2	D		Fact
3	A		Vocabulary
4	A		Negative Fact
5	C		Vocabulary
6	D		Fact
7	B		Vocabulary
8	C		Fact
9	A		Vocabulary
10	C		Vocabulary
11	B		Insert Text
12	Barbarossa: B, F. Napoleon: A, G. Both: C, D, H. Neither: E.		Table

Answer Key—4.5 The Kennewick Man

Question	Correct Answer	Right/Wrong	Category
1	D		Fact
2	B		Vocabulary
3	A		Inference
4	C		Negative Fact
5	C		Simplify Sentence
6	A		Vocabulary
7	C		Purpose
8	D		Vocabulary
9	A		Vocabulary
10	B		Inference
11	B		Vocabulary
12	D		Fact
13	D		Insert Text
14	B, C, D		Summary

Answer Key—4.6 Harriet Tubman

Question	Correct Answer	Right/Wrong	Category
1	C		Simplify Sentence
2	C		Inference
3	D		Purpose
4	C		Vocabulary
5	D		Vocabulary
6	A		Fact
7	A		Negative Fact
8	B		Purpose
9	A		Vocabulary
10	D		Fact
11	B		Vocabulary
12	C		Fact
13	B		Insert Text
14	A, B, F		Summary

Answer Key—4.7 The Sphinx

Question	Correct Answer	Right/Wrong	Category
1	C		Negative Fact
2	B		Purpose
3	C		Simplify Sentence
4	B		Vocabulary
5	C		Vocabulary
6	D		Fact
7	A		Fact
8	D		Fact
9	B		Reference
10	A		Vocabulary
11	A		Fact
12	D		Insert Text
13	C, E, F		Summary

Answer Key—4.8 The Man Who Would Not Be King

Question	Correct Answer	Right/Wrong	Category
1	B		Vocabulary
2	C		Fact
3	A		Purpose
4	A		Fact
5	C		Fact
6	B		Vocabulary
7	C		Fact
8	D		Vocabulary
9	D		Inference
10	B		Negative Fact
11	D		Simplify Sentence
12	A		Insert Text
13	A, E, F		Summary

Answer Key—4.9 Classroom Noise

Question	Correct Answer	Right/Wrong	Category
1	B		Vocabulary
2	C		Simplify Sentence
3	A		Inference
4	B		Vocabulary
5	D		Vocabulary
6	C		Fact
7	D		Purpose
8	A		Reference
9	B		Fact
10	B		Vocabulary
11	C		Inference
12	A, D		Fact
13	D		Insert Text
14	A, D, F		Summary

Answer Key—4.10 Urban Decay and Renewal

Question	Correct Answer	Right/Wrong	Category
1	D		Vocabulary
2	A		Inference
3	C		Purpose
4	A		Fact
5	B		Vocabulary
6	D		Negative Fact
7	C		Vocabulary
8	B		Fact
9	D		Fact
10	A		Vocabulary
11	C		Fact
12	B		Insert Text
13	Decay: A, C, F. Renewal: D, G. Neither: B, E.		Table

Answers and Explanations—
4.1 Cupule Rock Art

	Paragraph 1	Comments
S1	Parietal art is the archaeological term for human-made artwork—etchings, carvings, paintings, and drawings—typically done on cave walls or large blocks of stone.	Parietal (rock) art = human-made
2	Also called "cave art" or "rock art," parietal art is found in many culturally diverse regions of the world and has been produced in many contexts throughout human history.	Found through history and around world.
3	The oldest known rock art dates from the Upper Paleolithic period and has been found in Europe, Australia, Asia, and Africa.	
4	The purpose of these remains of the Paleolithic period (as well as many other periods of prehistoric art) is not known.	Purpose not known.
5	In the mid-1900s, however, researchers began to theorize that rock art was used as more than simple decoration.	
6	Archaeologists currently studying these artworks believe it likely that this art had religious and ritualistic significance.	Theory: religious/ritual purpose.

4

1. According to paragraph 1, recent archaeologists believe that rock art was

    FACT. Recent archaeologists are mentioned in S5–6. They believe that rock art is not only decorative, but also important in religious and ritualistic ways.

    ✗ (A) used primarily for decorative purposes.

    S5 indicates that more modern researchers and archaeologists believe the opposite.

    ✗ (B) found only in areas where the culture has remained constant over long periods of time.

    S2–3 note that rock art was found throughout history, around the world, and in culturally diverse areas.

    ✓ (C) probably an important aspect of a culture's religion or rituals.

    CORRECT. S6: "Archaeologists ... believe it likely that this art had religious and ritualistic significance."

    ✗ (D) more likely to be an etching or carving than a painting or drawing

    S1 lists all four of these types of parietal or rock art, but doesn't claim that any are more or less likely than others.

	Paragraph 2	**Comments**
S1	When discussing rock art, researchers delineate individual pieces into one of three forms: 1) petroglyphs, which are carved into the rock surface; 2) pictographs, which are painted onto the surface; and 3) earth figures, formed on the ground.	3 types of rock art.
2	Petroglyphs are considered the earliest known parietal art, and the most **prolific** petroglyphs are thought to be cup stones, also known as "cupules."	Most common petroglyph = cup stones = cupules.
3	Cupules have been found on every continent except Antarctica and were produced during all three eras of the Stone Age (Paleolithic, Mesolithic, and Neolithic).	Cupules are everywhere, were made all the time.
4	In fact, many tribal cultures continue to create cupules to this day.	Still made today.

2.   In paragraph 2, why does the author mention the three eras of the Stone Age?

PURPOSE. The three eras of the Stone Age are mentioned in S3: cupules were made in all three eras. S3 provides evidence for S2's assertion that cupules are the most prolific, or common, form of petroglyphs.

✓ (A) To support the claim that cupules are the most prolific petroglyphs.

CORRECT. The claim is in S2. Support for this claim is provided in S3.

✗ (B) To argue that cupules are a modern form of parietal art.

Opposite. S2 indicates that cupules are among the oldest known form of parietal art.

✗ (C) To show that the creation of cupules occured only during a very short time in history.

The three eras are introduced to show how long, not short, the history of cupules is.

✗ (D) To suggest further research into the reason prehistoric cultures created cupules.

The information about the three eras tells you when cupules were made, not why.

3.   The word "**prolific**" in the passage is closest in meaning to

VOCABULARY. "Prolific" = plentiful, present in large numbers or amounts.

✗ (A) valuable

Unrelated. Something in large quantities may or may not be valuable or worth much.

✗ (B) abnormal

In a way, this is the opposite. Something prolific (plentiful or present in large numbers) is more likely to be normal than abnormal.

✓ (C) abundant

CORRECT. "The most prolific petroglyphs" = the most common or abundant ones.

✗ (D) excessive

"Excessive" means "more than necessary" or "more than desirable." The word "prolific" does not convey this sense of "too much."

MANHATTAN PREP

4.   According to paragraph 2, the primary categori-
     zation of rock art is influenced by

FACT. S1 notes that researchers categorize rock art according to whether it was carved into a rock surface, painted on a surface, or formed on the ground. The process matters (carved, painted, or formed), and the surface matters (rock or ground).

✗   (A) the continent on which the art was
         produced.

S3 states that cupules (one type of rock art) can be found on almost all continents. But categories of rock art do not correspond to geography.

✗   (B) whether the art is a cup stone or other type
         of petroglyph.

S2 states that cupules are the most prolific type of petroglyph. But the three primary categories of rock art are laid out in S1.

✗   (C) the era of the Stone Age that the art dates
         from.

S3 notes that rock art was created in all three eras of the Stone Age. You are not told whether these eras provide categorizations for rock art.

✓   (D) the surface used and the process by which
         the art was created

CORRECT. This is the information about rock art categories that S1 provides.

Paragraph 3	Comments
S1 The actual term "cupule" was introduced in the early 1990s by Australian archaeologist Robert G. Bednarik.	
2 According to Bednarik and his colleagues, a cupule is a hemispherical petroglyph created by hammering the rock surface with another hard object, in a process called percussion.	Cupules = rock cups, half-spheres, made by hammering.
3 In order to be defined as a cupule, the indentation in the rock must be man-made, intentional, percussion-produced, and primarily symbolic or non-utilitarian in nature, although there may be secondary utilitarian functions present.	Primarily symbolic.

4

5. Each of the following corresponds to a requirement in the definition of cupules by Bednarik and his colleagues EXCEPT:

NEGATIVE FACT. S2 describes how cupules are hemisphere-shaped, hammered indentations in rock. S3 notes that in addition to being hammered into the rock, cupules must be man-made and created on purpose. Their primary purpose must be symbolic, but they can also serve a secondary utilitarian (useful) function. The three wrong answers will correspond to these features. The right answer will not.

✗ (A) If created accidentally, an indentation is not considered a cupule.

S3 says that cupules must be intentionally made.

✗ (B) The half-sphere indentation must have been created by hammering.

S2 says that cupules must be shaped like hemispheres and hammered.

✓ (C) To be classified as a cupule, the rock art cannot have any useful function.

CORRECT. S3 states that cupules can have a use, as long as that is not their primary function. So it is not necessary for a cupule to have absolutely zero useful function.

✗ (D) Cupules cannot be created by non-human forces such as erosion.

S3 notes that cupules must be man-made and so cannot be created by some other means.

Paragraph 4	**Comments**
S1 Cupules are typically found in large groups and often number in the hundreds (or even thousands) in a single location.	Cupules are found in large groups.
2 A recent series of research experiments conducted by the Indian archaeologist Giriraj Kumar has sought to understand the difficulty with which these large groupings of cupules were created.	Recent experiments to re-create.
3 Over the course of five experiments, Kumar's team attempted to replicate cupules found at Daraki-Chattan, India.	
4 For each replicated cupule, the team collected a variety of data, such as specific descriptions of the hammer-stones used, the time needed to create the cupule, and the number of percussion strikes required.	
5 The research found that the pounding of a single cupule out of hard rock required a colossal expenditure of energy: some cupules required upwards of 20,000 blows, an effort that would take several hours to complete.	Super hard to make just one.
6 Given that the Daraki-Chattan site includes over 500 cupules, creating such large formations would have required a great deal of time and dedication.	
7 Since cupules were chiefly symbolic, not practical, in nature, the immensity of the effort required to create them indicates the value these prehistoric cultures attached to certain non-utilitarian activities.	Difficult = important.

4

6.   According to paragraph 4, which of the following is thought to be true of the importance of cupules to prehistoric cultures?

FACT. S5 describes the immense effort required to produce a single cupule. S6 indicates that some locations where cupules are found have as many as 500 individual cupules. S7 reasons that such a great effort for something primarily symbolic must mean that whatever was symbolized must be of great importance to prehistoric cultures.

✗   (A) The hammering of cupule formations was a critical part of most prehistoric rituals.

S7 suggests that cupules were used in non-utilitarian activities. But S7 doesn't suggest that cupules were hammered or even used in most ritual activities, or that they were a necessary part of such activities.

✗   (B) Cupules were an early form of symbolic communication, allowing different prehistoric communities to signal their presence in an area.

S7 states that cupules were primarily symbolic. But there is no indication of their specific use.

✗   (C) Prehistoric cultures viewed cupules as primarily artistic and thus trivial in nature.

S5–6 indicates that cupules were not viewed as trivial (= unimportant), given the large effort that prehistoric cultures expended to create them.

✓   (D) Because they were so challenging to make, cupules signify the value of symbolic activities for prehistoric cultures.

CORRECT. S5–6 describe the immense effort necessary to create cupule formations. S7 notes that it logically follows that prehistoric cultures would only have exerted that effort if the symbolic activities were important.

7.   The word "**immensity**" in the passage is closest in meaning to

VOCABULARY. "Immensity" comes from the word "immense," meaning "large in size or scale." So "immensity" means "great size."

✓   (A) magnitude

CORRECT. "The immensity of the effort required to create [cupules]" = the great size or magnitude of that effort.

✗   (B) harshness

"Harsh" means "stern, strict, severe." The process of making cupules could be described this way, but "immensity" means something different.

✗   (C) insignificance

Opposite, or nearly so. Something that is insignificant is unimportant or small.

✗   (D) enjoyment

In a way, the opposite. The effort was considered to be extremely difficult; the joy or delight taken from the task would not be what was emphasized.

8. In paragraph 4, why does the author introduce Kumar's research?

PURPOSE. S2 introduces Kumar's research to determine how hard these cupules are to make. S3–4 describe the study. Finally, S5 finds that the effort was quite large, a fact that the author uses to highlight the apparent importance of these cupules in S6–7.

✓ (A) To provide support for the importance of cupules to prehistoric cultures

CORRECT. The work of Kumar and his team illustrated the difficulty with which cupules were made. The author uses this finding to support the theory that the creation of cupules must therefore be important.

✗ (B) To compare the various techniques used to create cupules

The specific techniques used by Kumar's team are not provided.

✗ (C) To demonstrate the effectiveness of researchers in replicating cupule production

Kumar's team was apparently effective in replicating the hammering of cupules, but this is not the point of the author. The re-creation of the cupules is described in order to point out how hard they must have been to create, and thus how important they must have been.

✗ (D) To explain why cupules were useful in a significant way to prehistoric cultures

Opposite. The author uses Kumar's findings to support the importance of this kind of *non*-utilitarian activity (since cupules were primarily symbolic in nature).

4

	Paragraph 5	Comments
S1	Experts have not yet agreed on a unified explanation of the cultural or artistic meaning of cupules.	Still don't all agree on single meaning.
2	However, a theory by archaeologist Charles P. Mountford in the early 1940s proposed that the creation of cupules might be associated with fertility rites.	But 1 idea = fertility rites.
3	To investigate this, Mountford studied an Aboriginal tribe who continued to create cupules.	Investigation.
4	Mountford witnessed the tribe hammering cupules as part of a fertility ritual for the pink cockatoo.	
5	The Aborigines pounded the cupules into a rock thought to contain the life essence of this bird.	
6	As the cupules were pounded out, the mineral dust that arose was thought to increase the female cockatoo's production of eggs, which were a valuable food source for the Aborigines.	

MANHATTAN PREP

9.   What did Mountford hope to evaluate with his research?

FACT. S2 states that Mountford proposed that the creation of cupules may be connected to fertility rites. S3: "To investigate this, Mountford …" S3–6 explain the investigation into this theory.

✗ (A) Whether the effort expended in creating cupules indicates their importance to prehistoric cultures

Mountford was interested in the purpose of cupules, not in the level of effort expended to create them.

✓ (B) Whether the creation of cupules was associated with fertility rites

CORRECT. This question is posed in S2. S3 begins with "To investigate this [question], Mountford …" The rest of the paragraph describes Mountford's research.

✗ (C) Whether the mineral dust created when cupules are pounded out has ritual purposes

Mountford noted the ritual purpose of the mineral dust, but the point of his research was to investigate the theory he proposed (as described in S2).

✗ (D) Whether the date of a cupule can be determined through experimentation

The passage never indicates that Mountford was interested in identifying when cupules were created.

10.   The word "**unified**" in the passage is closest in meaning to

VOCABULARY. "Unified" = united, brought together as one, combined.

✗ (A) popular

It might be easier to "unify" if something is popular, but this is unrelated in meaning.

✗ (B) simple

It might be easier to "unify" if the concept is simple, but this is unrelated in meaning.

✗ (C) thorough

People might be more willing to "unify" behind an explanation that was seen as thorough, but this is unrelated in meaning.

✓ (D) consolidated

CORRECT. "Experts have not yet agreed on a unified explanation" = they haven't agreed yet on a consolidated, combined explanation that they can all get behind.

4

Paragraph 6	**Comments**
S1 The earliest known examples of cupule art, dating back to between 290,000 and 700,000 B.C., were found in central India.	
2 It can be difficult for archaeologists to estimate the exact date of creation for many cupules, however, because some appear to have been reworked by later artists, sometimes thousands of years later.	Dating cupules is hard. They get reworked later.
3 For instance, one cupule at Moda Bhata, India, created around 7,000 B.C., was re-pounded around A.D. 200.	
4 Some researchers were initially surprised that all of the oldest known cupules appear on highly weatherproof and extremely hard rock, given the great physical effort clearly needed to create such formations.	Oldest = hard rock.
5 These same researchers questioned why easier, softer rocks were not chosen.	Why not use softer rock?
6 However, it is entirely possible that this pattern is the result of survivorship bias: cupules formed on hard and more weatherproof rock are more likely to survive to the present day.	Hard rock cupules survived better.
7 It is probable that archaeologists may one day discover even older cupules in weather-protected soft rock.	

11.   According to paragraph 6, the knowledge that some cupules were re-pounded suggests what difficulty for cupule research?

FACT. S2–3 discuss identifying the date of creation. Re-pounding (re-hammering an old cupule) could happen thousands of years after the cupule was initially created. This fact makes it difficult to date some cupules accurately.

✗   (A) It makes it tough to determine the purpose of the cupule.

S2–3 are not concerned with the purpose of cupules, as earlier paragraphs are.

✓   (B) It complicates efforts to estimate when cupules were created.

CORRECT. S2: "It can be difficult ... to estimate the exact date of creation for many cupules ... because some appear to have been reworked by later artists."

✗   (C) It undermines the belief that cupules are more difficult to create in hard rock.

Re-pounding makes it hard to estimate the date of creation. It doesn't have an impact on how people think about the difficulty of creating cupules under various conditions.

✗   (D) It indicates that survivorship bias had tainted the archaeological record.

This bias is mentioned later in the paragraph. But it is unrelated to the issue of estimating the date of creation.

12.   Which of the sentences below best expresses the essential information in the highlighted sentence in paragraph 6? Incorrect choices change the meaning in important ways or leave out essential information.

SIMPLIFY SENTENCE. S4 notes that some researchers were surprised to find the oldest cupules in hard rock, because cupules in such hard rock would have been very difficult to make.

✗ (A) Despite their initial surprise, several researchers confirmed that cupule formations are more difficult to create in hard rock, using the oldest known cupules.

This choice changes the meaning. Researchers did believe that cupule formations are more difficult to create in hard rock, but this fact was not confirmed in S4. If anything, this difficulty would help explain the researchers' surprise.

✓ (B) Finding the oldest cupules in extremely hard rock, which would have required immense labor to shape, was unexpected to some scientists.

CORRECT. This choice captures the same ideas as S4, although in a different order and with different wording. For example, "Some researchers were initially surprised" at the beginning of S4 becomes "was unexpected to some scientists" at the end of the rephrased sentence. The word "initially" is not so important here and can be safely dropped.

✗ (C) Researchers were surprised that the cupules that were most likely to survive the longest would be found in very hard, weatherproof rock, given the creation effort required.

S4 does not discuss survivorship bias (the cupules most likely to survive a long time would naturally be in harder rock). S6 is where this bias is explained.

✗ (D) Because cupules were extremely hard to make, scientists were astounded by the age of the oldest known cupules in weatherproof rock.

S4 does not say that the researchers were surprised by the age of the oldest cupules.

4

Paragraph 5	Comments
P5 S6 As the cupules were pounded out, the mineral dust that arose was thought to increase the female cockatoo's production of eggs, which were a valuable food source for the Aborigines.	

Paragraph 6	Comments
P6 **S1–2** [A] The earliest known examples of cupule art, dating back to between 290,000 and 700,000 B.C., were found in central India. It can be difficult for archaeologists to estimate the exact date of creation for many cupules, however, because some appear to have been reworked by later artists, sometimes thousands of years later.	The new sentence is in response to a specific doubt about how early cupules could have been hammered into hard rock. The sentence should be inserted after the doubt has been introduced. But that hasn't happened yet.
3–5 [B] For instance, one cupule at Moda Bhata, India, created around 7,000 B.C., was re-pounded around A.D. 200. Some researchers were initially surprised that all of the oldest known cupules appear on highly weatherproof and extremely hard rock, given the great physical effort clearly needed to create such formations. These same researchers questioned why easier, softer rocks were not chosen.	This position follows the issue of accurate dating, but not the issue of hammering early cupules in hard rock specifically. Again, the correct doubt hasn't been introduced yet.
6–7 [C] However, it is entirely possible that this pattern is the result of survivorship bias: cupules formed on hard and more weatherproof rock are more likely to survive to the present day. It is probable that archaeologists may one day discover even older cupules in weather-protected soft rock.	**CORRECT.** The right doubt is in S5, the previous sentence: why weren't these old cupules hammered out of soft rock, which would have been easier to work?
End [D]	This placement incorrectly indicates that the potential for finding old cupules in soft rock (in S7) is a "doubt." But S7 is a prediction.

13.   **This doubt arises from the expectation that as cultures advanced in history, their tools advanced as well, suggesting that the tools used to hammer early cupules were more rudimentary and would be less successful when used on hard rock.**

INSERT TEXT. "This doubt" should refer to a doubt expressed in the previous sentence. The doubt should be about why early cupules would be in hard rock, because the inserted sentence describes a reason for this doubt (namely, that early tools would not have worked as well as later tools did on hard rock).

Where would the sentence best fit?

✗ (A) Choice A

✗ (B) Choice B

✓ (C) Choice C   **CORRECT.**

✗ (D) Choice D

	Whole Passage	**Comments**
P1	Parietal art is the archaeological term for …	Parietal (Rock) art = human-made. Found through history and around world. Purpose not known. Theory: religious/ritual purpose.
P2	When discussing rock art, researchers delineate individual pieces …	3 types of rock art. Most common petroglyph = cup stones = cupules. Cupules are everywhere, were made all the time. Still made today.
P3	The actual term "cupule" was introduced …	Cupules = rock cups, half-spheres, made by hammering. Primarily symbolic.
P4	Cupules are typically found in large groups …	Cupules are found in large groups. Recent experiments to re-create. Super hard to make just one. Difficult = important.
P5	Experts have not yet agreed on …	Still don't all agree on single meaning. But 1 idea = fertility rites. Investigation.
P6	The earliest known examples of cupule art …	Dating cupules is hard. They get reworked later. Oldest = hard rock. Why not use softer rock? Hard rock cupules survived better.

14.   **Throughout history and around the globe, humans have created artwork known as rock art.**

SUMMARY. Correct answers must be clearly expressed in the passage. They must also be among the major points of the passage. They should tie as directly as possible to the summary given.

✓ ☐A   Cupules, the oldest and most prevalent form of rock art, are defined as serving a predominantly symbolic purpose.

CORRECT. Introduced in P2 and then defined in P3.

✗ ☐B   The effort to create cupules was often made easier by soft rock and therefore supports their purely decorative purpose.

Discussed in P6, the effort would likely have been easier in soft rock. But this point is never used as support for why cupules were created.

✗ ☐C   Cupules have been successfully used to better understand the utilitarian purpose of parietal art.

Opposite. Cupules are in fact defined as primarily non-utilitarian.

✓ ☐D   The effort to create the collections of cupules already discovered speaks to the importance that prehistoric cultures placed on symbolic activities.

CORRECT. Specifically presented as the core idea of P4.

✓ ☐E   Archaeologists continue to investigate the age of cupules and their potential symbolic significance to prehistoric and present-day cultures.

CORRECT. Specifically discussed in P5 (the study about fertility rites) and P6 (the difficulty of dating cupules well).

✗ ☐F   Recently, researchers and archaeologists have been able to come to an agreement on the specific meaning of cupules.

P5 S1 says the opposite is true.

Answers and Explanations—4.2 The Beaver Wars

	Paragraph 1	Comments
S1	The harsh aspects of globalization (international economic intertwining), including loss of livelihood and social disruption, have been the current focus of many pundits.	Globalization = international economic intertwining. Pundits (expert commentators) today focus on the harsh aspects.
2	Some condemn the suffering these dislocations have caused while others shrug off the human costs as an acceptable consequence in the service of progress, profit, and/or free-market principles.	
3	Unnoticed in this outcry is the general implicit agreement that the stresses of globalization are a modern, if not unique, crisis.	Most assume that globalization is modern.
4	However, the historical record proves that assumption to be utterly false.	But that's false.
5	Perhaps the only unique aspect is that technology has multiplied the rapidity with which these disruptions evolve; still, for hundreds of years, economic changes on one continent have dramatically altered societies on another continent—societies that were far more isolated from each other than groups at a similar geographic distance are today.	Yes, technology has accelerated impact. But globalization has been happening for centuries.
6	One notable historical example of this pattern would be the Beaver Wars.	Historical example: Beaver Wars.

1. The word "utterly" in the passage is closest in meaning to

    VOCABULARY. "Utterly" = completely, absolutely.

    ✗ (A) mistakenly

    Unrelated. "Mistakenly" = by accident or oversight.

    ✗ (B) partially

    Opposite. "Partially" = only in part or to a limited extent.

    ✗ (C) expressly

    Close but not quite. "Expressly" = explicitly or clearly, but this word emphasizes how *clear* it is that the assumption is false. "Utterly," however, emphasizes how *completely* or *entirely* false it is.

    ✓ (D) completely

    CORRECT. "The historical record proves that assumption to be utterly false" = the assumption is completely, 100% false.

2. According to paragraph 1, globalization today likely differs from earlier manifestations in what regard?

FACT. S5 suggests that "perhaps the only unique aspect" of globalization "is that technology has multiplied the rapidity with which these disruptions evolve."

✗ (A) Its effects are felt across greater distances than they previously were.

S5 contradicts this choice: "for hundreds of years, economic changes on one continent have dramatically altered societies on another continent."

✗ (B) It is now conducted for profit, progress, and/or in support of free-market principles.

S2 only states that these are motivations for globalization. It does not indicate that these motivations are new.

✗ (C) Its effects are more negative than they previously were.

S1 mentions the negative effects but does not indicate that these problems are worse than before.

✓ (D) Its effects occur more rapidly than they previously had.

CORRECT. S5: "the only unique aspect" = different from earlier manifestations. S5: "technology has multiplied the rapidity with which these disruptions evolve" = the effects occur more rapidly than before (because of technology).

Paragraph 2	**Comments**
S1	In the seventeenth century, fur pelts were much in demand in Europe for making both hats and garments; this burgeoning demand caused Dutch, French, and English traders to exploit the vast resources of the North American continent despite the many additional costs.	17th century: fur pelts in demand in Europe. So various European traders exploited North America for fur.
2	Many of these costs stemmed from the presence of the Iroquois Confederacy, a sophisticated political and social organization of tribes of Native Americans whose territory was centered in what is now much of New York State.	Iroquois Confederacy of Native American tribes in New York bordered European outposts.
3	By 1610, this territory bordered French trading outposts to the north and Dutch and English trading posts to the south and east.	
4	While the the French allied themselves with other largely Algonquin-speaking tribes of Native Americans, the Dutch and English supported their Iroquois trading partners.	Dutch/English allied with Iroquois, but French were allied with other tribes.
5	The ensuing competition for resources inflamed an already hostile relationship between the Algonquian and Iroquoian tribes into a full-blown war.	Competition turned into war between the two tribes.
6	Both sides launched raids that destroyed entire settlements, razing the structures, burning the crops, and killing or capturing all the inhabitants.	

4

3. According to paragraph 2, which of the following best characterizes the Iroquois Confederacy's relationship with the French traders?

FACT. S3–5 discuss the Iroquois's relationship with the European entities.

✓ (A) It devolved into a war over the fur trade.

CORRECT. S4 states that the Iroquois sided with the Dutch and English, while the French sided with other tribes. S5 notes that this strained relationship eventually devolved (fell or degenerated) into a full-blown war.

✗ (B) They eventually became allies in pursuit of profits from fur trading.

S4: "the French allied themselves with other largely Algonquin-speaking tribes of Native Americans." This led to war with the Iroquois.

✗ (C) They were exclusive trading partners, monopolizing the fur trade.

S3 indicates that the Iroquois also had trading contacts with the Dutch.

✗ (D) They learned how to create a sophisticated society from the French.

S2 says that the Iroquois had "a sophisticated political and social organization" before the arrival of European traders.

4. The word "**stemmed**" in the passage is closest in meaning to

VOCABULARY. As a verb, "stem from" = develop from, be caused by, originate in or from.

✗ (A) detached

These costs did not "detach" or become separated from the presence of the Confederacy. The costs were caused by it.

✓ (B) derived

CORRECT. "Derive from" = result from. "These costs stemmed from the presence of the Iroquois Confederacy" = the costs derived or resulted from the presence of this Confederacy. The Confederacy was the cause of the costs.

✗ (C) departed

These costs did not "depart" or deviate from the presence of the Confederacy. The costs were caused by it.

✗ (D) dispersed

These costs did not "disperse" or spread out from the presence of the Confederacy. The costs were caused by it.

Paragraph 3	**Comments**
S1 Beyond the direct stresses of war, the Iroquois Confederacy was profoundly changed by the economics of this European fashion trend.	Iroquois were deeply changed by the fur trade.
2 The introduction of European goods altered the way Iroquois tribes performed basic tasks; some of these goods soon became essentials.	Some European goods became essentials.
3 By 1640, the beaver population in traditional Iroquois lands had been exhausted.	Beavers disappeared locally.
4 To maintain their revenue flow, the Iroquois were forced to attempt to annex the territories of their Native American neighbors.	So Iroquois attacked neighbors with guns obtained from Dutch traders, which gave them military advantage.
5 Unlike the French, the Dutch traders were willing to exchange firearms for furs.	
6 Thus, the Iroquois had an advantage in weaponry over other tribes that led to their dominance over other tribes in the region.	

5. In paragraph 3, why does the author mention that "the Dutch traders were willing to exchange firearms for furs"?

Purpose. S4–6 describe the Iroquois territorial expansion undertaken to harvest furs.

  ✗ Ⓐ To indicate the advantage that the Iroquois acquired over beavers and other game

S5 notes that the Dutch traded firearms for furs. But S6 concludes that the advantage gained was in warfare. The author makes no mention of advantages gained in hunting.

  ✗ Ⓑ To emphasize how the Iroquois gained superiority in their battles with the French

S6 states that "the Iroquois had an advantage in weaponry over other tribes," not over the French.

  ✓ Ⓒ To explain a primary reason for the Iroquois's military success against neighboring tribes

CORRECT. S4 states that the Iroquois moved to annex territory. S6 concludes that the firearms mentioned in S5 were crucial to their military success.

  ✗ Ⓓ To provide an example of how basic tasks in the daily life of the Iroquois were changed by outside economic forces

While S1 states that Iroquois life was changed in this manner, S4–6 indicate that acquiring weaponry was relevant to warfare rather than to the basic tasks of daily life. It's true that the weaponry probably also altered daily tasks, but the author does not say so.

6. The word "annex" in the passage is closest in meaning to

VOCABULARY. "Annex" a neighboring place = take over control of it and add it to your own place.

✓ (A) conquer

CORRECT. "The Iroquois were forced to attempt to annex the territories of their ... neighbors" = they had to try to conquer their neighbors' lands. "Conquer" contains the idea of assuming control.

✗ (B) destroy

The Iroquois may have tried to destroy neighbors, but not the lands themselves. Rather, they wanted to preserve the lands and take over control of them.

✗ (C) surrender

Opposite. "Surrender [something]" = give it up or give it away. You can only surrender something that you own in the first place.

✗ (D) exploit

"Exploit" = use, take advantage of. It doesn't carry the meaning of taking over control from someone else.

Paragraph 4	**Comments**
S1 While the fortunes of this decades-long war ebbed and flowed, partly because of the intrigues of the European powers, by late in the seventeenth century the Iroquois had moved far beyond their original Hudson River lands.	Over time, Iroquois moved far beyond original lands.
2 They depopulated the entire Ohio Valley and Lower Peninsula of Michigan, defeating the Algonquin-speaking tribes, including the Shawnee, Miami, and Potawatomi, whose surviving members fled to the west.	Drove other tribes out.
3 In fact, this Iroquois offensive also drove the Lakota Sioux to the Dakotas, where they became nomadic mounted warriors, prominent in the United States frontier wars of the nineteenth century.	
4 To the north, the French effected a stalemate with the Iroquois only by committing a regiment of regulars, the Carignan-Salières regiment, to the fray in the 1660s.	French managed a stalemate.

4

7.   It can be inferred from paragraph 4 that forcing the Lakota Sioux to the Dakotas was primarily significant from the author's perspective because

✗   (A) the action forced the French to commit a regiment of regulars

✗   (B) as a result, the Lakota Sioux did not live in one place for long

✓   (C) the Lakota Sioux played an important role in nineteenth-century frontier wars of the United States

✗   (D) the Lakota Sioux learned how to create a partially urbanized society from the Iroquois

INFERENCE. S3 describes how the Lakota Sioux were forced to the Dakotas and what the implications of that event were.

S4 states that the French regiment safeguarded the north, not the west, from the Iroquois, not the Sioux.

S3 does state that the Lakota Sioux "became nomadic mounted warriors." The word "nomadic" indicates that they lived as nomads, moving from place to place. But the author's emphasis is on the "warriors" part. The rest of the sentence states that the Lakota Sioux were "prominent in the United States frontier wars of the nineteenth century." For the author, this last phrase has the greatest significance.

CORRECT. S3 notes that the Lakota Sioux were "prominent in the United States frontier wars of the nineteenth century." From the phrase's closing position in the sentence and the word "prominent," you can safely infer that from the author's perspective, this outcome had primary significance.

The passage does not comment on Sioux society, other than it became nomadic. "Partially urbanized" (living somewhat in cities) does not square with "nomadic" (moving from place to place). Moreover, the author never indicates anything that the Lakota Sioux learned from the Iroquois.

8.   Which of the following best describes the organization of paragraph 4?

✗   (A) A dubious claim is examined but rejected.

✓   (B) A statement of fact is followed by supporting details.

✗   (C) A previously unknown historical fact is documented.

✗   (D) A statement of fact is followed by the citation of parallel cases.

PURPOSE. P4 describes the course and consequences of the seventeenth-century Beaver Wars.

No sentence in the paragraph opposes the topic outlined in the first sentence.

CORRECT. S1 declares the Iroquois expansion. The following sentences provide details about their conquests, as well as some implications.

The paragraph never states that the information presented is new or otherwise unknown.

S2–4 present the details of the topic presented in the first sentence. The details are not about other, "parallel" (= similar) situations.

	Paragraph 5	**Comments**
S1	Fighting nonetheless continued for the rest of the seventeenth century, spurred both by economic concerns and the ongoing political rivalry between France and England, as the Dutch eventually ceded their North American interests to the English.	Fighting continued through 17th century for various reasons.
2	Horrific massacres, much like those of the ancient Greeks chronicled in the *Iliad,* were perpetrated by both the allegedly civilized Europeans and the Iroquois.	Massacres by both sides.
3	Four to five generations of Iroquois lived their entire lives in an era of constant warfare.	
4	Finally, in 1701, despite English efforts to prolong a war that burdened France, the French and Iroquois signed the Great Peace of Montreal.	Finally, the Great Peace in 1701.
5	This peace lasted for more than 20 years and allowed the dispossessed Algonquin tribes to slowly repopulate the Ohio Valley territory.	Algonquins repopulated Ohio Valley.
6	Meanwhile, the Iroquois Confederacy was able to further advance its economic and technological position, as well as **wield** influence over their European rivals.	Iroquois advanced their position.

4

9.   Which of the sentences below best expresses the essential information in the highlighted sentence in paragraph 5? Incorrect choices change the meaning in important ways or leave out essential information.

✗ Ⓐ In the wars between the supposedly civilized Europeans and the Iroquois, the Greeks were guilty of horrible massacres, comparable to those in the *Iliad.*

✗ Ⓑ The Europeans, who were alleged to be civilized, committed more atrocities like those recorded in the *Iliad* than the Iroquois did in the course of their wars.

✓ Ⓒ In the wars between the Iroquois and the Europeans (who were supposedly civilized), both sides committed terrible atrocities, like those reported in the *Iliad.*

✗ Ⓓ During the wars between the allegedly civilized Europeans and the Iroquois, dreadful massacres chronicled in the *Iliad* were committed by both sides.

SIMPLIFY SENTENCE. S2 is highlighted. Topic of paragraph: the wars continued throughout the seventeenth century. S2 states that both sides committed atrocities, much like those in the *Iliad.*

The Greeks were not present in these wars. The sentence instead says that these massacres were comparable to those recorded by the ancient Greeks in the *Iliad.*

S2 states that both sides were guilty, never claiming that one side was worse than the other.

CORRECT. S2 asserts that both sides were guilty of horrific massacres. These massacres or atrocities were like those reported in the *Iliad.*

S2 compares the massacres to other atrocities that were recorded in the *Iliad.* S2 does not say that the Beaver Wars massacres themselves were recorded in the *Iliad.*

10.   The word "wield" in the passage is closest in
       meaning to

VOCABULARY. "Wield" (something like influence) = use it, exercise it, apply it, much like a tool that you might physically wield.

✗   (A) retain

Close but not quite. "Retain" = hold onto something that is in danger of being lost. There's no indication that the influence might have gone away. Also, "retain" doesn't convey the emphasis of actually *using* the influence.

✓   (B) exert

CORRECT. "The Iroquois Confederacy was able to … wield influence over their European rivals" = the Confederacy could exert influence over their rivals. It could influence them in useful ways.

✗   (C) squander

Opposite. "Squander" = waste, misuse.

✗   (D) gain

Also close but not quite. "Gain" = increase or obtain (more). "Wield" influence = use it, not necessarily increase it or obtain more of it.

11.   All of the following are mentioned in paragraph 5
       as occurring before the Great Peace EXCEPT:

NEGATIVE FACT. Three answers are true and supported by the passage. One answer is false or just unsupported. The Great Peace is described in S4, and since the paragraph is in chronological order, S1–3 contain the events that occurred before the Great Peace.

✗   (A) Generations of Iroquois lived their entire
         lives at war.

S3: "Four to five generations of Iroquois lived their entire lives in an era of constant warfare."

✗   (B) The Iroquois committed horrific massacres.

S2 states that both the Iroquois and Europeans committed massacres.

✗   (C) The Dutch territories became English.

S1: "the Dutch eventually ceded their North American interests to the English."

✓   (D) Algonquin-speaking tribes repopulated the
         Ohio Valley.

CORRECT. Mentioned in S5 as occurring after, not before, the Great Peace.

4

Paragraph 6	Comments
S1 In sum, international trade and globalization hundreds of years ago caused profound and unforeseen economic consequences for peoples far removed from the initial catalyst.	
2 **A** Much like today, some prospered, some failed, and some died.	**CORRECT.** S1 discusses "international trade and globalization," which are the "forces" referred to in the new sentence. S1 also refers to the "economic consequences" these forces had. The start of the new sentence ("And along with economic gains and losses") builds well on that point. The new sentence also sets up S2 well: "much like today," which echoes "as always." Likewise, the clauses "some prospered, some failed, and some died" give vivid illustrations of the "powerful personal impacts." The insertion also works to tell you what "some" refers to: some of the "people involved" (in the inserted sentence).
3 **B** Furthermore, these same disruptive forces proved far more powerful than the will or policies of any of the entities involved.	This placement makes the inserted sentence redundant. The generality "powerful personal impacts" should come *before* the specific examples "some prospered, some failed," etc.
4 **C** Global economic currents arguably cut as wide a swath across societies in the seventeenth century as they do today.	This placement gives the sentence no relationship to the adjacent sentences. The prior sentence does not emphasize economic gains or losses, and the following sentence does not elaborate on the personal impacts of the forces.
End **D**	This placement does connect somewhat to the preceding sentence, which mentions "global economic currents." However, S4 works best as a closer for the whole passage. Moreover, the inserted sentence discusses "powerful personal impacts on the people involved," but if it is not followed by examples, then the power of the sentence is greatly lessened.

12.   **And along with economic gains and losses, these forces, as always, had powerful personal impacts on the people involved.**

Where would the sentence best fit?

INSERT TEXT. The start of the inserted sentence, "And along with economic gains and losses, these forces ..." signals that the prior sentence should discuss certain "forces" (whether that word is explicitly used or not) causing economic gains and losses. Since the whole passage is about a historical example of the impact of globalization, the "forces" are almost certainly those of globalization. So globalization should be the focus of the prior sentence. Finally, the following sentence should elaborate on "the powerful personal impacts" these forces had on people. The "as always" provides a reminder that these same patterns have been seen over and over. The following sentence ought to echo this point.

✓   (A) Choice A   **CORRECT.**

✗   (B) Choice B

✗   (C) Choice C

✗   (D) Choice D

Whole Passage	**Comments**
P1	The harsh aspects of globalization (international economic intertwining) …	Globalization = international economic intertwining. Pundits (expert commentators) today focus on the harsh aspects. Most assume that globalization is modern. But that's false. Yes, technology has accelerated impact. But globalization has been happening for centuries. Historical example: Beaver Wars.
P2	In the seventeenth century, fur pelts were much in demand in Europe …	17th century: fur pelts in demand in Europe. So various European traders exploited North America for fur. Iroquois Confederacy of Native American tribes in New York bordered European outposts. Dutch/English allied with Iroquois, but French were allied with other tribes. Competition turned into war between the two sides.
P3	Beyond the direct stresses of war, the Iroquois Confederacy was profoundly changed …	Iroquois were deeply changed by the fur trade. Some European goods became essentials. Beavers disappeared locally. So Iroquois attacked neighbors with guns obtained from Dutch traders, which gave them military advantage.
P4	While the fortunes of this decades-long war ebbed and flowed …	Over time, Iroquois moved far beyond original lands. Drove other tribes out. French managed a stalemate.
P5	Fighting nonetheless continued for the rest of the seventeenth century …	Fighting continued through 17th century for various reasons. Massacres by both sides. Finally, the Great Peace in 1701. Algonquins repopulated Ohio Valley. Iroquois advanced their position.
P6	In sum, international trade and globalization hundreds of years ago caused profound and unforeseen economic consequences …	Summary. Centuries ago, globalization had profound economic and personal impacts on people living far away. This is just like the situation today.

4

13. Select from the seven phrases below TWO that correctly characterize the Dutch during the Beaver Wars and THREE that correctly characterize the Iroquois, as described in the passage. Two of the phrases will NOT be used.

TABLE. Correct answers do not have to convey a main idea. They just have to be justified by the passage. If a choice corresponds to the Dutch or to the Iroquois, the passage must explicitly say so. There are no synonyms for "Dutch" or "Iroquois," so those keywords are useful as you scan the passage.

A | Became nomadic mounted warriors

NEITHER. Corresponds to P4 S3: it was the Lakota Sioux, not the Iroquois, who did so.

B | Conquered neighboring territories

THE IROQUOIS. Corresponds to P3 S4: "[they] were forced to attempt to annex the territories of their Native American neighbors." P4 S1: "[they] had moved far beyond their original ... lands." P4 S2: "[they] depopulated the entire Ohio Valley."

C | Waged and suffered through war for decades

THE IROQUOIS. Corresponds to P5 S3: "Four to five generations of Iroquois lived their entire lives in an era of constant warfare."

D | Provided firearms in exchange for furs

THE DUTCH. Corresponds to P3 S5: "Unlike the French, the Dutch traders were willing to exchange firearms for furs."

E | Allied with Algonquin-speaking tribes

NEITHER. P2 S4 says that it was the French who allied with Algonquin-speaking tribes.

F | Had a sophisticated political organization

THE IROQUOIS. P2 S2: "the Iroquois Confederacy, a sophisticated political and social organization of tribes of Native Americans."

G | Relinquished North American territories

THE DUTCH. Corresponds to P5 S1: "as the Dutch eventually ceded their North American interests to the English."

Answers and Explanations—4.3 The Flynn Effect

	Paragraph 1	**Comments**
S1	Since 1930, scores measuring intelligence quotients (IQs) have been increasing steadily across the globe.	IQs going up everywhere over time.
2	James Flynn first discovered this phenomenon in the 1980s in the United States.	
3	Ensuing analysis found that it was occurring in virtually every where such data was collected.	
4	This trend is referred to as "the Flynn Effect," a sustained increase in intelligence test scores worldwide with each passing year.	This is called the Flynn Effect.
5	Researchers have devoted a significant amount of study to the effect not only because of its geographic scope, but also because, mysteriously, the annual rise has occurred every year in more or less linear fashion over the past century.	Researchers are studying it because 1) it's everywhere and 2) it's going up linearly (at a steady rate) every year.

1. The word "ensuing" in the passage is closest in meaning to

    ✗ (A) confirmatory

    ✓ (B) later

    ✗ (C) broader

    ✗ (D) rigorous

VOCABULARY. "Ensuing" = following later, subsequent.

Unrelated. Although the analysis did "confirm" the occurrence of the phenomena described, these words are not related.

CORRECT. "Ensuing analysis" = later analysis, research that happened afterward.

Unrelated. The author is not saying that the analysis was more "broad."

Although the analysis might have been "rigorous" (thorough and accurate), this is unrelated to "ensuing."

2. According to paragraph 1, which of the following is true about the Flynn Effect?

    ✓ (A) It is taking place all over the planet.

    ✗ (B) It is unique to the United States.

    ✗ (C) It is occurring at a lesser rate than previously.

    ✗ (D) Researchers have been studying this phenomenon since 1930.

FACT. P1 is all about the Flynn Effect (although it's not named until S4). So the answer could be anywhere in the paragraph.

CORRECT. S1: "across the globe." S3: "in virtually every country."

Opposite. S1: "across the globe." S3: "in virtually every country."

Not mentioned in P1.

S1 states that the effect has been happening since 1930. But S2 states that Flynn discovered the effect "in the 1980s." So researchers have only been studying the phenomenon since then.

4

Paragraph 2	Comments
S1　Does this mean we are getting smarter?	Are we getting smarter?
2　The definition of "intelligence" is hotly debated, but generally speaking, IQ tests are designed to measure both **fluid intelligence** and **crystallized intelligence**.	IQ tests measure both fluid and crystallized intelligence.
3　Fluid intelligence refers to problem-solving abilities, such as looking for patterns, and using visual cues to solve problems.	Fluid = problem-solving.
4　Crystallized intelligence refers to learned skills, such as math and vocabulary.	Crystallized = learned skills.
5　When IQ tests are administered, the convention is to set the average of the test results to 100, with a standard deviation of 15 to 16 points.	Average IQ score = 100.
6　The test score distribution is restandardized with every new batch of test-takers, such that the number 100 consistently represents the average score of that year's test-takers.	Restandardized with every new batch of test-takers.
7　When younger subjects take older tests, their average score is higher than the previous group's average: the Flynn Effect.	Younger people do better on older tests = Flynn Effect.
8　The Flynn Effect is driven more by gains in fluid intelligence than in crystallized intelligence.	Driven more by gains in fluid.

3.　The word "batch" in the passage is closest in meaning to

　　　　VOCABULARY. "Batch" = group, often one group of many in a sequence.

✗　Ⓐ school

　　　A literal "school" is not what is meant here. The only context in which "school" means a less well-formed "group" is with artists following a particular philosophy (the "Impressionist school") or with fish (a "school of fish"). Neither meaning fits here.

✗　Ⓑ society

　　　A "society" is a group, but these words are not synonymous.

✗　Ⓒ country

　　　A "country" is populated by a group of people, but these words are not synonymous.

✓　Ⓓ group

　　　CORRECT. "With every new batch of test-takers" = with every new group or cohort of people taking the test.

4.   Which of the following can be inferred about crystallized intelligence from paragraph 2?

INFERENCE. S4 defines crystallized intelligence. S2 implies that fluid and crystallized intelligence are different.

✗ (A) Crystallized intelligence is less likely to be improved through teaching than fluid intelligence.

The paragraph does not imply this. If anything, you might infer the opposite is true, since crystallized intelligence refers to learned skills. Because fluid and crystallized intelligence are distinguished as categories in S2, you might conclude that fluid intelligence refers to skills that are not learned, or that cannot be learned.

✗ (B) Crystallized intelligence is more difficult to assess than fluid intelligence.

The paragraph does not suggest this. S2 states that IQ tests measure both types of intelligence. There is no indication that one is harder to measure than the other.

✓ (C) Higher crystallized intelligence scores demonstrate superior skills that have been taught to the test-taker.

CORRECT. S4: "Crystallized intelligence refers to learned skills." This means skills that have been taught. You can safely infer that higher scores on assessments of crystallized intelligence correspond to higher levels of skills that have been taught.

✗ (D) Worse performance on assessments of crystallized intelligence indicates greater fragility or fragmentation of thinking.

The term "crystallized" is never defined outside of S4, so you shouldn't read into it. The passage is not talking about literal or even metaphorical crystals, nor about thematically related concepts (fragility or fragmentation).

Paragraph 3	**Comments**
S1	While the cause of the Flynn Effect remains a mystery, scientists have been able to rule out some possible causes.	Cause of Flynn Effect = mystery. But some causes have been ruled out.
2	The time frame in which these increases have occurred, along with their geographic scope, seem to preclude the cause being genetic (genetic evolution takes a long time to take effect, as it occurs over many generations via reproduction).	Not genetic.
3	The Flynn Effect, by contrast, refers to steady increases in measured intelligence over much shorter time frames.	It's happening too fast for evolution.
4	Further, the population groups among whom it is occurring, often separated by great distances, do not interact extensively enough for reproduction to lead to shared genetic traits across the groups.	Not shared traits either. Populations don't interact enough.

5.   According to paragraph 3, what factors have led researchers to rule out genetics as a cause of the Flynn Effect?

FACT. S2–4 rule out genetics.

✗ (A) The extended distance and time over which the effect has occurred.

The time frame is short, according to S2 (by contrast with the "long time" needed for evolution to work).

✗ (B) The restriction of the effect to narrow geographic regions.

The geographic scope is wide. You already know this from P1, but S4 in this paragraph mentions again that the groups affected are "often separated by great distances."

✓ (C) The geographic scope of the effect, as well as its short time frame.

CORRECT. Both factors have helped rule out genetics as a cause. S2 indicates that the time frame is considered short, in comparison to the "long time" and "many generations" for evolution to take effect. S2 also credits the "geographic scope" of the effect. You are reminded in S4 that this scope is wide (with groups "separated by great distances").

✗ (D) The fact that the effect has occurred in one defined population group, but not in other groups.

S4 notes that the effect is occurring in more than one group around the world.

6.   Which of the following can be inferred from paragraph 3 about the Flynn Effect?

INFERENCE. P3 focuses on what is known *not* to cause the Flynn Effect.

✓ (A) Despite ruling out possible factors, researchers still do not know what causes the effect.

CORRECT. S1: "the cause of the Flynn Effect remains a mystery." That is, people don't know what the cause is.

✗ (B) Despite efforts to identify a single cause, multiple causes of the effect seem to be at work.

The paragraph does not discuss what causes the effect, even possibly. S1 says that the cause is a mystery. S2–4 notes that the cause is not genetic.

✗ (C) Despite some criticism, it appears that cultural factors may be driving the effect.

P3 does not discuss cultural factors.

✗ (D) Despite some findings to the contrary, it is likely that the effect does not actually exist.

Paragraph 3 does not question the existence of the Flynn Effect. S1 just asserts that its cause remains a mystery.

4

Paragraph 4	**Comments**
S1 Researchers attempting to identify the cause of the Flynn Effect have therefore been left with what seems to be the only alternative: a changing global culture.	Only possible cause seems to be a changing culture.
2 Research over the past 30 years has focused on identifying possible causes **rooted** in culture.	Research has focused on possible cultural causes.
3 These have included improvements in nutrition, education, testing methods, and so forth.	List of possibilities.
4 Further hypotheses have included increased complexity of social environments, changes in childrearing, advances in technology, and improved test-taking abilities.	

7.   Which one of the sentences below best expresses the essential information in the highlighted sentence of the passage? Incorrect choices change the meaning in important ways or leave out essential information.

SIMPLIFY SENTENCE. S1 (highlighted) says that researchers have been left with what seems to be the only possible cause of the Flynn Effect: a global culture that is changing. Notice that "alternative" means "choice, possibility" here.

✗   Ⓐ   Researchers are not certain that a changing global culture is responsible for the Flynn Effect.

It is true that researchers are not certain, but they are choosing to point to a changing global culture because of a lack of any other explanations.

✓   Ⓑ   Unable to definitively identify alternative causes, researchers seem to believe that a changing global culture might be responsible for the Flynn Effect.

CORRECT. This choice supports the uncertainty of the researchers as well as the idea that they are "left with" a changing global culture (in that other options have been ruled out).

✗   Ⓒ   Researchers have stopped looking for the cause of the Flynn Effect because a changing global culture is confusing the issue.

Researchers haven't stopped looking. The changing global culture is just what they have settled on at this point.

✗   Ⓓ   In their attempts to understand the Flynn Effect, a changing global culture has left researchers without an alternative.

This choice muddles words from the original sentence. They are not attempting to understand the effect itself, but rather its cause. Also, the changing global culture *is* the alternative.

8. The phrase "rooted in" in the passage is closest in meaning to

✓ (A) arising from

✗ (B) grown into

✗ (C) dug out of

✗ (D) distinct from

VOCABULARY. "Rooted in" = based on, caused by, fundamentally connected to.

CORRECT. "Possible causes rooted in culture" = possible causes arising from culture, or that spring out of culture.

"Grown from" might seem to be a better match. But that phrase wouldn't sound like natural English. And "grown into" does not have the right meaning.

The language of "root" and "dug" might make this choice tempting. However, "dug out of" means to be pulled from (as from the ground). This is not a synonym for "rooted in."

In a way, this is the opposite. If something is "distinct from," it is different, whereas something "rooted in" comes from that thing and is likely similar.

9. According to paragraph 4, why have researchers focused on improvements in nutrition, education, testing methods, and so forth?

✗ (A) These factors drive health and overall well-being globally.

✗ (B) These improvements are the reasons why the Flynn Effect exists.

✗ (C) These cultural factors are believed by researchers to vary by region.

✓ (D) These are cultural factors that could be causes of the Flynn Effect.

FACT. S3: "These have included improvements in nutrition..." S2 indicates that "these" refers to the "possible causes rooted in culture." In case you've forgotten, S1 reminds you that these causes would be of the Flynn Effect. S2 states that researchers have been focused on identifying possible cultural causes. That's why research has focused on the improvements listed in the question.

P4 does not say or imply this at all.

These are *possible* reasons for the Flynn Effect's existence. Researchers do not yet know whether these improvements are in fact causes of the effect.

Researchers are actually looking for "global" causes of the effect.

CORRECT. S2: "Research ... has focused on identifying possible causes [of the Flynn Effect, as S1 indicates] rooted in culture." S3 lists the improvements in nutrition and so on as some of the possible causes.

Paragraph 5	Comments
S1	A problem that researchers have faced in analyzing possible cultural factors is that the universality of the Flynn Effect seems in contradiction to the nature of culture itself, which by definition varies across time and space.	Problem: the Flynn Effect is universal, but culture varies across time and space.
2	In other words, different characteristics of places and population groups are what create divergence across cultures, and this diversity is a fundamental feature of the human population at large.	Diversity of cultures is fundamental.
3	Culture is different in Brazil than it is in Israel or Australia or Canada.	
4	But for cultural factors to be responsible for the Flynn Effect, they must essentially affect people across countries nearly identically.	But to cause the Flynn Effect, cultural factors must affect everyone the same way.
5	This would seem to be unlikely.	Unlikely.

10. The word "divergence" in the passage is closest in meaning to

VOCABULARY. "Divergence" = difference, separation between things, diversity. "Diverge" = move apart, deviate away from.

✗ (A) opposition

Close, but too extreme. "Divergence" just means difference. It does not necessarily mean that the cultures are actively opposing each other.

✗ (B) movement

The root verb "diverge" has a sense of movement. But it's always movement *apart*, or separation. By itself, the noun "movement" doesn't mean the same thing at all as "divergence."

✗ (C) alignment

Opposite. "Alignment" = arranged in a straight line or organized manner.

✓ (D) variation

CORRECT. "Different characteristics ... create divergence across cultures" = different features create variation, or differences, across those cultures.

Paragraph 5	Comments

P5
S4–5
But for cultural factors to be responsible for the Flynn Effect, they must essentially affect people across countries nearly identically. This would seem to be unlikely.

Paragraph 6	Comments

P6
S1–2
A Further, factors such as improved nutrition would seem to affect nutritionally impoverished regions more dramatically than regions where nutritional resources have been stable for decades. In other words, if better nutrition is driving improved fluid intelligence, areas that have seen the most improvement in nutrition should see the largest increase in IQ scores, while in areas where nutritional resources have been widely available for a long time, IQ scores should be leveling off.

It doesn't make sense to put the new sentence, which begins with the phrase "For example," at the beginning of the paragraph. The only good reason would be to elaborate on a point made at the end of the preceding paragraph. But that paragraph does not end with a contrast between high-nutrition regions and low-nutrition regions.

3
B But this is not the case.

CORRECT. The new sentence provides an example of the exact idea expressed in S1–2.

4
C Regions with poor nutritional resources and regions with high nutritional resources have both shown steady gains over time, regardless of how nutritional resources have changed.

Placement here puts "For example" after the sentence, "But this is not the case." But the inserted sentence is not an example of this not being the case. It is an example of the points made in S1–2.

End
D

S4 describes the actual state of affairs: all regions are increasing their IQ scores at a similar rate. So it doesn't work to put a hypothetical example of how regions might increase their scores at different rates.

11.   **For example, the Netherlands (a developed nation with high levels of nutrition generally) would not see as dramatic a rise in IQ scores as would, say, The Gambia or another developing nation.**

Where would the sentence best fit?

INSERT TEXT. The inserted sentence begins with "For example." So this sentence must provide an example of a more general point made in the previous sentence (or two). The example is of a developed country (the Netherlands) with high levels of nutrition and of a developing country (The Gambia), presumably with lower levels. The prior sentence should be contrasting places with high and low levels of nutrition. That sentence should point out that places with high levels of nutrition would see a smaller rise in IQ scores, if nutritional improvements were in fact a cause of the IQ rise. Notice that this is a hypothetical example ("would not see"), not a real example (which would not contain the verb "would"). This example would work *if* nutrition were a cause of IQ increases.

✗ (A) Choice A

✓ (B) Choice B   **CORRECT.**

✗ (C) Choice C

✗ (D) Choice D

	Whole Passage	**Comments**
P1	Since 1930, scores measuring intelligence quotients (IQs) have been increasing steadily across the globe …	IQs going up everywhere over time. This is called the Flynn Effect. Researchers are studying it because 1) it's everywhere and 2) it's going up linearly (at a steady rate) every year.
P2	Does this mean we are getting smarter? …	Are we getting smarter? IQ tests measure both fluid and crystallized intelligence. Fluid = problem-solving. Crystallized = learned skills. Average IQ score = 100. Restandardized with every new batch of test-takers. Younger people do better on older tests = Flynn Effect. Driven more by gains in fluid.
P3	While the cause of the Flynn Effect remains a mystery …	Cause of Flynn Effect = mystery. But some causes have been ruled out. Not genetic. It's happening too fast for evolution. Not shared traits either. Populations don't interact enough.
P4	Researchers attempting to identify the cause of the Flynn Effect …	Only possible cause seems to be a changing culture. Research has focused on possible cultural causes. List of possibilities.
P5	A problem that researchers have faced in analyzing possible cultural factors is that …	Problem: the Flynn Effect is universal, but culture varies across time and space. Diversity of cultures is fundamental. But to cause the Flynn Effect, cultural factors must affect everyone the same way. Unlikely.
P6	Further, factors such as improved nutrition would seem to affect nutritionally impoverished regions more dramatically …	If nutrition is a factor, then places that have gained the most in nutrition should also have gained the most in IQs. Those would be places starting off with poor nutrition, with the most gains made recently. But IQ gains everywhere are similar.
P7	The mystery of how culture could be causing the Flynn Effect …	Infant IQs are rising steadily, too. This further limits the possible impact of culture.

4

12.	This passage is developed primarily by	**PURPOSE.** This question focuses on the overall organization of the passage.
✗	(A) outlining reasons to support one theory of an observed pattern	More than one theory is discussed. Also, no single theory is well supported throughout the passage.
✗	(B) arguing for a particular cause of a global phenomenon	The author doesn't argue for one cause. At one point, cultural causes seem to be "the only alternative" (P4). But P5–7 point out problems with such cultural causes. The issue remains a mystery.
✓	(C) examining possible causes of a mysterious phenomenon	**CORRECT.** The "mysterious phenomenon" is the Flynn Effect. Several paragraphs "examine possible causes" of this effect.
✗	(D) discussing multiple problems with a single theory of an effect	Multiple theories are discussed. P5–7 do discuss multiple problems with possible cultural causes. But genetics are described and then dismissed as a possible cause in P3.

13.   Complete the table below by selecting THREE answer choices that are skills that would be representative of fluid intelligence and TWO that are skills that would be representative of crystallized intelligence.

TABLE. Correct answers in table questions do not have to convey a main idea. They just have to be justified by the passage. In P2, fluid intelligence and crystallized intelligence are defined. P2 S3: "Fluid intelligence refers to problem-solving abilities, such as looking for patterns, and using visual cues to solve problems." P2 S4: "Crystallized intelligence refers to learned skills, such as math and vocabulary."

| A | Solving a jigsaw puzzle by examining and putting together the pieces |

FLUID. Example of "problem-solving abilities" and "using visual cues to solve problems."

| B | Doing an algebra problem |

CRYSTALLIZED. Example of "learned skills, such as math."

| C | Winning a spelling bee |

CRYSTALLIZED. Example of "learned skills, such as… vocabulary."

| D | Matching shapes in a set of visual patterns |

FLUID. Example of "problem-solving abilities, such as looking for patterns" and "using visual cues to solve problems."

| E | Watching traffic to find a shortcut |

FLUID. Example of "problem-solving abilities" and "using visual cues to solve problems."

Answers and Explanations—
4.4 Operation Barbarossa and Napoleon

	Paragraph 1	**Comments**
S1	On June 22, 1941, one year to the day after the signing of an armistice following his successful invasion of France, Adolf Hitler launched Operation Barbarossa, the code name for Nazi Germany's invasion of Russia (then the dominant part of the Soviet Union).	Operation Barbarossa = Hitler's invasion of Russia in 1941.
2	Hitler had amassed an invading army of over 3 million soldiers, still the largest invading force in world history.	
3	What followed paralleled, in many ways, another failed invasion of Russia more than 100 years earlier by another tyrant: Napoleon Bonaparte, ruler of France.	Similar to another failed invasion of Russia: Napoleon's.
4	For both leaders, invading Russia would be the turning point in a war they had previously dominated, and would lead to their final defeat elsewhere in Europe.	For both leaders, invasion = turning point that led to final defeat.

MANHATTAN PREP

1. The author uses the phrase "What followed paralleled, in many ways, another failed invasion of Russia more than 100 years earlier" for which of the following reasons?

PURPOSE. S3 begins with "What followed paralleled, in many ways, another failed invasion of Russia more than 100 years earlier." This phrase is used to transition from the discussion of Operation Barbarossa to Napoleon's invasion, in order to draw a comparison between the two invasions. The verb "paralleled" indicates that similarities will be emphasized.

✗ (A) To point out that Napoleon's invasion and Hitler's invasion occurred in different centuries

S3 does point out that Napoleon's invasion of Russia occurred "more than 100 years earlier" than Hitler's. But the comparison is much broader than just the time difference. In fact, the author does not want to focus on differences but on similarities. S4 highlights the key parallel or similarity: for the invaders, both invasions crucially turned the course of each war for the worse.

✓ (B) To initiate a comparison between Operation Barbarossa and Napoleon's invasion of Russia

CORRECT. S1–2 begin the discussion of Operation Barbarossa. S3 initiates the comparison of this invasion with Napoleon's invasion over 100 years earlier.

✗ (C) To introduce a broad category of military actions consisting of failed invasions of Russia

This phrase opens a comparison between Operation Barbarossa and Napoleon's failed invasion, not a collection of failed invasions of Russia. No other such actions are alluded to.

✗ (D) To compare the size of Hitler's army with that of Napoleon's army

S2 does introduce the size of Hitler's army, but this is not the basis of comparison. The size of Napoleon's army is not mentioned in the paragraph.

2. According to paragraph 1, which of the following was true of both Operation Barbarossa and Napoleon's invasion of Russia?

FACT. S4 is the only sentence in P1 that discusses similarities between the two invasions: both were turning points in their respective wars, and both would ultimately lead to defeat elsewhere in Europe.

✗ (A) Both Hitler and Napoleon were considered tyrants.

S3 clearly states that both Napoleon and Hitler were tyrants. But this is a statement about the leaders themselves, not about their invasions of Russia.

✗ (B) Both invasions failed because of inadequate planning.

S4 implies that both invasions failed. They both turned the course of war and led to defeat elsewhere. But the paragraph never explains why these invasions might have failed.

✗ (C) Both invasions followed military victories in France.

S1 states that Hitler's invasion of the Soviet Union followed "his successful invasion of France." More than a century earlier, Napoleon was the ruler of France (S3). But the paragraph never states that Napoleon achieved military victory in France before invading Russia.

✓ (D) Both invasions precipitated events that eventually led to defeat.

CORRECT. S4: "For both leaders, invading Russia … would lead to their final defeat elsewhere in Europe." As a verb, "precipitate" = bring about, cause, trigger or even speed up.

	Paragraph 2	Comments
S1	Operation Barbarossa involved an invasion along three fronts.	Barbarossa: invasion on 3 fronts.
2	Army Group North was to conquer the Baltic countries and ultimately Leningrad.	
3	Army Group Center was to invade the heartland of present-day Russia and proceed to Moscow, the Soviet capital.	
4	Army Group South had orders to invade and conquer Ukraine and various southern cities in Russia to capture key economic resources, such as grain and oil.	
5	The conquest was one of **annihilation**: Nazi Germany viewed Soviet communism ("Bolshevism") as the mortal enemy of the Nazi's "National Socialist" political doctrine.	Goal was annihilation. Why.
6	Furthermore, National Socialism viewed Slavic and Jewish people—both predominant in Russia—as inferior to Germans.	
7	Therefore, the war was about conquest of land at all costs, and many civilians were targeted for forced labor or assassination.	

3. The word "**annihilation**" in the passage is closest in meaning to

VOCABULARY. "Annihilation" = total destruction, extermination, wiping a place (or a people) out of existence.

✓ (A) eradication

CORRECT. "The conquest was one of annihilation" = the conquest was focused on eradication, or total destruction (of the population).

✗ (B) dismissal

Not nearly strong enough. "Dismissal" is about asking someone to leave or having them removed. Not complete destruction.

✗ (C) introduction

Unrelated. To "introduce" is to bring into use or operation for the first time.

✗ (D) victory

The goal of the conquest, or of any conquest, is victory. But this term does not capture the harsh meaning intended by "annihilation."

 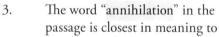

4.   All of the following are mentioned in paragraph 2 as places targeted by Operation Barbarossa EXCEPT:

NEGATIVE FACT. Three answers contain targets of the operation that are mentioned in the passage. S2–4 detail the targets and objectives of Army Group North, Army Group Center, and Army Group South, respectively. The remaining answer will not be mentioned as a place targeted by Operation Barbarossa.

✓ (A) France

CORRECT. P1 mentions Hitler's victory in France prior to Operation Barbarossa. But France is not described as a target of Operation Barbarossa.

✗ (B) Ukraine

S4: "Army Group South had orders to invade and conquer Ukraine and various southern cities in Russia to capture key economic resources, such as grain and oil."

✗ (C) cities in southern Russia

S4: "Army Group South had orders to invade and conquer Ukraine and various southern cities in Russia to capture key economic resources, such as grain and oil."

✗ (D) Leningrad

S2: "Army Group North was to conquer the Baltic countries and ultimately Leningrad."

Paragraph 3	**Comments**
S1 By contrast, Napoleon's invasion was based on a trade disagreement.	Napoleon's invasion: different reason. Trade disagreement.
2 The real enemy of Napoleon was Britain, with whom France was at war, and his invasion of Russia was intended to force the Russian nobility to stop trading with Britain.	Real enemy = Britain. Goal: force Russia to stop trading with Britain.
3 His goal was to use his *grande armée* (French for "great army") to swiftly defeat the inferior Russian defending forces, march to Moscow, and force Tsar Alexander I to sign an agreement ceasing all trade with Britain.	
4 This would culminate in Britain's inability to continue to wage war with France, Napoleon reasoned.	
5 Britain would have to seek peace, thereby ending the decade-long Napoleonic Wars.	Britain would seek peace.
6 Supposedly thus "fighting for an end to fighting," Napoleon's forces began the invasion on June 24, 1812, crossing the Neman River into Russia.	

4

5. The word "inferior" in the passage is closest in meaning to

    ✗ (A) exceptional

    ✗ (B) high-handed

    ✓ (C) substandard

    ✗ (D) derivative

VOCABULARY. "Inferior" = worse, lesser, lower, second-rate.

Opposite. "Exceptional" = unusual or not typical, particularly in terms of its outstanding or great nature.

Unrelated. "High-handed" = using one's power or authority without considering the feelings of others.

CORRECT. "Swiftly defeat the inferior Russian defending forces" = quickly defeat the substandard or second-rate forces defending Russia at that time.

"Derivative" = derived from something else, unoriginal. But this does not necessarily mean "inferior." Something derivative could be good or even better than the original. Moreover, "inferior" does not necessarily mean "derivative." Some things are inferior without being copied from a better original.

6. According to the paragraph, why did Napoleon believe that a successful invasion of Russia would lead Britain to "seek peace, thereby ending the decade-long Napoleonic Wars"?

    ✗ (A) Britain was supplying Russia with the means necessary to wage war against France.

    ✗ (B) Napoleon thought that Russia would be defeated if it were forced to sign a trade agreement ceasing all trade with Britain.

    ✗ (C) Both countries were trading with other countries in Europe, leading to the Napoleonic Wars.

    ✓ (D) Conquering Russia would force Russia to stop providing Britain with supplies for war against France.

FACT. S5 contains the highlighted phrase. The paragraph outlines Napoleon's rationale for the invasion. S1: Napoleon's invasion was predicated on a trade disagreement. S2: Napoleon's main enemy was Britain, which was trading with Russia. S3–4 claim that Napoleon intended his invasion to force the Tsar of Russia to agree not to trade with Britain, which would stop Britain from being able to wage war against France.

Opposite. The passage implies that trading with Russia enabled Britain to continue to wage war.

Opposite in another way. The goal of defeating Russia was to get Russia to sign a trade agreement ceasing all trade with Britain, not the other way around.

No mention is made in the paragraph of any countries besides Britain and Russia trading with each other.

CORRECT. S3–4: "His goal was to ... force Tsar Alexander I to sign an agreement ceasing all trade with Britain. This would culminate in Britain's inability to continue to wage war with France, Napoleon reasoned."

Paragraph 4	**Comments**
S1 For each leader, the invasion had substantial initial success but ultimately met disaster.	Invasions succeeded at first but then failed.
2 Russia is an enormous country geographically, and the distance to Moscow dwarfed that covered by any other invasion that either leader had successfully completed before.	Various challenges.
3 Supply lines for both invading armies quickly became stretched thin; troops and equipment were faced with exhaustion.	
4 To make matters worse, Russians engaged in scorched-earth tactics: as they retreated from the invading army, they burned or otherwise destroyed everything of value, so that no invading forces could use it.	
5 This dashed any hopes of living off the land.	
6 In addition, the Russian winter is exceptionally cold, and both leaders failed to make appropriate provisions for winter warfare, as both thought their invasion could be successfully completed before winter set in.	
7 Finally, while Russian armed resistance was light at first, it dramatically intensified as the invaders approached Moscow.	
8 By the end, invading troops met fierce Russian opposition while also combating hunger, privation, and extremely cold temperatures.	

7. The word "privation" in the passage is closest in meaning to

  ✗   (A)   expansion

  ✓   (B)   hardship

  ✗   (C)   bounty

  ✗   (D)   restlessness

VOCABULARY. "Privation" = extreme hardship, miserable deprivation of basic necessities.

Unrelated. "Expansion" = becoming larger or broader, taking up more space.

CORRECT. "Combating hunger, privation, and extremely cold temperatures" = combating hunger, hardship or deprivation of necessities, and extremely cold temperatures.

Opposite. "Bounty" = abundant supply (also reward for bringing in a fugitive or a predator).

Unrelated. "Restlessness" = the inability to rest or relax as a result of boredom or anxiety.

8. Which of the following does the author conclude was an important factor in the failure of Napoleon's invasion of Russia?

FACT. S2–8 detail many factors that led to the failure of Napoleon's invasion.

✗ (A) Napoleon's decision to begin his invasion in the middle of winter

S6 strongly implies that Napoleon, like Hitler, thought the invasion would be over *before* winter: "both leaders failed to make appropriate provisions for winter warfare, for both thought the invasion could be successfully completed before winter set in." So Napoleon's invasion had to have started *before* the middle of winter. In addition, the previous paragraph mentions that Napoleon's invasion began in late June, which is summer, not winter, in the northern hemisphere.

✗ (B) The relatively slight distances that invading troops were to cover

S2: "Russia is an enormous country geographically, and the distance to Moscow dwarfed that of any other invasion either leader had successfully completed before."

✓ (C) The scorched-earth response of the retreating defenders

CORRECT. S4: "To make matters worse, Russians engaged in scorched-earth tactics: as they retreated from the invading army, they burned or otherwise destroyed everything of value, so that no invading forces could use it."

✗ (D) Intense military resistance at the beginning of the invasion

S7–8 discuss the fact that Russian opposition eventually intensified. But S7 notes that "Russian armed resistance was light at first."

Paragraph 5	Comments
S1 Unlike Hitler, Napoleon did successfully reach Moscow, only to find it ablaze and vacated.	Napoleon reached Moscow, but it was burning and empty.
2 He waited with his army, trying to force the Russian tsar, now in exile, to sign a treaty.	
3 Meanwhile his army continued to starve, and the weather turned sharply colder.	
4 Napoleon was thus forced to leave Moscow to find provisions and shelter for his army, and this departure turned into an all-out retreat as appropriate provisions and shelter could not be found.	Starving & freezing army had to abandon Moscow.
5 As it attempted to flee Russia, Napoleon's army was massacred by hunger and temperatures of −25° Celsius much more than by Russian troops.	All-out retreat. Army was massacred by forces of nature.

9.   The word "ablaze" in the passage   **VOCABULARY.** "Ablaze" = burning, on fire. It can also mean
     is closest in meaning to   "lit up but not on fire" (for instance, with lights), but that
                                             meaning is not intended here.

✓   (A) burning   **CORRECT.** "Napoleon did successfully reach Moscow, only to
                                            find it ablaze" = Napoleon reached Moscow, but it was burning.

✗   (B) embattled   "Embattled" = involved in or prepared for war. Although this
                                            might have been true of Moscow, this is not related to
                                            "ablaze" or on fire.

✗   (C) deserted   The sentence says that Moscow was ablaze *and* vacated
                                            (deserted). These are two different concepts.

✗   (D) trashed   "Trashed" (damaged or wrecked) doesn't necessarily mean
                                            "on fire."

Paragraph 6	Comments
S1 Hitler's invasion took a somewhat different path to disaster.	Hitler's invasion: different path to disaster.
2 While Army Groups North and South succeeded in fulfilling their objectives, Hitler's Army Group Center was stopped about 15 miles short of Moscow by a Soviet counteroffensive.	Stopped short of Moscow.
3 Army Group Center successfully fended off the Soviets and survived the cold Russian winter, but had suffered heavy losses.	Survived winter but with heavy losses.
4 In 1942, German strategic objectives changed, and much of the strength of the invading force was redirected to southern Russia.	
5 The German advance to Moscow was thereby halted, and resounding defeats at the Battles of Stalingrad and Kursk permanently crippled the German war machine.	Defeats crippled German war machine.
6 It was only a matter of time before Soviet forces from the East and other Allied troops from the West could overwhelm and defeat Nazi Germany.	Just a matter of time before final defeat.

4

10.   The word "crippled" in the passage is closest in meaning to

VOCABULARY. "Cripple" = disable, impair, severely injure the functioning of something. This word is best used in a metaphorical way, as it is here. It can be considered offensive to describe a person this way.

✗   (A) surrendered

While these words might seem related, "crippled" is typically done *to* something (the army was impaired or injured) while "surrender" is a choice, even if under duress. "Surrender" = submit or stop fighting, stop resisting.

✗   (B) empowered

Opposite. "Empower" = give someone authority.

✓   (C) incapacitated

CORRECT. "Resounding defeats at the Battles of Stalingrad and Kursk permanently crippled the German war machine" = these defeats incapacitated (permanently impaired or weakened) the German war machine.

✗   (D) extinguished

Too extreme. "Extinguished" = completely destroyed, terminated, obliterated. But "crippled" means that the German war machine continued to limp along, incapacitated in many ways but not yet utterly destroyed.

Paragraph 3	**Comments**
S1 By contrast, Napoleon's invasion was based on a trade disagreement.	
2 **A** The real enemy of Napoleon was Britain, with whom France was at war, and his invasion of Russia was intended to force the Russian nobility to stop trading with Britain.	Placing the new sentence before S2 is confusing. No context has yet been given for why Britain is being discussed.
3 **B** His goal was to use his *grande armée* (French for "great army") to swiftly defeat the inferior Russian defending forces, march to Moscow, and force Tsar Alexander I to sign an agreement ceasing all trade with Britain.	**CORRECT.** S2 mentions Russia's trade with Britain. The new sentence explains why this trade angered Napoleon and articulates his intention to stop this trading. S3 then provides the specific plans and objectives for the invasion.
4-5 **C** This would culminate in Britain's inability to continue to wage war with France, Napoleon reasoned. Britain would have to seek peace, thereby ending the decade-long Napoleonic Wars.	Placement here puts the general intention (stop the shipments) *after* Napoleon's more specific plans in S3. This order makes less sense.
6 **D** Supposedly thus "fighting for an end to fighting," Napoleon's forces began the invasion on June 24, 1812, crossing the Neman River into Russia.	Likewise, placement here puts the general intention (stop the shipments) *after* Napoleon's more specific plans in S3–5. This order makes less sense.

11. **Napoleon correctly believed that the goods Russia was sending to Britain were helping Britain to wage war against France, and he felt it was imperative to stop these shipments.**

Where would the sentence best fit?

INSERT TEXT. This new sentence to insert provides more context as to why Russia's trade with Britain made Napoleon angry. So the sentence should come after the first mention of Russia's trade with Britain. Moreover, the new sentence also states that this anger became a broad intention: "he felt it was imperative to stop these shipments." So the sentence should come before Napoleon's specific plans, so that the broad intention can lead into those plans.

✗ (A) Choice A

✓ (B) Choice B   **CORRECT.**

✗ (C) Choice C

✗ (D) Choice D

Whole Passage	**Comments**
P1	On June 22, 1941, one year to the day after the signing of an armistice following his successful invasion of France, Adolf Hitler launched Operation Barbarossa …	Operation Barbarossa = Hitler's invasion of Russia in 1941. Similar to another failed invasion of Russia: Napoleon's. For both leaders, invasion = turning point that led to final defeat.
P2	Operation Barbarossa involved an invasion along three fronts …	Barbarossa: invasion on 3 fronts. Goal was annihilation. Why.
P3	By contrast, Napoleon's invasion was based on a trade disagreement …	Napoleon's invasion: different reason. Trade disagreement. Real enemy = Britain. Goal: force Russia to stop trading with Britain. Britain would seek peace.
P4	For each leader, the invasion had substantial initial success but ultimately met disaster …	Invasions succeeded at first but then failed. Various challenges.
P5	Unlike Hitler, Napoleon did successfully reach Moscow, only to find it ablaze and vacated …	Napoleon reached Moscow, but it was burning and empty. Starving & freezing army had to abandon Moscow. All-out retreat. Army was massacred by forces of nature.
P6	Hitler's invasion took a somewhat different path to disaster …	Hitler's invasion: different path to disaster. Stopped short of Moscow. Survived winter but with heavy losses. Defeats crippled German war machine. Just a matter of time before final defeat.

4

12. Select from the eight phrases below TWO that characterize Operation Barbarossa (Hitler's invasion) only, TWO that characterize Napoleon's invasion only, and THREE that characterize BOTH invasions. One of the phrases will NOT be used.

TABLE. Correct answers do not have to convey a main idea. They just have to be justified by the passage. Facts about each invasion are scattered throughout the passage. To complicate matters, three of the choices will relate to both Hitler's and Napoleon's invasions. One of the choices will relate to neither invasion.

| A | Succeeded in reaching Moscow |

NAPOLEON. P5 S1: "Unlike Hitler, Napoleon did successfully reach Moscow."

| B | Attempted to invade and conquer Ukraine |

BARBAROSSA. Invading and conquering Ukraine was a stated objective of Army Group South, according to P2 S4.

| C | Supply lines for the invading army became stretched thin |

BOTH. Mentioned for both in P4 S3: "Supply lines for both invading armies quickly became stretched thin."

| D | Met fierce Russian opposition |

BOTH. Mentioned in P4 S8: "By the end, invading troops met fierce Russian opposition."

| E | Army was destroyed in Moscow |

NEITHER. P5 S4–5 state that Napoleon's army was forced to leave Moscow before suffering its heaviest losses. According to P6 S5, Hitler never quite reached Moscow.

| F | Goal of invasion was annihilation |

BARBAROSSA. Mentioned in P2 S5 about Hitler's invasion. The goal was different for Napoleon (trade disagreement).

| G | Invasion was based on a trade disagreement |

NAPOLEON. Mentioned in P3 S1 about Napoleon's invasion, in contrast to Hitler's (annihilation).

| H | Failed to make appropriate provisions for winter warfare |

BOTH. Mentioned for both in P4 S6. "Russian winter is exceptionally cold, and both leaders failed to make appropriate provisions for winter warfare."

Answers and Explanations—4.5 The Kennewick Man

	Paragraph 1	**Comments**
S1	In 1996, while competing in a boating race in Columbia Park along the Columbia River near Kennewick, Washington, in the United States, Will Thomas stepped on something that felt like a large, round rock in the river bed.	
2	Upon inspection, this "rock" had teeth: Thomas had discovered a human skull.	Accidental discovery of a skull in Washington.
3	The bones of a nearly complete human skeleton were later unearthed at the site.	Almost a whole skeleton.
4	This accidental discovery of "The Kennewick Man" may shed new light on the development of the first human societies in North America.	"The Kennewick Man" may shed new light on first human societies in North America.

MANHATTAN PREP

1. According to paragraph 1, which of the following is true about the discovery of "The Kennewick Man"?

FACT. All of P1 discusses this discovery. The right answer must be supported in the text.

✗ (A) Its skeleton was discovered before the skull was found.

Opposite. S1–2: Will Thomas discovered the skull first. S3 says that the rest of the skeleton was "later unearthed."

✗ (B) It helped the first societies in North America to develop.

S4 states that the discovery may shed new light on the development of these societies, not help those societies to develop.

✗ (C) It was discovered after a purposeful search by an archaeologist.

Nothing in the paragraph indicates that Will Thomas, the finder of The Kennewick Man's skull, was an archaeologist, or that he was purposefully searching for the skull. In fact, the discovery appears to be accidental. At the time, the discoverer was "competing in a boating race."

✓ (D) At first, the finder thought he had stepped on a round rock.

CORRECT. S1: "Will Thomas stepped on something that felt like a large, round rock in the river bed."

2. The word "**inspection**" in the passage is closest in meaning to

VOCABULARY. "Inspection" = close look, examination, review of something (e.g., to form an opinion about it).

✗ (A) removal

Unrelated. "Removing" would mean taking it away.

✓ (B) scrutiny

CORRECT. "Upon inspection, this 'rock' had teeth" = upon scrutiny or a closer look, this supposed "rock" had teeth (it was actually a skull).

✗ (C) concealment

Opposite, or nearly so. "Concealment" = hiding or preventing something from being known.

✗ (D) deliberation

Unrelated. "Deliberation" = long and careful consideration or discussion.

4

	Paragraph 2	**Comments**
S1	Scientists have argued that the first humans came to North America during the last glacial period, or ice age, via "Beringia," commonly known as the Bering land bridge.	How humans came to North America during the last ice age: Beringia.
2	As in any glacial period, sea water levels were much lower than at other, more normal times; as a result, the waters of the present-day Bering Strait did not exist.	
3	Instead, present-day eastern Siberia in Russia and Alaska in North America were one continuous landmass.	Siberia and Alaska were connected by land.
4	Thus, possible human migration from Asia across this land bridge was unimpeded for thousands of years.	So human migration was possible across this land bridge.
5	It is known that at least several thousand humans migrated from Eastern Siberia to North America via Beringia during this time.	
6	The standard hypothesis has been that these migrators constituted a single group of people with a common ancestral background, and that they were the first humans to inhabit North America.	Standard hypothesis: a single migration of the first humans.
7	Indeed, evidence from many archaeological sites, including the original discovery in 1929 of ancient culture remains near Clovis, New Mexico, supports this "Clovis First" hypothesis.	Much evidence supports "Clovis First."

4

3. In paragraph 2, what does the author imply about the "Clovis First" hypothesis?

INFERENCE. S7 states that evidence discovered near Clovis, New Mexico, supports this "Clovis First" hypothesis. The only other hypothesis discussed in the paragraph is the "standard hypothesis" described in S6. Therefore, the "Clovis First" hypothesis must be the same as the standard hypothesis. According to S6, the standard hypothesis is that "these migrators constituted a single group of people with a common ancestral background, and that they were the first humans to inhabit North America."

✓ (A) It is synonymous with the standard hypothesis regarding migration to North America.

CORRECT. S7 begins with the word "indeed," suggesting that the contents of S7 support the ideas from the previous sentence. S6 tells what the "standard hypothesis" is. Together with the use of the word "this" in front of "Clovis First," the passage strongly suggests that the "Clovis First" hypothesis is the same as the standard hypothesis.

✗ (B) It suggests that most of the migrators to North America settled near present-day Clovis, New Mexico.

S7: "Indeed, evidence from many archaeological sites, including the original discovery in 1929 of ancient culture remains near Clovis, New Mexico." This suggests that Clovis was one of many sites producing evidence to support the "Clovis First" hypothesis. Nothing in the paragraph implies that most of the migrators to North America happened to settle at this one site, Clovis.

✗ (C) It suggests that some of the earliest settlers in North America migrated there in a manner other than by using Beringia.

Nothing in the paragraph even discusses alternate hypotheses about how migrations to North America happened.

✗ (D) It proposes that the first migration to North America likely consisted of people with multiple ancestral backgrounds.

Opposite. The standard hypothesis in S6 (which turns out to be the same as the "Clovis First" hypothesis in S7) is that the migration consisted of "a single group of people with a common ancestral background."

4

4.   According to paragraph 2, all of the following statements about the Bering land bridge migration are true EXCEPT:

NEGATIVE FACT. The entire paragraph discusses the Bering land bridge and hypotheses about migration patterns across it into North America. Three answer choices will be mentioned as relevant facts in P2. One answer choice will either be false or not discussed in the paragraph.

✗ (A) The land bridge only existed because an ice age was occurring at the time of the migrations.

S2: "the waters of the present-day Bering Strait did not exist" at the time because of the glacial period, or ice age.

✗ (B) The standard hypothesis states that this migration constituted the first arrival of human inhabitants in North America.

S6: "The standard hypothesis has been that these migrators … were the first humans to inhabit North America."

✓ (C) According to the standard hypothesis, the migration consisted of thousands of people over thousands of years in various groups.

CORRECT. The migration did consist of several thousand people (S5) and the bridge was "unimpeded for thousands of years" (S4). But according to S6: "The standard hypothesis has been that these migrators constituted a single group of people," not various groups.

✗ (D) It was made possible by the fact that Siberia and Alaska were, at the time, one single landmass.

S3–4: "present-day eastern Siberia in Russia and Alaska in North America were one continuous landmass. Thus, possible human migration from Asia across this land bridge was unimpeded for thousands of years."

4

5. Which of the sentences below best expresses the essential information in the highlighted sentence in paragraph 2? Incorrect choices change the meaning in important ways or leave out essential information.

SIMPLIFY SENTENCE. The first part of S2 states that sea water levels were lower than normal, as is usually the case during glacial periods. The second part states that as a result, the present-day waters of the Bering Strait didn't exist.

✗ (A) As in any glacial period, sea water levels were much lower than those of the Bering Strait normally at the time.

The Bering Strait did not exist at the time, so it is impossible for sea waters to be lower than "those of the Bering Strait normally at the time."

✗ (B) As in any glacial period, the waters of the present-day Bering Strait did not exist, leading to much lower sea water levels than normal at the time.

This choice reverses causality. Lower sea levels caused the Bering Strait not to exist, not the other way around.

✓ (C) The waters of the Bering Strait did not exist at that time because during any glacial period sea water levels are much lower than normal.

CORRECT. This choice says essentially the same thing as S2. The order of the ideas has been switched, but proper cause and effect have been preserved.

✗ (D) Sea water levels were much lower than during other, more normal glacial periods, so the waters of the present-day Bering Strait did not exist.

This version would be correct, except that it changes one very important idea. Nothing in the original sentence suggests that the glacial period in question led to "much lower" sea water levels than during other glacial periods. The comparison should be to more normal times, other than during glacial periods.

Paragraph 3	Comments
S1 New theories have emerged that the Beringia migration was not the only source of human migration to North America during the prehistoric period, and perhaps not even the first.	New theories: Beringia migration might not have been only, or first.
2 Advances in DNA testing have allowed scientists to group the discovered remains of Paleoamericans, or ancient Native Americans, according to five haplogroups, labeled A, B, C, D, and X.	
3 Among people in Northeast Asia and among Native Americans, haplogroups A, B, C, and D are all commonplace, supporting the theory of a single-migration model via Beringia.	Haplogroups found in Asia and among Native Americans support theory of single migration.
4 However, haplogroup X is different.	
5 It is found in only select locations in North America, and virtually does not exist in Siberia.	But haplogroup X is really only found in some places in North America.
6 Furthermore, genetic mutations among this haplogroup suggest that people in haplogroup X may have settled thousands of years earlier than populations from the other haplogroups.	And mutations suggest that X may have settled earlier.
7 This discovery gives weight to the possibility of earlier migrations to North America, possibly via coastal routes along the Pacific Ocean or even from Europe via the North Atlantic.	More support for possibility of earlier migrations.

6. The word "commonplace" in the passage is closest in meaning to

VOCABULARY. "Commonplace" = common, normal, unexceptional, frequently occurring.

✓ (A) unexceptional

CORRECT. "Haplogroups A, B, C, and D are all commonplace" = these haplogroups are all unexceptional, they're common.

✗ (B) reciprocal

Unrelated. "Reciprocal" = felt, done, or given in return.

✗ (C) parochial

"Parochial" = narrow-minded, provincial, only concerned with local matters. It is not a synonym for "commonplace."

✗ (D) extraordinary

Opposite.

7. Why does the author use the phrase "haplogroup X is different"?

PURPOSE. S3: "Among people in Northeast Asia and among Native Americans, haplogroups A, B, C, and D are all commonplace, supporting the theory of a single-migration model via Beringia." Then S4 indicates that "haplogroup X is different." The natural inference from this short, bold statement is that haplogroup X does not support the single-migration model. S5–7 provide more details.

✗ (A) To predict that new haplogroups will be discovered elsewhere in North America

Nothing in the paragraph discusses the possibility of new haplogroups being discovered.

✗ (B) To show that haplogroup X does not exist in Paleoamericans

S2: "Advances in DNA testing have allowed scientists to group the discovered remains of Paleoamericans ... according to five haplogroups, labeled A, B, C, D, and X." Although X exists only in "select locations in North America" (S5), it is not absent altogether.

✓ (C) To indicate that haplogroup X does not support the single-migration model

CORRECT. S4 provides a counterpoint to S3, in which the other haplogroups are said to support the single-migration model. S7 declares the end result: as a result of haplogroup X, there's more support for the possibility of earlier migrations.

✗ (D) To suggest that haplogroup X exhibits a greater rate of genetic mutations than other haplogroups

S6 states that "genetic mutations among this haplogroup suggest that people in haplogroup X may have settled thousands of years earlier than populations from the other haplogroups." However, this does not imply that mutations occur at a higher rate among haplogroup X than among other haplogroups.

8. The word "mutations" in the passage is closest in meaning to

VOCABULARY. "Mutations" = changes or transformations. Genetic mutations are particular kinds of changes to genetic material.

✗ (A) defections

This choice might be tempting as "defection" sounds like "defect," or an imperfection, however, mutations are not all defects. But a "defection" is deserting one's country, belief, or cause in favor of an opposing one. This is not related to mutation.

✗ (B) regulations

Unrelated. "Regulations" = a rule or directive.

✗ (C) inhibitions

Unrelated. "Inhibition" = restraining or prohibiting a behavior or action.

✓ (D) transformations

CORRECT. "Genetic mutations among this haplogroup" = genetic transformations or changes among this haplogroup.

Paragraph 4	**Comments**
S1 The Kennewick Man may help resolve these competing theories.	Kennewick Man may help resolve.
2 Anthropological analysis and carbon-dating techniques show that the skeleton is approximately 9,000 years old, but that the skeleton is distinctly different from most other Paleoamerican remains.	Different from most other Paleoamerican remains.
3 The Kennewick Man had a relatively small face with a long, narrow skull.	
4 In contrast, Paleoamericans and modern Native Americans tend to have larger faces with shorter, broader skulls and **prominent** cheekbones.	
5 Also, resin models of other important bones indicate key differences in size and structure from those of other Paleoamericans.	
6 Indeed, of all current peoples, the Kennewick Man possessed physical attributes most similar to Polynesians.	Most similar to Polynesians.
7 Present-day Polynesians, in turn, are most likely descended from the ancient Jōmon, the original inhabitants of the Japanese islands, who may have come into existence well over 15,000 years ago.	Polynesians probably descended from Jōmon people.

4

9. The word "**prominent**" in the passage is closest in meaning to

   ✓   (A) pronounced

   ✗   (B) flat

   ✗   (C) unfamiliar

   ✗   (D) unassuming

VOCABULARY. "Prominent" = obvious, noticeable, or even physically protruding. It can also mean famous or distinguished.

CORRECT. "Larger faces with ... prominent cheekbones" = larger faces with pronounced or noticeable cheekbones.

Opposite. Flat cheekbones would not be prominent, in the physical sense of "protruding."

Unrelated. "Unfamiliar" = not known or recognized.

Nearly opposite. "Unassuming" = modest, inconspicuous, not willing to stick out.

10. Which of the following can be inferred from paragraph 4 about the relationship between the Kennewick Man and the Jōmon people?

INFERENCE. S6–7: "The Kennewick Man possessed physical attributes most similar to Polynesians. Present-day Polynesians, in turn, are most likely descended from the ancient Jōmon."

✗ Ⓐ His physical features suggest that the Kennewick Man likely descended, not from the Jōmon, but from Polynesians.

S6 notes that the Kennewick Man's physical attributes are most similar to those of present-day Polynesians. However, S7 states that Polynesians were themselves most likely descendants of the Jōmon. So the Kennewick Man likely has a genetic connection to the Jōmon.

✓ Ⓑ Physical attributes of the Kennewick Man suggest that he may be a descendant of the Jōmon.

CORRECT. S6–7 link the Kennewick Man to Polynesians and in turn to the Jōmon people. Thus, based on the Kennewick Man's facial features, he may have descended from the Jōmon tribe.

✗ Ⓒ The 6,000-year gap between the birth of the Jōmon and the Kennewick Man indicates little connection between the two.

There is roughly a 6,000-year gap, or greater, between the two. The Kennewick Man is 9,000 years old (S2), whereas the Jōmon "may have come into existence well over 15,000 years ago" (S7). But this gap in time doesn't mean that the two are unconnected.

✗ Ⓓ Key differences in size and structure differentiate the Kennewick Man from his ancestral Jōmon people.

The "key differences in size and structure" mentioned in S5 apply to the comparison between the Kennewick Man and other Paleoamericans, not between the Kennewick Man and the Jōmon.

4

	Paragraph 5	**Comments**
S1	The Jōmon culture is known to have been dependent upon the oceans for survival, building primitive boats out of wood and using them for deep-sea fishing and exploration.	Jōmon used boats.
2	If new theories are correct, the Jōmon may have sailed along the coastline of Beringia, from Asia to Alaska, with plenty of natural resources available to support the journey.	They may have sailed along the coastline from Asia to Alaska, before the Beringia migration.
3	This ocean-based journey could have occurred before the migration across the Bering land bridge, with small Jōmon civilizations developing along the Pacific coast.	
4	Later, when the land-based migrators made their crossing, the resulting populations could have overwhelmed the established Jōmon population, eventually resulting in the societies that constitute the ancestors of modern Native Americans.	Later, that migration may have overwhelmed the Jōmon.

11. The word "overwhelmed" in the passage is closest in meaning to

   ✗ (A) undermined

   ✓ (B) overpowered

   ✗ (C) resisted

   ✗ (D) captivated

VOCABULARY. "Overwhelm" = overcome, overpower, conquer.

Not strong enough. "Undermine" = weaken, destabilize.

CORRECT. "The resulting populations could have overwhelmed the established Jōmon population" = the resulting populations could have overpowered the established Jōmon.

"Resist" conveys the concept of opposition, but it doesn't convey victory (and crushing defeat for the other side as "overwhelm" does.

"Captivate" = enchant, charm, fascinate. It does not mean to take someone captive in a literal sense.

12. According to paragraph 5, which of the following statements is true of Jōmon people?

   ✗ (A) They were native to the Pacific coast of North America.

   ✗ (B) They probably migrated to North America by crossing over the Bering land bridge.

   ✗ (C) If they sailed along the coastline of Beringia, they likely encountered a dearth of resources along the way.

   ✓ (D) They built wooden boats for fishing and exploration of the open seas.

FACT. Most of the paragraph discusses Jōmon people and culture. The correct answer needs direct support from the text.

Their origin is not described in this paragraph, although P4 says that they were the original inhabitants of the Japanese Islands. They may have migrated to the Pacific coast of North America via the coast of Beringia, but they were not native to that place.

S2 states that if the Jōmon culture did indeed migrate to North America, it likely would have done so by sailing along the coastline, not migrating over land.

Opposite. S2: "the Jōmon may have sailed along the coastline of Beringia, from Asia to Alaska, with plenty of natural resources available to support the journey." "Dearth" = lack, shortage, not enough of something.

CORRECT. S1 states that the Jōmon built boats out of wood and used them for deep-sea fishing and exploration.

Paragraph 4	**Comments**

S1–2 The Kennewick Man may help resolve these competing theories. Anthropological analysis and carbon dating techniques show that the skeleton is approximately 9,000 years old, but that the skeleton is distinctly different from most other Paleoamerican remains.

3–4 **A** The Kennewick Man had a relatively small face with a long, narrow skull. In contrast, Paleoamericans and modern Native Americans tend to have larger faces with shorter, broader skulls and prominent cheekbones.

> The Jōmon have not yet been introduced in the passage.

5–6 **B** Also, resin models of other important bones indicate key differences in size and structure from those of other Paleoamericans. Indeed, of all current peoples, the Kennewick Man possessed physical attributes most similar to Polynesians.

> The Jōmon have not yet been introduced in the passage.

7 **C** Present-day Polynesians, in turn, are most likely descended from the ancient Jōmon, the original inhabitants of the Japanese islands, who may have come into existence well over 15,000 years ago.

> The Jōmon have not yet been introduced in the passage.

End **D**

> **CORRECT.** The Jōmon have finally been introduced in the preceding sentence. The new conclusion is properly drawn after all the preceding evidence has been presented.

4

13. **This lends credence to the claim that the Kennewick Man may provide the first concrete evidence that members of the Jōmon people migrated to North America.**

Where would the sentence best fit?

INSERT TEXT. The new sentence begins with "This lends credence to (= this supports) the claim that …" So the previous sentence or sentences should lead to the claim or conclusion presented in this sentence. This claim is that the Kennewick Man (the primary subject of the passage) may provide evidence of Jōmon migration to North America. That's a big claim, so it should have sufficient prior support. A good clue to the proper position of the new sentence is the specialized term "Jōmon." This term must be introduced in the text before the insertion point, or the new sentence doesn't make sense as written.

✗ (A) Choice A

✗ (B) Choice B

✗ (C) Choice C

✓ (D) Choice D   **CORRECT.**

	Whole Passage	**Comments**
P1	In 1996, while competing in a boating race in Columbia Park along the Columbia River near Kennewick, Washington …	Accidental discovery of a skull in Washington. Almost a whole skeleton. "The Kennewick Man" may shed new light on first human societies in North America.
P2	Scientists have argued that the first humans came to North America during the last glacial period …	How humans came to North America during the last ice age: Beringia. Siberia and Alaska were connected by land. So human migration was possible across this land bridge. Standard hypothesis: a single migration of the first humans. Much evidence supports "Clovis First."
P3	New theories have emerged that the Beringia migration was not the only source of human migration to North America …	New theories: Beringia migration might not have been only, or first. Haplogroups found in Asia and among Native Americans support theory of single migration. But haplogroup X is really only found in some places in North America. And mutations suggest that X may have settled earlier. More support for possibility of earlier migrations.
P4	The Kennewick Man may help resolve these competing theories …	Kennewick Man may help resolve. Different from most other Paleoamerican remains. Most similar to Polynesians. Polynesians probably descended from Jōmon people.
P5	The Jomon culture is known to have been dependent upon the oceans for survival …	Jōmon used boats. They may have sailed along the coastline from Asia to Alaska, before the Beringia migration. Later, that migration may have overwhelmed the Jōmon.

4

14. **The discovery of the Kennewick Man has called into question long-standing theories about the migration patterns of the first human inhabitants of North America.**

SUMMARY. Correct answers must be clearly expressed in the passage. They must also be among the major points of the passage. They should tie as directly as possible to the summary given.

✗ [A] The Kennewick Man was recently discovered by accident in the river bed of the Columbia River near Kennewick, Washington.

Directly mentioned in P1. But this is a minor detail in the context of the passage as a whole.

✓ [B] The standard hypothesis has held that the first inhabitants of North America migrated there during the last ice age via a landmass located where the Bering Strait now lies.

CORRECT. P2 discusses this important conventional hypothesis at length.

✓ [C] New DNA analysis techniques have shown that while some genetic markers can be found in both Northeast Asia and Native American tribes, haplogroup X follows a different pattern.

CORRECT. P3 discusses this important finding and its implications.

✓ [D] The Kennewick Man's skeleton reveals physical features that are similar to those of Polynesians, who likely descended from the Jōmon people.

CORRECT. P4 discusses these facts as important evidence for a possible alternative source of early migrations to North America.

✗ [E] The Jōmon culture is known by anthropologists to have made use of wooden boats for both fishing and exploration.

Introduced at the beginning of P5. But this is actually a minor detail in the context of the passage as a whole. It does support the larger point that the Jōmon could have had outposts in North America. But many cultures have made use of wooden boats. By itself, this fact is not a main idea of the passage.

✗ [F] The Kennewick Man had a larger face and a shorter, broader skull with more prominent cheekbones than most Paleoamericans.

Not true. According to P4 S3, the Kennewick Man had a much smaller face and a longer, more narrow skull.

4

Answers and Explanations—4.6 Harriet Tubman

Paragraph 1	Comments
P1 S1 In April 2016, the United States Treasury Department announced that Harriet Tubman (1822–1913) would replace Andrew Jackson on the front of the $20 bill.	Harriet Tubman will appear on the US $20 bill.
2 This made her the first woman in over 100 years, and the first African American ever, to appear on paper currency issued by the United States.	Historic firsts.
3 This move was controversial, but Treasury Secretary Jacob Lew steadfastly supported the change, making it clear that he felt Tubman's life and accomplishments deserved to be celebrated.	Controversial, but Treasury Secretary was steadfast (= unwavering).
4 Indeed, while Tubman was a well-known anti-slavery activist, few people outside of the academic world are aware of the extent of her efforts and suffering to help bring about the abolition of slavery.	Few know the extent of her efforts to bring about end of slavery.
5 Perhaps this lack of modern-day awareness is best exemplified by the shortage of common knowledge about her efforts as a scout and spy supporting the Combahee River Raid during the American Civil War.	For instance, there's a shortage of common knowledge about her efforts to support a particular raid during the Civil War.

Paragraph 2	Comments
P2 S1 Harriet Tubman was born into slavery in southeastern Maryland.	Born into slavery.
2 Like most slave children, she was subject to violent punishment by her owners—even if no wrongdoing had been committed.	
3 She suffered a severe head injury at age 12 when a metal object was thrown by an owner at a slave he was attempting to punish.	Severe head injury in childhood.
4 The object struck Tubman instead.	
5 She suffered greatly for the rest of her life as a result of this injury, with frequent severe headaches, vertigo, seizures, and extreme drowsiness.	Resulted in health problems for the rest of her life.

1.   Which of the sentences below best expresses the essential information in the highlighted sentence in paragraph 1? Incorrect choices change the meaning in important ways or leave out essential information.

✗   (A) Feeling that Tubman's accomplishments deserved celebration, Secretary Lew supported the controversy over putting Tubman on the $20 bill.

✗   (B) Despite claims that Tubman's accomplishments deserved to be celebrated, Secretary Lew called the move to put Tubman on the $20 bill controversial.

✓   (C) Secretary Lew maintained his support for the controversial move to put Tubman on the $20 bill, which he felt celebrated her accomplishments deservedly.

✗   (D) Secretary Lew's support for putting Tubman on the $20 bill was made clear by the controversy around the move, but he felt her accomplishments deserved celebration.

SIMPLIFY SENTENCE. The first part of S3 states that the decision to put Harriet Tubman on the $20 bill was controversial. The second part states that Secretary Lew strongly supported the change, and it explains why he felt this way.

This sentence changes the meaning in a very important way. Lew supported the change itself, not the controversy behind this change.

The original version doesn't say that Lew was the one calling the move controversial. Moreover, this version *doesn't* clearly attribute to him what the original does: the claims that Tubman's accomplishments deserve recognition.

CORRECT. This version captures the core meaning of the original, while appropriately simplifying language (e.g., just mentioning "accomplishments" instead of "life and accomplishments").

The controversy was not what made Lew's support clear. He made it clear himself. The first part of the sentence (before the "but") does not match the original's meaning.

2.   It can be inferred from paragraph 1 that between 1916 and 2016

✗   (A) an African-American person appeared on United States paper currency

✗   (B) several women appeared on United States paper currency

✓   (C) no African-American woman appeared on United States paper currency

✗   (D) no bills other than the $20 bill were updated

INFERENCE. S2 is the only sentence to refer to "100 years," so the correct inference should be related to this sentence.

S2 states that no African American, male or female, has ever appeared on US paper currency.

S2: "This made her the first woman in over 100 years, and the first African American ever, to appear on paper currency issued by the United States."

CORRECT. S2: "This made her the first woman in over 100 years, and the first African American ever, to appear on paper currency issued by the United States."

There is no information about bills other than the $20 bill.

3. Which of the following best describes the relation of paragraph 1 to paragraph 2?

PURPOSE. P1 introduces Harriet Tubman, mentioning her forthcoming appearance on the US $20 bill. P1 also sets up a question for the passage to answer eventually: What were her extensive but little-known efforts to bring about the end of slavery? P2 pivots from these generalities about Harriet Tubman to specific descriptions of the early part of Tubman's life.

✗ (A) Paragraph 2 explains why the historical figure introduced in paragraph 1 deserves to be honored at a national level.

P2 provides certain tragic details of Tubman's life. But these details do not explain why Tubman deserves the national honors described in P1. This explanation comes later in the passage.

✗ (B) Paragraph 2 outlines the life and accomplishments of the historical figure who is introduced and celebrated in paragraph 1.

P2 starts to outline Tubman's life, but it does not mention any of her accomplishments, which are described generally in P1.

✗ (C) Paragraph 2 discusses reasons for a decision made about the historical figure who is introduced in paragraph 1.

Both of these topics are discussed in P1 only. The decision is about putting Tubman on the $20 bill. P2 is pure historical biography.

✓ (D) Paragraph 2 initiates a biography of the historical figure introduced in modern, general terms in paragraph 1.

CORRECT. P1 introduces the figure of Harriet Tubman by mentioning a modern-day fact about her: she will appear on the US $20 bill. P1 then makes general points about Tubman. P2 switches to a historical, biographical narrative, starting with Tubman's birth.

4. The word "exemplified" in the passage is closest in meaning to

VOCABULARY. "Exemplify" = show, illustrate, be an example of.

✗ (A) broadcast

Not quite. "Broadcast" = announce widely (especially via the media).

✗ (B) excused

This lack of awareness is not "excused" (forgiven).

✓ (C) illustrated

CORRECT. "This lack of modern-day awareness is best exemplified by the shortage of common knowledge about her efforts" = this lack of awareness is best illustrated or shown by the fact that few people know about her efforts (as a scout and a spy).

✗ (D) disguised

Opposite. This lack of awareness is not "disguised" (hidden).

Paragraph 3	**Comments**
S1 Tubman escaped enslavement in 1849, fleeing to Philadelphia about 150 miles to the north, where slavery was banned.	
2 Her freedom secured, she quickly made it her life's mission to support the abolitionist movement in any way she could.	Once she escaped slavery, she threw herself into supporting abolition.
3 She started by returning to Maryland to free her own family.	Freed her own family, then others.
4 Later, she continued this work, helping relatives, friends, and eventually any slave she could to flee to the North.	
5 After passage of the Fugitive Slave Act of 1850, assisting slaves who were attempting to escape **custody** became a serious criminal offense throughout the United States.	New law made this work criminal and dangerous.
6 This made Tubman's difficult work even more perilous.	
7 However, she continued it successfully—now, she would have to help escaped slaves flee all the way to Canada, all the while risking being arrested herself.	But she continued successfully.

5. The word "custody" in the passage is closest in meaning to

VOCABULARY. In the context of law enforcement, "custody" = captivity, imprisonment, detention. It can also mean having responsibility for a child.

✗ (A) liberty

Opposite. "Liberty" = a state of being free.

✗ (B) authority

Not quite. "Authority" = power to act or command. Especially in the plural form "the authorities," the word can also mean people who have authority in some way. But it is not a synonym for "custody."

✗ (C) encirclement

Not quite. "Encirclement" = barrier or obstacle that surrounds something, or the act of putting up such a barrier. While encirclements may be used to keep people in custody, it is not a synonym for "custody."

✓ (D) captivity

CORRECT. "Slaves who were attempting to escape custody" = slaves who were attempting to escape captivity, to escape being held against their will.

6. According to paragraph 3, the Fugitive Slave Act of 1850 made Tubman's work more dangerous because

FACT. S5 discusses this act. S6: "This made Tubman's difficult work even more perilous."

✓ (A) it made aiding slaves attempting to escape a criminal offense

CORRECT. S5: "After passage of the Fugitive Slave Act of 1850, assisting slaves who were attempting to escape custody became a serious criminal offense throughout the United States." This is what made her work more dangerous.

✗ (B) if she were caught, Tubman could be forced back into slavery

S5 clearly states that the act made her work a serious criminal offense. But the paragraph never claims that, as punishment for this crime, Tubman could be forced back into slavery.

✗ (C) slavery had not yet been banned in Philadelphia

S1 states that slavery had already been banned in Philadelphia.

✗ (D) it made it more difficult to return to Maryland to free her family and relatives

According to S3 and S4, one of Tubman's first acts in fighting slavery was to return to Maryland to free her own family, and then she freed other relatives. However, the paragraph implies that all this occurred before the Fugitive Slave Act of 1850. Also, this choice does not explain why the Fugitive Slave Act made her work more dangerous.

4

Paragraph 4	Comments
S1 In the late 1850s, she became more deeply involved with radical abolition efforts, helping John Brown plan his failed attack on the federal arsenal at Harpers Ferry in 1859.	Got more involved in radical efforts.
2 When the American Civil War broke out in 1861, Tubman immediately joined the Union army, as she felt that Union victory would almost certainly end slavery.	Civil War: she joined the Union army.
3 At first, she worked as a cook and field nurse, but later became involved in scouting and intelligence gathering.	Became a scout, gathered intelligence.
4 In January 1863, President Abraham Lincoln issued his Emancipation Proclamation, a wartime measure that freed slaves from bondage.	
5 Despite this, many African Americans remained in captivity in the South, as the slave owners there continued to rebel against Lincoln and the North.	
6 Because of her widespread reputation for anti-slavery work, Tubman was able to learn critical information from slaves still in bondage in exchange for helping them to freedom.	She learned critical information from slaves still in bondage.
7 The success of the Combahee River Raid in South Carolina in June 1863 is largely due to her effectiveness in gaining knowledge about the location of Confederate defensive positions.	Example: successful raid. She found out where the defenses were.
8 Tubman was able to help the Union gunboats avoid ambushes as they navigated the river, simultaneously guiding the ships to locations along the riverbank where runaway slaves awaited rescue.	
9 In total, over 700 slaves were rescued by the boats, and the military objective was achieved: numerous plantations owned by prominent secessionists were raided and destroyed, with the newly rescued slaves assisting the Union soldiers.	

4

7. According to paragraph 4, all of the following statements about Harriet Tubman's involvement with the Union Army are true EXCEPT:

NEGATIVE FACT. Three answer choices will be found in P4, which describes Tubman's involvement with the Union Army from S2 onward. One answer choice will not be found in P4. It could be false or just unsupported.

✓ (A) She questioned plantation owners to learn Confederate defenses.

CORRECT. S7: "The success of the Combahee River Raid … is largely due to her effectiveness in gaining knowledge about the location of Confederate defensive positions." However, she gained this information from slaves she helped to freedom. Nothing is mentioned in the paragraph about her questioning plantation owners.

✗ (B) She helped slaves escape from bondage in the South.

S5: "many African Americans remained in captivity in the South." S6: "Tubman was able to learn critical information from slaves still in bondage in exchange for helping them to freedom."

✗ (C) At first, she worked as a cook, but then became a scout.

S3: "At first, she worked as a cook … but later became involved in scouting."

✗ (D) She helped Union troops avoid potentially deadly traps.

S8: "Tubman was able to help the Union gunboats avoid ambushes as they navigated the river."

8. In paragraph 4, the author mentions Harriet Tubman's "widespread reputation for anti-slavery work" in order to

PURPOSE. S6 gives this phrase as a reason why Harriet Tubman was able to gather information from slaves to help the Union Army. They helped her "because of" her reputation.

✗ (A) predict that some people would oppose her efforts

In most cases of intelligence gathering during wartime, there will be people who oppose that effort. However, the author mentions Tubman's reputation to describe how it helped her overcome difficulties in gathering intelligence, rather than to indicate that some people might oppose her.

✓ (B) clarify that strangers knew of her and were willing to help her

CORRECT. S6: "Because of her widespread reputation for anti-slavery work, Tubman was able to learn critical information from slaves still in bondage." This indicates that some people who were initially strangers were aware of her because of her "widespread reputation." As a result of this reputation, they were more willing to help her.

✗ (C) demonstrate that not every Southern slave owner was her adversary

Nothing in the paragraph mentions slave owners who were not opposed to Tubman. "Adversary" = enemy, opponent.

✗ (D) explore the reasons many slaves remained in bondage

S5: "many African Americans remained in captivity in the South." But the mention of Tubman's reputation does not shed light on why this captivity continued.

9.   The phrase "intelligence gathering" in the passage is closest in meaning to

VOCABULARY. "Intelligence gathering"= collecting facts or news (especially on military opponents), investigating, scouting. In this context, the word "intelligence" is closer to "information" in meaning than it is to "intellect, brainpower" (how it is typically used).

✓ (A) conducting reconnaissance

CORRECT. "She … later became involved in scouting and intelligence gathering" = she later became involved in conducting reconnaissance. "Reconnaissance" = exploration for information, scouting.

✗ (B) attaining wisdom

Not quite. "Attaining wisdom" implies that Tubman herself reached a level of deep knowledge and general insight. "Gathering intelligence" refers to collecting important details and facts, often about a military enemy.

✗ (C) finding artifacts

"Artifacts" = physical objects made by humans in the past and left behind, generally with some cultural or historical significance. Tubman was not finding historical, physical artifacts. She was finding out current information, intangible but important to active military operations.

✗ (D) recruiting collaborators

Tubman was involved in recruiting collaborators among slaves still in captivity. In fact, the help they gave her was often in the form of intelligence about military matters. But "recruiting collaborators" is not synonymous with "intelligence gathering."

10.   According to paragraph 4, which of the following was true of many slaves in the South after the Emancipation Proclamation?

FACT. S4 mentions the Emancipation Proclamation as an 1863 "wartime measure that freed slaves from bondage." The rest of the paragraph describes slaves in the South several times.

✗ (A) They inadvertently helped defeat the Union army during the Combahee River Raid.

Opposite. S7–9 note that slaves helped the Union army win by giving critical information to Tubman and the Union army. Slaves also fought during the raid.

✗ (B) They were willingly set free by their owners in response to the Emancipation Proclamation.

Opposite. S4: "In January 1863, President Abraham Lincoln issued his Emancipation Proclamation." S5: "Despite this, many African Americans remained in captivity in the South, as the slave owners there continued to rebel."

✗ (C) They were skeptical about sharing information that could pose risks to their personal safety.

Opposite to at least some degree. S6: "Because of her widespread reputation for anti-slavery work, Tubman was able to learn critical information from slaves still in bondage in exchange for helping them to freedom." Sharing this information was certainly personally risky for these slaves, who would have been punished, harmed, or even killed by their owners in response.

✓ (D) They helped destroy a number of prominent plantations during the Combahee River Raid.

CORRECT. S9: "numerous plantations owned by prominent secessionists were raided and destroyed, with the newly rescued slaves assisting the Union soldiers."

Paragraph 5	Comments
S1 After the war ended in 1865, slavery had been completely abolished in the United States.	
2 Tubman retired to her property in upstate New York and tended to her family and personal affairs for several decades.	After the war, Tubman retired, focused on family for decades.
3 Later in life, she would continue her humanitarian work in different arenas.	Later she continued humanitarian work.
4 She became involved with the women's suffrage movement, fighting for women's right to vote, and she worked with the African Methodist church to provide assistance to elderly, poverty-stricken African Americans.	

11. The word "humanitarian" in the passage is closest in meaning to

VOCABULARY. "Humanitarian" = charitable, public-spirited, demonstrating particular compassion or care for humanity.

✗ (A) revolutionary

Not quite. Tubman's work was both humanitarian and revolutionary in many ways. But in general, humanitarian work does not have to be revolutionary, and revolutionary work does not have to be humanitarian.

✓ (B) charitable

CORRECT. "She would continue her humanitarian work in different arenas" = she would continue her charitable work helping others in different ways.

✗ (C) anthropological

"Anthropological" refers to the study of human cultures and development.

✗ (D) clandestine

"Clandestine" = secret, undercover.

12. According to paragraph 5, which of the following statements was true of Harriet Tubman after the war?

FACT. S2–4 provide an overview of Tubman's life after the war.

✗ (A) She continued to help slaves escape from bondage.

S1 makes it clear that slavery had ended. So this type of help was no longer needed.

✗ (B) She became a politician in upstate New York.

S2 mentions that Tubman moved to upstate New York after the war. S4 also describes how she became active in at least one political cause (the women's suffrage movement). But nothing in the paragraph mentions her becoming a politician.

✓ (C) She fought for women to gain the right to vote.

CORRECT. S4: "She became involved with the women's suffrage movement, fighting for women's right to vote."

✗ (D) She immediately began doing other kinds of socially oriented work.

S2–3: "Tubman retired to her property in upstate New York and tended to her family and personal affairs for several decades. Later in life, she would continue her humanitarian work in different arenas." That is, she did not begin doing socially oriented work right away after the war.

  MANHATTAN PREP

Paragraph 5	Comments
S1 After the war ended in 1865, slavery had been completely abolished in the United States.	
2 **A** Tubman retired to her property in upstate New York and tended to her family and personal affairs for several decades.	The new sentence almost fits in this position, but not quite. The "during this time" part might be forced to fit, but "in retreat" makes no sense here. It seems as if the author is talking about the retreat of slavery. But what is meant is retirement or seclusion from the world.
3 **B** Later in life, she would continue her humanitarian work in different arenas.	**CORRECT.** With the new sentence in this position, the phrase "during this time" cleanly refers to "several decades" after the war, while Tubman tended to her family in upstate New York. The phrase "in retreat" indicates Tubman's retirement from worldly matters, as described in S2. The meaning of the new sentence reinforces that of S2.
4 **C** She became involved with the women's suffrage movement, fighting for women's right to vote, and she worked with the African Methodist church to provide assistance to elderly, poverty-stricken African Americans.	Placing the new sentence here directly contradicts the previous sentence, S3, which moves the narrative forward to Tubman's return to humanitarian work.
End **D**	Likewise, placing the new sentence here contradicts the previous two sentences (S3–4), which describe Tubman's return to humanitarian work later in life.

13. **During this time in retreat, Tubman was much less active in public efforts of a political or benevolent nature.**

Where would the sentence best fit?

INSERT TEXT. The new sentence begins with "during this time in retreat." So the previous sentence should refer to actions that occur at the same time as those in the inserted sentence. The previous sentence should also clarify what "in retreat" means. It should refer to a withdrawal by Tubman from public affairs. According to the new sentence, Tubman was "much less active in public efforts." That statement should agree with the prior sentence.

✗ Ⓐ Choice A

✓ Ⓑ Choice B   **CORRECT.**

✗ Ⓒ Choice C

✗ Ⓓ Choice D

Whole Passage	**Comments**
P1 In April 2016, the United States Treasury Department announced that Harriet Tubman …	Harriet Tubman will appear on the US $20 bill. Historic firsts. Controversial, but Treasury Secretary was steadfast (= unwavering). Few know the extent of her efforts to bring about end of slavery. For instance, there's a shortage of common knowledge about her efforts to support a particular raid during the Civil War.
P2 Harriet Tubman was born into slavery in southeastern Maryland …	Born into slavery. Severe head injury in childhood. Resulted in health problems for the rest of her life.
P3 Tubman escaped enslavement in 1849, fleeing to Philadelphia about 150 miles to the north …	Once she escaped slavery, she threw herself into supporting abolition. Freed her own family, then others. New law made this work criminal and dangerous. But she continued successfully.
P4 In the late 1850s, she became more deeply involved with radical abolition efforts …	Got more involved in radical efforts. Civil War: she joined the Union army. Became a scout, gathered intelligence. She learned critical information from slaves still in bondage. Example: successful raid. She found out where the defenses were.
P5 After the war ended in 1865, slavery had been completely abolished in the United States …	After the war, Tubman retired, focused on family for decades. Later, she continued humanitarian work.

4

14.   **The decision to celebrate Harriet Tubman by putting her on the United States $20 bill honors her not only for her well-known efforts to free slaves but also for her less well-known efforts in the Union army to end slavery.**

SUMMARY. Correct answers must be clearly expressed in the passage. They must also be among the major points of the passage. They should tie as directly as possible to the summary given.

✓ A   Born into slavery, Tubman overcame considerable adversity to free herself and later to help others do the same.

CORRECT. P2–3 discuss these events in Tubman's life in detail.

✓ B   Tubman worked as a scout during the American Civil War, gathering critical information for the Union army.

CORRECT. P4 discusses these efforts by Tubman during the Civil War.

✗ C   Tubman is the first African American to appear on United States paper currency, but she is not the first woman.

P1 mentions the first fact and implies the second. But these are relatively minor details, mentioned only to highlight the particular honor being accorded to Tubman.

✗ D   Upon joining the Union army, Tubman first worked as a cook and as a field nurse during the Civil War.

This fact is mentioned in P4. But it is a minor detail, one that doesn't much support the main point about Tubman's extraordinary accomplishments.

✗ E   The Fugitive Slave Act, which criminalized assistance offered to slaves attempting to free themselves, was passed in 1850.

The Fugitive Slave Act upped the stakes for Tubman, making her work more dangerous. But the particular date is not so important. The passage of this act is only a supporting detail in the context of this passage.

✓ F   Tubman played a pivotal role in the successful Combahee River Raid, uncovering hidden defenses and rescuing hundreds of slaves.

CORRECT. Foreshadowed in P1 as one of Tubman's less well-known efforts to actually end slavery. The raid is described dramatically in P4.

Answers and Explanations—4.7 The Sphinx

	Paragraph 1	**Comments**
S1	The Sphinx, a mythical creature with a lion's body and human head, has become inextricably linked with ancient Egyptian culture, undoubtedly because of the fame of the Great Sphinx of Giza in Egypt.	Sphinx = linked with ancient Egypt.
2	However, in reality, sphinx-like creatures were prominent in many ancient cultures worldwide.	But prominent in many ancient cultures.
3	The sphinx's ubiquity and the relative constancy of its meaning and legend in many cultures points to a human commonality whose spread extends far beyond Giza and the Sahara Desert.	Some kind of human commonality.

1. According to paragraph 1, all of the following were true about sphinxes EXCEPT:

NEGATIVE FACT. S1 describes the association of sphinxes with Egypt. S2–3 mention their presence in many cultures. Three answer choices will be present in these sentences. One will not be.

✗ (A) Sphinxes had characteristics of both humans and other animals.

S1: "a mythical creature with a lion's body and human head."

✗ (B) In ancient times, sphinxes played a not insignificant role in cultures outside of Egypt.

S2: "sphinx-like creatures were prominent in many ancient cultures worldwide."

✓ (C) The Great Sphinx of Giza in Egypt is the first known example of its kind.

CORRECT. The paragraph never mentions or implies that the Great Sphinx was the first of its kind. Furthermore, the second paragraph says that it was not.

✗ (D) The symbolic meaning of sphinxes was roughly similar in several cultures.

S3: "the relative constancy of its meaning and legend in many cultures."

Paragraph 2	Comments
S1 The Egyptian sphinx sported a male human head and was apparently considered a **benevolent** god, although one that possessed great strength.	Characteristics of Egyptian sphinx.
2 As in many other cultures, sphinxes often guarded temple entrances.	
3 The famous Great Sphinx is generally not thought to be the oldest such Egyptian statue; many, but not all, scholars believe that one depicting Queen Hetepheres II, built in approximately 2600 BCE, is probably the oldest in Egypt.	Age of various sphinxes (old!).
4 However, further north in present-day Turkey, Neolithic sphinx-like figures dating to 9500 BCE have been found.	

4

2.   The author mentions present-day Turkey in paragraph 2 in order to

PURPOSE. S3 states that the Great Sphinx in Egypt is not the oldest sphinx in Egypt. The sentence goes on to name what is thought to be the oldest sphinx there. S4 points out that, in fact, there are far older sphinxes elsewhere in the world (namely, in what is now Turkey). This is the reason why present-day Turkey is mentioned.

✗   (A) indicate why the Great Sphinx is the oldest such Egyptian statue

S3 states that the Great Sphinx is *not* thought to be the oldest such Egyptian statue.

✓   (B) highlight the fact that there are even older sphinxes in the world than Egyptian ones

CORRECT. S4 states that some sphinxes found in what is present-day Turkey are far older than any found in Egypt.

✗   (C) emphasize the broad geographic spread of sphinxes in the ancient world

S4 does say "further north in present-day Turkey." But the purpose is not to argue how widespread sphinxes were in antiquity. Rather, the author mentions this particular example in order to make the point that sphinxes date back even further than S3 describes, to thousands of years before the oldest Egyptian sphinx.

✗   (D) point out the difference between sphinx-like figures and true sphinxes

S4 does not make any distinction between "sphinx-like figures" and any other kind of sphinx.

3.   Which of the sentences below best expresses the essential information in the highlighted sentence in paragraph 2? Incorrect choices change the meaning in important ways or leave out essential information.

SIMPLIFY SENTENCE. S3 discusses scholarly opinions about the relative ages of two Egyptian sphinxes.

✗   (A) The Great Sphinx is generally thought to be older than the one depicting Queen Hetepheres II, built in 2600 BCE.

Opposite. The Great Sphinx is generally thought to be *younger* than the other sphinx.

✗   (B) Many scholars believe that the Egyptian sphinx depicting a queen in 2600 BCE is likely to be about as old as the Great Sphinx.

Again, the Great Sphinx is likely younger than the other sphinx.

✓   (C) The oldest sphinx in Egypt is probably not the Great Sphinx but another made in 2600 BCE to depict a queen.

CORRECT. This version captures the proper relationship between the ages of the two sphinxes.

✗   (D) There is no Egyptian sphinx older than the one depicting Queen Hetepheres II, built in 2600 BCE, except for the Great Sphinx.

The exception at the end of the sentence invalidates this version.

4.   The word "benevolent" in the passage is closest in meaning to

    ✗ (A) sacred

    ✓ (B) kindhearted

    ✗ (C) powerful

    ✗ (D) vengeful

VOCABULARY. "Benevolent" = kind, generous, wishing well, disposed to doing good.

"Sacred" = connected with God (or the gods) or dedicated to a religious purpose. These words are not related.

CORRECT. "The Egyptian sphinx ... was apparently considered a benevolent god" = it appears that this sphinx was considered a kindhearted god.

Unrelated. "Powerful" = having great strength.

Nearly opposite. "Vengeful" = seeking to harm someone in return, seeking revenge.

Paragraph 3	**Comments**
S1 Like its Egyptian cousin, the Greek sphinx guarded temple entrances and had the body of a lion.	The Greek sphinx, in comparison.
2 However, Greek sphinxes had a female head and often wings.	
3 Furthermore, Greek sphinxes were far more malevolent.	More malevolent (= evil).
4 A prominent Greek myth tells of the Sphinx guarding Thebes; it would pose a riddle to passersby: "What walks on four feet in the morning, two in the afternoon, and three at night?"	Example in Greek myth.
5 It then killed the hapless travelers, who all failed to solve it.	
6 Finally, according to the myth, Oedipus, immortalized in Sophocles's ancient Greek play *Oedipus Rex*, solved the riddle: "Man.	
7 As an infant, he crawls on all fours; as an adult, he walks on two legs and in old age, he uses a 'walking' stick."	
8 The Sphinx then killed itself.	
9 This myth of this Sphinx still resonates in modern cultures; the French playwright Jean Cocteau reworked *Oedipus Rex* as *The Infernal Machine* in the twentieth century.	

5. The word "pose" in the passage is closest in meaning to

    ✗ (A) pretend

    ✗ (B) shout

    ✓ (C) present

    ✗ (D) answer

VOCABULARY. As a verb, "pose" = place, present, offer for attention.

"Pose as" can mean "pretend to be," but to pose a riddle is just to ask it or present it.

Too specific. You can pose a riddle without shouting it.

CORRECT. "It would pose a riddle to passersby" = it would present a riddle to passersby

In a way the opposite. To "pose" a question is to ask it, rather than answer it.

6. According to paragraph 3, how did Greek sphinxes differ from Egyptian sphinxes?

    ✗ (A) They had the body of a lion.

    ✗ (B) They were able to fly.

    ✗ (C) They confronted passersby with riddles.

    ✓ (D) They were more vicious or spiteful.

FACT. S1 lists similarities between Greek and Egyptian sphinxes. S2–3 discuss how Greek sphinxes differed from Egyptian sphinxes. The correct answer must be a feature that Greek sphinxes definitely had and that Egyptian sphinxes definitely did not have.

S1 lists a lion's body as a similarity, not as a difference, between the two types of sphinxes.

S2 states that Greek sphinxes often had wings. But the passage does not mention flying. Perhaps Greek sphinxes were like penguins or ostriches.

S4–8 recount the myth of a particular Greek sphinx that posed a riddle to passersby (= people who passed by). But you are never told that Egyptian sphinxes did not pose riddles. In fact, you're never told that Greek sphinxes posed riddles in general. So there's no way to call this feature a difference between the two types of sphinxes.

CORRECT. S3: "Furthermore, Greek sphinxes were far more malevolent." The implied comparison is to Egyptian sphinxes.

7. According to paragraph 3, which of the following is true about Oedipus?

    ✓ (A) He was famously portrayed in a Greek play.

    ✗ (B) He was killed by the Sphinx of Thebes.

    ✗ (C) He was acquainted with Jean Cocteau.

    ✗ (D) Upon solving the riddle, he slew the Sphinx of Thebes.

FACT. S4 begins the story of the Sphinx guarding Thebes. S6 introduces Oedipus.

CORRECT. S6: "Oedipus, immortalized in Sophocles's ancient Greek play *Oedipus Rex*."

S5 notes that travelers who failed to answer the riddle were killed. S6–7 say that Oedipus solved the riddle. S8 states that the Sphinx killed itself. It is never stated that this sphinx killed Oedipus.

This is impossible. S9 indicates that Cocteau lived in the twentieth century, whereas Oedipus supposedly lived in ancient times and may only be a mythical figure.

S8 states that the Sphinx killed itself. Oedipus did not slay the Sphinx directly, although his solution to the riddle seems to have caused the Sphinx to commit suicide.

Paragraph 4	Comments
S1 Sphinxes as gods are far from limited to Greece and the Middle East.	Sphinxes elsewhere in the world.
2 On the contrary, such figures have been depicted in myths and legends across the breadth of Asia.	Examples across Asia.
3 Creatures with human heads and the haunches of lions have particular names in the Sanskrit, Tamil, Pali, and Thai languages.	
4 They are known and respected throughout the Indian subcontinent, as well as in Myanmar, Sri Lanka, and Thailand.	
5 To this day, in parts of India, sphinxes guard temples and are worshiped in rituals.	
6 Even farther afield, there is a similar creature in the Philippines that is part man and part eagle.	
7 Interestingly enough, local lore has it that this sphinx also asks travelers a riddle and kills those who cannot answer it, much as in Thebes.	One example also asks deadly riddles.

8. Which of the following is named in paragraph 4 as a place in which a sphinx acts like the one in Thebes did?

FACT. S6–7 describe this sphinx.

✗ (A) Myanmar

S3–4 mention a sphinx with the head of a human and the haunches of a lion. No mention was made of its behavior.

✗ (B) Thailand

S3–4 mention a sphinx with the head of a human and the haunches of a lion. No mention was made of its behavior.

✗ (C) India

S5 notes that "sphinxes guard temples and are worshiped in rituals," but no mention is made of their behavior.

✓ (D) the Philippines

CORRECT. S6–7: "Even farther afield, there is similar creature in the Philippines that is part man and part eagle. Interestingly enough, local lore has it that this sphinx also asks travelers a riddle and kills those who cannot answer it, much as in Thebes."

9.   The word "They" in the passage refers to

REFERENCE. In theory, the pronoun "They" in S4 could refer to a couple of different nouns in the prior sentence. But the best candidate is the subject of S3: "Creatures" (specific ones that have human heads and the haunches of lions). This reference makes the most sense in S4 as well. The second best candidate would be the direct object in S3 ("names"). But the meaning of S4 and S5 strongly suggest that the pronoun should refer to "Creatures."

✗   (A) human heads

The noun phrase "human heads" is part of the larger noun phrase that can be considered the extended subject of S3: "Creatures with human heads and the haunches of lions." However, it is difficult for a later pronoun to refer back to a noun placed in such a junior position. Moreover, it makes more sense for the subject of S4 to be sphinxes: creatures with human heads (and other features), not human heads themselves.

✓   (B) creatures

CORRECT. S4 states that it is these creatures (namely, sphinxes) that are known throughout the Indian subcontinent and in other places. S5 also has sphinxes as its grammatical and topical subject.

✗   (C) lions

The noun "lions" is part of the noun phrase that can be considered the extended subject of S3: "Creatures with human heads and the haunches of lions." However, it is difficult for a later pronoun to refer back to a noun placed in such a junior position. Moreover, it makes more sense for the subject of S4 to be sphinxes: creatures with features of lions, not lions themselves.

✗   (D) languages

A list of languages immediately precedes the pronoun "They." However, a pronoun does not always have to refer to the closest previous noun. In fact, it's often better for a subject pronoun (such as "they") to refer back to the prior sentence's subject, which is usually more distant. Referring back to "Creatures" makes the pronoun "They" make the most sense.

Paragraph 5	**Comments**
S1 India is not the only place where interest in sphinxes survived antiquity.	Interest in sphinxes has continued, not just in India.
2 In Europe, an artistic fascination with sphinxes began around 1500 and continued into the 1700s.	
3 In Freemasonry, a guild organization that began in medieval times and still exists today, sphinxes as guardians of secrecy are often sculpted in front of temples and **adorn** several Masonic badges.	

10. The word "adorn" in the passage is closest in meaning to

  ✓ (A) decorate

  ✗ (B) entitle

  ✗ (C) shape

  ✗ (D) represent

VOCABULARY. "Adorn" = decorate, embellish, make more beautiful through ornamentation.

CORRECT. "Sphinxes ... adorn several Masonic badges" = they decorate those badges, they appear as ornamentation on those badges.

Unrelated. "Entitle" = give legal right or claim.

Not quite. To "shape" = form, create, or provide a form for. But sphinxes could adorn or decorate the Masonic badges without shaping them or giving them form.

Again, not quite. To say that "sphinxes represent several Masonic badges" would be to say that several of these badges *are* sphinxes. But sphinxes could adorn the badges without *being* those badges.

Paragraph 6	Comments
S1 While it is thus indisputable that the sphinx has had symbolic importance from prehistory to the present, uncertainty has arisen concerning the age of the most famous sphinx of all, the Great Sphinx of Giza in Egypt.	The age of the Great Sphinx of Giza in Egypt is still debated.
2 Most scholars still subscribe to the conventional view that the Great Sphinx was built by the pharaoh Khafra around 2500 BCE.	Conventional view of most scholars: 2500 BCE.
3 However, some point to stylistic features to argue that it must be one to two hundred years older.	Some think 100–200 years older.
4 More radically, one theory suggests that the Great Sphinx is several thousand years older than generally thought.	Another theory: thousands of years older, because of weathering pattern.
5 This hypothesis claims that the weathering pattern of the Great Sphinx indicates that extensive rainfall was the agent.	
6 As it is accepted that such rainfall ceased to be part of the Egyptian climate around 4000 BCE, this would mean that the Great Sphinx existed at least hundreds of years before that.	
7 While the majority opinion, with some scientific justification, argues that the damage to the stone could have been caused by wind erosion and that no other evidence of ancient Egyptians undertaking such constructions before 5000 BCE has surfaced, the rival theories have had enough credence to introduce uncertainty to the discussion.	
8 To this day, the exact age of the Great Sphinx remains a secret that it guards.	Issue is still uncertain.

11. According to paragraph 6, which of the following is evidence for the theory that the Great Sphinx was built closer to 5000 BCE?

FACT. S4–6 describe a theory that extensive rainfall caused the erosion of the Great Sphinx. Since there was little rain in Egypt after 4000 BCE, the Great Sphinx must date back to before this time, according to the theory.

✓ (A) A pattern of erosion seemingly caused by heavy rains

CORRECT. S5–6: "This hypothesis claims that the weathering pattern of the Great Sphinx indicates that extensive rainfall was the agent. As it is accepted that such rainfall ceased to be part of the Egyptian climate around 4000 BCE, this would mean that the Great Sphinx existed at least hundreds of years before that."

✗ (B) Certain stylistic aspects possibly indicating an older age

S3 describes stylistic features as evidence that the Sphinx is a few hundred years older than 2500 BCE, not 5000 BCE.

✗ (C) The lack of evidence of similar constructions in Egypt dating to that time

Opposite. S7 cites this lack of evidence as a point against the theory.

✗ (D) Accounts of the reign of the pharaoh Khafra

S2 mentions Khafra in reference to the conventional view that he built the Sphinx around 2500 BCE. No other historical details of his reign are provided.

4

	Paragraph 6	**Comments**
S1	While it is thus indisputable that the sphinx has had symbolic importance from prehistory to the present, uncertainty has arisen concerning the age of the most famous sphinx of all, the Great Sphinx of Giza in Egypt.	
2	**A** Most scholars still subscribe to the conventional view that the Great Sphinx was built by the pharaoh Khafra around 2500 BCE.	Insertion here actually works to some degree with the prior sentence (S1), which introduces the uncertainty around the Great Sphinx's age. The real problem, however, is that the following text doesn't follow. The rest of the paragraph never mentions anything about how the puzzle might be resolved with these new technologies.
3–6	**B** However, some point to stylistic features to argue that it must be one to two hundred years older. More radically, one theory suggests that the Great Sphinx is several thousand years older than generally thought. This hypothesis claims that the weathering pattern of the Great Sphinx indicates that extensive rainfall was the agent. As it is accepted that such rainfall ceased to be part of the Egyptian climate around 4000 BCE, this would mean that the Great Sphinx existed at least hundreds of years before that.	Insertion here fails in both directions. The previous sentence does not even allude to uncertainty around the Great Sphinx's age. Moreover, the following text does not discuss new technologies for resolving that uncertainty. Finally, insertion here would break the logical flow between S2 and S3.
7–8	**C** While the majority opinion, with some scientific justification, argues that the damage to the stone could have been caused by wind erosion and that no other evidence of ancient Egyptians undertaking such constructions before 5000 BCE has surfaced, the rival theories have had enough credence to introduce uncertainty to the discussion. To this day, the exact age of the Great Sphinx remains a secret that it guards.	Again, insertion here fails in both directions. The previous sentence does not mention the secret of the Great Sphinx's age. Moreover, the following text does not discuss new technologies for resolving any lingering uncertainty.
End	**D**	**CORRECT.** S8 mentions the secret of the Great Sphinx (its exact age), so the new sentence can refer to it. S8 also mentions that the secret remains to this day, so the "However" works. Finally, the allusion to new technologies is fine here as a concluding remark. Nothing further is required.

12.   **However, advances in laser technology and aerial surveying give hope that the Great Sphinx's secret may yet be discovered.**

Where would the sentence best fit?

INSERT TEXT. The prior sentence should clarify what "the Great Sphinx's secret" is, and the "However" (indicating contrast) suggests that the prior sentence should emphasize that the secret continues or something similar. The paragraph generally discusses the uncertainty around the Great Sphinx's age, so this is likely what the secret is (the exact age). Nevertheless, the previous sentence should make that point clear. Moreover, any text following the inserted sentence should build upon the subject introduced in this sentence ("advances in laser technology and aerial surveying").

✗ (A) Choice A

✗ (B) Choice B

✗ (C) Choice C

✓ (D) Choice D   **CORRECT.**

Whole Passage	**Comments**
P1 The Sphinx, a mythical creature with a lion's body and human head, has become inextricably linked with ancient Egyptian culture …	Sphinx = linked with ancient Egypt. But prominent in many ancient cultures. Some kind of human commonality.
P2 The Egyptian sphinx sported a male human head and was apparently considered a benevolent god …	Characteristics of Egyptian sphinx. Age of various sphinxes (old!).
P3 Like its Egyptian cousin, the Greek sphinx guarded temple entrances and had the body of a lion …	The Greek sphinx, in comparison. More malevolent (= evil). Example in Greek myth.
P4 Sphinxes as gods are far from limited to Greece and the Middle East …	Sphinxes elsewhere in the world. Examples across Asia. One example also asks deadly riddles.
P5 India is not the only place where interest in sphinxes survived antiquity …	Interest in sphinxes has continued, not just in India.
P6 While it is thus indisputable that the sphinx has had symbolic importance from prehistory to the present, uncertainty has arisen concerning the age of the most famous sphinx of all, the Great Sphinx of Giza in Egypt …	The age of the Great Sphinx of Giza in Egypt is still debated. Conventional view of most scholars: 2500 BCE. Some think 100–200 years older. Another theory: thousands of years older, because of weathering pattern. Issue is still uncertain.

4

13. **The mythical sphinx, while inevitably imagined as the Great Sphinx of Giza in Egypt, is a worldwide phenomenon of lasting importance.**

SUMMARY. Correct answers must be clearly expressed in the passage. They must also be among the major points of the passage. They should tie as directly as possible to the summary given.

✗ ☐A Both Greek and Thai sphinxes posed riddles.

P3 indicates that at least one Greek sphinx asked riddles. But it is not known whether Thai sphinxes did so as well. P5 attributes this characteristic to a sphinx in the Philippines.

✗ ☐B Sphinxes had a place in world cultures only until the 1700s.

P5 discusses a artistic trend ending around 1700. But P5 also mentions that sphinx symbolism continues to this day in Freemasonry. In addition, P3 S9 states that the "myth of this Sphinx still resonates in modern cultures; the French playwright Jean Cocteau reworked *Oedipus Rex* as *The Infernal Machine* in the twentieth century."

✓ ☐C Not limited to Egypt or Greece, sphinxes figure in legends throughout Asia.

CORRECT. P4 S2 emphasizes this point: "such figures have been depicted in myths and legends across the breadth of Asia."

✗ ☐D There are older sphinxes than the one thought to depict Queen Hetepheres II.

While this point is stated at the end of P2, it is a minor detail, not a major theme.

✓ ☐E The emblematic Great Sphinx of Giza in Egypt cannot be dated with absolute certainty.

CORRECT. This is the focus of P6. While a conventional view dominates, the paragraph explicitly states that this view is not completely proven.

✓ ☐F Egyptian and Greek sphinxes served certain similar functions, but differed in temperament.

CORRECT. P3 S1: "Like its Egyptian cousin, the Greek sphinx guarded temple entrances." Also, P3 S3: "Greek sphinxes were far more malevolent." The rest of P3 outlines a myth that illustrates the malevolence of Greek sphinxes.

Answers and Explanations—
4.8 The Man Who Would Not Be King

Passage		Comments
S1	Edward Albert Christian George Andrew Patrick David, known to his friends as David and, eventually, to the larger world as Edward VIII, was born in 1894.	Edward VIII: born in 1894.
2	He was the great-grandson of the legendary Queen Victoria, and both his grandfather, Edward VII, and his father, George V, preceded him to the throne.	Royalty.
3	Unlike his immediate predecessors, he reigned for less than a year.	Reigned < 1 year.
4	However, because he was the only British monarch to voluntarily abdicate the throne, and because of the racy circumstances of his abdication—it revolved around an American divorcée—he commanded the world stage in 1936 and nearly caused a constitutional crisis in the United Kingdom.	Abdicated the British throne. Huge news in 1936.

1. The word "racy" in the passage is closest in meaning to

VOCABULARY. "Racy" = suggestive, a little indecent or shocking, risqué.

✗ (A) bizarre

It is certainly "bizarre" (strange or unusual) for someone to abdicate (renounce or retire) the monarchy and no longer be king. However, these words are not related.

✓ (B) risqué

CORRECT. "The racy circumstances of his abdication" = the risqué or indecent circumstances of his abdication.

✗ (C) official

Unrelated. "Official" = done with authority or approval, or someone who has that authority.

✗ (D) political

Abdication (renouncing or leaving the throne) might be done for a "political" (governmental) reason but these words are not related.

2. According to paragraph 1, the reign of Edward VIII was especially distinctive for which of the following reasons?

FACT. The paragraph mentions several facts about Edward VIII. Some of these facts only provide biographical background. Only a few could be considered reasons for which Edward VIII's reign is especially distinctive or unique.

✗ (A) He was the great-grandson of Queen Victoria.

This fact is mentioned only as biographical background. It is true that few great-grandchildren of any particular British monarch would also rule the kingdom, but this fact of Edward VIII's descent is not presented as making his reign especially meaningful.

✗ (B) Both his father and grandfather were kings.

This fact is mentioned only as biographical background. The same pattern would hold for quite a few British monarchs, in fact.

✓ (C) He abdicated the British throne voluntarily.

CORRECT. S4: "he was the only British monarch to voluntarily abdicate the throne." This fact is cited as a unique, distinctive aspect of the reign of Edward VIII.

✗ (D) His reign was shorter than his father's.

Close but not quite. S3 says that his reign lasted for less than a year, unlike those of his immediate predecessors (his father and grandfather). But you are not told that no other British monarch reigned for less than a year, or that no other British monarch had a shorter reign than his or her father. So this fact is not presented as making the reign very distinctive. In comparison, Edward VIII's voluntary abdication is described as unique.

	Paragraph 2	**Comments**
S1	Like many royal heirs of that time, Edward had a haphazard education from private tutors.	Edward's haphazard education.
2	As a young man, aside from holding a military commission, he was confined to performing the ceremonial duties of his station as a prince.	Duties as prince.
3	During the First World War, his request to serve in combat was denied, since his death or capture was considered too serious a mishap to be chanced.	
4	After the war, he resumed a life of representing the monarchy on international and domestic tours.	
5	While his status and dashing appearance made him quite successful in this capacity, as well as a darling of high society, he grew weary of the pointlessness of his role as the heir to the throne.	Good at representing the throne, but he grew weary of it.
6	Consequently, he devoted much of his energy to partying and affairs with several married women.	Partied and had affairs.
7	His behavior disconcerted both the British politicians and his father, George V, who in fact accurately predicted that, as king, he would ruin himself within 12 months.	Disconcerted politicians and his father.

3.   The author mentions "status and dashing appearance" in support of which of the following?

PURPOSE. S5 contains this phrase. Referring back to S4 is also necessary to grasp the meaning.

✓ (A) Edward's success as an emissary of the British Crown

CORRECT. S5: "his status and dashing appearance made him quite successful in this capacity." What capacity? The answer is in S4: "representing the monarchy on international and domestic tours." Emissary = representative, someone sent on a mission. Crown = monarchy.

✗ (B) The denial of Edward's request to serve in combat

Edward's request was denied during the First World War (S3). The phrase "status and dashing appearance" has to do with his work after the war was over.

✗ (C) Edward's activities as a partier and womanizer

Edward's "status and dashing appearance" undoubtedly helped his activities as a partier and womanizer. But this is not what the passage specifically says. S6 mentions Edward's partying and womanizing as a distraction from his duties.

✗ (D) The concern that British politicians had about Edward's behavior

It was Edward's partying and womanizing, not his status and appearance, that disturbed British politicians (S7).

4.   According to paragraph 2, Edward did not serve in combat in the First World War because

FACT. S3 discusses Edward's wartime service.

✓ (A) the consequences of Edward becoming a casualty were too dire

CORRECT. S3: "During the First World War, his request to serve in combat was denied, since his death or capture was considered too serious a mishap to be chanced" (= risked, hazarded). This is why he did not serve in combat. Casualty = someone who has suffered death or injury in combat. Dire = extremely bad.

✗ (B) Edward was occupied with his ceremonial duties

What Edward actually did during the war is unclear. S4 states that Edward "resumed a life of representing the monarchy," implying that he had stepped away from this role during the war. Regardless, his ceremonial duties are not what is cited in the passage as the reason he was unable to serve in combat.

✗ (C) Edward's military training was haphazard

The discussion of Edward's education (S1) is not related to his wartime service.

✗ (D) Edward was unwilling to chance death or capture

S3 states that his superiors were unwilling, not Edward.

4

Paragraph 3	Comments
S1 Edward began a passionate affair with Wallis Simpson, who at the time was **estranged** from her second husband, in 1934.	Edward began an affair with Wallis Simpson.
2 Many accounts suggest that the relationship continued because she was the dominant figure and that he was utterly infatuated with her.	
3 In any case, this affair greatly disturbed George V, who refused to formally receive a divorcée, and his ministers.	Affair greatly disturbed George V.
4 King George V then died in January 1936, and Edward ascended to the throne.	Once he died, Edward became king.

5. According to paragraph 3, the affair between Edward and Wallis Simpson may have lasted because

   FACT. S1–2 directly address the relationship. S2 gives possible reasons for why the relationship continued.

   ✗ (A) it greatly upset his father, George V

   S3: "this affair greatly disturbed George V." However, this fact is not given as a reason for the relationship's continuation.

   ✗ (B) he finally managed to ascend to the throne

   Edward became king in 1936 (S4) two years after the relationship began in 1934 (S1). In any event, no connection is made between his ascension to the throne and the continuation of the affair.

   ✓ (C) Edward was deeply smitten with Wallis

   CORRECT. S2: "Many accounts suggest that the relationship continued because she was the dominant figure and that he was utterly infatuated with her." Smitten = infatuated, enamored, lovesick.

   ✗ (D) she was estranged from her second husband

   S1 notes that Wallis "at the time was estranged from her second husband." But this fact is not given as a reason why the relationship lasted.

6. The phrase "**estranged from**" in the passage is closest in meaning to

   VOCABULARY. "Estranged from" = separated or alienated from, no longer close to (or living with) a partner.

   ✗ (A) different from

   Not quite. Wallis might have felt that she was different from her husband, but "different" and "estranged" are not synonyms.

   ✓ (B) alienated from

   CORRECT. "Wallis Simpson … at the time was estranged from her second husband" = Wallis Simpson was alienated or separated (mentally and/or physically) from her husband.

   ✗ (C) confused by

   Confusion might have contributed to Wallis's feeling of estrangement or alienation. But "confused by" is not the same thing as "estranged from."

   ✗ (D) infuriated by

   Fury might have contributed to Wallis's feeling of estrangement or alienation. But "infuriated by" is not the same thing as "estranged from."

4

	Paragraph 4	**Comments**
S1	By summer, Edward decided to marry Wallis Simpson, but he faced **staunch** opposition from the Church of England, the Prime Minister, and the leaders of the Commonwealth nations.	They decided to marry, but many forces opposed them.
2	Edward had three choices: abdicate the throne, renounce Wallis Simpson, or marry her despite the opposition of his ministers, who would resign and thus create a constitutional crisis.	Edward's choices.
3	Edward eventually chose abdication, granting the throne to his brother George, as the combined power of church and state surpassed that of the king.	He chose to give up the throne.
4	For the moment, though, Edward triumphed in the court of public opinion, as he won worldwide sympathy from a radio broadcast during which he famously said, "I have found it impossible to carry the heavy burden of responsibility and to discharge my duties as king as I would wish to do without the help and support of the woman I love."	Public opinion was for him, for now.

7.	According to paragraph 4, at the time of his abdication, the general public viewed Edward's actions with	**FACT.** S4 describes how the general public ("the court of public opinion") viewed Edward's actions.
✗	(A) indifference	Opposite. They weren't "indifferent" (showing a lack of interest or concern). The paragraph says he won "sympathy."
✗	(B) disappointment	P4 suggests that government officials were disappointed by Edward's actions. But S4 states that the public was sympathetic.
✓	(C) sympathy	**CORRECT.** S4: "Edward triumphed in the court of public opinion, as he won worldwide sympathy."
✗	(D) alarm	It would seem natural for an abdication to be "alarming" (dangerous, worthy of warning), but the paragraph says that people actually felt sympathy (concern) for him.
8.	The word "**staunch**" in the passage is closest in meaning to	**VOCABULARY.** "Staunch" = firm, loyal, constant, resolute.
✗	(A) hesitant	Opposite. "Hesitant" = tentative, unsure.
✗	(B) surly	Not quite. "Surly" = bad-tempered, rude.
✗	(C) honorable	Not quite. "Honorable" = morally upright, worthy of honor. But "honorable" and "staunch" are not synonyms.
✓	(D) stalwart	**CORRECT.** "He faced staunch opposition" = he faced stalwart, dependable, resolute opposition.

9.   Which of the following can be inferred from paragraph 4 about the political power of the British monarchy at the time of Edward VIII?

INFERENCE. P4 discusses the political & institutional opposition to Edward's marriage, as well as the effectiveness of this opposition.

✗ (A) It was constitutionally absolute.

The paragraph points out the limits of Edward's power.

✗ (B) It was amplified in the court of public opinion.

S4 describes how the "court of public opinion" supported Edward himself during or just after his abdication. But that doesn't mean that the power of the monarchy itself (which he was abandoning) was itself amplified, or increased.

✗ (C) It was greater than that of Edward VIII's ministers.

It is possible that the political power of the monarchy was greater than that of the king's ministers. However, S3 only states that "the combined power of church and state surpassed that of the king."

✓ (D) It was less than that of church and state together.

CORRECT. S3: "the combined power of church and state surpassed (= was greater than) that of the king." In other words, the power of the king was less than the power of church and state, taken together.

Paragraph 5	**Comments**
S1 In the following years, the couple's fairy-tale romance took an unfortunate turn, as it was tarnished by conflict and suspicion stemming from both personal and political sources.	Afterwards, an unfortunate turn for the romance.
2 Edward and Wallis moved to the European continent following his abdication and, especially after a publicized visit with Adolf Hitler, were accused of being Nazi sympathizers and worse.	Moved elsewhere in Europe. Accused of Nazi sympathies.
3 While no concrete evidence ever surfaced, a cloud of suspicion about their ultimate loyalties remained over their heads: during the Second World War, Edward, now the Duke of Windsor, was made Governor of the (distant) Bahamas, largely to isolate him.	Cloud of suspicion remained. Made Governor of the Bahamas to isolate him.

10. According to paragraph 5, life for Edward and Wallis after the abdication included all of the following EXCEPT:

NEGATIVE FACT. Three answers will be found in P5 as true of the couple's life after Edward's abdication. One answer will not be supported in the text.

✗ (A) accusations of Nazi sympathies

S2 notes these accusations.

✓ (B) suspicions of infidelity

CORRECT. Infidelity (= lack of faithfulness within the couple) is never mentioned in P5.

✗ (C) residence outside of the United Kingdom in Europe

S2 states that the couple moved to the European continent.

✗ (D) formal leadership in the Bahamas

S3 states that Edward was named Governor of the Bahamas.

11. Which of the sentences below best expresses the essential information in the highlighted sentence in paragraph 5? Incorrect choices change the meaning in important ways or leave out essential information.

SIMPLIFY SENTENCE. S3 indicates that Edward's assignment to the distant Bahamas came about, at least in part, because his loyalty was suspect ("largely to isolate him"). The first part of the sentence points out the suspicions hanging over his head, although they were unproven.

✗ (A) Edward's wartime governorship of the Bahamas isolated him from the cloud of suspicions remaining over him.

Edward was not isolated *away from* the cloud of suspicions. He was isolated *because of* that cloud of suspicions.

✗ (B) No evidence ever arose to confirm the isolated suspicions that sent Edward to govern the remote Bahamas in wartime exile.

This version seems to come close. But it misuses the word "isolated" (in the original, Edward was isolated, not the suspicions). This inaccurately downplays the suspicions. The focus of the main clause ("No evidence ever arose") and the addition of "in exile" further de-emphasize those suspicions, hinting at sympathy for Edward. In contrast, the original is decidedly neutral about Edward and the suspicions.

✗ (C) In the face of unproven suspicions, Edward was named Duke of Windsor and Governor of the Bahamas during the war.

According to this version, Edward was given these titles and postings to *counteract* the suspicions ("in the face of unproven suspicions"). In fact, the opposite is true about his being named Governor of the Bahamas.

✓ (D) Edward was posted to the distant Bahamas during the war because of unresolved suspicions about his loyalties.

CORRECT. This version leaves out certain details (e.g., that he was named Governor, that he was already named Duke of Windsor). It also summarizes other details (e.g., "unresolved suspicions" indicates that no concrete evidence emerged either way). But this version captures the core meaning of the original sentence.

4

Paragraph 6	**Comments**
S1 — This estrangement only increased Edward's animosity towards his family; in the decades to come, he only saw members of his family on a handful of occasions.	
2 — **A** After the war, Edward and Wallis lived in France and were prominent in high society.	**CORRECT.** In this position, the new sentence elaborates on the topic of S1, which refers to occasions on which Edward saw his family, in the course of "decades." These are the years properly referred to in the phrase "through those years." That's when Edward was clearly standing by Wallis against the "perceived slights" of his family.
3 — **B** Such a lifestyle strained their financial means, and various speculative dealings caused some critics to deem them parasites, echoing past accusations of immorality and fascism.	This placement may seem okay: Edward probably stood by Wallis while they lived in France and took part in high society. But the connection to the "perceived slights" of his family is too weak. Placement here also unnaturally breaks the logical flow between S2 and S3, which begins "Such a lifestyle" (calling back to "high society" at the end of S2).
4 — **C** Following several years of health problems, Edward died in Paris in 1972; Wallis Simpson lived there for another 14 years.	Again, Edward seems to have stood by Wallis during the events described in S3. But again, the new sentence requires a strong connection to the actions of Edward's family in the prior sentence. S3 never mentions Edward's family.
5 — **D** In spite of all the family conflict, Edward and Wallis were accepted by the royal family in death, and the two were interred together in the Royal Burial Ground.	S4 discusses Edward's death and Wallis's survival for another 14 years. Edward could not have stood by Wallis "through those years," unless he was mummified in a standing position, and he certainly could not have resented the slights of his family, as the new sentence describes.

12. **As Edward stood by Wallis through those years, he must have resented perceived slights by his brother, George VI, and by other relatives.**

Where would the sentence best fit?

INSERT TEXT. The prior sentence needs to clarify which years the phrase "through those years" refers to. It should also make sense that during those years, Edward was standing by Wallis against his family's "perceived slights."

✓ (A) Choice A   **CORRECT.**

✗ (B) Choice B

✗ (C) Choice C

✗ (D) Choice D

Whole Passage	Comments
P1 Edward Albert Christian George Andrew Patrick David, known to his friends as David and, eventually, to the larger world as Edward VIII …	Edward VIII: born in 1894. Royalty. Reigned < 1 year. Abdicated the British throne. Huge news in 1936.
P2 Like many royal heirs of that time, Edward had a haphazard education from private tutors …	Edward's haphazard education. Duties as prince. Good at representing the throne, but he grew weary of it. Partied and had affairs. Disconcerted politicians and his father.
P3 Edward began a passionate affair with Wallis Simpson, who at the time was estranged from her second husband …	Edward began an affair with Wallis Simpson. Affair greatly disturbed George V. Once he died, Edward became king.
P4 By summer, Edward decided to marry Wallis Simpson, but he faced staunch opposition …	They decided to marry, but many forces opposed them. Edward's choices. He chose to give up the throne. Public opinion was for him, for now.
P5 In the following years, the couple's fairy-tale romance took an unfortunate turn …	Afterwards, an unfortunate turn for the romance. Moved elsewhere in Europe. Accused of Nazi sympathies. Cloud of suspicion remained. Made Governor of the Bahamas to isolate him.
P6 This estrangement only increased Edward's animosity towards his family …	Hostile toward family. Became prominent in French high society after the war. Strained their finances. After death, accepted and buried by family.

4

13. **Edward VIII, a twentieth-century British king, occupies a unique place in the annals of the United Kingdom's monarchy.**

SUMMARY. Correct answers must be clearly expressed in the passage. They must also be among the major points of the passage. They should tie as directly as possible to the summary given.

✓ ☐A As heir apparent, Edward successfully represented the monarchy, but many worried about his fitness for kingship.

CORRECT. Corresponds to P2 and P3.

✗ ☐B Edward's position allowed him to avoid combat duty in the First World War.

This is a minor point in the passage overall. As written, this choice also incorrectly implies that Edward wanted to avoid combat duty. P2 states that Edward requested such duty but was refused permission.

✗ ☐C After his abdication, Edward visited Adolf Hitler and secretly espoused Nazism.

Edward's meeting with Hitler is mentioned in P5. But the paragraph also states that there was no evidence that Edward was a Nazi.

✗ ☐D Wallis Simpson was considered an inappropriate spouse because she was an American.

P3 does not say this. P3 S3 implies that she was considered inappropriate by George V because she was a divorcée.

✓ ☐E Edward's short reign caused much political unrest because of his personal choices.

CORRECT. Corresponds to P4 as well as the end of P1.

✓ ☐F After abdicating, Edward lived the life he desired, but he was beset with personal, financial, and political difficulties.

CORRECT. Corresponds to P5 and much of P6.

Answers and Explanations—4.9 Classroom Noise

	Paragraph 1	**Comments**
S1	It should come as no surprise to any teacher or parent that noise in a classroom environment is distracting and may impact a student's ability to learn.	Classroom noise is distracting, of course.
2	But what types of noise are most distracting?	But what kinds? Other questions.
3	At what volume level does background noise begin to impact learning?	
4	How severe is the problem?	
5	Recent research can shed light on these important questions, and some of the results are surprising.	Research can shed light.

1. The phrase "shed light on" in the passage is closest in meaning to

    ✗ (A) enflame

    ✓ (B) clarify

    ✗ (C) decide

    ✗ (D) obscure

VOCABULARY. "Shed light on" = illuminate, clarify, make clear(er).

Once an issue has been made more clear, it might "enflame" (enrage or anger) people, but these words are not related.

CORRECT. "Recent research can shed light on these important questions" = research can clarify, or make clearer, these questions.

Too extreme. "Shed light on" does not typically mean that these questions are fully decided or resolved by the research.

Opposite. To "obscure" something is to make it less clear or uncertain.

Paragraph 2	Comments
S1 Perhaps the most consistent finding of the new research is the degree to which even low levels of noise can have a substantial impact on student performance.	Even low noise levels can impact student performance.
2 Noise levels are gauged in terms of a decibel scale—every increase of 10 decibels corresponds to a doubling of perceived loudness.	Decibel scale.
3 Adult conversation at a distance of 3 feet is roughly in the range of 55 to 65 decibels.	
4 Ninety decibels is roughly the loudness achieved by a train whistle at a distance of 500 feet (about 152 meters) or a lawn mower at a distance of 25 feet (8 meters).	
5 Both of these are certainly jarring enough to catch most people's attention.	
6 In fact, 90 decibels is the level at which hearing loss can begin, if people are exposed to it on a sustained basis.	90 decibels: hearing loss can begin.
7 Children are even more sensitive to loud sounds than adults.	Children are even more sensitive.
8 As a result, United States federal regulations mandate that all ambient classroom sounds above 90 decibels must be dampened; federal grants are made available for school districts to improve acoustics and soundproofing when these levels are exceeded.	So US regulations: classrooms must dampen sounds above 90 decibels. Grants to help.

4

2. Which of the sentences below best expresses the essential information in the highlighted sentence in paragraph 2? Incorrect choices change the meaning in important ways or leave out essential information.

SIMPLIFY SENTENCE. S1 states that new research consistently finds that even low levels of noise can impact student performance in a classroom.

✗ (A) A consistent finding of the new research is that low levels of noise can affect student performance more than loud noise.

The sentence does not state or imply that low levels of background noise in a classroom have a bigger impact than high levels of noise.

✗ (B) Research on student performance strongly suggests that high levels of noise have the most substantial impact.

This version is plausible. But the original sentence makes a claim only about what happens with *low* levels of noise.

✓ (C) Even low levels of noise can seriously affect student performance, new research shows.

CORRECT. This choice says essentially the same thing as P2 S1, but simplifies the language somewhat and reorders the wording.

✗ (D) Much new research claims that consistent levels of noise have a substantial impact on student performance.

This sentence changes the meaning in one very important way: it changes "even low levels" to "consistent levels."

3. It can be inferred from paragraph 2 that

INFERENCE. The question does not narrow down what the inference is about. So the correct answer could be supported by facts anywhere in the paragraph.

✓ (A) operating a lawn mower without hearing protection can lead to hearing loss

CORRECT. S4 states that lawn mowers emit a noise of approximately 90 decibels at a distance of 25 feet. A person operating a lawn mower is much closer than that. S6 states that sustained exposure to sounds measuring 90 decibels can lead to hearing loss. You can infer that lawn mower operators without protection are at risk of hearing loss.

✗ (B) federal regulations controlling excessive classroom noise eliminate declines in student performance

S1 asserts that even low levels of classroom noise can hinder student performance. The paragraph later states that 90 decibels, the cutoff for federal regulations, is quite loud. So the regulations do not eliminate the problem of declines in performance.

✗ (C) adults are not generally capable of speaking at a loudness of 90 decibels

S3 states that adult conversation is approximately 55 to 65 decimals. But nothing in the paragraph suggests that adults cannot speak much more loudly than that.

✗ (D) children are unlikely to suffer permanent damage caused by excessive classroom noise

According to P2, sustained exposure to 90 decibels can lead to hearing loss in adults, and children are more sensitive to loud sounds than adults. So children are in fact likely to suffer permanent damage if they are regularly subjected to excessive classroom noise.

MANHATTAN PREP

4.   The word "ambient" in the passage is closest in meaning to

    VOCABULARY. "Ambient" = nearby, in the immediate environment or surroundings.

✗ (A) remote

    Opposite. "Remote" = faraway or distant.

✓ (B) surrounding

    CORRECT. "All ambient classroom sounds above 90 decibels must be dampened" = all surrounding classroom sounds, all sounds in the classroom's environment, above this level must be dampened.

✗ (C) dissonant

    This word has two fairly common meanings, but both are unrelated. "Dissonant" when used with sounds means that something is lacking harmony, while "dissonant" when used with colors (or other items) means unsuitable, unusual, or not matching/combining well.

✗ (D) constant

    Close but not quite. An ambient sound might not be constant. It may fade in and out.

Paragraph 3	**Comments**
S1 New research, however, indicates that learning issues begin at a much lower noise level.	But much lower noise levels can hurt learning.
2 Even barely detectable noise, such as whispering behind a student, noise from a neighboring classroom, or the turning on and off of electric equipment such as a heater, can be **problematic**.	
3 These noises, while barely perceptible—at levels as low as 30 or 35 decibels—cause the cortisol level in many students to increase.	
4 Cortisol is a hormone released in response to low blood sugar levels, waking up, and most importantly, stress.	Even really quiet noises can increase cortisol, a "stress hormone."
5 The increase of this "stress hormone" produces difficulties with focus, can lead to physical exhaustion, and can impair the ability of a person to convert new information into long-term memory.	Cortisol can interfere with learning.
6 A 2013 study published in the *Journal of Urban Health* demonstrated that, after controlling for various other socioeconomic factors, among eight- and nine-year-old students a 10-decibel increase in background noise resulted in a predicted drop in test scores in both French and mathematics of about 5.5 percent.	
7 Many other studies conducted since 1980 have had similar findings: noisier classroom environments lead to **decreases in reading** aptitude, cognitive thinking skills, language acquisition, and even physical coordination.	Studies have linked noise to learning problems.

5. The word "problematic" in the passage is closest in meaning to

   ✗ (A) simplistic

   ✗ (B) deceptive

   ✗ (C) quizzical

   ✓ (D) troublesome

VOCABULARY. "Problematic" = challenging, difficult, causing problems.

Somewhat opposite. "Simplistic" = too simple, oversimplified.

Unrelated. "Deceptive" = misleading, false, or counterfeit.

Thinking of solving a problem might make "quizzical" sound tempting, but these words are not related. "Quizzical" = inquiring or questioning, curious.

CORRECT. "Even barely detectable noise ... can be problematic" = even barely detectable noise can be troublesome, it can cause trouble or problems.

6. According to paragraph 3, what is the relationship between cortisol and noise in the classroom?

   ✗ (A) Cortisol is a hormone produced upon waking and in times of stress.

   ✗ (B) Cortisol can make classroom noises seem louder than they actually are.

   ✓ (C) Even soft classroom noises can increase the production of cortisol.

   ✗ (D) Elevated levels of cortisol can impair memory and lead to exhaustion.

FACT. S3 introduces the relevant link between cortisol and classroom noise.

S4 points out these facts about cortisol production. But this does not clarify the relationship between classroom noise and cortisol.

Nothing in the paragraph suggests that higher levels of cortisol ever cause noises to seem louder than they actually are.

CORRECT. S3: "These noises, while barely perceptible—at levels as low as 30 or 35 decibels—cause the cortisol level in many students to increase."

S5 points out these facts about the effects of high cortisol levels. But this does not clarify the relationship between classroom noise and cortisol.

7.   Why does the author mention "decreases in reading aptitude, cognitive thinking skills, language acquisition, and even physical coordination"?

PURPOSE. S7 lists these findings from research about the effects of classroom noise.

✗ (A) To restrict the known problems associated with excessive classroom noise to a specified list

S7 lists these problems as associated with noisy classroom environments. But nothing in the sentence or paragraph states or suggests that this list is complete. Other problems not mentioned may be known.

✗ (B) To assert that these problems are not so important within the context of broader issues facing many students

Nothing in the paragraph compares these classroom performance issues with other problems students may be facing.

✗ (C) To encourage teachers to take action to limit the extent of classroom noise

The author would likely agree that limiting the extent of classroom noise would be beneficial. But the purpose of this list, and the entire paragraph, is to describe the problem, not to appeal to anyone in particular to take action.

✓ (D) To illustrate the breadth of problems that studies have associated with noisy classrooms

CORRECT. The paragraph details problems caused by even low levels of classroom noise. This sentence outlines some specific, known problems associated with noisier classrooms.

Paragraph 4	Comments
S1 Another interesting finding is that different types and levels of noise can have varying effects on different groups of children.	Different noises can have different effects on different children.
2 In a study conducted at the University of Southampton, England, differing levels of "white noise," which sounds roughly like running water or hissing, were introduced into multiple classrooms.	Study on white noise.
3 The study found that students with a higher ability to focus were most affected by the white noise at any volume, while students with attention difficulties actually performed better with low to moderate levels of white noise.	Students who could focus well: most affected. Students with attention difficulties: actually improved at low levels of noise.
4 Researchers speculate that this is true because the noise forced the students with attention difficulties to exert more effort to overcome the background noise, thereby temporarily improving their level of focus.	Possible reason: these students had to exert more effort to overcome noise. That improved focus.

8.   The word "**this**" in the passage refers to

✓ (A) what the study found

(X) (B) the study itself

(X) (C) the white noise

(X) (D) how students with attention difficulties performed

REFERENCE. S4: "this is true because ..." What can be true or not? What is the author trying to explain with "because"?

CORRECT. "This" refers back to what the study found. The rest of the sentence reveals that the author is specifically talking about the second finding (about students with attention difficulties). The author claims that this finding is true because of a particular reason outlined in S4.

"This" refers to what the study found, not the study itself. It would be strange to call a research study "true." You could call it accurate, revealing, etc., but the *findings* would be true.

The white noise that affected the students is neither "true" nor untrue. Rather, the findings about the white noise's effects are true.

How these students performed (that is, better with low levels of white noise) is not what "this" refers to. Their level of performance is neither "true" nor untrue.

9.   According to paragraph 4, an interesting finding from a research study conducted at the University of Southampton is that

(X) (A) white noise had no impact on students in the class who could focus their attention well

✓ (B) some students improved their performance with moderate levels of white noise

(X) (C) students in the class were affected roughly equally by different levels of white noise

(X) (D) students were more negatively affected by low levels of white noise than by higher levels

FACT. S2 introduces this study. S3 lists its findings. S4 discusses a possible reason for one of its findings.

S3: "The study found that students with a higher ability to focus were most affected by the white noise at any volume."

CORRECT. S3: "The study found that ... students with attention difficulties actually performed better with low to moderate levels of white noise."

S3 makes it clear that different groups of students were affected differently by the white noise.

Nothing in the paragraph mentions that low levels of white noise had worse effects than higher levels.

Paragraph 5   **Comments**

S1	Finally, increased noise can place <u>undue</u> burden on teachers.	Noise burdens teachers, too.
2	In order for a teacher to keep the attention of his or her students, they must speak about 15 to 20 decibels more loudly than any competing noise.	
3	In addition, for every doubling of distance, the perceived loudness drops by about 6 decibels.	
4	Thus, a student sitting 24 feet (about 8 meters) from a teacher will perceive reduced volume of about 12 decibels relative to a student sitting 6 feet (2 meters) away.	
5	In a typical classroom, the teacher must speak as much as 30 decibels more loudly than any background noise.	
6	If that background noise is high, teachers are forced to practically shout to be heard by students in the back of the classroom.	They have to shout over background noise.
7	Such a loud level of speaking for hours per day can lead to significant physical strain, high blood pressure, and, eventually, vocal-cord scarring.	Resulting problems.

10.   The word "**undue**" in the passage is closest in meaning to

    ✗ (A) invisible

    ✓ (B) excessive

    ✗ (C) moderate

    ✗ (D) uncompensated

VOCABULARY. "Undue" = extreme, unjustified, inappropriate.

Unrelated. "Invisible" = unable to be seen.

CORRECT. "Increased noise can place undue burden on teachers" = increased noise can place excessive, inappropriate burden on teachers.

Opposite. As an adjective (description), "moderate" = average or common. Be careful not to confuse this with the verb (action), "to moderate" = to control, calm, or lessen.

Too specific. "Uncompensated" = not paid for, so an uncompensated burden on a teacher would be undue or inappropriate. But not every undue burden is necessarily uncompensated.

4

11. It can be inferred from paragraph 5 that if the distance between a noise and a person is halved, the perceived loudness will

INFERENCE. S3 discusses the change in perceived loudness that accompanies change in distance.

✗ (A) decrease by about 12 decibels

This decline is mentioned in S4. But the situation in this question is different. In S4, the distance is quadrupled (multiplied by 4) to go from 6 feet to 24 feet. But in this question, the distance is halved.

✗ (B) decrease by about 6 decibels

This is the decline directly outlined in S3. However, this decline corresponds to a doubling of distance (multiplying by 2). But the question asks about a halving of distance (dividing by 2).

✓ (C) increase by about 6 decibels

CORRECT. Halving the distance between a noise and the person perceiving the noise is the opposite of doubling the distance. So it stands to reason that the change in perceived loudness should also be opposite. S3 says that if the distance is doubled, the perceived loudness declines by about 6 decibels. So if the distance is instead halved, you can infer that the perceived loudness increased by about 6 decibels. It's the same comparison, just in reverse.

✗ (D) increase by about 12 decibels

This choice overstates the increase in perceived loudness.

12. According to paragraph 5, why does background noise in the classroom increase the burden on teachers? To receive credit, you must select TWO answer choices.

FACT. P5 discusses the burden that background classroom noise places on teachers. Two reasons are given for this burden.

✓ [A] They must speak more loudly than any competing noise.

CORRECT. Discussed in S2.

✗ [B] Talking loudly tends to scar a teacher's vocal cords immediately.

S7 states that teachers' vocal cords can be scarred by talking loudly. However, S7 describes this effect as occurring "eventually" over a lengthy period, strongly suggesting that this scarring generally doesn't happen "immediately" after one bout of loud talking.

✗ [C] Classroom noise gives uninterested students an excuse for not paying attention.

This idea is plausible. But it is not suggested anywhere in P5.

✓ [D] Teachers must project their voices even more to reach the back of the room.

CORRECT. S3–4 describe the drop in volume that happens over distance. This means that teachers have to speak that much more loudly to reach all their students (as much as 30 decibels more loudly, according to S5). Without much background noise, this extra projection would still be necessary. But it wouldn't be as likely to put the teacher into a health danger zone. When this factor is combined with the need to talk above significant background noise, though, the teacher may wind up damaging his or her vocal cords or incurring other health issues.

Paragraph 2	**Comments**
S1 Perhaps the most consistent finding of the new research is the degree to which even low levels of noise can have a substantial impact on student performance.	
2–4 **A** Noise levels are gauged in terms of a decibel scale—every increase of 10 decibels corresponds to a doubling of perceived loudness. Adult conversation at a distance of 3 feet is roughly in the range of 55 to 65 decibels. Ninety decibels is roughly the loudness achieved by a train whistle at a distance of 500 feet (about 152 meters) or a lawn mower at a distance of 25 feet (8 meters).	Placing the new sentence here may work with the prior sentence, if the new research findings in S1 are the facts that "have caught the attention of the United States government." However, S2 doesn't follow up at all on the reference to the US government.
5–6 **B** Both of these are certainly jarring enough to catch most people's attention. In fact, 90 decibels is the level at which hearing loss can begin, if people are exposed to it on a sustained basis.	Placement here leaves the phrase "both of these" in S5 without a logical reference point. Also, S5 has no follow-up on the US government.
7 **C** Children are even more sensitive to loud sounds than adults.	Placing the new sentence here breaks the direct logical connection between S6 and S7. In addition, S7 doesn't refer to the US government.
8 **D** As a result, United States federal regulations mandate that all ambient classroom sounds above 90 decibels must be dampened; federal grants are made available for school districts to improve acoustics and soundproofing when these levels are exceeded.	**CORRECT.** "These facts" now refers to everything in the paragraph up to this point. Moreover, in this location, the new sentence provides an appropriate transition to S8, which describes the response of the US government to the issue.

13.   **In recent years, these facts have caught the attention of the United States government.**

INSERT TEXT. Wherever this new sentence is inserted, the prior sentence should refer to facts that are acted upon by the US government in the following sentence. Otherwise, the position of the new sentence will not make sense.

Where would the sentence best fit?

✗   (A) Choice A

✗   (B) Choice B

✗   (C) Choice C

✓   (D) Choice D   **CORRECT.**

	Whole Passage	**Comments**
P1	It should come as no surprise to any teacher or parent that noise in a classroom environment is distracting and may impact a student's ability to learn …	Classroom noise is distracting, of course. But what kinds? Other questions. Research can shed light.
P2	Perhaps the most consistent finding of the new research is the degree to which even low levels of noise can have a substantial impact on student performance …	Even low noise levels can impact student performance. Decibel scale. 90 decibels: hearing loss can begin. Children are even more sensitive. So US regulations: classrooms must dampen sounds above 90 decibels. Grants to help.
P3	New research, however, indicates that learning issues begin at a much lower noise level …	But much lower noise levels can hurt learning. Even really quiet noises can increase cortisol, a "stress hormone." Cortisol can interfere with learning. Studies have linked noise to learning problems.
P4	Another interesting finding is that different types and levels of noise can have varying effects on different groups of children …	Different noises can have different effects on different children. Study on white noise. Students who could focus well: most affected. Students with attention difficulties: actually improved at low levels of noise. Possible reason: these students had to exert more effort to overcome noise. That improved focus.
P5	Finally, increased noise can place undue burden on teachers …	Noise burdens teachers, too. They have to shout over background noise. Resulting problems.

4

14.   **That classroom noise is undesirable may seem to be uncontroversial, but recent research has illuminated aspects of the issue that may be surprising.**

SUMMARY. Correct answers must be clearly expressed in the passage. They must also be among the major points of the passage. They should tie as directly as possible to the summary given.

✓ ☐A United States law prevents background noise in classrooms from exceeding 90 decibels, but learning problems can begin at lower sound levels.

CORRECT. P2 discuss these facts in detail.

✗ ☐B Only a small number of students are affected by low or moderate levels of background noise.

Even low or moderate levels of noise have been shown to affect student performance in general.

✗ ☐C For every doubling of distance from a sound source, the perceived loudness drops by about 6 decibels.

This detail is mentioned in P5, but it is minor in the context of this passage as a whole.

✓ ☐D Even low levels of noise in a classroom can lead to difficulties in such areas as reading, thinking, and coordinated movement.

CORRECT. This description from the end of P3 S7 neatly distills many of the difficulties encountered by students because of classroom noise.

✗ ☐E Ninety decibels, the level at which hearing loss can begin, is roughly equal to the loudness of a lawn mower at a distance of 25 feet.

P2 mentions this fact, but it is a minor detail, meant as a concrete way to understand a particular noise level.

✓ ☐F To overcome classroom noise, teachers must speak much more loudly, potentially resulting in serious health consequences.

CORRECT. Corresponds to P5.

4

Answers and Explanations—
4.10 Urban Decay and Renewal

	Paragraph 1	**Comments**
S1	Urban decay is the process by which established cities, or parts of them, atrophy under the weight of any of several possible societal changes, falling into a state of dilapidation.	Urban decay is the decay of a city or a part of it.
2	Perhaps the most common reason for this process to begin is the loss of jobs due to a company closing or moving to another location.	Common reason: loss of jobs from a company closing.
3	For example, if a manufacturer in a particular city experiences financial hardship and closes down, thousands of jobs could be lost.	
4	People that work at the factory would no longer commute to it; small businesses such as restaurants and shopping centers near the factory may suffer a decline in business and close, and so on.	Cascade of bad effects.
5	Soon, many residences and businesses near the factory may be abandoned, triggering an exodus from that neighborhood to other locations where the economy is more vibrant.	
6	This further depletes the economic activity in that area, with the ultimate result being that large zones of the city now exhibit urban blight, or the ugly, neglected landscape of abandoned buildings that can attract gangs or criminals.	
7	These factors can be prohibitive for new residents and businesses to consider re-entering the area.	
8	Additionally, this process depletes the city of tax revenue, which can lead to a cut in services provided by the city, further incentivizing remaining residents to leave.	

1.	The word "atrophy" in the passage is closest in meaning to	**VOCABULARY.** "Atrophy" = waste away, weaken, shrivel.
✗	(A) flourish	Opposite. "Flourish" = grown, thrive, or prosper.
✗	(B) proliferate	Also opposite, or nearly so. "Proliferate" = increase rapidly in numbers, reproduce quickly.
✗	(C) revolt	Unrelated. "Revolt" = rise up, riot, or rebel.
✓	(D) wither	**CORRECT.** "Established cities, or parts of them, atrophy ... falling into a state of dilapidation" = established cities or parts of those cities wither or shrivel, becoming dilapidated.

 MANHATTAN PREP

2.   Which of the following statements about urban decay can be inferred from paragraph 1?

INFERENCE. P1 describes the process by which urban decay occurs or might occur. The whole paragraph is devoted to the topic of urban decay, so the facts to draw an inference from could be anywhere.

✓   (A) Events other than the closing or relocation of a company can cause urban decay.

CORRECT. S1 states that "Urban decay is the process by which established cities … atrophy under the weight of any of several possible societal changes." S2 discusses the closing of a company as one possible, very common example. But S1 makes it clear that other changes can cause urban decay.

✗   (B) Employees at an urban factory live far away from the factory itself.

S4: "People that work at the factory would no longer commute to it." But these people do not necessarily have to live far away for that to be the case.

✗   (C) Gangs and criminals do not pay taxes.

S6 mentions gangs and criminals. Some gangs or criminals probably do not pay taxes. But nothing in the paragraph supports this claim directly. The decline in tax revenue referred to in S8 could happen because so many residents and businesses that presumably do pay taxes leave.

✗   (D) New residents and businesses re-entering the area would compel gangs and criminals to leave.

S6–7 mention gangs and criminals as reasons why new residents and businesses may avoid re-entering the blighted area. But you cannot conclude that if these residents and businesses returned, they would actually compel or force the gangs and criminals to leave.

3.   In paragraph 1, why does the author mention small businesses closing after a factory has closed?

PURPOSE. S4 states that "small businesses such as restaurants and shopping centers near the factory may suffer a decline in business and close." This is an example of a possible consequence of the first step in the process: the closing of the factory. Later sentences then discuss how the closing of these small businesses can have other effects as well. The author's goal is to illustrate how the whole process can occur, step by step, leading up to urban decay.

✗   (A) To contrast small businesses with large companies in terms of their ability to survive economic hardship

The focus of S4 is describing follow-on consequences of the factory closing. The point of this sentence is not to show how large and small businesses are different but rather to indicate how they are interconnected.

✗   (B) To suggest that factory employees are to blame for changing their spending habits after the factory closes

Nothing in the paragraph is about assigning blame. Rather, the goal is to describe a step-by-step example of a process by which urban decay can occur.

✓   (C) To underscore that the factory closing is merely the first step in a process that can lead to urban decay

CORRECT. S3 describes a hypothetical example of a factory closing. The rest of the paragraph describes a series of possible consequences stemming from that factory closing.

✗   (D) To provide an example of an event that could interrupt the process of urban decay that might otherwise occur

If anything, the opposite is true. The closing of small businesses as a result of the loss of the factory is an important step in the urban decay process described in P1.

4

Paragraph 2	**Comments**
P2 S1 Other factors may be the primary cause of urban decay.	Other causes of urban decay.
2 One such phenomenon in the United States is "white flight," which began shortly after World War II.	White flight: mass migration of European Americans out of cities.
3 White flight refers to the mass migration of European Americans away from urban centers to more homogeneous, sometimes newer suburban or exurban communities.	
4 This migration was facilitated by the development of the Interstate Highway System, which was funded by the Federal Aid Highway Act of 1956.	Helped by Interstate Highway System, which enabled longer commutes.
5 The highway system made commuting longer distances to employment within urban centers much more practical.	
6 At the same time, the Second Great Migration, which describes a wave of over 5 million African Americans from Southern states migrating to urban centers in the North, Midwest, and Western United States, contributed to population pressures in urban centers.	Second Great Migration of African Americans probably also accelerated white flight.
7 This likely accelerated the trend of white flight.	

Paragraph 3	**Comments**
P3 S1 Another factor arguably contributing to urban decay is rent control, wherein tenants are guaranteed a relatively affordable price for renting apartments within a city.	Another potential factor: rent control.
2 Rent control can lead to an imbalance between the supply and demand for housing units.	
3 By keeping rents artificially low, the construction of new housing units is discouraged, and property owners may be forced to reduce expenditures on maintenance of existing homes.	Can keep rents artificially low and discourage neighborhood investment.
4 This can contribute to the deterioration of buildings within a neighborhood.	

4.   According to paragraph 2, which of the following is true of the Second Great Migration?

FACT. S6 describes The Second Great Migration and mentions that it contributed to population pressures in urban centers. S7 indicates that as a result, white flight was likely accelerated.

✓   (A) It probably played a contributory role in white flight.

CORRECT. S6–7 mention that the Second Great Migration "contributed to population pressures in urban centers" and "likely accelerated the trend of white flight."

✗   (B) It started to occur well before white flight began in earnest.

Nothing in the paragraph suggests that the Second Great Migration started to occur well before white flight. If anything, the paragraph implies that the two trends were occurring at the same time, with one possibly contributing to the other.

✗   (C) It was facilitated by the Federal Aid Highway Act of 1956.

The Federal Aid Highway Act of 1956 funded the Interstate Highway System, which contributed to the exodus of European Americans from urban centers to suburbs and exurbs (S4). However, nothing in the passage suggests that this act contributed to the Second Great Migration.

✗   (D) It caused a population shortage and related problems in the Southern United States.

S6 states that many African Americans left Southern states to move to other parts of the United States. But P2 does not discuss any problems occurring in the Southern states because of this mass departure.

5.   The word "accelerated" in the passage is closest in meaning to

VOCABULARY. "Accelerate" = speed up, quicken, make something go faster.

✗   (A) targeted

Unrelated. "Targeted" = single out, pick, or attack.

✓   (B) hastened

CORRECT. "This likely accelerated the trend of white flight" = this likely hastened or sped up white flight.

✗   (C) stressed

The situation might have added extra stressors (tensions, anxieties, worries), but these words are not related.

✗   (D) impeded

Opposite. To "impede" is to obstruct, delay, block, or slow down.

4

6. Paragraphs 2 and 3 mention all of the following as possible contributors to urban decay EXCEPT:

NEGATIVE FACT. Both paragraphs discuss factors that probably contribute or contributed to urban decay. Three answer choices will be listed as such factors. One answer choice will not be.

✗ (A) the development of the Interstate Highway System

P2 S4 states that the Interstate Highway System made commuting from towns outside of urban centers much easier. This facilitated white flight, which P2 claims was another cause of urban decay.

✗ (B) rent control

P3 is devoted to explaining how rent control can contribute to urban decay in some neighborhoods.

✗ (C) the Second Great Migration

P2 S6–7 explain how the Second Great Migration may have sped up the process of white flight, which P2 claims was a cause of urban decay.

✓ (D) the founding of exurban communities before World War II

CORRECT. S3 states that many European Americans moved to suburban and exurban communities during white flight. However, if some of these communities were founded before white flight began (after World War II), then the founding of these particular communities would not have been a cause of urban decay. The paragraph never mentions such events.

Paragraph 4		**Comments**
S1	How can the process of urban decay be prevented or reversed?	How to stop or reverse urban decay?
2	There are several potential mechanisms.	Several ways.
3	One is gentrification, which is effectively the process of urban decay in reverse.	Gentrification = urban decay in reverse.
4	With gentrification, wealthier outsiders become attracted to an urban area and move into it.	
5	This attracts investment and increases property values; new, lucrative businesses may emerge, and property owners have an incentive to invest in improvements.	
6	Tax revenues increase as the new residents with higher income populate the neighborhood.	
7	However, gentrification has its drawbacks.	Drawbacks of gentrification.
8	Pricing pressures created by the influx of new residents and businesses may render current residents unable to afford the neighborhood; existing businesses may experience hardship in the face of increased competition from new businesses.	
9	This displacement may create conflict between the "old guard" and the new residents of the neighborhood.	Newcomers vs. "old guard."

7. The word "lucrative" in the passage is closest in meaning to

VOCABULARY. "Lucrative" = profitable, money-making.

✗ (A) competitive

There are two common meanings of "competitive." It can be thought of as competition in a more aggressive sense (competitive players willing to be pushy or aggressive in order to win), or in terms of staying balanced (competitive prices are thought to be moderate or even low in order to draw customers). This second definition might seem related to making money, and therefore "lucrative," but they are not related.

✗ (B) growing

Not quite. A growing business might not make a profit, and a profitable business might not be growing.

✓ (C) profitable

CORRECT. "New, lucrative businesses may emerge" = new, profitable businesses may emerge.

✗ (D) unsuccessful

Opposite. Something that is "unsuccessful" would be a failure and likely unprofitable.

8. According to paragraph 4, which of the following statements about gentrification is true?

FACT. S3 and the following sentences discuss gentrification, along with its positives and negatives.

✗ (A) It creates conditions that discourage additional investment in the area.

S4 describes gentrification as a process by which "wealthier outsiders become attracted to an urban area and move into it." S5: "This attracts investment." So investment is not discouraged, but encouraged.

✓ (B) It can lead to displacements in a neighborhood, creating clashes among residents.

CORRECT. S9: "This displacement may create conflict between the 'old guard' and the new residents of the neighborhood."

✗ (C) It tends to be the result of promotion or facilitation by government agencies.

The paragraph does not state or imply that government plays a role in gentrification.

✗ (D) It can lead to declines in property prices in the face of increased competition.

S8: "Pricing pressures created by the influx of new residents and businesses may render current residents unable to afford the neighborhood." This implies that gentrification can cause prices to increase, not decrease.

Paragraph 5	**Comments**
S1 Another common mechanism for urban renewal is government-sponsored redevelopment projects.	Urban renewal can also happen through government redevelopment.
2 Large sections of a city may be acquired by the government, with existing structures refurbished or, more likely, demolished and replaced with new construction.	Government buys up parts of city, improves or demolishes and rebuilds.
3 This may include the development of commercial buildings, residential buildings, sporting venues, parks, bridges, or highways.	

9. According to paragraph 5, government-sponsored redevelopment projects

FACT. All of P5 is devoted to government-sponsored redevelopment projects. Fortunately, the paragraph is short.

✗ (A) often meet with unexpected problems

This is not stated anywhere in P5. Problems with government-sponsored redevelopment projects are discussed in the following paragraph.

✗ (B) usually involve renovating existing buildings or infrastructure

S2: "with existing structures refurbished or, more likely, demolished and replaced with new construction." So these projects do *not* usually involve renovating existing buildings or infrastructure.

✗ (C) require substantial investment from private entities

Nothing in the paragraph suggests that private investment is required.

✓ (D) may include the construction of sports facilities

CORRECT. S3: "This [construction] may include the development of ... sporting venues."

Paragraph 6	Comments
S1 — Many urban renewal projects have failed due to unintended consequences.	Unintended consequences can cause urban renewal projects to fail.
2 — For example, a highway or bridge construction project may leave an entire section of the city divided in half.	Examples.
3 — Residents displaced by the project may relocate to another neighborhood entirely, further exacerbating the population decline that the project was intended to reverse.	
4 — Traffic patterns may change, resulting in new opportunities for some businesses while severely impairing businesses that may now be bypassed because of the change in traffic flow.	
5 — These kinds of possible consequences subject many urban renewal projects to scrutiny by (and political pressure from) residents, existing business owners, and advocacy groups.	Scrutiny and political pressure.

10. The word "exacerbating" in the passage is closest in meaning to

   ✓ (A) intensifying

   ✗ (B) hindering

   ✗ (C) alleviating

   ✗ (D) signaling

VOCABULARY. "Exacerbate" = make worse, aggravate, amplify (something bad).

CORRECT. "Further exacerbating the population decline" = further intensifying or worsening the population decline. Although you can "intensify" good things as well, "intensifying" is an appropriate synonym for "exacerbating" in the context of this sentence.

Opposite. "Hinder" = obstruct, prevent from advancing.

Opposite in a different way. "Alleviate" = make better.

Unrelated. Displacement might have "signaled" (indicated, pointed to) the population decline, but it does not mean that it made it worse as "exacerbate" does.

11. Paragraph 6 supports which of the following statements about the unintended consequences of urban renewal projects?

   ✗ (A) They typically result from serious mistakes in the planning process.

   ✗ (B) They generally involve either subtle or dramatic changes in traffic patterns.

   ✓ (C) Residents and activists often pay close attention to urban renewal projects in order to avoid these consequences.

   ✗ (D) Government projects are more likely to experience unintended consequences than privately planned development projects.

FACT. Virtually all of P6 is devoted to unintended consequences from these projects.

In hindsight, some of these consequences may be viewed as the result of planning mistakes. This outcome seems plausible, in fact. But the passage never makes a hint in this direction.

S4 mentions changing traffic patterns as a possible result of these projects. But other examples of unintended consequences are given. Nothing in the paragraph suggests that traffic pattern changes are more likely than other consequences.

CORRECT. S5: "These kinds of possible consequences subject many urban renewal projects to scrutiny by (and political pressure from) residents, existing business owners, and advocacy groups." Scrutiny = close examination.

Nothing in the paragraph compares government and private development projects, or their consequences.

4

Paragraph 5		Comments
P5 S1	Another common mechanism for urban renewal is government-sponsored redevelopment projects.	
2–3	**A** Large sections of a city may be acquired by the government, with existing structures refurbished or, more likely, demolished and replaced with new construction. This may include the development of commercial buildings, residential buildings, sporting venues, parks, bridges, or highways.	Placing the new sentence here interrupts the logical flow, as indicated by the verb tenses. S1–3 are all in present tense, because they discuss and describe the phenomenon of government-sponsored redevelopment projects in *general*. But the new sentence in the past tense discusses a *particular* historical event (how many of these projects came about).
End	**B**	**CORRECT.** This placement allows "Many such large-scale construction projects" to refer to the development projects mentioned in S3. Also, tucking in the new sentence at the end of P5 allows the following text to be clearly separated, as the new paragraph starts.

Paragraph 6		Comments
P6 S1	Many urban renewal projects have failed due to unintended consequences.	
2–4	**C** For example, a highway or bridge construction project may leave an entire section of the city divided in half. Residents displaced by the project may relocate to another neighborhood entirely, further exacerbating the population decline that the project was intended to reverse. Traffic patterns may change, resulting in new opportunities for some businesses while severely impairing businesses that may now be bypassed because of the change in traffic flow.	Placing the new sentence here interrupts the logical connection between "unintended consequences" in S1 and the examples of these consequences in S2–4.
5	**D** These kinds of possible consequences subject many urban renewal projects to scrutiny by (and political pressure from) residents, existing business owners, and advocacy groups.	Placing the new sentence here breaks the logical flow. The subject of S5, "These kinds of possible consequences," needs to refer to the list of unintended consequences in S2-4, not the unrelated topic of the new sentence.

4

12.   **Many such large-scale construction projects were undertaken in the United States after passage of the Fair Housing Act of 1949, which provided for federal funds to help cities pay for them.**

Where would the sentence best fit?

✗   (A) Choice A

✓   (B) Choice B

✗   (C) Choice C

✗   (D) Choice D

INSERT TEXT. The prior sentence should clearly refer to large-scale construction projects. This new sentence introduces a historical event that isn't discussed elsewhere in the existing passage. So the sentence needs to function as an aside. The following text, if any, will need to transition away from this aside effectively.

CORRECT.

	Whole Passage	Comments
P1	Urban decay is the process by which established cities, or parts of them, atrophy under the weight of any of several possible societal changes, falling into a state of dilapidation …	Urban decay is the decay of a city or a part of it. Common reason: loss of jobs from a company closing. Cascade of bad effects.
P2	Other factors may be the primary cause of urban decay …	Other causes of urban decay. White flight: mass migration of European Americans out of cities. Helped by Interstate Highway System, which enabled longer commutes. Second Great Migration of African Americans probably also accelerated white flight.
P3	Another factor arguably contributing to urban decay is rent control, wherein tenants are guaranteed a relatively affordable price for renting apartments within a city …	Another potential factor: rent control. Can keep rents artificially low and discourage neighborhood investment.
P4	How can the process of urban decay be prevented or reversed? There are several potential mechanisms …	How to stop or reverse urban decay? Several ways. Gentrification = urban decay in reverse. Drawbacks of gentrification. Newcomers vs. "old guard."
P5	Another common mechanism for urban renewal is government-sponsored redevelopment projects …	Urban renewal can also happen through government redevelopment. Government buys up parts of city, improves or demolishes and rebuilds.
P6	Many urban renewal projects have failed due to unintended consequences …	Unintended consequences can cause urban renewal projects to fail. Examples. Scrutiny and political pressure.

4

13.   Select from the seven phrases below THREE that contribute to urban decay and TWO that contribute to urban renewal. Two of the phrases will NOT be used.

A	White flight	**TABLE.** Contribute to = help cause, support, reinforce. Correct answers do not have to be primary causes of urban decay or urban renewal. They just need to be potential and/or partial contributors to each phenomenon.

A	White flight	**URBAN DECAY.** Described in the first half of P2 as a cause of urban decay in some cities in the United States.
B	An increase in tax rates	**NEITHER.** Tax revenue decline is mentioned as a consequence of urban decay. But changes in tax rates are never discussed as a cause of either urban decay or urban renewal.
C	Rent control	**URBAN DECAY.** P3 discusses this potential source of urban decay in depth.
D	Gentrification	**URBAN RENEWAL.** Most of P4 discusses gentrification as a trigger for urban renewal.
E	The presence of small businesses such as restaurants	**NEITHER.** Small businesses are mentioned in P1 as potential victims if a large employer closes operations. But the presence of small businesses is not cited as a source of either urban decay or renewal.
F	Loss of manufacturing facilities	**URBAN DECAY.** Described in P1 S2–3 as an example of how urban decay can happen.
G	Government-sponsored construction	**URBAN RENEWAL.** P5 is devoted to this driver of urban renewal.

Chapter 5

Reading C: Natural Science

Reading passages and questions test your ability to comprehend and analyze academic information. Most questions are multiple-choice with four options (select one from A, B, C, or D). Some questions may ask you to select more than one option or to fill in a table.

Reading passages test your understanding of main ideas and details, as well as the organization of the passage or of specific parts of the passage. They also test your understanding of the relationship between different ideas and your ability to make inferences (messages implied by the passage).

How should you use this chapter? Here are some recommendations, according to the level you've reached in TOEFL Reading:

1. **Fundamentals**. Start with a topic-focused chapter, such as this one. Start with a topic that is a "medium weakness"—not your worst area but not your best either. At first, work untimed and check the answer after each question. Review the solutions closely, think carefully about the principles at work, and articulate what you've learned. Redo questions as necessary. As you improve, time yourself and do all of the questions for a passage at once, without stopping.

2. **Fixes**. Do one passage and set of questions untimed, examine the results, and learn your lessons. Next, test yourself with timed sets. When doing timed sets, don't check your answers until you're done with the whole set.

3. **Tweaks**. Confirm your mastery by doing a passage and question set under timed conditions. Concentrate on your weaker topic areas. Aim to improve the speed and ease of your process. As soon as you're ready, move to mixed-topic practice.

Good luck on Reading!

5.1 Lead in Gasoline (Petrol)

The element lead is a heavy, soft metal that has been known since ancient times to be poisonous in large quantities. More recently, it has been recognized that even low exposure to lead causes biological damage over long periods of time. For decades in the twentieth century, however, nearly every automobile produced exhaust laced with lead.

In the body, lead causes widespread damage by interfering with many enzymes (proteins that enable biological processes). The typical ion, or charged atomic form, of lead easily replaces calcium, iron, and zinc ions, which are necessary components of these enzymes. Lead ions are imperfect replacements, so the enzymes fail to function properly. Lead particularly damages the central nervous system, impeding the proper growth and working of brain cells. The element also displaces calcium in bone tissue, providing a reservoir for lead to reenter the rest of the body even when outside sources are removed. Children are particularly vulnerable to harm from lead exposure and can be impaired cognitively and behaviorally for life.

Easy to find, mine, and refine, lead has been in use for thousands of years. The word "plumbing" comes from *plumbum*, the Latin word for lead, because the ancient Romans ran drinking water through pipes made of the metal. Lead is now a crucial component of car batteries, radiation shields, and ammunition. The two forms of lead that have contributed the most to human exposure, however, are lead paint and tetraethyl lead (TEL), a gasoline additive that prevents a problem called engine knock.

Internal combustion engines depend upon the smooth burning of mixtures of fuel and air, so that the pistons inside the engines are driven in a steady way. When these mixtures ignite prematurely, however, unintended shock waves damage the pistons and other engine parts. This phenomenon is labeled "engine knock" for the loud metallic pinging that accompanies the shock waves. Engine knock is suppressed by changing the composition of the fuel itself or by adding other chemicals. Early automobile engines that ran on petroleum-based fuel suffered greatly from engine knock, because it was difficult and expensive to alter the makeup of the fuel itself to eliminate this issue.

Without the discovery of TEL's "antiknock" capabilities, automobiles may have had to run on non-petroleum-based fuel, such as ethanol. However, in 1919, TEL was identified as a potent additive to gasoline that eliminated knock and further lubricated engine valves. The United States oil industry quickly began to manufacture TEL and promote it as a means of improving both power and fuel economy in automobiles. Rapid expansion of industrial production of the additive resulted in several lethal accidents, as unprotected chemical plant workers were poisoned by contact with TEL. After a conference called by the chief United States health official, however, TEL was approved for countrywide use. Soon, automobiles in the United States and elsewhere were running almost exclusively on leaded gasoline.

In the late 1940s, geologist Clair Patterson analyzed the radioactive decay of uranium into lead in terrestrial rocks, as well as in meteorites, in order to determine the age of the Earth. In these investigations, however, Patterson had to overcome contamination resulting from lead pollution. The focus of his subsequent research was to show how widespread this contamination was and to advocate for restrictions on the use of TEL. His advocacy, as well as that of other scientists, was resisted by supporters of the lead and automobile industries. Under pressure to reduce general air pollution created by automobiles, however, manufacturers announced in the early 1970s that antipollution devices called catalytic converters would be installed on new cars. Since these devices would be ruined by lead, the use of TEL was to be phased out.

By 1986, the use of lead gasoline additives in the United States was prohibited. Since then, sharp reductions in blood-lead levels in the population have been observed, along with other improvements in public health. Nevertheless, TEL is still used in automobiles in a few countries, as well as in "avgas" (aviation gasoline) that fuels propeller airplanes around the world. In addition, the blanket of lead particles deposited globally by prior combustion of leaded gasoline will pose an environmental hazard for many years to come.

> Now answer the questions.

Paragraph 1

S1   The element lead is a heavy, soft metal that has been known since ancient times to be poisonous in large quantities.

2   More recently, it has been recognized that even low exposure to lead causes biological damage over long periods of time.

3   For decades in the twentieth century, however, nearly every automobile produced exhaust laced with lead.

1. The phrase "laced with" in the passage is closest in meaning to

    (A) improved by

    (B) deprived of

    (C) mixed with

    (D) obtained from

Paragraph 2

S1   In the body, lead causes widespread damage by interfering with many enzymes (proteins that enable biological processes).

2   The typical ion, or charged atomic form, of lead easily replaces calcium, iron, and zinc ions, which are necessary components of these enzymes.

3   Lead ions are imperfect replacements, so the enzymes fail to function properly.

4   Lead particularly damages the central nervous system, impeding the proper growth and working of brain cells.

5   The element also displaces calcium in bone tissue, providing a reservoir for lead to reenter the rest of the body even when outside sources are removed.

6   Children are particularly vulnerable to harm from lead exposure and can be impaired cognitively and behaviorally for life.

2. In paragraph 2, the author indicates that enzymes in the body do not work correctly when they contain lead ions because

    (A) lead ions easily replace calcium, iron, and zinc ions

    (B) calcium, iron, and zinc ions are necessary components of the enzymes

    (C) lead ions are flawed substitutes for calcium, iron, and zinc ions

    (D) lead ions cause particular damage to the central nervous system

3. Why does the author mention a "reservoir" in paragraph 2?

(A) To describe how lead could be re-released in the body

(B) To illustrate how lead displaces calcium in bone tissue

(C) To support the point that lead impedes the proper working of cells

(D) To provide an example of a location where lead is replaced by calcium ions

Paragraph 3

S1 Easy to find, mine, and refine, lead has been in use for thousands of years.

2   The word "plumbing" comes from *plumbum,* the Latin word for lead, because the ancient Romans ran drinking water through pipes made of the metal.

3   Lead is now a crucial component of car batteries, radiation shields, and ammunition.

4   The two forms of lead that have contributed the most to human exposure, however, are lead paint and tetraethyl lead (TEL), a gasoline additive that prevents a problem called engine knock.

4. Which of the sentences below best expresses the essential information in the highlighted sentence in paragraph 3? Incorrect choices change the meaning in important ways or leave out essential information.

(A) Tetraethyl lead, which is added to gasoline to prevent engine knock, contributes more than lead paint to human exposure.

(B) As a result of its anti-knock properties, the gasoline additive tetraethyl lead is the form of lead that contributes the most to human exposure.

(C) A gasoline additive and lead paint have contributed to human exposure to lead.

(D) Lead paint and a gasoline additive have contributed more to human exposure than any other forms of lead.

Paragraph 4

S1 Internal combustion engines depend upon the smooth burning of mixtures of fuel and air, so that the pistons inside the engines are driven in a steady way.

2   When these mixtures ignite prematurely, however, unintended shock waves damage the pistons and other engine parts.

3   This phenomenon is labeled "engine knock" for the loud metallic pinging that accompanies the shock waves.

4   Engine knock is suppressed by changing the composition of the fuel itself or by adding other chemicals.

5   Early automobile engines that ran on petroleum-based fuel suffered greatly from engine knock, because it was difficult and expensive to alter the makeup of the fuel itself to eliminate this issue.

  MANHATTAN PREP

5. The word "prematurely" in the passage is closest in meaning to

  (A) violently

  (B) early

  (C) unevenly

  (D) belatedly

6. It can be inferred from paragraph 4 that the primary reason to suppress engine knock is to

  (A) reduce the harm to various engine parts

  (B) muffle the loud metallic pings that result

  (C) improve the composition of the engine's fuel

  (D) promote the ignition of fuel–air mixtures

7. The phrase "this issue" in the passage refers to

  (A) engines running on petroleum-based fuel

  (B) engines suffering from knock

  (C) the difficulty and expense of fuel alterations

  (D) the addition of other chemicals to the fuel

Paragraph 5

5

S1	Without the discovery of TEL's "antiknock" capabilities, automobiles may have had to run on non-petroleum-based fuel, such as ethanol.
2	However, in 1919, TEL was identified as a potent additive to gasoline that eliminated knock and further lubricated engine valves.
3	The United States oil industry quickly began to manufacture TEL and promote it as a means of improving both power and fuel economy in automobiles.
4	Rapid expansion of industrial production of the additive resulted in several lethal accidents, as unprotected chemical plant workers were poisoned by contact with TEL.
5	After a conference called by the chief United States health official, however, TEL was approved for countrywide use.
6	Soon, automobiles in the United States and elsewhere were running almost exclusively on leaded gasoline.

8. When does paragraph 5 indicate that lethal accidents occurred in relation to other events described?

  (A) Before TEL was identified as a potent gasoline additive

  (B) After a conference that the chief United States health official called

  (C) Before the rapid expansion of industrial production of TEL

  (D) After the promotion of TEL as a way to improve automobile performance

9. The phrase "almost exclusively" in the passage is closest in meaning to

   (A) wholly and entirely

   (B) hardly at all

   (C) virtually privately

   (D) with few exceptions

Paragraph 6

S1   In the late 1940s, geologist Clair Patterson analyzed the radioactive decay of uranium into lead in terrestrial rocks, as well as in meteorites, in order to determine the age of the Earth.

2   In these investigations, however, Patterson had to overcome contamination resulting from lead pollution.

3   The focus of his subsequent research was to show how widespread this contamination was and to advocate for restrictions on the use of TEL.

4   His advocacy, as well as that of other scientists, was resisted by supporters of the lead and automobile industries.

5   Under pressure to reduce general air pollution created by automobiles, however, manufacturers announced in the early 1970s that antipollution devices called catalytic converters would be installed on new cars.

6   Since these devices would be ruined by lead, the use of TEL was to be phased out.

10. The word "subsequent" in the passage is closest in meaning to

    (A) later

    (B) minor

    (C) prior

    (D) principal

11. Paragraph 6 mentions all of the following as true of the activities of geologist Clair Patterson EXCEPT:

    (A) Patterson examined the way uranium decayed in terrestrial rocks and meteorites.

    (B) Patterson confronted the problem of lead contamination caused by pollution.

    (C) Patterson advocated for resistance by supporters of the lead and automobile industries.

    (D) Patterson studied how geographically wide-ranging the lead contamination was.

Paragraph 7

S1   By 1986, the use of lead gasoline additives in the United States was prohibited.

2   Since then, sharp reductions in blood-lead levels in the population have been observed, along with other improvements in public health.

3   Nevertheless, TEL is still used in automobiles in a few countries, as well as in "avgas" (aviation gasoline) that fuels propeller airplanes around the world.

4   In addition, the blanket of lead particles deposited globally by prior combustion of leaded gasoline will pose an environmental hazard for many years to come.

12. Which of the following statements is best supported by the reports on the current use of TEL described in paragraph 7?

(A) The continued worldwide presence of TEL in avgas makes differences in the use of TEL in automobile gasoline unimportant.

(B) Blood-lead levels in countries where TEL is still used in automobiles are likely higher than in the United States.

(C) Other improvements in public health have been observed in countries where TEL is still used in automobiles.

(D) Avgas use does not contribute to the blanket of lead particles deposited globally by combustion of leaded gasoline.

Paragraph 2

P2 S4–6   Lead particularly damages the central nervous system, impeding the proper growth and working of brain cells. The element also displaces calcium in bone tissue, providing a reservoir for lead to reenter the rest of the body even when outside sources are removed. Children are particularly vulnerable to harm from lead exposure and can be impaired cognitively and behaviorally for life.

Paragraph 3

P3 S1   **A** Easy to find, mine, and refine, lead has been in use for thousands of years.

2   **B** The word "plumbing" comes from *plumbum,* the Latin word for lead, because the ancient Romans ran drinking water through pipes made of the metal.

3   **C** Lead is now a crucial component of car batteries, radiation shields, and ammunition.

4   **D** The two forms of lead that have contributed the most to human exposure, however, are lead paint and tetraethyl lead (TEL), a gasoline additive that prevents a problem called engine knock.

> Look at the part of the passage that is displayed above. The letters [A], [B], [C], and [D] indicate where the following sentence could be added.

13. **Despite this potential for injury, the utilization of lead is widespread.**

Where would the sentence best fit?

(A) Choice A

(B) Choice B

(C) Choice C

(D) Choice D

An introductory sentence for a brief summary of the passage is provided below. Complete the summary by selecting the THREE answer choices that express the most important ideas in the passage. Some sentences do not belong in the summary because they express ideas that are not presented in the passage or are minor ideas in the passage. This question is worth 2 points.

---

14. **The poisonous metal lead was released by most cars for decades.**

A   Lead is now a key component of car batteries, as well as of radiation shields and ammunition.

B   Tetraethyl lead prevents knock from damaging automobile engines.

C   Geologist Clair Patterson analyzed the radioactive decay of uranium into lead.

D   The use of leaded gasoline was finally phased out in the United States in order to reduce blood-lead levels.

E   Health improvements have occurred since the elimination of lead in United States gasoline, but dangers remain worldwide.

F   Lead causes injury throughout the human body in various ways and is especially harmful to children.

5.2 The Golden Ratio

In math, simple relationships can often take on critical roles. One such relationship, the Golden Ratio, has captivated the imagination and appealed to mathematicians, architects, astronomers, and philosophers alike. The Golden Ratio has perhaps had more of an effect on civilization than any other well-known mathematical constant. To best understand the concept, start with a line and cut it into two pieces (as seen in the figure). If the pieces are cut according to the Golden Ratio, then the ratio of the length of the longer piece to the length of the shorter piece (A : B) would be the same as the ratio of the length of the entire line to the length of the longer piece (A+B : A). Rounded to the nearest thousandth, both of these ratios will equal 1.618 : 1.

The first recorded exploration of the Golden Ratio comes from the Greek mathematician Euclid in his 13-volume treatise on mathematics, *Elements*, published in approximately 300 BC. Many other mathematicians since Euclid have studied the ratio. It appears in various elements of certain "regular" geometric figures, which are geometric figures with all side lengths equal to each other and all internal angles equal to each other. Other regular or nearly regular figures that feature the ratio include the pentagram (a five-sided star formed by five crossing line segments, the center of which is a regular pentagon) and three-dimensional solids such as the dodecahedron (whose 12 faces are all regular pentagons).

The Fibonacci sequence, described by Leonardo Fibonacci, demonstrates one application of the Golden Ratio. The Fibonacci sequence is defined such that each term in the sequence is the sum of the previous two terms, where the first two terms are 0 and 1. The next term would be $0 + 1 = 1$, followed by $1 + 1 = 2$, $1 + 2 = 3$, $2 + 3 = 5$, etc. This sequence continues: 0, 1, 1, 2, 3, 5, 8, 13, 21, 34, 55, 89, and so on. As the sequence progresses, the ratio of any number in the sequence to the previous number gets closer to the Golden Ratio. This sequence appears repeatedly in various applications in mathematics.

The allure of the Golden Ratio is not limited to mathematics, however. Many experts believe that its aesthetic appeal may have been appreciated before it was ever described mathematically. In fact, ample evidence suggests that many design elements of the Parthenon building in ancient Greece bear a relationship to the Golden Ratio. Regular pentagons, pentagrams, and decagons were all used as design elements in its construction. In addition, several elements of the façade of the building incorporate the Golden Rectangle, whose length and width are in proportion to the Golden Ratio. Since the Parthenon was built over a century before *Elements* was published, the visual attractiveness of the ratio, at least for the building's designers, may have played a role in the building's engineering and construction.

Numerous studies indicate that many pieces of art now considered masterpieces may also have incorporated the Golden Ratio in some way. Leonardo da Vinci created drawings illustrating the Golden Ratio in numerous forms to supplement the writing of *De Divina Proportione*. This book on mathematics, written by Luca Pacioli, explored the application of various ratios, especially the Golden Ratio, in geometry and art. Analysts believe that the Golden Ratio influenced proportions in some of da Vinci's other works, including his *Mona Lisa* and *Annunciation* paintings. The ratio is also evident in certain elements of paintings by Raphael and Michelangelo. Swiss painter and architect Le Corbusier used the Golden Ratio in many design components of his paintings and buildings. Finally, Salvador Dalí intentionally made the dimensions of his work *Sacrament of the Last Supper* exactly equal to the Golden Ratio, and incorporated a large dodecahedron as a design element in the painting's background.

The Golden Ratio even appears in numerous aspects of nature. Philosopher Adolf Zeising observed that it was a frequently occurring relation in the geometry of natural crystal shapes. He also discovered a common recurrence of the ratio in the arrangement of branches and leaves on the stems of many forms of plant life. Indeed, the Golden Spiral, formed by drawing a smooth curve connecting the corners of Golden Rectangles repeatedly inscribed inside one another, approximates the arrangement or growth of many plant leaves and seeds, mollusk shells, and spiral galaxies.

> Now answer the questions.

Paragraph 1

S1   In math, simple relationships can often take on critical roles.

2   One such relationship, the Golden Ratio, has captivated the imagination and appealed to mathematicians, architects, astronomers, and philosophers alike.

3   The Golden Ratio has perhaps had more of an effect on civilization than any other well-known mathematical constant.

4   To best understand the concept, start with a line and cut it into two pieces (as seen in the figure).

5   If the pieces are cut according to the Golden Ratio, then the ratio of the length of the longer piece to the length of the shorter piece (A : B) would be the same as the ratio of the length of the entire line to the length of the longer piece (A+B : A).

6   Rounded to the nearest thousandth, both of these ratios will equal 1.618 : 1.

1. According to paragraph 1, which of the following is true about the Golden Ratio?
    (A) It was invented by mathematicians.
    (B) It has significantly impacted society in general.
    (C) It is most useful to astronomers and philosophers.
    (D) It is used to accurately calculate a length.

2. The phrase "appealed to" in the passage is closest in meaning to
    (A) interested
    (B) defended
    (C) requested
    (D) repulsed

Paragraph 2

S1   The first recorded exploration of the Golden Ratio comes from the Greek mathematician Euclid in his 13-volume treatise on mathematics, *Elements*, published in approximately 300 BC.

2   Many other mathematicians since Euclid have studied the ratio.

3   It appears in various elements related to certain "regular" geometric figures, which are geometric figures with all side lengths equal to each other and all internal angles equal to each other.

4   Other regular or nearly regular figures that feature the ratio include the pentagram (a five-sided star formed by five crossing line segments, the center of which is a regular pentagon) and three-dimensional solids such as the dodecahedron (whose 12 faces are all regular pentagons).

3. According to paragraph 2, all of the following are true of the Golden Ratio EXCEPT:

   (A) Its first known description occurred in approximately 300 BC.

   (B) It was studied by mathematicians after Euclid.

   (C) It only occurs in regular geometric figures.

   (D) It appears in some three-dimensional geometric figures.

Paragraph 3

S1   The Fibonacci sequence, described by Leonardo Fibonacci, demonstrates one application of the Golden Ratio.

2   The Fibonacci sequence is defined such that each term in the sequence is the sum of the previous two terms, where the first two terms are 0 and 1.

3   The next term would be $0 + 1 = 1$, followed by $1 + 1 = 2$, $1 + 2 = 3$, $2 + 3 = 5$, etc.

4   This sequence continues: 0, 1, 1, 2, 3, 5, 8, 13, 21, 34, 55, 89, and so on.

5   As the sequence progresses, the ratio of any number in the sequence to the previous number gets closer to the Golden Ratio.

6   This sequence appears repeatedly in various applications in mathematics.

4. According to paragraph 3, which of the following is true about the Fibonacci sequence?

   (A) It can be used to estimate the Golden Ratio.

   (B) It cannot be computed without the use of the Golden Ratio.

   (C) It was discovered by Euclid in approximately 300 BC.

   (D) No two terms in the sequence are equal to one another.

5. The word "progresses" in the passage is closest in meaning to

(A) calculates

(B) declines

(C) continues

(D) disintegrates

Paragraph 4

S1	The allure of the Golden Ratio is not limited to mathematics, however.
2	Many experts believe that its aesthetic appeal may have been appreciated before it was ever described mathematically.
3	In fact, ample evidence suggests that many design elements of the Parthenon building in ancient Greece bear a relationship to the Golden Ratio.
4	Regular pentagons, pentagrams, and decagons were all used as design elements in its construction.
5	In addition, several elements of the façade of the building incorporate the Golden Rectangle, whose length and width are in proportion to the Golden Ratio.
6	Since the Parthenon was built over a century before *Elements* was published, the visual attractiveness of the ratio, at least for the building's designers, may have played a role in the building's engineering and construction.

6. According to paragraph 4, which of the following is true about the construction of the Parthenon?

(A) It was based upon the writings of Euclid.

(B) Aesthetics may have played a role in the Parthenon's use of elements that exhibit the Golden Ratio.

(C) It is an example of mathematics being prioritized over aesthetics.

(D) The designer of the Parthenon is unknown.

7. Paragraph 4 supports the idea that the designers of the Parthenon

(A) were able to derive the Golden Ratio mathematically before it was formally recorded by Euclid

(B) were aware of the Golden Ratio on some level, even if they could not formally define it

(C) were mathematicians

(D) were more interested in aesthetic concerns than sound architectural principles

8. The word "elements" in the passage is closest in meaning to

   (A) origins

   (B) substances

   (C) drawings

   (D) components

Paragraph 5

S1	Numerous studies indicate that many pieces of art now considered masterpieces may also have incorporated the Golden Ratio in some way.
2	Leonardo da Vinci created drawings illustrating the Golden Ratio in numerous forms to supplement the writing of *De Divina Proportione*.
3	This book on mathematics, written by Luca Pacioli, explored the application of various ratios, especially the Golden Ratio, in geometry and art.
4	Analysts believe that the Golden Ratio influenced proportions in some of da Vinci's other works, including his *Mona Lisa* and *Annunciation* paintings.
5	The ratio is also evident in certain elements of paintings by Raphael and Michelangelo.
6	Swiss painter and architect Le Corbusier used the Golden Ratio in many design components of his paintings and buildings.
7	Finally, Salvador Dalí intentionally made the dimensions of his work *Sacrament of the Last Supper* exactly equal to the Golden Ratio, and incorporated a large dodecahedron as a design element in the painting's background.

9. Why does the author mention that Dalí "incorporated a large dodecahedron as a design element in the painting's background"?

   (A) To demonstrate Dalí's frequent use of geometric shapes

   (B) To illustrate the extent to which the Golden Ratio has influenced some works of art

   (C) To argue that certain style elements in art are more effective than others

   (D) To refer to works by other artists such as da Vinci and Le Corbusier

10. According to paragraph 5, da Vinci's illustrations in *De Divina Proportione* and two of his paintings, the *Mona Lisa* and *Annunciation*,

    (A) exhibit evidence that da Vinci's work was influenced by the Golden Ratio

    (B) illustrate that he had a higher commitment to the Golden Ratio than other artists

    (C) provide examples showing that Renaissance art was more influenced by the Golden Ratio than modern art

    (D) demonstrate that da Vinci's work was at least as influential as the work of mathematicians or architects

Paragraph 6

S1   The Golden Ratio even appears in numerous aspects of nature.

2   Philosopher Adolf Zeising observed that it was a frequently occurring relation in the geometry of natural crystal shapes.

3   He also discovered a common recurrence of the ratio in the arrangement of branches and leaves on the stems of many forms of plant life.

4   Indeed, the Golden Spiral, formed by drawing a smooth curve connecting the corners of Golden Rectangles repeatedly inscribed inside one another, approximates the arrangement or growth of many plant leaves and seeds, mollusk shells, and spiral galaxies.

11. By including the text "formed by drawing a smooth curve connecting the corners of Golden Rectangles repeatedly inscribed inside one another," the author is

    (A) emphasizing the importance of the Golden Spiral

    (B) providing the reader with instructions for creating a Golden Spiral

    (C) defining the Golden Spiral in relation to the Golden Ratio

    (D) providing illustrations of elements in nature that exhibit the Golden Ratio

12. According to paragraph 6, which of the following is an example from nature that demonstrates the Golden Spiral?

    (A) The arrangement of branches in some forms of plant life

    (B) The common recurrence of the spiral throughout nature

    (C) The geometry of natural crystal shapes

    (D) The arrangement or growth of some galaxies

Paragraph 3

S1   The Fibonacci sequence, described by Leonardo Fibonacci, demonstrates one application of the Golden Ratio.

2–4   **A** The Fibonacci sequence is defined such that each term in the sequence is the sum of the previous two terms, where the first two terms are 0 and 1. The next term would be $0 + 1 = 1$, followed by $1 + 1 = 2$, $1 + 2 = 3$, $2 + 3 = 5$, etc. This sequence continues: 0, 1, 1, 2, 3, 5, 8, 13, 21, 34, 55, 89, and so on.

5   **B** As the sequence progresses, the ratio of any number in the sequence to the previous number gets closer to the Golden Ratio.

6   **C** This sequence appears repeatedly in various applications in mathematics.

End   **D**

Look at the part of the passage that is displayed above. The letters [A], [B], [C], and [D] indicate where the following sentence could be added.

---

13. **For example, it can be shown that the sum of the entries in consecutive diagonals of Pascal's triangle, useful in calculating binomial coefficients and probabilities, correspond to consecutive terms in the Fibonacci sequence.**

Where would the sentence best fit?

- (A) Choice A
- (B) Choice B
- (C) Choice C
- (D) Choice D

5

An introductory sentence for a brief summary of the passage is provided below. Complete the summary by selecting the THREE answer choices that express the most important ideas in the passage. Some sentences do not belong in the summary because they express ideas that are not presented in the passage or are minor ideas in the passage. This question is worth 2 points.

14. **The Golden Ratio, a mathematical relationship that has been known for centuries, has numerous applications and associated examples in the fields of mathematics, architecture, art, and nature.**

   | A | The Fibonacci sequence has numerous applications in the field of mathematics.

   | B | The Golden Ratio appears in mathematical sequences and regular geometrical figures.

   | C | Some crystals have configurations that exhibit a relationship to the Golden Ratio.

   | D | The Golden Ratio influenced the work of many famous artists, including Da Vinci, Michelangelo, Le Corbusier, and Dalí.

   | E | The Golden Ratio appears in many examples from nature, ranging from crystal formations and plant structures to the shape of mollusk shells and spiral galaxies.

   | F | Although described by Euclid in approximately 300 BC, the Golden Ratio was formally defined at a much earlier date.

5.3 Pterosaurs

Scientists have long been fascinated with the evolution of pterosaurs—warm blooded, flying reptiles that flourished during the Jurassic and Cretaceous periods, the time of the dinosaurs. Pterosaurs were the first animal after insects to develop powered flight. This ability was enabled by the pterosaur's hollow bone structure, a structure more similar to modern birds than to ancient dinosaurs. Because of their ability to fly, pterosaurs were able to expand their range and fill many ecological niches[1], eventually evolving into dozens of different species that ranged in size from a small bird to a small airplane. However, hollow bones decay more easily than solid bones, making complete pterosaur fossils hard to find. Known fossils are difficult to categorize into evolutionary families. How did the pterosaur evolve over time into the many different species that roamed the Earth? Hidden from scientists' view were the linking fossils that would indicate how closely related many of the different species were.

Fossil discoveries allowed scientists to theorize that pterosaurs first split into two subgroups: short-tailed and long-tailed. Short-tailed pterosaurs are categorized into four distinct but evolutionarily related families. Theories about which species of pterosaur belonged in which family have changed over time as new evidence emerges. One of the four families, *Gallodactylidae*, was created specifically because the swan-beaked pterosaur was thought to be distinct from the members of the other three families. *Gallodactylidae* are characterized by having fewer than 50 teeth, all of which are present only in the tip of the jaw. As new fossils were found, it was determined that swan-beaked pterosaurs were, in fact, more similar to species from other families than was originally thought. As a result, the family *Gallodactylidae* was largely disregarded.

An exciting discovery in China soon reversed that trend. In 2012, a sword-headed pterosaur was discovered that also had teeth only in the front tip of the jaw. Swan-beaked and sword-headed pterosaurs were thought, for this reason, to be similar enough that they likely both directly evolved from a single common ancestor.

niches[1]: positions or functions of an organism in a community of plants and animals

The new discovery reenergized the belief that *Gallodactylidae* was its own unique family. Scientists quickly flocked back to the practice of classifying the swan-beaked pterosaur in the family *Gallodactylidae*, this time along with the sword-headed pterosaur. Like many pterosaur fossils, the 2012 sword-headed pterosaur fossil was incomplete; only the skull and lower jaw were recovered. By categorizing the sword-headed pterosaur as a close relative of the swan-beaked pterosaur, scientists vastly expanded the geographical range of this family. No specimen of *Gallodactylidae* had ever been discovered in China before this point. Researchers also concluded that the family was far more varied than was originally thought.

However, a major discovery in 2016 again forced scientists to reevaluate their classification of pterosaurs. Another specimen of the sword-headed pterosaur was discovered, but this time it was nearly complete. The entire skull was present, along with the jawbone and much of the postcranial skeleton[2]. The fossil was almost perfect, missing only one of the rear legs and two vertebrae[3]. Analysis of this new fossil had some surprising results. The sword-headed pterosaur was actually different from the swan-beaked pterosaur in important ways. In fact, researchers determined that the sword-headed pterosaur was far more similar to species located in other families than to the swan-beaked pterosaur, with which it had been previously paired.

Again, the families were reorganized. The sword-headed pterosaur was placed in an entirely different family called *Ctenochasmatoidea*. This family has been well-studied and is already known to have members in China. While a tentative organization of pterosaurs has helped to clarify which species evolved from a common ancestor and which are less closely related, it is apparent that the classification is far from final. Additional discoveries are likely to further alter scientists' perspectives on this reptile.

Now answer the questions.

Paragraph 1

S1	Scientists have long been fascinated with the evolution of pterosaurs—warm blooded, flying reptiles that flourished during the Jurassic and Cretaceous periods, the time of the dinosaurs.
2	Pterosaurs were the first animal after insects to develop powered flight.
3	This ability was enabled by the pterosaur's hollow bone structure, a structure more similar to modern birds than to ancient dinosaurs.
4	Because of their ability to fly, pterosaurs were able to expand their range and fill many ecological niches, eventually evolving into dozens of different species that ranged in size from a small bird to a small airplane.
5	However, hollow bones decay more easily than solid bones, making complete pterosaur fossils hard to find.
6	Known fossils are difficult to categorize into evolutionary families.
7	How did the pterosaur evolve over time into the many different species that roamed the Earth?
8	Hidden from scientists' view were the linking fossils that would indicate how closely related many of the different species were.

postcranial skeleton[2]: all or part of the bones behind the skull
vertebrae[3]: bones found in the spine

1. According to paragraph 1, all of the following are true statements about pterosaurs EXCEPT:

   (A) Pterosaurs were able to spread further because of their flight.

   (B) The bones of pterosaurs were hollow.

   (C) Pterosaurs varied in size notably.

   (D) Pterosaurs were the first animal to develop powered flight.

Paragraph 2

S1   Fossil discoveries allowed scientists to theorize that pterosaurs first split into two subgroups: short-tailed and long-tailed.

2   Short-tailed pterosaurs are categorized into four distinct but evolutionarily related families.

3   Theories about which species of pterosaur belonged in which family have changed over time as new evidence emerges.

4   One of the four families, *Gallodactylidae*, was created specifically because the swan-beaked pterosaur was thought to be **distinct** from the members of the other three families.

5   *Gallodactylidae* are characterized by having fewer than 50 teeth, all of which are present only in the tip of the jaw.

6   As new fossils were found, it was determined that swan-beaked pterosaurs were, in fact, more similar to species from other families than was originally thought.

7   As a result, the family *Gallodactylidae* was largely **disregarded**.

---

2. By stating that the swan-beaked pterosaur was "**distinct**" from the members of the other three families, the author means that

   (A) it was different from previously discovered pterosaurs

   (B) it fell into expected patterns for pterosaur fossils

   (C) the three families represented a comprehensive categorization of pterosaurs

   (D) it could have been categorized into any of the three families

3. The word "**disregarded**" in the passage is closest in meaning to

   (A) ignored

   (B) celebrated

   (C) known

   (D) hoped for

Paragraph 3

S1	An exciting discovery in China soon reversed that trend.
2	In 2012, a sword-headed pterosaur was discovered that also had teeth only in the front tip of the jaw.
3	Swan-beaked and sword-headed pterosaurs were thought, for this reason, to be similar enough that they likely both directly evolved from a single common ancestor.
4	The new discovery reenergized the belief that *Gallodactylidae* was its own unique family.
5	Scientists quickly flocked back to the practice of classifying the swan-beaked pterosaur in the family *Gallodactylidae*, this time along with the sword-headed pterosaur.
6	Like many pterosaur fossils, the 2012 sword-headed pterosaur fossil was incomplete; only the skull and lower jaw were recovered.
7	By categorizing the sword-headed pterosaur as a close relative of the swan-beaked pterosaur, scientists vastly expanded the geographical range of this family.
8	No specimen of *Gallodactylidae* had ever been discovered in China before this point.
9	Researchers also concluded that the family was far more varied than was originally thought.

4. According to paragraph 3, which of the following led scientists to reclassify the swan-beaked pterosaur as a member of the family *Gallodactylidae*?

   (A) The organizational structure of subgroups and families

   (B) The discovery of a new and seemingly similar fossil

   (C) The fact that sword-headed and swan-beaked pterosaurs evolved from different ancestors

   (D) The overwhelming scientific evidence that many pterosaurs belonged in a new family

5. Which of the following can be inferred from paragraph 3 about the theory that swan-beaked and sword-headed pterosaurs had the same ancestor?

   (A) It was based on comparison of completed fossils.

   (B) It tried to account for the pterosaur's ability to fly.

   (C) Researchers assumed that a partial fossil provided enough data for meaningful conclusions.

   (D) It challenged the 2012 discovery of a sword-headed pterosaur.

6. The word "ancestor" in the passage is closest in meaning to

   (A) location

   (B) predecessor

   (C) food source

   (D) time period

Paragraph 4

S1   However, a major discovery in 2016 again forced scientists to reevaluate their classification of pterosaurs.

2   Another specimen of the sword-headed pterosaur was discovered, but this time it was nearly complete.

3   The entire skull was present, along with the jawbone and much of the postcranial skeleton.

4   The fossil was almost perfect, missing only one of the rear legs and two vertebrae.

5   Analysis of this new fossil had some surprising results.

6   The sword-headed pterosaur was actually different from the swan-beaked pterosaur in important ways.

7   In fact, researchers determined that the sword-headed pterosaur was far more similar to species located in other families than to the swan-beaked pterosaur, with which it had been previously paired.

7. All of the following are mentioned in paragraph 4 as true about the 2016 discovery of a pterosaur fossil EXCEPT:

   (A) the fact that scientists focused their research on the skull

   (B) the presence of much of the postcranial skeleton

   (C) the classification of the fossil as a sword-headed pterosaur

   (D) the fact that the fossil was missing vertebrae

8. In paragraph 4, why does the author provide details about which parts of the fossil were discovered in 2016?

   (A) To evaluate the level of research done on sword-headed pterosaurs

   (B) To illustrate the effectiveness of new fossil discovery techniques

   (C) To demonstrate the difficulty of finding a complete pterosaur fossil

   (D) To emphasize that this fossil was more complete than previously discovered fossils

9. Which of the sentences below best expresses the essential information in the highlighted sentence of paragraph 4? Incorrect choices change the meaning in important ways or leave out essential information.

   (A) The swan-beaked pterosaur and the sword-headed pterosaur are considered identical by researchers.

   (B) Researchers now pair the swan-beaked pterosaur with the sword-headed pterosaur.

   (C) Researchers have located the sword-headed pterosaur in other families.

   (D) Researchers now consider the sword-headed pterosaur less like the swan-beaked pterosaur and more like species of other families.

Paragraph 5

S1   Again, the families were reorganized.

2   The sword-headed pterosaur was placed in an entirely different family called *Ctenochasmatoidea*.

3   This family has been well-studied and is already known to have members in China.

4   While a tentative organization of pterosaurs has helped to clarify which species evolved from a common ancestor and which are less closely related, it is apparent that the classification is far from final.

5   Additional discoveries are likely to further alter scientists' perspectives on this reptile.

10. The word "tentative" in the passage is closest in meaning to

    (A) adaptive

    (B) firm

    (C) provisional

    (D) controversial

11. According to paragraph 5, which of the following is NOT an accurate conclusion about the pterosaur classification system?

    (A) Additional discoveries will probably change what scientists believe about it.

    (B) The opinions of researchers will likely remain unchanged over time.

    (C) It includes at least one family that has been researched deeply.

    (D) It helps make clear the common ancestry of certain species.

12. Why does the author mention the family "*Ctenochasmatoidea*"?

    (A) To complete the list of pterosaur families

    (B) To emphasize the differences among the four pterosaur families

    (C) To illustrate a reorganization of the pterosaur classification system

    (D) To show that not all pterosaurs had the power of flight

Paragraph 3

S1–2   An exciting discovery in China soon reversed that trend. In 2012, a sword-headed pterosaur was discovered that also had teeth only in the front tip of the jaw.

3   **A** Swan-beaked and sword-headed pterosaurs were thought, for this reason, to be similar enough that they likely both directly evolved from a single common ancestor.

4–6   **B** The new discovery reenergized the belief that *Gallodactylidae* was its own unique family. Scientists quickly flocked back to the practice of classifying the swan-beaked pterosaur in the family *Gallodactylidae*, this time along with the sword-headed pterosaur. Like many pterosaur fossils, the 2012 sword-headed pterosaur fossil was incomplete; only the skull and lower jaw were recovered.

7–8   **C** By categorizing the sword-headed pterosaur as a close relative of the swan-beaked pterosaur, scientists vastly expanded the geographical range of this family. No specimen of *Gallodactylidae* had ever been discovered in China before this point.

9   **D** Researchers also concluded that the family was far more varied than was originally thought.

Look at the part of the passage that is displayed above. The letters [A], [B], [C], and [D] indicate where the following sentence could be added.

---

13. **Species that have common ancestors are generally categorized within the same evolutionary family.**

Where would the sentence best fit?

(A) Choice A

(B) Choice B

(C) Choice C

(D) Choice D

An introductory sentence for a brief summary of the passage is provided below. Complete the summary by selecting the THREE answer choices that express the most important ideas in the passage. Some sentences do not belong in the summary because they express ideas that are not presented in the passage or are minor ideas in the passage. This question is worth 2 points.

14. **The classification of pterosaurs is an area of interest to scientists.**

A   As new discoveries are unearthed, scientists continue to change the way they classify the families of short-tailed pterosaurs.

B   The most well-studied family of pterosaurs is the *Gallodactylidae* family, which continues to be a source of much debate among scientists.

C   The 2012 discovery of a sword-headed pterosaur was incomplete, containing only the skull and a portion of the jaw.

D   The number of teeth that a pterosaur has is critical to its correct classification.

E   Living in the time of the dinosaurs, pterosaurs were reptiles that had the power of flight, making their fossils particularly difficult to discover.

F   The discovery of two different fossils of sword-headed pterosaurs has led to recent reorganizations of the families of pterosaurs.

5.4 Why Humans Have Big Brains

Humans have the largest brain of any living primate. Our brain is exceptionally large in relation to our body size. While other social mammals—whales and elephants, for example—possess big brains, their brain size tends to correspond to their overall size. Human beings, on the other hand, are disproportionately small relative to their brain size. Furthermore, the human brain is the most rapidly changing organ in mammalian history. Why did the human brain evolve to be so large, so quickly? Evidence suggests that this enlargement happened because of the social advantages it conferred on our evolutionary ancestors.

For a trait to evolve, it must be handed down to future generations through processes of natural selection. Under standard Darwinian theory, a trait must be advantageous in order to spread throughout the population of a species. This is what it means to be "selected for." Big brains are believed to be advantageous because they store and process a great deal of information, enabling owners of big brains to be more socially successful. In other words, bigger brains improved our ability to relate to other members of our species—whether through cooperation or through competition.

Other evidence that our brains became big in order to improve our social skills can be found elsewhere in the animal kingdom. Other animals that have large brains tend to be the most social species on the planet. These include elephants, sperm whales, and dolphins—all highly social mammals. The sperm whale, with a brain that is the largest of any known current or extinct species, joins a social unit early in life and typically remains with it for a lifetime. Within social units, sperm whales spend a great deal of time devoted to socializing, emitting complex patterns of clicks called "codas."

Another indication that big brains probably evolved for social reasons is that sexual selection, a form of natural selection in which mating partners "choose" a particular variation of a trait by choosing a partner

that has that variation over other partners that do not, can progress much more quickly than nonsexual selection. The fact that the brain evolved over such a short period of time in evolutionary terms implies that sexual selection may have played a role in the rapid increase in human brain size. Given that mating and competition for mates are social phenomena, having an enhanced social skill set enabled by a larger brain may have made a member of a population more attractive for sexual selection.

Why else did humans evolve such a large brain despite our relatively petite body size? After all, having a large brain is costly. The human brain takes up approximately 2 percent of the human body but is responsible for a whopping 20 percent of the entire body's energy use (the proportion of blood and oxygen directed to the brain). Tool use may provide another cause, in addition to the development of social skills: the brain increased in size more rapidly after our ancestors learned to make tools. Early tools included not only weapons used for hunting, but also equipment such as the hand ax, which allowed early humans to break down the meat before they ate it. This would have eased the burden on the digestive system, freeing up valuable metabolic resources to fuel the operations of a larger brain.

Bizarrely, over the past 10,000 to 20,000 years, the human brain has actually shown a reverse trend: it is shrinking. Across the globe, our brains are getting smaller. Some scientists predict that if the brain continues to shrink at its current rate, it will soon approach the size of the brain of *Homo erectus*, our ancestral relative from 500,000 years ago. While some fear that this means we are becoming less intelligent, others point to the warming climate. They argue that a body of smaller stature is more efficiently cooled, and a smaller brain follows a smaller stature. Critics of the climatic theory, however, point to the fact that over the 2 million years during which the brain rapidly evolved to be larger, there were also periods of global warming. So the recent shrinkage of the brain remains a mystery.

Now answer the questions.

Paragraph 1

S1	Humans have the largest brain of any living primate.
2	Our brain is exceptionally large in relation to our body size.
3	While other social mammals—whales and elephants, for example—possess big brains, their brain size tends to correspond to their overall size.
4	Human beings, on the other hand, are disproportionately small relative to their brain size.
5	Furthermore, the human brain is the most rapidly changing organ in mammalian history.
6	Why did the human brain evolve to be so large, so quickly?
7	Evidence suggests that this enlargement happened because of the social advantages it conferred on our evolutionary ancestors.

1. According to paragraph 1, for which of the following animals is the ratio of brain size to body size exceptionally high?

   (A) Whales

   (B) Elephants

   (C) Humans

   (D) Non-human primates

2. The phrase "conferred on" is closest in meaning to

   (A) burdened with

   (B) displayed to

   (C) discussed with

   (D) given to

Paragraph 2

S1	For a trait to evolve, it must be handed down to future generations through processes of natural selection.
2	Under standard Darwinian theory, a trait must be advantageous in order to spread throughout the population of a species.
3	This is what it means to be "selected for."
4	Big brains are believed to be advantageous because they store and process a great deal of information, enabling owners of big brains to be more socially successful.
5	In other words, bigger brains improved our ability to relate to other members of our species—whether through cooperation or through competition.

3. According to paragraph 2, all of the following are true EXCEPT:

   (A) Advantageous traits are selected for.

   (B) Big brains can enhance one's competitive skills in relation to other humans.

   (C) Big brains evolved so that human beings could compete with other species.

   (D) For a trait to evolve, it must be inherited by future generations.

Paragraph 3

S1   Other evidence that our brains became big in order to improve our social skills can be found elsewhere in the animal kingdom.

2   Other animals that have large brains tend to be the most social species on the planet.

3   These include elephants, sperm whales, and dolphins—all highly social mammals.

4   The sperm whale, with a brain that is the largest of any known current or extinct species, joins a social unit early in life and typically remains with it for a lifetime.

5   Within social units, sperm whales spend a great deal of time devoted to socializing, emitting complex patterns of clicks called "codas."

4. According to paragraph 3, further evidence that humans developed large brains to improve social skills comes from

   (A) other animals that also have large brains and are highly social

   (B) the fact that sperm whales emit clicking sounds called "codas"

   (C) the socialization of dolphins with whales

   (D) the rate at which the sperm whale's brain evolved over its history

Paragraph 4

S1   Another indication that big brains probably evolved for social reasons is that sexual selection, a form of natural selection in which mating partners "choose" a particular variation of a trait by choosing a partner that has that variation over other partners that do not, can progress much more quickly than nonsexual selection.

2   The fact that the brain evolved over such a short period of time in evolutionary terms implies that sexual selection may have played a role in the rapid increase in human brain size.

3   Given that mating and competition for mates are social phenomena, having an enhanced social skill set enabled by a larger brain may have made a member of a population more attractive for sexual selection.

5. According to paragraph 4, the fact that sexual selection may have helped the human brain to grow quickly in size is suggested by

   (A) the rapid evolution of the human brain

   (B) the difficulty in finding suitable mating partners

   (C) the role of sexual selection in organ development

   (D) the societal importance of natural selection

6. Which of the sentences below best expresses the essential information in the highlighted sentence in the passage? Incorrect answer choices change the meaning in important ways or leave out essential information.

- (A) Because mating and competition aren't social, a larger brain was necessary to improve social skills.

- (B) Improved social skills enabled a larger brain and therefore better mating and sexual selection prospects.

- (C) Having a larger brain allowed for better social skills, probably enabling better mating and thus sexual selection.

- (D) Attractiveness for sexual selection may have been driven by mating and competition, social phenomena that were enabled by larger brains.

Paragraph 5

S1   Why else did humans evolve such a large brain despite our relatively petite body size?

2   After all, having a large brain is costly.

3   The human brain takes up approximately 2 percent of the human body but is responsible for a whopping 20 percent of the entire body's energy use (the proportion of blood and oxygen directed to the brain).

4   Tool use may provide another cause, in addition to the development of social skills: the brain increased in size more rapidly after our ancestors learned to make tools.

5   Early tools included not only weapons used for hunting, but also equipment such as the hand ax, which allowed early humans to break down the meat before they ate it.

6   This would have eased the burden on the digestive system, freeing up valuable metabolic resources to fuel the operations of a larger brain.

7. The word "whopping" in paragraph 5 is closest in meaning to
- (A) enormous
- (B) estimated
- (C) surprising
- (D) unjustified

8. All of the following are mentioned in paragraph 5 EXCEPT:
- (A) the general use of early tools
- (B) the hunting function of weapons
- (C) the operation of the digestive tract
- (D) the use of the hand ax in social competition

Paragraph 6

S1   Bizarrely, over the past 10,000 to 20,000 years, the human brain has actually shown a reverse trend: it is shrinking.

2   Across the globe, our brains are getting smaller.

3   Some scientists predict that if the brain continues to shrink at its current rate, it will soon approach the size of the brain of *Homo erectus*, our ancestral relative from 500,000 years ago.

4   While some fear that this means we are becoming less intelligent, others point to the warming climate.

5   They argue that a body of smaller stature is more efficiently cooled, and a smaller brain follows a smaller stature.

6   Critics of the climatic theory, however, point to the fact that over the 2 million years during which the brain rapidly evolved to be larger, there were also periods of global warming.

7   So the recent shrinkage of the brain remains a mystery.

9. According to paragraph 6, which of the following is true of the global climate during the time when the human brain was evolving to become larger?

   (A) It is responsible for the current shrinking of the human brain.

   (B) It was occasionally warm.

   (C) For the most part, it was not as warm as the climate is today.

   (D) It is shifting more now than it did historically.

10. The word "approach" in the passage is closest in meaning to

   (A) become like

   (B) make contact with

   (C) measure up to

   (D) infringe upon

11. What is the author's purpose in presenting the information in paragraph 6?

   (A) To explain how the human brain is now evolving to become even larger

   (B) To advocate for one hypothesis about current trends in brain size over another

   (C) To argue against a claim made elsewhere in the passage

   (D) To describe a phenomenon that opposes the pattern described in the rest of the passage

12. The word "stature" in the passage is closest in meaning to

   (A) intelligence

   (B) height

   (C) energy level

   (D) achievement

Paragraph 6

S1   Bizarrely, over the past 10,000 to 20,000 years, the human brain has actually shown a reverse trend: it is shrinking.

2–3   **A** Across the globe, our brains are getting smaller. Some scientists predict that if the brain continues to shrink at its current rate, it will soon approach the size of the brain of *Homo erectus*, our ancestral relative from 500,000 years ago.

4–5   **B** While some fear that this means we are becoming less intelligent, others point to the warming climate. They argue that a body of smaller stature is more efficiently cooled, and a smaller brain follows a smaller stature.

6   **C** Critics of the climatic theory, however, point to the fact that over the 2 million years during which the brain rapidly evolved to be larger, there were also periods of global warming.

7   **D** So the recent shrinkage of the brain remains a mystery.

> Look at the part of the passage that is displayed above. The letters [A], [B], [C], and [D] indicate where the following sentence could be added.

13. **This is not restricted to a single region or hemisphere.**

   Where would the sentence best fit?

   (A) Choice A

   (B) Choice B

   (C) Choice C

   (D) Choice D

An introductory sentence for a brief summary of the passage is provided below. Complete the summary by selecting the THREE answer choices that express the most important ideas in the passage. Some sentences do not belong in the summary because they express ideas that are not presented in the passage or are minor ideas in the passage. This question is worth 2 points.

14. **The human brain is one of the most rapidly evolving organs in mammalian history.**

[A] The most significant drain on energy in the human body is the brain.

[B] Since a trait that successfully evolves must benefit the organism, large brains were probably advantageous to human ancestors.

[C] Large brains are mostly restricted to marine life.

[D] Darwin's theory of natural selection can explain many traits of animals on Earth.

[E] Social species tend to have the largest brains, suggesting that humans evolved large brains for social reasons.

[F] The large human brain requires a significant amount of energy, which human ancestors accessed by using tools to aid in digestion.

5.5 Crystallization

When most people hear the word "crystal," they think of something cherished and rare. In fact, however, crystals are common occurrences in nature. A crystal, by definition, is any solid whose constituent parts (atoms, molecules, or ions, for example) are arranged in a highly ordered structure. This structure repeats, forming what's known as the "crystal lattice" that extends in all directions. Most inorganic solids are polycrystals—they are not each a single crystal. Rather, they are made up of many microscopic crystals fused together to make a single solid mass. Most metals and also ceramics fall into the polycrystal category. True crystals and polycrystals can be formed by a variety of natural forces, including heat and pressure deep underground, as well as cold on the earth's surface and even the flow of water.

Gems and minerals are the most widely recognized crystals. Although most mineral crystals form under similar conditions, their structures can be very different. As a general rule, a crystal's shape, perceptible to the naked eye, is a reflection of its microscopic structure. Because crystals are the repetition of a particular structure, they are defined by the "unit cell," which is the smallest group of particles containing the pattern that is then repeated to form the crystal lattice. A crystal with cubic unit cells can form a crystal that is, itself, a cube. Pyrite, known as "fool's gold" because of its resemblance to the precious metal, has a cubic structure and often forms in masses of interlocking cubes. Crystals with hexagonal unit cells, on the other hand, tend to form in barrel-shaped hexagonal prisms or pyramids. Corundum, the mineral best known for its gem varieties ruby and sapphire, is a hexagonal crystal. Some of the most prized specimens of corundum are bipyramidal sapphires, which are hexagonal prisms that are not barrel-shaped, but instead appear as though two pyramids are stuck together at the bottom. The middle of the crystal is its widest point, and it tapers sharply at each end, forming the tips of the pyramids.

Mineral crystals can form from magmatic processes. These processes occur when molten magma (also known as lava) solidifies and cools. The conditions under which the molten magma cools modify the type of crystal that is formed. Granite, for example, cools very slowly and under intense pressure, leading to complete crystallization. Many other magmatic rocks are formed when lava pours out onto the Earth's surface and cools very quickly, leaving small amounts of glassy material and never achieving full crystallization.

Fluids can also be an agent of crystallization. Suspended in a fluid solution, microscopic molecules, or even individual atoms, can begin to gather into clusters within the solution, forming stable, though still microscopic, structures. Once a cluster is large enough to be stable, it is called a nucleus. This nucleus will contain at least one unit cell and thus will define the crystal's structure, even in this microscopic state. Crystal growth will occur as more atoms or molecules are pulled out of the solution and join with the nucleus. In this way, crystallization is a solid-liquid separation technique.

When liquids evaporate, they form crystals from the sediment (solid materials) that remain after the evaporation has taken place. Water-based "aqueous" solutions often have suspended within them particles of minerals that can form crystals if the solution evaporates. Take, for example, the water of the ocean. Ocean water is saline, meaning that it contains relatively high concentrations of salt. When saline water evaporates, the salt cannot become gaseous. Instead, it is left behind in its solid form. When these solids make up a high enough volume of the evaporating fluid, they unite, forming the crystal halite, also known as rock salt. Vast expanses of halite can form when large bodies of saline water evaporate, giving rise to great deserts of salt like the one in Bonneville, Utah. The so-called "salt flat" is composed of 90 percent pure halite, with a surface so hard and flat that it has been used since 1914 to set land speed records for car and motorcycle racers.

5

Now answer the questions.

Paragraph 1

S1   When most people hear the word "crystal," they think of something cherished and rare.

2   In fact, however, crystals are common occurrences in nature.

3   A crystal, by definition, is any solid whose constituent parts (atoms, molecules, or ions, for example) are arranged in a highly ordered structure.

4   This structure repeats, forming what's known as the "crystal lattice" that extends in all directions.

5   Most inorganic solids are polycrystals—they are not each a single crystal.

6   Rather, they are made up of many microscopic crystals fused together to make a single solid mass.

7   Most metals and also ceramics fall into the polycrystal category.

8   True crystals and polycrystals can be formed by a variety of natural forces, including heat and pressure deep underground, as well as cold on the earth's surface and even the flow of water.

1. The word "cherished" in the passage is closest in meaning to

    (A) beautiful

    (B) cheap

    (C) treasured

    (D) extraordinary

2. Which of the following questions about crystals is NOT answered in paragraph 1?

    (A) Which natural forces can form true crystals and polycrystals?

    (B) What is the definition of a crystal?

    (C) What is a crystal lattice?

    (D) What is an inorganic solid?

3. The word "fused" in the passage is closest in meaning to

    (A) dispersed

    (B) joined

    (C) chosen

    (D) burned

Paragraph 2

S1   Gems and minerals are the most widely recognized crystals.

2   Although most mineral crystals form under similar conditions, their structures can be very different.

3   As a general rule, a crystal's shape, perceptible to the naked eye, is a reflection of its microscopic structure.

4   Because crystals are the repetition of a **particular** structure, they are defined by the "unit cell," which is the smallest group of particles containing the pattern that is then repeated to form the crystal lattice.

5   A crystal with cubic unit cells can form a crystal that is, itself, a cube.

6   Pyrite, known as "fool's gold" because of its resemblance to the precious metal, has a cubic structure and often forms in masses of interlocking cubes.

7   Crystals with hexagonal unit cells, on the other hand, tend to form in barrel-shaped hexagonal prisms or pyramids.

8   Corundum, the mineral best known for its gem varieties ruby and sapphire, is a hexagonal crystal.

9   Some of the most prized specimens of corundum are bipyramidal sapphires, which are hexagonal prisms that are not barrel-shaped, but instead appear as though two pyramids are stuck together at the bottom.

10   The middle of the crystal is its widest point, and it tapers sharply at each end, forming the tips of the pyramids.

4. The word "particular" in the passage is closest in meaning to

    (A) recurring

    (B) selective

    (C) atomic

    (D) specific

5. The author mentions pyrite, ruby, and sapphire in paragraph 2 in order to

    (A) distinguish between precious and semi-precious minerals

    (B) emphasize that not all crystals are necessarily rare

    (C) illustrate crystal forms with concrete gems and minerals

    (D) emphasize the underlying similarities between cubic and hexagonal crystals

6. According to paragraph 2, which of the following hexagonal crystals can exhibit a hexagonal prism that is not shaped like a barrel?

(A) Sapphire

(B) Ruby

(C) Non-gem corundum

(D) Pyrite

7. Paragraph 2 suggests which of the following about the relationship of pyrite to gold?

(A) Pyrite has a glossier appearance than gold.

(B) Pyrite is less valuable than gold.

(C) Pyrite has a cubic crystal structure, whereas gold does not.

(D) Pyrite is less common in the environment than gold.

8. According to paragraph 2, all of the following are true of the unit cell EXCEPT:

(A) It always gives rise to the same visible shape of the crystal.

(B) It contains the pattern that is repeated to form the crystal lattice.

(C) It can influence the appearance of the crystal as perceived by the naked eye.

(D) Its features determine the classification of the crystal.

Paragraph 3

S1	Mineral crystals can form from magmatic processes.
2	These processes occur when molten magma (also known as lava) solidifies and cools.
3	The conditions under which the molten magma cools modify the type of crystal that is formed.
4	Granite, for example, cools very slowly and under intense pressure, leading to complete crystallization.
5	Many other magmatic rocks are formed when lava pours out onto the Earth's surface and cools very quickly, leaving small amounts of glassy material and never achieving full crystallization.

9. The word "modify" in the passage is closest in meaning to

(A) influence

(B) exaggerate

(C) initiate

(D) degrade

Paragraph 4

S1   Fluids can also be an **agent** of crystallization.

2   Suspended in a fluid solution, microscopic molecules, or even individual atoms, can begin to gather into clusters within the solution, forming stable, though still microscopic, structures.

3   Once a cluster is large enough to be stable, it is called a nucleus.

4   This nucleus will contain at least one unit cell and thus will define the crystal's structure, even in this microscopic state.

5   Crystal growth will occur as more atoms or molecules are pulled out of the solution and join with the nucleus.

6   In this way, crystallization is a solid-liquid separation technique.

10. The word "agent" in the passage is closest in meaning to

  (A) barrier

  (B) instrument

  (C) purveyor

  (D) result

11. According to paragraph 4, which of the following is true of a nucleus in crystal formation?

  (A) It consists of unstable clusters within a fluid solution.

  (B) It determines the structure of the crystal.

  (C) It does not contain any unit cells of the crystal.

  (D) It repels the atoms or molecules drawn out of solution to form the crystal.

Paragraph 5

S1   When liquids evaporate, they form crystals from the sediment (solid materials) that remain after the evaporation has taken place.

2   Water-based "aqueous" solutions often have suspended within them particles of minerals that can form crystals if the solution evaporates.

3   Take, for example, the water of the ocean.

4   Ocean water is saline, meaning that it contains relatively high concentrations of salt.

5   When saline water evaporates, the salt cannot become gaseous.

6   Instead, it is left behind in its solid form.

7   When these solids make up a high enough volume of the evaporating fluid, they unite, forming the crystal halite, also known as rock salt.

8   Vast expanses of halite can form when large bodies of saline water evaporate, giving rise to great deserts of salt like the one in Bonneville, Utah.

9   The so-called "salt flat" is composed of 90 percent pure halite, with a surface so hard and flat that it has been used since 1914 to set land speed records for car and motorcycle racers.

12. According to the passage, which of the following is true of halite?

(A) Its largest deposit is found in Bonneville, Utah.

(B) Its crystal structure is cubic, based on its unit cell.

(C) It is formed from solids that combine in evaporating ocean water.

(D) It is generated when salt evaporates from saline water.

Paragraph 5

S1–2   When liquids evaporate, they form crystals from the sediment (solid materials) that remain after the evaporation has taken place. Water-based "aqueous" solutions often have suspended within them particles of minerals that can form crystals if the solution evaporates.

3   **A** Take, for example, the water of the ocean.

4   **B** Ocean water is saline, meaning that it contains relatively high concentrations of salt.

5–7   **C** When saline water evaporates, the salt cannot become gaseous. Instead, it is left behind in its solid form. When these solids make up a high enough volume of the evaporating fluid, they unite, forming the crystal halite, also known as rock salt.

8–9   **D** Vast expanses of halite can form when large bodies of saline water evaporate, giving rise to great deserts of salt like the one in Bonneville, Utah. The so-called "salt flat" is composed of 90 percent pure halite, with a surface so hard and flat that it has been used since 1914 to set land speed records for car and motorcycle racers.

Look at the part of the passage that is displayed above. The letters [A], [B], [C], and [D] indicate where the following sentence could be added.

13.   **These solutions can contain particles of multiple minerals, but when one mineral exists in significantly higher concentration than the others, the crystallization process is dominated by that mineral.**

Where would the sentence best fit?

(A) Choice A

(B) Choice B

(C) Choice C

(D) Choice D

5

An introductory sentence for a brief summary of the passage is provided below. Complete the summary by selecting the THREE answer choices that express the most important ideas in the passage. Some sentences do not belong in the summary because they express ideas that are not presented in the passage or are minor ideas in the passage. This question is worth 2 points.

14. **Crystals are solids with an orderly internal structure.**

   A   It is difficult to establish what determines the shape of the unit cell as it forms.

   B   Within the Earth's crust, crystallization depends largely on the application of heat and pressure.

   C   Crystallization is a common result of various natural forces, such as the cooling of magma.

   D   A crystal's shape is determined by its unit cell, a repeating microscopic building block.

   E   Crystals can be formed through evaporation of liquids, such as large bodies of water.

   F   Bipyramidal sapphire is a more valuable mineral than cubic pyrite.

5.6 Habitat Fragmentation

The habitats of terrestrial animals, which provide food, shelter, and places to bear and raise offspring, have been changing at an unnatural pace in recent centuries. The restriction of a once large, continuous habitat into smaller, segmented pieces is called **habitat fragmentation**. This process occurs over all types of habitats and is widely recognized as one of the major barriers to effective conservation efforts.

Habitat fragmentation occurs when the landscape is changed so that plants and animals no longer have access to all of the same areas they once did. In some cases, this process can occur because part of the habitat has been destroyed, leaving animals with less roaming space than they previously had. In other cases, the habitat still exists, but a barrier emerges that prevents animals from reaching all areas of their former habitat. Regardless of how it occurs, habitat fragmentation can be dangerous to both plants and animals. Plants are unable to respond quickly to change, so if they rely on an aspect of their habitat that no longer exists, there is often not enough time to adapt, and the plant will die off. Animals are more commonly able to move into the smaller habitat areas, but they suffer nonetheless. They may be cut off from food or shelter. Often, the resources remaining can support only a smaller population, leaving the animals vulnerable to disease.

While habitat fragmentation can be devastating to populations, it naturally occurs over time. Mountains will rise, volcanoes will erupt, and rivers will change course. Any of these changes and countless other natural progressions will segment large areas into smaller ones. It is widely accepted, however, that the primary source of habitat fragmentation in the modern world is human activity. As humans expand into new areas, they change the environment to suit their needs. Habitats are destroyed to make way for man-made buildings and are divided to connect those buildings. Plants and animals that encroach into areas where humans live are repelled or killed. Edge species, which live on the borders of habitats, expand as more borders are created and will compete with species that cannot live on edges. The increased competition in a decreased space endangers many species.

Four specific activities or structures are known as the most common causes of man-made habitat fragmentation: roads, housing developments, agriculture, and logging. Roads require an extensive expanse of land to be cleared, including the area surrounding the road. A single road will split a large habitat into two smaller ones and increase the edge area. Animals that attempt to traverse the road to reach land that may be essential for their survival are in additional danger from fast-moving cars.

Housing developments are necessary, as the population of humans continues to grow. Such development not only forces land to be cleared, but also creates competition between humans and edge species. Animal and pest control keep many native species from coming into housing developments. Non-native species, particularly plants, are regularly introduced into housing developments for the benefit of the occupants. Population growth also leads to the need for more agriculture. Consequently, large tracts of land are bulldozed and the natural plants destroyed to make way for crops. The cleared land has lost all its utility to the plants and animals that once called that area home. Finally, logging, whether for industrial uses or for firewood, destroys large trees that may be necessary for species' survival. Removing trees shrinks the habitat and could eliminate both food and shelter. At the same time, the presence of humans, their equipment, and the roads they need can imperil plants and animals in the area.

For a thriving and robust species, ample area, reasonable competition, and access to essentials are all necessary. If habitat fragmentation continues at the current pace, species will be restricted to areas in which only small populations can survive or will lose the ability to survive entirely. Conserving large tracts of land in a variety of areas is already underway and may help to slow this process.

> Now answer the questions.

Paragraph 1

S1   The habitats of terrestrial animals, which provide food, shelter, and places to bear and raise offspring, have been changing at an unnatural pace in recent centuries.

2   The restriction of a once large, continuous habitat into smaller, segmented pieces is called **habitat fragmentation**.

3   This process occurs over all types of habitats and is widely recognized as one of the major barriers to effective conservation efforts.

1. According to paragraph 1, what is true of habitat fragmentation?
    (A) It provides food and shelter to terrestrial animals.
    (B) It is a barrier to conservation efforts.
    (C) It occurs only in specific types of habitats.
    (D) It was widely recognized in recent centuries.

Paragraph 2

S1 Habitat fragmentation occurs when the landscape is changed so that plants and animals no longer have access to all of the same areas they once did.

2   In some cases, this process can occur because part of the habitat has been destroyed, leaving animals with less roaming space than they previously had.

3   In other cases, the habitat still exists, but a barrier emerges that prevents animals from reaching all areas of their former habitat.

4   Regardless of how it occurs, habitat fragmentation can be dangerous to both plants and animals.

5   Plants are unable to respond quickly to change, so if they rely on **an aspect** of their habitat that no longer exists, there is often not enough time to adapt, and the plant will die off.

6   Animals are more commonly able to move into the smaller habitat areas, but they suffer nonetheless.

7   They may be cut off from food or shelter.

8   Often, the resources remaining can support only a smaller population, leaving the animals vulnerable to disease.

2. The words "**an aspect**" in the passage are closest in meaning to

    (A) a food source

    (B) an advance

    (C) an attribute

    (D) another species

3. According to paragraph 2, which of the following occurs more with plants that suffer habitat fragmentation than with animals that suffer habitat fragmentation?

    (A) Plants cannot shift as easily into smaller areas.

    (B) Plants are more vulnerable to disease.

    (C) Plants respond more quickly to change.

    (D) Plants have less time to adapt to the absence of resources.

4. According to paragraph 2, a cause of habitat fragmentation is

    (A) the lack of access by plants and animals to previously available areas

    (B) the creation of physical obstacles within the habitat

    (C) the expansion of a habitat to increase access

    (D) the inability to adapt rapidly to changes in the landscape

Paragraph 3

S1	While habitat fragmentation can be devastating to populations, it naturally occurs over time.
2	Mountains will rise, volcanoes will erupt, and rivers will change course.
3	Any of these changes and countless other natural progressions will segment large areas into smaller ones.
4	It is widely accepted, however, that the primary source of habitat fragmentation in the modern world is human activity.
5	As humans expand into new areas, they change the environment to suit their needs.
6	Habitats are destroyed to make way for man-made buildings and are divided to connect those buildings.
7	Plants and animals that encroach into areas where humans live are repelled or killed.
8	Edge species, which live on the borders of habitats, expand as more borders are created and will compete with species that cannot live on edges.
9	The increased competition in a decreased space endangers many species.

5. The word "source" in the passage is closest in meaning to

   (A) objective

   (B) function

   (C) cause

   (D) center

6. According to paragraph 3, what currently has the greatest influence on habitat fragmentation?

   (A) The actions of human beings

   (B) Natural forces such as volcanic eruptions

   (C) Encroachment by plants and animals

   (D) Increased competition at habitat borders

7. The word "endangers" in the passage is closest in meaning to

   (A) includes

   (B) empowers

   (C) deters

   (D) jeopardizes

Paragraph 4

S1	Four specific activities or structures are known as the most common causes of man-made habitat fragmentation: roads, housing developments, agriculture, and logging.
2	Roads require an extensive expanse of land to be cleared, including the area surrounding the road.
3	A single road will split a large habitat into two smaller ones and increase the edge area.
4	Animals that attempt to traverse the road to reach land that may be essential for their survival are in additional danger from fast-moving cars.

8. Why does the author mention "roads," "housing developments," "agriculture," and "logging"?

   (A) To give examples of processes that can slow habitat fragmentation

   (B) To explain why habitat fragmentation is so dangerous

   (C) To list four specific activities or structures that are known to be man-made

   (D) To illustrate the ways that human activity most impacts habitat fragmentation

Paragraph 5

S1	Housing developments are necessary, as the population of humans continues to grow.
2	Such development not only forces land to be cleared, but also creates competition between humans and edge species.
3	Animal and pest control keep many native species from coming into housing developments.
4	Non-native species, particularly plants, are regularly introduced into housing developments for the benefit of the occupants.
5	Population growth also leads to the need for more agriculture.
6	Consequently, large tracts of land are bulldozed and the natural plants destroyed to make way for crops.
7	The cleared land has lost all its utility to the plants and animals that once called that area home.
8	Finally, logging, whether for industrial uses or for firewood, destroys large trees that may be necessary for species' survival.
9	Removing trees shrinks the habitat and could eliminate both food and shelter.
10	At the same time, the presence of humans, their equipment, and the roads they need can imperil plants and animals in the area.

MANHATTAN PREP

9. The word "utility" in the passage is closest in meaning to

    (A) value

    (B) nutrients

    (C) stability

    (D) energy

10. Why does the author mention "firewood"?

    (A) To emphasize the danger of fires to habitats

    (B) To clarify that human activity is not always undesirable

    (C) To provide an example of why logging may occur

    (D) To point out an easily eliminated cause of habitat fragmentation

Paragraph 6

S1   For a thriving and robust species, ample area, reasonable competition, and access to essentials are all necessary.

2   If habitat fragmentation continues at the current pace, species will be restricted to areas in which only small populations can survive or will lose the ability to survive entirely.

3   Conserving large tracts of land in a variety of areas is already underway and may help to slow this process.

11. Which of the sentences below best expresses the essential information in the highlighted sentence in paragraph 6? Incorrect choices change the meaning in important ways or leave out essential information.

    (A) Species will be eliminated or restricted to areas that can only support small populations if the current pace of habitat fragmentation continues to slow.

    (B) Habitat fragmentation, if not slowed, will be restricted to areas in which only small populations of species can survive, if at all.

    (C) The current pace of habitat fragmentation, if continued, will eradicate species or restrict them to small numbers in their remaining habitats.

    (D) Only small populations of species, or none at all, will survive in areas currently restricted from the continued pace of habitat fragmentation.

12. It can be inferred from paragraph 6 that compared with fragmented habitats, habitats that have not been fragmented

(A) are likely to be much rarer globally

(B) have probably benefited from conservation efforts

(C) provide access to all the essentials species need

(D) will likely support larger populations

Paragraph 5

S1–2   Housing developments are necessary, as the population of humans continues to grow. Such development not only forces land to be cleared, but also creates competition between humans and edge species.

3–4   **A** Animal and pest control keep many native species from coming into housing developments. Non-native species, particularly plants, are regularly introduced into housing developments for the benefit of the occupants.

5–6   **B** Population growth also leads to the need for more agriculture. Consequently, large tracts of land are bulldozed and the natural plants destroyed to make way for crops.

7–8   **C** The cleared land has lost all its utility to the plants and animals that once called that area home. Finally, logging, whether for industrial uses or firewood, destroys large trees that may be necessary for species' survival.

9–10   **D** Removing trees shrinks the habitat and could eliminate both food and shelter. At the same time, the presence of humans, their equipment, and the roads they need can imperil plants and animals in the area.

> Look at the part of the passage that is displayed above. The letters [A], [B], [C], and [D] indicate where the following sentence could be added.

13. **These species compete with native plants and often exacerbate habitat fragmentation.**

Where would the sentence best fit?

(A) Choice A

(B) Choice B

(C) Choice C

(D) Choice D

An introductory sentence for a brief summary of the passage is provided below. Complete the summary by selecting the THREE answer choices that express the most important ideas in the passage. Some sentences do not belong in the summary because they express ideas that are not presented in the passage or are minor ideas in the passage. This question is worth 2 points.

14. **Habitat fragmentation is a process that poses a threat to the survival of some plant and animal species.**

A   Habitat fragmentation can occur when part of the habitat is destroyed by the changed course of a river.

B   Despite the fact that habitat fragmentation occurs naturally, human activity is currently its principal cause.

C   Creation of roads is the most common human activity that results in habitat fragmentation.

D   The four major contributors to man-made habitat fragmentation impact species in various powerful ways.

E   Conservation efforts will be able to halt habitat fragmentation if implemented worldwide.

F   Without limiting the human impact on large areas of land, many species will shrink and possibly disappear over time.

5.7 Is Pluto a Planet?

Prior to 2006, the International Astronomical Union (IAU) had no formal definition of a planet, and it was generally assumed that the Solar System contained nine planets. Before the astronomical discoveries of the early twenty-first century, the definition of a planet seemed self-evident: a large body orbiting the Sun, readily distinguishable from moons, which orbit planets. In the early 1800s, smaller orbiting bodies were discovered; these were eventually classified as asteroids. Around the same time, astronomers also used increasingly powerful telescopes to identify additional planets beyond Saturn that were not readily visible to the naked eye. The first planet discovered was Uranus, sighted in 1781 by astronomer William Herschel. The charting of Uranus's unusual orbit then led scientists to predict the presence of another planet, whose gravitational pull would account for the irregularities in Uranus's movement around the sun. The resulting calculations of the new planet's position were so accurate that, in 1846, astronomer Johann Galle finally observed Neptune within a degree of its predicted location. Subsequently, additional observations of Uranus led astronomers to conclude that there was yet another planet in the outer reaches of the Solar System.

One of the early proponents of the existence of a new planet was Percival Lowell, a wealthy Bostonian who founded the Lowell Observatory in Arizona in 1894. He spearheaded extensive research into the existence of a ninth planet, known as "Planet X." This research was unsuccessful during Lowell's lifetime. After Lowell's death, the search stalled for over a decade, resuming only in 1929, when the young astronomer Clyde Tombaugh was tasked with finding the planet. Tombaugh systematically took pairs of photographs

of the night sky to look for a moving object, spending nearly a year on this painstaking task. His efforts were rewarded in January 1930, when he finally obtained evidence of Planet X's existence.

This planet was named Pluto and remained the ninth planet until the early twenty-first century, when new discoveries called its status as a planet into question. These discoveries included the sightings, starting in the early 1990s, of a number of other large objects near Pluto, which are now known as Kuiper Belt objects. Discovered in 2005, Eris is the largest of these. Eris is significantly more massive than Pluto and was briefly called the tenth planet by some. The lack of consensus on Eris's planetary status led the IAU to convene a meeting on the definition of a planet in 2006.

So is Pluto a planet? According to the definition produced by the IAU in 2006, it is not. A planet must meet three criteria: it orbits around the Sun; it is large enough to form itself into a sphere; and it is also large enough to clear other objects of significant size from its orbit. If one sticks rigorously to this definition, Pluto is not a planet; it meets only the first two criteria, as there are a number of other objects, like Eris, in its vicinity. However, not all astronomers agree with this definition; some believe that the presence of asteroids in the orbit of planets like Earth, Mars, and Jupiter would similarly disqualify them as planets.

Scientists continue to disagree about Pluto's status. Another debate on the subject was held in 2008, but the attendees did not reach agreement on the subject. Additionally, there was a wide public outcry, based largely on sentimental attachment, when Pluto's new classification as a "dwarf planet" was announced. Given the existence of a number of other large objects near Pluto, continuing to define Pluto as a planet could lead to the classification of many other entities as planets. Demoting Pluto seems like a simpler solution.

This is not to say that claims supporting Pluto's status as a planet don't have merit. Pluto does, in many respects, resemble other planets in the Solar System in its orbit and shape. Unlike these planets, though, Pluto is relatively small and has an unusual relationship with its large moon, Charon. Furthermore, the presence of many similar large bodies in Pluto's vicinity suggests that, without a clear standard definition such as the one decided upon by the IAU, we could find ourselves one day including dozens of planets in our Solar System, making for some extremely complicated school science projects.

> Now answer the questions.

Paragraph 1

S1   Prior to 2006, the International Astronomical Union (IAU) had no formal definition of a planet, and it was generally assumed that the Solar System contained nine planets.

2   Before the astronomical discoveries of the early twenty-first century, the definition of a planet seemed self-evident: a large body orbiting the Sun, readily distinguishable from moons, which orbit planets.

3   In the early 1800s, smaller orbiting bodies were discovered; these were eventually classified as asteroids.

4   Around the same time, astronomers also used increasingly powerful telescopes to identify additional planets beyond Saturn that were not readily visible to the naked eye.

5   The first planet discovered was Uranus, sighted in 1781 by astronomer William Herschel.

6   The charting of Uranus's unusual orbit then led scientists to predict the presence of another planet, whose gravitational pull would account for the irregularities in Uranus's movement around the sun.

7   The resulting calculations of the new planet's position were so accurate that, in 1846, astronomer Johann Galle finally observed Neptune within a degree of its predicted location.

8   Subsequently, additional observations of Uranus led astronomers to conclude that there was yet another planet in the outer reaches of the Solar System.

1.   The word "self-evident" in the passage is closest in meaning to

   (A) simplistic

   (B) obvious

   (C) paradoxical

   (D) qualified

2.   The author mentions planets "not readily visible to the naked eye" in order to

   (A) explain the usefulness of telescopes for the observation of these planets

   (B) assert that these planets could not have been discovered without increasingly powerful instruments

   (C) emphasize the fact that planets do not give off their own light, but instead reflect it

   (D) highlight specific technical improvements related to the manufacture of lenses

Paragraph 2

S1   One of the early **proponents of** the existence of a new planet was Percival Lowell, a wealthy Bostonian who founded the Lowell Observatory in Arizona in 1894.

2   He spearheaded extensive research into the existence of a ninth planet, known as "Planet X."

3   This research was unsuccessful during Lowell's lifetime.

4   After Lowell's death, the search stalled for over a decade, resuming only in 1929, when the young astronomer Clyde Tombaugh was tasked with finding the planet.

5   Tombaugh systematically took pairs of photographs of the night sky to look for a moving object, spending nearly a year on this painstaking task.

6   His efforts were rewarded in January 1930, when he finally obtained evidence of Planet X's existence.

3. The phrase "**proponents of**" in the passage is closest in meaning to:

   (A) explorers of

   (B) advocates for

   (C) skeptics of

   (D) oracles of

4. According to the passage, which of the following was true of Percival Lowell?

   (A) He is solely responsible for the successful effort to locate Pluto.

   (B) He tasked Clyde Tombaugh with continuing the search for Planet X.

   (C) He was originally from Boston.

   (D) He delayed efforts to find the planet by over a decade.

Paragraph 3

S1   This planet was named Pluto and remained the ninth planet until the early twenty-first century, when new discoveries called its status as a planet into question.

2   These discoveries included the sightings, starting in the early 1990s, of a number of other large objects near Pluto, which are now known as Kuiper Belt objects.

3   Discovered in 2005, Eris is the largest of these.

4   Eris is significantly more massive than Pluto and was briefly called the tenth planet by some.

5   The lack of **consensus** on Eris's planetary status led the IAU to convene a meeting on the definition of a planet in 2006.

5. The word "these" in the passage refers to

   (A) planets

   (B) asteroids

   (C) researchers

   (D) Kuiper Belt objects

6. According to the passage, what prompted astronomers to reconsider the definition of a planet?

   (A) Scientists did not agree on the existence of the Kuiper Belt.

   (B) Scientists convened a meeting of the International Astronomical Union.

   (C) An orbiting object larger than Pluto was discovered near Pluto.

   (D) Pluto remained the ninth planet for decades.

7. The word "consensus" in the passage is closest in meaning to

   (A) agreement

   (B) confirmation

   (C) discrepancy

   (D) emergence

Paragraph 4

S1	So is Pluto a planet?
2	According to the definition produced by the IAU in 2006, it is not.
3	A planet must meet three criteria: it orbits around the Sun; it is large enough to form itself into a sphere; and it is also large enough to clear other objects of significant size from its orbit.
4	If one sticks rigorously to this definition, Pluto is not a planet; it meets only the first two criteria, as there are a number of other objects, like Eris, in its vicinity.
5	However, not all astronomers agree with this definition; some believe that the presence of asteroids in the orbit of planets like Earth, Mars, and Jupiter would similarly disqualify them as planets.

8. According to the definition given in paragraph 4, which of the following must be true for something to be considered a planet?

   (A) It has no other large objects in its orbit.

   (B) It must have at least one moon.

   (C) It has a spherical orbit around the sun.

   (D) It has a mass at least as great as that of Pluto.

Paragraph 5

S1 Scientists continue to disagree about Pluto's status.

2 Another debate on the subject was held in 2008, but the attendees did not reach agreement on the subject.

3 Additionally, there was a wide public outcry, based largely on sentimental attachment, when Pluto's new classification as a "dwarf planet" was announced.

4 Given the existence of a number of other large objects near Pluto, continuing to define Pluto as a planet could lead to the classification of many other entities as planets.

5 Demoting Pluto seems like a simpler solution.

9. Which of the sentences below best expresses the essential information in the highlighted sentence in the passage? Incorrect choices change the meaning in important ways or leave out essential information.

(A) The announcement that Pluto was now a "dwarf planet" caused the public to feel sentimental attachment, based on the wide outcry.

(B) As a result of the wide public outcry, based largely on sentimental attachment, Pluto's new classification as a "dwarf planet" was announced.

(C) The wide outcry following the announcement of Pluto's "dwarf planet" status revealed the public's sentimental attachment to Pluto.

(D) Pluto's reclassification as a "dwarf planet" was based largely on sentimental attachment, as revealed in the wide public outcry following the announcement.

Paragraph 6

S1 This is not to say that claims supporting Pluto's status as a planet don't have merit.

2 Pluto does, in many respects, resemble other planets in the Solar System in its orbit and shape.

3 Unlike these planets, though, Pluto is relatively small and has an unusual relationship with its large moon, Charon.

4 Furthermore, the presence of many similar large bodies in Pluto's vicinity suggests that, without a clear standard definition such as the one decided upon by the IAU, we could find ourselves one day including dozens of planets in our Solar System, making for some extremely complicated school science projects.

10. The word "vicinity" in the passage is closest in meaning to

(A) path

(B) orbit

(C) gravitational pull

(D) neighborhood

11. According to paragraph 6, what is a characteristic of Pluto that makes it unlike other planets in the Solar System?

    (A) Its shape

    (B) Its orbit

    (C) The size of its moon

    (D) Its size

Paragraph 2

S1   One of the early proponents of the existence of a new planet was Percival Lowell, a wealthy Bostonian who founded the Lowell Observatory in Arizona in 1894.

2–3   **[A]** He spearheaded extensive research into the existence of a ninth planet, known as "Planet X." This research was unsuccessful during Lowell's lifetime.

4   **[B]** After Lowell's death, the search stalled for over a decade, resuming only in 1929, when the young astronomer Clyde Tombaugh was tasked with finding the planet.

5   **[C]** Tombaugh systematically took pairs of photographs of the night sky to look for a moving object, spending nearly a year on this painstaking task.

6   **[D]** His efforts were rewarded in January 1930, when he finally obtained evidence of Planet X's existence.

Look at the part of the passage that is displayed above. The letters [A], [B], [C], and [D] indicate where the following sentence could be added.

---

12. **However, Lowell did capture two images of Pluto in 1915, though these weren't identified as such until later.**

    Where would the sentence best fit?

    (A) Choice A

    (B) Choice B

    (C) Choice C

    (D) Choice D

> An introductory sentence for a brief summary of the passage is provided below. Complete the summary by selecting the THREE answer choices that express the most important ideas in the passage. Some sentences do not belong in the summary because they express ideas that are not presented in the passage or are minor ideas in the passage. This question is worth 2 points.

13. **Until the twenty-first century, astronomers did not have a standard definition of a planet.**

   A   Percival Lowell died before the discovery of Pluto.

   B   After its discovery, Pluto was initially called the ninth planet.

   C   By definition, planets occur in different shapes.

   D   The discovery of other large objects near Pluto led astronomers to formulate a new definition of a planet.

   E   Pluto is now officially classified as a "dwarf planet," though not all scientists agree on this.

   F   Kuiper Belt objects were discovered before Pluto was.

5.8 Turtle Navigation

Every 2 to 3 years, female leatherback sea turtles in their breeding years make their way to a beach, where they climb ashore to lay their eggs in the sand. Like other sea turtles, leatherbacks lay these eggs in a "clutch," or nest. A single clutch can contain as many as 85 eggs, although not all of them will have been fertilized. Of those that have been fertilized, however, the embryos will incubate in the sand for 50 to 60 days and then hatch, before which time the mother turtle will have already returned to the ocean. The baby turtles, or "hatchlings," collectively dig themselves out of the sand and onto the shore, where they must make their way to the sea in order to survive.

The stakes for finding the ocean quickly are extremely high. Hatchlings that do not quickly make their way from the clutch into the sea will die. During their sprints, they are at risk of predation by myriad creatures, from crabs to birds to snakes to native predators, that dwell on beaches worldwide. They are also exposed to possible dehydration should they remain out of the water for too long.

There are several factors involved in the navigation of these newborn reptiles to the sea. Light, however, is the most important factor. The hatchlings use visual cues to find their way into the lapping ocean water. In particular, they observe the reflection of the moon and stars in the night sky on the water, and the contrast of this reflection with the dark silhouettes of the dunes and trees on land.

Prior to modern times, this process was not made perilous by artificial light interfering with the turtles' seaward orientation. The turtles' innate sensitivity and attraction to light guided them where they needed to go: into the water. But nowadays, the brightest light often does not come from the moon and stars being reflected on the surface of the ocean. Instead, the bright lights of the lit structures that populate many beaches draw the baby turtles in the direction opposite of where they need to go: away from the ocean. As a result, and particularly because the leatherback turtle has been listed as an endangered species since 1970, efforts have been made to reduce the impact of artificial light on leatherback hatchlings.

Certain light-emitting diode (LED) lights that fall within set wavelengths have been found to interfere less with the navigation of baby turtles. These wavelengths are on the spectrum of light that ranges between

yellow/orange and red. Organizations such as the Florida Fish and Wildlife Conservation Commission have labeled these lights safe for use around turtles. In cooperation with wildlife advocates and organizations devoted to the protection of sea turtles, many coastal businesses worldwide have replaced problematic light fixtures with turtle-safe lighting.

Leatherbacks are "pelagic," meaning they live in open water (in contrast to staying near the shore or dwelling on the ocean bottom), and this includes the hatchlings; if they manage to make it to sea, they will venture into the open waters. Researchers have named the ensuing years the "lost years," as the turtles live in the open sea and are difficult to track. They have attempted to study their whereabouts and navigation patterns by tagging baby turtles and tracking them via satellite.

The turtles are known for their long-distance migrations and over the years will possibly travel tens of thousands of miles. When they are 15 to 25 years old, female leatherback turtles reach maturity and return to the different beaches where each was born to lay their own clutches of eggs. How does the mature leatherback find her way back to her natal beach, which is sometimes thousands of miles away? It is believed that the turtle uses the Earth's magnetic fields to accomplish this incredible feat. This magnetic sense is the same kind of "compass" used by a number of species that also navigate long distances, including monarch butterflies, yellow-fin tuna, and sockeye salmon.

> Now answer the questions.

Paragraph 1

S1	Every 2 to 3 years, female leatherback sea turtles in their breeding years make their way to a beach, where they climb ashore to lay their eggs in the sand.
2	Like other sea turtles, leatherbacks lay these eggs in a "clutch," or nest.
3	A single clutch can contain as many as 85 eggs, although not all of them will have been fertilized.
4	Of those that have been fertilized, however, the embryos will incubate in the sand for 50 to 60 days and then hatch, before which time the mother turtle will have already returned to the ocean.
5	The baby turtles, or "hatchlings," collectively dig themselves out of the sand and onto the shore, where they must make their way to the sea in order to survive.

1. According to paragraph 1, which of the following statements is true of baby leatherback turtles?

   (A) They compete with each other as they make their way to the sea.

   (B) They hatch on top of the sand of a beach.

   (C) They emerge from nests of typically just a few offspring.

   (D) By the time they hatch, their mother has returned to the sea.

2. The word "incubate" in the passage is closest in meaning to

(A) develop

(B) erupt

(C) degenerate

(D) burrow

Paragraph 2

S1   The stakes for finding the ocean quickly are extremely high.

2   Hatchlings that do not quickly make their way from the clutch into the sea will die.

3   During their sprints, they are at risk of predation by myriad creatures, from crabs to birds to snakes to native predators, that dwell on beaches worldwide.

4   They are also exposed to possible dehydration should they remain out of the water for too long.

3. Which of the sentences below best expresses the essential information in the highlighted sentence in the passage? Incorrect choices change the meaning in important ways or leave out essential information.

(A) As they race to the ocean, hatchings that avoid myriad predators on the beach are not at risk.

(B) The primary threat to hatchlings on their way to the sea is predation by various creatures that live on the beach.

(C) Numerous beach-dwelling predators are a threat to hatchlings rushing to the sea.

(D) Upon reaching the sea, hatchlings are vulnerable to a wide range of predators that live on beaches.

Paragraph 3

S1   There are several factors involved in the navigation of these newborn reptiles to the sea.

2   Light, however, is the most important factor.

3   The hatchlings use visual cues to find their way into the lapping ocean water.

4   In particular, they observe the reflection of the moon and stars in the night sky on the water, and the contrast of this reflection with the dark silhouettes of the dunes and trees on land.

4. Which of the following can be inferred from paragraph 3 about the dunes and trees?

(A) They largely fail to assist the newborn turtles in their navigation.

(B) By being uphill from the nests, they direct the hatchlings downhill toward the water.

(C) The dimness of their silhouettes causes the turtles to move away from them.

(D) They reflect the light of the moon and stars more effectively than the dark ocean water does.

Paragraph 4

S1   Prior to modern times, this process was not made perilous by artificial light interfering with the turtles' seaward orientation.

2   The turtles' innate sensitivity and attraction to light guided them where they needed to go: into the water.

3   But nowadays, the brightest light often does not come from the moon and stars being reflected on the surface of the ocean.

4   Instead, the bright lights of the lit structures that populate many beaches draw the baby turtles in the direction opposite of where they need to go: away from the ocean.

5   As a result, and particularly because the leatherback turtle has been listed as an endangered species since 1970, efforts have been made to reduce the **impact** of artificial light on leatherback hatchlings.

5.   According to paragraph 4, an important reason why baby turtles have difficulty nowadays navigating toward the sea is

    (A) the presence of distractingly illuminated buildings

    (B) the diminished brightness of the moon due to air pollution

    (C) the reduced influence of artificial light as a result of efforts since 1970

    (D) increased threats from scavenging predators, such as birds and snakes

6.   The word "**impact**" in the passage is most closest in meaning to

    (A) emphasis

    (B) effect

    (C) energy

    (D) esteem

Paragraph 5

S1   Certain light-emitting diode (LED) lights that fall within set wavelengths have been found to interfere less with the navigation of baby turtles.

2   These wavelengths are on the spectrum of light that ranges between yellow/orange and red.

3   Organizations such as the Florida Fish and Wildlife Conservation Commission have labeled these lights safe for use around turtles.

4   In cooperation with wildlife advocates and organizations devoted to the protection of sea turtles, many coastal businesses worldwide have replaced problematic light fixtures with turtle-safe lighting.

7. Why does the author mention "light-emitting diode (LED) lights" in the passage?

　　Ⓐ To contrast LED lights with lights that interfere less with the navigation of baby turtles

　　Ⓑ To suggest that LED lights be removed from existing installations near beaches

　　Ⓒ To argue that incandescent and fluorescent lights should not be permitted on coastal properties

　　Ⓓ To name a concrete example of a light that poses less of a threat to baby leatherback turtles

Paragraph 6

S1　Leatherbacks are "pelagic," meaning they live in open water (in contrast to staying near the shore or dwelling on the ocean bottom), and this includes the hatchlings; if they manage to make it to sea, they will venture into the open waters.

2　Researchers have named the ensuing years the "lost years," as the turtles live in the open sea and are difficult to track.

3　They have attempted to study their whereabouts and navigation patterns by tagging baby turtles and tracking them via satellite.

8. The word "venture" in the passage is closest in meaning to

　　Ⓐ be swept out

　　Ⓑ set out

　　Ⓒ tumble forth

　　Ⓓ linger around

Paragraph 7

S1　The turtles are known for their long-distance migrations and over the years will possibly travel tens of thousands of miles.

2　When they are 15 to 25 years old, female leatherback turtles reach maturity and return to the different beaches where each was born to lay their own clutches of eggs.

3　How does the mature leatherback find her way back to her natal beach, which is sometimes thousands of miles away?

4　It is believed that the turtle uses the Earth's magnetic fields to accomplish this incredible feat.

5　This magnetic sense is the same kind of "compass" used by a number of species that also navigate long distances, including monarch butterflies, yellow-fin tuna, and sockeye salmon.

9. The word "they" in the passage refers to

   (A) female leatherback turtles

   (B) long-distance migrations

   (C) 15 to 25 years

   (D) tens of thousands of miles

10. According to paragraph 7, which of the following is likely to be the method by which the adult female leatherback finds her way back to the beach where she was born?

   (A) Eventually reaching maturity

   (B) Using the Earth's magnetic fields

   (C) Tracking yellow-fin tuna and sockeye salmon

   (D) Laying her own clutch of eggs

Paragraph 7

S1–2   The turtles are known for their long-distance migrations and over the years will possibly travel tens of thousands of miles. When they are 15 to 25 years old, female leatherback turtles reach maturity and return to the different beaches where each was born to lay their own clutches of eggs.

3   **A** How does the mature leatherback find her way back to her natal beach, which is sometimes thousands of miles away?

4   **B** It is believed that the turtle uses the Earth's magnetic fields to accomplish this incredible feat.

5   **C** This magnetic sense is the same kind of "compass" used by a number of species that also navigate long distances, including monarch butterflies, yellow-fin tuna, and sockeye salmon.

End   **D**

> Look at the part of the passage that is displayed above. The letters [A], [B], [C], and [D] indicate where the following sentence could be added.

11. **An ability to perceive magnetic fields is in fact shared by animals such as these that may otherwise be quite different from one another.**

   Where would the sentence best fit?

   (A) Choice A

   (B) Choice B

   (C) Choice C

   (B) Choice D

> Select from the five phrases below THREE that characterize the behaviors of leatherback turtles and TWO that characterize the behaviors of people, according to the passage. This question is worth 2 points.

Behaviors of Leatherback Turtles	**Behaviors of People**
•	•
•	•
•	

12. ☐ A   Following reflective light on the ocean's surface

☐ B   Using magnetic fields for navigation

☐ C   Advancing the use of certain kinds of artificial light

☐ D   Tagging and tracking maturing leatherbacks

☐ E   Responding less to certain wavelengths of light and more to other wavelengths

5.9 Dyson Spheres

In the mid-twentieth century, the concept of "Dyson spheres" was introduced because of the growing awareness of the limitations of nonrenewable energy resources. It became apparent to many scientists that fossil fuels stores were decreasing while energy consumption was increasing. They were concerned about the growing possibility that the Earth would one day run out of usable fuel sources. Freeman Dyson, a theoretical physicist and mathematician, published a paper in 1960 that claimed that any energy-consuming civilization would eventually need more energy than its planet could provide, and that the only logical solution would be to capture all the energy emitted by its parent star[1] using Dyson spheres.

Dyson originally found the idea in the 1937 science fiction book *Star Maker*, written by Olaf Stapledon. This novel describes a fictional history of the universe in which alien civilizations build artificial structures to surround their parent star. These structures, later called Dyson spheres, mine the energy from the star. The fuel from the solar energy far surpasses anything available on a planet. Dyson recognized that the technology needed to create and place a Dyson sphere around the Sun was centuries away. However, he envisioned another practical use. He believed that creating a Dyson sphere would be an inevitable step in any civilization's development. All sufficiently advanced life forms, including those that originate on other planets, would attempt to create a Dyson sphere. If life exists beyond Earth, and if that life is technologically advanced enough, Dyson reasoned, those life forms must have created a Dyson sphere. If scientists could find that structure, they would find life.

But how can we discover an artificial structure thousands or millions of light years away? That was the question Dyson attempted to answer in his 1960 article. He presented the Dyson sphere as a thought experiment, not as something that humanity should attempt to create, so he did not go into many specifics. In essence, a Dyson sphere is an artificial structure or group of structures that surround a star. Most of the

parent star[1]: A star that produces a planet's heat and light, around which the planet orbits (e.g. the Sun is the parent star of the Earth)

  MANHATTAN PREP

structures are devoted to capturing the star's solar energy and transforming it into usable energy. The structures, Dyson hypothesized, would block or absorb much of the visible light coming from the star. From the perspective of the Earth, the star would seem to dim. However, the consolidation of all of the star's energy into the Dyson sphere would result in a measurable increase in infrared radiation. The decreased visible light and increased infrared radiation would significantly alter the star's emission spectrum[2]. Because the emission spectra of stars are easily and regularly monitored from Earth, the effects of the Dyson sphere would be observable. Scouring the heavens for stars with these characteristics would allow astronomers to predict that a Dyson sphere had been created—evidence, he felt, of alien life.

His idea caught on quickly, and searches for Dyson spheres continue to this day. There are currently two stars under investigation that have a reasonable possibility of being surrounded by a Dyson sphere. Several other causes of the anomalies observed in the emission spectra of these two stars have been proposed, but no definitive explanation has emerged. Currently, scientists cannot say definitively why these two stars appear less bright than they should.

Since the original publication, scientists have investigated the practicality of building a Dyson sphere around the Sun. They have ruled out the possibility of a Dyson sphere existing as a solid hollow ball surrounding a star. No known or theoretical material could endure the stress of the star's gravitational pull. Moreover, without constant correction, it would slowly drift until it collides with the star. To avoid these problems, thousands of smaller structures could be positioned around the Sun. Various theories on how to create and deploy these structures have been proposed. All theories agree, however, that a mass equivalent to all the planets within the inner Solar System—Mercury, Venus, Earth, and Mars—would be needed. Humans would live on the Dyson sphere itself, or on artificially created habitats within the sphere. While this would theoretically solve any energy crisis, it will be a very long time before humans could reasonably consider pursuing this option.

5

Now answer the questions.

Paragraph 1

S1   In the mid-twentieth century, the concept of "Dyson spheres" was introduced because of the growing awareness of the limitations of nonrenewable energy resources.

2   It became apparent to many scientists that fossil fuels stores were decreasing while energy consumption was increasing.

3   They were concerned about the growing possibility that the Earth would one day run out of usable fuel sources.

4   Freeman Dyson, a theoretical physicist and mathematician, published a paper in 1960 that claimed that any energy-consuming civilization would eventually need more energy than its planet could provide, and that the only logical solution would be to capture all the energy emitted by its parent star using Dyson spheres.

---

emission spectrum[2]: the spectrum of the electromagnetic radiation emitted by a source observable as bands of color on a spectrometer (plural: emission spectra)

1. The word "eventually" in the passage is closest in meaning to

    Ⓐ ultimately

    Ⓑ immediately

    Ⓒ accidentally

    Ⓓ intentionally

2. According to paragraph 1, which of the following is something that many scientists are concerned about?

    Ⓐ Solutions to the fossil fuels crisis that involve conservation are not being pursued adequately.

    Ⓑ Nonrenewable fuel sources will increase in quantity over time.

    Ⓒ The Earth may not always have enough fuel to support its demands.

    Ⓓ Dyson spheres may not be constructed as soon as they are needed.

Paragraph 2

S1   Dyson originally found the idea in the 1937 science fiction book *Star Maker*, written by Olaf Stapledon.

2   This novel describes a fictional history of the universe in which alien civilizations build artificial structures to surround their parent star.

3   These structures, later called Dyson spheres, mine the energy from the star.

4   The fuel from the solar energy far surpasses anything available on a planet.

5   Dyson recognized that the technology needed to create and place a Dyson sphere around the Sun was centuries away.

6   However, he envisioned another practical use.

7   He believed that creating a Dyson sphere would be an inevitable step in any civilization's development.

8   All sufficiently advanced life forms, including those that originate on other planets, would attempt to create a Dyson sphere.

9   If life exists beyond Earth, and if that life is technologically advanced enough, Dyson reasoned, those life forms must have created a Dyson sphere.

10   If scientists could find that structure, they would find life.

3. The phrase "far surpasses" in the passage is closest in meaning to

    Ⓐ falls far short of

    Ⓑ greatly overpowers

    Ⓒ largely eradicates

    Ⓓ vastly exceeds

4. In paragraph 2, Freeman Dyson supports his contention that a Dyson sphere could be used to find life beyond Earth by

   (A) reasoning that Dyson spheres must already exist elsewhere in the universe

   (B) indicating that Dyson spheres would be the primary artificial structures created by other life forms

   (C) presenting a rationale for why alien life forms would likely try to create a Dyson sphere

   (D) contrasting Dyson spheres with other potential means of technologically advanced energy extraction

5. The word "inevitable" in the passage is closest in meaning to

   (A) unavoidable

   (B) incredible

   (C) unremarkable

   (D) insurmountable

Paragraph 3

S1   But how can we discover an artificial structure thousands or millions of light years away?

2   That was the question Dyson attempted to answer in his 1960 article.

3   He presented the Dyson sphere as a thought experiment, not as something that humanity should attempt to create, so he did not go into many specifics.

4   In essence, a Dyson sphere is an artificial structure or group of structures that surround a star.

5   Most of the structures are devoted to capturing the star's solar energy and transforming it into usable energy.

6   The structures, Dyson hypothesized, would block or absorb much of the visible light coming from the star.

7   From the perspective of the Earth, the star would seem to dim.

8   However, the consolidation of all of the star's energy into the Dyson sphere would result in a measurable increase in infrared radiation.

9   The decreased visible light and increased infrared radiation would significantly alter the star's emission spectrum.

10   Because the emission spectra of stars are easily and regularly monitored from Earth, the effects of the Dyson sphere would be observable.

11   Scouring the heavens for stars with these characteristics would allow astronomers to predict that a Dyson sphere had been created—evidence, he felt, of alien life.

6. The word "perspective" in the passage is closest in meaning to

   (A) rotation

   (B) viewpoint

   (C) dimension

   (D) reverence

7. The words "these characteristics" in the passage refer to

   (A) effects of the consolidation of the star into the Dyson sphere

   (B) energy transformed from infrared radiation to visible light

   (C) decreased fuel stocks and increased energy consumption

   (D) increased infrared radiation and decreased visible light

8. Which of the sentences below best expresses the essential information in the highlighted sentence in paragraph 3? Incorrect choices change the meaning in important ways or leave out essential information.

   (A) The Dyson sphere was intended as a broad thought experiment, but Dyson provided specific instructions for how to create one.

   (B) In his article, Dyson described the Dyson sphere vaguely because it was meant as a concept to explore, not a plan to carry out.

   (C) Dyson presented the Dyson sphere as an experimental plan, one that he expected others to make more precise but not to execute.

   (D) The answer Dyson gave about Dyson spheres was a thought experiment that humanity should not attempt to create without specifics.

Paragraph 4

S1   His idea caught on quickly, and searches for Dyson spheres continue to this day.

2   There are currently **two stars under investigation** that have a reasonable possibility of being surrounded by a Dyson sphere.

3   Several other causes of the anomalies observed in the emission spectra of these two stars have been proposed, but no definitive explanation has emerged.

4   Currently, scientists cannot say definitively why these two stars appear less bright than they should.

9. According to paragraph 4, what is true about the two stars currently under investigation?

   (A) They are surrounded by Dyson spheres.

   (B) They appear less dim than they should.

   (C) Their emission spectra have not been conclusively explained.

   (D) They have been investigated more than most other stars.

10. In paragraph 4, why does the author mention the "two stars under investigation"?

  (A) To illustrate how Dyson's theory is still relevant and inspiring

  (B) To contend that these two stars probably have Dyson spheres surrounding them

  (C) To suggest that Dyson spheres around these stars may one day provide us energy

  (D) To explain why a Dyson sphere is less likely to be possible at present for our own star

Paragraph 5

S1 Since the original publication, scientists have investigated the practicality of building a Dyson sphere around the Sun.

2 They have ruled out the possibility of a Dyson sphere existing as a solid hollow ball surrounding a star.

3 No known or theoretical material could endure the stress of the star's gravitational pull.

4 Moreover, without constant correction, it would slowly drift until it collides with the star.

5 To avoid these problems, thousands of smaller structures could be positioned around the Sun.

6 Various theories on how to create and deploy these structures have been proposed.

7 All theories agree, however, that a mass equivalent to all the planets within the inner Solar System—Mercury, Venus, Earth, and Mars—would be needed.

8 Humans would live on the Dyson sphere itself, or on artificially created habitats within the sphere.

9 While this would theoretically solve any energy crisis, it will be a very long time before humans could reasonably consider pursuing this option.

11. According to paragraph 5, all of the following are considered challenges to building a Dyson sphere EXCEPT:

  (A) the stress on a hollow ball structure caused by the star's gravitational pull

  (B) the drift of a hollow ball structure

  (C) the quantity of mass that would be required

  (D) the ability of humans to live on a Dyson sphere

12. In paragraph 5, the solid hollow-ball structure is mentioned to illustrate

  (A) the possible existence of Dyson spheres outside the solar system

  (B) the potential difficulties of creating a Dyson sphere

  (C) the effects of a Dyson sphere on the star it surrounds

  (D) the amount of mass needed to create a Dyson sphere

Paragraph 3

S1–4   But how can we discover an artificial structure thousands or millions of light years away? That was the question Dyson attempted to answer in his 1960 article. He presented the Dyson sphere as a thought experiment, not as something that humanity should attempt to create, so he did not go into many specifics. In essence, a Dyson sphere is an artificial structure or group of structures that surround a star.

5   [A] Most of the structures are devoted to capturing the star's solar energy and transforming it into usable energy.

6–7   [B] The structures, Dyson hypothesized, would block or absorb much of the visible light coming from the star. From the perspective of the Earth, the star would seem to dim.

8   [C] However, the consolidation of all of the star's energy into the Dyson sphere would result in a measurable increase in infrared radiation.

9–11   [D] The decreased visible light and increased infrared radiation would significantly alter the star's emission spectrum. Because the emission spectra of stars are easily and regularly monitored from Earth, the effects of the Dyson sphere would be observable. Scouring the heavens for stars with these characteristics would allow astronomers to predict that a Dyson sphere had been created—evidence, he felt, of alien life.

Look at the part of the passage that is displayed above. The letters [A], [B], [C], and [D] indicate where the following sentence could be added.

---

13. **The increase in energy available to a civilization using the Dyson sphere would be exponential.**

Where would the sentence best fit?

(A) Choice A

(B) Choice B

(C) Choice C

(D) Choice D

An introductory sentence for a brief summary of the passage is provided below. Complete the summary by selecting the THREE answer choices that express the most important ideas in the passage. Some sentences do not belong in the summary because they express ideas that are not presented in the passage or are minor ideas in the passage. This question is worth 2 points.

14. **Dyson spheres were introduced in response to growing concerns about increased energy consumption on Earth.**

[A] A Dyson sphere is an artificial structure that surrounds a star, capturing as much of that star's energy as possible.

[B] In order to create a Dyson sphere around our sun, the planets Mercury, Venus, Earth, and Mars would all have to be used up.

[C] While it may one day be possible to build a Dyson sphere around the Earth's sun, they were proposed—and remain significant today—as a theoretical abstraction.

[D] The genesis of the concept of Dyson spheres in science fiction illustrates that scientific ideas and progress can grow from unexpected sources.

[E] Causes other than Dyson spheres may explain the anomalies in the emission spectra of two stars currently under observation.

[F] If a Dyson sphere surrounded a star visible from Earth, the star's altered emission spectrum would allow scientists to theorize that life existed elsewhere.

5.10 Southwestern Water Rights

Over the past century, the states of Utah, Nevada, New Mexico, Arizona, and California, forming the Southwestern United States, have experienced tremendous population growth. In the 1910 census, these five states accounted for less than 4 percent of the domestic population. In 2010, this figure was greater than 16 percent. Population growth in the Southwest continues to outstrip growth in the rest of the country, as the region receives positive net migration from other states as well as substantial immigration from foreign countries. Part of the appeal is the pleasant weather, with mild to hot temperatures all year, and low precipitation. However, therein lies the crux of a major problem—the ecosystems of the Southwest are not equipped to sustainably provide enough water for the increasing number of people that live there.

All five Southwestern states rely greatly on external water sources, plus groundwater sources, which are large but finite. Per-capita water consumption is also higher than the national average for two reasons. First, these states have a drier climate, so more water is needed for the watering of lawns and gardens. Second, all five states have a substantial farming industry and are exporters of agricultural products domestically and abroad. These states therefore use much more water for irrigation per person than the rest of the United States.

Water use has become much more efficient across the United States in recent decades. Since 1980, per-capita usage has fallen by about 40 percent. This decline is even more pronounced in the Southwest. However, it is

counterbalanced by a comparable growth in population, such that the total amount of water being consumed annually in the Southwest is basically unchanged. This level of usage is not sustainable over the long term.

The Southwestern states consumed a total of 61 million acre-feet[1] of water in 2010. About 35 percent of this water comes from groundwater, and the rest comes from surface water, such as lakes and streams. Most of the groundwater being used is not fully replenished. In California alone, the net withdrawal of groundwater, after replenishment from precipitation and surface water, is currently around 10 million acre-feet per year. At this rate, California's known usable groundwater supplies will be exhausted by the year 2060.

For surface water, these five states are heavily reliant on various sources. California has ample native freshwater supplies in the northern and central portions of the state. Excluding California, however, over half of the freshwater needs of the Southwest are met from a single source: the Colorado River. This river originates in the Rocky Mountains and meanders through Utah and Arizona before forming the border of Arizona and Nevada, plus parts of the Arizona–California border. The river then continues into Mexico.

Allocation of rights to this water has been a political flash point among the Southwestern states since the original Colorado River Compact, drafted in 1922. According to the present version of the Compact, 15 million acre-feet per year are allocated to seven Western states, of which the five Southwestern states receive about 10 million—Wyoming and Colorado receive the rest. Mexico also has an annual allotment of 1.5 million acre-feet. The river is dammed at various places, with the Hoover Dam on the border of Arizona and Nevada, forming Lake Mead, being the most well-known.

There are several problems with this allocation. First, the estimates for annual water flow in the Colorado River were based on a survey that occurred during a period of relatively heavy rainfall. It is unlikely that the Colorado River can continue to produce enough water to fill these allocations indefinitely. Evidence of this is seen by the water levels in Lake Mead, which are currently more than 150 feet below peak. Second, the agreement is a zero-sum game: any increase in allocation to one state must necessarily come at the expense of another. This puts pressure on high-growth states like Arizona and Nevada. Finally, there is the problem of the ongoing drought in the region. The drought puts pressure on all water sources, and the Colorado River is no exception. If the drought remains unabated, Lake Mead could eventually become unusable, and hydroelectric generating capacity in the Southwest could fall below minimum requirements as early as the year 2020.

acre-feet[1]: Units of volume used in the United States for large quantities of water. One acre-foot is equal to about 325,000 gallons, or 1.2 million liters.

Now answer the questions.

Paragraph 1

S1   Over the past century, the states of Utah, Nevada, New Mexico, Arizona, and California, forming the Southwestern United States, have experienced tremendous population growth.

2   In the 1910 census, these five states accounted for less than 4 percent of the domestic population.

3   In 2010, this figure was greater than 16 percent.

4   Population growth in the Southwest continues to outstrip growth in the rest of the country, as the region receives positive net migration from other states as well as substantial immigration from foreign countries.

5   Part of the appeal is the pleasant weather, with mild to hot temperatures all year, and low precipitation.

6   However, therein lies the crux of a major problem—the ecosystems of the Southwest are not equipped to sustainably provide enough water for the increasing number of people that live there.

1. According to paragraph 1, which of the following is true of population growth in the Southwestern United States?

    (A) A central reason for migration to the Southwest is the abundance of natural resources such as water and fertile soil.

    (B) Low annual rainfall totals provide a significant reason for people to migrate to the Southwest.

    (C) Population growth in the Southwest is driven primarily by foreign immigration.

    (D) Net migration from other states is the chief cause of Southwestern population growth.

2. The word "crux" in the passage is closest in meaning to

    (A) edge

    (B) answer

    (C) promise

    (D) core

Paragraph 2

P2 S1   All five Southwestern states rely greatly on external water sources, plus groundwater sources, which are large but finite.

2   Per-capita water consumption is also higher than the national average for two reasons.

3   First, these states have a drier climate, so more water is needed for the watering of lawns and gardens.

4   Second, all five states have a substantial farming industry and are exporters of agricultural products domestically and abroad.

5   These states therefore use much more water for irrigation per person than the rest of the United States.

Paragraph 3

P3 S1   Water use has become much more efficient across the United States in recent decades.

2   Since 1980, per-capita usage has fallen by about 40 percent.

3   This decline is even more pronounced in the Southwest.

4   However, it is counterbalanced by a comparable growth in population, such that the total amount of water being consumed annually in the Southwest is basically unchanged.

5   This level of usage is not sustainable over the long term.

3.   According to paragraphs 2 and 3, all of the following statements about water usage in the Southwestern United States are true EXCEPT:

(A) Since 1980, overall water usage in the Southwest has fallen substantially.

(B) More water is consumed per person in the Southwest than in the rest of the United States.

(C) More water is consumed annually in the Southwest than can be naturally replaced.

(D) As net exporters of agricultural products, the Southwestern states use more water per person for farming than most other states.

4.   The word "finite" in the passage is closest in meaning to

(A) isolated

(B) limited

(C) infected

(D) unending

5. Which of the sentences below best expresses the essential information in the highlighted sentence in paragraph 3? Incorrect choices change the meaning in important ways or leave out essential information.

(A) Population growth is supported by the decline in water use per person, leading to annually declining water consumption in the Southwest.

(B) The increase in per-person water consumption and population have balanced out the typical water usage in the Southwest.

(C) Declines in per-person water use have stunted population growth in the Southwest.

(D) The population has grown enough to offset the decline in per-capita water use, so the total amount of water used each year in the Southwest has remained about the same.

Paragraph 4

S1   The Southwestern states consumed a total of 61 million acre-feet of water in 2010.

2   About 35 percent of this water comes from groundwater, and the rest comes from surface water, such as lakes and streams.

3   Most of the groundwater being used is not fully replenished.

4   In California alone, the net withdrawal of groundwater, after replenishment from precipitation and surface water, is currently around 10 million acre-feet per year.

5   At this rate, California's known usable groundwater supplies will be **exhausted** by the year 2060.

6. According to paragraph 4, excessive use of groundwater in parts of the Southwest is noteworthy because

(A) the groundwater draws in contaminants from surface water, its ultimate source

(B) groundwater provides more than half of the water consumed in these regions

(C) groundwater will run out eventually if incomplete replenishment continues

(D) a high level of groundwater use is now illegal in certain areas

7. The word "exhausted" in the passage is closest in meaning to

(A) expended

(B) lessened

(C) ejected

(D) tainted

Paragraph 5

S1 For surface water, these five states are heavily reliant on various sources.

2   California has ample native freshwater supplies in the northern and central portions of the state.

3   Excluding California, however, over half of the freshwater needs of the Southwest are met from a single source: the Colorado River.

4   This river originates in the Rocky Mountains and meanders through Utah and Arizona before forming the border of Arizona and Nevada, plus parts of the Arizona–California border.

5   The river then continues into Mexico.

8. According to paragraph 5, one difference between water sources in California and the rest of the Southwestern United States is that

(A) California groundwater resources are being depleted at an alarming rate

(B) the Colorado River runs through or along all the Southwestern states except for California

(C) California uses surface water supplies, while the rest of the Southwest mostly relies on salt water from the ocean

(D) the states other than California depend largely on a particular river, whereas California does not

Paragraph 6

S1 Allocation of rights to this water has been a political flash point among the Southwestern states since the original Colorado River Compact, drafted in 1922.

2   According to the present version of the Compact, 15 million acre-feet per year are allocated to seven Western states, of which the five Southwestern states receive about 10 million—Wyoming and Colorado receive the rest.

3   Mexico also has an annual allotment of 1.5 million acre-feet.

4   The river is dammed at various places, with the Hoover Dam on the border of Arizona and Nevada, forming Lake Mead, being the most well-known.

9. Which of the following can be inferred from paragraph 6 about the Colorado River Compact?

(A) All of the water from the river is allocated to the Southwestern states.

(B) Most of the water from the river is allocated on an annual basis to Mexico.

(C) The original Compact did not fully resolve the political issues related to water rights.

(D) Among the seven Western states, Colorado is the largest recipient of Colorado River water rights.

Paragraph 7

S1   There are several problems with this allocation.

2   First, the estimates for annual water flow in the Colorado River were based on a survey that occurred during a period of relatively heavy rainfall.

3   It is unlikely that the Colorado River can continue to produce enough water to fill these allocations indefinitely.

4   Evidence of this is seen by the water levels in Lake Mead, which are currently more than 150 feet below peak.

5   Second, the agreement is a zero-sum game: any increase in allocation to one state must necessarily come at the expense of another.

6   This puts pressure on high-growth states like Arizona and Nevada.

7   Finally, there is the problem of the ongoing drought in the region.

8   The drought puts pressure on all water sources, and the Colorado River is no exception.

9   If the drought remains unabated, Lake Mead could eventually become unusable, and hydroelectric generating capacity in the Southwest could fall below minimum requirements as early as the year 2020.

10. All of the following are mentioned in paragraph 7 as problems with the Colorado River Compact allocation EXCEPT:

   (A) The allocations seem to be larger than the average amount of water carried by the river over time.

   (B) If more water is allocated to one state, less must be allocated to another state.

   (C) Changes in the compact itself are being driven by just a few high-growth states, such as Arizona and Nevada.

   (D) The region is currently experiencing a period of significantly less precipitation than normal.

11. The word "unabated" in the passage is closest in meaning to

   (A) persistent

   (B) uncontested

   (C) undiscussed

   (D) uneven

12. What is the author's purpose in presenting the information in paragraph 7?

   (A) To illustrate the importance of having enough water reserves for hydroelectricity generation

   (B) To highlight the problems with the Colorado River Compact and the scarcity of water sources in the Southwest

   (C) To advocate for reduced per-capita water consumption in the Southwest

   (D) To suggest that some residents of the Southwest consider moving to a different region of the country

Paragraph 6

S1 Allocation of rights to this water has been a political flash point among the Southwestern states since the original Colorado River Compact, drafted in 1922.

2 [A] According to the present version of the Compact, 15 million acre-feet per year are allocated to seven Western states, of which the five Southwestern states receive about 10 million—Wyoming and Colorado receive the rest.

3 [B] Mexico also has an annual allotment of 1.5 million acre-feet.

4 [C] The river is dammed at various places, with the Hoover Dam on the border of Arizona and Nevada, forming Lake Mead, being the most well-known.

End [D]

> Look at the part of the passage that is displayed above. The letters [A], [B], [C], and [D] indicate where the following sentence could be added.

13. **Among other things, this agreement somewhat naively divided the river region into two distinct basins—the Upper Basin and the Lower Basin—and attempted to allocate water to the two basins equally.**

   Where would the sentence best fit?

   (A) Choice A

   (B) Choice B

   (C) Choice C

   (D) Choice D

An introductory sentence for a brief summary of the passage is provided below. Complete the summary by selecting the THREE answer choices that express the most important ideas in the passage. Some sentences do not belong in the summary because they express ideas that are not presented in the passage or are minor ideas in the passage. This question is worth 2 points.

14. **The immense population growth enjoyed by the states of the Southwestern United States has stressed water resources in the region.**

    A | Immigration from other countries contributes to population growth in the Southwest.

    B | About one-third of the water allocation from the Colorado River Compact goes to states not considered part of the Southwest.

    C | Low rainfall in the area leads to both scarce water supplies and attractive weather, which drives population growth and further strain on those supplies.

    D | Groundwater sources can continue to be used sustainably to meet water demand in the Southwest.

    E | Allocation of surface water in the Southwest is a point of ongoing political contention, particularly with regard to the Colorado River.

    F | Despite declining per-capita water consumption, unchecked demand for water in the region can and will lead to severe consequences.

Answer Key—5.1 Lead in Gasoline (Petrol)

Question	Correct Answer	Right/Wrong	Category
1	C		Vocabulary
2	C		Fact
3	A		Purpose
4	D		Simplify Sentence
5	B		Vocabulary
6	A		Inference
7	B		Reference
8	D		Fact
9	D		Vocabulary
10	A		Vocabulary
11	C		Negative Fact
12	B		Inference
13	A		Insert Text
14	B, E, F		Summary

Answer Key—5.2 The Golden Ratio

Question	Correct Answer	Right/Wrong	Category
1	B		Fact
2	A		Vocabulary
3	C		Negative Fact
4	A		Fact
5	C		Vocabulary
6	B		Fact
7	B		Inference
8	D		Vocabulary
9	B		Purpose
10	A		Fact
11	C		Purpose
12	D		Fact
13	D		Insert Text
14	B, D, E		Summary

Answer Key—5.3 Pterosaurs

Question	Correct Answer	Right/Wrong	Category
1	D		Negative Fact
2	A		Vocabulary
3	A		Vocabulary
4	B		Fact
5	C		Inference
6	B		Vocabulary
7	A		Negative Fact
8	D		Purpose
9	D		Simplify Sentence
10	C		Vocabulary
11	B		Negative Fact
12	C		Purpose
13	B		Insert Text
14	A, E, F		Summary

Answer Key—5.4 Why Humans Have Big Brains

Question	Correct Answer	Right/Wrong	Category
1	C		Fact
2	D		Vocabulary
3	C		Negative Fact
4	A		Fact
5	A		Fact
6	C		Simplify Sentence
7	A		Vocabulary
8	D		Negative Fact
9	B		Fact
10	A		Vocabulary
11	D		Purpose
12	B		Vocabulary
13	A		Insert Text
14	B, E, F		Summary

Answer Key—5.5 Crystallization

Question	Correct Answer	Right/Wrong	Category
1	C		Vocabulary
2	D		Negative Fact
3	B		Vocabulary
4	D		Vocabulary
5	C		Purpose
6	A		Fact
7	B		Inference
8	A		Negative Fact
9	A		Vocabulary
10	B		Vocabulary
11	B		Fact
12	C		Fact
13	A		Insert Text
14	C, D, E		Summary

Answer Key—5.6 Habitat Fragmentation

Question	Correct Answer	Right/Wrong	Category
1	B		Fact
2	C		Vocabulary
3	A		Fact
4	B		Fact
5	C		Vocabulary
6	A		Fact
7	D		Vocabulary
8	D		Purpose
9	A		Vocabulary
10	C		Purpose
11	C		Simplify Sentence
12	D		Inference
13	B		Insert Text
14	B, D, F		Summary

Answer Key—5.7 Is Pluto a Planet?

Question	Correct Answer	Right/Wrong	Category
1	B		Vocabulary
2	A		Purpose
3	B		Vocabulary
4	C		Fact
5	D		Reference
6	C		Fact
7	A		Vocabulary
8	A		Fact
9	C		Simplify Sentence
10	D		Vocabulary
11	D		Fact
12	B		Insert Text
13	B, D, E		Summary

Answer Key—5.8 Turtle Navigation

Question	Correct Answer	Right/Wrong	Category
1	D		Fact
2	A		Vocabulary
3	C		Simplify Sentence
4	C		Inference
5	A		Fact
6	B		Vocabulary
7	D		Purpose
8	B		Vocabulary
9	A		Reference
10	B		Fact
11	D		Insert Text
12	Turtles: A, B, E. People: C, D.		Table

Answer Key—5.9 Dyson Spheres

Question	Correct Answer	Right/Wrong	Category
1	A		Vocabulary
2	C		Fact
3	D		Vocabulary
4	C		Fact
5	A		Vocabulary
6	B		Vocabulary
7	D		Reference
8	B		Simplify Sentence
9	C		Fact
10	A		Purpose
11	D		Negative Fact
12	B		Purpose
13	B		Insert Text
14	A, C, F		Summary

Answer Key—5.10 Southwestern Water Rights

Question	Correct Answer	Right/Wrong	Category
1	B		Fact
2	D		Vocabulary
3	A		Negative Fact
4	B		Vocabulary
5	D		Simplify Sentence
6	C		Fact
7	A		Vocabulary
8	D		Fact
9	C		Inference
10	C		Negative Fact
11	A		Vocabulary
12	B		Purpose
13	A		Insert Text
14	C, E, F		Summary

Answers and Explanations—5.1 Lead in Gasoline (Petrol)

Paragraph 1	Comments
S1 The element lead is a heavy, soft metal that has been known since ancient times to be poisonous in large quantities.	Lead is poisonous.
2 More recently, it has been recognized that even low exposure to lead causes biological damage over long periods of time.	
3 For decades in the twentieth century, however, nearly every automobile produced exhaust laced with lead.	But it came out of cars for a long time.

1.	The phrase "laced with" in the passage is closest in meaning to	**VOCABULARY.** "Laced (with)" = trimmed or fitted with (in terms of fabric lace or shoe laces), but in this context it means to be contaminated with a harmful substance but only in small amounts.
✗	(A) improved by	Unrelated. Something contaminated would not be improved (made better).
✗	(B) deprived of	Opposite. "Deprived" = without or withheld from.
✓	(C) mixed with	**CORRECT.** Exhaust "laced with" lead = exhaust mixed with (usually something bad, like poison) lead.
✗	(D) obtained from	Unrelated. Something that is "obtained" is acquired or gotten, but this is not necessarily the same as being contaminated (which has a distinctly negative meaning).

Paragraph 2	Comments
S1 In the body, lead causes widespread damage by interfering with many enzymes (proteins that enable biological processes).	How lead damages the body.
2 The typical ion, or charged atomic form, of lead easily replaces calcium, iron, and zinc ions, which are necessary components of these enzymes.	
3 Lead ions are imperfect replacements, so the enzymes fail to function properly.	
4 Lead particularly damages the central nervous system, impeding the proper growth and working of brain cells.	
5 The element also displaces calcium in bone tissue, providing a reservoir for lead to reenter the rest of the body even when outside sources are removed.	
6 Children are particularly vulnerable to harm from lead exposure and can be impaired cognitively and behaviorally for life.	

2.   In paragraph 2, the author indicates that enzymes in the body do not work correctly when they contain lead ions because

FACT. S3: "the enzymes fail to function properly" = the enzymes in the body do not work correctly.

✗ (A) lead ions easily replace calcium, iron, and zinc ions

True (S2), but on its own, this is not the reason. What if lead ions were perfect substitutes for calcium ions, etc.? The enzymes would still work.

✗ (B) calcium, iron, and zinc ions are necessary components of the enzymes

True (S2), but on its own, this is not the reason. What if the enzymes contained lead ions and calcium, iron, and zinc ions (the necessary components)? The enzymes would still work.

✓ (C) lead ions are flawed substitutes for calcium, iron, and zinc ions

CORRECT. S3: "Lead ions are imperfect replacements" = flawed substitutes (for the calcium ions, etc.) S3: "so" = therefore. Second part of the sentence (enzyme failure) is because of first part (imperfect replacements).

✗ (D) lead ions cause particular damage to the central nervous system

True (S4), but not the reason for the enzymes failing. If anything, this is a result of the enzymes failing.

3.   Why does the author mention a "reservoir" in paragraph 2?

PURPOSE. S5: "The element [lead] also displaces calcium in bone tissue, providing a reservoir for lead to reenter the rest of the body even when outside sources are removed."

✓ (A) To describe how lead could be re-released in the body

CORRECT. Reservoir = storage tank. S5: "a reservoir for lead to reenter the rest of the body." Re-release = release again = come out of storage and reenter the body.

✗ (B) To illustrate how lead displaces calcium in bone tissue

Lead does displace calcium, but how it does so exactly is not the point. What matters is the result: as a result of this displacement, there's a reservoir or storage tank for lead in the body.

✗ (C) To support the point that lead impedes the proper working of cells

Distracting language from S4.

✗ (D) To provide an example of a location where lead is replaced by calcium ions

Reversed (lead replaces calcium, not the other way around).

Paragraph 3	**Comments**
S1 Easy to find, mine, and refine, lead has been in use for thousands of years.	Lead is easy to use. It has been used for 1000s of years.
2 The word "plumbing" comes from *plumbum*, the Latin word for lead, because the ancient Romans ran drinking water through pipes made of the metal.	
3 Lead is now a crucial component of car batteries, radiation shields, and ammunition.	
4 The two forms of lead that have contributed the most to human exposure, however, are lead paint and tetraethyl lead (TEL), a gasoline additive that prevents a problem called engine knock.	Sets up discussion of use in gasoline.

4.   Which of the sentences below best expresses the essential information in the highlighted sentence in paragraph 3? Incorrect choices change the meaning in important ways or leave out essential information.

SIMPLIFY SENTENCE. S4 (highlighted) lists two forms of lead contributing most to human exposure: lead paint and TEL, a gasoline additive.

✗   (A) Tetraethyl lead, which is added to gasoline to prevent engine knock, contributes more than lead paint to human exposure.

No comparison is given between the 2 forms.

✗   (B) As a result of its anti-knock properties, the gasoline additive tetraethyl lead is the form of lead that contributes the most to human exposure.

You aren't told here that TEL contributes so much to human exposure because of its anti-knock properties. You only know that TEL has such properties.

✗   (C) A gasoline additive and lead paint have contributed to human exposure to lead.

This may be true, but what's lost is the comparison: these 2 forms have contributed the most to human exposure (in comparison to all other forms of lead).

✓   (D) Lead paint and a gasoline additive have contributed more to human exposure than any other forms of lead.

CORRECT. These 2 forms have contributed the most = more than any other forms.

Paragraph 4	Comments
S1 Internal combustion engines depend upon the smooth burning of mixtures of fuel and air, so that the pistons inside the engines are driven in a steady way.	P4 describes what engine knock is and why it's bad.
2 When these mixtures ignite prematurely, however, unintended shock waves damage the pistons and other engine parts.	
3 This phenomenon is labeled "engine knock" for the loud metallic pinging that accompanies the shock waves.	
4 Engine knock is suppressed by changing the composition of the fuel itself or by adding other chemicals.	
5 Early automobile engines that ran on petroleum-based fuel suffered greatly from engine knock, because it was difficult and expensive to alter the makeup of the fuel itself to eliminate this issue.	

5. The word "prematurely" in the passage is closest in meaning to

   ✗ (A) violently

   ✓ (B) early

   ✗ (C) unevenly

   ✗ (D) belatedly

VOCABULARY. Something that is "premature" is ahead of time or before expected.

Unrelated. "Violently" is something done through physical force with the intent to harm, damage, or destroy.

CORRECT. "mixtures ignite prematurely" = they ignite too early, before they're supposed to.

Unrelated. "Uneven" = not regular or consistent.

Opposite. "Belated" = coming or happening later than it should.

6. It can be inferred from paragraph 4 that the primary reason to suppress engine knock is to

   ✓ (A) reduce the harm to various engine parts

   ✗ (B) muffle the loud metallic pings that result

   ✗ (C) improve the composition of the engine's fuel

   ✗ (D) promote the ignition of fuel–air mixtures

INFERENCE. Look for the most negative effects of engine knock. Avoiding these negative effects would most likely be the primary reason to avoid engine knock.

CORRECT. S2: "unintended shock waves damage [= harm] the pistons and other engine parts." This harm is the most negative effect of engine knock that the passage describes.

These pings give engine knock its name, but they are not described in a very negative way. They're just loud.

S4 notes that changing the fuel composition is a way to reduce engine knock, not a reason to do so.

The ignition does not need to be "promoted" (supported or stimulated). In fact, when the ignition happens too quickly, the result is engine knock (S2–3).

MANHATTAN PREP

7.   The phrase "this issue" in the passage refers to

    ✗   (A)   engines running on petroleum-based fuel

    ✓   (B)   engines suffering from knock

    ✗   (C)   the difficulty and expense of fuel alterations

    ✗   (D)   the addition of other chemicals to the fuel

REFERENCE. S5: "to eliminate this issue." What issue? The problem of engine knock.

In fact, a lot of people wanted to eliminate knock so that engines could keep running on petroleum-based fuel.

CORRECT. S5: "Early automobile engines ... suffered greatly from engine knock."

The issue to eliminate is engine knock. It was difficult and expensive to alter the fuel in order to eliminate that issue.

S4 states that other chemicals are a way to suppress engine knock. They're not the issue to be eliminated.

Paragraph 5	Comments
S1 Without the discovery of TEL's "antiknock" capabilities, automobiles may have had to run on non-petroleum-based fuel, such as ethanol.	
2 However, in 1919, TEL was identified as a potent additive to gasoline that eliminated knock and further lubricated engine valves.	TEL eliminates knock.
3 The United States oil industry quickly began to manufacture TEL and promote it as a means of improving both power and fuel economy in automobiles.	
4 Rapid expansion of industrial production of the additive resulted in several lethal accidents, as unprotected chemical plant workers were poisoned by contact with TEL.	TEL is dangerous.
5 After a conference called by the chief United States health official, however, TEL was approved for countrywide use.	
6 Soon, automobiles in the United States and elsewhere were running almost exclusively on leaded gasoline.	But autos start using TEL.

8. When does paragraph 5 indicate that lethal accidents occurred in relation to other events described?

FACT. S4 discusses lethal accidents. These accidents happened after some events and before others. The paragraph generally follows chronological order.

✗ (A) Before TEL was identified as a potent gasoline additive

Described in S2. The accidents took place after TEL was identified this way.

✗ (B) After a conference that the chief United States health official called

Described in S5. The accidents took place before this conference.

✗ (C) Before the rapid expansion of industrial production of TEL

Described in S3. The accidents took place after this expansion.

✓ (D) After the promotion of TEL as a way to improve automobile performance

CORRECT. Described in S3: "promote it [TEL] as a means of improving both power and fuel economy in automobiles." The accidents took place afterwards, in S4.

9. The phrase "almost exclusively" in the passage is closest in meaning to

VOCABULARY. To say that something uses "exclusively" leaded gasoline is to say that is uses only that and nothing else. The addition of "almost" softens that meaning but still conveys that the vast majority of what they use is leaded gasoline. Anything else used would be infrequent.

✗ (A) wholly and entirely

Captures the meaning of "exclusively" but misses the softening from "almost."

✗ (B) hardly at all

Opposite. If something is used "hardly at all," it is almost never used.

✗ (C) virtually privately

This is trying to connect the meaning of "exclusive" that indicates the personal or private use of something (*the front entrance was for the owner's exclusive use*), but that is not the meaning of "almost exclusively" in this context.

✓ (D) with few exceptions

CORRECT. "automobiles … were running almost exclusively on leaded gasoline" = just a few autos were *not* running on it = with few exceptions.

Paragraph 6	**Comments**
S1 In the late 1940s, geologist Clair Patterson analyzed the radioactive decay of uranium into lead in terrestrial rocks, as well as in meteorites, in order to determine the age of the Earth.	Scientist Patterson investigates.
2 In these investigations, however, Patterson had to overcome contamination resulting from lead pollution.	
3 The focus of his **subsequent** research was to show how widespread this contamination was and to advocate for restrictions on the use of TEL.	
4 His advocacy, as well as that of other scientists, was resisted by supporters of the lead and automobile industries.	
5 Under pressure to reduce general air pollution created by automobiles, however, manufacturers announced in the early 1970s that antipollution devices called catalytic converters would be installed on new cars.	
6 Since these devices would be ruined by lead, the use of TEL was to be phased out.	TEL has to go.

10. The word "**subsequent**" in the passage is closest in meaning to

VOCABULARY. "Subsequent" = something that comes later or follows.

✓ (A) later

CORRECT. "His subsequent research" = following, later.

✗ (B) minor

Unrelated. "Minor" = slight, small, or unimportant.

✗ (C) prior

Opposite. "Prior" = before.

✗ (D) principal

Unrelated. "Principal" = chief, leading, or main.

11. Paragraph 6 mentions all of the following as true of the activities of geologist Clair Patterson EXCEPT:

NEGATIVE FACT. Three answers are true and supported by the passage. One answer is false or just unsupported. Facts on the activities of Patterson could be anywhere in P6.

✗ (A) Patterson examined the way uranium decayed in terrestrial rocks and meteorites.

S1: "Patterson analyzed the radioactive decay of uranium into lead in terrestrial rocks, as well as in meteorites."

✗ (B) Patterson confronted the problem of lead contamination caused by pollution.

S2: "Patterson had to overcome contamination resulting from lead pollution."

✓ (C) Patterson advocated for resistance by supporters of the lead and automobile industries.

CORRECT. S4: "His [Patterson's] advocacy … was resisted by supporters" of these industries. That's not the same thing as saying he advocated for resistance by them, as if he were on their side. Rather, they were opposed to Patterson.

✗ (D) Patterson studied how geographically wide-ranging the lead contamination was.

S3: "The focus of his [Patterson's] subsequent research was to show how widespread this contamination was." Widespread = geographically wide-ranging.

Paragraph 7	Comments
S1 By 1986, the use of lead gasoline additives in the United States was prohibited.	TEL banned in US cars.
2 Since then, sharp reductions in blood-lead levels in the population have been observed, along with other improvements in public health.	Positive results.
3 Nevertheless, TEL is still used in automobiles in a few countries, as well as in "avgas" (aviation gasoline) that fuels propeller airplanes around the world.	But hazards remain.
4 In addition, the blanket of lead particles deposited globally by prior combustion of leaded gasoline will pose an environmental hazard for many years to come.	

12. Which of the following statements is best supported by the reports on the current use of TEL described in paragraph 7?

INFERENCE. S3 focuses on current use. Might need information from elsewhere in passage.

✗ (A) The continued worldwide presence of TEL in avgas makes differences in the use of TEL in automobile gasoline unimportant.

"Unimportant" is a strong judgment that is not supported anywhere in the text.

✓ (B) Blood-lead levels in countries where TEL is still used in automobiles are likely higher than in the United States.

CORRECT. S1 states that TEL is prohibited in the US. S2 notes that since then, blood-lead levels have fallen sharply. The implication is that S1 caused or contributed to S2. So you would expect that blood-lead levels in countries still using TEL would be higher than in the US. The word "likely" in this answer choice makes the claim easier to support.

✗ (C) Other improvements in public health have been observed in countries where TEL is still used in automobiles.

The "other improvements in public health" (S2) have been observed in the US. You don't know whether these improvements have been observed in countries still using TEL. In fact, you'd expect they probably wouldn't be observed there.

✗ (D) Avgas use does not contribute to the blanket of lead particles deposited globally by combustion of leaded gasoline.

The "blanket of lead particles" (S4) was deposited by prior (earlier) combustion of leaded gasoline, but you aren't told that avgas does not further contribute to that blanket. In fact, you'd probably expect that the use of avgas in propeller planes would contribute further to that blanket.

5

Paragraph 2	Comments
P2 **S4–6** Lead particularly damages the central nervous system, impeding the proper growth and working of brain cells. The element also displaces calcium in bone tissue, providing a reservoir for lead to reenter the rest of the body even when outside sources are removed. Children are particularly vulnerable to harm from lead exposure and can be impaired cognitively and behaviorally for life.	

Paragraph 3	
P3 **S1** [A] Easy to find, mine, and refine, lead has been in use for thousands of years.	**CORRECT.** "This potential for injury" refers back to the damage described at the end of P2. "Despite" highlights the contrast between that damage and what's coming. The words "the utilization of lead is widespread" set up the rest of P3, which describes that use.
2 [B] The word "plumbing" comes from *plumbum*, the Latin word for lead, because the ancient Romans ran drinking water through pipes made of the metal.	"This potential for injury" doesn't fit with the prior sentence, which focuses on how easy lead is to find and refine.
3 [C] Lead is now a crucial component of car batteries, radiation shields, and ammunition.	Again, "this potential for injury" doesn't fit with the prior sentence, which focuses on the Roman use of lead in pipes (without mentioning any possible harm).
4 [D] The two forms of lead that have contributed the most to human exposure, however, are lead paint and tetraethyl lead (TEL), a gasoline additive that prevents a problem called engine knock.	Again, "this potential for injury" doesn't fit with the prior sentence.

13. **Despite this potential for injury, the utilization of lead is widespread.**

   Where would the sentence best fit?

   ✓ (A) Choice A

   ✗ (B) Choice B

   ✗ (C) Choice C

   ✗ (D) Choice D

INSERT TEXT. "Despite this potential for injury" tells you that the previous sentence must describe potential injury. The words "the utilization of lead is widespread" tell you that the next part of the text should provide more detail on the use of lead.

CORRECT.

	Whole Passage	Comments
P1	The element lead is a heavy, soft metal …	Lead is poisonous. But it came out of cars for a long time.
P2	In the body, lead causes widespread damage by interfering …	How lead damages the body.
P3	Unfortunately for human health, the metal is easy to find, mine, and refine …	Lead unfortunately is easy to use. Set up discussion of use in gasoline.
P4	Internal combustion engines depend upon the smooth burning of mixtures of fuel and air …	What engine knock is. Why it's bad.
P5	Without the discovery of TEL's "antiknock" capabilities …	TEL eliminates knock. TEL is dangerous. But autos start using TEL.
P6	In the late 1940s, geologist Clair Patterson analyzed the radioactive decay of uranium into lead in terrestrial rocks …	Scientist Patterson investigates. TEL has to go.
P7	By 1986, the use of lead gasoline additives in the United States was prohibited …	TEL banned in US cars. Positive results. But hazards remain.

14. **The poisonous metal lead was released by most cars for decades.**

SUMMARY. Correct answers must be clearly expressed in the passage. They must also be among the major points of the passage. They should tie as directly as possible to the summary given.

✗ | A | Lead is now a key component of car batteries, as well as of radiation shields and ammunition.

True but minor point in P3. Not related to use of lead in gasoline, the theme of the passage.

✓ | B | Tetraethyl lead prevents knock from damaging automobile engines.

CORRECT. Outlined in P3 and P5 as the reason lead was originally introduced into gasoline.

✗ | C | Geologist Clair Patterson analyzed the radioactive decay of uranium into lead.

True but minor point in P6. It's just background information about how Patterson came to be interested in studying lead contamination from the use of TEL in gasoline.

✗ | D | The use of leaded gasoline was finally phased out in the United States in order to reduce blood-lead levels.

Contradicted in P6. The use of leaded gasoline was phased out in order to protect new antipollution devices (catalytic converters). The reduction in blood-lead levels happened afterwards, but this was not the purpose of the phase-out, according to the passage.

✓ | E | Health improvements have occurred since the elimination of lead in United States gasoline, but dangers remain worldwide.

CORRECT. Outlined in P7 as the current state of affairs.

✓ | F | Lead causes injury throughout the human body in various ways and is especially harmful to children.

CORRECT. Outlined in P2 to emphasize how dangerous lead exposure is.

Answers and Explanations—5.2 The Golden Ratio

	Paragraph 1	Comments
S1	In math, simple relationships can often take on critical roles.	
2	One such relationship, the Golden Ratio, has captivated the imagination and appealed to mathematicians, architects, astronomers, and philosophers alike.	Golden Ratio = captivating.
3	The Golden Ratio has perhaps had more of an effect on civilization than any other well-known mathematical constant.	
4	To best understand the concept, start with a line and cut it into two pieces (as seen in the figure).	How to find = cut line in 2.
5	If the pieces are cut according to the Golden Ratio, then the ratio of the length of the longer piece to the length of the shorter piece (A : B) would be the same as the ratio of the length of the entire line to the length of the longer piece (A+B : A).	
6	Rounded to the nearest thousandth, both of these ratios will equal 1.618 : 1.	Ratio − 1.618 : 1.

5

1. According to paragraph 1, which of the following is true about the Golden Ratio?

FACT. S2–3 introduce the Golden Ratio and discusses the ratio's broad appeal and applications. S4–6 define it mathematically.

✗ (A) It was invented by mathematicians.

The paragraph does not discuss the invention of the ratio. If anything, the ratio would be discovered rather than invented.

✓ (B) It has significantly impacted society in general.

CORRECT. S3: "The Golden Ratio has perhaps had more of an effect on civilization than any other well-known mathematical constant."

✗ (C) It is most useful to astronomers and philosophers.

S2 states that the ratio has appeal to astronomers and philosophers. But S2 does not argue that the ratio is more useful to these groups than it is to mathematicians, philosophers, or others.

✗ (D) It is used to accurately calculate a length.

S4–6 explain the Golden Ratio using the example of a line cut into pieces, but the Golden Ratio is not used to accurately calculate a length. It is used to talk about a relationship.

2.   The phrase "appealed to" in the passage is closest in meaning to

VOCABULARY. In this context, "appealed" means to attract or to be interesting to someone or something.

✓ (A) interested

CORRECT. The Golden Ratio "appealed to" mathematicians = it attracted or interested them.

✗ (B) defended

Unrelated. "Defended" can either mean to protect or guard, or to support or justify.

✗ (C) requested

"Appealed to" can also mean "made a request to," but that does not make sense in context. The Golden Ratio isn't asking anything of mathematicians. Nor is it asking *for* mathematicians (which is what "requested mathematicians" means).

✗ (D) repulsed

Opposite. "Repulsed" = drive away or reject.

Paragraph 2	**Comments**
S1 The first recorded exploration of the Golden Ratio comes from the Greek mathematician Euclid in his 13-volume treatise on mathematics, *Elements*, published in approximately 300 BC.	First recorded discussion of the ratio.
2 Many other mathematicians since Euclid have studied the ratio.	
3 It appears in various elements related to certain "regular" geometric figures, which are geometric figures with all side lengths equal to each other and all internal angles equal to each other.	Examples of the ratio in mathematics.
4 Other regular or nearly regular figures that feature the ratio include the pentagram (a five-sided star formed by five crossing line segments, the center of which is a regular pentagon) and three-dimensional solids such as the dodecahedron (whose 12 faces are all regular pentagons).	

5

3. According to paragraph 2, all of the following are true of the Golden Ratio EXCEPT:

NEGATIVE FACT. Three answers are true and supported by the passage. One answer is false or just unsupported. Facts about the Golden Ratio could be anywhere in P2.

✗ (A) Its first known description occurred in approximately 300 BC.

S1 notes that the ratio was first recorded in a book published around 300 BC.

✗ (B) It was studied by mathematicians after Euclid.

S2: "Many other mathematicians since [= after] Euclid have studied the ratio."

✓ (C) It only occurs in regular geometric figures.

CORRECT. S3: the ratio shows up in "certain 'regular' geometric figures." It doesn't say that the ratio only occurs in them. In fact, S4 mentions that the Golden Ratio is featured in "nearly regular" figures.

✗ (D) It appears in some three-dimensional geometric figures.

S4 mentions that the Golden Ratio is featured in "three-dimensional solids such as the dodecahedron."

Paragraph 3	**Comments**
S1 The Fibonacci sequence, described by Leonardo Fibonacci, demonstrates one application of the Golden Ratio.	The Fibonacci sequence demonstrates the ratio.
2 The Fibonacci sequence is defined such that each term in the sequence is the sum of the previous two terms, where the first two terms are 0 and 1.	
3 The next term would be $0 + 1 = 1$, followed by $1 + 1 = 2$, $1 + 2 = 3$, $2 + 3 = 5$, etc.	
4 This sequence continues: 0, 1, 1, 2, 3, 5, 8, 13, 21, 34, 55, 89, and so on.	
5 As the sequence progresses, the ratio of any number in the sequence to the previous number gets closer to the Golden Ratio.	
6 This sequence appears repeatedly in various applications in mathematics.	

4. According to paragraph 3, which of the following is true about the Fibonacci sequence?

FACT. S1 introduces the Fibonacci sequence. S2–4 define the sequence. S5 explains how this sequence relates to the Golden Ratio. S6 mentions that the sequence is important in mathematics.

✓ (A) It can be used to estimate the Golden Ratio.

CORRECT. S5: "As the sequence progresses, the ratio of any number in the sequence to the previous number gets closer to the Golden Ratio." So you can estimate the Golden Ratio by computing many items in the sequence, then calculating the ratio of two consecutive terms in the sequence.

✗ (B) It cannot be computed without the use of the Golden Ratio.

S2–4 describe how to calculate the Fibonacci sequence without using the Golden Ratio.

✗ (C) It was discovered by Euclid in approximately 300 BC.

S1 notes that Fibonacci described the sequence. As discussed in P2, Euclid explored the Golden Ratio, not the Fibonacci sequence.

✗ (D) No two terms in the sequence are equal to one another.

S4 mentions the beginning of the sequence: 0, 1, 1, 2, 3 … The second and third terms are equal to one another.

5. The word "**progresses**" in the passage is closest in meaning to

VOCABULARY. "Progress" is about forward movement. In terms of a sequence or series of events, it means to advance, continue, or count up.

✗ (A) calculates

The sequence itself does not do any calculating. The person trying to determine the numbers in the sequence must calculate them (or look them up).

✗ (B) declines

Opposite in this case, because the sequence actually keeps getting bigger.

✓ (C) continues

CORRECT. The sequence "progresses" = the sequence continues.

✗ (D) disintegrates

Opposite. "Disintegrate" = to break up or fall apart

Paragraph 4	Comments
S1 The allure of the Golden Ratio is not limited to mathematics, however.	The ratio goes beyond math.
2 Many experts believe that its aesthetic appeal may have been appreciated before it was ever described mathematically.	Aesthetic/artistic appeal may have come first.
3 In fact, ample evidence suggests that many design elements of the Parthenon building in ancient Greece bear a relationship to the Golden Ratio.	The ratio is in the Parthenon in ancient Greece.
4 Regular pentagons, pentagrams, and decagons were all used as design elements in its construction.	
5 In addition, several elements of the façade of the building incorporate the Golden Rectangle, whose length and width are in proportion to the Golden Ratio.	
6 Since the Parthenon was built over a century before *Elements* was published, the visual attractiveness of the ratio, at least for the building's designers, may have played a role in the building's engineering and construction.	

6. According to paragraph 4, which of the following is true about the construction of the Parthenon?

    FACT. S3 notes that the Parthenon may be related to the Golden Ratio. S4–5 give examples. S6 provides a hypothesis about why this might have been the case.

✗ (A) It was based upon the writings of Euclid.

    P4 does not mention Euclid's writings, other than to state that the Parthenon was constructed more than 100 years before Euclid's publication of *Elements*.

✓ (B) Aesthetics may have played a role in the Parthenon's use of elements that exhibit the Golden Ratio.

    CORRECT. S2 states that the ratio's "aesthetic appeal may have been appreciated before it was ever described mathematically." S3: "many design elements of the Parthenon … bear a relationship to the Golden Ratio." S6: "the visual attractiveness of the ratio … may have played a role in the building's engineering and construction."

✗ (C) It is an example of mathematics being prioritized over aesthetics.

    S2 argues the opposite: aesthetics may have come before mathematics. P4 goes on to discuss the Parthenon as an example of this point.

✗ (D) The designer of the Parthenon is unknown.

    The paragraph does not mention the designer or designers of the Parthenon by name. But you can't conclude that the designer or designers are unknown.

7.   Paragraph 4 supports the idea that the designers of the Parthenon

   ✗   (A) were able to derive the Golden Ratio mathematically before it was formally recorded by Euclid

   ✓   (B) were aware of the Golden Ratio on some level, even if they could not formally define it

   ✗   (C) were mathematicians

   ✗   (D) were more interested in aesthetic concerns than sound architectural principles

INFERENCE. The designers of the Parthenon are mentioned only in S6. But the whole paragraph is concerned with design aspects of the Parthenon—in particular, the aesthetics of the Golden Ratio and its appearance in the Parthenon's design.

S4–5 describe Parthenon design elements that have a relationship to the Golden Ratio. However, you don't know that the designers were able to define the ratio formally or mathematically. The sentences only imply that they were aware of the ratio on some level.

CORRECT. S4–5 describe Parthenon design elements that have a relationship to the ratio. So the designers were probably aware of the ratio in some way. S6 mentions that the Parthenon was constructed well before the formal description of the ratio was published (in *Elements*, mentioned in P2). So the Parthenon designers may not have been able to define the ratio formally.

The paragraph does not provide any support for the idea that the designers were mathematicians.

The paragraph suggests that the aesthetic appeal of the Golden Ratio played a part in various design elements of the Parthenon. But nothing suggests that these aesthetic considerations were more important than "sound architectural principles."

8.   The word "elements" in the passage is closest in meaning to

   ✗   (A) origins

   ✗   (B) substances

   ✗   (C) drawings

   ✓   (D) components

VOCABULARY. The "elements" of something are its parts or components.

In some contexts, "elements" can mean "basics" or "fundamentals," which is similar to "origins." But here, the author means "parts" or "components."

In the context of chemistry, an "element" is a certain kind of basic substance or chemical. But here, the author means "parts" or "components."

Sketches or pictures are unrelated here.

CORRECT. "Many design elements of the Parthenon … bear a relationship to the Golden Ratio" = many components or parts of the building's design are related to the Golden Ratio.

Paragraph 5	**Comments**
S1 Numerous studies indicate that many pieces of art now considered masterpieces may also have incorporated the Golden Ratio in some way.	The Golden Ratio also seems to appear in great art.
2 Leonardo da Vinci created drawings illustrating the Golden Ratio in numerous forms to supplement the writing of *De Divina Proportione*.	Various examples.
3 This book on mathematics, written by Luca Pacioli, explored the application of various ratios, especially the Golden Ratio, in geometry and art.	
4 Analysts believe that the Golden Ratio influenced proportions in some of da Vinci's other works, including his *Mona Lisa* and *Annunciation* paintings.	
5 The ratio is also evident in certain elements of paintings by Raphael and Michelangelo.	
6 Swiss painter and architect Le Corbusier used the Golden Ratio in many design components of his paintings and buildings.	
7 Finally, Salvador Dalí intentionally made the dimensions of his work *Sacrament of the Last Supper* exactly equal to the Golden Ratio, and incorporated a large dodecahedron as a design element in the painting's background.	

9. Why does the author mention that Dalí "incorporated a large dodecahedron as a design element in the painting's background"?

PURPOSE. S7 discusses Dalí's painting *Sacrament of the Last Supper*. The sentence mentions two elements that have a relationship with the Golden Ratio. One of these elements is the dodecahedron mentioned in the highlighted text. Recall that P2 lists the regular dodecahedron as a geometric figure with a relationship to the Golden Ratio.

✗ (A) To demonstrate Dalí's frequent use of geometric shapes

S7 is the only sentence that discusses Dalí's work. You do not know that Dalí made "frequent use of geometric shapes," because you only have one example (the dodecahedron).

✓ (B) To illustrate the extent to which the Golden Ratio has influenced some works of art

CORRECT. P5 focuses on how the Golden Ratio is used in famous artwork. The Dalí painting discussed in S7 is an example of this use. The author mentions the dodecahedron in order to make a connection to the Golden Ratio. So the highlighted text illustrates the extent to which the Golden Ratio has influenced art.

✗ (C) To argue that certain style elements in art are more effective than others

The highlighted text does not argue or offer an opinion on anything. Also, the paragraph does not discuss the effectiveness of style elements in any way.

✗ (D) To refer to works by other artists such as da Vinci and Le Corbusier

The highlighted text does not refer to any aspects of the work of other artists. The only common thread among the works described in P5 is that all of them seem to have incorporated the Golden Ratio somehow.

10.   According to paragraph 5, da Vinci's illustrations in *De Divina Proportione* and two of his paintings, the *Mona Lisa* and *Annunciation*,

FACT. S2–4 discuss these works.

✓   (A) exhibit evidence that da Vinci's work was influenced by the Golden Ratio

CORRECT. S2 notes that da Vinci "created drawings illustrating the Golden Ratio" for *De Divina Proportione*. S4: "Analysts believe that the Golden Ratio influenced proportions in some of da Vinci's other works," including the paintings mentioned.

✗   (B) illustrate that he had a higher commitment to the Golden Ratio than other artists

Nothing in the paragraph suggests that da Vinci was more or less committed to the Golden Ratio than other artists discussed in P5.

✗   (C) provide examples showing that Renaissance art was more influenced by the Golden Ratio than modern art

Nothing in the passage tells you the historical category of art (Renaissance or modern) of the examples given. Moreover, you aren't told whether any artist is more or less influenced by the Golden Ratio than any other.

✗   (D) demonstrate that da Vinci's work was at least as influential as the work of mathematicians or architects

P5 mentions a mathematician (Pacioli) and an architect (Le Corbusier). But nothing states or implies that da Vinci's work was any more or less influential than work done by these or any other mathematicians or architects.

5

Paragraph 6	**Comments**
S1 The Golden Ratio even appears in numerous aspects of nature.	The ratio even appears in nature.
2 Philosopher Adolf Zeising observed that it was a frequently occurring relation in the geometry of natural crystal shapes.	Various examples.
3 He also discovered a common recurrence of the ratio in the arrangement of branches and leaves on the stems of many forms of plant life.	
4 Indeed, the Golden Spiral, formed by drawing a smooth curve connecting the corners of Golden Rectangles repeatedly inscribed inside one another, approximates the arrangement or growth of many plant leaves and seeds, mollusk shells, and spiral galaxies.	

11. By including the text "formed by drawing a smooth curve connecting the corners of Golden Rectangles repeatedly inscribed inside one another," the author is

PURPOSE. S4 discusses elements in nature that exhibit the Golden Spiral. The highlighted text defines the Golden Spiral in relation to the Golden Ratio (which is part of the Golden Rectangle).

✗ (A) emphasizing the importance of the Golden Spiral

The highlighted text makes no mention of the Golden Spiral's importance. It does not even mention any applications or examples.

✗ (B) providing the reader with instructions for creating a Golden Spiral

While the reader may be tempted to create a Golden Spiral based on the given description, that is not the purpose of the highlighted text. Rather, the author is just defining the Golden Spiral, so that the reader can loosely visualize it and understand how it relates to the Golden Ratio.

✓ (C) defining the Golden Spiral in relation to the Golden Ratio

CORRECT. The highlighted text defines the Golden Spiral in terms of Golden Rectangles, which themselves are related to the Golden Ratio (as defined in P4).

✗ (D) providing illustrations of elements in nature that exhibit the Golden Ratio

The highlighted text does not provide "illustrations" or examples of elements in nature. Instead, it defines the Golden Spiral mathematically.

12. According to paragraph 6, which of the following is an example from nature that demonstrates the Golden Spiral?

FACT. S4 is the only sentence that discusses the Golden Spiral. The correct answer must be found there.

✗ (A) The arrangement of branches in some forms of plant life

S3 discusses how the Golden Ratio occurs "in the arrangement of branches ... on the stems of many forms of plant life." But this is before the Golden Spiral is introduced. S4 specifically focuses on "plant leaves and seeds," not branches.

✗ (B) The common recurrence of the spiral throughout nature

The Golden Spiral may commonly recur throughout nature, according to S4, but just saying that it does so is not itself an example of the spiral.

✗ (C) The geometry of natural crystal shapes

S2 discusses how the Golden Ratio occurs "in the geometry of natural crystal shapes." But this is before the Golden Spiral is introduced.

✓ (D) The arrangement or growth of some galaxies

CORRECT. S4: "the Golden Spiral ... approximates the arrangement or growth of many ... spiral galaxies."

Paragraph 3	**Comments**

S1   The Fibonacci sequence, described by Leonardo Fibonacci, demonstrates one application of the Golden Ratio.

2-4   **A** The Fibonacci sequence is defined such that each term in the sequence is the sum of the previous two terms, where the first two terms are 0 and 1. The next term would be $0 + 1 = 1$, followed by $1 + 1 = 2$, $1 + 2 = 3$, $2 + 3 = 5$, etc. This sequence continues: 0, 1, 1, 2, 3, 5, 8, 13, 21, 34, 55, 89, and so on.

> Placement here would suggest that Pascal's triangle is an application of the Golden Ratio. But it is not—it is an application of the Fibonacci sequence.

5   **B** As the sequence progresses, the ratio of any number in the sequence to the previous number gets closer to the Golden Ratio.

> "For example" doesn't work here. Pascal's triangle is not an example of the way the Fibonacci sequence is built. Placement here interrupts the description of the Fibonacci sequence.

6   **C** This sequence appears repeatedly in various applications in mathematics.

> "For example" doesn't work here. Pascal's triangle is not an example of how the ratio of consecutive terms in the Fibonacci sequence gets closer to the Golden Ratio.

End   **D**

> **CORRECT.** "For example" works well. Pascal's triangle is an example of one of the "various applications in mathematics" (S6) of the Fibonacci sequence.

5

13.   **For example, it can be shown that the sum of the entries in consecutive diagonals of Pascal's triangle, useful in calculating binomial coefficients and probabilities, correspond to consecutive terms in the Fibonacci sequence.**

Where would the sentence best fit?

INSERT TEXT. "For example" tells you that this sentence must be an example of the idea in the previous sentence. The paragraph is about the Fibonacci sequence. This sentence describes something "new" that is related to that sequence (namely, some property of Pascal's triangle).

✗   (A) Choice A

✗   (B) Choice B

✗   (C) Choice C

✓   (D) Choice D   **CORRECT.**

	Whole Passage	Comments
P1	In math, simple relationships can often …	Golden Ratio = captivating. How to find = cut line in 2. Ratio = 1.618 : 1.
P2	The first recorded exploration of the Golden Ratio …	First recorded discussion of the ratio. Examples of the ratio in mathematics.
P3	The Fibonacci sequence, described by …	The Fibonacci sequence demonstrates the ratio.
P4	The allure of the Golden Ratio is not limited to …	The ratio goes beyond math. Aesthetic/artistic appeal may have come first. The ratio is in the Parthenon in ancient Greece.
P5	Numerous studies indicate that many pieces of art …	The Golden Ratio also seems to appear in great art. Various examples.
P6	The Golden Ratio even appears in …	The ratio even appears in nature. Various examples.

14. **The Golden Ratio, a mathematical relationship that has been known for centuries, has numerous applications and associated examples in the fields of mathematics, architecture, art, and nature.**

SUMMARY. Correct answers must be clearly expressed in the passage. They must also be among the major points of the passage. They should tie as directly as possible to the summary given.

✗ [A] The Fibonacci sequence has numerous applications in the field of mathematics.

P3 is devoted to the Fibonacci sequence as it relates to the Golden Ratio. But the fact that the Fibonacci sequence has applications in the field of mathematics does not fit in directly with the main idea. That main idea focuses on the breadth of areas related to the Golden Ratio. So this fact is a minor detail in the context of the passage as a whole.

✓ [B] The Golden Ratio appears in mathematical sequences and regular geometrical figures.

CORRECT. P2–P3 are devoted to discussing various examples of the appearance of the Golden Ratio in mathematics, including the Fibonacci sequence and various geometrical figures.

✗ [C] Some crystals have configurations that exhibit a relationship to the Golden Ratio.

Mentioned in P6. But this only one minor example of the Golden Ratio as found in nature.

✓ [D] The Golden Ratio influenced the work of many famous artists, including Da Vinci, Michelangelo, Le Corbusier, and Dalí.

CORRECT. P5 discusses the impact on the works of many famous artists.

✓ [E] The Golden Ratio appears in many examples from nature, ranging from crystal formations and plant structures to the shape of mollusk shells and spiral galaxies.

CORRECT. P6 discusses in detail these examples that illustrate the extent to which the Golden Ratio appears in nature.

✗ [F] Although described by Euclid in approximately 300 BC, the Golden Ratio was formally defined at a much earlier date.

Not supported by the passage. The author does not argue that the Golden Ratio was formally defined before Euclid. Rather, the author cites opinions that the ratio may have been appreciated aesthetically at an earlier date, before it was mathematically defined.

Answers and Explanations—5.3 Pterosaurs

	Paragraph 1	Comments
S1	Scientists have long been fascinated with the evolution of pterosaurs—warm blooded, flying reptiles that flourished during the Jurassic and Cretaceous periods, the time of the dinosaurs.	There were flying reptiles called pterosaurs.
2	Pterosaurs were the first animal after insects to develop powered flight.	
3	This ability was enabled by the pterosaur's hollow bone structure, a structure more similar to modern birds than to ancient dinosaurs.	
4	Because of their ability to fly, pterosaurs were able to expand their range and fill many ecological niches, eventually evolving into dozens of different species that ranged in size from a small bird to a small airplane.	Lots of varieties.
5	However, hollow bones decay more easily than solid bones, making complete pterosaur fossils hard to find.	It is difficult to find and categorize their fossils.
6	Known fossils are difficult to categorize into evolutionary families.	
7	How did the pterosaur evolve over time into the many different species that roamed the Earth?	
8	Hidden from scientists' view were the linking fossils that would indicate how closely related many of the different species were.	

1. According to paragraph 1, all of the following are true statements about pterosaurs EXCEPT:

   NEGATIVE FACT. Three answers are true and supported by the passage. One answer is false or just unsupported. Facts on pterosaurs could be anywhere in P1.

   ✗ (A) Pterosaurs were able to spread further because of their flight.

   S4: "Because of their ability to fly, pterosaurs were able to expand their range."

   ✗ (B) The bones of pterosaurs were hollow.

   S3: "the pterosaur's hollow bone structure."

   ✗ (C) Pterosaurs varied in size notably.

   S4: "dozens of different species that ranged in size from a small bird to a small airplane."

   ✓ (D) Pterosaurs were the first animal to develop powered flight.

   CORRECT. S2 says they were the second: "Pterosaurs were the first animal *after insects* to develop powered flight."

Paragraph 2   Comments

S1   Fossil discoveries allowed scientists to theorize that pterosaurs first split into two subgroups: short-tailed and long-tailed.

How pterosaurs are classified (2 subgroups, then 4 families within one subgroup).

2   Short-tailed pterosaurs are categorized into four distinct but evolutionarily related families.

3   Theories about which species of pterosaur belonged in which family have changed over time as new evidence emerges.

Classifications have changed over time.

4   One of the four families, *Gallodactylidae*, was created specifically because the swan-beaked pterosaur was thought to be distinct from the members of the other three families.

Example of one family.

5   *Gallodactylidae* are characterized by having fewer than 50 teeth, all of which are present only in the tip of the jaw.

6   As new fossils were found, it was determined that swan-beaked pterosaurs were, in fact, more similar to species from other families than was originally thought.

7   As a result, the family *Gallodactylidae* was largely disregarded.

2.   By stating that the swan-beaked pterosaur was "distinct" from the members of the other three families, the author means that

VOCABULARY. Something that is "distinct" is recognizably different from other potentially similar things. Here the author is saying that the swan-beaked pterosaur is different from the other pterosaur families.

✓ (A) it was different from previously discovered pterosaurs

CORRECT. "Distinct" = different from pterosaurs that had been categorized before.

✗ (B) it fell into expected patterns for pterosaur fossils

Opposite.

✗ (C) the three families represented a comprehensive categorization of pterosaurs

Opposite.

✗ (D) it could have been categorized into any of the three families

It could *not* be categorized into the other three families, so a new family had to be created.

3. The word "disregarded" in the passage is closest in meaning to

VOCABULARY. "Disregard" = pay no attention to or to ignore.

✓ (A) ignored

CORRECT. The pterosaur family was "disregarded" = it was ignored. Researchers stopped paying attention to it.

✗ (B) celebrated

Opposite. Something that is "celebrated" is greatly admired or renowned.

✗ (C) known

Not quite. The family was "known" in that researchers were familiar with it, but they no longer cared to distinguish it from other pterosaur families.

✗ (D) hoped for

Unrelated. The researchers had no feelings of expectation or desire.

Paragraph 3	**Comments**
S1 An exciting discovery in China soon reversed that trend.	A discovery changes things.
2 In 2012, a sword-headed pterosaur was discovered that also had teeth only in the front tip of the jaw.	
3 Swan-beaked and sword-headed pterosaurs were thought, for this reason, to be similar enough that they likely both directly evolved from a single common ancestor.	
4 The new discovery reenergized the belief that *Gallodactylidae* was its own unique family.	So people believed again that *Gallodactylidae* was its own family.
5 Scientists quickly flocked back to the practice of classifying the swan-beaked pterosaur in the family *Gallodactylidae*, this time along with the sword-headed pterosaur.	And they put the swan-beaked pterosaur back in that family.
6 Like many pterosaur fossils, the 2012 sword-headed pterosaur fossil was incomplete; only the skull and lower jaw were recovered.	
7 By categorizing the sword-headed pterosaur as a close relative of the swan-beaked pterosaur, scientists vastly expanded the geographical range of this family.	The family changed as a result.
8 No specimen of *Gallodactylidae* had ever been discovered in China before this point.	
9 Researchers also concluded that the family was far more varied than was originally thought.	

4.   According to paragraph 3, which of the following led scientists to reclassify the swan-beaked pterosaur as a member of the family *Gallodactylidae*?

FACT. S1–4 explain that the family *Gallodactylidae* was brought back into use for swan-beaked pterosaurs because of a new discovery.

✗ (A) The organizational structure of subgroups and families.

Pterosaurs are classified in subgroups and families. But this is not why the swan-beaked pterosaur was reclassified.

✓ (B) The discovery of a new and seemingly similar fossil.

CORRECT. S4: "The new discovery reenergized the belief that *Gallodactylidae* was its own unique family." That new discovery was the sword-headed pterosaur fossil.

✗ (C) The fact that sword-headed and swan-beaked pterosaurs evolved from different ancestors.

S3 mentions that the two were thought to have evolved from the same ancestor.

✗ (D) The overwhelming scientific evidence that many pterosaurs belonged in a new family.

The paragraph discussed only two pterosaurs, not "many." Also, the word "overwhelming" is extreme. The discovery of just one fossil is described. The effects of the discovery were dramatic, but it would be hard to claim that the evidence was "overwhelming" (= a lot of very convincing evidence).

5.   Which of the following can be inferred from paragraph 3 about the theory that swan-beaked and sword-headed pterosaurs had the same ancestor?

INFERENCE. S3: "Swan-beaked and sword-headed pterosaurs were thought, for this reason, to be similar enough that they likely both directly evolved from a single common ancestor." The reason is given in S2, which notes that the jaw of the sword-headed pterosaur "also" had certain features, features that resembled those of the swan-headed pterosaur.

✗ (A) It was based on comparison of completed fossils.

Contradicted in S6: "the 2012 sword-headed pterosaur fossil was incomplete."

✗ (B) It tried to account for the pterosaur's ability to fly.

Flight is not mentioned in relation to the ancestors of these pterosaurs.

✓ (C) Researchers assumed that a partial fossil provided enough data for meaningful conclusions.

CORRECT. S6: "the 2012 sword-headed pterosaur fossil was incomplete; only the skull and lower jaw were recovered." The theory explained in this paragraph is based solely on this partial fossil. If you can't draw meaningful conclusions from that fossil, then the theory falls apart.

✗ (D) It challenged the 2012 discovery of a sword-headed pterosaur.

There is no mention of challenging the discovery. In fact, the theory depended on this discovery.

6. The word "ancestor" in the passage is closest in meaning to

VOCABULARY. "Ancestor" is the person or thing from whom something is descended or evolved.

✗ (A) location

A place or position is unrelated.

✓ (B) predecessor

CORRECT. Common "ancestor" = predecessor = animal that both pterosaurs descended from.

✗ (C) food source

Unrelated. They didn't evolve from a single food source.

✗ (D) time period

Unrelated. They didn't evolve from a single time period.

Paragraph 4		**Comments**
S1	However, a major discovery in 2016 again forced scientists to reevaluate their classification of pterosaurs.	Another discovery changes things yet again.
2	Another specimen of the sword-headed pterosaur was discovered, but this time it was nearly complete.	A nearly complete sword-headed fossil is found.
3	The entire skull was present, along with the jawbone and much of the postcranial skeleton.	
4	The fossil was almost perfect, missing only one of the rear legs and two vertebrae.	
5	Analysis of this new fossil had some surprising results.	
6	The sword-headed pterosaur was actually different from the swan-beaked pterosaur in important ways.	Surprise: the sword-headed pterosaur is actually not like the swan-beaked one.
7	In fact, researchers determined that the sword-headed pterosaur was far more similar to species located in other families than to the swan-beaked pterosaur, with which it had been previously paired.	

5

7. All of the following are mentioned in paragraph 4 as true about the 2016 discovery of a pterosaur fossil EXCEPT:

NEGATIVE FACT. Three answers are true and supported by the passage. One answer is false or just unsupported. The discovery is discussed throughout P4.

✓ (A) the fact that scientists focused their research on the skull

CORRECT. Not mentioned in P4. S5 cites "analysis of this new fossil," but nothing is said about focus on the skull.

✗ (B) the presence of much of the postcranial skeleton

S3: "The entire skull was present along with ... much of the postcranial skeleton."

✗ (C) the classification of the fossil as a sword-headed pterosaur

S2: "Another specimen of the sword-headed pterosaur was discovered."

✗ (D) the fact that the fossil was missing vertebrae

S4: "missing ... two vertebrae."

8. In paragraph 4, why does the author provide details about which parts of the fossil were discovered in 2016?

PURPOSE. This find was "a major discovery" (S1) that led to a reclassification of pterosaurs. This reclassification resulted from analysis of the new fossil, which is described in S2 as "nearly complete" (and therefore valuable, because few pterosaur fossils are complete).

✗ (A) To evaluate the level of research done on sword-headed pterosaurs

S5 begins with analysis. But there's no evaluation of the level of research completed.

✗ (B) To illustrate the effectiveness of new fossil discovery techniques

There is no discussion of the methods of fossil discovery.

✗ (C) To demonstrate the difficulty of finding a complete pterosaur fossil

This difficulty is discussed earlier in the passage, but not as part of this paragraph. Here, parts of the fossil are listed to reinforce how complete the fossil is, so that its importance can be recognized.

✓ (D) To emphasize that this fossil was more complete than previously discovered fossils

CORRECT. S2 notes that the specimen is "nearly complete." S3–4 emphasize that point by providing details about which parts were present. S4 states that the fossil was "almost perfect."

9. Which of the sentences below best expresses the essential information in the highlighted sentence of paragraph 4? Incorrect choices change the meaning in important ways or leave out essential information.

SIMPLIFY SENTENCE. S7 (highlighted) indicates that the sword-headed (SH) pterosaur was actually more similar to other families than to the swan-beaked (SB) pterosaur, which had previously been considered its close relative. In shorthand, SH and SB used to be considered family. But the new discovery reveals that SH is actually closer to other families than it is to SB.

✗ (A) The swan-beaked pterosaur and the sword-headed pterosaur are considered identical by researchers.

They are never said to be identical, only similar. In fact, researchers now consider them less similar compared to the SH relationship to species in other families.

✗ (B) Researchers now pair the swan-beaked pterosaur with the sword-headed pterosaur.

This is the opposite. They used to pair the SB and SH, but have now started to compare the SH more closely to other species.

✗ (C) Researchers have located the sword-headed pterosaur in other families.

This sentence is about relating members of different pterosaur families, not whether the SH was actually located in a different family.

✓ (D) Researchers now consider the sword-headed pterosaur less like the swan-beaked pterosaur and more like species of other families.

CORRECT. This option doesn't directly mention the previous pairing, but the essence of the shift in similarity is clearly reflected.

Paragraph 5	Comments
S1 Again, the families were reorganized.	Another reorganization.
2 The sword-headed pterosaur was placed in an entirely different family called *Ctenochasmatoidea*.	Sword-headed went in a totally different family.
3 This family has been well-studied and is already known to have members in China.	
4 While a **tentative** organization of pterosaurs has helped to clarify which species evolved from a common ancestor and which are less closely related, it is apparent that the classification is far from final.	Not done yet!
5 Additional discoveries are likely to further alter scientists' perspectives on this reptile.	More studies may lead to additional changes.

10. The word "**tentative**" in the passage is closest in meaning to

VOCABULARY. "Tentative" = provisional, not certain or fixed.

✗ (A) adaptive

A tentative organization or structure is not necessarily adaptive (= flexible, responsive).

✗ (B) firm

Opposite. Something that is "firm" is fixed.

✓ (C) provisional

CORRECT. "Tentative" organization of pterosaurs = one that is current but not permanent = provisional.

✗ (D) controversial

A tentative structure is not necessarily controversial (= inspiring disagreement).

11. According to paragraph 5, which of the following is NOT an accurate conclusion about the pterosaur classification system?

NEGATIVE FACT. Three answers are true and supported by the passage. One answer is false or just unsupported. S4 lists overall conclusions from the classification system: "While a tentative organization of pterosaurs has helped to clarify which species evolved from a common ancestor and which are less closely related, it is apparent that the classification is far from final."

✗ (A) Additional discoveries will probably change what scientists believe about it.

S5: "Additional discoveries are likely to further alter scientists' perspectives on this reptile."

✓ (B) The opinions of researchers will likely remain unchanged over time.

CORRECT. S5 says the opposite: "Additional discoveries are likely to further alter scientists' perspectives on this reptile."

✗ (C) It includes at least one family that has been researched deeply.

S3: "This family has been well-studied" = researched deeply.

✗ (D) It helps make clear the common ancestry of certain species.

S4: "a tentative organization of pterosaurs has helped to clarify which species evolved from a common ancestor."

12. Why does the author mention the family "*Ctenochasmatoidea*"?

PURPOSE. S1–2 explain that sword-headed pterosaurs were again reclassified, this time into a different family called *Ctenochasmatoidea*. The reason for the reclassification was the 2016 discovery of a new fossil.

✗ (A) To complete the list of pterosaur families

The passage does not claim to provide a complete list of families.

✗ (B) To emphasize the differences among the four pterosaur families

While the families may be different, the passage never explains or emphasizes how they are different.

✓ (C) To illustrate a reorganization of the pterosaur classification system

CORRECT. The author mentions the new family in order to show that sword-headed pterosaurs were again reorganized because of the discovery.

✗ (D) To show that not all pterosaurs had the power of flight

The passage does not mention this point anywhere.

Paragraph 3   Comments

S1–2 An exciting discovery in China soon reversed that trend. In 2012, a sword-headed pterosaur was discovered that also had teeth only in the front tip of the jaw.

3 **A** Swan-beaked and sword-headed pterosaurs were thought, for this reason, to be similar enough that they likely both directly evolved from a single common ancestor.

Placement here doesn't link from common ancestry (before) to common family (after). The new sentence would also disrupt the connection between the evidence in S2 and the conclusion ("for this reason") about common ancestry in S3.

4–6 **B** The new discovery reenergized the belief that *Gallodactylidae* was its own unique family. Scientists quickly flocked back to the practice of classifying the swan-beaked pterosaur in the family *Gallodactylidae*, this time along with the sword-headed pterosaur. Like many pterosaur fossils, the 2012 sword-headed pterosaur fossil was incomplete; only the skull and lower jaw were recovered.

CORRECT. Placement here links common ancestry (S3) to common family (S4–5).

7–8 **C** By categorizing the sword-headed pterosaur as a close relative of the swan-beaked pterosaur, scientists vastly expanded the geographical range of this family. No specimen of *Gallodactylidae* had ever been discovered in China before this point.

Placement here doesn't link from common ancestry (before) to common family (after).

9 **D** Researchers also concluded that the family was far more varied than was originally thought.

Placement here doesn't link from common ancestry (before) to common family (after).

13.   **Species that have common ancestors are generally categorized within the same evolutionary family.**

Where would the sentence best fit?

INSERT TEXT. The subject of the sentence is "species that have common ancestors." So the text before this sentence should talk about having common ancestors. Next, the predicate of this sentence is "are generally categorized within the same evolutionary family." The sentence makes the logical link between having common ancestors and being in the same family. If species have common ancestors, then they are usually put in the same family. So the text after this sentence should focus on family classification. When placed in the paragraph, the sentence shouldn't interrupt existing logical connections and the flow of thought.

✗   (A) Choice A

✓   (B) Choice B   **CORRECT.**

✗   (C) Choice C

✗   (D) Choice D

Whole Passage	**Comments**
P1 Scientists have long been fascinated with …	There were flying reptiles called pterosaurs. Lots of varieties. It is difficult to find and categorize their fossils.
P2 Fossil discoveries allowed scientists to theorize …	How pterosaurs are classified. Classifications have changed over time. Example of one family.
P3 An exciting discovery in China …	A discovery changes things. So people believed again that *Gallodactylidae* was its own family. And they put the swan-beaked pterosaur back in that family. The family changed as a result.
P4 However, a major discovery in 2016 again forced scientists …	Another discovery changes things yet again. A nearly complete sword-headed fossil is found. Surprise: the sword-headed pterosaur is actually not like the swan-beaked one.
P5 Again, the families were reorganized …	Another reorganization. Sword-headed went in a totally different family. Not done yet! More studies may lead to additional changes.

14. **The classification of pterosaurs is an area of interest to scientists.**

SUMMARY. Correct answers must be clearly expressed in the passage. They must also be among the major points of the passage. They should tie as directly as possible to the summary given.

✓ [A] As new discoveries are unearthed, scientists continue to change the way they classify the families of short-tailed pterosaurs.

CORRECT. Corresponds to P5.

✗ [B] The most well-studied family of pterosaurs is the *Gallodactylidae* family, which continues to be a source of much debate among scientists.

The passage never claims that *Gallodactylidae* is well-studied. In fact, a lot more study seems to be needed.

✗ [C] The 2012 discovery of a sword-headed pterosaur was incomplete, containing only the skull and a portion of the jaw.

This detail is mentioned in P3, but it is not one of the main points of the passage.

✗ [D] The number of teeth that a pterosaur has is critical to its correct classification.

This is never stated. Sword-headed pterosaurs are eventually classified into the *Ctenochasmatoidea* family, despite the number of teeth they have (P5).

✓ [E] Living in the time of the dinosaurs, pterosaurs were reptiles that had the power of flight, making their fossils particularly difficult to discover.

CORRECT. Corresponds to P1.

✓ [F] The discovery of two different fossils of sword-headed pterosaurs has led to recent reorganizations of the families of pterosaurs.

CORRECT. Corresponds to P3, P4, and the beginning of P5.

Answers and Explanations—
5.4 Why Humans Have Big Brains

	Paragraph 1	**Comments**
S1	Humans have the largest brain of any living primate.	Humans have big brains relative to their bodies.
2	Our brain is exceptionally large in relation to our body size.	
3	While other social mammals—whales and elephants, for example—possess big brains, their brain size tends to correspond to their overall size.	
4	Human beings, on the other hand, are disproportionately small relative to their brain size.	
5	Furthermore, the human brain is the most rapidly changing organ in mammalian history.	Human brains have also evolved rapidly.
6	Why did the human brain evolve to be so large, so quickly?	Why?
7	Evidence suggests that this enlargement happened because of the social advantages it **conferred on** our evolutionary ancestors.	Social advantages.

1. According to paragraph 1, for which of the following animals is the ratio of brain size to body size exceptionally high?

   FACT. "Ratio of brain size to body size [is] exceptionally high" = the brain is big, compared to the body.

   ✗ (A) Whales

   S3 notes that whales have big brains, but the size of the brain corresponds to the size of the body.

   ✗ (B) Elephants

   S3 mentions that Elephants are like whales in this regard.

   ✓ (C) Humans

   CORRECT. S2: "Our brain is exceptionally large in relation to our body size." Also S4: "Human beings ... are disproportionately small relative to their brain size."

   ✗ (D) Non-human primates

   S1 suggests that other (living) primates have smaller brains. Nothing is directly said about the ratio of brain size to body size for these other primates, but humans are described as "exceptional" (S2), with "disproportionately small" bodies in comparison with their brains (S4). So you can safely conclude that other primates do not have the same kind of exceptionally large brains (relative to their bodies).

2. The phrase "conferred on" is closest in meaning to

✗ (A) burdened with

✗ (B) displayed to

✗ (C) discussed with

✓ (D) given to

VOCABULARY. "Conferred on" means "given to" or "bestowed upon." It is relatively neutral or slightly positive.

"Burdened with" has a negative connotation.

Something displayed or shown is not necessarily given.

"Confer with" means "discuss with," but "confer on" means "give to."

CORRECT. "The social advantages it [this brain enlargement] conferred on our evolutionary ancestors" = the advantages that the enlargement gave to our ancestors.

Paragraph 2	Comments
S1 For a trait to evolve, it must be handed down to future generations through processes of natural selection.	
2 Under standard Darwinian theory, a trait must be advantageous in order to spread throughout the population of a species.	For a trait to be passed down by natural selection, the trait must be advantageous.
3 This is what it means to be "selected for."	
4 Big brains are believed to be advantageous because they store and process a great deal of information, enabling owners of big brains to be more socially successful.	Big brains are advantageous, especially for social relationships.
5 In other words, bigger brains improved our ability to relate to other members of our species—whether through cooperation or through competition.	

3. According to paragraph 2, all of the following are true EXCEPT:

✗ (A) Advantageous traits are selected for.

✗ (B) Big brains can enhance one's competitive skills in relation to other humans.

✓ (C) Big brains evolved so that human beings could compete with other species.

✗ (D) For a trait to evolve, it must be inherited by future generations.

NEGATIVE FACT. Three answers are true and supported by the passage. One answer is false or just unsupported. Facts could be anywhere in P2.

S2–3: "a trait must be advantageous ... to be 'selected for.'"

S5: "bigger brains improved our ability to relate ... through competition."

CORRECT. S5 states that bigger brains would have improved our ability to interact with our own species, not a different species. It may be true that big brains helped us to compete with other species, but P2 never says so.

S1: "For a trait to evolve, it must be handed down to future generations."

Paragraph 3	Comments
S1 Other evidence that our brains became big in order to improve our social skills can be found elsewhere in the animal kingdom.	Other animals support this theory.
2 Other animals that have large brains tend to be the most social species on the planet.	Big-brained animals = very social.
3 These include elephants, sperm whales, and dolphins—all highly social mammals.	
4 The sperm whale, with a brain that is the largest of any known current or extinct species, joins a social unit early in life and typically remains with it for a lifetime.	
5 Within social units, sperm whales spend a great deal of time devoted to socializing, emitting complex patterns of clicks called "codas."	

4. According to paragraph 3, further evidence that humans developed large brains to improve social skills comes from

FACT. This paragraph is about other animals with large brains that are also very social.

  ✓ (A) other animals that also have large brains and are highly social

CORRECT. S2: "Other animals that have large brains tend to be the most social species on the planet."

  ✗ (B) the fact that sperm whales emit clicking sounds called "codas"

This fact in itself is not evidence of the claim that large brains improve social skills.

  ✗ (C) the socialization of dolphins with whales

The paragraph does not say that dolphins and whales socialize with one another.

  ✗ (D) the rate at which the sperm whale's brain evolved over its history

The rate at which the sperm whale's brain evolved is not discussed.

Paragraph 4	Comments
S1 Another indication that big brains probably evolved for social reasons is that sexual selection, a form of natural selection in which mating partners "choose" a particular variation of a trait by choosing a partner that has that variation over other partners that do not, can progress much more quickly than nonsexual selection.	Sexual selection can progress more quickly than nonsexual.
2 The fact that the brain evolved over such a short period of time in evolutionary terms implies that sexual selection may have played a role in the rapid increase in human brain size.	Rapid evolution of the brain may imply role of sexual selection.
3 Given that mating and competition for mates are social phenomena, having an enhanced social skill set enabled by a larger brain may have made a member of a population more attractive for sexual selection.	Mating is social, so if big brains help social skills, sexual selection could work here.

5. According to paragraph 4, the fact that sexual selection may have helped the human brain to grow quickly in size is suggested by

FACT. S2 says that the quick evolution of the human brain ("the brain evolved over such a short period of time in evolutionary terms") implies this fact (that "sexual selection may have played a role in the rapid increase in human brain size").

✓ (A) the rapid evolution of the human brain

CORRECT. S2: "The fact that the brain evolved over such a short period of time in evolutionary terms implies that sexual selection may have played a role in the rapid increase in human brain size."

✗ (B) the difficulty in finding suitable mating partners

There was no discussion of finding *suitable* partners nor of the difficulty in doing so.

✗ (C) the role of sexual selection in organ development

This discussion is about the brain, not other organs.

✗ (D) the societal importance of natural selection

The importance of natural selection would not explain why sexual selection (a subset) might be responsible for brain size increases.

6. Which of the sentences below best expresses the essential information in the highlighted sentence in the passage? Incorrect answer choices change the meaning in important ways or leave out essential information.

SIMPLIFY SENTENCE. S3 (highlighted) says that mating is social, so having good social skills (because of a big brain) may have made you a better candidate for mating and therefore sexual selection of your traits (such as having a big brain).

✗ (A) Because mating and competition aren't social, a larger brain was necessary to improve social skills.

S3 says mating and competition for mates *are* social phenomena.

✗ (B) Improved social skills enabled a larger brain and therefore better mating and sexual selection prospects.

Improved social skills were enabled by a larger brain, not the other way around.

✓ (C) Having a larger brain allowed for better social skills, probably enabling better mating and thus sexual selection.

CORRECT. The logical relationships in S3 are captured here. A larger brain led to better social skills, which may have led to better mating (because it's a social phenomenon), and ultimately sexual selection (which is natural selection of traits, such as having a big brain).

✗ (D) Attractiveness for sexual selection may have been driven by mating and competition, social phenomena that were enabled by larger brains.

This choice scrambles up the phrases from the original sentence, resulting in several unsupported assertions.

Paragraph 5	**Comments**
S1 Why else did humans evolve such a large brain despite our relatively petite body size?	Why did humans evolve large brains?
2 After all, having a large brain is costly.	Large brains are costly.
3 The human brain takes up approximately 2 percent of the human body but is responsible for a whopping 20 percent of the entire body's energy use (the proportion of blood and oxygen directed to the brain).	
4 Tool use may provide another cause, in addition to the development of social skills: the brain increased in size more rapidly after our ancestors learned to make tools.	Tool use is probably one reason.
5 Early tools included not only weapons used for hunting, but also equipment such as the hand ax, which allowed early humans to break down the meat before they ate it.	
6 This would have eased the burden on the digestive system, freeing up valuable metabolic resources to fuel the operations of a larger brain.	Tools allowed better digestion to fuel a big brain.

7. The word "whopping" in paragraph 5 is closest in meaning to

    VOCABULARY. "Whopping" is a somewhat informal word meaning "very large."

✓ (A) enormous

    CORRECT. S3: "The human brain … is responsible for a whopping 20 percent of the entire body's energy use" = that 20 percent is a really big number.

✗ (B) estimated

    Although the percent might be an estimate (rough calculation), this word is not related.

✗ (C) surprising

    "Whopping" may include an element of surprise. You could even argue that it means "surprisingly large." But "surprising" by itself isn't a good substitute, because it lacks the meaning of "large."

✗ (D) unjustified

    Unrelated. "Unjustified" = not right or reasonable, not justified.

8. All of the following are mentioned in paragraph 5 EXCEPT:

    NEGATIVE FACT. Paragraph 5 focuses on how much energy the human brain consumes and how our ancestors used tools to free up energy.

✗ (A) the general use of early tools

    S4 and S5 address early tool use.

✗ (B) the hunting function of weapons

    S5 addresses early weapons used for hunting.

✗ (C) the operation of the digestive tract

    S5–6 describe how breaking down meat "eased the burden on the digestive system."

✓ (D) the use of the hand ax in social competition

    CORRECT. S5 describes the use of equipment such as the hand ax, but in connection with cooking, not with social competition.

5

Paragraph 6	Comments
S1 Bizarrely, over the past 10,000 to 20,000 years, the human brain has actually shown a reverse trend: it is shrinking.	Now brains are getting smaller!
2 Across the globe, our brains are getting smaller.	
3 Some scientists predict that if the brain continues to shrink at its current rate, it will soon approach the size of the brain of *Homo erectus*, our ancestral relative from 500,000 years ago.	
4 While some fear that this means we are becoming less intelligent, others point to the warming climate.	One hypothesis = getting dumber; another one has to do with the warming climate.
5 They argue that a body of smaller stature is more efficiently cooled, and a smaller brain follows a smaller stature.	
6 Critics of the climatic theory, however, point to the fact that over the 2 million years during which the brain rapidly evolved to be larger, there were also periods of global warming.	
7 So the recent shrinkage of the brain remains a mystery.	Still a mystery.

9. According to paragraph 6, which of the following is true of the global climate during the time when the human brain was evolving to become larger?

   ✗ (A) It is responsible for the current shrinking of the human brain.

   ✓ (B) It was occasionally warm.

   ✗ (C) For the most part, it was not as warm as the climate is today.

   ✗ (D) It is shifting more now than it did historically.

FACT. S6 discusses the relevant time: "the 2 million years during which the brain rapidly evolved to be larger."

The question is about the climate in the past, not the climate in the present.

CORRECT. S6: "there were also periods of global warming."

This is not addressed in the passage.

This is not addressed in the passage.

10.   The word "approach" in the passage is closest in meaning to

   ✓   (A) become like

   ✗   (B) make contact with

   ✗   (C) measure up to

   ✗   (D) infringe upon

VOCABULARY. The verb "approach" in this context means "become more like" or "become closer to being like."

CORRECT. The brain "will soon approach the size of the brain of *Homo erectus*" = with respect to size, the human brain is becoming more like the brain of *Homo erectus*.

"Approach" can mean "make contact with" in a social setting ("she approached him about the issue" = "she came up to him and spoke to him about the issue.") But it is unnatural to say that one brain "made contact with" another brain, unless you are talking about physical touch or communication.

"Measure up to" implies a value comparison. "He tried to measure up to her" = "he tried to be as good as her in some way." Here, there's no value comparison.

To "infringe" is to limit, undermine, or even intrude. "By reading my diary, my sister had infringed upon my privacy."

11.   What is the author's purpose in presenting the information in paragraph 6?

   ✗   (A) To explain how the human brain is now evolving to become even larger

   ✗   (B) To advocate for one hypothesis about current trends in brain size over another

   ✗   (C) To argue against a claim made elsewhere in the passage

   ✓   (D) To describe a phenomenon that opposes the pattern described in the rest of the passage

PURPOSE. P6 presents a change in the trend (human brain sizes are now shrinking). The author concludes that the cause of the change remains a mystery.

Opposite. P6 describes how the human brain is now shrinking.

The author does not advocate for either hypothesis. Rather, the author believes that the phenomenon remains a mystery.

The author is not arguing against any claim. The trend in human brain size (now shrinking) is different than it was before, but presenting this fact is not the same thing as arguing against any previous points.

CORRECT. While the rest of the passage discusses how the brain evolved to become larger, this paragraph discusses a reversal of that trend.

5

12.   The word "stature" in the   **VOCABULARY.** "Stature" means "height of the body" in a
        passage is closest in meaning to   physical sense, or "social standing" in a non-physical sense.
                                            The context here indicates the physical meaning.

     ✗   (A) intelligence   Someone's mental capacity is not related to their height.

     ✓   (B) height   **CORRECT.** "A body of smaller stature" = a shorter person or
                                            body.

     ✗   (C) energy level   Someone's energy level is not necessarily related to their
                                            height.

     ✗   (D) achievement   "Stature" can mean "achievement," but only in a social context.

Paragraph 6	Comments
S1 Bizarrely, over the past 10,000 to 20,000 years, the human brain has actually shown a reverse trend: it is shrinking.	
2–3 **A** Across the globe, our brains are getting smaller. Some scientists predict that if the brain continues to shrink at its current rate, it will soon approach the size of the brain of *Homo erectus*, our ancestral relative from 500,000 years ago.	**CORRECT.** In the previous sentence you learn that human brains have been shrinking. The inserted sentence tells you that the phenomenon isn't restricted to one region. The next sentence goes on to say that this shrinkage is indeed occurring globally.
4–5 **B** While some fear that this means we are becoming less intelligent, others point to the warming climate. They argue that a body of smaller stature is more efficiently cooled, and a smaller brain follows a smaller stature.	Here, *Homo erectus* has just been mentioned in comparison to modern day humans. So "this" would have to refer to that comparison, but it doesn't make sense to say that this comparison is not restricted to a single region. The following sentence has nothing to do with the global nature of the phenomenon; that point was already made in S2, so it's strange to bring it back.
6 **C** Critics of the climatic theory, however, point to the fact that over the 2 million years during which the brain rapidly evolved to be larger, there were also periods of global warming.	Here, the relationship between brain size and body size is discussed. Again, it's strange to come back to the global nature of the phenomenon (human brain shrinkage) when it was mentioned in S2.
7 **D** So the recent shrinkage of the brain remains a mystery.	Once again, it's strange to come back to the global nature of the phenomenon (human brain shrinkage) when it was mentioned in S2.

13. **This is not restricted to a single region or hemisphere.**

Where would the sentence best fit?

INSERT TEXT. Although it is not perfectly clear what "this" is referring to, the sentence would make the most sense in a part of the paragraph where some phenomenon is being discussed as applying to the whole world (as opposed to just one "region or hemisphere.") The following text would ideally emphasize the global nature of the phenomenon.

✓ (A) Choice A

✗ (B) Choice B

✗ (C) Choice C

✗ (D) Choice D

CORRECT.

	Whole Passage	Comments
P1	Humans have the largest brain …	Humans have big brains relative to their bodies. Human brains have also evolved rapidly. Why? Social advantages.
P2	For a trait to evolve, it must be handed down …	For a trait to be passed down by natural selection, the trait must be advantageous. Big brains are advantageous, especially for social relationships.
P3	Other evidence that our brains became big in order to improve our social skills can be found …	Other animals support this theory. Big-brained animals = very social.
P4	Another indication that big brains probably evolved for social reasons is …	Sexual selection can progress more quickly than nonsexual. Rapid evolution of the brain may imply role of sexual selection. Mating is social, so if big brains help social skills, sexual selection could work here.
P5	Why else did humans evolve such a large brain …	Why else did humans evolve large brains? Large brains are costly. Tool use is probably one reason. Tools allowed better digestion to fuel a big brain.
P6	Bizarrely, over the past 10,000 to 20,000 years, the human brain has actually shown a reverse trend …	Now brains are getting smaller! One hypothesis = getting dumber; another one has to do with the warming climate. Still a mystery.

5

14. **The human brain is one of the most rapidly evolving organs in mammalian history.**

SUMMARY. Correct answers must be clearly expressed in the passage. They must also be among the major points of the passage. They should tie as directly as possible to the summary given.

✗ ☐ A The most significant drain on energy in the human body is the brain.

This is too extreme of a statement. You don't know that the brain is "the most significant drain" in this way. The statement is also too narrow in scope to capture a central idea of this passage.

✓ ☐ B Since a trait that successfully evolves must benefit the organism, large brains were probably advantageous to human ancestors.

CORRECT. This point is presented in P2 as the reason that large brains evolved. The passage as a whole explores the reasons for the evolution of large human brains.

✗ ☐ C Large brains are mostly restricted to marine life.

While dolphins and sperm whales are mentioned as having large brains, nowhere does the passage suggest that large brains are restricted to marine life.

✗ ☐ D Darwin's theory of natural selection can explain many traits of animals on Earth.

This statement is too broad and is not a central idea in the passage, which is specifically about large brains among humans and their ancestors.

✓ ☐ E Social species tend to have the largest brains, suggesting that humans evolved large brains for social reasons.

CORRECT. This core reason for the evolution of large human brains is explored in P2 and P3.

✓ ☐ F The large human brain requires a significant amount of energy, which human ancestors accessed by using tools to aid in digestion.

CORRECT. P5 presents tool use as an additional reason for the evolution of large human brains.

Answers and Explanations—5.5 Crystallization

	Paragraph 1	Comments
S1	When most people hear the word "crystal," they think of something cherished and rare.	
2	In fact, however, crystals are common occurrences in nature.	Crystals are actually common.
3	A crystal, by definition, is any solid whose constituent parts (atoms, molecules, or ions, for example) are arranged in a highly ordered structure.	Crystals are solids with an ordered structure.
4	This structure repeats, forming what's known as the "crystal lattice" that extends in all directions.	
5	Most inorganic solids are polycrystals—they are not each a single crystal.	
6	Rather, they are made up of many microscopic crystals fused together to make a single solid mass.	Polycrystals = many little crystals fused together.
7	Most metals and also ceramics fall into the polycrystal category.	
8	True crystals and polycrystals can be formed by a variety of natural forces, including heat and pressure deep underground, as well as cold on the earth's surface and even the flow of water.	Crystals are formed by various natural forces.

1.	The word "cherished" in the passage is closest in meaning to	**VOCABULARY.** "Cherished" = highly valued, treasured. To "cherish" something is to put great value on it.
✗	(A) beautiful	Something beautiful might also be cherished, but these are not necessarily related.
✗	(B) cheap	Opposite. "Cheap" = inexpensive or of poor quality.
✓	(C) treasured	**CORRECT.** "Something cherished" = something treasured or held dear.
✗	(D) extraordinary	Something may be cherished *because* it is extraordinary (unusual), but the two words are not synonyms.

2.   Which of the following questions about crystals is NOT answered in paragraph 1?

NEGATIVE FACT. Three answers are true and supported by the passage. One answer is false or just unsupported. Answers to these questions about crystals could be anywhere in P1.

✗ (A) Which natural forces can form true crystals and polycrystals?

S8 lists these forces (e.g., "heat and pressure deep underground").

✗ (B) What is the definition of a crystal?

S3 defines what crystals are: a solid with a highly ordered structure.

✗ (C) What is a crystal lattice?

S4 tells you what a crystal lattice is: the repeating structure of a crystal extending in all directions.

✓ (D) What is an inorganic solid?

CORRECT. S5 mentions "inorganic solids" (to say that most of them are polycrystals). But the paragraph never defines what an inorganic solid is.

3.   The word "fused" in the passage is closest in meaning to

VOCABULARY. "Fused" = bonded or joined together tightly into a whole. It can also mean "liquified, melted at a high temperature."

✗ (A) dispersed

Opposite. "Dispersed" = scattered, separated.

✓ (B) joined

CORRECT. "Many microscopic crystals fused together to make a single solid mass" = the little crystals are joined tightly together to make one whole.

✗ (C) chosen

Unrelated. "Chosen" = selected.

✗ (D) burned

Although the bonding may have taken place under conditions of extreme heat, "fused" does not mean that the crystals were burned or ignited.

	Paragraph 2	**Comments**
S1	Gems and minerals are the most widely recognized crystals.	
2	Although most mineral crystals form under similar conditions, their structures can be very different.	
3	As a general rule, a crystal's shape, perceptible to the naked eye, is a reflection of its microscopic structure.	Crystal shapes generally reflect the microscopic structure of the crystal.
4	Because crystals are the repetition of a **particular** structure, they are defined by the "unit cell," which is the smallest group of particles containing the pattern that is then repeated to form the crystal lattice.	Unit cell = tiny repeating part of the pattern.
5	A crystal with cubic unit cells can form a crystal that is, itself, a cube.	Various shapes, based on various unit cells.
6	Pyrite, known as "fool's gold" because of its resemblance to the precious metal, has a cubic structure and often forms in masses of interlocking cubes.	
7	Crystals with hexagonal unit cells, on the other hand, tend to form in barrel-shaped hexagonal prisms or pyramids.	
8	Corundum, the mineral best known for its gem varieties ruby and sapphire, is a hexagonal crystal.	
9	Some of the most prized specimens of corundum are bipyramidal sapphires, which are hexagonal prisms that are not barrel-shaped, but instead appear as though two pyramids are stuck together at the bottom.	
10	The middle of the crystal is its widest point, and it tapers sharply at each end, forming the tips of the pyramids.	

4. The word "particular" in the passage is closest in meaning to

VOCABULARY. "Particular" things = specific, individual, special, or unique things.

✗	(A) recurring	Unrelated. "Recur" = to happen repeatedly or periodically.
✗	(B) selective	This is an alternative meaning for the word "particular." This definition, however, only applies to people or other conscious beings who actively make choices. "He is very particular about his clothes" = he is very selective or picky about them.
✗	(C) atomic	"Particular" shares a root with "particle," but the meaning of "particular" doesn't have much to do with actual particles, such as atoms.
✓	(D) specific	**CORRECT.** "Crystals are the repetition of a particular structure" = crystals are formed by repeating a specific, special structure (the unit cell that captures the pattern).

5.   The author mentions pyrite, ruby, and sapphire in paragraph 2 in order to

PURPOSE. These minerals and gems are offered as concrete (= not abstract) examples of different crystal structures, which is cubic for pyrite and hexagonal for rubies and sapphires. The purpose is to link the technical, abstract terms (cubic and hexagonal) to physical examples of gems and minerals, which are likely to be more familiar to readers.

✗ (A) distinguish between precious and semi-precious minerals

You might already know that rubies and sapphires are much more precious than pyrite ("fool's gold"). But that is outside knowledge. The author never makes any distinction between precious and semi-precious minerals.

✗ (B) emphasize that not all crystals are necessarily rare

As an aside, the author mentions that pyrite is called "fool's gold" for its resemblance to real gold, implying that pyrite is much less rare than gold. But the rarity (or lack of rarity) of different crystals is not the point of the paragraph, which is to describe the various structures of crystals.

✓ (C) illustrate crystal forms with concrete gems and minerals

CORRECT. The crystal forms are cubic (described in S5–6) and hexagonal (described in S7–10). Pyrite, rubies, and sapphires provide tangible examples of these structures.

✗ (D) emphasize the underlying similarities between cubic and hexagonal crystals

These shapes are never described as similar. In fact, they're contrasted in S7: "on the other hand."

6.   According to paragraph 2, which of the following hexagonal crystals can exhibit a hexagonal prism that is not shaped like a barrel?

FACT. S9: "bipyramidal sapphires, which are hexagonal prisms that are not barrel-shaped."

✓ (A) Sapphire

CORRECT. S9 describes a certain kind of sapphire as exhibiting a hexagonal prism not shaped like a barrel.

✗ (B) Ruby

According to S7–8, rubies are hexagonal and tend to form in barrel-shaped prisms or pyramids. S9 mentions the bipyramidal sapphires as being "not barrel-shaped," but nothing is mentioned about this for rubies.

✗ (C) Non-gem corundum

S8 indicates that sapphires are a gem variety of the mineral corundum. Only a certain kind of sapphires are described as exhibiting the desired shape. You don't know whether non-gem varieties of corundum can exhibit this shape as well.

✗ (D) Pyrite

S6–7 indicate that pyrite is cubic rather than hexagonal.

7.   Paragraph 2 suggests which of the following about the relationship of pyrite to gold?

INFERENCE. S6 is the only sentence that mentions pyrite and gold: "Pyrite, known as 'fool's gold' because of its resemblance to the precious metal."

✗ (A) Pyrite has a glossier appearance than gold.

All you know about the appearance of the two substances is that they resemble each other. No difference in their appearances is given.

✓ (B) Pyrite is less valuable than gold.

CORRECT. The term "fool's gold" implies that you would be foolish to think that pyrite was the precious metal gold. You can safely deduce that pyrite's value is therefore less than that of gold.

✗ (C) Pyrite has a cubic crystal structure, whereas gold does not.

You aren't told anything about the crystal structure of gold, even whether it has one.

✗ (D) Pyrite is less common in the environment than gold.

If anything, you could be tempted to infer the opposite. From the text, you can safely draw the inference that pyrite is less valuable than gold. Bringing in a little outside knowledge about supply and demand, you might jump to the idea that pyrite is more common in the environment than gold. But even this inference is suspect, and you certainly can't infer that pyrite is *less* common than gold.

8.   According to paragraph 2, all of the following are true of the unit cell EXCEPT:

NEGATIVE FACT. S4 defines the unit cell as "the smallest group of particles containing the pattern that is then repeated to form the crystal lattice." S4 also says that crystals are defined by the unit cell they contain. Later sentences describe the different shapes and structures of crystals, all dependent on their unit cell.

✓ (A) It always gives rise to the same visible shape of the crystal.

CORRECT. S7 describes hexagonal unit cells that give rise to barrel-shaped hexagonal prisms. But according to S8–9, corundum is a hexagonal crystal, but one of its forms (bipyramidal sapphire) is not barrel-shaped.

✗ (B) It contains the pattern that is repeated to form the crystal lattice.

Definition of unit cell in S4.

✗ (C) It can influence the appearance of the crystal as perceived by the naked eye.

S5–10 indicate how different unit cells influence the visible shape and appearance of the crystal.

✗ (D) Its features determine the classification of the crystal.

S4 notes that crystals are defined by the unit cell. That is, the type of unit cell, such as cubic or hexagonal defines the crystal as cubic or hexagonal, etc. Examples are given in S5–10.

5

Paragraph 3	Comments
S1 Mineral crystals can form from magmatic processes.	Magma/lava can crystallize in various ways.
2 These processes occur when molten magma (also known as lava) solidifies and cools.	
3 The conditions under which the molten magma cools modify the type of crystal that is formed.	Depends on how the magma cools.
4 Granite, for example, cools very slowly and under intense pressure, leading to complete crystallization.	
5 Many other magmatic rocks are formed when lava pours out onto the Earth's surface and cools very quickly, leaving small amounts of glassy material and never achieving full crystallization.	

9.   The word "modify" in the passage is closest in meaning to

VOCABULARY. "Modify" = change, alter, affect.

✓ (A) influence

CORRECT. "The conditions ... modify the type of crystal that is formed" = the conditions affect or influence the crystal type.

✗ (B) exaggerate

"Exaggerate" = amplify a great deal or even too much. This is too specific a form of influence.

✗ (C) initiate

Unrelated. "Initiate" = to cause or begin (a process).

✗ (D) degrade

"Degrade" = make worse. Again, this is too specific a form of influence.

Paragraph 4	Comments
S1 Fluids can also be an agent of crystallization.	Fluids can also cause crystals to form.
2 Suspended in a fluid solution, microscopic molecules, or even individual atoms, can begin to gather into clusters within the solution, forming stable, though still microscopic, structures.	Molecules gather into clusters.
3 Once a cluster is large enough to be stable, it is called a nucleus.	Stable cluster = nucleus.
4 This nucleus will contain at least one unit cell and thus will define the crystal's structure, even in this microscopic state.	
5 Crystal growth will occur as more atoms or molecules are pulled out of the solution and join with the nucleus.	Crystal grows around nucleus.
6 In this way, crystallization is a solid-liquid separation technique.	

10. The word "agent" in the passage is closest in meaning to

✗ (A) barrier

✓ (B) instrument

✗ (C) purveyor

✗ (D) result

VOCABULARY. A thing described as an "agent" is something that causes or helps cause an effect, or is a means to that end.

Opposite. An agent helps make something happen, whereas a barrier would be an obstacle to that event.

CORRECT. "Fluids can also be an agent of crystallization" = fluids can help make crystallization happen = they are an instrument or means for this to occur.

"Purveyor" can mean "supplier, transmitter, source," but this word is only used for people or companies.

Opposite in another sense. An agent is a cause of some effect, not the effect or result itself.

11. According to paragraph 4, which of the following is true of a nucleus in crystal formation?

✗ (A) It consists of unstable clusters within a fluid solution.

✓ (B) It determines the structure of the crystal.

✗ (C) It does not contain any unit cells of the crystal.

✗ (D) It repels the atoms or molecules drawn out of solution to form the crystal.

FACT. S3 defines the nucleus as a stable cluster. S4–5 give more facts about the nucleus.

Opposite. S3: the nucleus = a cluster "large enough to be stable."

CORRECT. S4: "This nucleus … will define the crystal's structure."

Opposite. S4: "This nucleus will contain at least one unit cell."

Opposite. S5: "Crystal growth will occur as more atoms or molecules are pulled out of the solution and join with the nucleus." The nucleus does not repel the atoms or molecules; it evidently attracts them.

5

Paragraph 5   **Comments**

S1   When liquids evaporate, they form crystals from the sediment (solid materials) that remain after the evaporation has taken place.

Crystals form out of what's left behind when liquids evaporate.

2   Water-based "aqueous" solutions often have suspended within them particles of minerals that can form crystals if the solution evaporates.

3   Take, for example, the water of the ocean.

Example: when ocean water evaporates, rock salt is left behind.

4   Ocean water is saline, meaning that it contains relatively high concentrations of salt.

5   When saline water evaporates, the salt cannot become gaseous.

6   Instead, it is left behind in its solid form.

7   When these solids make up a high enough volume of the evaporating fluid, they unite, forming the crystal halite, also known as rock salt.

8   Vast expanses of halite can form when large bodies of saline water evaporate, giving rise to great deserts of salt like the one in Bonneville, Utah.

9   The so-called "salt flat" is composed of 90 percent pure halite, with a surface so hard and flat that it has been used since 1914 to set land speed records for car and motorcycle racers.

12.   According to the passage, which of the following is true of halite?

FACT. Halite is first mentioned by name in S7, but the example of ocean water evaporating starts in S3. S8–9 also discuss halite.

✗ (A) Its largest deposit is found in Bonneville, Utah.

S8 states that a large deposit (a "great desert of salt") is found in Bonneville, Utah, but you aren't told that this is the largest deposit of halite.

✗ (B) Its crystal structure is cubic, based on its unit cell.

The author never tells you the crystal structure of halite. By the way, the structure is in fact cubic, but the passage never says so.

✓ (C) It is formed from solids that combine in evaporating ocean water.

CORRECT. S3–7 describe this process. S7: "When these solids make up a high enough volume of the evaporating fluid, they unite, forming the crystal halite, also known as rock salt."

✗ (D) It is generated when salt evaporates from saline water.

S5–6 note that the salt itself doesn't evaporate or "become gaseous." Rather, it is left behind when the water evaporates.

Paragraph 5	**Comments**
S1–2 When liquids evaporate, they form crystals from the sediment (solid materials) that remain after the evaporation has taken place. Water-based "aqueous" solutions often have suspended within them particles of minerals that can form crystals if the solution evaporates.	
3 **A** Take, for example, the water of the ocean.	**CORRECT.** The subject of S2 is "water-based 'aqueous' solutions." The subject of the inserted sentence ("these solutions") easily refers back to S2. The following sentences (S3–7) describe an example of a high-concentration mineral (salt) dominating the crystallization that happens in evaporating ocean water.
4 **B** Ocean water is saline, meaning that it contains relatively high concentrations of salt.	The subject "these solutions" in the inserted sentence doesn't follow well from "the water of the ocean" in the previous sentence. Placement here also would interrupt the logical flow of the ocean water example from S3 to S4.
5–7 **C** When saline water evaporates, the salt cannot become gaseous. Instead, it is left behind in its solid form. When these solids make up a high enough volume of the evaporating fluid, they unite, forming the crystal halite, also known as rock salt.	Same problems as in B. The subject "these solutions" doesn't follow well from "ocean water." Placement here also would interrupt the logical flow of the ocean water example from S4 to S5.
8–9 **D** Vast expanses of halite can form when large bodies of saline water evaporate, giving rise to great deserts of salt like the one in Bonneville, Utah. The so-called "salt flat" is composed of 90 percent pure halite, with a surface so hard and flat that it has been used since 1914 to set land speed records for car and motorcycle racers.	Same problems as in B and C. The subject "these solutions" doesn't follow well from "these solids" (which are not solutions) or "the evaporating fluid." In addition, placement here would interrupt the discussion of halite.

13.   **These solutions can contain particles of multiple minerals, but when one mineral exists in significantly higher concentration than the others, the crystallization process is dominated by that mineral.**

     Where would the sentence best fit?

     ✓   (A) Choice A

     ✗   (B) Choice B

     ✗   (C) Choice C

     ✗   (D) Choice D

INSERT TEXT. "These solutions" should refer to solutions discussed in the previous sentence. The following sentence should continue the main thought in this sentence: namely, a mineral in high concentration (higher than that of others) should dominate the crystallization process.

CORRECT.

Whole Passage	**Comments**
P1 When most people hear the word "crystal," they think …	Crystals are actually common. Crystals are solids with an ordered structure. Polycrystals = many little crystals fused together. Crystals are formed by various natural forces.
P2 Gems and minerals are the most widely recognized crystals …	Crystal shapes generally reflect the microscopic structure of the crystal. Unit cell = tiny repeating part of the pattern. Various shapes, based on various unit cells.
P3 Mineral crystals can form from magmatic processes …	Magma/lava can crystallize in various ways. Depends on how the magma cools.
P4 Fluids can also be an agent of crystallization …	Fluids can also cause crystals to form. Molecules gather into clusters. Stable cluster = nucleus. Crystal grows around nucleus.
P5 When liquids evaporate, they form crystals …	Crystals form out of what's left behind when liquids evaporate. Example: when ocean water evaporates, rock salt is left behind.

14.   **Crystals are solids with an orderly internal structure.**

SUMMARY. Correct answers must be clearly expressed in the passage. They must also be among the major points of the passage. They should tie as directly as possible to the summary given.

✗ ☐ A   It is difficult to establish what determines the shape of the unit cell as it forms.

This difficulty (if it exists) is mentioned nowhere.

✗ ☐ B   Within the Earth's crust, crystallization depends largely on the application of heat and pressure.

P1 S8 does mention "heat and pressure deep underground" as one of the natural forces that form crystals. However, you aren't told that these two forces are the primary forces for crystallization within the Earth's crust. P3 discusses crystallization of cooling magma (which would involve the removal of heat and probably pressure).

✓ ☐ C   Crystallization is a common result of various natural forces, such as the cooling of magma.

CORRECT. This key point is made at the end of P1 to introduce the rest of the passage. The cooling of magma is the example that is the topic of P3.

✓ ☐ D   A crystal's shape is determined by its unit cell, a repeating microscopic building block.

CORRECT. P2 defines the unit cell and explains how it determines the visible shape and appearance of crystals.

✓ ☐ E   Crystals can be formed through evaporation of liquids, such as large bodies of water.

CORRECT. P5 discusses how crystals can be formed via evaporation.

✗ ☐ F   Bipyramidal sapphire is a more valuable mineral than cubic pyrite.

As an aside, you are told that pyrite is "fool's gold." You can infer that pyrite is not as valuable as real gold, but you are not told how the value of any kind of sapphire compares. Moreover, even if this point were made, it would be a minor detail in the passage.

Answers and Explanations—5.6 Habitat Fragmentation

	Paragraph 1	Comments
S1	The habitats of terrestrial animals, which provide food, shelter, and places to bear and raise offspring, have been changing at an unnatural pace in recent centuries.	Habitats have been changing.
2	The restriction of a once large, continuous habitat into smaller, segmented pieces is called **habitat fragmentation**.	Habitat fragmentation = restriction into smaller segments.
3	This process occurs over all types of habitats and is widely recognized as one of the major barriers to effective conservation efforts.	This is a barrier to effective conservation.

1.   According to paragraph 1, what is true of habitat fragmentation?

    FACT. S2 defines habitat fragmentation. S3 provides additional information about the phenomenon.

✗ (A) It provides food and shelter to terrestrial animals.

    S1 says this about habitats, not habitat fragmentation.

✓ (B) It is a barrier to conservation efforts.

    CORRECT. S3: "This process … is widely recognized as one of the major barriers to effective conservation efforts."

✗ (C) It occurs only in specific types of habitats.

    Opposite. S3: "This process occurs over all types of habitats."

✗ (D) It was widely recognized in recent centuries.

    This mixes up language from S3 ("widely recognized") and S1 ("in recent centuries"). The mash-up isn't necessarily true.

5

	Paragraph 2	**Comments**
S1	Habitat fragmentation occurs when the landscape is changed so that plants and animals no longer have access to all of the same areas they once did.	Habitat fragmentation occurs when landscape changes so there's no more access.
2	In some cases, this process can occur because part of the habitat has been destroyed, leaving animals with less roaming space than they previously had.	Some cases: part of habitat is destroyed.
3	In other cases, the habitat still exists, but a barrier emerges that prevents animals from reaching all areas of their former habitat.	Other cases: barrier emerges.
4	Regardless of how it occurs, habitat fragmentation can be dangerous to both plants and animals.	Dangerous to both plants and animals.
5	Plants are unable to respond quickly to change, so if they rely on an aspect of their habitat that no longer exists, there is often not enough time to adapt, and the plant will die off.	Explains how.
6	Animals are more commonly able to move into the smaller habitat areas, but they suffer nonetheless.	
7	They may be cut off from food or shelter.	
8	Often, the resources remaining can support only a smaller population, leaving the animals vulnerable to disease.	

2. The words "an aspect" in the passage are closest in meaning to

VOCABULARY. "Aspect" = feature, characteristic, property or quality.

✗ (A) a food source

A food source is an example of what an aspect could be, but it's too narrow a replacement. Many more kinds of things could be aspects of a habitat (e.g., its average temperature or its elevation above sea level).

✗ (B) an advance

Again, this is too specific. An "advance" of a habitat would mean its physical progression into neighboring areas. A possible aspect of a habitat could be that it is advancing, but that possibility excludes all other potential aspects.

✓ (C) an attribute

CORRECT. "They rely on an aspect of their habitat" = they depend on some attribute, feature, or characteristic of their habitat.

✗ (D) another species

Again, this is too specific.

3.   According to paragraph 2, which of the following occurs more with plants that suffer habitat fragmentation than with animals that suffer habitat fragmentation?

FACT. S5 discusses the impact on plants. S6–8 discuss the impact on animals.

✓ (A) Plants cannot shift as easily into smaller areas.

CORRECT. S6: "Animals are *more* commonly able to move into the smaller habitat areas." The comparison "more" comes after S5, which describes plant behavior. So the comparison is to plants, which are therefore *less* able to shift or move into those areas.

✗ (B) Plants are more vulnerable to disease.

S8 mentions only that animals in smaller populations are vulnerable to disease.

✗ (C) Plants respond more quickly to change.

Opposite, if anything. S5: "Plants are unable to respond quickly to change."

✗ (D) Plants have less time to adapt to the absence of resources.

Not supported. S5 mentions that plants often do not have enough time to adapt when a necessary aspect of their habitat disappears. But that doesn't mean plants have less time than animals do to adapt.

4.   According to paragraph 2, a cause of habitat fragmentation is

FACT. S1–3 outline causes of habitat fragmentation. S1 explains the general cause: the landscape changes in such a way as to limit access by plants and animals. The change could be destruction of part of the habitat (S2) or the emergence of a barrier (S3).

✗ (A) the lack of access by plants and animals to previously available areas

This is the result of habitat fragmentation, not the cause of it. In fact, this result is what defines the change in a landscape as habitat fragmentation, according to S1.

✓ (B) the creation of physical obstacles within the habitat

CORRECT. S3: "a barrier emerges." The phrase "the creation of physical obstacles" means the same thing.

✗ (C) the expansion of a habitat to increase access

This would be the opposite of habitat fragmentation.

✗ (D) the inability to adapt rapidly to changes in the landscape

S5 mentions that this inability to adapt quickly is a property of plants. It is not a cause of habitat fragmentation.

Paragraph 3	Comments
S1 While habitat fragmentation can be devastating to populations, it naturally occurs over time.	Habitat fragmentation occurs naturally.
2 Mountains will rise, volcanoes will erupt, and rivers will change course.	
3 Any of these changes and countless other natural progressions will segment large areas into smaller ones.	
4 It is widely accepted, however, that the primary source of habitat fragmentation in the modern world is human activity.	But human activity is now the primary source.
5 As humans expand into new areas, they change the environment to suit their needs.	Why and how.
6 Habitats are destroyed to make way for man-made buildings and are divided to connect those buildings.	
7 Plants and animals that encroach into areas where humans live are repelled or killed.	
8 Edge species, which live on the borders of habitats, expand as more borders are created and will compete with species that cannot live on edges.	
9 The increased competition in a decreased space endangers many species.	

5. The word "source" in the passage is closest in meaning to

VOCABULARY. "Source" = cause, reason, the place where something comes from.

✗ (A) objective

"Objective" = goal, purpose, object, result.

✗ (B) function

"Function" = purpose, role, way in which something operates.

✓ (C) cause

CORRECT. S4: the primary source of habitat fragmentation ... is human activity" = the main cause of habitat fragmentation, or the biggest reason for it, is human activity.

✗ (D) center

Not exactly. A center of some phenomenon doesn't have to be its source or cause. A center is just where it happens a lot.

6.   According to paragraph 3, what currently has the greatest influence on habitat fragmentation?

FACT. S4 describes "the primary source of habitat fragmentation."

✓ (A) The actions of human beings

CORRECT. S4: "the primary source of habitat fragmentation ... is human activity."

✗ (B) Natural forces such as volcanic eruptions

S2 mentions volcanic eruptions as an example of a natural cause of habitat fragmentation. But they are not described as having the greatest influence.

✗ (C) Encroachment by plants and animals

Described in S7 as an effect of habitat fragmentation caused by humans.

✗ (D) Increased competition at habitat borders

Described in S8–9 as an effect of habitat fragmentation caused by humans.

7.   The word "endangers" in the passage is closest in meaning to

VOCABULARY. "Endangers" = threatens, puts in danger or at risk.

✗ (A) includes

Unrelated. "Includes" = contains.

✗ (B) empowers

Opposite. "Empowers" = makes stronger or more confident.

✗ (C) deters

Unrelated. "Deter" = to discourage or instill doubt or fear of consequences.

✓ (D) jeopardizes

CORRECT. "The increased competition ... endangers many species" = this competition jeopardizes, or puts in danger, many species.

Paragraph 4	**Comments**
S1 Four specific activities or structures are known as the most common causes of man-made habitat fragmentation: roads, housing developments, agriculture, and logging.	Habitat fragmentation by humans has 4 common causes.
2 Roads require an extensive expanse of land to be cleared, including the area surrounding the road.	Explains one cause (roads).
3 A single road will split a large habitat into two smaller ones and increase the edge area.	
4 Animals that attempt to traverse the road to reach land that may be essential for their survival are in additional danger from fast-moving cars.	

8. Why does the author mention "roads," "housing developments," "agriculture," and "logging"?

PURPOSE. S1 lists these "four specific activities or structures."

✗ (A) To give examples of processes that can slow habitat fragmentation

Opposite. These are all specific causes of habitat fragmentation.

✗ (B) To explain why habitat fragmentation is so dangerous

The paragraph does mention the danger to animals attempting to cross roads, but this is not the primary reason the list of four items is given.

✗ (C) To list four specific activities or structures that are known to be man-made

In fact, the four items do form a list of specific human activities or man-made structures. But the reason for this list is omitted. The purpose is not just to list four human activities or structures, but to assert that these are the most common causes of habitat fragmentation.

✓ (D) To illustrate the ways that human activity most impacts habitat fragmentation

CORRECT. S1 notes that these activities or structures are the "most common causes of man-made habitat fragmentation."

Paragraph 5		**Comments**
S1	Housing developments are necessary, as the population of humans continues to grow.	Explains other 3 causes (housing, agriculture, & logging)
2	Such development not only forces land to be cleared, but also creates competition between humans and edge species.	
3	Animal and pest control keep many native species from coming into housing developments.	
4	Non-native species, particularly plants, are regularly introduced into housing developments for the benefit of the occupants.	
5	Population growth also leads to the need for more agriculture.	
6	Consequently, large tracts of land are bulldozed and the natural plants destroyed to make way for crops.	
7	The cleared land has lost all its utility to the plants and animals that once called that area home.	
8	Finally, logging, whether for industrial uses or for firewood, destroys large trees that may be necessary for species' survival.	
9	Removing trees shrinks the habitat and could eliminate both food and shelter.	
10	At the same time, the presence of humans, their equipment, and the roads they need can imperil plants and animals in the area.	

9. The word "utility" in the passage is closest in meaning to

VOCABULARY. "Utility" = usefulness, use, value.

✓ (A) value

CORRECT. "The cleared land has lost all its utility to the plants and animals" = the cleared land has lost all its value to these species.

✗ (B) nutrients

Too specific. Nutrients can be a form of utility or value, but "utility" is a much broader term.

✗ (C) stability

Again, too specific. Stability can be a form of utility or value, but "utility" is a much broader term.

✗ (D) energy

Again, too specific. Not all forms of utility or value can be called energy.

10. Why does the author mention "firewood"?

PURPOSE. S8: "logging, whether for industrial uses or for firewood, destroys large trees." The two phrases "for industrial uses" and "for firewood" describe reasons for logging. "Whether ... or" indicates that the particular reason doesn't matter, with regard to the effect logging has on habitat fragmentation.

✗ (A) To emphasize the danger of fires to habitats

Not mentioned here.

✗ (B) To clarify that human activity is not always undesirable

The author does not pass judgment on human activity, declaring any of it undesirable or desirable. Rather, the author is explaining the effects of that activity.

✓ (C) To provide an example of why logging may occur

CORRECT. S8: "for firewood" is an example of a reason for logging.

✗ (D) To point out an easily eliminated cause of habitat fragmentation

The passage never states that cutting firewood is easily eliminated as a cause of habitat fragmentation.

Paragraph 6	Comments
S1 For a thriving and robust species, ample area, reasonable competition, and access to essentials are all necessary.	Ample habitats are necessary for species to thrive.
2 If habitat fragmentation continues at the current pace, species will be restricted to areas in which only small populations can survive or will lose the ability to survive entirely.	If habitat fragmentation continues, species will shrink in numbers or vanish.
3 Conserving large tracts of land in a variety of areas is already underway and may help to slow this process.	Conserving large tracts may help slow habitat fragmentation.

11. Which of the sentences below best expresses the essential information in the highlighted sentence in paragraph 6? Incorrect choices change the meaning in important ways or leave out essential information.

✗ (A) Species will be eliminated or restricted to areas that can only support small populations if the current pace of habitat fragmentation continues to slow.

SIMPLIFY SENTENCE. S2 is a conditional prediction: if habitat fragmentation continues at the current rate, Y or Z will happen. Namely, species will shrink in numbers (by being restricted to areas that can only support small populations) or die off altogether.

Opposite. This choice would be fine if the last part of the sentence were "if the pace of habitat fragmentation does *not* slow."

✗ (B) Habitat fragmentation, if not slowed, will be restricted to areas in which only small populations of species can survive, if at all.

It's not the habitat fragmentation that will be restricted to certain areas, but the species themselves.

✓ (C) The current pace of habitat fragmentation, if continued, will eradicate species or restrict them to small numbers in their remaining habitats.

CORRECT. "The current pace of habitat fragmentation, if continued, will eradicate species" is equivalent to the original phrasing: "species ... will lose the ability to survive entirely" (if the current pace is continued). The rest of the rephrased sentence captures the original meaning.

✗ (D) Only small populations of species, or none at all, will survive in areas currently restricted from the continued pace of habitat fragmentation.

Also somewhat opposite. "Restricted from" would mean that the areas would *not* be subject to continued habitat fragmentation. You would expect species to do better in areas without habitat fragmentation.

12. It can be inferred from paragraph 6 that compared with fragmented habitats, habitats that have not been fragmented

INFERENCE. P6 (as well as preceding paragraphs) discuss the damaging effects of fragmented habitats. Specifically, S2 mentions the effects of continued habitat fragmentation: species will be eliminated or restricted to areas that can only support small populations. You can make inferences about unfragmented habitats by comparison.

✗ (A) are likely to be much rarer globally

Notice that you are asked to compare unfragmented habitats with fragmented habitats. You aren't told anything about their comparative size or numbers geographically. Unfragmented habitats are likely to become rarer over time, but that could be starting from a high proportion.

✗ (B) have probably benefited from conservation efforts

S3 remarks on conservation efforts, indicating that large tracts of land are being conserved now. But you can't conclude that unfragmented habitats worldwide have all or mostly benefited from these conservation efforts.

✗ (C) provide access to all the essentials species need

Extreme. You could say that unfragmented habitats are more likely to provide species with access to at least some essentials. But you can't infer that these habitats actually provide access to all the essentials.

✓ (D) will likely support larger populations

CORRECT. S1 discusses the "ample area, reasonable competition, and access to essentials" that are necessary for "thriving and robust species." It can be inferred that these features apply to habitats that have not been fragmented.

Paragraph 5	Comments
S1–2 Housing developments are necessary, as the population of humans continues to grow. Such development not only forces land to be cleared, but also creates competition between humans and edge species.	
3–4 [A] Animal and pest control keep many native species from coming into housing developments. Non-native species, particularly plants, are regularly introduced into housing developments for the benefit of the occupants.	"Edge species" in S2 are not clearly non-native plants.
5–6 [B] Population growth also leads to the need for more agriculture. Consequently, large tracts of land are bulldozed and the natural plants destroyed to make way for crops.	**CORRECT.** S4 mentions "non-native species, particularly plants" that are brought into housing developments. The inserted sentence appropriately refers back to these non-native plants.
7–8 [C] The cleared land has lost all its utility to the plants and animals that once called that area home. Finally, logging, whether for industrial uses or firewood, destroys large trees that may be necessary for species' survival.	"Natural plants" in S6 would be native plants, not non-native ones.
9–10 [D] Removing trees shrinks the habitat and could eliminate both food and shelter. At the same time, the presence of humans, their equipment, and the roads they need can imperil plants and animals in the area.	"Large trees" in S8 are not non-native plants.

13. **These species compete with native plants and often exacerbate habitat fragmentation.**

Where would the sentence best fit?

INSERT TEXT. "These species" needs to refer properly to species mentioned in the previous sentence. According to the inserted sentence, these species "compete with native plants." So these species should *not* be native plants, but they should still be plants (in order to compete with them). You are looking for *non*-native plants or a synonymous expression in the prior sentence.

✗ (A) Choice A

✓ (B) Choice B   **CORRECT.**

✗ (C) Choice C

✗ (D) Choice D

Whole Passage	**Comments**
P1 The habitats of terrestrial animals, which provide food, shelter, and places to bear and raise offspring …	Habitats have been changing. Habitat fragmentation = restriction into smaller segments. This is a barrier to effective conservation.
P2 Habitat fragmentation occurs when the landscape is changed so that plants and animals no longer have access …	Habitat fragmentation occurs when landscape changes so there's no more access. Some cases: part of habitat is destroyed. Other cases: barrier emerges. Dangerous to both plants and animals. Explains how.
P3 While habitat fragmentation can be devastating to populations, it naturally occurs over time …	Habitat fragmentation occurs naturally. But human activity is now the primary source. Why and how.
P4 Four specific activities or structures are known as the most common causes of man-made habitat fragmentation …	Habitat fragmentation by humans has 4 common causes. Explains one cause (roads).
P5 Housing developments are necessary, as the population of humans continues to grow …	Explains other 3 causes (housing, agriculture, & logging).
P6 For a thriving and robust species, ample area, reasonable competition, and access to essentials are all necessary …	Ample habitats are necessary for species to thrive. If habitat fragmentation continues, species will shrink in numbers or vanish. Conserving large tracts may help slow habitat fragmentation.

5

MANHATTAN PREP

14. **Habitat fragmentation is a process that poses a threat to the survival of some plant and animal species.**

SUMMARY. Correct answers must be clearly expressed in the passage. They must also be among the major points of the passage. They should tie as directly as possible to the summary given.

✗ A Habitat fragmentation can occur when part of the habitat is destroyed by the changed course of a river.

True but minor detail. P3 S2 mentions that "rivers will change course," but this is just a quick example of how nature can cause habitat fragmentation. Moreover, the focus of the passage is on habitat fragmentation caused by humans.

✓ B Despite the fact that habitat fragmentation occurs naturally, human activity is currently its principal cause.

CORRECT. This is the main point of P3.

✗ C Creation of roads is the most common human activity that results in habitat fragmentation.

Roads are listed as the first of the four specific causes of human-generated habitat fragmentation. But nothing in the passage tells you that this is the most common of the four causes.

✓ D The four major contributors to man-made habitat fragmentation impact species in various powerful ways.

CORRECT. P4–5 describe these four causes in detail.

✗ E Conservation efforts will be able to halt habitat fragmentation if implemented worldwide.

Extreme. The last sentence of P6 gives some hope by mentioning conservation efforts. But the sentence only claims that these efforts "may help to slow" habitat fragmentation, not halt or stop it altogether.

✓ F Without limiting the human impact on large areas of land, many species will shrink and possibly disappear over time.

CORRECT. P6 S2 delivers this final, culminating thought as a clear warning about the future.

5

Answers and Explanations—5.7 Is Pluto a Planet?

	Paragraph 1	Comments
S1	Prior to 2006, the International Astronomical Union (IAU) had no formal definition of a planet, and it was generally assumed that the Solar System contained nine planets.	Old ideas: 9 planets, no formal definition.
2	Before the astronomical discoveries of the early twenty-first century, the definition of a planet seemed self-evident: a large body orbiting the Sun, readily distinguishable from moons, which orbit planets.	Old definition: large body orbiting sun.
3	In the early 1800s, smaller orbiting bodies were discovered; these were eventually classified as asteroids.	Smaller bodies are discovered: asteroids.
4	Around the same time, astronomers also used increasingly powerful telescopes to identify additional planets beyond Saturn that were not readily visible to the naked eye.	Additional planets are discovered.
5	The first planet discovered was Uranus, sighted in 1781 by astronomer William Herschel.	
6	The charting of Uranus's unusual orbit then led scientists to predict the presence of another planet, whose gravitational pull would account for the irregularities in Uranus's movement around the sun.	
7	The resulting calculations of the new planet's position were so accurate that, in 1846, astronomer Johann Galle finally observed Neptune within a degree of its predicted location.	
8	Subsequently, additional observations of Uranus led astronomers to conclude that there was yet another planet in the outer reaches of the Solar System.	Yet another planet is predicted.

1.	The word "self-evident" in the passage is closest in meaning to	**VOCABULARY.** "Self-evident" = obvious, indisputable, plain for all to see and understand without additional explanation.
✗	(A) simplistic	Unrelated. Something that is "simplistic" is treating a complex issue or problem as if it were much simpler than it really is.
✓	(B) obvious	**CORRECT.** "The definition of a planet seemed self-evident" = the definition seemed obvious.
✗	(C) paradoxical	Opposite. "Paradoxical" = inconsistent, self-contradictory.
✗	(D) qualified	Opposite in another sense. "Qualified" = limited, restricted.

2. The author mentions planets "not readily visible to the naked eye" in order to

    ✓ Ⓐ explain the usefulness of telescopes for the observation of these planets

    ✗ Ⓑ assert that these planets could not have been discovered without increasingly powerful instruments

    ✗ Ⓒ emphasize the fact that planets do not give off their own light, but instead reflect it

    ✗ Ⓓ highlight specific technical improvements related to the manufacture of lenses

PURPOSE. S4 discusses the use of "increasingly powerful telescopes to identify additional planets ... that were not readily visible to the naked eye."

CORRECT. The phrase in question explains why telescopes would be helpful in the search for these particular planets—namely, because they are difficult to see with the naked eye.

Extreme. The sentence only claims that these planets were "not readily visible," not that they were invisible and could absolutely not be discovered without telescopes.

This point is nowhere discussed in the passage.

S4 mentions that the telescopes are "increasingly powerful." But these improvements are not themselves the focus of the sentence. No specific improvements are mentioned.

5

Paragraph 2	**Comments**
S1 One of the early proponents of the existence of a new planet was Percival Lowell, a wealthy Bostonian who founded the Lowell Observatory in Arizona in 1894.	
2 He spearheaded extensive research into the existence of a ninth planet, known as "Planet X."	Lowell spearheads research into Planet X.
3 This research was unsuccessful during Lowell's lifetime.	Unsuccessful until after Lowell's death.
4 After Lowell's death, the search stalled for over a decade, resuming only in 1929, when the young astronomer Clyde Tombaugh was tasked with finding the planet.	
5 Tombaugh systematically took pairs of photographs of the night sky to look for a moving object, spending nearly a year on this painstaking task.	
6 His efforts were rewarded in January 1930, when he finally obtained evidence of Planet X's existence.	Tombaugh uses photographs of night sky to identify Pluto in 1930.

3.   The phrase "proponents of" in the passage is closest in meaning to:

VOCABULARY. "Proponents of" something = supporters of that thing, advocates of or for it.

✗   (A) explorers of

Unrelated. Supporters are not necessarily those exploring.

✓   (B) advocates for

CORRECT. "One of the early proponents of the existence of a new planet" = one of the early advocates for its existence.

✗   (C) skeptics of

Opposite. "Skeptic" = someone who doubts or disbelieves.

✗   (D) oracles of

Not quite. "Oracle" = seer, prophet, someone who transmits divine wisdom. Even if you ignore the supernatural element, this word isn't an appropriate substitute for "proponent."

4.   According to the passage, which of the following was true of Percival Lowell?

FACT. S1–3 discuss Lowell directly.

✗   (A) He is solely responsible for the successful effort to locate Pluto.

"Solely" makes this choice too extreme. Lowell "spearheaded extensive research" into finding Pluto (S2), but his search was unsuccessful (S3). Tombaugh was the one to find Pluto at last (S6).

✗   (B) He tasked Clyde Tombaugh with continuing the search for Planet X.

Not stated. S4 states that "Clyde Tombaugh was tasked with finding the planet," but the sentence does not say by whom. In fact, it was almost certainly not Lowell, because this assignment was given over a decade after Lowell's death.

✓   (C) He was originally from Boston.

CORRECT. S1: "Percival Lowell, a wealthy Bostonian."

✗   (D) He delayed efforts to find the planet by over a decade.

The reason for the 10-year delay is not given. Although "the search stalled" after Lowell died (S4), you cannot conclude that Lowell actually "delayed efforts" to find the planet with his death or with any other action.

	Paragraph 3	**Comments**
S1	This planet was named Pluto and remained the ninth planet until the early twenty-first century, when new discoveries called its status as a planet into question.	Pluto was named as the 9th planet. But new discoveries called this into question.
2	These discoveries included the sightings, starting in the early 1990s, of a number of other large objects near Pluto, which are now known as Kuiper Belt objects.	Kuiper Belt objects.
3	Discovered in 2005, Eris is the largest of these.	
4	Eris is significantly more massive than Pluto and was briefly called the tenth planet by some.	Eris is bigger than Pluto. Some called Eris the 10th planet.
5	The lack of consensus on Eris's planetary status led the IAU to convene a meeting on the definition of a planet in 2006.	Disagreement led to a meeting about the definition of a planet.

5. The word "these" in the passage refers to

   ✗ (A) planets

   ✗ (B) asteroids

   ✗ (C) researchers

   ✓ (D) Kuiper Belt objects

REFERENCE. Look in the current sentence (S3) or in the prior sentence (S2) for an appropriate plural noun that "these" could refer to. What is Eris the largest of?

Although Eris was called the tenth planet in a later sentence, the use of "these" is pointing back to the "other large objects near Pluto, which are known as Kuiper Belt objects" (S2).

Asteroids are not mentioned in this paragraph.

Eris was discovered, presumably by researchers, but there is no specific reference to them that this could point back to.

CORRECT. S2: "a number of other large objects near Pluto, which are now known as Kuiper Belt objects." The phrase "Kuiper Belt objects" is the last noun phrase in the sentence, so it can supply meaning easily to the pronoun "these" in the next sentence. Logically, it makes sense that Eris is the largest of these Kuiper Belt objects.

6. According to the passage, what prompted astronomers to reconsider the definition of a planet?

   ✗ (A) Scientists did not agree on the existence of the Kuiper Belt.

   ✗ (B) Scientists convened a meeting of the International Astronomical Union.

   ✓ (C) An orbiting object larger than Pluto was discovered near Pluto.

   ✗ (D) Pluto remained the ninth planet for decades.

FACT. S5 discusses the meeting that was called about the definition of a planet. S5 also states what prompted the meeting: "the lack of consensus on Eris's planetary status."

Not stated anywhere.

Scientists convened this meeting in order to reconsider the definition of a planet. The meeting was not the cause of the reconsideration.

CORRECT. S3–4 note that Eris, an object "more massive than Pluto," was discovered. S5 mentions that the "lack of consensus" about Eris's possible status as a planet triggered the meeting.

This does not answer the question. S1 states that Pluto was named the ninth planet and remained so for decades (from 1930 until the early twenty-first century). But this event did not cause astronomers to reconsider their definition of a planet.

7. The word "consensus" in the passage is closest in meaning to

   ✓ (A) agreement

   ✗ (B) confirmation

   ✗ (C) discrepancy

   ✗ (D) emergence

VOCABULARY. "Consensus" = agreement, mutual consent.

CORRECT. "Agreement" and "consensus" are almost exact synonyms.

Not quite. "Confirmation" = validation, proof. But this does not necessarily mean "agreement."

Almost opposite. "Discrepancy" = difference.

Unrelated. "Emergence" = process of coming into view or becoming exposed.

	Paragraph 4	**Comments**
S1	So is Pluto a planet?	
2	According to the definition produced by the IAU in 2006, it is not.	By 2006 definition, Pluto is not a planet.
3	A planet must meet three criteria: it orbits around the Sun; it is large enough to form itself into a sphere; and it is also large enough to clear other objects of significant size from its orbit.	3 criteria to be a planet.
4	If one sticks rigorously to this definition, Pluto is not a planet; it meets only the first two criteria, as there are a number of other objects, like Eris, in its vicinity.	Pluto only meets first 2.
5	However, not all astronomers agree with this definition; some believe that the presence of asteroids in the orbit of planets like Earth, Mars, and Jupiter would similarly disqualify them as planets.	But not all astronomers agree with definition.

8.	According to the definition given in paragraph 4, which of the following must be true for something to be considered a planet?	**FACT.** S3 lists the three criteria that define planets according to the definition produced in 2006.
✓	(A) It has no other large objects in its orbit.	**CORRECT.** The third criterion in S3 states that "it is … large enough to clear other objects of significant size from its orbit."
✗	(B) It must have at least one moon.	Not mentioned as a criterion in S3.
✗	(C) It has a spherical orbit around the sun.	This choice incorrectly mashes up the first two criteria, which are that the object must orbit around the Sun and that the object is large enough to form itself into a sphere.
✗	(D) It has a mass at least as great as that of Pluto.	Not mentioned as a criterion in S3.

	Paragraph 5	Comments
S1	Scientists continue to disagree about Pluto's status.	Scientists still disagree.
2	Another debate on the subject was held in 2008, but the attendees did not reach agreement on the subject.	2008 debate didn't reach agreement.
3	Additionally, there was a wide public outcry, based largely on sentimental attachment, when Pluto's new classification as a "dwarf planet" was announced.	Public outcry against Pluto as "dwarf planet."
4	Given the existence of a number of other large objects near Pluto, continuing to define Pluto as a planet could lead to the classification of many other entities as planets.	But keeping Pluto would have meant including a lot more things as planets.
5	Demoting Pluto seems like a simpler solution.	Simpler to demote Pluto.

9.   Which of the sentences below best expresses the essential information in the highlighted sentence in the passage? Incorrect choices change the meaning in important ways or leave out essential information.

SIMPLIFY SENTENCE. The core ideas in S3 are these: Pluto was reclassified as a "dwarf planet." As a result, there was a wide public outcry. This outcry was based on "sentimental attachment," or strong, almost romantic feelings toward Pluto.

✗   Ⓐ The announcement that Pluto was now a "dwarf planet" caused the public to feel sentimental attachment, based on the wide outcry.

The original sentence doesn't claim that the public's "sentimental attachment" *begins* after the announcement. If anything, the sentimental attachment probably existed well before the announcement. It was just revealed or expressed afterward.

✗   Ⓑ As a result of the wide public outcry, based largely on sentimental attachment, Pluto's new classification as a "dwarf planet" was announced.

Reverses the order and causation. The outcry happened as a result of the announcement, not the other way around.

✓   Ⓒ The wide outcry following the announcement of Pluto's "dwarf planet" status revealed the public's sentimental attachment to Pluto.

CORRECT. This choice omits certain words (such as "based largely in"), expressing the logical relationships in other ways. But those relationships are preserved here.

✗   Ⓓ Pluto's reclassification as a "dwarf planet" was based largely on sentimental attachment, as revealed in the wide public outcry following the announcement.

The reclassification was not based on sentimental attachment. According to earlier sentences, it was based on the results of a scientific debate. What was "based largely on sentimental attachment" was the wide public outcry, according to S3.

5

	Paragraph 6	**Comments**
S1	This is not to say that claims supporting Pluto's status as a planet don't have merit.	
2	Pluto does, in many respects, resemble other planets in the Solar System in its orbit and shape.	Pluto does resemble planets in many ways.
3	Unlike these planets, though, Pluto is relatively small and has an unusual relationship with its large moon, Charon.	But other things about Pluto make it unusual among planets.
4	Furthermore, the presence of many similar large bodies in Pluto's vicinity suggests that, without a clear standard definition such as the one decided upon by the IAU, we could find ourselves one day including dozens of planets in our Solar System, making for some extremely complicated school science projects.	Classifying Pluto as something other than a planet prevents us from including dozens of planets.

10. The word "vicinity" in the passage is closest in meaning to

VOCABULARY. "Vicinity" = neighborhood, area, locality. Being in something's vicinity means being near it.

✗ (A) path — Too specific. You can be in an object's vicinity without being in its path (as it moves).

✗ (B) orbit — Again, too specific. Whether being "in Pluto's orbit" means being in the same orbit as Pluto is in or being in orbit *around* Pluto, either description is too narrow.

✗ (C) gravitational pull — "Gravitational pull" is never mentioned or described in the passage. You don't know whether an object in Pluto's vicinity (i.e., near Pluto) would be subject to its gravitational pull. Regardless, the two concepts do not mean the same thing.

✓ (D) neighborhood — **CORRECT.** "Many similar large bodies in Pluto's vicinity" = many similar bodies near Pluto, in Pluto's neighborhood.

11. According to paragraph 6, what is a characteristic of Pluto that makes it unlike other planets in the Solar System?

FACT. S3 mentions ways in which Pluto is not like other planets.

✗ (A) Its shape — Opposite. S2: "Pluto does ... resemble other planets in the Solar System in its ... shape."

✗ (B) Its orbit — Also opposite. S2: "Pluto does ... resemble other planets in the Solar System in its orbit."

✗ (C) The size of its moon — S3 does assert that one of Pluto's extraordinary characteristics is that it has "an unusual relationship with its large moon." But the relationship is what is unusual," according to this sentence. The moon is described as "large," but not as "unusually large" or "excessively large."

✓ (D) Its size — **CORRECT.** S3: "Unlike these planets ... Pluto is relatively small."

  MANHATTAN PREP

	Paragraph 2	**Comments**
S1	One of the early proponents of the existence of a new planet was Percival Lowell, a wealthy Bostonian who founded the Lowell Observatory in Arizona in 1894.	
2-3	**A** He spearheaded extensive research into the existence of a ninth planet, known as "Planet X." This research was unsuccessful during Lowell's lifetime.	S1 describes an accomplishment of Lowell: he founded an observatory. That doesn't contrast well with the accomplishment in the inserted sentence (which is also about Pluto).
4	**B** After Lowell's death, the search stalled for over a decade, resuming only in 1929, when the young astronomer Clyde Tombaugh was tasked with finding the planet.	**CORRECT.** This choice refers to Lowell, and the "However" creates the proper contrast between the lack of success in finding Pluto (S3) and the actual capture of images of the planet (in the inserted sentence).
5	**C** Tombaugh systematically took pairs of photographs of the night sky to look for a moving object, spending nearly a year on this painstaking task.	Too late to insert a sentence about Lowell. Tombaugh is the focus of the action now.
6	**D** His efforts were rewarded in January 1930, when he finally obtained evidence of Planet X's existence.	Too late.

5

12. **However, Lowell did capture two images of Pluto in 1915, though these weren't identified as such until later.**

Where would the sentence best fit?

INSERT TEXT. "However" indicates that this inserted sentence should contrast with the previous sentence. Since the subject is "Lowell," you should focus on S1–3, which describe Lowell's actions. The main clause of the sentence is "Lowell did capture two images of Pluto in 1915." This is a positive accomplishment that evidently ought to be contrasted with the prior sentence.

✗ (A) Choice A

✓ (B) Choice B   **CORRECT.**

✗ (C) Choice C

✗ (D) Choice D

		Whole Passage	**Comments**
P1		Prior to 2006, the International Astronomical Union (IAU) had no formal definition of a planet …	Old ideas: 9 planets, no formal definition. Old definition: large body orbiting Sun. Smaller bodies are discovered: asteroids. Additional planets are discovered. Yet another planet is predicted.
P2		One of the early proponents of the existence of a new planet was Percival Lowell …	Lowell spearheads research into Planet X. Unsuccessful until after Lowell's death. Tombaugh uses photographs of night sky to identify Pluto in 1930.
P3		This planet was named Pluto and remained the ninth planet until the early twenty-first century …	Pluto was named as the 9th planet. But new discoveries called this into question. Kuiper Belt objects. Eris is bigger than Pluto. Some called Eris the 10th planet. Disagreement led to a meeting about the definition of a planet.
P4		So is Pluto a planet? According to the definition produced by the IAU in 2006 …	By 2006 definition, Pluto is not a planet. 3 criteria to be a planet. Pluto only meets first 2. But not all astronomers agree with definition.
P5		Scientists continue to disagree about Pluto's status …	Scientists still disagree. 2008 debate didn't reach agreement. Public outcry against Pluto as "dwarf planet." But keeping Pluto would have meant including a lot more things as planets. Simpler to demote Pluto.
P6		This is not to say that claims supporting Pluto's status as a planet don't have merit …	Pluto does resemble planets in many ways. But other things about Pluto make it unusual among planets. Classifying Pluto as something other than a planet prevents us from including dozens of planets.

5

13. **Until the twenty-first century, astronomers did not have a standard definition of a planet.**

SUMMARY. Correct answers must be clearly expressed in the passage. They must also be among the major points of the passage. They should tie as directly as possible to the summary given.

✗ A   Percival Lowell died before the discovery of Pluto.

True, according to P2 S3. But this detail is too specific to be a main idea of the passage.

✓ B   After its discovery, Pluto was initially called the ninth planet.

CORRECT. The passage as a whole is about whether Pluto should be called a planet. So the occasion of naming Pluto a planet counts as a major idea.

✗ C   By definition, planets occur in different shapes.

Not true. P4 S3: planets must be spheres. At any rate, this is a minor point within the passage.

✓ D   The discovery of other large objects near Pluto led astronomers to formulate a new definition of a planet.

CORRECT. P3 describes the new discoveries that called Pluto's status into question. This is a key twist in the story.

✓ E   Pluto is now officially classified as a "dwarf planet," though not all scientists agree on this.

CORRECT. P5 and P6 describe this current classification and the lack of full scientific agreement.

✗ F   Kuiper Belt objects were discovered before Pluto was.

Not true. P3 S2 states that Kuiper Belt objects were discovered in the early 1990s, after the discovery of Pluto in 1930. Regardless, the exact order of discovery is not as important as the implication of the Kuiper Belt objects: at least one (Eris) is larger than Pluto and made a claim to be a planet as well.

5

Answers and Explanations—5.8 Turtle Navigation

	Paragraph 1	Comments
S1	Every 2 to 3 years, female leatherback sea turtles in their breeding years make their way to a beach, where they climb ashore to lay their eggs in the sand.	Leatherback sea turtles lay eggs on a beach every 2–3 years.
2	Like other sea turtles, leatherbacks lay these eggs in a "clutch," or nest.	
3	A single clutch can contain as many as 85 eggs, although not all of them will have been fertilized.	1 clutch = up to 85 eggs.
4	Of those that have been fertilized, however, the embryos will incubate in the sand for 50 to 60 days and then hatch, before which time the mother turtle will have already returned to the ocean.	Eggs hatch after 50–60 days.
5	The baby turtles, or "hatchlings," collectively dig themselves out of the sand and onto the shore, where they must make their way to the sea in order to survive.	Baby turtles dig out and head toward the sea.

1. According to paragraph 1, which of the following statements is true of baby leatherback turtles?

    FACT. S4–5 discuss the baby turtles most directly.

    ✗ (A) They compete with each other as they make their way to the sea.

    S5 states that they make their way to the sea, but never mentions anything about competition.

    ✗ (B) They hatch on top of the sand of a beach.

    S4–5: "the embryos will incubate in the sand ... and then hatch ... The baby turtles ... dig themselves out of the sand." In other words, the baby turtles hatch *in* or within the sand, not on top of it.

    ✗ (C) They emerge from nests of typically just a few offspring.

    S3: "A single clutch can contain as many as 85 eggs." This number is substantially higher than "just a few."

    ✓ (D) By the time they hatch, their mother has returned to the sea.

    CORRECT. S4: "the embryos ... hatch, before which time the mother turtle will have already returned to the ocean."

2. The word "incubate" in the passage is closest in meaning to

    VOCABULARY. "Incubate" = literally, sit on eggs to keep them warm, so they can develop. More generally, "incubate" = develop or grow something at an early stage. You can also say that something "incubates" on its own, meaning that it develops or grows while it is in an early stage.

    ✓ (A) develop

    CORRECT. "The embryos will incubate in the sand for 50 to 60 days" = they will develop in the sand for that period of time, within the eggs.

    ✗ (B) erupt

    "Erupt" = break out violently. "Incubate" does not imply that speed or violence at all. Also, S4 says that the embryos incubate and *then* hatch, or break out of their shells.

    ✗ (C) degenerate

    Opposite. "Degenerate" = become worse or weaker.

    ✗ (D) burrow

    Unrelated. "Burrow" = to dig a hole or tunnel.

Paragraph 2	Comments
S1 The stakes for finding the ocean quickly are extremely high.	Stakes are high.
2 Hatchlings that do not quickly make their way from the clutch into the sea will die.	Turtles that are slow die.
3 During their sprints, they are at risk of predation by myriad creatures, from crabs to birds to snakes to native predators, that dwell on beaches worldwide.	Predators.
4 They are also exposed to possible dehydration should they remain out of the water for too long.	Dehydration.

3. Which of the sentences below best expresses the essential information in the highlighted sentence in the passage? Incorrect choices change the meaning in important ways or leave out essential information.

SIMPLIFY SENTENCE. S3 explains one of the risks to hatchlings on their way to the ocean: predators.

✗ (A) As they race to the ocean, hatchings that avoid myriad predators on the beach are not at risk.

S3 presents the risk of predators. But you cannot conclude that if hatchlings avoid predators, they are not at risk. After all, S4 explains another risk (dehydration).

✗ (B) The primary threat to hatchlings on their way to the sea is predation by various creatures that live on the beach.

S3 does not claim that predators are the primary threat, just that they are a threat.

✓ (C) Numerous beach-dwelling predators are a threat to hatchlings rushing to the sea.

CORRECT. This rephrasing captures the essence of S3. The omission of specific examples of the predators is fine.

✗ (D) Upon reaching the sea, hatchlings are vulnerable to a wide range of predators that live on beaches.

S3: "During their sprints ..." That is, S3 refers to the time *during* which the hatchlings are sprinting toward the sea. This rephrasing incorrectly puts the threat afterwards.

Paragraph 3	**Comments**
S1	There are several factors involved in the navigation of these newborn reptiles to the sea.	Several factors help the baby turtles navigate.
2	Light, however, is the most important factor.	Light = most important.
3	The hatchlings use visual cues to find their way into the lapping ocean water.	How that works.
4	In particular, they observe the reflection of the moon and stars in the night sky on the water, and the contrast of this reflection with the dark silhouettes of the dunes and trees on land.	

4.   Which of the following can be inferred from paragraph 3 about the **dunes and trees**?

INFERENCE. S4 describes the "dark silhouettes of the dunes and trees." These dark silhouettes are contrasted with the brighter water, which shows "the reflection of the moon and stars in the night sky." The turtles observe this contrast and use it to move in the right direction.

✗ (A) They largely fail to assist the newborn turtles in their navigation.

Opposite. Their "dark silhouettes" contrast with the brighter water to help the turtles find their way to the ocean.

✗ (B) By being uphill from the nests, they direct the hatchlings downhill toward the water.

The passage never mentions the difference in elevation between the ocean and the dunes or trees.

✓ (C) The dimness of their silhouettes causes the turtles to move away from them.

CORRECT. The hatchlings sprint toward the brighter "reflection of the moon and stars ... on the water" (S4), which is contrasted with the "dark silhouettes of the dunes and trees." S4 is meant to illustrate the key point of S2, which states that "light ... is the most important factor" in guiding the turtles to the ocean. So you can infer that the turtles move toward the water *because* it is brighter, and away from the dunes and trees *because* they are darker or dimmer.

✗ (D) They reflect the light of the moon and stars more effectively than the dark ocean water does.

Opposite. S4 indicates that the reflection of the moon and stars is visible in the water, not in the dunes and trees.

Paragraph 4	**Comments**
S1 Prior to modern times, this process was not made perilous by artificial light interfering with the turtles' seaward orientation.	Artificial light was not a problem before modern times.
2 The turtles' innate sensitivity and attraction to light guided them where they needed to go: into the water.	
3 But nowadays, the brightest light often does not come from the moon and stars being reflected on the surface of the ocean.	
4 Instead, the bright lights of the lit structures that populate many beaches draw the baby turtles in the direction opposite of where they need to go: away from the ocean.	But now, bright lights on shore can draw baby turtles in the wrong direction.
5 As a result, and particularly because the leatherback turtle has been listed as an endangered species since 1970, efforts have been made to reduce the **impact** of artificial light on leatherback hatchlings.	So efforts have been made to reduce this problem, especially because leatherbacks are endangered.

5.   According to paragraph 4, an important reason why baby turtles have difficulty nowadays navigating toward the sea is

FACT. P4 describes the modern-day problem of artificial light on shore. This light can cause the turtles to go in the wrong direction.

✓ (A) the presence of distractingly illuminated buildings

CORRECT. S4: "the bright lights of the lit structures that populate many beaches draw the baby turtles" in the wrong direction.

✗ (B) the diminished brightness of the moon due to air pollution

Not mentioned in the text.

✗ (C) the reduced influence of artificial light as a result of efforts since 1970

Opposite. S5 states that these efforts to reduce the impact of artificial light are a result of the problems described in S3 and S4.

✗ (D) increased threats from scavenging predators, such as birds and snakes

Threats from predators were mentioned earlier in the passage. They are not discussed in P4.

6.   The word "impact" in the passage is most closest in meaning to

VOCABULARY. "Impact" = influence, effect.

✗ (A) emphasis

"Emphasis" = importance or stress. That's not the same as impact, influence, or effect.

✓ (B) effect

CORRECT. "Reduce the impact of artificial light on leatherback hatchlings" = reduce the effect that artificial light has on these hatchlings.

✗ (C) energy

Unrelated. Stamina or drive is not the same as having an effect.

✗ (D) esteem

Unrelated. Although someone or something with influence might also be held in high "esteem" (respected or admired), it is not necessarily the case.

Paragraph 5	**Comments**
S1 Certain light-emitting diode (LED) lights that fall within set wavelengths have been found to interfere less with the navigation of baby turtles.	Certain lights interfere less.
2 These wavelengths are on the spectrum of light that ranges between yellow/orange and red.	
3 Organizations such as the Florida Fish and Wildlife Conservation Commission have labeled these lights safe for use around turtles.	These lights have been labeled safe for turtles.
4 In cooperation with wildlife advocates and organizations devoted to the protection of sea turtles, many coastal businesses worldwide have replaced problematic light fixtures with turtle-safe lighting.	Many coastal businesses have put in these lights.

7. Why does the author mention "light-emitting diode (LED) lights" in the passage?

PURPOSE. S1 includes the mention of these lights, which "have been found to interfere less with the navigation of baby turtles." The description "light-emitting diode (LED)" is there to provide the name of a specific example.

✗ (A) To contrast LED lights with lights that interfere less with the navigation of baby turtles

LED lights *are* the lights that interfere less with turtles.

✗ (B) To suggest that LED lights be removed from existing installations near beaches

Again, these LED lights are actually the turtle-safe kind.

✗ (C) To argue that incandescent and fluorescent lights should not be permitted on coastal properties

These other kinds of lights are not named. More importantly, the author never suggests banning outright other kinds of lights from coastal properties.

✓ (D) To name a concrete example of a light that poses less of a threat to baby leatherback turtles

CORRECT. This concrete example in S1 allows the author to discuss the impact of this kind of lighting in the rest of the paragraph.

Paragraph 6	**Comments**
S1 Leatherbacks are "pelagic," meaning they live in open water (in contrast to staying near the shore or dwelling on the ocean bottom), and this includes the hatchlings; if they manage to make it to sea, they will **venture** into the open waters.	Leatherbacks live in open water, including the hatchlings.
2 Researchers have named the ensuing years the "lost years," as the turtles live in the open sea and are difficult to track.	"Lost years" in the open sea.
3 They have attempted to study their whereabouts and navigation patterns by tagging baby turtles and tracking them via satellite.	Researchers have tried to study with tagging.

8. The word "venture" in the passage is closest in meaning to

VOCABULARY. As a verb of motion, "venture into" something = go forward into it, usually at some risk.

✗ (A) be swept out

"Be swept out" would mean that the turtles are not moving on their own. "Venture" = go forward of your own free will.

✓ (B) set out

CORRECT. "They will venture into the open waters" = they will set out or go forward into those (dangerous) waters.

✗ (C) tumble forth

Like "be swept out," the word "tumble" implies involuntary action, a lack of power and choice on the turtles' part. This is not what "venture" signifies.

✗ (D) linger around

Opposite. "Linger" = stay, delay going forward.

Paragraph 7	Comments
S1 The turtles are known for their long-distance migrations and over the years will possibly travel tens of thousands of miles.	Turtles travel very far.
2 When they are 15 to 25 years old, female leatherback turtles reach maturity and return to the different beaches where each was born to lay their own clutches of eggs.	At maturity, female returns to beach where she was born.
3 How does the mature leatherback find her way back to her natal beach, which is sometimes thousands of miles away?	How?
4 It is believed that the turtle uses the Earth's magnetic fields to accomplish this incredible feat.	Maybe Earth's magnetic fields, like some other traveling species.
5 This magnetic sense is the same kind of "compass" used by a number of species that also navigate long distances, including monarch butterflies, yellow-fin tuna, and sockeye salmon.	

9.   The word "they" in the passage refers to

REFERENCE. S2: "When they are 15 to 25 years old, female leatherback turtles …" Here, the word "they" in the short introductory clause actually refers forward to the subject of the sentence, "female leatherback turtles." (If that subject didn't make sense, "they" would most likely then refer back to the subject of the previous sentence, "the turtles.")

✓ (A) female leatherback turtles

CORRECT. S2: "When they are 15 to 25 years old, female leatherback turtles reach maturity" = when female leatherback turtles are this old, they reach maturity.

✗ (B) long-distance migrations

It would not make sense to say "When [long-distance migrations] are 15 to 25 years old."

✗ (C) 15 to 25 years

It would not make sense to say "When [15 to 25 years] are 15 to 25 years old."

✗ (D) tens of thousands of miles

It would not make sense to say "When [tens of thousands of miles] are 15 to 25 years old."

5

10. According to paragraph 7, which of the following is likely to be the method by which the adult female leatherback finds her way back to the beach where she was born?

FACT. S3 essentially asks this same question. S4–5 provide the answer.

✗ (A) Eventually reaching maturity

S2 mentions that once the turtles reach maturity, they return to the beaches where they were born. But reaching maturity is not presented as the method. S3 poses the question of how this navigation is done, and S4–5 provide the answer.

✓ (B) Using the Earth's magnetic fields

CORRECT. S4–5 describe how the female turtle "uses the Earth's magnetic fields to accomplish this incredible feat" = find her way back to her natal beach, according to S3.

✗ (C) Tracking yellow-fin tuna and sockeye salmon

S5 mentions these fish as examples of other species that likely use a magnetic "compass" as well.

✗ (D) Laying her own clutch of eggs

For the turtle, this is not the method of finding her way back. This is the goal of finding her way back.

Paragraph 7	**Comments**
S1-2 The turtles are known for their long-distance migrations and over the years will possibly travel tens of thousands of miles. When they are 15 to 25 years old, female leatherback turtles reach maturity and return to the different beaches where each was born to lay their own clutches of eggs.	
3 A How does the mature leatherback find her way back to her natal beach, which is sometimes thousands of miles away?	S2 does not list different species of animals that could be referenced by the key phrase "such as these."
4 B It is believed that the turtle uses the Earth's magnetic fields to accomplish this incredible feat.	Likewise, S3 does not list different species of animals that could be referenced by the key phrase "such as these."
5 C This magnetic sense is the same kind of "compass" used by a number of species that also navigate long distances, including monarch butterflies, yellow-fin tuna, and sockeye salmon.	Likewise, S4 does not list different species of animals that could be referenced by the key phrase "such as these."
End D	**CORRECT.** Finally, S5 contains the critical list: "a number of species that also navigate long distances, including monarch butterflies, yellow-fin tuna, and sockeye salmon." The inserted sentence fits here.

11.   **An ability to perceive magnetic fields is in fact shared by animals such as these that may otherwise be quite different from one another.**

Where would the sentence best fit?

INSERT TEXT. The telling phrase in the inserted sentence is "animals such as these." This phrase indicates that the previous sentence must list types of animals that have an ability to perceive magnetic fields and that "may otherwise be quite different from one another."

✗ Ⓐ Choice A

✗ Ⓑ Choice B

✗ Ⓒ Choice C

✓ Ⓓ Choice D   **CORRECT.**

Whole Passage	**Comments**
P1 — Every 2 to 3 years, female leatherback sea turtles in their breeding years make their way to a beach …	Leatherback sea turtles lay eggs on a beach every 2–3 years. 1 clutch = up to 85 eggs. Eggs hatch after 50–60 days. Baby turtles dig out and head toward the sea.
P2 — The stakes for finding the ocean quickly are extremely high …	Stakes are high. Turtles that are slow die. Predators. Dehydration.
P3 — There are several factors involved in the navigation of these newborn reptiles to the sea …	Several factors help the baby turtles navigate. Light = most important. How that works.
P4 — Prior to modern times, this process was not made perilous by artificial light …	Artificial light was not a problem before modern times. But now, bright lights on shore can draw baby turtles in the wrong direction. So efforts have been made to reduce this problem, especially because leatherbacks are endangered.
P5 — Certain light-emitting diode (LED) lights that fall within set wavelengths have been found to interfere less …	Certain lights interfere less. These lights have been labeled safe for turtles. Many coastal businesses have put in these lights.
P6 — Leatherbacks are "pelagic," meaning they live in open water …	Leatherbacks live in open water, including the hatchlings. "Lost years" in the open sea. Researchers have tried to study with tagging.
P7 — The turtles are known for their long-distance migrations …	Turtles travel very far. At maturity, female returns to beach where she was born. How? Maybe Earth's magnetic fields, like some other traveling species.

12.   Select from the five phrases below THREE that characterize the behaviors of leatherback turtles and TWO that characterize the behaviors of people, according to the passage.

TABLE. Unfortunately, the passage is not neatly divided according to these two categories. Using the knowledge you've gained from reading the passage and answering questions so far, try to classify the answers without necessarily finding proof. Only go back to the passage if you are stuck.

| A | Following reflective light on the ocean's surface | **TURTLES.** P3 describes this turtle behavior. |

| B | Using magnetic fields for navigation | **TURTLES.** P7 describes this turtle behavior. |

| C | Advancing the use of certain kinds of artificial light | **PEOPLE.** P4 describes how people are making efforts to replace artificial lighting hazardous to turtles with other kinds of artificial light that is more turtle-friendly. |

| D | Tagging and tracking maturing leatherbacks | **PEOPLE.** P6 describes this human behavior. |

| E | Responding less to certain wavelengths of light and more to other wavelengths | **TURTLES.** P5 describes certain kinds of lights that are safer for turtles. It is strongly implied that these lights are safer *because* the lights "fall within set wavelengths." So the turtles must respond to those wavelengths less than they do to the wavelengths in typical lights. |

Answers and Explanations—5.9 Dyson Spheres

	Paragraph 1	Comments
S1	In the mid-twentieth century, the concept of "Dyson spheres" was introduced because of the growing awareness of the limitations of nonrenewable energy resources.	Idea for Dyson spheres came from limits of nonrenewable energy.
2	It became apparent to many scientists that fossil fuels stores were decreasing while energy consumption was increasing.	
3	They were concerned about the growing possibility that the Earth would one day run out of usable fuel sources.	Scientists were concerned: Earth could run out of fuel.
4	Freeman Dyson, a theoretical physicist and mathematician, published a paper in 1960 that claimed that any energy-consuming civilization would eventually need more energy than its planet could provide, and that the only logical solution would be to capture all the energy emitted by its parent star using Dyson spheres.	Dyson proposed a logical long-term solution: Dyson sphere captures all the parent star's energy.

1. The word "eventually" in the passage is closest in meaning to

    VOCABULARY. "Eventually" = finally, in the end.

    ✓ (A) ultimately

    CORRECT. "Any energy-consuming civilization would eventually need more energy" = any such civilization would ultimately, or finally, need more energy.

    ✗ (B) immediately

    Opposite. "Immediately" = at once or right away.

    ✗ (C) accidentally

    Unrelated. "Accidentally" = by chance, not on purpose.

    ✗ (D) intentionally

    Unrelated. "Intentionally" = on purpose.

2. According to paragraph 1, which of the following is something that many scientists are concerned about?

    FACT. S3 describes the concerns of many scientists, with context given in S1–2.

    ✗ (A) Solutions to the fossil fuels crisis that involve conservation are not being pursued adequately.

    Not supported in the text.

    ✗ (B) Nonrenewable fuel sources will increase in quantity over time.

    Opposite. S1: "the limitations of nonrenewable energy resources."

    ✓ (C) The Earth may not always have enough fuel to support its demands.

    CORRECT. S3: "[Many scientists] were concerned about the growing possibility that the Earth would one day run out of usable fuel sources."

    ✗ (D) Dyson spheres may not be constructed as soon as they are needed.

    Some scientists who are concerned about the Earth running out of fuel may have the further concern that Dyson spheres may not be constructed as soon as they are needed. But this second possible concern is never mentioned in P1.

5

Paragraph 2	Comments
S1 Dyson originally found the idea in the 1937 science fiction book *Star Maker*, written by Olaf Stapledon.	Dyson got idea from science fiction.
2 This novel describes a fictional history of the universe in which alien civilizations build artificial structures to surround their parent star.	
3 These structures, later called Dyson spheres, mine the energy from the star.	Dyson sphere = structure around star to mine its energy.
4 The fuel from the solar energy **far surpasses** anything available on a planet.	
5 Dyson recognized that the technology needed to create and place a Dyson sphere around the Sun was centuries away.	Technology is centuries away.
6 However, he envisioned another practical use.	But we can use the idea to search for life outside Earth.
7 He believed that creating a Dyson sphere would be an **inevitable** step in any civilization's development.	Why.
8 All sufficiently advanced life forms, including those that originate on other planets, would attempt to create a Dyson sphere.	
9 If life exists beyond Earth, and if that life is technologically advanced enough, Dyson reasoned, those life forms must have created a Dyson sphere.	
10 If scientists could find that structure, they would find life.	

3.   The phrase "**far surpasses**" in the passage is closest in meaning to

VOCABULARY. "Surpass" = exceed, go beyond or above or better than something. "Far surpass" = exceed by far, go beyond by a great amount.

✗   (A) falls far short of

Opposite. To "fall short" of something means to fail to meet the goal, be deficient or inadequate.

✗   (B) greatly overpowers

"Overpower" = subdue, overwhelm (someone) in a physical or mental way. You don't use "overpower" to compare two quantities, even if one vastly exceeds the other.

✗   (C) largely eradicates

"Eradicate" = destroy, remove completely, eliminate. Similar problem as with "overpower."

✓   (D) vastly exceeds

CORRECT. "The fuel from the solar energy far surpasses anything available on a planet" = the fuel from the solar energy vastly exceeds, or goes beyond by far, anything available on a planet.

4.   In paragraph 2, Freeman Dyson supports his contention that a Dyson sphere could be used to find life beyond Earth by

FACT. S6–10 discuss Dyson's idea about how Dyson spheres could be used to find life.

✗   (A) reasoning that Dyson spheres must already exist elsewhere in the universe

Dyson spheres are only discussed as theories. Dyson argues that if sufficiently advanced life exists elsewhere, then Dyson spheres must exist elsewhere too. But that is a big if.

✗   (B) indicating that Dyson spheres would be the primary artificial structures created by other life forms

Dyson never says these would be the primary structures created by other life forms.

✓   (C) presenting a rationale for why alien life forms would likely try to create a Dyson sphere

CORRECT. S8–10: "All sufficiently advanced life forms ... would attempt to create a Dyson sphere. If life exists beyond Earth, and if that life is technologically advanced enough, Dyson reasoned, those life forms must have created a Dyson sphere. If scientists could find that structure, they would find life."

✗   (D) contrasting Dyson spheres with other potential means of technologically advanced energy extraction

No other means of energy extraction are discussed.

5.   The word "inevitable" in the passage is closest in meaning to

VOCABULARY. "Inevitable" = unavoidable, inescapable, certain to happen.

✓   (A) unavoidable

CORRECT. "Creating a Dyson sphere is an inevitable step in any civilization's development" = any civilization, if it develops far enough, must unavoidably create a Dyson sphere.

✗   (B) incredible

Unrelated. "Incredible" = impossible or difficult to believe, extraordinary.

✗   (C) unremarkable

Unrelated. "Unremarkable" = not interesting or surprising.

✗   (D) insurmountable

An "insurmountable" obstacle = one that cannot be surmounted or overcome.

Paragraph 3	**Comments**
S1 But how can we discover an artificial structure thousands or millions of light years away?	How can we see Dyson spheres far away in space?
2 That was the question Dyson attempted to answer in his 1960 article.	Dyson tried to answer.
3 He presented the Dyson sphere as a thought experiment, not as something that humanity should attempt to create, so he did not go into many specifics.	
4 In essence, a Dyson sphere is an artificial structure or group of structures that surround a star.	
5 Most of the structures are devoted to capturing the star's solar energy and transforming it into usable energy.	
6 The structures, Dyson hypothesized, would block or absorb much of the visible light coming from the star.	A Dyson sphere would block the light from the star it surrounds.
7 From the perspective of the Earth, the star would seem to dim.	So the star would seem to dim.
8 However, the consolidation of all of the star's energy into the Dyson sphere would result in a measurable increase in infrared radiation.	Also, infrared radiation would increase.
9 The decreased visible light and increased infrared radiation would significantly alter the star's emission spectrum.	
10 Because the emission spectra of stars are easily and regularly monitored from Earth, the effects of the Dyson sphere would be observable.	Astronomers could see the changes from Earth.
11 Scouring the heavens for stars with these characteristics would allow astronomers to predict that a Dyson sphere had been created—evidence, he felt, of alien life.	That would indicate alien life.

6. The word "perspective" in the passage is closest in meaning to

VOCABULARY. "Perspective" = a place from which to see something, a point of view. Like the term "point of view," a perspective can also be an opinion or judgment.

✗ (A) rotation

It might be tempting to think about the "rotation" (spin) of the Earth. But that is not what the sentence is trying to say.

✓ (B) viewpoint

CORRECT. "From the perspective of the Earth, the star would seem to dim" = from our viewpoint, the star would look dimmer.

✗ (C) dimension

It might be tempting to think about the "dimension" (size) of the Earth. But that is not what the sentence is trying to say.

✗ (D) reverence

Unrelated. "Reverence" = deep respect.

7.   The words "these characteristics" in the passage refer to

REFERENCE. S11: "Scouring the heavens for stars with these characteristics would allow astronomers to predict that a Dyson sphere had been created." Which observable characteristics would a star have if a Dyson sphere were built around it? S6–10 describe the effects: visible light would decrease, while infrared radiation would increase.

✗ (A) effects of the consolidation of the star into the Dyson sphere

S8 mentions the consolidation of all of the star's *energy* into the Dyson sphere. The star itself is not ever "consolidated" into the Dyson sphere, as if the star became part of it.

✗ (B) energy transformed from infrared radiation to visible light

Opposite. In effect, what we could see from the Earth is the transformation of the star's visible light into infrared radiation.

✗ (C) decreased fuel stocks and increased energy consumption

These items are described in P1. They concerned scientists and prompted Dyson to think about ways to capture solar energy.

✓ (D) increased infrared radiation and decreased visible light

CORRECT. S9–10 discuss how scientists are looking for the effects of Dyson spheres. These effects are described in S9 as "decreased visible light and increased infrared radiation," which we would see in the star's emission spectrum.

8.   Which of the sentences below best expresses the essential information in the highlighted sentence in paragraph 3? Incorrect choices change the meaning in important ways or leave out essential information.

SIMPLIFY SENTENCE. S3 describes how Dyson presented the idea of the Dyson sphere: as a "thought experiment" (an idea to explore) rather than as something we should actually try to build.

✗ (A) The Dyson sphere was intended as a broad thought experiment, but Dyson provided specific instructions for how to create one.

This version strongly suggests that Dyson intended for humans to build a Dyson sphere at some point. That intention is not present in the original.

✓ (B) In his article, Dyson described the Dyson sphere vaguely because it was meant as a concept to explore, not a plan to carry out.

CORRECT. This rephrased sentence captures the sense of the original. "A concept to explore" = "thought experiment."

✗ (C) Dyson presented the Dyson sphere as an experimental plan, one that he expected others to make more precise but not to execute.

The original never indicates that Dyson expected others to make his idea more precise.

✗ (D) The answer Dyson gave about Dyson spheres was a thought experiment that humanity should not attempt to create without specifics.

Dyson did not say that humanity should not attempt to create Dyson spheres without specifics, as if the addition of specifics would give the go-ahead.

Paragraph 4	Comments
S1 His idea caught on quickly, and searches for Dyson spheres continue to this day.	Searches for Dyson spheres continue.
2 There are currently two stars under investigation that have a reasonable possibility of being surrounded by a Dyson sphere.	Two stars have potential.
3 Several other causes of the anomalies observed in the emission spectra of these two stars have been proposed, but no definitive explanation has emerged.	
4 Currently, scientists cannot say definitively why these two stars appear less bright than they should.	They appear dimmer than they should. No one knows why.

9. According to paragraph 4, what is true about the two stars currently under investigation?

FACT. S2–4 describe these stars.

✗ (A) They are surrounded by Dyson spheres.

S2 notes that they may be. But there's no proof.

✗ (B) They appear less dim than they should.

Opposite. S4 states that these stars "appear less bright."

✓ (C) Their emission spectra have not been conclusively explained.

CORRECT. S3: "no definitive explanation has emerged" for the anomalies (= unusual features) of their emission spectra.

✗ (D) They have been investigated more than most other stars.

Not supported. These stars are "under investigation" (S2), but you don't know whether they have been studied more than most, or even many, other stars.

10.   In paragraph 4, why does the author mention the "two stars under investigation"?

✓   (A)   To illustrate how Dyson's theory is still relevant and inspiring

✗   (B)   To contend that these two stars probably have Dyson spheres surrounding them

✗   (C)   To suggest that Dyson spheres around these stars may one day provide us energy

✗   (D)   To explain why a Dyson sphere is less likely to be possible at present for our own star

PURPOSE. S2 mentions these stars as a follow-up to S1: "His idea caught on quickly, and searches for Dyson spheres continue to this day."

CORRECT. S1 expresses the idea that Dyson's theory is still relevant and inspiring. The two stars described in S2–4 illustrate this point.

The author does not contend, or argue, that these stars definitely or even *probably* have Dyson spheres. S2 just says that there's a "reasonable possibility." That's a much lower standard than "probably."

The paragraph never makes this suggestion. Scientists are only trying to find out whether Dyson spheres exist around these stars.

The author would likely agree that a Dyson sphere is less likely to be possible right now around our own sun than around either of these two stars. After all, a Dyson sphere is certainly not around our sun right now, and it wouldn't be possible to build one for centuries, at best. In contrast, Dyson spheres *could* be around these two other stars. But what's important for the question is this: the author does not mention these two stars *in order to* contrast their situation with our own.

5

Paragraph 5	Comments
S1 Since the original publication, scientists have investigated the practicality of building a Dyson sphere around the Sun.	Scientists have looked at how practical Dyson spheres would be to build.
2 They have ruled out the possibility of a Dyson sphere existing as a solid hollow ball surrounding a star.	Can't be a hollow ball.
3 No known or theoretical material could endure the stress of the star's gravitational pull.	
4 Moreover, without constant correction, it would slowly drift until it collides with the star.	
5 To avoid these problems, thousands of smaller structures could be positioned around the Sun.	Instead, thousands of smaller structures.
6 Various theories on how to create and deploy these structures have been proposed.	
7 All theories agree, however, that a mass equivalent to all the planets within the inner Solar System—Mercury, Venus, Earth, and Mars—would be needed.	Would need mass of all inner planets.
8 Humans would live on the Dyson sphere itself, or on artificially created habitats within the sphere.	
9 While this would theoretically solve any energy crisis, it will be a very long time before humans could reasonably consider pursuing this option.	Very long time before we could do.

11. According to paragraph 5, all of the following are considered challenges to building a Dyson sphere EXCEPT:

NEGATIVE FACT. Three of the answers must be presented as challenges to building a Dyson sphere. One answer is not presented this way, or at all.

✗ (A) the stress on a hollow ball structure caused by the star's gravitational pull

S2–3: "... ruled out the possibility of a Dyson sphere existing as a solid hollow ball ... No known or theoretical material could endure the stress of the star's gravitational pull."

✗ (B) the drift of a hollow ball structure

S4: "without constant correction, it would slowly drift until it collides with the star."

✗ (C) the quantity of mass that would be required

S7: "a mass equivalent to all the planets within the inner Solar System—Mercury, Venus, Earth, and Mars—would be needed."

✓ (D) the ability of humans to live on a Dyson sphere

CORRECT. S8: "Humans would live on the Dyson sphere." But this is not posed as a challenge to the concept.

12. In paragraph 5, the solid hollow-ball structure is mentioned to illustrate

PURPOSE. S2 rules out this possible type of structure. S3–4 give reasons why: we can't imagine any material that could stand the stress, and the ball would drift into the star if not constantly maneuvered.

✗ (A) the possible existence of Dyson spheres outside the solar system

The hollow ball structure is not mentioned to illustrate the possible existence of Dyson spheres elsewhere. This paragraph does not focus on the possible existence of the spheres elsewhere, but on the challenges involved in creating them.

✓ (B) the potential difficulties of creating a Dyson sphere

CORRECT. The reasons given in S3–4 provide a sense of scale for the immense challenges of building a Dyson sphere.

✗ (C) the effects of a Dyson sphere on the star it surrounds

The paragraph never discusses such effects. An earlier paragraph describes the effect on radiation from the star. No other effects on the star are ever mentioned.

✗ (D) the amount of mass needed to create a Dyson sphere

S7 outlines the amount of mass required, but specifically for the "thousands of smaller structures" (S5) that could make up a Dyson sphere, not the solid hollow-ball structure discussed in S2–4.

5

Paragraph 3	**Comments**
S1–4 But how can we discover an artificial structure thousands or millions of light years away? That was the question Dyson attempted to answer in his 1960 article. He presented the Dyson sphere as a thought experiment, not as something that humanity should attempt to create, so he did not go into many specifics. In essence, a Dyson sphere is an artificial structure or group of structures that surround a star.	
5 **A** Most of the structures are devoted to capturing the star's solar energy and transforming it into usable energy.	The prior sentence, S4, doesn't discuss how energy is obtained from the Dyson sphere.
6–7 **B** The structures, Dyson hypothesized, would block or absorb much of the visible light coming from the star. From the perspective of the Earth, the star would seem to dim.	**CORRECT.** The prior sentence (S5) ends with "usable energy." The inserted sentence then describes the benefit: a huge increase in the amount of energy that a civilization can use.
8 **C** However, the consolidation of all of the star's energy into the Dyson sphere would result in a measurable increase in infrared radiation.	The prior sentence doesn't discuss obtaining useful energy from the Dyson sphere, but rather how energy would be blocked from reaching the Earth.
9–11 **D** The decreased visible light and increased infrared radiation would significantly alter the star's emission spectrum. Because the emission spectra of stars are easily and regularly monitored from Earth, the effects of the Dyson sphere would be observable. Scouring the heavens for stars with these characteristics would allow astronomers to predict that a Dyson sphere had been created—evidence, he felt, of alien life.	Again, the previous sentence doesn't discuss the *useful* energy that the Dyson sphere gathers. The story has moved on to the effects that we could observe from the Earth.

13.   **The increase in energy available to a civilization using the Dyson sphere would be exponential.**

Where would the sentence best fit?

INSERT TEXT. This sentence should be inserted right after the paragraph describes how useful energy would be obtained from the Dyson sphere. In this position, it would be natural then to discuss "increase in energy available to a civilization using the Dyson sphere," as the new sentence does.

✗ (A) Choice A

✓ (B) Choice B   **CORRECT.**

✗ (C) Choice C

✗ (D) Choice D

	Whole Passage	**Comments**
P1	In the mid-twentieth century, the concept of "Dyson spheres" was introduced ...	Idea for Dyson spheres came from limits of nonrenewable energy. Scientists were concerned: Earth could run out of fuel. Dyson proposed a logical long-term solution: Dyson sphere captures all the parent star's energy.
P2	Dyson originally found the idea in the 1937 science fiction book *Star Maker* ...	Dyson got idea from science fiction. Dyson sphere = structure around star to mine its energy. Technology is centuries away. But we can use the idea to search for life outside Earth. Why.
P3	But how can we discover an artificial structure thousands or millions of light years away? ...	How can we see Dyson spheres far away in space? Dyson tried to answer. A Dyson sphere would block the light from the star it surrounds, so the star would seem to dim. Also, infrared radiation would increase. Astronomers could see the changes from Earth. That would indicate alien life.
P4	His idea caught on quickly, and searches for Dyson spheres continue to this day ...	Searches for Dyson spheres continue. Two stars have potential. They appear dimmer than they should. No one knows why.
P5	Since the original publication, scientists have investigated the practicality of building a Dyson sphere around the Sun ...	Scientists have looked at how practical Dyson spheres would be to build. Can't be a hollow ball. Instead, thousands of smaller structures. Would need mass of all inner planets. Very long time before we could do.

5

14. **Dyson spheres were introduced in response to growing concerns about increased energy consumption on Earth.**

   ✓ | A | A Dyson sphere is an artificial structure that surrounds a star, capturing as much of that star's energy as possible.

   ✗ | B | In order to create a Dyson sphere around our sun, the planets Mercury, Venus, Earth, and Mars would all have to be used up.

   ✓ | C | While it may one day be possible to build a Dyson sphere around the Earth's sun, they were proposed—and remain significant today—as a theoretical abstraction.

   ✗ | D | The genesis of the concept of Dyson spheres in science fiction illustrates that scientific ideas and progress can grow from unexpected sources.

   ✗ | E | Causes other than Dyson spheres may explain the anomalies in the emission spectra of two stars currently under observation.

   ✓ | F | If a Dyson sphere surrounded a star visible from Earth, the star's altered emission spectrum would allow scientists to theorize that life existed elsewhere.

SUMMARY. Correct answers must be clearly expressed in the passage. They must also be among the major points of the passage. They should tie as directly as possible to the summary given.

CORRECT. The definition of a Dyson sphere (given in P1 and reiterated more than once along the way) is crucial to the passage.

It's not clear that these planets themselves would actually be used to create a Dyson sphere around our own sun, or just an equivalent mass. More importantly, this idea in P5 is just a small detail, an illustration of one of the enormous hurdles involved in ever creating a Dyson sphere.

CORRECT. P1–3 describe how Dyson proposed these spheres as theoretical constructs, or "thought experiments" (P3 S3). P4 discusses how the concept has remained significant.

The conclusion of this sentence, that "scientific ideas and progress can grow from unexpected sources," is a very broad idea that is never explored in the passage.

This is true, but it's a minor point made in P4 to support a larger idea: Dyson spheres have not yet been proven to exist.

CORRECT. This point, outlined in P3, is how Dyson spheres remain relevant today: in the search for extraterrestrial life.

Answers and Explanations—
5.10 Southwestern Water Rights

	Paragraph 1	**Comments**
S1	Over the past century, the states of Utah, Nevada, New Mexico, Arizona, and California, forming the Southwestern United States, have experienced tremendous population growth.	Southwestern U.S. has grown a lot in population.
2	In the 1910 census, these five states accounted for less than 4 percent of the domestic population.	
3	In 2010, this figure was greater than 16 percent.	
4	Population growth in the Southwest continues to outstrip growth in the rest of the country, as the region receives positive net migration from other states as well as substantial immigration from foreign countries.	Faster than rest of country.
5	Part of the appeal is the pleasant weather, with mild to hot temperatures all year, and low precipitation.	One reason is pleasant weather.
6	However, therein lies the **crux** of a major problem—the ecosystems of the Southwest are not equipped to sustainably provide enough water for the increasing number of people that live there.	But that's a problem: not enough water.

5

1.   According to paragraph 1, which of the following is true of population growth in the Southwestern United States?

FACT. Almost all of P1 discusses the Southwest's population growth.

✗ (A) A central reason for migration to the Southwest is the abundance of natural resources such as water and fertile soil.

Opposite, if anything. S6: "the ecosystems of the Southwest are not equipped to sustainably provide enough water for the increasing number of people that live there." That is, water is *not* an abundant resource in the Southwest. Other natural resources may be plentiful, but the point about water is enough to disqualify this choice.

✓ (B) Low annual rainfall totals provide a significant reason for people to migrate to the Southwest.

CORRECT. S5: "Part of the appeal is the pleasant weather ... and low precipitation."

✗ (C) Population growth in the Southwest is driven primarily by foreign immigration.

S4 mentions foreign immigration as a key source of population growth. But S4 does not state that it is the *primary* driver.

✗ (D) Net migration from other states is the chief cause of Southwestern population growth.

S4 mentions net migration from other states as a key source of population growth. But S4 does not state that it is the *chief* cause.

2. The word "crux" in the passage is closest in meaning to

VOCABULARY. "Crux" = central issue, heart of the matter.

✗ Ⓐ edge

Opposite.

✗ Ⓑ answer

Unrelated. The central issue is not the same as the answer.

✗ Ⓒ promise

Unrelated. The central issue is not the same as a promise.

✓ Ⓓ core

CORRECT. "Therein lies the crux of a major problem" = that's where the core or heart of a major problem lies.

Paragraph 2	Comments
P2 S1 All five Southwestern states rely greatly on external water sources, plus groundwater sources, which are large but finite.	Southwest relies on external sources and groundwater.
2 Per-capita water consumption is also higher than the national average for two reasons.	Two reasons for higher water consumption per person.
3 First, these states have a drier climate, so more water is needed for the watering of lawns and gardens.	Drier climate = thirsty gardens.
4 Second, all five states have a substantial farming industry and are exporters of agricultural products domestically and abroad.	Irrigation for farming industry.
5 These states therefore use much more water for irrigation per person than the rest of the United States.	

Paragraph 3	Comments
P3 S1 Water use has become much more efficient across the United States in recent decades.	Water use has become more efficient, especially in the Southwest.
2 Since 1980, per-capita usage has fallen by about 40 percent.	
3 This decline is even more pronounced in the Southwest.	
4 However, it is counterbalanced by a comparable growth in population, such that the total amount of water being consumed annually in the Southwest is basically unchanged.	But population growth there counterbalances.
5 This level of usage is not sustainable over the long term.	Water use is not sustainable.

3. According to paragraphs 2 and 3, all of the following statements about water usage in the Southwestern United States are true EXCEPT:

NEGATIVE FACT. Three answer choices are somewhere in P2–3, which focus on water usage patterns in the Southwest. So those facts could be almost anywhere. One answer will not be supported in the paragraphs. It could be contradicted or just not mentioned.

✓ (A) Since 1980, overall water usage in the Southwest has fallen substantially.

CORRECT. P3 S4 mentions that the decline in per-capita water usage is "counterbalanced by a comparable growth in population, such that the total amount of water being consumed annually in the Southwest is basically unchanged." Overall water usage has not fallen substantially.

✗ (B) More water is consumed per person in the Southwest than in the rest of the United States.

P2 S2: "Per capita water consumption is also higher than the national average for two reasons."

✗ (C) More water is consumed annually in the Southwest than can be naturally replaced.

P3 S5: "This level of usage is not sustainable over the long term."

✗ (D) As net exporters of agricultural products, the Southwestern states use more water per person for farming than most other states.

P2 S2 and S4: "Per capita water consumption is also higher than the national average for two reasons … Second, all five states have a substantial farming industry and are exporters of agricultural products."

4. The word "finite" in the passage is closest in meaning to

VOCABULARY. "Finite" = limited, restricted, fixed at a certain amount. Finite is the opposite of infinite.

✗ (A) isolated

Not quite. "Isolated" = remote, separated, difficult or impossible to access. That's not the same as "finite" = limited.

✓ (B) limited

CORRECT. "Groundwater sources … are large but finite" = they are large but still limited. They're not infinite.

✗ (C) infected

Unrelated. "Infected" = contaminated.

✗ (D) unending

Opposite. "Unending" = never ending.

5

5. Which of the sentences below best expresses the essential information in the highlighted sentence in paragraph 3? Incorrect choices change the meaning in important ways or leave out essential information.

SIMPLIFY SENTENCE. The first part of P3 S4 states that population growth has counterbalanced, or offset, the per-capita water usage decline mentioned in S3. The second part of S4 gives the net result: total water usage has remained about the same. The rephrased sentence must preserve these meanings.

✗ (A) Population growth is supported by the decline in water use per person, leading to annually declining water consumption in the Southwest.

The total amount of water consumed each year in the Southwest is not declining. It is "basically unchanged" according to the original sentence.

✗ (B) The increase in per-person water consumption and population have balanced out the typical water usage in the Southwest.

Per-person water consumption has fallen.

✗ (C) Declines in per-person water use have stunted population growth in the Southwest.

The declines in water use have not stunted (prevented) population growth. The population has been growing.

✓ (D) The population has grown enough to offset the decline in per-capita water use, so the total amount of water used each year in the Southwest has remained about the same.

CORRECT. This choice means the same thing as P3 S4, but simplifies the language and uses synonyms.

	Paragraph 4	**Comments**
S1	The Southwestern states consumed a total of 61 million acre-feet of water in 2010.	Total amount of water consumed in Southwest.
2	About 35 percent of this water comes from groundwater, and the rest comes from surface water, such as lakes and streams.	Where it comes from.
3	Most of the groundwater being used is not fully replenished.	Groundwater is dropping.
4	In California alone, the net withdrawal of groundwater, after replenishment from precipitation and surface water, is currently around 10 million acre-feet per year.	Net withdrawal in California.
5	At this rate, California's known usable groundwater supplies will be **exhausted** by the year 2060.	Will exhaust groundwater by 2060.

6.   According to paragraph 4, excessive use of groundwater in parts of the Southwest is noteworthy because

FACT. S2–5 discuss groundwater as a water source. S4–5 focus specifically on groundwater depletion that is happening in California.

✗ (A) the groundwater draws in contaminants from surface water, its ultimate source

While groundwater must come from the surface at some point, this fact is not mentioned in the passage. Neither are possible contaminants of groundwater.

✗ (B) groundwater provides more than half of the water consumed in these regions

Opposite. S2: "About 35 percent of this water comes from groundwater." That's less than half.

✓ (C) groundwater will run out eventually if incomplete replenishment continues

CORRECT. S3–5: "Most of the groundwater being used is not fully replenished ... California's known usable groundwater supplies will be exhausted by the year 2060."

✗ (D) a high level of groundwater use is now illegal in certain areas

Nothing in the passage mentions the legality of groundwater usage anywhere in the Southwest.

7.   The word "exhausted" in the passage is closest in meaning to

VOCABULARY. In the context of supplies or resources, "exhausted" = used up, drained or spent completely.

✓ (A) expended

CORRECT. "California's known usable groundwater supplies will be exhausted by the year 2060" = the supplies will be expended, or used up, by then.

✗ (B) lessened

Not quite. "Lessen" = make or get smaller. But "lessen" doesn't convey that the supplies will be exhausted (= completely gone, used up). If anything, "lessen" suggests that the supplies would be smaller, but still there.

✗ (C) ejected

Again, not quite. "Eject" = throw out, expel violently. That's not the same as "exhaust supplies" = use them up. If anything, "eject supplies" = throw them out and *not* use them.

✗ (D) tainted

"Taint" = pollute, contaminate. That's not the same as "exhaust."

5

Paragraph 5	Comments
S1 For surface water, these five states are heavily reliant on various sources.	States rely a lot on various sources for surface water.
2 California has ample native freshwater supplies in the northern and central portions of the state.	California has enough in north and center.
3 Excluding California, however, over half of the freshwater needs of the Southwest are met from a single source: the Colorado River.	But the other states get over half from Colorado River alone.
4 This river originates in the Rocky Mountains and meanders through Utah and Arizona before forming the border of Arizona and Nevada, plus parts of the Arizona California border.	
5 The river then continues into Mexico.	

8. According to paragraph 5, one difference between water sources in California and the rest of the Southwestern United States is that

FACT. S2–3 highlight a contrast between California and the rest of the Southwest. S2 mentions that California has plentiful surface water of its own. S3 notes that the rest of the Southwest relies heavily on one source: the Colorado River.

✗ (A) California groundwater resources are being depleted at an alarming rate

This fact is mentioned in P4, not P5. Moreover, you are never told that the rest of the Southwest is *not* experiencing groundwater depletion.

✗ (B) the Colorado River runs through or along all the Southwestern states except for California

S4 states that the Colorado River runs along the Arizona California border. Also, the passage does not indicate that the river runs through New Mexico, which is part of the Southwest.

✗ (C) California uses surface water supplies, while the rest of the Southwest mostly relies on salt water from the ocean

All sources mentioned in P5 are surface water sources. Ocean water is never discussed.

✓ (D) the states other than California depend largely on a particular river, whereas California does not

CORRECT. S3: "Excluding California, however, over half of the freshwater needs of the Southwest are met from a single source: the Colorado River." According to S2, California has enough other supplies of surface water.

Paragraph 6	Comments
S1 Allocation of rights to this water has been a political flash point among the Southwestern states since the original Colorado River Compact, drafted in 1922.	How water from the Colorado River is allocated (shared) is political.
2 According to the present version of the Compact, 15 million acre-feet per year are allocated to seven Western states, of which the five Southwestern states receive about 10 million—Wyoming and Colorado receive the rest.	Who gets what.
3 Mexico also has an annual allotment of 1.5 million acre-feet.	
4 The river is dammed at various places, with the Hoover Dam on the border of Arizona and Nevada, forming Lake Mead, being the most well-known.	

9. Which of the following can be inferred from paragraph 6 about the Colorado River Compact?

INFERENCE. S1–3 discuss the division of water rights according to the Compact.

✗ (A) All of the water from the river is allocated to the Southwestern states.

S2 states that Colorado and Wyoming, which are not Southwestern states, receive about 5 million acre-feet. Mexico (also not a Southwestern state) receives 1.5 million acre-feet (S3).

✗ (B) Most of the water from the river is allocated on an annual basis to Mexico.

S3 mentions that Mexico gets a 1.5 million acre-feet allotment. This is only 10% of the allotment (15 million acre-feet) granted to the seven Western states.

✓ (C) The original Compact did not fully resolve the political issues related to water rights.

CORRECT. S1: "Allocation of rights to this water has been a political flash point among the Southwestern states since the original Colorado River Compact, drafted in 1922." Since the allocation remained a political flash point (= a source of controversy), the original Compact, must not have fully resolved the political issues surrounding water rights.

✗ (D) Among the seven Western states, Colorado is the largest recipient of Colorado River water rights.

This is possible—for example, Colorado could receive 3 million acre-feet while all other states mentioned receive 2 million. But exact amounts are not given for any single state in the agreement. So you can't infer that Colorado gets the most.

	Paragraph 7	Comments
S1	There are several problems with this allocation.	Problems with this allocation.
2	First, the estimates for annual water flow in the Colorado River were based on a survey that occurred during a period of relatively heavy rainfall.	1: Estimates for water flow in the river are too high.
3	It is unlikely that the Colorado River can continue to produce enough water to fill these allocations indefinitely.	
4	Evidence of this is seen by the water levels in Lake Mead, which are currently more than 150 feet below peak.	
5	Second, the agreement is a zero-sum game: any increase in allocation to one state must necessarily come at the expense of another.	2: Agreement is zero-sum (win-lose).
6	This puts pressure on high-growth states like Arizona and Nevada.	
7	Finally, there is the problem of the ongoing drought in the region.	3: Ongoing drought.
8	The drought puts pressure on all water sources, and the Colorado River is no exception.	
9	If the drought remains unabated, Lake Mead could eventually become unusable, and hydroelectric generating capacity in the Southwest could fall below minimum requirements as early as the year 2020.	Lake Mead could become unusable.

10.   All of the following are mentioned in paragraph 7 as problems with the Colorado River Compact allocation EXCEPT:

NEGATIVE FACT. The entire paragraph describes the water allocation and its problems. Three answer choices will be somewhere in P7, in some form. One answer will not be.

✗ (A) The allocations seem to be larger than the average amount of water carried by the river over time.

S2–3: "the estimates for annual water flow in the Colorado River were based on ... a period of relatively heavy rainfall. It is unlikely that the Colorado River can continue to produce enough water to fill these allocations indefinitely."

✗ (B) If more water is allocated to one state, less must be allocated to another state.

S5: "the agreement is a zero-sum game: any increase in allocation to one state must necessarily come at the expense of another."

✓ (C) Changes in the compact itself are being driven by just a few high-growth states, such as Arizona and Nevada.

CORRECT. S6: "This puts pressure on high-growth states like Arizona and Nevada." But the paragraph never mentions changes to the Compact being driven by anyone, let alone these two states in particular.

✗ (D) The region is currently experiencing a period of significantly less precipitation than normal.

S7: "Finally, there is the problem of the ongoing drought in the region." Drought = systematic water shortage driven by reduced rainfall or other precipitation.

11.   The word "unabated" in the passage is closest in meaning to

VOCABULARY. "Unabated" = constant, endless, without any decrease in intensity over time.

✓ (A) persistent

CORRECT. "If the drought remains unabated" = if it remains persistent, if it continues without any reduction.

✗ (B) uncontested

Not quite. "Uncontested" = not opposed or challenged. That's not exactly the same as "unabated." The drought could abate by itself, without ever being opposed or challenged.

✗ (C) undiscussed

Unrelated. "Undiscussed" = not discussed.

✗ (D) uneven

Almost opposite. "Uneven" = not regular or consistent.

5

12. What is the author's purpose in presenting the information in paragraph 7?

PURPOSE. P7 describes several problems with the Colorado River Compact that persist to this day. S2–8 discuss these problems and the consequences that follow from them. S9 delves into specific issues with Lake Mead that could lead to its failure as a source of water and electricity.

✗ (A) To illustrate the importance of having enough water reserves for hydroelectricity generation

S9 states that hydroelectric generating capacity in the Southwest could fall below minimum requirements if Lake Mead's water levels continue to drop. This is an important aspect of the discussion. But it is not the primary purpose of the whole paragraph. Electricity generation is mentioned as just one function of the water supply.

✓ (B) To highlight the problems with the Colorado River Compact and the scarcity of water sources in the Southwest

CORRECT. P7 discusses the problem of water scarcity in the Southwest through the lens of the Colorado River Compact itself. It also discusses the ongoing difficulties with water management that the Southwest faces.

✗ (C) To advocate for reduced per-capita water consumption in the Southwest

Reduced water consumption would likely help with the problems discussed in the paragraph. But nothing in the paragraph actually advocates or argues for reductions in water consumption.

✗ (D) To suggest that some residents of the Southwest consider moving to a different region of the country

The paragraph never suggests that anyone move away from the Southwest.

Paragraph 6	Comments
S1 Allocation of rights to this water has been a political flash point among the Southwestern states since the original Colorado River Compact, drafted in 1922.	
2 [A] According to the present version of the Compact, 15 million acre-feet per year are allocated to seven Western states, of which the five Southwestern states receive about 10 million—Wyoming and Colorado receive the rest.	**CORRECT.** With the new sentence in this position, the subject "this agreement" now clearly refers to "the original Colorado River Compact, drafted in 1922" in S1.
3 [B] Mexico also has an annual allotment of 1.5 million acre-feet.	Placing the new sentence here makes it unclear what "this agreement" refers to.
4 [C] The river is dammed at various places, with the Hoover Dam on the border of Arizona and Nevada, forming Lake Mead, being the most well-known.	Placing the new sentence here makes it seem as if "this agreement" refers to the allotment given to Mexico. That reference is incorrect.
End [D]	In this position, the new sentence would not be anchored to the previous sentence, which discusses the damming of the river, not the overall agreement.

13.   **Among other things, this agreement somewhat naively divided the river region into two distinct basins—the Upper Basin and the Lower Basin—and attempted to allocate water to the two basins equally.**

Where would the sentence best fit?

✓   (A) Choice A

✗   (B) Choice B

✗   (C) Choice C

✗   (D) Choice D

INSERT TEXT. The subject of the inserted sentence is "this agreement." So the previous sentence should make it clear which agreement is meant. The paragraph introduces the Colorado River Compact, which is an agreement about water rights. Moreover, the new sentence describes the sweeping action of "this agreement." So "this agreement" almost certainly refers to that Compact, and the new sentence should probably go right after that introduction.

CORRECT.

Whole Passage	**Comments**
P1 Over the past century, the states of Utah, Nevada, New Mexico, Arizona, and California …	Southwestern U.S. has grown a lot in population. Faster than rest of country. One reason is pleasant weather. But that's a problem: not enough water.
P2 All five Southwestern states rely greatly on external water sources …	Southwest relies on external sources and groundwater. Two reasons for higher water consumption per person. Drier climate = thirsty gardens. Irrigation for farming industry.
P3 Water use has become much more efficient across the United States …	Water use has become more efficient, especially in the Southwest. But population growth there counterbalances. Water use is not sustainable.
P4 The Southwestern states consumed a total of 61 million acre-feet of water …	Total amount of water consumed in Southwest. Where it comes from. Groundwater is dropping. Net withdrawal in California. Will exhaust groundwater by 2060.
P5 For surface water, these five states are heavily reliant on various sources …	States rely a lot on various sources for surface water. California has enough in north and center. But the other states get over half from Colorado River alone.
P6 Allocation of rights to this water has been a political flash point among the Southwestern states…	How water from the Colorado River is allocated (shared) is political. Who gets what.
P7 There are several problems with this allocation …	Problems with this allocation. 1. Estimates for water flow in the river are too high. 2. Agreement is zero-sum (win-lose). 3. Ongoing drought. Lake Mead could become unusable.

5

14. **The immense population growth enjoyed by the states of the Southwestern United States has stressed water resources in the region.**

SUMMARY. Correct answers must be clearly expressed in the passage. They must also be among the major points of the passage. They should tie as directly as possible to the summary given.

✗ [A] Immigration from other countries contributes to population growth in the Southwest.

P1 mentions this fact. But it is a minor detail that helps explain why there is immense population growth in the region. This point is never explored further; it is not a major idea in the passage.

✗ [B] About one-third of the water allocation from the Colorado River Compact goes to states not considered part of the Southwest.

This specific aspect of the Colorado River allocation is mentioned in P6. But it is just a minor detail in the broader picture.

✓ [C] Low rainfall in the area leads to both scarce water supplies and attractive weather, which drives population growth and further strain on those supplies.

CORRECT. P1 explains why there is both population growth and scarcity of water in the Southwest: there's not much rainfall. This fact underpins the rest of the passage, as it explores groundwater depletion and battles over surface water.

✗ [D] Groundwater sources can continue to be used sustainably to meet water demand in the Southwest.

P1, P3, and P4 say otherwise. Groundwater resources are not being used sustainably; they are not replenished as quickly as they are used. California, for example, faces the possibility of exhausting its groundwater resources before the end of the 21st century.

✓ [E] Allocation of surface water in the Southwest is a point of ongoing political contention, particularly with regard to the Colorado River.

CORRECT. P5–7 describe the difficulties surrounding the allocation of surface water in the Southwest. The Colorado River Compact, along with its issues, is the subject of P6 and P7.

✓ [F] Despite declining per-capita water consumption, unchecked demand for water in the region can and will lead to severe consequences.

CORRECT. This choice makes an overall point that summarizes much of the passage well.

Chapter 6
Reading D: Mixed

Reading passages and questions test your ability to comprehend and analyze academic information. Most questions are multiple-choice with four options (select one from A, B, C, or D). Some questions may ask you to select more than one option or to fill in a table.

Reading passages test your understanding of main ideas and details, as well as the organization of the passage or of specific parts of the passage. They also test your understanding of the relationship between different ideas and your ability to make inferences (messages implied by the passage).

How should you use this chapter? Here are some recommendations, according to the level you've reached in TOEFL Reading:

1. **Fundamentals**. When you feel comfortable with the individual topics, move on to "mixed" practice, which you'll find in this chapter. Because you already practiced by topic in the earlier chapters, time yourself in this chapter and do all of the questions for a passage at once, without stopping.

2. **Fixes**. Test yourself with timed sets (a passage and all of its associated questions). Review the answers carefully to learn how to improve.

3. **Tweaks**. Confirm your mastery by doing a passage and question set under timed conditions. Concentrate on your weaker topic areas. Aim to improve the speed and ease of your process.

Good luck on Reading!

6.1 Developmental Plasticity

An organism's biology—its living properties, functions, and behaviors—is partially determined by its evolutionary history, which typically proceeds over the course of millions of years. The biology of an organism is also, however, shaped by its unique and much shorter developmental history, which begins when it is conceived and which unfolds over time, accruing particular and relevant events throughout the organism's lifetime.

The developmental history of an organism is subject to changes in its environment. This is nature's way of allowing an organism to be adaptive more quickly than through genetic evolution, which occurs at a very slow pace. In the early 1890s, German-American anthropologist Franz Boas (1858–1942) coined the term "developmental plasticity" to describe this concept of rapid non-evolutionary adaptation.

Developmental plasticity takes place from the very beginning of an organism's development; for mammals, it starts inside the womb, or *in utero*. An example of *in utero* developmental plasticity occurs among field mice. Signals that the mouse receives from its mother while it is still unborn will determine the thickness of the mouse's fur coat. It is conjectured that these signals are communicating to the unborn mouse what season it is in order to prepare it for its future environment. Such signaling would improve the survival rates of the offspring.

Human beings also experience developmental plasticity in the womb. If a human fetus is deprived of nutrition *in utero*, the fetus will respond by channeling vital energy to the heart and brain while deprioritizing the development of other, less vital organs. The result is that the development of these other features, such as limbs and overall size, is slowed down, and the child is born smaller. Smaller newborns have higher rates of mortality. This particular example illustrates that sometimes, what promotes survival during one developmental stage can become damaging, or "maladaptive," later on.

Perhaps the most notorious example of developmental plasticity comes from the Dutch Hunger Winter of 1944. Children born to women who experienced the six-month famine while pregnant were smaller, as their development in the womb had prioritized vital organs over other, less vital ones. But the reason this particular example is so well known is that the effect on birth size did not stop at one generation; the children of the Dutch famine children were also smaller than average.

While developmental plasticity—the idea that an organism's life experience can alter its biology—is well-established, the idea that a trait derived from the lived experience of a parent can be passed down to its child (and even further, passed down to its grandchild), known as "Lamarckian inheritance," had been dismissed as unfounded until recently. It was originally introduced by Jean-Baptiste Lamarck in 1801 but largely abandoned following publication of Charles Darwin's *On the Origin of Species* in 1859.

The concept of Lamarckian inheritance has reemerged in recent years, however, as phenomena such as that exhibited by the grandchildren of the Dutch Hunger Winter have come to light and subsequent research has confirmed that acquired traits can, in fact, be passed down to offspring. Researchers, for example, exposed male rats to acetophenone, a chemical that smells very sweet to the animal. In conjunction with the substance, the rats received a mild but painful shock to the foot. After several days of this treatment, the rats had been conditioned to fear the smell—when they were exposed to the smell, they froze. Both their offspring and their offspring's offspring also demonstrated specific fear of the smell. In addition, all three generations also had larger than normal structures that process smell in the brain.

A similar phenomenon has been observed in red-eyed fruit flies. Researchers in Japan found that when fruit fly embryos were exposed to heat shock, the stress of the shock caused them to be hatched lacking a certain protein involved in gene regulation. The lack of this protein furnished the flies with particular observable qualities, including red eyes. The offspring of the male fruit flies who had been exposed to the heat (and who therefore lacked the protein) also lacked the protein, and consequently, these offspring also had red eyes.

> Now answer the questions.

Paragraph 1

S1   An organism's biology—its living properties, functions, and behaviors—is partially determined by its evolutionary history, which typically proceeds over the course of millions of years.

2   The biology of an organism is also, however, shaped by its unique and much shorter developmental history, which begins when it is conceived and which unfolds over time, **accruing** particular and relevant events throughout the organism's lifetime.

1. The word "accruing" in the passage is closest in meaning to

   (A) accumulating

   (B) celebrating

   (C) repeating

   (D) recounting

2. According to paragraph 1, in comparison with an organism's evolutionary history, its developmental history

   (A) shapes the organism's biology to a greater degree

   (B) takes millions of years to unfold

   (C) is typically more universal

   (D) lasts for much less time

Paragraph 2

S1   The developmental history of an organism is subject to changes in its environment.

2   This is nature's way of allowing an organism to be adaptive more quickly than through genetic evolution, which occurs at a very slow pace.

3   In the early 1890s, German-American anthropologist Franz Boas (1858–1942) **coined** the term "developmental plasticity" to describe this concept of rapid non-evolutionary adaptation.

3. The word "coined" in paragraph 2 is closest in meaning to

   (A) understood

   (B) quoted

   (C) employed

   (D) created

Paragraph 3

S1 Developmental plasticity takes place from the very beginning of an organism's development; for mammals, it starts inside the womb, or *in utero*.

2   An example of *in utero* developmental plasticity occurs among field mice.

3   Signals that the mouse receives from its mother while it is still unborn will determine the thickness of the mouse's fur coat.

4   It is conjectured that these signals are communicating to the unborn mouse what season it is in order to prepare it for its future environment.

5   Such signaling would improve the survival rates of the offspring.

4. The word "conjectured" in the passage is closest in meaning to

    (A) known

    (B) reported

    (C) theorized

    (D) contrived

Paragraph 4

S1 Human beings also experience developmental plasticity in the womb.

2   If a human fetus is deprived of nutrition *in utero*, the fetus will respond by channeling vital energy to the heart and brain while deprioritizing the development of other, less vital organs.

3   The result is that the development of these other features, such as limbs and overall size, is slowed down, and the child is born smaller.

4   Smaller newborns have higher rates of mortality.

5   This particular example illustrates that sometimes, what promotes survival during one developmental stage can become damaging, or "maladaptive," later on.

5. Paragraph 4 indicates that being born smaller

    (A) is typically the result of poor nutrition *in utero*

    (B) deprives vital organs of critical nutrition

    (C) puts infants at greater risk of death

    (D) can lead to health problems in adulthood

6. The last sentence of paragraph 4 supports which of the following statements?

   (A) When an organism is born, it has attributes that will later prove to be maladaptive.

   (B) The suffering of an organism through a difficult stage of life makes it more capable of handling later challenges.

   (C) Organisms cannot distinguish between what they need and what they do not need in order to survive.

   (D) An organism's survival needs may change over the course of its lifetime.

Paragraph 5

P5 S1   Perhaps the most notorious example of developmental plasticity comes from the Dutch Hunger Winter of 1944.

2   Children born to women who experienced the six-month famine while pregnant were smaller, as their development in the womb had prioritized vital organs over other, less vital ones.

3   But the reason this particular example is so well known is that the effect on birth size did not stop at one generation; the children of the Dutch famine children were also smaller than average.

Paragraph 6

P6 S1   While developmental plasticity—the idea that an organism's life experience can alter its biology—is well-established, the idea that a trait derived from the lived experience of a parent can be passed down to its child (and even further, passed down to its grandchild), known as "Lamarckian inheritance," had been dismissed as unfounded until recently.

2   It was originally introduced by Jean-Baptiste Lamarck in 1801 but largely abandoned following publication of Charles Darwin's *On the Origin of Species* in 1859.

6

7. It can be inferred from paragraphs 5 and 6 that Lamarckian inheritance

   (A) is the subject of Charles Darwin's 1801 book *On the Origin of Species*

   (B) was regarded as incorrect by the scientific community for over a century

   (C) now is viewed as more legitimate than Charles Darwin's theory of evolution

   (D) denies that acquired traits can be passed down through generations

8. In paragraphs 5 and 6, what evidence supports the claim that Lamarckian inheritance may not be unfounded after all?

   (A) The smaller size of children who were *in utero* in women who experienced the Dutch Hunger Winter

   (B) The publication of Charles Darwin's *On the Origin of Species*

   (C) The prioritization of vital organs over less vital organs in the womb

   (D) The effects of the Dutch famine on birth size endured to the next generation

Paragraph 7

S1 The concept of Lamarckian inheritance has reemerged in recent years, however, as phenomena such as that exhibited by the grandchildren of the Dutch Hunger Winter have come to light, and subsequent research has confirmed that acquired traits can, in fact, be passed down to offspring.

2 Researchers, for example, exposed male rats to acetophenone, a chemical that smells very sweet to the animal.

3 In conjunction with the substance, the rats received a mild but painful shock to the foot.

4 After several days of this treatment, the rats had been conditioned to fear the smell—when they were exposed to the smell, they froze.

5 Both their offspring and their offspring's offspring also demonstrated specific fear of the smell.

6 In addition, all three generations also had larger than normal structures that process smell in the brain.

9. The word "reemerged" in the passage is closest in meaning to

   (A) become dominant again

   (B) regained prominence

   (C) been reinterpreted

   (D) been recombined with other theories

10. The word "conditioned" in the passage is closest in meaning to

    (A) trained

    (B) unable

    (C) forbidden

    (D) permitted

11. According to paragraph 7, which of the following explains why the rats froze when exposed to the smell of acetophenone?

    (A) Previous experience had associated the smell with pain.

    (B) Acetophenone has a very sweet, attractive aroma.

    (C) Multiple generations of their offspring displayed the same reaction to the smell.

    (D) They were taught to connect the smell with the provision of food.

Paragraph 8

S1   A similar phenomenon has been observed in red-eyed fruit flies.

2   Researchers in Japan found that when fruit fly embryos were exposed to heat shock, the stress of the shock caused them to be hatched lacking a certain protein involved in gene regulation.

3   The lack of this protein furnished the flies with particular observable qualities, including red eyes.

4   The offspring of the male fruit flies who had been exposed to the heat (and who therefore lacked the protein) also lacked the protein, and consequently, these offspring also had red eyes.

12. The word "furnished" in the passage is closest in meaning to

   (A) endangered

   (B) supplied

   (C) encumbered

   (D) disguised

Paragraph 3

S1   Developmental plasticity takes place from the very beginning of an organism's development; for mammals, it starts inside the womb, or *in utero*.

2   **A** An example of *in utero* developmental plasticity occurs among field mice.

3   **B** Signals that the mouse receives from its mother while it is still unborn will determine the thickness of the mouse's fur coat.

4–5   **C** It is conjectured that these signals are communicating to the unborn mouse what season it is in order to prepare it for its future environment. Such signaling would improve the survival rates of the offspring.

End   **D**

> Look at the part of the passage that is displayed above. The letters [A], [B], [C], and [D] indicate where the following sentence could be added.

13. **If the season of the year is colder, the mouse will be born with a thicker coat; on the other hand, if the season is warmer, the mouse's coat at birth will not be as thick.**

Where would the sentence best fit?

   (A) Choice A

   (B) Choice B

   (C) Choice C

   (D) Choice D

An introductory sentence for a brief summary of the passage is provided below. Complete the summary by selecting the THREE answer choices that express the most important ideas in the passage. Some sentences do not belong in the summary because they express ideas that are not presented in the passage or are minor ideas in the passage. This question is worth 2 points.

14. **Developmental plasticity refers to the way an organism's biology adjusts to its environment during its lifetime.**

A It seems that certain acquired traits can be passed down to the offspring of an organism.

B Various species exhibit developmental plasticity, including in early stages of growth after conception.

C Fruit flies are more developmentally plastic than most other insects.

D Field mice fetuses are unlikely to grow coats of fur at all unless they receive signals from their mothers to do so.

E During the Dutch Hunger Winter of 1944, a six-month famine occurred in which many people starved.

F Once banished, Lamarckian inheritance has resurfaced as a result of new research, including studies of animals and humans.

6.2 Depletion of California's Aquifers

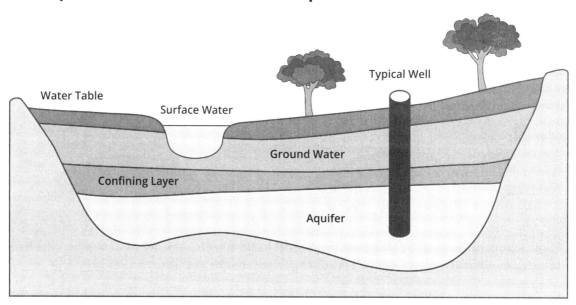

California became an important center of agriculture in the United States in the second half of the nineteenth century, as the gold rush of the 1850s faded and residents discovered that the land was ideal for growing wheat and, later, a variety of crops. California now produces more than half of the fresh fruit and vegetables grown in the United States. Most of the industry is located in the Central Valley, which covers approximately 57,000 square kilometers and spans more than half the state. The Central Valley and

most of the coastal regions of California have a Mediterranean climate, with ample sunshine and warm temperatures. These attributes are ideal for most types of farming. However, Mediterranean climates usually have relatively low rainfall. While the Central Valley has an enormous watershed[1], the massive amount of food produced there, to say nothing of California's large population and industry, requires more water than is available from rainfall and snowfall.

As a result, much of California's water demand is met via groundwater, which can be found in hundreds of pools located in layers of rock beneath the land surface. These reserves are known as aquifers. Aquifers in California have slowly accumulated for thousands of years and are enormous—geological studies indicate that California has over 850 million acre-feet[2] of water in its known groundwater reserves. About half of this is usable, and the usable portion is, in total, larger than Lake Erie.

However, the water in these aquifers is being consumed much more rapidly than nature can replenish it. In a year with typical rainfall and snowfall, only about 2 million acre-feet of groundwater is replaced. Meanwhile, overdrafting (the amount by which water is removed from aquifers beyond the rate at which it is replenished) has risen substantially. Some estimates place recent overdrafting at 10 million acre-feet per year. The amount of annual overdrafting can vary significantly, and it is difficult to control.

There are two reasons for the variable and unruly nature of the overdrafting. The first is a severe drought in California that started in 2012. Normally, about 30 percent of the water consumed in California comes from groundwater sources. However, since 2012 the figure has been closer to 60 percent. Farmers and residents are able to curb their consumption of water somewhat during a drought, but there is a limit to how much reduction can actually be attained. In January 2014, California Governor Jerry Brown declared a state of emergency, targeting a 20 percent reduction in water consumption while simultaneously seeking to make more water sources available. However, consumption of water has fallen by far less than that target and in some areas has actually increased. The second reason is that there are no statewide laws governing the use of groundwater. Each reservoir has different regulations that determine usage rights. In many cases, there is little restriction on how quickly water may be pumped out. Groundwater can be removed practically without limitation, provided that it is removed by the owner of the land above it.

Should California's groundwater crisis continue unabated, it could become a disaster. Depleted aquifers can give rise to a lowering of the water table, which makes groundwater harder to access. They can also cause land subsidence, the physical drop of land because of the removal of water beneath; this phenomenon can destroy bridges, buildings, and roads. Water costs could skyrocket, drastically affecting crop prices and yields. Because California is such a prominent agricultural producer, these shocks could have far-reaching effects economically and socially.

Numerous attempts to improve management of California's scarce groundwater resources have been made, dating back to 1873, when the first "California Water Plan" was drafted. Completed in 2013, the most recent version of this document calls for an integrated approach to managing the state's water resources and preserving groundwater supplies. The plan suggests improvements in water conservation, recycling of waste water, and provision of financial incentives to reduce usage. However, the plan barely forces users to change consumption habits and does virtually nothing to simplify the complex legal web surrounding groundwater extraction.

watershed[1]: a region of land from which all surface water flows into a single location, typically a river or lake
acre-feet[2]: unit of volume used in the United States for large bodies of water

> Now answer the questions.

Paragraph 1

S1 California became an important center of agriculture in the United States in the second half of the nineteenth century, as the gold rush of the 1850s faded and residents discovered that the land was ideal for growing wheat and, later, a variety of crops.

2 California now produces more than half of the fresh fruit and vegetables grown in the United States.

3 Most of the industry is located in the Central Valley, which covers approximately 57,000 square kilometers and spans more than half the state.

4 The Central Valley and most of the coastal regions of California have a Mediterranean climate, with ample sunshine and warm temperatures.

5 These attributes are ideal for most types of farming.

6 However, Mediterranean climates usually have relatively low rainfall.

7 While the Central Valley has an enormous watershed, the massive amount of food produced there, to say nothing of California's large population and industry, requires more water than is available from rainfall and snowfall.

1. The word "massive" in the passage is closest in meaning to

    (A) cumbersome

    (B) colossal

    (C) diminutive

    (D) precipitous

2. According to paragraph 1, agriculture in California is especially important today for which of the following reasons?

    (A) When the gold rush of the 1850s faded, many people turned to agriculture in California, especially in the Central Valley.

    (B) The amount of water consumed by agriculture is larger than that consumed by the rest of California's population and industry.

    (C) California has bountiful sunshine and warm temperatures, which are ideal for most types of farming.

    (D) More than half of the fresh fruit and vegetables grown in the United States come from there.

Paragraph 2

S1 As a result, much of California's water demand is met via groundwater, which can be found in hundreds of pools located in layers of rock beneath the land surface.

2 These reserves are known as aquifers.

3 Aquifers in California have slowly accumulated for thousands of years and are enormous—geological studies indicate that California has over 850 million acre-feet of water in its known groundwater reserves.

4 About half of this is usable, and the usable portion is, in total, larger than Lake Erie.

3. The author mentions "Lake Erie" in the passage for what reason?

(A) To explain the source of the underground water

(B) To demonstrate the amount of water that cannot be used

(C) To emphasize the immensity of underground water available in California

(D) To provide an example of one well-known aquifer in California

4. According to paragraph 2, which of the following is true of aquifers in general?

(A) They accumulate in pools beneath layers of rock.

(B) They collect above ground before seeping uselessly beneath underground rock.

(C) Almost all of California's water needs are met by aquifers.

(D) They are typically enormous, comparable in size to large lakes.

Paragraph 3

S1 However, the water in these aquifers is being consumed much more rapidly than nature can replenish it.

2 In a year with typical rainfall and snowfall, only about 2 million acre-feet of groundwater is replaced.

3 Meanwhile, overdrafting (the amount by which water is removed from aquifers beyond the rate at which it is replenished) has risen substantially.

4 Some estimates place recent overdrafting at 10 million acre-feet per year.

5 The amount of annual overdrafting can vary significantly, and it is difficult to control.

5. According to paragraph 3, which of the following is currently true of overdrafting in California?

   (A) It is roughly consistent from year to year.

   (B) It is caused by excess rainfall and snowfall.

   (C) Its current rate is approximately 2 million acre-feet per year.

   (D) Government or other entities cannot easily constrain it.

6. The word "replenish" in the passage is closest in meaning to

   (A) recollect

   (B) replace

   (C) retrieve

   (D) remove

Paragraph 4

S1	There are two reasons for the variable and unruly nature of the overdrafting.
2	The first is a severe drought in California that started in 2012.
3	Normally, about 30 percent of the water consumed in California comes from groundwater sources.
4	However, since 2012 the figure has been closer to 60 percent.
5	Farmers and residents are able to curb their consumption of water somewhat during a drought, but there is a limit to how much reduction can actually be attained.
6	In January 2014, California Governor Jerry Brown declared a state of emergency, targeting a 20 percent reduction in water consumption while simultaneously seeking to make more water sources available.
7	However, consumption of water has fallen by far less than that target and in some areas has actually increased.
8	The second reason is that there are no statewide laws governing the use of groundwater.
9	Each reservoir has different regulations that determine usage rights.
10	In many cases, there is little restriction on how quickly water may be pumped out.
11	Groundwater can be removed practically without limitation, provided that it is removed by the owner of the land above it.

7. According to paragraph 4, which of the following is true of groundwater usage rights?

    (A) They are subject to a universal set of regulations from a central government agency.

    (B) They are not governed by laws that cover the entire state.

    (C) The owner of land with groundwater underneath has little control over that water.

    (D) The rate at which groundwater can be removed is strictly limited.

8. According to paragraph 4, groundwater preservation in California has been made more difficult by all of the following EXCEPT:

    (A) The California governor declared a state of emergency to reduce water consumption.

    (B) California has been experiencing a serious drought for years.

    (C) Government control of groundwater extraction is incomplete and inconsistent.

    (D) Farmers can reduce their use of groundwater only up to a certain point.

9. Which of the following can be inferred from paragraph 4 regarding Governor Brown's emergency declaration?

    (A) It temporarily halted groundwater depletion.

    (B) It rewrote California regulations concerning groundwater extraction.

    (C) It failed to achieve the governor's water preservation goals.

    (D) It coincided with the ending of the previously mentioned drought.

6

Paragraph 5

S1	Should California's groundwater crisis continue unabated, it could become a disaster.
2	Depleted aquifers can give rise to a lowering of the water table, which makes groundwater harder to access.
3	They can also cause land subsidence, the physical drop of land because of the removal of water beneath; this phenomenon can destroy bridges, buildings, and roads.
4	Water costs could skyrocket, **drastically** affecting crop prices and yields.
5	Because California is such a prominent agricultural producer, these shocks could have far-reaching effects economically and socially.

10. The phrase "drastically" in the passage is closest in meaning to

    (A) immediately

    (B) adversely

    (C) modestly

    (D) radically

Paragraph 6

S1   Numerous attempts to improve management of California's scarce groundwater resources have been made, dating back to 1873, when the first "California Water Plan" was drafted.

2   Completed in 2013, the most recent version of this document calls for an integrated approach to managing the state's water resources and preserving groundwater supplies.

3   The plan suggests improvements in water conservation, recycling of waste water, and provision of financial incentives to reduce usage.

4   However, the plan barely forces users to change consumption habits and does virtually nothing to simplify the complex legal web surrounding groundwater extraction.

11. Which of the sentences below best expresses the essential information in the highlighted sentence in paragraph 6? Incorrect choices change the meaning in important ways or leave out essential information.

    (A) Since the first "California Water Plan" was drafted in 1873, many attempts to better conserve the state's groundwater have been made.

    (B) Many attempts to increase use of scarce groundwater resources have been foiled since 1873, the date of the first "California Water Plan."

    (C) When the first "California Water Plan" was drafted, several attempts to better manage the state's groundwater resources were made.

    (D) Many attempts to improve management of the "California Water Plan," the state's groundwater resources, have been made since 1873.

Paragraph 2

P2
S3–4
Aquifers in California have slowly accumulated for thousands of years and are enormous—geological studies indicate that California has over 850 million acre-feet of water in its known groundwater reserves. About half of this is usable, and the usable portion is, in total, larger than Lake Erie.

Paragraph 3

P3 S1
[A] However, the water in these aquifers is being consumed much more rapidly than nature can replenish it.

2
[B] In a year with typical rainfall and snowfall, only about 2 million acre-feet of groundwater is replaced.

3–4
[C] Meanwhile, overdrafting (the amount by which water is removed from aquifers beyond the rate at which it is replenished) has risen substantially. Some estimates place recent overdrafting at 10 million acre-feet per year.

5
[D] The amount of annual overdrafting can vary significantly, and it is difficult to control.

Look at the part of the passage that is displayed above. The letters [A], [B], [C], and [D] indicate where the following sentence could be added.

---

12. **Because of the drought in California, this figure is less than 1 million acre-feet in recent years.**

Where would the sentence best fit?

(A) Choice A

(B) Choice B

(C) Choice C

(D) Choice D

An introductory sentence for a brief summary of the passage is provided below. Complete the summary by selecting the THREE answer choices that express the most important ideas in the passage. Some sentences do not belong in the summary because they express ideas that are not presented in the passage or are minor ideas in the passage. This question is worth 2 points.

13. **California's nationally important agricultural industry depends to an alarming degree on the use of rapidly decreasing supplies of water underground.**

   [A] The California drought that began in 2012 caused Governor Jerry Brown to declare a state of emergency in early 2014.

   [B] Depletion of the state's groundwater could lead to dire outcomes, such as land subsidence, reduced crop yields, and infrastructure destruction.

   [C] As evidenced by its vast production of fruits and vegetables, California has an ideal agricultural climate, except for its low rainfall.

   [D] California now has proven, usable groundwater reserves that are smaller, in total, than the volume of Lake Erie.

   [E] Farming in California is heavily dependent on groundwater reserves that are threatened by uncontrolled overdrafting.

   [F] Under normal usage and precipitation patterns, about 30 percent of the water consumed in California comes from groundwater sources.

6.3 Difference and Analytical Engines

The shift in processing power and information storage from human beings to computers over the past several decades represents the most significant change in productivity since the Industrial Revolution. Despite all of the obvious technological improvements in production, manufacturing technique, materials, and engineering, no other innovation can rival computers in terms of their overall impact on the economy. The most basic dichotomy in information processing today lies between computers on the one hand and human beings on the other.

Interestingly, if a person today were asked, "When was the first computer program ever written?", he or she would probably miss the mark by over a century. Many might think of the Electronic Numerical Integrator and Computer (ENIAC). Completed in 1946 at the University of Pennsylvania, ENIAC was the first completely electronic general-use computer. Others may think of the Universal Automatic Computer (UNIVAC), the first commercially used electronic computer, built in 1951 by the inventors of ENIAC. Or perhaps one would think of the electromechanical machines that preceded ENIAC, such as those that controlled telephone exchanges in the first half of the twentieth century. In fact, the first completed computer program dates back to 1843. It was written by Ada Lovelace (1815–1852), a mathematician and colleague of Charles Babbage (1791–1871), inventor of the "difference engine" and, later, the "analytical engine."

Babbage was an English mathematician, inventor, and engineer. He is regarded by many as the father of modern-day computing. He began work designing the first version of his difference engine in 1822. This mechanical engine was to compute the value of polynomial functions using a mathematical process known as "finite differences." Using this method, the difference engine would only be capable of adding and subtracting. Unfortunately, Babbage ran into difficulties both with funding his project and with the builder of the initial prototype of his design, and the project was abandoned partway through. Eventually, Babbage shifted to designing what he called the "analytical engine," which drew on his designs for the difference engine but was intended as a more general computing machine.

The analytical engine featured a new concept called "punched cards," which would contain coded information that the engine would accept as inputs. The machine would then produce outputs in the form of a drawn curve, printed output, or additional punched cards to be used later. The machine would have a unit designed to perform computation and another unit to store information. Though the design of these units was mechanical rather than electronic, they are directly analogous to the processor and memory found in computers today.

Lovelace's computer program, designed for use on the analytical engine once it was built, was modest by modern standards. It simply entailed a written, step-by-step description of how a machine might compute a mathematical series known as the Bernoulli numbers. However, as simple as it was, it had all of the traits of a modern-day computer algorithm: a set of instructions to be followed by a computer, operating upon a set of inputs, in order to arrive at a desired set of outputs.

Like the original difference engine, Babbage's analytical engine was never completely built. The combination of financial resources and available technology to implement Babbage's blueprint was simply insufficient during his lifetime. In fact, Babbage worked for decades to simplify his design so that building it would be feasible; he was only able to finish building a small portion of it before his death in 1871. Babbage's son, Henry, continued to work on building the analytical engine, and was able to produce some of the desired outputs from the machine. However, Henry never came close to realizing his father's complete vision.

It was not until 1991, in Australia, that a complete version of Babbage's difference engine was produced. The completed "Difference Engine No. 2" implemented Babbage's designs, correcting for some errors (which may have been intentional), and was constructed using only methods that might have been available in the nineteenth century. The finished machine works exactly as Babbage would have hoped. To this day, though, no analytical engine that matches Babbage's later designs has ever been fully built.

> Now answer the questions.

Paragraph 1

S1 The shift in processing power and information storage from human beings to computers over the past several decades represents the most significant change in productivity since the Industrial Revolution.

2 Despite all of the obvious technological improvements in production, manufacturing technique, materials, and engineering, no other innovation can rival computers in terms of their overall impact on the economy.

3 The most basic **dichotomy** in information processing today lies between computers on the one hand and human beings on the other.

1. The word "dichotomy" in the passage is closest in meaning to

   (A) comparison

   (B) contrast

   (C) contradiction

   (D) confluence

2. Which of the sentences below best expresses the essential information in the highlighted sentence in paragraph 1? Incorrect choices change the meaning in important ways or leave out essential information.

   (A) Despite technological improvements in computers, innovations in such areas as production and manufacturing rival them with regard to their economic impact.

   (B) The economic impact of computers is unmatched by that of any technological innovation in other areas such as manufacturing and production.

   (C) In spite of developments in production, manufacturing technique, materials, and engineering, none of these are as economically innovative as computers.

   (D) Despite technological improvements in their production, computers cannot match other inventions in terms of their overall impact on the economy.

Paragraph 2

S1   Interestingly, if a person today were asked, "When was the first computer program ever written?", he or she would probably miss the mark by over a century.

2   Many might think of the Electronic Numerical Integrator and Computer (ENIAC).

3   Completed in 1946 at the University of Pennsylvania, ENIAC was the first completely electronic general-use computer.

4   Others may think of the Universal Automatic Computer (UNIVAC), the first commercially used electronic computer, built in 1951 by the inventors of ENIAC.

5   Or perhaps one would think of the electromechanical machines that preceded ENIAC, such as those that controlled telephone exchanges in the first half of the twentieth century.

6   In fact, the first completed computer program dates back to 1843.

7   It was written by Ada Lovelace (1815–1852), a mathematician and colleague of Charles Babbage (1791–1871), inventor of the "difference engine" and, later, the "analytical engine."

3. According to paragraph 2, which of the following statements about the first computer program is true?

(A) It was written in the nineteenth century.

(B) It was written by Charles Babbage.

(C) It was written for ENIAC at the University of Pennsylvania.

(D) It was written for a completely electronic general-use computer.

4. According to paragraph 2, all of the following statements about UNIVAC are true EXCEPT:

(A) It was built by the creators of ENIAC.

(B) It was the first electronic computer used commercially.

(C) It was an electromechanical machine that preceded ENIAC.

(D) It was created after machines to control telephone exchanges were developed.

Paragraph 3

S1   Babbage was an English mathematician, inventor, and engineer.

2   He is regarded by many as the father of modern-day computing.

3   He began work designing the first version of his difference engine in 1822.

4   This mechanical engine was to compute the value of polynomial functions using a mathematical process known as "finite differences."

5   Using this method, the difference engine would only be capable of adding and subtracting.

6   Unfortunately, Babbage ran into difficulties both with funding his project and with the builder of the initial prototype of his design, and the project was **abandoned** partway through.

7   Eventually, Babbage shifted to designing what he called the "analytical engine," which drew on his designs for the difference engine but was intended as a more general computing machine.

5. The word "abandoned" in the passage is closest in meaning to

   (A) corrected

   (B) continued

   (C) shackled

   (D) scrapped

6. In paragraph 3, why does the author provide the information regarding funding for the initial prototype of the difference engine?

   (A) To assert that the difference engine would have been completed with better funding

   (B) To acknowledge the resources that made completing the prototype of the difference engine possible

   (C) To explain, at least in part, why the prototype of the difference engine was abandoned

   (D) To highlight a factor that would be useful as focus shifted to the analytical engine

Paragraph 4

S1   The analytical engine featured a new concept called "punched cards," which would contain coded information that the engine would accept as inputs.

2   The machine would then produce outputs in the form of a drawn curve, printed output, or additional punched cards to be used later.

3   The machine would have a unit designed to perform computation and another unit to store information.

4   Though the design of these units was mechanical rather than electronic, they are directly analogous to the processor and memory found in computers today.

7.   The phrase "analogous to" in the passage is closest in meaning to

   (A) coupled with

   (B) comparable to

   (C) opposed to

   (D) descended from

8.   According to paragraph 4, all of the following are design features of the analytical engine EXCEPT:

   (A) It would produce punched cards as output.

   (B) It would receive instructions via punched cards.

   (C) It would store information and perform calculations.

   (D) It would contain a basic electronic processor.

Paragraph 5

S1   Lovelace's computer program, designed for use on the analytical engine once it was built, was modest by modern standards.

2   It simply entailed a written, step-by-step description of how a machine might compute a mathematical series known as the Bernoulli numbers.

3   However, as simple as it was, it had all of the traits of a modern-day computer algorithm: a set of instructions to be followed by a computer, operating upon a set of inputs, in order to arrive at a desired set of outputs.

9.   According to paragraph 5, Lovelace's computer program

   (A) appeared ill-suited to compute a mathematical series

   (B) was eventually used on modern computers

   (C) was employed to discover the Bernoulli numbers

   (D) had the core features of modern algorithms

Paragraph 6

S1   Like the original difference engine, Babbage's analytical engine was never completely built.

2   The combination of financial resources and available technology to implement Babbage's blueprint was simply insufficient during his lifetime.

3   In fact, Babbage worked for decades to simplify his design so that building it would be feasible; he was only able to finish building a small portion of it before his death in 1871.

4   Babbage's son, Henry, continued to work on building the analytical engine, and was able to produce some of the desired outputs from the machine.

5   However, Henry never came close to realizing his father's complete vision.

10. The word "feasible" in the passage is closest in meaning to

    (A) comprehensible

    (B) postponable

    (C) achievable

    (D) impossible

11. Paragraph 6 mentions which of the following as a difficulty facing the construction of Babbage's analytical engine?

    (A) Adequate technology was not available.

    (B) Babbage's son did not fully understand the design.

    (C) Babbage's son produced some intended outputs from the machine.

    (D) Babbage died prematurely in 1871.

Paragraph 7

S1   It was not until 1991, in Australia, that a complete version of Babbage's difference engine was produced.

2   The completed "Difference Engine No. 2" implemented Babbage's designs, correcting for some errors (which may have been intentional), and was constructed using only methods that might have been available in the nineteenth century.

3   The finished machine works exactly as Babbage would have hoped.

4   To this day, though, no analytical engine that matches Babbage's later designs has ever been fully built.

12. According to paragraph 7, which of the following is true of the completed "Difference Engine No. 2"?

   (A) It corrected intentional design flaws.

   (B) It was built in a fashion that would have been possible in the 1800s.

   (C) It did not perform as Babbage would have wanted.

   (D) It followed the completion of a version of Babbage's analytical engine.

Paragraph 3

S1–2   Babbage was an English mathematician, inventor, and engineer. He is regarded by many as the father of modern-day computing.

3–4   **A** He began work designing the first version of his difference engine in 1822. This mechanical engine was to compute the value of polynomial functions using a mathematical process known as "finite differences."

5–6   **B** Using this method, the difference engine would only be capable of adding and subtracting. Unfortunately, Babbage ran into difficulties both with funding his project and with the builder of the initial prototype of his design, and the project was abandoned partway through.

7   **C** Eventually, Babbage shifted to designing what he called the "analytical engine," which drew on his designs for the difference engine but was intended as a more general computing machine.

End   **D**

Look at the part of the passage that is displayed above. The letters [A], [B], [C], and [D] indicate where the following sentence could be added.

13. **This prototype engine, known as "Difference Engine No. 1," would never be fully constructed.**

   Where would the sentence best fit?

   (A) Choice A

   (B) Choice B

   (C) Choice C

   (D) Choice D

An introductory sentence for a brief summary of the passage is provided below. Complete the summary by selecting the THREE answer choices that express the most important ideas in the passage. Some sentences do not belong in the summary because they express ideas that are not presented in the passage or are minor ideas in the passage. This question is worth 2 points.

14. **Although the nineteenth-century inventions of Charles Babbage were not completed in his lifetime, they foreshadow the modern computer.**

   A   The first known computer program was written by Ada Lovelace to be used on Babbage's analytical engine.

   B   Babbage is acknowledged as the inventor of ENIAC and UNIVAC, the first fully electronic computing machines.

   C   The recent completion of one of Babbage's designs showed that his machines could work as "computation engines," as intended.

   D   Babbage's mechanical machines provided models for many features of modern electronic computing.

   E   Henry Babbage, Charles's son, was never able to turn his father's vision into reality.

   F   Modern computing power is unlikely to be the most important economic innovation in history.

6.4 The Black Death

Bubonic plague is caused by the *Yersinia pestis* bacterium, which is endemic in wild rodents, including rats. When these animals are present in great numbers and density, a "plague reservoir" provides a springboard for epidemics. As the infected rat population dies, their fleas migrate to humans and spread the disease. Such a reservoir has long existed in the central steppes of Asia. Consequently, China, India, and much of the Middle East have long endured epidemics, including the Justinian plague, which ravaged the Byzantine Empire in 541. However, Europe was spared, at least on a grand scale, for another 800 years.

In 1346, the central steppes of Asia were part of the Mongol Khanate of the Golden Horde; a Mongol army besieged the Italian trading outpost in Kaffa, a Black Sea port. The Mongol force suffered from plague, and during the siege the bodies of those dead were catapulted into the town. The following spring, the Italians fled home by ship and brought the plague to Europe. At that time, Europe was exceedingly vulnerable to such an epidemic. Burgeoning medieval trade networks allowed the disease to spread rapidly by ship, up to several hundred kilometers a week. The lack of modern medical knowledge ensured that no effective measures were taken to curb its spread. In 1347, the Adriatic Italian seaports were infected, and from there the plague followed the sailing routes to Sicily and then Marseilles; after a lull during the winter, when cold temperatures inhibit the flea population, 1348 saw the plague spread to Spain, the rest of France, and then England and northern Europe. From Norway, the trading ships of the Hanseatic League carried it to the

Baltic cities and Russia. By the time the epidemic had run its course in 1353, all of Europe had been significantly ravaged.

While the fragmentary nature of medieval records has hindered scholars, recent research has caused an upward revision in the already horrific estimate of the mortality rate. It is now thought that more than half of the population perished. While some more northern or isolated regions were less afflicted, the Italian cities may have lost as many as 80 percent of their people. All told, perhaps 50 million died, a number comparable with global deaths caused by the Second World War. One of the first acknowledged great books of Western literature, *The Decameron*, chronicles the impact as it describes the plight of a group of Italian gentry that fled to the countryside in a vain attempt to avoid infection. The cities became cemeteries, in which streets were littered with unburied dead, and houses were abandoned or occupied only by the dying.

It would be 300 years before the population returned to its 1347 peak. Thus, it is little wonder that this plague, named the Black Death, remains in the human consciousness hundreds of years later, as the disruption of such depopulation greatly affected the development of European society. Some of the changes actually brought unforeseen benefits: the resulting labor shortage raised wages and the standard of living for the surviving peasantry, many of whom then acquired land left vacant by the deaths of the previous owners and tenants. It has also been theorized that this disruption spurred the development of modern capitalism, since labor-intensive feudal organization was no longer practical.

Other consequences were much darker. The epidemic struck swiftly and terribly; people sickened within days of infection and died within a week. Naturally enough, panic, fear, and anger quickly tore the social fabric apart. As neither government nor religious leaders had any factual understanding of the terrifying malady that had befallen them, these leaders did not oppose the inevitable scapegoating of members of religious or ethnic minorities, beggars, foreigners, or those with disfiguring diseases other than plague. In 1349, authority figures condoned, or even encouraged, the extermination of many Jewish communities in central Europe.

Today, in developed countries, it is easy to view the plague as a relic of the medieval past, especially since the disease can be treated with modern antibiotics. However, less celebrated outbreaks regularly occurred in Europe into the eighteenth century. In the nineteenth century, another bubonic plague epidemic killed tens of millions. Much more recently, panic reminiscent of the fourteenth century quickly asserted itself when many quickly succumbed during the Ebola outbreak from 2014 to 2016.

Now answer the questions.

Paragraph 1

S1   Bubonic plague is caused by the *Yersinia pestis* bacterium, which is endemic in wild rodents, including rats.

2   When these animals are present in great numbers and density, a "plague reservoir" provides a springboard for epidemics.

3   As the infected rat population dies, their fleas migrate to humans and spread the disease.

4   Such a reservoir has long existed in the central steppes of Asia.

5   Consequently, China, India, and much of the Middle East have long endured epidemics, including the Justinian plague, which ravaged the Byzantine Empire in 541.

6   However, Europe was spared, at least on a grand scale, for another 800 years.

1.   According to paragraph 1, humans contract bubonic plague most directly when

  (A) a plague reservoir is present nearby

  (B) infected fleas migrate from rats to humans

  (C) they live in the central steppes of Asia

  (D) they are bitten by rats

2.   The word "springboard" in the passage is closest in meaning to

  (A) cure

  (B) damper

  (C) foundation

  (D) explanation

3.   Paragraph 1 presents a fact and then goes on to

  (A) detail how an epidemic from the Byzantine Empire infected the whole Middle East

  (B) discuss how plague epidemics ultimately reached Europe

  (C) provide additional facts that clash and a theory to reconcile them all

  (D) describe how plague is transmitted and cite historical examples

MANHATTAN PREP

Paragraph 2

S1   In 1346, the central steppes of Asia were part of the Mongol Khanate of the Golden Horde; a Mongol army besieged the Italian trading outpost in Kaffa, a Black Sea port.

2   The Mongol force suffered from plague, and during the siege the bodies of those dead were catapulted into the town.

3   The following spring, the Italians fled home by ship and brought the plague to Europe.

4   At that time, Europe was exceedingly vulnerable to such an epidemic.

5   Burgeoning medieval trade networks allowed the disease to spread rapidly by ship, up to several hundred kilometers a week.

6   The lack of modern medical knowledge ensured that no effective measures were taken to curb its spread.

7   In 1347, the Adriatic Italian seaports were infected, and from there the plague followed the sailing routes to Sicily and then Marseilles; after a lull during the winter, when cold temperatures inhibit the flea population, 1348 saw the plague spread to Spain, the rest of France, and then England and northern Europe.

8   From Norway, the trading ships of the Hanseatic League carried it to the Baltic cities and Russia.

9   By the time the epidemic had run its course in 1353, all of Europe had been significantly ravaged.

4. The word "**burgeoning**" in the passage is closest in meaning to
    - (A) flourishing
    - (B) unraveling
    - (C) dwindling
    - (D) branching

5. Paragraph 2 supports the idea that the spread of the plague throughout Europe was facilitated by which of the following factors?
    - (A) Ineffective medical countermeasures
    - (B) Low temperatures in wintertime
    - (C) The exclusion of plague-ridden corpses from Kaffa
    - (D) Europe's proximity to the central steppes of Asia

6. Which of the sentences below best expresses the essential information in the highlighted sentence in paragraph 2? Incorrect choices change the meaning in important ways or leave out essential information.

(A) In 1347, after a winter lull due to inactivated fleas, plague infected Italian seaports and then spread to Sicily, Marseilles, and the rest of France, Spain, England, and northern Europe.

(B) Plague, after landing in Adriatic Italian seaports in 1347, followed sailing routes to Sicily, Marseilles, then Spain, the rest of France, and finally England and northern Europe.

(C) Even with winter briefly inactivating the fleas, plague swept through several European countries within a year of landing in Italian seaports in 1347, following travel routes and spreading north.

(D) After infecting Italian seaports in 1347, plague blazed through cities, islands, and countries of Europe following well-traveled routes, only to be halted by winter, which leveled the flea population.

Paragraph 3

S1   While the fragmentary nature of medieval records has hindered scholars, recent research has caused an upward revision in the already horrific estimate of the mortality rate.

2   It is now thought that more than half of the population perished.

3   While some more northern or isolated regions were less afflicted, the Italian cities may have lost as many as 80 percent of their people.

4   All told, perhaps 50 million died, a number comparable with global deaths caused by the Second World War.

5   One of the first acknowledged great books of Western literature, *The Decameron*, chronicles the impact as it describes the plight of a group of Italian gentry that fled to the countryside in a vain attempt to avoid infection.

6   The cities became cemeteries, in which streets were littered with unburied dead, and houses were abandoned or occupied only by the dying.

7. The main purpose of paragraph 3 is to

(A) emphasize and illustrate the decimation of Europe

(B) explain why German principalities fared better than the Italian cities

(C) support the claim that *The Decameron* is a literary classic

(D) downplay the losses of the Second World War by comparison with those caused by plague

Paragraph 4

S1   It would be 300 years before the population returned to its 1347 peak.

2   Thus, it is little wonder that this plague, named the Black Death, remains in the human consciousness hundreds of years later, as the disruption of such depopulation greatly affected the development of European society.

3   Some of the changes actually brought unforeseen benefits: the resulting labor shortage raised wages and the standard of living for the surviving peasantry, many of whom then acquired land left vacant by the deaths of the previous owners and tenants.

4   It has also been theorized that this disruption spurred the development of modern capitalism, since labor-intensive feudal organization was no longer practical.

8. The word "spurred" in the passage is closest in meaning to

    (A) accompanied

    (B) halted

    (C) affected

    (D) promoted

9. According to paragraph 4, which of the following is mentioned as an unexpected benefit of the plague?

    (A) Feudalism recovered as a social structure.

    (B) Many peasants subsequently acquired real estate.

    (C) The epidemic left a lasting impact on human consciousness.

    (D) Overcrowded urban areas were reduced in population.

Paragraph 5

S1   Other consequences were much darker.

2   The epidemic struck swiftly and terribly; people sickened within days of infection and died within a week.

3   Naturally enough, panic, fear, and anger quickly tore the social fabric apart.

4   As neither government nor religious leaders had any factual understanding of the terrifying malady that had befallen them, these leaders did not oppose the inevitable scapegoating of members of religious or ethnic minorities, beggars, foreigners, or those with disfiguring diseases other than plague.

5   In 1349, authority figures condoned, or even encouraged, the extermination of many Jewish communities in central Europe.

10. The word "**disfiguring**" in the passage is closest in meaning to

(A) debilitating

(B) marring

(C) infectious

(D) incurable

11. According to paragraph 5, which of the following is true about government and religious leaders at the time of the Black Death?

(A) Their comprehension of the disease was based on hard facts.

(B) They allowed vulnerable, marginal groups to be victimized.

(C) Their mortality rate was lower than that of ordinary citizens.

(D) They strove to preserve social tranquility and justice.

Paragraph 6

S1   Today, in developed countries, it is easy to view the plague as a relic of the medieval past, especially since the disease can be treated with modern antibiotics.

2   However, less celebrated outbreaks regularly occurred in Europe into the eighteenth century.

3   In the nineteenth century, another bubonic plague epidemic killed tens of millions.

4   Much more recently, panic **reminiscent of** the fourteenth century quickly asserted itself when many quickly succumbed during the Ebola outbreak from 2014 to 2016.

12. The phrase "**reminiscent of**" in the passage is closest in meaning to

(A) suspicious of

(B) sensitive to

(C) commemorative of

(D) suggestive of

Paragraph 3

S1   While the fragmentary nature of medieval records has hindered scholars, recent research has caused an upward revision in the already horrific estimate of the mortality rate.

2–3   **A** It is now thought that more than half of the population perished. While some more northern or isolated regions were less afflicted, the Italian cities may have lost as many as 80 percent of their people.

4   **B** All told, perhaps 50 million died, a number comparable with global deaths caused by the Second World War.

5   **C** One of the first acknowledged great books of Western literature, *The Decameron*, chronicles the impact as it describes the plight of a group of Italian gentry that fled to the countryside in a vain attempt to avoid infection.

6   **D** The cities became cemeteries, in which streets were littered with unburied dead, and houses were abandoned or occupied only by the dying.

> Look at the part of the passage that is displayed above. The letters [A], [B], [C], and [D] indicate where the following sentence could be added.

13. **The fictional stories presented therein run the gamut from erotica to tragedy, but most contrast the bucolic countryside to the urban horror.**

Where would the sentence best fit?

(A) Choice A

(B) Choice B

(C) Choice C

(D) Choice D

An introductory sentence for a brief summary of the passage is provided below. Complete the summary by selecting the THREE answer choices that express the most important ideas in the passage. Some sentences do not belong in the summary because they express ideas that are not presented in the passage or are minor ideas in the passage. This question is worth 2 points.

14. **The Black Death, the outbreak of bubonic plague that ravaged Europe in the fourteenth century, not only caused horrific suffering but also altered the course of social history.**

   A The Black Death inspired the poets and writers of the period, spurring a renaissance of Western literature.

   B The plague's devastation created both positive and negative reverberations throughout the social order.

   C When plague-ridden Italians returned from war, trade networks and medical ignorance enabled the epidemic's rapid sweep through Europe.

   D Some areas of Europe, such as Italian cities, were far more afflicted than other areas.

   E More recent plague outbreaks and parallel epidemics imply that modern society is not immune to similar disruptions.

   F In medieval European cities, rats were far more numerous than they are today, and their fleas spread the disease to humans.

6.5 South Asian Carnivores

Large cats, honey badgers, and ants—what do these animals have in common? They dominate their respective subsets of the food chain as carnivores in the jungles of South and Southeast Asia. Among these, cats are probably the most majestic, the most dangerous, and the most vulnerable to extinction. All cats are carnivores and "apex predators," meaning that they are at the top of the food chain in their own ecosystem and have no predators themselves. Perhaps the most impressive of the wild cats in Asia are the tigers. With red-orange fur, vertical black stripes, and a white underbelly, tigers are easily recognizable as distinct from other cat species. Their size is also a factor: most tiger species grow to 9 to 11 feet (about 275 to 335 centimeters) in length, and can weigh up to 600 pounds (about 275 kilograms). Tigers may be the most admired of what are known as the "charismatic megafauna"—large animals with broad popular appeal, such as pandas, polar bears, elephants, and lions. As a result, the declining population of tigers is frequently used by environmentalists to call attention to the problem of endangered species.

As recently as a century ago, tigers were commonplace throughout Asia, excluding the Middle East and western Russia. Today, they are found only in small pockets of India, Southeast Asia, and the southeastern edge of Russia. Most of the loss in tiger population and habitat is due to the expansion of the activities of

civilization, such as mining and farming, and to the deforestation that happens concurrently. Still, a significant portion of the population decline is a consequence of the ongoing hunting of both tigers and their prey. Indeed, the Bengal tiger, the most populous of all tiger subspecies, only numbers about 2,500 animals in the wild, though that number has increased slightly in recent years.

Other prominent cat species in South Asia include the leopard, found scattered throughout India, Malaysia, and Thailand, and the snow leopard, found in parts of India, southern China, and Central Asia. Both leopards and snow leopards are strong, powerful animals with a yellowish-grey coat with rosette markings, or dark rings encircled around dots of lighter-colored fur. These cats are typically 4 to 6 feet (about 120 to 180 centimeters) in length, and weigh about as much as a typical adult human. Both animals are ferocious in attacking prey, which consists primarily of smaller mammals: they bite the throat of victims until they suffocate. Like the tiger, the snow leopard is considered an endangered species. By contrast, the leopard has the largest global distribution of any wild cat. It is not yet considered endangered, but many subspecies are considered threatened.

The honey badger is perhaps the most fascinating of all the South Asian carnivores. A misnamed species, the honey badger has little in common with the badgers that are widely distributed in North America, Africa, and Asia; it is much more closely related to weasels. Found throughout India and other parts of Asia, the honey badger is long from head to tail, short in stature, and broad in build, with fast reflexes and thick skin, leaving it with few known predators. A common sighting is that of a honey badger attacking a populated beehive, eating all of the honey available, and escaping completely unscathed. Honey badgers are fast enough to snap the neck of a venomous snake unharmed, with jaws strong enough to easily crack the shell of a tortoise. They can live comfortably anywhere from sea level up to elevations of 13,000 feet (about 4,000 meters).

Finally, despite their small size, weaver ants are a dominant carnivorous species in tropical parts of South and Southeast Asia. Worker ants construct unique canopy nests by connecting leaves with spun silk. These nests can become enormous, with as many as a million worker ants living in a single colony that spans dozens of trees. Interestingly, there is almost no overlap between the two groups of worker ants in a colony: "major workers" are typically about 0.4 inches (1 centimeter) in length, and "minor workers" are about half that size. The division of labor is very clear, as major workers are responsible for expanding the colony and hunting for smaller insect prey, while minor workers tend to the colony's offspring and collect nutritious excretions from smaller insects in or near the colony, in a process known as "milking" or "farming."

> Now answer the questions.

Paragraph 1

S1   Large cats, honey badgers, and ants—what do these animals have in common?

2   They dominate their respective subsets of the food chain as carnivores in the jungles of South and Southeast Asia.

3   Among these, cats are probably the most majestic, the most dangerous, and the most **vulnerable** to extinction.

4   All cats are carnivores and "apex predators," meaning that they are at the top of the food chain in their own ecosystem and have no predators themselves.

5   Perhaps the most impressive of the wild cats in Asia are the tigers.

6   With red-orange fur, vertical black stripes, and a white underbelly, tigers are easily recognizable as distinct from other cat species.

7   Their size is also a factor: most tiger species grow to 9 to 11 feet (about 275 to 335 centimeters) in length, and can weigh up to 600 pounds (about 275 kilograms).

8   Tigers may be the most admired of what are known as the "charismatic megafauna"—large animals with broad popular appeal, such as pandas, polar bears, elephants, and lions.

9   As a result, the declining population of tigers is frequently used by environmentalists to call attention to the problem of endangered species.

1. The word "vulnerable" in the passage is closest in meaning to
    - (A) related
    - (B) susceptible
    - (C) condemned
    - (D) resistant

2. Why does the author mention "charismatic megafauna"?
    - (A) To identify a class of animals that are dissimilar to tigers
    - (B) To call attention to other popular animals
    - (C) To explain why tigers are so popular
    - (D) To explain why environmentalists often refer to them

3. Which of the sentences below best expresses the essential information in the highlighted sentence in paragraph 1? Incorrect choices change the meaning in important ways or leave out essential information.

    (A) Environmentalists call attention to the falling tiger population to raise awareness of species endangerment.

    (B) To highlight the issues of charismatic megafauna, environmentalists draw attention to declines in tiger numbers.

    (C) The population of tigers is falling as a result of the attention directed toward species endangerment by environmentalists.

    (D) The most admired of the charismatic megafauna, tigers call attention to their declining numbers, and more broadly to the problem of endangered species.

Paragraph 2

S1 As recently as a century ago, tigers were commonplace throughout Asia, excluding the Middle East and western Russia.

2   Today, they are found only in small pockets of India, Southeast Asia, and the southeastern edge of Russia.

3   Most of the loss in tiger population and habitat is due to the expansion of the activities of civilization, such as mining and farming, and to the deforestation that happens concurrently.

4   Still, a significant portion of the population decline is a consequence of the ongoing hunting of both tigers and their prey.

5   Indeed, the Bengal tiger, the most **populous** of all tiger subspecies, only numbers about 2,500 animals in the wild, though that number has increased slightly in recent years.

4. Which of the following is NOT mentioned in paragraph 2 as a reason for the decline in the population of wild tigers in Asia?

    (A) The hunting of tiger prey

    (B) Human conflict in the region

    (C) Expanded mining and farming

    (D) Destruction of forested areas

5. The word "populous" in the passage is closest in meaning to

    (A) beloved

    (B) predatory

    (C) numerous

    (D) sparse

Paragraph 3

S1   Other prominent cat species in South Asia include the leopard, found scattered throughout India, Malaysia, and Thailand, and the snow leopard, found in parts of India, southern China, and Central Asia.

2   Both leopards and snow leopards are strong, powerful animals with a yellowish-grey coat with rosette markings, or dark rings encircled around dots of lighter-colored fur.

3   These cats are typically 4 to 6 feet (about 120 to 180 centimeters) in length, and weigh about as much as a typical adult human.

4   Both animals are ferocious in attacking prey, which consists primarily of smaller mammals: they bite the throat of victims until they suffocate.

5   Like the tiger, the snow leopard is considered an endangered species.

6   By contrast, the leopard has the largest global distribution of any wild cat.

7   It is not yet considered endangered, but many subspecies are considered threatened.

6.   Paragraph 3 indicates what about the conservation status of leopards and snow leopards?

   (A) At present, their conservation status is not clearly known to researchers.

   (B) Snow leopards are endangered, while leopards on the whole are not.

   (C) Both species are considered threatened, but not endangered.

   (D) Their status is imperiled by a lack of available prey in the form of smaller mammals.

7.   What is the author's primary purpose in paragraph 3?

   (A) To highlight key differences between the leopard and snow leopard

   (B) To illustrate the importance of the leopard and snow leopard in the food chain

   (C) To outline significant characteristics of two dominant carnivore cats

   (D) To warn of the potential extinction of the snow leopard

8.   The word "ferocious" in the passage is closest in meaning to

   (A) fierce

   (B) coldblooded

   (C) adept

   (D) precise

Paragraph 4

S1   The honey badger is perhaps the most fascinating of all the South Asian carnivores.

2   A misnamed species, the honey badger has little in common with the badgers that are widely distributed in North America, Africa, and Asia; it is much more closely related to weasels.

3   Found throughout India and other parts of Asia, the honey badger is long from head to tail, short in stature, and broad in build, with fast reflexes and thick skin, leaving it with few known predators.

4   A common sighting is that of a honey badger attacking a populated beehive, eating all of the honey available, and escaping completely unscathed.

5   Honey badgers are fast enough to snap the neck of a venomous snake unharmed, with jaws strong enough to easily crack the shell of a tortoise.

6   They can live comfortably anywhere from sea level up to elevations of 13,000 feet (about 4,000 meters).

9. Paragraph 4 mentions all of the following as features of the honey badger EXCEPT:

(A) Its broad build, thick skin, and fast reflexes leave the honey badger with few predators.

(B) It can live at a variety of different altitudes.

(C) It is closely related to the badgers found in North America, Africa, and Asia.

(D) It is capable of raiding a beehive and escaping virtually unharmed.

10. Which of the following facts is most clearly used in paragraph 4 to illustrate the speed of the honey badger?

(A) They can crack a tortoise's shell.

(B) They can kill a poisonous snake while avoiding injury.

(C) They are known to attack full beehives for their honey.

(D) They are found throughout India and other parts of Asia.

6

Paragraph 5

S1   Finally, despite their small size, weaver ants are a dominant carnivorous species in tropical parts of South and Southeast Asia.

2   Worker ants construct unique canopy nests by connecting leaves with spun silk.

3   These nests can become enormous, with as many as a million worker ants living in a single colony that spans dozens of trees.

4   Interestingly, there is almost no overlap between the two groups of worker ants in a colony: "major workers" are typically about 0.4 inches (1 centimeter) in length, and "minor workers" are about half that size.

5   The division of labor is very clear, as major workers are responsible for expanding the colony and hunting for smaller insect prey, while minor workers tend to the colony's offspring and collect nutritious excretions from smaller insects in or near the colony, in a process known as "milking" or "farming."

11. In paragraph 5, what does the author suggest about major workers vs. minor workers among the weaver ant?

    (A) Minor workers are regularly longer than 1 centimeter.

    (B) Minor workers stay within a single tree for most of their lives.

    (C) Major workers ignore the offspring of the colony.

    (D) Building canopy nests is done more by major workers than by minor workers.

12. Paragraph 5 indicates that weaver ants

    (A) use other insects for nourishment in more than one way

    (B) often have difficulty distinguishing between major and minor workers

    (C) use no external materials in constructing their canopy nests

    (D) typically number around one million within a single tree

Paragraph 5

S1–2 Finally, despite their small size, weaver ants are a dominant carnivorous species in tropical parts of South and Southeast Asia. Worker ants construct unique canopy nests by connecting leaves with spun silk.

3 **A** These nests can become enormous, with as many as a million worker ants living in a single colony that spans dozens of trees.

4 **B** Interestingly, there is almost no overlap between the two groups of worker ants in a colony: "major workers" are typically about 0.4 inches (1 centimeter) in length, and "minor workers" are about half that size.

5 **C** The division of labor is very clear, as major workers are responsible for expanding the colony and hunting for smaller insect prey, while minor workers tend to the colony's offspring and collect nutritious excretions from smaller insects in or near the colony, in a process known as "milking" or "farming."

End **D**

Look at the part of the passage that is displayed above. The letters [A], [B], [C], and [D] indicate where the following sentence could be added.

13. **Because the major workers are so effective at their job of killing other insects, weaver ants have been used as a natural form of pest control to protect valuable crop trees for thousands of years.**

Where would the sentence best fit?

(A) Choice A

(B) Choice B

(C) Choice C

(D) Choice D

An introductory sentence for a brief summary of the passage is provided below. Complete the summary by selecting the THREE answer choices that express the most important ideas in the passage. Some sentences do not belong in the summary because they express ideas that are not presented in the passage or are minor ideas in the passage. This question is worth 2 points.

14. **Carnivore cats, honey badgers, and weaver ants have each carved out dominant roles in their South and Southeast Asian habitats.**

   A The tiger, leopard, and snow leopard are at the top of their food chains, but human activities threaten their existence in the wild.

   B The number of Bengal tigers living in the wild has increased in recent years, although only slightly.

   C Weaver ants are exceptional builders with an organized social hierarchy and job specialization.

   D Leopards and snow leopards have a distinctive appearance produced by their circular rosette markings.

   E Honey badgers are strong, fast, fearless, and capable of surviving in many different environments.

   F Honey badgers are dwindling in number in some parts of Asia because of predation by several different species.

6.6 Coal Mining

Coal is an ignitable, or burnable, black or dark brown rock that is generally found within deep layers of sedimentary rock. Coal is formed from peat bogs, or bogs containing dead plant material, that became buried due to flooding, landslides, or earthquakes. Over many years, additional soil and mud gradually layer on top of them, causing both the pressure upon and the temperature of the trapped material to rise. This process eventually transforms it into the hard rock known as coal.

As coal forms, it progresses through a series of stages, called grades, ranging from peat, which is considered the predecessor to coal, to lignite, bituminous, and finally anthracite coal. Each grade of coal is progressively harder and blacker, with a higher carbon content and a lower hydrogen and oxygen content. Peat and lignite coal have a few special applications, while bituminous coal is mostly used in electric power generation and the production of coke, a low-impurity fuel that burns very hot and is thus suitable for smelting metals. Anthracite coal is primarily used as an indoor heating fuel.

For at least 6,000 years, coal has been used for various purposes, starting with the use of black lignite for carving into ornaments in China. In Britain, coal has been used at least to some extent as a fuel source for over 5,000 years. Today, about half of the coal produced globally comes from China, with most of the rest produced in the United States, India, Australia, and Europe. In total, about 8 billion metric tons (8 trillion kilograms) of coal is produced and consumed annually worldwide.

Coal is extracted from the ground via coal mining, which can be divided into two categories: surface mining and underground mining. Strip, or "open cut," mining is primarily used for surface mining,

because it recovers a larger proportion of the available coal deposits. With this method, deep chunks of earth are razed, with the "overburden," or rock and soil covering the deposits, removed via explosives, power shovels, and trucks. Once the coal is exposed, it is then ruptured into strips and transported to coal refineries or directly to sites where it will be consumed. Contour mining and mountaintop removal mining are surface mining techniques that are comparable to strip mining, but are typically directed toward coal deposits found underneath the slope of a hill or inside a mountain.

Underground mining is more prevalent than strip mining, as most coal deposits are too far below the surface to make strip mining practical. In underground mining, deep vertical shafts are drilled, with coal miners and equipment descending down the shafts to extract the coal in the horizontal deposits found between and around the shafts. As coal is removed, the weight of the rock and soil above the coal deposits, known as the "mine roof," becomes supported more and more tenuously. Thus, hydraulic "roof supports" are positioned to buttress the ground above the mines in order to prevent dangerous cave-ins. Once the mining operation is completed, these roof supports are removed, and in most cases the mine roof eventually collapses.

While safety measures have evolved considerably over the past century, coal mining is still considered a dangerous occupation. Between 1900 and 1999, over 100,000 coal miners perished in the United States alone. Roof collapse, gas explosions, gas poisoning, wall failure, coal dust explosions, and suffocation are among the many reasons for these deaths. Moreover, the use of coal causes a number of serious health and environmental problems. Lung cancer and "black lung" can be caused by the burning and mining of coal, while the ashes from burnt coal contain poisonous heavy metals that can leak into the ground and atmosphere. Coal-fired power plants contaminate soil and groundwater and can lead to acid rain, which can harm ecosystems hundreds of miles away. Coal is also a primary contributor to the rise of "greenhouse gases," such as carbon dioxide, which can lead to global climate change. While "clean coal" technologies can reduce or remove some of these threats, many such technologies will take decades to implement, and questions remain about whether it will ever be economically or politically possible to do so.

6

Now answer the questions.

Paragraph 1

S1   Coal is an ignitable, or burnable, black or dark brown rock that is generally found within deep layers of sedimentary rock.

2   Coal is formed from peat bogs, or bogs containing dead plant material, that became buried due to flooding, landslides, or earthquakes.

3   Over many years, additional soil and mud gradually layer on top of them, causing both the pressure upon and the temperature of the trapped material to rise.

4   This process eventually transforms it into the hard rock known as coal.

1. According to paragraph 1, how does the material of peat bogs turn into coal?

    (A) The material becomes trapped on top of the soil, and low pressure and high temperatures turn it into coal.

    (B) The material becomes trapped on top of the soil, and high pressure and temperatures turn it into coal.

    (C) The material becomes trapped under the soil, and high pressure and temperatures turn it into coal.

    (D) The material becomes trapped under the soil, and low pressure and temperatures turn it into coal.

Paragraph 2

P2 S1 As coal forms, it progresses through a series of stages, called grades, ranging from peat, which is considered the predecessor to coal, to lignite, bituminous, and finally anthracite coal.

2 Each grade of coal is progressively harder and blacker, with a higher carbon content and a lower hydrogen and oxygen content.

3 Peat and lignite coal have a few special applications, while bituminous coal is mostly used in electric power generation and the production of coke, a low-impurity fuel that burns very hot and is thus suitable for smelting metals.

4 Anthracite coal is primarily used as an indoor heating fuel.

Paragraph 3

P3 S1 For at least 6,000 years, coal has been used for various purposes, starting with the use of black lignite for carving into ornaments in China.

2 In Britain, coal has been used at least to some extent as a fuel source for over 5,000 years.

3 Today, about half of the coal produced globally comes from China, with most of the rest produced in the United States, India, Australia, and Europe.

4 In total, about 8 billion metric tons (8 trillion kilograms) of coal is produced and consumed annually worldwide.

2. According to paragraphs 2 and 3, all of the following are true of various grades of coal EXCEPT:

    (A) Peat and lignite coal are used in electric power generation.

    (B) The first known use of coal was of lignite found in China.

    (C) Anthracite is the hardest and darkest form of coal.

    (D) Coke, used in smelting, is made using bituminous coal.

3. According to paragraph 3, what role does China play in worldwide coal consumption and production?

    (A) China is the leading global exporter of coal.

    (B) China is the global leader in coal production but not coal consumption.

    (C) China consumes about 4 billion metric tons (4 trillion kilograms) of coal annually.

    (D) China produces about 4 billion metric tons (4 trillion kilograms) of coal annually.

4. The word "progressively" in the passage is closest in meaning to

    (A) gradually

    (B) liberally

    (C) markedly

    (D) sharply

Paragraph 4

S1   Coal is extracted from the ground via coal mining, which can be divided into two categories: surface mining and underground mining.

2   Strip, or "open cut," mining is primarily used for surface mining, because it recovers a larger proportion of the available coal deposits.

3   With this method, deep chunks of earth are razed, with the "overburden," or rock and soil covering the deposits, removed via explosives, power shovels, and trucks.

4   Once the coal is exposed, it is then ruptured into strips and transported to coal refineries or directly to sites where it will be consumed.

5   Contour mining and mountaintop removal mining are surface mining techniques that are comparable to strip mining, but are typically directed toward coal deposits found underneath the slope of a hill or inside a mountain.

6

5. The word "ruptured" in the passage is closest in meaning to

    (A) mended

    (B) arranged

    (C) cracked

    (D) fashioned

6. The phrase "this method" in the passage refers to

    (A) coal mining

    (B) underground mining

    (C) surface mining

    (D) strip mining

Paragraph 5

S1 Underground mining is more prevalent than strip mining, as most coal deposits are too far below the surface to make strip mining practical.

2   In underground mining, deep vertical shafts are drilled, with coal miners and equipment descending down the shafts to extract the coal in the horizontal deposits found between and around the shafts.

3   As coal is removed, the weight of the rock and soil above the coal deposits, known as the "mine roof," becomes supported more and more tenuously.

4   Thus, hydraulic "roof supports" are positioned to buttress the ground above the mines in order to prevent dangerous cave-ins.

5   Once the mining operation is completed, these roof supports are removed, and in most cases the mine roof eventually collapses.

7. Which of the sentences below best expresses the essential information in the highlighted sentence in paragraph 5? Incorrect choices change the meaning in important ways or leave out essential information.

    (A) The weight of the "mine roof," or rock and soil above the coal deposits, becomes increasingly unsupported as coal is removed.

    (B) As coal is removed, rock and soil overhead becomes supported more and more weakly, in a process known as the "mine roof."

    (C) As it is removed, the coal becomes more shakily supported because of the weight of the "mine roof," or rock and soil above.

    (D) As the weight of rock and soil above the deposits is removed, coal from the "mine roof" becomes less solidly supported.

8. According to paragraph 5, risk of collapse of the mine roof during underground mining is

    (A) eliminated by permanent hydraulic roof supports

    (B) temporarily mitigated by hydraulic roof supports

    (C) buttressed by hydraulic roof supports

    (D) increased by positioning hydraulic roof supports

Paragraph 6

S1   While safety measures have evolved considerably over the past century, coal mining is still considered a dangerous occupation.

2   Between 1900 and 1999, over 100,000 coal miners perished in the United States alone.

3   Roof collapse, gas explosions, gas poisoning, wall failure, coal dust explosions, and suffocation are among the many reasons for these deaths.

4   Moreover, the use of coal causes a number of serious health and environmental problems.

5   Lung cancer and "black lung" can be caused by the burning and mining of coal, while the ashes from burnt coal contain poisonous heavy metals that can leak into the ground and atmosphere.

6   Coal-fired power plants contaminate soil and groundwater and can lead to acid rain, which can harm ecosystems hundreds of miles away.

7   Coal is also a primary contributor to the rise of "greenhouse gases," such as carbon dioxide, which can lead to global climate change.

8   While "clean coal" technologies can reduce or remove some of these threats, many such technologies will take decades to implement, and questions remain about whether it will ever be economically or politically possible to do so.

6

9.   The author mentions coal dust explosions in paragraph 6 in order to
   (A) introduce a possible use for coal
   (B) provide an example of an occupational hazard
   (C) explain how coal-fired power plants operate
   (D) surface a reason for concern about greenhouse gases

10. The word "contaminate" in the passage is closest in meaning to
   (A) fertilize
   (B) extract
   (C) pollute
   (D) exhaust

11. Which of the following is mentioned in paragraph 6 as one of the ways in which the combustion of coal can cause health problems?
   (A) Greenhouse gas release
   (B) Heavy metal leakage
   (C) Suffocation
   (D) Failure of mine walls

Paragraph 5

S1–2   Underground mining is more prevalent than strip mining, as most coal deposits are too far below the surface to make strip mining practical. In underground mining, deep vertical shafts are drilled, with coal miners and equipment descending down the shafts to extract the coal in the horizontal deposits found between and around the shafts.

3   **A** As coal is removed, the weight of the rock and soil above the coal deposits, known as the "mine roof," becomes supported more and more tenuously.

4   **B** Thus, hydraulic "roof supports" are positioned to buttress the ground above the mines in order to prevent dangerous cave-ins.

5   **C** Once the mining operation is completed, these roof supports are removed, and in most cases the mine roof eventually collapses.

End   **D**

> Look at the part of the passage that is displayed above. The letters [A], [B], [C], and [D] indicate where the following sentence could be added.

12. **This breakdown can lead to earthquakes and an increased likelihood that the ground above the mine could give way.**

   Where would the sentence best fit?

   (A) Choice A

   (B) Choice B

   (C) Choice C

   (D) Choice D

An introductory sentence for a brief summary of the passage is provided below. Complete the summary by selecting the THREE answer choices that express the most important ideas in the passage. Some sentences do not belong in the summary because they express ideas that are not presented in the passage or are minor ideas in the passage. This question is worth 2 points.

13. **Coal, the well-known fuel, is formed as plant material is crushed over many years under deep, growing layers of rock.**

   A | First used for carving ornaments over 6,000 years ago, coal is now produced in vast quantities worldwide for fuel consumption.

   B | Coal's hardest and darkest grade, anthracite, is now principally used as an indoor heating fuel.

   C | Coal is extracted either at the surface by stripping away ground above the deposit or deep underground via vertical shafts.

   D | Coal mining is very dangerous, and society's use of coal has led to serious health and environmental consequences.

   E | China is the leading global producer of coal, with much of the rest coming from the United States, India, Australia, and Europe.

   F | It is probable that clean coal technologies will soon reduce the health and environmental threats posed by coal.

6.7 The Sixth Amendment

The Sixth Amendment to the United States Constitution provides a set of rights to people accused of crimes—including, most famously, the right to counsel. This right specifies that people accused of crimes are entitled to be represented by an attorney. It is the most well-known right granted by the Sixth Amendment, and the reason may be that, according to the Supreme Court, it is the most important of the Sixth Amendment rights. In the 1984 case *United States v. Cronic*, which was a case about how to interpret the Sixth Amendment's right to counsel, the Supreme Court wrote, "Of all the rights that an accused person has, the right to be represented by counsel is by far the most pervasive, for it affects his ability to assert any other rights he may have."

Today, the Sixth Amendment entitles all people of any age (including juveniles, or children under the age of 18) to legal representation (an attorney) when they face potential imprisonment through criminal proceedings. The attorney must be available at every "critical stage" of the person's legal case, and the attorney must also provide "effective representation." In the 1963 case *Gideon v. Wainwright*, the Supreme Court ruled that this right must be provided by the states. The states may delegate the obligation to smaller governmental entities within, such as counties and cities, but they must make sure that the counties and cities are able to fulfill their duty, so that the right is not violated by any level of government.

The Sixth Amendment changed the landscape of criminal justice in the United States. Prior to its adoption, criminal cases looked very different. Victims, not government officials (prosecutors), typically brought cases against the people they accused of committing a crime against them. Now, it is the government that brings a criminal case—the victim may be a witness who testifies, but he or she is not one of the two "parties" to

the case. Before the adoption of the Sixth Amendment, typically neither side was represented by a lawyer in a criminal case. Finally, criminal trials were much shorter prior to the Sixth Amendment. Instead of weeks or even months, such trials lasted only minutes or hours. It was when lawyers became integral to the process that trials became longer and increased in complexity.

As the United States criminal justice system expanded and grew more complicated, trials became more expensive to conduct, and the system became congested by the number of cases. It is at least in part for this reason—to save time and money—that the "plea bargain" emerged. A plea bargain is an agreement between the prosecution and the defense. Under the "plea," the defendant agrees to plead guilty or "no contest" in exchange for sentencing for a lesser offense, which generally results in a shorter sentence or less severe penalty.

The trend toward plea bargaining began in the 1800s, but it was in the 1900s that plea bargains began to dominate the criminal justice process in the United States. By the 1930s, 90 percent of convictions were achieved through plea bargains. At that time, federal prosecutions under the Prohibition Act, which outlawed alcohol consumption (among other related things), had become so numerous that the only way of moving cases through the system seemed to be to encourage those accused of minor offenses to accept lighter penalties. Today, that percentage is even higher and includes all levels of offenses, not just minor ones. In 2013, more than 97 percent of federal cases that were not dismissed were resolved through plea bargaining. That means less than 3 percent went to trial. When state cases are added, the combined percentage of cases that are resolved through plea bargains hovers around 90 to 95 percent.

| Now answer the questions. |

6

Paragraph 1

S1 The Sixth Amendment to the United States Constitution provides a set of rights to people accused of crimes—including, most famously, the right to counsel.

2   This right specifies that people accused of crimes are entitled to be represented by an attorney.

3   It is the most well-known right granted by the Sixth Amendment, and the reason may be that, according to the Supreme Court, it is the most important of the Sixth Amendment rights.

4   In the 1984 case *United States v. Cronic*, which was a case about how to interpret the Sixth Amendment's right to counsel, the Supreme Court wrote, "Of all the rights that an accused person has, the right to be represented by counsel is by far the most pervasive, for it affects his ability to assert any other rights he may have."

1. In paragraph 1, what does the author claim about the right to counsel in the United States Constitution?
    - (A) It is the most pervasive of the rights guaranteed by the Sixth Amendment.
    - (B) It is provided both to people accused of crimes and to people suspected of crimes.
    - (C) It is the most important of all the rights guaranteed by the Constitution.
    - (D) It is the most well-known right of those guaranteed by the Sixth Amendment.

2. Which of the following can be inferred from paragraph 1 about the right to counsel?

    (A) Is it only considered important because of a Supreme Court ruling.

    (B) At times, it can be interpreted by a court.

    (C) It typically depends on the other Sixth Amendment rights.

    (D) It is the primary cause of employment for attorneys.

Paragraph 2

S1 Today, the Sixth Amendment entitles all people of any age (including juveniles, or children under the age of 18) to legal representation (an attorney) when they face potential imprisonment through criminal proceedings.

2   The attorney must be available at every "critical stage" of the person's legal case, and the attorney must also provide "effective representation."

3   In the 1963 case *Gideon v. Wainwright*, the Supreme Court ruled that this right must be provided by the states.

4   The states may delegate the obligation to smaller governmental entities within, such as counties and cities, but they must make sure that the counties and cities are able to fulfill their duty, so that the right is not violated by any level of government.

6

3. The word "delegate" in the passage is closest in meaning to

    (A) adjust

    (B) justify

    (C) explain

    (D) assign

4. According to *Gideon v. Wainwright*, the Supreme Court determined that the obligation to provide counsel

    (A) fell to the states, which could in turn delegate it

    (B) had to be directly carried out by the states themselves

    (C) could be met by counties but not by cities

    (D) was primarily a responsibility of federal courts

5. The word "they" in the passage refers to

    (A) states

    (B) counties

    (C) smaller governmental entities

    (D) cities

	Paragraph 3
S1	The Sixth Amendment changed the landscape of criminal justice in the United States.
2	Prior to its adoption, criminal cases looked very different.
3	Victims, not government officials (prosecutors), typically brought cases against the people they accused of committing a crime against them.
4	Now, it is the government that brings a criminal case—the victim may be a witness who testifies, but he or she is not one of the two "parties" to the case.
5	Before the adoption of the Sixth Amendment, typically neither side was represented by a lawyer in a criminal case.
6	Finally, criminal trials were much shorter prior to the Sixth Amendment.
7	Instead of weeks or even months, such trials lasted only minutes or hours.
8	It was when lawyers became integral to the process that trials became longer and increased in complexity.

6. The phrase "integral to" in the passage is closest in meaning to

   (A) committed to

   (B) involved in

   (C) essential to

   (D) ideal for

7. Paragraph 3 states that since the adoption of the Sixth Amendment, the victim of a crime may

   (A) bring a criminal case against the accused

   (B) testify as a witness in the case

   (C) be one of the two parties to the case

   (D) not accuse the possible criminal of committing a crime

8. Which of the following can be inferred from paragraph 3?

   (A) Lawyers were more common in criminal cases after the Sixth Amendment than before it.

   (B) Criminal trials were longer prior to the Sixth Amendment.

   (C) If not for the Sixth Amendment, people accused of crimes would have few rights.

   (D) Lawyers were not at all present in criminal cases prior to the Sixth Amendment.

Paragraph 4

S1 As the United States criminal justice system expanded and grew more complicated, trials became more expensive to conduct, and the system became congested by the number of cases.

2   It is at least in part for this reason—to save time and money—that the "plea bargain" emerged.

3   A plea bargain is an agreement between the prosecution and the defense.

4   Under the "plea," the defendant agrees to plead guilty or "no contest" in exchange for sentencing for a lesser offense, which generally results in a shorter sentence or less severe penalty.

9. Why does the author use the word "generally" in mentioning that pleas result in shorter sentences?

(A) Penalties can be less severe without sentences being shorter.

(B) Exceptions to the rule are more numerous than might be expected.

(C) Shorter sentences are typical but not certain.

(D) Longer sentences are in fact more likely in certain states.

Paragraph 5

S1 The trend toward plea bargaining began in the 1800s, but it was in the 1900s that plea bargains began to dominate the criminal justice process in the United States.

2   By the 1930s, 90 percent of convictions were achieved through plea bargains.

3   At that time, federal prosecutions under the Prohibition Act, which outlawed alcohol consumption (among other related things), had become so numerous that the only way of moving cases through the system seemed to be to encourage those accused of minor offenses to accept lighter penalties.

4   Today, that percentage is even higher and includes all levels of offenses, not just minor ones.

5   In 2013, more than 97 percent of federal cases that were not dismissed were resolved through plea bargaining.

6   That means less than 3 percent went to trial.

7   When state cases are added, the combined percentage of cases that are resolved through plea bargains hovers around 90 to 95 percent.

10. Which of the sentences below best expresses the essential information in the highlighted portion of the passage? Incorrect choices change the meaning in important ways or leave out essential information.

(A) Because of the nature of the Prohibition Act, it became no longer feasible to offer lighter penalties to those accused under it.

(B) Offering lighter penalties to some accused people was used to reduce the large number of prosecutions created under the Prohibition Act.

(C) Under the Prohibition Act, it became impossible to conduct prosecutions, given their number, so offering shorter penalties became necessary.

(D) To fight court congestion, anyone prosecuted under the Prohibition Act was given the option of a lighter penalty via a plea bargain.

11. The word "hovers" in the passage is closest in meaning to

(A) exceeds

(B) increases

(C) drops

(D) remains

Paragraph 5

| S1 | The trend toward plea bargaining began in the 1800s, but it was in the 1900s that plea bargains began to dominate the criminal justice process in the United States. |

2   **A** By the 1930s, 90 percent of convictions were achieved through plea bargains.

3   **B** At that time, federal prosecutions under the Prohibition Act, which outlawed alcohol consumption (among other related things), had become so numerous that the only way of moving cases through the system seemed to be to encourage those accused of minor offenses to accept lighter penalties.

4   **C** Today, that percentage is even higher and includes all levels of offenses, not just minor ones.

5–7   **D** In 2013, more than 97 percent of federal cases that were not dismissed were resolved through plea bargaining. That means less than 3 percent went to trial. When state cases are added, the combined percentage of cases that are resolved through plea bargains hovers around 90 to 95 percent.

> Look at the part of the passage that is displayed above. The letters [A], [B], [C], and [D] indicate where the following sentence could be added.

12. **In fact, even individuals accused of society's most serious crimes are often pressured nowadays to accept plea bargains in order to save cost.**

Where would the sentence best fit?

(A) Choice A

(B) Choice B

(C) Choice C

(D) Choice D

> An introductory sentence for a brief summary of the passage is provided below. Complete the summary by selecting the THREE answer choices that express the most important ideas in the passage. Some sentences do not belong in the summary because they express ideas that are not presented in the passage or are minor ideas in the passage. This question is worth 2 points.

13. **The Sixth Amendment, especially its declaration of the right to counsel, changed criminal justice in the United States.**

A | Prior to the Sixth Amendment, only some people were represented by attorneys, and trials tended to be longer.

B | A famous Sixth Amendment right is the right of a person accused of a crime to be represented by an attorney.

C | The longer a criminal trial goes on, the more costly it is for the government.

D | Today, the vast majority of United States prosecutions end in plea bargains, with defendants accepting lesser penalties.

E | With the Sixth Amendment, criminal trials changed, lengthening as lawyers became involved and the government took over the role of prosecution.

F | In the course of their work, courts must decide how to interpret the Sixth Amendment.

6.8 Signaling Theory

There is a history of controversy within evolutionary biology over why honesty exists in animal communication. All animals, humans included, engage in communication that involves both a sender and a receiver, and this communication occurs both within and across species. The sender communicates a signal to a receiver, who then acts upon that signal. Male peacocks seek to signal their worthiness to females of the species by growing vibrant tail feathers, and gazelles engage in spectacular leaping displays, called stotting, upon seeing approaching predators in order to indicate their athletic prowess and therefore dissuade the predator from attacking.

In some cases, a signal may be honest, meaning that the sender is conveying accurate information, but signals can also be dishonest when the sender is providing false information to a receiver. All signals, however, share the additional feature of being costly to produce and send. A peacock's tail feathers have significant weight and take excessive energy to produce. A bird chirping to alert others in the flock of a nearby predator has now exposed its own location to that same predator, potentially making it more vulnerable to attack.

Biologists have found that, in general, animals communicate with honest signals, but why? Deception would seem to provide short-term gains. For example, the male fiddler crab is known for its one large fighting claw, which it uses to compete for a mate with other male crabs. If a fiddler crab loses its claw in the fight, another claw that is lighter in weight and therefore less effective grows in its place. Although the crab can still scare off other mates with its new claw that is similar in size to the original, it is sending the dishonest signal to other males that it is strong and able to fight, although if challenged it would likely lose. Scientists theorize that signals must be honest on average, at least to a certain degree. If not, the intended receiver would eventually evolve to ignore the signal, rendering it useless. In the early 1970s, biologist Amotz Zahavi proposed the handicap principle: honesty is maintained through handicaps, or high-cost signals, which are naturally more believable.

The handicap principle relies on the assumption that prominent signals of fighting ability or selection may be impossible, or impossibly costly, to fake. For example, a full-grown bull elk's rack of antlers may weigh in excess of 40 pounds, a weight greater than a young, weak, or sickly individual could hope to carry. Therefore, an elk able to grow a large rack of antlers is honestly signaling its ability to defend itself in a fight. Male peacock tail feathers present the same honest signal to females about the male's strength and desirability as a mate. The long tail not only takes significant effort to produce, but also creates issues for survival. The bright colors are more attractive to predators, and the length of the tail somewhat restricts flight and therefore the bird's ability to escape pursuit. As with the elk, a weaker or sicklier bird could not afford to produce such ornamentation. In both examples, the signal of strength is, in actuality, a handicap to the animal sending it.

Thus, these revealing handicaps are honest signals of strength in the sense that some members of the species are better equipped to handle the costs of these handicaps. While most biologists agree on the power of handicaps to maintain honest signaling, the question still debated is that of choice. Are handicaps the result of a genetic condition that allows only certain members of the species to express the handicap fully? Or do they happen when a more capable individual actively chooses to take on a visible hardship and therefore signal to others its underlying strength or abilities?

The condition-dependent model suggests that the level of display of a behavior or trait is directly proportional to genetic quality and environmental conditions and therefore cannot be faked. Some point to bright, iridescent plumage of some bird species as a condition-dependent, and therefore honest, handicap. Without limited physical wear, low parasite load, and a nutritious diet, these shiny feathers are impossible to maintain. The choice model, alternatively, was advocated in 1990 by biologist Alan Grafen, who claimed that all animals have the option to display a large handicap, but each must choose whether and to what extent to display that handicap, according to its knowledge of its own ability level. The optional signal remains honest because low-quality individuals will never signal at a level that is higher than would be advantageous for them, because of the increased cost of those signals.

Now answer the questions.

Paragraph 1

S1   There is a history of controversy within evolutionary biology over why honesty exists in animal communication.

2   All animals, humans included, engage in communication that involves both a sender and a receiver, and this communication occurs both within and across species.

3   The sender communicates a signal to a receiver, who then acts upon that signal.

4   Male peacocks seek to signal their worthiness to females of the species by growing vibrant tail feathers, and gazelles engage in spectacular leaping displays, called stotting, upon seeing approaching predators in order to indicate their athletic prowess and therefore dissuade the predator from attacking.

1. According to paragraph 1, what is true of animal communication?

   (A) It often indicates the athletic prowess of the sender.

   (B) It involves a receiver who acts upon the communication sent.

   (C) Senders and receivers must be of the same species.

   (D) Evolutionary biologists agree on the reasons why it is honest.

Paragraph 2

S1   In some cases, a signal may be honest, meaning that the sender is conveying accurate information, but signals can also be dishonest when the sender is providing false information to a receiver.

2   All signals, however, share the additional feature of being costly to produce and send.

3   A peacock's tail feathers have significant weight and take excessive energy to produce.

4   A bird chirping to alert others in the flock of a nearby predator has now exposed its own location to that same predator, potentially making it more vulnerable to attack.

2. Why does the author mention "a bird chirping to alert others"?

   (A) To point out an example of a dishonest signal

   (B) To illustrate cross-species communication

   (C) To outline the requirements of an honest signal

   (D) To show how some signals are costly to send

3. The word "conveying" in the passage is closest in meaning to

   (A) transmitting

   (B) interpreting

   (C) withholding

   (D) manufacturing

Paragraph 3

S1 Biologists have found that, in general, animals communicate with honest signals, but why?

2 Deception would seem to provide short-term gains.

3 For example, the male fiddler crab is known for its one large fighting claw, which it uses to compete for a mate with other male crabs.

4 If a fiddler crab loses its claw in the fight, another claw that is lighter in weight and therefore less effective grows in its place.

5 Although the crab can still scare off other mates with its new claw that is similar in size to the original, it is sending the dishonest signal to other males that it is strong and able to fight, although if challenged it would likely lose.

6 Scientists theorize that signals must be honest on average, at least to a certain degree.

7 If not, the intended receiver would eventually evolve to ignore the signal, rendering it useless.

8 In the early 1970s, biologist Amotz Zahavi proposed the handicap principle: honesty is maintained through handicaps, or high-cost signals, which are naturally more believable.

---

4. According to paragraph 3, all of the following are characteristics of the replacement claw grown by a fiddler crab EXCEPT:

   (A) It is similar in size to the original claw.

   (B) It is not as heavy as the original claw.

   (C) It is no less effective than the original claw.

   (D) It functions as a dishonest signal.

Paragraph 4

S1   The handicap principle relies on the assumption that prominent signals of fighting ability or selection may be impossible, or impossibly costly, to fake.

2   For example, a full-grown bull elk's rack of antlers may weigh in excess of 40 pounds, a weight greater than a young, weak, or sickly individual could hope to carry.

3   Therefore, an elk able to grow a large rack of antlers is honestly signaling its ability to defend itself in a fight.

4   Male peacock tail feathers present the same honest signal to females about the male's strength and desirability as a mate.

5   The long tail not only takes significant effort to produce, but also creates issues for survival.

6   The bright colors are more attractive to predators, and the length of the tail somewhat restricts flight and therefore the bird's ability to escape pursuit.

7   As with the elk, a weaker or sicklier bird could not afford to produce such ornamentation.

8   In both examples, the signal of strength is, in actuality, a handicap to the animal sending it.

5. According to paragraph 4, the antlers of a full-grown bull elk are useful because

   (A) large, heavy antlers act as an authentic signal of strength

   (B) they allow scientists to estimate the age of the bull elk

   (C) they can be faked by sickly elks, which can then avoid costly fights

   (D) they restrict the elk's ability to escape pursuit

6. The phrase "**in actuality**" in the passage is closest in meaning to

   (A) in theory

   (B) intentionally

   (C) in reality

   (D) unfortunately

Paragraph 5

S1   Thus, these revealing handicaps are honest signals of strength in the sense that some members of the species are better **equipped** to handle the costs of these handicaps.

2   While most biologists agree on the power of handicaps to maintain honest signaling, the question still debated is that of choice.

3   Are handicaps the result of a genetic condition that allows only certain members of the species to express the handicap fully?

4   Or do they happen when a more capable individual actively chooses to take on a visible hardship and therefore signal to others its **underlying** strength or abilities?

7.   The word "equipped" in the passage is closest in meaning to

   (A) exposed

   (B) evolved

   (C) prepared

   (D) disarmed

8.   According to paragraph 5, biologists continue to argue over which of the following with regard to handicaps?

   (A) Whether handicaps are an effective way to maintain honest signaling

   (B) Whether some individuals are better able to handle the costs of handicaps

   (C) Whether all handicaps are honest signals

   (D) Whether capable individuals choose to take on handicaps

9.   The word "underlying" in the passage is closest in meaning to

   (A) tremendous

   (B) physical

   (C) relative

   (D) inherent

Paragraph 6

S1   The condition-dependent model suggests that the level of display of a behavior or trait is directly proportional to genetic quality and environmental conditions and therefore cannot be faked.

2   Some point to bright, iridescent plumage of some bird species as a condition-dependent, and therefore honest, handicap.

3   Without limited physical wear, low parasite load, and a nutritious diet, these shiny feathers are impossible to maintain.

4   The choice model, alternatively, was advocated in 1990 by biologist Alan Grafen, who claimed that all animals have the option to display a large handicap, but each must choose whether and to what extent to display that handicap, according to its knowledge of its own ability level.

5   The optional signal remains honest because low-quality individuals will never signal at a level that is higher than would be advantageous for them, because of the increased cost of those signals.

10. What can be inferred from paragraph 6 about certain birds with shiny, iridescent feathers?

   (A) They are choosing to maintain such feathers as a display.

   (B) They are honestly signaling their good health.

   (C) They are handicapped by low-nutrient diets.

   (D) It is a low-cost signal that can be feigned.

11. Which of the sentences below best expresses the essential information in the highlighted sentence in paragraph 3? Incorrect choices change the meaning in important ways or leave out essential information.

   (A) Because weaker individuals will not choose costly signals, such signals must be honest.

   (B) Higher-quality individuals are the only ones capable of choosing and producing honest signals.

   (C) Weaker individuals will not survive if they choose to display costly signals.

   (D) A chosen signal cannot be considered honest if it does not have an increased cost.

12. The passage mentions which of the following as a dishonest signal?

   (A) A male peacock's long ornamental tail feathers

   (B) The stotting behavior of a gazelle

   (C) A bird chirping in response to a predator

   (D) A fiddler crab's regrown fighting claw

Paragraph 3

S1–2 Biologists have found that, in general, animals communicate with honest signals, but why? Deception would seem to provide short-term gains.

3 [A] For example, the male fiddler crab is known for its one large fighting claw, which it uses to compete for a mate with other male crabs.

4–5 [B] If a fiddler crab loses its claw in the fight, another claw that is lighter in weight and therefore less effective grows in its place. Although the crab can still scare off other mates with its new claw that is similar in size to the original, it is sending the dishonest signal to other males that it is strong and able to fight, although if challenged it would likely lose.

6–7 [C] Scientists theorize that signals must be honest on average, at least to a certain degree. If not, the intended receiver would eventually evolve to ignore the signal, rendering it useless.

8 [D] In the early 1970s, biologist Amotz Zahavi proposed the handicap principle: honesty is maintained through handicaps, or high-cost signals, which are naturally more believable.

> Look at the part of the passage that is displayed above. The letters [A], [B], [C], and [D] indicate where the following sentence could be added.

13. **This dishonest signal, however, appears to be the exception.**

Where would the sentence best fit?

(A) Choice A

(B) Choice B

(C) Choice C

(D) Choice D

An introductory sentence for a brief summary of the passage is provided below. Complete the summary by selecting the THREE answer choices that express the most important ideas in the passage. Some sentences do not belong in the summary because they express ideas that are not presented in the passage or are minor ideas in the passage. This question is worth 2 points.

14. **Why animal signaling is typically honest is a question that many evolutionary biologists have tried to understand.**

[A] Because a weak individual is likely to have a less nutritious diet, its ability to produce a high-cost signal is reduced.

[B] All animals communicate with one another, both within and across species, through signals that carry some cost to send.

[C] It is unclear whether individuals choose to exhibit specific handicaps or whether only some individuals are genetically capable of so doing.

[D] One typical purpose of signals that animals send to other members of their species is to indicate mating desirability.

[E] According to the handicap principle, honest signaling dominates because high-cost signals are more believable.

[F] By 1990, much of the debate over the issue of choice in animal signaling was resolved in favor of the condition-dependent model.

6

Answer Key—6.1 Developmental Plasticity

Question	Correct Answer	Right/Wrong	Category
1	A		Vocabulary
2	D		Fact
3	D		Vocabulary
4	C		Vocabulary
5	C		Fact
6	D		Inference
7	B		Inference
8	D		Fact
9	B		Vocabulary
10	A		Vocabulary
11	A		Fact
12	B		Vocabulary
13	C		Insert Text
14	A, B, F		Summary

Answer Key—6.2 Depletion of California's Aquifers

Question	Correct Answer	Right/Wrong	Category
1	B		Vocabulary
2	D		Fact
3	C		Purpose
4	A		Fact
5	D		Fact
6	B		Vocabulary
7	B		Fact
8	A		Negative Fact
9	C		Inference
10	D		Vocabulary
11	A		Simplify Sentence
12	C		Insert Text
13	B, C, E		Summary

MANHATTAN PREP

Answer Key—6.3 Difference and Analytical Engines

Question	Correct Answer	Right/Wrong	Category
1	B		Vocabulary
2	B		Simplify Sentence
3	A		Fact
4	C		Negative Fact
5	D		Vocabulary
6	C		Purpose
7	B		Vocabulary
8	D		Negative Fact
9	D		Fact
10	C		Vocabulary
11	A		Fact
12	B		Fact
13	C		Insert Text
14	A, C, D		Summary

Answer Key—6.4 The Black Death

Question	Correct Answer	Right/Wrong	Category
1	B		Fact
2	C		Vocabulary
3	D		Purpose
4	A		Vocabulary
5	A		Inference
6	C		Simplify Sentence
7	A		Purpose
8	D		Vocabulary
9	B		Fact
10	B		Vocabulary
11	B		Fact
12	D		Vocabulary
13	D		Insert Text
14	B, C, E		Summary

Answer Key—6.5 South Asian Carnivores

Question	Correct Answer	Right/Wrong	Category
1	B		Vocabulary
2	D		Purpose
3	A		Simplify Sentence
4	B		Negative Fact
5	C		Vocabulary
6	B		Fact
7	C		Purpose
8	A		Vocabulary
9	C		Negative Fact
10	B		Fact
11	D		Inference
12	A		Fact
13	D		Insert Text
14	A, C, E		Summary

Answer Key—6.6 Coal Mining

Question	Correct Answer	Right/Wrong	Category
1	C		Fact
2	A		Negative Fact
3	D		Fact
4	A		Vocabulary
5	C		Vocabulary
6	D		Reference
7	A		Simplify Sentence
8	B		Fact
9	B		Purpose
10	C		Vocabulary
11	B		Fact
12	D		Insert Text
13	A, C, D		Summary

Answer Key—6.7 The Sixth Amendment

Question	Correct Answer	Right/Wrong	Category
1	D		Fact
2	B		Inference
3	D		Vocabulary
4	A		Fact
5	A		Reference
6	C		Vocabulary
7	B		Fact
8	A		Inference
9	C		Purpose
10	B		Simplify Sentence
11	D		Vocabulary
12	D		Insert Text
13	B, D, E		Summary

Answer Key—6.8 Signaling Theory

Question	Correct Answer	Right/Wrong	Category
1	B		Fact
2	D		Purpose
3	A		Vocabulary
4	C		Negative Fact
5	A		Fact
6	C		Vocabulary
7	C		Vocabulary
8	D		Fact
9	D		Vocabulary
10	B		Inference
11	A		Simplify Sentence
12	D		Fact
13	C		Insert Text
14	B, C, E		Summary

6

Answers and Explanations—6.1 Developmental Plasticity

	Paragraph 1	Comments
S1	An organism's biology—its living properties, functions, and behaviors—is partially determined by its evolutionary history, which typically proceeds over the course of millions of years.	Biology of an organism: partly determined by evolutionary history (long).
2	The biology of an organism is also, however, shaped by its unique and much shorter developmental history, which begins when it is conceived and which unfolds over time, accruing particular and relevant events throughout the organism's lifetime.	But also by its developmental history (birth to death).

1. The word "accruing" in the passage is closest in meaning to

    ✓ (A) accumulating

    ✗ (B) celebrating

    ✗ (C) repeating

    ✗ (D) recounting

VOCABULARY. "Accruing" = collecting, gathering up, adding to a collection.

CORRECT. S2: "developmental history ... unfolds over time, accruing particular and relevant events throughout the organism's lifetime" = developmental history unfolds over time, accumulating or gathering up these events throughout the organism's lifetime.

"Celebrate" conveys an unwarranted sense of happiness about the events.

"Repeating" = say again or restate. Events might repeat throughout an organism's life, but that is not the meaning the author intends here.

"Recount" = tell, narrate. The developmental history of an organism doesn't really recount or narrate the relevant events in the organism's life. You would need a person to do so. "Accrue" and "recount" are fairly far apart in meaning.

2. According to paragraph 1, in comparison with an organism's evolutionary history, its developmental history

    ✗ (A) shapes the organism's biology to a greater degree

    ✗ (B) takes millions of years to unfold

    ✗ (C) is typically more universal

    ✓ (D) lasts for much less time

FACT. S1 focuses on evolutionary history; S2 focuses on developmental history. Both affect the biology of an organism.

According to P1, both evolutionary history and developmental history "shape" or "determine" the organism's biology. But no comparison is made. You are not told whether one type of history shapes the organism more.

S1 states that this is true of evolutionary history. No such claim is made about developmental history.

S2 points out that an organism's developmental history is unique. In other words, it is not universal. No such adjective is used to describe the organism's evolutionary history.

CORRECT. S2: "its ... much shorter developmental history." The comparison is to the organism's evolutionary history from S1.

  MANHATTAN PREP

Paragraph 2	Comments
S1 The developmental history of an organism is subject to changes in its environment.	Developmental history depends on environment.
2 This is nature's way of allowing an organism to be adaptive more quickly than through genetic evolution, which occurs at a very slow pace.	Allows more rapid adaptation than evolution does.
3 In the early 1890s, German-American anthropologist Franz Boas (1858–1942) coined the term "developmental plasticity" to describe this concept of rapid non-evolutionary adaptation.	"Developmental plasticity."

3.   The word "coined" in paragraph 2 is closest in meaning to

VOCABULARY. "Coin" (a term or phrase) = invent it, think it up.

✗ (A) understood

Boas certainly "understood" the term, because he invented it, but these words are not related.

✗ (B) quoted

"Quoted" would mean that someone *else* thought up the term.

✗ (C) employed

"Coin" and "employ" (= use) are not synonyms. You can employ a phrase you didn't coin, and you can coin a phrase that you don't later employ.

✓ (D) created

CORRECT. "Franz Boas … coined the term 'developmental plasticity'" = he created the term.

Paragraph 3	Comments
S1 Developmental plasticity takes place from the very beginning of an organism's development; for mammals, it starts inside the womb, or *in utero*.	Developmental plasticity starts in the womb for mammals.
2 An example of *in utero* developmental plasticity occurs among field mice.	Example: field mice.
3 Signals that the mouse receives from its mother while it is still unborn will determine the thickness of the mouse's fur coat.	Signals tell the fetus how thick its fur coat should be.
4 It is conjectured that these signals are communicating to the unborn mouse what season it is in order to prepare it for its future environment.	It's thought that this prepares the mouse for its future environment.
5 Such signaling would improve the survival rates of the offspring.	Improves survival rate.

4.   The word "conjectured" in the passage is closest in meaning to

   ✗ (A) known

   ✗ (B) reported

   ✓ (C) theorized

   ✗ (D) contrived

VOCABULARY. "Conjecture" = guess in an educated way, hypothesize.

Too strong. "Conjecture" means "guess using evidence," not "know for sure."

A conjecture and a report are both somewhat uncertain, but in different ways.

CORRECT. "It is conjectured" = it is theorized or hypothesized.

"Contrive" = create or fabricate, implying that the idea is completely made up.

Paragraph 4	Comments
S1 Human beings also experience developmental plasticity in the womb.	Developmental plasticity also starts for humans in the womb.
2 If a human fetus is deprived of nutrition *in utero*, the fetus will respond by channeling vital energy to the heart and brain while deprioritizing the development of other, less vital organs.	Fetus deprived of nutrition channels energy to heart and brain away from less vital organs.
3 The result is that the development of these other features, such as limbs and overall size, is slowed down, and the child is born smaller.	Smaller child.
4 Smaller newborns have higher rates of mortality.	Higher mortality (= death rate).
5 This particular example illustrates that sometimes, what promotes survival during one developmental stage can become damaging, or "maladaptive," later on.	What can help you survive one stage can hurt you later.

5.   Paragraph 4 indicates that being born smaller

   ✗ (A) is typically the result of poor nutrition *in utero*

   ✗ (B) deprives vital organs of critical nutrition

   ✓ (C) puts infants at greater risk of death

   ✗ (D) can lead to health problems in adulthood

FACT. S3 describes a child being born smaller. S2 gives a reason, and S3 outlines a consequence.

The passage says that poor fetal nutrition can lead to smaller size at birth. But you don't know whether smaller size is always or even typically the result of poor fetal nutrition.

On the contrary, the passage says that children are born smaller when vital organs are prioritized.

CORRECT. S4: "Smaller newborns have higher rates of mortality" = smaller newborns have greater risk of death.

Adulthood is not mentioned.

MANHATTAN PREP

6. The last sentence of paragraph 4 supports which of the following statements?

INFERENCE. S5 states that what is good for survival at one stage in a lifetime can sometimes be bad for survival later on. The correct answer must be clearly supported by this idea.

✗ (A) When an organism is born, it has attributes that will later prove to be maladaptive.

This outcome may sometimes occur in specific instances. But S5 does not support the claim that this is *always* the case.

✗ (B) The suffering of an organism through a difficult stage of life makes it more capable of handling later challenges.

This popular idea ("what doesn't kill you makes you stronger") is not supported by S5. If anything, S5 argues the opposite: what doesn't kill you (e.g., poor nutrition *in utero*) can wind up hurting you later.

✗ (C) Organisms cannot distinguish between what they need and what they do not need in order to survive.

S5 does not support this point. Even if S5 is true, it's not necessarily the case that organisms cannot distinguish between survival needs and non-needs.

✓ (D) An organism's survival needs may change over the course of its lifetime.

CORRECT. If S5 is true, then it must be the case that an organism's survival needs can change. S5 indicates that the same factor that caused survival at one stage can be damaging later on. Thus, the needs of the organism must have changed.

Paragraph 5	Comments
P5 S1 Perhaps the most notorious example of developmental plasticity comes from the Dutch Hunger Winter of 1944.	Dutch Hunger Winter: notorious example.
2 Children born to women who experienced the six-month famine while pregnant were smaller, as their development in the womb had prioritized vital organs over other, less vital ones.	Smaller children.
3 But the reason this particular example is so well known is that the effect on birth size did not stop at one generation; the children of the Dutch famine children were also smaller than average.	Also smaller grandchildren. That's why this is a famous example.

Paragraph 6	Comments
P6 S1 While developmental plasticity—the idea that an organism's life experience can alter its biology—is well-established, the idea that a trait derived from the lived experience of a parent can be passed down to its child (and even further, passed down to its grandchild), known as "Lamarckian inheritance," had been dismissed as unfounded until recently.	"Lamarckian inheritance" (passing down the results of lived experience) had been dismissed until recently.
2 It was originally introduced by Jean-Baptiste Lamarck in 1801 but largely abandoned following publication of Charles Darwin's *On the Origin of Species* in 1859.	Introduced in 1801 but mostly abandoned after Darwin.

7.   It can be inferred from paragraphs 5 and 6 that Lamarckian inheritance

INFERENCE. Lamarckian inheritance is introduced as a term in P6 S1. But the example in P5 illustrates the concept well. So the right answer could be anywhere.

✗ (A) is the subject of Charles Darwin's 1801 book *On the Origin of Species*

First, the book was published in 1859. Second, it is true that Darwin's book led to Lamarckian inheritance being discredited. But that does not mean that Lamarckian inheritance is necessarily the *subject* of Darwin's book.

✓ (B) was regarded as incorrect by the scientific community for over a century

CORRECT. P6 states that Lamarckian inheritance was regarded as unfounded after publication of Darwin's book in 1859. This did not change "until recently" (P6 S1). Even with a generous look backwards a couple of decades to "recently," the elapsed time would still be well over a century.

✗ (C) now is viewed as more legitimate than Charles Darwin's theory of evolution

The theory is now viewed more positively than it used to be. But the passage does not state that Lamarckian inheritance is viewed as better than Darwin's theory. Such a comparison is not made.

✗ (D) denies that acquired traits can be passed down through generations

In fact, Lamarckian inheritance embraces the idea of passing down acquired traits (P6 S1).

8.   In paragraphs 5 and 6, what evidence supports the claim that Lamarckian inheritance may not be unfounded after all?

FACT. P5 includes evidence that supports Lamarckian inheritance.

✗ (A) The smaller size of children who were *in utero* in women who experienced the Dutch Hunger Winter

It's not the smaller size of these children that supports Lamarckian inheritance. These children experienced the famine directly and were born smaller as a result of their own lived experience. It's the smaller size of *their* children that's famously interesting (P5 S3) and that supports Lamarckian inheritance.

✗ (B) The publication of Charles Darwin's *On the Origin of Species*

The publication of this book isn't evidence for the possible validity of Lamarckian inheritance.

✗ (C) The prioritization of vital organs over less vital organs in the womb

This prioritization is not given as an example of Lamarckian inheritance, but as an example of developmental plasticity. Lamarckian inheritance would be this same development pattern being passed down to the next generation.

✓ (D) The effects of the Dutch famine on birth size endured to the next generation

CORRECT. P5 S3: "the effect on birth size did not stop at one generation; the children of the Dutch famine children were also smaller than average." This evidence supports Lamarckian inheritance.

Paragraph 7	**Comments**
S1 The concept of Lamarckian inheritance has **reemerged** in recent years, however, as phenomena such as that exhibited by the grandchildren of the Dutch Hunger Winter have come to light, and subsequent research has confirmed that acquired traits can, in fact, be passed down to offspring.	Lamarckian inheritance has reemerged. Dutch example. Also subsequent research has confirmed.
2 Researchers, for example, exposed male rats to acetophenone, a chemical that smells very sweet to the animal.	
3 In conjunction with the substance, the rats received a mild but painful shock to the foot.	
4 After several days of this treatment, the rats had been **conditioned** to fear the smell—when they were exposed to the smell, they froze.	Example: rats learned to fear a specific smell.
5 Both their offspring and their offspring's offspring also demonstrated specific fear of the smell.	Same fear in children and grandchildren.
6 In addition, all three generations also had larger than normal structures that process smell in the brain.	Larger brain areas for smell.

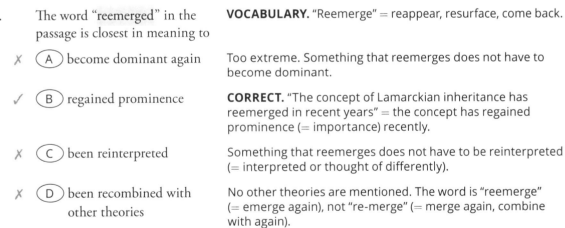

9.   The word "**reemerged**" in the passage is closest in meaning to   **VOCABULARY.** "Reemerge" = reappear, resurface, come back.

✗   (A) become dominant again   Too extreme. Something that reemerges does not have to become dominant.

✓   (B) regained prominence   **CORRECT.** "The concept of Lamarckian inheritance has reemerged in recent years" = the concept has regained prominence (= importance) recently.

✗   (C) been reinterpreted   Something that reemerges does not have to be reinterpreted (= interpreted or thought of differently).

✗   (D) been recombined with other theories   No other theories are mentioned. The word is "reemerge" (= emerge again), not "re-merge" (= merge again, combine with again).

10. The word "conditioned" in the passage is closest in meaning to

VOCABULARY. "Condition" (as a verb) = prepare, train, get ready.

✓ (A) trained

CORRECT. "The rats had been conditioned to fear the smell" = they had been trained to fear it.

✗ (B) unable

This is in a way the opposite. "Conditioned" mice were trained to fear the smell, meaning that not only were they *able* to fear it, they were more likely to do so.

✗ (C) forbidden

Again, this is in a way the opposite. "Conditioned" mice were trained to fear the smell, meaning that not only were they *allowed* to fear it, they were more likely to do so.

✗ (D) permitted

The issue of conditioning or learning is not quite the same as being "permitted" or allowed to do something. It is stronger in a way. They weren't just allowed to feel it, the feeling of fear was actually reinforced.

11. According to paragraph 7, which of the following explains why the rats froze when exposed to the smell of acetophenone?

FACT. S4 states the fact that the rats froze in reaction to the smell. S2–3 describe the experiment.

✓ (A) Previous experience had associated the smell with pain.

CORRECT. S3: "In conjunction with the substance, the rats received a mild but painful shock to the foot." This occurred for several days (S4), in order to strengthen the association between the smell and pain.

✗ (B) Acetophenone has a very sweet, attractive aroma.

This fact about acetophenone (S2) does not explain why the rats froze.

✗ (C) Multiple generations of their offspring displayed the same reaction to the smell.

This is a consequence of the behavior, not the reason for it.

✗ (D) They were taught to connect the smell with the provision of food.

The smell was not connected with food, but with pain.

Paragraph 8	**Comments**
S1 A similar phenomenon has been observed in red-eyed fruit flies.	Another example: red-eyed fruit flies.
2 Researchers in Japan found that when fruit fly embryos were exposed to heat shock, the stress of the shock caused them to be hatched lacking a certain protein involved in gene regulation.	Heat caused embryos to be born without a certain protein.
3 The lack of this protein furnished the flies with particular observable qualities, including red eyes.	This gave them such features as red eyes.
4 The offspring of the male fruit flies who had been exposed to the heat (and who therefore lacked the protein) also lacked the protein, and consequently, these offspring also had red eyes.	Offspring also had red eyes.

12. The word "furnished" in the passage is closest in meaning to

   ✗ Ⓐ endangered

   ✓ Ⓑ supplied

   ✗ Ⓒ encumbered

   ✗ Ⓓ disguised

VOCABULARY. "Furnish" = provide, supply, equip.

"Endanger" = put something at risk. This changes the meaning of the sentence drastically. Saying that "the lack of this protein *furnished* the flies with particular observable qualities" is very different from saying that same lack of protein put those flies in danger.

CORRECT. "The lack of this protein furnished the flies with particular observable qualities" = the lack of the protein supplied the flies with particular qualities.

"Encumber" = burden, hamper. The word has a clearly negative meaning. But "furnish" is neutral to positive. The qualities provided to the fruit flies were not necessarily burdens.

Observable traits could make the flies unrecognizable, but that is not the meaning of "furnish." These words are unrelated.

6

Paragraph 3	**Comments**

S1 Developmental plasticity takes place from the very beginning of an organism's development; for mammals, it starts inside the womb, or *in utero*.

2 **A** An example of *in utero* developmental plasticity occurs among field mice.

Nothing about "the mouse" or the situation in general has been clarified yet.

3 **B** Signals that the mouse receives from its mother while it is still unborn will determine the thickness of the mouse's fur coat.

"Mice" have been introduced, but the situation has still not been clarified. Introducing seasons would be confusing here.

4–5 **C** It is conjectured that these signals are communicating to the unborn mouse what season it is in order to prepare it for its future environment. Such signaling would improve the survival rates of the offspring.

CORRECT. S3 states that the mother sends signals to the fetus about the season of the year, which will determine the thickness of its coat. That is the situation. The new sentence fits well immediately afterward, where it can elaborate on what those signals specifically are.

End **D**

This position is too separated from the specific description in S3 (the mouse fetus receiving signals about how thick its coat should be).

13. **If the season of the year is colder, the mouse will be born with a thicker coat; on the other hand, if the season is warmer, the mouse's coat at birth will not be as thick.**

INSERT TEXT. The previous text should make the context of this new sentence make sense. Terms that imply prior knowledge on the part of the reader, such as "the mouse," need to be introduced earlier. Moreover, the new sentence delineates two cases (colder season and warmer season). What is the situation that these two cases are cases *of*? That should be clear immediately before the insertion.

Where would the sentence best fit?

✗ (A) Choice A

✗ (B) Choice B

✓ (C) Choice C   **CORRECT.**

✗ (D) Choice D

Whole Passage	Comments
P1 An organism's biology—its living properties, functions, and behaviors—is partially determined by its evolutionary history …	Biology of an organism: partly determined by evolutionary history (long). But also by its developmental history (birth to death).
P2 The developmental history of an organism is subject to changes in its environment …	Developmental history depends on environment. Allows more rapid adaptation than evolution does. "Developmental plasticity."
P3 Developmental plasticity takes place from the very beginning of an organism's development; for mammals, it starts inside the womb, or *in utero* …	Developmental plasticity starts in the womb for mammals. Example: field mice. Signals tell the fetus how thick its fur coat should be. It's thought that this prepares the mouse for its future environment. Improves survival rate.
P4 Human beings also experience developmental plasticity in the womb …	Developmental plasticity also starts for humans in the womb. Fetus deprived of nutrition channels energy to heart and brain away from less vital organs. Smaller child. Higher mortality (= death rate). What can help you survive one stage can hurt you later.
P5 Perhaps the most notorious example of developmental plasticity comes from the Dutch Hunger Winter of 1944 …	Dutch Hunger Winter: notorious example. Smaller children. Also smaller grandchildren. That's why this is a famous example.
P6 While developmental plasticity—the idea that an organism's life experience can alter its biology—is well-established …	"Lamarckian inheritance" (passing down the results of lived experience) had been dismissed until recently. Introduced in 1801 but mostly abandoned after Darwin.
P7 The concept of Lamarckian inheritance has reemerged in recent years, however, as phenomena such as that exhibited by the grandchildren of the Dutch Hunger Winter have come to light …	Lamarckian inheritance has reemerged. Dutch example. Also subsequent research has confirmed. Example: rats learned to fear a specific smell. Same fear in children and grandchildren. Larger brain areas for smell.
P8 A similar phenomenon has been observed in red-eyed fruit flies …	Another example: red-eyed fruit flies. Heat caused embryos to be born without a certain protein. This gave them such features as red eyes. Offspring also had red eyes.

6

14. **Developmental plasticity refers to the way an organism's biology adjusts to its environment during its lifetime.**

SUMMARY. Correct answers must be clearly expressed in the passage. They must also be among the major points of the passage. They should tie as directly as possible to the summary given.

✓ [A] It seems that certain acquired traits can be passed down to the offspring of an organism.

CORRECT. This important idea (Lamarckian inheritance) is discussed through the last several paragraphs of the passage.

✓ [B] Various species exhibit developmental plasticity, including in early stages of growth after conception.

CORRECT. The passage discusses how field mice (P3), humans (P4–5), rats (P7), and even fruit flies (P8) display developmental plasticity, in many cases even before they are born or hatched.

✗ [C] Fruit flies are more developmentally plastic than most other insects.

This point is not made in the passage at all.

✗ [D] Field mice fetuses are unlikely to grow coats of fur at all unless they receive signals from their mothers to do so.

While the thickness of the coat of fur is determined by signals from the mother, you are not told that fur would not grow at all based on these signals (P3).

✗ [E] During the Dutch Hunger Winter of 1944, a six-month famine occurred in which many people starved.

This information is provided in the passage as background for an important example (P7). But in and of itself, it is not a central idea of this passage.

✓ [F] Once banished, Lamarckian inheritance has resurfaced as a result of new research, including studies of animals and humans.

CORRECT. This core idea occupies much of the passage. P6 introduces Lamarckian inheritance and states that it was dismissed for a long time. P7 describes its reemergence through examination of human phenomena (the Dutch Hunger Winter) and through animal research (rats exposed to a smell). P8 gives another animal example (fruit flies).

6

Answers and Explanations—
6.2 Depletion of California's Aquifers

	Paragraph 1	Comments
S1	California became an important center of agriculture in the United States in the second half of the nineteenth century, as the gold rush of the 1850s faded and residents discovered that the land was ideal for growing wheat and, later, a variety of crops.	California became agricultural center in 19th century.
2	California now produces more than half of the fresh fruit and vegetables grown in the United States.	Now produces >1/2 of US fruit & vegetables.
3	Most of the industry is located in the Central Valley, which covers approximately 57,000 square kilometers and spans more than half the state.	
4	The Central Valley and most of the coastal regions of California have a Mediterranean climate, with ample sunshine and warm temperatures.	
5	These attributes are ideal for most types of farming.	Ideal sunshine, warmth.
6	However, Mediterranean climates usually have relatively low rainfall.	But low rainfall.
7	While the Central Valley has an enormous watershed, the massive amount of food produced there, to say nothing of California's large population and industry, requires more water than is available from rainfall and snowfall.	Need more water than available from rain & snow.

6

1. The word "massive" in the passage is closest in meaning to

VOCABULARY. "Massive" = enormous, immense, having a lot of mass or size.

✗ (A) cumbersome

"Cumbersome" = burdensome, complicated. A heavy or bulky amount of something can be cumbersome, because it is awkward to move. But that is not the sense intended here.

✓ (B) colossal

CORRECT. "The massive amount of food produced there" = the colossal or enormous amount of food produced in California.

✗ (C) diminutive

Opposite. "Diminutive" = extremely or unusually small.

✗ (D) precipitous

Unrelated. "Precipitous" = sudden and dramatic, dangerously high or steep.

2. According to paragraph 1, agriculture in California is especially important today for which of the following reasons?

FACT. S1–3 briefly discuss the history and importance of California's agriculture.

✗ (A) When the gold rush of the 1850s faded, many people turned to agriculture in California, especially in the Central Valley.

S1–4 discuss this history, which explains the importance of agriculture in California in the second half of the nineteenth century. But the question asks about agriculture's present-day importance.

✗ (B) The amount of water consumed by agriculture is larger than that consumed by the rest of California's population and industry.

S7 mentions agriculture, population, and industry as the consumers of water resources. But the paragraph does not indicate the relative amounts consumed by each.

✗ (C) California has bountiful sunshine and warm temperatures, which are ideal for most types of farming.

These points, conveyed in S4–5, explain why California has so much agriculture. They do not explain why that agriculture is so important.

✓ (D) More than half of the fresh fruit and vegetables grown in the United States come from there.

CORRECT. S2–3: "California now produces more than half of the fresh fruit and vegetables grown in the United States." That is, the country depends on Californian agriculture.

Paragraph 2	**Comments**
S1 As a result, much of California's water demand is met via groundwater, which can be found in hundreds of pools located in layers of rock beneath the land surface.	Groundwater meets much of the demand.
2 These reserves are known as aquifers.	Aquifers.
3 Aquifers in California have slowly accumulated for thousands of years and are enormous—geological studies indicate that California has over 850 million acre-feet of water in its known groundwater reserves.	Huge, accumulated over thousands of years.
4 About half of this is usable, and the usable portion is, in total, larger than Lake Erie.	

3. The author mentions "Lake Erie" in the passage for what reason?

PURPOSE. S3–4 state that "California has over 850 million acre-feet of water in its known groundwater reserves. About half of this is usable, and the usable portion is, in total, larger than Lake Erie." Whether you are familiar with this particular lake or not, this "Lake Erie" reference helps highlight the enormous amount of usable water underground in California.

✗ (A) To explain the source of the underground water

Nothing in the paragraph indicates that the underground water in California is in any way physically connected to Lake Erie.

✗ (B) To demonstrate the amount of water that cannot be used

S4 does mention that about half of the underground water is unusable. But the emphasis of the paragraph is the amount of underground water that *can* be used.

✓ (C) To emphasize the immensity of underground water available in California

CORRECT. S3–4: "Aquifers ... have slowly accumulated for thousands of years and are enormous ... the usable portion is, in total, larger than Lake Erie." This comparison provides a concrete benchmark by which to grasp the total size of California's aquifers.

✗ (D) To provide an example of one well-known aquifer in California

Aquifers are found underground, as defined in the paragraph. From the name alone, you can safely assume that Lake Erie is above ground. More importantly, whether you know that Lake Erie is not in California, it would make no sense to compare the usable portion of California's aquifers (if you assumed it *was* an aquifer) to one of its own aquifers.

4. According to paragraph 2, which of the following is true of aquifers in general?

FACT. S1–2 define what aquifers are. S3–4 discuss California's aquifers.

✓ (A) They accumulate in pools beneath layers of rock.

CORRECT. S1–2: "Groundwater ... can be found in hundreds of pools located in layers of rock beneath the land surface. These reserves are known as aquifers."

✗ (B) They collect above ground before seeping uselessly beneath underground rock.

Aquifers are below ground. You are not told that they collect above ground first. Moreover, at least some water in aquifers is useful, not useless. For instance, S4 indicates that about half of the water in California's known underground reserves is usable.

✗ (C) Almost all of California's water needs are met by aquifers.

S1 states that "much" of California's water demand is met by aquifers, not almost all of that demand.

✗ (D) They are typically enormous, comparable in size to large lakes.

S3 states that "aquifers in California have slowly accumulated for thousands of years and are enormous." But this does not mean that aquifers are typically enormous—only the ones found in California.

	Paragraph 3	**Comments**
S1	However, the water in these aquifers is being consumed much more rapidly than nature can replenish it.	But water is being used up too fast.
2	In a year with typical rainfall and snowfall, only about 2 million acre-feet of groundwater is replaced.	
3	Meanwhile, overdrafting (the amount by which water is removed from aquifers beyond the rate at which it is replenished) has risen substantially.	"Overdrafting" has increased.
4	Some estimates place recent overdrafting at 10 million acre-feet per year.	
5	The amount of annual overdrafting can vary significantly, and it is difficult to control.	Hard to control.

5. According to paragraph 3, which of the following is currently true of overdrafting in California?

  FACT. P3 discusses the problem and severity of overdrafting in California.

✗ (A) It is roughly consistent from year to year.

  S3: "overdrafting ... has risen substantially." S5: "The amount of annual overdrafting can vary significantly, and it is difficult to control."

✗ (B) It is caused by excess rainfall and snowfall.

  S2–3: "In a year with typical rainfall and snowfall, only about 2 million acre-feet of groundwater is replaced. Meanwhile, overdrafting ... has risen substantially." Excess rainfall and snowfall would actually reduce overdrafting.

✗ (C) Its current rate is approximately 2 million acre-feet per year.

  S2 states that about 2 million acre-feet are *replaced* each year. S4: "Some estimates place recent overdrafting at 10 million acre-feet per year."

✓ (D) Government or other entities cannot easily constrain it.

  CORRECT. S5: "The amount of annual overdrafting ... is difficult to control."

6. The word "replenish" in the passage is closest in meaning to

  VOCABULARY. "Replenish" = refill, restock, bring back (a stored amount) to full.

✗ (A) recollect

  "Recollect" does not mean "collect again," unless you are referring to thoughts or memories. "Recollect" means to recall something, to bring it back in your mind.

✓ (B) replace

  CORRECT. "The water in these aquifers is being consumed much more rapidly than nature can replenish it" = the water is being consumed faster than nature can replace it.

✗ (C) retrieve

  "Retrieve" = find and bring back a particular item that was lost or misplaced. That's not what's going on with the water in these aquifers.

✗ (D) remove

  Opposite, in some sense. To replace or add something back is the opposite of removing it (taking it away).

MANHATTAN PREP

	Paragraph 4	Comments
S1	There are two reasons for the variable and unruly nature of the overdrafting.	2 reasons.
2	The first is a severe drought in California that started in 2012.	1) Recent severe drought.
3	Normally, about 30 percent of the water consumed in California comes from groundwater sources.	
4	However, since 2012 the figure has been closer to 60 percent.	
5	Farmers and residents are able to curb their consumption of water somewhat during a drought, but there is a limit to how much reduction can actually be attained.	Can't curb water use too much.
6	In January 2014, California Governor Jerry Brown declared a state of emergency, targeting a 20 percent reduction in water consumption while simultaneously seeking to make more water sources available.	
7	However, consumption of water has fallen by far less than that target and in some areas has actually increased.	Have missed 2014 reduction target.
8	The second reason is that there are no statewide laws governing the use of groundwater.	2) No statewide laws.
9	Each reservoir has different regulations that determine usage rights.	
10	In many cases, there is little restriction on how quickly water may be pumped out.	Little restriction on pumping out groundwater.
11	Groundwater can be removed practically without limitation, provided that it is removed by the owner of the land above it.	

7. According to paragraph 4, which of the following is true of groundwater usage rights?

FACT. S8–11 discuss the regulation of groundwater usage.

✗ (A) They are subject to a universal set of regulations from a central government agency.

S9: "Each reservoir has different regulations that determine usage rights." No mention is made of a central government agency.

✓ (B) They are not governed by laws that cover the entire state.

CORRECT. S8: "there are no statewide laws governing the use of groundwater."

✗ (C) The owner of land with groundwater underneath has little control over that water.

S11: "Groundwater can be removed practically without limitation, provided that it is removed by the owner of the land above it." The owner actually has a lot of control over the groundwater.

✗ (D) The rate at which groundwater can be removed is strictly limited.

S10: "In many cases, there is little restriction on how quickly water may be pumped out."

8.   According to paragraph 4, groundwater preservation in California has been made more difficult by all of the following EXCEPT:

NEGATIVE FACT. The entire paragraph details problems that make it harder to preserve groundwater in California. Three answer choices are provided in the paragraph as problems with groundwater preservation in California. One answer choice is either not mentioned or does not support the question.

✓ (A) The California governor declared a state of emergency to reduce water consumption.

CORRECT. The opposite motivation for this behavior is true. S6 mentions this declaration, but it did not make it harder to preserve groundwater. The goal of this declaration was in fact to try to preserve groundwater or slow its rate of depletion.

✗ (B) California has been experiencing a serious drought for years.

S1 directly mentions this fact as a problem for groundwater preservation.

✗ (C) Government control of groundwater extraction is incomplete and inconsistent.

This problem is discussed at length in S8–11.

✗ (D) Farmers can reduce their use of groundwater only up to a certain point.

S5: "Farmers and residents are able to curb their consumption of water somewhat during a drought, but there is a limit to how much reduction can actually be attained."

9.   Which of the following can be inferred from paragraph 4 regarding Governor Brown's emergency declaration?

INFERENCE. S6–7 state that Governor Brown's declaration targeted "a 20 percent reduction in water consumption while simultaneously seeking to make more water sources available. However, consumption of water has fallen by far less than that target and in some areas has actually increased." A reasonable inference is that this declaration failed to achieve its objectives.

✗ (A) It temporarily halted groundwater depletion.

Nothing in the paragraph indicates that this might be the case. If anything, S6–7 indicate that the declaration had less of an effect than hoped.

✗ (B) It rewrote California regulations concerning groundwater extraction.

S8–11 discuss the regulation of groundwater extraction, but this discussion is separate from Governor Brown's declaration. Furthermore, the discussion in S8–11 indicate that restrictions on groundwater extraction in California are relatively lenient. During the emergency declaration, it's possible that certain regulations were temporarily altered (if at all). But they certainly weren't rewritten in any kind of permanent sense.

✓ (C) It failed to achieve the governor's water preservation goals.

CORRECT. S7: "However, consumption of water has fallen by far less than that target and in some areas has actually increased." The direct implication is that the emergency declaration did not achieve the Governor's goals for water preservation.

✗ (D) It coincided with the ending of the previously mentioned drought.

Nowhere in the paragraph is it mentioned or implied that the drought ended during the time discussed.

Paragraph 5	Comments
S1 Should California's groundwater crisis continue unabated, it could become a disaster.	If the crisis continues, it could be a disaster.
2 Depleted aquifers can give rise to a lowering of the water table, which makes groundwater harder to access.	Lowered water table.
3 They can also cause land subsidence, the physical drop of land because of the removal of water beneath; this phenomenon can destroy bridges, buildings, and roads.	Land subsidence (physical drop).
4 Water costs could skyrocket, **drastically** affecting crop prices and yields.	Water costs could skyrocket.
5 Because California is such a prominent agricultural producer, these shocks could have far-reaching effects economically and socially.	Far-reaching effects.

10. The phrase "**drastically**" in the passage is closest in meaning to

VOCABULARY. "Drastically" = radically, powerfully, severely.

✗ (A) immediately

"Immediately" implies that the price change would be sudden. But this is not necessarily the case. The change in prices and yields could be very large but occur over a long time.

✗ (B) adversely

Not quite. It's true that in this case, the drastic effects would almost certainly be adverse (= negative, unfavorable) ones, at least from some people's points of view. And "drastic" usually implies something negative. But "drastic" and "adverse" are not synonyms. Adverse effects can be small; they don't have to be drastic.

✗ (C) modestly

Opposite. "Modest" = small, moderate, limited.

✓ (D) radically

CORRECT. "Water costs could skyrocket, drastically affecting crop prices" = water costs could skyrocket, radically affecting crop prices.

6

Paragraph 6	Comments
S1 Numerous attempts to improve management of California's scarce groundwater resources have been made, dating back to 1873, when the first "California Water Plan" was drafted.	Many attempts over the years to improve management.
2 Completed in 2013, the most recent version of this document calls for an integrated approach to managing the state's water resources and preserving groundwater supplies.	Most recent "California Water Plan."
3 The plan suggests improvements in water conservation, recycling of waste water, and provision of financial incentives to reduce usage.	Various suggestions.
4 However, the plan barely forces users to change consumption habits and does virtually nothing to simplify the complex legal web surrounding groundwater extraction.	But it can't really force changes in consumption or legal complexities.

11. Which of the sentences below best expresses the essential information in the highlighted sentence in paragraph 6? Incorrect choices change the meaning in important ways or leave out essential information.

   SIMPLIFY SENTENCE. The first part of S1 states that many attempts have been made to better manage the state's groundwater resources, going back to 1873. The second part of S1 mentions that this original attempt was the first "California Water Plan."

✓   (A) Since the first "California Water Plan" was drafted in 1873, many attempts to better conserve the state's groundwater have been made.

   CORRECT. This version says essentially the same thing as P6 S1, but simplifies the language somewhat.

✗   (B) Many attempts to increase use of scarce groundwater resources have been foiled since 1873, the date of the first "California Water Plan."

   This version changes the core meaning. It states that attempts to increase use of the water have been foiled (= stopped). But the original talks about attempts to conserve the water that have been made.

✗   (C) When the first "California Water Plan" was drafted, several attempts to better manage the state's groundwater resources were made.

   This version implies that the attempts to improve water management occurred at the same time as the "California Water Plan." This changes the meaning of the original sentence, which strongly suggests that the attempts were made over a long period of time.

✗   (D) Many attempts to improve management of the "California Water Plan," the state's groundwater resources, have been made since 1873.

   This version claims that the "California Water Plan" is the same thing as the water resources themselves. That claim is not correct.

Paragraph 2	Comments

P2
S3–4

Aquifers in California have slowly accumulated for thousands of years and are enormous—geological studies indicate that California has over 850 million acre-feet of water in its known groundwater reserves. About half of this is usable, and the usable portion is, in total, larger than Lake Erie.

Paragraph 3	Comments

P3 S1

A However, the water in these aquifers is being consumed much more rapidly than nature can replenish it.

Placing the new sentence here would leave the phrase "this figure" without a noun it can easily refer to in the previous text. At best, you might argue that the figure quantifies the usable portion of California's aquifers ("about half" of 850 million acre-feet). But even that figure makes little sense in the inserted sentence.

2

B In a year with typical rainfall and snowfall, only about 2 million acre-feet of groundwater is replaced.

Placement here would make "this figure" ambiguous. It could refer to either consumption or the rate of replenishment of aquifers.

3–4

C Meanwhile, overdrafting (the amount by which water is removed from aquifers beyond the rate at which it is replenished) has risen substantially. Some estimates place recent overdrafting at 10 million acre-feet per year.

CORRECT. "This figure" logically refers to the amount of annual groundwater replacement. This position also nicely highlights the contrast between the "typical" situation in S2 and the unusual drought situation in the new sentence. In the drought situation, less water is replaced.

5

D The amount of annual overdrafting can vary significantly, and it is difficult to control.

Placing the sentence here creates a contradiction. S4 says that overdrafting is 10 million acre-feet in recent years. But then the new sentence would say that this figure is less than 1 million acre-feet in recent years. This doesn't make sense.

6

12. **Because of the drought in California, this figure is less than 1 million acre-feet in recent years.**

INSERT TEXT. The prior sentence needs to present a quantity that "this figure" can refer to. The numbers should make sense as well. You don't have to do any math, but the figures should not contradict each other, for instance.

Where would the sentence best fit?

✗ (A) Choice A

✗ (B) Choice B

✓ (C) Choice C   **CORRECT.**

✗ (D) Choice D

	Whole Passage	**Comments**
P1	California became an important center of agriculture in the United States in the second half of the nineteenth century …	California became agricultural center in 19th century. Now produces >1/2 of US fruit & vegetables. Ideal sunshine, warmth. But low rainfall. Need more water than available from rain & snow.
P2	As a result, much of California's water demand is met via groundwater, which can be found in hundreds of pools found in layers of rock beneath the land surface …	Groundwater meets much of the need. Aquifers. Huge, accumulated over thousands of years.
P3	However, the water in these aquifers is being consumed much more rapidly than nature can replenish it …	But water is being used up too fast. "Overdrafting" has increased. Hard to control.
P4	There are two reasons for the variable and unruly nature of the overdrafting …	2 reasons. 1) Recent severe drought. Can't curb water use too much. Have missed 2014 reduction target. 2) No statewide laws. Little restriction on pumping out groundwater.
P5	Should California's groundwater crisis continue unabated, it could become a disaster …	If the crisis continues, it could be a disaster. Lowered water table. Land subsidence (physical drop). Water costs could skyrocket. Far-reaching effects.
P6	Numerous attempts to improve management of California's scarce groundwater resources have been made, dating back to 1873, when the first "California Water Plan" was drafted …	Many attempts over the years to improve management. Most recent "California Water Plan." Various suggestions. But it can't really force changes in consumption or legal complexities.

13. **California's nationally important agricultural industry depends to an alarming degree on the use of rapidly decreasing supplies of water underground.**

✗ A The California drought that began in 2012 caused Governor Jerry Brown to declare a state of emergency in early 2014.

✓ B Depletion of the state's groundwater could lead to dire outcomes, such as land subsidence, reduced crop yields, and infrastructure destruction.

✓ C As evidenced by its vast production of fruits and vegetables, California has an ideal agricultural climate, except for its low rainfall.

✗ D California now has proven, usable groundwater reserves that are smaller, in total, than the volume of Lake Erie.

✓ E Farming in California is heavily dependent on groundwater reserves that are threatened by uncontrolled overdrafting.

✗ F Under normal usage and precipitation patterns, about 30 percent of the water consumed in California comes from groundwater sources.

SUMMARY. Correct answers must be clearly expressed in the passage. They must also be among the major points of the passage. They should tie as directly as possible to the summary given.

This event is mentioned in P4. But in the context of the whole passage, it is a single, minor detail.

CORRECT. P5 discusses these serious problems in detail.

CORRECT. P1 presents these facts, which have led to the groundwater depletion problem.

Contradicted in P2 S4: "About half of this [groundwater supply] is usable, and the usable portion is, in total, larger than Lake Erie."

CORRECT. Corresponds to the core of P2 and P3.

This point is mentioned in P4, but it is a relatively minor detail in the context of the whole passage. For instance, it ignores the fact that in recent years, this figure has been closer to 60%.

6

Answers and Explanations—
6.3 Difference and Analytical Engines

Paragraph 1	Comments
S1 The shift in processing power and information storage from human beings to computers over the past several decades represents the most significant change in productivity since the Industrial Revolution.	Shift from humans to computers = biggest change in work since Industrial Revolution.
2 Despite all of the obvious technological improvements in production, manufacturing technique, materials, and engineering, no other innovation can rival computers in terms of their overall impact on the economy.	
3 The most basic dichotomy in information processing today lies between computers on the one hand and human beings on the other.	

1.   The word "dichotomy" in the passage is closest in meaning to

  ✗ (A) comparison

  ✓ (B) contrast

  ✗ (C) contradiction

  ✗ (D) confluence

VOCABULARY. "Dichotomy" = contrast, opposition, or separation between two different things.

"Comparison" emphasizes similarity, not difference.

CORRECT. "The most basic dichotomy in information processing today lies between computers on the one hand and human beings on the other" = the most basic contrast, opposition, or separation in information processing lies between computers and humans.

In a few circumstances, "dichotomy" might go so far as to mean "contradiction" (= logical inconsistency between two things). But here, the dichotomy between humans and computers is not one of literal, logical contradiction. Rather, it is a contrast or opposition.

"Confluence" = the flowing together of two things.

2. Which of the sentences below best expresses the essential information in the highlighted sentence in paragraph 1? Incorrect choices change the meaning in important ways or leave out essential information.

SIMPLIFY SENTENCE. The first part of S2 acknowledges the technological advances in production, manufacturing technique, materials, and engineering that have occurred. The second part of S2 states that they cannot compare to computers in terms of their overall economic impact.

✗ (A) Despite technological improvements in computers, innovations in such areas as production and manufacturing rival them with regard to their economic impact.

This version claims that the other listed items can rival computers in terms of economic impact. The original sentence claims the opposite.

✓ (B) The economic impact of computers is unmatched by that of any technological innovation in other areas such as manufacturing and production.

CORRECT. This choice says essentially the same thing as S2, but changes the order of ideas and simplifies the language.

✗ (C) In spite of developments in production, manufacturing technique, materials, and engineering, none of these are as economically innovative as computers.

The comparison in the original sentence is about overall impact on the economy. But in this version, the comparison is about the degree of "economic innovation," which means something different.

✗ (D) Despite technological improvements in their production, computers cannot match other inventions in terms of their overall impact on the economy.

In the original sentence, computers surpass other inventions with regard to economic impact. Moreover, this version relates the "Despite" part to computers ("their production"), whereas in the original sentence, the contrasted technological improvements were about the other inventions.

6

Paragraph 2	Comments
S1 Interestingly, if a person today were asked, "When was the first computer program ever written?", he or she would probably miss the mark by over a century.	First computer program was written over a century before you might expect.
2 Many might think of the Electronic Numerical Integrator and Computer (ENIAC).	Various early computers.
3 Completed in 1946 at the University of Pennsylvania, ENIAC was the first completely electronic general-use computer.	
4 Others may think of the Universal Automatic Computer (UNIVAC), the first commercially used electronic computer, built in 1951 by the inventors of ENIAC.	
5 Or perhaps one would think of the electromechanical machines that preceded ENIAC, such as those that controlled telephone exchanges in the first half of the twentieth century.	
6 In fact, the first completed computer program dates back to 1843.	But actual first program was written in 1843.
7 It was written by Ada Lovelace (1815–1852), a mathematician and colleague of Charles Babbage (1791–1871), inventor of the "difference engine" and, later, the "analytical engine."	Ada Lovelace. Charles Babbage, who invented the difference & analytical engines.

3. According to paragraph 2, which of the following statements about the first computer program is true?

FACT. S3–5 discuss the first electronic computers ever built. S6–7 point out that the first completed computer program predates those electronic computers by over 100 years.

✓ (A) It was written in the nineteenth century.

CORRECT. S6–7: "the first completed computer program dates back to 1843. It was written by Ada Lovelace (1815–1852)." These dates were in the nineteenth century.

✗ (B) It was written by Charles Babbage.

S7 states that Ada Lovelace was a colleague of Charles Babbage (and the rest of the passage is devoted to discussing Babbage's inventions). But S6–7 clearly state that it was Lovelace who wrote the first computer program.

✗ (C) It was written for ENIAC at the University of Pennsylvania.

S3 states that ENIAC was the first completely electronic general-use computer, but S6–7 later clarify that the first completed computer program came over 100 years before that.

✗ (D) It was written for a completely electronic general-use computer.

S3: "ENIAC was the first completely electronic general-use computer." The first computer program was written over 100 years earlier.

4.   According to paragraph 2, all of the following statements about UNIVAC are true EXCEPT:

NEGATIVE FACT. S4 discusses the background of UNIVAC. Three answer choices will be referenced in the paragraph. One answer choice will not be.

✗ (A) It was built by the creators of ENIAC.

S4: "Others may think of the Universal Automatic Computer (UNIVAC) ... built in 1951 by the inventors of ENIAC."

✗ (B) It was the first electronic computer used commercially.

S4: "Others may think of the Universal Automatic Computer (UNIVAC), the first commercially used electronic computer."

✓ (C) It was an electromechanical machine that preceded ENIAC.

CORRECT. S4 states that UNIVAC was built in 1951, while S3 states ENIAC was built in 1946. Furthermore, nothing in the paragraph indicates that it was "electromechanical," rather than fully electronic.

✗ (D) It was created after machines to control telephone exchanges were developed.

S4 states that UNIVAC was built in 1951, while S3 states ENIAC was built in 1946. S5 mentions "electromechanical machines that preceded ENIAC, such as those that controlled telephone exchanges." Therefore, these machines were developed before UNIVAC was invented.

Paragraph 3	Comments
S1 Babbage was an English mathematician, inventor, and engineer.	
2 He is regarded by many as the father of modern-day computing.	Babbage = father of modern computing.
3 He began work designing the first version of his difference engine in 1822.	1822: started working on difference engine.
4 This mechanical engine was to compute the value of polynomial functions using a mathematical process known as "finite differences."	Mechanical engine to compute math values.
5 Using this method, the difference engine would only be capable of adding and subtracting.	
6 Unfortunately, Babbage ran into difficulties both with funding his project and with the builder of the initial prototype of his design, and the project was **abandoned** partway through.	But he ran into difficulties.
7 Eventually, Babbage shifted to designing what he called the "analytical engine," which drew on his designs for the difference engine but was intended as a more general computing machine.	Shifted to more general "analytical engine."

6

5. The word "**abandoned**" in the passage is closest in meaning to

✗ (A) corrected

✗ (B) continued

✗ (C) shackled

✓ (D) scrapped

VOCABULARY. "Abandon" = leave behind, give up, walk away from permanently.

The project wasn't corrected (fixed) but rather abandoned (given up).

Opposite. To continue is to keep going, while abandon means to quit.

Not quite. "Shackle" = constrain, restrict, restrain. This is not the same as "abandon."

CORRECT. "The project was abandoned partway through" = the project was scrapped or given up partway through.

6. In paragraph 3, why does the author provide the information regarding funding for the initial prototype of the difference engine?

✗ (A) To assert that the difference engine would have been completed with better funding

✗ (B) To acknowledge the resources that made completing the prototype of the difference engine possible

✓ (C) To explain, at least in part, why the prototype of the difference engine was abandoned

✗ (D) To highlight a factor that would be useful as focus shifted to the analytical engine

PURPOSE. S6: "Unfortunately, Babbage ran into difficulties both with funding his project and with the builder of the initial prototype of his design, and the project was abandoned partway through." The author is strongly implying that difficulties with funding (as well as with the builder) led to Babbage's abandonment of the difference engine and his shift in focus to the analytical engine.

S6 indicates that Babbage had difficulties with funding. But nothing in the passage suggests that he could have completed the work with better funding. S6 also notes that Babbage also had separate difficulties with the builder of the prototype.

The prototype of the difference engine was never completed.

CORRECT. S6 directly implies that difficulties with funding led to, or at least contributed to, the fact that Babbage abandoned development of the difference engine.

Perhaps Babbage recognized that he would need better funding sources for his next project. But the passage never makes this claim.

Paragraph 4	**Comments**
S1 The analytical engine featured a new concept called "punched cards," which would contain coded information that the engine would accept as inputs.	"Punched card" inputs.
2 The machine would then produce outputs in the form of a drawn curve, printed output, or additional punched cards to be used later.	Various outputs.
3 The machine would have a unit designed to perform computation and another unit to store information.	Computation and storage.
4 Though the design of these units was mechanical rather than electronic, they are directly **analogous to** the processor and memory found in computers today.	Mechanical, but analogous to electronic components of today's computers.

7.   The phrase "**analogous to**" in the passage is closest in meaning to

    VOCABULARY. "Analogous" = similar, parallel, comparable.

✗   (A) coupled with

    Not quite. "Coupled" = attached, joined. The use of this word would imply physical attachment in this case.

✓   (B) comparable to

    CORRECT. "They are directly analogous to the processor and memory" = they are directly comparable to these parts.

✗   (C) opposed to

    In some ways the opposite. "Antithetical" = opposing, contradictory.

✗   (D) descended from

    These mechanical elements may have been ancestors of components of modern computers. But "ancestral" and "analogous" are not synonyms.

8.   According to paragraph 4, all of the following are design features of the analytical engine EXCEPT:

    NEGATIVE FACT. The entire paragraph is devoted to describing the design of the analytical engine. Three answer choices will be contained in the paragraph. One answer choice will not be.

✗   (A) It would produce punched cards as output.

    S2: "The machine would then produce outputs in the form of ... additional punched cards to be used later."

✗   (B) It would receive instructions via punched cards.

    S1: "The analytical engine featured ... 'punched cards,' which would contain coded information that the engine would accept as inputs."

✗   (C) It would store information and perform calculations.

    S3: "The machine would have a unit designed to perform computation and another unit to store information."

✓   (D) It would contain a basic electronic processor.

    CORRECT. S4: "the design of these units was mechanical rather than electronic."

Paragraph 5	**Comments**
S1 Lovelace's computer program, designed for use on the analytical engine once it was built, was modest by modern standards.	Lovelace's program for the engine: modest to our eyes.
2 It simply entailed a written, step-by-step description of how a machine might compute a mathematical series known as the Bernoulli numbers.	Step-by-step description of how to compute certain numbers.
3 However, as simple as it was, it had all of the traits of a modern-day computer algorithm: a set of instructions to be followed by a computer, operating upon a set of inputs, in order to arrive at a desired set of outputs.	Simple. But all the traits of a modern algorithm.

9. According to paragraph 5, Lovelace's computer program

FACT. S1 states that Lovelace's program was "modest by modern standards." S2 describes its simple purpose. S3 indicates, however, that "it had all of the traits of a modern-day computer algorithm."

✗ (A) appeared ill-suited to compute a mathematical series

S2 states that it was a step-by-step description of how to compute a mathematical series. The paragraph never claims that Lovelace's program was ill-suited to carry out this task.

✗ (B) was eventually used on modern computers

The passage does not state that Lovelace's program was ever used on a modern computer.

✗ (C) was employed to discover the Bernoulli numbers

Lovelace's program was designed to work on the analytical engine once it was built. But with the use of "would" throughout, the paragraph implies that it never was built. Furthermore, the Bernoulli numbers seem to have already been known before she wrote the program. Nothing indicates that her program enabled their discovery.

✓ (D) had the core features of modern algorithms

CORRECT. S3: "it had all of the traits of a modern-day computer algorithm."

Paragraph 6	Comments
S1 Like the original difference engine, Babbage's analytical engine was never completely built.	Analytical engine was never completed.
2 The combination of financial resources and available technology to implement Babbage's blueprint was simply insufficient during his lifetime.	
3 In fact, Babbage worked for decades to simplify his design so that building it would be feasible; he was only able to finish building a small portion of it before his death in 1871.	He built just a small part before he died.
4 Babbage's son, Henry, continued to work on building the analytical engine, and was able to produce some of the desired outputs from the machine.	Son kept working on. Produced some outputs.
5 However, Henry never came close to realizing his father's complete vision.	But never realized the vision.

10. The word "feasible" in the passage is closest in meaning to

VOCABULARY. "Feasible" = possible, practical.

✗ (A) comprehensible

Not quite. Comprehension of the plans would have been necessary for them to be carried out. But comprehension would not have been sufficient. In general, "comprehensible" and "feasible" are not synonyms.

✗ (B) postponable

Unrelated. To "postpone" is to put off or delay.

✓ (C) achievable

CORRECT. "Babbage worked for decades to simplify his design so that building it would be feasible" = he worked to simplify his design so that building it would be achievable or possible.

✗ (D) impossible

Opposite.

11.   Paragraph 6 mentions which of the following as a difficulty facing the construction of Babbage's analytical engine?

FACT. S2 outlines difficulties that Babbage faced in this task.

✓ (A) Adequate technology was not available.

CORRECT. S2: "The combination of financial resources and available technology to implement Babbage's blueprint was simply insufficient during his lifetime."

✗ (B) Babbage's son did not fully understand the design.

Nothing in the paragraph indicates that Henry had difficulty understanding his father's design. In fact, Henry was able to complete portions of it that his father never did.

✗ (C) Babbage's son produced some intended outputs from the machine.

S4 states that Henry was able to do this, but this fact did not impede construction of the analytical engine.

✗ (D) Babbage died prematurely in 1871.

Nothing in the paragraph suggests that Babbage's death was "premature," or that a few additional years of life would necessarily have enabled Babbage to complete construction of the analytical engine. Indeed, Babbage "was only able to finish building a small portion of it before his death."

	Paragraph 7	**Comments**
S1	It was not until 1991, in Australia, that a complete version of Babbage's difference engine was produced.	1991: an actual version of the difference engine was built.
2	The completed "Difference Engine No. 2" implemented Babbage's designs, correcting for some errors (which may have been intentional), and was constructed using only methods that might have been available in the nineteenth century.	Corrected some errors, used only 19th-century methods.
3	The finished machine works exactly as Babbage would have hoped.	It worked!
4	To this day, though, no analytical engine that matches Babbage's later designs has ever been fully built.	No analytical engine has been fully built.

6

MANHATTAN PREP

12.   According to paragraph 7, which of the following is true of the completed "Difference Engine No. 2"?

FACT. S1–3 discuss the completed version of this difference engine in Australia in 1991.

✗ (A) It corrected intentional design flaws.

S2 states that the design flaws *may have been* intentional. But they were not *necessarily* intentional.

✓ (B) It was built in a fashion that would have been possible in the 1800s.

CORRECT. S2 states that the machine "was constructed using only methods that might have been available in the nineteenth century."

✗ (C) It did not perform as Babbage would have wanted.

S3: "The finished machine works exactly as Babbage would have hoped."

✗ (D) It followed the completion of a version of Babbage's analytical engine.

S4: "To this day, though, no analytical engine that matches Babbage's later designs has ever been fully built."

Paragraph 3	**Comments**

S1–2	Babbage was an English mathematician, inventor, and engineer. He is regarded by many as the father of modern-day computing.	
3–4	**A** He began work designing the first version of his difference engine in 1822. This mechanical engine was to compute the value of polynomial functions using a mathematical process known as "finite differences."	Placement of the new sentence here does not provide a previous noun (in S2) for "This prototype engine" to refer to.
5–6	**B** Using this method, the difference engine would only be capable of adding and subtracting. Unfortunately, Babbage ran into difficulties both with funding his project and with the builder of the initial prototype of his design, and the project was abandoned partway through.	Placing the new sentence here does give "This prototype engine" a good reference point in S4. But this placement improperly disrupts the direct connection between S4 (which describes a "mathematical process") and S5 ("Using this method").
7	**C** Eventually, Babbage shifted to designing what he called the "analytical engine," which drew on his designs for the difference engine but was intended as a more general computing machine.	**CORRECT.** The modifier "This prototype engine" refers to the abandoned machine discussed above. The rest of the paragraph follows the fact that the difference engine prototype was not built.
End	**D**	Placing the new sentence here implies that "Difference Engine No. 1" was the name of the "analytical engine." However, these two kinds of engines are distinguished carefully in the passage.

6

13. **This prototype engine, known as "Difference Engine No. 1," would never be fully constructed.**

INSERT TEXT. The previous sentence needs to refer to an engine, so that "This prototype engine" makes sense. Given the content of the new sentence, this engine ought to be a difference engine that Babbage was trying to build. Wherever the new sentence is placed, it should not interrupt the logical flow of existing sentences.

Where would the sentence best fit?

✗ (A) Choice A

✗ (B) Choice B

✓ (C) Choice C   **CORRECT.**

✗ (D) Choice D

	Whole Passage	Comments
P1	The shift in processing power and information storage from human beings to computers over the past several decades represents the most significant change in productivity since the Industrial Revolution …	Shift from humans to computers = biggest change in work since Industrial Revolution.
P2	Interestingly, if a person today were asked, "When was the first computer program ever written?", he or she would probably miss the mark by over a century …	First computer program was written over a century before you might expect. Various early computers. But actual first program was written in 1843. Ada Lovelace. Charles Babbage, who invented the difference & analytical engines.
P3	Babbage was an English mathematician, inventor, and engineer …	Babbage = father of modern computing. 1822: started working on difference engine. Mechanical engine to compute math values. But he ran into difficulties. Shifted to more general "analytical engine."
P4	The analytical engine featured a new concept called "punched cards," which would contain coded information that the engine would accept as inputs …	"Punched card" inputs. Various outputs. Computation and storage. Mechanical, but analogous to electronic components of today's computers.
P5	Lovelace's computer program, designed for use on the analytical engine once it was built, was modest by modern standards …	Lovelace's program for the engine: modest to our eyes. Step-by-step description of how to compute certain numbers. Simple. But all the traits of a modern algorithm.
P6	Like the original difference engine, Babbage's analytical engine was never completely built …	Analytical engine was never completed. He built just a small part before he died. Son kept working on. Produced some outputs. But never realized the vision.
P7	It was not until 1991, in Australia, that a complete version of Babbage's difference engine was produced …	1991: an actual version of the difference engine was built. Corrected some errors, used only 19th-century methods. It worked! No analytical engine has been fully built.

14.   **Although the nineteenth-century inventions of Charles Babbage were not completed in his lifetime, they foreshadow the modern computer.**

SUMMARY. Correct answers must be clearly expressed in the passage. They must also be among the major points of the passage. They should tie as directly as possible to the summary given.

✓ | A | The first known computer program was written by Ada Lovelace to be used on Babbage's analytical engine.

CORRECT. P2 and P4 discuss the historical significance of Lovelace's program in the context of Babbage's inventions and the development of modern computer programming.

✗ | B | Babbage is acknowledged as the inventor of ENIAC and UNIVAC, the first fully electronic computing machines.

P2 states that ENIAC and UNIVAC were completed nearly a century after Babbage's death (1871, from P6). Babbage's influence on those projects was probably significant. But the passage never states that Babbage is acknowledged as the inventor of these computing machines.

✓ | C | The recent completion of one of Babbage's designs showed that his machines could work as "computation engines," as intended.

CORRECT. This is a significant event in P7, especially in light of the difficulties Babbage had in building his machines during his lifetime (and the difficulties others had after his death). His designs didn't just signal to later inventors the features that computers should have. His designs actually contained mechanical models of those features, models that would work as expected if built.

✓ | D | Babbage's mechanical machines provided models for many features of modern electronic computing.

CORRECT. Various "computer" features (such as printed output, storing information, and performing mathematical computations) are outlined in P4.

✗ | E | Henry Babbage, Charles's son, was never able to turn his father's vision into reality.

This detail is mentioned in P6. However, it is relatively minor in the scheme of this passage.

✗ | F | Modern computing power is unlikely to be the most important economic innovation in history.

P1 makes an opposing point, although not in as stark and extreme a fashion.

6

Answers and Explanations—6.4 The Black Death

	Paragraph 1	Comments
S1	Bubonic plague is caused by the *Yersinia pestis* bacterium, which is endemic in wild rodents, including rats.	Bubonic plague is caused by a bacterium carried by rats.
2	When these animals are present in great numbers and density, a "plague reservoir" provides a **springboard** for epidemics.	"Plague reservoir" = lots of rats.
3	As the infected rat population dies, their fleas migrate to humans and spread the disease.	Fleas jump to humans.
4	Such a reservoir has long existed in the central steppes of Asia.	Reservoir in Asian steppes.
5	Consequently, China, India, and much of the Middle East have long endured epidemics, including the Justinian plague, which ravaged the Byzantine Empire in 541.	So there have been many epidemics in China, India, Middle East.
6	However, Europe was spared, at least on a grand scale, for another 800 years.	But not Europe until 800 years after 541.

1. According to paragraph 1, humans contract bubonic plague most directly when

   ✗ (A) a plague reservoir is present nearby

   ✓ (B) infected fleas migrate from rats to humans

   ✗ (C) they live in the central steppes of Asia

   ✗ (D) they are bitten by rats

FACT. P1 discusses how and where bubonic plague spreads. The question asks for the direct cause of bubonic plague in humans.

S2 states that "a 'plague reservoir' provides a springboard for epidemics." Without a plague reservoir, it's doubtful that humans will contract plague. But the presence of this reservoir is not sufficient. It is not actually the direct mechanism by which humans contract plague.

CORRECT. S3: "As the infected rat population dies, their fleas migrate to humans and spread the disease."

The central steppes of Asia is the historical location of a plague reservoir. But the paragraph doesn't imply that all or even most humans contract plague when they live in those steppes.

Perhaps being bitten by plague-infected rats will pass plague to humans (although only if the plague bacterium is present in rat saliva). But this possible method is never mentioned in P1.

MANHATTAN PREP

2.   The word "springboard" in the passage is closest in meaning to

VOCABULARY. "Springboard" = foundation, launching pad, or catalyst.

✗ (A) cure

Opposite. In this context, a cure for an epidemic would be something that might bring it to an end. A "springboard" would be a jumping off point (meaning it would likely get worse).

✗ (B) damper

Opposite in another sense. "Damper" = obstacle, something that hinders or obstructs. This would be the opposite of a catalyst.

✓ (C) foundation

CORRECT. "A 'plague reservoir' provides a springboard for epidemics" = a plague reservoir provides a foundation or a launching pad for epidemics.

✗ (D) explanation

Unrelated. Understanding the meaning of or cause of an epidemic is not the same as catalyzing or initiating it.

3.   Paragraph 1 presents a fact and then goes on to

PURPOSE. S1 contains the basic fact about what causes bubonic plague. The paragraph continues by outlining how plague is spread. The last part of the paragraph provides historical illustrations.

✗ (A) detail how an epidemic from the Byzantine Empire infected the whole Middle East

S5 only mentions that the Byzantine Empire suffered an epidemic in 541. It is implied that this empire was part of the Middle East. In any event, transmission from this empire to the "whole Middle East" is never mentioned.

✗ (B) discuss how plague epidemics ultimately reached Europe

P1 only discusses how plague kept recurring in Asia and the Middle East. S6: "However, Europe was spared, at least on a grand scale, for another 800 years."

✗ (C) provide additional facts that clash and a theory to reconcile them all

No set of clashing facts are presented, let alone a theory that might reconcile them. The broad picture of how plague spreads is logically coherent.

✓ (D) describe how plague is transmitted and cite historical examples

CORRECT. S2–3 discuss how plague is transmitted. S4–5 provide examples.

6

Paragraph 2	Comments
S1 In 1346, the central steppes of Asia were part of the Mongol Khanate of the Golden Horde; a Mongol army besieged the Italian trading outpost in Kaffa, a Black Sea port.	1346: Mongol army besieged Kaffa, an Italian outpost.
2 The Mongol force suffered from plague, and during the siege the bodies of those dead were catapulted into the town.	Dead bodies with plague in them are catapulted in.
3 The following spring, the Italians fled home by ship and brought the plague to Europe.	Next spring, Italians flee, bringing plague home.
4 At that time, Europe was exceedingly vulnerable to such an epidemic.	Europe was very vulnerable.
5 Burgeoning medieval trade networks allowed the disease to spread rapidly by ship, up to several hundred kilometers a week.	Why.
6 The lack of modern medical knowledge ensured that no effective measures were taken to curb its spread.	
7 In 1347, the Adriatic Italian seaports were infected, and from there the plague followed the sailing routes to Sicily and then Marseilles; after a lull during the winter, when cold temperatures inhibit the flea population, 1348 saw the plague spread to Spain, the rest of France, and then England and northern Europe.	How plague spread.
8 From Norway, the trading ships of the Hanseatic League carried it to the Baltic cities and Russia.	
9 By the time the epidemic had run its course in 1353, all of Europe had been significantly ravaged.	Ravaged all of Europe.

4. The word "burgeoning" in the passage is closest in meaning to

VOCABULARY. "Burgeoning" = growing, flourishing, proliferating, prospering.

✓ (A) flourishing

CORRECT. "Burgeoning medieval trade networks" = flourishing medieval trade networks.

✗ (B) unraveling

If the trade routes were "unraveling," they would be collapsing or falling apart. The opposite is true here.

✗ (C) dwindling

Opposite.

✗ (D) branching

"Branching" does not necessarily convey the growth that "burgeoning" does. "Branching" could describe static, unchanging networks that just have a lot of branches.

5.   Paragraph 2 supports the idea that the spread of the plague throughout Europe was facilitated by which of the following factors?

INFERENCE. S1–3 describe how the Italians in Kaffa were exposed to plague and brought it home. S4 states that Europe was very vulnerable (= at risk). S5–6 describe why.

✓   (A)   Ineffective medical countermeasures

CORRECT. S6: "The lack of modern medical knowledge ensured that no effective measures were taken to curb its spread."

✗   (B)   Low temperatures in wintertime

S7: "after a lull during the winter, when cold temperatures inhibit the flea population." In fact, low winter temperatures seem to slow down the spread of plague.

✗   (C)   The exclusion of plague-ridden corpses from Kaffa

In fact, plague-ridden corpses were apparently not excluded all that effectively from Kaffa (they were catapulted into the town).

✗   (D)   Europe's proximity to the central steppes of Asia

S1 states that these central steppes (which harbored plague) were part of the Mongol Khanate. But geographical proximity at most only indirectly facilitated the spread of plague throughout Europe. After all, the steppes did not physically get any closer to Europe in the 1300s.

6.   Which of the sentences below best expresses the essential information in the highlighted sentence in paragraph 2? Incorrect choices change the meaning in important ways or leave out essential information.

SIMPLIFY SENTENCE. The sentence is long and fact-filled. Fortunately, there are few logical twists. The right answer can leave out some or even many details, but it must get the core story straight. Wrong answers will mix up the facts or otherwise change the meaning fundamentally.

6

✗   (A)   In 1347, after a winter lull due to inactivated fleas, plague infected Italian seaports and then spread to Sicily, Marseilles, and the rest of France, Spain, England, and northern Europe.

Plague infected the Italian seaports before winter, not after.

✗   (B)   Plague, after landing in Adriatic Italian seaports in 1347, followed sailing routes to Sicily, Marseilles, then Spain, the rest of France, and finally England and northern Europe.

This version leaves out the winter lull altogether, which is an important detail. It also gives no time frame for the spread of the disease. Its rapid advance is key to the story.

✓   (C)   Even with winter briefly inactivating the fleas, plague swept through several European countries within a year of landing in Italian seaports in 1347, following travel routes and spreading north.

CORRECT. This version leaves out much of the geographic detail but captures the central meaning of the original sentence. It emphasizes the rapidity of the spread northward along travel routes and the temporary nature of the winter lull (as well as why there was a lull at all).

✗   (D)   After infecting Italian seaports in 1347, plague blazed through cities, islands, and countries of Europe following well-traveled routes, only to be halted by winter, which leveled the flea population.

This version places the winter pause at the end of the sentence and rephrases it with more extreme language ("level" a population = flatten it = destroy it). So this version overemphasizes that winter pause, turning it into a force that was able to stop plague completely. But according to the original sentence, winter was only able to slow the devastation down briefly.

Paragraph 3	Comments
S1 While the fragmentary nature of medieval records has hindered scholars, recent research has caused an upward revision in the already horrific estimate of the mortality rate.	Recent research: death rate even worse.
2 It is now thought that more than half of the population perished.	More than half the people died.
3 While some more northern or isolated regions were less afflicted, the Italian cities may have lost as many as 80 percent of their people.	
4 All told, perhaps 50 million died, a number comparable with global deaths caused by the Second World War.	50 million deaths.
5 One of the first acknowledged great books of Western literature, *The Decameron*, chronicles the impact as it describes the plight of a group of Italian gentry that fled to the countryside in a vain attempt to avoid infection.	One story: described in *The Decameron*.
6 The cities became cemeteries, in which streets were littered with unburied dead, and houses were abandoned or occupied only by the dying.	Cities = cemeteries. Houses were abandoned.

7. The main purpose of paragraph 3 is to

PURPOSE. P3 discusses the terrible mortality rate of the plague, with an illustration that comes down through an Italian work of literature.

✓ (A) emphasize and illustrate the decimation of Europe

CORRECT. S1–4 detail the deaths resulting from the plague. S5–6 illustrate the effects of this decimation.

✗ (B) explain why German principalities fared better than the Italian cities

S3 mentions that some northern locations were less afflicted. But this is only a minor qualification. Furthermore, these locations are not identified as German.

✗ (C) support the claim that *The Decameron* is a literary classic

The book is only cited to illustrate of the effects of the plague. S5 calls it "one of the first acknowledged great books of Western literature," but making this declaration is not the primary purpose of the paragraph.

✗ (D) downplay the losses of the Second World War by comparison with those caused by plague

S4 mentions the losses of the Second World War to show how enormous the casualties from plague were, not to downplay or soften the losses of the war.

Paragraph 4	Comments
S1 It would be 300 years before the population returned to its 1347 peak.	300 years for population to come back.
2 Thus, it is little wonder that this plague, named the Black Death, remains in the human consciousness hundreds of years later, as the disruption of such depopulation greatly affected the development of European society.	Black Death: still in our minds. Greatly affected how European society developed.
3 Some of the changes actually brought unforeseen benefits: the resulting labor shortage raised wages and the standard of living for the surviving peasantry, many of whom then acquired land left vacant by the deaths of the previous owners and tenants.	Even some unforeseen benefits. Labor shortage, higher wages.
4 It has also been theorized that this disruption spurred the development of modern capitalism, since labor-intensive feudal organization was no longer practical.	May have even spurred capitalism to develop.

8.   The word "spurred" in the passage is closest in meaning to

     VOCABULARY. "Spur" = encourage, stimulate, provoke, urge.

✗   (A) accompanied

     Not quite. "Accompanied" would indicate just that they occurred together, not that one caused or encouraged the other.

✗   (B) halted

     Opposite. "Halted" = stopped or curbed.

✗   (C) affected

     Not quite. "Affect" = influence, but this influence could be positive or negative.

✓   (D) promoted

     CORRECT. "This disruption spurred the development of modern capitalism" = this disruption promoted or encouraged the development of modern capitalism.

9. According to paragraph 4, which of the following is mentioned as an unexpected benefit of the plague?

FACT. S3 lists "unforeseen benefits" of the plague. S4 may or may not be continuing this list.

✗ (A) Feudalism recovered as a social structure.

S4 suggests that feudalism actually declined in the wake of the devastation, "since labor-intensive feudal organization was no longer practical." Moreover, it's not clear that S4 is actually listing benefits of the plague.

✓ (B) Many peasants subsequently acquired real estate.

CORRECT. S3: "many of whom then acquired land left vacant by the deaths of the previous owners and tenants."

✗ (C) The epidemic left a lasting impact on human consciousness.

S2 mentions the impact to stress the magnitude of the depopulation, not to enumerate a benefit of the disease.

✗ (D) Overcrowded urban areas were reduced in population.

This idea is not mentioned in the paragraph.

Paragraph 5		Comments
S1	Other consequences were much darker.	Other, much darker consequences.
2	The epidemic struck swiftly and terribly; people sickened within days of infection and died within a week.	Swift and terrible death.
3	Naturally enough, panic, fear, and anger quickly tore the social fabric apart.	Panic, fear, and anger.
4	As neither government nor religious leaders had any factual understanding of the terrifying malady that had befallen them, these leaders did not oppose the inevitable scapegoating of members of religious or ethnic minorities, beggars, foreigners, or those with **disfiguring** diseases other than plague.	Inevitable scapegoating (= blaming) minorities & others.
5	In 1349, authority figures condoned, or even encouraged, the extermination of many Jewish communities in central Europe.	Extermination of many Jewish communities.

6

10. The word "**disfiguring**" in the passage is closest in meaning to

VOCABULARY. "Disfigure" = mar, deface, mutilate, spoil the appearance.

✗ (A) debilitating

Not quite. "Debilitate" = weaken, incapacitate. But this does not necessarily mean that the patient's appearance is marred.

✓ (B) marring

CORRECT. "Marring" = disfiguring, mutilating, scarring.

✗ (C) infectious

Unrelated. An "infectious" disease is one that can be spread. The author is talking about diseases that damage or impair rather than those that are easily spread.

✗ (D) incurable

The diseases might have been "incurable" (untreatable), but this word is not related to "disfigure."

11. According to paragraph 5, which of the following is true about government and religious leaders at the time of the Black Death?

FACT. S4 discusses how these leaders, otherwise helpless, allowed or encouraged violence against minority groups.

✗ (A) Their comprehension of the disease was based on hard facts.

S4: "neither government nor religious leaders had any factual understanding of the terrifying malady that had befallen them."

✓ (B) They allowed vulnerable, marginal groups to be victimized.

CORRECT. S4: "these leaders did not oppose the inevitable scapegoating of members of religious or ethnic minorities, beggars, foreigners, or those with disfiguring diseases other than plague." The scapegoated groups were vulnerable and marginal (= outsider).

✗ (C) Their mortality rate was lower than that of ordinary citizens.

This might well be true. But it was not mentioned in the paragraph.

✗ (D) They strove to preserve social tranquility and justice.

S4 indicates the opposite.

Paragraph 6	**Comments**
S1 Today, in developed countries, it is easy to view the plague as a relic of the medieval past, especially since the disease can be treated with modern antibiotics.	Easy to view plague as relic of medieval past.
2 However, less celebrated outbreaks regularly occurred in Europe into the eighteenth century.	But outbreaks continued into 18th century.
3 In the nineteenth century, another bubonic plague epidemic killed tens of millions.	Another epidemic in 19th century.
4 Much more recently, panic **reminiscent** of the fourteenth century quickly asserted itself when many quickly succumbed during the Ebola outbreak from 2014 to 2016.	Much more recent panic around Ebola in 2014-2016. Reminiscent of 14th century.

12. The phrase "reminiscent of" in the passage is closest in meaning to

VOCABULARY. "Reminiscent of" = suggestive of, resembling, awakening memories.

✗ (A) suspicious of

Unrelated. No one was "suspicious of" (doubtful or unsure of) the fourteenth century.

✗ (B) sensitive to

Unrelated. No one was "sensitive to" (aware of or even thoughtful of) the fourteenth century.

✗ (C) commemorative of

"Commemorative of" would mean that the panic was consciously celebrating the memory of the Black Death. This is not the intended meaning. "Commemorative" and "reminiscent" are not synonyms.

✓ (D) suggestive of

CORRECT. "Panic reminiscent of the fourteenth century" = panic suggestive of the fourteenth century, panic that could remind one of that time.

Paragraph 3	**Comments**
S1 While the fragmentary nature of medieval records has hindered scholars, recent research has caused an upward revision in the already horrific estimate of the mortality rate.	
2–3 **A** It is now thought that more than half of the population perished. While some more northern or isolated regions were less afflicted, the Italian cities may have lost as many as 80 percent of their people.	S1 doesn't refer to anything that could reasonably contain the "fictional stories" of the new sentence. The "recent research" in S1 wouldn't contain such fiction.
4 **B** All told, perhaps 50 million died, a number comparable with global deaths caused by the Second World War.	S3 also does not relate at all to fictional stories.
5 **C** One of the first acknowledged great books of Western literature, *The Decameron*, chronicles the impact as it describes the plight of a group of Italian gentry that fled to the countryside in a vain attempt to avoid infection.	Placement here still doesn't work. It is illogical to address "fictional stories presented therein" before the book has been mentioned.
6 **D** The cities became cemeteries, in which streets were littered with unburied dead, and houses were abandoned or occupied only by the dying.	**CORRECT.** The new sentence clearly refers to *The Decameron* in S5. This book can contain the "fictional stories" referred to in the new sentence, which also leads well into S6.

13. **The fictional stories presented therein run the gamut from erotica to tragedy, but most contrast the bucolic country-side to the urban horror.**

INSERT TEXT. "Therein" means "in or within that place or thing," which had to have been mentioned already. So the previous sentence must contain something that itself can contain the fictional stories described in this new sentence.

Where would the sentence best fit?

✗ (A) Choice A

✗ (B) Choice B

✗ (C) Choice C

✓ (D) Choice D   **CORRECT.**

	Whole Passage	**Comments**
P1	Bubonic plague is caused by the *Yersinia pestis* bacterium, which is endemic in wild rodents, including rats …	Bubonic plague is caused by a bacterium carried by rats. "Plague reservoir" = lots of rats. Fleas jump to humans. Reservoir in Asian steppes. So there have been many epidemics in China, India, Middle East. But not Europe until 800 years after 541.
P2	In 1346, the central steppes of Asia were part of the Mongol Khanate of the Golden Horde; a Mongol army besieged the Italian trading outpost in Kaffa, a Black Sea port …	1346: Mongol army besieged Kaffa, an Italian outpost. Dead bodies with plague in them are catapulted in. Next spring, Italians flee, bringing plague home. Europe was very vulnerable. Why. How plague spread. Ravaged all of Europe.
P3	While the fragmentary nature of medieval records has hindered scholars, recent research has caused an upward revision in the already horrific estimate of the mortality rate …	Recent research: death rate even worse. More than half the people died. 50 million deaths. One story: described in *The Decameron*. Cities = cemeteries. Houses were abandoned.
P4	It would be 300 years before the population returned to its 1347 peak …	300 years for population to come back. Black Death: still in our minds. Greatly affected how European society developed. Even some unforeseen benefits. Labor shortage, higher wages. May have even spurred capitalism to develop.
P5	Other consequences were much darker. The epidemic struck swiftly and terribly; people sickened within days of infection and died within a week …	Other, much darker consequences. Swift and terrible death. Panic, fear, and anger. Inevitable scapegoating (= blaming) minorities & others. Extermination of many Jewish communities.
P6	Today, in developed countries, it is easy to view the plague as a relic of the medieval past, especially since the disease can be treated with modern antibiotics …	Easy to view plague as relic of medieval past. But outbreaks continued into 18th century. Another epidemic in 19th century. Much more recent panic around Ebola in 2014–2016. Reminiscent of 14th century.

14. **The Black Death, the outbreak of bubonic plague that ravaged Europe in the fourteenth century, not only caused horrific suffering but also altered the course of social history.**

SUMMARY. Correct answers must be clearly expressed in the passage. They must also be among the major points of the passage. They should tie as directly as possible to the summary given.

✗ | A | The Black Death inspired the poets and writers of the period, spurring a renaissance of Western literature.

The passage does not claim that the plague caused a literary renaissance. The only related reference is that *The Decameron*, an acknowledged masterpiece, chronicles the plague.

✓ | B | The plague's devastation created both positive and negative reverberations throughout the social order.

CORRECT. P4–5 discuss the positive and negative consequences of the plague at length.

✓ | C | When plague-ridden Italians returned from war, trade networks and medical ignorance enabled the epidemic's rapid sweep through Europe.

CORRECT. P2 gives a detailed history of the origin and spread of the plague in Europe. This choice summarizes that paragraph.

✗ | D | Some areas of Europe, such as Italian cities, were far more afflicted than other areas.

Mentioned in P3. But this is a minor detail in the context of the passage as a whole.

✓ | E | More recent plague outbreaks and parallel epidemics imply that modern society is not immune to similar disruptions.

CORRECT. This is the core point of the concluding paragraph.

✗ | F | In medieval European cities, rats were far more numerous than they are today, and their fleas spread the disease to humans.

The first part, while true, is never mentioned. The second part is discussed in P1, but it is a minor detail in the context of the whole passage.

6

Answers and Explanations—6.5 South Asian Carnivores

	Paragraph 1	**Comments**
S1	Large cats, honey badgers, and ants—what do these animals have in common?	
2	They dominate their respective subsets of the food chain as carnivores in the jungles of South and Southeast Asia.	3 carnivores in S/SE Asia: large cats, honey badgers, & ants.
3	Among these, cats are probably the most majestic, the most dangerous, and the most **vulnerable** to extinction.	Cats: most majestic, dangerous, and vulnerable.
4	All cats are carnivores and "apex predators," meaning that they are at the top of the food chain in their own ecosystem and have no predators themselves.	Apex predators.
5	Perhaps the most impressive of the wild cats in Asia are the tigers.	Tigers.
6	With red-orange fur, vertical black stripes, and a white underbelly, tigers are easily recognizable as distinct from other cat species.	Easily recognizable by appearance.
7	Their size is also a factor: most tiger species grow to 9 to 11 feet (about 275 to 335 centimeters) in length, and can weigh up to 600 pounds (about 275 kilograms).	Huge size.
8	Tigers may be the most admired of what are known as the "charismatic megafauna"—large animals with broad popular appeal, such as pandas, polar bears, elephants, and lions.	Example of "charismatic megafauna."
9	As a result, the declining population of tigers is frequently used by environmentalists to call attention to the problem of endangered species.	So tigers are used to highlight problem of endangered species.

1.   The word "vulnerable" in the passage is closest in meaning to

    VOCABULARY. "Vulnerable" = exposed, at risk, defenseless.

   ✗ (A) related

    Although they are most at risk of extinction, this does not mean the same as saying that they are the most "related" (connected) to extinction.

   ✓ (B) susceptible

    CORRECT. "Cats are ... the most vulnerable to extinction" = cats are the most susceptible to extinction, they are most at risk of dying off completely.

   ✗ (C) condemned

    Too extreme. "Condemned to extinction" = sentenced to extinction. There's no way out. But "vulnerable to extinction" means "at risk of extinction," which may or may not happen.

   ✗ (D) resistant

    Opposite. "Resistant" = immune or unaffected by.

2.   Why does the author mention "charismatic megafauna"?

PURPOSE. The term "charismatic megafauna" is introduced and defined in S8. The following sentence begins with "As a result," meaning that the purpose of introducing this term is likely to be found in S9.

✗ (A) To identify a class of animals that are dissimilar to tigers

According to S8, tigers are explicitly part of the "charismatic megafauna" category of animals. In this regard, these animals are alike, not dissimilar.

✗ (B) To call attention to other popular animals

S8 mentions other popular animals, such as pandas and polar bears, in order to define and illustrate the term "charismatic megafauna." However, the author does not continue discussing these other animals, but returns to tigers in S9.

✗ (C) To explain why tigers are so popular

S5–7 list several reasons why tigers are so popular. The fact that tigers are in the "charismatic megafauna" category indicates *that* they are popular. But being in this category does not explain why the author introduces the "charismatic megafauna" term. And it does not explain why tigers are popular.

✓ (D) To explain why environmentalists often refer to them

CORRECT. S9 indicates that environmentalists call attention to the declining tiger population to illustrate the problem of endangered species. Why do they do this? Because tigers may be the most popular and admired of well-known, beloved animals in the "charismatic megafauna" class. The author introduces the term in order to put the environmentalists' actions in context.

3.   Which of the sentences below best expresses the essential information in the highlighted sentence in paragraph 1? Incorrect choices change the meaning in important ways or leave out essential information.

SIMPLIFY SENTENCE. The first part of S9 states that the declining population of tigers is used by environmentalists. The second part of the sentence explains that this use is to raise awareness of (call attention to) species endangerment.

✓ (A) Environmentalists call attention to the falling tiger population to raise awareness of species endangerment.

CORRECT. This choice says essentially the same thing as S9, but with simpler phrasing in most cases.

✗ (B) To highlight the issues of charismatic megafauna, environmentalists draw attention to declines in tiger numbers.

This version changes the purpose to "highlight the issues of charismatic megafauna." Whatever issues these may be, they're not necessarily the same as the problem of endangered species.

✗ (C) The population of tigers is falling as a result of the attention directed toward species endangerment by environmentalists.

The original sentence doesn't claim that the tiger population is falling because of the actions of environmentalists.

✗ (D) The most admired of the charismatic megafauna, tigers call attention to their declining numbers, and more broadly to the problem of endangered species.

By leaving out "environmentalists" altogether and making "tigers" the grammatical subject, this version makes it sound as if tigers are the ones doing all the work. In some sense, they are doing the real work. But this omission of environmentalists and their deliberate use of the tiger example changes the meaning too much.

Paragraph 2	**Comments**
S1 As recently as a century ago, tigers were commonplace throughout Asia, excluding the Middle East and western Russia.	Tigers used to be more common in Asia.
2 Today, they are found only in small pockets of India, Southeast Asia, and the southeastern edge of Russia.	Now found only in small pockets.
3 Most of the loss in tiger population and habitat is due to the expansion of the activities of civilization, such as mining and farming, and to the deforestation that happens concurrently.	Why? Mining, farming, deforestation.
4 Still, a significant portion of the population decline is a consequence of the ongoing hunting of both tigers and their prey.	But also hunting.
5 Indeed, the Bengal tiger, the most populous of all tiger subspecies, only numbers about 2,500 animals in the wild, though that number has increased slightly in recent years.	Now only ~2,500 Bengal tigers in the wild.

4.   Which of the following is NOT mentioned in paragraph 2 as a reason for the decline in the population of wild tigers in Asia?

NEGATIVE FACT. P2 outlines the current state of the wild tiger population. S3–4 focus on reasons for the declines in that population. Three answer choices will be found in P2. One will not.

✗   (A) The hunting of tiger prey

S4: "a significant portion of the population decline is a consequence of the ongoing hunting of both tigers and their prey."

✓   (B) Human conflict in the region

CORRECT. The paragraph never mentions human conflict as a cause of tiger population loss.

✗   (C) Expanded mining and farming

S3: "Most of the loss in tiger population and habitat is due to the expansion of the activities of civilization, such as mining and farming."

✗   (D) Destruction of forested areas

S3: "Most of the loss in tiger population and habitat is due to ... the deforestation that happens concurrently."

5.   The word "populous" in the passage is closest in meaning to

VOCABULARY. In reference to an animal or other species, "populous" = large in number. It can also describe an area as crowded or heavily populated.

✗   (A) beloved

"Beloved" means "well-liked" or "popular," not "populous."

✗   (B) predatory

Unrelated. "Predatory" = hunting prey.

✓   (C) numerous

CORRECT. "The most populous of all tiger subspecies" = the most numerous of all tiger subspecies.

✗   (D) sparse

Opposite. "Sparse" = infrequent, scarce, in short supply.

	Paragraph 3	**Comments**
S1	Other prominent cat species in South Asia include the leopard, found scattered throughout India, Malaysia, and Thailand, and the snow leopard, found in parts of India, southern China, and Central Asia.	Other cats: leopard & snow leopard.
2	Both leopards and snow leopards are strong, powerful animals with a yellowish-grey coat with rosette markings, or dark rings encircled around dots of lighter-colored fur.	Characteristics.
3	These cats are typically 4 to 6 feet (about 120 to 180 centimeters) in length, and weigh about as much as a typical adult human.	
4	Both animals are ferocious in attacking prey, which consists primarily of smaller mammals: they bite the throat of victims until they suffocate.	
5	Like the tiger, the snow leopard is considered an endangered species.	Snow leopard is endangered, too.
6	By contrast, the leopard has the largest global distribution of any wild cat	Leopard is not. Large global distribution.
7	It is not yet considered endangered, but many subspecies are considered threatened.	But many subspecies are threatened.

6. Paragraph 3 indicates what about the conservation status of leopards and snow leopards?

FACT. S5–7 discuss the conservation status of these cats (how endangered or not they are).

✗ (A) At present, their conservation status is not clearly known to researchers.

S5–7 declare the conservation status of leopards and snow leopards. This status must be clearly known to researchers.

✓ (B) Snow leopards are endangered, while leopards on the whole are not.

CORRECT. S5: "the snow leopard is considered an endangered species." S7: "It [the leopard] is not yet considered endangered, but many subspecies are considered threatened."

✗ (C) Both species are considered threatened, but not endangered.

S5 indicates that snow leopards are endangered.

✗ (D) Their status is imperiled by a lack of available prey in the form of smaller mammals.

S4 states that the primary form of prey for both animals is smaller mammals. However, nothing in the passage suggests that there is a shortage of available prey for these animals.

7.   What is the author's primary purpose in paragraph 3?

PURPOSE. S1 introduces the leopard and the snow leopard, placing them geographically. S2–4 outline the physical characteristics of these animals. S4 describes their behavior, and S5–6 describe the conservation status of both animals. The paragraph is factual in content and tone.

✗ (A) To highlight key differences between the leopard and snow leopard

Differences between the two animals are pointed out in several places. But much of the paragraph is devoted to discussing the similarities.

✗ (B) To illustrate the importance of the leopard and snow leopard in the food chain

Nothing in the paragraph focuses on the importance of these animals in the food chain. The only passing mention of anything related to this concept is in S4, which describes how the animals kill their prey.

✓ (C) To outline significant characteristics of two dominant carnivore cats

CORRECT. The leopard and the snow leopard are dominant carnivore species. This answer choice neatly summarizes the content and purpose of this paragraph.

✗ (D) To warn of the potential extinction of the snow leopard

S5: "Like the tiger, the snow leopard is considered an endangered species." However, this point is made too briefly to be the primary purpose of the paragraph.

8.   The word "**ferocious**" in the passage is closest in meaning to

VOCABULARY. "Ferocious" = fierce, savage, vicious, aggressive.

✓ (A) fierce

CORRECT. "Both animals are ferocious in attacking prey" = both animals are fierce or savage in attacking prey.

✗ (B) coldblooded

Not quite. "Coldblooded" = without pity, mercy, or warmth. The ferocious attack of a snow leopard may also lack mercy. But "coldblooded" implies none of the wild savagery that "ferocious" does, but rather a calculated, almost civilized assault.

✗ (C) adept

While it is true that both animals are "adept" or skillful in attacking prey, "ferocious" focuses on the fierce and aggressive nature of those attacks.

✗ (D) precise

While it is true that both animals are likely "precise" or accurate and careful in attacking prey, "ferocious" focuses on the fierce and aggressive nature of those attacks.

6

Paragraph 4	Comments
S1 The honey badger is perhaps the most fascinating of all the South Asian carnivores.	Honey badger.
2 A misnamed species, the honey badger has little in common with the badgers that are widely distributed in North America, Africa, and Asia; it is much more closely related to weasels.	More like weasels than badgers.
3 Found throughout India and other parts of Asia, the honey badger is long from head to tail, short in stature, and broad in build, with fast reflexes and thick skin, leaving it with few known predators.	Characteristics.
4 A common sighting is that of a honey badger attacking a populated beehive, eating all of the honey available, and escaping completely unscathed.	
5 Honey badgers are fast enough to snap the neck of a venomous snake unharmed, with jaws strong enough to easily crack the shell of a tortoise.	
6 They can live comfortably anywhere from sea level up to elevations of 13,000 feet (about 4,000 meters).	

9. Paragraph 4 mentions all of the following as features of the honey badger EXCEPT:

NEGATIVE FACT. The entire paragraph discusses features of the honey badger. Three answer choices will be listed. One will not be.

✗ (A) Its broad build, thick skin, and fast reflexes leave the honey badger with few predators.

S3: "the honey badger is long from head to tail, short in stature, and broad in build, with fast reflexes and thick skin, leaving it with few known predators."

✗ (B) It can live at a variety of different altitudes.

S6: "They can live comfortably anywhere from sea level up to elevations of 13,000 feet (about 4,000 meters)."

✓ (C) It is closely related to the badgers found in North America, Africa, and Asia.

CORRECT. S2: "A misnamed species, the honey badger has little in common with the badgers that are widely distributed in North America, Africa, and Asia."

✗ (D) It is capable of raiding a beehive and escaping virtually unharmed.

S4: "A common sighting is that of a honey badger attacking a populated beehive, eating all of the honey available, and escaping completely unscathed."

10. Which of the following facts is
     most clearly used in paragraph 4
     to illustrate the speed of the
     honey badger?

FACT. S5 brings up an example to illustrate the honey badger's speed.

✗ (A) They can crack a tortoise's
        shell.

S5 mentions this fact as a demonstration of the strength of the honey badger's jaws, not its speed. Tortoises are not known for their quickness.

✓ (B) They can kill a poisonous
        snake while avoiding
        injury.

CORRECT. S5: "Honey badgers are fast enough to snap the neck of a venomous snake unharmed."

✗ (C) They are known to attack
        full beehives for their
        honey.

S4 mentions this fact, but their attacks are not explicitly attributed to the honey badger's speed. If anything, the fact as stated would illustrate the fearlessness and ferocity of the honey badger. A reasonable inference is that speed would help the honey badger take the honey with little or no injury. But the success of the attacks is not mentioned in the answer choice.

✗ (D) They are found throughout
        India and other parts of
        Asia.

The geographic distribution of the honey badger is in part because the animal has few known predators, which is in part due to its fast reflexes. However, there are plenty of animal species that have large populations that are not fast. The author does not use this fact to illustrate the honey badger's speed.

Paragraph 5	**Comments**
S1	Finally, despite their small size, weaver ants are a dominant carnivorous species in tropical parts of South and Southeast Asia.	Weaver ants.
2	Worker ants construct unique canopy nests by connecting leaves with spun silk.	Huge canopy nests.
3	These nests can become enormous, with as many as a million worker ants living in a single colony that spans dozens of trees.	
4	Interestingly, there is almost no overlap between the two groups of worker ants in a colony: "major workers" are typically about 0.4 inches (1 centimeter) in length, and "minor workers" are about half that size.	Two groups of worker ants.
5	The division of labor is very clear, as major workers are responsible for expanding the colony and hunting for smaller insect prey, while minor workers tend to the colony's offspring and collect nutritious excretions from smaller insects in or near the colony, in a process known as "milking" or "farming."	

6

11. In paragraph 5, what does the author suggest about major workers vs. minor workers among the weaver ant?

INFERENCE. S4–5 discuss the different features of major workers vs. minor workers.

✗ (A) Minor workers are regularly longer than 1 centimeter.

S4: "'major workers' are typically about 0.4 inches (1 centimeter) in length, and 'minor workers' are about half that size." Therefore, minor workers will rarely be much longer than half a centimeter.

✗ (B) Minor workers stay within a single tree for most of their lives.

Weaver ant colonies can span dozens of trees, but minor workers are not responsible for building the canopy nests. Rather, minor workers tend to offspring and milk or farm smaller insects. However, these facts do not imply that minor workers are stationary—they might move from tree to tree in performing their tasks.

✗ (C) Major workers ignore the offspring of the colony.

S5: "major workers are responsible for expanding the colony and hunting for smaller insect prey, while minor workers tend to the colony's offspring." But this does not necessarily mean that major workers completely ignore the offspring. For example, the major workers might share with offspring some of the food collected from hunting prey.

✓ (D) Building canopy nests is done more by major workers than by minor workers.

CORRECT. S2: "Worker ants construct unique canopy nests by connecting leaves with spun silk." S3: "a single colony ... spans dozens of trees." S5: "The division of labor is very clear, as major workers are responsible for expanding the colony and hunting for smaller insect prey, while minor workers tend to the colony's offspring and collect nutritious excretions from smaller insects in or near the colony." Since major workers expand the colony, it is reasonable to infer that major workers are more responsible than minor workers are for building canopy nests that extend over dozens of trees. Growth of the nest corresponds to growth of the colony.

MANHATTAN PREP

12.   Paragraph 5 indicates that weaver ants

FACT. All of paragraph 5 discusses the weaver ant.

✓   (A) use other insects for nourishment in more than one way

CORRECT. S5 states that major workers hunt smaller insects as prey, while minor workers "collect nutritious excretions from smaller insects in or near the colony, in a process known as 'milking' or 'farming.'" So weaver ants both eat smaller insects directly and milk them for nutritious excretions.

✗   (B) often have difficulty distinguishing between major and minor workers

S4: "there is almost no overlap between the two groups of worker ants in a colony: 'major workers' are typically about 0.4 inches (1 centimeter) in length, and 'minor workers' are about half that size." There is no reason to believe that weaver ants would have trouble distinguishing between the two groups.

✗   (C) use no external materials in constructing their canopy nests

S2: "Worker ants construct unique canopy nests by connecting leaves with spun silk." Leaves qualify as "external materials."

✗   (D) typically number around one million within a single tree

S3: "These nests can become enormous, with as many as a million worker ants living in a single colony that spans dozens of trees." However, this figure of one million represents the total amount in a colony that is spread across dozens of trees—not necessarily or even typically a single tree.

Paragraph 5	**Comments**
S1–2 Finally, despite their small size, weaver ants are a dominant carnivorous species in tropical parts of South and Southeast Asia. Worker ants construct unique canopy nests by connecting leaves with spun silk.	
3 [A] These nests can become enormous, with as many as a million worker ants living in a single colony that spans dozens of trees.	Placement here doesn't work. Major workers have not yet been introduced.
4 [B] Interestingly, there is almost no overlap between the two groups of worker ants in a colony: "major workers" are typically about 0.4 inches (1 centimeter) in length, and "minor workers" are about half that size.	Placement here doesn't work. Major workers have not yet been introduced.
5 [C] The division of labor is very clear, as major workers are responsible for expanding the colony and hunting for smaller insect prey, while minor workers tend to the colony's offspring and collect nutritious excretions from smaller insects in or near the colony, in a process known as "milking" or "farming."	Major workers have just been introduced (in S4). But their job of killing other insects has not yet been mentioned. Placing the new sentence here would also interrupt the flow of logic from S4 to S5. S4 introduces the two types of worker ants, while S5 describes their different roles.
End [D]	**CORRECT.** Both major workers themselves and their job of killing other insects ("hunting for smaller insect prey" in S5) have been introduced by now.

13. **Because the major workers are so effective at their job of killing other insects, weaver ants have been used as a natural form of pest control to protect valuable crop trees for thousands of years.**

INSERT TEXT. The inserted sentence assumes a lot of prior knowledge: what or who are "the major workers"? Likewise, "their job of killing other insects" ought to have been brought up previously.

Where would the sentence best fit?

✗ (A) Choice A

✗ (B) Choice B

✗ (C) Choice C

✓ (D) Choice D   **CORRECT.**

Whole Passage		Comments
P1	Large cats, honey badgers, and ants—what do these animals have in common? …	3 carnivores in S/SE Asia: large cats, honey badgers, & ants. Cats: most majestic, dangerous, & vulnerable. Apex predators. Tigers. Easily recognizable by appearance. Huge size. Example of "charismatic megafauna." So tigers are used to highlight problem of endangered species.
P2	As recently as a century ago, tigers were commonplace throughout Asia, excluding the Middle East and western Russia …	Tigers used to be more common in Asia. Now found only in small pockets. Why? Mining, farming, deforestation. But also hunting. Now only ~2,500 Bengal tigers in the wild.
P3	Other prominent cat species in South Asia include the leopard, found scattered throughout India, Malaysia, and Thailand, and the snow leopard, found in parts of India, southern China, and Central Asia …	Other cats: leopard & snow leopard. Characteristics. Snow leopard is endangered, too. Leopard is not. Large global distribution. But many subspecies are threatened.
P4	The honey badger is perhaps the most fascinating of all the South Asian carnivores …	Honey badger. More like weasels than badgers. Characteristics.
P5	Finally, despite their small size, weaver ants are a dominant carnivorous species in tropical parts of South and Southeast Asia …	Weaver ants. Huge canopy nests. Two groups of worker ants.

14. **Carnivore cats, honey badgers, and weaver ants have each carved out dominant roles in their South and Southeast Asian habitats.**

SUMMARY. Correct answers must be clearly expressed in the passage. They must also be among the major points of the passage. They should tie as directly as possible to the summary given.

✓ | A | The tiger, leopard, and snow leopard are at the top of their food chains, but human activities threaten their existence in the wild.

CORRECT. P1–3 elaborate on this major theme.

✗ | B | The number of Bengal tigers living in the wild has increased in recent years, although only slightly.

P2 mentions this fact. But it is a minor detail in the context of this passage.

✓ | C | Weaver ants are exceptional builders with an organized social hierarchy and job specialization.

CORRECT. Summarizes P5.

✗ | D | Leopards and snow leopards have a distinctive appearance produced by their circular rosette markings.

This detail, mentioned in P3, is minor.

✓ | E | Honey badgers are strong, fast, fearless, and capable of surviving in many different environments.

CORRECT. Summarizes P4.

✗ | F | Honey badgers are dwindling in number in some parts of Asia because of predation by several different species.

No decline in number is mentioned. Moreover, P4 states that honey badgers have "few known predators."

6

Answers and Explanations—6.6 Coal Mining

	Paragraph 1	Comments
S1	Coal is an ignitable, or burnable, black or dark brown rock that is generally found within deep layers of sedimentary rock.	Coal is a burnable rock found in deep rock layers.
2	Coal is formed from peat bogs, or bogs containing dead plant material, that became buried due to flooding, landslides, or earthquakes.	Formed from buried plant material.
3	Over many years, additional soil and mud gradually layer on top of them, causing both the pressure upon and the temperature of the trapped material to rise.	Gradually build up layers on top.
4	This process eventually transforms it into the hard rock known as coal.	Eventually makes coal.

1. According to paragraph 1, how does the material of peat bogs turn into coal?

    FACT. S2: "Coal is formed from peat bogs ... that became buried due to flooding." S3–4 describe how these bogs are transformed into coal. The answer choices differ only slightly from each other, so small differences matter.

✗ (A) The material becomes trapped on top of the soil, and low pressure and high temperatures turn it into coal.

    S3 states that the mud and soil form layers on top of the peat bogs, not under them. Furthermore, both the pressure and the temperature rise.

✗ (B) The material becomes trapped on top of the soil, and high pressure and temperatures turn it into coal.

    S3 states that the mud and soil form layers on top of the peat bogs, not under them.

✓ (C) The material becomes trapped under the soil, and high pressure and temperatures turn it into coal.

    CORRECT. S3: "Over many years, additional soil and mud gradually layer on top of them, causing both the pressure upon and the temperature of the trapped material to rise."

✗ (D) The material becomes trapped under the soil, and low pressure and temperatures turn it into coal.

    S3 states that the mud and soil cause the pressure and temperature to rise, not fall.

Paragraph 2	Comments
P2 S1 As coal forms, it progresses through a series of stages, called grades, ranging from peat, which is considered the predecessor to coal, to lignite, bituminous, and finally anthracite coal.	Different grades of coal.
2 Each grade of coal is progressively harder and blacker, with a higher carbon content and a lower hydrogen and oxygen content.	Progressively harder and blacker.
3 Peat and lignite coal have a few special applications, while bituminous coal is mostly used in electric power generation and the production of coke, a low-impurity fuel that burns very hot and is thus suitable for smelting metals.	Uses of the different grades.
4 Anthracite coal is primarily used as an indoor heating fuel.	

Paragraph 3	Comments
P3 S1 For at least 6,000 years, coal has been used for various purposes, starting with the use of black lignite for carving into ornaments in China.	Coal has been used since ancient times.
2 In Britain, coal has been used at least to some extent as a fuel source for over 5,000 years.	
3 Today, about half of the coal produced globally comes from China, with most of the rest produced in the United States, India, Australia, and Europe.	Current sources.
4 In total, about 8 billion metric tons (8 trillion kilograms) of coal is produced and consumed annually worldwide.	Total amount produced and used.

2.   According to paragraphs 2 and 3, all of the following are true of various grades of coal EXCEPT:

NEGATIVE FACT. All of P2 is devoted to describing the different grades of coal. Lignite is mentioned in P3 as the first form of coal found and used in China. Three answer choices will appear in the paragraphs. One will not.

✓ (A) Peat and lignite coal are used in electric power generation.

CORRECT. P2 S3 states that bituminous coal is used in electric power generation. But it is not mentioned whether the same is true of peat or lignite coal.

✗ (B) The first known use of coal was of lignite found in China.

P3 S1: "For at least 6,000 years, coal has been used for various purposes, starting with the use of black lignite for carving into ornaments in China."

✗ (C) Anthracite is the hardest and darkest form of coal.

P2 S1–2: "As coal forms, it progresses through a series of stages, called grades, ranging from peat … [to] anthracite coal. Each grade of coal is progressively harder and blacker."

✗ (D) Coke, used in smelting, is made using bituminous coal.

P2 S3: "bituminous coal is mostly used in electric power generation and the production of coke, a low-impurity fuel that burns very hot and is thus suitable for smelting metals."

3.   According to paragraph 3, what role does China play in worldwide coal consumption and production?

FACT. S1 mentions China in the context of the history of coal mining and usage. S3 discusses modern day production—specifically, the countries that are leading producers of coal. S4 discusses the total amount of coal currently produced and consumed.

✗ (A) China is the leading global exporter of coal.

The paragraph does not give any information about the importing or exporting of coal.

✗ (B) China is the global leader in coal production but not coal consumption.

The paragraph does not mention any breakdown of coal consumption by country.

✗ (C) China consumes about 4 billion metric tons (4 trillion kilograms) of coal annually.

S3 mentions that China accounts for about half of global coal *production*, but does not discuss consumption. S4 discusses overall global production and consumption, but does not break down consumption by country. So China may not consume as much coal as it produces, and it might be exporting the rest. Or it may consume more than it produces. That is, it would import the difference.

✓ (D) China produces about 4 billion metric tons (4 trillion kilograms) of coal annually.

CORRECT. S3 mentions that China accounts for about half of global coal production. S4 states that annual production and consumption are each about 8 billion metric tons. So China produces about half of 8 billion, or 4 billion, metric tons annually.

6

4. The word "progressively" in the passage is closest in meaning to

   ✓ (A) gradually

   ✗ (B) liberally

   ✗ (C) markedly

   ✗ (D) sharply

VOCABULARY. "Progressively" = gradually increasing, advancing in a steady, step-by-step way, "more and more."

CORRECT. "Each grade of coal is progressively harder and blacker" = each grade of coal is gradually harder and blacker.

In political contexts, "progressive" and "liberal" can mean nearly the same thing. But in this neutral context, "liberally" = freely, generously, substantially. That's not the same as "increasingly." The meaning of "liberally" may even be opposed to the idea of progressive, *gradual* increase.

"Marked" = noticeable. This is opposed to the gradual sense of "progressively."

Even more opposed to the gradual sense of "progressively."

	Paragraph 4	Comments
S1	Coal is extracted from the ground via coal mining, which can be divided into two categories: surface mining and underground mining.	Coal mining = surface or underground.
2	Strip, or "open cut," mining is primarily used for surface mining, because it recovers a larger proportion of the available coal deposits.	Strip mining — type of surface mining.
3	With **this method**, deep chunks of earth are razed, with the "overburden," or rock and soil covering the deposits, removed via explosives, power shovels, and trucks.	How it is done.
4	Once the coal is exposed, it is then **ruptured** into strips and transported to coal refineries or directly to sites where it will be consumed.	
5	Contour mining and mountaintop removal mining are surface mining techniques that are comparable to strip mining, but are typically directed toward coal deposits found underneath the slope of a hill or inside a mountain.	Other surface mining techniques: contour and mountaintop removal.

5. The word "ruptured" in the passage is closest in meaning to

   ✗ (A) mended

   ✗ (B) arranged

   ✓ (C) cracked

   ✗ (D) fashioned

VOCABULARY. "Ruptured" = broken, burst, cracked, shattered.

Opposite. "Mended" = repaired or fixed.

"Arranged" = positioned, organized in some particular way. This does not convey the meaning of "ruptured," which is more explosive and chaotic.

CORRECT. "It is then ruptured into strips" = the coal is then cracked or broken into strips.

"Fashioned" = made with skill and care. This also does not imply the chaotic meaning of "ruptured."

6.   The phrase "this method" in the passage refers to

REFERENCE. The phrase "this method" occurs at the beginning of S3. It refers to subject of the previous sentence: strip mining, also called "open cut" mining.

✗   (A) coal mining

This paragraph and following paragraphs broadly discuss coal mining. But at this stage in the paragraph, the passage is discussing a very specific subcategory of coal mining: strip mining.

✗   (B) underground mining

Underground mining is mentioned in S1 as one of the two main categories of coal mining. But this paragraph focuses on the other category: surface mining. This specific part of the paragraph discusses the subcategory of surface mining called strip mining.

✗   (C) surface mining

Surface mining is mentioned at the end of S1, and strip mining is indeed a form of surface mining. But according to the paragraph, surface mining is a category of techniques. Strip mining is one subcategory of surface mining (others are described in S5). Strip mining is what "this method" refers to.

✓   (D) strip mining

CORRECT. S2–3: "Strip, or 'open cut,' mining is primarily used for surface mining, because it recovers a larger proportion of the available coal deposits. With this method ..." = with strip mining.

Paragraph 5	**Comments**
S1 Underground mining is more prevalent than strip mining, as most coal deposits are too far below the surface to make strip mining practical.	Underground mining is more common.
2 In underground mining, deep vertical shafts are drilled, with coal miners and equipment descending down the shafts to extract the coal in the horizontal deposits found between and around the shafts.	How it is done. Vertical shafts. Horizontal deposits.
3 As coal is removed, the weight of the rock and soil above the coal deposits, known as the "mine roof," becomes supported more and more tenuously.	
4 Thus, hydraulic "roof supports" are positioned to buttress the ground above the mines in order to prevent dangerous cave-ins.	Roof supports are put in place as coal is removed.
5 Once the mining operation is completed, these roof supports are removed, and in most cases the mine roof eventually collapses.	Supports are taken out afterwards.

7. Which of the sentences below best expresses the essential information in the highlighted sentence in paragraph 5? Incorrect choices change the meaning in important ways or leave out essential information.

SIMPLIFY SENTENCE. The first part of S3 discusses the removal of coal from a mine; the second part defines "mine roof," and the third part is what happens to this mine roof due to the removal of coal.

✓ (A) The weight of the "mine roof," or rock and soil above the coal deposits, becomes increasingly unsupported as coal is removed.

CORRECT. This choice says essentially the same thing as S3, but simplifies the language somewhat. "Tenuous" = weak, fragile, shaky.

✗ (B) As coal is removed, rock and soil overhead becomes supported more and more weakly, in a process known as the "mine roof."

"Mine roof" does not refer to the process of rock and soil becoming supported more weakly. It refers to the rock and soil itself.

✗ (C) As it is removed, the coal becomes more shakily supported because of the weight of the "mine roof," or rock and soil above.

The rock and soil overhead, or "mine roof," becomes supported more tenuously—not the coal itself, as in this version.

✗ (D) As the weight of rock and soil above the deposits is removed, coal from the "mine roof" becomes less solidly supported.

Coal is being removed, not the rock and soil above it.

8. According to paragraph 5, risk of collapse of the mine roof during underground mining is

FACT. S3 introduces the concept of a mine roof and describes how its weight becomes supported more tenuously (= weakly) after coal underneath is removed. S4–5 discuss what is done to remedy the risk of "dangerous cave-ins."

✗ (A) eliminated by permanent hydraulic roof supports

According to S5, once mining is completed, these roof supports are removed, and mines often collapse eventually. So the risk of roof collapse is not eliminated forever, and the supports are not permanently in place.

✓ (B) temporarily mitigated by hydraulic roof supports

CORRECT. According to S5, once mining is completed, these roof supports are removed, and mines often eventually collapse. "Mitigate" = partially lessen, alleviate, or diminish something bad.

✗ (C) buttressed by hydraulic roof supports

S4 states that hydraulic roof supports are brought in to "prevent dangerous cave-ins." The roof itself is buttressed (= supported, reinforced) by the hydraulic roof supports. The risk of roof collapse is lessened.

✗ (D) increased by positioning hydraulic roof supports

S4 states that hydraulic roof supports are brought in to "prevent dangerous cave-ins," not increase the risk of such cave-ins.

Paragraph 6	Comments
S1 While safety measures have evolved considerably over the past century, coal mining is still considered a dangerous occupation.	Coal mining is dangerous.
2 Between 1900 and 1999, over 100,000 coal miners perished in the United States alone.	Many deaths.
3 Roof collapse, gas explosions, gas poisoning, wall failure, coal dust explosions, and suffocation are among the many reasons for these deaths.	Many reasons.
4 Moreover, the use of coal causes a number of serious health and environmental problems.	Also, health and environmental problems.
5 Lung cancer and "black lung" can be caused by the burning and mining of coal, while the ashes from burnt coal contain poisonous heavy metals that can leak into the ground and atmosphere.	
6 Coal-fired power plants contaminate soil and groundwater and can lead to acid rain, which can harm ecosystems hundreds of miles away.	
7 Coal is also a primary contributor to the rise of "greenhouse gases," such as carbon dioxide, which can lead to global climate change.	
8 While "clean coal" technologies can reduce or remove some of these threats, many such technologies will take decades to implement, and questions remain about whether it will ever be economically or politically possible to do so.	Clean coal technologies may help. But they will take decades. May never be possible.

6

9. The author mentions coal dust explosions in paragraph 6 in order to

PURPOSE. S3 mentions coal dust explosions in a list of causes of death among coal miners.

✗ (A) introduce a possible use for coal

Coal dust explosions are listed as a cause of death, not as a possible use for coal.

✓ (B) provide an example of an occupational hazard

CORRECT. S3: "Roof collapse, gas explosions, gas poisoning, wall failure, coal dust explosions, and suffocation are among the many reasons for these deaths" (from coal mining).

✗ (C) explain how coal-fired power plants operate

S6 discusses coal-fired power plants, but coal dust explosions are not part of this discussion.

✗ (D) surface a reason for concern about greenhouse gases

S7 discusses greenhouse gases, but coal dust explosions is not part of this discussion.

10.   The word "**contaminate**" in the passage is closest in meaning to

   ✗ (A) fertilize

   ✗ (B) extract

   ✓ (C) pollute

   ✗ (D) exhaust

VOCABULARY. "Contaminate" = pollute, make unclean or unusable by adding something poisonous.

Nearly opposite. "Fertilize" = feed, enrich.

Unrelated. "Extract" = remove or release (physically). While this might eventually contaminate the soil and groundwater, the soil and groundwater are not themselves removed.

CORRECT. "Coal-fired power plants contaminate soil and groundwater" = they pollute soil and groundwater.

"Exhaust" = use up, consume. Again, this is not a precise synonym for "contaminate."

11.   Which of the following is mentioned in paragraph 6 as one of the ways in which the combustion of coal can cause health problems?

   ✗ (A) Greenhouse gas release

   ✓ (B) Heavy metal leakage

   ✗ (C) Suffocation

   ✗ (D) Failure of mine walls

FACT. Much of S4–8 is devoted to the health risks of mining and burning coal, while the rest discusses environmental impacts. The question focuses on health issues caused by burning (combusting) coal.

S7 states that greenhouse gases can come from the burning of coal. But this is described as an environmental concern much more than as a direct health concern.

CORRECT. S5: "the ashes from burnt coal contain poisonous heavy metals that can leak into the ground and atmosphere."

S3 mentions suffocation as a potential cause of death from mining coal, not burning it.

S3 mentions wall failure as a potential cause of death from mining coal, not burning it.

Paragraph 5	Comments
S1–2 Underground mining is more prevalent than strip mining, as most coal deposits are too far below the surface to make strip mining practical. In underground mining, deep vertical shafts are drilled, with coal miners and equipment descending down the shafts to extract the coal in the horizontal deposits found between and around the shafts.	
3 **A** As coal is removed, the weight of the rock and soil above the coal deposits, known as the "mine roof," becomes supported more and more tenuously.	S2 does not provide a suitable reference for "This breakdown."
4 **B** Thus, hydraulic "roof supports" are positioned to buttress the ground above the mines in order to prevent dangerous cave-ins.	S3 does not provide a suitable reference for "This breakdown."
5 **C** Once the mining operation is completed, these roof supports are removed, and in most cases the mine roof eventually collapses.	"Dangerous cave-ins" in S4 seems like a good reference for "This breakdown." However, one noun is singular, while the other noun is plural. This reference doesn't work grammatically.
End **D**	**CORRECT.** Placing the new sentence here properly links the eventual collapse of the mine roof to "This breakdown," which can lead to earthquakes and the ground possibly giving way.

12. **This breakdown can lead to earthquakes and an increased likelihood that the ground above the mine could give way.**

   Where would the sentence best fit?

   ✗ (A) Choice A
   ✗ (B) Choice B
   ✗ (C) Choice C
   ✓ (D) Choice D

INSERT TEXT. The sentence before the insertion needs to provide a reference for "This breakdown." That is, in the previous sentence, something must break down. It also should be reasonable that this breakdown can lead to the consequences described.

CORRECT.

	Whole Passage	Comments
P1	Coal is an ignitable, or burnable, black or dark brown rock that is generally found within deep layers of sedimentary rock …	Coal is a burnable rock found in deep rock layers. Formed from buried plant material. Gradually build up layers on top. Eventually makes coal.
P2	As coal forms, it progresses through a series of stages, called grades, ranging from peat, which is considered the predecessor to coal, to lignite, bituminous, and finally anthracite coal …	Different grades of coal. Progressively harder and blacker. Uses of the different grades.
P3	For at least 6,000 years, coal has been used for various purposes, starting with the use of black lignite for carving into ornaments in China …	Coal has been used since ancient times. Current sources. Total amount produced and used.
P4	Coal is extracted from the ground via coal mining, which can be divided into two categories: surface mining and underground mining …	Coal mining = surface or underground. Strip mining = type of surface mining. How it is done. Other surface mining techniques: contour and mountaintop removal.
P5	Underground mining is more prevalent than strip mining, as most coal deposits are too far below the surface to make strip mining practical …	Underground mining is more common. How it is done. Vertical shafts. Horizontal deposits. Roof supports are put in place as coal is removed. Supports are taken out afterwards.
P6	While safety measures have evolved considerably over the past century, coal mining is still considered a dangerous occupation …	Coal mining is dangerous. Many deaths. Many reasons. Also, health and environmental problems. Clean coal technologies may help. But they will take decades. May never be possible.

6

13.   **Coal, the well-known fuel, is formed as plant material is crushed over many years under deep, growing layers of rock.**

SUMMARY. Correct answers must be clearly expressed in the passage. They must also be among the major points of the passage. They should tie as directly as possible to the summary given.

✓ ☐A First used for carving ornaments over 6,000 years ago, coal is now produced in vast quantities worldwide for fuel consumption.

CORRECT. The use of coal through history, culminating in the enormous amounts produced and consumed worldwide today, is the central point of P3.

✗ ☐B Coal's hardest and darkest grade, anthracite, is now principally used as an indoor heating fuel.

P2 mentions this specific detail. But it is minor in the context of the passage.

✓ ☐C Coal is extracted either at the surface by stripping away ground above the deposit or deep underground via vertical shafts.

CORRECT. The methods of extracting coal from the ground are detailed in P4–5. This sentence summarizes those paragraphs.

✓ ☐D Coal mining is very dangerous, and society's use of coal has led to serious health and environmental consequences.

CORRECT. This is the focus of P6.

✗ ☐E China is the leading global producer of coal, with much of the rest coming from the United States, India, Australia, and Europe.

This detail is mentioned in P3. In the scope of the whole passage, it is minor.

✗ ☐F It is probable that clean coal technologies will soon reduce the health and environmental threats posed by coal.

P6 asserts that many of these technologies would take decades to implement, and questions remain about whether it will ever be possible to do so.

6

Answers and Explanations—6.7 The Sixth Amendment

	Paragraph 1	Comments
S1	The Sixth Amendment to the United States Constitution provides a set of rights to people accused of crimes—including, most famously, the right to counsel.	Sixth Amendment: rights to people accused of crimes.
2	This right specifies that people accused of crimes are entitled to be represented by an attorney.	Right to counsel (attorney).
3	It is the most well-known right granted by the Sixth Amendment, and the reason may be that, according to the Supreme Court, it is the most important of the Sixth Amendment rights.	Most well-known right. Supreme Court: may be most important Sixth Amendment right.
4	In the 1984 case *United States v. Cronic*, which was a case about how to interpret the Sixth Amendment's right to counsel, the Supreme Court wrote, "Of all the rights that an accused person has, the right to be represented by counsel is by far the most pervasive, for it affects his ability to assert any other rights he may have."	Affects ability to assert any other rights.

1. In paragraph 1, what does the author claim about the right to counsel in the United States Constitution?

    FACT. S1 introduces the right to counsel as a Sixth Amendment right. This right is defined in S2 and commented on through the rest of P1.

    ✗ (A) It is the most pervasive of the rights guaranteed by the Sixth Amendment.

    S4 quotes the opinion of the Supreme Court that the right to counsel is "the most pervasive" of the Sixth Amendment rights. But this is not necessarily the *author's* claim.

    ✗ (B) It is provided both to people accused of crimes and to people suspected of crimes.

    The right is provided to "people accused of crimes" (S2). But the passage never states that it is provided to people who are just suspected of crimes.

    ✗ (C) It is the most important of all the rights guaranteed by the Constitution.

    In S3, the author writes that "according to the Supreme Court," the right to counsel is "the most important of the Sixth Amendment rights." However, this does not indicate that is actually is the most important right in that Amendment or in the Constitution as a whole.

    ✓ (D) It is the most well-known right of those guaranteed by the Sixth Amendment.

    CORRECT. S3: "It is the most well-known right granted by the Sixth Amendment." The author is making this statement on his or her own.

MANHATTAN PREP

2. Which of the following can be inferred from paragraph 1 about the right to counsel?

INFERENCE. Every sentence in P1 discusses the right to counsel in some way. So the correct answer could be anywhere. Regardless, it must be clearly supported by the text.

✗ (A) Is it only considered important because of a Supreme Court ruling.

It is presented that the Supreme Court found the right to counsel is the most important Sixth Amendment right. But there is no evidence that it is only considered important because of this.

✓ (B) At times, it can be interpreted by a court.

CORRECT. S4 states that the Supreme Court heard a case about how to interpret the right.

✗ (C) It typically depends on the other Sixth Amendment rights.

The Supreme Court stated the opposite in the quote in S4. The other Sixth Amendment rights depend on the right to counsel.

✗ (D) It is the primary cause of employment for attorneys.

The right to counsel guarantees representation by an attorney for people accused of crimes. But that does not mean that this right is the primary reason that attorneys are employed.

Paragraph 2	Comments
S1	Today, the Sixth Amendment entitles all people of any age (including juveniles, or children under the age of 18) to legal representation (an attorney) when they face potential imprisonment through criminal proceedings.	How the Sixth Amendment works today to provide right to counsel.
2	The attorney must be available at every "critical stage" of the person's legal case, and the attorney must also provide "effective representation."	How the attorney must work.
3	In the 1963 case *Gideon v. Wainwright*, the Supreme Court ruled that this right must be provided by the states.	States must provide the right.
4	The states may delegate the obligation to smaller governmental entities within, such as counties and cities, but they must make sure that the counties and cities are able to fulfill their duty, so that the right is not violated by any level of government.	They can delegate to counties/cities but must ensure fulfillment.

6

3. The word "delegate" in the passage is closest in meaning to

VOCABULARY. "Delegate" = give, assign, hand over (a task or authority) to someone or something.

✗ (A) adjust

Not quite. "Adjust" = change to fit. The word "delegate" does not imply that the obligation itself was changed at all.

✗ (B) justify

Unrelated. If the state was only "justifying" the obligation to cities or counties, it would mean that they would defend it or give reasons for its importance. This is not the same as handing it over to them.

✗ (C) explain

Unrelated. "Explaining" the obligation to cities or counties is not the same as handing it over to them.

✓ (D) assign

CORRECT. "The states may delegate the obligation to smaller governmental entities" = the states may assign the obligation to smaller governmental entities.

4. According to *Gideon v. Wainwright*, the Supreme Court determined that the obligation to provide counsel

FACT. S3 introduces this case and states its central finding. S4 elaborates on how the obligation could be fulfilled.

✓ (A) fell to the states, which could in turn delegate it

CORRECT. S3: "In the 1963 case *Gideon v. Wainwright*, the Supreme Court ruled that this right must be provided by the states." S4: "The states may delegate the obligation."

✗ (B) had to be directly carried out by the states themselves

S4 mentions that states can assign the obligation to other entities.

✗ (C) could be met by counties but not by cities

S4: "The states may delegate the obligation to smaller governmental entities within, such as counties and cities."

✗ (D) was primarily a responsibility of federal courts

The only federal court mentioned is the Supreme Court. S3–4 describe how this obligation is primarily a responsibility of the states, even if they delegate it to cities and counties.

5. The word "they" in the passage refers to

REFERENCE. In the latter part of S4, the pronoun "they" refers back to the subject of the same sentence: "states." This is the most important noun in S4.

✓ (A) states

CORRECT. "The states may delegate the obligation to smaller governmental entities within, such as counties and cities, but they (= the states) must make sure that the counties and cities are able to fulfill their duty." This is the only reading that makes sense.

✗ (B) counties

The pronoun "they" does not have to refer to a close prior noun. In this case, it refers back to the most distant prior noun in S4, "states," which is the subject of the sentence.

✗ (C) smaller governmental entities

Again, the pronoun "they" does not have to refer to a close prior noun.

✗ (D) cities

Again, the pronoun "they" does not have to refer to a close prior noun, even one that is just a couple of words away.

Paragraph 3	**Comments**
S1 The Sixth Amendment changed the landscape of criminal justice in the United States.	Sixth Amendment changed US criminal justice.
2 Prior to its adoption, criminal cases looked very different.	
3 Victims, not government officials (prosecutors), typically brought cases against the people they accused of committing a crime against them.	Before, victims brought criminal cases.
4 Now, it is the government that brings a criminal case—the victim may be a witness who testifies, but he or she is not one of the two "parties" to the case.	Now the government does.
5 Before the adoption of the Sixth Amendment, typically neither side was represented by a lawyer in a criminal case.	Neither side used to use lawyers.
6 Finally, criminal trials were much shorter prior to the Sixth Amendment.	Trials used to be much shorter.
7 Instead of weeks or even months, such trials lasted only minutes or hours.	
8 It was when lawyers became **integral to** the process that trials became longer and increased in complexity.	

6. The phrase "**integral to**" in the passage is closest in meaning to

VOCABULARY. "Integral to" = essential to, vitally important to, a fundamental part of.

✗ (A) committed to

Not quite. The lawyers are not "committed to" (devoted or dedicated to) the trials in this sentence. They are a necessary or required part of them.

✗ (B) involved in

Not quite. "Involved in" doesn't convey the idea of necessity that "integral to" does.

✓ (C) essential to

CORRECT. "Lawyers became integral to the process" = lawyers became essential to the process, they became an essential part of the process.

✗ (D) ideal for

Unrelated. The lawyers are "ideal for" trials, in that it is the definition of their job. However, this sentence is indicating that lawyers had become a necessary or essential part of the process (this is stronger than just saying they were well suited).

7. Paragraph 3 states that since the adoption of the Sixth Amendment, the victim of a crime may

FACT. S3–4 discuss how the role of the crime victim in the criminal justice process changed with the Sixth Amendment.

✗ (A) bring a criminal case against the accused

S4: "Now, it is the government that brings a criminal case," not the victim as was typical before the Sixth Amendment.

✓ (B) testify as a witness in the case

CORRECT. S4: "The victim may be a witness who testifies."

✗ (C) be one of the two parties to the case

S4: "The victim … is not one of the two 'parties' to the case."

✗ (D) not accuse the possible criminal of committing a crime

The Sixth Amendment gives rights to the accused. But nothing in the passage suggests that a victim cannot accuse a possible criminal of committing the crime in question. It's just that this accusation would not necessarily be a formal part of the government's case.

8. Which of the following can be inferred from paragraph 3?

INFERENCE. The question doesn't provide any direction about where to look in the paragraph.

✓ (A) Lawyers were more common in criminal cases after the Sixth Amendment than before it.

CORRECT. S1: the Sixth Amendment changed the criminal justice system. S4: "Before the adoption of the Sixth Amendment, typically neither side was represented by a lawyer in a criminal case." You can infer that after the Sixth Amendment, lawyers were more common in criminal cases.

✗ (B) Criminal trials were longer prior to the Sixth Amendment.

S5 states the opposite.

✗ (C) If not for the Sixth Amendment, people accused of crimes would have few rights.

The paragraph outlines how the Sixth Amendment changed the process of criminal justice. The passage as a whole discusses the rights granted by the Sixth Amendment to people accused of crimes. But that does not mean that the passage is anywhere suggesting that, without the Sixth Amendment, people accused of crimes would have few rights in general. After all, their other constitutional rights would still be present.

✗ (D) Lawyers were not at all present in criminal cases prior to the Sixth Amendment.

While lawyers were less common before the Sixth Amendment, "not at all" is extreme.

Paragraph 4	**Comments**
S1 As the United States criminal justice system expanded and grew more complicated, trials became more expensive to conduct, and the system became congested by the number of cases.	Criminal justice system grew. Trials became more expensive. More cases.
2 It is at least in part for this reason—to save time and money—that the "plea bargain" emerged.	So the "plea bargain" emerged.
3 A plea bargain is an agreement between the prosecution and the defense.	
4 Under the "plea," the defendant agrees to plead guilty or "no contest" in exchange for sentencing for a lesser offense, which **generally** results in a shorter sentence or less severe penalty.	Agreement: defendant pleads guilty or "no contest" in return for a less severe penalty.

9.   Why does the author use the word "**generally**" in mentioning that pleas result in shorter sentences?

    PURPOSE. "Generally" = usually, typically, in general. The author uses this word in S4 to make a claim that is less than absolute about something that "generally" happens.

✗ (A) Penalties can be less severe without sentences being shorter.

    These are the general results of a plea bargain. They are not the reason *why* the author mentions it.

✗ (B) Exceptions to the rule are more numerous than might be expected.

    There is no discussion about exceptions to a rule.

✓ (C) Shorter sentences are typical but not certain.

    CORRECT. S4 notes that sentencing for a lesser offense "generally results in a shorter sentence or less severe penalty." So, this outcome typically happens, but it is not certain.

✗ (D) Longer sentences are in fact more likely in certain states.

    There is no indication about sentencing in different states.

6

	Paragraph 5	Comments
S1	The trend toward plea bargaining began in the 1800s, but it was in the 1900s that plea bargains began to dominate the criminal justice process in the United States.	History of plea bargains.
2	By the 1930s, 90 percent of convictions were achieved through plea bargains.	90% of convictions by 1930s.
3	At that time, federal prosecutions under the Prohibition Act, which outlawed alcohol consumption (among other related things), had become so numerous that the only way of moving cases through the system seemed to be to encourage those accused of minor offenses to accept lighter penalties.	Prohibition created many prosecutions. Plea bargains were used to lessen the congestion.
4	Today, that percentage is even higher and includes all levels of offenses, not just minor ones.	Even higher percentage today.
5	In 2013, more than 97 percent of federal cases that were not dismissed were resolved through plea bargaining.	Federal cases: 97%.
6	That means less than 3 percent went to trial.	
7	When state cases are added, the combined percentage of cases that are resolved through plea bargains hovers around 90 to 95 percent.	With state cases: 90-95%.

10.   Which of the sentences below best expresses the essential information in the highlighted portion of the passage? Incorrect choices change the meaning in important ways or leave out essential information.

SIMPLIFY SENTENCE. The major ideas of S3 can be separated. 1) The Prohibition Act outlawed alcohol consumption in the 1930s (this is background). 2) Federal prosecutions became very numerous. 3) As a result, to move cases through the system, people accused of minor offenses were encouraged to accept lighter penalties. It was thought that this maneuver was the only way to achieve the goal. This is the meaning of "the only way … seemed to be." Not all of these ideas can be kept as they are compressed into a simpler sentence. But the core story should remain.

✗ (A) Because of the nature of the Prohibition Act, it became no longer feasible to offer lighter penalties to those accused under it.

The original version states the opposite.

✓ (B) Offering lighter penalties to some accused people was used to reduce the large number of prosecutions created under the Prohibition Act.

CORRECT. This version preserves the central meaning of S3.

✗ (C) Under the Prohibition Act, it became impossible to conduct prosecutions, given their number, so offering shorter penalties became necessary.

"Impossible to conduct prosecutions" is extreme. It was more difficult, but not necessarily impossible. Also, "necessary" is unjustified. To some people, it seemed necessary to offer plea bargains, but the author of the sentence is not saying so.

✗ (D) To fight court congestion, anyone prosecuted under the Prohibition Act was given the option of a lighter penalty via a plea bargain.

"Anyone" is extreme and not supported in the text. Ninety percent of convictions were achieved under plea bargains, but that doesn't mean that everyone was given the option.

11.   The word "hovers" in the passage is closest in meaning to

VOCABULARY. "Hover" = float in place, stay near with only little variation.

✗ (A) exceeds

The number does not "exceed" (surpass or greater than) 90 to 95 percent, it stays in that range.

✗ (B) increases

If the number increases 90 to 95 percent, then adding the state cases would nearly double the number of plea bargains. The federal rate was 97 percent while the combined rate "hovers" (stays close to) 90 to 95 percent. This is actually lower by combining them. And "increases" is not a synonym for "hover."

✗ (C) drops

If the number drops 90 to 95 percent, then adding the state cases would significantly reduce the number of plea bargains. The percent does drop slightly, but it doesn't drop by 90 to 95 percent. Rather it drops to. And "drops" is not a synonym for "hover."

✓ (D) remains

CORRECT. "The combined percentage of cases that are resolved through plea bargains hovers around 90 to 95 percent" = the combined percentage remains around 90 to 95 percent.

	Paragraph 5	**Comments**
S1	The trend toward plea bargaining began in the 1800s, but it was in the 1900s that plea bargains began to dominate the criminal justice process in the United States.	
2	**A** By the 1930s, 90 percent of convictions were achieved through plea bargains.	S1 is about the 1900s, while the new sentence is about the present. Then S2 switches back to the 1930s. This temporal flow would be jarring.
3	**B** At that time, federal prosecutions under the Prohibition Act, which outlawed alcohol consumption (among other related things), had become so numerous that the only way of moving cases through the system seemed to be to encourage those accused of minor offenses to accept lighter penalties.	Again, the flow of time does not work if the new sentence is inserted here. S2 and S3 ("At that time") are both about the 1930s. But the new sentence is about the present day.
4	**C** Today, that percentage is even higher and includes all levels of offenses, not just minor ones.	S3 is still about the 1930s, so the inserted sentence doesn't properly extend it. Moreover, it breaks the logic flow from S2–3 to S4 (which focuses on "that percentage," referring back to the percentage cited in S2).
5–7	**D** In 2013, more than 97 percent of federal cases that were not dismissed were resolved through plea bargaining. That means less than 3 percent went to trial. When state cases are added, the combined percentage of cases that are resolved through plea bargains hovers around 90 to 95 percent.	**CORRECT.** S4 brings the discussion to the present. With "all levels of offenses, not just minor ones," S4 provides a good launching point for the new sentence, which can then extend the idea of S4.

12. **In fact, even individuals accused of society's most serious crimes are often pressured nowadays to accept plea bargains in order to save cost.**

INSERT TEXT. The "In fact" means that this sentence is extending an idea presented in the previous sentence. In this case, it will have to do with even people accused of the most serious crimes being pressured to plea bargain. So the prior sentence will likely focus on more minor crimes. "Nowadays" also places the time of the sentence in the present.

Where would the sentence best fit?

✗ (A) Choice A

✗ (B) Choice B

✗ (C) Choice C

✓ (D) Choice D   **CORRECT.**

Whole Passage	**Comments**
P1 The Sixth Amendment to the United States Constitution provides a set of rights to people accused of crimes—including, most famously, the right to counsel …	Sixth Amendment: rights to people accused of crimes. Right to counsel (attorney). Most well-known right. Supreme Court: may be most important Sixth Amendment right. Affects ability to assert any other rights.
P2 Today, the Sixth Amendment entitles all people of any age (including juveniles, or children under the age of 18) to legal representation (an attorney) when they face potential imprisonment through criminal proceedings …	How the Sixth Amendment works today to provide right to counsel. How the attorney must work. States must provide the right. They can delegate to counties/cities but must ensure fulfillment.
P3 The Sixth Amendment changed the landscape of criminal justice in the United States …	Sixth Amendment changed US criminal justice. Before, victims brought criminal cases. Now the government does. Neither side used to use lawyers. Trials used to be much shorter.
P4 As the United States criminal justice system expanded and grew more complicated, trials became more expensive to conduct, and the system became congested by the number of cases …	Criminal justice system grew. Trials became more expensive. More cases. So the "plea bargain" emerged. Agreement: defendant pleads guilty or "no contest" in return for a less severe penalty.
P5 The trend toward plea bargaining began in the 1800s, but it was in the 1900s that plea bargains began to dominate the criminal justice process in the United States …	History of plea bargains. 90% of convictions by 1930s. Prohibition created many prosecutions. Plea bargains were used to lessen the congestion. Even higher percentage today. Federal cases: 97%. With state cases: 90-95%.

6

13. **The Sixth Amendment, especially its declaration of the right to counsel, changed criminal justice in the United States.**

SUMMARY. Correct answers must be clearly expressed in the passage. They must also be among the major points of the passage. They should tie as directly as possible to the summary given.

✗ ☐ A   Prior to the Sixth Amendment, only some people were represented by attorneys, and trials tended to be longer.

The second part of this sentence is incorrect. The passage states that trials used to be shorter.

✓ ☐ B   A famous Sixth Amendment right is the right of a person accused of a crime to be represented by an attorney.

CORRECT. This is the focus of P1. Indeed, this right to counsel is the focus of the entire passage.

✗ ☐ C   The longer a criminal trial goes on, the more costly it is for the government.

While true (P4 S1), this particular detail is too specific to be a central idea of this passage.

✓ ☐ D   Today, the vast majority of United States prosecutions end in plea bargains, with defendants accepting lesser penalties.

CORRECT. This is the culmination of P5.

✓ ☐ E   With the Sixth Amendment, criminal trials changed, lengthening as lawyers became involved and the government took over the role of prosecution.

CORRECT. This idea is the core of P3.

✗ ☐ F   In the course of their work, courts must decide how to interpret the Sixth Amendment.

Only one moment in the passage (in P1) alludes to courts interpreting the Sixth Amendment.

Answers and Explanations—6.8 Signaling Theory

	Paragraph 1	Comments
S1	There is a history of controversy within evolutionary biology over why honesty exists in animal communication.	Why is animal communication honest?
2	All animals, humans included, engage in communication that involves both a sender and a receiver, and this communication occurs both within and across species.	All animals communicate.
3	The sender communicates a signal to a receiver, who then acts upon that signal.	Communication = send + receive signals.
4	Male peacocks seek to signal their worthiness to females of the species by growing vibrant tail feathers, and gazelles engage in spectacular leaping displays, called stotting, upon seeing approaching predators in order to indicate their athletic prowess and therefore dissuade the predator from attacking.	Examples.

MANHATTAN PREP

1. According to paragraph 1, what is true of animal communication?

FACT. All of P1 discusses animal communication. The correct answer must be supported in the text.

✗ (A) It often indicates the athletic prowess of the sender.

S4 mentions that gazelles communicate their athletic prowess in a certain way. But this is not necessarily the case with all or even most animal communication.

✓ (B) It involves a receiver who acts upon the communication sent.

CORRECT. S3: "The sender communicates a signal to a receiver, who then acts upon that signal."

✗ (C) Senders and receivers must be of the same species.

S2: "this communication occurs both within and across species."

✗ (D) Evolutionary biologists agree on the reasons why it is honest.

S1: "There is a history of controversy within evolutionary biology over why honesty exists in animal communication."

Paragraph 2	**Comments**
S1 In some cases, a signal may be honest, meaning that the sender is conveying accurate information, but signals can also be dishonest when the sender is providing false information to a receiver.	Honest and dishonest signals.
2 All signals, however, share the additional feature of being costly to produce and send.	All signals are costly.
3 A peacock's tail feathers have significant weight and take excessive energy to produce.	Examples.
4 A bird chirping to alert others in the flock of a nearby predator has now exposed its own location to that same predator, potentially making it more vulnerable to attack.	

2. Why does the author mention "a bird chirping to alert others"?

PURPOSE. The chirping (in S4) is an example of a signal that has a cost to the signaler. The general point is made in S2.

✗ (A) To point out an example of a dishonest signal

Both examples in this paragraph are honest signals.

✗ (B) To illustrate cross-species communication

This signal is not cross-species. It is prompted by a predator (almost certainly of a different species), but the bird is chirping to alert other birds in its flock, which are of the same species.

✗ (C) To outline the requirements of an honest signal

This example is of an honest signal. But it does not describe any particular requirements of an honest signal.

✓ (D) To show how some signals are costly to send

CORRECT. S2 makes the point that all signals are costly to the sender. The example of the bird chirping in S4 illustrates this point. This chirping helps other birds but can put the chirping bird in even more danger.

3. The word "**conveying**" in the
    passage is closest in meaning to

    ✓ (A) transmitting

    ✗ (B) interpreting

    ✗ (C) withholding

    ✗ (D) manufacturing

VOCABULARY. "Convey" = transmit, communicate, send.

CORRECT. "The sender is conveying accurate information" = the sender is transmitting or communicating accurate information.

The sender is sending the messages, not "interpreting" (explaining) them.

Opposite. "Withholding" = retaining or refusing to give.

Not quite. "Manufacturing" signals would mean to create, devise, or even invent signals. The sender isn't necessarily making up new signals. They are communicating signals that might already exist.

	Paragraph 3	Comments
S1	Biologists have found that, in general, animals communicate with honest signals, but why?	Why are animals honest?
2	Deception would seem to provide short-term gains.	Lying seems useful (in short run).
3	For example, the male fiddler crab is known for its one large fighting claw, which it uses to compete for a mate with other male crabs.	Example of dishonest fiddler crab.
4	If a fiddler crab loses its claw in the fight, another claw that is lighter in weight and therefore less effective grows in its place.	
5	Although the crab can still scare off other mates with its new claw that is similar in size to the original, it is sending the dishonest signal to other males that it is strong and able to fight, although if challenged it would likely lose.	
6	Scientists theorize that signals must be honest on average, at least to a certain degree.	Scientists: signals must generally be honest or they'll stop working.
7	If not, the intended receiver would eventually evolve to ignore the signal, rendering it useless.	
8	In the early 1970s, biologist Amotz Zahavi proposed the handicap principle: honesty is maintained through handicaps, or high-cost signals, which are naturally more believable.	Handicap = high-cost signal = more believable.

4. According to paragraph 3, all of the following are characteristics of the replacement claw grown by a fiddler crab EXCEPT:

NEGATIVE FACT. S3–5 contain the fiddler crab example. S4–5 focus on the replacement claw. Three answer choices will be mentioned in the paragraph. One answer choice will not be.

✗ (A) It is similar in size to the original claw.

S5: "Its new claw ... is similar in size to the original."

✗ (B) It is not as heavy as the original claw.

S4: "another claw that is lighter in weight ... grows in its place."

✓ (C) It is no less effective than the original claw.

CORRECT. S4: "Another claw that is ... less effective grows in its place."

✗ (D) It functions as a dishonest signal.

S5: "it is sending the dishonest signal to other males."

	Paragraph 4	**Comments**
S1	The handicap principle relies on the assumption that prominent signals of fighting ability or selection may be impossible, or impossibly costly, to fake.	Handicap principle: prominent signals can't be faked.
2	For example, a full-grown bull elk's rack of antlers may weigh in excess of 40 pounds, a weight greater than a young, weak, or sickly individual could hope to carry.	Example of elk antlers. Only strong can grow.
3	Therefore, an elk able to grow a large rack of antlers is honestly signaling its ability to defend itself in a fight.	
4	Male peacock tail feathers present the same honest signal to females about the male's strength and desirability as a mate.	Example of peacock tail. Only strong can deal with the handicap.
5	The long tail not only takes significant effort to produce, but also creates issues for survival.	
6	The bright colors are more attractive to predators, and the length of the tail somewhat restricts flight and therefore the bird's ability to escape pursuit.	
7	As with the elk, a weaker or sicklier bird could not afford to produce such ornamentation.	
8	In both examples, the signal of strength is, in actuality, a handicap to the animal sending it.	Both examples: the signal of strength is the costly handicap.

6

5.   According to paragraph 4, the antlers of a full-grown bull elk are useful because

FACT. S2–3 discuss the example of a bull elk's antlers.

✓ (A) large, heavy antlers act as an authentic signal of strength

CORRECT. S3: "An elk able to grow a large rack of antlers is honestly signaling its ability to defend itself in a fight."

✗ (B) they allow scientists to estimate the age of the bull elk

This point is not mentioned in the paragraph.

✗ (C) they can be faked by sickly elks, which can then avoid costly fights

S2 indicates that sickly elks cannot carry such heavy racks of antlers.

✗ (D) they restrict the elk's ability to escape pursuit

This point is made in S6 about a peacock's tail feathers, not about the elk's antlers.

6.   The phrase "in actuality" in the passage is closest in meaning to

VOCABULARY. "Actuality" = reality, the real world.

✗ (A) in theory

Opposite. When talking about something "in theory," the speaker is hypothesizing rather than saying it is definitely true.

✗ (B) intentionally

The signal would not be an "intentional" (deliberate or calculated) handicap.

✓ (C) in reality

CORRECT. "The signal of strength is, in actuality, a handicap" = the signal is, in reality, a handicap.

✗ (D) unfortunately

While the handicap is likely unfortunate for the animal, these words are not synonyms.

Paragraph 5	Comments
S1 Thus, these revealing handicaps are honest signals of strength in the sense that some members of the species are better **equipped** to handle the costs of these handicaps.	Handicaps are honest signals.
2 While most biologists agree on the power of handicaps to maintain honest signaling, the question still debated is that of choice.	Is it a choice to use handicaps?
3 Are handicaps the result of a genetic condition that allows only certain members of the species to express the handicap fully?	Genetic condition?
4 Or do they happen when a more capable individual actively chooses to take on a visible hardship and therefore signal to others its **underlying** strength or abilities?	Or active choice?

7. The word "equipped" in the passage is closest in meaning to

    ✗ (A) exposed

    ✗ (B) evolved

    ✓ (C) prepared

    ✗ (D) disarmed

VOCABULARY. "Equipped" = prepared, enabled, armed.

Opposite to a large degree. "Exposed" = unprotected, unsheltered, vulnerable.

"Evolved" would mean that evolution did the preparing. That may be true in this case, but things can be equipped or prepared in other ways. "Evolved" is not a precise synonym for "equipped."

CORRECT. "Some members of the species are better equipped to handle the costs" = some members are better prepared to handle the costs.

Also somewhat opposite. "Disarmed" = deprived of weapons (arms).

8. According to paragraph 5, biologists continue to argue over which of the following with regard to handicaps?

    ✗ (A) Whether handicaps are an effective way to maintain honest signaling

    ✗ (B) Whether some individuals are better able to handle the costs of handicaps

    ✗ (C) Whether all handicaps are honest signals

    ✓ (D) Whether capable individuals choose to take on handicaps

FACT. S2 indicates that the debate is about whether there is the choice behind the handicaps. S3–4 discuss the options: either genetics dictate who can display this kind of signal or individuals themselves choose to display on the basis of their own strength and ability.

Opposite. S2 says that biologists agree on this.

Biologists agree on this point as well, which is made in S1.

Biologists do not seem to be debating this point, also made in S1.

CORRECT. S2: "the question still debated is that of choice." S3 poses one side of the debate (it's genetically determined to use handicaps as signals), while S4 poses the other side (it's an individual choice to do so).

6

9.   The word "underlying" in the passage is closest in meaning to

VOCABULARY. "Underlying" = fundamental, perhaps hidden under the surface but essential and real.

✗ (A) tremendous

Not quite. The individual would likely want to show "tremendous" (great or excessive) strength. However, great strength is not always hidden. These words are not synonyms.

✗ (B) physical

The individuals in question are likely indicating physical strength (as opposed to mental), but these words are not synonyms.

✗ (C) relative

Unrelated. When used as an adjective, the word "relative" typically means comparable, corresponding, or proportional.

✓ (D) inherent

CORRECT. "a more capable individual actively chooses to … signal to others its underlying strength" = a more capable individual chooses to signal its inherent or essential strength.

Paragraph 6	**Comments**
S1 The condition-dependent model suggests that the level of display of a behavior or trait is directly proportional to genetic quality and environmental conditions and therefore cannot be faked.	Condition-dependent model: genetics + environment = cannot be faked.
2 Some point to bright, iridescent plumage of some bird species as a condition-dependent, and therefore honest, handicap.	Feather example.
3 Without limited physical wear, low parasite load, and a nutritious diet, these shiny feathers are impossible to maintain.	
4 The choice model, alternatively, was advocated in 1990 by biologist Alan Grafen, who claimed that all animals have the option to display a large handicap, but each must choose whether and to what extent to display that handicap, according to its knowledge of its own ability level.	Choice model: all have option, but not all take it.
5 The optional signal remains honest because low-quality individuals will never signal at a level that is higher than would be advantageous for them, because of the increased cost of those signals.	Honest because signals are costly.

10. ✗ What can be inferred from paragraph 6 about certain birds with shiny, iridescent feathers?

INFERENCE. S2–3 discuss this example of shiny bird feathers.

✗ (A) They are choosing to maintain such feathers as a display.

S2: "Some point to bright, iridescent plumage of some bird species as a condition-dependent ... handicap." According to the passage, the condition-dependent model is opposed to the choice model (which is embraced in this answer choice).

✓ (B) They are honestly signaling their good health.

CORRECT. S2 states that these shiny feathers are a condition-dependent and honest handicap. S3 indicates that limited physical wear, low parasite load, and good nutrition support the bird's ability to maintain these feathers. These attributes are all indicators of good health.

✗ (C) They are handicapped by low-nutrient diets.

Their diets are in fact "nutritious" (S3). In addition, the handicap is actually the display of feathers. This is a specialized meaning of "handicap" that is developed in the passage: a handicap is a visible, costly signal of strength that cannot be faked because it is so costly to maintain.

✗ (D) It is a low-cost signal that can be feigned.

S2: This signal is honest. That is, it cannot be feigned (= faked). Also, it is not low-cost.

11. Which of the sentences below best expresses the essential information in the highlighted sentence in paragraph 3? Incorrect choices change the meaning in important ways or leave out essential information.

SIMPLIFY SENTENCE. S5 explains why a signal that is chosen is still honest. The reason is that weaker individuals will not choose high-cost signals.

✓ (A) Because weaker individuals will not choose costly signals, such signals must be honest.

CORRECT. This version properly simplifies the core ideas of S5.

✗ (B) Higher-quality individuals are the only ones capable of choosing and producing honest signals.

The original does not claim that only higher-quality individuals can choose and produce honest signals. Perhaps low-quality individuals can send other kinds of honest signals (besides these costly ones involving handicaps).

✗ (C) Weaker individuals will not survive if they choose to display costly signals.

This version exaggerates the impact on weaker individuals. The original states that weaker individuals will not choose to display costly signals. It never says that such individuals would actually die if they do make that choice.

✗ (D) A chosen signal cannot be considered honest if it does not have an increased cost.

The increased cost of a signal is a major reason why it can be considered honest. But the idea of the original sentence is not as general as it is presented in this version. The original is only justifying why chosen costly signals *can* be considered honest.

	Whole Passage	Comments
P1	There is a history of controversy within evolutionary biology over why honesty exists in animal communication …	Why is animal communication honest? All animals communicate. Communication = send + receive signals. Examples.
P2	In some cases, a signal may be honest, meaning that the sender is conveying accurate information, but signals can also be dishonest when the sender is providing false information to a receiver …	Honest and dishonest signals. All signals are costly. Examples.
P3	Biologists have found that, in general, animals communicate with honest signals, but why? …	Why are animals honest? Lying seems useful (in short run). Example of dishonest fiddler crab. Scientists: signals must generally be honest, or they'll stop working. Handicap = high-cost signal = more believable.
P4	The handicap principle relies on the assumption that prominent signals of fighting ability or selection may be impossible, or impossibly costly, to fake …	Handicap principle: prominent signals can't be faked. Example of elk antlers. Only strong can grow. Example of peacock tail. Only strong can deal with the handicap. Both examples: the signal of strength is the costly handicap.
P5	Thus, these revealing handicaps are honest signals of strength in the sense that some members of the species are better equipped to handle the costs of these handicaps …	Handicaps are honest signals. Is it a choice to use handicaps? Genetic condition? Or active choice?
P6	The condition-dependent model suggests that the level of display of a behavior or trait is directly proportional to genetic quality and environmental conditions and therefore cannot be faked …	Condition-dependent model: genetics + environment = cannot be faked. Feather example. Choice model: all have option, but not all take it. Honest because signals are costly.

6

  **MANHATTAN** PREP

12. The passage mentions which of the following as a dishonest signal?

FACT. The only mention of a dishonest signal is that of the fiddler crab's replacement claw in P3.

✗ (A) A male peacock's long ornamental tail feathers

These feathers are mentioned in P1 and P2. In P3, they are described as an "honest signal."

✗ (B) The stotting behavior of a gazelle

This stotting behavior (= "spectacular leaping") is mentioned in P1. It is not specifically described as either honest or dishonest. But the behavior is meant to indicate athletic prowess, and it seems impossible to engage in this behavior without actually having such prowess.

✗ (C) A bird chirping in response to a predator

This chirping is not described specifically as honest. But according to P2, it happens in response to the true presence of a predator. Faking is never mentioned. So this signal appears honest as well.

✓ (D) A fiddler crab's regrown fighting claw

CORRECT. In P3, the short-term gains of deception are illustrated with the example of the fiddler crab's claw. This is specifically described as a dishonest signal (S5).

Paragraph 3	Comments
S1–2 Biologists have found that, in general, animals communicate with honest signals, but why? Deception would seem to provide short-term gains.	
3 **A** For example, the male fiddler crab is known for its one large fighting claw, which it uses to compete for a mate with other male crabs.	Insertion here doesn't work. No particular dishonest signal has been introduced yet.
4–5 **B** If a fiddler crab loses its claw in the fight, another claw that is lighter in weight and therefore less effective grows in its place. Although the crab can still scare off other mates with its new claw that is similar in size to the original, it is sending the dishonest signal to other males that it is strong and able to fight, although if challenged it would likely lose.	Inserting the new sentence here won't work either. So far, the paragraph has not mentioned whether the claw is dishonest.
6–7 **C** Scientists theorize that signals must be honest on average, at least to a certain degree. If not, the intended receiver would eventually evolve to ignore the signal, rendering it useless.	**CORRECT.** S5 introduces the idea that the regrown claw is a dishonest signal. The new sentence can now refer back to that signal. Moreover, S6 can pick up from the new sentence, making the point that signals must be, on average, honest.
8 **D** In the early 1970s, biologist Amotz Zahavi proposed the handicap principle: honesty is maintained through handicaps, or high-cost signals, which are naturally more believable.	In this location, the "however" does not make sense. S6–7 agree with the inserted sentence: dishonest signals are rare, and honest ones are common.

13. **This dishonest signal, however, appears to be the exception.**

Where would the sentence best fit?

INSERT TEXT. The inserted sentence begins with "This dishonest signal." So the previous text must refer to this kind of signal. The new sentence also contains a "however," meaning that the new sentence introduces a permanent turn in the road about dishonest signals: namely, that they "appear to be the exception." So the prior sentence or sentences ought to be presenting a dishonest signal, and the following text should be discussing how most signals are actually honest.

✗ (A) Choice A

✗ (B) Choice B

✓ (C) Choice C   **CORRECT.**

✗ (D) Choice D

14. **Why animal signaling is typically honest is a question that many evolutionary biologists have tried to understand.**

SUMMARY. Correct answers must be clearly expressed in the passage. They must also be among the major points of the passage. They should tie as directly as possible to the summary given.

✗ [A] Because a weak individual is likely to have a less nutritious diet, its ability to produce a high-cost signal is reduced.

This particular case may hold for the example of a bird's shiny feathers (P6). But having a less nutritious diet is a minor point in this passage.

✓ [B] All animals communicate with one another, both within and across species, through signals that carry some cost to send.

CORRECT. This is the main idea of P1 and P2.

✓ [C] It is unclear whether individuals choose to exhibit specific handicaps or whether only some individuals are genetically capable of so doing.

CORRECT. This is the primary question discussed in P5 and P6.

✗ [D] One typical purpose of signals that animals send to other members of their species is to indicate mating desirability.

Indicating mating desirability might be one reason for signals, but not necessarily "typically." Moreover, this point is minor within the passage.

✓ [E] According to the handicap principle, honest signaling dominates because high-cost signals are more believable.

CORRECT. This is the main topic of discussion for P3 and P4.

✗ [F] By 1990, much of the debate over the issue of choice in animal signaling was resolved in favor of the condition-dependent model.

P6 indicates that the choice model was advocated in 1990, but not that the debate was resolved in either direction.

Chapter 7

Lectures A: Humanities

Listening lectures test your ability to comprehend academic-level spoken English. You'll listen to a short lecture (about 3 to 5 minutes long) from a professor. Occasionally, a student may also speak. You will only be able to listen to the lecture once. You will not be able to pause the recording or to replay any part of it (though some questions will replay a specific part of the lecture for you). You can take notes as you listen.

You will then answer six questions for that lecture. Most questions are multiple-choice with four options (select one from A, B, C, or D). Some questions may ask you to select more than one option or to fill in a table. You will have to answer the questions in order. You cannot return to a question once you have moved on to the next question.

Listening lectures test your understanding of main ideas, contrasts, the lecturer's tone and degree of certainty about the information, and why the lecturer relates certain information or examples. They also test your understanding of the organization of the lecture and the relationship between different ideas. Finally, they test your ability to make inferences or draw conclusions.

How should you use this chapter? Here are some recommendations, according to the level you've reached in TOEFL Listening:

1. **Fundamentals.** Start with a topic-focused chapter, such as this one. Start with a topic that is a "medium weakness"—not your worst area but not your best either. At first, listen to the lecture once, then work on the questions untimed and check the answer after each question. Review the solutions closely, think carefully about the principles at work, and articulate what you've learned. Redo questions as necessary. As you get better, time yourself and do all of the questions for a lecture at once, without stopping.

2. **Fixes.** Do an entire lecture and its associated questions under timed conditions. Don't replay any part of the lecture while you are still answering the questions! Examine the results, learn your lessons, then test yourself with another lecture and question set.

3. **Tweaks.** Confirm your mastery by doing two or three lectures in a row under timed conditions. Work your way up to doing four lectures and two conversations in one sitting. Aim to improve the speed and ease of your process.

Good luck on Listening!

7.1

1. What does the professor mainly discuss?

    (A) The history of costuming in theater

    (B) A writer's new perspective on theatrical costuming

    (C) The kind of costumes most popular in Shakespearean plays

    (D) A prominent playwright of the nineteenth century

2. According to the professor, how did Planché change traditional Shakespearean plays of the time? *Choose 2 answers.*

    [A] He modernized the costumes.

    [B] He expanded the number of costumes available to actors.

    [C] He introduced historically accurate costumes.

    [D] He rejected unrealistic costumes.

3. What can be inferred about the actors' views of Planché's work on *King John*?

    (A) They refused to wear historically accurate costumes.

    (B) Most of them preferred to wear costumes ironically.

    (C) They had complete control over their costumes.

    (D) Some of them initially thought that historically accurate costumes would not be well received.

4. What is the professor's opinion about the relationship between James Planché and later playwrights?

    (A) He thinks later playwrights met more resistance than Planché did when they tried to change costumes.

    (B) He thinks Planché distrusted the research of later playwrights.

    (C) He thinks later playwrights copied Planché's costuming practices.

    (D) He thinks Planché had less influence than has been attributed to later playwrights.

5. Why does the professor mention *Hamlet*?

    (A) To demonstrate that Planché respected the playwright's vision

    (B) To illustrate that Planché costumed plays with precise historical accuracy

    (C) To provide context for how plays were produced at the time

    (D) To explain how Planché researched his costuming

6. What are two notable features of Planché's costuming preferences? *Choose 2 answers.*

    [A] Planché preferred fantastical costumes to modern costumes.

    [B] Planché preferred accurate costumes to modern costumes.

    [C] Planché preferred Shakespearean costumes to historically accurate costumes.

    [D] Planché preferred the playwright's vision to historical accuracy.

7.2

 Listen to Track 11.

Now answer the questions.

1. What aspect of acting does the professor mainly discuss?

    (A) How to keep the audience's interest

    (B) How to create believable characters

    (C) Why bad actors mostly focus on the preparation that occurs long before the performance

    (D) Techniques for memorizing lines

2. Why does the professor ask the students to think about living truthfully?

    (A) Because the professor wants to point out that, in reality, people are concerned with achieving objectives, not their motivations for doing so

    (B) Because it is easier to understand the tactics people use than to understand the goals they are trying to achieve

    (C) Because the professor wants to point out that people are selfish

    (D) Because the professor wants to help the students obtain information, money, love, or sex from others

3. The professor says that "to play Hitler, you have to think you're right." What point does that example illustrate?

    (A) Actors must make their characters' objectives urgent to make their work believable.

    (B) Actors must display self-indulgence to make their work believable.

    (C) Historical villains are often the most interesting characters.

    (D) Historical villains are usually self-indulgent.

4. What warning does the professor give about emotional preparation when he daydreams about his mother's death?

   (A) That daydreaming about the death of a relative is inappropriate

   (B) That daydreaming will make an actor broadly emotional

   (C) That preparing by daydreaming is inferior to using "sense memory"

   (D) That successful preparation must be specific

5. What does the professor imply about most sit-com actors?

   (A) They cannot thread a needle properly.

   (B) They are unable to make a cappuccino.

   (C) They only pretend to do things.

   (D) They are not as good as movie actors.

 Listen to Track 12.

Now answer the question.

6. (A) To suggest that the students study music or athletics

   (B) To remind the students that becoming a musician or athlete is more difficult than becoming an actor

   (C) To encourage the students, because the work can be difficult

   (D) To caution the students that most actors do not earn much money

7.3

 Listen to Track 13.

Now answer the questions.

1. What is the lecture mainly about? *Choose 2 answers.*

   A   The origin and evolution of the novel

   B   Reasons why novels are not true to bourgeois values

   C   Reasons for the differences between Western and Asian novels

   D   Similarities between heroes of novels and films

2. According to the professor, what was the advantage of prose rather than verse in novel writing?

   (A) Only novels are written using prose.

   (B) Prose is less static and thus more suited to writing novels.

   (C) Prose lends itself to shorter works.

   (D) Prose was easier for most people to read.

3. Why does the professor mention Japanese and Chinese cultures?

   (A) To give reasons why Asian novels predate *Don Quixote*

   (B) To describe the differences between Western and Asian novels

   (C) To point out reasons for the relative lack of novel creation in those cultures

   (D) To explain why Western novels were not popular in those cultures

4. What does the professor say about the differentiation of novels from histories starting around 1700?

   (A) It allowed writers to create fantasies.

   (B) It made novels more interesting to the public.

   (C) It allowed writers to produce shorter works than Asian novels.

   (D) It allowed writers more choice of topic by alleviating the fear of lawsuits.

 Listen to Track 14.

Now answer the question.

5. (A) To show differences between Asian and European novels with regard to their content

   (B) To illustrate one reason for the smaller number of new novels in Asia

   (C) To discuss the popularity of Asian novels

   (D) To emphasize the wisdom of this Chinese proverb about writing while reading

 Listen to Track 15.

Now answer the question.

6. (A) Bourgeois culture does not involve adventures and quests.

   (B) Books and films are essentially the same.

   (C) Bourgeois culture should pursue wealth and love.

   (D) A knight's search for adventure is more noble than most bourgeois pursuits.

7.4

 Listen to Track 16.

Now answer the questions.

1. What is the lecture mainly about?

    (A) How plots shape storytelling

    (B) What a story arc is and different types of story arcs

    (C) The definition of stories

    (D) The Cinderella story arc

2. What does the professor mean when she says that story arcs and plots are not the same thing?

    (A) A story arc is more important than a plot.

    (B) There are many more story arcs than plots.

    (C) A plot is more about emotional states, while a story arc is more about specific, unemotional facts.

    (D) A story arc is more general, while a plot is more specific.

3. Why does the professor clarify what she means when she discusses the "features" of a story, including the beginning, middle, and end?

    (A) To stress that she is referring to the structure of the story

    (B) To establish the origin of the term "features"

    (C) To claim that all stories have different features

    (D) To challenge the idea of developing a universal definition of a story

4. What does the professor say about stories that follow the tragedy story arc?

    (A) They ultimately lead to the main character's triumph.

    (B) They go from sad to happy to sad to happy.

    (C) They go from happy to sad.

    (D) They involve characters who overstep their bounds.

5. In the lecture, the professor discusses the characteristics of story arcs and plots. Select from the five statements below THREE that characterize story arcs and TWO that characterize plots. This question is worth 2 points.

Story Arcs	**Plots**
•	•
•	•
•	

A	There are thousands of variations.
B	There are only a handful of common ones.
C	They can be shown on an emotional spectrum.
D	They involve specific facts and details.
E	Of the common types, popularity varies across time and culture.

 Listen to Track 17.

Now answer the question.

6. (A) To remind students of a story they have likely forgotten

    (B) To show that the best stories tend to follow a tragedy story arc

    (C) To illustrate the Cinderella story arc

    (D) To illustrate a specific type of story arc not yet discussed

7.5

 Listen to Track 18.

Now answer the questions.

1. What is the lecture mainly about?

    (A) The immorality inherent in art forgery

    (B) Methods of creating a forged painting

    (C) Ways to determine the purpose of an artwork

    (D) Aspects of art authentication and forgery

2. According to the professor, what is one problem with provenance?

    (A) The fragility of paper

    (B) The translation of ancient languages

    (C) The costliness of evaluating the accuracy of provenance

    (D) Reliance on feelings in evaluating provenance

3. Why does the professor talk about the 1930s Van Gogh forgery case in Berlin?

    (A) To suggest that the conviction was unjust

    (B) To illustrate a problem with expert authentication

    (C) To lament the short prison sentence associated with the case

    (D) To demonstrate that provenance is superior to expert opinion

4. Why does the professor mention undocumented restorations?

    (A) To claim that these restorations make forgery impossible to detect

    (B) To warn against the restoration of aging artwork

    (C) To point out a problem with scientific analysis

    (D) To argue for verification using provenance rather than scientific analysis

5. The professor mentions four aspects of art authentication. Indicate the order in which they are presented in the lecture: first, second, third, or fourth.

    [A] Scientific methods for analyzing artwork _____

    [B] Paper provenance _____

    [C] Expert opinion _____

    [D] Objective criteria for the certification of art experts _____

    🎧 Listen to Track 19.

    Now answer the question.

    ---

6. (A) Art museums use their power to collect as many masterpieces as they can.

    (B) Top art museums exert every effort to avoid exhibiting forgeries, with little regard for cost.

    (C) Art museums do not always make determining the authenticity of artwork their top priority.

    (D) Top art museums, such as the Getty and Metropolitan, cooperate to suppress scandals.

7.6

 Listen to Track 20.

Now answer the questions.

1. What is the lecture mainly about?

   (A) The history of the National Park Service in the United States

   (B) Popular and unpopular national parks and monuments

   (C) Different ways that governments can protect natural resources

   (D) Reasons why the National Park Service has been unsuccessful

2. According to the discussion, in what three ways was the creation of a unified National Park Service advantageous? *Choose 3 answers.*

   [A] It prevented individual parks from having to face government pressure alone.

   [B] It could perform inventory and track park resources.

   [C] It allowed the military to utilize park resources more efficiently during the war.

   [D] It was able to develop criteria for "irreplaceable treasures."

   [E] It allowed the National Park Service to designate Yellowstone as a national park.

3. The class discusses several events related to the National Park Service in the United States. Put the events in chronological order: first, second, third, or fourth.

   [A] The National Park Service was created. _____

   [B] The National Park Service started issuing free passes to active-duty military. _____

   [C] Parks were used for military training programs during World War II. _____

   [D] Yellowstone was designated a national park. _____

4. Why does the professor mention Civil War cannons?

   (A) To show an example of popular historic artifacts

   (B) To illustrate the support that the National Park Service was willing to give to the military during the war

   (C) To give an example of a resource that the military wanted to take from national parks

   (D) To explain why the National Park Service was created

5. What does the professor say about some people's objection to designating land as a national park?

(A) They feared that the "irreplaceable treasures" in such parks might be lost.

(B) They wanted to ensure that the military had complete access to the resources found on the land.

(C) They were concerned about the number of potential visitors to the park each year.

(D) They were concerned about having their own rights to the land taken away.

 Listen to Track 21.

Now answer the question.

6. (A) The student did not understand what was explained in an earlier discussion.

(B) Most of the class would disagree with this student's opinion.

(C) Not everyone is supportive of the creation of national parks.

(D) National parks are extremely popular in the United States.

7.7

 Listen to Track 22.

Now answer the questions.

1. What is the main purpose of the lecture?

(A) To describe the work of an influential musician

(B) To discuss the importance of avant-garde art forms

(C) To explain what minimalism is

(D) To describe Philip Glass's impact on advertising

2. How were La Monte Young's compositions different from those of his contemporaries?

(A) They were experimental.

(B) They were about dreams.

(C) They were influential.

(D) They were very minimal.

3. According to the professor, why was Young's music less popular than other minimalist music?

   (A) It could be difficult to listen to.

   (B) It used unusual instruments.

   (C) It was only performed outdoors.

   (D) It wasn't performed very often.

4. Why does the professor mention the *Dream House* installation?

   (A) To contrast his work with Philip Glass's

   (B) To show how difficult minimalist music could be to make

   (C) To illustrate Young's interest in pieces of long duration

   (D) To explain Young's creative process

5. Why does the professor compare the work of Philip Glass and La Monte Young?

   (A) To explain how Young influenced Glass

   (B) To emphasize how groundbreaking Young's work was

   (C) To emphasize the musical innovation of Glass's work

   (D) To demonstrate the superiority of Young's creative process

---

 Listen to Track 23.

Now answer the question.

---

6. What does the student imply when he says this?

   (A) He does not like Young's music.

   (B) He thinks the professor should focus more on the works of Philip Glass.

   (C) He believes that Young should be more famous than Glass.

   (D) He believes that Young's works might deserve greater recognition.

7.8

 Listen to Track 24.

Now answer the questions.

1. What does the professor mainly talk about?
   - (A) How Francis Picabia became a Dadaist
   - (B) Art immediately before World War I
   - (C) The features of Dadaism in contrast with Surrealism
   - (D) The artistic career of Francis Picabia

2. Why does the professor reference her discovery of Picabia while she was an art history student?
   - (A) To emphasize that the trajectory of Picabia's career was surprising to her
   - (B) To explain the historical appeal of Picabia's paintings
   - (C) To argue that Picabia was as misunderstood then as he is today
   - (D) To help describe her own philosophy as a student of art

3. What are two techniques that were invented during the Dadaism movement? *Choose 2 answers.*
   - [A] Readymades
   - [B] Assemblages
   - [C] Collages
   - [D] Abstract painting

4. According to the professor, what is true of other painters who worked at the same time as Picabia?
   - (A) They resented Picabia and the other Dadaists.
   - (B) They leaned more toward abstract painting than figurative painting.
   - (C) They did not change styles at all over the course of their careers.
   - (D) They did not commonly alternate between abstract painting and figurative painting.

5. Compared with other painters living at the same time, what was unusual about Francis Picabia?
   - (A) He could paint better abstractly than he could figuratively.
   - (B) He was part of the Dadaism movement.
   - (C) He worked in a true mix of styles throughout his career.
   - (D) He made assemblages.

MANHATTAN PREP

6. What is the professor's opinion about "readymades" in the Dadaism movement?

   (A) They were offensive and therefore not art.

   (B) Among other things, they were intended to offend people.

   (C) They were probably the most powerful part of the Dadaism movement.

   (D) They were considered more valuable than they should have been.

7.9

 Listen to Track 25.

Now answer the questions.

1. What aspect of architecture is this lecture primarily about?

   (A) The different challenges to consider when constructing different types of buildings

   (B) The reasons for the timing of a particular type of building

   (C) The variations in architecture in the 1860s and 1870s

   (D) The reasons why skyscrapers can have larger windows than traditional buildings

 Listen to Track 26.

Now answer the question.

2. (A) To indicate that the student's answer is incorrect

   (B) To determine whether the students understood the original question

   (C) To point out that there is no way to know which skyscraper was completed first

   (D) To ask for a more specific answer

3. Why does the woman refer to where her parents are from?

   (A) To explain why she is so interested in architecture

   (B) To explain how architectural design can vary within a city

   (C) To explain how she knows where the first skyscraper was built

   (D) To explain where steel is mass-produced

4. What is mentioned in the lecture as a challenge architects faced when designing the first skyscrapers?

   (A) Occupants were unwilling to walk up a large number of stairs to reach the top floors.

   (B) The additional weight from taller buildings had to be supported.

   (C) Culturally, wooden buildings were still preferred to steel ones.

   (D) The cost of obtaining the needed materials was sometimes excessive.

5. According to the professor, what contributed to the increased demand for skyscrapers in some cities?

   (A) The desire for cities to be on the forefront of technological development

   (B) The increased weight resting on a taller building's base

   (C) The population increase in urban city centers

   (D) The push for family members to live and work in locations near to each other

6. According to the lecture, what are two features of skyscrapers that were possible because of the steel skeleton frame? *Choose 2 answers.*

   A   The elevator

   B   The thinner walls

   C   The number of hallways

   D   The larger windows

   E   The higher ceilings

7.10

 Listen to Track 27.

Now answer the questions.

1. What is the main purpose of the lecture?

   (A) To investigate Renaissance poetry

   (B) To explain why Sicilian School poetry involves role reversals

   (C) To explain how romantic relationships changed in the thirteenth century

   (D) To compare two different types of poetry using an example from each period

2. What does the professor say about Occitan poetry written during the Medieval Period?

   (A) It was more popular than Sicilian School poetry.

   (B) It was primarily sung, rather than read.

   (C) It was a tool court jesters could use to raise their status.

   (D) It developed from Sicilian School poetry.

3. Why does the professor mention the start of the Renaissance?

   (A) To emphasize the growing popularity of poetry in this time

   (B) To explain one of the differences between the two poems being discussed

   (C) To point out similarities between poems written during this time period

   (D) To provide evidence that Occitan poets were attempting to change traditional mindsets of the time

4. According to the professor, what topics were forbidden to Sicilian School poets? *Choose 2 answers.*

   [A] Politics

   [B] Romance

   [C] Religion

   [D] Courtship

5. According to the professor, what is true of the romance described in the Occitan poem and the romance described in the Sicilian School poem? Classify each of the following phrases as applying either to 1. Occitan Poetry or 2. Sicilian School Poetry.

   [A] Is conducted in secret _____

   [B] Features a woman as the aggressor _____

   [C] Involves the woman's family _____

   [D] Is used as social commentary _____

   > 🎧 Listen to Track 28.
   >
   > Now answer the question.

6. (A) To invite members of the class to answer directly

   (B) To emphasize that this question cannot be answered

   (C) To introduce a rhetorical question that he is about to answer

   (D) To remind students of the importance of thinking critically about poetry

7

Answer Key—7.1

Question	Correct Answer	Right/Wrong	Category
1	B		Gist-content
2	C, D		Detail
3	D		Inference
4	C		Speaker's Attitude
5	A		Organization
6	B, D		Detail

Answer Key—7.2

Question	Correct Answer	Right/Wrong	Category
1	B		Gist-content
2	A		Organization
3	A		Detail
4	D		Detail
5	C		Inference
6	C		Function of What Is Said

Answer Key—7.3

Question	Correct Answer	Right/Wrong	Category
1	A, C		Gist-content
2	B		Detail
3	C		Organization
4	D		Detail
5	B		Function of What Is Said
6	A		Inference

Answer Key—7.4

Question	Correct Answer	Right/Wrong	Category
1	B		Gist-content
2	D		Detail
3	A		Inference
4	C		Detail
5	Story Arc: B, C, E. Plot: A, D.		Connecting Content
6	D		Function of What Is Said

Answer Key—7.5

Question	Correct Answer	Right/Wrong	Category
1	D		Gist-content
2	A		Detail
3	B		Organization
4	C		Purpose
5	A: Fourth. B: First. C: Second. D: Third.		Connecting Content
6	C		Inference

Answer Key—7.6

Question	Correct Answer	Right/Wrong	Category
1	A		Gist-content
2	A, B, D		Detail
3	A: Second. B: Fourth. C: Third. D: First.		Connecting Content
4	C		Organization
5	D		Detail
6	C		Inference

Answer Key—7.7

Question	Correct Answer	Right/Wrong	Category
1	A		Gist-purpose
2	D		Detail
3	A		Detail
4	C		Organization
5	B		Organization
6	D		Function of What Is Said

Answer Key—7.8

Question	Correct Answer	Right/Wrong	Category
1	D		Gist-content
2	A		Organization
3	A, B		Detail
4	D		Inference
5	C		Detail
6	B		Speaker's Attitude

Answer Key—7.9

Question	Correct Answer	Right/Wrong	Category
1	B		Gist-content
2	A		Function of What Is Said
3	C		Organization
4	B		Detail
5	C		Detail
6	B, D		Detail

Answer Key—7.10

Question	Correct Answer	Right/Wrong	Category
1	D		Gist-purpose
2	B		Detail
3	B		Organization
4	A, C		Detail
5	Occitan: A, C. Sicilian: B, D.		Connecting Content
6	C		Function of What Is Said

Answers and Explanations—7.1

Historical Costumes—Track 10

NARRATOR: Listen to part of a lecture in a theater class.

PROFESSOR: As we've seen, over the course of the nineteenth century, British theater changed dramatically. Despite your studies, you've probably never heard of James Planché. He was an individual who had one of the most profound, and least recognized, impacts on British theater.

Planché was born in 1796 in Piccadilly, London. By the age of 14, he had already written several amateur plays, and was apprenticing with a bookseller in an attempt to sell them. By chance, an actor happened upon one of Planché's early plays and recognized the potential it contained. This actor performed the play at Drury Lane, and Planché's writing career began. However, most of his early plays were described as unremarkable. Until 1820, his most notable play, called *The Vampire*, was known most for the presence of a trapdoor which allowed actors to seem to disappear beneath the stage and reappear as if from nowhere.

This play, however, was not notable for what Planché would later become famous for—*costuming*. As was typical in other plays of the time, *The Vampire* used costuming that was not realistic to the situation. The play was set in Scotland, and the actors wore costumes that would clearly convey to the audience that they were Scottish, but in stereotypical or unrealistic ways. For example, in the opening scene, a woman is shown hiding in a cave. She has been forced into it because of a storm that began raging while she was on a hunting trip, yet she is wearing a formal Scottish ball gown, complete with jewels.

Planché realized that this was… was ridiculous. The costumes were not realistic to the situation the actor was supposed to be in. In other plays, actors would wear modern clothing, despite the play being based in the past. Planché believed that costumes should be accurate to a play's situation. In 1823, he published an article saying that more attention should be paid to the time period of the play—particularly Shakespearean plays. At the time, actors in these plays would wear modern clothing, despite the fact that the plays were written over 300 years prior.

Finally, people were beginning to recognize him as something outside the ordinary. He was given control over the Shakespearean play *King John*. He kept the actors and sets relatively unchanged, but spent an

incredible amount of time planning the costumes. His publications… before the play was produced, he published a 22-costume book which detailed, with historical accuracy, the costumes of all of the major characters. The book was remarkable because it made no reference to the theater, the actors… the Shakespearean text. It just went into significant detail about how the costumes should be constructed and how they should appear. Planché was not just creating costumes tailored to the actor, but also tailored to the *play itself*.

Though the actors in *King John* seemed to think that this adaptation of Shakespeare might be a flop, it enjoyed great success. The accurate costuming made it easier for audiences to imagine the setting of the play. His time-period costuming was so successful that Planché went on to design historically accurate costumes for all of Shakespeare's histories, and seven of his non-histories. You know, his style of costuming with historical accuracy, rather than using unrealistic costumes, became the standard for Shakespearean plays for the next century.

Planché's desire for historical accuracy in costuming seemed almost obsessive. He would extensively research the appropriate time period for each play, and clearly stated that he preferred accurate costuming to fanciful costuming. But his loyalty was to the play over the time period. For example, in researching *Hamlet*, Planché determined that the appropriate setting was eighth-century Denmark. A Danish prince of that time would have worn scarlet, which is a brilliant red-orange. Yet one of Shakespeare's characters remarks that Hamlet, the Danish prince, is wearing sable, which is a dark brown-black. Planché wrote of this problem and said he wished… he wished the contradiction wasn't there, but in the end, he costumed Hamlet in sable, keeping with Shakespeare's original vision.

From Shakespeare, he moved on to using historically accurate costumes in new genres. When he transitioned to Greek and Roman mythology, he used his costumes for comedic effect. He produced a play in which the characters were dressed in completely accurate Greek costumes, yet played a modern British card game. The irony of seeing realistically ancient costumes juxtaposed with the modern actions of the actors was a hit, and soon other writers began copying the technique.

The amount of time and research Planché put into all his costumes was widely recognized. Historians consulted him about the correct placement of armor and other artifacts well into his retirement. Playwrights continued their attempt to create historically accurate costumes for the next 100 years.

1. What does the professor mainly discuss?

    GIST-CONTENT. The professor primarily discusses James Planché and his efforts involving costuming.

    ✗ (A) The history of costuming in theater

    This choice is too broad—the lecture is focused on Planché's costuming only.

    ✓ (B) A writer's new perspective on theatrical costuming

    CORRECT. Planché introduced realistic costuming.

    ✗ (C) The kind of costumes most popular in Shakespearean plays

    The lecture is mostly about Planché. It is also unclear that his costumes for Shakespearean plays are still the most popular.

    ✗ (D) A prominent playwright of the nineteenth century

    It is not clear that Planché was prominent as a playwright, and this choice ignores his innovations in costuming.

2. According to the professor, how did Planché change traditional Shakespearean plays of the time? *Choose 2 answers.*

    DETAIL. Planché introduced costuming that was realistic for the setting of the plays.

  ✗ ☐ A He modernized the costumes.

    This is the opposite of what he did—he replaced inappropriately modern or fancy costumes with realistic ones.

  ✗ ☐ B He expanded the number of costumes available to actors.

    The professor never discusses the number of costumes available.

  ✓ ☐ C He introduced historically accurate costumes.

    CORRECT. This was his primary goal.

  ✓ ☐ D He rejected unrealistic costumes.

    CORRECT. This was his original objection to traditional costumes.

3. What can be inferred about the actors' views of Planché's work on *King John*?

    INFERENCE. The professor notes that the actors were concerned that a play using Planché's costumes "might be a flop."

  ✗ Ⓐ They refused to wear historically accurate costumes.

    They did wear the costumes, but were concerned that audiences would not receive the play well as a result.

  ✗ Ⓑ Most of them preferred to wear costumes ironically.

    The actors' preferences are not discussed, aside from their concern that the play "might be a flop."

  ✗ Ⓒ They had complete control over their costumes.

    If they had this control, Planché would have been unlikely to be able to introduce the costuming changes that he did.

  ✓ Ⓓ Some of them initially thought that historically accurate costumes would not be well received.

    CORRECT. The actors suspected that the play may not be successful because of the historical costumes.

7

4.   What is the professor's opinion about the relationship between James Planché and later playwrights?

SPEAKER'S ATTITUDE. The professor notes: "Playwrights continued their attempt to create historically accurate costumes for the next 100 years," implying that he believes that Planché influenced them.

✗ (A) He thinks later playwrights met more resistance than Planché did when they tried to change costumes.

The professor does not discuss any resistance that later playwrights met.

✗ (B) He thinks Planché distrusted the research of later playwrights.

This idea is not mentioned in the lecture.

✓ (C) He thinks later playwrights copied Planché's costuming practices.

CORRECT. He states that Planché started a new movement of historical costuming that was replicated for the next 100 years.

✗ (D) He thinks Planché had less influence than has been attributed to later playwrights.

The professor thinks Planché had a significant influence, and there is no mention of anyone doubting that perspective.

5.   Why does the professor mention *Hamlet*?

ORGANIZATION. The professor notes that, in a costuming choice in that play, Planché deferred to the playwright's choice, even though Planché thought it was technically incorrect.

✓ (A) To demonstrate that Planché respected the playwright's vision

CORRECT. This is the only example of Planché being historically inaccurate, and he did so to defer to the playwright's vision.

✗ (B) To illustrate that Planché costumed plays with precise historical accuracy

Planché did the opposite in this example.

✗ (C) To provide context for how plays were produced at the time

There is no general discussion of a play's production in the lecture.

✗ (D) To explain how Planché researched his costuming

While he did research this play, the focus of this example is not to illustrate Planché's method of research.

6. What are two notable features of Planché's costuming preferences? *Choose 2 answers.*

DETAIL. The professor states that Planché preferred realistic costuming, and that when there was a discrepancy, he deferred to the playwright's vision over historical accuracy.

✗ [A] Planché preferred fantastical costumes to modern costumes.

Fantastical costumes are not mentioned.

✓ [B] Planché preferred accurate costumes to modern costumes.

CORRECT. This is one of Planché's basic beliefs about how to costume actors.

✗ [C] Planché preferred Shakespearean costumes to historically accurate costumes.

Planché did feel that the playwright's vision was more important than historical accuracy, if one had to be chosen over the other. But the term "Shakespearean costumes" refers to costumes often associated with Shakespeare's plays. It doesn't necessarily mean that they were part of Shakespeare's vision. Also, this choice implies that Planché preferred Shakespearean costumes even when they would not be historically accurate.

✓ [D] Planché preferred the playwright's vision to historical accuracy.

CORRECT. This idea is illustrated in the example of Hamlet's costuming.

Answers and Explanations—7.2

Building a Character—Track 11

NARRATOR: Listen to part of a lecture in an acting class.

PROFESSOR: Okay, everybody… settle down… C'mon guys, I know all the world's a stage, but right now this is a classroom… Okay then, let's get started.

Maybe you think that as actors, your job is to memorize lines and go out and act. And maybe that's true in a simplistic sense, but thinking about it that way produces bad acting. Your job isn't to act, it's to live on stage. Acting isn't acting—it's living truthfully under imaginary circumstances.

How do you do that? How do you "build a character," as they say? Well, I'd say there are three components: what you do long before the performance, what you do right before the performance, and what you do during the performance. Most bad actors only do the first properly, if that.

So what do you do long before the performance? Besides memorize lines. I can see what you're thinking—you're preparing to be bored while I drone on about writing your character's biography and other stuff you already know. Well, I suppose it's true that you need to know the person you're playing. But that's really a very small part of it. You know, when I was your age—when I was young and pretty—I went to a very serious acting school. And on the first day, the founder, a renowned teacher, said, "The problem with college actors is they worry about *why* they're doing things instead of worrying about *what* they're doing."

Think about "living truthfully" again. In life, do you worry about why you're at the grocery store? Or the laundry, or the audition, for that matter? No, you're thinking about what you want to accomplish. What you want to do. And when you're with another person, you're thinking about what you want from them, whether it's information or money or love or sex. And that's how it should be on stage. So, while you do have to know your character, you should spend most of your preparation and rehearsal time figuring what you need to *do*

or *accomplish* in each scene. And how are you going to make the other people give you what you want. That's what you're on stage for… not to prance around and display your emotional or physical beauty.

And you'll notice I said "need." If you want your work to be believable, which is to say good, it's not about self-display or self-indulgence, it's about giving your needs *urgency*. Make it important to you. An acting coach once told me, "If you're going to play Hitler, you have to think you're right."

But what about that emotion? That's the work you do *right before* you go on stage. Emotional preparation, which means being in the right mood for the scene. Perhaps you've heard of "sense memory?" Recalling events in your life that put you in the appropriate frame of mind. Another approach, which I was taught, involves fantasizing, or daydreaming, about the appropriate situation. In theory that approach makes you more accessible instead of withdrawn.

But you have to be specific. If I want to be sad, I don't just repeat "my mother died." I dream about how I saw her walking up the street when this car—an old, banged up, red Mustang—skidded off the road and the grill plowed into her in the small of her back, and her body… See? I'm getting all choked up.

Now, you're on stage for your scene. And this might sound funny… but *let go* of your preparation. Trust that it will be there. Remember this: in life, people don't try to be upset. In life, people don't try to cry— they try not to cry.

So what are you supposed to do on stage? You're supposed to *really do* things. Watching anyone *really do* something is interesting. Haven't you ever watched someone thread a needle or make a cappuccino? It was fascinating, right? What's not interesting is watching people *pretend* to do things. Like most sit-com actors. So. Instead of hanging on to your preparation, just do what you're supposed to do. Really shake hands, really threaten someone, really pour the tea, really ask the question, and—this is the hard part—really *listen* to the answer, even though you've heard it a hundred times before.

OK. That's what you want to work on this week with your partner. Really doing things. Quit acting. Just listen to them and answer them. It takes a lot of energy at first. People forget that acting is a craft and an art. If we were here to learn to play the violin, or throw a slider for that matter, you'd expect to practice for years before someone paid you a lot of money to perform. So don't get discouraged. And break a leg!

1. What aspect of acting does the professor mainly discuss?	**GIST-CONTENT.** The professor primarily discusses techniques for improving the believability of the characters that actors portray.
✗ (A) How to keep the audience's interest	The professor's purpose is to discuss a component of good acting, which will lead to holding interest, but that is not the main focus of the discussion.
✓ (B) How to create believable characters	**CORRECT.** Relatively early in the lecture, the professor states the purpose explicitly: "building a character."
✗ (C) Why bad actors mostly focus on the preparation that occurs long before the performance	The professor briefly mentions that bad actors tend to do this, but this is a minor detail in the lecture as a whole.
✗ (D) Techniques for memorizing lines	Memorization is only briefly mentioned.

2.   Why does the professor ask the students to think about living truthfully?

ORGANIZATION. The professor points out that, in real life, people worry about accomplishing their objectives, not *why* they do things.

✓ (A) Because the professor wants to point out that, in reality, people are concerned with achieving objectives, not their motivations for doing so

CORRECT. The professor goes on to point out that in life, people worry about their objectives, not why they do things.

✗ (B) Because it is easier to understand the tactics people use than to understand the goals they are trying to achieve

The professor never makes such a claim.

✗ (C) Because the professor wants to point out that people are selfish

The professor discusses human behavior, but does not judge it.

✗ (D) Because the professor wants to help the students obtain information, money, love, or sex from others

The professor's point is only that this is how people act in life.

3.   The professor says that "to play Hitler, you have to think you're right." What point does that example illustrate?

DETAIL. The professor says that the actor must give the needs of the character urgency for the acting to be believable.

✓ (A) Actors must make their characters' objectives urgent to make their work believable.

CORRECT. The professor says that making the character's objectives important makes the acting believable.

✗ (B) Actors must display self-indulgence to make their work believable.

This is the opposite of the professor's point.

✗ (C) Historical villains are often the most interesting characters.

This example relates to the need for urgency, not the type of character.

✗ (D) Historical villains are usually self-indulgent.

This example relates to the need for urgency, not the type of character.

4. What warning does the professor give about emotional preparation when he daydreams about his mother's death?

DETAIL. The professor is discussing emotional preparation in this example. He emphasizes using concrete, specific examples in this process.

✗ (A) That daydreaming about the death of a relative is inappropriate

On the contrary—the professor does so to give an appropriate, effective demonstration.

✗ (B) That daydreaming will make an actor broadly emotional

The goal is creating *appropriate* emotion. The warning given was about the need for something *specific*.

✗ (C) That preparing by daydreaming is inferior to using "sense memory"

The professor does not rank the two approaches.

✓ (D) That successful preparation must be specific

CORRECT. His daydream is an example of making the preparation specific to a situation.

5. What does the professor imply about most sit-com actors?

INFERENCE. The professor's remark indicates that most sit-com actors only pretend to do things. This is intended to be an example of what not to do.

✗ (A) They cannot thread a needle properly.

The professor uses this example to illustrate that watching someone really doing something is interesting. But it is not implied that sit-com actors cannot do this task.

✗ (B) They are unable to make a cappuccino.

The professor uses this example to illustrate that watching someone really doing something is interesting. But it is not implied that sit-com actors cannot do this task.

✓ (C) They only pretend to do things.

CORRECT. The professor says, "What's not interesting is watching people *pretend* to do things. Like most sit-com actors."

✗ (D) They are not as good as movie actors.

The professor does not discuss movie actors or make any such comparison.

Track 12

NARRATOR: Listen again to part of the lecture. Then answer the question.

PROFESSOR: It takes a lot of energy at first. People forget that acting is a craft and an art. If we were here to learn to play the violin, or throw a slider for that matter, you'd expect to practice for years before someone paid you a lot of money to perform.

NARRATOR: Why does the professor say this:

PROFESSOR: If we were here to learn to play the violin, or throw a slider for that matter, you'd expect to practice for years before someone paid you a lot of money to perform.

6.   **FUNCTION OF WHAT IS SAID.** The professor's point is to both encourage the students' efforts and remind them of the dedication required to become successful at acting.

✗ (A) To suggest that the students study music or athletics

Studying music or athletics was a metaphor. The subject of the talk is acting.

✗ (B) To remind the students that becoming a musician or athlete is more difficult than becoming an actor

The professor's metaphor implies that they are similarly difficult to perfect.

✓ (C) To encourage the students, because the work can be difficult

CORRECT. The professor makes a metaphor involving other skills that also require much practice.

✗ (D) To caution the students that most actors do not earn much money

The subject of earning potential from acting is not discussed or implied.

Answers and Explanations—7.3

The Novel—Track 13

NARRATOR: Listen to part of a lecture in a literature class.

PROFESSOR: The word novel means "new." Or, really, it derives from the Italian "*novella*," which can mean "short story of something new." Interestingly, most European languages use a version of the French word "*roman*," derived from "romance," and an allusion to the medieval epics that fathered them. Actually, "fathered" is a controversial point—while some scholars agree that *Don Quixote*, written in 1605, was the first novel, others argue that that is an ethnocentric view that ignores a rich and older tradition in Asia. We'll return to that point in a bit.

So what is a *novel*? Fairly or not, the classical and medieval European epics of knightly heroism, quests, and courtly love do not meet the modern definition of a novel, which is said to have an individual perspective, rounded characters, and some sort of psychological insight. Note that the use of prose instead of verse is not a criterion as, despite the popular misconception, the shift to prose came long before *Don Quixote*. However, prose lent itself to novel writing because each sentence leads to the next, while verse is a much more static form, partly because it is so much more symmetrical.

Changing socioeconomic factors also encouraged academics to trace the birth of the novel back to the seventeenth century. A simple assumption would be to attribute this to the rise in literacy. However, while that was certainly a contributing factor, in the 200 years after *Don Quixote*, the publication, and presumably the readership, of novels increased far faster than the literacy rate did. One reason for this is that printing and paper itself became much cheaper. However, a less obvious factor was the evolving legal system, particularly changes in libel laws. Before roughly 1700, novels were not differentiated from histories. That distinction came about afterwards, allowing an author to be much freer in the choice of topic and plot if it were a *fiction* that was being presented instead of a *fact*. And, thus, he or she was much freer from being *sued* by someone. Consequently, novels delved further and further into realism.

By the nineteenth century, the novelistic interest in realism led to in-depth portrayals of all classes of society, seemingly a far cry from stories exclusively about knights and damsels in distress. Authors such as Charles Dickens and Emile Zola were famed for such explorations of lower-class life. Of course, this was not a requirement, and one need look no further than the Bronte sisters to find works that retained a romantic focus. These works remain accessible to modern readers, as shown not only by their sales, but also by their use as sources for popular motion pictures. The final feature of the modern novel emerged in the beginning of the twentieth century. Following the lead of D. H. Lawrence, modern novels now usually portray the inner monologues of their characters. Previously, novelists largely used the device of a narrator to advance their stories.

Let's return to the issue of Japanese and Chinese novels. The Japanese work, *The Tale of the Genji*, meets the previously mentioned standards for a novel. And it was published in the year 1010! Furthermore, many works that should be considered novels were written in China before the fourteenth century. So, besides narrow-mindedness, why have these works been ignored? One reason is that just as novels proliferated in Europe, production declined in Asia. Another possible reason was that Japanese and Chinese cultures at the time valued permanence and the status quo rather than change and progress like in Europe. Thus, Asians read and re-read their classics—there was much less demand for fresh creations.

There is another cultural reason that might prove more interesting. There were fewer new works created in Asia because novels commanded more respect as *art*. Let me explain. As high art, these books were meant to be studied, as one might study philosophical or theological works—not raced through, for, say, enjoyment purposes only. In fact, many Chinese novels were published with accompanying commentaries that rivaled the books in length. And even though these were long books, editions without such notes were unpopular! An old Chinese proverb roughly said, "Without a pen, it's not really reading." Obviously, such an approach dampened demand.

Speaking of demand, one quick final thought for you to consider. In Europe, and of course in the United States, novels came to be thought of as an embodiment of the bourgeois, or middle class, culture of merchants and entrepreneurs. In a way, that is very ironic because, despite the evolution we have discussed, the heroes of Western literature are usually not bourgeois. They remain nobles, and much like the heroes of medieval epics. Think about it this week—most protagonists of books, and films, are modern knights, needing adventures and undertaking quests to find wealth or love.

1.	What is the lecture mainly about? *Choose 2 answers.*	**GIST-CONTENT.** The lecture traces the development of novels and the differences between them on different continents.
✓ A	The origin and evolution of the novel	**CORRECT.** The professor states that that is the main purpose of the lecture.
✗ B	Reasons why novels are not true to bourgeois values	This refers to the very end of the lecture, which was only a digression.
✓ C	Reasons for the differences between Western and Asian novels	**CORRECT.** The last half of the lecture devotes itself to this.
✗ D	Similarities between heroes of novels and films	These similarities are mentioned only at the very end of the lecture.

2.   According to the professor, what
      was the advantage of prose
      rather than verse in novel
      writing?

DETAIL. The professor states that prose is more forward-moving, rather than static.

✗   (A) Only novels are written
         using prose.

The professor states that this is not true.

✓   (B) Prose is less static and thus
         more suited to writing
         novels.

CORRECT. The professor explicitly makes this point.

✗   (C) Prose lends itself to shorter
         works.

The issue of the length of works is not discussed.

✗   (D) Prose was easier for most
         people to read.

The issue of readability is not mentioned.

3.   Why does the professor mention
      Japanese and Chinese cultures?

ORGANIZATION. The professor discusses them to explain the difference in the evolution of novels across continents.

✗   (A) To give reasons why Asian
         novels predate *Don Quixote*

The professor's point is about why there were fewer Asian novels, not their relative age.

✗   (B) To describe the differences
         between Western and
         Asian novels

The discussion concerns the effect on the number of novels written, not the works themselves.

✓   (C) To point out reasons for
         the relative lack of novel
         creation in those cultures

CORRECT. The professor says that cultural values influenced the number of novels that were written.

✗   (D) To explain why Western
         novels were not popular in
         those cultures

The popularity of Western novels in Asia is not discussed.

4.   What does the professor say about
      the differentiation of novels from
      histories starting around 1700?

DETAIL. The professor says that differentiating novels from histories gave writers freedom from libel suits.

✗   (A) It allowed writers to create
         fantasies.

On the contrary—this differentiation allowed writers to explore more realistic topics.

✗   (B) It made novels more
         interesting to the public.

This might be true, but this part of the lecture revolves around the legal concerns surrounding novels.

✗   (C) It allowed writers to
         produce shorter works
         than Asian novels.

Neither relative length nor Asian novels are mentioned in this part of the lecture.

✓   (D) It allowed writers more
         choice of topic by alleviating
         the fear of lawsuits.

CORRECT. The professor says that this differentiation gave writers freedom from libel suits.

Track 14

NARRATOR: Why does the professor say this:

PROFESSOR: An old Chinese proverb roughly said, "Without a pen, it's not really reading."

5.   **FUNCTION OF WHAT IS SAID.** This quote refers to the Asian custom of studying and notating novels.

   ✗ Ⓐ To show differences between Asian and European novels with regard to their content
      The substance of the quote involves the mode of reading novels, not the novels themselves.

   ✓ Ⓑ To illustrate one reason for the smaller number of new novels in Asia
      CORRECT. The professor later says that this mode of reading limited demand for new novels.

   ✗ Ⓒ To discuss the popularity of Asian novels
      The point of this quote is the pace and mode of reading, not the popularity of the books.

   ✗ Ⓓ To emphasize the wisdom of this Chinese proverb about writing while reading
      The content of the proverb itself is not the point the professor is trying to illustrate.

Track 15

NARRATOR: What does the professor imply when he says this:

PROFESSOR: In a way, that is very ironic because, despite the evolution we have discussed, the heroes of Western literature are usually not bourgeois. They remain nobles, and much like the heroes of medieval epics. Think about it this week—most protagonists of books, and films, are modern knights, needing adventures and undertaking quests to find wealth or love.

6.   **INFERENCE.** The professor is discussing the irony that while novels are thought to be bourgeois, the heroes in them usually are not.

   ✓ Ⓐ Bourgeois culture does not involve adventures and quests.
      CORRECT. The irony is that the culture depicted in novels is actually much different from what it is perceived to be.

   ✗ Ⓑ Books and films are essentially the same.
      He is giving two examples—books and movies—and only indicates that they are related, not identical.

   ✗ Ⓒ Bourgeois culture should pursue wealth and love.
      The professor doesn't make any claims about what bourgeois culture should or shouldn't do. He only says that in pursuing wealth and love, the heroes of Western literature are not behaving in a bourgeois way.

   ✗ Ⓓ A knight's search for adventure is more noble than most bourgeois pursuits.
      The professor does not judge the merits of the two cultures.

Answers and Explanations—7.4

Story Arcs—Track 16

NARRATOR: Listen to part of a lecture in a literature class.

PROFESSOR: Now, we can't really discuss story arcs without first talking about what a story is… because to understand an arc, you have to understand what you're talking about in the first place. So what is a story? How would you define a story, Carlos?

MALE STUDENT: Well, a story is something, I think… that has a beginning, middle, and an end. Apart from that, I would say that it's about something that happens to a person, or a group of people. And within these rules, I think stories can be very different.

PROFESSOR: That's right, stories vary in terms of what their beginnings, middles, and ends are but what they have in common is that all stories share these features. By "features," I mean the *structure* of a story— that it can be divided into these three parts. So any story could be broken down into its three main components. Beginning, middle, and end. Um, OK… so what about story *arcs*? Because we've talked now about the structure of a story, and the three pieces that make it up, but we haven't talked about how those pieces connect to one another in a meaningful way. Lindsey?

FEMALE STUDENT: Well, I think a story arc would probably refer to what the plot of the story is. Like, what actually *happens* in the three parts. For example, a common story arc is the Cinderella story arc—she's sad and alone, then a really good thing happens to her at the beginning because she gets to go to the royal ball, which is a dream come true. But then in the middle, it gets bad again when she has to flee from the ball at midnight, and the prince can't find her. She has lost her love… they're separated. Then at the end, it's happy again when he does find her. So the arc of the story is sad-happy-sad-happy.

PROFESSOR: Good description. The Cinderella story arc—sad-happy-sad-happy—is a common one in literature. There are a handful of common story arcs like this one…five or six that repeat themselves in great novels. How do we describe a story arc that does the opposite of the Cinderella story, that starts happy and ends sad? Actually, that story arc… we will come back to in a few minutes.

MALE STUDENT: I thought a story arc was the same thing as the plot. And there are more than six plots in the world.

PROFESSOR: Good point—they are not exactly the same thing, although the plot follows the story arc. The story arc is going to be a more general description of the emotional state of the person the story is about. Like Lesley said, when she described it as happy and sad—you might think of story arcs on a spectrum from happy to sad. The story arc is how you would graph the character's journey. Where were they the happiest, and where were they the saddest?

Plots, on the other hand, are more specific. There are as many possible plots as there are specific details that you can dream up in your mind. The plots in modern Western literature are extremely varied. There are thousands and thousands of them. They mostly, however, conform to standard story arcs. One of the standard story arcs we have identified: the Cinderella story arc.

Another common arc—the one I hinted at a moment ago—is the *tragedy*. In a tragedy, things start out fine, but by the end, something so terrible has happened that it is heartbreaking. Tragic. Obviously, this is why it's called a tragedy.

If you think about some classic stories, you can come up with what other ones might be, right? There's what we call "rags to riches," which starts sad and builds to a happy ending. That title is based on the legend of a person working his way up in the world, from wearing rags to owning riches. Then there's the arc we refer to as "Icarus," based on the famous Greek myth. Icarus was imprisoned with his father on the island of Crete. To escape, his father created wings out of wax and feathers for them to use to fly out of the prison. His father warned him not to fly too close to the sun, but he didn't listen. He flew so close to the sun that his wax wings melted, and he could no longer fly. He fell into the sea and perished. So this is a type of tragic story arc that starts off sad, then becomes happy, then ends sad again.

An interesting phenomenon to study is how some story arcs are more popular during certain times, in certain cultures. The Icarus story arc, for example, is not nearly as popular in contemporary America as the Cinderella story arc. Why do you think that is?

1. What is the lecture mainly about?

GIST-CONTENT. The lecture primarily discusses the definition of story arcs and several examples of them.

✗ (A) How plots shape storytelling

The professor differentiates between plots and story arcs, but plots are not the main focus of the lecture.

✓ (B) What a story arc is and different types of story arcs

CORRECT. The professor defines what a story arc is and discusses several examples of them.

✗ (C) The definition of stories

The professor discusses this definition in the beginning with the class, but this is not the primary focus of the lecture.

✗ (D) The Cinderella story arc

This story arc is defined in the lecture and discussed a fair amount, but it is not the central topic of the lecture.

2. What does the professor mean when she says that story arcs and plots are not the same thing?

DETAIL. The professor illustrates the difference between story arcs and plots—that plots are varied and much more specific, while story arcs are more general and reflect the emotional states of the audience or characters in the story.

✗ (A) A story arc is more important than a plot.

The professor does not imply this at any point in the lecture.

✗ (B) There are many more story arcs than plots.

The professor indicates that the opposite is true—there are many more potential plots than there are story arcs.

✗ (C) A plot is more about emotional states, while a story arc is more about specific, unemotional facts.

The professor indicates that the opposite is true—that plots are more specific and fact-driven, while story arcs reflect emotional states and are more general.

✓ (D) A story arc is more general, while a plot is more specific.

CORRECT. The professor notes that plots are much more specific, but typically follow some standard, general story arc.

3. Why does the professor clarify what she means when she discusses the "features" of a story, including the beginning, middle, and end?

INFERENCE. The professor says: "By 'features,' I mean the *structure* of a story—that it can be divided into these three parts."

✓ (A) To stress that she is referring to the structure of the story

CORRECT. This is precisely the clarification that the professor gives in the quote.

✗ (B) To establish the origin of the term "features"

The professor does not discuss this at any point in the lecture.

✗ (C) To claim that all stories have different features

In the context of discussing the "features" of a story, the professor says that all stories have the same features: a beginning, middle, and end.

✗ (D) To challenge the idea of developing a universal definition of a story

The professor does not discuss this concept at any point in the lecture.

4. What does the professor say about stories that follow the tragedy story arc?

DETAIL. The professor states that in a tragedy arc, the situation starts off happily but ends sadly.

✗ (A) They ultimately lead to the main character's triumph.

The professor does not mention this idea in the lecture.

✗ (B) They go from sad to happy to sad to happy.

This defines the Cinderella story arc, not the tragedy story arc.

✓ (C) They go from happy to sad.

CORRECT. The standard tragedy story arc goes from happy to sad.

✗ (D) They involve characters who overstep their bounds.

The professor describes the Icarus arc, in which the character of Icarus oversteps his bounds by flying too close to the sun. But the professor does not claim that this theme is common to all tragedy story arcs.

7

5. In the lecture, the professor discusses the characteristics of story arcs and plots. Select from the five statements below THREE that characterize story arcs and TWO that characterize plots. This question is worth 2 points.

CONNECTING CONTENT. According to the professor, plots are specific, fact-based, and separate from emotional states. Meanwhile, story arcs are general, and they relate to the emotional state of the reader or characters in the story.

A   There are thousands of variations.

PLOT. Plots are fact-specific, and therefore many thousands of potential plots exist.

B   There are only a handful of common ones.

STORY ARC. Story arcs are more general, and therefore only a handful of them exist.

C   They can be shown on an emotional spectrum.

STORY ARC. Story arcs deal with emotional states, while plots are fact-driven.

D   They involve specific facts and details.

PLOT. Plots are driven by specific facts and details, while story arcs relate to emotional states of the reader or characters in the story.

E   Of the common types, popularity varies across time and culture.

STORY ARC. The professor indicates that some story arcs are more prevalent or popular at certain times or in certain cultures.

Track 17

NARRATOR: Listen again to part of the lecture. Then answer the question.

PROFESSOR: Icarus was imprisoned with his father on the island of Crete. To escape, his father created wings out of wax and feathers for them to use to fly out of the prison. His father warned him not to fly too close to the sun, but he didn't listen. He flew so close to the sun that his wax wings melted, and he could no longer fly. He fell into the sea and perished. So this is a type of tragic story arc that starts sad, then becomes happy, then ends sad again.

NARRATOR: Why does the professor say this:

PROFESSOR: So this is a type of tragic story arc that starts sad, then becomes happy, then ends sad again.

6.   **FUNCTION OF WHAT IS SAID.** This quote is used to demonstrate a particular story arc that has not yet been discussed (the Icarus story arc), but that is based upon a broader type of arc (the tragedy story arc) already defined.

✗	(A)	To remind students of a story they have likely forgotten	The story is used to provide detail about the origins of this new story arc, not to remind students of the original story itself.
✗	(B)	To show that the best stories tend to follow a tragedy story arc	The professor does not indicate that any one type of story arc tends to produce better stories than others.
✗	(C)	To illustrate the Cinderella story arc	This example does not follow the Cinderella story arc.
✓	(D)	To illustrate a specific type of story arc not yet discussed	**CORRECT.** The Icarus story arc is based on the tragedy story arc, with the added feature of a sad beginning state.

Answers and Explanations—7.5

Art Forgery—Track 18

NARRATOR: Listen to part of a lecture in an art history class.

PROFESSOR: Today we're going to talk about evaluating works of art in a special way—we're going to discuss *art forgery*. Art forgery is a special kind of crime… it's not like, um… murder, and not even that much like robbery—that is, if it goes undetected, there isn't really a monetary loss. And if it is detected, it often damages only reputations, not people or property. And forgery itself is not a crime—the crime is usually fraud. Furthermore, convicted forgers get off relatively lightly, usually serving only a few years in prison. This is partly because they are not viewed with the same contempt as other criminals. In fact, the general public often admires them because they fooled members of the cultural and financial elite. Almost like… like a "cultural Robin Hood." Not only that, many find fame and fortune after their… again, short sentence… they either live off their exploits or even find an audience for their own work.

I can see that some of you are finding this an attractive proposition. Well, there's some truth to that. Aside from the points I just mentioned, the reality of the art world is that it is very vulnerable to such schemes. To understand that, we have to discuss aesthetics and art evaluation on the business side of the art world. Art has been copied and forged since ancient times, starting with classic Greek vases in Roman days, continuing through fake religious relics in medieval times… and, yes, there's the forgery of paintings, which I'm sure was your first thought.

But even though the value of a work of art is tied to its genuineness, the art world isn't very good at *establishing authenticity*. Although, in all fairness, there are big problems. One method of determining whether a piece is authentic is through evaluating *provenance*—that is, the paper trail of ownership. But paper is fragile—a lot of it is destroyed by fires, wars, and other catastrophes. Sometimes it disintegrates or disappears over the course of a few hundred years. And, of course, paper itself is easier to forge than artwork. On top of that, it has been suggested that at least half the works of masters before, say, um, 1800,

have been lost. We know they existed from diaries, contracts, and such like... so maybe some of them will turn up. But, of course, they will be without provenance.

OK. So, expert appraisal is another theoretical safeguard. But that has problems, too. Lately, experts in a variety of fields have been denounced or had their expertise called into question. Well, in the art world, there's some justification for that. Until very recently—a few decades ago, really—there were no objective criteria for certifying experts in art appraisal. Scientific methods such as laser and x-ray examinations of artwork are an even more recent development. So, in some ways, expert appraisal was a confidence game. And even legitimate and honest practitioners partly based their opinion on feelings as much as on brush strokes, pigments, and so forth. But, keep in mind that many painters, notably during the Renaissance, had studios where assistants and apprentices also contributed to the master's work. So often it was practically a guessing game.

In the 1930s, there was a famous forgery case in Berlin involving Van Gogh paintings. Not only did different experts hold different positions, but some of them changed their views diametrically back and forth during the course of the investigation and trial. Typically enough, the eventually convicted forger, a fellow named Otto Wacker... I kid you not... received a sentence of less than two years. This trial, though, was one of the first cases where scientific evidence—a chemical analysis of the pigment—was employed.

Ok, so you might think that since then, employing scientific methods has pretty much solved this uncertainty... right? Yes and no. Without a doubt, advancement and utilization of science has improved the accuracy of authentication. But there's a problem there too. Over time, wood panels and canvases age, and the paint itself can crack. So, many verifiable masterpieces have been subjected to undocumented restorations—of varying quality—hundreds of years ago, but also hundreds of years after the originals were created. In these cases, scientific analysis of the composition, age, and origin of the materials can be confusing—even deceptive. As recently as 1993, some works purchased by the Getty Museum in Los Angeles were found to almost certainly have been forgeries, despite appropriate scrutiny. Modern art museums are powerful institutions and, thus, they vigorously protect their reputations. Consequently, the Getty on that occasion—and the Metropolitan in New York on another—stonewalled the authentication process and sued to prevent the unmasking of expensive purchases as dubious. So, to this day, the Latin cliché certainly still applies to art purchases—*caveat emptor*... you know, "buyer beware."

1.	What is the lecture mainly about?	**GIST-CONTENT.** The lecture is about art forgery and the difficulty of authenticating artwork.
✗	(A) The immorality inherent in art forgery	The lecture does not discuss the morality of art forgery.
✗	(B) Methods of creating a forged painting	The lecture does not get into specifics on how to create a forgery.
✗	(C) Ways to determine the purpose of an artwork	The lecture covers how art forgery occurs, not the purpose of the artwork.
✓	(D) Aspects of art authentication and forgery	**CORRECT.** The lecture covers exactly these points.

2.   According to the professor, what is one problem with provenance?

   ✓ (A) The fragility of paper

   ✗ (B) The translation of ancient languages

   ✗ (C) The costliness of evaluating the accuracy of provenance

   ✗ (D) Reliance on feelings in evaluating provenance

DETAIL. The professor says that provenance paperwork can be destroyed, lost, or easily forged.

CORRECT. The professor says that provenance paperwork can be destroyed, lost, and easily forged.

This idea is not mentioned in the lecture.

This idea is not mentioned in the lecture.

Reliance on feelings was discussed as a problem with expert opinion, not with provenance.

3.   Why does the professor talk about the 1930s Van Gogh forgery case in Berlin?

   ✗ (A) To suggest that the conviction was unjust

   ✓ (B) To illustrate a problem with expert authentication

   ✗ (C) To lament the short prison sentence associated with the case

   ✗ (D) To demonstrate that provenance is superior to expert opinion

ORGANIZATION. This case exemplifies the problems with expert opinions.

The professor's point is that experts can be unreliable, but there is no opinion given about the conviction.

CORRECT. It is an example of the lack of accuracy of experts.

The mention of the length of the sentence is merely a digression, not the main point.

The professor does not rank these two aspects of authentication.

4.   Why does the professor mention undocumented restorations?

   ✗ (A) To claim that these restorations make forgery impossible to detect

   ✗ (B) To warn against the restoration of aging artwork

   ✓ (C) To point out a problem with scientific analysis

   ✗ (D) To argue for verification using provenance rather than scientific analysis

PURPOSE. The professor says that undocumented restorations make scientific analysis less useful.

Undocumented restoration makes scientific analysis less useful in detecting forgery, but not useless.

This idea is not mentioned in the lecture.

CORRECT. The professor says, "In these cases, scientific analysis of the composition, age, and origin of the materials can be confusing—even deceptive."

The professor does not rank different authentication methods.

5. The professor mentions four aspects of art authentication. Indicate the order in which they are presented in the lecture: first, second, third, or fourth.

CONNECTING CONTENT. The professor discusses paper provenance, expert opinion, certification of experts, and scientific analysis, in that order.

| A | Scientific methods for analyzing artwork _____ |

FOURTH. The professor says, "Scientific methods such as laser and x-ray examinations of artwork are an even more recent development." This mention comes last.

| B | Paper provenance _____ |

FIRST. The professor discusses provenance before any of the other aspects of art authentication.

| C | Expert opinion _____ |

SECOND. The professor discusses expert opinion before certification or the use of science.

| D | Objective criteria for the certification of art experts _____ |

THIRD. The professor says, "Until very recently—a few decades ago, really—there were no objective criteria for certifying experts in art appraisal." Scientific methods are mentioned afterwards.

Track 19

NARRATOR: What does the professor imply when he says this:

PROFESSOR: Modern art museums are powerful institutions and, thus, they vigorously protect their reputations.

6. **INFERENCE.** The professor says this before describing museum efforts to block such investigations.

✗ (A) Art museums use their power to collect as many masterpieces as they can.

The use of power to collect masterpieces was not discussed.

✗ (B) Top art museums exert every effort to avoid exhibiting forgeries, with little regard for cost.

If anything, the professor implies the opposite.

✓ (C) Art museums do not always make determining the authenticity of artwork their top priority.

CORRECT. The professor says this before describing museum efforts to block such investigations.

✗ (D) Top art museums, such as the Getty and Metropolitan, cooperate to suppress scandals.

This may be possible in the real world. But the professor mentions them as two separate examples and does not imply any cooperation between these two museums or any others.

Answers and Explanations—7.6

National Parks—Track 20

NARRATOR: Listen to part of a lecture in a United States history class.

PROFESSOR: OK, last class we talked about the history of national parks, a–and the *National Park Service* here in the United States. Can anyone give a summary of what we covered? Angela?

FEMALE STUDENT: Well, let's see, the first national park was Yellowstone, which is located in, um, parts of several states—I think Wyoming, Idaho, and um, Montana, right? Congress established it as a national park in, um, 1872, but the National Park Service came later, after several more national parks were established.

PROFESSOR: Exactly. What about the National Park Service… what details do you remember?

FEMALE STUDENT: Um… it was started in the early 1900s, um, 1916 I think. There were a lot more national parks and monuments established by that time and, well, each originally had its own management agencies.

PROFESSOR: Right, but why create the National Park Service? What do you think Luis?

MALE STUDENT: Well, it was probably difficult to track that many different agencies, and since parks and monuments were constantly being added, right?—it would be a… well, a better idea to have a single managing group for them all.

PROFESSOR: Exactly.

FEMALE STUDENT: Yeah. But you mentioned last time that there was a campaign to, ah, convince the government to protect certain areas or sites. Wouldn't people want to preserve natural lands and historic monuments?

PROFESSOR: Ah, okay… well, we might think that preservation is a goal for everyone, but, actually, that isn't necessarily true. Why might some resist giving land a park designation, restricting it like that?

FEMALE STUDENT: Well, I mean, establishing it as a park, a national park, would mean that the land couldn't be used for something else later, something profitable, right?

PROFESSOR: Yes, and people who wanted to farm or develop that land, well they were likely going to resist the government—resist having those rights taken away. But it wasn't always individuals or even corporations who fought, or tried to, ah… challenge the distinction of a national park… and, um… the limits on use. As a matter of fact, an interesting case was in the 1940s, during World War II. During the war, Congress and, um, the military needed resources for the war effort, things like meat and water and, uh, even wood. Many of these things could be found in national parks but, because of the restrictions, they couldn't be used freely… some military units even came looking for metal, asking to melt down items like Civil War cannons! Without the National Park Service, many of these artifacts might be lost—gone forever. In fact, having a, um, single National Park Service, rather than, say, all under separate control, likely saved many park resources from destruction and overharvesting, overuse.

FEMALE STUDENT: Wait, why would having them under a single organization be helpful?

PROFESSOR: Well, you see, there arc actually a few key reasons why a unified National Park Service was advantageous. Alone, it would have been harder for a single park to push back against a government, um, or, a m–military request. The war effort was extremely popular with the public. Any one park, standing

alone, risked losing public support if they resisted. By, ah, banding… joining together, they could create a unified front. The larger system was also able to develop a single criteria for what they called "irreplaceable treasures," and only allow their use when all other sources were completely exhausted. And finally, as a large body, it could do inventory and track park resources, as well as who was attempting to use them.

MALE STUDENT: But you mentioned support… public support for the war effort. Just because the NPS was able to push back against other governmental, and, um… military agencies, how did it deal with the public? Was this an issue?

PROFESSOR: Well, as a matter of fact, the National Park Service eventually worked, well… with the military in order to… move attention away from its protected resources, and… instead, to its role in supporting the military during a time of crisis. During this time, several national parks were used for military training exercises because of the… the harsh and rough terrain, er… mountains or deserts they provided. The park system even created programs specifically for members of the military coming home from service… using nature to help soldiers heal from the stresses of war. In fact, this relationship with the military continues. In 2012, the National Park Service began issuing free annual passes to all 397 parks for active-duty military and their families.

1.	What is the lecture mainly about?	**GIST-CONTENT.** The lecture focuses mainly on the National Park Service and some aspects of its history.
✓	(A) The history of the National Park Service in the United States	**CORRECT.** This is the primary focus of the lecture.
✗	(B) Popular and unpopular national parks and monuments	Nothing is stated about the popularity of parks or monuments.
✗	(C) Different ways that governments can protect natural resources	The lecture does mention ways that the National Park Services worked to protect park resources, but this is not the main point of the discussion.
✗	(D) Reasons why the National Park Service has been unsuccessful	The opposite is true—several successful endeavors by the National Park Service are discussed.

2. According to the discussion, in what three ways was the creation of a unified National Park Service advantageous? *Choose 3 answers.*

DETAIL. This question addresses a student's question about how it would help to have individual parks managed by a single organization. The professor mentions the organization's ability to stand up to government, to designate "irreplaceable treasures," and to track park resources.

✓ A It prevented individual parks from having to face government pressure alone.

CORRECT. This point is mentioned explicitly in the lecture.

✓ B It could perform inventory and track park resources.

CORRECT. This point is mentioned explicitly in the lecture.

✗ C It allowed the military to utilize park resources more efficiently during the war.

The opposite it true—the unified system allowed parks to refuse some military requests.

✓ D It was able to develop criteria for "irreplaceable treasures."

CORRECT. This point is mentioned explicitly in the lecture.

✗ E It allowed the National Park Service to designate Yellowstone as a national park.

According to the lecture, Yellowstone was designated a national park before the National Park Service was created.

3. The class discusses several events related to the National Park Service in the United States. Put the events in chronological order: first, second, third, or fourth.

CONNECTING CONTENT. The professor says that Yellowstone was established first, and then the National Park Service was created. Next, national parks were used for military training in World War II, and finally, in recent times, free passes have been issued to active-duty military.

A The National Park Service was created. _____

SECOND. The student mentions that this came after several parks, including Yellowstone, had already been designated. This choice therefore might not be first.

B The National Park Service started issuing free passes to active-duty military.
_____

FOURTH. This would have to occur after the National Park Service was created. The professor mentions this as a recent development.

C Parks were used for military training programs during World War II.
_____

THIRD. This occurred after the creation of the National Park Service, but before the free passes were issued.

D Yellowstone was designated a national park. _____

FIRST. This occurred before the creation of the National Park Service, and therefore it comes first.

7

4. Why does the professor mention Civil War cannons?

ORGANIZATION. The professor mentions that "some military units even came looking for metal, asking to melt down items like Civil War cannons!" She mentions this as an example of the National Park Service protecting monuments and artifacts from military requests.

✗ (A) To show an example of popular historic artifacts

The professor never mentions the popularity of cannons, just the National Park Service's work to preserve them.

✗ (B) To illustrate the support that the National Park Service was willing to give to the military during the war

The opposite is true. This is an example of something the National Park Service wanted to keep from military use unless absolutely necessary.

✓ (C) To give an example of a resource that the military wanted to take from national parks

CORRECT. The Civil War cannons were an example of artifacts that the military wanted to take and melt down for metal.

✗ (D) To explain why the National Park Service was created

This was not given as a reason why the National Park Service was originally created.

5. What does the professor say about some people's objection to designating land as a national park?

DETAIL. According to the professor, one reason some people object to this designation is that it prevents the land from being used for economic purposes.

✗ (A) They feared that the "irreplaceable treasures" in such parks might be lost.

This was a fear of those in the National Park Service, not those who opposed park designation.

✗ (B) They wanted to ensure that the military had complete access to the resources found on the land.

This was not mentioned as a concern at this point in the lecture.

✗ (C) They were concerned about the number of potential visitors to the park each year.

This was never mentioned as a concern in the lecture.

✓ (D) They were concerned about having their own rights to the land taken away.

CORRECT. Rights such as future farming and development were mentioned specifically.

Track 21

NARRATOR: Listen again to part of the lecture. Then answer the question.

FEMALE STUDENT: Yeah. But you mentioned last time that there was a campaign to, ah, convince the government to protect certain areas or sites. Wouldn't people want to preserve natural lands and historic monuments?

PROFESSOR: Ah, okay… well, we might think that preservation is a goal for everyone, but, actually, that isn't necessarily true.

NARRATOR: What does the professor imply when she says this:

PROFESSOR: Ah, okay… well, we might think that preservation is a goal for everyone, but, actually, that isn't necessarily true.

6.   **INFERENCE.** In this quote, the professor is rejecting the idea that everyone would want to protect some lands by designating them as national parks.

✗ (A) The student did not understand what was explained in an earlier discussion. | This quote does not address an earlier discussion.

✗ (B) Most of the class would disagree with this student's opinion. | The opposite is more likely true—the professor thinks that many people would think the way this student does.

✓ (C) Not everyone is supportive of the creation of national parks. | **CORRECT.** The professor states that it isn't necessarily true that everyone has the goal of preservation.

✗ (D) National parks are extremely popular in the United States. | The professor is pointing out that some might not want the parks—not that they are or are not generally popular.

Answers and Explanations—7.7

Minimalism in Music—Track 22

NARRATOR: Listen to part of a lecture in a music history class.

PROFESSOR: Okay, we've been talking about avant-garde music in the United States in the 1950s and '60s, and, um, how, at that time, composers were experimenting with a lot of new techniques in their music. We, um, saw composers bringing in all kinds of new sounds, recorded sounds, ambient noise, trying out different processes of putting things together… like using chance processes to make decisions. And today we're going to talk about one person who came out of this period, who was very influential, in terms of founding an entire new school—minimalism. His name was La Monte Young.

La Monte Young was born in 1935 in a log cabin in Idaho. He started out playing jazz in Los Angeles as a teenager. But he quickly moved beyond that, and by the mid-1950s he was exploring a lot of the new experimental techniques we talked about. But Young took things further. He wanted to reduce music to its, uh, most basic elements, long held tones, drones, heavily, uh, influenced by the sounds of his childhood in Idaho. He really started exploring this with his 1958 *Trio for Strings*—which some people say is the beginning of minimalist music.

Young was the, the first composer to really commit to this kind of extremely, uh, reduced music. *Trio for Strings*, for example, consists entirely of a few tones, sustained for a very long time. After this, he started moving more and more into the *conceptual* realm, influenced by people like John Cage and the so-called "twelve-tone composers." He'd take a single idea, some conception, say, that we have about how music works, or what makes something music, for example, the idea that music is linear, that it moves forward in time. And then he'd isolate that idea, and pursue it to its logical extreme. For example, one composition from the 1960s just has the instructions "draw a straight line and follow it." That sort of thing. He was really interested in duration, too, in seeing how long something could be drawn out, just sustained without the kind of direction, or climaxes, that we normally, uh, look for in Western music. He had one installation, *Dream House*, that ran for four years, more or less continuously. And today there's still a version of *Dream House* running, in New York. He and his wife even tried to live this way, too, keeping up an extended schedule of waking and sleeping, in periods longer than 24 hours.

Tanya? You have a question?

FEMALE STUDENT: Yeah, it sounds like what he was doing was pretty normal for that time, right? I mean, a lot of other people were exploring the same kinds of techniques?

PROFESSOR: Well, he was influenced by work being done by other artists at the time. But at the same time, he was pushing these things in really new directions.

FEMALE STUDENT: But what about someone like Philip Glass? Wasn't he doing the same kind of stuff, with minimalism and all that?

PROFESSOR: Yes, yes, Philip Glass. OK, so, Young and Glass were both experimenting with similar things, and both are recognized as key minimalist composers, but that's where the similarities end. First of all, Young got there first, in terms of minimalism… um, Glass was still working with much more, uh, traditional ideas, when Young wrote *Trio for Strings*… and Glass also stayed a lot, uh, closer to tonal music, and to the usual kinds of instrumentation, and arrangements. He was much more of, uh, a classical musician, really, than Young, who started off in jazz. Young got into classical stuff much later, while Glass started out, you know, at Juilliard. Young was a lot more, um, out there, in terms of unusual instrumentation, and durations, and pushing the, uh, boundaries of what could be done. While Glass was, you know, experimental, but still working with traditional forms, like opera, and the symphony.

Mark, you have a question?

MALE STUDENT: Well, um, maybe this question is inappropriate… but, if Young was such an innovator, if he was such an important influence, then why haven't we heard more of his music? I mean, we all know who Philip Glass is…

PROFESSOR: That's a reasonable thing to ask. Uh, the short answer is that a lot of Young's works aren't written down, or recorded. It goes back to the, um, deeply experimental nature of the work. A lot of his stuff is also just, um, harder to listen to. By contrast, Glass did, you know, things that sound a lot nicer to the ear, if you've grown up listening to classical music. But Young influenced a lot of musicians, and a lot of really well-known people cite him as an influence—not just classical musicians, but people like Lou Reed, Brian Eno, and Andy Warhol.

1.   What is the main purpose of the lecture?

GIST-PURPOSE. The main purpose of this lecture is to discuss the work of La Monte Young.

✓ (A) To describe the work of an influential musician

CORRECT. This lecture is primarily focused on the contributions made by one person and his influence on other musicians and artists.

✗ (B) To discuss the importance of avant-garde art forms

This choice is too broad for the scope of this passage.

✗ (C) To explain what minimalism is

While the passage does discuss minimalism, it does so primarily in the context of the work done by one particular musician.

✗ (D) To describe Philip Glass's impact on advertising

This idea is not mentioned in the lecture.

2.   How were La Monte Young's compositions different from those of his contemporaries?

DETAIL. The professor states that Young was "the first composer to really commit to this kind of extremely... reduced music." Young's work focused on simple, minimalist outputs much more than the work of his peers did.

✗ (A) They were experimental.

The lecture says that La Monte Young was one of many experimental composers at the time, and connects him to other experimental musicians.

✗ (B) They were about dreams.

While Young did have a project called *Dream House*, his work didn't specifically describe dreams.

✗ (C) They were influential.

This is true, but not necessarily something that makes him different from others.

✓ (D) They were very minimal.

CORRECT. The lecture says that Young "took things further" than other experimental composers and that he tried to make music that was extremely minimal and reduced.

3.   According to the professor, why was Young's music less popular than other minimalist music?

DETAIL. The professor states that Young's work was more difficult to listen to, and much more dissimilar to music people would be familiar with than was the music of other minimalist composers.

✓ (A) It could be difficult to listen to.

CORRECT. This is mentioned toward the end of the lecture, in comparison with the music of Philip Glass.

✗ (B) It used unusual instruments.

The professor mentions that Philip Glass used more standard instrumentation than Young did, but this is not given as a reason for Young's work being less popular.

✗ (C) It was only performed outdoors.

This idea is not mentioned in the lecture.

✗ (D) It wasn't performed very often.

This idea is not mentioned in the lecture.

4. Why does the professor mention the *Dream House* installation?

    ✗ Ⓐ To contrast his work with Philip Glass's

    ✗ Ⓑ To show how difficult minimalist music could be to make

    ✓ Ⓒ To illustrate Young's interest in pieces of long duration

    ✗ Ⓓ To explain Young's creative process

ORGANIZATION. The professor mentions this installation as an illustration of Young's interest in exploring duration.

This contrast happens later in the lecture.

This idea is not mentioned in the lecture.

CORRECT. This detail appears just after the professor's mention of Young's obsession with exploring duration.

The professor mentions *Dream House* as an example of Young's interest in exploring duration, not to explain Young's creative process overall.

5. Why does the professor compare the work of Philip Glass and La Monte Young?

    ✗ Ⓐ To explain how Young influenced Glass

    ✓ Ⓑ To emphasize how groundbreaking Young's work was

    ✗ Ⓒ To emphasize the musical innovation of Glass's work

    ✗ Ⓓ To demonstrate the superiority of Young's creative process

ORGANIZATION. The professor compares the work of these two artists after questions from students.

This idea is not discussed in the lecture.

CORRECT. The professor emphasizes how "out there" Young's work was, in contrast with Glass's work.

Glass's work is described as somewhat more conservative than Young's work.

This choice adds a value judgment where none is explicitly given by the professor.

Track 23

NARRATOR: What does the student imply when he says this:

MALE STUDENT: Well, um, maybe this question is inappropriate… but, if Young was such an innovator, if he was such an important influence, then why haven't we heard more of his music? I mean, we all know who Philip Glass is…

MANHATTAN PREP

6. What does the student imply when he says this?

FUNCTION OF WHAT IS SAID. The student is implying that, if Young was very influential, he should possibly also be more widely recognized. Another possible interpretation is that, because Young is not well-known, perhaps he was not that influential.

✗ (A) He does not like Young's music.

This makes inappropriate assumptions about the student's intentions or opinions.

✗ (B) He thinks the professor should focus more on the works of Philip Glass.

This idea is outside the scope of this lecture, which is more about Young than Glass.

✗ (C) He believes that Young should be more famous than Glass.

Nothing in the student's quote suggests that this is the case.

✓ (D) He believes that Young's works might deserve greater recognition.

CORRECT. This matches most closely with the student's likely intention: if Young were so influential, then perhaps he should be more widely recognized.

Answers and Explanations—7.8

Francis Picabia—Track 24

NARRATOR: Listen to part of a lecture in an art history class.

PROFESSOR: Francis Picabia is not a household name, like Picasso or Matisse. But he, uh… he was truly a force in the world of art throughout the twentieth century. He sort of, uh… defies classification, though, in a way, because of how varied his career was.

You know, I remember when I discovered Picabia as a student of art history. I assumed that he was a standard member of the *Dadaism movement*, because the first thing I learned about him was that he was called "Papa Dada," as in Dadaism. The Dadaism movement, you may remember, was a movement in art that took place in Europe during and after World War I. Not just Europe, but mainly Europe. It reached North America as well. And mainly, well… mainly it took place after the war. It was a response to the war, really, and all that was happening at the time. The ideas at the root of this movement were about challenging… protesting… the accepted definitions of art. If you've ever heard the term "anti-art," that was a term that came up during this time. I believe it was coined by the famous Dadaist, Marcel Duchamp. You may have heard of him.

But really, Dadaism was about more than just challenging art. It was about questioning the cultural and political forces that Dadaists believed led to the war. Dadaists rejected the established idea that there were, you know, only certain ways that art could and should be. They opposed the idea that there's logic behind what art is. Dadaism was the opposite of logic! No logic. No reason. Just feeling, intuition… chaos.

Some people were really horrified by this, you know. They found it offensive. You can probably see why. I mean, it was meant to offend. That was sort of the point.

Now, what did this art actually look like? Well, you probably recall that collage was a technique that developed during the Cubism movement, which came before, and it means, uh… pasting pieces of paper

onto the canvas. Actually cutting them out, of newspapers or magazines or whatever, and pasting them on. Dadaism used collage, but took it to a whole new level… instead of just using paper to create a piece of art, they were assembling actual objects. An *assemblage* is a collection of everyday objects fastened together. The objects are things that you'd just find sitting around—nothing particularly special. Assemblages would become a big thing later in the twentieth century, but the idea of an assemblage originated in Dadaism. And finally, another Dada technique was called "*readymades*." These were, for some, the most controversial kind of Dada art… maybe because they were really just, well… already-made objects—like a toilet, by itself—that the artists tried to get away with calling "art." Again, if that sounds offensive, it's because that was part of the point.

But to get back to Francis Picabia… he was called Papa Dada, but he wasn't only a Dadaist. After the Dada movement and its dominant styles sort of passed, and the art world had moved on to Surrealism, and then to conceptual art… Picabia? He did not follow the trend. He was unusual in that he would continue to work in a variety of styles—a true mix—when other artists were at least sticking generally to a particular style at a particular time. You'll see in a moment, when I show you slides of his work over time… well, it was all over the place. Some people have even described his style as incoherent. He would make work that was figurative and work that was abstract—so by that, I mean, not figurative, meaning not recognizable as being pulled from life, like a person or a tree. He really defied categorization. Picabia was… it was almost like he was determined not to stick to a particular style. He went back and forth. He was making more figurative work in the 1920s and mid-1940s, but in his last years making art, in the late 1940s and early 1950s, he returned to abstractionism. And throughout his entire career, I don't think you could say that he was any one thing, because that's just not how he thought about it. When he talked about what inspired him, he talked about what he felt in the deepest part of his mind… his intuition. Let me show you these slides so you'll see what I mean…

1. What does the professor mainly talk about?

   ✗ (A) How Francis Picabia became a Dadaist

   ✗ (B) Art immediately before World War I

   ✗ (C) The features of Dadaism in contrast with Surrealism

   ✓ (D) The artistic career of Francis Picabia

GIST-CONTENT. The professor mainly discusses Francis Picabia and what makes him unique as an artist.

The professor does not discuss how Picabia became a Dadaist.

While art after World War I is discussed, art beforehand is only briefly mentioned.

Surrealism is briefly mentioned, but a comparison with Dadaism is not made in the lecture.

CORRECT. The lecture is about one artist in particular, his career as a whole, and the art movement associated with him.

2.   Why does the professor reference her discovery of Picabia while she was an art history student?

  ✓ (A) To emphasize that the trajectory of Picabia's career was surprising to her

  ✗ (B) To explain the historical appeal of Picabia's paintings

  ✗ (C) To argue that Picabia was as misunderstood then as he is today

  ✗ (D) To help describe her own philosophy as a student of art

ORGANIZATION. The professor states, "I remember when I discovered Picabia as a student of art history. I assumed that he was a standard member of the Dadaism movement."

CORRECT. As an art student, the professor assumed that Picabia was a "standard member of the Dadaism movement," but in fact his career was more varied.

The professor does not discuss the historical appeal of Picabia's work.

The professor does not argue that Picabia was, or is, misunderstood.

The professor does not discuss her philosophy as an art student.

3.   What are two techniques that were invented during the Dadaism movement? *Choose 2 answers.*

  ✓ [A] Readymades

  ✓ [B] Assemblages

  ✗ [C] Collages

  ✗ [D] Abstract painting

DETAIL. The professor mentions that both assemblages and readymades were styles invented during the Dadaism movement.

CORRECT. Readymades are essentially previously-made objects. This is a technique created by Dadaists.

CORRECT. Assemblages are collage-like collections of everyday objects. This is a technique created by Dadaists.

The professor states that collage was invented beforehand, during the Cubism movement.

The professor does not mention in the lecture when abstract painting was invented.

4.   According to the professor, what is true of other painters who worked at the same time as Picabia?

  ✗ (A) They resented Picabia and the other Dadaists.

  ✗ (B) They leaned more toward abstract painting than figurative painting.

  ✗ (C) They did not change styles at all over the course of their careers.

  ✓ (D) They did not commonly alternate between abstract painting and figurative painting.

INFERENCE. The professor states that other artists at the time "were at least sticking generally to a particular style at a particular time."

The professor does not mention this idea in the lecture.

The professor implies that these painters worked in either of these two styles.

The professor only states that they generally stuck to a particular style during a particular time. "At all" is too strong.

CORRECT. It was in this way that Picabia was unusual.

5. Compared with other painters living at the same time, what was unusual about Francis Picabia?

    DETAIL. The professor states that Picabia was working in "a true mix" of styles, and that this is what made him unusual.

    ✗ (A) He could paint better abstractly than he could figuratively.

    The professor does not mention this idea in the lecture.

    ✗ (B) He was part of the Dadaism movement.

    Picabia's inclusion in the Dadaism movement is not what made him unique.

    ✓ (C) He worked in a true mix of styles throughout his career.

    CORRECT. This is the main point of the lecture.

    ✗ (D) He made assemblages.

    The professor does not mention Picabia making assemblages in the lecture.

6. What is the professor's opinion about "readymades" in the Dadaism movement?

    SPEAKER'S ATTITUDE. The professor addresses "readymades" in her explanation of Dadaism. They were objects that were already made—Dadaists then labeled them as "art." She notes that they were especially controversial.

    ✗ (A) They were offensive and therefore not art.

    The professor does not argue or imply that because readymades were controversial, they weren't art.

    ✓ (B) Among other things, they were intended to offend people.

    CORRECT. The professor states that people taking offense at readymades was "part of the point."

    ✗ (C) They were probably the most powerful part of the Dadaism movement.

    The professor does not claim they were the most powerful part of the Dadaism movement.

    ✗ (D) They were considered more valuable than they should have been.

    The professor does not offer a personal opinion of the value of readymades.

Answers and Explanations—7.9

US Skyscrapers—Track 25

NARRATOR: Listen to part of a lecture in an architecture class.

PROFESSOR: Up until now, we've been talking, uh… talking mostly about traditional residential structures. Today we're going to look at high-rises, or skyscrapers. Since high-rises are so different from traditional one and two-story buildings, I… I think this will help us see the relationship between culture and engineering in new building design.

Uh, but before we get into the details of that, I want you to think about where in the United States skyscrapers first started to appear. Can anyone take a guess? John?

MALE STUDENT: New York has huge skyscrapers. And there's a lot of them, so I bet it's New York.

PROFESSOR: Some early skyscrapers were built in New York—but was the first one there? Yeah, Mary?

FEMALE STUDENT: How about where my parents are from? They're from Chicago and they always say it was the home of the first skyscraper.

PROFESSOR: That's it. Here's an image of a… of what a typical—what an early skyscraper may have looked like.

These first examples were maybe 14, 15 stories tall. Now, of course, skyscrapers are a lot taller… uh, but it was a major architectural feat for the time. What structural problems would architects at the time have had to consider? Someone give me an example of something that is more challenging because of the height of this building. What problems would they have encountered when they tried to build anything that tall?

FEMALE STUDENT: Well… if the building is taller, it's heavier. And… well… that weight has to go somewhere. So the… the architect would have to design a really strong base—something that could hold all that weight.

PROFESSOR: Good! And, at the time, buildings were supported by their walls. So the walls would have to be thicker to support a, uh, a heavier building. The tallest buildings at the time had walls that were so thick that there was limited space, and architects actually had trouble finding people interested in using them. But society was pushing for taller and taller buildings.

Who knows what was going on in the United States in the 1860s and 1870s?

MALE STUDENT: People were moving from farms to the cities.

FEMALE STUDENT: And weren't there some fires in the big cities that destroyed the downtown areas?

PROFESSOR: Yes. Both Chicago and New York saw many of their traditional wooden buildings destroyed, and they wanted to rebuild with new materials. At the same time, these cities' populations were growing at an incredible rate. So, um… so many people arrived at Chicago during this time that the city couldn't hold them. In 1830, Chicago had only about 100 people living in it. In 1850, that number was up to 30,000. And by 1870 nearly 300,000 people lived in Chicago. In 1871, the Great Chicago fire destroyed many of the traditional buildings downtown. Reconstructed buildings had to be taller just to… just to house everyone!

Now. What changed that made skyscrapers possible? Think about technological advancements.

FEMALE STUDENT: Well there's mass-produced steel… Because… Wouldn't mass producing steel help… I mean, since… tall buildings need a lot of steel.

MALE STUDENT: Yeah, steel's a lot stronger and sturdier than what they used to use, right?

PROFESSOR: Exactly. Steel girders were… were strong, and architects could make a skeleton frame in the center of the building that could support the building's weight. Remember they used to support all the weight with the walls? Now, the walls, floors, and ceilings could be suspended from the steel frame. Column-frame construction, as this was called, completely changed the way architects designed buildings. The weight wasn't put on the walls anymore; it was on the interior frame.

FEMALE STUDENT: So now the walls could be thinner, and, you know… cheaper.

PROFESSOR: Good point. So these buildings were more economical to construct. And taking the weight off the walls let architects design with more windows and bigger windows. The availability of natural light because less space was taken up by walls made these buildings far more attractive. So the cultural conditions, combined with the material advances of the time, inspired the invention of skyscrapers, and encouraged the building of taller and taller structures.

1.   What aspect of architecture is this lecture primarily about?

GIST-CONTENT. It's mainly about why skyscrapers emerged when they did and what conditions helped their emergence.

✗ (A) The different challenges to consider when constructing different types of buildings

Only the challenges to one building type are mentioned.

✓ (B) The reasons for the timing of a particular type of building

CORRECT. The particular type of building discussed is the skyscraper, and the passage is about its initial creation and early developments.

✗ (C) The variations in architecture in the 1860s and 1870s

Variations at that time are not mentioned in the lecture.

✗ (D) The reasons why skyscrapers can have larger windows than traditional buildings

This is merely a supporting detail given near the end of the lecture.

Track 26

NARRATOR: Listen again to part of the lecture. Then answer the question.

PROFESSOR: Uh, but before we get into the details of that, I want you to think about where in the United States skyscrapers first started to appear. Can anyone take a guess? John?

MALE STUDENT: New York has huge skyscrapers. And there's a lot of them, so I bet it's New York.

PROFESSOR: Some early skyscrapers were built in New York—but was the first one there?

NARRATOR: Why does the professor say this:

PROFESSOR: But was the first one there?

2.   **FUNCTION OF WHAT IS SAID.** The students soon learn that the first skyscraper was constructed in Chicago.

✓ (A) To indicate that the student's answer is incorrect

CORRECT. The professor is asking someone in the class to correct John's guess.

✗ (B) To determine whether the students understood the original question

He is seeking another answer to the same question, not trying to clarify the question.

✗ (C) To point out that there is no way to know which skyscraper was completed first

On the contrary—the professor knows which skyscraper was the first to be built.

✗ (D) To ask for a more specific answer

The student's answer is not too general. It is simply incorrect.

3. Why does the woman refer to where her parents are from?

     ✗ (A) To explain why she is so interested in architecture

     ✗ (B) To explain how architectural design can vary within a city

     ✓ (C) To explain how she knows where the first skyscraper was built

     ✗ (D) To explain where steel is mass-produced

ORGANIZATION. They're from Chicago, home of the first skyscraper.

The student never mentions her interests.

Variations within a city are not mentioned.

CORRECT. Her parents were from Chicago and have told her that the first skyscraper was built there.

The location of steel production is not mentioned.

4. What is mentioned in the lecture as a challenge architects faced when designing the first skyscrapers?

     ✗ (A) Occupants were unwilling to walk up a large number of stairs to reach the top floors.

     ✓ (B) The additional weight from taller buildings had to be supported.

     ✗ (C) Culturally, wooden buildings were still preferred to steel ones.

     ✗ (D) The cost of obtaining the needed materials was sometimes excessive.

DETAIL. The primary challenge first faced by architects of skyscrapers was how to handle the additional weight of the building.

The professor does not mention this idea.

CORRECT. The skeleton frame eventually solved this problem, but this challenge was difficult to solve before steel became mass-produced.

The professor implies that some people wanted to *stop* creating wooden buildings because of the risk of fire.

The professor does not mention this idea.

5. According to the professor, what contributed to the increased demand for skyscrapers in some cities?

     ✗ (A) The desire for cities to be on the forefront of technological development

     ✗ (B) The increased weight resting on a taller building's base

     ✓ (C) The population increase in urban city centers

     ✗ (D) The push for family members to live and work in locations near to each other

DETAIL. A migration of people from rural areas to cities was causing explosive urban population growth. At the same time, fires burned down many of the existing housing structures in several cities.

The professor does not mention this idea.

This is cited as a problem for architects at the time, not as a cause for increased demand of skyscrapers.

CORRECT. Chicago in particular is cited as a city that saw a large influx of residents and had to create more structures to house them.

The professor does not mention this idea.

6. According to the lecture, what are two features of skyscrapers that were possible because of the steel skeleton frame? *Choose 2 answers.*

DETAIL. The steel frame was a turning point in building skyscrapers. The weight of the building could now be carried by the frame, not the walls.

✗ ☐ A The elevator

The professor does not mention this feature.

✓ ☐ B The thinner walls

CORRECT. Thick walls had only been necessary to support the weight of the building. Once the steel frame carried the weight, the walls could be thinned.

✗ ☐ C The number of hallways

The professor does not mention this feature.

✓ ☐ D The larger windows

CORRECT. Because they didn't need to support the weight of the building, walls could now contain more fragile material. This made more windows and bigger windows possible.

✗ ☐ E The higher ceilings

The professor mentions that ceilings could be suspended from the steel frame, but there's no discussion of whether they could be higher as a result.

Answers and Explanations—7.10

Occitan and Sicilian School Poetry—Track 27

NARRATOR: Listen to part of a lecture in a poetry class. The professor is discussing thirteenth century poetry.

PROFESSOR: Okay, so, today we're looking at two poems, both written around, uh… the thirteenth century. What was going on in history around that time?

FEMALE STUDENT: That was around the start of the Renaissance, right?

PROFESSOR: Yes that's right. It was the end of the Medieval Period and the very start of the Renaissance…

FEMALE STUDENT: But professor, I don't understand how these could be written at about the same time. The occ—ox—however it's pronounced… that one has a lot of repetition and really simple lines. The other one is more… more poetic. I mean, they're just so different!

PROFESSOR: Well, think about the different features of the poetry we've studied so far in class.

FEMALE STUDENT: Uh-huh.

PROFESSOR: Poems that are meant to be heard are written differently than poems that are meant to be read. Sicilian School poetry was the first poetry type that was written instead of sung, and it was a very early Renaissance poetry. Occitan poetry was a little earlier—in fact it's considered Medieval—so it was typically presented orally, uh… was sung. But there are even—even more important differences. Let's start with the earlier, Medieval, one first. That's Occitan.

Occitan poems were written just before the Renaissance began, and they were on a variety of topics— from… from romance, to politics, to historical lessons. For the most part, they were written for landholders, who were the only ones with much leisure time. In fact, some theorize that Occitan poetry

was started by the court jesters, the, uh… comedians for nobility. They wrote songs, musical poetry, and this whole genre of poetry was born. How would… could someone summarize the main features of the Occitan poem you read?

MALE STUDENT: Well, there's the man and woman who are in love. And the woman's family that the man has to convince… has to show that he's a good guy. When the family doesn't, uh… doesn't like him, doesn't approve of him, he and the woman start a romance in secret.

PROFESSOR: Okay, now… given that the intended audience was landholders, why do you think these poems might have been written? What purpose might they have served?

FEMALE STUDENT: Well I guess it was probably meant to be entertaining. It tells a story, and you really want to know how it ends. So it was just something they could listen to and have fun with?

PROFESSOR: Good. And because these were supposed to be sung, there's a lot of repetition—maybe so people could sing along. There were also interchangeable lines so singers could, uh… adapt on the spot. The other poem, the Renaissance one from the Sicilian School, also involves a love story. But what makes this romance different from the romance in the Occitan poem?

Well, first, the roles of the characters are different. In the older, Occitan poem, the man is the aggressor. He pursues the woman and he eventually is able to, well… create a romantic relationship with her. But in the Sicilian School poem, it's the woman who gets her way. She knows what she wants, and she is the instigator in the relationship. Throughout this poem, the traditional roles of men and women seem to be reversed. And remember when this was written—this is in the thirteenth century, so women didn't have much power. They were expected to obey men in almost all aspects of their lives.

What explains this role reversal? Well, digging into the society in the Sicilian School at the time explains a lot. The Renaissance was just starting, and new ideas about society were beginning to appear. But the royals still had complete control over poetry. The only topics that poets were, uh—that poets were allowed to write about, um… to compose poetry about—were courtship and romance. Politics, religion—all of that—could not be mentioned in poems. At least, not openly.

Undoubtedly, this was at least partly because this time period was so volatile politically! The kings and queens, the monarchy, the traditional source of power… was losing power. And at the same time the middle class was gaining power. Poets sensed a dramatic change was coming, but they weren't allowed to write about it.

So how did they get around that? They wrote about love… love stories that had role reversals and power reversals. The men, and by analogy the king and royalty, were placed in lower roles. And the women, the traditionally less powerful group, were given the power. In their own way, these poets were talking about the rise of the middle class and the transfer of power to those who traditionally had none. While seemingly restricted in what they could write, these Sicilian School poets were speaking to their time and to what was starting to go on around them.

1.   What is the main purpose of the lecture?

     GIST-PURPOSE. The professor discusses two poems. One is a traditional, medieval poem, and the other reflects the transition to the Renaissance.

     ✗ (A) To investigate Renaissance poetry

     Only one poem is from the Renaissance, and the lecture doesn't cover any other types of Renaissance poetry.

     ✗ (B) To explain why Sicilian School poetry involves role reversals

     This choice overgeneralizes about Sicilian School poetry, and doesn't address the Occitan poem.

     ✗ (C) To explain how romantic relationships changed in the thirteenth century

     Romance was the topic of the poems, but not the topic of the lecture.

     ✓ (D) To compare two different types of poetry using an example from each period

     CORRECT. Occitan and Sicilian School poems are compared.

2.   What does the professor say about Occitan poetry written during the Medieval Period?

     DETAIL. The professor discusses the Occitan poem at length. It features a secret romance and was likely meant for entertainment purposes, to name a few characteristics.

     ✗ (A) It was more popular than Sicilian School poetry.

     This comparison is not made in the lecture.

     ✓ (B) It was primarily sung, rather than read.

     CORRECT. The earlier Occitan poetry was mostly sung. The Sicilian School poetry is named as one of the first types of poetry meant to be read.

     ✗ (C) It was a tool court jesters could use to raise their status.

     There is no discussion of raising the status of court jesters.

     ✗ (D) It developed from Sicilian School poetry.

     The lecture contradicts this—Occitan poetry was from an earlier period.

3.   Why does the professor mention the start of the Renaissance?

     ORGANIZATION. The two poems were both written around this time. The Occitan poem was written just before the Renaissance, and the Sicilian School poem was written just after it.

     ✗ (A) To emphasize the growing popularity of poetry in this time

     The professor does not discuss whether the popularity of poetry changed over time.

     ✓ (B) To explain one of the differences between the two poems being discussed

     CORRECT. One was written at the beginning of the Renaissance, while the other was written beforehand.

     ✗ (C) To point out similarities between poems written during this time period

     The focus is on contrasting the two poems much more than noting their similarities.

     ✗ (D) To provide evidence that Occitan poets were attempting to change traditional mindsets of the time

     The professor does not mention this idea.

4.   According to the professor, what topics were forbidden to Sicilian School poets? *Choose 2 answers.*

✓ | A | Politics

✗ | B | Romance

✓ | C | Religion

✗ | D | Courtship

DETAIL. The only topics these poets were allowed to write about were courtship and romance.

CORRECT. The professor explicitly states that politics were forbidden in poems written at that time.

This topic is mentioned as permissible.

CORRECT. The professor explicitly states that religion was a forbidden topic in poems written at that time.

This topic is mentioned as permissible.

5.   According to the professor, what is true of the romance described in the Occitan poem and the romance described in the Sicilian School poem? Classify each of the following phrases as applying either to 1. Occitan Poetry or 2. Sicilian School Poetry.

| A | Is conducted in secret _____

| B | Features a woman as the aggressor _____

| C | Involves the woman's family _____

| D | Is used as social commentary _____

CONNECTING CONTENT. The Occitan poem is described as a more traditional, albeit secretive, romance. The Sicilian School poem illustrates a reversal of traditional gender roles.

1. OCCITAN POETRY. The student explains that when the family does not approve of the romance, it becomes a secret romance.

2. SICILIAN SCHOOL POETRY. Reversal of traditional gender roles is one of the ways that poets were able to comment on the changing social norms of the time.

1. OCCITAN POETRY. The man initially tries to win the approval of the woman's family in the Occitan poem.

2. SICILIAN SCHOOL POETRY. Though it is intentionally hidden, political and social commentary is featured in the Sicilian School poem.

Track 28

NARRATOR: Listen again to part of the lecture. Then answer the question.

PROFESSOR: Throughout this poem, the traditional roles of men and women seem to be reversed. And remember when this was written—this is in the thirteenth century, so women didn't have much power. They were expected to obey men in almost all aspects of their lives.

What explains this role reversal?

NARRATOR: Why does the professor say this:

PROFESSOR: What explains this role reversal?

6.   **FUNCTION OF WHAT IS SAID.** The professor is going into the social commentary developed in the Sicilian School poem. He later answers his own question by saying that the role reversal reflected the reversal of power dynamics that was beginning to occur in society at that time.

✗   (A) To invite members of the class to answer directly

There is no student response—the question is rhetorical.

✗   (B) To emphasize that this question cannot be answered

He subsequently answers this rhetorical question.

✓   (C) To introduce a rhetorical question that he is about to answer

CORRECT. This introduces the topic that follows in the lecture.

✗   (D) To remind students of the importance of thinking critically about poetry

The professor does not mention this idea.

Chapter 8
Lectures B: Humanities

Listening lectures test your ability to comprehend academic-level spoken English. You'll listen to a short lecture (about 3 to 5 minutes long) from a professor. Occasionally, a student may also speak. You will only be able to listen to the lecture once. You will not be able to pause the recording or to replay any part of it (though some questions will replay a specific part of the lecture for you). You can take notes as you listen.

You will then answer six questions for that lecture. Most questions are multiple-choice with four options (select one from A, B, C, or D). Some questions may ask you to select more than one option or to fill in a table. You will have to answer the questions in order. You cannot return to a question once you have moved on to the next question.

Listening lectures test your understanding of main ideas, contrasts, the lecturer's tone and degree of certainty about the information, and why the lecturer relates certain information or examples. They also test your understanding of the organization of the lecture and the relationship between different ideas. Finally, they test your ability to make inferences or draw conclusions.

How should you use this chapter? Here are some recommendations, according to the level you've reached in TOEFL Listening:

1. **Fundamentals.** Start with a topic-focused chapter, such as this one. Start with a topic that is a "medium weakness"—not your worst area but not your best either. At first, listen to the lecture once, then work on the questions untimed and check the answer after each question. Review the solutions closely, think carefully about the principles at work, and articulate what you've learned. Redo questions as necessary. As you get better, time yourself and do all of the questions for a lecture at once, without stopping.

2. **Fixes.** Do an entire lecture and its associated questions under timed conditions. Don't replay any part of the lecture while you are still answering the questions! Examine the results, learn your lessons, then test yourself with another lecture and question set.

3. **Tweaks.** Confirm your mastery by doing two or three lectures in a row under timed conditions. Work your way up to doing four lectures and two conversations in one sitting. Aim to improve the speed and ease of your process.

Good luck on Listening!

8.1

 Listen to Track 29.

Now answer the questions.

1. What is the main purpose of this talk?
   - (A) To discuss filmmakers who helped to revitalize the film industry
   - (B) To contrast the style of two young filmmakers
   - (C) To discuss the Golden Age of the Hollywood studio system
   - (D) To describe Cassavetes's influence on Scorsese

2. Why does the professor mention that *Faces* was nominated for three major Academy Awards?
   - (A) To bemoan Cassavetes's lack of financial backing
   - (B) To complain that *Faces* did not win any of the awards it was nominated for
   - (C) To support the claim that Cassavetes's new approach was successful
   - (D) To refute criticism of *Faces*

3. Why did Cassavetes's *Faces* succeed when studio films were failing?
   - (A) It was filmed in New York.
   - (B) It reflected the fact that English was not Cassavetes's first language.
   - (C) It used a hand-held camera and improvisation.
   - (D) It embraced realism rather than traditional, happy-ending plots.

4. According to the professor, what is one reason that Scorsese is better known than Cassavetes?
   - (A) Scorsese is considered more talented than Cassavetes was.
   - (B) Scorsese's films have had stars and advertising support.
   - (C) Scorsese is ethnically Italian, whereas Cassavetes was ethnically Greek.
   - (D) Scorsese made movies about organized crime.

5. Why does the professor mention that Cassavetes was a contrarian?
   - (A) To explain how Cassavetes influenced Scorsese
   - (B) To explain why Scorsese is more famous than Cassavetes today
   - (C) To criticize Cassavetes's behavior
   - (D) To explain why Cassavetes favored unknown actors

Listen to Track 30.

Now answer the question.

6. (A) He wants to discuss Scorsese only.

    (B) He somewhat dislikes Cassavetes's films.

    (C) He thinks that great filmmakers are usually well-known.

    (D) He thinks that Cassavetes's films were suppressed.

8.2

 Listen to Track 31.

Now answer the questions.

1. What are two points that reflect Pyrrho's belief about facts? *Choose 2 answers.*

    [A] They must be fully understood before they can be acted upon.

    [B] They can be argued from multiple perspectives.

    [C] They cannot be understood with certainty.

    [D] Learning them is fundamental to the attainment of tranquility.

 Listen to Track 32.

Now answer the question.

2. (A) It is more complex than it may appear.

    (B) It has already been discussed in a prior class.

    (C) It does not warrant further discussion.

    (D) It is too formal for students in the class to understand.

Listen to Track 33.

Now answer the question.

3. What point does the professor make when she says this?

   (A) To imply that the first question that Pyrrho asked is too basic to need explanation

   (B) To suggest that the students might incorrectly assume Pyrrho's belief applied only to broad concepts

   (C) To express disagreement with a point made by Pyrrho

   (D) To explain why students should always look for the deeper meaning in philosophy

4. Why does the professor talk about horse-drawn carriages?

   (A) To explain why it is challenging to achieve tranquility

   (B) To point out a flaw in typical Greek philosophy of the time

   (C) To introduce students to a common occurrence in ancient times

   (D) To illustrate Pyrrho's commitment to uncertainty

5. According to Pyrrho, what attitude should a person adopt?

   (A) Indifference, because it is impossible to know whether one choice is better than any other

   (B) Excitement, because every choice provides new opportunities

   (C) Caution, because one never knows what dangers may appear

   (D) Reflection, because every choice is important and needs to be considered carefully

6. Based on information given in the lecture, select the statement(s) below that reflect beliefs held by Pyrrho.

   A Skepticism allows one to find absolute truth.

   B Skepticism can be applied to both abstract and concrete ideas.

   C Skepticism can lead to tranquility.

8.3

 Listen to Track 34.

Now answer the questions.

1. What aspect of creative writing does the professor focus on in this lecture?

    (A) Techniques for revealing rules in a story to the reader

    (B) How to create a world that feels believable

    (C) Differences between a realist story and a science fiction story

    (D) How to write a story that readers will enjoy

2. Why does the professor suggest that students imagine themselves walking around in the world of their story?

    (A) Students can use the knowledge of their story's world to create clear, consistent rules.

    (B) This exercise helps students to describe the sights and sounds of their world.

    (C) Observing a neighborhood can inspire settings for stories.

    (D) It is easier to set a story in a familiar place.

3. The professor mentions an example of a friend who breaks her ankle. What point does the professor use this example to illustrate?

    (A) The rules of the world allow people to predict the consequences of events or actions.

    (B) Accidents can have a major impact on the development of a story.

    (C) A real-world friend's experiences can inspire events in a story.

    (D) A single event can have many unexpected results.

4. What, according to the professor, can make creating rules difficult?

    (A) Many of our world's rules are hard to identify.

    (B) The rules of a story cannot be too similar to the rules of the real world.

    (C) Too many rules can bore the reader.

    (D) Rules must be consistent with one another.

5. What role does the professor suggest breaking rules can have?

    (A) Breaking rules can allow the writer to create multiple worlds within the same story.

    (B) Breaking rules encourages the reader to pay close attention to the text of a story.

    (C) Breaking rules can create opportunities to develop a new plotline in a story.

    (D) Breaking rules helps to clarify where those rules originated.

Listen to Track 35.

Now answer the question.

6. Why does the professor say this?

   (A) To illustrate that cars can have an important function in a story

   (B) To illustrate that the world generally operates in predictable ways

   (C) To clarify that transportation helps characters to navigate their world

   (D) To show that a car failing to start would alarm a reader

8.4

 Listen to Track 36.

Now answer the questions.

1. What is the main purpose of this lecture?

   (A) To provide a partial biography of Kafka

   (B) To prepare students to read a story by Kafka

   (C) To compare different translations of Kafka's story

   (D) To show how Kafka influenced other authors

2. What is a common misconception about Kafka's *The Metamorphosis*?

   (A) It took Kafka a full decade to write the story.

   (B) Kafka's story was not at all popular when first published.

   (C) Kafka personally drew the image on the cover of the first edition.

   (D) The narrator of the story turns into a cockroach.

3. How is Kafka's story different from other transformation myths?

   (A) Kafka doesn't show the actual transformation.

   (B) Kafka's character undergoes a series of transformations.

   (C) Kafka's story is much longer and more psychologically complex.

   (D) In other transformation myths, people usually turn into plants, not animals.

4. Why does the professor mention that Kafka didn't want a picture of the creature on the cover of the book?

    Ⓐ To illustrate that Kafka was picky about his cover designs in general

    Ⓑ To clarify the importance of cover art in speculative fiction

    Ⓒ To emphasize that Kafka wasn't interested in the details of the transformation

    Ⓓ To prove that Kafka was willfully deceiving his readers

5. What does the professor imply about himself when he mentions some of his own struggles at the end of the lecture? *Choose 2 answers.*

    A   He tends to miss important deadlines.

    B   He sometimes focuses too much on everyday concerns.

    C   He believes that everyday responsibilities are not important.

    D   He should work to pay attention to the important things happening around him.

     Listen to Track 37.

    Now answer the question.

6. Why does the professor say this?

    Ⓐ To illustrate that translating from German to English can be difficult

    Ⓑ To demonstrate that English and German are similar languages

    Ⓒ To highlight that the word "metamorphosis" isn't the most accurate translation for the title

    Ⓓ To complain about the impact of inaccurate translations

8.5

 Listen to Track 38.

Now answer the questions.

1. What is the lecture mainly about? *Choose 2 answers.*

    A   The historical development of the symphony

    B   The decline of Italy as a musical center

    C   Composers who influenced symphonic composition

    D   Contemporary trends in classical music

2. According to the professor, what happened as symphony orchestras became more versatile and sophisticated?

   (A) Musicians who performed symphonies began being paid more.

   (B) More composers wanted to write symphonies.

   (C) Symphony orchestras increased in size.

   (D) Audience attendance improved.

3. Why does the professor mention the Greek word "symphonia"?

   (A) To assert that the ancient Greeks wrote the first symphonies

   (B) To emphasize the importance of Greek themes in symphonic compositions

   (C) To underscore the two meanings of the word "symphony"

   (D) To provide evidence that the symphony was introduced to Italy by ancient Greeks

4. According to the professor, what was Haydn's main contribution to the development of the symphony?

   (A) He increased the number of musicians performing in an orchestra.

   (B) He wrote only a few symphonies.

   (C) He introduced choral music to the symphony.

   (D) He added a fourth movement to his compositions.

 Listen to Track 39.

Now answer the question.

5. Why does the professor say this?

   (A) To celebrate the work of Paul Hindemith

   (B) To emphasize that twentieth-century audiences continued to attend symphonies, even with these changes

   (C) To argue against using electronic sounds in classical music

   (D) To provide examples of composers who used dissonance

Listen to Track 40.

Now answer the question.

6. What does the professor imply when he says this?

  (A) He believes that the symphony is still important today.

  (B) He believes that contemporary symphonies are more interesting than older ones.

  (C) He thinks composers should write more symphonies.

  (D) He hopes that composers continue writing symphonies well into the future.

8.6

 Listen to Track 41.

Now answer the questions.

1. What is this lecture primarily about?

  (A) How to decide whether a poem is well-written

  (B) Methods for analyzing the structure of a poem

  (C) Ways to identify rhetorical devices in poetry

  (D) How to most effectively approach reading a poem

2. According to the professor, what is the purpose of rhetoric?

  (A) To decorate a piece of writing

  (B) To simplify complicated ideas

  (C) To persuade others

  (D) To entertain the reader

3. Why does the professor make a comparison to puzzles?

  (A) To emphasize that poems are easy to solve

  (B) To clarify how not to read a poem

  (C) To suggest that reading a poem and solving a puzzle are similar

  (D) To encourage students to see hidden messages in poems

4. Why does the professor mention similes and metaphors?

   (A) To criticize poets who use too many comparisons

   (B) To illustrate the sophistication of ancient Greek poetry

   (C) To give examples of rhetorical devices

   (D) To encourage students to use similes and metaphors in their own poems

5. The professor mentions four steps to follow when reading a poem. Put the steps in the order he mentions: first, second, third, or fourth.

   [A] Think about the purpose and meaning of the poem _____

   [B] Pay attention to images and feelings _____

   [C] Read the poem out loud _____

   [D] Analyze the poem for structure and rhetorical devices _____

 Listen to Track 42.

Now answer the question.

---

6. What does the professor imply when he says this?

   (A) Emotion is the most important part of a poem.

   (B) Good poets raise interesting questions.

   (C) Not all poems are written for the same reason.

   (D) The reader's experience is a poet's primary concern.

8.7

 Listen to Track 43.

Now answer the questions.

---

1. What is the main purpose of the lecture?

   (A) To discuss trade between Europe and China on the Silk Road

   (B) To describe the effects of gunpowder on European history

   (C) To describe the flaws of primitive guns

   (D) To explore the effects of the Mongol invasion of Europe

2. What does the professor imply about the strength of the first gunpowder made in Europe?

   (A) It was stronger in the Duchy of Burgundy than elsewhere.

   (B) It was weaker than Chinese gunpowder.

   (C) Its strength led to the success of the Mongol invasion of Europe.

   (D) Its strength indicated that it was not invented in Europe.

3. Why does the professor mention the nineteenth-century saying about Colonel Colt?

   (A) To indicate that use of a gun offset the advantages of training with other weapons

   (B) To suggest that the United States has long been a violent place

   (C) To illustrate the greater level of equality found in European nations

   (D) To assert that Colt's weapons were superior to harquebuses

4. According to the professor, what was a long-term effect of the introduction of gunpowder to Europe?

   (A) It tilted the balance of world power away from China.

   (B) It advantaged wealthier European states that adopted gunpowder use.

   (C) It had a negative effect on international relations within Europe.

   (D) It led to popular revolutions and the decline of European nobility.

5. According to the professor, why were Taoist monks interested in gunpowder?

   (A) It was a way to transform materials.

   (B) It gave them defensive military benefits.

   (C) They believed it warded off unhealthy spirits.

   (D) It was a component of fireworks for ritual use.

    Listen to Track 44.

   Now answer the question.

6. What can be inferred about the professor when she says this?

   (A) She does not know the answer to her own question.

   (B) She is criticizing the student.

   (C) She is exploring the extent of the student's knowledge.

   (D) She is suggesting that the student's first answer was incorrect.

8

8.8

> Listen to Track 45.
>
> Now answer the questions.

1. What is the lecture mainly about?

    (A) Reasons why the United States did not support communism

    (B) United States policies concerning the Spanish Civil War

    (C) The illegal activities of the Abraham Lincoln Brigade

    (D) Ways in which the United States helped the Spanish Fascists

2. According to the discussion, what are two reasons why African Americans joined the Abraham Lincoln Brigade? *Choose 2 answers.*

    A   An opportunity to fight in an integrated combat unit

    B   Hitler's racism at the 1936 Olympics in Berlin

    C   Protests against racial discrimination in the United States

    D   Mussolini's invasion of Ethiopia

3. The lecture discusses important events related to the Spanish Civil War and the Abraham Lincoln Brigade. Put the events in chronological order: first, second, third, or fourth.

    A   Abraham Lincoln Brigade members were declared "premature anti-fascists." _____

    B   Abraham Lincoln Brigade members were blacklisted by the House Un-American Activities Committee. _____

    C   The Great Depression began. _____

    D   Oliver Law died in combat. _____

4. Why does the professor mention the United States government's embrace of the Flying Tiger volunteers?

    (A) To provide a contrast to the treatment given to Abraham Lincoln Brigade volunteers

    (B) To illustrate the fairness of the United States government in a comparable situation

    (C) To show that it was common for United States citizens to volunteer for foreign combat

    (D) To highlight the United States government's opposition to integrated units

5. What does the professor say about the Abraham Lincoln Brigade volunteers?

   (A) Most were African Americans.

   (B) Some were communist spies.

   (C) Most were primarily interested in fighting fascists.

   (D) Most were killed in action.

 Listen to Track 46.

Now answer the question.

---

6. (A) The government proclamation was twice as strong as most similar declarations were.

   (B) The government proclamation was meant to support the fascists.

   (C) George Orwell was supportive of the fascists.

   (D) The government proclamation was deliberately misleading.

8.9

 Listen to Track 47.

Now answer the questions.

---

1. What does the professor mainly discuss?

   (A) The pioneering work of artist Richard Prince

   (B) The history of rephotography

   (C) The new meaning of art in the twenty-first century

   (D) Innovations in the early days of photography

2. According to the professor, how did Richard Prince challenge common notions of what constitutes art?
   Choose 2 answers.

   [A] By taking photographs of photographs

   [B] By filing a lawsuit against a fellow photographer

   [C] By refusing to sign his work

   [D] By disowning a piece of art he had made and sold

3. What can be inferred about Prince's future career as an artist?

  (A) Prince's work will likely revolve around how to maintain popularity.

  (B) Prince's work will probably lead to many more lawsuits.

  (C) Prince's work will likely raise more political and social questions.

  (D) Prince's work will probably answer more questions than it raises.

4. What is the professor's opinion of Richard Prince?

  (A) He thinks that criticisms of Prince are unfair and unwarranted.

  (B) He believes that Prince has made valuable contributions to how the definition of art has evolved.

  (C) He thinks that photographer Patrick Cariou should have prevailed in court.

  (D) He believes that Prince breaks rules and expectations in the art community that should not be violated.

5. What are two key features of appropriation as discussed by the professor in the context of rephotography? *Choose 2 answers.*

  [A] Asking for permission to use one's work

  [B] Taking someone else's work for one's own use

  [C] Refusing to grant permission to someone who wants to use one's work

  [D] Using someone else's work without permission

6. Why does the professor describe Prince's revocation of his signature on a work of art as "unheard of in the art world"?

  (A) It was problematic for the art world.

  (B) It angered art critics.

  (C) It had likely never been done before.

  (D) It was an action that was performed silently.

8.10

 Listen to Track 48.

Now answer the questions.

1. What does the professor mainly discuss?

  (A) The construction of the oldest church in the Americas

  (B) The development of the medieval ivory trade

  (C) Theories about the disappearance of a settlement

  (D) Key differences between Viking and Inuit communities

2. Why does the professor mention holding a sword from 1495?

- (A) To emphasize how close in history the sword's manufacture was to Columbus's voyage
- (B) To emphasize how warlike the Vikings were
- (C) To demonstrate Viking techniques of swordsmanship
- (D) To illustrate to the class the age of the Viking colony

3. What is the professor's opinion about the Viking settlements during the Medieval Warm Period?

- (A) He believes they were successful.
- (B) He regards their inhabitants as very religious.
- (C) He is distressed that their inhabitants starved to death.
- (D) He is mildly shocked that their inhabitants conquered the Inuits.

4. According to the professor, what is the significance of the change from beef to seal in the Viking diet?

- (A) It demonstrates that the Vikings were starving.
- (B) It demonstrates that their society was adaptable.
- (C) It is provided as evidence of the effect of globalization.
- (D) It shows that the Inuit taught them how to hunt seals.

5. What does the professor say about the Viking walrus hunts?

- (A) From a modern point of view, they were inhumane.
- (B) They were very profitable at first.
- (C) They were very dangerous for participants.
- (D) They required competing with the Portuguese for prey.

6. What are two questions about the Gardar Vikings that the professor definitively answers?
Choose 2 answers.

- A What happened to the Vikings in the 1400s
- B Why the Vikings did not leave Gardar to go to Iceland or Norway
- C When the Vikings colonized Greenland
- D Whether the Vikings adapted to climate change in any way

Answer Key—8.1

Question	Correct Answer	Right/Wrong	Category
1	A		Gist-purpose
2	C		Organization
3	D		Organization
4	B		Detail
5	B		Connecting Content
6	C		Function of What Is Said

Answer Key—8.2

Question	Correct Answer	Right/Wrong	Category
1	B, C		Gist-content
2	A		Inference
3	B		Function of What Is Said
4	D		Detail
5	A		Detail
6	B, C		Connecting Content

Answer Key—8.3

Question	Correct Answer	Right/Wrong	Category
1	B		Gist-content
2	A		Organization
3	A		Organization
4	D		Detail
5	C		Inference
6	B		Function of What Is Said

Answer Key—8.4

Question	Correct Answer	Right/Wrong	Category
1	B		Gist-purpose
2	D		Detail
3	A		Detail
4	C		Detail
5	B, D		Inference
6	C		Function of What Is Said

Answer Key—8.5

Question	Correct Answer	Right/Wrong	Category
1	A, C		Gist-content
2	B		Detail
3	C		Organization
4	D		Detail
5	B		Function of What Is Said
6	A		Inference

Answer Key—8.6

Question	Correct Answer	Right/Wrong	Category
1	D		Gist-content
2	C		Detail
3	B		Organization
4	C		Organization
5	A: Fourth. B: Second. C: First. D: Third.		Connecting Content
6	C		Inference

Answer Key—8.7

Question	Correct Answer	Right/Wrong	Category
1	B		Gist-purpose
2	D		Inference
3	A		Organization
4	B		Detail
5	A		Detail
6	C		Function of What Is Said

Answer Key—8.8

Question	Correct Answer	Right/Wrong	Category
1	B		Gist-content
2	B, D		Detail
3	A: Third. B: Fourth. C: First. D: Second.		Connecting Content
4	A		Organization
5	C		Detail
6	D		Inference

Answer Key—8.9

Question	Correct Answer	Right/Wrong	Category
1	A		Gist-content
2	A, D		Detail
3	C		Inference
4	B		Speaker's Attitude
5	B, D		Detail
6	C		Organization

Answer Key—8.10

Question	Correct Answer	Right/Wrong	Category
1	C		Gist-content
2	D		Organization
3	A		Speaker's Attitude
4	B		Detail
5	B		Detail
6	C, D		Detail

Answers and Explanations—8.1

Raging Bulls—Track 29

NARRATOR: Listen to part of a lecture in a film history class.

PROFESSOR: Okay, we've been talking about the rise and reign of the Hollywood studio system in the Golden Age of the 1930s and 1940s. In those days the studios essentially, ah… had a monopoly on the film business, and a huge chunk of the overall entertainment business. Back then, many people went to–to the movies at least three times a week. And they saw pictures made by the studios, with stars under contract with the studios, and in theaters owned by the studios. But then, in the 1950s and 1960s, it all… well, I guess it didn't collapse, but it greatly contracted, and some of the studios did go bankrupt or otherwise disappeared. How did that happen? Ellie, you have an idea?

FEMALE STUDENT: Isn't that when television began? I mean, I always heard television hurt the movies.

PROFESSOR: Well, to an extent, that's true. People could see–could see motion pictures without leaving their houses, and that did cut into movie attendance. But there were other problems. Legally, the monopoly they had got them into trouble. They were forced to divest themselves of their theater interests, which cut into their revenue. And, similarly, the actors were freed from those, um… onerous contracts that bound them to a studio and obligated them to appear in whatever movies the studio heads decided. But the biggest problem was rot and complacency, just as with other empires. The studio heads, as well as their producers and directors, were all much older than in their glory days, and they lost touch with their audience. In other words, they, ah… basically, made too many movies that people didn't want to see. The Baby Boomers were your age then, and they rejected the establishment in film as well as politics. Out of desperation, cracks opened in the studio system, and some young mavericks seized that opportunity… and arguably saved the industry.

One such filmmaker was John Cassavetes. Cassavetes was a Greek American, and didn't speak English until he was seven. As a–a young man, he fell into acting, and–and worked in television, largely in New York instead of Hollywood. Using the money he earned that way, he began to write, direct, and produce movies. His second film, *Faces*, which came out in 1968, took him three years to make—on a shoestring budget—and was mostly shot in his home. It was a well-received, realistic view of the disintegration of a marriage—very different from the sugar-coated, happy-ending studio offerings of the time. Cassavetes also

favored hand-held cameras and improvisational work—both of which were a far cry from polished studio productions and dictatorial directors. Despite this, it was nominated for three major Academy Awards. And so began the ascendance of a new generation of filmmakers. This new generation created what is today considered a second Hollywood Golden Age.

FEMALE STUDENT: But what about Martin Scorsese? Didn't he break new ground around then?

PROFESSOR: Ah, Martin Scorsese. Well, like Cassavetes, Scorsese grew up in New York in an immigrant family from Southern Europe. Italy, in his case. And in fact, Cassavetes was a mentor and friend to Scorsese, and encouraged his artistic vision. But Scorsese was about 15 years younger. And his first important film, *Mean Streets*, didn't come out until, um, 1973, five years later than *Faces*. Furthermore, many felt that its–its rough-hewn style owed a debt to Cassavetes. And if you're thinking about *Taxi Driver*, that wasn't until 1976. So... Will, you want to ask about something?

MALE STUDENT: Yeah, I guess maybe this is disrespectful, but if Cassavetes was so brilliant, how come we've never heard of him? I mean, everybody here knows who Scorsese is.

PROFESSOR: No, no… not disrespectful… fair enough. There's a simple, sad, human answer. Cassavetes died in 1989 at the age of 59. On the other hand, Scorsese is not only alive today—he's about 74—but he's stayed active professionally. Since he turned 59, he's directed six major films, along with some documentaries and television projects. More artistically though, Scorsese's lifelong ambition was to become a Hollywood filmmaker. And he succeeded. But that means that, while he was a great and innovative talent, many of his projects had a–a broad enough appeal to command not only large shooting budgets and big stars but lavish amounts for advertising and other support. Cassavetes, though, was a true contrarian, and it showed in his work. He made films on, um… on quirky, intimate topics, and preferred to use largely unknown actors in many roles. Consequently, his films had far less distribution and he is less known today. Nonetheless, serious students of film cherish his work and consider him an equally great artist.

1. What is the main purpose of this talk?	**GIST-PURPOSE.** The main purpose is to discuss the contributions of Cassavetes and Scorsese to film history.	
✓ (A) To discuss filmmakers who helped to revitalize the film industry	**CORRECT.** The professor summarizes the studio system and its decline before focusing on his main point—filmmakers who helped reverse the decline.	
✗ (B) To contrast the style of two young filmmakers	The professor only contrasts them at the end of the lecture. His main focus is to discuss how they helped revitalize the film industry.	
✗ (C) To discuss the Golden Age of the Hollywood studio system	The point of the lecture is the decline of the Golden Age and a subsequent rebirth of Hollywood filmmaking.	
✗ (D) To describe Cassavetes's influence on Scorsese	While the professor mentions this, the main focus of the lecture is on how both men helped to revitalize Hollywood filmmaking.	

2. Why does the professor mention that *Faces* was nominated for three major Academy Awards?

ORGANIZATION. The professor says that the success of *Faces* helped mark the ascent of a new generation of filmmakers.

✗ (A) To bemoan Cassavetes's lack of financial backing

The Academy Awards are cited as evidence of Cassavetes's success, not of problems caused by a lack of financial backing.

✗ (B) To complain that *Faces* did not win any of the awards it was nominated for

The nominations themselves are presented as evidence of success.

✓ (C) To support the claim that Cassavetes's new approach was successful

CORRECT. This is mentioned to describe the success of the unorthodox *Faces*.

✗ (D) To refute criticism of *Faces*

No criticism of *Faces* is mentioned.

3. Why did Cassavetes's *Faces* succeed when studio films were failing?

ORGANIZATION. The professor indicates that Cassavetes rejected some established conventions that had fallen out of favor.

✗ (A) It was filmed in New York.

The professor does not mention where *Faces* was filmed. He only mentions that Cassavetes's television work was primarily in New York.

✗ (B) It reflected the fact that English was not Cassavetes's first language.

It is true that English was not Cassavetes's first language, but this is not mentioned as an important factor in *Faces*.

✗ (C) It used a hand-held camera and improvisation.

These facts are mentioned, but the success of *Faces* is not attributed to those aspects of Cassavetes's work. In fact, the professor says: "despite this, it was nominated for three major Academy Awards."

✓ (D) It embraced realism rather than traditional, happy-ending plots.

CORRECT. The professor mentions that *Faces* was well-received for being realistic, rather than a "happy-ending" film.

8

4. According to the professor, what is one reason that Scorsese is better known than Cassavetes?

    ✗ (A) Scorsese is considered more talented than Cassavetes was.

    ✓ (B) Scorsese's films have had stars and advertising support.

    ✗ (C) Scorsese is ethnically Italian, whereas Cassavetes was ethnically Greek.

    ✗ (D) Scorsese made movies about organized crime.

DETAIL. The professor says that Scorsese picked projects that commanded big budgets and stars. Scorsese's longevity also played a role.

The professor implies that he feels they were equally gifted.

CORRECT. The professor cites Scorsese's desire to make big films, with big stars and large advertising budgets, as reasons for his fame.

Scorsese's ethnicity is not cited as a reason for his popularity.

This idea is not mentioned in the lecture.

5. Why does the professor mention that Cassavetes was a contrarian?

    ✗ (A) To explain how Cassavetes influenced Scorsese

    ✓ (B) To explain why Scorsese is more famous than Cassavetes today

    ✗ (C) To criticize Cassavetes's behavior

    ✗ (D) To explain why Cassavetes favored unknown actors

CONNECTING CONTENT. The professor mentions this to contrast him with Scorsese and to help explain Scorsese's greater fame.

Cassavetes did influence Scorsese, but the professor's comment about Cassavetes being a contrarian is meant to contrast the two filmmakers.

CORRECT. This comment is part of a contrast between the two to answer a student's question about Cassavetes's relative lack of fame.

There is no criticism of Cassavetes implied by the professor's comment.

Cassavetes's contrarian nature and his preference for unknown actors are given as parallel reasons for his relative lack of fame.

Track 30

NARRATOR: What does the student imply when he says this:

MALE STUDENT: Yeah, I guess maybe this is disrespectful, but if Cassavetes was so brilliant, how come we've never heard of him? I mean, everybody here knows who Scorsese is.

6.   **FUNCTION OF WHAT IS SAID.** The student is puzzled that Cassavetes was a brilliant filmmaker, but yet the student and others were unaware of Cassavetes.

  ✗ (A) He wants to discuss Scorsese only.   The student's comment does not imply this.

  ✗ (B) He somewhat dislikes Cassavetes's films.   The student is unaware of Cassavetes, and thus is unlikely to be aware of his films.

  ✓ (C) He thinks that great filmmakers are usually well-known.   **CORRECT.** The student is surprised that he has not heard of such a great filmmaker. This implies that he believes that great filmmakers are almost always well-known.

  ✗ (D) He thinks that Cassavetes's films were suppressed.   Nothing in the lecture suggests that Cassavetes's films were suppressed.

Answers and Explanations—8.2

Pyrrho—Track 31

NARRATOR: Listen to part of a lecture in a philosophy class. The professor has been talking about happiness.

PROFESSOR: Achieving personal satisfaction—peace, tranquility, happiness, however you define it—is the ultimate goal of many schools of thought. We've already discussed how some ancient philosophers viewed this. In ancient Greece, the endeavor for peace often involved religion, rationalism, or trying to achieve some kind of balance. Most of these ideas were organized around a central dogma or foundational belief. Today I want to introduce the philosophy of someone who rejected the idea of dogmatic belief. So we're going to talk about Pyrrho.

Pyrrho was an ancient Greek philosopher who is considered the founder of skepticism. So, what is skepticism? Well, you probably already know the answer, so I won't bore you with a formal definition. In essence, a skeptic is someone who does not automatically believe what he is told. He questions, he argues, he debates. But I wouldn't bring this up if we all already knew everything there is to know about this topic. And in fact, it is the idea of knowledge itself that Pyrrho challenged. He introduced the ancient Greeks to three questions that must be asked. First, what are things like naturally? Second, what attitude should we adopt towards them? And third, what will be the outcome for those who have this attitude?

It is in answering, or I should say trying to answer, the first question that Pyrrho introduced something novel to the ancient Greeks. Pyrrho believed that the nature of things could not be determined. So, when answering the question what things are like naturally, Pyrrho would have to answer, "I'm not sure." Now, I know that this attitude is completely understandable for the broadest questions. When debating religion, morality, or the nature of existence, many of you might also conclude that you are not sure. But Pyrrho

believed this was true about all things. There is no such thing as truth or lies. Every belief can be argued from a different perspective that would reasonably produce a different belief. Because of this we cannot say with certainty that anything is definitively true. You cannot, therefore, trust your own beliefs or perceptions.

One anecdote about Pyrrho suggests that he was so devoted to the idea that he could know nothing that he would put himself in dangerous situations. According to the story, he once walked in front of a horse-drawn carriage because he could not be sure that the carriage was really there. It is unlikely that this is a true story, but it does illustrate one of the fundamental notions of Pyrrhonism.

With that perspective, the second question has a fairly straightforward answer. What attitude should we adopt toward things? Well, if we cannot know what things are with any certainty, then we cannot determine what attitude we should adopt toward them. So the appropriate way to react to anything is with indifference. Deciding to turn left instead of right implies that for some reason, left is preferable to right. But we cannot know anything with certainty about left or right, so we cannot prefer one to the other.

The outcome for those who adopted this belief was meant to be tranquility. Without the oppression of judgments and beliefs, peace would follow.

One thing I find particularly interesting about this philosophy is the difficulty of teaching it. Its core belief is that there is no truth or knowledge. A follower of Pyrrho would later be famously quoted as saying "nothing can be known, not even this." Pyrrho himself created no writings, presumably because he believed that he neither should nor shouldn't pass on his teachings. It is only through the notes of his followers that we know of his beliefs.

1.   What are two points that reflect Pyrrho's belief about facts? *Choose 2 answers.*

GIST-CONTENT. According to the professor, Pyrrho believed that even facts cannot be known with certainty, and that every belief "can be argued from a different perspective that would reasonably produce a different belief."

✗   A   They must be fully understood before they can be acted upon.

The opposite is true. Pyrrho believed that facts can never be fully understood.

✓   B   They can be argued from multiple perspectives.

CORRECT. This is stated in the lecture, and is one of the reasons that Pyrrho believed that there is no such thing as truth.

✓   C   They cannot be understood with certainty.

CORRECT. This is one of the fundamental tenets of Pyrrho's philosophy.

✗   D   Learning them is fundamental to the attainment of tranquility.

Pyrrho argued that one should reject the idea of truth, or facts, in order to attain tranquility.

Track 32

NARRATOR: Listen again to part of the lecture. Then answer the question.

PROFESSOR: So, what is skepticism? Well, you probably already know the answer, so I won't bore you with a formal definition. In essence, a skeptic is someone who does not automatically believe what he is told. He questions, he argues, he debates. But I wouldn't bring this up if we all already knew everything there is to know about this topic.

NARRATOR: What does the professor imply about skepticism when she says this:

PROFESSOR: But I wouldn't bring this up if we all already knew everything there is to know about this topic.

2.   **INFERENCE.** In this quote, the professor starts with a basic definition of skepticism. This allows her to elaborate on the specifics of Pyrrhonism later in the lecture.

✓ (A) It is more complex than it may appear.

CORRECT. The rest of the lecture is a discussion of Pyrrho's philosophy of skepticism. The professor is implying that there is significantly more to be discussed than the students are likely aware of.

✗ (B) It has already been discussed in a prior class.

The professor does not suggest that skepticism has already been discussed in class.

✗ (C) It does not warrant further discussion.

The opposite is true. The rest of the lecture is a further discussion of skepticism.

✗ (D) It is too formal for students in the class to understand.

Nothing in this quote suggests that the professor believes this. The professor implies that students do understand skepticism at a basic level, and is attempting to explain an aspect of skepticism they may not yet understand.

8

Track 33

NARRATOR: Listen again to part of the lecture. Then answer the question.

PROFESSOR: Pyrrho believed that the nature of things could not be determined. So, when answering the question what things are like naturally, Pyrrho would have to answer, "I'm not sure." Now, I know that this attitude is completely understandable for the broadest questions.

NARRATOR: What point does the professor make when she says this:

PROFESSOR: Now, I know that this attitude is completely understandable for the broadest questions.

3.   What point does the professor make when she says this?

FUNCTION OF WHAT IS SAID. The fundamental tenet of Pyrrhonism is that nothing can be known for certain. This includes the broadest questions that the professor refers to, such as religion and philosophy, but also basic facts, such as whether objects actually exist.

✗ (A) To imply that the first question that Pyrrho asked is too basic to need explanation

The opposite is true. The professor spends most of the lecture explaining Pyrrho's answer to the first question he posed.

✓ (B) To suggest that the students might incorrectly assume Pyrrho's belief applied only to broad concepts

CORRECT. The professor elaborates by saying that Pyrrho also doubted what might be considered the most basic of concepts.

✗ (C) To express disagreement with a point made by Pyrrho

The professor does not indicate that she believes that Pyrrho is inaccurate in any aspect of his philosophy.

✗ (D) To explain why students should always look for the deeper meaning in philosophy

The professor is explaining one particular philosopher. She is not making generalizations about what students should do when studying philosophy in general.

4.   Why does the professor talk about horse-drawn carriages?

DETAIL. The professor gives an anecdote claiming that Pyrrho was so committed to the idea that he could know nothing that he walked in front of a carriage, putting himself in danger, because he could not know whether the danger was real. She notes that this is likely a fictional story, but it illustrates the degree of Pyrrho's skepticism.

✗ (A) To explain why it is challenging to achieve tranquility

The overarching goal of Pyrrhonism is to achieve tranquility, but the carriage story has nothing to do with this pursuit.

✗ (B) To point out a flaw in typical Greek philosophy of the time

No "typical Greek philosophy" is mentioned in the lecture.

✗ (C) To introduce students to a common occurrence in ancient times

There is no discussion about what was common during ancient times.

✓ (D) To illustrate Pyrrho's commitment to uncertainty

CORRECT. Pyrrho is said to have walked into the path of a carriage because he could not be sure that carriages actually existed. This anecdote is used to demonstrate Pyrrho's belief that nothing could be known with certainty.

5. According to Pyrrho, what attitude should a person adopt?

DETAIL. This is the second question Pyrrho asked. The professor states that, in Pyrrho's view, "if we cannot know what things are with any certainty, then we cannot determine what attitude we should adopt toward them."

✓ (A) Indifference, because it is impossible to know whether one choice is better than any other

CORRECT. According to the professor, Pyrrho believed that "the appropriate way to react to anything is with indifference."

✗ (B) Excitement, because every choice provides new opportunities

The professor does not mention this idea.

✗ (C) Caution, because one never knows what dangers may appear

On the contrary—danger seems to be something that Pyrrho does not fear, as demonstrated by the story about him stepping in front of a carriage.

✗ (D) Reflection, because every choice is important and needs to be considered carefully

The opposite is true. Pyrrho believed that no decision is better than any other decision.

6. Based on information given in the lecture, select the statement(s) below that reflect beliefs held by Pyrrho.

CONNECTING CONTENT. Pyrrho believed that truth was unknowable, and it is through accepting this, and treating different decisions with indifference, that one can achieve tranquility.

✗ [A] Skepticism allows one to find absolute truth.

Pyrrho does not believe that absolute truth exists.

✓ [B] Skepticism can be applied to both abstract and concrete ideas.

CORRECT. Pyrrho believed that one should be skeptical about all things. This includes basic ideas, like whether a carriage actually exists.

✓ [C] Skepticism can lead to tranquility.

CORRECT. According to Pyrrho, the outcome for people who held this philosophy is tranquility.

Answers and Explanations—8.3

Rules and World Building—Track 34

NARRATOR: Listen to part of a lecture in a creative writing class.

PROFESSOR: Hey everyone, okay. Today, we're going to talk about how to make your stories feel more real. We do this by building our world... the world the story happens in. Now this doesn't have to be the same as the world we live in, though it could be... I guess you all know that. But... either way, some rules apply.

Let's talk about rules. Rules are how we navigate our world... essentially, they're expectations—how we trust that we can expect certain things—like, um... that our car will start when we turn the key... we hope, anyway. Even if we're writing something that happens on Mars, that setting has rules too, right?

Sometimes people think that when we're writing a story, especially if it's fantastic in some way, we can have anything we want happen. But that's not... well, not necessarily true. The reader needs rules to, uh... know how to make sense of our story. And the reader needs to trust us, too... we can have a few surprises, or sometimes a rule can change, but our reader still wants to... well... have some sense that they know how this world works, right?

That's what makes a story feel real. Because it has order, and rules... like our world. So when you start making up a setting for your story, begin by writing down the rules for that world. Think about the kinds of rules our world has... then figure out how these rules would be the same or different in your created world.

You want to make sure you're really clear on how and why everything in your world works the way it does—you'll need to keep this consistent in your story. You also have to communicate these rules to the reader. Not that you should state them up front, but more by... by showing the way people interact with that world.

You should be able to imagine yourself walking around in the world of your story like you'd walk around your own neighborhood. You know your neighborhood well enough to know what the consequences of different actions would be, right? Say your friend is walking to class one day, and she falls and breaks her ankle. Well, you can probably imagine what will happen next. People will see or hear her and come to help. Someone might call an ambulance that will take her to the hospital. At the hospital, she'll wait, get an x ray... eventually get a cast. You know enough about how the world generally works to predict what's going to happen next for her. You need to know the same kinds of things about the world in your story... that way, whenever one of your characters does something, you know what the results of that action are going to be. And when your reader reads that, it feels realistic—because each action plays out according to consistent rules. No matter how crazy your world is, it's the rules that make it believable.

When you're coming up with the rules of your world, be clear and be detailed. Ask yourself questions, even about things that may not happen in your story—like, what happens in this world if someone gets sick? Do people help them? Do they get treatment? Does that treatment happen at home, or in an institution? Is it expensive? Write this stuff down—the sketches of different events and their consequences.

Now, this is where things can get a little tricky. Not only do you have to know what the rules are, and make actions consistent with those... but, well... the rules also have to match with each other. So if, um... you have a world where no one gets sick, then it doesn't make sense to also have a world where people are really obsessed with, say, washing their hands. Each rule connects to other rules. So you should start with a few, and then build outward from there. When you add new rules, ask yourself what those rules now make necessary.

Alright. So I mentioned that sometimes you can break or change a rule. And I want to say something more about that. If you're really clear on your rules, and your reader is too, then you can play around with them a little. Let's say we have a world where the sky is always green. Then one day, people wake up and the sky is starting to turn pink. Now, if we know up front that the sky is always green, that change is a big deal. We've surprised our reader—and now we have to do something with that surprise. We have to have our characters react to that change. And maybe the way they react starts to change them. Or maybe it changes some other rules in the world... maybe society becomes more chaotic. So I can have these big breaks in rules, but usually that's going to happen so that I can... well, move the plot or the characters forward, somehow.

1. What aspect of creative writing does the professor focus on in this lecture?

    ✗   (A) Techniques for revealing rules in a story to the reader

    ✓   (B) How to create a world that feels believable

    ✗   (C) Differences between a realist story and a science fiction story

    ✗   (D) How to write a story that readers will enjoy

GIST-CONTENT. The main focus of this lecture is on how to make a story feel believable by establishing clear rules for the world in which the story is based.

The professor does mention the importance of revealing rules to the reader, but does not discuss specific techniques for doing so.

CORRECT. The professor devotes most of the lecture to strategies for developing a world that "feels real" to the reader.

The professor does not explicitly discuss differences between any literary genres.

The lecture is not specifically concerned with appealing to readers. Instead, it is concerned with establishing rules that allow a story to be believable.

2. Why does the professor suggest that students imagine themselves walking around in the world of their story?

    ✓   (A) Students can use the knowledge of their story's world to create clear, consistent rules.

    ✗   (B) This exercise helps students to describe the sights and sounds of their world.

    ✗   (C) Observing a neighborhood can inspire settings for stories.

    ✗   (D) It is easier to set a story in a familiar place.

ORGANIZATION. The professor says this in order to clarify that writers should know the world of their story as well as they know their own neighborhood. If they do, then they can identify clear and consistent rules for their world.

CORRECT. The professor uses this exercise to illustrate how students can create detailed rules for their world.

The professor uses this example to illustrate how to create consistent rules, not to provide a source of sensory detail.

The professor does not directly suggest using real-life observations as settings for stories.

The professor does not discuss what makes story settings easier or harder to create.

8

3.   The professor mentions an example of a friend who breaks her ankle. What point does the professor use this example to illustrate?

ORGANIZATION. This example is used to illustrate how the rules of the world allow people to predict the consequences of events or actions. The rules of a story should create consequences that are similarly predictable to its characters.

✓   (A) The rules of the world allow people to predict the consequences of events or actions.

CORRECT. The professor uses this example to explain how thorough knowledge of how a world works allows a writer to create realistic consequences of actions.

✗   (B) Accidents can have a major impact on the development of a story.

The professor does not discuss the role accidents play in story development.

✗   (C) A real-world friend's experiences can inspire events in a story.

The professor does not suggest that students use real-world events as inspiration for story events.

✗   (D) A single event can have many unexpected results.

The professor is focused on the predictable consequences of events, not on unexpected ones.

4.   What, according to the professor, can make creating rules difficult?

DETAIL. The professor states that what makes creating rules tricky is that "the rules ... have to match with each other."

✗   (A) Many of our world's rules are hard to identify.

The professor suggests the opposite—that real-world rules are usually readily known.

✗   (B) The rules of a story cannot be too similar to the rules of the real world.

The professor does not make this claim. Rather, he suggests that rules can be the same as, or parallel to, the rules of the real world.

✗   (C) Too many rules can bore the reader.

This idea is not mentioned in the lecture.

✓   (D) Rules must be consistent with one another.

CORRECT. In the lecture the professor explicitly states that "the rules ... have to match with each other."

5. What role does the professor suggest breaking rules can have?

INFERENCE. The professor implies that breaking rules can be a good way to advance the plot or character development in a story.

✗ (A) Breaking rules can allow the writer to create multiple worlds within the same story.

This idea is not mentioned in the lecture.

✗ (B) Breaking rules encourages the reader to pay close attention to the text of a story.

This idea is not mentioned in the lecture.

✓ (C) Breaking rules can create opportunities to develop a new plotline in a story.

CORRECT. The professor states that rule-breaking can help move the plot forward. One example of this could be the development of a new plotline.

✗ (D) Breaking rules helps to clarify where those rules originated.

This idea is not mentioned in the lecture.

Track 35

NARRATOR: Listen again to part of the lecture. Then answer the question.

PROFESSOR: Let's talk about rules. Rules are how we navigate our world… essentially, they're expectations—how we trust that we can expect certain things—like, um… that our car will start when we turn the key… we hope, anyway. Even if we're writing something that happens on Mars, that setting has rules too, right?

NARRATOR: Why does the professor say this:

PROFESSOR: Like, um… that our car will start when we turn the key…

6. Why does the professor say this?

FUNCTION OF WHAT IS SAID. The professor is illustrating what he means when he says that people expect their actions to have predictable consequences.

✗ (A) To illustrate that cars can have an important function in a story

The professor does not discuss the use of cars in stories.

✓ (B) To illustrate that the world generally operates in predictable ways

CORRECT. The professor is pointing out that his car starting is an example of a predictable rule in the world.

✗ (C) To clarify that transportation helps characters to navigate their world

In this quote, the professor is discussing a real-world example. He is not discussing characters in a story.

✗ (D) To show that a car failing to start would alarm a reader

The professor is not discussing readers' reactions.

Answers and Explanations—8.4

Kafka's Metamorphosis—Track 36

NARRATOR: Listen to part of a lecture in a literature class.

PROFESSOR: So, to conclude today's class, I want to give you a few things to think about while you do this week's assignment. We're reading a very famous work—Franz Kafka's *The Metamorphosis*, or just *Metamorphosis*. If you haven't read it before, you probably still know about it—the cockroach and all—but I think all of us will… find something interesting, something useful in it. I want you to think about it in relation to some of the other works we've read recently—myths and poems… works that are about transformation.

We're going to read an English translation of *Metamorphosis*, so I think knowing a couple things about the original German will help you when you read it. And the first thing is the original title, which means, literally, "transformation." German has a word that's very similar to our "metamorphosis," but it's not the word Kafka uses.

Another thing is the word he uses to describe the creature the guy turns into. The description may make you think of a cockroach, but that's not actually stated. Kafka just says it's some kind of monstrous creature—maybe "vermin" is a better word—something that's unclean in some way.

So why is this important to know? Well, first, this is one of those stories a lot of us are going to come to with a lot of expectations… ideas about what it is. And I want you to be prepared to be surprised. Pay attention to how the thing you read isn't necessarily what you thought you were going to read.

Also, I want to point out how this is different from the transformation myths we've read. Those are mostly, well… they deal a lot with the actual changing-into-something-else part, like describing how a woman turns into a tree. Kafka isn't so interested in that. He just starts out right with the change—this happens, no explanation given. And then he explores what the results, the consequences of that, might be.

He also doesn't tell us exactly what kind of creature we're dealing with either—you might want to think about why that is. He describes what the creature looks like, but not in a very definite way. Actually, you know, one of Kafka's early publishers wanted to put a picture of the creature on the cover, and Kafka was like, "Absolutely not!" He was really adamant about that… that they not show what it looked like.

So that's something else to, um, think about. Why he doesn't want us to, or thinks we shouldn't, uh… see this creature as a whole… or be able to, um… put a label on what it is.

Alright, so, why isn't Kafka interested in the change? And why don't we get to see the creature? These should be, well… the most interesting parts, right? That's what we want in these transformation stories, isn't it… to see how one thing becomes another? What's the point of skipping over all that stuff? Well, Kafka's saying, in a way, that it isn't the why or the how that's so important… that, well… maybe these aren't the most interesting questions to ask. Because, in our daily lives, how often do we really get into the how or the why—in a way, what Kafka's doing is closer to the way we live our own lives. Things happen, unexpected things, big changes and transformations, and maybe they surprise us at first, but then really quickly, we adjust to them. Even really drastic changes… we tend to normalize them pretty fast. And the everyday routines of our lives take over. And I think what Kafka goes on to say, what you might see as you read the whole text, is that really this is maybe where our worst cruelty is. Not in the really bad things people do, but in the way the everyday—social norms, routines, that kind of stuff—sweeps over everything else.

So, I'll be interested to see what you all make of this. But I think you might find there's something useful in it for you, in one way or the other. I know for me, this is something I think about a lot… something I struggle with. How not to let my own concerns, which are mostly kind of small, but feel really pressing, too, you know—what deadlines I have to meet, or what I'm going to eat—not to let that stuff keep me from noticing important things going on around me. Anyway, I think you'll see what I mean, I hope, when you read the story.

1.   What is the main purpose of this lecture?

     GIST-PURPOSE. This lecture provides students with information about Kafka's *The Metamorphosis* that will help them as they complete their reading assignment for the week.

   ✗   (A) To provide a partial biography of Kafka

     Kafka's biography is not discussed in the lecture.

   ✓   (B) To prepare students to read a story by Kafka

     CORRECT. The professor is giving students information that will help guide them as they read this story.

   ✗   (C) To compare different translations of Kafka's story

     The professor discusses the translation of the story's title, but does not compare translations of the story itself.

   ✗   (D) To show how Kafka influenced other authors

     The professor does not mention other authors influenced by Kafka.

2.   What is a common misconception about Kafka's *The Metamorphosis*?

     DETAIL. This lecture discusses the fact that, while many people think the main character turns into a cockroach, this is not necessarily the case. Kafka does not specify what kind of animal the narrator turns into.

   ✗   (A) It took Kafka a full decade to write the story.

     This is not discussed in the lecture.

   ✗   (B) Kafka's story was not at all popular when first published.

     This is not discussed in the lecture.

   ✗   (C) Kafka personally drew the image on the cover of the first edition.

     On the contrary—the professor explicitly states that Kafka protested against including an image of the creature from his story on the cover.

   ✓   (D) The narrator of the story turns into a cockroach.

     CORRECT. The professor states that, while many people think the narrator turns into a cockroach, Kafka didn't actually specify what kind of creature he becomes.

3.   How is Kafka's story different from other transformation myths?

DETAIL. The professor states that other transformation myths and stories focus on discussing the transformation itself. Kafka essentially leaves this part out of his story.

✓   (A) Kafka doesn't show the actual transformation.

CORRECT. The professor emphasizes that the transformation is mentioned very quickly, and then the main focus of the story begins.

✗   (B) Kafka's character undergoes a series of transformations.

The main character only changes once, at the beginning of the story. Other transformations aren't mentioned.

✗   (C) Kafka's story is much longer and more psychologically complex.

The professor doesn't mention the length of *The Metamorphosis*.

✗   (D) In other transformation myths, people usually turn into plants, not animals.

The professor barely mentions the specifics of other transformation myths.

4.   Why does the professor mention that Kafka didn't want a picture of the creature on the cover of the book?

DETAIL. The professor wants to make it clear that it was important to Kafka not to define exactly what animal the creature was. This was a deliberate choice, not a mistake.

✗   (A) To illustrate that Kafka was picky about his cover designs in general

The professor doesn't discuss Kafka's general attitude about cover designs. He only discusses Kafka's attitude toward the cover of *The Metamorphosis*.

✗   (B) To clarify the importance of cover art in speculative fiction

The professor does not discuss cover art in general.

✓   (C) To emphasize that Kafka wasn't interested in the details of the transformation

CORRECT. The professor mentions this just before he discusses why Kafka didn't want to explain the transformation itself.

✗   (D) To prove that Kafka was willfully deceiving his readers

This idea is not mentioned in the lecture.

5. What does the professor imply about himself when he mentions some of his own struggles at the end of the lecture? *Choose 2 answers.*

INFERENCE. The professor mentions that he sometimes gets overwhelmed by petty details and forgets to pay attention to the bigger, more important things going on around him.

✗ ☐ A He tends to miss important deadlines.

The professor does not suggest that this is the case.

✓ ☐ B He sometimes focuses too much on everyday concerns.

CORRECT. The professor mentions that thinking too much about everyday details can distract him from bigger concerns.

✗ ☐ C He believes that everyday responsibilities are not important.

The professor does not imply that he believes everyday responsibilities are not important. He is simply suggesting that they are not the only things that are important.

✓ ☐ D He should work to pay attention to the important things happening around him.

CORRECT. The professor states that one of the points of Kafka's story is that people should pay attention to larger concerns. He then says that he sometimes fails to do this, suggesting that he should try to do so more often.

Track 37

NARRATOR: Listen again to part of the lecture. Then answer the question.

PROFESSOR: We're going to read an English translation of *Metamorphosis*, so I think knowing a couple things about the original German will help you when you read it. And the first thing is the original title, which means, literally, "transformation." German has a word that's very similar to our "metamorphosis," but it's not the word Kafka uses.

NARRATOR: Why does the professor say this:

PROFESSOR: German has a word that's very similar to our "metamorphosis," but it's not the one Kafka uses.

6. Why does the professor say this?

FUNCTION OF WHAT IS SAID. The professor is talking about the accuracy of the translation of the word "metamorphosis." He points out that "metamorphosis" is not the best English equivalent, and that the word Kafka chose is closer in meaning to "transformation."

✗ Ⓐ To illustrate that translating from German to English can be difficult

The professor doesn't mention or suggest that translating from German to English is difficult.

✗ Ⓑ To demonstrate that English and German are similar languages

The professor doesn't generally compare the two languages.

✓ Ⓒ To highlight that the word "metamorphosis" isn't the most accurate translation for the title

CORRECT. The professor wants to stress that Kafka could have chosen a word very similar to "metamorphosis," but didn't.

✗ Ⓓ To complain about the impact of inaccurate translations

The professor does not discuss inaccurate translations in general and does not complain about translation accuracy.

Answers and Explanations—8.5

The Symphony—Track 38

NARRATOR: Listen to part of a lecture in a music history class. The professor has been discussing symphonies.

PROFESSOR: The word "symphony" comes from the Greek word *symphonia*. This refers both to a harmonious arrangement of sounds and to music performed by a group. Today, we use the term "symphony" to refer both to large-scale pieces of music and the groups that perform them.

We're going to talk about these pieces—symphonies—today. The earliest ancestor of what we think of as a symphony showed up in Milan in the 1730s. These early pieces came from the overtures of operas. They were short—about 10 to 20 minutes in length. They were also written for fairly small groups, um… about 25 to 30 people. Known as the "Italian" style of symphony, these early pieces usually had three sections, or movements. The first one was fast, the second slow, and the third fast and dance-like.

Initially, these pieces were just for string instruments—things like the violin, viola, cello, and bass. But soon wind instruments—the bassoon, oboe, and flute—started to be added. Later, drums—usually the timpani or kettle drum—were added too. And, uh… while this was happening, the center of symphonic music also migrated from Italy to Mannheim, Germany. The orchestras there were famous for being able to play a wide range of sounds and pieces. Since the orchestras—like the one in Mannheim—were getting better and better, more and more composers got interested in writing symphonies.

Franz Josef Haydn, sometimes called "Papa Haydn"—because he was really the father of our modern symphony—wrote over 100 symphonies in the second half of the eighteenth century. He also standardized a new form of symphony—Haydn's works tended to have a pattern of four movements, rather than the traditional three.

The first movement was fast paced, with a regular structure. The second movement was slower, at *andante*, or walking speed. The third movement was a dance, and the fourth was fast again. Sometimes the fourth movement would be a *rondo*, meaning "round." Haydn's contemporary, Wolfgang Amadeus Mozart, also adopted this form, as did Ludwig van Beethoven. Writing at the start of the nineteenth century, Beethoven transformed the symphony into a major, lengthy composition. His symphonies are still some of our most popular orchestral works today. His ninth symphony also includes a large chorus in the last movement, making it one of the first choral symphonies.

The legacy of writing symphonies continued as most of the major romantic composers of the nineteenth century—people like Brahms, Schubert, Schumann—wrote symphonies. People thought of the symphony as the peak achievement of a composer's career. It was, uh… how he demonstrated all of his skill, and, uh… his artistry.

By the twentieth century, the orchestra had gotten a lot larger. In the early twentieth century, Gustav Mahler took this large orchestra to its extreme. He wrote one symphony—his eighth—that required over 1,000 instrumentalists and singers. Composers also began experimenting more. Some added or subtracted movements. Others wrote "programmatic" music, or symphonies that told some kind of story.

Even when composers began getting very experimental—exploring things like electronic, recorded, or dissonant sounds—the symphony remained popular. Innovators like Arnold Schoenberg and Paul Hindemith still composed symphonies.

While the symphony got its start in Italy, by the twentieth century composers all over the world were creating symphonies. Composers from many different traditions outside of Europe—in Asia, Africa, and North and South America—continue to integrate their cultural style into symphonies today. The Chinese composer Tan Dun is one example. His symphonies are influenced by traditional Chinese theatre and music. So the symphony has proven that it's very versatile—very adaptable—across a lot of different times and places.

The orchestra and the music written for it have changed a lot in the last 300 years, but the symphony still remains popular in concert halls around the world. The symphony's length, complexity, and flexibility make it challenging and appealing for contemporary performers, audiences, and composers alike.

1. **What is the lecture mainly about?** *Choose 2 answers.*

GIST-CONTENT. This lecture covers the development of the symphony as a musical genre from the 1730s to present day. It touches on composers who had a major influence on the development of the symphony.

✓ [A] The historical development of the symphony

CORRECT. The main topic of the lecture is how the symphony has evolved since the early eighteenth century.

✗ [B] The decline of Italy as a musical center

The professor mentions that "the center of symphonic music also migrated from Italy to Mannheim, Germany," but this does not indicate that Italy declined as a musical center in general. Also, this is not the main focus of the lecture.

✓ [C] Composers who influenced symphonic composition

CORRECT. The lecture discusses a number of composers whose symphonies were influential.

✗ [D] Contemporary trends in classical music

Classical music as a broad category is not discussed in the lecture.

2. **According to the professor, what happened as symphony orchestras became more versatile and sophisticated?**

DETAIL. The professor states that "Since the orchestras—like the one in Mannheim—were getting better and better, more and more composers got interested in writing symphonies."

✗ (A) Musicians who performed symphonies began being paid more.

This idea is not mentioned in the lecture.

✓ (B) More composers wanted to write symphonies.

CORRECT. The lecture states that as symphony orchestras became better, "more and more composers got interested in writing symphonies."

✗ (C) Symphony orchestras increased in size.

The lecture does discuss the fact that symphonies increased in size. However, this is not claimed to be a result of improved skill or versatility.

✗ (D) Audience attendance improved.

Increased attendance at symphony performances is not mentioned as a result of orchestras becoming more versatile or sophisticated.

3. Why does the professor mention the Greek word "symphonia"?

ORGANIZATION. The professor uses this word to illustrate that "symphony" can refer both to a piece of music and to the group that performs it.

✗ (A) To assert that the ancient Greeks wrote the first symphonies

This idea is not mentioned in the lecture.

✗ (B) To emphasize the importance of Greek themes in symphonic compositions

This idea is not mentioned in the lecture.

✓ (C) To underscore the two meanings of the word "symphony"

CORRECT. The Greek word "symphonia" has two meanings that parallel the two modern meanings of "symphony"—both the composition and the group performing it.

✗ (D) To provide evidence that the symphony was introduced to Italy by ancient Greeks

The professor does not indicate that Greeks played a role in the development of symphonies in Italy.

4. According to the professor, what was Haydn's main contribution to the development of the symphony?

DETAIL. Haydn's symphonies had four movements instead of three. This change became standard practice for composers afterward.

✗ (A) He increased the number of musicians performing in an orchestra.

This idea is not mentioned in the lecture.

✗ (B) He wrote only a few symphonies.

The opposite is true. Haydn wrote nearly 100 symphonies.

✗ (C) He introduced choral music to the symphony.

The professor states that Beethoven, not Haydn, was the first to do this.

✓ (D) He added a fourth movement to his compositions.

CORRECT. The professor states that Haydn switched from three to four movements, a change that others adopted afterward.

Track 39

NARRATOR: Why does the professor say this:

PROFESSOR: Even when composers began getting very experimental—exploring things like electronic, recorded, or dissonant sounds—the symphony remained popular. Innovators like Arnold Schoenberg and Paul Hindemith still composed symphonies.

5.   Why does the professor say this?

FUNCTION OF WHAT IS SAID. The professor is saying that, even as classical music evolved and became more experimental, the symphony remained popular with composers and audiences.

✗ (A) To celebrate the work of Paul Hindemith

The professor mentions Hindemith, but does not celebrate his work specifically.

✓ (B) To emphasize that twentieth-century audiences continued to attend symphonies, even with these changes

CORRECT. The professor states that symphonies remained popular, even as the music changed dramatically.

✗ (C) To argue against using electronic sounds in classical music

The professor does not give an opinion regarding electronic sounds.

✗ (D) To provide examples of composers who used dissonance

The professor does not specifically state whether the composers mentioned used dissonance. He only notes that they were innovators of some kind.

Track 40

NARRATOR: What does the professor imply when he says this:

PROFESSOR: The orchestra and the music written for it have changed a lot in the last 300 years, but the symphony still remains popular in concert halls around the world. The symphony's length, complexity, and flexibility make it challenging and appealing for contemporary performers, audiences, and composers alike.

8

6.   What does the professor imply when he says this?

INFERENCE. Even though the symphony has changed substantially, it remains popular. The professor is suggesting that he believes that the symphony is still an interesting and important musical genre today.

✓ (A) He believes that the symphony is still important today.

CORRECT. The professor is emphasizing that the symphony continues to attract musicians and audiences today.

✗ (B) He believes that contemporary symphonies are more interesting than older ones.

In this quote, the professor is not comparing the quality of works from different time periods.

✗ (C) He thinks composers should write more symphonies.

In this quote, the professor does not suggest that composers should write more symphonies.

✗ (D) He hopes that composers continue writing symphonies well into the future.

The professor does not consider the future developments of the symphony in this lecture.

Answers and Explanations—8.6

How to Read a Poem—Track 41

NARRATOR: Listen to part of a lecture in a literature class.

PROFESSOR: Today we're going to talk about how to read a poem. Now, most of us are a lot more comfortable reading prose, but that's really different from reading a poem. Even though poems often contain fewer words, they take a lot longer to read *effectively*, because they're more condensed. In some ways, they're closer to music than to prose.

So when we sit down to read a poem, the first thing we want to think about is how it sounds. And that's where a knowledge of rhetorical devices can come in handy.

Rhetoric is the art of speaking effectively—to persuade people, or get some kind of emotional response. The study of rhetoric started with classical authors—the Ancient Greeks and the Romans. They developed and named a lot of the devices that we still use today, like "metaphor" and "simile." They also named a whole lot of techniques that have to do with sound, things like repeating words at the beginning of phrases, or playing around with the *order* of words.

Now, because poems don't have to be written in complete sentences, poets have a lot more freedom. So poets can use these devices *way* more effectively than prose writers can. And poets use these devices not just to make their poem sound fancy, but to convey some kind of feeling or meaning. In a poem, the order of the words, the way they sound, the rhyme—assuming it's a poem that rhymes—these things are just as important as the content or meaning.

We'll talk a lot more about how to identify rhetorical devices when we start analyzing individual poems. One thing to keep in mind—a lot of us, when we first learned about poems, were told that a poem has some kind of message, or point. And our job is to decipher all the tricky language and *figure out* that message. Like it's some kind of puzzle.

Now, poems do often have different kinds of messages or points. Some more than others. That's definitely *one* layer. But they have a lot of *other* layers too. And if we can reduce a poem to just a simple statement, something that could be said more clearly in prose, then why bother writing poems in the first place? They would just be unnecessarily frustrating.

Instead, I think it's a lot more interesting to think about poems as, first and foremost, *experiences*. So when we read a poem, before we start thinking about what it means, we should just spend a little time *living* in it. For this reason, I always start by reading the poem out loud. That way, I get a feel for the sound of the words. Then I think about the *visual* world of the poem. What kinds of images do I see? What are the colors like? People? Objects? I try to imagine everything described in the poem as fully as I can. As I do that, I pay attention to how I *feel* at different points in the poem. I read it a few times, trying to see where I feel what, and where that feeling changes.

Once I've done that, then I can start doing a more structured analysis. This is where I look for rhetoric, for anything unusual about the words the poet chose or how she arranged them. I might also look at the structure and think about how the poem is organized, what *patterns* there are. I then try to connect all these unusual things I've noticed back to the feelings and images from my first couple of reads. How does the structure, or rhetoric, or rhyme, create or reinforce these feelings?

Finally, I might start thinking about meaning or *purpose*. Remember that the poet chose each word *very* carefully. If you think about why she made each choice, then you start getting closer to why the poet wrote the poem. And that's always an interesting question. It might have been to get some kind of message across. But it also might just be to give the reader an interesting experience, or to convey a particular feeling.

So. Reading a poem has a *lot* of layers. But I think, if you try this out the next time you read a poem, you'll start to find it makes poetry a lot more fun. A lot more *engaging*. Though you'll definitely find you're spending a lot longer on each poem.

Alright, so now let's see this in action. I'll put a poem up on the screen, and we'll read it together.

1. What is this lecture primarily about?

   GIST-CONTENT. The lecture is about techniques for reading a poem that will allow the reader to better understand and enjoy it.

   ✗ (A) How to decide whether a poem is well-written

   The lecture does not talk about making value judgments regarding poems.

   ✗ (B) Methods for analyzing the structure of a poem

   The lecture does not cover specific tools for analyzing structure.

   ✗ (C) Ways to identify rhetorical devices in poetry

   The lecture discusses rhetorical devices, but does not mention how to identify them.

   ✓ (D) How to most effectively approach reading a poem

   CORRECT. The main focus of the lecture is to describe techniques for reading and better understanding a poem.

2. According to the professor, what is the purpose of rhetoric?

   DETAIL. The professor states that rhetoric is used to persuade people or elicit an emotional response from people.

   ✗ (A) To decorate a piece of writing

   The professor does not discuss the decoration of writing.

   ✗ (B) To simplify complicated ideas

   The professor does not claim that rhetoric is used for this purpose.

   ✓ (C) To persuade others

   CORRECT. The professor states that rhetoric "is the art of speaking effectively—to persuade people, or get some kind of emotional response."

   ✗ (D) To entertain the reader

   The professor does not mention entertainment as a goal of the use of rhetoric.

3.   Why does the professor make a comparison to puzzles?

ORGANIZATION. The professor mentions puzzles in describing how not to read a poem. His point is that a poem is not a puzzle that, when deciphered, yields a simple point.

✗ (A) To emphasize that poems are easy to solve

The professor does not make this suggestion.

✓ (B) To clarify how not to read a poem

CORRECT. The professor states that seeing a poem as a puzzle is not the most effective way to read a poem.

✗ (C) To suggest that reading a poem and solving a puzzle are similar

The opposite is true. The professor is claiming that reading a poem is not like solving a puzzle.

✗ (D) To encourage students to see hidden messages in poems

The professor emphasizes that many poems don't contain "hidden messages."

4.   Why does the professor mention similes and metaphors?

ORGANIZATION. The professor mentions similes and metaphors as examples of rhetorical devices.

✗ (A) To criticize poets who use too many comparisons

The professor does not criticize poets for using rhetorical devices.

✗ (B) To illustrate the sophistication of ancient Greek poetry

The professor does not mention sophistication and is not focused on ancient Greek poetry specifically.

✓ (C) To give examples of rhetorical devices

CORRECT. Similes and metaphors are mentioned as examples of rhetorical devices.

✗ (D) To encourage students to use similes and metaphors in their own poems

The lecture does not discuss poems written by students.

5. The professor mentions four steps to follow when reading a poem. Put the steps in the order he mentions: first, second, third, or fourth.

CONNECTING CONTENT. The process that the professor outlines is as follows: 1. Read the poem out loud and pay attention to the sound of the words. 2. Read the poem again, paying attention to images and feelings. 3. Analyze the poem's structure and rhetorical devices, thinking about how they connect to feelings. 4. Think about the meaning or purpose of the poem.

A   Think about the purpose and meaning of the poem _____

FOURTH. The professor emphasizes that this step should come last, after the student has read the poem several times and has analyzed structure and rhetorical devices.

B   Pay attention to images and feelings _____

SECOND. After reading out loud, the professor asks students to "live in" the world of the poem, imagining how it looks, sounds, and feels.

C   Read the poem out loud _____

FIRST. The professor states that the first thing to do is to read the poem out loud, paying attention to how the words sound.

D   Analyze the poem for structure and rhetorical devices _____

THIRD. Once readers have thought about sounds and images, the professor states that they are ready to perform a more structured analysis.

Track 42

NARRATOR: What does the professor imply when he says this:

PROFESSOR: If you think about why she made each choice, then you start getting closer to why the poet wrote the poem. And that's always an interesting question. It might have been to get some kind of message across. But it also might just be to give the reader an interesting experience, or to convey a particular feeling.

6. What does the professor imply when he says this?

INFERENCE. The professor is explaining that poems are written for many different reasons. Some may have a point or message, but others do not.

✗ (A) Emotion is the most important part of a poem.

The professor does not state that one purpose of a poem is more important than any other.

✗ (B) Good poets raise interesting questions.

The professor does not state what makes a poet "good" or "not good."

✓ (C) Not all poems are written for the same reason.

CORRECT. The professor describes several reasons why someone might write a poem.

✗ (D) The reader's experience is a poet's primary concern.

The professor does not suggest what poets are primarily concerned with.

Answers and Explanations—8.7

Gunpowder—Track 43

NARRATOR: Listen to part of a lecture in a European history class.

PROFESSOR: OK, so last week we discussed how certain foodstuffs, such as potatoes, changed European geopolitical history. And even though we often associate them with Ireland or Germany, potatoes are not indigenous to Europe. Well, today we'll talk about another substance whose arrival in Europe changed European history—gunpowder. But, even though you might associate gunpowder with Europe—or the United States for that matter—it was not invented there. Does anyone know where it was invented?

MALE STUDENT: Well… I heard that it was from Asia—China, I think.

PROFESSOR: Right. And do you know who invented it there?

MALE STUDENT: I guess it would have been the Emperor. Well, not him, but the warriors… the samurai.

PROFESSOR: Not quite. And, by the way… the samurai were the nobility of the Japanese military—they were not Chinese warriors. Actually—and this might surprise you—gunpowder was invented by Taoist monks. I'm not saying that the Tao is not a religion of peace. The monks were investigating how to change one material into another as part of their search for eternal life. So the combustive quality of gunpowder attracted them. They were not interested in its military application, but that happened soon enough. As a matter of fact, you might also be surprised by how long ago that was. There are at least implied references to gunpowder in Taoist tracts long before the year 1000. And Chinese documents record the use of gunpowder-based weapons by the early 1200s. In Europe, this was the time of the Crusades—warfare with knights using swords, lances, and arrows. How do you think it got to Europe?

FEMALE STUDENT: My grandmother loved history, especially Marco Polo. So I bet that he brought it back on the Silk Road.

PROFESSOR: Interesting—there's a lot of uncertainty, but the written evidence and archaeological results from Silk Road excavations don't really support that theory.

FEMALE STUDENT: Oh. Then maybe the early Portuguese and Spanish explorers brought it back.

PROFESSOR: That's a good thought too, but really, their journeys were too late. The most likely view is that the Mongol invasion of Europe introduced gunpowder there. The evidence for that is more logical than it might appear. You see, the original Chinese gunpowder was very weak—more useful for combustion than for propelling projectiles. It took them centuries to adjust the mixture to make it the lethal force that the Mongols probably used in their invasion. But European gunpowder was immediately suitable for military applications when its first use was recorded around 1330. That leads to the conclusion that the Europeans copied it during or after the invasion.

MALE STUDENT: They must have been pretty excited about it. Now that I think about it, didn't Columbus have some primitive guns?

PROFESSOR: Actually, just like potatoes, Europeans didn't immediately embrace guns. The reasons for that might seem almost contradictory. On the one hand, there were practical considerations. As John said, those guns—commonly called *harquebuses*—were primitive. Originally, they had about the same effective range as a decent archer, but were slower and less reliable. Additionally, the establishment elite opposed them as a disruption of the status quo. Religious leaders called them inhumane and blasphemous. Why was that? Well, guns were cheaper to make than swords and suits of armor. On top of that, unlike the extensive training and practice required for swords and bows, one could easily master firing a gun. There was a saying in the nineteenth century in the United States—"God may have created all men, but it was Colonel Colt who made them equal." Needless to say, the nobility was not particularly in favor of equality. But, resistance faded as the technology rapidly improved. Soon guns could penetrate suits of armor, making these suits obsolete, and before long, guns and cannons dominated European battlefields.

Then what happened? The first European entity to capitalize on this technology was the Duchy of Burgundy. It developed large siege cannons that could destroy medieval castles and city walls, and became a huge power in the late medieval period. Then, a new type of fortress was developed to withstand these cannons, turning warfare in Europe largely into a series of protracted sieges. This lasted for 300 years, and shifted the balance of power to wealthier states. It also contributed to the ascent of France and the Habsburg Empire. So gunpowder had a crucial effect on the European political order. The new order was relatively stable from, say 1500, to the unification of Germany in 1870. And that German—really Prussian—military prowess stemmed from the excellence of their Krupp weapons.

1.   What is the main purpose of the lecture?

GIST-PURPOSE. In his introduction, the professor indicates that the purpose of the lecture is to describe the effects that the introduction of gunpowder had on Europe.

✗ (A) To discuss trade between Europe and China on the Silk Road

Trade in general is not discussed in the lecture. The focus is on the introduction of gunpowder in Europe.

✓ (B) To describe the effects of gunpowder on European history

CORRECT. At the beginning of the lecture, the professor says that "today we'll talk about another substance whose arrival in Europe changed European history—gunpowder."

✗ (C) To describe the flaws of primitive guns

This is a supporting detail, not the main purpose of the lecture.

✗ (D) To explore the effects of the Mongol invasion of Europe

The Mongol invasion is only mentioned as a possible cause of the arrival of gunpowder in Europe. This is a supporting detail, not the main purpose of the lecture.

8

2.   What does the professor imply about the strength of the first gunpowder made in Europe?

   ✗   (A) It was stronger in the Duchy of Burgundy than elsewhere.

   ✗   (B) It was weaker than Chinese gunpowder.

   ✗   (C) Its strength led to the success of the Mongol invasion of Europe.

   ✓   (D) Its strength indicated that it was not invented in Europe.

INFERENCE. The professor states that "European gunpowder was immediately suitable for military applications when its first use was recorded around 1330. That leads to the conclusion that the Europeans copied it during or after the invasion."

The professor talks about the strength of the Duchy of Burgundy and its cannons, but not about the quality of its gunpowder.

On the contrary—according to the professor, European gunpowder was immediately suitable for the military, implying that it was strong.

Nothing in the lecture suggests that the strength of European gunpowder would have aided the success of the Mongol invasion of Europe.

CORRECT. The professor stated that it took centuries for the Chinese to refine the mix. The implication is that Europeans must have borrowed that knowledge in some way to create such strong gunpowder immediately.

3.   Why does the professor mention the nineteenth-century saying about Colonel Colt?

   ✓   (A) To indicate that use of a gun offset the advantages of training with other weapons

   ✗   (B) To suggest that the United States has long been a violent place

   ✗   (C) To illustrate the greater level of equality found in European nations

   ✗   (D) To assert that Colt's weapons were superior to harquebuses

ORGANIZATION. The professor mentions the saying, "God may have created all men, but It was Colonel Colt who made them equal." He does so in discussing early opposition to the use of guns. This opposition came from those who wished to preserve an unequal system that gave advantage to those who trained with older traditional weapons.

CORRECT. The professor mentions that "unlike the extensive training and practice required for swords and bows, one could easily master firing a gun."

The professor does not discuss the history of violence in the United States.

This idea is not discussed in the lecture.

While this is true, this is not why the professor mentions the saying.

4. According to the professor, what was a long-term effect of the introduction of gunpowder to Europe?

DETAIL. The professor claims that it changed the balance of power, and the resulting arrangement continued for centuries.

✗ (A) It tilted the balance of world power away from China.

The balance of power between China and other parts of the world is not discussed in the lecture.

✓ (B) It advantaged wealthier European states that adopted gunpowder use.

CORRECT. The professor says that gunpowder led to siege warfare, which gave wealthier nations an advantage for centuries.

✗ (C) It had a negative effect on international relations within Europe.

The professor only addresses changes in the balance of power among European nations. She does not discuss international relations.

✗ (D) It led to popular revolutions and the decline of European nobility.

This is not mentioned or suggested anywhere in the lecture.

5. According to the professor, why were Taoist monks interested in gunpowder?

DETAIL. The professor describes the monks' interest as non-military, in fact.

✓ (A) It was a way to transform materials.

CORRECT. The professor says, "The monks were investigating how to change one material into another as part of their search for eternal life. So the combustive quality of gunpowder attracted them."

✗ (B) It gave them defensive military benefits.

On the contrary, the professor states that the monks were not interested in the military applications of gunpowder.

✗ (C) They believed it warded off unhealthy spirits.

This idea is not mentioned in the lecture.

✗ (D) It was a component of fireworks for ritual use.

While this may be true, fireworks are not mentioned in the lecture.

Track 44

NARRATOR: Listen again to part of the lecture. Then answer the question.

PROFESSOR: But, even though you might associate gunpowder with Europe—or the United States for that matter—it was not invented there. Does anyone know where it was invented?

MALE STUDENT: Well… I heard that it was from Asia—China, I think.

PROFESSOR: Right. And do you know who invented it there?

NARRATOR: What can be inferred about the professor when she says this:

PROFESSOR: And do you know who invented it there?

6.　　What can be inferred about the professor when she says this?

FUNCTION OF WHAT IS SAID. The professor is exploring the extent of the student's knowledge about the history of gunpowder.

✗　(A) She does not know the answer to her own question.

The professor doesn't indicate in any way that she does not know the answer to her question.

✗　(B) She is criticizing the student.

The professor is asking the student a follow-up question. She does not intend any criticism.

✓　(C) She is exploring the extent of the student's knowledge.

CORRECT. The student answered the professor's first question correctly. She is asking a follow-up question to see whether the student also knows the answer to that question.

✗　(D) She is suggesting that the student's first answer was incorrect.

The student answered the first question correctly. The professor is merely asking that student a follow-up question.

Answers and Explanations—8.8

Abraham Lincoln Brigade—Track 45

NARRATOR: Listen to part of a lecture in a United States government class.

PROFESSOR: Okay, you've been reading about the actions of the United States during the Spanish Civil War in the 1930s. Can anyone summarize the main points of that conflict? Alan?

MALE STUDENT: Well, uh… the Fascists under General Francisco Franco revolted against the elected Spanish government. And Hitler and Mussolini helped them. And, uh… Stalin helped the government.

PROFESSOR: Right. And what about the United States?

MALE STUDENT: The United States tried to stay neutral, but really that helped Franco, because it was the government that needed supplies and stuff.

PROFESSOR: That pretty accurately sums it up. Heather, do you think that was a good policy?

FEMALE STUDENT: I'm not sure. I mean, Franco was rebelling against an elected government. And I read that lots of Americans wanted to help Spain. And some even went there to fight.

PROFESSOR: It's true, there were a lot of drives to raise money and donate medical supplies to the Spanish government, and some people went and fought with them.

MALE STUDENT: Yeah, but Professor, weren't they communists? Especially the ones that went? Plus, Stalin was on that side.

PROFESSOR: Yes, a lot of the volunteers were communists. But you have to remember that this was during the Great Depression. So, for one thing, communism didn't sound as bad to a lot of ordinary people as it may to you now, because they were interested in helping workers. And because of the Depression, right-wing dictators—fascists, I suppose—were taking power in lots of places. These volunteers were more interested in fighting fascists than supporting communism.

MALE STUDENT: I guess maybe that's true, but how do we know for sure?

PROFESSOR: Good question. We can't know anything for sure, but the letters and essays these men wrote indicate they were sincere. Also, there was a great documentary made back in the 1980s—*The Good Fight*—that interviewed survivors, and they still said the same thing. They also talked about the mistakes the government made, mostly afterwards. A little background that wasn't in your reading. Americans were forbidden to travel to Spain then, but about 3,000 went to France and snuck in. Other volunteers came from France, the United Kingdom, from all over Europe—even anti-Nazis from Germany. Under the communists—that's true—they formed "International Brigades." The main American one was called the "*Abraham Lincoln Brigade.*" These soldiers came from all walks of life—there were students, artists, sailors, steelworkers… and quite a few Jewish men who wanted to fight Hitler any way they could. And speaking of their sincerity, the "Abraham Lincoln Brigade" was the first American integrated military unit, allowing different races to fight side-by-side. A significant number of African Americans went because of Hitler's racism—remember, this was right after Jesse Owens won medals at the 1936 Berlin Olympics—or because of Mussolini's attack on Ethiopia. Not only that, Oliver Law was the first African American to command an American military unit… until he was killed in action. Even though the soldiers were given very little training, they fought bravely. But they were outnumbered and outgunned, partly because of the United States embargo. And almost a quarter of them died there. That's a lot.

MALE STUDENT: But you said that the United States government made mistakes. What mistakes?

PROFESSOR: Well, once the United States entered World War II in 1941, the surviving men—communists or not—mostly volunteered for military service. You would think the government would have welcomed combat veterans. But the government called them ineligible. It called them *premature anti-fascists*, which, if you ask me, is the kind of doublespeak George Orwell talked about. Some of them managed to serve anyway, but the unwritten policy pushed by J. Edgar Hoover, head of the Federal Bureau of Investigations, was that they should not be decorated or made officers.

FEMALE STUDENT: But isn't it the government's responsibility to worry about… you know… spies?

PROFESSOR: Well, of course it is, although the suspicion seems pretty unfounded in this case. In fact, some actually served the United States as spies because of their anti-fascist connections in Europe. Anyway, it gets worse. After the war, many of them were blacklisted by the House Un-American Activities Committee—the same Red Scare that blacklisted Hollywood types. These were ordinary people—not celebrities—who then lost their jobs. They were denied housing, and refused passports for years and years. And, really, they were just idealists. Idealists like the men who fought in the Chinese Air Force against Japan in the Flying Tigers. But those volunteers were embraced by the United States government. Anyway, even a well-meaning government can make mistakes, especially if some of the people in government are not well-meaning. This week you'll read about the safeguards that the United States government has written into law in an attempt to avoid such mistakes and unfairness.

1. What is the lecture mainly about?

    GIST-CONTENT. The lecture covers activity of the United States during the Spanish Civil War, and questions some of its related policies.

    ✗ (A) Reasons why the United States did not support communism

    The reasons that the United States government opposed communism—before, during, or after the Spanish Civil War—are not discussed in the lecture.

    ✓ (B) United States policies concerning the Spanish Civil War

    CORRECT. The lecture discusses policies of the United States government concerning the Spanish Civil War and some United States citizens who fought in it.

    ✗ (C) The illegal activities of the Abraham Lincoln Brigade

    The lecture does not mention any illegal activities of the Abraham Lincoln Brigade.

    ✗ (D) Ways in which the United States helped the Spanish Fascists

    Some United States policies benefited the Spanish Fascists, but not intentionally. This also is not the main focus of the lecture.

2. According to the discussion, what are two reasons why African Americans joined the Abraham Lincoln Brigade? *Choose 2 answers.*

    DETAIL. The reasons stated in the lecture were Hitler's racism during the 1936 Olympics and Mussolini's invasion of Ethiopia.

    ✗ A An opportunity to fight in an integrated combat unit

    While this did take place, it is not mentioned as a reason that African Americans chose to join the brigade.

    ✓ B Hitler's racism at the 1936 Olympics in Berlin

    CORRECT. This reason is stated directly by the professor.

    ✗ C Protests against racial discrimination in the United States

    This idea is not mentioned in the lecture.

    ✓ D Mussolini's invasion of Ethiopia

    CORRECT. This reason is stated directly by the professor.

3. The lecture discusses important events related to the Spanish Civil War and the Abraham Lincoln Brigade. Put the events in chronological order: first, second, third, or fourth.

CONNECTING CONTENT. The chronological order of the events mentioned by the professor are as follows: 1. Brigade members volunteered during the Great Depression. 2. Oliver Law died in combat during the Spanish Civil War. 3. Punitive actions were taken against brigade members at the beginning of World War II. 4. Punitive actions were taken against brigade members after World War II.

- [A] Abraham Lincoln Brigade members were declared "premature anti-fascists." _____

THIRD. This declaration was made shortly after the beginning of United States involvement in World War II in 1941.

- [B] Abraham Lincoln Brigade members were blacklisted by the House Un-American Activities Committee. _____

FOURTH. The professor mentions that this took place after World War II, and therefore is the most recent event.

- [C] The Great Depression began. _____

FIRST. The professor mentions that US citizens volunteering to help the Spanish government did so during the Great Depression. Therefore, this event came first.

- [D] Oliver Law died in combat. _____

SECOND. Oliver Law was the first African American to command an American military unit. His death occurred during the Spanish Civil War in the 1930s.

4. Why does the professor mention the United States government's embrace of the Flying Tiger volunteers?

ORGANIZATION. The professor mentions this embrace as an example that contrasts with the government's treatment of Abraham Lincoln Brigade members.

- ✓ (A) To provide a contrast to the treatment given to Abraham Lincoln Brigade volunteers

CORRECT. The professor implies that the US government displayed a double standard in its treatment of these two groups of veterans.

- ✗ (B) To illustrate the fairness of the United States government in a comparable situation

The opposite is true. The professor implies that the United States government treated members of the Abraham Lincoln Brigade unfairly.

- ✗ (C) To show that it was common for United States citizens to volunteer for foreign combat

The professor is not implying that volunteering for foreign combat was common for US citizens.

- ✗ (D) To highlight the United States government's opposition to integrated units

This issue is not discussed in the lecture.

5.   What does the professor say about the Abraham Lincoln Brigade volunteers?

DETAIL. The only comment that the professor makes about the volunteers as a whole is that they wanted to fight Fascism.

✗ (A) Most were African Americans.

The professor notes that a significant number of the volunteers were African Americans, but does not suggest that *most* were.

✗ (B) Some were communist spies.

The professor implies that the United States government was worried about that possibility, but does not imply that any of the volunteers actually *were* spies.

✓ (C) Most were primarily interested in fighting fascists.

CORRECT. The professor clearly says that the volunteers "were more interested in fighting fascists than supporting communism."

✗ (D) Most were killed in action.

The professor states that almost one-fourth of the volunteers were killed in action—a substantial percentage, but not *most* of them.

Track 46

NARRATOR: Listen again to part of the lecture. Then answer the question.

PROFESSOR: You would think the government would have welcomed combat veterans. But the government called them ineligible. It called them *premature anti-fascists*, which, if you ask me, is the kind of doublespeak George Orwell talked about.

NARRATOR: What does the professor imply when he says this:

PROFESSOR: … which, if you ask me, is the kind of doublespeak George Orwell talked about.

6.   **INFERENCE.** In this quote, the professor implies that the government declaration of combat veterans as "premature anti-fascists" was deliberately misleading and insincere.

✗ (A) The government proclamation was twice as strong as most similar declarations were.

The term "doublespeak" implies dishonesty, not declaring something twice, or declaring it twice as strongly as usual.

✗ (B) The government proclamation was meant to support the fascists.

The proclamation was not meant to support the fascists. The professor is talking instead about the inherent dishonesty of the proclamation.

✗ (C) George Orwell was supportive of the fascists.

The professor does not make any reference to George Orwell's political views.

✓ (D) The government proclamation was deliberately misleading.

CORRECT. The term "doublespeak" means language that is deliberately misleading.

Answers and Explanations—8.9

Richard Prince—Track 47

NARRATOR: Listen to part of a lecture in an art theory class.

PROFESSOR: As we've seen, the second half of the twentieth century was a pivotal period in art history. It was a time of pushing the definition of what art is, and crossing boundaries that had never before been crossed. Among the artists who were pioneers in this regard is Richard Prince.

Richard Prince is an American painter and photographer who became known for his work in copying the work of other artists. It was 1975 when he created his first "*rephotograph*," or photograph of a photograph, that would become a highly valued piece of art. It was a photograph of a photograph, the latter of which had been featured in a cigarette ad. Prince's rephotograph sold at auction for over a million dollars in 2005.

He was not the only person creating rephotographs at the time, however. Rephotography was actually a movement in the art world in the 1970s. The nature of it is *appropriation*, which means taking something from someone else to use yourself—usually without permission. In this case, it meant taking the photography of others to use in one's own photography. Prince, in particular, was interested in how photographing a photograph immediately created a new history for it—like beginning its life as a piece of art again, from scratch. He was fascinated with how photographic film was a kind of automatic appropriation device, since it was able to do this in an instant.

His most famous pieces are of cowboys from those Marlboro cigarette ads, like the one I mentioned a moment ago. It's like… by taking a picture of a picture someone else took, he's asking, "What makes a work of art real, or not?"

Now, you may not be surprised to learn that this didn't go over well with a lot of the photographers whose work Prince appropriated. It was only a matter of time before one of them sued him. In 2008, a photographer named Patrick Cariou sued Prince for copyright violation. The suit involved 35 photographs of Cariou's. The question for the court was really whether Prince had transformed Cariou's work into something new, or if he hadn't transformed it enough for it to count as different. The question was the *degree of transformation*. We have to acknowledge here that this is a very subjective question to ask about a piece of art. Could we say, for example, that even just knowing that a photograph is actually a rephotograph makes us have a different experience of it than we would have if we thought it was just a plain old photograph? Can it count as "transformation" if the change is just conceptual, in the mind of the viewer, or does it need to be visually obvious?

The court agreed with Cariou—it ruled that Richard Prince had violated Cariou's copyright. But then, a higher court reversed this ruling for most of the photos, so the question wasn't ever fully resolved.

Prince wasn't done raising the question of what constitutes art. In 2017, nine years after the Cariou lawsuit, he asked this question again, in a different way. The daughter of a prominent politician had purchased one of Prince's works—a rephotograph—years before her father ran for office. She still owns it—it's apparently featured in her home, and worth a fair amount of money. It was an original Richard Prince rephotograph, after all. But then Prince did something unheard of in the art world. As an act of political protest against her father, he declared publicly that this piece—the one this woman bought from him—was not his. He disowned it, and returned the money she paid him. So that raised the question—does a piece of art exist apart from its creator's views of it? Can an artist rescind his or her signature on the piece? Or maybe there is something special about art that makes it separate from its maker once it's made. And then there is the

question of what the nature of the art is to begin with, and whether that matters. Would we feel differently if it were, say, a painting, instead of a photograph of a photograph?

One thing is for sure: Richard Prince has not shied away from controversy and social commentary throughout his career, and he continues to contribute to public discourse on the definition of art.

1.	What does the professor mainly discuss?	**GIST-CONTENT.** The professor mainly discusses the artist Richard Prince, and how he has challenged the definition of art.
✓	(A) The pioneering work of artist Richard Prince	**CORRECT.** Pioneering means "advancing new ideas or values." That is what Prince has done in his career, and his work is the main topic of the lecture.
✗	(B) The history of rephotography	This is discussed to some extent, but is not the main focus of the lecture.
✗	(C) The new meaning of art in the twenty-first century	The lecture is also about art theory in the twentieth century. Also, it is focused primarily on one specific form of art, not art in general.
✗	(D) Innovations in the early days of photography	The professor does not discuss the early days of photography. Also, the primary form of art discussed is rephotography, not photography.

2.	According to the professor, how did Richard Prince challenge common notions of what constitutes art? *Choose 2 answers*.	**DETAIL.** The professor discusses Prince's rephotographs at length. Also discussed is Prince's decision to rescind—or take back—his signature on a previous work, out of political protest.
✓	[A] By taking photographs of photographs	**CORRECT.** Rephotographs represent a challenge to the accepted definition of art.
✗	[B] By filing a lawsuit against a fellow photographer	The lawsuit discussed was filed *against* Prince, not by Prince.
✗	[C] By refusing to sign his work	Prince disowned a piece of his own artwork, which is different from refusing to sign it in the first place.
✓	[D] By disowning a piece of art he had made and sold	**CORRECT.** Prince revoked his signature, raising the question of what that implies about the status of the work he disowned.

3.   What can be inferred about Prince's
     future career as an artist?

INFERENCE. The professor references Prince's present and future work at the end of the lecture, when he states that Prince continues not to "shy away" from controversy.

✗ (A) Prince's work will likely revolve
        around how to maintain
        popularity.

There is no mention of Prince's broad popularity, nor his level of interest in maintaining it or focusing on it as a subject.

✗ (B) Prince's work will probably lead to
        many more lawsuits.

While this possibility exists, it is not mentioned or suggested in the lecture.

✓ (C) Prince's work will likely raise more
        political and social questions.

CORRECT. By noting that Prince continues not to "shy away" from controversy, the professor suggests that Prince's work will continue to raise political and social questions.

✗ (D) Prince's work will probably answer
        more questions than it raises.

If anything, the opposite is true. The professor suggests that Prince's work raises questions, but does not necessarily answer them.

4.   What is the professor's opinion of
     Richard Prince?

SPEAKER'S ATTITUDE. The professor does not criticize Prince. If anything, the professor seems impressed with Prince's contributions to art theory.

✗ (A) He thinks that criticisms of Prince
        are unfair and unwarranted.

The professor offers no personal opinion on criticisms of Prince made by others.

✓ (B) He believes that Prince has made
        valuable contributions to how the
        definition of art has evolved.

CORRECT. The professor devotes the lecture to a discussion of Prince's contributions to art theory, noting in particular the questions Prince raises about what constitutes a work of art.

✗ (C) He thinks that photographer
        Patrick Cariou should have
        prevailed in court.

The professor offers no personal opinion on this lawsuit, other than to suggest that its result did not definitively answer important questions about the definition of art.

✗ (D) He believes that Prince breaks
        rules and expectations in the art
        community that should not be
        violated.

While the professor does discuss the ways in which Prince violates rules and expectations, he doesn't criticize these actions.

8

5. What are two key features of appropriation as discussed by the professor in the context of rephotography? *Choose 2 answers.*

✗ ☐A Asking for permission to use one's work

DETAIL. The professor describes appropriation as using someone else's work in one's own work, often without permission.

The professor states the opposite. Appropriation is using someone else's work without permission.

✓ ☐B Taking someone else's work for one's own use

CORRECT. This is the main feature of appropriation as defined in the lecture.

✗ ☐C Refusing to grant permission to someone who wants to use one's work

Appropriation is an action taken by a person using someone *else's* work, not by the person whose work is potentially being reused by someone else.

✓ ☐D Using someone else's work without permission

CORRECT. This is often a feature of appropriation, especially within the context of the professor's discussion of rephotography.

6. Why does the professor describe Prince's revocation of his signature on a work of art as "unheard of in the art world"?

ORGANIZATION. The expression "unheard of" is used to describe something as very uncommon. Quite often, it refers to something that has never happened before.

✗ Ⓐ It was problematic for the art world.

There is no direct suggestion that Prince's revocation of his signature was problematic for the art world.

✗ Ⓑ It angered art critics.

Responses by art critics were not discussed in the lecture.

✓ Ⓒ It had likely never been done before.

CORRECT. "Unheard of" is an idiom meaning that something has never happened before, or at least is extremely unusual.

✗ Ⓓ It was an action that was performed silently.

"Unheard of" does not mean "silent"—it means exceptionally rare, or possibly unprecedented.

Answers and Explanations—8.10

Greenland Vikings—Track 48

NARRATOR: Listen to part of a lecture in an anthropology class.

PROFESSOR: If I asked you where the oldest Christian church in the New World was, that is, in the Americas, some of you might impulsively say Massachusetts—uh… the Pilgrims and all. But if you thought about it more, you'd probably think of Spanish conquistadors in South America. Or even the West Indies, after all… Columbus landed there in 1492. And you know, 1492 was a long time ago. More than

500 years. I really understood that when I was a boy and held a medieval sword belonging to my great-uncle, which was made in 1495—that year was engraved on the blade. And I thought, "Wow, three years after Columbus," which seemed like the oldest thing I knew. Well, the oldest Christian Church in the New World was built around 1140 CE. That's 350 years before Columbus! And it's in Greenland, in a place that was called Gardar. That's right, the Vikings built it. I'll show you some pictures in a little bit.

The Vikings colonized Greenland in 985 CE, and 150 years later, they were doing well enough to build a stone cathedral with stained glass windows and a bronze bell. They even had their own archbishop then. And that society went on for centuries until it just disappeared in the early 1400s. The last written records, from around 1420, don't refer to any trouble—they involve a wedding. Now, everyone doesn't agree about how such a stable society suddenly disappeared. I mean, there wasn't an earthquake or a volcanic eruption, like there was with Vesuvius in Pompeii. Discussing those theories is a good place to begin our discussion of social organization.

These Viking settlements, as I said, had prospered for centuries—they had farms and solid homes. There weren't more than a few thousand Vikings there, but their lives were much like other Scandinavians of the medieval period. Here's the old consensus about what happened. Interestingly enough, it involves climate change. Perhaps you've heard of the Medieval Warm Period, from about 900 to 1300 CE, when in the north, the growing season got longer and sea voyages got easier.

But then the Little Ice Age began. The theory holds that the Greenland Vikings no longer could successfully farm or feed their herds, and the growing ice packs made seafaring treacherous. Scholars had believed that the Vikings clung to their ways instead of adapting… and starved to death. Icelanders and Norwegians were very literate peoples, and their archives give no evidence of any notable influx of Vikings returning to Europe. Why did they stay? Why didn't they evacuate? Some historians have speculated that a lack of wood, due to colder conditions and overuse, prevented them from maintaining their boats, or that perhaps they were lost at sea. Others held that the exodus back to Iceland was gradual and thus unrecorded.

But, uh… more recent field work, along with advances in the available scientific tools, has significantly undermined the idea that this stable society's unwillingness to adapt doomed them. Analysis of Viking skeletons has determined that they did in fact switch from a beef and sheep-based diet to one based on seals, much like the Greenland Inuits, who live in the same area to this day. Furthermore, the seal bones found in archaeological digs indicate that the Vikings did not hunt the local harbor seals out of existence, but sailed north instead to harvest the plentiful harp seals. So what is the new theory? The new theory—even more interestingly—suggests that, aside from colder temperatures, *globalization* was the undoing of the Greenland Vikings. These historians argue that the Vikings did not colonize Greenland just to farm in a less favorable climate than Iceland or Norway. They say the Vikings came primarily to hunt walruses, because the medieval ivory trade was incredibly lucrative. Records show that one longship from Greenland delivered a cargo of ivory to the Norwegian king that was worth more than all the wool sent from Iceland that year. Well, around 1300, not only did the fashion for ivory somewhat decline, but Portuguese traders began importing elephant ivory, which was of better quality and less expensive, from Africa. The collapse of this industry, along with the more dangerous seas, made the Greenland settlements financially unviable.

So what to make of this? Well, it is our starting point to explore the effects throughout history of climate change and globalization on previously prosperous societies. And what really happened to the Greenland Vikings? Again, some think that economic hardship caused a gradual emigration. Others still hold out for extinction, noting that these small Viking communities, like small whaling towns in New England, were vulnerable to maritime disasters. If a large number of able-bodied men were lost at sea, the community would destabilize. The condition of the archaeological evidence argues against a violent end from some war with the Inuit. We don't know. But let's look at some pictures from Gardar.

1.   What does the professor mainly discuss?

GIST-CONTENT. After mentioning the oldest church in the Americas, the professor discusses theories about the dissolution of the Viking settlement of Gardar, in Greenland.

✗ (A) The construction of the oldest church in the Americas

The professor only mentions this as an introduction to the Viking settlement in Gardar.

✗ (B) The development of the medieval ivory trade

This is mentioned only as a supporting detail about the Viking settlement.

✓ (C) Theories about the disappearance of a settlement

CORRECT. After mentioning the oldest church in the Americas, the professor discusses theories about the dissolution of Gardar.

✗ (D) Key differences between Viking and Inuit communities

Inuits are only briefly mentioned in the lecture.

2.   Why does the professor mention holding a sword from 1495?

ORGANIZATION. The professor tells this story to emphasize how long ago the year 1495 was. This in turn emphasizes that Gardar was hundreds of years older than *that*.

✗ (A) To emphasize how close in history the sword's manufacture was to Columbus's voyage

The professor's point is how *old* the sword is, not how close the timing of the sword's manufacture was to Columbus's voyage.

✗ (B) To emphasize how warlike the Vikings were

The professor never mentions the warlike nature of Vikings.

✗ (C) To demonstrate Viking techniques of swordsmanship

The professor's point concerns the age of the sword, not the issue of swordsmanship.

✓ (D) To illustrate to the class the age of the Viking colony

CORRECT. The professor tells that story ultimately to emphasize how old the Gardar church was—and thus how old Gardar itself was.

3. What is the professor's opinion about the Viking settlements during the Medieval Warm Period?

SPEAKER'S ATTITUDE. The professor referred to these settlements as stable and prosperous at the time.

✓ (A) He believes they were successful.

CORRECT. The professor calls them stable and prosperous—doing well enough that the inhabitants built a church featuring stained glass.

✗ (B) He regards their inhabitants as very religious.

The inhabitants did build a church, but the professor does not discuss the extent of their religiousness.

✗ (C) He is distressed that their inhabitants starved to death.

The possible starvation, if it happened, would have occurred later, during the Little Ice Age.

✗ (D) He is mildly shocked that their inhabitants conquered the Inuits.

The professor does not discuss any such conquest.

4. According to the professor, what is the significance of the change from beef to seal in the Viking diet?

DETAIL. It is mentioned as evidence of the Vikings' adaptability to changing conditions.

✗ (A) It demonstrates that the Vikings were starving.

The dietary change is provided as evidence of adaptability, not starvation.

✓ (B) It demonstrates that their society was adaptable.

CORRECT. The professor cites this as evidence to discredit the idea that the Vikings were unwilling to adapt.

✗ (C) It is provided as evidence of the effect of globalization.

This dietary change is mentioned in relation to climate change, not globalization.

✗ (D) It shows that the Inuit taught them how to hunt seals.

This idea is not mentioned or suggested anywhere in the lecture.

5. What does the professor say about the Viking walrus hunts?

DETAIL. The professor states that they were very lucrative at first, although it is implied that this changed later, when the Portuguese began importing elephant ivory from Africa.

✗ (A) From a modern point of view, they were inhumane.

This idea is not mentioned in the lecture.

✓ (B) They were very profitable at first.

CORRECT. The professor states that they were very lucrative before Portuguese elephant ivory emerged as a substitute to walrus ivory.

✗ (C) They were very dangerous for participants.

The professor mentions the dangers of seafaring, but he does not explicitly mention danger from these hunts.

✗ (D) They required competing with the Portuguese for prey.

Portuguese ivory came from elephants, not walruses. Therefore, the Portuguese did not compete with the Vikings for walrus prey.

6. What are two questions about the Gardar Vikings that the professor definitively answers? *Choose 2 answers.*

DETAIL. The professor is definitive about the date of the Viking arrival in Gardar (985 CE) and the Viking's adaptations to climate change.

✗ [A] What happened to the Vikings in the 1400s

At the end of the lecture, the professor states that it is not known for certain.

✗ [B] Why the Vikings did not leave Gardar to go to Iceland or Norway

The professor cites theories about why they may have stayed in Gardar—such as farming or walrus hunting—but he does not give a definitive answer.

✓ [C] When the Vikings colonized Greenland

CORRECT. The professor states that they arrived in 985 CE.

✓ [D] Whether the Vikings adapted to climate change in any way

CORRECT. The professor explicitly mentions the shift in diet from beef to seals as an example of the Vikings adapting to changes in climate.

Chapter 9
Lectures C: Social Science

Listening lectures test your ability to comprehend academic-level spoken English. You'll listen to a short lecture (about 3 to 5 minutes long) from a professor. Occasionally, a student may also speak. You will only be able to listen to the lecture once. You will not be able to pause the recording or to replay any part of it (though some questions will replay a specific part of the lecture for you). You can take notes as you listen.

You will then answer six questions for that lecture. Most questions are multiple-choice with four options (select one from A, B, C, or D). Some questions may ask you to select more than one option or to fill in a table. You will have to answer the questions in order. You cannot return to a question once you have moved on to the next question.

Listening lectures test your understanding of main ideas, contrasts, the lecturer's tone and degree of certainty about the information, and why the lecturer relates certain information or examples. They also test your understanding of the organization of the lecture and the relationship between different ideas. Finally, they test your ability to make inferences or draw conclusions.

How should you use this chapter? Here are some recommendations, according to the level you've reached in TOEFL Listening:

1. **Fundamentals.** Start with a topic-focused chapter, such as this one. Start with a topic that is a "medium weakness"—not your worst area but not your best either. At first, listen to the lecture once, then work on the questions untimed and check the answer after each question. Review the solutions closely, think carefully about the principles at work, and articulate what you've learned. Redo questions as necessary. As you get better, time yourself and do all of the questions for a lecture at once, without stopping.

2. **Fixes.** Do an entire lecture and its associated questions under timed conditions. Don't replay any part of the lecture while you are still answering the questions! Examine the results, learn your lessons, then test yourself with another lecture and question set.

3. **Tweaks.** Confirm your mastery by doing two or three lectures in a row under timed conditions. Work your way up to doing four lectures and two conversations in one sitting. Aim to improve the speed and ease of your process.

Good luck on Listening!

9.1

 Listen to Track 49.

Now answer the questions.

1. What is the main topic of the lecture?

   (A) New ways of implementing bike-sharing programs

   (B) Critical factors for creating a successful bike-sharing program

   (C) Where bike-sharing programs first started

   (D) The importance of bike-sharing programs in reducing congestion

2. According to the professor, what is the primary reason for introducing a bike-sharing program in major cities?

   (A) To encourage people to purchase their own bikes

   (B) To improve access to shopping centers and attractions

   (C) To reduce car congestion and noise

   (D) To increase tourist activity in city centers

3. When determining whether a city is "bike-friendly," what are two considerations that must be addressed? *Choose 2 answers.*

   [A] The physical terrain of the city

   [B] The number of popular tourist sites

   [C] Access to safe places to ride bikes

   [D] Availability of helmets and other biking accessories

4. Why does the professor explain the recommendations for the location and number of bikes in a bike-sharing system?

   (A) To illustrate why city governments have decided to start bike-sharing programs

   (B) To explain the differences between bike sharing and public transportation

   (C) To point out how access to bikes is more important than physical terrain

   (D) To show their importance in creating a successful bike-sharing system

5. Why does the professor discuss the Toronto bike-sharing program?

   (A) To provide an example of a typical North American bike-sharing program

   (B) To illustrate how poor planning can impact the success of a bike-sharing program

   (C) To discuss which bike-sharing program she likes best

   (D) To show how a bike-sharing program can be more effective than public transportation

Listen to Track 50.

Now answer the question.

6. What does the professor mean when she says this?

  (A) Only athletic people can use a bike-sharing program.

  (B) The terrain of a city is of little importance when considering a bike-sharing program.

  (C) Steep roads and uneven surfaces are dangerous for cyclists and should be avoided.

  (D) The effort required to travel by bike is an important consideration for a bike-sharing program.

9.2

 Listen to Track 51.

Now answer the questions.

1. What does the professor mainly discuss?

  (A) The evolution of dreaming in human beings

  (B) How dreaming occurs in the brain

  (C) Theories from two psychoanalysts about dreaming

  (D) One scientist's research into how people dream

 Listen to Track 52.

Now answer the question.

2. Why does the professor say this?

  (A) To describe how the human brain is physically organized

  (B) To illustrate Freud's distinct categories of consciousness

  (C) To explain why Freud became a psychoanalyst

  (D) To remind students of a previous point

3. What does the professor say about art and religion?

  (A) That it is not possible to understand why they exist, according to Freud

  (B) That they are the opposite of dreaming, according to Jung

  (C) That Freud studied them to better understand dreams

  (D) That they are part of the collective unconscious, according to Jung

4. What point does the professor make when he refers to introverts and extroverts?
    A Jung was the one who created these terms.
    B Students should become aware of which category they fall in.
    C All people are chiefly one or the other, but not both.
    D The concepts of introversion and extroversion introduced him to Jung.

5. The professor describes the collective unconscious to the class. What is this description about?
    A How Freud invented psychoanalysis
    B How the collective unconscious is the tip of the iceberg for human thinking
    C Why Freud did not believe in a collective unconscious
    D Jung's belief that this is how humans feel connected to one another

6. What is the professor's opinion of dream interpretation?
    A Jung is more in line with scientific perspectives than Freud is.
    B Developing a perfect understanding of the nature of dreaming may not be possible.
    C Freud's work is more applicable to modern dreaming than Jung's work is.
    D It is more valid to believe in a collective unconscious than to not believe in one.

9.3

 Listen to Track 53.

Now answer the questions.

1. What is the main purpose of the talk?
    A To discuss possible ways infants learn
    B To describe key considerations of learning language
    C To explain processes used to test learning in infants
    D To discuss why it is so difficult to learn a language after infancy

2. Why does the professor ask students about the first thing they learned?
    A To engage students in the topic she is about to discuss
    B To establish that everyone learns similar things in infancy
    C To introduce the difficulty of learning a language
    D To illustrate that learning stages can occur at different times for different people

3. What does the professor imply about some of the theories for how infants begin learning?

   (A) They cannot be scientifically proven or disproven.

   (B) They do not have scientific evidence to support them.

   (C) They explain only how a child learns language.

   (D) They have been disproven by her research.

4. The professor mentions a number of theories for early learning methods. Select each of the following that is one of the theories she mentions.

   A   When children are born, they are inherently good.

   B   Learning occurs at a constant rate over a lifetime.

   C   Children are born with some innate knowledge.

   D   Learning occurs in progressive stages.

   E   All children master stages of learning at essentially the same time.

5. How was advanced reasoning studied in infants?

   (A) By recording how often infants made reasonable decisions

   (B) By observing how children interacted with one another

   (C) By having children repeat the actions of the researchers who conducted the experiments

   (D) By monitoring the attention levels of infants to possible and seemingly impossible events

6. The professor mentioned a study that tested the ability of children to understand a seemingly dangerous fall. What did the researchers conclude from this study?

   (A) Infants learn by progressing through different stages of understanding.

   (B) Infants sometimes show more advanced reasoning than is suggested by Piaget's theories.

   (C) Infants typically demonstrate reasoning starting at about nine months.

   (D) Advanced reasoning skill development is dependent upon rational thought.

9.4

 Listen to Track 54.

Now answer the questions.

1. What is the main subject of the lecture?

   (A) The rise of shopping malls in ancient Rome

   (B) The current decline of shopping malls in the United States

   (C) How to design a successful shopping mall

   (D) Reasons why shopping malls can be detrimental to civic life

2. According to the professor, why did shopping malls appear in America when and where they did?

(A) The migration of people to the suburbs, coupled with the proliferation of automobiles

(B) The movement of the population to urban areas from suburban ones

(C) The desire of city planners to improve social life for suburban residents

(D) The pressure placed on city planners by citizens to create shopping centers like the ones in Europe

3. What are two theories that the professor mentions as to why shopping malls are struggling in the 21st century? *Choose 2 answers.*

A Most malls are not large enough to accommodate the required foot traffic.

B There are too many malls close to one another in some areas.

C People are now moving back into cities, away from suburbs.

D Many people are now shopping online.

4. Why does the professor discuss the Mall of America?

(A) To demonstrate how the success or failure of a shopping mall depends on its size

(D) To provide an example of a specific type of American shopping mall

(C) To illustrate the trend in American shopping malls in the 21st century

(D) To show how designing a mall that is too large can lead to problems later

5. Why does the professor mention Real Estate Investment Trusts, or REITs?

(A) To discuss her least favorite aspect of city planning

(B) To give an example of a challenge that investors in shopping malls faced

(C) To provide context for the rise of American shopping malls in the 1960s

(D) To argue that, if not for REITs, shopping malls would not exist

 Listen to Track 55.

Now answer the question.

6. What does the professor mean when she says this?

(A) Shopping malls stopped being built largely because of the Great Recession.

(B) The Great Recession began earlier than 2008, along with the decline in shopping malls.

(C) The Great Recession alone cannot explain the decline in shopping malls.

(D) Most malls did not survive the impact of the Great Recession.

9.5

 Listen to Track 56.

Now answer the questions.

1. What is the lecture primarily about?

   (A) A management strategy in business that improves employee morale

   (B) An approach to product development and why it can be useful

   (C) Two methods for maximizing efficiency in business

   (D) A tool that customers can use in evaluating whether to buy a product

2. According to the professor, what is a potential benefit of the MVP strategy?

   (A) It can contribute to the design of a nearly perfect product early in the development process.

   (B) It can help product developers avoid many wasted hours of work.

   (C) It can relieve anxiety among product developers.

   (D) It drives engineers to work more quickly.

3. What does the professor say about customers that use the MVP?

   (A) An MVP should appeal to the largest possible number of potential customers.

   (B) An MVP is created solely for the purpose of hypothetical distribution and will not be shown to actual customers.

   (C) An MVP is designed for release to a small number of select customers.

   (D) An MVP evaluation always produces conflicting requests from different customers that must be resolved.

4. Why does the professor mention that in sports, MVP is used to mean "Most Valuable Player?"

   (A) To give an example of another industry that uses an MVP

   (B) To illustrate the usefulness of the concept across multiple industries

   (C) To emphasize that MVP means essentially the same thing in both sports and product development

   (D) To explain that the meaning of MVP in the context of product development is different

5. Why does the professor use the term "visionaries"?

   (A) To identify the kind of customers an MVP should target

   (B) To name a group of customers who would prefer an MVP over a more developed product

   (C) To offer an example of how an MVP can originate from anywhere within a company

   (D) To emphasize the importance of inspired engineers in product development

Listen to Track 57.

Now answer the question.

6. What does the professor imply when she says this?

   (A) The MVP is exclusively designed by the product manager.

   (B) It is unlikely that anyone but the product manager would have a strong opinion on the number of customers targeted by an MVP.

   (C) The MVP approach can be customized by whoever is managing product development.

   (D) It is concerning that the MVP would be released to more than a few customers, but ultimately that is the product manager's decision.

9.6

Listen to Track 58.

Now answer the questions.

1. What is the main purpose of this lecture?

   (A) To compare the study of sociology with the study of literature

   (B) To explain the value of studying literature as a serious endeavor

   (C) To explore the traditional model of literature study and how that study has changed

   (D) To explain the origins of the study of literature in the United States

2. Why does the professor mention the "Canon of Western Literature?"

   (A) To explain why she prefers the traditional model

   (B) To describe the traditional model of literature study

   (C) To correct a student's description of a model of literature study

   (D) To compare literature courses to sociology courses

3. According to the professor, what is an advantage of the more recent model of literature study?

   (A) It includes transgressive material such as pornography.

   (B) It is more ethnocentric than prior models.

   (C) It includes works from a more diverse group of writers.

   (D) It focuses almost entirely on women and minority authors.

4. What types of writers is the professor likely to discuss in the course?

   (A) A group composed of "dead, white males"

   (B) A group composed of Caucasian women and men

   (C) A group composed primarily of men

   (D) A group composed of at least one woman, one male, and one non-Caucasian

5. Match each of the following works of literature with the model of literature study in which it would most likely be included: Traditional Model, Horizontally Expanded Model, or Vertically Expanded Model. Each model will only be used once.

Traditional Model	**Horizontally Expanded Model**	**Vertically Expanded Model**
•	•	•

A	*One Hundred Years of Solitude*
B	*Women*
C	*Moby Dick*

 Listen to Track 59.

Now answer the question.

6. (A) She is somewhat reluctant to condemn ethnocentricity.

   (B) She is displeased that the traditional model excluded certain authors.

   (C) She is worried that students were not in the right to protest over this issue.

   (D) She feels express admiration for the game of baseball.

9.7

 Listen to Track 60.

Now answer the questions.

1. What does the professor mainly talk about?

   (A) The findings of studies on bird chirping and singing

   (B) A hypothesis about the evolution of human language

   (C) The various ways that animals use expressive communication

   (D) The differences between hand gestures and vocal communication

2. Why does the student mention the animal communication that he is studying in his biology class?

   (A) To question the professor's claim that some animal communication does not send a specific message

   (B) To point out the difference between a bird's chirping and a bird's singing

   (C) To explain why he is interested in learning about language

   (D) To prove that he applied his understanding of linguistics to another course

3. What is the professor's opinion of recent research on the singing of the silvery gibbon?

   (A) She takes issue with the researchers' methods.

   (B) She sees the study as proof that human language is unique.

   (C) She thinks the study may help explain how human language first evolved.

   (D) She finds the study interesting, but believes its results are flawed.

4. According to the professor, a bird singing is most comparable to what aspect of human communication?

   (A) Gesturing

   (B) Grammar

   (C) Singing

   (D) Words

5. According to the professor, what two communication systems are uniquely combined in human language? *Choose 2 answers.*

   [A] Lexical communication

   [B] Cross-cultural communication

   [C] Nonverbal communication

   [D] Expressive communication

    Listen to Track 61.

   Now answer the question.

6. (A) To determine whether the student has done the assigned homework

   (B) To express disappointment at having to explain an issue for a second time

   (C) To clarify the use of certain terminology, at least for the present

   (D) To recommend that the student do further research on the topic

9.8

 Listen to Track 62.

Now answer the questions.

1. What is the main purpose of the lecture?

    (A) To introduce ways for students to optimize their social networks

    (B) To describe the characteristics of networks and provide examples

    (C) To explain the differences between social and neurological networks

    (D) To explain the differences between networks of fish, birds, and the brain

2. Why does the professor talk about bees?

    (A) To emphasize the importance of environmental conservation

    (B) To draw an analogy between the farming industry and naturally occurring networks

    (C) To provide an example of a keystone species in a larger network

    (D) To show how networks can change over time

3. According to the professor, which of the following are examples of networks? *Choose 2 answers.*

    [A] A football team

    [B] A neurotransmitter

    [C] A police department

    [D] A school of fish

 Listen to Track 63.

Now answer the question.

4. (A) To connect the previous examples to the main topic of the lecture

    (B) To ask students for examples of social networks

    (C) To acknowledge that she has strayed off topic

    (D) To encourage students to draw from their own experiences

5. What does the professor compare to serotonin, a neurotransmitter that impacts mood?

    (A) A company working to manufacture a product

    (B) A school of fish avoiding a predator

    (C) Vitamins C and B6 ingested as supplements

    (D) A team member who is assigned an appropriate task

6. What example of a network's resources does the professor provide?

   (A) A neurotransmitter

   (B) A football team's equipment

   (C) A school of fish

   (D) Winning a game

9.9

 Listen to Track 64.

Now answer the questions.

1. What does the professor mainly discuss?

   (A) The impact of lesions in Wernicke's Area

   (B) How scientists today relate cognition to brain activity

   (C) A theory about the localization of cognitive functions in the brain

   (D) A study on people with speech disorders

 Listen to Track 65.

Now answer the question.

2. (A) To explain why Broca decided to study this area of the brain

   (B) To describe a crucial discovery in Broca's research

   (C) To provide an alternative explanation for what was observed

   (D) To connect this observation with what Wernicke discovered

3. What does the professor say about people who have lost the ability to speak?

   (A) They often have brain abnormalities present from birth.

   (B) They are sometimes able to recover their speaking capabilities.

   (C) Many of them have lesions in Broca's Area.

   (D) Some of them have cognitive function that is not localized within parts of the brain.

4. The professor describes a speech disorder in which people cannot understand speech. What does this disorder illustrate?

    (A) An impairment not caused by damage to Broca's Area

    (B) A type of disorder that can be corrected through speech therapy

    (C) The most common type of speech disorder

    (D) Speech centers in the brain are unique compared to other cognitive functions

5. What is the professor's opinion of the cognitive functioning of the brain?

    (A) There has been little or no research on this topic.

    (B) It can only be observed in adult brains.

    (C) With further research, scientists will conclude that cognition is not localized in the brain.

    (D) It is more complex than early scientists generally believed.

6. What point does the professor make when he mentions connections between different regions of the brain?

    (A) Regions of the brain are interchangeable as long as the relevant connections stay active.

    (B) Students should continue to study connections of different areas of the brain throughout the class.

    (C) Scientists need to continue to study how cognition works before arriving at definitive conclusions.

    (D) When connections between areas of the brain are damaged, there will be no noticeable effect.

9

9.10

 Listen to Track 66.

Now answer the questions.

1. What is the main purpose of the lecture?

    (A) To elaborate on the purpose of a college education

    (B) To explain a way of framing personal and social transitions

    (C) To elaborate on the different ways in which societies celebrate coming of age

    (D) To explain the differences between adolescence and adulthood

2. Why does the professor discuss Mardi Gras and Carnaval?

    (A) To emphasize that celebrations are an important part of all societies

    (B) To draw an analogy between carnival celebrations and college graduation

    (C) To give examples of liminal time periods in different cultures

    (D) To show how carnivals have evolved differently in different places

3. According to the lecture, which of the following are examples of liminal moments? *Choose 2 answers.*

    [A] A birthday celebration

    [B] A serious accident

    [C] An election

    [D] A long-term illness

4. What example does the professor give of a rite of incorporation?

    (A) Graduating from college

    (B) Returning from a trip

    (C) Completing a large project

    (D) Attending Mardi Gras

5. Why does the professor mention the change from winter to spring?

    (A) To illustrate the annual occurrence of all liminal events

    (B) To give an example of a rite of passage

    (C) To provide an example of an entire society going through a transition

    (D) To give an example of a liminal event that makes people happy

 Listen to Track 67.

Now answer the question.

6. Why does the professor say this?

    (A) To describe death as yet another transition all people make

    (B) To conclude that liminal states are traumatic

    (C) To illustrate a rite of incorporation

    (D) To emphasize that liminal periods begin with the ending of what has come before

Answer Key—9.1

Question	Correct Answer	Right/Wrong	Category
1	B		Gist-content
2	C		Detail
3	A, C		Detail
4	D		Organization
5	B		Organization
6	D		Function of What Is Said

Answer Key—9.2

Question	Correct Answer	Right/Wrong	Category
1	C		Gist-content
2	B		Function of What Is Said
3	D		Detail
4	A		Organization
5	D		Detail
6	B		Speaker's Attitude

Answer Key—9.3

Question	Correct Answer	Right/Wrong	Category
1	A		Gist-purpose
2	A		Organization
3	B		Inference
4	A, C, D		Connecting Content
5	D		Detail
6	B		Detail

Answer Key—9.4

Question	Correct Answer	Right/Wrong	Category
1	B		Gist-content
2	A		Detail
3	B, D		Detail
4	B		Organization
5	C		Organization
6	C		Function of What Is Said

Answer Key—9.5

Question	Correct Answer	Right/Wrong	Category
1	B		Gist-content
2	B		Detail
3	C		Detail
4	D		Organization
5	A		Organization
6	C		Inference

Answer Key—9.6

Question	Correct Answer	Right/Wrong	Category
1	C		Gist-purpose
2	B		Organization
3	C		Detail
4	D		Inference
5	A: Horizontally Expanded. B: Vertically Expanded. C: Traditional.		Connecting Content
6	B		Speaker's Attitude

Answer Key—9.7

Question	Correct Answer	Right/Wrong	Category
1	B		Gist-Content
2	A		Organization
3	C		Speaker's Attitude
4	B		Detail
5	A, D		Detail
6	C		Function of What Is Said

Answer Key—9.8

Question	Correct Answer	Right/Wrong	Category
1	B		Gist-purpose
2	C		Organization
3	A, D		Detail
4	A		Function of What Is Said
5	D		Detail
6	B		Detail

Answer Key—9.9

Question	Correct Answer	Right/Wrong	Category
1	C		Gist-content
2	B		Function of What Is Said
3	C		Detail
4	A		Connecting Content
5	D		Speaker's Attitude
6	C		Organization

Answer Key—9.10

Question	Correct Answer	Right/Wrong	Category
1	B		Gist-purpose
2	C		Inference
3	A, C		Detail
4	A		Detail
5	C		Detail
6	D		Function of What Is Said

Answers and Explanations—9.1

Bike Sharing—Track 49

NARRATOR: Listen to part of a lecture in an urban planning class.

PROFESSOR: Over the last 15 to 20 years, uh, there has a been a large… push to make American cities less reliant on automobile traffic. Car congestion and noise are problems, but, uh, it is expensive and time-consuming to build the… systems for better public transportation, right? Things like buses, light rail, subways, and so on. Even with public transportation options… uh, there is also a problem known as the "last mile." So, essentially, the idea is that a bus or train can only take you so far, right? Getting that, uh, "last mile" from the bus depot or train station to your destination… like, maybe a shopping center or office… that might be difficult or frustrating. If that last bit is too much of a hassle, people might, uh… avoid public transport completely. So, well, what are cities doing about it? Well, many are turning to a program of, uh, bike sharing.

Now, the basic idea of bike sharing is to put affordable, and, uh, public… access to bicycles in urban areas. People could then travel short distances by bike rather than, say, bus or rail. It can even help with "last mile" issue, right? You take the bus part of the way, then take a bike for the final distance. So, not only does this help city visitors and residents get around, but, well… it also helps reduce traffic congestion, noise, and even air pollution. Bicycle "hubs"—basically these are large bike racks where bikes can be borrowed or returned—are placed throughout an urban area… and subscribers, or users, can rent them for, uh, short times or distances. They can even, er, borrow from one hub and return to another… they can travel between locations without going back to an earlier rental location.

Well, so bike sharing isn't actually a new idea, although, um… the version used in cities today depends on technology that didn't really exist until the mid 2000s. Old systems had no way of tracking users or bikes, so, um, at some point, many bikes were lost, stolen, or vandalized. All modern systems now track users and bikes, and many are very successful. Why?

Well, there are two essential factors to consider—bike-friendly cities and access to bikes. And both of these are equally important. Ok, now let's start with the city itself and how friendly it is for bike traffic. To be thought of as "bike friendly," there are two considerations. The physical terrain—um, that would be like…

the layout of streets, or even how hilly the city is—and access to safe spaces to ride bikes, which we'll get to in just a moment.

Now for physical terrain. What if the things people want to see in the city aren't easily connected by bike traffic—or even, what if the city has a lot of hills or uneven terrain? If, um… people find it difficult to go where they want, either, because, um, the routes are bad, or the roads are very steep, then using a bike will not be a good choice.

But what if the terrain is good? Well, this is where bike lanes come in. A bike lane is a, well, a portion of the road separated for only bike traffic. I-If cities—if roads in a city don't have lanes exclusively for bike traffic, people might not use the bike-share, w-which makes sense, because if people don't feel safe on a bike in traffic, well… they won't choose to use a bike.

OK. So that's bike friendliness, but–but what about access to the actual bikes? Well, access isn't just the number of bikes but also the location of hubs… how spread out are they… are they in good locations? So, successful systems recommend 10 to 30 bikes for every 1,000 residents in the city. The higher end is, uh, for cities with more commuters, or tourists, coming into the city—this would be additional demand beyond the actual city residents. Also, if a bike-share system, well, only covers a small corner of a city—there are only hubs in a small area—or if the hubs are spaced too far apart, it won't be as successful. Riders need to be able to find and return bikes in locations where they want to travel, without having to go extra distances.

Er, but, now, what if one component of this is missing? A city might have a system that fails to gain riders… people just don't use it. And, eh, I think a good example of this is the bike-share system in Toronto, Canada.

So, well, Toronto was already a bike-friendly city before the bike-share was introduced. They tried to space the hubs around the city, and not just in one neighborhood, b-but they didn't install enough bikes. Anyways, advisors recommended 3,000 bikes. B-but, well… the Toronto system… only installed 1,000 bikes. Well, you can imagine that people looking for bikes were often frustrated and the system almost collapsed. It wasn't until the city added an additional 1,000 bikes, umm… that the bike-share program started to be successful.

1. What is the main topic of the lecture?

GIST-CONTENT. The lecture discusses bike-sharing systems in cities, including factors that help determine whether the system will be successful.

✗ (A) New ways of implementing bike-sharing programs

New methods of implementation are alluded to, but this is not the main focus of the talk.

✓ (B) Critical factors for creating a successful bike-sharing program

CORRECT. The lecture primarily focuses on factors that determine whether a bike-sharing system is likely to succeed.

✗ (C) Where bike-sharing programs first started

This detail is mentioned, but is not the primary topic of the lecture.

✗ (D) The importance of bike-sharing programs in reducing congestion

This is mentioned as a motivation for implementing a bike-sharing program, but is not the primary topic of the lecture.

2. According to the professor, what is the primary reason for introducing a bike-sharing program in major cities?

   ✗   (A) To encourage people to purchase their own bikes

   ✗   (B) To improve access to shopping centers and attractions

   ✓   (C) To reduce car congestion and noise

   ✗   (D) To increase tourist activity in city centers

DETAIL. The professor indicates that car congestion and noise are problems that should be addressed.

The opposite is true. A bike share would mean that people do not need their own bikes.

While access to shopping centers is mentioned as an example of the "last-mile" problem, access to these destinations is not the primary reason for implementing bike sharing.

CORRECT. These reasons are explicitly stated by the professor.

Tourists are only mentioned to explain why some cities may need more shared bikes per 1,000 residents than others do.

3. When determining whether a city is "bike-friendly," what are two considerations that must be addressed? *Choose 2 answers.*

   ✓   [A] The physical terrain of the city

   ✗   [B] The number of popular tourist sites

   ✓   [C] Access to safe places to ride bikes

   ✗   [D] Availability of helmets and other biking accessories

DETAIL. The professor mentions terrain (hills and street layout) and access to safe places to ride a bike.

CORRECT. This is the primary issue in the first consideration discussed.

The professor mentions the desire to access tourist sites, but this does not affect whether a city is considered "bike-friendly."

CORRECT. This is the second consideration discussed.

These are never mentioned in the lecture.

4. Why does the professor explain the recommendations for the location and number of bikes in a bike-sharing system?

   ✗   (A) To illustrate why city governments have decided to start bike-sharing programs

   ✗   (B) To explain the differences between bike sharing and public transportation

   ✗   (C) To point out how access to bikes is more important than physical terrain

   ✓   (D) To show their importance in creating a successful bike-sharing system

ORGANIZATION. To create a successful bike-sharing program, there must be enough bikes, and those bikes must be in accessible locations.

The recommendations are not motivations to implement a bike-sharing program. They are requirements for success once a city has decided to implement one.

This comparison is never made in the lecture.

No direct comparison between access to bikes and terrain was mentioned.

CORRECT. If there are not enough bikes, or if the bike hubs are not in the right locations, people are unlikely to use them.

 MANHATTAN PREP

5. Why does the professor discuss the Toronto bike-sharing program?

ORGANIZATION. Toronto was a system that initially failed because it did not follow recommendations for the number of bikes to have available.

✗ (A) To provide an example of a typical North American bike-sharing program

It is not clear whether Toronto's program was typical of other North American programs.

✓ (B) To illustrate how poor planning can impact the success of a bike-sharing program

CORRECT. By not making enough bikes available originally, the bike-sharing program there was not successful at first.

✗ (C) To discuss which bike-sharing program she likes best

The professor never indicates her preferences.

✗ (D) To show how a bike-sharing program can be more effective than public transportation

The professor mentions that bike sharing is less expensive to set up than many other forms of public transportation, but never compares their effectiveness.

Track 50

NARRATOR: What does the professor mean when she says this:

PROFESSOR: Now for physical terrain. What if the things people want to see in the city aren't easily connected by bike traffic—or even, what if the city has a lot of hills or uneven terrain? If, um… people find it difficult to go where they want, either, because, um, the routes are bad, or the roads are very steep, then using a bike will not be a good choice.

6. What does the professor mean when she says this?

FUNCTION OF WHAT IS SAID. Here the professor is discussing the negative aspects of terrain that would make riding a bike less desireable as a means of travel a city. Therefore, she is illustrating that terrain *is* important in the decision to implement a bike-sharing program.

✗ (A) Only athletic people can use a bike-sharing program.

Not all bike-sharing programs will be in cities with difficult terrain, and the professor never claims that being athletic is a requirement for using the system.

✗ (B) The terrain of a city is of little importance when considering a bike-sharing program.

This is the opposite of what the professor indicates.

✗ (C) Steep roads and uneven surfaces are dangerous for cyclists and should be avoided.

This might be true, but it is not the meaning the professor was attempting to convey.

✓ (D) The effort required to travel by bike is an important consideration for a bike-sharing program.

CORRECT. The amount of effort required to ride a bike in a city is a consideration in whether to implement bike sharing.

909

Answers and Explanations—9.2

Freud and Jung—Track 51

NARRATOR: Listen to part of a psychology lecture. The professor is discussing psychoanalysis.

PROFESSOR: Now, many people consider Sigmund Freud to be the creator of psychoanalysis. And, just like psychoanalysts today, he believed that the solution to mental anguish lies in the subconscious mind. Many of the terms that are commonly used in psychology today—ego, libido, repression, catharsis, and neurosis—we can attribute to Freud. He ushered these and other major, commonly used terms into the field of psychology. The basic idea is that… Freud believed that while many human beings are clearly adept at lying to other human beings, the people we're really good at lying to? Yep—ourselves.

Freud believed that we rationalize why we do things, but that doesn't mean we're right about our motivations. We come up with reasons for what we do, but often, those aren't the real reasons for why we behave the way we behave. He believed that we do this because our true motivations can be difficult to face.

A metaphor that Freud used to describe the human mind was an iceberg. On the surface of the iceberg is consciousness. These are the thoughts that we are aware of. Ever heard the phrase "tip of the iceberg?" That's what our conscious thoughts are—only the tip. The second level, below the surface, are thoughts that we can pull from memory, but that we may have to work to remember. Sometimes, it takes effort. The third, and deepest, level is the unconscious mind, and this is where he believed our true motivations are stored. According to Freud, it's where our behavior originates, and where our most "primitive" desires live. He claims that, sometimes, these desires are so frightening or painful that our minds refuse to let them rise out of this bottom layer. That's why we aren't even aware of them! This phenomenon he called "repression."

FEMALE STUDENT: Professor Frank, um, did Freud consider how dreams factor in? Because we don't control our dreams. And when you're asleep, you're unconscious.

PROFESSOR: Um, he did, actually, and um… to skip a bit ahead, Freud believed that dreams are the key—the doorway—to understanding the unconscious mind. The reason for this is precisely what you seem to be suggesting… when we are asleep, our conscious mind is not repressing our unconscious mind. So it's easier for our unconscious thoughts to make their way into awareness… he called dreams "the royal road" to the unconscious.

A related theory about dreaming was developed by Carl Jung. Other than Freud, no one has had a bigger impact on dream studies than Carl Jung, who was also a psychoanalyst. Jung himself was a friend of Freud's. Their theories about dreaming overlap in important ways. They both believe that dreams can reveal much about what goes on in the unconscious mind… but unlike Freud, Jung did not believe that dreams necessarily bring up things that we are trying to repress. For Jung, the way that dreams are useful isn't that they should be interpreted to discover true motivations… but that the point of them is to integrate the conscious and unconscious minds. They are the brain's attempt to feel "whole," in other words.

Another major difference between Jung and Freud is that Jung didn't just believe that individuals have an unconscious. He also believed in something he called the "collective unconscious." It's the collection of all human experiences and knowledge, like a sort of, ah, atmosphere, in which people exist… the collective unconscious is why we feel connected to each other, according to Jung. For him, things like art, and religion, and even myths and stories… these are all a part of this collective unconscious.

  **MANHATTAN** PREP

There's more that Jung is known for—ever hear of the terms *introvert* and *extrovert*? These days, the terms are used to describe personality types. Introverts are said to draw energy from the internal world, within themselves, and extroverts do so more from the outside world. It's become a popular distinction in recent years. There are personality tests that will tell you whether you are an introvert or an extrovert… well, Jung created the ideas of extroversion and introversion. That was him.

But back to dreaming. To recap, Freud believed that dreams are about unearthing repressed ideas. And Jung believed that dreams are the way that our minds create a sense of wholeness. Is one right and one wrong? I think the answer is that we don't know. It's probably impossible to definitively understand the nature of dreaming.

1.	What does the professor mainly discuss?	**GIST-CONTENT.** The lecture is about two different psychoanalysts and how their theories compare, particularly with respect to dreaming.
✗ (A)	The evolution of dreaming in human beings	The professor does not discuss the evolution of dreaming.
✗ (B)	How dreaming occurs in the brain	The professor does not discuss the mechanisms of dreaming in the brain.
✓ (C)	Theories from two psychoanalysts about dreaming	**CORRECT.** The professor describes Freud's theory of dreaming, then follows it with a description of Jung's theory.
✗ (D)	One scientist's research into how people dream	The lecture is about two psychoanalysts—Freud and Jung.

9

Track 52

NARRATOR: Listen again to part of the lecture. Then answer the question.

PROFESSOR: He believed that we do this because our true motivations can be difficult to face.

A metaphor that Freud used to describe the human mind was an iceberg. On the surface of the iceberg is consciousness. These are the thoughts that we are aware of. Ever heard the phrase "tip of the iceberg?" That's what our conscious thoughts are—only the tip. The second level, below the surface, are thoughts that we can pull from memory, but that we may have to work to remember. Sometimes, it takes effort. The third, and deepest, level is the unconscious mind, and this is where he believed our true motivations are stored. According to Freud, it's where our behavior originates, and where our most "primitive" desires live.

NARRATOR: Why does the professor say this:

PROFESSOR: A metaphor that Freud used to describe the human mind was an iceberg.

2.   Why does the professor say this?

   ✗ Ⓐ To describe how the human brain is physically organized

   ✓ Ⓑ To illustrate Freud's distinct categories of consciousness

   ✗ Ⓒ To explain why Freud became a psychoanalyst

   ✗ Ⓓ To remind students of a previous point

FUNCTION OF WHAT IS SAID. The professor mentions the iceberg as a metaphor that Freud used to describe his theory of consciousness.

The professor is not arguing that the human brain is physically organized like an iceberg.

CORRECT. The iceberg metaphor is used to illustrate levels of consciousness, according to Freud.

The professor never discussed why Freud became a psychoanalyst.

The discussion of the iceberg is meant to illustrate a new idea, not a previous point.

3.   What does the professor say about art and religion?

   ✗ Ⓐ That it is not possible to understand why they exist, according to Freud

   ✗ Ⓑ That they are the opposite of dreaming, according to Jung

   ✗ Ⓒ That Freud studied them to better understand dreams

   ✓ Ⓓ That they are part of the collective unconscious, according to Jung

DETAIL. The professor states that Jung viewed art and religion as part of a "collective unconscious."

The professor does not discuss art or religion in relation to Freud.

The professor does not state that Jung believed this.

The professor does not discuss art or religion in relation to Freud.

CORRECT. This is the context in which art and religion are mentioned by the professor.

4.   What point does the professor make when he refers to introverts and extroverts?

   ✓ Ⓐ Jung was the one who created these terms.

   ✗ Ⓑ Students should become aware of which category they fall in.

   ✗ Ⓒ All people are chiefly one or the other, but not both.

   ✗ Ⓓ The concepts of introversion and extroversion introduced him to Jung.

ORGANIZATION. The professor states that Jung created these categories.

CORRECT. The point the professor is making is that Jung created these categories.

The professor does not mention this idea in the lecture.

The professor does not state this in the lecture.

The professor does not state this in the lecture.

9

5. The professor describes the collective unconscious to the class. What is this description about?

   ✗ (A) How Freud invented psychoanalysis

   ✗ (B) How the collective unconscious is the tip of the iceberg for human thinking

   ✗ (C) Why Freud did not believe in a collective unconscious

   ✓ (D) Jung's belief that this is how humans feel connected to one another

DETAIL. The professor describes the collective unconscious as a cultural "atmosphere," which includes art and religion as institutions that connect people to one another.

The professor does not discuss the collective unconscious in relation to Freud.

The professor does not discuss the collective unconscious in relation to the iceberg metaphor.

The professor does not discuss the collective unconscious in relation to Freud.

CORRECT. The professor describes Jung's view of the collective unconscious as institutions that connect people.

6. What is the professor's opinion of dream interpretation?

   ✗ (A) Jung is more in line with scientific perspectives than Freud is.

   ✓ (B) Developing a perfect understanding of the nature of dreaming may not be possible.

   ✗ (C) Freud's work is more applicable to modern dreaming than Jung's work is.

   ✗ (D) It is more valid to believe in a collective unconscious than to not believe in one.

SPEAKER'S ATTITUDE. The professor believes that while Jung and Freud held different views of dreaming, whether one is more correct than the other is unknown and perhaps cannot be known. He expresses this view at the end of the lecture.

The professor does not state or imply this.

CORRECT. This is the view expressed by the professor at the conclusion of the lecture.

The professor does not state or imply this. There was also no discussion of "modern dreaming" as distinct from other kinds of dreaming.

The professor does not state or imply this.

Answers and Explanations—9.3

Childhood Cognitive Development—Track 53

NARRATOR: Listen to part of a lecture in a psychology class.

PROFESSOR: Ok, each of you is here to learn, to further your cognitive development. But what was the very first thing you learned? Before high school, you knew basic math and language. Before elementary school, you knew how to speak and maybe even how to read, right? Well, how–how does a child first start this process of cognitive development?

Before the eighteenth century, there were, um… a few speculations on what knowledge was already present within a newborn child. Some thought children were born evil, others thought they were naturally good, and still others thought they were a blank slate, waiting to be taught. And… and these theories were based on… well–well, they're based on a combination of religion and philosophy, not the scientific

processes that I want to talk about today. So—so let's focus on when childhood development started to be studied scientifically. OK? It—it could be that there is some innate knowledge every child is born with, and it builds on that as it grows up. That's one theory. Another option is that children are born with, um, with no knowledge, but learn from their environment. And that idea… um, that children learn exclusively from interactions, um… that was the original scientific theory of childhood cognitive development introduced by Jean Piaget.

Jean Piaget hypothesized that there were four cognitive stages that every child had to go through. So… Piaget thought that a newborn would start interacting with his or her environment, learn everything it could at that stage, then move on to the next stage, building on the previous experiences. Everybody understand? While each child could reach these different stages at different ages, Piaget believed that the stages must be completed in order. Modern theories have broadened that to allow for some… for some overlap of the stages. These theories also include the possibility that different domains, like language and mathematics, could advance at different rates. So—so for example, a child could be at stage three of language learning, but only stage one of mathematical reasoning. And this model is still in use and heavily re–relied upon today.

Well, later theories have questioned this progression of stages. Studies have shown that infants—as young as a few months—do have the ability to reason at the supposedly advanced stages. Studies show children separating models of living things from models of inanimate things. They act surprised when an inanimate object moves, but not when a living object moves. They even seem to understand the basic laws of physics. Adults created a room that was half covered with glass, with what appeared to be a drop of a few feet to the room below. At a certain age, children refuse to crawl over the glass floor, believing it would let them fall. But how could they have that knowledge? Presumably, they have never experienced a fall from that height. This inductive reasoning should only exist after years of learning in Piaget's model. Similarly, infants were shown two solid objects that seemed to approach each other, but stop before colliding, then an illusion of the same two solid objects seeming to move through each other. Infants were more attentive to the apparently impossible situation. Even children as young as five months old! Now, if they haven't had time to advance through the lower stages, how can they be showing advanced stage reasoning? That's a hard question to answer, since our knowledge is generally built from the bottom up. I guess I should add that it is very hard to assess a child's reasoning when it's less than a few months old, so we don't have studies on children at the earliest stages of life. But that's not the main issue here…

Some reasoning, especially with language, seems impossible to learn as completely as infants do with the inputs that they have. Even if you assume they start to hear and learn language while still in the womb, there doesn't seem to be enough time and exposure to language for an infant to become fluent. How do children understand sentences they have never heard? Some theorize that children must be born with some innate ability to perceive and translate a grammatical structure… sort of a skeleton on which a child can build a language. But how would we test for that? Current scientific thinking is that there must be some mix between innate and staged learning, but we'll need much more study to say for sure.

1.   What is the main purpose of the talk?

   ✓ (A) To discuss possible ways infants learn

   ✗ (B) To describe key considerations of learning language

   ✗ (C) To explain processes used to test learning in infants

   ✗ (D) To discuss why it is so difficult to learn a language after infancy

GIST-PURPOSE. The primary focus of the lecture is different theories about the cognitive development of children.

CORRECT. The lecture touches on multiple theories and studies related to how children learn.

The lecture is not limited to learning language, but is about childhood learning in general.

While studies are discussed, the main purpose is not to talk about the studies, but to talk about what they imply.

No learning after infancy is discussed. Moreover, the lecture is not restricted to languages.

2.   Why does the professor ask students about the first thing they learned?

   ✓ (A) To engage students in the topic she is about to discuss

   ✗ (B) To establish that everyone learns similar things in infancy

   ✗ (C) To introduce the difficulty of learning a language

   ✗ (D) To illustrate that learning stages can occur at different times for different people

ORGANIZATION. This was asked in the first part of the lecture.

CORRECT. This introductory question is never answered, but is used to get students to start thinking about the topic of the lecture—childhood learning.

This is never suggested in the lecture.

Language is not brought up until later, and the students' experience with learning language is never discussed.

This is stated later, but not in reference to the students' experiences.

3.   What does the professor imply about some of the theories for how infants begin learning?

   ✗ (A) They cannot be scientifically proven or disproven.

   ✓ (B) They do not have scientific evidence to support them.

   ✗ (C) They explain only how a child learns language.

   ✗ (D) They have been disproven by her research.

INFERENCE. Several theories are discussed. Piaget's is the only one discussed in depth, but others are mentioned and dismissed or described as needing further study.

This is too extreme. The professor thinks some of them haven't yet been proven or disproven, but doesn't comment on whether they could be.

CORRECT. This is why she dismisses the theories based on the innate morality of a child. They are based on religion and philosophy, not scientific evidence.

None of the theories focus on any particular learning area.

The professor never discusses her own research.

9

4. The professor mentions a number of theories for early learning methods. Select each of the following that is one of the theories she mentions.

CONNECTING CONTENT. The professor mentions a variety of theories about learning throughout the lecture. Most theories mentioned are either dismissed as unproven or are noted as being worthy of further study.

✓ ☐A When children are born, they are inherently good.

CORRECT. This is dismissed as scientifically unproven, but this theory is presented.

✗ ☐B Learning occurs at a constant rate over a lifetime.

This idea is never mentioned in the lecture.

✓ ☐C Children are born with some innate knowledge.

CORRECT. This is presented as a possible explanation for how language learning occurs.

✓ ☐D Learning occurs in progressive stages.

CORRECT. This is Piaget's theory on how childhood learning occurs.

✗ ☐E All children master stages of learning at essentially the same time.

This is contradicted in the lecture. Different stages start and end at different times for each child.

5. How was advanced reasoning studied in infants?

DETAIL. The professor mentions several studies conducted to assess advanced reasoning capabilities in children.

✗ Ⓐ By recording how often infants made reasonable decisions

There was no decision-making testing discussed in the lecture.

✗ Ⓑ By observing how children interacted with one another

This idea was never mentioned in the lecture.

✗ Ⓒ By having children repeat the actions of the researchers who conducted the experiments

This idea was never mentioned in the lecture.

✓ Ⓓ By monitoring the attention levels of infants to possible and seemingly impossible events

CORRECT. Different objects were moved in front of children, and the children were more engaged in those that seemed to violate the laws of physics.

6. The professor mentioned a study that tested the ability of children to understand a seemingly dangerous fall. What did the researchers conclude from this study?

DETAIL. This refers to the study of infants who refused to crawl over a glass floor, believing they would fall.

✗ Ⓐ Infants learn by progressing through different stages of understanding.

This is Piaget's theory, but the described study does not support it.

✓ Ⓑ Infants sometimes show more advanced reasoning than is suggested by Piaget's theories.

CORRECT. This study showed an understanding of basic laws of physics and advanced reasoning techniques that should only be present at the highest of Piaget's stages.

✗ Ⓒ Infants typically demonstrate reasoning starting at about nine months.

The age of the children in the study is not mentioned.

✗ Ⓓ Advanced reasoning skill development is dependent upon rational thought.

Rational thought is not mentioned, and there's no discussion about what the understanding of the situation depends upon.

Answers and Explanations—9.4

Shopping Malls—Track 54

NARRATOR: Listen to part of a lecture in a city planning class.

PROFESSOR: As you may know, many American cities now have what are referred to as "dead malls." These are shopping malls built during the latter half of the twentieth century that have, um, started to struggle… or even have closed. By 2014, around one out of every five malls had vacancies of 10 percent or more. And 3 percent of them are considered "dying," which is defined as, um… being over 40 percent vacant, or empty.

But well into the 1990s, shopping malls were still being built. And at a pretty high rate—140 malls a year! So what happened? Because by, um, 2007… there was not a single mall built that year. And you may not remember, but that was actually just before the Great Recession really got underway in 2008, so we can't say that that's the cause of it.

There are some different theories about the decline of malls, but what may help us understand is if we go back to why the shopping mall was created in the first place. When I talk about a shopping mall, I'm talking about an enclosed space, where people can come and shop from a collection of different merchants who sell different things… this kind of shopping mall is one you'd find in any suburban area, these days. It may not surprise you that this phenomenon didn't really explode in the United States until after automobile use became widespread. Why? Because malls are often in locations that you have to drive to. So their appearance overlaps with, um… the spread of suburban culture—people moving out of cities, into the suburbs, and relying on their cars more to get around.

American shopping malls began popping up in the 1950s and 1960s. In 1960, legislation was passed by the United States government that allowed for something called REITs—that stands for Real Estate Investment Trusts. Under these REITs, people could come together and invest directly in commercial property construction. So REITs became a way of gathering capital, or money, to build income-generating real estate. Now, these could be hotels, office buildings, even hospitals… and, most importantly for our discussion today, shopping malls. Centers for retail.

This is not to say that shopping malls are an American invention. I mean, they've actually been around, well… there were even public shopping centers comparable to malls in Ancient Rome. There's a market in Rome called Trajan's Market that was built thousands of years ago—it was called an arcade, meaning, a shopping structure ringed by arches. It is believed to be the world's oldest shopping mall. Ever since, shopping centers have appeared in civilizations all over the world—India, Turkey, England…I could go on. Human beings are social, and creating places to congregate and also shop seems to be a pretty universal practice.

But the American version of malls became its own kind of distinct phenomenon in the late twentieth century. The "mega-mall," or giant mall, was created. The Mall of America, in Bloomington, Minnesota, is the largest mall in the United States. It opened in 1992. In total, it has just over 450,000 square meters of floor space. For reference…that is big enough to fit 9 Yankee Stadiums, or more than 40 Boeing 747 airplanes. Crazy, right? It's huge.

This mall is still operational. It is not a dead mall. But the Mall of America, in this regard, is not representative of the trend for American shopping malls in the twenty-first century. Is it that people aren't shopping as much? Or something else?

One theory is that the invention of the internet changed the retail business model—as it has changed so many other business models. People are buying things online now. They aren't getting in their cars and

driving across town to get to a mall to buy a t-shirt—they're just ordering the t-shirt online, then waiting for it to show up at their door. This certainly seems plausible.

Another theory is that shopping malls simply became too numerous. Perhaps at some point, there was just no way all of them were going to survive. If people have one or two malls to choose from, well, that's one thing. But if there are five or six within driving distance… that makes it more difficult for all of them to attract enough customers to survive.

So, uh, many of these dead malls are closing down. And so you end up having these… these big, hollowed-out buildings—almost like ghost towns—that are peppering the outer edges of cities all over the United States.

1.	What is the main subject of the lecture?	**GIST-CONTENT.** The lecture primarily discusses shopping malls in the United States, and why they are experiencing a decline.
✗	(A) The rise of shopping malls in ancient Rome	While a shopping mall from ancient Rome is mentioned, this is not the main topic of the lecture.
✓	(B) The current decline of shopping malls in the United States	**CORRECT.** The professor opens and closes the lecture by discussing the decline of malls in the United States.
✗	(C) How to design a successful shopping mall	The lecture is not focused on how to design a successful mall.
✗	(D) Reasons why shopping malls can be detrimental to civic life	The professor does not make this argument.

2.	According to the professor, why did shopping malls appear in America when and where they did?	**DETAIL.** The professor states that shopping malls appeared once automobile use was widespread, and people were moving to the suburbs.
✓	(A) The migration of people to the suburbs, coupled with the proliferation of automobiles	**CORRECT.** The professor states this directly in the lecture.
✗	(B) The movement of the population to urban areas from suburban ones	The professor describes a trend in the opposite direction.
✗	(C) The desire of city planners to improve social life for suburban residents	The desires of city planners are not discussed in the lecture.
✗	(D) The pressure placed on city planners by citizens to create shopping centers like the ones in Europe	The professor does not discuss pressure from citizens on city planners in the lecture.

3. What are two theories that the professor mentions as to why shopping malls are struggling in the 21st century? *Choose 2 answers.*

    ✗   A Most malls are not large enough to accommodate the required foot traffic.

    ✓   B There are too many malls close to one another in some areas.

    ✗   C People are now moving back into cities, away from suburbs.

    ✓   D Many people are now shopping online.

DETAIL. The professor describes the impact of the internet on people's shopping habits. She also mentions that there may be too many malls competing for the same customers.

The size of malls is not given as a reason that malls are declining.

CORRECT. The professor mentions this in the lecture.

This idea is not discussed in the lecture.

CORRECT. The professor mentions this in the lecture.

4. Why does the professor discuss the Mall of America?

    ✗   (A) To demonstrate how the success or failure of a shopping mall depends on its size

    ✓   (B) To provide an example of a specific type of American shopping mall

    ✗   (C) To illustrate the trend in American shopping malls in the 21st century

    ✗   (D) To show how designing a mall that is too large can lead to problems later

ORGANIZATION. The professor mentions the Mall of America as an example of a "mega-mall," or giant mall.

This is not the purpose for discussing this mall. While it is a notably large mall that hasn't struggled like many other large malls, the professor does not suggest that the reason for its success is its size.

CORRECT. It is mentioned as an example of a "mega-mall," or giant mall.

The Mall of America does *not* follow this trend, according to the professor.

This was not suggested in the lecture.

9

5. Why does the professor mention Real Estate Investment Trusts, or REITs?

    ✗   (A) To discuss her least favorite aspect of city planning

    ✗   (B) To give an example of a challenge that investors in shopping malls faced

    ✓   (C) To provide context for the rise of American shopping malls in the 1960s

    ✗   (D) To argue that, if not for REITs, shopping malls would not exist

ORGANIZATION. The professor mentions REITs as context for the appearance of American shopping malls. REITs provided the capital, or financing, needed to build them.

The professor does not express a personal opinion about REITs.

REITs were not a challenge to shopping mall investors—rather, they provided a vehicle for investing directly in shopping malls.

CORRECT. The professor mentions REITs to provide context for the rise of shopping malls.

The professor does not make this argument in the lecture. REITs facilitated the development of malls, but malls existed before REITs were invented.

Track 55

NARRATOR: What does the professor mean when she says this:

PROFESSOR: By, um, 2007… there was not a single mall built that year. And you may not remember, but that was actually just before the Great Recession really got underway in 2008…

6. What does the professor mean when she says this?

FUNCTION OF WHAT IS SAID. This quote lays out the timeline of when malls began to decline in the United States relative to the Great Recession of 2008. Specifically, shopping malls began to decline before the recession.

✗ (A) Shopping malls stopped being built largely because of the Great Recession.

The professor is making the opposite point—that malls were already declining before the recession.

✗ (B) The Great Recession began earlier than 2008, along with the decline in shopping malls.

This is not what the professor is arguing or suggesting.

✓ (C) The Great Recession alone cannot explain the decline in shopping malls.

CORRECT. The professor's point is that the recession is not what caused the decline in shopping malls to begin. The recession really started after the decline in shopping malls began.

✗ (D) Most malls did not survive the impact of the Great Recession.

This is not a point made in the lecture.

Answers and Explanations—9.5

Minimum Viable Product—Track 56

NARRATOR: Listen to part of a lecture in a business class.

PROFESSOR: OK, as we've talked about, when developing a new product, it's important to make sure that you aren't wasting dollars creating something that customers don't actually want. In order to avoid doing this, you want to make sure you have a solid understanding of what customers actually want before you pour a lot of money into designing a product. So with this as our goal, I want to tell you about an approach to product development that helps address this concern. It is called MVP, or Minimum Viable Product.

Now, you may have heard "MVP" before in relation to sports. In sports, it means "Most Valuable Player." But in business, it's different. In fact, it's almost the opposite. The idea is that you design a product that is not at all sophisticated or fancy. It only has the minimum number of features necessary to distribute to a small number of customers, so that you can learn from them. You test this very basic product with a small number of customers in order to discover what they want, and you continue development from there. 'Cause this is great way to discover what your product's needs are before you invest a lot of money designing features that aren't essential… features that your customers may not want or need.

FEMALE STUDENT: But don't you think it is kind of dangerous to do that? People aren't going to want a product that is so basic, it isn't special. Maybe they won't even understand what about it is different from other, similar products, or see what about it should attract them.

PROFESSOR: That's a good point. Here is the key—you are not trying to sell this product to a large number of customers. The MVP is not a strategy to attract to every potential customer in your market. That is not the point. The point is that you're targeting a small set of customers who you think of as… visionaries. People who can help you envision what other features this product should have.

And you need to remember what the goal is, here. The MVP is not about selling a finished product. It is not about perfection. It's about combating perfectionism early in the process of product development, because attempting perfection early on can be detrimental. First, because trying to design the perfect product before you've done user research can lead to many wasted hours of work. For example, your engineers spend hours and hours creating a feature that may not be very valuable to customers, or that they don't even care about at all! And second, trying to create the perfect product typically lengthens the amount of time you spend working on the product. This delays actually getting the product into the hands of customers so that you can learn from them. Again—I don't mean all customers. I mean select ones.

MALE STUDENT: Well, I would expect that customers don't always know what they want anyway. I mean, how do you trust such a small sample size? If it's only a small group of customers, they may not represent the desires of all of your customers, right?

PROFESSOR: Let's remember that you are listening to how your visionary customers respond to your MVP so that you can decide whether to implement their ideas into future versions of your product. You aren't obliged to do anything you don't want to do. The point of releasing an MVP, which again, means Minimum Viable Product, is to gather information for your benefit. And also remember… if we're talking about the number of customers you release the MVP to… that's up to you! You want to balance considerations… how many customers do you want to hear from to feel you can rely on their responses? You don't want to go too small, as you say, but you also don't want to go bigger than you need to, because you aren't trying to sell the MVP to all potential customers. That comes later. It's important to keep in mind what your goal is when deploying an MVP.

1.   What is the lecture primarily about?

    GIST-CONTENT. The lecture is about a product development method called the Minimum Viable Product, or MVP.

✗ (A) A management strategy in business that improves employee morale

    The lecture is not about a employee morale. It is about a product development strategy.

✓ (B) An approach to product development and why it can be useful

    CORRECT. This is the main topic of the lecture.

✗ (C) Two methods for maximizing efficiency in business

    The lecture is only about one method.

✗ (D) A tool that customers can use in evaluating whether to buy a product

    The MVP isn't a tool that customers buying a product use. It's a tool for managing product development.

2.   According to the professor, what is a
       potential benefit of the MVP strategy?

   DETAIL. The MVP strategy is a method of releasing an early version of a product to a small number of customers to learn from them before investing more resources in developing the product.

✗ (A) It can contribute to the design of a
       nearly perfect product early in the
       development process.

   The professor says the opposite is true—MVP is used to combat perfectionism early in the product development cycle.

✓ (B) It can help product developers avoid
       many wasted hours of work.

   CORRECT. The professor states that it can save developers from spending time working on features that may not ultimately be included in the product.

✗ (C) It can relieve anxiety among product
       developers.

   The professor does not discuss anxiety.

✗ (D) It drives engineers to work more
       quickly.

   The professor does not suggest that the MVP increases the rate at which engineers work.

3.   What does the professor say about customers
       that use the MVP?

   DETAIL. The professor says that customers to whom an MVP is released can help a product developer make decisions about the future vision of the product.

✗ (A) An MVP should appeal to the largest
       possible number of potential
       customers.

   The professor states the opposite in the lecture—the MVP is designed to provide the minimum number of required features to allow early users to help decide what other features to include.

✗ (B) An MVP is created solely for the
       purpose of hypothetical distribution
       and will not be shown to actual
       customers.

   The MVP is meant to be released to actual customers, not hypothetical ones.

✓ (C) An MVP is designed for release to a
       small number of select customers.

   CORRECT. The professor is clear that an MVP is not meant to appeal to a large number of customers, but is meant to be released to a targeted group.

✗ (D) An MVP evaluation always produces
       conflicting requests from different
       customers that must be resolved.

   While users of the MVP may have different ideas about what features to add, it is not the case that conflicting requests "always" occur.

4. Why does the professor mention that in sports, MVP is used to mean "Most Valuable Player?"

   ✗ (A) To give an example of another industry that uses an MVP

   ✗ (B) To illustrate the usefulness of the concept across multiple industries

   ✗ (C) To emphasize that MVP means essentially the same thing in both sports and product development

   ✓ (D) To explain that the meaning of MVP in the context of product development is different

ORGANIZATION. At the beginning of the lecture, the professor mentions that in sports, MVP means "Most Valuable Player." This definition is given to contrast its meaning in a business context.

The question asks *why* the professor mentions the definition of MVP in sports. The reason is not merely to show that MVP is a term used in another industry as well.

The professor's point is that MVP is a different concept in the sports industry than it is in product development.

The professor states the opposite—MVP in sports has a very different meaning from MVP in product development.

CORRECT. The professor's point is that in business, MVP means something very different than it does in sports.

5. Why does the professor use the term "visionaries"?

   ✓ (A) To identify the kind of customers an MVP should target

   ✗ (B) To name a group of customers who would prefer an MVP over a more developed product

   ✗ (C) To offer an example of how an MVP can originate from anywhere within a company

   ✗ (D) To emphasize the importance of inspired engineers in product development

ORGANIZATION. The professor describes the select group of customers to whom the MVP is released as "visionaries," in that they can assist in furthering the vision of the product.

CORRECT. These are the people that should be targeted by an MVP.

The point is not that these customers prefer an MVP over a more developed product.

MVP is a product that is released to visionary customers.

Engineering is not relevant to this part of the lecture.

Track 57

NARRATOR: What does the professor imply when she says this:

PROFESSOR: And also remember… if we're talking about the number of customers you release the MVP to… that's up to you!

6.   What does the professor imply when she says this?

   ✗   (A) The MVP is exclusively designed by the product manager.

   ✗   (B) It is unlikely that anyone but the product manager would have a strong opinion on the number of customers targeted by an MVP.

   ✓   (C) The MVP approach can be customized by whoever is managing product development.

   ✗   (D) It is concerning that the MVP would be released to more than a few customers, but ultimately that is the product manager's decision.

INFERENCE. In this quote, the professor is reminding students that the number of customers to whom an MVP is released is not predetermined.

"Exclusively" is a strong word. Furthermore, this quote is about the decision of how many customers to distribute the MVP to, not who designs the MVP.

The professor does not contrast various roles within a project, and does not imply that only the product manager would have an opinion on this issue.

CORRECT. The specific decisions within the MVP approach, such as how many customers to target, is up to product developers.

She does not convey concern about the issue of MVP customer group size. She is making a more neutral point.

Answers and Explanations—9.6

Models of Literary Study—Track 58

NARRATOR: Listen to part of a lecture in a sociology class.

PROFESSOR: So, this course is called Models of Literary Study, hosted by the Sociology department. I know that, for one, you are here because it is a required course. But maybe some of you spent a little time thinking about what this course would be like. Besides a lot of reading and a lot of work. Does anyone have any idea?

FEMALE STUDENT: Well… um… about great writers—like, like Hemingway, uh, or F. Scott Fitzgerald or Mark Twain. And about books like… I don't know… the books everybody should read. Like *Moby Dick!* That's one.

PROFESSOR: I see. Yes, the books everybody—at least everybody educated in literature—should read. That's a pretty good description of the traditional model of literature study. That's the way I studied it in high school and college. Of course, that was so long ago that we had to stop and push the horseless carriages when we were walking five miles to school in the snow. Ha ha.

In fact, I would say that that was the model for studying literature at the first United States universities when they were founded, and it remained that way for a couple of hundred years thereafter. There was this concept called the "Canon of Western Literature." Do you know what that was? It's what Beth said—the books everybody should read. Now this list has changed, but very, very slowly—over many years. When I was in school we read books like, um, *You Can't Go Home Again, Tender Is the Night, The Sound and the Fury, The Ambassadors…* and yes, *Moby Dick*. Books by authors such as Thomas Wolfe, F. Scott Fitzgerald, William Faulkner, Henry James, Herman Melville. Back then, literature was probably a bigger part of popular culture—there weren't very many television channels, and nothing like video games or the internet. So studying these works imparted a uniform set of values, norms, and expectations.

Now, don't get me wrong. There was some good stuff there. And noble sentiments. But eventually, in the 1960s, people—especially students—started to question the virtue of cultural uniformity. You see, the student population had become more diverse and found the canon kind of narrow. Did anyone notice anything about the names I mentioned? They're all men. They're all Caucasian men. Students began to protest—they called them "dead white males." And it represented ethnocentricity, or a belief that one's own ethnicity or culture is better than others. This ethnocentricity was pretty deeply embedded in society until this awakening. I mean, it was the same mindset that named the United States professional baseball championship "The *World* Series." In any case, works by women and minorities just weren't given the same respect, on the whole.

Before too long, and to their credit, the universities changed. The canon was largely abandoned as the standard, and a new model inserted other worthy and long-neglected works in literature courses. So, here, while we will look at Wolfe and Sinclair Lewis, because they're my favorite "dead white males," we're going to study *One Hundred Years of Solitude* by Gabriel Garcia Marquez and *Play It as It Lays* by Joan Didion, just to name a couple. And I'd like each of you to submit a favorite of yours and we'll include one of those too.

So to sum up the ground we've covered, the model of literature study became horizontally bigger, as the range of authors included greatly expanded. In the time we have left, I'd like to also discuss what I call a vertical expansion of the model. What do I mean by that? I mean that the uniform culture also enforced informal and formal censorship—sometimes concerning political matters, but mostly concerning sexual topics. Publishers were very quick to refuse material that violated polite conventions for moral as well as commercial motives. Governments, including those of the United States and United Kingdom, banned some such books well into the twentieth century. James Joyce's *Ulysses*, now part of the established canon we teach today, was banned for obscenity. As were novels by Henry Miller and others.

However, the formation of a more diverse society, especially after the Second World War, led to a rejection—or relaxation—of the moral code commonly associated with the Victorian period in the nineteenth century. Formerly taboo topics were now discussed at social gatherings and in acclaimed literature. We are not speaking of pornography, which admittedly became more prominent as well, but of writers like, uh, Charles Bukowski, whose work—such as his novel *Women*—was very… frank. Mirroring society, the model of literature study began to include such works as well. Thus, I call it a vertical expansion. I hope that this course, then, will vertically *and* horizontally expand your experience with classic literature.

9

1.   What is the main purpose of this lecture?

   GIST-PURPOSE. The lecture discusses the traditional model of literature study in US universities, and how it has changed.

   ✗   (A) To compare the study of sociology with the study of literature

   The professor notes that the course covers literature, even though it is hosted by the sociology department. She does not compare literature study with any other field.

   ✗   (B) To explain the value of studying literature as a serious endeavor

   The lecture discusses the scope of literature covered, not the value of studying it.

   ✓   (C) To explore the traditional model of literature study and how that study has changed

   CORRECT. The professor begins with a discussion of the original model based on the "Canon of Western Literature." She goes on to explain that it has been largely replaced by a new, expanded model that covers more subjects and more authors.

   ✗   (D) To explain the origins of the study of literature in the United States

   This is only briefly mentioned by the professor.

2.   Why does the professor mention the "Canon of Western Literature?"

ORGANIZATION. She does so to describe the traditional model of literature study.

✗   (A) To explain why she prefers the traditional model

The opposite is true. The professor implies that she prefers the new, expanded model.

✓   (B) To describe the traditional model of literature study

CORRECT. The professor notes that the traditional model is based on the "Canon of Western Literature."

✗   (C) To correct a student's description of a model of literature study

On the contrary—the professor mostly agrees with the student's description, as it applies to the traditional model.

✗   (D) To compare literature courses to sociology courses

The professor does not compare different types of courses.

3.   According to the professor, what is an advantage of the more recent model of literature study?

DETAIL. It includes works from a more diverse group of authors, covering more diverse subjects.

✗   (A) It includes transgressive material, such as pornography.

The professor mentions pornography only to imply that it is *not* included in the more recent model.

✗   (B) It is more ethnocentric than prior models.

The opposite is true. The professor states that the traditional model was ethnocentric.

✓   (C) It includes works from a more diverse group of writers.

CORRECT. The professor describes the inclusion of authors from diverse backgrounds as a virtue.

✗   (D) It focuses almost entirely on women and minority authors.

The professor says that the more recent model includes women and minority authors. She does not state that it focuses *almost entirely* on them.

4.   What types of writers is the professor likely to discuss in the course?

INFERENCE. In previewing the authors to be discussed, the professor lists two white men, a woman, and, by inference, a non-Caucasian man. She notes that the course will also include an author selected by the class.

✗   (A) A group composed of "dead, white males"

This refers to the traditional model, not the current model that the professor intends to use.

✗   (B) A group composed of Caucasian women and men

The professor implies that the writers discussed will include minorities.

✗   (C) A group composed primarily of men

While the list of books she mentions includes mostly male authors, she does not give the full list of books for the course, so this is not certain.

✓   (D) A group composed of at least one woman, one male, and one non-Caucasian

CORRECT. In previewing the authors to be discussed, the professor lists two white men, a woman, and, by inference, a non-Caucasian man.

5. Match each of the following works of literature with the model of literature study in which it would most likely be included: Traditional Model, Horizontally Expanded Model, or Vertically Expanded Model. Each model will only be used once.

    | A | *One Hundred Years of Solitude* |

    | B | *Women* |

    | C | *Moby Dick* |

CONNECTING CONTENT. *Moby Dick* is mentioned as part of the traditional model. *One Hundred Years of Solitude* is mentioned as part of the "horizontally expanded" model. *Women* is mentioned as part of the "vertically expanded" model.

HORIZONTALLY EXPANDED MODEL. *One Hundred Years of Solitude* is mentioned when the professor discusses the "horizontally expanded" model.

VERTICALLY EXPANDED MODEL. *Women* is mentioned when the professor discusses the "vertically expanded" model.

TRADITIONAL MODEL. The professor notes that *Moby Dick*, mentioned by a student, fits into the traditional model of literature study.

Track 59

NARRATOR: Listen again to part of the lecture. Then answer the question.

PROFESSOR: Did anyone notice anything about the names I mentioned? They're all men. They're all Caucasian men. Students began to protest—they called them "dead white males." And it represented ethnocentricity, or a belief that one's own ethnicity or culture is better than others. This ethnocentricity was pretty deeply embedded in society until this awakening. I mean, it was the same mindset that named the United States professional baseball championship "The *World* Series."

NARRATOR: What is the professor's attitude?

6. **SPEAKER'S ATTITUDE.** The professor emphasizes how exclusionary the traditional model was, and uses the naming of "The World Series" as an example of the ethnocentricity of society at the time.

    ✗ (A) She is somewhat reluctant to condemn ethnocentricity.

    The opposite is true. In this quote, the professor implies that ethnocentricity is unfair to certain groups.

    ✓ (B) She is displeased that the traditional model excluded certain authors.

    CORRECT. The professor's quote focuses on the lack of non-Caucasian authors and lack of female authors. It also implicitly criticizes the ethnocentricity of society at the time.

    ✗ (C) She is worried that students were not in the right to protest over this issue.

    The opposite is true. The professor is expressing grounds for viewing the traditional model of literature as exclusionary.

    ✗ (D) She feels express admiration for the game of baseball.

    The professor's point in mentioning "The World Series" is not to express her admiration for baseball.

Answers and Explanations—9.7

Integrated Hypothesis—Track 60

NARRATOR: Listen to part of a lecture in a linguistics class. The professor has been talking about the origins of human language systems.

PROFESSOR: OK, last week we finished our discussion about the way various human languages spread throughout the world, and, um… at the end of our last class, I mentioned the idea that human language is, uh, in many ways, different from any other communication system found in nature. Today, I want to continue discussing human language… oh, yes, Morgan?

FEMALE STUDENT: Professor, when you say language, do you mean vocal or, like, sounds only, or does language also include something like body language or hand gestures?

PROFESSOR: Ah, OK… I should definitely be more clear. If we are talking about human language, then that is, let's say for now, just verbal communication… talking or writing, right? For now, let's put aside sign language, or rather sign languages, which are a whole nother, very interesting topic that we'll cover later. So while it is true that communication, even in humans, can include all sorts of nonverbal aspects, today we will focus exclusively on the verbal communication systems that animals have.

FEMALE STUDENT: Okay, that makes sense… so you're saying that no other animals talk like humans? But isn't something like a bird chirping, maybe, just the bird version of talking?

PROFESSOR: Yes, I can see how they do seem similar. It might help to understand a recent theory about the evolution of human language. Actually, your suggestion about a bird chirping or singing plays a part here. One group of researchers has proposed that there are, well—animals can engage in two different types of vocal communication. The example of a bird's vocalizations can represent both.

The distinction between a bird song and a bird call—or, uh, in your words, a "chirp"—is based on length, complexity, and most importantly, meaning or context. When a bird sings, it is typically engaging in a courtship activity… trying to attract a mate. Studies of several bird species that sing have found that these songs do not convey any specific message… instead, they are intended to simply impress other birds, with, uh, the volume or even the variety of notes and pitches, or sounds that they can make. This is an example of an *expressive system* of communication.

On the other hand, a bird call is functional… it serves to send a message of warning or alarm. In other words, a specific sound is used to convey a specific meaning—you can think of this like it's a word. This type of communication represents a *lexical system*.

MALE STUDENT: Wait, but if a bird song sends a signal about mating, is that still sending a message? Is that le… lexical?

PROFESSOR: Well, hold on, hold on, I see the confusion and…

MALE STUDENT: I mean, I was actually thinking about something we're covering in my biology class, that even individual animals communicate in different ways for different messages. Like, dogs, for example, they might make a whining noise for some messages, but then might howl or growl for something else. Just because a song sounds different than a chirp, how are they actually different types of communication? You said that they sing to attract a mate, right? Isn't that a message?

PROFESSOR: OK, w—wait, let me explain. In a lexical system, each specific sound, say chirp or howl, has a specific meaning. But that is not true with a bird song. There is no meaning behind a specific sound or

pattern of sounds or notes. The signal is not a specific meaning but rather, well… the bird showing off how pretty it can sound. Think of this like a person playing the piano. Well, I'm sure you would admit that the music might convey a feeling or impress a listener, but it doesn't really mean anything specific.

And we already discussed that humans are lexical—we use words. In fact, all animals that vocalize… engage in lexical communication. But in non-humans, expressive and lexical communication don't happen at the same time. For example, the bird is either singing or sending an alarm, but never both at the same time.

So let's bring this back to, uh, the evolution of language that I mentioned before. In something called the *Integration Hypothesis*, scientists theorize that lexical and expressive communication merged in humans, and created what we now call language. The lexical words are obvious enough, but according to scientists… well, expressive communication developed in the form of grammar.

See, every sentence in the human language conveys a message through the specific words, but it also has an expressive shape. Essentially that shape is the sentence structure or organization of the words. The shape can indicate the emotion or the tone or purpose of the speaker—say, angry or sad… or is the speaker asking or telling? No other animal does this. The question remains, how? All of our primate relatives have lexical communication, but where did the expressive system come from? But there is some exciting new research on the silvery gibbon—one of very few primates that actually sings—that might indicate that these gibbons are singing something more like actual words… combining lexical and expressive communication.

1. What does the professor mainly talk about?	**GIST-CONTENT.** The lecture focuses on different forms of communication and the Integration Hypothesis, which suggests that lexical and expressive communication uniquely merged in humans to form language.
✗ (A) The findings of studies on bird chirping and singing	Several studies involving bird singing are mentioned, but this is only a supporting detail.
✓ (B) A hypothesis about the evolution of human language	**CORRECT.** The professor introduces the structure of human language and then discusses a hypothesis about its evolution.
✗ (C) The various ways that animals use expressive communication	Examples of expressive communication among animals are given, but this is not the main focus of the lecture.
✗ (D) The differences between hand gestures and vocal communication	The fact that they are different is briefly discussed, but this is only a supporting detail.

9

2. Why does the student mention the animal communication that he is studying in his biology class?

✓ (A) To question the professor's claim that some animal communication does not send a specific message

✗ (B) To point out the difference between a bird's chirping and a bird's singing

✗ (C) To explain why he is interested in learning about language

✗ (D) To prove that he applied his understanding of linguistics to another course

ORGANIZATION. The student is questioning a previous statement made by the professor.

CORRECT. The professor had stated that a bird singing is an example of expressive communication, which does not send a specific message. The student is questioning that claim.

The student is not pointing out differences, but rather similarities, in the different forms of communication used by animals.

This statement by the student doesn't indicate his interest. It simply demonstrates that he has been exposed elsewhere to the topic being discussed.

The student is not attempting to prove anything to the professor.

3. What is the professor's opinion of recent research on the singing of the silvery gibbon?

✗ (A) She takes issue with the researchers' methods.

✗ (B) She sees the study as proof that human language is unique.

✓ (C) She thinks the study may help explain how human language first evolved.

✗ (D) She finds the study interesting, but believes its results are flawed.

SPEAKER'S ATTITUDE. The professor remarks that "there is some exciting new research on the silvery gibbon," indicating her interest in its findings. She says this directly after presenting the question of how expressive communication developed in humans.

The methods used in this research are not mentioned.

On the contrary—the professor indicates that the research might show that silvery gibbons are also capable of using lexical and expressive communication at the same time. This combination has been thought to only exist in humans.

CORRECT. She implies that the study might show that human language developed from a communication style similar to one used by the silvery gibbon.

There is no suggestion in the lecture that she finds any flaws in the study.

4. According to the professor, a bird singing is most comparable to what aspect of human communication?

DETAIL. The professor notes that bird singing is a form of expressive, rather than lexical, communication. She also states that, in humans, "expressive communication developed in the form of grammar."

✗ (A) Gesturing

A bird singing is a form of vocal communication, while gesturing is not.

✓ (B) Grammar

CORRECT. A bird singing is an example expressive communication. The professor notes that grammar is also considered expressive communication.

✗ (C) Singing

Human singing is not mentioned in the lecture.

✗ (D) Words

Words are an example of lexical communication, while a bird singing is an example of expressive communication.

5. According to the professor, what two communication systems are uniquely combined in human language? *Choose 2 answers.*

DETAIL. According to the professor, the Integration Hypothesis states that "lexical and expressive communication merged in humans, and created what we now call language."

✓ [A] Lexical communication

CORRECT. The professor states that this is one of the two types of communication uniquely combined in human language.

✗ [B] Cross-cultural communication

Cross-cultural communication is not mentioned in the lecture.

✗ [C] Nonverbal communication

Human language is verbal communication, not nonverbal.

✓ [D] Expressive communication

CORRECT. The professor states that this is one of the two types of communication uniquely combined in human language.

Track 61

NARRATOR: Listen again to part of the lecture. Then answer the question.

FEMALE STUDENT: Professor, when you say language, do you mean vocal or, like, sounds only, or does language also include something like body language or hand gestures?

PROFESSOR: Ah, OK… I should definitely be more clear. If we are talking about human language, then that is, let's say for now, just verbal communication… talking or writing, right?

NARRATOR: Why does the professor say this:

PROFESSOR: If we are talking about human language, then that is, let's say for now, just verbal communication… talking or writing, right?

6.   **FUNCTION OF WHAT IS SAID.** In this quote, the professor indicates that the student's use of a term is inexact. She then clarifies the issue for the student by focusing on a particular definition for the present time ("let's say for now").

✗   (A) To determine whether the student has done the assigned homework

The professor is not trying to determine whether the student is prepared. She is making sure the student is clear on the specifics of what is being discussed.

✗   (B) To express disappointment at having to explain an issue for a second time

The professor does not indicate any disappointment.

✓   (C) To clarify the use of certain terminology, at least for the present

CORRECT. The student is unclear about the use of the term "language." The professor clarifies the issue by restricting "for now" the use of the term "language" to verbal communication.

✗   (D) To recommend that the student do further research on the topic

The professor is not recommending that the student do further research.

Answers and Explanations—9.8

Networking—Track 62

NARRATOR: Listen to part of a lecture in a sociology class.

PROFESSOR: You've heard about how important bees are, right? There are theories that if bees go extinct, humans may not survive. Consider this: bees are responsible for the pollination of 70 percent of the crops that feed 90 percent of the world. Honey bees alone help produce $30 billion in crops annually. If they die out, so could much of our food supply, along with all the animals that depend on that supply. Did you realize bees were that important? They're what we call a keystone species, because they're essential to the functioning of a large network.

Or, how about schools of fish? You've seen them moving around, acting like they all have one mind. They seem to turn in unison, with no one fish appearing to lead. It's just a large group working together. But there must be some kind of communication occurring. One fish sees danger, food—something that's important—then alerts the rest of the school… and every fish immediately steers clear of the danger or heads for the attractive food source.

Well, these, as unrelated as they may seem, are examples of *networks*. A network is a collection of people, animals, computers, companies—basically anything—that are interconnected in some way. There are both natural and man-made networks… this definition explains why companies say they have "networked computers."

So what does this have to do with sociology? Everything! Our day-to-day lives, our career aspirations, our families, are all created and comprised of social networks. These networks can shift over time, and one person may use different networks to achieve different goals… I doubt you think of your high school network as the one that's going to get you a job. I want to use the social networks you're already familiar with to draw an analogy with neurological networks… the networks in your brain.

You already know that our brain controls our thoughts, our emotions, even our physical feelings. But how? Through the relationships… the networks… created there. Whenever we learn something new, we change the neural networks in our brains. Sometimes those changes are permanent… sometimes they are temporary. By analogy, meeting someone new changes your social networks, if only for a moment. To describe these complex and dynamic interactions, there are three domains to consider: individuals, tasks, and resources.

First, *individuals*. A network, by definition, is composed of interconnected individuals. The brain has small entities, called neurotransmitters, that can be considered individuals. A neurotransmitter is the chemical messenger used to send signals throughout the brain. They talk to each other and allow parts of the brain to communicate. Each neurotransmitter can be activated in response to different stimuli, or different conditions. For a social network, an individual can be one person, groups of people, or even large entities like a company or a country. You can consider the United States to be networked with the United Kingdom, China, and basically every other country. You are networked with your family, your friends, and this college, and you have many other networks.

Second, *tasks*. Based on the skills and materials each individual possesses, they will be assigned appropriate tasks. Each neurotransmitter is designed to produce a particular reaction. The neurotransmitter serotonin, for example, works to affect your mood, appetite, and sleep. Its particular composition is designed to make it perfect for these tasks. Other neurotransmitters would be assigned other, more appropriate tasks. Similarly, a team may work to win a football game, with each individual assigned a task, and the whole network working to achieve a larger task.

Finally, *resources*. To produce serotonin, the brain needs Vitamin C and an amino acid derivative known as 5-HTP. For dopamine, another neurotransmitter that impacts mood, the brain needs Vitamins C and B6 and a different amino acid derivative. People who have vitamin deficiencies might feel depressed because the brain does not have enough resources available to complete the task of feeling happy. Similarly, a football team is unlikely to win without the appropriate sports equipment and the right coach to teach them how to play the game effectively.

So you see how the complex relationships seen throughout the world can be described in terms of relatively simple concepts? The trick is making sure you track all the different relationships. A single person, or a single neurotransmitter, can be part of an incredibly large network, or, even more likely, several large networks.

1.	What is the main purpose of the lecture?	**GIST-PURPOSE.** The professor defines the term "network" and a network's three key characteristics, using a comparison between social and neural networks.
✗ (A)	To introduce ways for students to optimize their social networks	The professor mentions social networks, but does not discuss how to optimize them.
✓ (B)	To describe the characteristics of networks and provide examples	**CORRECT.** The professor uses two types of networks—social and neurological—to describe the characteristics of a network.
✗ (C)	To explain the differences between social and neurological networks	The professor does not focus on the differences between social and neurological networks. She focuses on their similarities to explain networks in general.
✗ (D)	To explain the differences between networks of fish, birds, and the brain	The focus of the lecture is not the differences among different networks. It is on their similarities.

2.   Why does the professor talk about bees?

  ✗ (A) To emphasize the importance of environmental conservation

  ✗ (B) To draw an analogy between the farming industry and naturally occurring networks

  ✓ (C) To provide an example of a keystone species in a larger network

  ✗ (D) To show how networks can change over time

ORGANIZATION. Bees are one of two examples that the professor mentions early in the lecture to introduce the concept of networks.

The professor does not discuss environmental conservation.

The professor does not discuss the farming industry directly. She only refers to farming concepts to illustrate the importance of bees in a much larger network.

CORRECT. The professor discusses networks in a variety of fields. She uses the example of bees as a keystone species at the beginning of the lecture to pique the students' interest in the topic of networks.

The professor's discussion of bees does not focus on changes to any network.

3.   According to the professor, which of the following are examples of networks? *Choose 2 answers.*

  ✓ [A] A football team

  ✗ [B] A neurotransmitter

  ✗ [C] A police department

  ✓ [D] A school of fish

DETAIL. The professor mentions several examples of networks throughout the lecture, including both social and neurological networks.

CORRECT. A football team is one of the examples the professor gives of a social network.

The professor compares a neurotransmitter to an individual in a social network. Both a neurotransmitter and an individual are described as components of a network, not networks themselves.

Police departments are not mentioned in the lecture.

CORRECT. A school of fish is given as an example of a social network from the animal kingdom.

Track 63

NARRATOR: Listen again to part of the lecture. Then answer the question.

PROFESSOR: A network is a collection of people, animals, computers, companies—basically anything—that are interconnected in some way. There are both natural and man-made networks… this definition explains why companies say they have "networked computers."

So what does this have to do with sociology?

NARRATOR: Why does the professor say this:

PROFESSOR: So what does this have to do with sociology?

4. **FUNCTION OF WHAT IS SAID.** The professor defines and gives examples of networks in the beginning of her lecture. In this quote, she pivots to speaking more directly about social networks, using neural networks as an analogy.

✓ (A) To connect the previous examples to the main topic of the lecture

CORRECT. The professor later answers her own question by saying that the examples she has mentioned have "everything" to do with sociology. The rest of her lecture uses social network examples to help describe networks generally.

✗ (B) To ask students for examples of social networks

The professor is not asking the students for examples. Her question is rhetorical.

✗ (C) To acknowledge that she has strayed off topic

This is not the purpose of the professor's question.

✗ (D) To encourage students to draw from their own experiences

In this quote, the professor is not asking the students for details of their own experiences.

5. What does the professor compare to serotonin, a neurotransmitter that impacts mood?

DETAIL. Serotonin and other neurotransmitters are examples of individuals in a larger network. Serotonin specifically is used to describe the assignment of tasks based on the ability of the individual.

✗ (A) A company working to manufacture a product

This example is not given in the lecture.

✗ (B) A school of fish avoiding a predator

The school of fish is described as an entire network. It is not comparable to serotonin, because serotonin is compared to an individual in this lecture.

✗ (C) Vitamins C and B6 ingested as supplements

Vitamins are examples of resources that are needed to produce neurotransmitters. They are not given as examples of individuals in a network.

✓ (D) A team member who is assigned an appropriate task

CORRECT. Just as serotonin is "assigned" to affect the chemistry of the brain in a specific way, an individual is assigned an appropriate task to complete as part of the larger goals of the network as a whole.

6. What example of a network's resources does the professor provide?

DETAIL. The professor mentions vitamins and amino acid derivatives as resources for neurological networks, and a football team's coaching and equipment as resources for that team.

✗ (A) A neurotransmitter

The professor uses neurotransmitters as examples of individuals, not resources.

✓ (B) A football team's equipment

CORRECT. A football team needs equipment and coaching. Both are given as examples of the network's resources.

✗ (C) A school of fish

A school of fish is an example of an entire network, not a network resource.

✗ (D) Winning a game

Winning a game is a task, not a network resource.

Answers and Explanations—9.9

Neuropsychology—Track 64

NARRATOR: Listen to part of a psychology lecture. The professor is discussing neuropsychology.

PROFESSOR: While there's a lot of debate around the exact start of the field, many people consider Paul Broca to be the father of neuropsychology. Like modern neuropsychologists and some psychologists of his time, Broca believed that different regions of the brain were involved in different cognitive processes. Today we use technologies like EEG and fMRI—don't worry about those acronyms, they're not important—to watch what happens in the brain when different actions are performed. Broca, however, did not have those technological advantages.

During his time, a great debate was raging. Some, like Broca, argued that mental processes, meaning cognition, were localized within brain regions. Others thought that cognition was diffused—spread out—across the entire brain. A few even maintained that the mind was actually located in the heart—the brain was there to support physical, not mental, functions. In Broca's time, phrenology—the idea that the shape of a person's skull reflected that person's personality—was still widely believed.

So Broca, a well-respected surgeon already, set out to prove that cognitive processes are localized in specific parts of the brain. He was particularly interested in speech—both understanding and producing speech—and he was confident that speech came from a particular region in the brain. Now around this time, he heard of… yes?

FEMALE STUDENT: Professor Abbott, um, what about people who can't speak? Not babies… people who have some kind of brain damage.

PROFESSOR: Uh, that's very astute. For an undamaged brain, it would have been nearly impossible for, um… for people at the time to tell what was causing speech. That's why there was so much debate surrounding the topic. Paul Broca had the same idea as you. Now, remember, it wasn't feasible to perform studies on a living brain at the time, so Broca's work focused on physically inspecting the brains of deceased patients… those who had passed away. He studied the brains of people who had lost the ability to speak. In every case, Broca found that the person had a lesion—a sign of an injury—on the same part of the brain. That part, now called Broca's Area, is considered the brain's speech center.

So Broca was the first to prove that one particular area of the brain is associated with a particular cognitive function. His work was expanded upon by Carl Wernicke, who realized that not all people with speech problems showed lesions in Broca's Area.

Some people suffer from a type of speech disorder that allows them to form words, but they cannot understand speech. This can be mild, and only become problematic when talking to people with heavy accents or those who speak very quickly. But Carl Wernicke was interested in more extreme cases. In these cases, a person will produce words that follow a logical grammar and intonation… they'll put emphasis on some words, pause in all the right places… but the words they're using won't make any sense. And they generally don't realize there's a problem because they can't understand the words that they're saying.

For these people, the Broca's Area was typically healthy, but there was another area, closer to the back of the head, that consistently showed lesions. This area, appropriately enough, is called Wernicke's Area. Wernicke showed that the brain is even more complicated than Broca believed. One area of the brain might be associated with producing speech, but another area was there for comprehending speech.

Ok, so both scientists helped to prove that the mind was definitively localized within the brain. Today, brain-imaging studies agree with that conclusion, but there are still problems with studying the mind. While we can assign general areas to most cognitive functions, there's no way to clearly define boundaries between one area and another one. The functional regions of the brain can differ somewhat from person to person. So while we can approximate where both Broca's and Wernicke's Areas are, we can't universally pinpoint either.

Well, Broca correctly assumed that each cognitive function has its own area of the brain. But given the separation of different aspects of language, and what we've talked about with some functions needing multiple areas of the brain, one has to ask—how else could the mind work? Could it be more about the connections between different regions, rather than the regions themselves? Neural connections are clearly a factor, and sometimes damage to the connections is more impactful than damage to the area under study itself. Are we able to come to definite conclusions on this yet? I think it's pretty clear that we are not.

1.	What does the professor mainly discuss?	**GIST-CONTENT.** The lecture is about both Broca's and Wernicke's studies into cognition. The professor uses their early work to explain how researchers were first able to conclude that different areas of the brain were responsible for different mental functions.
✗ (A)	The impact of lesions in Wernicke's Area	This is mentioned, but only to help support the idea of localization of cognitive functions.
✗ (B)	How scientists today relate cognition to brain activity	The focus of the lecture is not on current scientists, and there's little discussion about how modern scientists conduct their work.
✓ (C)	A theory about the localization of cognitive functions in the brain	**CORRECT.** The theory is that different regions of the brain are responsible for different cognitive processes. Broca and Wernicke both contributed to proving that theory correct.
✗ (D)	A study on people with speech disorders	Multiple studies are cited, but they serve to support the main focus of the lecture—localization of cognitive functions in the brain.

Track 65

NARRATOR: Listen again to part of the lecture. Then answer the question.

PROFESSOR: Now, remember, it wasn't feasible to perform studies on a living brain at the time, so Broca's work focused on physically inspecting the brains of deceased patients… those who had passed away. He studied the brains of people who had lost the ability to speak. In every case, Broca found that the person had a lesion—a sign of an injury—on the same part of the brain.

NARRATOR: Why does the professor say this:

PROFESSOR: In every case, Broca found that the person had a lesion—a sign of an injury—on the same part of the brain.

2.   **FUNCTION OF WHAT IS SAID.** The area of the brain referred to in this quote, Broca's Area, is the brain's speech center. When it is sufficiently damaged, a person can lose the ability to speak.

✗	(A) To explain why Broca decided to study this area of the brain	The professor mentions that Broca was particularly interested in speech. However, this quote highlights Broca's finding that one type of cognitive function is localized. This is what the professor's quote focuses on.
✓	(B) To describe a crucial discovery in Broca's research	**CORRECT.** Based on his discovery, Broca was able to conclude that the part of the brain mentioned in the quote was responsible for speech.
✗	(C) To provide an alternative explanation for what was observed	No explanation for what caused the lesions is given, and only one explanation for their interpretation is presented.
✗	(D) To connect this observation with what Wernicke discovered	While it is true that both scientists observed lesions, that's not what the professor is discussing in this quote.

3.   What does the professor say about people who have lost the ability to speak?

		DETAIL. In Broca's examinations, all such people had lesions present in the same area of the brain.
✗	(A) They often have brain abnormalities present from birth.	This idea is not mentioned, and it is implied in the lecture that this idea is untrue. The brain abnormalities, or lesions, are said to be caused by injury, not present from birth.
✗	(B) They are sometimes able to recover their speaking capabilities.	Recovery is not mentioned. Both Broca's study and Wernicke's study involved analysis performed on people after they were deceased, so the subjects would have still have had speech problems at their time of death.
✓	(C) Many of them have lesions in Broca's Area.	**CORRECT.** People who can no longer speak were the basis of Broca's study. In each case that he examined, he found that the brain was damaged in the same area.
✗	(D) Some of them have cognitive function that is not localized within parts of the brain.	The opposite is true. Both scientists demonstrated that cognitive functions are localized within parts of the brain.

4.   The professor describes a speech disorder in which people cannot understand speech. What does this disorder illustrate?

CONNECTING CONTENT. This is what caused Wernicke to investigate beyond Broca's Area. This type of speech disorder was not associated with lesions in Broca's Area.

✓ (A) An impairment not caused by damage to Broca's Area

CORRECT. This impairment is characterized by injury to Wernicke's Area, not Broca's Area.

✗ (B) A type of disorder that can be corrected through speech therapy

Correcting this disorder is not discussed in the lecture.

✗ (C) The most common type of speech disorder

The professor did not indicate which, if any, of the discussed disorders is the most common.

✗ (D) Speech centers in the brain are unique compared to other cognitive functions

Nothing is discussed in the lecture other than speech disorders, so there is no reason to believe that speech centers are unique.

5.   What is the professor's opinion of the cognitive functioning of the brain?

SPEAKER'S ATTITUDE. The professor lists some early theories that were too simplistic. Additionally, he implies that even Broca did not have a complex enough view. Broca believed that there was a single speech center of the brain, though Wernicke showed that at least two separate centers are involved. In the conclusion of the lecture, the professor implies that it may be even more complicated than that.

✗ (A) There has been little or no research on this topic.

The lecture discusses various studies completed on cognitive functioning. Therefore, there has been significant research done on this topic.

✗ (B) It can only be observed in adult brains.

The professor does not discuss current limitations on who can be observed, especially with the modern technology he mentions.

✗ (C) With further research, scientists will conclude that cognition is not localized in the brain.

The opposite is true. All of the research he presents suggests that cognition is localized.

✓ (D) It is more complex than early scientists generally believed.

CORRECT. This summarizes the professor's opinion of cognitive functioning in the brain.

9

6. What point does the professor make when he mentions connections between different regions of the brain?

ORGANIZATION. Connections are discussed in the conclusion of the lecture. The professor suggests that cognition may not only be localized to different areas of the brain, but may also involve the connections between those areas. He states that scientists have not yet reached a full conclusion about how the mind functions.

✗ (A) Regions of the brain are interchangeable as long as the relevant connections stay active.

The professor does not suggest this idea anywhere in the lecture.

✗ (B) Students should continue to study connections of different areas of the brain throughout the class.

While later in the class, the professor may discuss this topic further, he is not recommending that the students pursue such study independently.

✓ (C) Scientists need to continue to study how cognition works before arriving at definitive conclusions.

CORRECT. This is the professor's summation of the current state of understanding cognitive function in humans.

✗ (D) When connections between areas of the brain are damaged, there will be no noticeable effect.

This idea is refuted by the professor in the conclusion of the lecture when he says that "sometimes damage to the connections is more impactful than damage to the area under study itself."

Answers and Explanations—9.10

Liminality—Track 66

NARRATOR: Listen to part of a lecture in a sociology class.

PROFESSOR: Many of you are probably familiar with Mardi Gras in New Orleans or *Carnaval* in Rio. But these are just two of many, many carnival celebrations that take place around the world each winter. There are all kinds of interesting traditions linked to carnival celebrations like these. In Ivrea, Italy, people pelt each other with 400 tons of oranges. In parts of Spain and Latin America, people hold elaborate funerals for sardines. And in the Rhineland of Germany, women take over the town and cut off men's ties.

What's the point of all this? Well, you may not have been to Carnaval, but you've probably taken part in something like one. A graduation ceremony, a sweet sixteen or quinceañera party, or even just going to college. These are all examples of something called *liminality*, which is what we're going to talk about today.

Liminality is defined as the period of uncertainty that occurs when you pass from one state to another. A lot of the things we celebrate—birthdays, graduations, and so on—are markers of liminal times. And the same holds true on a bigger scale—things like a carnival, or an election, or even a war. These are all liminal moments.

Why is this important? We go through transitions all the time. What's interesting is that these transitions tend to have the same structure and purpose in societies all around the world, throughout history.

During a liminal period, many normal rules and boundaries are dissolved. People have the freedom to explore and change. When a person or group finishes a liminal stage, they often emerge with new ideas, rules, or even institutions. Liminality is important part of how humans move forward.

The idea of liminality came from studies of rites of passage—the events we have to help people move from one state to another. Most societies have these, most often to help young people transition to adulthood. In our society, going to college is one rite of passage that helps young people move toward adult lives. Like all liminal rites, going to college has three phases: rites of separation, transition rites, and reincorporation rites. Let's talk a bit more about each phase.

First, *rites of separation*. This phase starts a liminal period. Some theorists call it a kind of "metaphorical death." At this point, the person or group makes a break with their past. This can be a literal change of place or stopping a routine—things like that. So leaving home to move into a dorm, this is a rite of separation. You're leaving your home and family behind. This marks the end of your childhood, so that you can begin preparing for an adult life.

Second, *transition rites* happen during the period of liminality. During this phase, one is between things. You're not who you were before, but you haven't become who you will be. Rules and structure are more fluid. There's room to experiment. Often this period is overseen by an older, more experienced person or group. Sounds kind of like college, right? You have a lot more freedom, and you live mostly with people your own age. Although with some guidance from teachers and other adults. And, like all transition rites, it only lasts for a limited time.

Finally, *rites of incorporation*. In this phase, people come back to established structures and settings. Now, they are different people, with roles that are different from before. Everything that was learned during the transition phase can now be applied to a new adult life. Often there's a celebration. In an ideal world, this is what will happen when you graduate—a big party, and then you'll probably start a job… maybe get your own apartment. You begin living an adult life, different from the one you had before. So in college, we have whole groups of people going through this transition together. Sometimes entire societies go through liminal rites, too. Like Rio's Carnaval, when all kinds of crazy things happen to mark the beginning of Lent or the change from winter to spring. And sometimes individuals go through these rites alone, often around major life events, like a birth or a death. These liminal periods last different lengths of time—a single day or a few years… like the four years you spend in college.

1.	What is the main purpose of the lecture?	**GIST-PURPOSE.** The main purpose of the lecture is to explain a framework for how individuals and societies structure transitions, particularly for young people growing up.
✗	(A) To elaborate on the purpose of a college education	While the lecture uses college as an example of a liminal state, the main focus of the lecture is not on college but on the larger issue of liminality.
✓	(B) To explain a way of framing personal and social transitions	**CORRECT.** "Liminality," the topic of the lecture, is one way of organizing the many social practices surrounding transitional states.
✗	(C) To elaborate on the different ways in which societies celebrate coming of age	Coming of age celebrations are briefly mentioned, but only as examples of liminal events.
✗	(D) To explain the differences between adolescence and adulthood	The lecture does not focus on how these states differ. Rather, it is focused on the transition between these, and other, states.

9

2.   Why does the professor discuss Mardi Gras and Carnaval?

INFERENCE. At the beginning of the lecture, the professor uses Mardi Gras and Carnaval as well-known examples to illustrate the celebrations associated with liminality.

✗ Ⓐ To emphasize that celebrations are an important part of all societies

The professor does not discuss the purpose of celebrations generally. The lecture focuses on liminal states.

✗ Ⓑ To draw an analogy between carnival celebrations and college graduation

While both celebrations are connected to liminal states, the lecture does not explicitly compare the two.

✓ Ⓒ To give examples of liminal time periods in different cultures

CORRECT. The lecture uses these examples to introduce some of the ways liminal events are celebrated in different cultures.

✗ Ⓓ To show how carnivals have evolved differently in different places

The lecture does not discuss the evolution of different carnival celebrations.

3.   According to the lecture, which of the following are examples of liminal moments? *Choose 2 answers.*

DETAIL. The professor says, "A lot of the things we celebrate—birthdays, graduations, and so on—are markers of liminal times. And the same holds true on a bigger scale—things like a carnival, or an election, or even a war. These are all liminal moments."

✓ Ⓐ A birthday celebration

CORRECT. The lecture mentions birthdays as well as sweet sixteen and quinceañera celebrations as examples of liminal moments.

✗ Ⓑ A serious accident

Accidents are not mentioned in the lecture.

✓ Ⓒ An election

CORRECT. The lecture includes elections in its list of liminal moments.

✗ Ⓓ A long-term illness

Long-term illnesses are not mentioned in the lecture.

4.   What example does the professor give of a rite of incorporation?

DETAIL. The professor discusses rites of incorporation in the final segment of the lecture, stating that these rites mark the end of a liminal period. College graduation is included as an example of this rite.

✓ Ⓐ Graduating from college

CORRECT. The lecture uses college graduation as an example of a rite of incorporation.

✗ Ⓑ Returning from a trip

Returning from a trip is not mentioned in the lecture.

✗ Ⓒ Completing a large project

Completing a large project is not mentioned in the lecture.

✗ Ⓓ Attending Mardi Gras

Mardi Gras is given as an example of a liminal celebration, not a rite of incorporation.

5. Why does the professor mention the change from winter to spring?

   ✗ (A) To illustrate the annual occurrence of all liminal events

   ✗ (B) To give an example of a rite of passage

   ✓ (C) To provide an example of an entire society going through a transition

   ✗ (D) To give an example of a liminal event that makes people happy

DETAIL. The professor includes this example as part of a list of times when an entire society goes through a liminal event.

The professor does not indicate that all liminal events occur annually.

The professor does not describe the change from winter to spring as a rite of passage.

CORRECT. This example is given immediately after the professor explains that entire societies can experience liminal periods.

This is not the purpose of the professor mentioning the transition from winter to spring.

Track 67

NARRATOR: Listen again to part of the lecture. Then answer the question.

PROFESSOR: This phase starts a liminal period. Some theorists call it a kind of "metaphorical death." At this point, the person or group makes a break with their past. This can be a literal change of place or stopping a routine—things like that.

NARRATOR: Why does the professor say this:

PROFESSOR: Some theorists call it a kind of "metaphorical death."

6. Why does the professor say this?

   ✗ (A) To describe death as yet another transition all people make

   ✗ (B) To conclude that liminal states are traumatic

   ✗ (C) To illustrate a rite of incorporation

   ✓ (D) To emphasize that liminal periods begin with the ending of what has come before

FUNCTION OF WHAT IS SAID. The professor is describing rites of separation. The "metaphorical death" emphasizes that a liminal phase begins with a definitive break from the initial state.

The professor is talking about a "metaphorical death," not a literal death.

Trauma is not mentioned in the lecture.

In this quote, the professor is discussing rites of separation, not rites of incorporation.

CORRECT. This statement emphasizes that liminal periods start when something ends.

Chapter 10

Lectures D: Social Science

Listening lectures test your ability to comprehend academic-level spoken English. You'll listen to a short lecture (about 3 to 5 minutes long) from a professor. Occasionally, a student may also speak. You will only be able to listen to the lecture once. You will not be able to pause the recording or to replay any part of it (though some questions will replay a specific part of the lecture for you). You can take notes as you listen.

You will then answer six questions for that lecture. Most questions are multiple-choice with four options (select one from A, B, C, or D). Some questions may ask you to select more than one option or to fill in a table. You will have to answer the questions in order. You cannot return to a question once you have moved on to the next question.

Listening lectures test your understanding of main ideas, contrasts, the lecturer's tone and degree of certainty about the information, and why the lecturer relates certain information or examples. They also test your understanding of the organization of the lecture and the relationship between different ideas. Finally, they test your ability to make inferences or draw conclusions.

How should you use this chapter? Here are some recommendations, according to the level you've reached in TOEFL Listening:

1. **Fundamentals.** Start with a topic-focused chapter, such as this one. Start with a topic that is a "medium weakness"—not your worst area but not your best either. At first, listen to the lecture once, then work on the questions untimed and check the answer after each question. Review the solutions closely, think carefully about the principles at work, and articulate what you've learned. Redo questions as necessary. As you get better, time yourself and do all of the questions for a lecture at once, without stopping.

2. **Fixes.** Do an entire lecture and its associated questions under timed conditions. Don't replay any part of the lecture while you are still answering the questions! Examine the results, learn your lessons, then test yourself with another lecture and question set.

3. **Tweaks.** Confirm your mastery by doing two or three lectures in a row under timed conditions. Work your way up to doing four lectures and two conversations in one sitting. Aim to improve the speed and ease of your process.

Good luck on Listening!

10.1

 Listen to Track 68.

Now answer the questions.

1. What is the lecture mainly about?
   - (A) A review of the "prisoner's dilemma" game example
   - (B) Contrasting the game of poker with stock market investing
   - (C) A topic within game theory called "zero-sum games"
   - (D) Explaining theories developed by von Neumann and Morgenstern

2. Why does the professor talk about poker and stock market investing?
   - (A) To avoid expanding on a topic brought up by a student
   - (B) To illustrate examples of zero-sum games
   - (C) To demonstrate different payouts to participants in a prisoner's dilemma game
   - (D) To explain why zero-sum games don't exist in real life

 Listen to Track 69.

Now answer the question.

3. Why does the professor say this?
   - (A) To stress the level of mutual cooperation that the prisoners need to maintain
   - (B) To note that each side individually is better off not confessing
   - (C) To point out that without trust, neither side is likely to confess
   - (D) To indicate how the situation is likely to turn into a zero-sum game

4. What is an example of a zero-sum game?
   - (A) A worker's hourly wage is determined by his productivity in the prior quarter.
   - (B) The stock market goes up, increasing the value of the holdings of most owners of company stock.
   - (C) Two countries in a peace agreement each have an incentive to violate the terms of the agreement.
   - (D) Only three gifts are available to be distributed among four children.

5. According to the professor, how can non-zero-sum games be modeled as zero-sum games?

   (A) By turning the game into a prisoner's dilemma

   (B) By increasing transaction costs

   (C) By temporarily removing a player from the game

   (D) By adding a player to the game

6. Classify each statement below as describing a prisoner's dilemma or a zero-sum game.

   A   The two sides in the game are better off cooperating.

   B   One side cannot gain without the other side losing.

   C   Cooperation requires high levels of trust.

   D   It can be dangerous to society as a whole.

10.2

 Listen to Track 70.

Now answer the questions.

1. What is the main purpose of this talk?

   (A) To evaluate the causes of market crashes in the twentieth century

   (B) To explore the dot-com crash as a way to understand boom-and-bust cycles in general

   (C) To argue in favor of better regulation to reduce the likelihood or severity of market crashes

   (D) To predict that boom-and-crash cycles will become less common in the future

2. What is the speaker's opinion about the housing bubble and credit crisis?

   (A) Most people were ignoring the ability of borrowers to repay the loans given to them.

   (B) The investment banks would have preferred that lenders were more selective in choosing homebuyers to lend money to.

   (C) Investors believed that the loans being given to homebuyers were safer than United States Treasury bonds.

   (D) The increase in home values during the housing bubble was justified.

3. According to the professor, when did the dot-com bubble "mania" reach its peak?

   (A) In 2008

   (B) In 2001

   (C) In 1998 and 1999

   (D) In 1997

4. Why does the professor mention "other investors from other areas" that began to invest in dot-com companies?

   (A) To highlight the relative inexperience of these investors

   (B) To emphasize that traditional investors in technology were not interested in dot-com companies

   (C) To argue that the dot-com crash had already begun before these other investors got involved

   (D) To suggest that these investors lacked attractive opportunities in areas they typically invested in

5. According to the professor, which of the following factors contributed to the dot-com crash in 2000–2002? *Choose 3 answers.*

   [A] A lack of competition among investors in technology businesses

   [B] A high demand to invest in dot-com companies relative to the amount of investment funds being sought

   [C] The development of a new product or innovation with great potential

   [D] A great deal of uncertainty about which companies will succeed and which will fail

   [E] A loss of interest in pursuing non-technology investments

6. The professor mentions that the investment landscape for a new, promising innovation often becomes overcrowded. What does this fact explain? *Choose 2 answers.*

   [A] Why having a solid business plan becomes less important to prospective investors

   [B] Why a general "mania" or "euphoria" overcomes the investing public

   [C] Why there will often be many investments made in fundamentally unsound businesses

   [D] Why the companies working on developing this innovation typically need cash from investors to grow

10.3

 Listen to Track 71.

Now answer the questions.

1. What is this lecture primarily about?

   (A) The economic impact of telecommuting technology in recent decades

   (B) The advantages and disadvantages of being a telecommuter

   (C) The management of telecommuters

   (D) The reasons why some managers dislike telecommuters

2. According to the professor, what is a potential drawback of allowing telecommuting?

   (A) Some telecommuters lose focus without direct oversight.

   (B) Some telecommuters dislike having their outputs tracked.

   (C) Telecommuters are more likely to have children, which means they will tend to work less and be distracted more.

   (D) Employees who are forced to work from an office often become resentful of telecommuters, causing morale to drop.

3. What does the professor say about the software used to track the productivity of telecommuters?

   (A) It can be very expensive to set up and maintain across a distributed network.

   (B) Much of it is focused on tracking inputs, like time spent working on a project, rather than outputs.

   (C) Much of it lacks important features like email and video conferencing capabilities.

   (D) Frequently it lacks safeguards like password protection and encryption.

4. Why does the professor mention the announcement made by a particular technology CEO?

   (A) To demonstrate that some managers do not like, or are uncomfortable with, telecommuting

   (B) To explain why telecommuters are more productive than regular employees

   (C) To argue that most companies should not allow the practice of telecommuting

   (D) To indicate that telecommuting is becoming far less common in the technology industry

5. Why does the professor discuss telecommuters being "scattered all over the place"?

   (A) To assert that having a broad geographic exposure of a company's employee base can be beneficial for creating new marketing opportunities

   (B) To point out that telecommuters are much more likely to live far from a company's office than non-telecommuters

   (C) To provide reasons why a telecommuter may be reluctant to come into a company's office

   (D) To underscore a disadvantage of telecommuting, particularly when business needs change rapidly

---

 Listen to Track 72.

Now answer the question.

---

6. What does the professor imply when she says this?

   (A) The company in question is not a prominent technology company.

   (B) The CEO herself was generally unpopular with her employees.

   (C) Other technology companies are likely to follow suit and eliminate their "work-from-home" programs.

   (D) If given a choice between telecommuting and working from an office, some employees would choose to telecommute.

10.4

 Listen to Track 73.

Now answer the questions.

1. What is the main purpose of the lecture?
   - (A) To discuss how a sense of self develops in humans
   - (B) To describe methods of testing whether a child has a sense of self
   - (C) To argue that the notion of a sense of self is only fully developed in humans
   - (D) To explain why animals other than humans do not have a sense of self

2. Why does the professor predict that she knows how students will respond if she asks whether they have a "self"?
   - (A) To point out that she has gotten to know her students well
   - (B) To illustrate that a sense of self is universal among humans
   - (C) To point out that she expects some students to respond incorrectly
   - (D) To establish that a sense of self does not develop until adulthood

3. What does the professor say about the reasons why humans have a sense of self and other animals appear not to?
   - (A) These reasons are unlikely to ever be discovered.
   - (B) Researchers have yet to begin trying to discover these reasons.
   - (C) Studies into this issue that have been completed show contradictory findings.
   - (D) The reasons are not yet understood.

4. What does the experiment using a pencil in a box reveal about children?
   - (A) Whether they are able to imitate the actions of another person
   - (B) Whether they can comprehend how objects interact with one another in space
   - (C) Whether they can reason from the perspective of another person
   - (D) Whether they understand that they are children

5. The professor mentions a child who is only several months old and whose mother leaves the room. What is true about this child's perception of the world?

    (A) The child does not understand that her mother still exists somewhere outside of the room.

    (B) The child understands that her mother is somewhere else, but does not yet understand that her mother has her own perspective.

    (C) The child is certain that her mother will return, although the child cannot express this certainty.

    (D) The child believes and hopes that her mother might return, but is not certain.

6. The professor mentions several abilities that typically appear at specific stages of cognitive development. Classify each of the following abilities as typically occurring either 1. Under the Age of Three or 2. Around Age Four or Older.

    [A] Awareness that its mother is elsewhere if not in the room _____

    [B] Ability to view the world from its mother's perspective _____

    [C] Ability to understand object relations _____

    [D] Ability to pass the "false belief" test _____

10.5

 Listen to Track 74.

Now answer the questions.

1. What is the main topic of this lecture?

    (A) How to improve bargaining power with suppliers and buyers

    (B) How to create barriers to entry

    (C) How to eliminate substitute products from the marketplace

    (D) How to analyze industry dynamics for strategic decision-making

2. According to the professor, what might be two sources of barriers to entry? *Choose 2 answers.*

    [A] A lack of pricing coordination among suppliers

    [B] Patent protection

    [C] A high degree of competitive rivalry

    [D] High fixed costs to begin operations

3. Why does the professor talk about Walmart?

    (A) To emphasize the importance of selling to large retailers

    (B) To provide an example of a buyer with significant bargaining power

    (C) To illustrate the difference between a supplier and a buyer

    (D) To give an example of a company with significant barriers to entry

4. In the discussion of barriers to entry, what does the professor imply about new competitors when barriers to entry are low?

    (A) They will tend to avoid entering a market that has low barriers to entry.

    (B) They will deliver a product that is superior to the original.

    (C) They will reduce the potential profitability for companies in the market they enter.

    (D) They will seek to develop new barriers to entry, often by seeking patent protection.

5. What is the professor's point when she discusses the example of the butter manufacturer?

    (A) Even the simplest products can sometimes produce strong profits.

    (B) Threats from new entrants and substitute products are less important than the degree of competitive rivalry.

    (C) It is often difficult to make strong profits without patent protection.

    (D) The threat of substitutes by itself can limit a business's profit-making potential.

 Listen to Track 75.

Now answer the question.

---

6. What does the professor mean when she says this?

    (A) The drug manufacturer has significant pricing power due to its lack of substitutes.

    (B) Some people may balk at paying high prices for a drug, even if it does help save lives.

    (C) Some people may be more interested in helping others than saving their own lives.

    (D) The drug manufacturer's ability to charge high prices will be limited by its ability to create barriers to entry.

10

10.6

Listen to Track 76.

Now answer the questions.

1. What is the talk primarily about?

    (A) Why absolute advantage is a flawed framework for evaluating international trade

    (B) Ways to restrict the expansion of international trade

    (C) Lessons learned from history about manufacturing advantages in one country compared with another

    (D) The theory of comparative advantage and why it supports international trade

2. According to the professor, under what circumstances should one country trade with another country?

    (A) When costs of trading abroad are high

    (B) When one country is more productive generally than another

    (C) When one country has significantly more labor power available than another

    (D) When one country can make a product more efficiently than another country, relative to a different product

3. According to the professor, what is the main difference between absolute advantage and comparative advantage?

    (A) Comparative advantage involves the relative production efficiency in one country, compared with another country, at making different products.

    (B) Comparative advantage involves the production efficiency in one country compared with another at making one specific product.

    (C) Comparative advantage only holds when one country is more efficient at making several products than is another country.

    (D) Comparative advantage only holds when one country is more efficient at making at least one product than is another country.

4. What does the professor imply about comparative advantage when there are more than two products available for trade?

    (A) Countries will be more likely to not benefit from trade.

    (B) Countries will still be able to benefit from international trade in most circumstances.

    (C) Trading costs will be higher than when there are only two products available for trade.

    (D) Trading costs will be less important than when there are only two products available for trade.

5. What does the professor imply about the trade example given between Country X and Country Y?

   (A) The trading ratio of socks-to-shoes can affect whether trading will be beneficial to both countries.

   (B) Both countries will benefit from trade irrespective of the cost of shipping socks and shoes to one another.

   (C) Only Country X will benefit from trade because it has an absolute advantage in production.

   (D) Only Country Y will benefit from trade because it has an absolute disadvantage in production.

6. What is the professor's viewpoint regarding trade protection?

   (A) Trade barriers should only be put in place if one country has an absolute advantage over another in production.

   (B) Trade protection is valuable in some circumstances—particularly to help people avoid losing their jobs to foreign workers.

   (C) He believes that if two countries have economic reasons for trading with one another, trade barriers are harmful to both countries.

   (D) He believes that if two countries have economic reasons for trading with one another, trade barriers are harmful only to the country with an absolute advantage in production.

10.7

 Listen to Track 77.

Now answer the questions.

1. What is the talk primarily about?

   (A) Explaining an economic theory that frequently proves to be inaccurate

   (B) Exploring ways to make a riskless profit through international trade

   (C) Discussing the pricing of the Big Mac sandwich

   (D) Providing information about how services can be traded internationally

2. What does the professor imply about possible reasons why Big Macs sell for a higher price in Switzerland than in many other places?

   (A) There is a high demand for Big Macs among Swiss citizens.

   (B) Switzerland is close to Egypt.

   (C) Real estate in Switzerland is expensive.

   (D) Switzerland lacks some materials needed to make Big Macs.

3. According to the professor, what is a reason that services often violate the Law of One Price?

    (A) Most services are granted using a barter system, with prices that vary from country to country.

    (B) Many services are difficult to trade across long distances.

    (C) Services often require raw materials that are expensive to purchase.

    (D) Some services can be provided over the telephone or internet.

4. What does the professor imply about the prices of goods sold in New York and London?

    (A) They are likely to be higher than in most other places.

    (B) They are likely to be similar to those in Egypt.

    (C) They are likely to be higher in New York than in London.

    (D) They are likely to be equal to the prices found in other major cities worldwide.

5. What does the professor imply about trade barriers?

    (A) They allow international prices for a product to converge.

    (B) They can cause the Law of One Price to be violated.

    (C) They reduce the cost of shipping internationally.

    (D) They are usually implemented for political reasons.

6. What is the professor's viewpoint regarding the accuracy of the Law of One Price?

    (A) It is a helpful method for finding the average price of a product worldwide.

    (B) It is an effective way to generate arbitrage opportunities.

    (C) It is accurate in most cases.

    (D) It holds in certain circumstances, but there are many reasons why it will never hold for some products.

10.8

 Listen to Track 78.

Now answer the questions.

1. What is the lecture mainly about?

    (A) A discussion of efficient ways to wash a car

    (B) A contributor to management theory and one of the processes he invented

    (C) The differences between the original form of scientific management and modern versions of it

    (D) Worker dissatisfaction with automation in the workplace

2. Why does the professor discuss washing a car?

  (A) To give an example of conducting a time and motion study

  (B) To explore the case of a task that may normally be considered menial

  (C) To contrast the views of two different schools of management theory

  (D) To demonstrate the degree to which certain tasks can be automated

---

 Listen to Track 79.

Now answer the question.

---

3. Why does the professor say this?

  (A) To answer his own question, after no student was able to answer it correctly

  (B) To point out that the student's response did not identify the right person

  (C) To indicate that the student was essentially correct, despite making a slight error

  (D) To ask the rest of the class whether the given response was correct

4. What is an example of a component of a time and motion study?

  (A) The use of a stopwatch to see how long completing a step in an overall process takes

  (B) Tracking the speed of individual employees so that they can be ranked in terms of efficiency

  (C) Eliminating steps that had previously been considered essential to a process

  (D) Making inventory lists to ensure that a task can be completed

5. According to the professor, where may a potential conflict arise as a result of applying scientific management in a workplace?

  (A) From other managers who feel that scientific management principles are obsolete

  (B) From competitors who can replicate the efficiency gains achieved from scientific management

  (C) From civil rights advocates who claim that some scientific management principles violate worker rights

  (D) From laborers and unions who are concerned about workers being replaced by machines

6. Select the description(s) below that apply to time and motion studies, as described in the lecture. *Select all that apply.*

  ☐ A   A list of steps needed to complete a task is drafted.

  ☐ B   Ways to train workers to move faster through each step are found.

  ☐ C   Workers who fail to complete assignments quickly may be subjected to penalties.

  ☐ D   Steps to complete a task may be reordered to achieve greater efficiency.

10.9

 Listen to Track 80.

Now answer the questions.

1. What is the primary purpose of this lecture?

    (A) To introduce a new perspective on United States history and an author who exemplifies that perspective

    (B) To compare the study of United States history to the study of literature

    (C) To explain the opinions of an author they have read about in a different class

    (D) To detail the political turmoil of many periods of United States history

2. Why does the professor mention the "establishment view" used in most schools?

    (A) To refer to Howard Zinn's book

    (B) To refer to the standard historical accounts often found in high school textbooks

    (C) To correct a known error found in many historical accounts

    (D) To offer legitimacy to stories that are considered dubious by many

3. According to the professor, what is an advantage of the "minority view" of United States history?

    (A) It is generally well-known.

    (B) It disproves many themes found in the "establishment view" of United States history.

    (C) It accounts for the perspectives of people that may have been oppressed.

    (D) It was written primarily by the social elite.

4. What aspect of history does the professor imply could be discussed in the course?

    (A) Efforts by civic leaders to overcome male politicians' opposition to a woman's right to vote

    (B) Key battles won by United States soldiers during World War II

    (C) Biographical information about contributors to the writing of the United States Constitution

    (D) Immigrants from foreign countries who became successful businesspeople in the United States

5. Classify each topic below according to the professor's descriptions. Indicate whether each topic below would likely relate more to 1. Establishment View or 2. Minority View.

    | A | Descriptions of the education of each United States President _____ |
    | B | Job discrimination experienced by recent immigrants from a variety of nations _____ |
    | C | Debates among wealthy delegates as the United States Bill of Rights was written _____ |
    | D | Personal struggles of African-American leaders during the 1960s Civil Rights Movement _____ |

10

Listen to Track 81.

Now answer the question.

6. What is the professor's attitude?

    (A) She believes high school history textbooks provide an accurate, fair representation of historical events.

    (B) She doubts that most students in the course have been taught history before.

    (C) She is uncertain whether some students have enrolled in the correct course.

    (D) She hopes that students are willing to question things they think they know about history.

10.10

Listen to Track 82.

Now answer the questions.

1. What is the main topic of this lecture?

    (A) How to determine the appropriate pricing for a luxury product

    (B) Factors to consider in developing a marketing strategy

    (C) Why some marketing strategies fail

    (D) The differences between mass-market products and specialty products

2. According to the professor, what might be two examples of a poor marketing strategy?
    Choose 2 answers.

    [A] Selling products at a price lower than competitors' products

    [B] Using a mass-market distribution strategy for a luxury product

    [C] Failing to consider the quality of a product in an advertising campaign

    [D] Using promotions to encourage existing customers to repeat purchases

3. Why does the professor talk about breakfast cereal?

    (A) To provide an example of a product for which a broad placement strategy is appropriate

    (B) To illustrate the difference between a perishable product and a nonperishable product

    (C) To demonstrate how effective sales promotions can be

    (D) To show that marketing encompasses much more than just advertising

4. In the example about designer jewelry, what does the professor imply about offering price discounts?

   (A) It is an effective way to generate new, profitable customers.

   (B) It may result in opportunities to sell additional products to existing customers.

   (C) It works against the image of the product being special.

   (D) It can provide insight about which customers are likely to recommend the product to their friends.

5. What is the professor's point when she discusses advertising?

   (A) It is only one of a variety of promotional techniques.

   (B) Most people are not familiar with the tactics used in advertising to persuade people to buy products.

   (C) No product can be sold successfully without advertising.

   (D) It should not be used if the product is dangerous for some people.

 Listen to Track 83.

Now answer the question.

---

6. What does the professor mean when she says this?

   (A) She is asking students what their preferred pricing strategies are.

   (B) She is uncertain whether the point she is discussing is relevant to marketing strategy.

   (C) She is trying to illustrate that pricing strategy involves more than just determining what consumers are willing to pay.

   (D) She believes that some pricing strategies are always superior to others.

Answer Key—10.1

Question	Correct Answer	Right/Wrong	Category
1	C		Gist-content
2	B		Organization
3	A		Function of What Is Said
4	D		Detail
5	D		Detail
6	Prisoner's Dilemma: A, C. Zero-Sum Game: B, D.		Connecting Content

Answer Key—10.2

Question	Correct Answer	Right/Wrong	Category
1	B		Gist-purpose
2	A		Speaker's Attitude
3	C		Detail
4	A		Organization
5	B, C, D		Detail
6	A, C		Detail

Answer Key—10.3

Question	Correct Answer	Right/Wrong	Category
1	C		Gist-content
2	A		Detail
3	B		Detail
4	A		Organization
5	D		Organization
6	D		Function of What Is Said

Answer Key—10.4

Question	Correct Answer	Right/Wrong	Category
1	A		Gist-purpose
2	B		Organization
3	D		Detail
4	C		Detail
5	A		Detail
6	1. Under Three: A, C. 2. Four or Older: B, D.		Connecting Content

Answer Key—10.5

Question	Correct Answer	Right/Wrong	Category
1	D		Gist-content
2	B, D		Detail
3	B		Organization
4	C		Inference
5	D		Organization
6	A		Function of What Is Said

Answer Key—10.6

Question	Correct Answer	Right/Wrong	Category
1	D		Gist-content
2	D		Detail
3	A		Detail
4	B		Inference
5	A		Inference
6	C		Speaker's Attitude

Answer Key—10.7

Question	Correct Answer	Right/Wrong	Category
1	A		Gist-content
2	C		Inference
3	B		Detail
4	A		Inference
5	B		Inference
6	D		Speaker's Attitude

Answer Key—10.8

Question	Correct Answer	Right/Wrong	Category
1	B		Gist-content
2	A		Organization
3	C		Function of What Is Said
4	A		Detail
5	D		Detail
6	A, D		Connecting Content

Answer Key—10.9

Question	Correct Answer	Right/Wrong	Category
1	A		Gist-purpose
2	B		Organization
3	C		Detail
4	A		Inference
5	1. Establishment: A, C. 2. Minority: B, D.		Connecting Content
6	D		Speaker's Attitude

Answer Key—10.10

Question	Correct Answer	Right/Wrong	Category
1	B		Gist-content
2	B, C		Detail
3	A		Organization
4	C		Inference
5	A		Organization
6	C		Function of What Is Said

MANHATTAN PREP

Answers and Explanations—10.1

Zero-Sum Games—Track 68

NARRATOR: Listen to part of a lecture in a business management class.

PROFESSOR: All right, last week we started talking about game theory, and how it applies to management of companies. Does anyone remember the name of the example we talked about?

MALE STUDENT: Was it the *prisoner's dilemma*?

PROFESSOR: Yes… and what did it prove?

FEMALE STUDENT: Rational agents sometimes may not cooperate with each other.

PROFESSOR: That's right. And why is that?

MALE STUDENT: It's because, um… it might be in their interest to not cooperate.

PROFESSOR: Exactly. In a prisoner's dilemma, each prisoner has an incentive to cooperate with the police—in other words, to not cooperate with each other—because if they do, they will receive a lighter punishment. So, cooperating with police basically means confessing. But if neither confesses, they will be much better off than if both of them confess. The worst case for either prisoner is to not confess, when the other prisoner *does* confess.

So it leads to a dilemma. Do I confess, or do I honor my commitment to the other prisoner not to confess? This requires, absolutely, that the prisoners trust each other entirely. They each trust that the other one will not confess. Otherwise, there's no point—both sides will confess and both sides will be ruined. But, if the trust is there, then there is still incentive to cheat on the agreement to cooperate—to go ahead and confess when the other prisoner doesn't. Because in that case, the prisoner who confesses may get off scot-free.

So now, today, we are going to pivot to a new way of looking at game theory situations, and how this impacts business decision-making. Today, we will talk about zero-sum games.

OK, so can anyone tell me what a *zero-sum game* is? Yes?

FEMALE STUDENT: It's a game in which the total profit is fixed.

PROFESSOR: OK… and?

FEMALE STUDENT: And?

PROFESSOR: Listen, you're right, the total profit is fixed. So what does that—

FEMALE STUDENT: It means that… let's say I make a decision that improves my profit…

PROFESSOR: Right, so you're acting in your own best interest, trying to maximize your own profit. What does that do to the other player in the zero-sum game? And when would this come up?

FEMALE STUDENT: It reduces that other person's by the same amount.

PROFESSOR: Yes, that's true… Also, I asked… I asked when this would come up. I wanna know what this has to do with business decision-making. Yes.

MALE STUDENT: Well, for example, if we're talking about acquiring a customer, and there's only one possible customer, then whichever firm gets that customer… the other firm loses that potential customer.

PROFESSOR: OK. And… the point is—a zero-sum game—it–it is a "winner and loser" game. If someone gains, someone else has to lose something. So these games model highly competitive situations. Ones in which you cannot gain without someone else taking a hit.

FEMALE STUDENT: So this would be like, say, poker or trading in the stock market?

PROFESSOR: Yes, that's *exactly*… that's exactly what I'm getting at. If I win a pot in a poker game, it must be because someone else failed to win that pot. In a sense, I can only profit by taking someone else's money. Likewise, in the stock market, I can only make a profit in a stock by buying it from someone at a low price, and selling it to someone else at a high price—thereby denying the original holder of the stock of the profit he could have made by selling it to the other party at the price I sold it. Now, these are interesting games because in both cases, there can be *transaction costs*. Say I'm playing poker in a casino. How does the casino make money?

MALE STUDENT: Don't they take a small amount out of every pot?

PROFESSOR: That's precisely what happens. So in effect, the casino does not care who wins the pot. They care about…

FEMALE STUDENT: …They want to play as many hands as possible.

PROFESSOR: Right. So, is that still a zero-sum game?

FEMALE STUDENT: …No.

PROFESSOR: Well, it depends on how you frame it. If you're only talking about the poker players at the table, then no, it is no longer a zero-sum game. But what if we include the casino as a player in this game?

Then in that case, it still is a zero-sum game, but the number of players has increased by one. A couple of game-theory experts named von Neumann and Morgenstern proved years ago that any non-zero-sum game can be modeled as a zero-sum game by adding one additional player. This player represents the net profits, or losses, of the other players.

In business, zero-sum games occur frequently. They can be dangerous. And recent research has shown that over time, zero-sum games can cause damage to society as a whole. Think about two businesses that spend all their resources fighting to steal customers from each other, rather than focusing on higher goals, such as innovation of products, or environmental sustainability. How do we avoid falling into the short-term, zero-sum trap? We've run out of time, so we will get into this discussion next week.

1.　　　What is the lecture mainly about?

　　✗　Ⓐ A review of the "prisoner's dilemma" game example

　　✗　Ⓑ Contrasting the game of poker with stock market investing

　　✓　Ⓒ A topic within game theory called "zero-sum games"

　　✗　Ⓓ Explaining theories developed by von Neumann and Morgenstern

GIST-CONTENT. The main discussion of this lecture is zero-sum games, although there is a substantial review of the prisoner's dilemma at the beginning.

While this takes up a fair portion of the lecture, this review is primarily used to pivot to a new topic—zero-sum games.

The lecture compares the two, rather than contrasting them. Furthermore, these are merely examples used to illustrate zero-sum games.

CORRECT. The main discussion of the lecture is about zero-sum games.

The von Neumann and Morgenstern finding involved how to model non-zero-sum games as zero-sum games. This is not the main point of the lecture.

  MANHATTAN PREP

2.   Why does the professor talk about poker and stock market investing?

   ✗ (A) To avoid expanding on a topic brought up by a student

   ✓ (B) To illustrate examples of zero-sum games

   ✗ (C) To demonstrate different payouts to participants in a prisoner's dilemma game

   ✗ (D) To explain why zero-sum games don't exist in real life

ORGANIZATION. When a student brings up poker and stock market investing, the professor goes on to explain why they are good examples of zero-sum games.

On the contrary, while these examples were given by a student, the professor points out that they are good examples. He then furthers the discussion by explaining why they are good examples of zero-sum games.

CORRECT. The examples were given by a student, but the professor uses them as examples to illustrate what zero-sum games are and what characteristics they have.

Poker and stock-market investing are given as examples of zero-sum games, not prisoner's dilemma games.

On the contrary, the professor explains that zero-sum games do exist, and that all non-zero-sum games can be modeled as zero-sum games by adding an additional player.

Track 69

NARRATOR: Listen again to part of the lecture. Then answer the question.

PROFESSOR: In a prisoner's dilemma, each prisoner has an incentive to cooperate with the police—in other words, to not cooperate with each other—because if they do, they will receive a lighter punishment. So, cooperating with police basically means confessing. But if neither confesses, they will be much better off than if both of them confess. The worst case for either prisoner is to not confess, when the other prisoner *does* confess.

So it leads to a dilemma. Do I confess, or do I honor my commitment to the other prisoner not to confess? This requires, absolutely, that the prisoners trust each other entirely. They each trust that the other one will not confess.

NARRATOR: Why does the professor say this:

PROFESSOR: This requires, absolutely, that the prisoners trust each other entirely. They each trust that the other one will not confess.

3. Why does the professor say this?

FUNCTION OF WHAT IS SAID. In this quote, the professor describes the structure of a prisoner's dilemma situation in detail, explaining that each prisoner is better off confessing, but in total, the two prisoners are better off not confessing. The highlighted phrase is used to illustrate the importance of trust in achieving their ultimate goal, which is for neither of the prisoners to confess.

✓ (A) To stress the level of mutual cooperation that the prisoners need to maintain

CORRECT. The prisoners must trust each other strongly in order for both of them to overcome the temptation to confess. This is the only way to avoid a harsh penalty for one or both.

✗ (B) To note that each side individually is better off not confessing

The opposite is true. Each side, individually, is better off confessing, irrespective of what the other party does.

✗ (C) To point out that without trust, neither side is likely to confess

The opposite is true. Without trust, each side is likely to confess.

✗ (D) To indicate how the situation is likely to turn into a zero-sum game

In this discussion, the professor is talking about a prisoner's dilemma, not a zero-sum game.

4. What is an example of a zero-sum game?

DETAIL. Zero-sum games are ones in which the total combined profit (or loss) of both sides is fixed. Therefore, one side cannot gain without the other side losing.

✗ (A) A worker's hourly wage is determined by his productivity in the prior quarter.

This is not a "winners and losers" situation and thus not an example of a zero-sum game.

✗ (B) The stock market goes up, increasing the value of the holdings of most owners of company stock.

This is an example in which nearly everyone profits, and thus not an example of a zero-sum game.

✗ (C) Two countries in a peace agreement each have an incentive to violate the terms of the agreement.

This is a cooperative game with incentives to not cooperate. In other words, this is a prisoner's dilemma example, not a zero-sum game example.

✓ (D) Only three gifts are available to be distributed among four children.

CORRECT. Once three children get their gifts (the "winners"), the other child must necessarily not get one (the "loser"). This child cannot take a gift without causing an equivalent loss for one of the other children. Therefore, this is a standard example of a zero-sum game.

5. According to the professor, how can non-zero-sum games be modeled as zero-sum games?

    DETAIL. The professor explains that von Neumann and Morgenstern proved that non-zero-sum games can be modeled as a zero-sum game by adding an additional player. That player represents the net profits or losses to the other players.

  ✗ (A) By turning the game into a prisoner's dilemma

This possibility is not mentioned in the lecture.

  ✗ (B) By increasing transaction costs

If anything, any transaction costs must be reduced (to zero) to turn the non-zero-sum-game into a zero-sum game.

  ✗ (C) By temporarily removing a player from the game

Removing a player is never mentioned in the lecture.

  ✓ (D) By adding a player to the game

CORRECT. This new player represents the net combined profits or losses of the other players.

6. Classify each statement below as describing a prisoner's dilemma or a zero-sum game.

    CONNECTING CONTENT. Prisoner's dilemma games are discussed at the beginning of the lecture. Zero-sum games are discussed throughout the rest of the lecture.

  [A] The two sides in the game are better off cooperating.

PRISONER'S DILEMMA. This is one of the key features of a prisoner's dilemma.

  [B] One side cannot gain without the other side losing.

ZERO-SUM GAME. This is a key feature of zero-sum games.

  [C] Cooperation requires high levels of trust.

PRISONER'S DILEMMA. This is one of the requirements of avoiding the "confession trap" of a prisoner's dilemma.

  [D] It can be dangerous to society as a whole.

ZERO-SUM GAME. This is mentioned near the end of a lecture as a potential consequence of zero-sum games.

10

Answers and Explanations—10.2

The Dot-com Crash—Track 70

NARRATOR: Listen to part of a lecture in an economics class.

PROFESSOR: Good morning class. I hope you had an enjoyable weekend. Now, last week we discussed the housing bubble and credit crisis that nearly destroyed the global economy in 2008. Can anyone recall what the primary cause of that bubble was?

FEMALE STUDENT: Credit that was far too easy to access?

PROFESSOR: Right, and it was specifically credit to buy homes that was extended to people who could not afford it. People who had no hope of ever repaying the loans they were taking out. This was driven by speculation on Wall Street—people wanted to invest in fixed income assets that promised a higher return

than safer securities, like United States Treasury Bonds. And the investment banks provided them. More and more and more to fill the demand. Unfortunately, everyone was asleep at the wheel and the situation disintegrated to the point where almost no one had any idea just how bad the credit characteristics of these fixed income products had become. Meanwhile, home prices soared, as all this new money was chasing a relatively fixed number of homes on the market. Eventually, the whole thing collapsed.

There are quite a few similarities between this crash and the one before it. Does anyone know what that crash was?

FEMALE STUDENT: The Asian crisis?

PROFESSOR: Oh, you mean the financial crisis in Asia, in 1997? Actually… yes, that's a good one, you can definitely argue that was caused by credit that was too easy. Credit boom, then credit bust, in, uh, Thailand, South Korea, and Indonesia especially. But I was actually thinking of another crash, a little closer to home. Yes?

MALE STUDENT: The internet crash?

PROFESSOR: Yes. Most people call it the "*dot-com crash*" or the "dot-com bubble." But that's exactly right. This bubble was actually quite short-lived, much like the housing bubble—it took less than 10 years from the beginning of the bubble to the end of the crash. Some bubbles can last for much longer. But what caused it in the first place?

Well, to understand this, you have to understand a bit about psychology. The psychology of investing. See, whenever a new innovation comes along, there is a lot of excitement about it. Innovation means something new; it means business opportunities. For the dot-com crash, it meant new companies sprang up, and these companies needed cash to grow, before they earned any profit. So they needed investors.

Often when this happens, virtually no one has any idea what ideas are going to work. It means that some companies will get overvalued, and some valuable ideas will be ignored. It means that people have no real idea how big the new innovation could be, how big the mature industry will be, and so on. It also means that, if people are making money on these stocks, other investors from other areas are going to see all this money being made in this new area, and they are going to allocate their capital to investing in that new area. Even if they have no idea what's going on there. A type of "blind mania" takes over.

So—the landscape for investing in this new arena is going to become overcrowded very easily. Many investment dollars will be chasing the relatively few investments that are truly sound and promising. What's the result? Well, fundamentals get overlooked. Having a solid business plan becomes less important than having a "snappy idea" that you can convince others to buy into. You're going to get a ton of investments in businesses that are almost certain to fail.

That's exactly what happened in the late 1990s. And it can take time before people return to their senses—in this case, really, the peak of the "mania" was in roughly 1998 and 1999, and the market for internet companies began sagging in mid-2000. By 2001, the party was over, and trillions of dollars worth of investment capital, at least on paper, was totally wiped out. In fact, by late 2002, the NASDAQ Index, which is heavily technology-weighted, lost nearly 80 percent of its value from its peak only two years earlier. This sounds terrible, and indeed it was, but believe it or not, plenty of crashes in the past have been much, much worse.

So, you have the classic symptoms of a boom-and-crash cycle: a new product or innovation, a large demand to invest in it, a lot of uncertainty about the final outcome—who the winners and losers will be—and a general "mania" or "euphoria" that overcomes the investing public. Once all of these things come together,

you have the perfect recipe for a crash. Once the crash starts, this "mania" turns into terror and panic, and everything falls apart. Next week, however, we will see how you can profit from this irrational fear that grows out of the initial, irrational mania.

1.   What is the main purpose of this talk?

   ✗ (A) To evaluate the causes of market crashes in the twentieth century

   ✓ (B) To explore the dot-com crash as a way to understand boom-and-bust cycles in general

   ✗ (C) To argue in favor of better regulation to reduce the likelihood or severity of market crashes

   ✗ (D) To predict that boom-and-crash cycles will become less common in the future

GIST-PURPOSE. The main discussion of this lecture is market crashes—in particular, the dot-com crash of the early 2000s.

The lecture is primarily focused on the dot-com crash, which occurred in 2000–2002 (mostly in the twenty-first century). It does not discuss all twentieth-century market crashes.

CORRECT. Roughly half of the lecture is devoted to the specifics of the dot-com crash. Much of the rest explains other crashes or market crashes in general, and how the dot-com crash is a typical example of them.

While the professor would likely agree that reducing the severity or frequency of crashes would be a good thing, she does not indicate that regulation could help prevent or diminish them.

Nothing in the lecture indicates that the professor believes this to be the case.

2.   What is the speaker's opinion about the housing bubble and credit crisis?

   ✓ (A) Most people were ignoring the ability of borrowers to repay the loans given to them.

   ✗ (B) The investment banks would have preferred that lenders were more selective in choosing homebuyers to lend money to.

   ✗ (C) Investors believed that the loans being given to homebuyers were safer than United States Treasury bonds.

   ✗ (D) The increase in home values during the housing bubble was justified.

SPEAKER'S ATTITUDE. This is discussed briefly at the beginning of the lecture. The speaker's attitude is that no one was paying attention to borrowers' ability to repay the loans.

CORRECT. The key line in the lecture is that "everyone was asleep at the wheel." That is, the professor believes that people in general (most or all of them) must have been ignoring the ability of borrowers to repay the loans.

The professor mentions that investment banks provided higher-return investment opportunities, which necessitated more loans being given out. Therefore, it is not clear that the investment banks wanted more selectivity.

The professor does indicate that investors wanted higher-return investment options. However, she does not go so far as to say that investors believed such investments were safer than United States Treasury bonds.

The professor believes that the opposite is true. She believes that the increase in home values was unjustified and that the crash was inevitable.

10

3. According to the professor, when did the dot-com bubble "mania" reach its peak?

DETAIL. The professor mentions the timing of three major boom-and-crash cycles: the Asian financial crisis, the dot-com crash, and the housing bubble and credit crisis.

✗ (A) In 2008

This is when the housing bubble collapsed after the credit crisis began.

✗ (B) In 2001

This is when the dot-com *crash* was occurring.

✓ (C) In 1998 and 1999

CORRECT. The professor states that "the peak of the 'mania' was in roughly 1998 and 1999."

✗ (D) In 1997

According to the professor, this is when the Asian financial crisis happened.

4. Why does the professor mention "other investors from other areas" that began to invest in dot-com companies?

ORGANIZATION. This is mentioned to explain some of the factors that contribute to market bubbles, using the dot-com crash as an example. Specifically, the professor mentions these naïve investors to highlight the fact that some were not skilled at investing in this new area.

✓ (A) To highlight the relative inexperience of these investors

CORRECT. The lack of experience on the part of these investors—at least in technology companies—contributes to the idea that bad investments were bound to be made.

✗ (B) To emphasize that traditional investors in technology were not interested in dot-com companies

This is not indicated anywhere in the lecture.

✗ (C) To argue that the dot-com crash had already begun before these other investors got involved

If anything, the dot-com crash began after this. The inexperienced new investors were a contributing factor to the crash that came later.

✗ (D) To suggest that these investors lacked attractive opportunities in areas they typically invested in

It is possible that investors experienced at investing in other areas may have been suffering from a lack of interesting opportunities in their typical industries of focus. But nothing in the lecture suggests that this was the case.

5.   According to the professor, which of the following factors contributed to the dot-com crash in 2000–2002? *Choose 3 answers.*

DETAIL. Toward the end of the lecture, the professor explains several factors that contributed to the dot-com crash.

✗ ☐ A   A lack of competition among investors in technology businesses

If anything, the opposite is true. The space was "overcrowded" with investors, which generally leads to increased competition.

✓ ☐ B   A high demand to invest in dot-com companies relative to the amount of investment funds being sought

CORRECT. The professor strongly implies that there was much more money available for investment into dot-com companies than could be productively used by these companies. This led to bad investments, as is typical in a boom-and-crash cycle.

✓ ☐ C   The development of a new product or innovation with great potential

CORRECT. This is mentioned directly in the lecture as a contributing factor to the dot-com crash.

✓ ☐ D   A great deal of uncertainty about which companies will succeed and which will fail

CORRECT. This uncertainty is mentioned directly in the lecture as a contributing factor to the dot-com crash.

✗ ☐ E   A loss of interest in pursuing non-technology investments

The professor never suggests that investors lost interest in investing in non-technology companies.

6.   The professor mentions that the investment landscape for a new, promising innovation often becomes overcrowded. What does this fact explain? *Choose 2 answers.*

DETAIL. In the middle of the lecture, the professor mentions that the investing space for a new, promising innovation can become overcrowded. This can lead to too many investments being made, and therefore some poor investments being made.

✓ ☐ A   Why having a solid business plan becomes less important to prospective investors

CORRECT. The professor mentions this in describing a primary factor behind the development of market bubbles. Specifically, investment opportunities in the new area are so highly sought that at some point, investors may begin ignoring the fundamentals of a company and are seduced by attractive sales pitches instead.

✗ ☐ B   Why a general "mania" or "euphoria" overcomes the investing public

While this occurrence is true of most boom-and-crash cycles, it is not caused by the investment area becoming overcrowded. If anything, the reverse is true—a general "mania" causes investors to flood into the new area, resulting in overcrowding.

✓ ☐ C   Why there will often be many investments made in fundamentally unsound businesses

CORRECT. Because the space is overcrowded, there are more investment dollars seeking a company to invest in than there are strong companies seeking investment. As a result, some bad investments usually are made.

✗ ☐ D   Why the companies working on developing this innovation typically need cash from investors to grow

Growing companies typically need cash from investors to grow, but this fact is not explained by the investment space in a market bubble becoming overcrowded.

Answers and Explanations—10.3

Managing Telecommuters—Track 71

NARRATOR: Listen to part of a lecture in a business class.

PROFESSOR: OK so… we've talked about technology, and how rapidly it has changed in the past generation or so. We've discussed the economic benefits this has had for businesses. Now we're going to talk about the impact technology has had on businesses from, um… a new angle. A different, you know, perspective.

Technology has sharply increased the productivity of office workers, but it's also changed the way that these workers have, have interacted with their job. In fact, with technology, many office tasks can now be done from anywhere. This has led to a significant increase in people working full-time outside of a formal office space. We call these people "telecommuters," and we're going to talk about how to manage them— *managing telecommuters.*

Now, this is a big benefit to many employees. They save money and time, by not having to dress up every day, and by not having to commute to work. But it presents a new, ah… wrinkle that some managers don't like. In fact… did you hear about it? Um, that company… let's just call it a technology company. Anyway, the CEO of this company surprised everyone by announcing that their "work from home" program was going to be eliminated. In the technology industry especially, a lot of people work from home, because they can. But she said that, while people tend to be more productive when they work alone, they tend to actually be more creative and collaborative when they are working from–from the same location. They talk to each other more, ah, bounce ideas, you know, off of one another. Soon after she made this announcement, several other companies followed her lead. Yes, Jonathan?

MALE STUDENT: Well I think maybe that's a bit too harsh—I mean, maybe for some jobs you need that sort of thing, but maybe for others, productivity is more important than collaborating, right?

PROFESSOR: You know, that's a good point. And, er… I'm going to have to agree with you. But if the executive's viewpoint is that, as a company, more collaboration and innovation is needed, then, uh, well… you know—she can't very easily make a new policy that only applies to *some* of the employees. The employees being affected will wonder why others don't have to follow the new rules. I mean, wouldn't you feel that way? So look, at the time she felt it was what the company needed. She also admitted that the way she made the announcement, ah… you know—it could have been handled better.

But let's assume that you work for a company that has telecommuters. Maybe just a few, maybe a lot of people who can't or–or won't physically convene in the same office space. What are some things your company will need to do to make sure that this setup works well for the company's needs?

Well, studies have shown that, indeed, telecommuters tend to be more productive. They use some of the time they'd spend traveling to and from work, well—they spend it working instead. They call in sick less often, and are usually happier with their job—especially if they have children. And also, it can cut down on office expenses—especially rent, because you need less space with fewer people in the office.

But, there are problems. Some people do not work as efficiently if there is not direct oversight. They get distracted, or lose focus, or focus on the wrong things. Or, for some jobs, the needs can change rapidly, and

it can be difficult, to, you know—gather the resources of a team to shift focus to something new if they're scattered all over the place. Yes, Angela?

FEMALE STUDENT: But how can you really tell whether someone is being less productive when working from home? I mean, I can get distracted just as easily in an office with lots of people, plus with the internet, and for me, at home… it's much easier to drown out all the distractions and focus on what I need to.

PROFESSOR: Well, then you are an ideal candidate for telecommuting! See the problem, ah, is that it is very difficult to measure this… the, um… well, how productive people are from home relative to in an office. I mean, there's software designed to help managers track this, but a lot of them are focused on inputs—how many hours did John say he worked on XYZ project?—rather than outputs—was XYZ project completed on time, and was it done properly? So it really does take experience, not just software, to learn how to manage telecommuters effectively.

There are a few things I can offer, though, that will make the task much easier. First, make sure everyone has a phone and email address so you can–can check in with them regularly. Second, set up a conference calling system that everyone uses frequently. Communication via video conferencing, for example, can be just as effective as in-person meetings. Third, make sure everyone has laptops, so they can bring their work into the office easily, and ensure they have backups and encryption. Finally, um… make sure to track the performance—the outputs—of your telecommuters. Be sure they meet your expectations, or match the performance of other employees who work from the office.

1. What is this lecture primarily about?

    GIST-CONTENT. The main topic of the lecture is simply the management of telecommuters.

    ✗ (A) The economic impact of telecommuting technology in recent decades

    Telecommuting has become much more prevalent in the past several decades thanks to technology, but this is not the main focus of the lecture.

    ✗ (B) The advantages and disadvantages of being a telecommuter

    Some of these are mentioned, but the lecture is more focused on managing telecommuters than on the perspective of the telecommuter himself or herself.

    ✓ (C) The management of telecommuters

    CORRECT. Virtually everything discussed in the lecture falls under the umbrella of managing telecommuters.

    ✗ (D) The reasons why some managers dislike telecommuters

    The professor mentions reasons why some managers dislike the practice of telecommuting, not the telecommuters themselves. Furthermore, this is not the main focus of the lecture.

2. According to the professor, what is a potential drawback of allowing telecommuting?

    ✓ (A) Some telecommuters lose focus without direct oversight.

    ✗ (B) Some telecommuters dislike having their outputs tracked.

    ✗ (C) Telecommuters are more likely to have children, which means they will tend to work less and be distracted more.

    ✗ (D) Employees who are forced to work from an office often become resentful of telecommuters, causing morale to drop.

DETAIL. Several potential drawbacks are stated in the lecture.

CORRECT. This is stated as one potential drawback of telecommuting for some employees.

This idea is not mentioned in the lecture.

If anything, the opposite is true. While the professor states that employees with children do tend to prefer telecommuting, she also states that telecommuters in general tend to work *more* than employees who work from an office.

This idea is not mentioned in the lecture.

3. What does the professor say about the software used to track the productivity of telecommuters?

    ✗ (A) It can be very expensive to set up and maintain across a distributed network.

    ✓ (B) Much of it is focused on tracking inputs, like time spent working on a project, rather than outputs.

    ✗ (C) Much of it lacks important features like email and video conferencing capabilities.

    ✗ (D) Frequently it lacks safeguards like password protection and encryption.

DETAIL. The professor mentions productivity tracking software for telecommuters toward the end of the lecture. She states that this can help in managing telecommuters, but that it has drawbacks.

This idea is not mentioned in the lecture.

CORRECT. The professor notes that, frequently, software designed to help manage telecommuters is too focused on employee inputs rather than outputs.

Email and video conferencing are mentioned, but this functionality need not be part of the same software package as telecommuter performance tracking.

This idea is not mentioned in the context of telecommuter performance tracking. Encryption is mentioned later, but only with respect to employee laptops.

4.   Why does the professor mention the announcement made by a particular technology CEO?

ORGANIZATION. The decision regarding telecommuting at this technology company is used to illustrate the pushback against telecommuting from some managers and begin a discussion about the reasons for this pushback.

✓ (A) To demonstrate that some managers do not like, or are uncomfortable with, telecommuting

CORRECT. The CEO announced that telecommuting at the company would no longer be allowed. This case is used as an example of some managers not being comfortable with telecommuting.

✗ (B) To explain why telecommuters are more productive than regular employees

While the lecture indicates that this may be true, the CEO's decision discussed by the professor does not explain this in any way.

✗ (C) To argue that most companies should not allow the practice of telecommuting

If anything, the professor believes the opposite is true. The CEO example introduces reasons why some managers may not like telecommuting, but the professor is clearly an advocate of telecommuting under the right circumstances.

✗ (D) To indicate that telecommuting is becoming far less common in the technology industry

According to the professor, telecommuting in the technology industry is a widespread practice, the CEO's decision notwithstanding.

5.   Why does the professor discuss telecommuters being "scattered all over the place"?

ORGANIZATION. In the middle of the lecture, the professor enumerates some of the advantages and disadvantages of telecommuting. She states that telecommuters being "scattered all over the place" is a disadvantage when work circumstances change rapidly and the team's resources need to be redirected.

✗ (A) To assert that having a broad geographic exposure of a company's employee base can be beneficial for creating new marketing opportunities

This idea is not mentioned in the lecture.

✗ (B) To point out that telecommuters are much more likely to live far from a company's office than non-telecommuters

While this may indeed be the case, this is not why the professor mentions the phrase "scattered all over the place."

✗ (C) To provide reasons why a telecommuter may be reluctant to come into a company's office

The idea of telecommuters being reluctant to come into a company's office is not discussed in the lecture.

✓ (D) To underscore a disadvantage of telecommuting, particularly when business needs change rapidly

CORRECT. The professor claims that when the needs of a job change rapidly, having a "scattered" workforce can make adapting to those changes more difficult.

Track 72

NARRATOR: What does the professor imply when she says this:

PROFESSOR: Anyway, the CEO of this company surprised everyone by announcing that their "work-from-home" program was going to be eliminated. In the technology industry especially, a lot of people work from home, because they can.

6.   What does the professor imply when she says this?

FUNCTION OF WHAT IS SAID. In this quote, the professor cites the CEO's decision to eliminate the "work-from-home" program at the company. She then explains that working from home is common in the technology industry, and states why that is the case.

✗   (A) The company in question is not a prominent technology company.

If anything, the implication is that the company is prominent. The professor does not seem to want to mention the name of the company.

✗   (B) The CEO herself was generally unpopular with her employees.

While the CEO's *decision* may have been unpopular with some employees, nothing in the lecture indicates that the CEO *herself* was unpopular.

✗   (C) Other technology companies are likely to follow suit and eliminate their "work-from-home" programs.

The professor states later in the lecture that other companies did follow this company's lead, but does not indicate that they were technology companies. Furthermore, nothing in the quoted portion of the lecture implies anything about other technology companies.

✓   (D) If given a choice between telecommuting and working from an office, some employees would choose to telecommute.

CORRECT. The professor states that "in the technology industry especially, a lot of people work from home, because they can." This implies that a lot of people choose to work from home.

Answers and Explanations—10.4

The Notion of "Self"—Track 73

NARRATOR: Listen to part of a lecture in a psychology class.

PROFESSOR: OK, if I ask you whether or not you have a "self," I am going to assume that all of you would say "yes." Right? What distinguishes humans from other, um… creatures in the animal kingdom is this idea that we have a *"sense of self."* It is so fundamental to what it means to be a human being that you probably can't even imagine what it would feel like not to have a "self."

As I said, I assume all of you would say "yes," that you have a self, because the sense of self in human beings is, it's safe to say, universal. Of course, there will be some exceptions—people who have brain damage and so forth—but in general, human beings perceive themselves as separate from the world around them, and thus, as individual entities. Now, where does our sense of self come from? It's… um, well… it's helpful to think of how a sense of self develops over time in a human child. When an infant is only a few months old, for instance, the infant will believe that anything he or she cannot see… just isn't there. There is no notion of, "Maybe I can't see it, but it still exists somewhere." If the baby's mother leaves the room? As far as that

baby is concerned, the mother has ceased to exist. During this period, the baby does not have an understanding of self, of course. But the child is learning *object relations*, meaning, how objects relate to one another. Like, I can reach out and touch this ball, and it moves.

Now, after a year or two of life, something changes in the child's brain. At this age, the child becomes able to understand herself as a reference point… she knows that she has a point of view, and that it's only one point of view. So, to get back to our example of the mother leaving the room… now when the mom leaves, the child knows the mom is just in another room. Does the child have a notion of self at this point? Arguably, yes, but it's not yet as fully developed as it will become. Because you can ask the child, "Where's mommy?" And she'll know that mommy is somewhere else that isn't "here." But if you ask the child, "What does your mom think you're doing right now?" the child would have no idea how to answer. Because even though the child understands that she represents just one perspective, she cannot yet imagine viewing herself from someone else's perspective.

So… when does that develop? Around four years of age, maybe a little older… four and a half or so. There have been some studies showing how, at this age, children begin to be able to see themselves from other people's points of view, by imagining themselves in someone else's shoes. This is called *theory of mind*, and it is the highest level of self, in the sense that, this is what distinguishes humans from other species. Now, at this age, children can not only distinguish themselves from other people, but they can also imagine how other people are thinking! Just like all of you can… like we all take for granted every day.

How do we know that children become able to do this around age four, or four and a half? There is a study called the *false belief* test. This test is designed to measure whether a child is capable of reasoning about the mental states of other people. The way that it works is this: someone puts an object—like, say, a pencil—into a box, closes the box, and leaves the room. The child is just watching this happen, OK? The child is now sitting there, and the person has left the room. Next, a new person enters. The new person opens the box, takes the pencil out of the box, closes the box, and puts the pencil in another location. The experimenter will then ask the child, "If we bring the first person back into the room, where will they look for the pencil?" The reason this test works is that the child must be able to distinguish her knowledge—that the pencil is no longer in the box—from the other person's expectation that the pencil will still be in the box. If the child can do this, we know that she is able to actually reason from another person's perspective. And again, for the most part, children can't do this until the age of four or older. By age six, most children can do it.

So… back to our question of where the self comes from. We now know when it develops in humans during childhood. But why do we have this ability while other organisms do not seem to? That question is one that people are still trying to answer.

1. What is the main purpose of the lecture?

    ✓ (A) To discuss how a sense of self develops in humans

    ✗ (B) To describe methods of testing whether a child has a sense of self

    ✗ (C) To argue that the notion of a sense of self is only fully developed in humans

    ✗ (D) To explain why animals other than humans do not have a sense of self

GIST-PURPOSE. The purpose of the lecture is to explain the phases through which a sense of self develops in children.

CORRECT. The lecture discusses this process as it occurs in children.

The professor mentions only one such method. Also, it is a supporting detail, not the overall focus of the lecture.

This is mentioned in the lecture, but it is not the main purpose of the lecture.

The professor only mentions, at the end of the lecture, that the reasons why other organisms do not have a sense of self are not fully understood.

2. Why does the professor predict that she knows how students will respond if she asks whether they have a "self"?

    ✗ (A) To point out that she has gotten to know her students well

    ✓ (B) To illustrate that a sense of self is universal among humans

    ✗ (C) To point out that she expects some students to respond incorrectly

    ✗ (D) To establish that a sense of self does not develop until adulthood

ORGANIZATION. The professor makes this point in order to illustrate that a sense of self is universal in humans. Therefore, she knows what the students' response will be.

This is not why the professor makes this prediction.

CORRECT. She can make this prediction because the sense of self is considered universal among humans.

Nothing in the lecture indicates that the professor believes any students will respond incorrectly.

On the contrary—the professor states that a sense of self almost always develops by age six.

3. What does the professor say about the reasons why humans have a sense of self and other animals appear not to?

    ✗ (A) These reasons are unlikely to ever be discovered.

    ✗ (B) Researchers have yet to begin trying to discover these reasons.

    ✗ (C) Studies into this issue that have been completed show contradictory findings.

    ✓ (D) The reasons are not yet understood.

DETAIL. At the end of the lecture, the professor notes that the question of why humans have a sense of self and other animals apparently do not is one that researchers are still trying to answer.

The professor does not state or imply this at any point in the lecture.

The professor does not imply this at any point in the lecture. In fact, the professor's final comments imply that researchers are currently studying this issue.

The professor does not mention the results of any such studies.

CORRECT. This is the point made by the professor at the end of the lecture.

4.   What does the experiment using a pencil in a box reveal about children?

   ✗ (A) Whether they are able to imitate the actions of another person

   ✗ (B) Whether they can comprehend how objects interact with one another in space

   ✓ (C) Whether they can reason from the perspective of another person

   ✗ (D) Whether they understand that they are children

DETAIL. The experiment is used to determine whether a child is able to reason from the point of view of another person.

The purpose of the experiment is not to determine whether children can imitate the actions of others.

The purpose of the experiment is not to determine whether children understand how objects interact in space.

CORRECT. The professor explicitly states that this is the purpose of the experiment.

The purpose of the experiment is not to determine whether children understand that they are children.

5.   The professor mentions a child who is only several months old and whose mother leaves the room. What is true about this child's perception of the world?

   ✓ (A) The child does not understand that her mother still exists somewhere outside of the room.

   ✗ (B) The child understands that her mother is somewhere else, but does not yet understand that her mother has her own perspective.

   ✗ (C) The child is certain that her mother will return, although the child cannot express this certainty.

   ✗ (D) The child believes and hopes that her mother might return, but is not certain.

DETAIL. According to the professor, when a child is only several months old, she does not understand that when her mother is not visible, her mother still exists somewhere.

CORRECT. At this very young age, the child has not yet developed an understanding that she has access to only one perspective in the world.

The ability to understand that the child's mother exists somewhere else does not develop until one to two years of age.

At this age, the child does not understand that her absent mother still exists somewhere. Therefore, the child is not capable of expecting her mother to return.

At this age, the child does not understand that her absent mother still exists somewhere. Therefore, the child is not capable of expecting her mother to return.

10

6. The professor mentions several abilities that typically appear at specific stages of cognitive development. Classify each of the following abilities as typically occurring either 1. Under the Age of Three or 2. Around Age Four or Older.

| A | Awareness that its mother is elsewhere if not in the room _____ |

| B | Ability to view the world from its mother's perspective _____ |

| C | Ability to understand object relations _____ |

| D | Ability to pass the "false belief" test _____ |

CONNECTING CONTENT. According to the professor, "object relations," or understanding how objects interact in space, is something that children start learning after several months of life. At one to two years old, children understand that they represent only one perspective, but cannot yet reason from another person's perspective. That ability develops around age four or older.

1. UNDER THE AGE OF THREE. This ability develops at one to two years of age.

2. AROUND AGE FOUR OR OLDER. This ability does not typically develop until age four or older.

1. UNDER THE AGE OF THREE. This ability begins developing soon after birth, when an infant is several months old.

2. AROUND AGE FOUR OR OLDER. This test measures one's ability to view the world from another person's perspective, which typically does not develop until age four or older.

Answers and Explanations—10.5

Porter's Five Forces—Track 74

NARRATOR: Listen to part of a lecture in a business management class.

PROFESSOR: OK, let's begin—there's a lot to cover today. Last week, we talked about different frameworks for strategic decision-making. We mentioned PESTEL, which is an acronym that stands for "political, economic, social, technological, environmental, and legal" factors. This is a kind of a laundry list of external factors, meaning factors that arise outside of a company, that shape business opportunities and therefore strategic decision-making. Next, we talked about SWOT analysis, which stands for "strengths, weaknesses, opportunities, and threats." SWOT takes into account both internal factors—the strengths and weaknesses of a company—and external ones—the opportunities and threats.

What we did not get into last week is Michael Porter's Five Forces. This is probably the most well-known strategic framework used in business today. It was published in 1979, in the Harvard Business Review, and has radically changed the way executives think about competitiveness in their industries. We are going to spend a while talking about this framework, because it is so commonly used.

The five forces: bargaining power of suppliers… bargaining power of customers… the threat of new entrants… the threat of substitute products or services… and competitive rivalry. Basically, what Porter said is that these five forces dictate the level of competitiveness in any industry. They are all essential components of an industry landscape for any business executive to understand, before making any strategic decisions. Stamp these forces into your memory! OK. Let's start by talking about the two "bargaining" forces.

When either suppliers or buyers hold a powerful position, it leads to increased competitiveness. For example, think about Walmart. For most mainstream consumer goods companies, Walmart will be a buyer for your products. It is a massive company, will purchase your goods in very large quantities, and therefore will be able to dictate the terms of pricing and delivery much more than, say, a thousand mom-and-pop shops that all buy their product from you. Likewise, if a supplier produces a unique product that your company needs, or has a dominant market share, that supplier can exert a lot of pricing pressure on your company. Powerful suppliers or buyers increase competition in your industry, and this reduces your profitability.

Now, let's look at the threats. The threat of new entrants. Let's say, for example, that your company makes a product that has patent protection. This will create something known as a "barrier to entry" from competitors. In other words, it will be difficult for a competitor to enter the market and fill the demand that your product fulfills. Now, patents can be circumvented, but still, it provides something of a barrier—a, a form of protection—against aggressive competition. Other things can be barriers to entry, like government regulation or high fixed costs to begin operations. Or, what's called "economies of scale," which means that production costs decrease the bigger a company gets. Any of these barriers to entry tend to decrease competition and improve profits. A lack of barriers means that strong profits will not last very long, because new competition will quickly enter the market.

Next, the threat of substitutes. So, a simple example here. Let's say you own a company that has a very profitable business producing extremely high-quality butter. Never mind other butter manufacturers—just assume for a moment that your company produces the world's best butter, and also has an insurmountable barrier to entry. OK? This should be great for your company's bottom line, right? Really strong profits? Well, maybe. But, consider this—people aren't going to pay a ridiculous amount of money for your butter. Why? Because at some point, they will just switch to a different product instead. A substitute product. Maybe olive oil… maybe heavy cream… maybe even soy milk. It just depends on what the butter is used for. There is a reasonable substitute for practically every use of butter. So your ability to raise prices, and thereby generate large profits, is limited. Now, contrast this with, say, a company that has developed a life-saving drug. No other drug has the same effectiveness—in that case, there are no reasonable substitutes. So while the world's best butter manufacturer will hit a limit, the drug manufacturer—assuming it has proper barriers to entry—will be able to charge just about anything for this drug. I mean, what people are going to skimp on paying for a drug that will save their own lives?

We're almost out of time. So, next time we will discuss competitive rivalry—which is fine, because that topic is important enough to merit an entire lecture. Competitive rivalry simply refers to the degree to which existing companies in an industry compete with each other. So, for next time, think of an industry in which competitive rivalry is very high. And think of one in which competitive rivalry is relatively low. We will share these examples next week, and talk about factors that can cause an industry to have very high or very low competitive rivalry.

1.   What is the main topic of this lecture?

GIST-CONTENT. The lecture primarily focuses on Porter's Five Forces, a framework for strategic analysis of an industry and competitive decision-making.

✗   (A) How to improve bargaining power with suppliers and buyers

Bargaining power of suppliers and buyers are two of the five forces, but this is only a subset of what's covered in the lecture. Also, Porter's Five Forces is more focused on understanding bargaining power dynamics, rather than improving them.

✗   (B) How to create barriers to entry

While barriers to entry can be very helpful for protecting a company's profitability, this is not the main focus of the lecture. Also, Porter's Five Forces is more focused on understanding barriers to entry, rather than creating them.

✗   (C) How to eliminate substitute products from the marketplace

The threat of substitutes is one of the five forces, but this only a subset of what's covered in the lecture. Also, Porter's Five Forces is more focused on understanding substitutes, rather than eliminating them.

✓   (D) How to analyze industry dynamics for strategic decision-making

CORRECT. This encompasses all of the topics discussed in the lecture.

2.   According to the professor, what might be two sources of barriers to entry? *Choose 2 answers.*

DETAIL. In the middle of the lecture, the professor discusses a number of sources of barriers to entry, including government regulation, high fixed costs to begin operations, and patent protection.

✗   [A] A lack of pricing coordination among suppliers

Suppliers are not mentioned in the lecture as having anything to do with barriers to entry.

✓   [B] Patent protection

CORRECT. The professor mentions this as a possible barrier to entry.

✗   [C] A high degree of competitive rivalry

Competitive rivalry is one of Porter's Five Forces, but is not mentioned in the lecture as having anything to do with barriers to entry.

✓   [D] High fixed costs to begin operations

CORRECT. The professor mentions this point in the lecture.

3.   Why does the professor talk about Walmart?

ORGANIZATION. The professor mentions Walmart as a very large retailer that will be a powerful buyer for many products that companies produce—particularly consumer products. This will enable Walmart to exert heavy influence on companies that it buys from.

✗ Ⓐ To emphasize the importance of selling to large retailers

This idea is not mentioned anywhere in the lecture.

✓ Ⓑ To provide an example of a buyer with significant bargaining power

CORRECT. Because Walmart will purchase such a large amount of any product it carries, it can exert significant pressure on manufacturers.

✗ Ⓒ To illustrate the difference between a supplier and a buyer

This is not the reason Walmart is mentioned in the lecture.

✗ Ⓓ To give an example of a company with significant barriers to entry

While barriers to entry are discussed in the lecture, this is not the reason Walmart is mentioned.

4.   In the discussion of barriers to entry, what does the professor imply about new competitors when barriers to entry are low?

INFERENCE. The professor states that "barriers to entry tend to decrease competition and improve profits. A lack of barriers means that strong profits will not last very long, because new competition will quickly enter the market." The implication is that the new entrants reduce profitability in the market, presumably by reducing pricing.

✗ Ⓐ They will tend to avoid entering a market that has low barriers to entry.

The opposite is true. The professor states that new competition will enter a market when barriers to entry are low.

✗ Ⓑ They will deliver a product that is superior to the original.

This idea is not mentioned or implied in the lecture.

✓ Ⓒ They will reduce the potential profitability for companies in the market they enter.

CORRECT. This professor says that "strong profits will not last very long, because new competition will quickly enter the market." This implies that the new competition will cause reduced profit potential for everyone in the market.

✗ Ⓓ They will seek to develop new barriers to entry, often by seeking patent protection.

This idea is not mentioned or implied in the lecture.

10

5.   What is the professor's point when she discusses the example of the butter manufacturer?

ORGANIZATION. The professor grants this hypothetical butter manufacturer strong market position and barriers to entry, but notes that profit making potential will be limited because of the existence of substitute products.

✗   (A) Even the simplest products can sometimes produce strong profits.

While this may be the case, this idea is not discussed in the lecture.

✗   (B) Threats from new entrants and substitute products are less important than the degree of competitive rivalry.

The professor directly states that threats from new entrants and substitute products are important, and is using the butter manufacturer example to illustrate the threat of substitutes.

✗   (C) It is often difficult to make strong profits without patent protection.

While patent protection often leads to barriers to entry, that is not the purpose of the discussion of the hypothetical butter manufacturer.

✓   (D) The threat of substitutes by itself can limit a business's profit-making potential.

CORRECT. The professor assumes very strong market position and barriers to entry for this butter manufacturer, but states: "There is a reasonable substitute for practically every use of butter. So your ability to raise prices, and thereby generate large profits, is limited."

Track 75

NARRATOR: Listen again to part of the lecture. Then answer the question.

PROFESSOR: So while the world's best butter manufacturer will hit a limit, the drug manufacturer—assuming it has proper barriers to entry—will be able to charge just about anything for this drug. I mean, what people are going to skimp on paying for a drug that will save their own lives?

NARRATOR: What does the professor mean when she says this:

PROFESSOR: I mean, what people are going to skimp on paying for a drug that will save their own lives?

6.   What does the professor mean when she says this?

FUNCTION OF WHAT IS SAID. In this quote, the professor delivers the point about substitute products threatening profit potential. The highlighted quote reinforces the idea that pricing power is much stronger for a life-saving drug than for a product like butter that has substitutes.

✓ (A) The drug manufacturer has significant pricing power due to its lack of substitutes.

CORRECT. Because the drug fills an important need and has no realistic substitutes, very high prices for the drug can be charged.

✗ (B) Some people may balk at paying high prices for a drug, even if it does help save lives.

In this case, the professor is asserting the exact opposite. She is saying that people will pay very high prices for a life-saving drug.

✗ (C) Some people may be more interested in helping others than saving their own lives.

This is not the professor's intention from this statement.

✗ (D) The drug manufacturer's ability to charge high prices will be limited by its ability to create barriers to entry.

The professor does make this caveat—she states that she's assuming the drug maker has proper barriers to entry. However, this is not the main point of her statement.

Answers and Explanations—10.6

Comparative Advantage—Track 76

NARRATOR: Listen to part of a lecture in an economics class.

PROFESSOR: Probably you've thought about why countries may decide to trade internationally, or not, for certain products. Some countries even put up barriers to try to limit trading—um, imposing import or export tariffs, for example, or setting quotas—to try to prevent job losses at home. Just about every economist I know would agree that these barriers are a bad idea. Current political trends, however, may suggest that many people feel otherwise.

Regardless, I hope I can convince you, future business leaders, of the value of trade—with a simple argument based on a very simple principle. And that principle is called the theory of *comparative advantage*. Note that it's not really a theory—it's more of a mathematical fact.

First, a little history. Adam Smith made reference, back in the eighteenth century, to the idea of absolute advantage. Now, this is a bit different—Smith said that if we can buy something more cheaply abroad than we can make it home, it makes sense for us to, um, basically... to pocket the difference by just buying the cheaper foreign product. Then, we can turn around and sell a product in that country where we have an advantage. So he's looking at price differences on an absolute basis. But—what if, say, one economy is just much more efficient at producing everything? Should it just not trade at all?

No! Comparative advantage says that it should, in fact, trade... if it has a relative advantage in one product, and a relative disadvantage in another. So, here's where I will attempt to explain this mathematically, using a very simple situation that I hope will be easy to understand.

Let's say there are only two countries—Country X and Country Y—and there are only two products. Products that relate to one another—let's say, socks and shoes. OK. Now, suppose Country X is much more advanced. Let's say that in Country X, a worker can make 12 pairs of shoes, or 8 pairs of socks, in a day. By contrast, let's say that a worker in Country Y can only make 3 pairs of shoes, or 4 pairs of socks, in a day. You would think that Country Y should just trade for both products with Country X, because both products should be cheaper to make in Country X. Is that right?

Well, actually… comparative advantage says that both of these countries can be made better off by trading, assuming they can do so cheaply—meaning shipping costs aren't much of an issue. The reason is, Country X has a relative advantage in making shoes, and Country Y has a relative advantage in making socks. What do I mean? Well, Country X can make more shoes each day than it can make socks, and Country Y can make more socks than shoes.

So… the optimal outcome for both countries is for all the labor in Country X to make shoes, for all the labor in Country Y to make socks, and for them to trade with each other for the footwear they do not produce domestically. As long as they trade in a ratio that is in between Country X's shoes-to-socks ratio and Country Y's shoes-to-socks ratio, both countries will profit. Both!

So let's do the math here. Assume they trade at a ratio of one-to-one: Country X exports one pair of shoes to Country Y in exchange for every pair of socks it imports. Assume that Country X has two workers and Country Y has eight workers—it makes the math easy. In Country X, if one worker makes shoes and one makes socks, it will have 12 pairs of shoes and 8 pairs of socks in a day. But if both workers make shoes, it will have 24 pairs of shoes. It can then trade 12 pairs of shoes and receive 12 pairs of socks. Now, Country X is left with 12 pairs of shoes, but instead of 8 pairs of socks, now it has 12!

Now, let's focus on Country Y. It has eight workers, and if they are divided evenly between making socks and shoes, Country Y would have 12 pairs of shoes and 16 pairs of socks. But, if instead they all made socks, now Country Y would have 32 pairs of socks. Country Y can then trade 12 pairs of socks with Country X, receiving 12 pairs of shoes in return… and like magic, it now has 12 pairs of shoes but 20 pairs of socks instead of 16.

Um, so, both countries profited by specializing in their relative, or comparative, advantage, and trading with the other country. Even though one country was much more productive than the other at, um, making both products. This idea can be extended to more sophisticated examples, but the principle always holds—countries are better off by specializing in some products and exchanging for others, so long as a comparative advantage exists, trading costs are low, and there are no barriers to trade. I hope this proves to you that, while protecting jobs by restricting trade may be politically attractive, in the long run, trade barriers are harmful to both sides.

1.   What is the talk primarily about?

    ✗ (A) Why absolute advantage is a flawed framework for evaluating international trade

    ✗ (B) Ways to restrict the expansion of international trade

    ✗ (C) Lessons learned from history about manufacturing advantages in one country compared with another

    ✓ (D) The theory of comparative advantage and why it supports international trade

GIST-CONTENT. The lecture primarily focuses on comparative advantage, and a mathematical example explaining how it affects international trade decisions.

The professor makes it clear that comparative advantage is the proper metric to use, but the lecture is not devoted to exposing flaws in absolute advantage.

The professor is arguing *against* restricting international trade.

While the professor does mention the historical principle of absolute advantage, this is not the primary focus of the talk.

CORRECT. The professor focuses on comparative advantage, and uses a mathematical example to explain why comparative advantage implies that international trade is beneficial.

2.   According to the professor, under what circumstances should one country trade with another country?

    ✗ (A) When costs of trading abroad are high

    ✗ (B) When one country is more productive generally than another

    ✗ (C) When one country has significantly more labor power available than another

    ✓ (D) When one country can make a product more efficiently than another country, relative to a different product

DETAIL. According to the lecture, the countries should trade whenever one country has a relative advantage at making one product over another product, relative to the other country (provided that trading costs are low).

The opposite is true. Trade should be considered when such costs are low.

This is called "absolute advantage," and the professor explains why this should *not* be the basis for international trade decision-making.

This idea is not discussed in the lecture.

CORRECT. "Comparative advantage" states that when one country has a relative advantage in producing one product over another, relative to the production capabilities in a different country, those countries should trade.

10

3.   According to the professor, what is the main difference between absolute advantage and comparative advantage?

     DETAIL. The professor makes it clear that absolute advantage is simply one country producing a product more efficiently than another, while comparative advantage involves a country being relatively more efficient at producing one good than another good.

   ✓   (A)   Comparative advantage involves the relative production efficiency in one country, compared with another country, at making different products.

     CORRECT. This is the definition of "comparative advantage."

   ✗   (B)   Comparative advantage involves the production efficiency in one country compared with another at making one specific product.

     This is the definition of "absolute advantage."

   ✗   (C)   Comparative advantage only holds when one country is more efficient at making several products than is another country.

     This is "absolute advantage" across multiple products, not "comparative advantage."

   ✗   (D)   Comparative advantage only holds when one country is more efficient at making at least one product than is another country.

     The example given by the professor shows the opposite. One country is more efficient at making both goods than is the other country, but trade would still benefit both countries.

4.   What does the professor imply about comparative advantage when there are more than two products available for trade?

     INFERENCE. Near the end of the lecture, the professor mentions that there are more "sophisticated examples, but the principle always holds—countries are better off by specializing in some products and exchanging for others, so long as a comparative advantage exists, trading costs are low, and there are no barriers to trade."

   ✗   (A)   Countries will be more likely to not benefit from trade.

     This opposite is true. The more products there are that are available for trading, the more likely some form of comparative advantage exists.

   ✓   (B)   Countries will still be able to benefit from international trade in most circumstances.

     CORRECT. This idea is precisely what is implied in the quote mentioned above.

   ✗   (C)   Trading costs will be higher than when there are only two products available for trade.

     This idea is not mentioned or implied in the lecture.

   ✗   (D)   Trading costs will be less important than when there are only two products available for trade.

     This idea is not mentioned or implied in the lecture. In fact, the professor even repeats the idea that benefit from trade may be contingent upon "trading costs [being] low."

5. What does the professor imply about the trade example given between Country X and Country Y?

INFERENCE. The professor discusses a scenario in which Country X should make shoes, Country Y should make socks, and the two countries should trade, even though Country X has an absolute advantage at making both products.

✓ (A) The trading ratio of socks-to-shoes can affect whether trading will be beneficial to both countries.

CORRECT. The professor states: "As long as they trade in a ratio that is in between Country X's shoes-to-socks ratio and Country Y's shoes-to-socks ratio, both countries will profit." The implication is that if the trading ratio is outside of that range, one or both countries may fail to gain from trade.

✗ (B) Both countries will benefit from trade irrespective of the cost of shipping socks and shoes to one another.

The professor directly states that when there is comparative advantage, trading should occur "assuming [the countries] can do so cheaply—meaning shipping costs aren't much of an issue." This implies that if shipping costs are high, one or both countries may fail to benefit.

✗ (C) Only Country X will benefit from trade because it has an absolute advantage in production.

The professor states that both countries will benefit.

✗ (D) Only Country Y will benefit from trade because it has an absolute disadvantage in production.

The professor states that both countries will benefit.

6. What is the professor's viewpoint regarding trade protection?

SPEAKER'S ATTITUDE. The professor makes it clear that he feels trade barriers are harmful from an economic perspective.

✗ (A) Trade barriers should only be put in place if one country has an absolute advantage over another in production.

This idea is not discussed in the lecture.

✗ (B) Trade protection is valuable in some circumstances—particularly to help people avoid losing their jobs to foreign workers.

The professor does not agree with this sentiment, which is the rationale used by some countries for implementing trade restrictions. Instead, he argues that trade restrictions are harmful rather than helpful.

✓ (C) He believes that if two countries have economic reasons for trading with one another, trade barriers are harmful to both countries.

CORRECT. At the end of the lecture the professor says "while protecting jobs by restricting trade may be politically attractive, in the long run, trade barriers are harmful to both sides."

✗ (D) He believes that if two countries have economic reasons for trading with one another, trade barriers are harmful only to the country with an absolute advantage in production.

On the contrary, at the end of the lecture, the professor says that "while protecting jobs may be politically attractive, in the long run, trade barriers are harmful to both sides."

10

Answers and Explanations—10.7

Law of One Price—Track 77

NARRATOR: Listen to part of a lecture in an economics class.

PROFESSOR: One of the most interesting aspects of international trade is the pricing of goods and services in different places. Has anyone heard of the Big Mac Index? …Yes, a few of you? This is a clever index, published by *The Economist* magazine, that shows how much a McDonald's hamburger costs—depending on exactly where you are buying it. It sounds silly, but actually there's a very important macroeconomic principle behind it.

That principle is called the Law of One Price. Basically, this "Law" states that a product must sell for the same price in different locations… once the exchange rate, um… is taken into account. But that's not what the Big Mac Index shows. Last time I checked, the spread in prices worldwide was substantial. Would you believe, if you bought a Big Mac in, say, Switzerland, you would have to pay more than four times what you'd pay in Egypt? Again, adjusting for exchange rates… but… how–how can this be? Well, if… if the Law of One Price actually held, then it couldn't. So let's talk about where the "Law" comes from, and what factors can cause it not to hold.

First, let's talk about *arbitrage*. Yes, this is a fancy word. People on Wall Street love to use it. But "arbitrage" means something very simple—it means "an opportunity to make a profit without taking any risk." Much of economic theory is built on the idea that arbitrage opportunities don't exist. Or, that if they do, buyers and sellers will move quickly to extract that profit from the marketplace. If the Law of One Price does not hold, someone could make a riskless profit by buying in one location and selling elsewhere.

So, can you "arbitrage" a Big Mac? Do you want to buy a Big Mac in Egypt, then fly to Switzerland and find a buyer there? Of course not. The flight alone would be too expensive. But maybe corporations could do so? Well, if it were that easy, wouldn't McDonald's already be doing so? Or someone else?

Clearly, that is one reason why the Law of One Price doesn't hold. For most products, the situation is this: it's a useful theory to help explain the long-run balance in the worldwide market for a tradeable product, but often in the short term it does not hold. And there are reasons why it may never hold.

The first reason, as you might have deduced from my example, is shipping costs. The Law of One Price assumes no shipping costs, and… no trade barriers. Well, first, there's the Mediterranean Sea between Egypt and Switzerland. Then, you have to find a way up the mountains of Switzerland to find your Big Mac buyer. And you have to do all this nearly instantly, before the Big Mac goes bad. So there goes the theory of no shipping costs!

Another reason is that some goods are not tradeable. Here's an example. Can you export a haircut? Think about it… How would you sell a haircut to someone many kilometers away? You can't. And this is true of all services—unless they can be done remotely, say over the telephone, or internet… there, uh… there's no way to sell that service to someone elsewhere. Think about dry cleaning, or window repair, or performing marriage ceremonies—you can't ship these services, so you can't trade them. And when a product can't be traded, the Law of One Price may not hold.

Want another asset that's not tradeable? Land. Land cannot be shipped elsewhere. And some land—some real estate—is much more valuable than others. This is a big reason why Big Macs are more expensive in Switzerland than many other places. It's like in certain cities, like New York and London—real estate is extremely expensive, because the demand to live or work there is very high, while the supply of land is never

really going to increase. And when you're talking about nearly any product, real estate costs will factor into the price of any goods sold there. You have to lease or buy the land for the restaurant that serves the Big Mac, right? You also must pay people more money to live in an expensive town to sell those Big Macs. And you must store some of the ingredients, in freezers or refrigerators or warehouses, located on or near this expensive land.

Um, it's interesting to note that there's one more reason why the Law of One Price may not hold… that is imperfect information. This comes up in economics all the time. The point is that if producers are unaware of customers in other places that are willing to pay more for a product—or if buyers don't know about cheaper ways to buy the product elsewhere—then the Law of One Price can be violated indefinitely. This used to be a much bigger issue, but with communication capabilities today, it's becoming less and less important.

1.	What is the talk primarily about?	**GIST-CONTENT.** The lecture primarily focuses on the Law of One Price, and reasons why it may not hold in the real world.
✓	(A) Explaining an economic theory that frequently proves to be inaccurate	**CORRECT.** In the lecture, the professor notes many reasons why the Law of One Price may not hold.
✗	(B) Exploring ways to make a riskless profit through international trade	The professor explains that arbitrage means a way to make a profit without taking any risk. But the professor but does not explore ways to do so.
✗	(C) Discussing the pricing of the Big Mac sandwich	This example is used heavily at the beginning of the lecture to explain the Law of One Price, but it is not the primary focus of the lecture.
✗	(D) Providing information about how services can be traded internationally	The professor only discusses services specifically to point out that many of them cannot be traded across long distances.

10

2.	What does the professor imply about possible reasons why Big Macs sell for a higher price in Switzerland than in many other places?	**INFERENCE.** According to the lecture, selling Big Macs in areas where real estate is expensive increases the price of Big Macs. Additionally, high shipping costs can prevent prices in different locations from converging. Both of these factors imply that Big Macs may remain more expensive in Switzerland than in other locations.
✗	(A) There is a high demand for Big Macs among Swiss citizens.	The professor does not mention anything about Swiss citizens having a high demand for Big Macs.
✗	(B) Switzerland is close to Egypt.	If anything, the professor implies the opposite: there are physical barriers between Egypt and Switzerland, and these barriers prevent prices from converging.
✓	(C) Real estate in Switzerland is expensive.	**CORRECT.** The professor states: "Land cannot be shipped elsewhere. And some land—some real estate—is much more valuable than others. This is a big reason why Big Macs are more expensive in Switzerland than many other places."
✗	(D) Switzerland lacks some materials needed to make Big Macs.	This idea is not mentioned in the lecture.

3.   According to the professor, what is a reason that services often violate the Law of One Price?

DETAIL. The professor makes it clear that the Law of One Price applies in the long-run to tradeable products only, and that many services cannot be traded long distances.

✗ (A) Most services are granted using a barter system, with prices that vary from country to country.

This idea is not mentioned in the lecture.

✓ (B) Many services are difficult to trade across long distances.

CORRECT. Because these services are difficult to trade over long distances, pricing differentials are difficult to exploit, so they can persist.

✗ (C) Services often require raw materials that are expensive to purchase.

This idea is not mentioned in the lecture.

✗ (D) Some services can be provided over the telephone or internet.

It is implied that this is a reason why some services may adhere to the Law of One Price, rather than violate it.

4.   What does the professor imply about the prices of goods sold in New York and London?

INFERENCE. The professor compares Switzerland to New York and London—two cities with very high real estate prices—to explain how high real estate costs can affect the prices of goods sold there.

✓ (A) They are likely to be higher than in most other places.

CORRECT. This is implied as a result of real estate being expensive in both cities.

✗ (B) They are likely to be similar to those in Egypt.

This idea is not mentioned or implied in the lecture.

✗ (C) They are likely to be higher in New York than in London.

This idea is not mentioned or implied in the lecture.

✗ (D) They are likely to be equal to the prices found in other major cities worldwide.

The professor does not discuss other major cities worldwide.

5.   What does the professor imply about trade barriers?

INFERENCE. The professor states: "The Law of One Price assumes no shipping costs, and ... no trade barriers." The implication is that trade barriers can cause the Law of One Price not to hold.

✗ (A) They allow international prices for a product to converge.

If anything, the professor argues that the opposite is true—trade barriers can interfere with the Law of One Price.

✓ (B) They can cause the Law of One Price to be violated.

CORRECT. The professor states that the Law of One Price assumes no trading costs and no trade barriers. This implies that trade barriers can cause the Law of One Price not to hold.

✗ (C) They reduce the cost of shipping internationally.

This idea is not mentioned or implied in the lecture.

✗ (D) They are usually implemented for political reasons.

The professor does not discuss or imply anything about why trade barriers are implemented.

6.   What is the professor's viewpoint regarding the accuracy of the Law of One Price?

SPEAKER'S ATTITUDE. The professor makes it clear that the Law of One Price often does not hold, especially in the short term.

✗   (A) It is a helpful method for finding the average price of a product worldwide.

This idea is not discussed in the lecture.

✗   (B) It is an effective way to generate arbitrage opportunities.

The professor states that if the Law of One Price holds, then no arbitrage opportunities will exist.

✗   (C) It is accurate in most cases.

The professor claims that the Law of One Price holds for some products in the long run, but it's frequently wrong for a number of reasons.

✓   (D) It holds in certain circumstances, but there are many reasons why it will never hold for some products.

CORRECT. According to the professor, the Law of One Price is useful for understanding pricing tendencies in the long run, for certain products, under a series of conditions.

Answers and Explanations—10.8

Time and Motion Studies—Track 78

NARRATOR: Listen to part of a lecture in a business management class.

PROFESSOR: Alright, we have been talking about the history of management theory—specifically focusing on the end of nineteenth century. Can anyone remind me… who we were discussing?

MALE STUDENT: Frederick Winthrop Taylor?

PROFESSOR: Frederick *Winslow* Taylor. And he invented…?

FEMALE STUDENT: Scientific management.

PROFESSOR: That's right. What is that?

MALE STUDENT: It's basically, um… it's a system for analyzing how work is done, and for organizing work processes, to maximize efficiency.

PROFESSOR: Very good. Organizing work processes, or what Taylor called workflows. In scientific management, the focus is primarily on one thing—how to do work in the most efficient way possible. Taylor was obsessed with this concept—to the point where many of his workers thought he didn't care about them at all, or merely viewed them as machines who were alive to make products in his factories as efficiently as possible. And they weren't wrong—Taylor was notorious for his lack of respect toward workers.

But let's stay focused on his contributions to management theory. Taylor was considered the inventor of the original form of scientific management—in fact, it's sometimes referred to as Taylorism. And he contributed substantially to the study of management as an empirical, data-driven discipline—much like biology or physics. Scientific management eventually became obsolete, but that's really because many of his ideas were incorporated into other schools of thought that came around later.

One of his focuses was improving the efficiency of manual labor. Can anyone tell me what process he came up with, for studying manual labor and making it more efficient? Jenelle?

FEMALE STUDENT: Time and motion studies.

PROFESSOR: Yes, time and motion studies. And how did those work?

FEMALE STUDENT: How?

PROFESSOR: Yes, let's say we were going to design a time and motion study for… I don't know… how to wash your car. How would we do that?

FEMALE STUDENT: Well, what assumptions are we going to make? Are we assuming this is part of an industrial process, or… say, if you worked at a car wash?

PROFESSOR: Well… well for this example, let's just assume that you're in a garage—one that is large enough for washing a car, and you have all the supplies you need.

FEMALE STUDENT: Well, we would need to go through step by step and measure how long each step takes, and what actions are needed in each.

PROFESSOR: Good. Let's go further. I want to know exactly what that would look like. Peter?

MALE STUDENT: Alright, well first we would need a stopwatch, to time each component of work required. Then, we would draw up a list of all the pieces of work that need to be done—unrolling the hose, for example… filling a bucket with soap and water… rinsing the car, and so on. The we would record how long each step took, and make adjustments for the worker's efficiency—let's say the person washing the car was overall pretty efficient, but took too long drying the windows… we might want to estimate a time reduction for that.

PROFESSOR: OK. That… that is exactly what a time and motion study is. Once it's been completed, you would have a full, detailed list of every step in the car washing process, the amount of time it took to perform every task, and then an adjusted time, as you put it, for what you believe should be the right amount of time. Now, there is one final piece we are missing.

FEMALE STUDENT: You would then analyze that list to see if there is a more efficient order to do things, how the tasks could be distributed more efficiently among workers if there's more than one…

PROFESSOR: Exactly right. At the end of the study, you analyze the data to determine which task should come first, which should follow, and so on—sometimes rearranging them to get a more efficient car washing process. And then this process would be considered the "best practice" for car washing—if you did it right, Taylor himself would agree!

I'm sure you can see how this approach received a lot of resistance. Many workers didn't like the idea of having their job reduced to a series of instructions, each with an expected amount of time to complete them. But this paved the way for a more rigorous understanding of how exactly to improve productivity in many tasks that require labor. Of course, as this science advanced, managers realized that many human tasks could be performed by machines instead… and this paved the way for automation—which continues to be a source of conflict for workers and workers' unions today.

1.   What is the lecture mainly about?

    ✗   (A) A discussion of efficient ways to wash a car

    ✓   (B) A contributor to management theory and one of the processes he invented

    ✗   (C) The differences between the original form of scientific management and modern versions of it

    ✗   (D) Worker dissatisfaction with automation in the workplace

GIST-CONTENT. The main discussion of this lecture is Taylor and the time and motion study process he invented.

The professor uses the example of washing a car to illustrate the main topic of the lecture—time and motion studies.

CORRECT. The lecture discusses Frederick Winslow Taylor and his invention, time and motion studies.

This idea is alluded to in the lecture, but is not the primary focus.

This issue is only mentioned at the very end of the lecture.

2.   Why does the professor discuss washing a car?

    ✓   (A) To give an example of conducting a time and motion study

    ✗   (B) To explore the case of a task that may normally be considered menial

    ✗   (C) To contrast the views of two different schools of management theory

    ✗   (D) To demonstrate the degree to which certain tasks can be automated

ORGANIZATION. The professor mentions this example to explain how a time and motion study works.

CORRECT. The car wash example is used to explain how a time and motion study is organized.

This idea is not presented in the lecture.

This is not the purpose of the car wash example.

The professor discusses automation at the end of the lecture, but the purpose of the car wash example is to explain how to make a work process more efficient, not how to automate it.

10

Track 79

NARRATOR: Listen again to part of the lecture. Then answer the question.

PROFESSOR: Alright, we have been talking about the history of management—specifically focusing on the end of nineteenth century. Can anyone remind me... who we were discussing?

MALE STUDENT: Frederick Winthrop Taylor?

PROFESSOR: Frederick *Winslow* Taylor.

NARRATOR: Why does the professor say this:

PROFESSOR: Frederick *Winslow* Taylor.

3.   Why does the professor say this?

FUNCTION OF WHAT IS SAID. In this quote, the professor corrects the student's use of the wrong middle name for Frederick Winslow Taylor, but implies that he identified the right person.

✗ (A) To answer his own question, after no student was able to answer it correctly

The student who responded to the question did identify the correct person, but got his middle name wrong.

✗ (B) To point out that the student's response did not identify the right person

The student who responded to the question did identify the right person, but got his middle name wrong.

✓ (C) To indicate that the student was essentially correct, despite making a slight error

CORRECT. The student named the correct person, but got that person's middle name wrong.

✗ (D) To ask the rest of the class whether the given response was correct

This was not the professor's intention.

4.   What is an example of a component of a time and motion study?

DETAIL. In the lecture, the steps for completing a time and motion study are discussed using the example of a car wash.

✓ (A) The use of a stopwatch to see how long completing a step in an overall process takes

CORRECT. Each step required to complete a task is timed.

✗ (B) Tracking the speed of individual employees so that they can be ranked in terms of efficiency

This idea is not mentioned in the lecture.

✗ (C) Eliminating steps that had previously been considered essential to a process

The professor talks about potentially reordering tasks, not eliminating them.

✗ (D) Making inventory lists to ensure that a task can be completed

This idea is not mentioned in the lecture.

5.   According to the professor, where may a potential conflict arise as a result of applying scientific management in a workplace?

DETAIL. The professor mentions that laborers are generally against it, and that laborers and labor unions are particularly against the automation that may result from it.

✗ (A) From other managers who feel that scientific management principles are obsolete

The idea that some scientific management principles are considered obsolete is hinted at in the lecture, but the potential for conflict with other managers is not implied in any way.

✗ (B) From competitors who can replicate the efficiency gains achieved from scientific management

Competitors are not mentioned in the lecture.

✗ (C) From civil rights advocates who claim that some scientific management principles violate worker rights

This idea is never mentioned in the lecture.

✓ (D) From laborers and unions who are concerned about workers being replaced by machines

CORRECT. At the end of the lecture, the professor mentions that "managers realized that many human tasks could be performed by machines instead... and this paved the way for automation," which many laborers and unions are against.

6.   Select the description(s) below that apply to time and motion studies, as described in the lecture. *Select all that apply.*

CONNECTING CONTENT. In a time and motion study, tasks are broken down into steps needed for completion. Each step is then timed, and afterward, adjustments to the recorded times are potentially made. Steps are then potentially reordered to make the overall process for completing the task as efficient as possible.

10

✓ [A] A list of steps needed to complete a task is drafted.

CORRECT. This is one of the key components of a time and motion study.

✗ [B] Ways to train workers to move faster through each step are found.

This idea is not mentioned in the lecture. Time reductions for individual steps that may take too long (e.g., "drying the windows") may be estimated, but the lecture never mentions actual training for workers to speed up their drying process or other steps that may be slow.

✗ [C] Workers who fail to complete assignments quickly may be subjected to penalties.

This idea is not mentioned in the lecture.

✓ [D] Steps to complete a task may be reordered to achieve greater efficiency.

CORRECT. This is mentioned as a final step in completing a time and motion study.

Answers and Explanations—10.9

Zinn and A People's History—Track 80

NARRATOR: Listen to part of a lecture in a United States history class.

PROFESSOR: Whenever you study a work of history, it's important to ask yourself, "Who wrote this history? What perspective do they bring to this account?" We've all been exposed to the standard stories about United States history that were written in our high school textbooks… but–but were they accurate? …Anyone?

MALE STUDENT: Well, I suppose… I mean, most of the stories we've heard seemed to make sense… They fit the model I know—the United States stands for freedom and democracy, leads the way in social and economic achievement, it's the land of opportunity… that kind of thing. But sometimes I've wondered… I mean, was there another side, maybe?

PROFESSOR: OK. So now, what you're thinking about is the possibility of an alternative version of history. One that you didn't read about in your textbooks. And that brings us to Howard Zinn. Howard Zinn was born in New York City, the son of Jewish immigrants who fled the Austro-Hungarian Empire just before World War I. Throughout his childhood, Zinn harbored communist and socialist inclinations and connections. Later in life, when asked about his political affiliation, he described himself as "something of an anarchist, something of a socialist. Maybe a democratic socialist." Keep in mind that at the time during the Cold War saying you were a communist was an absolute no-no in the United States. This undoubtedly influenced his worldview.

Uh… Zinn got a Ph.D. in history from Columbia, and became a history professor at several institutions—most notably Boston University. He was also a prolific writer. Suffice it to say that his political leanings, um… influenced his writing. And his viewpoint on history is often substantially different from what I would call the "establishment view."

OK… so… his most influential work is undoubtedly *A People's History of the United States*, originally published in 1980… but with more chapters added over time. To summarize this book …this book challenged just about everything that you know—or thought you knew—about United States history. What do I mean? Well, Winston Churchill once famously said, "History is written by the victors." The idea being that the groups who are conquered often don't get their version of history told.

Zinn sought to correct that. In chapter after chapter, Zinn challenges the wisdom of the established view of United States history. This "establishment view" is, in fact, relatively limited—often excluding major events and movements because they do not fit the establishment storyline. Zinn's account, on the other hand, recounts the untold stories from groups that generally lost the major conflicts—usually people that were oppressed in some way. African Americans, Native Americans, women, the working class, and so on. This is a second view of United States history. Zinn would probably call it the "people's view," although I like to think of it as the "minority view."

So Zinn tells an untold history of the United States—although in all fairness, there are times he possibly goes too far in rejecting the establishment viewpoint. I think of his work as a complementary text, not a definitive source that automatically overrules perceptions or beliefs that Zinn himself rejects.

I should also note that many critics believe Zinn's account is too dark, bleak… even cynical. And on occasion, they may have a point—but Zinn didn't see it that way. He wanted to tell this alternative history as he saw it, however ugly at times it might be. He felt that change was always possible—that oppression could be overcome if the people worked together to bring about change. He was greatly encouraged by the rise of organized labor, for example, or the Civil Rights Movement and anti-war demonstrations that took place in

the 1960s and 1970s. In fact, he took part in those himself. But he also felt that it was important for people to know about the struggles that took place in the past—to know history from the perspective of common men and women. With this knowledge, he believed people might be able to lead what he called a "quiet revolution"—not a violent overthrow, but the gaining of power through the institutions that already exist.

So in this course, we are going to spend a lot of time talking about Zinn… talking about an alternative view of United States history. Hearing stories that are largely brushed over in the "establishment view." We will use Zinn's stories to challenge our ideas about past events and the reasons they happened. Our broad goal is true enlightenment—a deep, balanced understanding of the events that have made the United States the country it is today.

1. What is the primary purpose of this lecture?

    GIST-PURPOSE. The lecture discusses Howard Zinn and his "alternative view" of United States history.

    ✓ (A) To introduce a new perspective on United States history and an author who exemplifies that perspective

    CORRECT. The author focuses on Howard Zinn, an author with a different perspective on United States history, and introduces him by talking about the possibility of different accounts, or perspectives, on historical events.

    ✗ (B) To compare the study of United States history to the study of literature

    The professor does not discuss literature in this lecture.

    ✗ (C) To explain the opinions of an author they have read about in a different class

    The professor is introducing a new author, not necessarily one they have read about in a different class.

    ✗ (D) To detail the political turmoil of many periods of United States history

    While one might infer that such turmoil might be discussed later in her class, she does not go into much—if any—detail during this lecture.

10

2. Why does the professor mention the "establishment view" used in most schools?

ORGANIZATION. The professor introduces Howard Zinn by saying that "his viewpoint on history is often substantially different from what I would call the 'establishment view.'" She implies that this view is the source of "the standard stories about United States history that were written in our high school textbooks."

✗ (A) To refer to Howard Zinn's book

Zinn's writings are the exact opposite of the "establishment view," from the professor's perspective.

✓ (B) To refer to the standard historical accounts often found in high school textbooks

CORRECT. The professor is attempting to clarify the difference between the "establishment view," as portrayed by most high school textbooks and other standard accounts, and Zinn's "people's view," or "minority view."

✗ (C) To correct a known error found in many historical accounts

The professor is not attempting to correct any errors. She is laying a foundation for differing perspectives of historical events by separating them into different camps—the "establishment view" and the "minority view."

✗ (D) To offer legitimacy to stories that are considered dubious by many

This concept is not discussed in the lecture.

3. According to the professor, what is an advantage of the "minority view" of United States history?

DETAIL. The professor discusses several advantages of the "minority view," but emphasizes that it takes into account the perspective of groups of people who may have been oppressed or unheard.

✗ (A) It is generally well-known.

The opposite is true. The professor argues that often, the "minority view" has been mostly forgotten.

✗ (B) It disproves many themes found in the "establishment view" of United States history.

While the "minority view" may disagree with many such themes, the professor does not claim that it necessarily disproves them.

✓ (C) It accounts for the perspectives of people that may have been oppressed.

CORRECT. The professor states: "Zinn's account... recounts the untold stories from groups that generally lost the major conflicts—usually people that were oppressed in some way."

✗ (D) It was written primarily by the social elite.

It is implied in the lecture that the "establishment view" was primarily written by the social elite—not the "minority view."

10

4. What aspect of history does the professor imply could be discussed in the course?

INFERENCE. The professor states that "in this course, we are going to spend a lot of time talking about Zinn... talking about an alternative view of United States history. Hearing stories that are largely brushed over in the 'establishment view.'" Therefore, she will likely discuss stories regarding people who were oppressed in some way.

✓ (A) Efforts by civic leaders to overcome male politicians' opposition to a woman's right to vote

CORRECT. The professor notes that the "minority view" often tells the story from the perspective of people who have been oppressed, such as women. This example fits that description.

✗ (B) Key battles won by United States soldiers during World War II

These battles would be well-documented in many "establishment view" textbooks.

✗ (C) Biographical information about contributors to the writing of the United States Constitution

These contributors would be well-documented in many "establishment view" textbooks.

✗ (D) Immigrants from foreign countries who became successful businesspeople in the United States

Many such individuals would be chronicled by "establishment view" textbooks—and those who aren't chronicled there are not more likely to be chronicled in "minority view" publications, because there is no indication that they were oppressed.

5. Classify each topic below according to the professor's descriptions. Indicate whether each topic below would likely relate more to 1. Establishment View or 2. Minority View.

CONNECTING CONTENT. "Establishment view" relates to standard accounts of United States history from the perspective of the majority and/or the social elite. "Minority view" relates to lesser-known stories, often from the perspective of groups that have suffered oppression of some kind.

A   Descriptions of the education of each United States President _____

1. ESTABLISHMENT VIEW. This is standard information likely to be covered in an "establishment view" textbook.

B   Job discrimination experienced by recent immigrants from a variety of nations _____

2. MINORITY VIEW. Groups facing job discrimination are facing a form of oppression, and therefore qualify as "minority view" subjects.

C   Debates among wealthy delegates as the United States Bill of Rights was written _____

1. ESTABLISHMENT VIEW. This is standard information likely to be covered in an "establishment view" textbook.

D   Personal struggles of African-American leaders during the 1960s Civil Rights Movement _____

2. MINORITY VIEW. African Americans are listed as a group facing oppression in the United States. The struggles of African-American leaders during the Civil Rights Movement, although perhaps covered in establishment textbooks, would relate more to the "minority view" in the professor's classification.

Track 81

NARRATOR: Listen again to part of the lecture. Then answer the question.

PROFESSOR: Whenever you study a work of history, it's important to ask yourself, "Who wrote this history? What perspective do they bring to this account?" We've all been exposed to the standard stories about United States history that were written in our high school textbooks... but–but were they accurate?

NARRATOR: What is the professor's attitude?

6.   What is the professor's attitude?

| | **SPEAKER'S ATTITUDE.** In this quote, the professor calls upon students to question the author, and the perspective of the author, for any piece of history they might read. In so doing, they might begin to question the accuracy, or completeness, of the author's account. |

✗ Ⓐ She believes high school history textbooks provide an accurate, fair representation of historical events.

The opposite is true. She is encouraging students to question whether these textbooks were accurate and fair.

✗ Ⓑ She doubts that most students in the course have been taught history before.

Nothing in the quote suggests that this is what she thinks.

✗ Ⓒ She is uncertain whether some students have enrolled in the correct course.

Nothing in the quote suggests that she is uncertain about this.

✓ Ⓓ She hopes that students are willing to question things they think they know about history.

CORRECT. By asking students to question who the author of an account was, and what his or her perspective was, she is challenging the idea that the stories told by them are perfectly accurate, or at least, perfectly complete.

Answers and Explanations—10.10

The 4 P's of Marketing—Track 82

NARRATOR: Listen to part of a lecture in a business class.

PROFESSOR: OK, let's start! Now, in yesterday's class, we talked about what marketing actually is... connecting your target market—your prospective buyers—with the goods and services you are selling. Today, we will talk about what is called the "marketing mix"—the components you need to successfully market your product offering. The "marketing mix" is a core concept in marketing—it provides a systematic, uh... framework for proper decision-making... ensuring that you have a well-developed plan to reach your potential customer base.

So, what does this marketing mix framework look like? Well, it can be summarized with the Four P's of Marketing.

Alright, as you can see, the four P's—product, price, promotion, and place—they can be in any order, really, although usually "product" is listed first. The four P's are the things you need to focus on in developing your marketing mix.

So let's start with product. This one is easy—you have to know what it is you're selling. And there are many attributes to understand about your product—or service—and the better you understand them, the more successful you will be at marketing that product. Things to know include… your product's features, quality level, design, uses, branding, advantages, packaging, cost to produce, and so on. Now, keep in mind that this framework can also be used to help develop new products—so in that case, feedback from previous marketing endeavors can help you redesign an existing product, or create a new product—to fill a demand that hasn't been filled yet.

Second, let's look at price. This is not as simple as "how much do we charge for this product?" That is certainly part of it… but pricing is more complex than just the sticker price you see when you buy something at the store. Of course, you must consider the price consumers are willing to pay… but you also need retailers to put the items on the shelf in the first place. Do you offer volume discounts? Do you expect payment up front, or do you allow credit purchases, and if so, on what terms? Often, decisions about pricing can influence whether consumers or vendors opt to buy your products, rather than a competitor's products.

Next up… promotion. This is usually what people think about when they hear the word "marketing"— they think "advertising." But really, promotion is much more than just advertising. It's about using some or all of the channels—ads, publicity, public relations… even direct marketing—to connect with your target customer base. Promotion also includes decisions about when and how to use sales—you know, reduced prices or other special offers—to motivate consumers to buy your product. Now, here's an example of what not to do… let's say you're running a marketing campaign for a luxury product. Something like… designer jewelry. Now, this is an expensive product category, and usually the customers buying these kinds of products will be most interested in product differentiation—the idea that they are buying something precious and unique. So your promotions should not consist of giving a bunch of price discounts—this will not attract the right customers. In fact, it may even turn off some of the customers you hope to connect with. They don't want less expensive jewelry, they want better jewelry. So, you should focus on what makes your product offering different and special.

The final P, then, is place. This refers to how you deliver your products to your customer. For example… it's no good to have a great product everyone wants to buy, if they don't know where to buy it! So, place refers having an appropriate distribution strategy for your products. Again, using the example of designer jewelry… this is a differentiated, elite product, and when customers by it, they want to feel they are buying something exceptional. So, you do not want to use a mass-market distribution strategy for your jewelry— you want distribution to be focused on a select few locations, like stores in premier shopping districts in major cities. Conversely, if you're marketing a breakfast cereal, you're more likely to want to develop a broad placement strategy, partnering with the biggest grocery chains and food distributors to get your cereal stocked on as many supermarket shelves as possible.

Alright, I have an assignment for you. I want you to break into teams of four. Each team will develop a marketing strategy for a hypothetical product that I will assign to you. Remember the four P's of the marketing mix—product, price, promotion, and place—and next time we meet, each team will give a five-minute presentation on your ideas for a successful marketing strategy tailored for that product.

1. What is the main topic of this lecture?

    ✗ (A) How to determine the appropriate pricing for a luxury product

    ✓ (B) Factors to consider in developing a marketing strategy

    ✗ (C) Why some marketing strategies fail

    ✗ (D) The differences between mass-market products and specialty products

GIST-CONTENT. The lecture is about the Four P's of Marketing, a framework for making decisions about marketing strategy.

Pricing in general is discussed in the lecture, but this is not the main focus.

CORRECT. The Four P's of Marketing is a framework for marketing strategy decision-making.

The professor discusses some mistakes to avoid while developing a marketing strategy, but this is not the main topic discussed.

This topic comes up in several places when examples are being discussed, but this is not the primary focus of the lecture.

2. According to the professor, what might be two examples of a poor marketing strategy? *Choose 2 answers.*

    ✗ [A] Selling products at a price lower than competitors' products

    ✓ [B] Using a mass-market distribution strategy for a luxury product

    ✓ [C] Failing to consider the quality of a product in an advertising campaign

    ✗ [D] Using promotions to encourage existing customers to repeat purchases

DETAIL. Throughout the lecture, the professor indicates that it is important to understand many aspects of the product and the target customer base when developing an appropriate marketing strategy.

The professor does not indicate that pricing below a competitor's product price point would necessarily be bad. It might depend on a number of factors.

CORRECT. In discussing the example of designer jewelry, a luxury product, the professor says that "distribution [should] be focused on a select few locations, like stores in premier shopping districts in major cities."

CORRECT. One aspect of the "product" component of the 4 P's is understanding the product's quality, and how that impacts all marketing decisions.

Repeat purchasers are not discussed in the lecture.

3. Why does the professor talk about breakfast cereal?

ORGANIZATION. The professor mentions breakfast cereal in discussing "place," meaning the placement or distribution strategy for a product. Breakfast cereal is an example of a mass-market product for which the goal is getting the "cereal stocked on as many supermarket shelves as possible."

✓ (A) To provide an example of a product for which a broad placement strategy is appropriate

CORRECT. This is the reason breakfast cereal is discussed by the professor.

✗ (B) To illustrate the difference between a perishable product and a nonperishable product

Perishable and nonperishable products are not discussed in the lecture.

✗ (C) To demonstrate how effective sales promotions can be

Breakfast cereal is discussed in the context of placement and distribution, not sales promotions.

✗ (D) To show that marketing encompasses much more than just advertising

The professor implies this in the lecture, but breakfast cereal is discussed to make a different, more specific point.

4. In the example about designer jewelry, what does the professor imply about offering price discounts?

INFERENCE. The professor states that it would be a mistake, noting that "it may even turn off some of the customers you hope to connect with."

✗ (A) It is an effective way to generate new, profitable customers.

The professor actually says that price discounts for this product may attract the wrong kind of customers, and could turn off customers for whom the product is intended.

✗ (B) It may result in opportunities to sell additional products to existing customers.

This idea is not mentioned or implied in the lecture.

✓ (C) It works against the image of the product being special.

CORRECT. This professor states that potential customers of designer jewelry "don't want less expensive jewelry, they want better jewelry. So, you should focus on what makes your product offering different and special." This implies that offering price discounts diminishes the idea of the product being special.

✗ (D) It can provide insight about which customers are likely to recommend the product to their friends.

This idea is not mentioned or implied in the lecture.

5.   What is the professor's point when she discusses advertising?

ORGANIZATION. The professor mentions advertising during the discussion of promotions. Her point is that promotion covers many more techniques than just advertising.

✓ (A) It is only one of a variety of promotional techniques.

CORRECT. The professor mentions direct marketing, sales, public relations, and publicity as other ways of promoting a product.

✗ (B) Most people are not familiar with the tactics used in advertising to persuade people to buy products.

This idea is not discussed in the lecture.

✗ (C) No product can be sold successfully without advertising.

The professor indicates that there are several different means of promoting a product, including advertising. She does not indicate that a successful promotion strategy must include advertising.

✗ (D) It should not be used if the product is dangerous for some people.

This idea is not mentioned in the lecture.

Track 83

NARRATOR: Listen again to part of the lecture. Then answer the question.

PROFESSOR: Of course, you must consider the price consumers are willing to pay… but you also need retailers to put the items on the shelf in the first place. Do you offer volume discounts? Do you expect payment up front, or do you allow credit purchases, and if so, on what terms?

NARRATOR: What does the professor mean when she says this:

PROFESSOR: Do you offer volume discounts? Do you expect payment up front, or do you allow credit purchases, and if so, on what terms?

6.   What does the professor mean when she says this?

FUNCTION OF WHAT IS SAID. In this quote, the professor discusses decisions that must be made about pricing, including options for how the product is purchased, and methods for enticing retailers to carry the product.

✗ (A) She is asking students what their preferred pricing strategies are.

These questions are rhetorical. They are intended to illustrate the types of decisions about pricing that need to be made in a marketing campaign.

✗ (B) She is uncertain whether the point she is discussing is relevant to marketing strategy.

The professor is claiming the opposite. The decisions implied by the questions she asks are critical parts of a marketing strategy.

✓ (C) She is trying to illustrate that pricing strategy involves more than just determining what consumers are willing to pay.

CORRECT. The professor's questions give examples of pricing decisions beyond the issue of what consumers are willing to pay.

✗ (D) She believes that some pricing strategies are always superior to others.

The professor does not indicate that she prefers any particular pricing strategy to others.

Chapter 11

Lectures E: Natural Science

Listening lectures test your ability to comprehend academic-level spoken English. You'll listen to a short lecture (about 3 to 5 minutes long) from a professor. Occasionally, a student may also speak. You will only be able to listen to the lecture once. You will not be able to pause the recording or to replay any part of it (though some questions will replay a specific part of the lecture for you). You can take notes as you listen.

You will then answer six questions for that lecture. Most questions are multiple-choice with four options (select one from A, B, C, or D). Some questions may ask you to select more than one option or to fill in a table. You will have to answer the questions in order. You cannot return to a question once you have moved on to the next question.

Listening lectures test your understanding of main ideas, contrasts, the lecturer's tone and degree of certainty about the information, and why the lecturer relates certain information or examples. They also test your understanding of the organization of the lecture and the relationship between different ideas. Finally, they test your ability to make inferences or draw conclusions.

How should you use this chapter? Here are some recommendations, according to the level you've reached in TOEFL Listening:

1. **Fundamentals.** Start with a topic-focused chapter, such as this one. Start with a topic that is a "medium weakness"—not your worst area but not your best either. At first, listen to the lecture once, then work on the questions untimed and check the answer after each question. Review the solutions closely, think carefully about the principles at work, and articulate what you've learned. Redo questions as necessary. As you get better, time yourself and do all of the questions for a lecture at once, without stopping.

2. **Fixes.** Do an entire lecture and its associated questions under timed conditions. Don't replay any part of the lecture while you are still answering the questions! Examine the results, learn your lessons, then test yourself with another lecture and question set.

3. **Tweaks.** Confirm your mastery by doing two or three lectures in a row under timed conditions. Work your way up to doing four lectures and two conversations in one sitting. Aim to improve the speed and ease of your process.

Good luck on Listening!

11.1

> Listen to Track 84.
>
> Now answer the questions.

1. What is Kepler's First Law?
   - (A) A fundamental law of nature
   - (B) A prediction of when a comet would return
   - (C) A description of how comet tails form
   - (D) A statement about the shapes of planetary orbits

2. Why does the professor explain Edmond Halley's work to the class?
   - (A) To highlight how long in the historical record Halley's Comet has been observed
   - (B) To explain how Halley's Comet got its name
   - (C) To walk through detailed calculations that use Newton's Laws
   - (D) To emphasize the eccentricity of cometary orbits

3. How does the professor introduce comets to the class?
   - (A) By asking which objects have a certain kind of orbit
   - (B) By discussing the composition of comets
   - (C) By drawing attention to meteors first
   - (D) By describing the effects of a hypothetical orbit of the Earth

> Listen to Track 85.
>
> Now answer the question.

4. Why does the professor say this?
   - (A) To argue that Kepler's Laws are essentially flawed
   - (B) To point out how comets do not obey Kepler's Laws
   - (C) To suggest how Kepler's Laws may be applied more broadly
   - (D) To contrast Kepler's Laws with more fundamental laws of nature

5. According to the professor, why did no one before Halley know that various historical observations of Halley's Comet were of the same comet? *Choose 2 answers.*

   A   The comet looked different every time it was observed.

   B   Whenever the comet was observed, its orbit had a different size and shape.

   C   The historical observations were not precise enough.

   D   There were many other observations of other comets.

6. What does the professor imply about Halley's Comet?

   (A) Newton could not have identified the comet first.

   (B) The comet has a more eccentric orbit than most other comets.

   (C) No other comet has the same orbital elements.

   (D) Halley's Comet was not observed before 240 BC.

11.2

 Listen to Track 86.

Now answer the questions.

1. What is the lecture mainly about?

   (A) Factors involved in the decline of Piñon pine populations

   (B) How unseasonably cold winters might be affecting Piñon pines

   (C) Why the population of bark beetles has been declining

   (D) Reasons that Piñon pines are expanding their range

2. According to the professor, what are two features of masting events for Piñon pines? *Choose 2 answers.*

   A   They occur only in cold climates.

   B   The rate at which they occur depends on the age of the pine trees.

   C   They are influenced by changes in temperature.

   D   They involve the release of pine cones.

3. What is one reason for the decrease in Piñon pine populations in the Sonoran Desert?

   (A) Decreases in the amount of nutrients in the soil have increased competition among Piñon pines.

   (B) Increases in the number of bark beetles have left them more susceptible to drought.

   (C) Increases in the average temperature have caused masting events to occur more frequently.

   (D) Increases in rainfall have altered the natural environment of the Piñon pine

4. Why are humans NOT intervening to protect Piñon pines?

   (A) Most Piñon pines are in locations that humans cannot easily reach.

   (B) The actions humans would need to take could be controversial.

   (C) The bark beetle also needs to be protected by human intervention.

   (D) Masting events have decreased in recent years.

5. Why does the professor mention the 1950s drought, which did not severely affect most of the Piñon pines?

   (A) To suggest that healthy Piñon pines can survive in dry environments

   (B) To explain how Piñon pines can expand to wetter environments

   (C) To cite a similarity between Piñon pines and other types of pine trees

   (D) To explain how increasing temperatures can encourage the growth of bark beetle populations.

> Listen to Track 87.
>
> Now answer the question.

6. (A) The adaptability of Piñon pines is an important enough theme to be repeated.

   (B) Climate scientists should not bother studying the impact of a temperature increase on Piñon pines.

   (C) The climate change she is describing involves more factors that have not yet been discussed.

   (D) Students should be able to answer this question quickly.

11.3

> Listen to Track 88.
>
> Now answer the questions.

1. What does the professor mainly discuss?

   (A) The changing basis for defining standard units of measurement

   (B) The controversial belief that standards should be uniform across the world

   (C) Examples of differences in units of measurement across countries

   (D) Why people believe in the importance of standards units of measurement

2. The professor discusses units of measurement and how the standards on which they are based have changed. What can be inferred about the professor's opinion regarding these changes?

    (A) She is sure that the cylinder is a better standard for the kilogram than Planck's constant.

    (B) She believes that changing the standards to natural constants is an improvement.

    (C) She thinks that the kilogram as a unit of measurement is obsolete.

    (D) She admits that the old ways of standardizing measurements were better than the new ways.

3. According to the professor, what is one problem with the weighted cylinder in France on which the kilogram is based?

    (A) It can no longer be adequately secured in its vault.

    (B) It is no longer useful.

    (C) It was created before modern physics.

    (D) It is losing weight.

4. According to the professor, which is the standard unit of measurement that has not been updated since the nineteenth century?

    (A) The second

    (B) The meter

    (C) The kilogram

    (D) The candela

5. What will the kilogram be based on once it is no longer based on the cylinder?

    (A) The circumference of the Earth

    (B) A new standard yet to be determined

    (C) A new cylinder with constant weight

    (D) Planck's constant

6. How does the professor organize the lecture?

    (A) By defining the kilogram, then listing all of the reasons why it has been impossible to standardize

    (B) By speaking about how the kilogram will be redefined, then describing how it has been defined since the nineteenth century

    (C) By discussing how the kilogram is currently defined, then noting that other units have been redefined and that the kilogram will be redefined soon

    (D) By emphasizing the importance of standardizing the meter before redefining the kilogram and the second

11.4

1. What is the lecture mainly about?
    - (A) Reasons that finding ancient rivers is important to the study of climate change
    - (B) A comparison of ancient and modern-day rivers in the Sahara Desert
    - (C) Satellite evidence of climate change in deserts
    - (D) A hypothesis for what the geology of the Sahara Desert was at one point in the past

2. What is the professor's opinion about the amount of plant growth in the modern Saharan climate?
    - (A) It will be crucial to monitoring the continuing climate change in the Sahara.
    - (B) It is abnormally bountiful considering the current climate.
    - (C) It explains the dry season that the Sahara is currently experiencing.
    - (D) It is limited, especially compared to growth during the African Humid Period.

3. What factors could have contributed to the creation of the climates that existed during the African Humid Period? *Choose 2 answers.*
    - [A] The tilt of the Earth relative to the Sun
    - [B] The increase of greenhouse gases in the atmosphere
    - [C] The presence of water-dependent vegetation
    - [D] The drying of Lake Victoria

4. What does the professor imply about the Southern Hemisphere during the African Humid Period?
    - (A) The level of greenhouse gases in the atmosphere was enough to increase the temperature in Southern Africa.
    - (B) The rivers in the Southern Hemisphere were larger and more common than they were in the Northern Hemisphere.
    - (C) The vegetation in the Southern Hemisphere was more varied at that time than it is today.
    - (D) Observation satellites have been unable to detect as many ancient rivers from that time period in the Southern Hemisphere.

5. According to the professor, what was an observation satellite recently able to confirm?

   (A) The degree of precipitation increase during the African Humid Period

   (B) The presence of an ancient river in the Sahara Desert

   (C) The position of ancient jungles relative to ancient rivers

   (D) Differences in levels of greenhouse gases between the Northern and Southern Hemispheres

6. What possible prediction does the professor give for the future of the 500 kilometer riverbed that was discovered?

   (A) The riverbed could alter the area's vegetation.

   (B) The riverbed could itself bring about local climate change.

   (C) The riverbed could start to flow again.

   (D) A completely new riverbed could be carved in the Sahara Desert.

11.5

 Listen to Track 90.

Now answer the questions.

1. What does the professor mainly discuss?

   (A) When and why some animals engage in hibernation or torpor

   (B) Animal defense mechanisms in cold climates

   (C) The navigation techniques of species that migrate

   (D) Hormonal shifts that control an animal's internal calendar

2. According to the professor, why do smaller mammals typically hibernate rather than migrate?

   (A) They are more likely to be caught by predators if they migrate.

   (B) They are skilled at building underground dens.

   (C) They are less likely to find food if they migrate.

   (D) They need less energy to stay warm than to travel long distances.

3. In order to determine whether an animal is in a state of hibernation or torpor, which of the following questions needs to be answered?

   (A) Whether the animal is large or small

   (B) Whether the act is voluntary or involuntary

   (C) The amount of food available

   (D) The current weather conditions

11

4. According to the professor, what are two triggers that determine when an animal enters into or awakens from hibernation? *Choose 2 answers.*

    ☐ A Food availability

    ☐ B Hormonal shifts

    ☐ C Length of the day

    ☐ D Snowstorm frequency

     Listen to Track 91.

    Now answer the question.

5. What does the professor mean when she says this?

    Ⓐ She has already covered the details in an earlier class.

    Ⓑ She is not confident enough about the details to explain them.

    Ⓒ She does not want to discuss details that are not relevant to her main point.

    Ⓓ She believes that the explanation is too complicated for the students to understand.

     Listen to Track 92.

    Now answer the question.

6. What point does the professor make when she says this?

    Ⓐ It is not clear how animals know whether to hibernate or migrate.

    Ⓑ Different animals hibernate at different times of the year.

    Ⓒ The changing temperature might prevent animals from migrating.

    Ⓓ Animals might hibernate at the wrong time if they only use weather signals.

11.6

 Listen to Track 93.

Now answer the questions.

1. What is the lecture mainly about?

    Ⓐ How domesticated dogs communicate with humans

    Ⓑ The difference between domesticated dogs and wolves

    Ⓒ The possible meaning of different dog barks

    Ⓓ How humans can misunderstand the meaning of a dog wagging its tail

2. According to the professor, what did researchers learn by having people listen to recordings of dogs barking?

   Ⓐ People are unable to distinguish one dog from another.

   Ⓑ People can learn how to give their own dogs more praise.

   Ⓒ People are often able to correctly identify the meaning of a dog's bark.

   Ⓓ People are able to imitate a dog's bark accurately.

3. What does the professor imply about feral dogs?

   Ⓐ They communicate with pet dogs by barking.

   Ⓑ They wag their tails to communicate with wolves.

   Ⓒ They are a type of wolf.

   Ⓓ They do not bark because they do not need to communicate with humans.

4. Why does the professor mention her former student's dog, Rocky?

   Ⓐ To give her students an example of doing research at home

   Ⓑ To encourage students to study something that interests them

   Ⓒ To help her students choose a graduate program

   Ⓓ To inform students of the difficulty of experiments involving animals

5. According to the professor, which two of the following are true of tail wagging in dogs?
   Choose 2 answers.

   ☐ A Dogs only use tail wagging for balance.

   ☐ B Tail wagging is the most important way dogs communicate with one another.

   ☐ C Dogs use tail wagging to communicate with other dogs.

   ☐ D Tail wagging is often misunderstood by humans.

    Listen to Track 94.

   Now answer the question.

6. What does this finding illustrate?

   Ⓐ That dogs interpret some forms of human communication much like humans interpret each other

   Ⓑ The difference between speaking to a dog and using hand gestures

   Ⓒ The importance of using scientific research methods

   Ⓓ One way that dogs communicate differently with humans than with one another

11.7

  Listen to Track 95.

Now answer the questions.

1. What does the professor mainly talk about?
    - (A) Changes in the migration patterns of chimney swifts
    - (B) Causes of the decline in chimney swift populations
    - (C) Where chimney swifts nest in rainforests
    - (D) Health risks of residential pesticides

2. What does the professor imply might be causing a decline in the chimney swift population?
    - (A) Deforestation along their migration routes
    - (B) An increase in hunting activity
    - (C) A decrease in the number of homes with uncapped or unsealed chimneys
    - (D) A change in the birds' migration patterns

3. What does the professor say about how the use of pesticides affects chimney swift populations?
    - (A) Pesticides are poisoning chimney swift populations.
    - (B) Pesticides are an effective way to reduce parasites that are harmful to chimney swifts.
    - (C) Pesticides have little or no impact on chimney swift populations.
    - (D) Pesticides kill the primary food sources of chimney swifts, making food harder to find.

4. According to the professor, how are some scientists estimating the decline in the chimney swift population?
    - (A) Counting the swifts that return to suitable nests each year
    - (B) Collecting estimates from people who report seeing a chimney swift nest
    - (C) Tracking the birds with radio-frequency identification tags
    - (D) Constructing swift "towers" to attract the birds

5. What does the professor imply about bird perching?
    - (A) Most birds only perch in a nest.
    - (B) A bird is more vulnerable to attack when perched.
    - (C) Perching is essential for migrating chimney swifts.
    - (D) The majority of birds can perch.

Listen to Track 96.

Now answer the question.

6. What does the professor imply when she says this?

    (A) She does not think her next point is important enough to share.

    (B) Students are likely to find her next point obvious.

    (C) She is unsure about her next point.

    (D) She believes the next point will confuse students.

11.8

Listen to Track 97.

Now answer the questions.

1. What is the main purpose of the talk?

    (A) To discuss how to minimize the impact of humans on the sulfur cycle

    (B) To describe sulfur compounds found in gunpowder and fireworks

    (C) To illustrate why life on Earth could not exist without sulfur

    (D) To explain how sulfur moves in and out of the atmosphere

Listen to Track 98.

Now answer the question.

2. (A) She wants to emphasize that sulfur can take on a variety of forms.

    (B) She anticipates that students will struggle with this concept.

    (C) She is reassuring students that fertilizer is not as dangerous as gunpowder and fireworks are.

    (D) She is explaining that the components of fertilizer are more complex than those that make up gunpowder and fireworks.

3. Which processes that release sulfur into the atmosphere does the professor mention? *Choose 2 answers.*

    [A] Plant death

    [B] Deep sea mining

    [C] Burning fossil fuels

    [D] Acid rain

11

4. What can be inferred about the professor's view on the burning of fossil fuels?

   (A) She thinks that it will benefit plants because of increased access to sulfur.

   (B) She believes that it has directly contributed to an increase in the amount of sulfur released into the atmosphere.

   (C) She is concerned that there is no way to reduce the amount of sulfur released by this process.

   (D) She is encouraged by the fact that most of her students want to help end this practice.

5. Why does the professor discuss acid rain?

   (A) To describe a consequence of excess sulfur in the atmosphere

   (B) To emphasize the importance of continuing the study of environmental science

   (C) To point out one of the many natural dangers present because of the Earth's environment

   (D) To illustrate that sulfur is just one of many elements under investigation

6. What comparison does the professor make involving sulfur and nitrogen?

   (A) Burning fossil fuels releases more nitrogen than sulfur into the atmosphere.

   (B) The atmosphere contains more nitrogen than sulfur.

   (C) One element is a component of acid rain, and the other is not.

   (D) Plants require less nitrogen than sulfur to survive.

11.9

 Listen to Track 99.

Now answer the questions.

1. What aspect of plants does the professor mainly describe in her talk?

   (A) Their use in cleaning water and air

   (B) Their use as houseplants

   (C) The density of their root systems

   (D) Their use as building materials

Listen to Track 100.

Now answer the question.

2. Why does the professor mention her graduate research assistant's family emergency?

    (A) To tell the students an interesting story

    (B) To provide support for the topic of the lecture

    (C) To explain why the grading of an assignment will not be completed on time

    (D) To encourage students to volunteer at the lab

3. What does the professor imply about city streets without trees?

    (A) They are less expensive to maintain than streets with trees.

    (B) They are less attractive than streets with trees.

    (C) They are safer than streets with trees.

    (D) They have more pollution than city streets with trees.

4. Why does the professor mention the executive in New Delhi?

    (A) To show that companies do not care about air quality

    (B) To provide an example of apparently effective phytoremediation

    (C) To demonstrate the cost of phytoremediation

    (D) To illustrate the dangers of poor air quality

5. According to the professor, what was the main reason for using bamboo, rather than other plants, in a water treatment system?

    (A) It is cheaper than other options.

    (B) It has a dense root system.

    (C) It is readily available.

    (D) It quickly regenerates after cutting.

6. According to the lecture, what are two reasons that scientists are investigating non-chemical alternatives for treating greywater? *Choose 2 answers.*

    [A] The growing concern over clean, available, drinking water

    [B] The bad taste of chemically treated water

    [C] The expense of moving water between homes and treatment centers

    [D] The difficulty of storing chemicals for long periods of time

11.10

 Listen to Track 101.

Now answer the questions.

1. What is the lecture primarily about?

    (A) Illustrating how planets orbit the Sun

    (B) Exploring the concept of the "Goldilocks zone"

    (C) Describing the plan to colonize other planets in the future

    (D) Explaining the development of solar systems

2. According to the professor, what is true of Goldilocks planets?

    (A) They are roughly the same size as Earth.

    (B) They are located between other planets in a solar system.

    (C) They do not have a substantial atmosphere.

    (D) They can potentially support liquid water.

3. What does the professor imply about the planet Venus? *Choose 2 answers.*

    [A] Its core is likely composed of lead.

    [B] It is too hot to sustain life as we know it.

    [C] It is sometimes located in the habitable zone.

    [D] It has an insignificant atmosphere.

4. According to the lecture, what is the possible significance of several of the planets recently found orbiting the star TRAPPIST-1?

    (A) They demonstrate how advanced telescopes have become.

    (B) They are useful for studying the atmosphere of distant planets.

    (C) They are in the habitable zone.

    (D) They are the only known Goldilocks planets other than Earth.

Listen to Track 102.

Now answer the question.

5. Why does the professor say this?

   (A) To explain that being in the habitable zone is not the only requirement for life to exist on a planet

   (B) To stress the importance of the position of the Goldilocks planets orbiting TRAPPIST-1

   (C) To explain why life on Earth is able to exist

   (D) To describe how researchers determine the size of a habitable zone

Listen to Track 103.

Now answer the question.

6. Why does the student say this?

   (A) To share his opinion on the issue at hand

   (B) To remind the professor of an earlier question

   (C) To express his disapproval of the professor's comment

   (D) To verify his understanding of a previous statement

11

Answer Key—11.1

Question	Correct Answer	Right/Wrong	Category
1	D		Detail
2	B		Gist-purpose
3	A		Organization
4	D		Function of What Is Said
5	A, D		Detail
6	C		Inference

Answer Key—11.2

Question	Correct Answer	Right/Wrong	Category
1	A		Gist-content
2	C, D		Detail
3	B		Detail
4	B		Detail
5	A		Organization
6	C		Function of What Is Said

Answer Key—11.3

Question	Correct Answer	Right/Wrong	Category
1	A		Gist-content
2	B		Speaker's Attitude
3	D		Detail
4	C		Detail
5	D		Detail
6	C		Organization

Answer Key—11.4

Question	Correct Answer	Right/Wrong	Category
1	D		Gist-content
2	D		Speaker's Attitude
3	A, B		Inference
4	A		Inference
5	B		Detail
6	C		Detail

Answer Key—11.5

Question	Correct Answer	Right/Wrong	Category
1	A		Gist-content
2	D		Detail
3	B		Inference
4	B, C		Detail
5	C		Speaker's Attitude
6	D		Function of What Is Said

Answer Key—11.6

Question	Correct Answer	Right/Wrong	Category
1	A		Gist-content
2	C		Detail
3	D		Inference
4	B		Speaker's Attitude
5	C, D		Detail
6	A		Organization

Answer Key—11.7

Question	Correct Answer	Right/Wrong	Category
1	B		Gist-content
2	C		Inference
3	D		Detail
4	A		Detail
5	D		Inference
6	B		Function of What Is Said

Answer Key—11.8

Question	Correct Answer	Right/Wrong	Category
1	D		Gist-purpose
2	C		Function of What Is Said
3	A, C		Detail
4	B		Inference
5	A		Organization
6	B		Detail

Answer Key—11.9

Question	Correct Answer	Right/Wrong	Category
1	A		Gist-content
2	C		Function of What Is Said
3	D		Inference
4	B		Organization
5	B		Detail
6	A, C		Detail

Answer Key—11.10

Question	Correct Answer	Right/Wrong	Category
1	B		Gist-content
2	D		Detail
3	B, C		Inference
4	C		Detail
5	A		Function of What Is Said
6	D		Function of What Is Said

Answers and Explanations—11.1

Comets—Track 84

NARRATOR: Listen to part of a lecture in an astronomy class.

PROFESSOR: OK. Today, I'm going to tell you about how a famous object in the Solar System got its name. Let's start with Kepler. Remember from the reading Kepler's First Law?… Uh, planetary orbits are in the shapes of…

FEMALE STUDENT: Ellipses.

PROFESSOR: Right. An ellipse is basically an oval, uh, a stretched-out circle. How much it's stretched is called the eccentricity. A circle is actually an ellipse with zero eccentricity, and if the eccentricity is just say 2 percent, the circle is stretched just a bit. But if you push the eccentricity towards 100 percent, the ellipse gets really stretched out and skinny.

Um, how eccentric do you think the Earth's orbit is?

MALE STUDENT: I'd say like 1 or 2 percent.

PROFESSOR: Good, it's between 1 and 2 percent. That's a very good thing for us, by the way, because if we were on a really eccentric orbit, it'd be a lot hotter in the summer, like oceans boiling, and in the winter they might freeze completely solid.

Mercury has a kind of elliptical orbit, 20 percent or so. But there are other objects in the Solar System with even more elliptical orbits. Know what they are?

MALE STUDENT: Meteors?

PROFESSOR: Well… not necessarily. Meteors are usually just little chunks of rock that enter the Earth's atmosphere and burn up. But out in the Solar System, they're mostly just, uh, randomly kicked around. The things I'm thinking about are bigger—not as big as a planet, but several miles across—and more importantly they follow more regular orbits, just… eccentric ones. They swoop in near the Sun and go back out again…

FEMALE STUDENT: Comets.

PROFESSOR: Yes, comets. Comets travel in pretty eccentric orbits. Now… when comets get in close to the Sun, what do they do?

MALE STUDENT: They grow a tail.

PROFESSOR: Exactly, they grow tails. Think of comets as dirty snowballs. Radiation from the Sun boils off some water and other stuff, and that's what makes up the tail.

All right, here's the story of a famous comet. It wasn't first seen by the person it's named after. In fact, this comet was seen back in 240 BC by Chinese astronomers, who called comets "broom stars." The tail is the broom, the brush part.

So then this comet gets seen in 164 BC by astronomers in Babylon, and every 75 or 76 years after that it's in Chinese records. But no one seemed to know it was the same comet. For one thing, it looked different every time. Sometimes it was close to the Earth, sometimes it was pretty far away. And there are a lot of other comets in the meantime, all kinds of broom stars.

Then in 1607 Kepler himself even observes this particular comet, but he doesn't connect the dots. He's figuring out his laws of planetary orbits, which were just observational, by the way, just patterns. He never proved why the orbits were ellipses. He just said, planets move in elliptical orbits, that's what we see but who knows why. So Kepler's Laws weren't fundamental laws of nature.

Next comes Isaac Newton. He publishes the Principia in 1687, which lays out the laws of motion and gravitation—these are the fundamental laws of nature that give rise to Kepler's Laws, or maybe I should say Kepler's Patterns. So in the Principia, Newton also explains how to calculate cometary orbits from observations, because comets follow Newton's Laws along with planets and everything else.

Finally, Newton's buddy Edmond Halley applies the Principia method to a bunch of historical records of comets—

FEMALE STUDENT: Halley's Comet.

PROFESSOR: Yes! Hold that thought. Halley calculates all these cometary orbits using Newton's Laws, and he finds that the comet Kepler saw in 1607, and another one seen in 1531 and a third one in 1682, all three comets have the same size orbit, the same shape orbit, the same orientation in the sky. The numbers that describe the orbit are called orbital elements, and these three comets all have the same orbital elements.

So Halley says, these are all the same comet, reappearing every 75 to 76 years. And he predicts this comet will come back in late 1758. He dies in 1742, but sure enough, in December 1758 the comet shows back up.

That's why we call it Halley's Comet—not because Halley was the first one to ever see it. People had been seeing it for hundreds and hundreds of years. But Halley was the first one to make use of scientific laws, he was the first one to prove it was all the same comet, and he even predicted its return.

1.	What is Kepler's First Law?	**DETAIL.** This is the first question the professor poses the class.
✗ (A)	A fundamental law of nature	Later the professor specifically says that Kepler's Laws are *not* fundamental. She even calls them Kepler's Patterns.
✗ (B)	A prediction of when a comet would return	Halley made the prediction of when a comet would return, using Newton's Laws.
✗ (C)	A description of how comet tails form	The professor describes how comet tails form, but she does not associate that process with Kepler's First Law.
✓ (D)	A statement about the shapes of planetary orbits	**CORRECT.** After asking what Kepler's First Law is, the professor prompts the class: "Planetary orbits are in the shapes of…" A student responds, "Ellipses," and the professor says, "Right." The point that planets move in elliptical orbits is repeated later.

2. Why does the professor explain Edmond Halley's work to the class?

GIST-PURPOSE. Edmond Halley's work is explained toward the end of the lecture. Halley identifies three separate observations as one comet and predicts its return. As a result, the comet is named for him.

✗ (A) To highlight how long in the historical record Halley's Comet has been observed

Halley's work comes toward the end of a long historical record of sightings of the comet. But the professor explains Halley's work without emphasizing the length of this historical record.

✓ (B) To explain how Halley's Comet got its name

CORRECT. The professor begins by saying: "Today, I'm going to tell you about how a famous object in the Solar System got its name." This object is Halley's Comet. Toward the end of the lecture, the professor explains Halley's work and then says: "That's why we call it Halley's Comet."

✗ (C) To walk through detailed calculations that use Newton's Laws

The professor emphasizes that Newton's Laws made Halley's work (his calculations) possible, but she never demonstrates any actual calculations to the class.

✗ (D) To emphasize the eccentricity of cometary orbits

Midway through the lecture, the professor describes comets as objects that "travel in pretty eccentric orbits." But this is not why she explains Halley's work later on. In that explanation, she never emphasizes how eccentric cometary orbits are.

3. How does the professor introduce comets to the class?

ORGANIZATION. The professor talks about elliptical orbits in general, mentions that Earth's orbit is not very elliptical, and then asks the class which objects in the Solar System have very elliptical orbits. The correct response, given by a student, is comets. The professor then goes on to describe comets further.

✓ (A) By asking which objects have a certain kind of orbit

CORRECT. To introduce comets, the professor asks which objects have "even more elliptical orbits" than Mercury.

✗ (B) By discussing the composition of comets

The professor describes comets as "dirty snowballs" *after* introducing comets.

✗ (C) By drawing attention to meteors first

The professor does not bring up meteors or try to draw attention to them. A student gives "meteors" as an incorrect response, so the professor has to describe them briefly and draw a contrast to the objects she's thinking of (comets). But this was not her original intent.

✗ (D) By describing the effects of a hypothetical orbit of the Earth

The professor mentions the "oceans boiling" that might happen if the Earth were in a very eccentric orbit (hypothetically). But this mention is an aside. The professor says "by the way" as she makes this aside.

11

Track 85

NARRATOR: Listen again to part of the lecture. Then answer the question.

PROFESSOR: So Kepler's Laws weren't fundamental laws of nature. Next comes Isaac Newton. He publishes the Principia in 1687, which lays out the laws of motion and gravitation—these are the fundamental laws of nature that give rise to Kepler's Laws, or maybe I should say Kepler's Patterns.

NARRATOR: Why does the professor say this:

PROFESSOR: …or maybe I should say Kepler's Patterns.

4.   Why does the professor say this?

    FUNCTION OF WHAT IS SAID. Look for the purpose of the professor's specific words. By saying "Kepler's Patterns," the professor is emphasizing that Kepler's Laws are not like Newton's Laws, which are "fundamental laws of nature."

✗   (A) To argue that Kepler's Laws are essentially flawed

    The professor is not arguing that the laws are wrong, or flawed. Rather, they are just not fundamental, in the way that Newton's Laws are.

✗   (B) To point out how comets do not obey Kepler's Laws

    The professor never says that comets do not obey any of Kepler's Laws. According to the professor, comets follow elliptical orbits, just as Kepler's First Law says that planets do.

✗   (C) To suggest how Kepler's Laws may be applied more broadly

    By calling Kepler's Laws "patterns," the professor is not trying to apply these laws more broadly. Rather, she is indicating that these laws are not fundamental laws.

✓   (D) To contrast Kepler's Laws with more fundamental laws of nature

    CORRECT. The professor changes the name to "Kepler's Patterns" to highlight the contrast between these "patterns" and "fundamental laws of nature," which Kepler's Laws are not.

5.   According to the professor, why did no one before Halley know that various historical observations of Halley's Comet were of the same comet? *Choose 2 answers.*

    DETAIL. As the professor describes various observations of Halley's Comet through history, she says "But no one seemed to know it was the same comet." She immediately gives two reasons.

✓   [A] The comet looked different every time it was observed.

    CORRECT. The professor says: "For one thing, it looked different every time. Sometimes it was close to the Earth, sometimes it was pretty far away."

✗   [B] Whenever the comet was observed, its orbit had a different size and shape.

    The professor does not cite this reason. In fact, Halley found that the comet's orbit each time had the *same* size and shape. That's why he claimed that the same comet had been observed each time.

✗   [C] The historical observations were not precise enough.

    The professor never describes how precise or not the historical observations were.

✓   [D] There were many other observations of other comets.

    CORRECT. The professor also says: "And there are a lot of other comets in the meantime, all kinds of broom stars."

6.   What does the professor imply about Halley's Comet?

INFERENCE. The professor discusses the comet itself in the latter part of the lecture.

✗ (A) Newton could not have identified the comet first.

The professor never implies that Newton could not have identified the comet first. In fact, Newton provided the method that Halley used to identify the comet. So, if anything, Newton probably could have identified the comet first, in theory.

✗ (B) The comet has a more eccentric orbit than most other comets.

The professor never discusses how eccentric the orbit of Halley's comet is. Nor does she compare its eccentricity to that of any other comets. All you can assume is that Halley's Comet has an eccentric orbit. After all, it is a comet, and according to the professor, comets have "pretty eccentric orbits."

✓ (C) No other comet has the same orbital elements.

CORRECT. If another comet had the same orbital elements (the numbers describing the orbit) as Halley's Comet, then Halley could not have made his claim. He could not have argued that the various observations were all of the same single comet. The professor implies that Halley's Comet (as well as every other comet) has a unique set of orbital elements describing its orbit.

✗ (D) Halley's Comet was not observed before 240 BC.

The professor describes the first known and recorded observation, which occurred in 240 BC. But you can't infer that before that time, no one had ever observed the comet at all.

Answers and Explanations—11.2

Piñon Pines—Track 86

NARRATOR: Listen to part of a lecture in an environmental science class.

PROFESSOR: So we've been talking about the way climate change can impact plant and animal species. In particular, in the Sonoran Desert, in the Southwestern United States, over the last… oh, hundred years or so, temperatures have increased by about 2 degrees Fahrenheit. And scientists have been studying the effect of this change on Piñon pines.

Piñon pines are a pine tree native to the Sonoran Desert. They have adapted to a hot, dry environment. Piñons are… really interesting. Like other pines, they reproduce by shedding their pine cones, which can then grow into new pine trees. But instead of reproducing on a set schedule, Piñons wait until the climactic conditions are just right for reproduction. They tend to shed their pine cones every three to seven years. In years when the climate is hotter and dryer, and the pine cones might have trouble growing, the Piñon pines will delay shedding their pine cones.

FEMALE STUDENT: So, because of the climate and the fact that Piñon pines can change their reproduction, they should be really adaptable to climate change, right?

PROFESSOR: Yes, that's right. Piñon pines are perfect for an environment that varies from year to year. In fact, in the 1950s, there was a large drought, but most of the Piñon pines were unaffected. The oldest and weakest pines did not survive, but the vast majority of the Piñon pines made it made it through with basically no trouble. The process of shedding their pine cones, which is called a masting event… well, the Piñons reduced their masting events.

MALE STUDENT: Um, I'm sorry, when you say reduced their "masting events," do you mean that they didn't have as many or that when they had masting events, they shed fewer pine cones?

PROFESSOR: Good question. Actually both. The Piñons didn't have as many masting events as they would have had in normal years. And the masting events that they did have produced fewer pine cones than usual. So the Piñon pines were able to survive and wait until the timing was right to reproduce in large amounts.

Okay, so why are we talking about these sturdy plants in regard to climate change? It seems like a small temperature increase is something these pines can deal with. Well, the problem is there are many other factors that come into play. Climate change is a long-term shift, so Piñons can't just wait for it to stop before their next masting event. But the hotter environment reduces the masting events anyway, so we have fewer new pines growing. And some insects that feed on the Piñon pines are thriving in this hot environment.

One type of insect, the bark beetle, flourishes in hot environments. And because the pine trees are not reproducing frequently, they are more susceptible to the bark beetle's invasion. Fewer pine trees are being created, and those that are created tend to be more sickly as a result.

Not to mention, Piñon pines use unseasonably low temperatures in late summer as the sign to start their masting event. And when the temperature doesn't get unseasonably low, the masting events don't occur. What's worse is that in the midst of this climate change, there are still droughts. In the 2000s, a drought that was even worse than the one in the 1950s hit the Sonoran Desert. It affected all ages of Piñon pines. The sickly Piñons were already infested with bark beetles, and now, they did not have enough water. So many Piñons did not survive. It's estimated that the population fell by about 40 percent.

FEMALE STUDENT: What about human intervention? Can't we use, I don't know… insect repellent or something? There has to be a way to get the bark beetles away from the Piñon pines.

PROFESSOR: Well, human intervention is controversial. Probably the best thing we could do for them is start controlled wildfires. Piñon pines group so closely together that it's easy for the beetles to migrate from one tree to another. A wildfire would thin the groups of pines, making it harder for bark beetles to expand their range. At the same time, the wildfire would reduce the grasses and shrubs growing around the Piñon pines, so there'd be less competition for nutrients. But starting a forest fire isn't something most people would support.

FEMALE STUDENT: But if we know it would help the pines, shouldn't we be able to convince people who are against wildfires?

PROFESSOR: Maybe. But we're not completely sure what the effect would be. Maybe thinning the groups of pines would allow more sunlight to reach the bases of the trees, which could be harmful to them, for example. We have to proceed very carefully when we consider intervention.

1.   What is the lecture mainly about?

GIST-CONTENT. The professor discusses the reproduction process of Piñon pines, and the factors currently threatening them.

✓ (A) Factors involved in the decline of Piñon pine populations

CORRECT. Temperature variations, droughts, and infestation are are discussed to explain why the Piñon pines are experiencing difficulty.

✗ (B) How unseasonably cold winters might be affecting Piñon pines

This idea is not mentioned in the lecture.

✗ (C) Why the population of bark beetles has been declining

The lecture contradicts this idea.

✗ (D) Reasons that Piñon pines are expanding their range

The population of Piñon pines is diminishing. The professor does not discuss Piñon pines expanding their range.

2.   According to the professor, what are two features of masting events for Piñon pines? *Choose 2 answers.*

DETAIL. A masting event is the process by which Piñon pines shed their pine cones for reproduction.

✗ [A] They occur only in cold climates.

This is contradicted by the lecture. Piñon pines grow in the hot, dry environment of the Sonoran Desert.

✗ [B] The rate at which they occur depends on the age of the pine trees.

Age of the pine trees is not discussed in relation to masting events.

✓ [C] They are influenced by changes in temperature.

CORRECT. Masting events are triggered when the temperature is appropriate for reproduction, and delayed when the weather is too hot and dry.

✓ [D] They involve the release of pine cones.

CORRECT. A masting event is defined as a period when the Piñon pines shed their pine cones.

3.   What is one reason for the decrease in Piñon pine populations in the Sonoran Desert?

DETAIL. The professor mentions several factors that threaten Piñon pines, but specifically states that one combination led to a decrease in population: bark beetles and a drought.

✗ (A) Decreases in the amount of nutrients in the soil have increased competition among Piñon pines.

This idea is not discussed in the lecture.

✓ (B) Increases in the number of bark beetles have left them more susceptible to drought.

CORRECT. The drought in the 2000s is cited as so deadly for Piñon pines largely because they were weakened by bark beetles.

✗ (C) Increases in the average temperature have caused masting events to occur more frequently.

There have been increases in temperature, but this has resulted in a decrease in masting events.

✗ (D) Increases in rainfall have altered the natural environment of the Piñon pine

This idea is not mentioned in the lecture.

4. Why are humans NOT intervening to protect Piñon pines?

DETAIL. The professor mentions that some people may disagree with intervention, and that any intervention would need to be carefully thought through.

✗ (A) Most Piñon pines are in locations that humans cannot easily reach.

This idea is not mentioned in the lecture.

✓ (B) The actions humans would need to take could be controversial.

CORRECT. The professor directly says this.

✗ (C) The bark beetle also needs to be protected by human intervention.

This idea is not mentioned in the lecture.

✗ (D) Masting events have decreased in recent years.

If anything, this fact argues in favor of human intervention, not against it.

5. Why does the professor mention the 1950s drought, which did not severely affect most of the Piñon pines?

ORGANIZATION. The professor mentions this event in response to a student's question about how adaptable the pines are to hot, dry environments.

✓ (A) To suggest that healthy Piñon pines can survive in dry environments

CORRECT. This drought is also used to contrast with the 2000s drought, in which many pines did not survive.

✗ (B) To explain how Piñon pines can expand to wetter environments

Piñon pines survived, but did not expand, and there is no discussion of moving to wetter environments.

✗ (C) To cite a similarity between Piñon pines and other types of pine trees

Other types of trees are not mentioned in this example.

✗ (D) To explain how increasing temperatures can encourage the growth of bark beetle populations.

This fact is unrelated to the 1950s drought.

Track 87

NARRATOR: What does the professor imply when she says this:

PROFESSOR: Okay, so why are we talking about these sturdy plants in regard to climate change? It seems like a small temperature increase is something these pines can deal with.

6.   **FUNCTION OF WHAT IS SAID.** The professor is indicating that there is a reason to discuss the topic beyond what has already been mentioned. Note that "these sturdy plants" refers to Piñon pines.

✗ (A) The adaptability of Piñon pines is an important enough theme to be repeated.

Piñon pines can adapt to temperature changes up to a point. But this question sets up a discussion about *limits* to their adaptability.

✗ (B) Climate scientists should not bother studying the impact of a temperature increase on Piñon pines.

The professor implies that such a study would be useful.

✓ (C) The climate change she is describing involves more factors that have not yet been discussed.

CORRECT. The professor goes on to talk about the various ways that an increase in temperature, over the long term, can weaken the pines and potentially threaten their population.

✗ (D) Students should be able to answer this question quickly.

There is still much that needs to be discussed before this question can be answered.

Answers and Explanations—11.3

Units of Measurement—Track 88

NARRATOR: Listen to part of a lecture in a physics class.

PROFESSOR: OK, so, I want to begin today by talking about units of measurement. I know, you're probably thinking, this is not going to be very interesting, right? But seriously, the next time you take a measurement, I'd like you to remember something. Whether it's the passing of time, or traveling a certain distance, or weighing the ingredients in a recipe—these are pretty common things we do, right? We are constantly taking measurements. And we all have a pretty intuitive sense of how to do these by now, I imagine. On any particular day, we might measure how much time to, say, heat up a dish in the microwave, in seconds. And based on seconds, we have minutes and hours. We can measure distance—under the International System of Units, also called *SI*—by meter or by kilometer. And we measure weight in the SI by the kilogram. There are seven base units of measurement in SI. Three of these are the meter, the second and the kilogram, which I just mentioned. The others are the candela, the ampere, the kelvin, and the mole.

Does anyone know what the kilogram is based on? How it's defined? *(pause)* No?… OK. The kilogram is set to be equivalent to the weight of a cylinder made of platinum-iridium that is stored in a vault in France. Its specific location is a secret, only known by a few scientists living today. That is how important this cylinder is.

Isn't that wild? The universal unit of measurement, the kilogram, is based on the weight of this one special cylinder. Once every 30 or so years, it's removed from the vault so that it can be cleaned... and while it's out, it's also weighed. And here is the really strange part... the last two times it has been weighed, right after World War II and again in 1992, the cylinder had lost weight. That's right, the cylinder whose only purpose is to define how much weight is in a kilogram? It is losing weight.

Now, why this is? No one knows. But what it makes clear is that when standard units of measurement are based on particular *tangible things*, like the cylinder in the vault in France... it introduces the risk of variation. And variation when what you want is for something to be standard, constant, and universal? This... this is bad.

So the International Committee of Weights and Measures, which is the group of people that oversees standard units of measurement, has been working to replace particular tangible objects as the basis of units with *natural constants* in physics. That means, constants that don't change at all under earthly conditions and that don't depend on one particular random object. Take the meter, for instance... in the late 1700s, when the metric system was created, the meter was defined based on the Earth's circumference. Specifically, it was defined as one ten-millionth of one-fourth of the Earth's circumference. But that was a measurement based on the Earth, which, again, *metrologists*—the people who study this stuff—didn't like because of possible variation. So in 1983, the meter was redefined as the distance that light travels in a fraction of a second... it's a giant, messy fraction, and you don't need to know it. The point is that the meter was redefined so that it wouldn't be dependent on the Earth's features.

Another unit of measurement whose definition has already been changed from having a tangible object as its basis to a natural constant? The second. It used to be based on the timing of the Earth's rotation around the Sun. Now it's based on a property of certain radiation that's the same anywhere, theoretically, in the universe.

The other four standard units—do you remember what they are? Candela, ampere, kelvin, and mole... these were also redefined in the twentieth century, just as the meter and the second were. It's *only* the kilogram that hasn't been redefined since the nineteenth century... so it's been well over 100 years. And so fairly soon, that is what is going to happen... I mean, it's especially important in the case of the kilogram— it needs to be based on a standard that cannot alter, given that that cylinder in France is actually losing weight. What is the kilogram going to be based on? It will be based on "Planck's constant," which is a concept from quantum theory. Does anyone know what Planck's constant is?... No? It defines the amount of energy carried by a single particle of light. Once this change happens, there won't be a need for this high-security vault in France anymore.

1.		What does the professor mainly discuss?	**GIST-CONTENT.** The lecture is about standard units of measurement, and how they are being redefined so that they are based on natural constants, not particular tangible objects.
✓	(A)	The changing basis for defining standard units of measurement	**CORRECT.** This is the primary focus of the lecture.
✗	(B)	The controversial belief that standards should be uniform across the world	The professor does not suggest that the belief that standards should be uniform is controversial.
✗	(C)	Examples of differences in units of measurement across countries	This issue is not discussed in the lecture.
✗	(D)	Why people believe in the importance of standards units of measurement	The lecture only peripherally touches upon why standard units are important.

2.   The professor discusses units of measure-ment and how the standards on which they are based have changed. What can be inferred about the professor's opinion regarding these changes?

SPEAKER'S ATTITUDE. The professor regards these as positive changes, as they remove the possibility of variation from standards that should not vary.

✗ (A) She is sure that the cylinder is a better standard for the kilogram than Planck's constant.

She believes the opposite of this. In her opinion, natural constants are a better basis for standard units than are particular tangible things.

✓ (B) She believes that changing the standards to natural constants is an improvement.

CORRECT. The professor speaks about how tangible bases for units can lead to variation, while natural constants are not susceptible to variation and are therefore preferred.

✗ (C) She thinks that the kilogram as a unit of measurement is obsolete.

She believes that the cylinder on which the kilogram is based is obsolete, but she does not think the kilogram as a unit of measurement is obsolete.

✗ (D) She admits that the old ways of standardizing measurements were better than the new ways.

She does not believe or admit this. She believes the new ways are preferable to the old ways.

3.   According to the professor, what is one problem with the weighted cylinder in France on which the kilogram is based?

DETAIL. The professor states that the cylinder is losing weight.

✗ (A) It can no longer be adequately secured in its vault.

The professor does not state or suggest this.

✗ (B) It is no longer useful.

The cylinder is still useful, as long as the kilogram is still based upon it.

✗ (C) It was created before modern physics.

The professor does not state or suggest this.

✓ (D) It is losing weight.

CORRECT. The professor explicitly states that this is the problem with the weighted cylinder in France.

4.   According to the professor, which is the standard unit of measurement that has not been updated since the nineteenth century?

DETAIL. The professor states in the lecture that the kilogram is the unit that hasn't been updated since the nineteenth century.

✗ (A) The second

The professor states that only the kilogram hasn't been redefined since the nineteenth century.

✗ (B) The meter

The professor states that only the kilogram hasn't been redefined since the nineteenth century.

✓ (C) The kilogram

CORRECT. This is the unit the professor states has not been updated since the nineteenth century.

✗ (D) The candela

The professor states that only the kilogram hasn't been redefined since the nineteenth century.

5.   What will the kilogram be based on once it is no longer based on the cylinder?

DETAIL. The kilogram will be based on Planck's constant.

✗   (A) The circumference of the Earth

This is the particular tangible thing previously used to define the meter.

✗   (B) A new standard yet to be determined

The professor mentions what the new standard will be.

✗   (C) A new cylinder with constant weight

The intention behind the change in standards is to move away from tangible things as the basis of units, not to replace one tangible thing with another.

✓   (D) Planck's constant

CORRECT. This is what the professor states in the lecture.

6.   How does the professor organize the lecture?

ORGANIZATION. The author focuses mainly on the kilogram at first. Then, she discusses how other units of measurement have been redefined. Later, she returns to the kilogram and explains how it will be redefined soon.

✗   (A) By defining the kilogram, then listing all of the reasons why it has been impossible to standardize

The professor does not state or suggest that the kilogram is impossible to standardize.

✗   (B) By speaking about how the kilogram will be redefined, then describing how it has been defined since the nineteenth century

The professor does not state how the kilogram will be redefined until the end of the lecture.

✓   (C) By discussing how the kilogram is currently defined, then noting that other units have been redefined and that the kilogram will be redefined soon

CORRECT. This is how the professor organizes this lecture.

✗   (D) By emphasizing the importance of standardizing the meter before redefining the kilogram and the second

The professor does not suggest that redefining the kilogram or the second depends upon standardizing the meter.

Answers and Explanations—11.4

African Humid Period—Track 89

NARRATOR: Listen to part of a lecture in a geology class.

PROFESSOR: So, continuing our discussion of desert rivers, now I want to focus on the Sahara Desert.

The Sahara Desert is the largest hot desert on Earth. In its wettest areas, it receives only 100 to 250 millimeters of precipitation—rainfall and snowfall—per year. Its driest areas have absolutely no precipitation. There are some fertile areas around the Nile River and the Mediterranean Sea, but most of the Sahara Desert has very limited plant growth, and few animal species can survive there. However, in ancient times, the climate of the Sahara was substantially different. Starting about 11,000 years ago and

continuing to about 5,000 years ago—this was known as the African Humid Period—the Sahara might have actually been a jungle-like environment.

FEMALE STUDENT: Excuse me, Professor, but I'm confused. How could it be that a desert was ever a jungle? Doesn't a jungle need a lot of precipitation?

PROFESSOR: Good question. You're right that the modern climate of the Sahara could never support a jungle. But climates *can* change significantly over the course of thousands of years. Some periods are hot and humid. Others cover the planet in ice. These changes are periodic, and a single area can change from a desert to a jungle and back again several times.

Why does this occur? There are two major theories—one well known, and the other just beginning to get support. Um, first, the wobbling of the Earth is known to have a direct impact on the climate. The Earth is tilted, and as it revolves around the Sun, sometimes the Northern Hemisphere is tilted slightly towards the Sun, and sometimes the Southern Hemisphere is instead. Whichever hemisphere is tilted toward the Sun gets more sunlight. Getting more or less sunlight, as you know, can change the temperature, causing substantial climate change. Second, greenhouse gases build up and increase the amount of solar radiation present in some areas. Even though you may think that greenhouse gases are a product of industrialization, they are not limited to that… humans have been affecting greenhouse gases substantially since we mastered agriculture. And plants and animals also use carbon dioxide, a common greenhouse gas. So it can build up or diminish over time, changing the climate significantly.

Now, the tilt of the Earth—the more studied phenomenon—is fairly predictable. So in the African Humid Period, the Northern Hemisphere was tilted towards the Sun, and received more direct sunlight. As a result, the land was hotter, and stronger winds were brought in from the ocean, so precipitation increased. Lakes and rivers were formed, and it was much more fertile land. However, if you look at just 10,000 years before that… about 21,000 years ago… the Northern Hemisphere was at the peak of an ice age, and the Sahara Desert was actually drier than it is today. Lake Victoria, which today is a massive lake, was almost completely dry. It existed only as swampy marshlands.

As for greenhouse gases, recent modeling studies suggest they were the primary driver of the climate of the Southern Hemisphere. Keep in mind, when the North is tilted toward the Sun, the South is tilted away. So we should expect the Southern Hemisphere to have been cold and dry during the African Humid Period… except it wasn't. Southern Africa experienced the same increase in precipitation as Northern Africa. Why? An increase in greenhouse gases could account for it. If they built up in the Southern Hemisphere, they could have offset the impact of the Earth's tilt.

But what happens to the dried-up rivers? The water is gone, but it has already carved out a trench and forever changed the geology of the land. The only problem is that these dried riverbeds, over time, get buried under sand or dirt. But recently, an observation satellite imaged a huge ancient river in the Sahara Desert. It used radar to photograph several meters below the sand, and discovered a riverbed that ran over 500 kilometers across the Sahara.

Based on these images and other observations, scientists suspect that this river flows freely during wet periods and dries up when there is less rainfall. It has likely alternated between flowing and being dry several times over the last 125,000 years.

Interestingly, if the Earth's tilt was all that affected the Sahara Desert's climate, we could predict that this river would become active again in a few thousand years. Uh, but with the rapidly changing greenhouse gas levels… that's impossible to predict. Maybe that river will never flow again. Maybe it will start to flow and never dry up. Only time will tell for sure.

1. What is the lecture mainly about?

GIST-CONTENT. The professor mainly discusses the variability in climate in the Sahara Desert over the course of thousands of years, and evidence to suggest that it was much wetter during the African Humid Period than it is currently.

✗ (A) Reasons that finding ancient rivers is important to the study of climate change

This idea is not mentioned in the lecture.

✗ (B) A comparison of ancient and modern-day rivers in the Sahara Desert

No direct comparison is made between the two groups of rivers.

✗ (C) Satellite evidence of climate change in deserts

The satellite evidence is mentioned only to support a specific example of the Sahara's climate change.

✓ (D) A hypothesis for what the geology of the Sahara Desert was at one point in the past

CORRECT. The lecture talks about the causes of a different climate in the African Humid Period, as well as evidence that the landscape at that time was different.

2. What is the professor's opinion about the amount of plant growth in the modern Saharan climate?

SPEAKER'S ATTITUDE. He states that it is much drier, hotter, and less friendly to plant growth than it was during the African Humid Period.

✗ (A) It will be crucial to monitoring the continuing climate change in the Sahara.

The professor does not suggest that studying these plants will help to better understand Saharan climate change.

✗ (B) It is abnormally bountiful considering the current climate.

He never suggests there is anything abnormal about the current plant growth there.

✗ (C) It explains the dry season that the Sahara is currently experiencing.

The plants grow as a *result* of the climate. The professor does not suggest they *caused* the current climate.

✓ (D) It is limited, especially compared to growth during the African Humid Period.

CORRECT. The professor states this explicitly, going on to say that the current climate could never support the jungle-like conditions of the past.

3. What factors could have contributed to the creation of the climates that existed during the African Humid Period? *Choose 2 answers.*

INFERENCE. The professor mentions two primary factors that could drive long-term climate change: the Earth's tilt and greenhouse gases.

✓ ☐A The tilt of the Earth relative to the Sun

CORRECT. The Northern Hemisphere's tilt toward the Sun caused the temperature of the Sahara to increase, contributing to an increase in precipitation in the area.

✓ ☐B The increase of greenhouse gases in the atmosphere

CORRECT. This is stated as the primary driver of the hotter climate in the Southern Hemisphere and as a factor in changing climates.

✗ ☐C The presence of water-dependent vegetation

This factor is not mentioned in the lecture.

✗ ☐D The drying of Lake Victoria

This didn't occur during the African Humid Period, and was not a *cause* of *increased* precipitation, but rather a *result* of *decreased* precipitation.

4. What does the professor imply about the Southern Hemisphere during the African Humid Period?

INFERENCE. The professor notes that precipitation increased during this period. He adds as a potential explanation that "an increase in greenhouse gases could account for it. If they built up in the Southern Hemisphere, they could have offset the impact of the Earth's tilt."

✓ Ⓐ The level of greenhouse gases in the atmosphere was enough to increase the temperature in Southern Africa.

CORRECT. The Southern Hemisphere was tilted away from the Sun, which should have made it cooler and drier. However, the professor says that there was actually *more* precipitation in Southern Africa. He states that increased greenhouse gases could account for this by causing warming. Therefore, he implies that the greenhouse gases warmed the Southern Hemisphere relative to what would otherwise have been expected.

✗ Ⓑ The rivers in the Southern Hemisphere were larger and more common than they were in the Northern Hemisphere.

Rivers in the Southern Hemisphere were not mentioned in the lecture.

✗ Ⓒ The vegetation in the Southern Hemisphere was more varied at that time than it is today.

This comparison is not mentioned in the lecture.

✗ Ⓓ Observation satellites have been unable to detect as many ancient rivers from that time period in the Southern Hemisphere.

This idea is not mentioned in the lecture.

11

5. According to the professor, what was an observation satellite recently able to confirm?

DETAIL. Toward the end of the lecture, the professor states that an "observation satellite imaged a huge ancient river in the Sahara Desert. It used radar to photograph several meters below the sand, and discovered a riverbed that ran over 500 kilometers across the Sahara."

✗ (A) The degree of precipitation increase during the African Humid Period

The satellite did not discover this.

✓ (B) The presence of an ancient river in the Sahara Desert

CORRECT. The satellite imaged a dried river several meters below the Saharan sand that ran for over 500 kilometers.

✗ (C) The position of ancient jungles relative to ancient rivers

No such evidence was discussed.

✗ (D) Differences in levels of greenhouse gases between the Northern and Southern Hemispheres

No such difference has been established from any source.

6. What possible prediction does the professor give for the future of the 500 kilometer riverbed that was discovered?

DETAIL. The professor makes it clear that the future of this riverbed is uncertain—it may start flowing again, or it may not.

✗ (A) The riverbed could alter the area's vegetation.

This idea is not mentioned in the lecture.

✗ (B) The riverbed could itself bring about local climate change.

This idea is not mentioned in the lecture.

✓ (C) The riverbed could start to flow again.

CORRECT. This was directly stated by the professor.

✗ (D) A completely new riverbed could be carved in the Sahara Desert.

This idea is not mentioned in the lecture.

Answers and Explanations—11.5

Hibernation—Track 90

NARRATOR: Listen to part of a lecture in a biology class.

PROFESSOR: Yesterday, we were talking about survival techniques that animals use to endure harsh conditions. Today, um, I want to talk more specifically about *hibernation*—um, why some animals, mainly mammals, sleep through the winter. Now, many animals hibernate as a way to cope with food scarcity, but this isn't the only way. Some animals have other adaptations, you know, such as migrating to warmer climates for the winter. Or, for example, the red fox actually grows a thicker coat and changes its diet.

Interestingly enough, what many think of as hibernation, in some species, is actually *torpor*, which is something like a light hibernation. They look similar, but they're actually different. So, uh, what is it that

signals an animal to hibernate? Can anyone name one thing that might signal to an animal that it's time to start hibernating?

MALE STUDENT: Uh, the temperature? You know, the animal starts to get cold, or its food supply dies with the season?

PROFESSOR: Good guess. That would seem like the obvious signal, right? The animal's food supply dies or migrates and it knows to, well, gather up what it can and prepare its den or nest where it will stay. However, studies have shown that, uh, the length of the day and hormonal shifts are actually what trigger hibernation. So, well, as days get shorter, the animal knows that winter is approaching. In fact, hibernating animals enter hibernation at, um, around the same time every year. Regardless of the temperature or other external factors. We're not going to go into the specific details right now, but these scientists point to an internal calendar that signals hormone shifts in the body.

MALE STUDENT: I don't understand—if there is still food available, why would the animal hibernate? Or if, say, it got colder earlier, why wouldn't the animal hibernate then?

PROFESSOR: Right. Those would seem to be smart things for an animal to do, but consider how unpredictable weather can be. If hibernating and waking were completely weather-dependent, what would happen with an early frost in the fall or a warm day in the spring? It's not like the hibernating mammal has a weather forecast that allows it to see that cold weather might continue even after the warm day. However, the length of day is a much more reliable indicator of the exact time of year, unlike the weather.

Okay, so these factors might be how the animal knows when to hibernate, but what about the why? We're back to our original question. We know that hibernation is an adaptation to scarce resources, but why hibernate as opposed to say, migrating? Any ideas? No?

The key is the energy requirement for each option. A lot of energy is used in order for an animal to travel far enough to escape the winter climate, and then return, right? In fact, this is often why smaller mammals typically hibernate while larger ones often migrate. A larger animal can cover more distance with less effort, while a smaller animal doesn't need as much energy to keep its small body warm during hibernation. Evolution, therefore, favors these advantages. Sarah, you have a question?

FEMALE STUDENT: Um, yes, the idea that smaller animals are more likely to hibernate doesn't make sense to me. Didn't we discuss yesterday that many large bear species do not migrate. Why did they evolve to hibernate?

PROFESSOR: That's a great question, and it comes back to a point I made earlier. Bears don't actually hibernate, they enter torpor. Many of the processes of hibernation and torpor are the same, which is why they are often confused. Both, um, involve a reduction in body temperature, slowed heart rate and breathing, and even a restriction of blood to the main organs. However, a main difference seems to be whether the act is voluntary or involuntary.

Hibernation is actually a voluntary state, one, uh, that we know is triggered by hormones and day length, right? But, torpor appears to be involuntary—weather conditions seem to dictate this, and typically it will last for a short period of time, maybe just during the day or through the evening—depending on when the animal needs to be awake to hunt or forage for food. OK?

Now, before we move on, we need to examine one more activity similar to hibernation… and that is *estivation*. It is similar to the others… estivating animals become inactive and have lower heart and breathing rates. However, estivation is used by animals, such as, um… tortoises or even hedgehogs… to

survive extremely hot and dry climates, not cold ones. Rather than staying warm and maintaining fat stores, this behavior can help keep an animal cool and preserve water stores.

1.　What does the professor mainly discuss?

GIST-CONTENT. The professor is discussing sleep adaptations, mostly hibernation and torpor, and why these occur.

✓ (A) When and why some animals engage in hibernation or torpor

CORRECT. The professor primarily discusses long-term, deep forms of sleeping, such as hibernation and torpor, that are adaptations to changes in an animal's environment.

✗ (B) Animal defense mechanisms in cold climates

The forms of sleeping discussed in the lecture are not defense mechanisms, and they are reactions to hormonal shifts and changes in day length, not weather or climates.

✗ (C) The navigation techniques of species that migrate

This issue is briefly mentioned by the professor, but is not the main focus of the lecture.

✗ (D) Hormonal shifts that control an animal's internal calendar

This concept is discussed by the professor, but is not the main point of the lecture.

2.　According to the professor, why do smaller mammals typically hibernate rather than migrate?

DETAIL. According to the professor, the basis of this choice was the amount of energy required. To travel far enough to migrate takes a lot of energy for small animals, but they do not need as much energy to keep themselves warm if they hibernate.

✗ (A) They are more likely to be caught by predators if they migrate.

Nothing stated by the professor indicates that this would be the case.

✗ (B) They are skilled at building underground dens.

This idea is not mentioned in the lecture.

✗ (C) They are less likely to find food if they migrate.

This idea is not mentioned in the lecture.

✓ (D) They need less energy to stay warm than to travel long distances.

CORRECT. The professor explicitly states this in the lecture.

3.　In order to determine whether an animal is in a state of hibernation or torpor, which of the following questions needs to be answered?

INFERENCE. The professor states that the primary difference is whether the state is entered into voluntarily or involuntarily.

✗ (A) Whether the animal is large or small

Size plays a role in the choice between hibernation and *migration*, not between hibernation and *torpor*.

✓ (B) Whether the act is voluntary or involuntary

CORRECT. This is the primary difference noted by the professor.

✗ (C) The amount of food available

Hibernation and torpor are *both* adaptations to food availability, among other factors.

✗ (D) The current weather conditions

Hibernation and torpor are *both* adaptations to weather conditions, among other factors.

4. According to the professor, what are two triggers that determine when an animal enters into or awakens from hibernation? *Choose 2 answers.*

DETAIL. The professor says that hormonal shifts and day length are the two triggers. She explicitly says it was not weather conditions or food availability, although those are primary reasons for the adaptation.

✗ [A] Food availability

This is a reason for the adaptation of hibernation, but not a *trigger* for it.

✓ [B] Hormonal shifts

CORRECT. The professor said that hormonal shifts and day length are the two triggers.

✓ [C] Length of the day

CORRECT. The professor said that hormonal shifts and day length are the two triggers.

✗ [D] Snowstorm frequency

This idea is not mentioned in the lecture.

Track 91

NARRATOR: Listen again to part of the lecture. Then answer the question.

PROFESSOR: Studies have shown that, uh, the length of the day and hormonal shifts are actually what trigger hibernation. So, well, as days get shorter, the animal knows that winter is approaching. In fact, hibernating animals enter hibernation at, um, around the same time every year. Regardless of the temperature or other external factors. We're not going to go into the specific details right now, but these scientists point to an internal calendar that signals hormone shifts in the body.

NARRATOR: What does the professor mean when she says this:

PROFESSOR: We're not going to go into the specific details right now, but these scientists point to an internal calendar that signals hormone shifts in the body.

5. What does the professor mean when she says this?

SPEAKER'S ATTITUDE. In the highlighted quote, the professor has decided not to provide certain specific details. Instead, she focuses more on a general point.

✗ (A) She has already covered the details in an earlier class.

The professor does not indicate that this is the case.

✗ (B) She is not confident enough about the details to explain them.

Nothing in the lecture suggests that the professor is not confident about the details of hibernation triggers.

✓ (C) She does not want to discuss details that are not relevant to her main point.

CORRECT. The professor does not state her reasons. But it is implied that she would rather conclude this specific point and move on than provide more detail.

✗ (D) She believes that the explanation is too complicated for the students to understand.

This is possibly a reason for the professor not continuing. But it is not certain. What is known is that the professor wishes to move on to discussing her more general point.

Track 92

NARRATOR: Listen again to part of the lecture. Then answer the question.

MALE STUDENT: I don't understand—if there is still food available, why would the animal hibernate? Or if, say, it got colder earlier, why wouldn't the animal hibernate then?

PROFESSOR: Right. Those would seem to be smart things for an animal to do, but consider how unpredictable weather can be. If hibernating and waking were completely weather-dependent, what would happen with an early frost in the fall or a warm day in the spring?

NARRATOR: What point does the professor make when she says this:

PROFESSOR: If hibernating and waking were completely weather dependent, what would happen with an early frost in the fall or a warm day in the spring?

6. What point does the professor make when she says this?	**FUNCTION OF WHAT IS SAID.** In this quote, the professor is indicating that weather is an unreliable guide for when to begin, or end, hibernation, because weather can vary substantially from day to day.
✗ (A) It is not clear how animals know whether to hibernate or migrate.	On the contrary, the professor has explained this earlier in the lecture.
✗ (B) Different animals hibernate at different times of the year.	This might be the case, but this is not the point the professor is making.
✗ (C) The changing temperature might prevent animals from migrating.	This quote is not about migration. It is about the timing of hibernation.
✓ (D) Animals might hibernate at the wrong time if they only use weather signals.	**CORRECT.** Because weather can vary substantially from day to day, animals may enter into or end hibernation at the wrong time if weather is the basis for the decision.

Answers and Explanations—11.6

Canine–Human Interactions—Track 93

NARRATOR: Listen to part of a lecture in a biology class.

PROFESSOR: We've been talking about the various ways that animals communicate with one another, but, um, today we're also going to talk about something related but slightly different. We will talk about interspecies communication… specifically, how domesticated and socialized, ah, pet dogs, communicate with humans.

Now, dogs communicate with one another through a variety of signals—ah, visual cues, vocalization, and even through smell. If you have been around a dog, you know they make a wide variety of sounds—growls, barks, howls… they even whimper or whine. There is one interesting finding about dog vocalizations when communicating with one another versus wh-when, communicating with humans. *Barking*… the, uh, the sound most frequently associated with dogs… well, there is no clear evidence that barking plays any role in dog-to-dog communication. Interesting, right?

  **MANHATTAN** PREP

Mature wolves, the ancestors to our pet dogs, do not bark. Very young wolves do make some bark-like sounds, but the behavior is very limited. However, because dogs have evolved to become quite genetically different from wolves, researchers studied feral dogs—these are essentially domesticated dogs that are not socialized to humans… so do not live around humans—basically, wild dogs. Even feral dogs don't bark. Andrew?

MALE STUDENT: So… if wild dogs and wolves don't bark to one another, is a pet dog trying to talk to a person when it barks?

PROFESSOR: Well, that's actually something that some researchers wanted to test. In order for a vocalization to be used for effective communication, the speaker, in this case the dog, must be understood by the listener, or human. And, if this was not the case, then the bark likely would not have survived evolution. Dogs and humans have been evolving together for at least 15,000 years, after all. In initial research, they–they recorded the barks of dogs in a variety of distinct scenarios—afraid, excited, angry, sad—and then played the recordings for humans. The researchers found that regardless of gender, age, or even experience with dogs, the humans were able to identify the correct feeling of each bark without any visual clues, more often than random chance alone would suggest.

The pitch, length of the sound, or even number of repeats within a short interval all conveyed information to the human. For example, low pitch barks indicated aggression, while longer sounds appear to indicate a more confident dog. And quickly repeated sounds indicated urgency, or more immediate demand for a human's attention.

Ah, and what's interesting is that dogs interpret our vocal communication in the same way that humans understand one another—ah, by combining the tone with the specific word used.

Using an MRI—magnetic resonance imaging technology—researchers found that when a dog's owner would say a praise word or phrase—like "good boy"—in a positive tone, like "Good boy!", the reward center of the dog's brain would activate. However, if only one was given, either just the tone or just the word, no activity would register in that part of the brain.

But remember, dogs use more than just vocal communication with one another. Um, does anyone remember other dog-to-dog signals?

FEMALE STUDENT: Last week, we talked about how dogs use body language. I thought it was interesting that they communicate with their tails. Oh, and… they even use facial expressions… like ah… when they show teeth, or look away from a more aggressive dog.

PROFESSOR: Yes… *tail wagging* is an interesting example. The primary purpose of a tail is for balance, but puppies do begin using, er… wagging their tail at around one to two months to communicate with their mother or litter mates. But tail wagging is actually a very ineffective means of communicating with humans—it, well… it is often misunderstood. I have a former student who has been doing her graduate research on human–dog signaling. It turns out that many people are actually bitten because they thought a certain tail wag meant "*happy*."

My former student is, uh, actually a great example that I'd like to share with you all. She has, well, always had pet dogs. When doing research for this class, she found a study where dogs were better at reading human hand signals than even apes. That night, she… she said she tried out the same experiment on her dog Rocky, and was so excited by the result that, well, she knew what she wanted to do her thesis research on. But, that is what makes good research—studying something that really interests you. I hope you all are able to do the same.

1.　What is the lecture mainly about?

　　✓　(A) How domesticated dogs communicate with humans

　　✗　(B) The difference between domesticated dogs and wolves

　　✗　(C) The possible meaning of different dog barks

　　✗　(D) How humans can misunderstand the meaning of a dog wagging its tail

GIST-CONTENT. The lecture talks about several aspects of dog communication—particularly with humans.

CORRECT. The lecture discusses various ways that domesticated dogs communicate with humans.

This detail is mentioned, but is not the main focus of the lecture.

This detail is mentioned, but is not the main focus of the lecture.

This detail is mentioned, but is not the main focus of the lecture.

2.　According to the professor, what did researchers learn by having people listen to recordings of dogs barking?

　　✗　(A) People are unable to distinguish one dog from another.

　　✗　(B) People can learn how to give their own dogs more praise.

　　✓　(C) People are often able to correctly identify the meaning of a dog's bark.

　　✗　(D) People are able to imitate a dog's bark accurately.

DETAIL. According to the professor, an essential component of communication is that the listener can understand what message is being conveyed. In this example, humans were able to understand different dog barks and their meaning.

People were asked to compare different types of barks, not necessarily from different dogs.

Praising a dog with words and tone is mentioned, but not with respect to this study.

CORRECT. This research found that humans did a good job understanding the meaning behind the bark, even without visual clues, and regardless of age, gender, or experience with dogs.

People were not asked to imitate a dog's bark in this study.

3.　What does the professor imply about feral dogs?

　　✗　(A) They communicate with pet dogs by barking.

　　✗　(B) They wag their tails to communicate with wolves.

　　✗　(C) They are a type of wolf.

　　✓　(D) They do not bark because they do not need to communicate with humans.

INFERENCE. Feral dogs and wolves are mentioned early in the lecture as examples of canines who do not bark as adults. This was used to set up the finding that only socialized adult dogs bark.

There is no discussion of communication between feral and pet dogs.

Tail wagging was mentioned in the lecture, but not in relation to feral dogs.

The lecture indicates that they are similar to wolves in some ways, but not that they are a type of wolf.

CORRECT. Feral dogs are domesticated, but not socialized, meaning they do not live in contact with humans. The professor indicates that feral dogs do not bark because they do not need to communicate with humans.

4. Why does the professor mention her former student's dog, Rocky?

SPEAKER'S ATTITUDE. The professor mentions Rocky to point out that the former student discovered her thesis topic by conducting an informal communication experiment with her dog. This led to the professor advising students to choose a research topic that appeals to them.

✗ (A) To give her students an example of doing research at home

Although this student was doing research at home, that was not the professor's motivation for sharing the story.

✓ (B) To encourage students to study something that interests them

CORRECT. The student decided on a research topic because of her interest in her own dog, Rocky. The professor tells the students that it's important to study a topic that interests them.

✗ (C) To help her students choose a graduate program

The professor recommends that students study a topic that interests them, but she never mentions choosing graduate programs.

✗ (D) To inform students of the difficulty of experiments involving animals

She never discusses the difficulty of any experiments with animals.

5. According to the professor, which two of the following are true of tail wagging in dogs? *Choose 2 answers.*

DETAIL. The professor discusses tail wagging later in the lecture. During that discussion, the professor mentions the use of the tail for balance and for communicating with other dogs. However, the professor also mentions that tail wagging signals can easily be misunderstood by humans.

✗ [A] Dogs only use tail wagging for balance.

The professor says that a dog uses its tail for balance, but not necessarily through tail *wagging*. Also, the professor explicitly states that tail wagging is used to communicate with other dogs.

✗ [B] Tail wagging is the most important way dogs communicate with one another.

Several forms of canine-to-canine communication are discussed. The professor never suggests that tail wagging is the *most* important form.

✓ [C] Dogs use tail wagging to communicate with other dogs.

CORRECT. This is the primary reason given for a dog wagging its tail.

✓ [D] Tail wagging is often misunderstood by humans.

CORRECT. The professor explains that humans sometimes confuse the signals sent by tail wagging and have been bitten as a result.

Track 94

NARRATOR: Listen again to part of the lecture. Then answer the question.

PROFESSOR: Using an MRI—magnetic resonance imaging technology—researchers found that when a dog's owner would say a praise word or phrase—like "good boy"—in a positive tone, like "Good boy!", the reward center of the dog's brain would activate. However, if only one was given, either just the tone or just the word, no activity would register in that part of the brain.

NARRATOR: What does this finding illustrate?

6. What does this finding illustrate?

ORGANIZATION. Earlier the professor explains that humans communicate with each other through a combination of the *meaning* of words and the *tone* used when speaking. This finding indicates that dogs might understand humans in the same way.

✓ (A) That dogs interpret some forms of human communication much like humans interpret each other

CORRECT. This is an example of how dogs can communicate with humans, which is similar to the way humans communicate with one another.

✗ (B) The difference between speaking to a dog and using hand gestures

This discussion is about vocal communication only.

✗ (C) The importance of using scientific research methods

The specific scientific methods used in the study are not the focus of the professor's quote.

✗ (D) One way that dogs communicate differently with humans than with one another

This quote is about communication between dogs and humans, and how it can be similar to communication between humans—not how it can be different from communication between dogs.

Answers and Explanations—11.7

Chimney Swift Nesting—Track 95

NARRATOR: Listen to part of a lecture in an environmental science class.

PROFESSOR: So, last week we covered issues regarding, um, how humans impact animal habitats, specifically the negative impact… how habitats are declining or have been destroyed completely. For example, deforestation—cutting down acres of trees where some animals hunt and live—has an obvious impact on an animal population. There are, of course, unexpected impacts, um… that might not be obvious—impacts that can occur either before or after an animal population has declined. Today, I want to talk about a specific example of this type of… unexpected—and, honestly strange—way that humans have affected a species… the *chimney swift*.

Well, chimney swifts… you might not have heard of these birds, but they are—well were—common in the Eastern United States and Canada during the summer. During the winter months, they migrate to South, um… South America… to the upper Amazon basin of Ecuador, Brazil, Chile, and Peru. They're most common in, um, areas with many chimneys, as this is where they nest, um… hence the name—chimney swift. However, when traveling across rural areas you might find them nesting in trees, especially hollow trees, or even caves.

Now, nesting for chimney swifts is a very unique experience—get this—they actually can't perch! That is, they can't sit or stand on branches. In fact, um, they can't even stand or walk at all, not even on the ground! They spend almost all their lives airborne… they eat, and even bathe, while flying. The only time they are not in flight is when they are nesting or roosting. Remember that a nest is for incubating… hatching eggs and raising young, while a roost is a place where a bird sleeps. But when they are nesting or roosting, chimney swifts must cling to the side of an enclosure… which is why a chimney is such a perfect home, right?

Well, chimney swifts have been in a long-term decline throughout their migration range. In fact, in 2010, they were added to the list of near-threatened bird species in North America. But why the decline? Would you guess that it is partially because more and more houses and apartment buildings are being built without chimneys? And, um, even those older homes with chimneys, well… their owners are often capping or sealing off the chimneys.

Those chimneys that are being built… they're just not made the same as they used to be. Old chimneys were typically brick or some type of masonry, maybe concrete, so there was a surface that the bird could attach itself and its nest to. But newer construction—newer chimneys—are often lined with metal… and the birds cannot cling to that smooth surface. And I don't need to tell you, but… a population that cannot find places to live and nest will struggle to survive.

But changing fireplaces isn't the only thing that's had an unexpected impact on the chimney swift population. Some scientists have started to study the roosting and nesting locations of the swifts. See, these birds will return to the same nesting site year after year… the young will even return to the nest where they were born to set up their own nest. These scientists have noticed that even when nesting locations are still suitable—no chimney cap or liner has been added—fewer and fewer birds are returning. These researchers blame pesticides, especially residential pesticides. You see, chimney swifts are actually quite useful because they feed on all sorts of flying and biting insects—particularly, um, mosquitos, biting flies, wasps, and even fire ants. However, people don't like getting bitten while trying to enjoy a backyard barbeque. With more people buying supplies at the local lawn and garden store to kill these pests, well… I'm sure you can guess what happens to chimney swifts when they don't have enough insects to feed on.

Remember that these birds spend essentially all their time flying—an activity, uh, that uses a considerable amount of energy. And yes, they are quite small—most weigh about an ounce—but they eat over a third of their weight in insects each day!

Most of the focus on conservation of the species is, well… on habitat. Many municipalities are trying to encourage homeowners to leave their chimneys uncapped, at least during summer, when the swifts are nesting. Some places are even building chimney swift "towers" and placing them in fields and parks.

In general, the conservation efforts have focused on informing the general population of this species—showing how useful they can be at pest control, for example. Across their habitat range, groups are even setting up annual chimney swift "sits" to get people interested in the bird. People report the presence of a roost or nest, and then get together with friends to sit and watch the swifts coming and going—a nice excuse to spend a pleasant evening outdoors.

1.   What does the professor mainly talk about?

GIST-CONTENT. The professor primarily talks about the chimney swift and challenges it is currently facing due to changes in human activities.

✗ (A) Changes in the migration patterns of chimney swifts

Specifics of their migration patterns are never mentioned.

✓ (B) Causes of the decline in chimney swift populations

CORRECT. This lecture focuses on the loss of suitable nesting sites and the reduction of food sources due to pesticide use.

✗ (C) Where chimney swifts nest in rainforests

There was no discussion of rainforests in the lecture.

✗ (D) Health risks of residential pesticides

Residential pesticides are possibly diminishing food sources for chimney swifts, but nothing is mentioned about health risks.

2.   What does the professor imply might be causing a decline in the chimney swift population?

✗ (A) Deforestation along their migration routes

✗ (B) An increase in hunting activity

✓ (C) A decrease in the number of homes with uncapped or unsealed chimneys

✗ (D) A change in the birds' migration patterns

INFERENCE. The professor notes two likely causes: changes in the number of chimneys and how they are built, and residential pesticides.

Deforestation along migration routes was never mentioned.

Human hunting was never mentioned in the lecture.

CORRECT. The professor mentions that a possible cause of the population decline is that "more and more houses and apartment buildings are being built without chimneys," and that existing chimneys are often being capped or sealed off.

A change in migration patterns was never mentioned.

3.   What does the professor say about how the use of pesticides affects chimney swift populations?

✗ (A) Pesticides are poisoning chimney swift populations.

✗ (B) Pesticides are an effective way to reduce parasites that are harmful to chimney swifts.

✗ (C) Pesticides have little or no impact on chimney swift populations.

✓ (D) Pesticides kill the primary food sources of chimney swifts, making food harder to find.

DETAIL. The professor states that it may be reducing the food supply of the chimney swift.

Pesticides are killing the prey of chimney swifts, not the birds themselves.

Chimney swift parasites are never mentioned in the lecture.

On the contrary, pesticides are likely responsible for reducing the bird's natural food supply.

CORRECT. The professor lists wasps, ants, mosquitos, and other yard pests as the primary food sources for chimney swifts. She also notes that many residents are using pesticides to kill them off.

4.   According to the professor, how are some scientists estimating the decline in the chimney swift population?

✓ (A) Counting the swifts that return to suitable nests each year

✗ (B) Collecting estimates from people who report seeing a chimney swift nest

✗ (C) Tracking the birds with radio-frequency identification tags

✗ (D) Constructing swift "towers" to attract the birds

DETAIL. Chimney swifts usually return to the same nesting locations each year, so scientists are tracking the number of birds that return to known nesting sites.

CORRECT. The professor states that, because chimney swifts return to the same nesting sites year after year, scientists count the number of birds that return to each nest to estimate population changes.

The professor indicates that people are setting up chimney swift "sits" to increase interest in the bird, but not to track population numbers.

This practice is never mentioned in the lecture.

People are building swift "towers" to provide new places for the swifts to nest or roost in response to the loss of suitable chimneys, but scientists are not doing this to track population numbers.

5. What does the professor imply about bird perching?

INFERENCE. The professor states that "nesting for chimney swifts is a very unique experience… they actually can't perch!" The implication is that the inability to perch is unusual for a bird.

✗ (A) Most birds only perch in a nest.

The common locations for birds to perch in general are not mentioned.

✗ (B) A bird is more vulnerable to attack when perched.

There is no discussion about what leaves a bird vulnerable to attack.

✗ (C) Perching is essential for migrating chimney swifts.

There is little discussion about the migration of chimney swifts.

✓ (D) The majority of birds can perch.

CORRECT. The professor mentions that nesting for chimney swifts is unique in that they cannot perch. This implies that most birds are able to perch.

Track 96

NARRATOR: Listen again to part of the lecture. Then answer the question.

PROFESSOR: Those chimneys that are being built… they're just not made the same as they used to be. Old chimneys were typically brick or some type of masonry, maybe concrete, so there was a surface that the bird could attach itself and its nest to. But newer construction—newer chimneys—are often lined with metal… and the birds cannot cling to that smooth surface. And I don't need to tell you, but… a population that cannot find places to live and nest will struggle to survive.

NARRATOR: What does the professor imply when she says this:

PROFESSOR: And I don't need to tell you, but…

6. What does the professor imply when she says this?

FUNCTION OF WHAT IS SAID. The phrase "and I don't need to tell you, but…" means that the speaker believes that what she is about to say is an obvious consequence of what she just finished saying.

✗ (A) She does not think her next point is important enough to share.

This expression does not indicate importance, or lack thereof. It indicates that what follows is obvious.

✓ (B) Students are likely to find her next point obvious.

CORRECT. She uses this phrase because she believes that her students probably could already figure out what she says next.

✗ (C) She is unsure about her next point.

This comment has nothing to do with her confidence in her next point.

✗ (D) She believes the next point will confuse students.

On the contrary, she believes they probably could already figure out what she says next.

Answers and Explanations—11.8

Sulfates—Track 97

NARRATOR: Listen to part of a lecture in an ecology class.

PROFESSOR: So we've been talking about the various reactions that occur in Earth's atmosphere. These reactions are essential to life, because elements react differently in the atmosphere than they do down here on the ground. These reactions are so important, they've become a part of the natural cycle of life that every organism needs. The cycle of nutrients—elements that living things on Earth need to survive, reacting in the atmosphere, coming back to the ground, feeding life forms, and returning to the atmosphere again and again—allows life to continue, and even helps to control the weather.

Many compounds react in the atmosphere. You've probably heard of carbon monoxide, nitrates, and even the one we're going to talk about today: *sulfates.*

Sulfur, the key element in sulfates, starts where many other essential elements start: in the ground. It is present in rocks and minerals, and throughout the ocean floor. Over time, those rocks wear down, exposing the sulfur to the air. That's where the reactions begin. Plants and animals can't use sulfur in the form it takes—it takes within rocks. How does sulfur become useful? The air reacts with the sulfur, combining it with oxygen, which changes sulfur into sulfates. At that point, plants and small organisms can start absorbing and using the sulfur, in the form of sulfate, as a nutrient.

FEMALE STUDENT: So that's why sulfates are used in fertilizer? To give the plants the nutrients they need?

PROFESSOR: Yep. Plants can't survive without sulfates, so adding them to fertilizer is a good way to keep plants healthy. In fact, we use sulfur for many different things. It's used as a component of gunpowder, or in fireworks. Don't worry though—that's not the same form as what is used in fertilizers.

The sulfates in plants will eventually return to the atmosphere. When plants die, or when the animals that ate the plants—or even the animals that ate those animals—die, the sulfates become available again. Can anyone guess what happens to them? Joanne?

FEMALE STUDENT: Um, well, after death, the bacteria and… and other small things start to eat away at the nutrients. So it must go back to the microorganisms, and then to new plants, right?

PROFESSOR: Yes. A large amount of it does exactly that. The sulfates will travel from one organism to another, giving each one an essential nutrient. But some of it never reaches the microorganisms… it gets released directly into the air.

Once in the atmosphere, the sulfates can react in different ways. One of the most common outcomes is the sulfate will react with other molecules to form sulfate salts. Those salts attach themselves to the water vapor in the atmosphere, and when it rains, they come down with the water. So even sulfates in the air will find their way back to plants and animals that need them to survive.

If this was the only source of atmospheric sulfates, the cycle of ground to atmosphere to ground again should continue without change. But there are several other places that sulfates come from. Naturally, volcanic eruptions and the breakdown of organic compounds in swamps release high concentrations of sulfates into the atmosphere. That's at least part of the reason why the air can be toxic in the area around a volcanic eruption.

But remember, we use sulfates too. And we're releasing more and more of it into the atmosphere every day. It's released every time we burn fossil fuels, and whenever we process metals. Both of these processes bring sulfur from underground into the atmosphere much faster than would otherwise happen. In fact, one-third of all the sulfur that enters the atmosphere, and about 90 percent of all sulfates, come directly from human activities. The result is more sulfate salt in the atmosphere than would naturally be present, and it comes down in concentrated forms. This is what many people refer to as *acid rain*.

MALE STUDENT: But what about… I mean, if sulfates are constantly going up into the atmosphere and coming back down, aren't there other things that do that too? Like, does nitrogen cycle through the atmosphere too?

PROFESSOR: Good question, David. There are a lot of nutrients that undergo cycles very similar to this one. And nitrogen, in particular, is a major nutrient for life, as well as a component in acid rain. In fact, there's more nitrogen in the atmosphere than sulfur. But sulfur is the biggest cause of acid rain, which is why it has the attention of a lot of ecologists.

1. What is the main purpose of the talk?

    GIST-PURPOSE. The professor discusses the natural uses of sulfates, their cycle from the ground to the atmosphere and back, and their presence in acid rain.

    ✗ (A) To discuss how to minimize the impact of humans on the sulfur cycle

    The professor does not discuss this idea.

    ✗ (B) To describe sulfur compounds found in gunpowder and fireworks

    The professor does not discuss the details of these sulfur compounds.

    ✗ (C) To illustrate why life on Earth could not exist without sulfur

    It is true sulfur is an essential nutrient, but there's no discussion of why.

    ✓ (D) To explain how sulfur moves in and out of the atmosphere

    CORRECT. This lesson is a continuation of a discussion about reactions in the Earth's atmosphere, according to the professor, and it focuses on the sulfur cycle.

Track 98

NARRATOR: Listen again to part of the lecture. Then answer the question.

FEMALE STUDENT: So that's why sulfates are used in fertilizer? To give the plants the nutrients they need?

PROFESSOR: Yep. Plants can't survive without sulfates, so adding them to fertilizer is a good way to keep plants healthy. In fact, we use sulfur for many different things. It's used as a component of gunpowder, or in fireworks. Don't worry though—that's not the same form as what is used in fertilizers.

NARRATOR: What does the professor mean when she says this:

PROFESSOR: Don't worry though—that's not the same form as what is used in fertilizers.

2.   **FUNCTION OF WHAT IS SAID.** In this quote, the professor explains some of the benefits of using sulfur, but reassures students that the sulfur compounds used in fertilizer are not the same as those used in gunpowder or fireworks.

✗ (A) She wants to emphasize that sulfur can take on a variety of forms.

This is not the point being made by the professor in this quote.

✗ (B) She anticipates that students will struggle with this concept.

The concept is expressed clearly, and there is no reason to believe the professor expects students to struggle with it.

✓ (C) She is reassuring students that fertilizer is not as dangerous as gunpowder and fireworks are.

CORRECT. The connection among fertilizer, gunpowder, and fireworks is that all contain sulfur. The implication could be that fertilizers are therefore explosive. The professor is indicating, somewhat jokingly, that this is not the case.

✗ (D) She is explaining that the components of fertilizer are more complex than those that make up gunpowder and fireworks.

The professor does not mention this idea.

3.   Which processes that release sulfur into the atmosphere does the professor mention? *Choose 2 answers.*

DETAIL. Sulfur is naturally released into the atmosphere when dead plants and animals decompose. Humans can also release sulfur by burning fossil fuels and processing metals.

✓ [A] Plant death

CORRECT. Sulfur from decaying plants is absorbed by microorganisms, and some of it is released directly into the atmosphere.

✗ [B] Deep sea mining

The professor does not mention this activity.

✓ [C] Burning fossil fuels

CORRECT. This is one of the major contributors to sulfur release that the professor mentions.

✗ [D] Acid rain

This process actually removes sulfur from the atmosphere.

4.   What can be inferred about the professor's view on the burning of fossil fuels?

INFERENCE. The burning of fossil fuels is mentioned as one of the human activities that releases a large amount of sulfur into the atmosphere.

✗ (A) She thinks that it will benefit plants because of increased access to sulfur.

The professor does not mention this concept.

✓ (B) She believes that it has directly contributed to an increase in the amount of sulfur released into the atmosphere.

CORRECT. She claims that this activity has significantly increased the amount of sulfur released into the atmosphere.

✗ (C) She is concerned that there is no way to reduce the amount of sulfur released by this process.

The professor does not mention this idea.

✗ (D) She is encouraged by the fact that most of her students want to help end this practice.

There is no indication that the students feel this way.

5.   Why does the professor discuss acid rain?

ORGANIZATION. Acid rain forms when there is a high concentration of sulfate in the atmosphere. The sulfate forms sulfate salts, which attach to water vapor. In high enough concentrations, this can form acid rain.

✓ (A) To describe a consequence of excess sulfur in the atmosphere

CORRECT. This is exactly how acid rain relates to sulfur.

✗ (B) To emphasize the importance of continuing the study of environmental science

This choice is much too general. The professor is only discussing studying the sulfur cycle.

✗ (C) To point out one of the many natural dangers present because of the Earth's environment

There is no discussion of dangers in the Earth's environment.

✗ (D) To illustrate that sulfur is just one of many elements under investigation

Acid rain is discussed in reference to the sulfur cycle. The purpose of mentioning it is not to broaden the scope of the lecture to include other elements.

6.   What comparison does the professor make involving sulfur and nitrogen?

DETAIL. Both elements are involved in acid rain, and both are present in the atmosphere. Although there is more nitrogen in the atmosphere, sulfur is a bigger cause of acid rain.

✗ (A) Burning fossil fuels releases more nitrogen than sulfur into the atmosphere.

The professor does not mention this idea.

✓ (B) The atmosphere contains more nitrogen than sulfur.

CORRECT. The professor directly states this.

✗ (C) One element is a component of acid rain, and the other is not.

Both sulfur and nitrogen are named as components of acid rain.

✗ (D) Plants require less nitrogen than sulfur to survive.

The professor does not mention this idea.

Answers and Explanations—11.9

Phytoremediation—Track 99

NARRATOR: Listen to part of a lecture from a botany class.

PROFESSOR: Well this is a surprise… I didn't expect so many of you to be here this morning, as your research assignment is due to me by 5pm today. Actually, I wanted to let you know… I was planning to get those graded and back to you by Monday, but, well my weekend plans have changed. One of my graduate research assistants had a family emergency and can no longer monitor the lab over the weekend. My other graduate student assistant won't be back from her off-site research project. All that means I'm stuck working at the lab through the weekend and won't have time for other work. Regardless, I'll make

sure that I have your grades to you by the middle of next week. You can also come by the lab this weekend if you have specific questions about the assignment, since that is where I'll be.

Okay, let's turn our attention to today's lecture. So you're all familiar with photosynthesis… a plant's natural process of absorbing carbon dioxide from the air and converting it into oxygen. Today we're going to talk about how we can use this natural process to help clean up pollution… has anyone heard of *phytoremediation*? The term comes from the Greek word for plants, "phyto-"… and the word "remediate," which means to remedy… as in to fix… or in this case, to clean. Phyto… remediation… cleaning with plants.

Of course, we have long known that the rainforests are critical to air quality all over the world… scientists have found that plants don't just absorb carbon dioxide, they actually absorb a long list of gases, including many thought to be major pollutants or that pose serious health risks like asthma or cancer. A recent study showed that having trees and bushes on city streets reduced the levels of two of the worst common pollutants by 40 to 60 percent… this was eight times more than earlier research had found!

But what about on a smaller scale? Does the houseplant in my office actually make the air in my office better? One executive in New Delhi, the city with the world's worst air pollution, decided to test out exactly that idea. The air inside his multi-story, 50,000 square foot facility is filtered from the outside through a rooftop greenhouse of 400 plants, and he has another 800 plants spread throughout inside spaces. His office building does have very clean air… the air quality is equivalent to that in the United States. However, researchers warn that this is not a successful test of efficacy, as it wasn't a controlled experiment. He was also using an extensive system of air scrubbers and other filtration devices.

But phytoremediation isn't just about cleaning the air. Some of the, well… most successful projects have targeted soil and water. A great example is *greywater* treatment. Wastewater generated from bathing, cooking, washing clothes, washing dishes, and so on is called greywater… essentially any wastewater other than sewage, which is called blackwater. For the most part, greywater and blackwater are mixed in the pipes that carry them from our houses to the same sewage treatment plants. However, given growing concern over clean, available drinking water, and the expense to move water from homes to treatment facilities and back through the system… some are looking for ways of dealing with the greywater that don't require chemical treatments.

The intervention here would be to filter greywater through a mass of plant or tree roots. See, the roots can actually remove any excess nutrients… say from food matter in the water. The roots can even remove toxic substances. A recent project, funded by the European Union, uses bamboo. This bamboo treatment system is really just a small bamboo plantation. The greywater and blackwater are kept separate, and the greywater is run through the soil of the bamboo forest. The scientists responsible for the study chose bamboo because of its extremely dense root system, which proved to be extremely effective compared with vegetation that has a less dense root system.

1. What aspect of plants does the professor mainly describe in her talk?

    GIST-CONTENT. The professor mainly talks about the use of plants for cleaning air and water.

    ✓ (A) Their use in cleaning water and air

    CORRECT. The discussion is about phytoremediation, or the use of plants to clean air, water, and soil. However, only the cleaning of water and air are discussed in detail.

    ✗ (B) Their use as houseplants

    Houseplants are mentioned only briefly in the context of purifying air.

    ✗ (C) The density of their root systems

    This issue is mentioned in relation to a greywater treatment facility, but this is not the primary aspect of plants that is discussed.

    ✗ (D) Their use as building materials

    This use is not mentioned in the lecture.

Track 100

NARRATOR: Listen again to part of the lecture. Then answer the question.

PROFESSOR: Well this is a surprise… I didn't expect so many of you to be here this morning, as your research assignment is due to me by 5pm today. Actually, I wanted to let you know… I was planning to get those graded and back to you by Monday, but, well my weekend plans have changed. One of my graduate research assistants had a family emergency and can no longer monitor the lab over the weekend. My other graduate student assistant won't be back from her off-site research project. All that means I'm stuck working at the lab through the weekend and won't have time for other work.

NARRATOR: Why does the professor mention her graduate research assistant's family emergency?

2. Why does the professor mention her graduate research assistant's family emergency?

    FUNCTION OF WHAT IS SAID. The professor is explaining why she will not be able to grade research assignments over the weekend, and thus the return of graded assignments will be delayed.

    ✗ (A) To tell the students an interesting story

    Although the story might be interesting to some, this is not the reason she is sharing the story.

    ✗ (B) To provide support for the topic of the lecture

    This information is unrelated to the topic of the lecture.

    ✓ (C) To explain why the grading of an assignment will not be completed on time

    CORRECT. The family emergency means that the graduate assistant cannot work in the lab, and the professor must work in her place. Therefore, the professor will not have the time she planned to grade the class's assignments.

    ✗ (D) To encourage students to volunteer at the lab

    There is no indication that she would like the students to volunteer at the lab.

3.   What does the professor imply about city streets without trees?

    ✗ (A) They are less expensive to maintain than streets with trees.

    ✗ (B) They are less attractive than streets with trees.

    ✗ (C) They are safer than streets with trees.

    ✓ (D) They have more pollution than city streets with trees.

INFERENCE. The professor notes a study that found that trees on city streets help reduce the levels of two major pollutants.

There is no discussion of the expense of maintaining streets, with or without trees.

There is no discussion of the aesthetics of city streets, with or without trees.

There is no discussion of the safety of city streets, with or without trees.

CORRECT. In the lecture, the professor mentions a study that found that planting trees on city streets reduced the levels of two pollutants. This implies that streets without trees would have worse pollution.

4.   Why does the professor mention the executive in New Delhi?

    ✗ (A) To show that companies do not care about air quality

    ✓ (B) To provide an example of apparently effective phytoremediation

    ✗ (C) To demonstrate the cost of phytoremediation

    ✗ (D) To illustrate the dangers of poor air quality

ORGANIZATION. The professor discusses this example to illustrate an uncontrolled experiment in which it appears that the use of plants helped purify the air in the executive's office building.

On the contrary, the executive was trying to improve the air quality in his office building.

CORRECT. The executive used plants to filter the air in his office building.

There was no mention of the executive's cost to purify his office building's air as described in the lecture.

Although the professor implies that poor air quality in New Delhi is a concern, she never specifically describes the dangers.

5.   According to the professor, what was the main reason for using bamboo, rather than other plants, in a water treatment system?

    ✗ (A) It is cheaper than other options.

    ✓ (B) It has a dense root system.

    ✗ (C) It is readily available.

    ✗ (D) It quickly regenerates after cutting.

DETAIL. According to the professor, bamboo is preferred because it has a particularly dense root system.

Nothing is mentioned about the cost of using bamboo.

CORRECT. The professor mentions that the scientists responsible chose bamboo for its dense root system.

Nothing is mentioned about the availability of bamboo.

The professor does not say anything about the regenerative powers of bamboo.

6. According to the lecture, what are two reasons that scientists are investigating non-chemical alternatives for treating greywater? *Choose 2 answers.*

DETAIL. The professor mentions the availability of clean drinking water and the cost of transporting water from homes to a treatment center and back again.

✓ ☐A☐ The growing concern over clean, available, drinking water

CORRECT. The professor directly mentions this as a motivation for investigating alternatives to chemical treatments.

✗ ☐B☐ The bad taste of chemically treated water

The taste of chemically treated water is not mentioned in the lecture.

✓ ☐C☐ The expense of moving water between homes and treatment centers

CORRECT. The professor directly mentions this as a motivation for investigating alternatives to chemical treatments.

✗ ☐D☐ The difficulty of storing chemicals for long periods of time

Chemical storage is not discussed in the lecture.

Answers and Explanations—11.10

Goldilocks Zone—Track 101

NARRATOR: Listen to part of a lecture in an astronomy class.

PROFESSOR: It's an exciting time to be studying astronomy right now… Who has heard of the star TRAPPIST-1… or what have you heard in the news about it?

MALE STUDENT: Well, I read something about scientists finding several Earth-like planets nearby, and something about… do they think there might actually be life there?

PROFESSOR: That would be exciting, and you're close! So, scientists did prove the existence of seven Earth-sized planets orbiting the star TRAPPIST-1, but at this point only three are clearly in what is called the *habitable zone* around a star… the distance from a star that allows a planet to support liquid water. How does this work? Well, a planet that is too close to a star is too hot… any water evaporates into space… But get too far from the star, and you have the opposite problem… water stays frozen. This is critical because a planet needs to be able to maintain liquid water in order for life… at least as we know it… to live there.

It shouldn't be surprising that this habitable zone is often called the "*Goldilocks zone*"… and the planets there… well, Goldilocks planets. This name is based on the childhood story "Goldilocks and the Three Bears." You know, the one where the little girl, Goldilocks, has to keep choosing between three things… like a bed or even a bowl of soup… and she always avoids the extremes… she picks the bed that is not too hard or too soft… or the soup that is not too hot or too cold… she always picks the one that is…

FEMALE STUDENT: Just right! In the middle! Okay, but what do we hope, or expect to, uh, find on Goldilocks planets? Life already living there… or just that life could exist there?

PROFESSOR: Great question, and it's both actually, or at least scientists look for Goldilocks planets for both reasons. We have been searching for intelligent life in the universe… extraterrestrial intelligence… for years. In the earliest days of the invention of the radio, scientists wondered whether they could use radio waves to find and communicate with life on other planets. But scientists have another reason for searching

for Goldilocks zone… the possibility that humans on Earth would need another home in the event that something happened to Earth. Maybe another ice age, or an asteroid, or even nuclear war.

But let's move on. We can talk about why we want to find Goldilocks planets later. So, these planets around TRAPPIST-1 aren't the only Goldilocks planets out there. In fact, we have a few closer to home. Any ideas?

FEMALE STUDENT: Well, our Solar System neighbors are Venus and Mars, right? Are either of those in the Goldilocks zone?

PROFESSOR: Nice guess! In many current calculations, Earth sits closer to the hot edge of our Sun's habitable zone, which means that Venus, our very near neighbor, is sometimes in and sometimes out. Mars, on the other hand, appears to sit just inside the far, or cold, edge of the habitable zone.

MALE STUDENT: Wait, so you're saying that Mars is in the habitable zone? So do scientists think there could be life on Mars?

PROFESSOR: No, although some science fiction movies and books might make you think otherwise!

Just because a planet is in the habitable zone around a star doesn't mean life as we know it exists there. Remember, "habitable zone" just means that liquid water is possible, because it is a requirement for life to exist. But there are other requirements, too.

In order for a planet to be habitable by life that we would recognize… this even means bacteria or a very basic plant… it can't just be in the habitable zone. We need to include *atmospheric pressure* into the equation. A planet's atmosphere consists of a layer of gases held in place by gravity, and higher gravity increases the atmospheric pressure… which makes the atmosphere more dense. If the atmosphere is too thin, then the planet will undergo big swings in temperature, especially to the cold side… And if the atmosphere is too dense, especially with what are called greenhouse gases, then it will trap too much energy from the star and heat up… a lot. Of course, you want some heat, but too much… Well, Venus is a great example. Even though Venus isn't the closest planet to the Sun, it is the hottest! Venus's atmosphere is far more dense than Earth's, with runaway greenhouse gases… and so it has a surface temperature of about 460 degrees Celsius, or hot enough to melt lead! Mars, on the other hand, has almost no atmosphere and therefore can't maintain enough heat to keep water from staying permanently frozen.

1.   What is the lecture primarily about?

GIST-CONTENT. The lecture describes the Goldilocks zone, a range of temperatures for a planet in which life could potentially be supported.

✗ (A) Illustrating how planets orbit the Sun

There is no discussion about how a planet orbits the Sun in the lecture.

✓ (B) Exploring the concept of the "Goldilocks zone"

CORRECT. The professor introduces this topic and spends the rest of the lecture discussing the specifics of the Goldilocks zone and its importance.

✗ (C) Describing the plan to colonize other planets in the future

Although the idea of colonization is raised, this is not the main focus of the lecture.

✗ (D) Explaining the development of solar systems

The professor never explains the development of a solar system.

  MANHATTAN PREP

2.   According to the professor, what is true of Goldilocks planets?

      DETAIL. Goldilocks planets are ones that are located an appropriate distance from the stars they orbit, so that they can support water in liquid form.

✗   (A) They are roughly the same size as Earth.

      This point is not supported by the lecture.

✗   (B) They are located between other planets in a solar system.

      There is no evidence given in the lecture to support this idea.

✗   (C) They do not have a substantial atmosphere.

      This is contradicted in the lecture. Earth is a Goldilocks planet with an atmosphere. Venus also has an atmosphere and is sometimes in the Goldilocks zone.

✓   (D) They can potentially support liquid water.

      CORRECT. The Goldilocks planets are those within a specific distance of their star—not so close that water evaporates, and not so far that water stays frozen. In this zone, it is possible for such planets to support liquid water.

3.   What does the professor imply about the planet Venus?
Choose 2 answers.

      INFERENCE. The professor notes that while Venus is sometimes within the Goldilocks zone, it also has a very dense atmosphere with a lot of greenhouse gases, which causes excessive heat to be trapped, making the planet far too hot to sustain life.

✗   A   Its core is likely composed of lead.

      The discussion mentions that the surface is hot enough to melt lead, not that the core of the planet is possibly made of lead.

✓   B   It is too hot to sustain life as we know it.

      CORRECT. The professor says that the surface of Venus is hot enough to melt lead. This is far too hot to sustain life as we know it.

✓   C   It is sometimes located in the habitable zone.

      CORRECT. The professor says that Venus is sometimes in the Goldilocks zone, or habitable zone, and sometimes outside of it.

✗   D   It has an insignificant atmosphere.

      This is contradicted in the lecture. Venus has a very dense atmosphere.

11

4. According to the lecture, what is the possible significance of several of the planets recently found orbiting the star TRAPPIST-1?

DETAIL. The professor opens the lecture by discussing these planets orbiting TRAPPIST-1, because they are located within the habitable zone, or Goldilocks zone.

✗ (A) They demonstrate how advanced telescopes have become.

Although this is potentially true, there is no evidence to support it in the lecture.

✗ (B) They are useful for studying the atmosphere of distant planets.

Atmosphere is later mentioned as a necessity for life, but it is not referenced in the discussion about planets orbiting TRAPPIST-1.

✓ (C) They are in the habitable zone.

CORRECT. The star TRAPPIST-1 and the planets orbiting it are mentioned to help introduce the concept of Goldilocks planets.

✗ (D) They are the only known Goldilocks planets other than Earth.

This is contradicted in the lecture. Mars and sometimes Venus are other Goldilocks planets mentioned.

Track 102

NARRATOR: Why does the professor say this:

PROFESSOR: Just because a planet is in the habitable zone around a star doesn't mean life as we know it exists there. Remember, "habitable zone" just means that liquid water is possible, because it is a requirement for life to exist. But there are other requirements, too.

5. Why does the professor say this?

FUNCTION OF WHAT IS SAID. In this quote, the professor explains that a planet's location in the habitable zone is a necessary, but not sufficient, condition for life as we know it to exist.

✓ [A] To explain that being in the habitable zone is not the only requirement for life to exist on a planet

CORRECT. By saying that there are other requirements for life to exist, the professor is indicating that distance, defined by the "habitable zone," is not the only requirement.

✗ [B] To stress the importance of the position of the Goldilocks planets orbiting TRAPPIST-1

These Goldilocks planets are the ones located in the habitable zone around TRAPPIST-1. Here, the professor is introducing the idea that other requirements for sustaining life are important as well.

✗ [C] To explain why life on Earth is able to exist

This explanation is not about Earth specifically, but about the various requirements for life as we know it to be possible on a planet.

✗ [D] To describe how researchers determine the size of a habitable zone

The methods scientists use to estimate the size of a habitable zone is never mentioned in the lecture.

Track 103

NARRATOR: Listen again to part of the lecture. Then answer the question.

PROFESSOR: Nice guess! In many current calculations, Earth sits closer to the hot edge of our Sun's habitable zone, which means that Venus, our very near neighbor, is sometimes in and sometimes out. Mars, on the other hand, appears to sit just inside the far, or cold, edge of the habitable zone.

MALE STUDENT: Wait, so you're saying that Mars is in the habitable zone? So do scientists think there could be life on Mars?

NARRATOR: Why does the student say this:

MALE STUDENT: Wait, so you're saying that Mars is in the habitable zone? So do scientists think there could be life on Mars?

6.   Why does the student say this?

FUNCTION OF WHAT IS SAID. The professor explains the status of Venus and Mars as Goldilocks planets. The student is surprised by part of the professor's explanation, and asks a question to confirm that he understood correctly.

✗ (A) To share his opinion on the issue at hand

The student is asking a question to confirm understanding. He is not providing an opinion.

✗ (B) To remind the professor of an earlier question

The student is asking the professor for more clarification, not providing a reminder.

✗ (C) To express his disapproval of the professor's comment

The student is asking for clarification, not indicating disapproval.

✓ (D) To verify his understanding of a previous statement

CORRECT. The student is checking with the professor to make sure his understanding of the professor's explanation is correct.

11

Chapter 12

Lectures F: Natural Science

Listening lectures test your ability to comprehend academic-level spoken English. You'll listen to a short lecture (about 3 to 5 minutes long) from a professor. Occasionally, a student may also speak. You will only be able to listen to the lecture once. You will not be able to pause the recording or to replay any part of it (though some questions will replay a specific part of the lecture for you). You can take notes as you listen.

You will then answer six questions for that lecture. Most questions are multiple-choice with four options (select one from A, B, C, or D). Some questions may ask you to select more than one option or to fill in a table. You will have to answer the questions in order. You cannot return to a question once you have moved on to the next question.

Listening lectures test your understanding of main ideas, contrasts, the lecturer's tone and degree of certainty about the information, and why the lecturer relates certain information or examples. They also test your understanding of the organization of the lecture and the relationship between different ideas. Finally, they test your ability to make inferences or draw conclusions.

How should you use this chapter? Here are some recommendations, according to the level you've reached in TOEFL Listening:

1. **Fundamentals.** Start with a topic-focused chapter, such as this one. Start with a topic that is a "medium weakness"—not your worst area but not your best either. At first, listen to the lecture once, then work on the questions untimed and check the answer after each question. Review the solutions closely, think carefully about the principles at work, and articulate what you've learned. Redo questions as necessary. As you get better, time yourself and do all of the questions for a lecture at once, without stopping.

2. **Fixes.** Do an entire lecture and its associated questions under timed conditions. Don't replay any part of the lecture while you are still answering the questions! Examine the results, learn your lessons, then test yourself with another lecture and question set.

3. **Tweaks.** Confirm your mastery by doing two or three lectures in a row under timed conditions. Work your way up to doing four lectures and two conversations in one sitting. Aim to improve the speed and ease of your process.

Good luck on Listening!

12.1

 Listen to Track 104.

Now answer the questions.

1. What is the lecture mainly about?

    (A) The defense mechanisms of a variety of animals

    (B) The benefits of the schooling behavior of fish

    (C) The importance of schooling behavior during migration

    (D) The ways in which predators target fish that are prey

2. Select each of the activities below that describes an advantage given in the lecture of schooling behavior in fish. *Choose all that apply.*

    [A] A fish that sees danger can signal to other fish.

    [B] The rapid movement of a school can confuse predators.

    [C] Swimming in a school formation is efficient for traveling long distances.

    [D] Staying close together reduces the likelihood of detection.

3. How does the professor define the "encounter dilution effect"?

    (A) Schooling increases a fish's chances of finding a mate.

    (B) Schooling allows predators to find fish more easily.

    (C) Individual fish are less likely to be detected in a school.

    (D) Schooling permits quicker detection of predators that are encountered.

4. According to the lecture, what is one possible benefit arising from a school of fish consisting of nearly identical fish?

    (A) Improved efficiency from the group swimming in unison

    (B) Fish with better vision capabilities can act as scouts to help protect the other fish

    (C) Increased safety, because predators typically target a fish that stands out

    (D) The reduced likelihood of individual fish becoming separated from the school

5. Why does the professor mention the humpback whale's ability to consume a "bait ball"?

    (A) To explain how different types of predators locate fish

    (B) To contrast schooling with the defense mechanisms of other animals

    (C) To give an example of a swimming technique used by whales

    (D) To point out a disadvantage of schooling

Listen to Track 105.

Now answer the question.

6. Ⓐ The student's logic has led him to the wrong final conclusion.

   Ⓑ She is impressed with the creativity of the student.

   Ⓒ The student should investigate a different question.

   Ⓓ She thinks that she has confused the student.

12.2

Listen to Track 106.

Now answer the questions.

1. What aspect of global warming is the lecture primarily about?

   Ⓐ Human behavior that has led to the increase in greenhouse gases

   Ⓑ The sharp decline in many endangered species

   Ⓒ The impact of global temperatures on sea ice formation

   Ⓓ Factors influencing global ocean currents

2. According to the professor, why do geologists track the amount of sea ice over time?

   Ⓐ To determine the reflective quality of ice

   Ⓑ To understand how the greenhouse effect impacts global temperatures

   Ⓒ To study how sea ice and glaciers are related

   Ⓓ To track global warming

3. What is the greenhouse effect, according to the professor?

   Ⓐ The reflective quality of snow and ice

   Ⓑ The trapping of the Sun's energy by the atmosphere

   Ⓒ The melting and refreezing of sea ice

   Ⓓ The pattern of ocean currents around the globe

4. According to the professor, what is one unique aspect of sea ice?

    (A) It forms in the ocean rather than on land.

    (B) It is the main way for scientists to track global warming.

    (C) It indicates that the North and South polar regions should not be compared.

    (D) It provides an example of a natural phenomenon of less interest to scientists.

5. Why are scientists confused by sea ice in the Antarctic?

    (A) It forms on land rather than in the ocean.

    (B) There is much less sea ice in the Antarctic than in the Arctic.

    (C) It is experiencing a trend similar to that of Arctic sea ice.

    (D) It is increasing in volume even as global temperatures rise.

 Listen to Track 107.

Now answer the question.

6. (A) To provide evidence that proves his point

    (B) To use a potentially familiar concept to help explain a new concept

    (C) To encourage students to visit greenhouses to experience the effect directly

    (D) To point to a flaw in the theory of global warming

12.3

 Listen to Track 108.

Now answer the questions.

1. What is this lecture mainly about?

    (A) Recent research connecting whales to ray-finned fish

    (B) Differences between mammals and other tetrapods

    (C) Discussing the evolution of tetrapods

    (D) The importance of DNA evidence in evolutionary research

2. According to the professor, what are two evolutionary changes that occurred in the ancestors of tetrapods? *Choose 2 answers.*

   A   Their swimming ability improved dramatically.

   B   They developed lobe fins.

   C   They became more like ray-finned fish.

   D   Their air sacs developed into a more advanced lung.

3. According to the professor, what was surprising about the discovery of a living coelacanth?

   Ⓐ Its DNA did not match that found in earlier fossils.

   Ⓑ Coelacanths were thought to have become extinct 66 million years ago.

   Ⓒ The fisherman who caught the coelacanth was testing out a new method of net fishing.

   Ⓓ Researchers had not previously thought to search fish markets for coelacanth specimens.

4. What evidence suggests that modern, land-dwelling mammals are descended from lobe-finned fish?

   Ⓐ Lobe-finned fish are able to walk on land, even if only awkwardly.

   Ⓑ The coelacanth moves by "walking" on the ocean floor.

   Ⓒ Lobe fins include a bone extending from the body with smaller, finger-like bones attached.

   Ⓓ No lobe-finned fish use lungs to breathe air.

5. What is the professor's opinion about the studies investigating the DNA of lungfish, coelacanths, and tetrapods?

   Ⓐ She is disappointed that DNA research is relatively new.

   Ⓑ She is excited to discover what conclusions may arise from such studies.

   Ⓒ She hopes that future researchers will be more accurate in their reporting.

   Ⓓ She does not agree with the findings of most studies.

6. What does DNA evidence indicate about the ancestral relationship among lungfish, coelacanths, and tetrapods?

   Ⓐ It is not clear which of the three are most closely related.

   Ⓑ Earlier beliefs about the relationships among the three were proven incorrect.

   Ⓒ Lungfish and tetrapods have the highest degree of similarity among the three.

   Ⓓ The DNA of tetrapods is too varied to study effectively.

12.4

Listen to Track 109.

Now answer the questions.

1. What is the lecture mainly about?

   (A) The use of a defense mechanism by various animals

   (B) Predators that threaten the African crested porcupine

   (C) One way that animals avoid detection by predators

   (D) The application of animal toxins in medicine

2. According to the lecture, what are three weapons used by animals to protect themselves from attack?
   Choose 3 answers.

   [A] Quick evasion

   [B] Toxins

   [C] A poisonous sea anemone

   [D] Avoidance of detection

   [E] Spines

3. According to the lecture, when do African crested porcupines attack?

   (A) Only when faced with predators larger than themselves

   (B) Only once they are fully grown

   (C) When their attempts to scare a predator away fail

   (D) Whenever they are startled by a potential predator

Listen to Track 110.

Now answer the question.

4. (A) To admit a flaw in her own logic

   (B) To express momentary confusion

   (C) To ask students to describe how animal weapons look

   (D) To introduce the next topic

Listen to Track 111.

Now answer the question.

5. (A) To question whether a fascinating theory should be trusted

   (B) To emphasize the importance of further study in this area

   (C) To explain how certain animals use fangs effectively

   (D) To present an unexpected type of defense mechanism

 Listen to Track 112.

Now answer the question.

6. (A) The porcupine is typically successful at scaring off predators.

   (B) The porcupine prefers to escape detection or run away from predators.

   (C) The porcupine is likely to attempt to scare a potential predator away before attacking.

   (D) The porcupine has few natural predators.

12.5

 Listen to Track 113.

Now answer the questions.

1. What is the lecture primarily about?

   (A) How astronomers debated and found the correct interpretation for an observed phenomenon

   (B) The discovery of various underlying causes of an astronomical phenomenon

   (C) What astrologers first saw when they began to use telescopes

   (D) An unresolved question about a phenomenon originally observed less than 1,000 years ago

2. According to the lecture, how did sunspots appear to early astronomers?

   (A) Like orbiting bodies

   (B) Like dark areas

   (C) Like short flares of light

   (D) Like brighter regions

12

3. What does the professor imply was a consideration that may have led to Scheiner's initial interpretation of sunspots?

   (A) An observation of numerous satellites orbiting the Sun

   (B) A centuries-old understanding of sunspots

   (C) A belief that the heavens could not change

   (D) An analogy drawn from observations of other stars

 Listen to Track 114.

Now answer the question.

---

4. (A) To correct a different student's error

   (B) To encourage the student to elaborate on his answer

   (C) To help the student recognize an error he has made

   (D) To help the professor understand what this student meant.

5. According to the professor, what was a result of the debate between Galileo and Scheiner?

   (A) In the end, Scheiner rejected his original theory.

   (B) The public began believing that the heavens were unchanging.

   (C) Later astronomers showed more interest in studying the surface of stars.

   (D) Galileo became known as the foremost astronomer of his time.

6. During a year in which the Sun has a large number of sunspots, what impact is felt on Earth?

   (A) Sunspots will exhibit faster movement than usual.

   (B) There will be less variation in global climate change.

   (C) There will be more satellites between the Earth and the Sun.

   (D) Temperatures on Earth will be higher than normal.

12.6

 Listen to Track 115.

Note: The actual lecture contains color images. The colors from one image are discussed by the professor. You do not need to see the colors to understand the lecture or to answer the questions.

Now answer the questions.

1. What is the main purpose of the lecture?
    - (A) To explain why scientists disagree about the formation of Mount Sharp
    - (B) To present a feature of Mars that should continue to be studied
    - (C) To describe the goals of the Mars rover *Curiosity*
    - (D) To review the atmospheric conditions of Mars in an effort to track its water loss

2. What does the professor imply about the Mars rover *Curiosity*?
    - (A) It took the first images of Mars's surface.
    - (B) It uses both solar and wind energy.
    - (C) It landed a great distance away from the Gale Crater.
    - (D) It has the ability to take mineral samples.

3. Why is the image of the Gale Crater that the professor displays color-coded?
    - (A) To illustrate that Mount Sharp is taller than any mountain on Earth
    - (B) To compensate for the poor quality of images sent by *Curiosity*
    - (C) To indicate more clearly what areas of the crater are at a high elevation and what areas are at a low elevation
    - (D) To prove that the crater was formed by a meteor impact

4. Why does the professor mention the composition of Mount Sharp?
    - (A) To explain how craters are formed
    - (B) To provide evidence to support theories about how it was created
    - (C) To explain that clay is uncommon in mountains that are not formed from ancient lakes
    - (D) To imply that Mount Sharp was formed at the same time as the Gale Crater

5. Why does the professor believe that there may have once been water on Mars? *Choose 2 answers.*

   A The clay sediment at the base of Mount Sharp could have come from an ancient lake bed.

   B Some of the minerals on Mount Sharp can probably only be formed in the presence of running water.

   C The atmosphere of Mars contains traces of water.

   D *Curiosity* has found water molecules embedded in rocks within the Gale Crater.

    Listen to Track 116.

   Now answer the question.

6. A The student should be paying more attention to the lecture than he is.

   B The push to explore other worlds has directly led to an improvement in technology on Earth.

   C Without continuing to push the boundaries of knowledge, scientific progress will decline.

   D Understanding the history of Mars may help reveal aspects of the Earth's history.

12.7

 Listen to Track 117.

Now answer the questions.

1. What is the main topic of the lecture?
   A Variations in types of roots
   B Methods of transpiration
   C The function of taproots
   D Improving the water intake of plants

    Listen to Track 118.

   Now answer the question.

2. A She wants to elicit examples from the students.
   B She does not believe that taproots are common.
   C She is trying to trick her students by talking about other kinds of roots.
   D She forgot what she was about to say.

3. The professor mentions that plant root systems are typically observed in water. Why does she mention this?

   Ⓐ To demonstrate that it doesn't matter what material plants are grown in

   Ⓑ To explain why the typical setup for this type of experiment would not work in this case

   Ⓒ To remind students of the importance of using the scientific method

   Ⓓ To reinforce the point that taproots are generally used to store nutrients.

4. According to the professor, why did the researchers grow a species of pine trees in sand?

   Ⓐ To add specific fertilizer types

   Ⓑ To remove the branching roots

   Ⓒ To monitor the intake of water

   Ⓓ To control the size of the taproot

5. According to the professor, what similarity exists between loblolly pines and carrot plants?

   Ⓐ Both can be grown in sand.

   Ⓑ Both have been extensively studied.

   Ⓒ Both rely exclusively on branching roots for transpiration.

   Ⓓ Both use taproots to absorb water.

    Listen to Track 119.

   Now answer the question.

6. Ⓐ To imply that the conclusions reached by the lab were incorrect

   Ⓑ To emphasize that structure and storage are the most important roles of a taproot

   Ⓒ To indicate that the researchers discovered that taproots play a broader role than previously thought

   Ⓓ To suggest that MRI technology was not the best tool for this lab to use

12.8

 Listen to Track 120.

Now answer the questions.

1. What does the class mainly discuss?
   - (A) How fungi choose certain plants with which to form mutualistic relationships
   - (B) The impact that human beings have on plant life
   - (C) The role of a particular plant species in an ecosystem
   - (D) How organisms in an ecosystem are affected by one another

2. According to the professor, which of the following is true of the mycorrhizal relationship between fungi and plants?
   - (A) It is uncommon in plant life.
   - (B) The mycorrhizal relationship is widespread among the Earth's plants.
   - (C) The mycorrhizal relationship between fungi and plants is not well understood.
   - (D) The fungi not involved in a mycorrhizal relationship die more readily.

3. Which of the following is an example of mutualism?
   - (A) Fungi and plants occupying separate environments in an ecosystem.
   - (B) Plants benefit from the presence of fungi, but fungi do not benefit from the presence of plants.
   - (C) Plants provide oxygen to fungi, while the fungi provide benefits to a different organism.
   - (D) Plants provide carbohydrates to fungi, while the fungi provide plants with access to water and nutrients.

4. According to the professor, what is a possible impact of human behavior on ecosystems?
   - (A) It can influence relationships between other organisms.
   - (B) It often leads to the destruction of entire ecosystems.
   - (C) It is the cause of an overall decrease in biodiversity.
   - (D) It can encourage new species to develop.

Listen to Track 121.

Now answer the question.

5. Why does the professor say this?

    (A) To suggest that human beings are rarely destructive toward plants

    (B) To defend human behavior with regard to caring for plants

    (C) To introduce a theoretical situation for the purpose of discussion

    (D) To illustrate a way human behavior might benefit plants

 Listen to Track 122.

Now answer the question.

6. What does the professor imply when she says this?

    (A) Plants would benefit from humans in lieu of fungi.

    (B) The death of plants would cause land to become uninhabitable for humans.

    (C) The elimination of fungi could damage plants, unless plants find another source of nutrition.

    (D) The most efficient way to destroy plants is to remove fungi from their habitats.

12.9

 Listen to Track 123.

Now answer the questions.

1. What does the professor mainly talk about?

    (A) The types of signals used by humans to prevent inbreeding

    (B) How animals reproduce

    (C) The mechanisms primates use to prevent inbreeding

    (D) The findings of a study on how mammals prevent inbreeding

2. Why does the student mention that male monkeys leave their group when they are young?

   (A) To point out ways in which young male monkeys are similar to young male humans

   (B) To mention a behavior she knows of that can prevent inbreeding in monkeys

   (C) To explain why she is majoring in biology

   (D) To demonstrate that she knows how inbreeding is prevented in non-primates

3. What is the professor's attitude toward the social cues that non-human primates use to prevent certain behaviors?

   (A) She believes that these social cues have not been adequately researched.

   (B) She believes that these social cues are ineffective.

   (C) She finds them distinctly different from taboos among humans.

   (D) She finds them similar in function to human taboos.

4. According to the professor, which of the following is a way that some apes prevent inbreeding?

   (A) Abstention from mating

   (B) Mating outside of their species

   (C) Social dominance

   (D) Cultural taboos

5. The professor discusses hormones in two contexts. What are they? *Choose 2 answers.*

   A   Dominance

   B   Taboo development

   C   Physical separation

   D   Reproductive behavior

 Listen to Track 124.

Now answer the question.

---

6. Why does the professor say this?

   (A) To see whether other students agree or disagree with the student's response

   (B) To express that the student has misunderstood an important concept

   (C) To indicate that the student has frustrated her by failing to do the assigned reading

   (D) To ascertain whether she is understanding the student's point correctly or not

MANHATTAN PREP

12.10

 Listen to Track 125.

Now answer the questions.

1. What is the lecture primarily about?

   (A) Different methods to determine the helium content of a star

   (B) How Henrietta Leavitt became a notable astronomer

   (C) How astronomers measure the distance between stars and the Earth

   (D) Why Cepheid variables display a pulsing pattern

2. According to the professor, what is one application of spectroscopy?

   (A) To measure the distance between some stars and the Earth

   (B) To study the composition of nearby planets

   (C) To determine the luminosity of a Cepheid variable

   (D) To measure the lifespan of a star

 Listen to Track 126.

Now answer the question.

3. (A) He wants to start the explanation by using an analogous situation that is easy to understand.

   (B) He is using an example to prove that distance often cannot be precisely determined.

   (C) He has gotten temporarily distracted by talking about mountains at various distances from an observer.

   (D) He believes that the methods used for measuring distances on Earth can be applied to stars.

 Listen to Track 127.

Now answer the question.

4. (A) To imply that he does not believe the students are doing their assigned work

   (B) To indicate that his next question was answered in the assigned homework

   (C) To emphasize the importance of understanding astronomers throughout history

   (D) To remind students about their upcoming homework assignments

5. What does the professor explain to one of the students about the term "pulsing star"?
   - (A) It is a rather misleading term.
   - (B) It is a term no longer used by astronomers.
   - (C) It is a complete description of a phenomenon.
   - (D) It is another term for a Cepheid variable.

6. What can be inferred about two Cepheid variables if their pulsing periods are the same?
   - (A) They are the same distance from the Earth.
   - (B) They have equal luminosities.
   - (C) They are likely to be difficult to tell apart.
   - (D) They are approximately the same age.

Answer Key—12.1

Question	Correct Answer	Right/Wrong	Category
1	B		Gist-content
2	A, B, D		Connecting Content
3	C		Detail
4	C		Detail
5	D		Organization
6	A		Function of What Is Said

Answer Key—12.2

Question	Correct Answer	Right/Wrong	Category
1	C		Gist-content
2	D		Detail
3	B		Detail
4	A		Detail
5	D		Detail
6	B		Function of What Is Said

Answer Key—12.3

Question	Correct Answer	Right/Wrong	Category
1	C		Gist-content
2	B, D		Detail
3	B		Detail
4	C		Detail
5	B		Speaker's Attitude
6	A		Detail

Answer Key—12.4

Question	Correct Answer	Right/Wrong	Category
1	A		Gist-content
2	B, C, E		Detail
3	C		Detail
4	D		Function of What Is Said
5	D		Function of What Is Said
6	C		Inference

Answer Key—12.5

Question	Correct Answer	Right/Wrong	Category
1	A		Gist-content
2	B		Detail
3	C		Inference
4	B		Function of What Is Said
5	A		Detail
6	D		Detail

Answer Key—12.6

Question	Correct Answer	Right/Wrong	Category
1	B		Gist-purpose
2	D		Inference
3	C		Detail
4	B		Organization
5	A, B		Detail
6	D		Inference

Answer Key—12.7

Question	Correct Answer	Right/Wrong	Category
1	C		Gist-content
2	A		Function of What Is Said
3	B		Organization
4	C		Detail
5	D		Detail
6	C		Function of What Is Said

Answer Key—12.8

Question	Correct Answer	Right/Wrong	Category
1	D		Gist-content
2	B		Detail
3	D		Detail
4	A		Detail
5	C		Function of What Is Said
6	C		Inference

Answer Key—12.9

Question	Correct Answer	Right/Wrong	Category
1	C		Gist-content
2	B		Organization
3	D		Speaker's Attitude
4	C		Detail
5	A, D		Detail
6	B		Function of What Is Said

Answer Key—12.10

Question	Correct Answer	Right/Wrong	Category
1	C		Gist-content
2	A		Detail
3	A		Function of What Is Said
4	B		Function of What Is Said
5	D		Detail
6	B		Inference

Answers and Explanations—12.1

Schooling Fish—Track 104

NARRATOR: Listen to part of a lecture in a biology class. The class is discussing animal behavior.

PROFESSOR: Ok, now I want to talk about an animal behavior that many of you are likely familiar with. You may have seen a video of, or if you have ever been diving or snorkeling actually seen, fish swimming together in extremely tight formations, or schools.

If each fish is uniform in appearance—um… similar looking—and the movements are coordinated—say they are move in the same direction or at the same speed—the fish are said to be *schooling*. There are many benefits to schooling. For example, it is easier to find a potential mate within a school.

So, what might another benefit of schooling be?

MALE STUDENT: Well, I was thinking safety, but it would seem like having more fish together would make them an easier target, right? If that is true, then safety is not a benefit.

PROFESSOR: That is an interesting conclusion, Sebastian, but your original thought was correct. It turns out that safety is a major benefit of schooling, even though it might seem counterintuitive at first. There are

several theories about why safety in numbers might occur in schools of fish. First, there's the "*many eyes hypothesis.*" If a fish is swimming alone, it can only rely on what it sees, but in a school, any fish that sees danger can signal to all of the other fish. Predator detection is therefore enhanced, allowing the school to escape predators more quickly, or even avoid them altogether.

Why else might schooling be safer for fish? Elaine?

FEMALE STUDENT: I remember reading about the way a school of fish can confuse a predator. I think I read once that predators were more likely to choose a fish that stood out… looked different. So by staying in schools where they all move very quickly and look the same, it should be harder for a predator to choose just one. That would improve safety, right?

PROFESSOR: Exactly—that is another reason suggested for the safety of schools. In fact, some experiments have shown that this effect, called the "*confusion effect,*" isn't just on visually-oriented predators, meaning those that hunt primarily by sight. Some predators rely on movement, and the rapid movement of a school can also confuse those predators.

But we haven't talked about the most interesting idea that suggests the safety of a school. It is called the "*encounter dilution effect.*"

Now, when you consider the likelihood of detection of a school—how visible it is to predators—you might initially come to the same conclusion as Sebastian. A small fish might be nearly invisible to a predator, but certainly a large school must be very easy to see… highly visible. But this is actually false. We won't get into the details here, but visibility underwater is very limited… even in the clearest conditions, an object is only visible from about 200 meters away, regardless of size.

Can anyone suggest why the lowered visibility underwater might make a large school of fish less likely to be seen than individual fish?

MALE STUDENT: Well, if fish are spread out over an area, a predator would be fairly likely to encounter one, right? So if they all gather together, the predator would have to find the entire school to find any of them. And since the predators can't see far, it would be easier for the group to, uh… avoid being seen.

FEMALE STUDENT: Professor, isn't it possible, though, that for some huge predators, that the whole school of fish could be consumed? I know that some whales are large enough to fit an entire school in their mouths at once.

PROFESSOR: You're exactly right, although that behavior isn't terribly common. The one well-known example is the lunge feeding of a humpback whale. Essentially they accelerate from below a very dense school, often called a bait ball, and engulf the entire school as they move toward the surface.

1.   What is the lecture mainly about?

    ✗ (A) The defense mechanisms of a variety of animals

    ✓ (B) The benefits of the schooling behavior of fish

    ✗ (C) The importance of schooling behavior during migration

    ✗ (D) The ways in which predators target fish that are prey

GIST-CONTENT. The lecture focuses primarily on the benefits of the schooling behavior of fish.

This lecture focuses exclusively on a defense mechanism of fish.

CORRECT. The professor introduces schooling behavior, then discusses benefits associated with that behavior.

Migration is never mentioned in the lecture.

This topic is discussed briefly, but it is not the main point of the lecture.

2.   Select each of the activities below that describes an advantage given in the lecture of schooling behavior in fish. *Choose all that apply.*

    ✓ [A] A fish that sees danger can signal to other fish.

    ✓ [B] The rapid movement of a school can confuse predators.

    ✗ [C] Swimming in a school formation is efficient for traveling long distances.

    ✓ [D] Staying close together reduces the likelihood of detection.

CONNECTING CONTENT. The professor explores the safety benefits of schooling at length. She also mentions that schooling makes it easier for fish to find mates.

CORRECT. This is called the "many eyes hypothesis." One fish can only detect a predator that it itself sees, but in a group, all of the fish can detect threats and send signals to each other.

CORRECT. This is called the "confusion effect." Rapid movement can confuse predators that rely on detecting the movement of an individual fish.

This idea is never mentioned in the lecture.

CORRECT. This is called the "encounter dilution effect." If fish are spread out, predators are more likely to find one of the fish. In a group, the predator will only find one if it finds the entire group.

3.   How does the professor define the "encounter dilution effect"?

    ✗ (A) Schooling increases a fish's chances of finding a mate.

    ✗ (B) Schooling allows predators to find fish more easily.

    ✓ (C) Individual fish are less likely to be detected in a school.

    ✗ (D) Schooling permits quicker detection of predators that are encountered.

DETAIL. The professor explains that by forming a school, fish can reduce the chance that any particular fish in that school is detected by a predator.

This is a benefit of schooling, but it is not the "encounter dilution effect."

The opposite is true. The "encounter dilution effect" states that schooling fish are less likely to be detected than fish that are scattered.

CORRECT. The "encounter dilution effect" states that if fish are spread out, predators are more likely to find one of the fish. In a group, the predator will only find one if it finds the entire group.

This is a benefit of schooling ("many eyes"), but it is not the "encounter dilution effect."

4.   According to the lecture, what is one possible benefit arising from a school of fish consisting of nearly identical fish?

DETAIL. According to the professor, there are several benefits from the fish in a school being nearly identical.

✗   (A) Improved efficiency from the group swimming in unison

Nothing is mentioned regarding efficiency gained from swimming in unison.

✗   (B) Fish with better vision capabilities can act as scouts to help protect the other fish

This idea is not mentioned in the lecture.

✓   (C) Increased safety, because predators typically target a fish that stands out

CORRECT. This is directly mentioned in the lecture.

✗   (D) The reduced likelihood of individual fish becoming separated from the school

This idea is not mentioned in the lecture.

5.   Why does the professor mention the humpback whale's ability to consume a "bait ball"?

ORGANIZATION. The professor mentions this ability as a disadvantage of schooling.

✗   (A) To explain how different types of predators locate fish

The professor's point about the humpback whale's ability to consume a bait ball is not related to how predators locate fish.

✗   (B) To contrast schooling with the defense mechanisms of other animals

No other animal's defense mechanisms are mentioned.

✗   (C) To give an example of a swimming technique used by whales

The professor briefly describes the way a humpback whale swims when attacking a bait ball. However, this is not the reason the professor mentions this ability of the humpback whale.

✓   (D) To point out a disadvantage of schooling

CORRECT. The professor mentions that the humpback whale's ability to eat a large group of fish, or "bait ball," is an example of a drawback to schooling.

Track 105

NARRATOR: Listen again to part of the lecture. Then answer the question.

MALE STUDENT: Well, I was thinking safety, but it would seem like having more fish together would make them an easier target, right? If that is true, then safety is not a benefit.

PROFESSOR: That is an interesting conclusion, Sebastian, but your original thought was correct.

NARRATOR: What does the professor mean when she says this:

PROFESSOR: That is an interesting conclusion, Sebastian, but your original thought was correct.

6.   **FUNCTION OF WHAT IS SAID.** In the selected quote, the professor points out that Sebastian's instinctual first answer was correct, but not his second answer.

✓ (A) The student's logic has led him to the wrong final conclusion.

CORRECT. The professor is pointing out that the student was correct originally, and that his later reasoning has led him to a conclusion that was incorrect.

✗ (B) She is impressed with the creativity of the student.

She is not commenting on his creativity.

✗ (C) The student should investigate a different question.

This is not the message the professor intends to convey in this quote.

✗ (D) She thinks that she has confused the student.

She does not indicate that she believes she is to blame for the student's incorrect conclusion.

Answers and Explanations—12.2

Sea Ice—Track 106

NARRATOR: Listen to this part of a lecture in a geology class.

PROFESSOR: OK, since the 1970s, geologists have been using images from satellites to track glaciers, sea ice, and other ice formations around the globe… and, um… have started to notice an interesting trend with sea ice. So let's back up a moment and discuss what we mean when we say *sea ice*.

Now, sea ice is obviously not the only ice we find around the globe, but it is unique. There are glaciers, icebergs, ice sheets, and even ice shelves, many I'm sure, um, some of you may have heard of. We won't go into the individual distinctions of all these other ice formations today, but… just note that they all form on land, while sea ice actually forms in the water. Sea ice is essentially frozen ocean water that develops during the winter months, and that partially melts during the summer. At any given time, sea ice covers 15 percent of the world's oceans… so you can see, it is widespread.

There is sea ice at both poles… North and South. In the Northern Hemisphere, sea ice is actually more abundant, meaning, um, it can be found stretching quite far south… For example, sea ice can form in Bohai Bay, China… which is actually slightly closer to the Equator than to the North Pole! However, in the Southern Hemisphere, this isn't the case… sea ice only forms around Antarctica, and doesn't extend nearly as far from the pole.

So… geologists have been tracking the amount of sea ice over time. But why do we even care how much ice there is in the oceans? The issue is part of an attempt to track *global warming*, which is the gradual increase in the Earth's temperature over the last hundred years or so. You might be wondering, though… since the world's ice is primarily at the poles, what should that matter for the areas where most of us live—closer to the Equator?

Well, don't forget that air and water currents flow around the globe. What happens to the temperature—or the weather—in one part of the world… see, that impacts us all.

Now, the Earth's atmosphere… dense air… is what helps hold in some of the energy, if you want to call it heat, okay… from the Sun's rays. This is known as the "*greenhouse effect*." If you've been in an actual greenhouse, you will know what this means. Light energy from the sun hits the Earth's surface, and while

12

some bounces off and escapes, the rest essentially turns into infrared rays and gets trapped by the atmosphere. That warms the atmosphere up, and it maintains a comfortable temperature for us—for life as we know it—to exist.

You probably didn't think about it this way, but remember that ice and snow are usually a very bright white in color… they act as a giant reflector of sunlight. That reflective quality means that it helps bounce much of the Sun's radiation right back out into space, in a form that isn't trapped by greenhouse gases. In contrast, dark water or ground absorbs visible light and turns that energy into infrared, which is what gets trapped by greenhouse gases. Just like a dark shirt is hotter to wear than a white shirt in the summertime. So the amount of ice we have helps regulate the amount of heat that escapes versus what winds up being retained. As the temperature rises, it melts more and more ice, allowing the temperatures to rise even further, melting even more ice, and so on. Because of this effect, you can think of global warming as a cycle that feeds itself.

As temperatures rise, areas in the tropics… near the Equator… might become too hot to be habitable. And as ice melts, the sea level rises. Even just a few meters can be enough to leave entire coastal areas… or even small islands… underwater.

So what scientists expected to see, when they tracked sea ice, was that warmer overall temperatures meant that less sea ice would form. And this is what they did see… at the North Pole. In the Arctic, sea ice formation is declining sharply. But then, the surprise—the same wasn't true at the South Pole. Antarctic sea ice was actually growing year after year. And, in the last decade, sea ice in the Antarctic has hit record highs. Why?

Scientists are still working with several hypotheses. Some compare the differing amounts of salt in the water or the amount of snow versus ice in the region. A recently proposed theory points to the differences in geography. The Arctic is a giant ocean with the North Pole sitting in the middle. The Arctic Ocean is surrounded on all sides by the giant frozen landmasses of the Northern Hemisphere—Canada, Alaska, Greenland, and Russia. At the South Pole, however, the opposite is true. Sea ice forms as a fringe around the continent of Antarctica. Regardless of the specifics, essentially all current hypotheses hinge on the fact that comparing the Arctic to the Antarctic isn't an apples-to-apples comparison… they just aren't the same.

1.	What aspect of global warming is the lecture primarily about?	**GIST-CONTENT.** The lecture primarily focuses on sea ice formation and how sea ice is related to global warming.
✗	(A) Human behavior that has led to the increase in greenhouse gases	Nothing is mentioned about the human behavior contributing to global warming.
✗	(B) The sharp decline in many endangered species	Endangered species are not mentioned in the lecture.
✓	(C) The impact of global temperatures on sea ice formation	**CORRECT.** The lecture is primarily about sea ice and its relationship to global warming.
✗	(D) Factors influencing global ocean currents	Global currents are mentioned briefly, but they are not the main topic of the lecture.

2.   According to the professor, why do geologists track the amount of sea ice over time?

DETAIL. The amount of sea ice both influences and is influenced by global warming. Therefore, geologists have been tracking the amount of sea ice as part of an effort to track global warming.

✗ (A) To determine the reflective quality of ice

The fact that ice has a reflective quality is mentioned, but this is not the reason geologists track sea ice levels.

✗ (B) To understand how the greenhouse effect impacts global temperatures

Although the greenhouse effect is discussed, it is not mentioned as the direct reason for tracking sea ice levels.

✗ (C) To study how sea ice and glaciers are related

The relationship between sea ice and glaciers is not discussed.

✓ (D) To track global warming

CORRECT. The professor notes that geologists have been tracking the volume of sea ice over time to help track global warming.

3.   What is the greenhouse effect, according to the professor?

DETAIL. The greenhouse effect is the process by which the Sun's radiation is trapped by the atmosphere, causing the atmosphere's temperature to rise.

✗ (A) The reflective quality of snow and ice

This is not what the term "greenhouse effect" refers to.

✓ (B) The trapping of the Sun's energy by the atmosphere

CORRECT. Light from the Sun hits the Earth's surface, and while some bounces off and escapes, the rest of the energy gets trapped by the atmosphere, thereby warming the atmosphere.

✗ (C) The melting and refreezing of sea ice

This is not what the term "greenhouse effect" refers to.

✗ (D) The pattern of ocean currents around the globe

This is not what the term "greenhouse effect" refers to.

4.   According to the professor, what is one unique aspect of sea ice?

DETAIL. The professor mentions that unlike other natural forms of ice, sea ice forms in the ocean rather than on land.

✓ (A) It forms in the ocean rather than on land.

CORRECT. The professor notes that all other global ice formations occur on land.

✗ (B) It is the main way for scientists to track global warming.

There is no evidence presented in the lecture to support this idea.

✗ (C) It indicates that the North and South polar regions should not be compared.

At the end of the lecture, the professor says that "comparing the Arctic to the Antarctic isn't an apples-to-apples comparison… they just aren't the same," but this comment has nothing to do with the unique aspects of sea ice.

✗ (D) It provides an example of a natural phenomenon of less interest to scientists.

The professor directly states that scientists are studying sea ice.

12

5. Why are scientists confused by sea ice in the Antarctic?

DETAIL. Because of global warming, the scientists expected to find that sea ice formations in the Antarctic were declining, but they found the opposite.

✗ (A) It forms on land rather than in the ocean.

This is incorrect. By definition, all sea ice forms in the ocean.

✗ (B) There is much less sea ice in the Antarctic than in the Arctic.

This is implied to be true in the lecture, and it is not surprising, because the Arctic is composed primarily of ocean and the Antarctic is composed primarily of Antarctica.

✗ (C) It is experiencing a trend similar to that of Arctic sea ice.

The opposite is true. The scientists found that while Arctic sea ice is declining, Antarctic sea ice is actually increasing.

✓ (D) It is increasing in volume even as global temperatures rise.

CORRECT. Sea ice in the Arctic is decreasing in volume as expected. However, sea ice in the Antarctic has actually been increasing in volume recently.

Track 107

NARRATOR: Listen again to part of the lecture. Then answer the question.

PROFESSOR: Now, the Earth's atmosphere… dense air… is what helps hold in some of the energy, if you want to call it heat, okay… from the Sun's rays. This is known as the *greenhouse effect*. If you've been in an actual greenhouse, you will know what this means.

NARRATOR: Why does the professor say this:

PROFESSOR: If you've been in an actual greenhouse, you will know what this means.

6. **FUNCTION OF WHAT IS SAID.** The professor implies that greenhouses retain heat, and that it can be noticed by anyone who has been in a greenhouse. Therefore, to students who may have experienced a greenhouse, the meaning of "greenhouse effect" should be obvious.

✗ (A) To provide evidence that proves his point

The professor is using the example of a greenhouse to help explain the term "greenhouse effect," not to provide evidence to prove a point.

✓ (B) To use a potentially familiar concept to help explain a new concept

CORRECT. The professor is attempting to use some students' knowledge of an actual greenhouse to help explain how the atmosphere creates a heating effect similar to the one created by a greenhouse.

✗ (C) To encourage students to visit greenhouses to experience the effect directly

This is not the purpose of the professor's quote.

✗ (D) To point to a flaw in the theory of global warming

Flaws in the theory of global warming are not discussed in the lecture.

Answers and Explanations—12.3

Tetrapods—Track 108

NARRATOR: Listen to part of a lecture in a marine biology class.

PROFESSOR: So we've already talked about the evolution of aquatic mammals… say, how whales and dolphins evolved from land-dwelling mammals, making their way into the water. But our next question takes us back a step—how did a whale's ancestors… our ancestors… end up on land in the first place? Remember that all life initially started in the sea.

Mammals are actually a form of tetrapod… this comes from the Greek *tetra*, meaning "four," and *pous*, meaning "foot." So the tetrapods are any animals with four "feet," or limbs. This includes humans and other mammals, but also includes birds, reptiles, and amphibians. Early tetrapods appeared in the fossil record about 400 million years ago, but were all aquatic. It took another 25 million years before they made their way onto land. In fact, there is still a lot of debate on exactly how this happened.

But let's start with where these tetrapods came from… this is actually pretty interesting. It turns out that fish and tetrapods both evolved from early vertebrates, or animals with spines. These early animals had bony fins and gills like a fish, but they also had air sacs that were connected to the back of their throats, which meant they could breathe air, not just pull oxygen out of the water. They could also use this air sac to control their ability to float at different water depths—this ability is called buoyancy.

Now over time, fish and our tetrapod ancestors took two different evolutionary paths. Some fish kept their gills, but the air sacs lost connection to the throat and became exclusively for buoyancy control. Others developed a more advanced lung that started to look more and more like what you and I have today. One example is a lungfish… this is, uh… a modern freshwater fish with lungs that allow it to breathe air at the water's surface. Eventually, many of these fish would completely lose the gills and buoyancy control. Of course, there are modern tetrapods, like amphibians, that still have gills… or at least start off with gills that they shed as they move into adulthood.

Another notable difference occurred in the fins. The fish that you're probably familiar with are considered ray-finned, in that there are a lot of little bones that create a web or ray shape in the fin. Their early aquatic ancestors had the same fin shape. But our tetrapod ancestors began to develop lobe fins… the lungfish is a lobe-finned fish. These lobe fins are different from ray fins in that there is a single bone extending from the fish's body that then connects to almost finger-like bones. As you can see, the early needs for living on land were starting to appear… feet to walk around on and lungs in order to breathe air.

Um…so most lobe-finned fish are actually extinct. Scientists thought the lungfish was the last remaining one. But in 1938 a fisherman caught a different kind of fish—a *coelacanth*… bet you didn't think that was how to pronounce that word! Scientists had already been studying fossils of the coelacanth, but it was thought to have gone extinct 66 million years ago! So, of course, the fisherman had no idea that he'd caught something so rare, but a museum curator happened to be at a fish market in South Africa, where it was caught, and noticed it. I bet you can imagine her surprise!

So the puzzle of how our early lobe-finned ancestors made their way to land is still unsolved. There are only two living species of lobe-finned fish… the coelacanth and the lungfish. The question stands—how are we all related? Recent studies of DNA, which is the carrier of all genetic information in a living organism, focus on the three groups—coelacanths, lungfish, and tetrapods. How are we all related, and are some of us more related than others? For example, are coelacanths and lungfish closely tied, while the tetrapods represent a different evolutionary lineage? Or maybe we are evolved from one of the other ancient lines of

12

fish? It is an exciting question to try to answer, but unfortunately, the DNA evidence of several studies hasn't yet been able to provide support for any of these hypotheses!

1.   What is this lecture mainly about?

   ✗ (A) Recent research connecting whales to ray-finned fish

   ✗ (B) Differences between mammals and other tetrapods

   ✓ (C) Discussing the evolution of tetrapods

   ✗ (D) The importance of DNA evidence in evolutionary research

GIST-CONTENT. The lecture is primarily concerned with the question of how tetrapods ended up becoming land-based.

Whales are mentioned at the start of the lecture, but no recent research about them is discussed.

There is no contrast made between mammals and other tetrapods.

CORRECT. The question of how mammals and many other tetrapods evolved from ocean-dwelling animals into land-dwelling animals is the central idea of the lecture.

DNA research is only mentioned near the end of the lecture.

2.   According to the professor, what are two evolutionary changes that occurred in the ancestors of tetrapods? *Choose 2 answers.*

   ✗ [A] Their swimming ability improved dramatically.

   ✓ [B] They developed lobe fins.

   ✗ [C] They became more like ray-finned fish.

   ✓ [D] Their air sacs developed into a more advanced lung.

DETAIL. The professor cites the development of lungs and the development of lobe fins as two evolutionary changes among tetrapod ancestors.

Swimming ability is not discussed in the lecture.

CORRECT. Tetrapod ancestors developed lobe fins. These lobe fins are implied to be the predecessors of hands and feet.

The opposite is true. While the ancestors of modern fish were ray-finned, tetrapod ancestors developed lobe fins.

CORRECT. The air sacs in tetrapod ancestors became better-developed to support breathing air, while the air sacs in ray-finned fish evolved to primarily support buoyancy.

3.   According to the professor, what was surprising about the discovery of a living coelacanth?

  ✗ (A) Its DNA did not match that found in earlier fossils.

  ✓ (B) Coelacanths were thought to have become extinct 66 million years ago.

  ✗ (C) The fisherman who caught the coelacanth was testing out a new method of net fishing.

  ✗ (D) Researchers had not previously thought to search fish markets for coelacanth specimens.

DETAIL. The surprise derives from the fact that scientists had previously believed that coelacanths became extinct millions of years ago.

The DNA of living and fossil specimens of coelacanths is not discussed in the lecture.

CORRECT. The professor indicates that this was the cause of the surprise.

Nothing is mentioned about the methods used by the fisherman to catch the living coelacanth.

Prior searches for coelacanth specimens are not discussed in the lecture.

4.   What evidence suggests that modern, land-dwelling mammals are descended from lobe-finned fish?

  ✗ (A) Lobe-finned fish are able to walk on land, even if only awkwardly.

  ✗ (B) The coelacanth moves by "walking" on the ocean floor.

  ✓ (C) Lobe fins include a bone extending from the body with smaller, finger-like bones attached.

  ✗ (D) No lobe-finned fish use lungs to breathe air.

DETAIL. The professor notes that the structure of the lobe fin is "a single bone extending from the fish's body that then connects to almost finger-like bones." This is implied to be comparable to the structure of a hand or foot.

This idea is not presented in the lecture.

This idea is not presented in the lecture.

CORRECT. The professor implies that this structure of the lobe fin is similar to that of a hand or foot.

On the contrary, the lungfish is given as an example of a lobe-finned fish with lungs that allow it to breathe air.

12

5. What is the professor's opinion about the studies investigating the DNA of lungfish, coelacanths, and tetrapods?

    SPEAKER'S ATTITUDE. The professor mentions these studies in the context of determining the degree of ancestral relationship among lungfish, coelacanths, and tetrapods. She states: "It is an exciting question to try to answer."

    ✗ (A) She is disappointed that DNA research is relatively new.

    She does not express disappointment about how new the DNA research is.

    ✓ (B) She is excited to discover what conclusions may arise from such studies.

    CORRECT. She calls the issue an exciting one, but indicates that no conclusive evidence has yet been found.

    ✗ (C) She hopes that future researchers will be more accurate in their reporting.

    Accuracy of the researchers involved in completed studies is never called into question in the lecture.

    ✗ (D) She does not agree with the findings of most studies.

    The professor does not indicate her disagreement with the results of any studies.

6. What does DNA evidence indicate about the ancestral relationship among lungfish, coelacanths, and tetrapods?

    DETAIL. The professor notes that no definitive conclusions have yet been reached about these relationships.

    ✓ (A) It is not clear which of the three are most closely related.

    CORRECT. The professor states that "the DNA evidence of several studies hasn't yet been able to provide support for any" of the hypotheses about the relationships among the three groups.

    ✗ (B) Earlier beliefs about the relationships among the three were proven incorrect.

    The professor never mentions earlier beliefs about these relationships. Furthermore, she notes that any hypotheses about these relationships are not yet proven or disproven.

    ✗ (C) Lungfish and tetrapods have the highest degree of similarity among the three.

    The studies have not yet been able to conclude which relationships are the strongest.

    ✗ (D) The DNA of tetrapods is too varied to study effectively.

    On the contrary, tetrapod DNA has been researched in these studies, but no definitive conclusions have yet been drawn from them.

12

Answers and Explanations—12.4

Animal Weapons—Track 109

NARRATOR: Listen to part of a lecture in a biology class. The class has been learning about animal adaptations.

PROFESSOR: Alright, let's continue the discussion from last class… we were talking about defense mechanisms, or means of self-protection, that animals have developed to defend themselves. These anti-predator adaptations come in a wide variety of forms… and serve many purposes.

For example, some mechanisms might allow an animal to avoid detection… others might startle or distract a predator… or even help the animal escape quickly. And, well… some animals have developed ways of fighting back or physically defending themselves when attacked. Some even have their own "weapons"… now what might those look like?

The most obvious are probably the physical structures you see… say, horns… or claws. Of course, most of these are used by predators to attack prey, but these features can also be used for defense, um—used as *defense mechanisms*! Take spines—sharp, needle-like structures—a good example here is the African crested porcupine. These rodents are only about 75 centimeters in length, but they are almost entirely covered with spines. The spines covering the animal's sides—and back—are each over 30 centimeters long, and they are extremely sturdy.

Now, porcupines are herbivores… which means, well… they only eat plants. So the spines are clearly not for attacking prey. But they definitely know how to use them to defend themselves! When disturbed, the porcupine initially tries to "puff up"… to appear larger, to scare off the predator. But if that doesn't work, well… they attack. The porcupine will actually run backwards toward the attacker, trying to stab them with the sturdier spines found on their backside. Now, remember, these animals aren't even 1 meter long, and weigh no more than 25 or 30 kilograms… but they are able to kill leopards, lions, and even humans if they need to defend themselves.

OK… but not all defense mechanisms are visible, like spines or horns. Some animals use chemical warfare… venom or other poisonous chemicals. These toxins might be housed inside structures already made for defense… fangs and spines are great examples. But sometimes the venom might simply cover the skin of the animal… an attacker would taste the chemical before actually eating the animal.

Here is something really fascinating though. There are a couple of animals that use other animals as weapons. One such animal is the *blanket octopus*.

So, a fully mature female can grow to be almost 2 meters long. However, the males only grow to be a few centimeters long… it actually took scientists decades to figure out that there even were males, because no one could ever find them! Now, the full grown females can spread out their blanket-like body to scare off potential predators, but the smaller males and the immature females need a little more help. As it turns out, the blanket octopus is immune to the venom found in the highly poisonous Portuguese man-of-war. The octopus actually hunts the man-of-war for its poisonous tentacles—a Portuguese man-of-war has several of them. The octopus tears off a tentacle, and then carries it around to whip anything that tries to attack.

And if you thought that was an innovative weapon, then you'll appreciate the boxer crab, also called the *pom-pom crab*. They get their name because they carry a certain stinging sea anemone— a Triactis producta—around in each claw. The anemones look like little pom-poms, or puffy boxing gloves, but are actually thought to be among the most poisonous of the sea anemone family. The crab uses these living

pom-poms to sting its attackers. The sea anemone gets a pretty good deal too—by getting carried around, it has better access to floating food particles.

1.   What is the lecture mainly about?

   GIST-CONTENT. The professor discusses the use of weapons by animals as a defense mechanism.

✓ (A) The use of a defense mechanism by various animals

   CORRECT. The lecture primarily discusses the use of weapons by animals in self-defense.

✗ (B) Predators that threaten the African crested porcupine

   Some potential predators of the African crested porcupine are mentioned, but this is not the focus of the lecture.

✗ (C) One way that animals avoid detection by predators

   Avoiding detection is mentioned, but this is not the main topic discussed in the lecture.

✗ (D) The application of animal toxins in medicine

   This topic is not mentioned in the lecture.

2.   According to the lecture, what are three weapons used by animals to protect themselves from attack? *Choose 3 answers.*

   DETAIL. Various animal weapons are discussed throughout the lecture.

✗ [A] Quick evasion

   This is mentioned as a defense mechanism, but not as a weapon.

✓ [B] Toxins

   CORRECT. The presence of toxins in spines, in fangs, or even on the skin was discussed.

✓ [C] A poisonous sea anemone

   CORRECT. The example of the boxer crab using a poisonous sea anemone as a weapon was given.

✗ [D] Avoidance of detection

   This is mentioned as a defense mechanism, but not as a weapon.

✓ [E] Spines

   CORRECT. The example of the African crested porcupine using its spines to stab predators was given.

3.   According to the lecture, when do African crested porcupines attack?

   DETAIL. The professor notes that generally, African crested porcupines first attempt to "puff up," to appear larger than they are, in an attempt to scare off predators. If that doesn't work, the porcupine will attack the predator.

✗ (A) Only when faced with predators larger than themselves

   The size of the African crested porcupine is discussed, but not the size of its predators.

✗ (B) Only once they are fully grown

   The age at which the African crested porcupine attacks was not mentioned in the lecture.

✓ (C) When their attempts to scare a predator away fail

   CORRECT. The first defense is to puff up, in order to scare the predator away. If this does not work, they will attack.

✗ (D) Whenever they are startled by a potential predator

   The professor indicates that they generally attempt to scare the predator away first, by puffing up.

Track 110

NARRATOR: Why does the professor say this:

PROFESSOR: And, well… some animals have developed ways of fighting back or physically defending themselves when attacked. Some even have their own "weapons"… now what might those look like?

4.   **FUNCTION OF WHAT IS SAID.** In this quote, the professor explains the use of weapons by animals in self-defense. She then rhetorically asks what these weapons might look like, in order to pivot to introducing examples of such weapons.

    ✗   (A) To admit a flaw in her own logic   She is not pointing out any flaws in her own logic in this quote.

    ✗   (B) To express momentary confusion   The professor does not indicate any confusion in this quote.

    ✗   (C) To ask students to describe how animal weapons look   By asking "now what might those look like?", the professor is not actually inviting students to give a physical description of animal weapons. She is rhetorically introducing her next topic.

    ✓   (D) To introduce the next topic   **CORRECT.** The professor is asking the question rhetorically, as a way to introduce her next topic of discussion—some examples of animal weapons.

Track 111

NARRATOR: Why does the professor say this:

PROFESSOR: Here is something really fascinating though. There are a couple of animals that use other animals as weapons.

5.   **FUNCTION OF WHAT IS SAID.** In this quote, the professor is introducing an unusual concept—the use, by animals, of other animals as weapons.

    ✗   (A) To question whether a fascinating theory should be trusted   The professor is not discussing the issue of whether to trust this fascinating theory.

    ✗   (B) To emphasize the importance of further study in this area   She is not emphasizing any need for further study.

    ✗   (C) To explain how certain animals use fangs effectively   The professor has previously discussed fangs, and is now transitioning to a new topic.

    ✓   (D) To present an unexpected type of defense mechanism   **CORRECT.** The professor indicates that it is "fascinating," and thus unexpected, that some animals use other animals as a weapon.

Track 112

NARRATOR: Listen again to part of the lecture. Then answer the question.

PROFESSOR: Now, porcupines are herbivores… which means, well… they only eat plants. So the spines are clearly not for attacking prey. But they definitely know how to use them to defend themselves! When disturbed, the porcupine initially tries to "puff up" … to appear larger, to scare off the predator.

NARRATOR: What does the professor imply when she says this:

PROFESSOR: When disturbed, the porcupine initially tries to "puff up"… to appear larger, to scare off the predator.

6. **INFERENCE.** In this quote, the professor begins by talking about a porcupine's spines, but then says that "the porcupine initially tries to 'puff up'… to appear larger, to scare off the predator." The implication is that these porcupines will generally try to scare a predator away initially, and will only attack with their spines if that tactic fails.

✗ (A) The porcupine is typically successful at scaring off predators.

The degree of success of this initial tactic is not mentioned.

✗ (B) The porcupine prefers to escape detection or run away from predators

Escaping detection and running away are not mentioned as defense mechanisms used by the porcupine.

✓ (C) The porcupine is likely to attempt to scare a potential predator away before attacking.

CORRECT. In this quote, the professor indicates that the first line of defense is to "puff up" to scare the predator. The professor implies that the porcupine will only tend to attack if this scare tactic does not work.

✗ (D) The porcupine has few natural predators.

No information is given regarding the number of natural predators the porcupine has.

Answers and Explanations—12.5

Sunspots—Track 113

NARRATOR: Listen to part of a lecture in an astronomy class.

PROFESSOR: I want to relate a story about how astronomers began to solve a longstanding puzzle. For more than 1,000 years, astronomers observed a phenomenon, without knowing what it was. And even though today we can start to answer it, there are still lingering questions. But what we know about this phenomenon started with the creation of the telescope. So imagine you were an early astronomer, and you have just created one of the first telescopes. Tell me, what would you be interested in observing? Anyone?

FEMALE STUDENT: The Moon…

PROFESSOR: Right…

MALE STUDENT: And, maybe, the motion of the planets?

PROFESSOR: Yes…

FEMALE STUDENT: Stars.

PROFESSOR: Okay. What else? What about something you see every day? How about the Sun? I'm sure you've heard of something called *sunspots*. Well, so had astronomers at the time. They just didn't know what they were.

You can see sunspots by looking carefully towards the Sun. They are areas that are darker than the rest of the Sun. They can look black, but really they're just dark relative to the bright Sun surrounding them. Because the largest ones are visible without a telescope, they have been documented since the year 807 CE, and probably seen even before that. Sunspots can appear for hours, or even days. Some years a lot of sunspots are observed, and other years it's hard to find even one.

What could these mysterious dark spots be? At the time, the school of thought founded by Aristotle claimed that the heavens—what we now think of as outer space—were unchanging. So, this school of thought believed the Sun couldn't be changing. Instead, these dark spots were simply satellites of the Sun, and we observed them when their revolution brought them between the Sun and the Earth. But others believed that these were actually spots on the Sun that appeared and disappeared.

Which of these two theories, at least initially, was more believable?

MALE STUDENT: The satellite theory.

PROFESSOR: And why?

MALE STUDENT: Well, most people probably believed the Sun couldn't change. And the satellite theory supported that, right?

PROFESSOR: Right. But there was still some debate. Christoph Scheiner was one of the first to hypothesize that sunspots were satellites—and he wrote to Galileo Galilei asking for his input. Galileo thought that these sunspots appeared on the Sun. There were several letters back and forth in which these two astronomers debated their theories. These letters were published in newspapers, so the public could evaluate both sides. Both men were using telescopes to observe sunspots, and for the most part, they agreed on what they were observing. But they disagreed on what it meant.

But what could be done to resolve the debate? How can you measure something so far away? Any thoughts? Jamie?

FEMALE STUDENT: Well, what about watching the movement of the sunspots? Because, if a sunspot is orbiting the Sun, we should be able to watch its revolution.

PROFESSOR: Yes, but there's an issue. The Sun itself is rotating, and the sunspots themselves would therefore move across the surface of the Sun. So if you see a sunspot that migrates from one end of the Sun the other, it can mean a few things.

FEMALE STUDENT: Oh… it could be a satellite or not.

PROFESSOR: And it's hard to tell which. But Galileo had an idea. Instead of just making observations, he tracked the sunspots at particular times of the day to see whether a regular revolution was occurring. Without going too much into the details, he found pretty good evidence that the sunspots were not orbiting, but were appearing and disappearing.

So what do you think Scheiner's reaction was?

MALE STUDENT: Well, he could have changed his mind, or maybe he was just stubborn.

PROFESSOR: Right. Fortunately, Galileo's and Scheiner's letters were very polite and collegial, so when Galileo presented what was nearly irrefutable evidence that the sunspots were on the Sun, Scheiner changed his mind. He began publishing articles which suggested that, in fact, the heavens could change. That they weren't perfect.

So there are two lessons to take from this. One is that collaboration is essential. In science, you have to keep testing and challenging your theories, and one of the best ways to do that is to work with somebody who has a different opinion. Two is that you want to keep an open mind. Sometimes the assumptions we hold are false.

Now, another reason why I brought this up today is that there is still debate surrounding sunspots. During years when there are fewer sunspots… it tends to produce a cooling effect on the Earth. Years with more sunspots cause higher temperatures. And there is evidence that the Sun is about to enter a period of fewer sunspots.

How does that impact our debate? Well, think about global climate change. There's intense debate about what causes it. And if the Sun itself is going to change in a way that affects the global temperature, it will be much harder to argue with certainty what is causing the climate to change, and to what degree.

1. What is the lecture primarily about?

GIST-CONTENT. The professor is discussing a debate about sunspots and the eventual consensus that was reached about what they are.

✓ (A) How astronomers debated and found the correct interpretation for an observed phenomenon

CORRECT. The lecture focuses on the debate about sunspots. It was eventually determined that they are darker spots on the surface of the Sun, not orbiting satellites blocking parts of the Sun.

✗ (B) The discovery of various underlying causes of an astronomical phenomenon

There was no discovery of "various" causes of the astronomical phenomenon. The debate was about what might cause the appearance of dark areas on or in front of the Sun. But there was only one cause that was finally determined: actual sunspots on the Sun itself. As for the underlying cause or causes of those spots on the Sun itself, the lecture never discusses the issue.

✗ (C) What astrologers first saw when they began to use telescopes

There's no mention of what astronomers first saw using telescopes.

✗ (D) An unresolved question about a phenomenon originally observed less than 1,000 years ago

The question about what sunspots represent has been resolved. Also, the professor indicates that sunspots were first observed more than 1,000 years ago.

2. According to the lecture, how did sunspots appear to early astronomers?

    ✗ (A) Like orbiting bodies

    ✓ (B) Like dark areas

    ✗ (C) Like short flares of light

    ✗ (D) Like brighter regions

DETAIL. The professor indicates that sunspots were first observed as dark areas on the Sun's surface.

This was a theory to explain what early astronomers saw, not a description of what they saw.

CORRECT. The professor describes sunspots as dark areas on the Sun's surface.

This idea is not mentioned in the lecture.

This idea is not mentioned in the lecture.

3. What does the professor imply was a consideration that may have led to Scheiner's initial interpretation of sunspots?

    ✗ (A) An observation of numerous satellites orbiting the Sun

    ✗ (B) A centuries-old understanding of sunspots

    ✓ (C) A belief that the heavens could not change

    ✗ (D) An analogy drawn from observations of other stars

INFERENCE. Scheiner theorized that sunspots were caused by bodies orbiting the Sun. The professor implies that this theory was fed by the Aristotelian belief that the heavens were unchanging.

These satellites were theorized, but never observed.

The earliest theory mentioned regarding the source of sunspots is Scheiner's theory.

CORRECT. Scheiner originally theorized that sunspots were caused by bodies orbiting the sun. This rejected the idea that sunspots existed on the surface of the sun. The professor implies that Scheiner's theory was fed by the Aristotelian belief that the heavens were unchanging.

Observations of other stars are not discussed in the lecture.

Track 114

NARRATOR: Listen again to part of the lecture. Then answer the question.

PROFESSOR: So, this school of thought believed the sun couldn't be changing. Instead, these dark spots were simply satellites of the Sun, and we observed them when their revolution brought them between the Sun and the Earth. But others believed that these were actually spots on the sun that appeared and disappeared.

Which of these two theories, at least initially, was more believable?

MALE STUDENT: The satellite theory.

PROFESSOR: And why?

NARRATOR: Why does the professor say this:

PROFESSOR: And why?

4. **FUNCTION OF WHAT IS SAID.** In this quote, the professor describes the two theories about sunspots, and asks the class which of the theories was more believable at the time.

   ✗   (A) To correct a different student's error

There are no other students involved in this discussion.

   ✓   (B) To encourage the student to elaborate on his answer

CORRECT. The student is correct, the professor is simply looking for more detail.

   ✗   (C) To help the student recognize an error he has made

On the contrary, the student is correct. The professor simply wants the student to elaborate on why he answered as he did.

   ✗   (D) To help the professor understand what this student meant.

The student's meaning was clear to the professor.

5. According to the professor, what was a result of the debate between Galileo and Scheiner?

DETAIL. Scheiner's theory was proven incorrect. He therefore rejected his own theory and accepted Galileo's findings.

   ✓   (A) In the end, Scheiner rejected his original theory.

CORRECT. Galileo was able to prove his own theory, and through his letters, convinced Scheiner to change his mind.

   ✗   (B) The public began believing that the heavens were unchanging.

This was the original assumption behind Scheiner's theory. It was eventually refuted by Galileo's findings.

   ✗   (C) Later astronomers showed more interest in studying the surface of stars.

The professor does not mention this idea in the lecture.

   ✗   (D) Galileo became known as the foremost astronomer of his time.

The professor does not mention this idea in the lecture.

6. During a year in which the Sun has a large number of sunspots, what impact is felt on Earth?

DETAIL. The professor states that years with fewer sunspots have a cooling effect on the Earth, and that years "with more sunspots cause higher temperatures."

   ✗   (A) Sunspots will exhibit faster movement than usual.

The professor does not mention this idea in the lecture.

   ✗   (B) There will be less variation in global climate change.

The professor does not claim that an increase in the number of sunspots will reduce variation in global climate change. Instead, he argues that the variability caused by changes in sunspot activity makes determining the causes of climate change harder to separate and measure.

   ✗   (C) There will be more satellites between the Earth and the Sun.

This choice aligns with Schreiner's original theory, which was proven false.

   ✓   (D) Temperatures on Earth will be higher than normal.

CORRECT. As the professor notes, "more sunspots cause higher temperatures."

Answers and Explanations—12.6

The Gale Crater—Track 115

NARRATOR: Listen to part of a lecture in an astronomy class.

PROFESSOR: This semester, we've been talking about the pros and cons of exploring Mars. We already know that it would be expensive, the practical benefits are uncertain, and it could be very dangerous. But, um… there are a lot of reasons to explore Mars. Let's start with the Gale Crater. The Gale Crater is a massive crater on the surface of Mars. It's somewhere between 3.5 and 3.8 billion years old. And right in the center of the Gale Crater is a huge mountain. Here's an image of both the mountain and the crater.

This image is an elevation map of the Gale Crater. The Mars rover *Curiosity* first landed on Mars in the Gale Crater, specifically in the oval you see there, and it has been maneuvering around it, taking samples and pictures. The picture you see has been, ah… color-coded to show the different elevations. Obviously, the crater isn't actually these colors, um, but it is easier to see the different elevations using this color-coded map. The deep blue shows the bottom of the crater… very low elevations. The orange-red in the center is the peak of the mountain, often referred to as Mount Sharp. Mount Sharp is approximately 5 kilometers high. This height is comparable to some of the Earth's taller mountains. The Gale Crater has a diameter of about 150 kilometers… it's a little bigger than Rhode Island and Connecticut combined.

Because both the crater and the mountain are so large and so old, they offer a huge amount of information to scientists. The mountain itself is made up of two different kinds of sediment. The base is mostly clay. Why? Well, the crater was originally made by a meteor hitting the surface of Mars. Some scientists theorize that the resulting crater filled with water, making it a giant lake, and this clay sediment comes from the lake bed. Above the clay, the sediment is composed of oxygen and sulfur-containing minerals. These are likely dirt and rocks that were blown into the crater by the wind after the lake dried up. Um, Lisa?

FEMALE STUDENT: How do they know that part came from the lake bed and part was just blown in?

PROFESSOR: Um, well, the form and composition of each rock depends on its environment. Y'know, there are some types of rocks that can only be formed in water, and some that can only be formed in the atmosphere. After analyzing the rock samples, um, much of the minerals in the higher portion of Mount Sharp can really only be formed by running water. Several areas on Mount Sharp look like ancient river and stream beds, which, um… would explain the origin of the oxygen and sulfur minerals.

MALE STUDENT: But if Mars had water, where is it now?

PROFESSOR: Most scientists theorize that the water evaporated into space. There is a study underway that would measure the elements in the atmosphere and compare them with the minerals on the ground. Scientists will be able to predict not only how much water was on the ground, but also when and how quickly it left the surface of the planet.

FEMALE STUDENT: But… I thought Mars didn't have an atmosphere?

PROFESSOR: It doesn't have much of one, that's true. The atmosphere on Mars has about 1 percent of the atmospheric pressure on Earth. But there's enough of it left that we can take measurements of the elements there.

MALE STUDENT: Why does all this ancient history matter? I mean, shouldn't we be studying the Earth and not some distant planet?

PROFESSOR: Oh, there's lots we can learn from this. For instance, if Mars did have water, it likely had it before Earth did. And that water might have supported life. Now, if it did, that means one of two things is true. Maybe the life that formed on Mars was the same as the life that formed on Earth, which means our ancestors—our bacterial ancestors—originally came from Mars, and arrived on Earth by meteors... so in a way, then we'd all be Martians. Or, maybe the life on Mars was different from ours. That would be definitive proof that we were not alone in the universe.

1.   What is the main purpose of the lecture?

GIST-PURPOSE. The professor discusses the Gale Crater, a feature of Mars that he believes is particularly interesting. He uses it as an example of why exploring Mars is worthwhile.

✗ (A) To explain why scientists disagree about the formation of Mount Sharp

Mount Sharp is discussed, but there is no disagreement mentioned about how it was formed.

✓ (B) To present a feature of Mars that should continue to be studied

CORRECT. The professor primarily focuses on discussing the Gale Crater, and Mount Sharp at the center of the crater. Early in the lecture, the professor cites the Gale Crater as a reason to continue to study Mars.

✗ (C) To describe the goals of the Mars rover *Curiosity*

Curiosity is being used to learn more about the Gale Crater, but the focus of the lecture is not *Curiosity's* goals.

✗ (D) To review the atmospheric conditions of Mars in an effort to track its water loss

This is mentioned as one of the goals of scientists studying the Gale Crater, but this is not the main focus of the lecture.

2.   What does the professor imply about the Mars rover *Curiosity*?

INFERENCE. *Curiosity* is the rover that is currently taking samples from and exploring the Gale Crater.

✗ (A) It took the first images of Mars's surface.

This idea is not mentioned in the lecture.

✗ (B) It uses both solar and wind energy.

The power source of *Curiosity* is not mentioned in the lecture.

✗ (C) It landed a great distance away from the Gale Crater.

On the contrary, the professor said that *Curiosity* landed within the Gale Crater.

✓ (D) It has the ability to take mineral samples.

CORRECT. The professor notes that *Curiosity* is "taking samples and pictures." Those samples are later described as being used for mineral analysis. The implication is that *Curiosity* must be capable of taking mineral samples.

3. Why is the image of the Gale Crater that the professor displays color-coded?

DETAIL. The professor states that it has been color-coded to make it easier for the students to see the different elevations of the crater and the mountain.

✗ (A) To illustrate that Mount Sharp is taller than any mountain on Earth

Nothing stated in the lecture supports this idea.

✗ (B) To compensate for the poor quality of images sent by *Curiosity*

The professor never mentions anything about the quality of images sent by *Curiosity*.

✓ (C) To indicate more clearly what areas of the crater are at a high elevation and what areas are at a low elevation

CORRECT. The professor says that "it is easier to see the different elevations using this color-coded map."

✗ (D) To prove that the crater was formed by a meteor impact

The professor does not claim that the color-coding is related to how the crater was formed.

4. Why does the professor mention the composition of Mount Sharp?

ORGANIZATION. The professor states that Mount Sharp has base consisting of clay and an upper layer consisting of oxygen and sulfur-containing minerals.

✗ (A) To explain how craters are formed

The professor doesn't talk about craters in general. His lecture is about the Gale Crater specifically.

✓ (B) To provide evidence to support theories about how it was created

CORRECT. Because the bottom layer is clay, it is theorized that there was an ancient lake in that location. The oxygen and sulfur-containing minerals suggest that dirt and rocks were later swept in by wind after the lake dried up.

✗ (C) To explain that clay is uncommon in mountains that are not formed from ancient lakes

This idea is not mentioned in the lecture.

✗ (D) To imply that Mount Sharp was formed at the same time as the Gale Crater

On the contrary, the professor states that the crater was possibly filled by an ancient lake at first, and that the mountain probably developed later.

12

5. Why does the professor believe that there may have once been water on Mars? *Choose 2 answers.*

✓ ☐A The clay sediment at the base of Mount Sharp could have come from an ancient lake bed.

✓ ☐B Some of the minerals on Mount Sharp can probably only be formed in the presence of running water.

✗ ☐C The atmosphere of Mars contains traces of water.

✗ ☐D *Curiosity* has found water molecules embedded in rocks within the Gale Crater.

DETAIL. The professor mentions that the Gale Crater was believed to be filled by a lake at one point, and that what appear to be ancient river beds are still present on the higher elevations of Mount Sharp.

CORRECT. A theorized ancient lake would imply that water was present on Mars at that time.

CORRECT. The professor notes this, and adds that there are also what appear to be ancient river and stream beds on the mountain.

According to the professor, the atmosphere of Mars still needs to be studied. He does not discuss the composition of Mars's atmosphere.

This is idea is not mentioned in the lecture.

Track 116

NARRATOR: Listen again to part of the lecture. Then answer the question.

MALE STUDENT: Why does all this ancient history matter? I mean, shouldn't we be studying the Earth and not some distant planet?

PROFESSOR: Oh, there's lots we can learn from this.

NARRATOR: What does the professor imply when he says this:

PROFESSOR: Oh, there's lots we can learn from this.

6. **INFERENCE.** The professor seems excited about the idea of what studying the Gale Crater might reveal.

✗ Ⓐ The student should be paying more attention to the lecture than he is.

✗ Ⓑ The push to explore other worlds has directly led to an improvement in technology on Earth.

✗ Ⓒ Without continuing to push the boundaries of knowledge, scientific progress will decline.

✓ Ⓓ Understanding the history of Mars may help reveal aspects of the Earth's history.

The professor is not criticizing the student. He is answering the student's question.

The professor does not mention or imply this idea.

The professor does not mention or imply this idea.

CORRECT. The professor goes on to give an example in which hypothetical life on Mars might lead to information about how life on Earth began.

Answers and Explanations—12.7

Taproots—Track 117

NARRATOR: Listen to part of a talk in a botany class.

PROFESSOR: OK. We've been discussing the various kinds of roots systems that plants have. We've even seen slides of some incredibly extensive roots that, I have to admit, are pretty cool. Now I want to talk about a particular type of root—the *taproot*. There have been some studies that are pretty eye opening. In the past, scientists thought that taproots—those long, thick roots that some plants have that grow straight down, you know—like beets or… or what else?

MALE STUDENT: Carrots. Maybe also, um, turnips and radishes, right?

PROFESSOR: Right. So the thought was that these taproots were there just to support other roots and store nutrients. A thick taproot would grow, then small branches would grow out of it, and smaller branches would come from those, and so on. The taproots were there to give the branches a base—the branches were what the plant really needed to get water and nutrients. So these scientists in North Carolina decided to investigate—to actually see what role taproots play. Normally, when we want to observe roots, where do we need to grow them?

FEMALE STUDENT: Um… in water so we can see them, right?

PROFESSOR: That's right. But these scientists had a problem. They wanted to watch the root system absorb water, and that's really hard to do if the plant's completely immersed in water. By the way, what's it called when a plant takes in water from its roots?

MALE STUDENT: Transpiration?

PROFESSOR: Transpiration… they transpire… basically, they drink. All living things need water, so transpiration is a crucial process. To study it, we need to limit the amount of water, so we can see the areas… the parts of the roots… that attract and absorb water. So this group decided to grow plants in sand. Any ideas why the scientists thought sand would be helpful?

FEMALE STUDENT: Well, sand doesn't hold on to water, right? That's why there aren't that many plants that can grow in deserts.

PROFESSOR: Exactly. So this group of scientists had complete control over how much water they added and how much water they removed. OK. So this group—this lab—started growing loblolly pine trees… these trees grow taproots when they're young… they started growing these pine trees in sand. They added water, waited for some of the water to be absorbed by the roots, then drained the excess water. They used magnetic resonance imaging—MRI—technology to image where in the plant the water was. I was so surprised by their results! Remember, taproots supposedly just add structure and store nutrients. They're thick—too thick, we thought, to help with transpiration. It's the branches that grow from them that were supposed bring water to the rest of the plant. I say supposedly, because… well, can you guess?

MALE STUDENT: Were the taproots holding the water?

PROFESSOR: Yes! At least it was mostly the taproots. Not only that, but it looked like there were particular compartments that were made to store water. Some areas of the taproot had more water and some had less… it's like it was made for this. But that's just water storage. We want to focus on transpiration… on the uptake of water from the environment. Since we've always thought that taproots were just there for

structure, maybe the transpiration actually occurs at the branches, and the water moves to the taproots where it gets stored. So if you removed all the branches, the plant should stop transpiring, right?

FEMALE STUDENT: Nope!

PROFESSOR: I think I heard the right answer. I can't fool you guys. The answer is a definitive no. This group removed the branches, and still saw the normal amount of transpiration and water storage occurring. So what can we conclude from this study?

MALE STUDENT: That the taproot is doing the transpiration!

PROFESSOR: Exactly. So taproots are far more important than we used to think. They help the plant get the water it needs, and maybe the nutrition as well.

1. What is the main topic of the lecture?	**GIST-CONTENT.** The professor starts by introducing and describing taproots. She then discusses an experiment that showed that taproots are involved in transpiration.
✗ (A) Variations in types of roots	Although two types of roots are discussed—taproots and branching roots—the focus of the lecture is on taproots, not on the differences between the types of roots.
✗ (B) Methods of transpiration	Transpiration is discussed in the lecture, but is a supporting detail to the main topic—the function of taproots.
✓ (C) The function of taproots	**CORRECT.** The experiment discussed at length in the lecture supports the idea that taproots are used for transpiration.
✗ (D) Improving the water intake of plants	This idea is not mentioned in the lecture.

Track 118

NARRATOR: Listen again to part of the lecture. Then answer the question.

PROFESSOR: In the past, scientists thought that taproots—those long, thick roots that some plants have that grow straight down, you know—like beets or… or what else?

NARRATOR: Why does the professor say this:

PROFESSOR: … like beets or… or what else?

2. **FUNCTION OF WHAT IS SAID.** The professor pauses in the middle of listing examples of taproots to see whether the students can provide additional examples of taproots.	
✓ (A) She wants to elicit examples from the students.	**CORRECT.** A student later continues the list of examples that the professor began.
✗ (B) She does not believe that taproots are common.	The professor does not believe that taproots are uncommon.
✗ (C) She is trying to trick her students by talking about other kinds of roots.	The professor is only discussing taproots. There is no indication that she is trying to trick her students.
✗ (D) She forgot what she was about to say.	There's no evidence to suggest that the professor forgot what she was about to say.

 MANHATTAN PREP

3.   The professor mentions that plant root systems are typically observed in water. Why does she mention this?

ORGANIZATION. The professor mentions that it would be difficult to track the water uptake in a root system if the roots were immersed in water.

✗   (A) To demonstrate that it doesn't matter what material plants are grown in

The opposite is true. For the purposes of the experiment, immersing the taproots in water would make it difficult to study the water uptake of the plant's roots.

✓   (B) To explain why the typical setup for this type of experiment would not work in this case

CORRECT. The experimenters decided to grow their plants in sand rather than water, because immersing the plants in water would make it difficult to study the water uptake of the plant's roots.

✗   (C) To remind students of the importance of using the scientific method

This not the purpose of the professor mentioning that plant root systems are typically observed in water.

✗   (D) To reinforce the point that taproots are generally used to store nutrients.

This fact has nothing to do with whether the experiment should feature plants immersed in water.

4.   According to the professor, why did the researchers grow a species of pine trees in sand?

DETAIL. In this experiment, researchers wanted to observe water uptake in different parts of the root system. The advantage of using sand is that it does not hold on to water.

✗   (A) To add specific fertilizer types

The professor does not mention fertilizers in the lecture.

✗   (B) To remove the branching roots

While this procedure was performed later in the experiment, it is not why the researchers grew the pine trees in sand.

✓   (C) To monitor the intake of water

CORRECT. Sand allowed the scientists to control the level of water present outside the root, making it easier to observe water uptake in different parts of the root system.

✗   (D) To control the size of the taproot

This idea is not mentioned in the lecture.

5.   According to the professor, what similarity exists between loblolly pines and carrot plants?

DETAIL. Loblolly pines were used in the main experiment discussed in the lecture. Carrots were given as an example of a taproot.

✗   (A) Both can be grown in sand.

The professor doesn't claim that carrots can be grown in sand.

✗   (B) Both have been extensively studied.

The professor doesn't make this claim about either plant.

✗   (C) Both rely exclusively on branching roots for transpiration.

The loblolly pines are shown to rely on taproots for transpiration, not branching roots.

✓   (D) Both use taproots to absorb water.

CORRECT. Both plants have taproots, and according to the professor, the experiment demonstrated that taproots are used for transpiration.

Track 119

NARRATOR: Listen again to part of the lecture. Then answer the question.

PROFESSOR: OK. So this group—this lab—started growing loblolly pine trees… these trees grow taproots when they're young… they started growing these pine trees in sand. They added water, waited for some of the water to be absorbed by the roots, then drained the excess water. They used magnetic resonance imaging—MRI—technology to image where in the plant the water was. I was so surprised by their results! Remember, taproots supposedly just add structure and store nutrients.

NARRATOR: Why does the professor say this:

PROFESSOR: Remember, taproots supposedly just add structure and store nutrients.

6.   **FUNCTION OF WHAT IS SAID.** In this quote, the professor is describing the experiment that determined that taproots are involved in transpiration. By emphasizing that taproots were believed to be limited in function, she is implying that the experiment produced an unexpected result.

✗ (A) To imply that the conclusions reached by the lab were incorrect

The professor agrees with the conclusions of the lab. She just finds them surprising.

✗ (B) To emphasize that structure and storage are the most important roles of a taproot

The professor never talks about which roles of a taproot are most important.

✓ (C) To indicate that the researchers discovered that taproots play a broader role than previously thought

CORRECT. In this quote, the professor is implying that the experiment discovered a previously unknown function of taproots.

✗ (D) To suggest that MRI technology was not the best tool for this lab to use

This idea is not mentioned in the lecture.

Answers and Explanations—12.8

Fungi and Plants—Track 120

NARRATOR: Listen to part of a lecture in an ecology class.

PROFESSOR: Mutualism is a relationship between two organisms in which both organisms benefit in some way. They may share resources—one may provide water while the other provides food. For example, our bodies have bacteria in our guts that break down food and provide us with essential vitamins and nutrients, while the bacteria is nourished by that very food. Let's take what you read for this week and see if we can apply mutualism to it. Who can give me a couple of examples of mutualism? Tom?

MALE STUDENT: Well, uh, how about fungus… plants and fungus?

PROFESSOR: Good example. Please, go on.

MALE STUDENT: Well, like, the mycorrhiza… the symbiotic relationship between a fungus and a plant. There is a mutualistic relationship between the fungus and the plant, right?

PROFESSOR: Nice. Mycorrhiza is a mutualistic relationship that exists between fungi and a vast majority of plant species on Earth. Good. Can you name another kind of mutualistic relationship that a plant can have with a fungus?

FEMALE STUDENT: OK, well, I'm not sure if algae are plants or not… but don't fungi interact with algae? I think it's called a lichen.

PROFESSOR: And that relationship does what? Tell me more.

FEMALE STUDENT: The fungus needs food. So it benefits from the sugar that the algae create through photosynthesis. And then the algae benefit from the stable structure that the fungus provides through its, um… filaments.

PROFESSOR: Good. That's great. So now, let's return to the first kind of mutualism that Tom mentioned—the mycorrhizal relationship that exists between fungus and most of the Earth's plants. In this relationship, the fungus provides access to water, or moisture, because the fungus is highly absorbent. And also, it provides access to nutrients that aren't available to the plant unless the fungus is there. In exchange, the fungus receives carbohydrates from the plant. So what do you think happens if you own a plant, and you give your plant soil and water? If there is fungus in the soil, will it still have a mutualistic relationship with the plant?

FEMALE STUDENT: Well, not necessarily. It won't if the plant no longer needs to have a mutualistic relationship with the fungus, because it's already being provided water and nutrients.

PROFESSOR: OK, good. So this is a great example of how humans can alter relationships and ecosystems—by changing the relationships between organisms, including microorganisms. Hypothetically, what might happen if we created a product that killed all fungi?

MALE STUDENT: Maybe a lot of plants would die?

PROFESSOR: Maybe. Or at least, they'd have to find another way to obtain the water and nutrients that the fungi were making available to them. Let's move on… what other kinds of relationships can exist between organisms? We've talked about mutualism… there were two more kinds of relationships mentioned in your reading this week.

MALE STUDENT: Commensalism and parasitism.

PROFESSOR: Can you define those terms for me? And maybe give an example of each, please?

MALE STUDENT: Commensalism is when one organism benefits without harming or helping the other one. So an example would be, um, those fish that ride on sharks. The sharks provide the fish with transportation, but the fish don't hurt or help the sharks. And parasitism is when an organism benefits at the expense of the other. So one organism is getting something out of the relationship, which harms the other. An example of that… hmm… well, like a bad bacteria? In humans? Anything that would make you sick, I guess. Say, malaria.

PROFESSOR: Nice work. So to sum up what we covered today, when we're looking at how organisms relate, it's important not to see microorganisms like bacteria or fungi as all good or all bad. It depends on the nature of their interactions, and many of those relationships are necessary for the survival of entire species. In this way they're actually—they can be—critical to maintaining ecological balance.

1.   What does the class mainly discuss?

   ✗ (A) How fungi choose certain plants with which to form mutualistic relationships

   ✗ (B) The impact that human beings have on plant life

   ✗ (C) The role of a particular plant species in an ecosystem

   ✓ (D) How organisms in an ecosystem are affected by one another

GIST-CONTENT. The class discusses three different kinds of relationships that organisms can have with one another—mutualism, commensalism, and parasitism.

The professor does not cover differences among specific plants, or fungi choosing among these plants.

This issue is discussed in an example given in the lecture, but it is not the main focus of discussion.

The discussion is not about a particular plant species.

CORRECT. The discussion is about the ways in which organisms in an ecosystem can affect each other.

2.   According to the professor, which of the following is true of the mycorrhizal relationship between fungi and plants?

   ✗ (A) It is uncommon in plant life.

   ✓ (B) The mycorrhizal relationship is widespread among the Earth's plants.

   ✗ (C) The mycorrhizal relationship between fungi and plants is not well understood.

   ✗ (D) The fungi not involved in a mycorrhizal relationship die more readily.

DETAIL. The professor states that the mycorrhizal relationship exists between fungi and "a vast majority" of the world's plants.

The opposite is true. The professor states that this relationship exists between fungi and "a vast majority" of the world's plants.

CORRECT. The phrase "a vast majority" means that the phenomenon is widespread.

The professor does not suggest this in the lecture.

The professor does not suggest this in the lecture.

3.   Which of the following is an example of mutualism?

   ✗ (A) Fungi and plants occupying separate environments in an ecosystem.

   ✗ (B) Plants benefit from the presence of fungi, but fungi do not benefit from the presence of plants.

   ✗ (C) Plants provide oxygen to fungi, while the fungi provide benefits to a different organism.

   ✓ (D) Plants provide carbohydrates to fungi, while the fungi provide plants with access to water and nutrients.

DETAIL. According to the professor, mutualism is a relationship between two organisms in which both organisms benefit from the relationship.

This is not an example of mutualism.

This is an example of commensalism, not mutualism.

This three-part relationship is not an example of mutualism.

CORRECT. This is an example of mutualism that is discussed in the lecture.

 MANHATTAN PREP

4. According to the professor, what is a possible impact of human behavior on ecosystems?

DETAIL. The professor states that human behavior can affect the balance of ecosystems by influencing the relationships between other organisms.

✓ (A) It can influence relationships between other organisms.

CORRECT. The example the professor gives is of a human providing a plant with soil and water. She notes that this can influence the relationship between the plant and fungi in the soil.

✗ (B) It often leads to the destruction of entire ecosystems.

The professor does not indicate anything this extreme in the lecture.

✗ (C) It is the cause of an overall decrease in biodiversity.

This idea is not mentioned in the lecture.

✗ (D) It can encourage new species to develop.

This idea is not mentioned in the lecture.

Track 121

NARRATOR: Listen again to part of the lecture. Then answer the question.

PROFESSOR: So this is a great example of how humans can alter relationships and ecosystems—by changing the relationships between organisms, including microorganisms. Hypothetically, what might happen if we created a product that killed all fungi?

NARRATOR: Why does the professor say this:

PROFESSOR: Hypothetically, what might happen if we created a product that killed all fungi?

5. Why does the professor say this?

FUNCTION OF WHAT IS SAID. In this quote, the professor discusses human intervention in a relationship between organisms. She mentions this in order to invite the students to consider one possible outcome of this intervention.

✗ (A) To suggest that human beings are rarely destructive toward plants

The professor does not suggest this in the highlighted quote.

✗ (B) To defend human behavior with regard to caring for plants

The professor does not suggest this in the highlighted quote.

✓ (C) To introduce a theoretical situation for the purpose of discussion

CORRECT. The word "hypothetical" means it has not happened, although it could.

✗ (D) To illustrate a way human behavior might benefit plants

Nothing in the lecture suggests that this hypothetical situation might *benefit* plants.

Track 122

NARRATOR: Listen again to part of the lecture. Then answer the question.

PROFESSOR: Hypothetically, what might happen if we created a product that killed all fungi?

MALE STUDENT: Maybe a lot of plants would die?

PROFESSOR: Maybe. Or at least, they'd have to find another way to obtain the water and nutrients that the fungi were making available to them.

NARRATOR: What does the professor imply when she says this:

PROFESSOR: Or at least, they'd have to find another way to obtain the water and nutrients that the fungi were making available to them.

6. What does the professor imply when she says this?

   ✗ (A) Plants would benefit from humans in lieu of fungi.

   ✗ (B) The death of plants would cause land to become uninhabitable for humans.

   ✓ (C) The elimination of fungi could damage plants, unless plants find another source of nutrition.

   ✗ (D) The most efficient way to destroy plants is to remove fungi from their habitats.

INFERENCE. In this quote, the professor suggests that killing fungi could have a negative impact on plants. This could especially be true in the absence of an alternative source of water and nutrients.

The professor's statement does not imply that plants would benefit from humans in any way.

Nothing in the lecture suggests this possibility.

CORRECT. The professor implies that killing fungi could indirectly cause damage to plants that depend upon fungi for water and nutrients.

The professor does not suggest anything about the efficiency of different methods of destroying plants.

Answers and Explanations—12.9

Primates and Taboos—Track 123

NARRATOR: Listen to part of a lecture in a biology class.

PROFESSOR: OK, last time we discussed the way in which "taboos" are maintained among humans… We know that taboos are behaviors that are prohibited by social custom or by culture. And in humans, it is believed that taboos against incest help prevent inbreeding. Today, I'd like to look at–at how other primates that are not humans prevent, um… mating within the same gene pool… um, yes, Lucas?

MALE STUDENT: Pardon me, professor, but when you talk about mating within the same gene pool, do you mean like, two members of the species reproducing, or—

PROFESSOR: OK, OK, let's hold up for a second—two organisms that are capable of reproducing fertile, viable offspring—meaning they can have offspring that can also have offspring—belong to the same species by definition, right? That is the definition of a species.

MALE STUDENT: Oh, sorry… right. But then in that case, could you clarify what you mean?

PROFESSOR: Of course. We know that genetic variation is important to a species's ability to survive and thrive. Diversity is… it's important. OK? So we know that much. And we know that inbreeding, which refers to breeding among individuals who are closely related genetically… this does not contribute to diversity.

Among humans, there are cultural taboos that may help prevent inbreeding. We've been talking about how taboos guide behavior, and what function they serve in this regard. And taboos are cultural phenomena. That's why they vary from culture to culture. But other primates—like, say, chimpanzees—don't have culture. Which means they can't rely on the same kind of social pressures, such as taboos, that humans, uh… use. So how do chimps ensure that inbreeding does not lead to a deficiency in genetic diversity? What kind of behaviors would help with this? We're talking about behaviors here. Karen?

FEMALE STUDENT: Maybe it has something to do with how they form groups? Um…

PROFESSOR: OK, that's close to what—

FEMALE STUDENT: I mean, I'm thinking, like, about how we learned earlier in this course that male monkeys, like… leave their group when they are pretty young so that they end up mating with female monkeys from a different group. I'm pretty sure that is how it works.

PROFESSOR: OK, I see what you're saying, and you're somewhat correct. There are some species of monkeys in which a young, mature monkey will be driven from his group to join another group, or form a new group of his own. In other kinds of primates, it's the females who leave the group upon reaching reproductive maturity. This kind of splintering is fairly common… it's, well, we can think of it simply as physical separation. So, we're talking about physical separation from closely related genetic conspecifics—for those who don't know, that means, members of the same species. Conspecifics. Conspecifics sometimes disperse. And this kind of physical separation is one way that inbreeding is prevented among primates.

Another way involves behaviors that occur within a group. If we are talking about apes, for example… we see that all adult apes are dominant over all juvenile apes. This is true regardless of the gender of the apes. So whether the adult ape is male or female, they're still dominant over the juveniles. You know what I mean by "dominant," right? It's a superior standing within a social hierarchy, and it forms a kind of barrier to certain forms of inbreeding. Because of hormones, which are a vital part of reproduction, male apes of subordinate status are usually unable to reproduce with dominant females.

Hormones are also very important in enabling a more general kind of suppression—reproductive suppression, which is when members of a species that can reproduce are actually prevented from doing so because of stimuli within the group that are somehow suppressing their breeding. Sometimes this is useful because it can prevent them from inbreeding if, say, the only potential mates available are too closely related to them, genetically. It can ensure that the timing of their reproductive activity is in line with having genetically different mating partners. What's really fascinating is that even though we wouldn't say that non-human primates, like apes and monkeys, have "culture," what this shows is that they can often still rely on social cues to deter certain behaviors, much like human cultures rely on taboos.

1. What does the professor mainly talk about?

    ✗ (A) The types of signals used by humans to prevent inbreeding

    ✗ (B) How animals reproduce

    ✓ (C) The mechanisms primates use to prevent inbreeding

    ✗ (D) The findings of a study on how mammals prevent inbreeding

GIST-CONTENT. The professor mainly discusses how inbreeding is prevented among primates other than human beings.

The focus of the lecture is non-human primates, not humans.

The lecture is not about how animals reproduce, in general. It is about mechanisms to prevent inbreeding.

CORRECT. This choice accurately summarizes the main topic of the lecture.

The lecture is about how non-human primates avoid inbreeding in general. It is not about a specific study on that topic.

2. Why does the student mention that male monkeys leave their group when they are young?

    ✗ (A) To point out ways in which young male monkeys are similar to young male humans

    ✓ (B) To mention a behavior she knows of that can prevent inbreeding in monkeys

    ✗ (C) To explain why she is majoring in biology

    ✗ (D) To demonstrate that she knows how inbreeding is prevented in non-primates

ORGANIZATION. The student is providing an example of a method by which monkeys prevent inbreeding among conspecifics.

The student does not make this comparison.

CORRECT. The student is providing an example of a method by which monkeys prevent inbreeding.

The student does not state that she is majoring in biology.

This is not the student's purpose, as monkeys are primates.

3. What is the professor's attitude toward the social cues that non-human primates use to prevent certain behaviors?

    ✗ (A) She believes that these social cues have not been adequately researched.

    ✗ (B) She believes that these social cues are ineffective.

    ✗ (C) She finds them distinctly different from taboos among humans.

    ✓ (D) She finds them similar in function to human taboos.

SPEAKER'S ATTITUDE. In her lecture, the professor notes that social cues among non-human primates function similarly to the way taboos do among humans.

This idea is not mentioned in the lecture.

Nothing in the lecture suggests that the professor believes this.

The opposite is true. The professor believes that these social cues function in ways that are similar to taboos among humans.

CORRECT. The professor explicitly states this near the end of the lecture.

4. According to the professor, which of the following is a way that some apes prevent inbreeding?

DETAIL. The professor mentions physical separation, dominance, and general reproductive suppression as ways that non-human primates prevent inbreeding.

  ✗ (A) Abstention from mating

This idea is not mentioned in the lecture.

  ✗ (B) Mating outside of their species

Apes mate outside of their *social groups*. According to the professor, animals are not capable of successfully mating and reproducing outside of their species.

  ✓ (C) Social dominance

CORRECT. Social dominance is mentioned as a method used to prevent inbreeding.

  ✗ (D) Cultural taboos

Humans, not apes, use cultural taboos to prevent inbreeding.

5. The professor discusses hormones in two contexts. What are they? *Choose 2 answers.*

DETAIL. The professor discusses hormones in relation to social dominance, and more generally, as a method of suppressing certain reproductive behaviors.

  ✓ [A] Dominance

CORRECT. The professor mentions hormones in her discussion of social dominance among apes.

  ✗ [B] Taboo development

The professor discusses hormones within the context of non-human primates. Taboos apply only to humans.

  ✗ [C] Physical separation

The professor does not discuss hormones in relation to physical separation, which is a separate method of preventing inbreeding.

  ✓ [D] Reproductive behavior

CORRECT. The professor discusses hormones in relation to the circumstances under which reproductive behavior is stimulated or suppressed.

Track 124

NARRATOR: Listen again to part of the lecture. Then answer the question.

PROFESSOR: Today I'd like to look at–at how other primates that are not humans prevent, um… mating within the same gene pool… um, yes, Lucas?

MALE STUDENT: Pardon me, professor, but when you talk about mating within the same gene pool, do you mean like, two members of the species reproducing, or—

PROFESSOR: OK, OK, let's hold up for a second—

NARRATOR: Why does the professor say this:

PROFESSOR: OK, OK, let's hold up for a second—

6.   Why does the professor say this?

    ✗ (A) To see whether other students agree or disagree with the student's response

    ✓ (B) To express that the student has misunderstood an important concept

    ✗ (C) To indicate that the student has frustrated her by failing to do the assigned reading

    ✗ (D) To ascertain whether she is understanding the student's point correctly or not

FUNCTION OF WHAT IS SAID. In this quote, the professor stops a student from continuing, because the student has misunderstood an important concept.

This is not the professor's purpose in interrupting the student.

CORRECT. The professor goes on to clarify that by saying "within the same gene pool," she does not mean "within the same species."

The professor does not express frustration or mention any failure to complete an assignment.

The professor does not give any indication that she may have misunderstood the student's point.

Answers and Explanations—12.10

Cepheid Variables—Track 125

NARRATOR: Listen to part of a lecture in an astronomy class.

PROFESSOR: Astronomy is, in many ways, an amalgamation—a mixture—of many different sciences. Astronomers can measure the distance of a few nearby stars using simple math, specifically, um… trigonometry and geometry. As the Earth revolves around the Sun… we can track changes in the relative position of a single star in the night sky. And geometry will allow us to use those changes to calculate the distance from the Earth to that star. This method works for anything within about 500 light-years of Earth. A light-year is exactly what it sounds like… the distance light can travel in one year, which is far—over 9 trillion kilometers!

Beyond 500 light-years, astronomers use spectroscopy… which, in this case, is the study of the light from stars. They can use spectroscopy to measure the different wavelengths of radiation—of light—coming from the star. Based on the wavelengths, we determine the temperature, size, and distance from Earth. This covers stars up to about 160,000 light-years away. But what about beyond that? The key is *Cepheid variables*. But let's back up a bit before we dive into what those are.

OK, picture a set of mountains you're looking at from a great distance. Some of the mountains are closer to you, and some are farther away. How might you tell which ones are the closest and which are the farthest?

FEMALE STUDENT: What about comparing the sizes? The ones that look smallest are really far away, right?

PROFESSOR: It's certainly possible. But those mountains might actually be smaller. You'd have to know which ones are smaller to begin with before you can compare the distance. Astronomers had the same problem. A nearby star should look brighter than a distant star. But what if one is *naturally* brighter than the other? If the farther star is more *luminous*, or intrinsically, inherently brighter, it could appear to us that the two stars are the same brightness, right? Then we'd incorrectly assume they're the same distance away.

Because I know you've all done the assigned homework, I know you already have a suspicion of how astronomers solved this. What did Henrietta Leavitt determine in the early 1900s?

MALE STUDENT: Didn't she find pulsing stars? And she used that to figure out distances?

PROFESSOR: You're right, but it's a bit more complicated than that. Leavitt's focus was the Cepheid variable stars—what you called "pulsing stars." A Cepheid variable is a type of star that is very near death. We'll cover the science of that in a later class, but for now we'll focus on the pulsing of this type of star. A Cepheid variable has lots of the gas… helium. And when that helium gets hot—very, very hot—it expands, and the star gets brighter. As it continues to expand, the helium gets farther away from the center of the star, which cools it down. This causes the star to contract and dim. But that makes the helium heat again, so the star re-expands… and contracts, then expands, and… well, I'm sure you see the pattern here. From Earth, this looks like this star is pulsing. If you charted the brightness over time, it would look something like this.

Notice that the time it takes to expand and contract repeats itself… that's the period of the star… it's always the same! How does this regular pattern help us determine its distance from Earth?

FEMALE STUDENT: Didn't the book say that the longer the period, the brighter the star was? Now you can calculate the actual brightness of the star, right?

PROFESSOR: That's right! So if astronomers compare two Cepheid variables that, from Earth, look equally bright, but one has a longer pulsing period than the other, they'll know that the stars aren't *actually* equally bright. The one with the longer period is actually more *luminous*, inherently. They only appear the same because the one that's more luminous is farther away. Mathematically, we can determine the exact distance. So no matter how far away a star is, if there is a nearby Cepheid variable, we can find its distance from the Earth.

12

1.	What is the lecture primarily about?	**GIST-CONTENT.** The professor discusses Cepheid variables in order to explain to students how astronomers calculate a star's distance from the Earth.

✗ (A) Different methods to determine the helium content of a star

Helium is mentioned only to explain why Cepheid variables display the pulsing pattern that they do. The lecture does not discuss methods to measure helium content of a star.

✗ (B) How Henrietta Leavitt became a notable astronomer

The professor states that Leavitt's focus was Cepheid variables, which are important to astronomers, but does not mention whether she became a notable astronomer. Also, Leavitt is not the focus of the lecture.

✓ (C) How astronomers measure the distance between stars and the Earth

CORRECT. The lecture focuses primarily on one method of measuring distances—namely, the use of Cepheid variables. Spectroscopy, trigonometry, and geometry are also discussed as methods to compute stellar distances.

✗ (D) Why Cepheid variables display a pulsing pattern

The pulsing pattern of Cepheid variables helps astronomers to measure the distance between distant stars and the Earth. The professor explains why this pulsing pattern occurs, but this is only a supporting detail.

2. According to the professor, what is one application of spectroscopy?

DETAIL. The professor describes spectroscopy as one of the techniques scientists use to compute the distance between stars and the Earth.

✓ (A) To measure the distance between some stars and the Earth

CORRECT. Spectroscopy can be used to measure the distance to stars that are up to 160,000 light-years from the Earth.

✗ (B) To study the composition of nearby planets

This lecture exclusively talks about studying stars. Planets are not mentioned.

✗ (C) To determine the luminosity of a Cepheid variable

The professor relates the pulsing period of Cepheid variables to their luminosity. He does not suggest that spectroscopy could be used to measure luminosity.

✗ (D) To measure the lifespan of a star

The professor does not discuss any method to measure a star's lifespan.

Track 126

NARRATOR: Listen again to part of the lecture. Then answer the question.

PROFESSOR: The key is *Cepheid variables*. But let's back up a bit before we dive into what those are.

OK, picture a set of mountains you're looking at from a great distance. Some of the mountains are closer to you, and some are farther away. How might you tell which ones are the closest and which are the farthest?

NARRATOR: Why does the professor say this:

PROFESSOR: How might you tell which ones are the closest and which are the farthest?

3. **FUNCTION OF WHAT IS SAID.** Mountains are discussed as an analogy to help illustrate the idea that scientists need some understanding of a star's properties before they can measure its distance from the Earth.

✓ (A) He wants to start the explanation by using an analogous situation that is easy to understand.

CORRECT. Students are likely to have an easier time understanding how hard it would be to evaluate which mountain in a range is farthest away. This analogy facilitates the professor's explanation of the use of Cepheid variables.

✗ (B) He is using an example to prove that distance often cannot be precisely determined.

The professor does not suggest this. His lecture explains how absolute distances between stars and the Earth are measured.

✗ (C) He has gotten temporarily distracted by talking about mountains at various distances from an observer.

This topic of mountains is relevant because it is a helpful analogy. Nothing in the lecture suggests that the professor is distracted.

✗ (D) He believes that the methods used for measuring distances on Earth can be applied to stars.

The lecture does not support this idea. The methods used to measure stellar distances are different from those used to measure distances on the Earth.

Track 127

NARRATOR: Why does the professor say this:

PROFESSOR: Because I know you've all done the assigned homework, I know you already have a suspicion of how astronomers solved this.

4.   **FUNCTION OF WHAT IS SAID.** The professor has established that a star's brightness is not a reliable indicator of how far it is from the Earth. He is reminding students that they have already read that this problem was solved by using the pulsing periods of Cepheid variables—assuming that the students did the assigned reading.

    ✗   (A) To imply that he does not believe the students are doing their assigned work | It's unlikely that the professor believes this, because he later asks a question that students would likely only be able to answer by having done the assigned reading.

    ✓   (B) To indicate that his next question was answered in the assigned homework | **CORRECT.** The professor follows this quote with a question about a specific detail of the reading, which the students would likely only know if they had completed the assigned reading.

    ✗   (C) To emphasize the importance of understanding astronomers throughout history | This idea is not mentioned or suggested in the lecture.

    ✗   (D) To remind students about their upcoming homework assignments | The professor is not referring to upcoming homework. He is indicating that his next question was answered in previously assigned homework.

5.   What does the professor explain to one of the students about the term "pulsing star"? | **DETAIL.** The term "pulsing star" refers to a Cepheid variable. The professor builds on a student's answer to a question by explaining how Cepheid variables are used to measure distance between stars and the Earth.

    ✗   (A) It is a rather misleading term. | While the professor says that the answer is more complicated than it appears, the term itself is not misleading, because "pulsing stars" do in fact appear to pulse.

    ✗   (B) It is a term no longer used by astronomers. | The lecture does not state or imply that the term "pulsing star" is no longer used by astronomers.

    ✗   (C) It is a complete description of a phenomenon. | The opposite is true. The professor states that the situation is more complicated than the explanation given by the student.

    ✓   (D) It is another term for a Cepheid variable. | **CORRECT.** The professor states this in his explanation, and explains why Cepheid variables appear to "pulse."

6. What can be inferred about two Cepheid variables if their pulsing periods are the same?

INFERENCE. The professor uses the example of two Cepheid variables that appear to be equally bright, but have different pulsing patterns. The one with the longer period must actually be brighter inherently, and thus must be farther away. If Cepheid variable periods are the same, scientists can infer that their brightness is also the same.

✗ (A) They are the same distance from the Earth.

The pulsing pattern is proportional to luminosity, or inherent brightness—not to distance.

✓ (B) They have equal luminosities.

CORRECT. The pulsing period directly relates to a star's inherent brightness, or luminosity. Two stars with the same period must have the same luminosity, or true, inherent brightness.

✗ (C) They are likely to be difficult to tell apart.

This idea is not mentioned in the lecture.

✗ (D) They are approximately the same age.

The professor states that all Cepheid variables are near death, but doesn't give any information about determining their ages.

12

Chapter 13

Conversations A

In the Listening section, conversations test your ability to comprehend everyday spoken English. You'll listen to a short conversation (about 2 to 3 minutes long) between a student and someone else—a professor or another university staff member—about a campus situation. You will be able to listen to the conversation only once. You will not be able to pause the recording or to replay any part of it (though some questions will replay a specific part of the lecture for you). You can take notes as you listen.

You will then answer five questions for that conversation. Most questions are multiple-choice with four options (select one from A, B, C, or D). Some questions may ask you to select more than one option or to fill in a table. You will have to answer the questions in order. You cannot return to a question once you have moved on to the next question.

Conversations test your understanding of main ideas, contrasts, and the speaker's tone and attitude toward the topic. They also test your ability to compare and contrast information, understand cause and effect, make connections between different parts of the conversation, and make inferences or draw conclusions.

How should you use this chapter? Here are some recommendations, according to the level you've reached in TOEFL Listening:

1. **Fundamentals.** At first, listen to the conversation once, then work on the questions untimed and check the answer after each question. Review the solutions closely, think carefully about the principles at work, and articulate what you've learned. Redo questions as necessary. As you get better, time yourself and do all of the questions for a conversation at once, without stopping.

2. **Fixes.** Do an entire conversation and its associated questions under timed conditions. Don't replay any part of the conversation while you are still answering the questions! Examine the results, learn your lessons, then test yourself with another conversation and question set.

3. **Tweaks.** Confirm your mastery by doing two conversations (plus the associated questions) in a row under timed conditions. Work your way up to doing four lectures and two conversations in one sitting. Aim to improve the speed and ease of your process.

Good luck on Listening!

13.1

Listen to Track 128.

Now answer the questions.

1. Why does the student go to see the professor?

    (A) To find out about jobs in sustainable agriculture

    (B) To debate different sales channels that farmers can use

    (C) To get guidance on the topic of a project

    (D) To ask whether meal kit services are a good idea

2. In the brochure for the student's meal kit service, why do the farmers say they like to participate?

    (A) They made more money with the meal kit service than selling in a CSA.

    (B) They liked being able to grow unusual crops for customers.

    (C) They enjoyed supplying the right amounts of ingredients with little waste.

    (D) They loved being part of an innovative and growing sales channel.

3. Why does the professor mention his previous employment?

    (A) To support a statement the student made about jobs in agricultural science

    (B) To indicate that government jobs can lead to becoming a professor

    (C) To explain why the student should remain engaged in class conversations

    (D) To recommend that the student look for a position with the United States government

4. What does the professor imply about the farm near the university?

    (A) The farm prefers to supply local customers, such as restaurants.

    (B) At least some of the farm's workers studied at the university.

    (C) He helped the farm try different crop rotations to increase productivity.

    (D) People who work at the farm might have useful insights to share.

Listen to Track 129.

Now answer the question.

5. (A) The student has evidently not spent much time so far at the university.

    (B) The student has just been accepted into the broader world of academic research.

    (C) The problem that the student confronts is common in academic research.

    (D) The student should not complain about the challenges of narrowing down early-stage research.

13.2

 Listen to Track 130.

Now answer the questions.

1. Why does the student go to see the professor?

   (A) To ask the professor which high school class he should observe for his teacher observation assignment

   (B) To discuss which subject he might want to learn to teach

   (C) To ask about the professor's experience with teaching

   (D) To explain why he was absent from the last class

2. What does the professor suggest that the student do in order to decide which teacher to observe?

   (A) Observe a math class

   (B) Ask his sister which of her teachers she likes the best

   (C) Talk with another professor at the college

   (D) Talk with some of the teachers at the local high school

3. Why does the student mention that he was president of his high school math club?

   (A) To show that he likes math

   (B) To show that math is not difficult for him

   (C) To indicate that he does not want to observe a math class

   (D) To explain his interest in math

4. What does the professor want the student to learn from his teacher observation?

   (A) What the high school teachers will be teaching next week

   (B) How much money teachers get paid

   (C) Which subject the student might want to eventually teach

   (D) Why each teacher likes teaching

 Listen to Track 131.

Now answer the question.

5. (A) The professor is offering to arrange a discussion with the high school teachers.

   (B) The student should be careful about talking with the high school teachers.

   (C) The high school teachers will be happy to talk with the student about which class he should observe.

   (D) The high school teachers will not want to talk with the student.

13.3

 Listen to Track 132.

Now answer the questions.

1. Why does the student go to see the professor?
   - (A) To ask the professor where she should send her story for publication
   - (B) To ask about his experience getting his own story published
   - (C) To ask for the professor's advice about getting her first story published
   - (D) To tell the professor that her story has been published

2. What does the professor say is the first step the student should take?
   - (A) Research magazines that might publish her story.
   - (B) Call his friend at a magazine.
   - (C) Write a cover letter.
   - (D) Visit the website he showed in class.

3. What does the professor imply about some of his former students?
   - (A) They had good memories.
   - (B) They did not get their stories published.
   - (C) They did not ask for his advice.
   - (D) They failed to write cover letters.

4. What does the professor suggest that the student include in her cover letter? *Choose 2 answers.*
   - [A] That she has never been published before
   - [B] That she is a student
   - [C] Information about her story
   - [D] A list of magazines she thinks might publish her story

 Listen to Track 133.

Now answer the question.

5.
   - (A) It is hard for her to remember things.
   - (B) She applied to a large number of colleges.
   - (C) She wants to tell him which colleges she applied to.
   - (D) She has a good memory.

13.4

 Listen to Track 134.

Now answer the questions.

1. Why does the student go to the Bursar's office?

    (A) To update her email address

    (B) To ask why she is no longer enrolled in class

    (C) To register for class

    (D) To find out why her class was canceled

2. Why is the student no longer enrolled in class?

    (A) The class was canceled.

    (B) She didn't get an email reminder about the first class.

    (C) She failed to meet the prerequisites for the class.

    (D) She didn't pay for the class on time.

3. Why didn't the student know about the payment deadline?

    (A) She has been out of the country.

    (B) The Bursar's office sent the reminders about the payment deadline to her old apartment.

    (C) She didn't get the emails about the payment deadline.

    (D) The deadline was recently changed.

4. What does the receptionist suggest that the student do every semester?

    (A) Visit the Bursar's office in person.

    (B) Change her password.

    (C) Call to make sure she is enrolled in class.

    (D) Check the Bursar's office website for the payment deadline.

 Listen to Track 135.

Now answer the question.

5. (A) The student should update her email address herself.

    (B) The student should not provide her new email address.

    (C) The Bursar's office needs more than one email address from the student.

    (D) Reminders about the payment deadline will no longer be sent via email.

13.5

 Listen to Track 136.

Now answer the questions.

1. Why does the student go to see the professor?

   (A) To get help in understanding and overcoming unexpected trouble

   (B) To build a personal relationship in the hope that it will impact his grades

   (C) To discuss and debate the purpose of classes at different levels

   (D) To request a chance to retake a recent exam

2. What does the student imply about her experience with the "two totally different kinds of classes"?

   (A) She did not realize that both types of classes might be possible in the same subject area.

   (B) She has always earned much better grades in one type than in the other.

   (C) She was unaware of this distinction before university, but she is now benefiting from having learned about it.

   (D) At the university level, this is no longer a meaningful distinction.

3. According to the professor, how seriously will this exam affect the student's overall grade for the course, and why?

   (A) It will have a significant effect, since this is the only exam for the course.

   (B) It will have a significant effect, since this specific exam is weighted more heavily than the others.

   (C) It will have only a slight effect, since so many other items will also be included in the course grade.

   (D) It will probably have no effect at all, since it will likely be dropped entirely from the calculation.

4. Why does the professor mention that words and math tables are commonly memorized in elementary school?

   (A) To complain that today's university students are lacking certain extremely basic skills

   (B) To explain how many topics start as memorization and then move to problem-solving

   (C) To give examples of material at different levels of difficulty

   (D) To show that school courses have changed very little in the past several decades

5. Which of the following statements are true in the conversation you just heard? *Choose 2 answers.*

   A The student is too busy to study for her exams.

   B The student prepared for this exam in largely inappropriate ways.

   C The professor is personally disappointed in the student's performance.

   D Many other students performed as badly on this exam.

13

13.6

 Listen to Track 137.

Now answer the questions.

1. Why does the student go to the Student Health Clinic?
    - (A) To find out the requirements for joining the tennis team
    - (B) To obtain a physical exam from a doctor
    - (C) To get some tennis playing advice from a doctor
    - (D) To cancel the appointment he had made for that day

2. What does the student say about his teammates on the tennis team?
    - (A) They urged him to make an appointment sooner.
    - (B) They were supposed to have set up an appointment for him.
    - (C) They told him that the Student Health Clinic had great doctors.
    - (D) They thought the form could be filled out without an appointment.

3. Why doesn't the student set up an appointment for the following week?
    - (A) He needs to have his form signed sooner than that.
    - (B) He will be busy with tennis tryouts the following week.
    - (C) He decides to just get a physical from the tennis team's doctor instead.
    - (D) He forgot to bring his student ID, which is required to make an appointment.

4. How will the student attempt to get his form signed in time?
    - (A) By skipping the blood test
    - (B) By having the receptionist sign the form
    - (C) By hoping for a canceled appointment
    - (D) By scheduling an appointment online

 Listen to Track 138.

Now answer the question.

5. Why does the receptionist say this to the student?
    - (A) To accuse his teammates of playing a joke on him
    - (B) To warn him about the effects of getting older
    - (C) To tell him she will make an exception for him.
    - (D) To indicate that he received the wrong impression

13.7

 Listen to Track 139.

Now answer the questions.

1. What are the speakers mainly discussing?
    (A) How to become an Art College student
    (B) The artists featured in the library's collection
    (C) What is required for a student to be able to access the Art Library
    (D) The library's book borrowing policies

2. Why does the student become frustrated partway through the conversation?
    (A) She is told that she needs to pay a fee in order to access the library.
    (B) She discovers that the art collections are no longer at this library.
    (C) She learns that there are no art classes she can take.
    (D) She finds out that art students are not allowed to visit the main libraries.

3. What does the employee imply about the art students?
    (A) They have already paid for access to the Art Library in their school fees.
    (B) They are not allowed to visit the main libraries.
    (C) They spend most of their time off campus.
    (D) They don't usually use the Art Library.

4. Why does the student need to go to see the art professor?
    (A) To be interviewed for a project on art criticism
    (B) To get approved as a "visiting student"
    (C) To ask to join her art class
    (D) To complain that art students are coming to the main libraries

 Listen to Track 140.

Now answer the question.

5. (A) He needs the student to tell him where Kimmer Hall is.
    (B) He is trying to point out how far away Kimmer Hall is.
    (C) He wants to know if he needs to explain where Kimmer Hall is.
    (D) He is suggesting that the student should have been to Kimmer Hall already.

13.8

 Listen to Track 141.

Now answer the questions.

1. What do the speakers mainly discuss?

    (A) The food her family likes to cook

    (B) How the student can resolve a dispute with her sister

    (C) The student's relationship with her family

    (D) Different methods available for the student to travel home

2. Why does the student mention her four brothers and sisters?

    (A) To emphasize that she has a large and close family

    (B) To acknowledge that she is comfortable in large groups

    (C) To indicate that some of her siblings are planning on attending this university

    (D) To draw a contrast with other student's families

3. What does the student imply about family weekend?

    (A) It is an event that she will likely not be able to participate in.

    (B) It would allow her to see her family on a daily basis.

    (C) It would help take her mind off her problems about cooking.

    (D) It would be an opportunity to see her family sooner than expected.

4. What does the student imply about helping her sister learn to cook?

    (A) She was embarrassed because she taught an inaccurate cooking method.

    (B) She was upset because she didn't get a chance to finish teaching her sister.

    (C) She was confused by her mother's contradictory expectations.

    (D) She was disappointed that her sister was unable to learn as quickly as expected.

5. According to the counselor, what could the student do before family weekend? *Choose 2 answers.*

    A Do a video call with her mother

    B Write letters to her aunt

    C Watch movies with her siblings

    D Visit home more frequently

Answer Key—13.1

Question	Correct Answer	Right/Wrong	Category
1	C		Gist-purpose
2	B		Detail
3	A		Function of What Is Said
4	D		Inference
5	C		Function of What Is Said

Answer Key—13.2

Question	Correct Answer	Right/Wrong	Category
1	A		Gist-purpose
2	D		Detail
3	B		Function of What Is Said
4	C		Detail
5	C		Inference

Answer Key—13.3

Question	Correct Answer	Right/Wrong	Category
1	C		Gist-purpose
2	A		Detail
3	B		Inference
4	B, C		Detail
5	D		Function of What Is Said

Answer Key—13.4

Question	Correct Answer	Right/Wrong	Category
1	B		Gist-purpose
2	D		Detail
3	C		Connecting Content
4	D		Detail
5	A		Function of What Is Said

Answer Key—13.5

Question	Correct Answer	Right/Wrong	Category
1	A		Gist-purpose
2	A		Inference
3	D		Detail
4	B		Function of What Is Said
5	B, D		Detail

Answer Key—13.6

Question	Correct Answer	Right/Wrong	Category
1	B		Gist-purpose
2	D		Detail
3	A		Detail
4	C		Connecting Content
5	D		Function of What Is Said

Answer Key—13.7

Question	Correct Answer	Right/Wrong	Category
1	C		Gist-content
2	A		Speaker's Attitude
3	A		Inference
4	B		Detail
5	C		Function of What Is Said

Answer Key—13.8

Question	Correct Answer	Right/Wrong	Category
1	C		Gist-content
2	A		Gist-purpose
3	D		Inference
4	B		Function of What Is Said
5	A, C		Detail

Answers and Explanations—13.1

Sustainable Agriculture Project—Track 128

NARRATOR: Listen to conversation between a student and her professor.

PROFESSOR: I know our appointment is short, but I just wanted to say, you always seem so engaged in the conversation in class.

STUDENT: Yeah, I'm really interested in working in agricultural science after graduation. There's gotta be opportunity. I mean, we're always gonna have to find better ways to grow food.

PROFESSOR: That's true. Lots of progress has been made, as you know, but there's so much more to do. I, um, before I became a professor, I worked with the US government to find more efficient ways to grow crops. I even worked with some local farms. We tried different crop rotations to help the farm stay productive for years.

STUDENT: That's so interesting. I'd love to work in sustainable agriculture. Farms should be run for generations, not just a few years.

PROFESSOR: Well, it's a tough balance to strike. Farmers want to think long term, but they also have to pay the bills right now.

STUDENT: I know! I keep finding stories about farms that have grown one type of crop so much the soil can't keep up. They're making less money each year, but they're kind of stuck.

PROFESSOR: Yeah, it's risky for farmers to change to a brand-new crop 'cause they don't know how strong the demand will be.

STUDENT: That's what… that's what I actually wanted to ask you about, to use for my project. I wanted to write about how to help farmers decide which crops to grow. Do you think that's a good idea?

PROFESSOR: Yes, it's a great topic! There's a lot you could explore. Crop rotation, fertilization, irrigation, leaving fields fallow…

STUDENT: Exactly… Help!

PROFESSOR: How much research have you done so far?

STUDENT: Well, some, but everything I read leads me five more places.

PROFESSOR: Welcome to academia! Let's see… has anything you've read jumped out at you as, um, connected to your own life?

STUDENT: You know… well, it wasn't in the research. It's that my roommates and I just decided to try a meal kit service. You know, where you get a kit of ingredients each week, with all the little packages of herbs and stuff?

PROFESSOR: Yes! Those are getting big.

STUDENT: Yeah, we love it. They give you just the right amounts of everything, so there's no waste. And there were quotes from farmers, they loved participating, because they can grow unusual crops. But… you know, it was just the brochure saying that.

PROFESSOR: But it sparked an idea that you can definitely follow up on. Are these meal kits helping farmers make crop decisions or not?

STUDENT: Well, there's not much real research yet that I could find. These things are so new.

PROFESSOR: Hmm… You know, there's a farm near here that I think supplies one of these meal kit places. They sell to agribusiness in general. But they also supply some local restaurants, and I'm pretty sure they even do a CSA on the side.

STUDENT: Oh yeah, I've heard of CSAs—that's where you sign up directly with a farm and they give you a big box of vegetables every week, right?

PROFESSOR: Right, Community Supported Agriculture boxes. You know, all these channels are different ways for farmers to sell their crops, and they all influence the crop decision.

STUDENT: Yeah, that's super interesting. Maybe I can talk to the people at this farm and do a comparison.

PROFESSOR: Just be sure to keep focusing on that main decision for the farmer—which crops should I grow this year? There are pros and cons to each sales channel.

STUDENT: Right, that makes sense.

13

1. Why does the student go to see the professor?

    ✗ (A) To find out about jobs in sustainable agriculture

    ✗ (B) To debate different sales channels that farmers can use

    ✓ (C) To get guidance on the topic of a project

    ✗ (D) To ask whether meal kit services are a good idea

GIST-PURPOSE. What did the student want? Why did she set up the appointment?

She expresses interest in working in sustainable agriculture after graduation. However, she doesn't ask for guidance in this direction.

The student and the professor wind up discussing a few sales channels for farmers. But this is because the student is looking for guidance on her project. And they certainly don't debate, or argue about, the different sales channels.

CORRECT. The student actually has an appointment with the professor. They discuss some related issues first, but then the student describes the question she wants to write about. She asks whether that's a good idea for a topic. This is the purpose of the appointment.

The student never asks this question. She personally loves her meal kit service, and she wants to use it in her project. But she doesn't ask the professor whether these services are a good idea.

2. In the brochure for the student's meal kit service, why do the farmers say they like to participate?

    ✗ (A) They made more money with the meal kit service than selling in a CSA.

    ✓ (B) They liked being able to grow unusual crops for customers.

    ✗ (C) They enjoyed supplying the right amounts of ingredients with little waste.

    ✗ (D) They loved being part of an innovative and growing sales channel.

DETAIL. The student mentions the brochure as she describes, in positive terms, the meal kit service that she and her roommates are using.

This connection is never made, and there is no discussion about how much money is made through the various sales channels.

CORRECT. The student says that "there were quotes from farmers, they loved participating, because they can grow unusual crops. But... you know, it was just the brochure."

The student talks about how great it is from her point of view that she receives the right amounts of ingredients. This was not something the farmers said.

While the student does mention that this sales channel is growing, this is never mentioned as a reason that farmers like participating.

3. Why does the professor mention his previous employment?

FUNCTION OF WHAT IS SAID. The professor brings up his previous employment (with the US government) early in the conversation. He and the student are discussing job opportunities in agricultural science.

✓ (A) To support a statement the student made about jobs in agricultural science

CORRECT. The student says: "There's gotta be opportunity [to work in agricultural science]... we're always gonna have to find better ways to grow food." The professor agrees and then describes his employment with the government on improving the long-term productivity of farms. This story reinforces his support for her statements about opportunities in the field.

✗ (B) To indicate that government jobs can lead to becoming a professor

It's true for this professor that his government job happened before he became a professor. But that doesn't mean he's saying the government job led to his later position.

✗ (C) To explain why the student should remain engaged in class conversations

Right at the start, the professor praises the student for her engagement in class conversations. But he never returns to that theme in any way.

✗ (D) To recommend that the student look for a position with the United States government

The professor never recommends to the student that she follow in his footsteps.

4. What does the professor imply about the farm near the university?

INFERENCE. Near the end of the conversation, the student indicates that there isn't much research out there on meal kit services and their impact on participating farmers. In response, the professor brings up the farm.

✗ (A) The farm prefers to supply local customers, such as restaurants.

The farm supplies some local restaurants and runs a CSA (directly supplying local citizens). But the professor never suggests that the farm prefers these local customers over more distant customers, such as meal kit services and agribusiness in general.

✗ (B) At least some of the farm's workers studied at the university.

The professor gives no hint in this direction.

✗ (C) He helped the farm try different crop rotations to increase productivity.

Early in his career, the professor worked with some local farms, trying different crop rotations. The professor tells this story near the beginning of the conversation. But the professor never suggests that the farm he refers to later is one of the farms he worked on.

✓ (D) People who work at the farm might have useful insights to share.

CORRECT. The farm is the professor's answer to the lack of available research. He implies that the student could talk with people at the farm. The student picks up on this implication. Later on, she says: "Maybe I can talk to the people at this farm and do a comparison."

Track 129

NARRATOR: Listen again to part of the conversation. Then answer the question.

PROFESSOR: How much research have you done so far?

STUDENT: Well, some, but everything I read leads me five more places.

PROFESSOR: Welcome to academia!

NARRATOR: What does the professor mean when he says this:

PROFESSOR: Welcome to academia!

5.   **FUNCTION OF WHAT IS SAID.** This segment takes place roughly in the middle of the conversation, after the student has asked whether the topic is good for the project and the professor has agreed. But now the student is overwhelmed by the specific possibilities. After saying, "Welcome to academia!", the professor asks a question to help the student narrow down the options.

✗ (A) The student has evidently not spent much time so far at the university.

The professor is not saying that the student is new to the university itself.

✗ (B) The student has just been accepted into the broader world of academic research.

The professor is not literally welcoming the student to the world of "academia," e.g. as a researcher.

✓ (C) The problem that the student confronts is common in academic research.

CORRECT. The professor is offering some sympathy. He is basically saying, "I know how you feel! This is what happens in academia a lot."

✗ (D) The student should not complain about the challenges of narrowing down early-stage research.

The professor is not making a value judgment of any kind. He is not suggesting that the student shouldn't complain.

Answers and Explanations—13.2

Teacher Observation Assignment—Track 130

NARRATOR: Listen to a conversation between a student and his professor.

PROFESSOR: Hello Rahul, how are you today?

STUDENT: I'm feeling better. Thanks for meeting with me after I missed class. Um, I want to talk to you about the assignment—the directions say we're supposed to decide by tomorrow which subject we want to observe, right? I mean, which teacher, but I am wondering about which subject I should choose.

PROFESSOR: Alright. Yes, you do need to decide by tomorrow. You will need to observe one of the teachers at the high school. Do you want to observe a math teacher, a science teacher, or an English teacher?

STUDENT: Well, yeah, that's my problem. Which one should I do?

PROFESSOR: I can't answer that for you. It depends on which subject you like the most and want to focus on for your final class assignment. You should pick the subject that you think you might want to learn to teach yourself.

STUDENT: I, uh… I don't know which one will be best for me. I am trying to decide between two, I guess, math or English.

PROFESSOR: Are you worried that math will be too difficult?

STUDENT: Well, I was the president of my math club when I was in high school. I just… well, I want to observe the best one. Maybe… you can tell me which one will be the best for the class?

PROFESSOR: No, I can't tell you which class to observe, that is up to you. But I can suggest some ideas that might help you decide. Uh, do you know any of the teachers at the high school?

STUDENT: Yeah… uh, my sister is a student there.

PROFESSOR: Great, so why don't you talk with the math teacher and the English teacher, and see what they have to say? That might help you decide which class to observe.

STUDENT: Do you think that's OK… to just ask them?

PROFESSOR: Sure, I think that's fine. I want you to observe a class so that you can learn something about how to teach and which subject you might want to teach. The teachers at the high school will understand that and will probably be happy to talk to you.

STUDENT: What do I ask them?

PROFESSOR: Let's see… you could ask them what they are going to be teaching next week, how they like teaching their subject. Tell them you are my student and that you are thinking about becoming a teacher.

STUDENT: Really?

PROFESSOR: Yes, I think that is fine. Teachers like to help people who want to become teachers, believe me. You could also ask them why they decided to teach their subject.

STUDENT: Like why, um, they teach math instead of something else?

PROFESSOR: Sure, that sounds like a good question to ask.

STUDENT: Yeah, ok.

PROFESSOR: Just make sure you do it quickly. I need your decision by tomorrow.

13

1. Why does the student go to see the professor?

GIST-PURPOSE. How does the student start the conversation? What does he want from the professor?

✓ (A) To ask the professor which high school class he should observe for his teacher observation assignment

CORRECT. The students tells the professor that he is having trouble deciding which class to observe for his assignment. He asks the professor to tell him which one he should observe.

✗ (B) To discuss which subject he might want to learn to teach

The professor does ask the student which subject he thinks he might want to learn to teach. But the professor only asks this to help the student think about which class to observe for his assignment.

✗ (C) To ask about the professor's experience with teaching

The professor suggests that the student ask some of the high school teachers about their experiences. They do not discuss the professor's own teaching experience.

✗ (D) To explain why he was absent from the last class

The student does mention that he missed the last class and implies that he was sick, but they don't discuss it further. He does not explain why he missed class, but instead asks for advice about the assignment.

2. What does the professor suggest that the student do in order to decide which teacher to observe?

DETAIL. The student notes that he is trying to decide whether to observe a math class or an English class.

✗ (A) Observe a math class

The professor does mention math, but she does not suggest that the student observe a math class. She says she cannot tell the student which class to observe.

✗ (B) Ask his sister which of her teachers she likes the best

The student does mention that his sister goes to the local high school, but only to imply that he knows some of the teachers there. They do not discuss which of the teachers his sister likes the best.

✗ (C) Talk with another professor at the college

The professor does suggest that the student talk with others. But the professor and the student do not discuss talking with another professor. Instead, the professor suggests that the student talk with high school teachers.

✓ (D) Talk with some of the teachers at the local high school

CORRECT. The professor says that she cannot tell the student which class to observe. Instead, the professor suggests that he talk with some of the teachers at the high school to help him decide which one of their classes to observe for his assignment.

3. Why does the student mention that he was president of his high school math club?

FUNCTION OF WHAT IS SAID. The professor asks the student whether he thinks math is difficult for him.

✗ (A) To show that he likes math

You might want to assume that the student likes math, since he was president of his high school math club. But the student does not indicate whether he likes or dislikes math. And he only mentions the math club in response to the professor's question about whether he finds math difficult.

✓ (B) To show that math is not difficult for him

CORRECT. The student mentions his high school math club in response to the professor's question about whether he thinks math will be too difficult. It is safe to assume that the student is saying that math is not difficult for him, since he was president of the math club.

✗ (C) To indicate that he does not want to observe a math class

The student says that he is trying to decide between observing a math class and an English class. He does not know which one he wants to observe.

✗ (D) To explain his interest in math

While the student mentions that he is considering observing a math class, he does not talk with the professor about his interest in math. He only mentions the math club in response to the professor's question about math being difficult.

4. What does the professor want the student to learn from his teacher observation?

DETAIL. Near the end of the conversation, the professor talks about why she is asking students to complete the teacher observation assignment.

✗ (A) What the high school teachers will be teaching next week

The professor does mention that the student can ask the high school teachers what they will be teaching next week. But she suggests this as a question to help the student decide which class to observe. Later in the conversation, the professor mentions what she wants the student to learn.

✗ (B) How much money teachers get paid

The professor and the student do not discuss teacher salaries or money.

✓ (C) Which subject the student might want to eventually teach

CORRECT. Near the end of the conversation, the professor mentions what she wants the student to learn from observing the teachers. She says that she wants the student to learn something about teaching and the subject he might want to teach.

✗ (D) Why each teacher likes teaching

The professor does suggest that the student ask the high school teachers what they like about teaching their subject. But she suggests this to help the student decide which class to observe. The professor does not mention why teachers like teaching when she discusses what she wants the student to learn from the assignment.

Track 131

NARRATOR: Listen again to part of the conversation. Then answer the question.

PROFESSOR: Tell them you are my student and that you are thinking about becoming a teacher.

STUDENT: Really?

PROFESSOR: Yes, I think that is fine. Teachers like to help people who want to become teachers, believe me.

NARRATOR: What does the professor imply?

5. **INFERENCE.** This segment takes place after the professor suggests that the student talk with some of the high school teachers to help him decide which class to observe. The student seems worried about talking with the teachers.

✗ (A) The professor is offering to arrange a discussion with the high school teachers.

The professor is not offering to arrange a discussion. She suggests that he mention he is her student so the high school teachers will know he is studying to become a teacher and want to help him.

✗ (B) The student should be careful about talking with the high school teachers.

The professor is trying to help the student feel better about talking with the teachers. She is giving him suggestions about how to talk with them.

✓ (C) The high school teachers will be happy to talk with the student about which class he should observe.

CORRECT. The professor is encouraging the student to talk with the teachers. She mentions that teachers like to help other people who want to become teachers to help him feel confident that they will want to talk with him.

✗ (D) The high school teachers will not want to talk with the student.

The professor is implying the opposite: that the high school teachers will want to talk with the student.

Answers and Explanations—13.3

Getting First Story Published—Track 132

NARRATOR: Listen to a conversation between a student and her professor.

PROFESSOR: Ok, Sonja, what did you want to talk about?

STUDENT: Thanks for seeing me. So, do you remember the story I wrote for workshop last month?

PROFESSOR: Yes, the… uh, the one about the space ship?

STUDENT: Yes, that one. So, I rewrote it like you said, and I think it's really good. But, what do I do with it now? I think… I should try to get it published, right? I've never had anything published before.

PROFESSOR: That's the next step. You can… um, you should do a little bit of research about which magazines publish the kinds of stories you like, and which ones… might want to publish your story. That is really the first step. You should make a list. And, uh, be very organized about it. Make sure you know exactly where you sent your story and when. Remember, it can take a long time for a magazine to get back to you, and you want to make sure you remember where you submitted it.

STUDENT: Oh, I'll remember where I sent it, don't worry. I remember every single college that I applied to.

PROFESSOR: That's good. This is, uh, a little different than your college applications, though. This is the beginning of your career as a writer, and you want to… you need to make sure that you start out on the right foot. You might have a long relationship with some of these magazines and meet people who will help you get your stories published for a long time.

STUDENT: Sure, I know. So…

PROFESSOR: Listen, I have had several, uh, former students who sent their story to so many places that they forgot where they sent it. And then… they ended up submitting their story to the same place twice, and that looks really bad. It's not very professional… and it makes a poor first impression that people will remember.

STUDENT: I see, ok. So, um, any other advice?

PROFESSOR: Oh, of course. That is… it seems like such a basic thing, but it's a big problem I've seen.

STUDENT: I understand.

PROFESSOR: Ok, so after you know where you are going to submit your story, you want to think about a cover letter. There's a good example on our website… uh, the one I showed you in class. You can use that as a model. Make sure you introduce yourself, tell them you are a student here, and, um, tell them a little bit about your story. Just a little bit. You shouldn't write more than one page.

STUDENT: Yeah, ok. Thanks Professor. I'll get started.

PROFESSOR: Good luck. Happy to talk again.

13

1. Why does the student go to see the professor?

GIST-PURPOSE. What does the student want to discuss with the professor?

✗ (A) To ask the professor where she should send her story for publication

The professor does mention magazines, but the student does not ask him where she should send her story. He simply advises her to do her own research.

✗ (B) To ask about his experience getting his own story published

The professor and the student do not discuss his own experience getting published. He only mentions the experience of some of his other students.

✓ (C) To ask for the professor's advice about getting her first story published

CORRECT. The student mentions a story that the professor read in class. Then, she asks him what she should do with it now that is finished. She specifically asks him about getting it published.

✗ (D) To tell the professor that her story has been published

The student's story has not been published. She says she has never been published. She is asking for the professor's advice about how to get her first story published.

2. What does the professor say is the first step the student should take?

✓ (A) Research magazines that might publish her story.

✗ (B) Call his friend at a magazine.

✗ (C) Write a cover letter.

✗ (D) Visit the website he showed in class.

DETAIL. Where should the student start? What does the professor suggest that she do first?

CORRECT. The professor makes several suggestions to the student. The first thing he mentions is that the student should do research into magazines that she thinks might want to publish her story. He says that is the first step.

The professor does not mention a friend at a magazine.

The professor does suggest that the student write a cover letter, but he does not say it is the first step.

The professor does mention the website he showed in class, but it is not the first step. He suggests that the student go there to find a model cover letter.

3. What does the professor imply about some of his former students?

✗ (A) They had good memories.

✓ (B) They did not get their stories published.

✗ (C) They did not ask for his advice.

✗ (D) They failed to write cover letters.

INFERENCE. The professor tells a story about his former students who forgot where they sent their stories for publication.

The professor doesn't say anything about their memories. Maybe they had good memories, maybe not. All we know is that they forgot where they sent their stories.

CORRECT. The professor says that several of his former students forgot where they sent their stories for publication. He says doing this makes a bad impression and is not very professional. He is warning the student not to follow this example if she wants to get her story published.

It's not clear whether the professor's former students asked for his advice. The professor does not say.

The professor mentions his former students in the middle of the conversation. He is talking about the consequences of forgetting where a story is sent. He talks about cover letters in a different part of the conversation, near the end.

4. What does the professor suggest that the student include in her cover letter? *Choose 2 answers.*

✗ [A] That she has never been published before

✓ [B] That she is a student

✓ [C] Information about her story

✗ [D] A list of magazines she thinks might publish her story

DETAIL. Near the end of the conversation, the professor recommends that the student write a cover letter.

This might be information that the student would include in her cover letter. However, the professor does not suggest that she do so.

CORRECT. The professor suggests telling potential publishers that she is a student at the university.

CORRECT. The professor suggests that the student "tell them a little bit about your story." He is recommending that she include information about her story in the cover letter.

The professor does suggest that she make a list of magazines that might publish her story, but he does not recommend that she include the list in her cover letter.

Track 133

NARRATOR: Listen again to part of the conversation. Then answer the question.

STUDENT: Oh, I'll remember where I sent it, don't worry. I remember every single college that I applied to.

PROFESSOR: That's good.

NARRATOR: What does the student mean when she says that she remembers every single college she applied to?

5.   **FUNCTION OF WHAT IS SAID.** This segment takes place after the professor cautions the student about making sure that she keeps track of where she sent her story, so she doesn't forget.

  ✗ (A) It is hard for her to remember things.   The student is implying the opposite: that she has a good memory. Otherwise, she would not remember every college she applied to.

  ✗ (B) She applied to a large number of colleges.   We don't know how many colleges she applied to, and it doesn't matter in the context of the conversation. They are not talking about college applications.

  ✗ (C) She wants to tell him which colleges she applied to.   The student and the professor are not discussing which colleges she applied to. The context is sending her story to magazines.

  ✓ (D) She has a good memory.   **CORRECT.** The professor is warning her not to forget where she sends her story. She is telling him she has a good memory, so she won't forget.

Answers and Explanations—13.4

Class Dropped—Track 134

NARRATOR: Listen to a conversation between a student and a receptionist at the Bursar's office.

RECEPTIONIST: Yes?

STUDENT: Hi, so… um, I went to my first class this morning, and the professor told me that I am no longer enrolled. She said I should come to the Bursar's office and ask you.

RECEPTIONIST: About why you are not enrolled?

STUDENT: Yes. I registered two months ago, and I know I was enrolled.

RECEPTIONIST: Ok, well… you probably didn't pay for your class on time. We just dropped classes for several students who hadn't paid. Um… ok, what is your name?

STUDENT: Amalia Sieve.

RECEPTIONIST: Amalia… Sieve… ok, um, here we go. Yeah, ok, you didn't pay for your class by the deadline, so your class was dropped.

STUDENT: So I am no longer enrolled in the class?

RECEPTIONIST: That's right, yeah. You are no longer enrolled. The payment deadline was… yesterday. If you don't pay on time, you can't attend class.

STUDENT: But… I didn't know the deadline was yesterday. I can pay for the class now. Then can I be enrolled again?

RECEPTIONIST: Yes, you can pay now and enroll again. Then you can attend the class next week. Just make sure this doesn't happen again. You need to pay for the class by the deadline. We sent out, uh, we sent out several reminders.

STUDENT: I didn't know the deadline was yesterday. I didn't see any reminders.

RECEPTIONIST: Well… uh, you need to check your email.

STUDENT: I check it every day.

RECEPTIONIST: Ok, well, we sent three reminders about the payment deadline. Maybe we have the wrong email for you?

STUDENT: Oh. I did cancel my old email address… I got too many ad messages. I'm using a new one now, I will give it to you.

RECEPTIONIST: Yeah, OK… or you can, um, go online and update your email address. Just… uh, make sure we have it so you don't miss important information.

STUDENT: Ok. When is the payment deadline for next semester? I want to make sure to pay on time.

RECEPTIONIST: Well, um, we don't have the specific date yet. You can… you can check online to see what the deadline will be before the semester starts. You just… uh, go to the university homepage, and click on… Bursar.

STUDENT: So the payment deadline will be posted there?

RECEPTIONIST: Yes… you can't miss it. You should write it down… remind yourself to check the deadline every semester. That will save you a lot of trouble.

STUDENT: Yeah, ok.

RECEPTIONIST: And update your email address.

STUDENT: Yes, I will go online and do that as soon as I get home.

RECEPTIONIST: Ok. So, do you want to pay for your class now?

STUDENT: Yeah, let's do that.

1.	Why does the student go to the Bursar's office?	**GIST-PURPOSE.** Who sent the student to the Bursar's office? What is the problem with her class?
✗ (A)	To update her email address	While the student and the receptionist discuss updating her email address, that is not why she goes to the Bursar's office. They only discuss her email address later on, after the student finds out why she is no longer enrolled in class.
✓ (B)	To ask why she is no longer enrolled in class	**CORRECT.** The student says she went to class, and her professor told her she was not enrolled. The professor sent her to the Bursar's office to find out why.
✗ (C)	To register for class	The student mentions that she registered for class two months ago. They do not talk about class registration again.
✗ (D)	To find out why her class was canceled	The student's class has not been canceled. In fact, the student tried to attend the class, but was told that she was not enrolled.

2.   Why is the student no longer
      enrolled in class?

   ✗ (A) The class was canceled.

   ✗ (B) She didn't get an email
         reminder about the first
         class.

   ✗ (C) She failed to meet the
         prerequisites for the class.

   ✓ (D) She didn't pay for the class
         on time.

DETAIL. What does the receptionist tell the student about her class?

The class has not been canceled—instead, the student has been dropped from the class. The student mentions that she tried to attend the first class and was told she wasn't enrolled.

They discuss email reminders, but not about the first class. The email reminders were about the payment deadline. The student also mentions that she tried to attend the first class.

The student and the receptionist don't discuss prerequisites. They only discuss failure to pay the class fee as the reason the student is no longer enrolled.

CORRECT. The receptionist tells the students that the Bursar's office just dropped classes for those who didn't pay by the deadline. He tells the student that she is no longer enrolled in class because she missed the payment deadline.

3.   Why didn't the student know
      about the payment deadline?

   ✗ (A) She has been out of the
         country.

   ✗ (B) The Bursar's office sent the
         reminders about the
         payment deadline to her
         old apartment.

   ✓ (C) She didn't get the emails
         about the payment
         deadline.

   ✗ (D) The deadline was recently
         changed.

CONNECTING CONTENT. What does the student say in response to the receptionist when he mentions that the Bursar's office sent reminders about the deadline?

The student might have been out of the country, but that is not part of the discussion. We don't know whether she has been traveling.

The student didn't get the reminders about the payment deadline, but it wasn't because the Bursar's office sent them to the wrong apartment. The receptionist implies that the reminders were sent via email, and the student realizes that the school doesn't have her new email address.

CORRECT. The receptionist says that the Bursar's office sent reminders about the payment deadline, and then mentions that the student needs to check her email. He is implying that the reminders were sent via email. The student then realizes that she hasn't given the school her new email address, so she didn't get the emails about the payment deadline.

There is no mention of the deadline being changed. And the receptionist also notes that the Bursar's office sent reminders to the students about the deadline.

4. What does the receptionist suggest that the student do every semester?

DETAIL. Near the end of the conversation, the receptionist directs the student to the school's website.

✗ (A) Visit the Bursar's office in person.

The receptionist does not suggest that she visit the Bursar's office in person every semester. Instead, he directs her to the website.

✗ (B) Change her password.

While the receptionist does suggest that the student update her email address online, he does not suggest that she update her password.

✗ (C) Call to make sure she is enrolled in class.

The receptionist does not suggest that she call. Nor does he suggest that the student make sure she is enrolled her class. Instead, he advises her to make sure she knows when the payment deadline is so her classes won't be dropped again.

✓ (D) Check the Bursar's office website for the payment deadline.

CORRECT. The student asks about the payment deadline for the next semester, and the receptionist says that there is not a specific date yet. He recommends that the student go to the Bursar's office website every semester to check the payment deadline.

Track 135

NARRATOR: Listen again to part of the conversation. Then answer the question.

STUDENT: Oh. I did cancel my old email address… I got too many ad messages. I'm using a new one now, I will give it to you.

RECEPTIONIST: Yeah, OK… or you can, um, go online and update your email address …

NARRATOR: What is the receptionist implying?

5. **FUNCTION OF WHAT IS SAID.** Why does the receptionist mention this option rather than just changing the email address for the student?

✓ (A) The student should update her email address herself.

CORRECT. The student offers to give her new email address to the receptionist. Rather than taking it from her, he tells her that she can update it online. He is implying that she should do it herself.

✗ (B) The student should not provide her new email address.

The receptionist tells her that she should update her email address; in other words, provide the school with the new address. He just tells her that she can do it online.

✗ (C) The Bursar's office needs more than one email address from the student.

The receptionist does not imply that the student should provide more than one email address. They are discussing updating her old email address to her new one.

✗ (D) Reminders about the payment deadline will no longer be sent via email.

Earlier in the conversation, the receptionist implies that reminders about the payment deadline are normally sent via email. He does not imply that this will stop in the future. Rather, he implies that the reminders will continue to be sent via email, which is why the student should update her email address.

Answers and Explanations—13.5

Hard Biology Tests—Track 136

NARRATOR: Listen to a conversation between a student and her biology professor.

STUDENT: Um… I'm sorry… excuse me, Professor Novak? I… I mean, if you're busy I understand. But, I was hoping I could speak to you for a moment.

PROFESSOR: Sure, Irene, come on in. What's up?

STUDENT: Well, this is embarrassing, but… I… well, you know already. This midterm we just took… I… I'm sorry to disappoint you, Professor. I've never done so badly on a test before.

PROFESSOR: Well … if every student in the class aced the test, I'd be over the moon. But, also, if that happened… I mean, I'd just have to make the next midterm more challenging! You see what I mean? It's my job to make exams that are just right—not too easy, not too hard. So, I'm not "disappointed" at all. Actually, this is kind of good news, because… well, you know, it means you're really learning. Believe me, I know it's not a good feeling to score lower than you'd anticipated, but… at some point that's going to happen. That's why you're even here in the first place!

STUDENT: Well… I'm not even slacking on studying. In fact, I've been studying even harder than usual.

PROFESSOR: Well, maybe that's part of the problem. Are you getting enough sleep?

STUDENT: Oh, yeah… yes, definitely. I'm very aware of that. And it's easier to get a good night's sleep here, because I don't have to take care of my baby brother.

PROFESSOR: I'm glad to hear that. Honestly, just sleeping enough hours, you're already ahead of the game. But… ok. So, then… what do you think might be the issue?

STUDENT: Well… it's the way your tests work. They're just… um… I've never taken tests like yours.

PROFESSOR: How do you mean?

STUDENT: Well… I'm used to… like, basically having two totally different kinds of classes. Like… in most of my classes, the main point has always been just learning and remembering stuff. Basically just memorization. But then there's math, and chemistry and physics… and also some of my English classes where they'd give us new stuff to read on the tests, that we'd never seen before. In other words, those were… you know, problem-solving classes.

PROFESSOR: I think I understand. But just to be sure—the problem is, you're thinking of biology as one of the "memorization" classes.

STUDENT: Exactly. So I just wasn't ready for this midterm. I was trying to remember pretty much everything.

PROFESSOR: Well, don't forget there are three midterms. And we only count your best two out of three for your course grade. In other words, everyone gets to mess up one test as bad as they want to. And honestly, I don't think you're alone here. I've—

STUDENT: Heh, no… people were definitely talking about this class all over campus that day. And plenty of other really smart kids were pretty upset.

PROFESSOR: You bet they were. And that's a big part of what I'm doing here. See, when you take biology in high school, you have to memorize lots of facts. In the same way you have to memorize words, or math

tables, when you're in elementary school. I mean, you can't really start to think until you have a decent set of ideas to think with. So, that's the point of your high school biology. But now, you're at the next level, and it's time to start using that knowledge.

1.   Why does the student go to see the professor?

GIST-PURPOSE. Why did the student come to see the professor? What was her concern?

✓ (A) To get help in understanding and overcoming unexpected trouble

CORRECT. The student has scored poorly on a biology exam for the very first time ever. She wants help figuring out why.

✗ (B) To build a personal relationship in the hope that it will impact his grades

There is nothing to indicate that the student has any interest in developing a personal friendship—let alone that she wants to do such a thing so that she'll be given artificially good grades.

✗ (C) To discuss and debate the purpose of classes at different levels

The professor talks about different levels of classes to help the student understand why her exams differ from what the student has seen before. However, there is no evidence that she comes with the intention of discussing (or debating) such a thing.

✗ (D) To request a chance to retake a recent exam

Although the student might wish she had a chance to retake the exam, she mentions no such possibility anywhere.

2.   What does the student imply about her experience with the "two totally different kinds of classes"?

INFERENCE. Her experience is that some classes are more concerned with memorization while others focus on "problem-solving." Her experience is that certain subjects, such as biology, are always memorization, while other subjects, such as English, are always problem-solving.

✓ (A) She did not realize that both types of classes might be possible in the same subject area.

CORRECT. The student says that biology has always been a "memorization" course, and this is why she's having difficulty. What's different is that biology has become a "problem-solving class," and the student was not prepared for the switch.

✗ (B) She has always earned much better grades in one type than in the other.

The student says nothing to imply a consistent difference in her performance. In fact, it's most likely that she has always earned high grades across both types.

✗ (C) She was unaware of this distinction before university, but she is now benefiting from having learned about it.

The student makes nearly the opposite point: the distinction has worked very well until right now.

✗ (D) At the university level, this is no longer a meaningful distinction.

The student is troubled by the fact that biology has "jumped" from one category to the other. But she still clearly believes that the same two categories still exist.

3. According to the professor, how seriously will this exam affect the student's overall grade for the course, and why?

DETAIL. The professor indicates that her performance is fine and that only two of her three exam grades will count. Therefore, she should not be worried about this low score.

✗ Ⓐ It will have a significant effect, since this is the only exam for the course.

There are, in fact, three midterm exams.

✗ Ⓑ It will have a significant effect, since this specific exam is weighted more heavily than the others.

The professor says nothing to suggest that any exam might be worth more or less than any other. (In fact, the professor's policy—dropping any one of the three exams—very strongly suggests that all three exams have exactly the same weight.)

✗ Ⓒ It will have only a slight effect, since so many other items will also be included in the course grade.

The only grading items discussed are the three midterm exams. Furthermore, this choice misses the most important idea, namely, that one of those three will be dropped.

✓ Ⓓ It will probably have no effect at all, since it will likely be dropped entirely from the calculation.

CORRECT. After the professor explains her policy of dropping one exam from the course grade, she even remarks that "everyone gets to mess up one test as bad as they want to".

4. Why does the professor mention that words and math tables are commonly memorized in elementary school?

FUNCTION OF WHAT IS SAID. The professor says that high school science classes are primarily memorization and then says the same was true of math and words in elementary school. What is the comparison she is trying to make?

✗ Ⓐ To complain that today's university students are lacking certain extremely basic skills

The professor says nothing about how well university students have learned basic fundamentals.

✓ Ⓑ To explain how many topics start as memorization and then move to problem-solving

CORRECT. The professor uses basic words and math tables as an analogy for basic biology facts: both must be memorized before a student can begin true problem-solving.

✗ Ⓒ To give examples of material at different levels of difficulty

The professor points out similarities between these types of material, to make an analogy that explains how biology courses are structured. Differences (including differences in difficulty) are not discussed.

✗ Ⓓ To show that school courses have changed very little in the past several decades

The professor makes an analogy using only the present versions of these courses. She does not mention their history.

5. Which of the following statements are true in the conversation you just heard? *Choose 2 answers.*

   ✗   A   The student is too busy to study for her exams.

   ✓   B   The student prepared for this exam in largely inappropriate ways.

   ✗   C   The professor is personally disappointed in the student's performance.

   ✓   D   Many other students performed as badly on this exam.

DETAIL. The student is discussing a poor grade on her biology exam. She also shares with her professor that she studied incorrectly because she did not realize that biology could be about problem-solving rather than memorization alone.

The student says she has "been studying even harder than usual," so she must have the time to do so. Also, she says she is getting plenty of sleep and has fewer family obligations than at home.

CORRECT. The student studied in ways that would have been appropriate for a memorization-based exam, but that were not well suited to a problem-solving exam like this one.

The professor explicitly states that she is not disappointed. Furthermore, she says, if she is doing her job properly then at least some students will score poorly on the first exam.

CORRECT. When the professor says, "I don't think you're alone," this means many other students scored just as low as this student did. This is confirmed by the student's statement that "plenty of … smart kids were pretty upset," and by the professor's next response.

Answers and Explanations—13.6

Tennis Physical—Track 137

NARRATOR: Listen to a conversation between a student and a university employee.

RECEPTIONIST: Hi, there… what can I help you with?

STUDENT: I'm… actually… not even sure I'm in the right place.

RECEPTIONIST: Where are you hoping to be?

STUDENT: I'm looking for the… uh… Student Health Clinic. I heard you could get a free physical here.

RECEPTIONIST: This is, indeed, the clinic. And you can indeed get a physical, assuming you have your student ID—but wait, were you hoping to get one today?

STUDENT: Yeah, preferably.

RECEPTIONIST: Oh. Sorry, we don't do walk-ins for physicals. You have to make an appointment in advance. Do you want to put something on the calendar for next week?

STUDENT: Ugh… I don't think that would work… the tennis team needs all my paperwork turned in by Thursday.

RECEPTIONIST: Are you saying that you need to have a physical on record in order to join the tennis team?

STUDENT: Yeah, we need to have a form that says… that's signed by a doctor that says we're healthy.

RECEPTIONIST: Well, unfortunately, this is a busy clinic and so we have to use an appointment system or else we would get overwhelmed at peak times.

STUDENT: Yeah, I understand. I checked online and saw there weren't any appointments until next week, so I thought I'd come by and see if you could squeeze me in. It should really just take under 5 minutes. I basically just need my height, weight, and vision measured.

RECEPTIONIST: An appointment for a physical is usually at least 30 minutes, because we also draw some blood.

STUDENT: Right… but I'm not worried about my blood levels. My family is real healthy. I've always been healthy. I just need this form filled out so that I can join the team.

RECEPTIONIST: Why didn't you come set up this appointment sooner?

STUDENT: Some of the other guys who are already on the team did this last year and they said you could basically just walk in to the Student Health Clinic and get the form filled out.

RECEPTIONIST: Well, I guess sometimes our memories don't tell the truth.

STUDENT: So there's no way to just get you, or a doctor, to fill out the quick parts of this form so that I can turn it in?

RECEPTIONIST: I'm sorry, no. Only doctors can sign it, and doctors will only sign it if they've conducted a proper examination. I can put you on the waiting list and we can call you in the next couple days if any of our scheduled appointments cancel.

STUDENT: Thanks. I guess I'll have to hope for that, then.

1.	Why does the student go to the Student Health Clinic?	**GIST-PURPOSE.** What was the student hoping to achieve or find out?
✗	(A) To find out the requirements for joining the tennis team	The student already knew that he needed a physical exam form signed by a doctor to join the tennis team.
✓	(B) To obtain a physical exam from a doctor	**CORRECT.** The student needs a physical so that he can get a form signed that allows him to join the tennis team.
✗	(C) To get some tennis playing advice from a doctor	There's no indication that the student wants to discuss tennis with a doctor.
✗	(D) To cancel the appointment he had made for that day	The student doesn't have an appointment scheduled.
2.	What does the student say about his teammates on the tennis team?	**DETAIL.** The student's teammates were the ones that suggested it would be fine to go to the clinic without an appointment.
✗	(A) They urged him to make an appointment sooner.	This is the opposite of what was said.
✗	(B) They were supposed to have set up an appointment for him.	There is no indication that his teammates tried to set up an appointment.
✗	(C) They told him that the Student Health Clinic had great doctors.	There were no comments about the quality of doctors at the clinic.
✓	(D) They thought the form could be filled out without an appointment.	**CORRECT.** The student says he got the impression from other members of the tennis team that he could get the form quickly signed; these other players claim to have done so the previous year.

3. Why doesn't the student set up an appointment for the following week?

DETAIL. When the receptionist learns that he doesn't have an appointment, she offers to schedule him one for the following week.

✓ (A) He needs to have his form signed sooner than that.

CORRECT. The man says that the form is due that Thursday, so an appointment the following week wouldn't help solve his problem.

✗ (B) He will be busy with tennis tryouts the following week.

There is no information about when the tennis team has practice or tryouts, only when a certain form is due.

✗ (C) He decides to just get a physical from the tennis team's doctor instead.

Nothing is said about the tennis team having its own doctor.

✗ (D) He forgot to bring his student ID, which is required to make an appointment.

The man never says whether he has his student ID with him.

4. How will the student attempt to get his form signed in time?

CONNECTING CONTENT. Did the man reach any solution to his problem?

✗ (A) By skipping the blood test

Although the student would be happy to skip the blood test, the receptionist says that would not be allowable.

✗ (B) By having the receptionist sign the form

The student inquires about this possibility, but the receptionist says no.

✓ (C) By hoping for a canceled appointment

CORRECT. The receptionist offers to put him on the waitlist, in case an appointment cancels, and he indicates that he will have to hope for that.

✗ (D) By scheduling an appointment online

The student mentions that he tried this approach but the next available appointments were too late.

Track 138

NARRATOR: Listen again to part of the conversation. Then answer the question.

RECEPTIONIST: Why didn't you come set up this appointment sooner?

STUDENT: Some of the other guys who are already on the team did this last year and they said you could basically just walk in to the Student Health Clinic and get the form filled out.

RECEPTIONIST: Well, I guess sometimes our memories don't tell the truth.

NARRATOR: Why does the receptionist say this to the student:

RECEPTIONIST: Well, I guess sometimes our memories don't tell the truth.

5.   Why does the receptionist say this to the student?

FUNCTION OF WHAT IS SAID. This segment takes place as the receptionist asks why the student waited so long to make his appointment. He says that other people on the tennis team gave him the impression he didn't need to schedule in advance.

✗ (A) To accuse his teammates of playing a joke on him

She is only suggesting that his teammates remember their experience from the previous year incorrectly.

✗ (B) To warn him about the effects of getting older

She is only talking about memories in order to politely say that his teammates were wrong.

✗ (C) To tell him she will make an exception for him.

This is the opposite of what she is saying. She is denying that it is possible to just walk in and get the form signed.

✓ (D) To indicate that he received the wrong impression

CORRECT. The receptionist continues to hold her position that you need an appointment to have a physical.

Answers and Explanations—13.7

Access to the Art Library—Track 139

NARRATOR: Listen to a conversation between a student and a university employee.

STUDENT: Hi! I'm wondering if you could help me. I was told I just needed to swipe my student ID to enter the library, but the card reader seems not to be working.

EMPLOYEE: Is this your first time here?

STUDENT: Yeah. I just started classes a few days ago. My name is Irene Miller.

EMPLOYEE: Ah, well that explains it. We'll have to set you up in the system. It'll just take a moment.

STUDENT: Oh, good! I'm so excited to finally be able to see all the collections of printing and paintings! I just transferred here from Beckett University, and we didn't have anything like this there.

EMPLOYEE: Oh, I know. It's a treasure trove of art history. The collection has been a long time in the making, I can tell you that.

STUDENT: I bet! Most schools don't have a fraction of what you guys have here.

EMPLOYEE: Hmm… I can't seem to find you in our system. You are a student in the Art College, right?

STUDENT: Um… No. I'm actually in the School of Arts & Sciences.

EMPLOYEE: Oh, no. I'm afraid your student ID doesn't automatically give you access to this library.

STUDENT: What? Really? But… but I've been looking forward to this ever since I got accepted to transfer! And I thought library fees were part of the tuition payment each semester.

EMPLOYEE: Yes, but the fee you paid just entitles you to use the main university libraries—there are quite a few: Robst Library right in the center of campus, Bammel Library, and the Business Library.

STUDENT: But how can I get into this library, too?

EMPLOYEE: You'll have to register as a "visiting student," and pay a small fee each semester.

STUDENT: Another fee! But the art students don't have to pay extra to use the Arts & Sciences libraries, do they?

EMPLOYEE: Well, no, but—

STUDENT: Then it seems unfair that I need to pay an extra fee to use this one, doesn't it?

EMPLOYEE: I see what you're saying, but it's not the same. Everyone can use the main libraries, but the Art Library is highly specialized, with extra staff on hand to assist with all the materials available. And the art students have a totally different set of fees they pay already.

STUDENT: So, to be able to study here…

EMPLOYEE: We'll need to get you registered and paid. Did you say you were a graduate student or an undergraduate?

STUDENT: Undergraduate.

EMPLOYEE: Okay, so this is the form you'll need to fill out, then there's the $50 fee.

STUDENT: I still don't think the libraries should be separate like this, but, if this is the only way… Can I fill it out right now and give it back to you?

EMPLOYEE: First, you'll need an Art College professor to approve your request. If you're taking an art class, just ask that professor. If not, you'll need to arrange to see Professor Alma—she'll want to know what your art experience is.

STUDENT: You mean she's going to test me on my knowledge of art?

EMPLOYEE: No, not really—she'll mostly want to know what you're interested in, why you'd like to visit this library, if you're planning to take art classes in the future, that kind of thing.

STUDENT: So, where do I find Professor Alma?

EMPLOYEE: Do you know where Kimmer Hall is?

STUDENT: Yeah.

EMPLOYEE: Professor Alma's office is on the third floor. If she's not there when you stop by, you should be able to make an appointment with the student services staff outside her office.

STUDENT: Okay.

EMPLOYEE: Then, after she's approved it and signed it, bring it back here with your fee. Once you do, we can change your Student ID to reflect your access to this library.

STUDENT: Thanks a lot.

1.   What are the speakers mainly discussing?

GIST-CONTENT. The student asks for help accessing the art library. The resulting conversation covers how to gain access and the fee involved.

✗ (A) How to become an Art College student

The student wants to access the Art Library, but does not indicate that she wishes to become an art student.

✗ (B) The artists featured in the library's collection

The student is interested in the library's collection, but she and the employee never discuss the artists represented there.

✓ (C) What is required for a student to be able to access the Art Library

CORRECT. The student assumes she has already done everything required for access, but the employee informs her that there is more she has to do: pay a fee and get a form approved.

✗ (D) The library's book borrowing policies

The borrowing policies of the library are never discussed.

2.   Why does the student become frustrated partway through the conversation?

SPEAKER'S ATTITUDE. The student starts the conversation believing she has access to the library, but that her card is malfunctioning. She becomes frustrated when the she realizes that's not the case.

✓ (A) She is told that she needs to pay a fee in order to access the library.

CORRECT. The student thought that she already had access to the library. When she finds out she must pay a fee, she is unhappy.

✗ (B) She discovers that the art collections are no longer at this library.

There is no discussion of any of the collections having been removed from the library.

✗ (C) She learns that there are no art classes she can take.

The student and the employee never discuss the possibility of her taking an art class.

✗ (D) She finds out that art students are not allowed to visit the main libraries.

On the contrary, the art students are allowed to access these libraries. That is part of what the student thinks is unfair.

3.   What does the employee imply about the art students?

INFERENCE. The employee does not think that it would be fair to require the art students to pay additional fees to use the main libraries on campus.

✓ (A) They have already paid for access to the Art Library in their school fees.

CORRECT. The employee says the art students have "a totally different set of fees they pay already" to contradict the student's claim that the situation is unfair. The fees make the situation fair, as everyone must pay for access to the library—the two groups of students simply pay for it differently.

✗ (B) They are not allowed to visit the main libraries.

Everyone, including the art students, is allowed to visit the main libraries.

✗ (C) They spend most of their time off campus.

There is no discussion of where the art students spend their time.

✗ (D) They don't usually use the Art Library.

There is no mention of how often the art students use the Art Library.

4. Why does the student need to go to see the art professor?

  ✗ Ⓐ To be interviewed for a project on art criticism

  ✓ Ⓑ To get approved as a "visiting student"

  ✗ Ⓒ To ask to join her art class

  ✗ Ⓓ To complain that art students are coming to the main libraries

DETAIL. The student wants to fill out the form right away. The employee tells her there is something she needs to do first.

While Professor Alma will want to question the student about her art experience, this is not for a project. It is simply to be approved to use the library.

CORRECT. The student needs an art professor to approve the request and sign the form. The employee suggests that if the student is not in an art class, she should ask Professor Alma for this approval.

The employee suggests that if the student is already taking an art class, she could ask that art professor to approve her form. Professor Alma is offered as an alternative to sign the form, not as a way to take an art class.

While the student complains to the employee that the art students can come to the main library without paying extra fees, she does so in order to argue that she should not have to pay a fee for the Art Library. There is no indication that she will further argue the policy with Professor Alma.

Track 140

NARRATOR: Listen again to part of the conversation. Then answer the question.

STUDENT: So, where do I find Professor Alma?

EMPLOYEE: Do you know where Kimmer Hall is?

NARRATOR: Why does the employee ask the student if she knows where Kimmer Hall is?

5. **FUNCTION OF WHAT IS SAID.** This segment takes place after the student has accepted that she must complete the form to gain access to the library. After the employee asks "Do you know where Kimmer Hall is?", she goes on to explain how the student should go about seeing the professor once inside Kimmer Hall.

  ✗ Ⓐ He needs the student to tell him where Kimmer Hall is.

  ✗ Ⓑ He is trying to point out how far away Kimmer Hall is.

  ✓ Ⓒ He wants to know if he needs to explain where Kimmer Hall is.

  ✗ Ⓓ He is suggesting that the student should have been to Kimmer Hall already.

While often people ask where something is when they themselves need to know, that's not what's happening here. The employee is trying to explain where the professor is, not ask for information himself.

The context surrounding the quote does not indicate that there is any sort of information being conveyed about how far away the hall is, just whether the student is aware of its location.

CORRECT. The employee is explaining where and how to find the professor at Kimmer Hall. Once the student indicates that she does know where the hall is, the employee simply continues with the instructions.

The employee is not indicating that the student has done anything wrong. There was no reason that the student would have known prior to coming to the library that she needed to go to Kimmer Hall.

Answers and Explanations—13.8

Missing Family—Track 141

NARRATOR: Listen to a conversation between a student and a counselor at the university counseling center.

STUDENT: Hi, I hope you don't mind me dropping in like this.

COUNSELOR: That's what I'm here for. What can I do for you?

STUDENT: Well, I'm having a lot of trouble being away from home.

COUNSELOR: Yeah, that's a pretty common problem.

STUDENT: It's just, my family and I have always been so close. I come from a really big family, I have four brothers and sisters, and my aunt and her family live with us too. It's really hard knowing I'll only get to see them on school holidays.

COUNSELOR: That's a big adjustment, going from a close family to living in a community where no one is related.

STUDENT: Yeah, that's absolutely right. I mean, I still talk to my mom every day, but it's just not the same.

COUNSELOR: Yeah, of course. Did you know that the school has a family weekend every fall?

STUDENT: No, I hadn't heard of that.

COUNSELOR: It's a really fun weekend. Tours are set up so that the family can explore campus, some professors make themselves available to meet parents, and a lot of the nearby restaurants have specials for family members of students. The next one is coming up at the end of next month.

STUDENT: Oh, that sounds really great. I'll have to tell my family about it so they can visit. But it still feels like it's a long way away. I'm not sure what to do until then.

COUNSELOR: Hmm, well, when you think about missing your family, what's the thing that first comes to mind?

STUDENT: My mom's cooking. I can shut my eyes and almost smell her delicious food.

COUNSELOR: I know what you mean. I still get cravings for my mom's Sunday night dinners.

STUDENT: It just feels like it's going to be such a long time before I can taste that again.

COUNSELOR: Well, maybe we can see this as an opportunity. Do you enjoy cooking?

STUDENT: Oh yeah! It was one of my favorite things to do with my mom and aunt. The three of us would just chat together, and the whole family would come together and we all eat. I was just starting to help my sister learn how to cook her favorite meal when I had to leave for college.

COUNSELOR: I can see why it means so much to you. This is a big part of your identity. Have you tried to cook anything in the kitchen space in the dorms?

STUDENT: I've tried, but it's just not the same.

COUNSELOR: Well, what if you called your mom while you were cooking? You can even do a video call.

STUDENT: I don't know, I wouldn't want to distract her while she's spending time with my aunt and sister.

COUNSELOR: Don't you think she misses you, too? I'm sure that she wants to be cooking with you as much as you want to cook with her. You two could set it up so that you're cooking at the same time, and maybe even cooking the same dish. That way it's more like you're working together.

STUDENT: You're right! That's a really good idea!

COUNSELOR: And it doesn't need to be limited to cooking. You can think about things that you like to do with your siblings or with your aunt, and make it a point to still do those things, but from two different locations.

STUDENT: Oh yeah, now that I'm thinking about it, there's lots of things that we can do besides talking over the phone. I mean we could even watch a movie together. I think this will really help. Thanks for your advice!

COUNSELOR: Not a problem.

1.   What do the speakers mainly discuss?

       GIST-CONTENT. The student misses her family so she and the counselor try to come up with ways to still feel connected to them.

    ✗   (A) The food her family likes to cook

       Cooking is certainly mentioned. However, the focus is not on the specific food, but on the fact that the student misses her family.

    ✗   (B) How the student can resolve a dispute with her sister

       No dispute is mentioned.

    ✓   (C) The student's relationship with her family

       CORRECT. The student has a very strong relationship with her family and is upset because she can't see them as often as she used to while on campus. The counselor is able to suggest some solutions.

    ✗   (D) Different methods available for the student to travel home

       This is not discussed.

2.   Why does the student mention her four brothers and sisters?

       GIST-PURPOSE. She's describing her family to illustrate that she's used to being around a lot of people she cares about. It helps to show how disconnected she's feeling now that she's at school.

    ✓   (A) To emphasize that she has a large and close family

       CORRECT. She mentions her siblings in the context of describing her big family and explaining how unusual and uncomfortable it feels to be in a campus environment.

    ✗   (B) To acknowledge that she is comfortable in large groups

       The discussion is about the student's discomfort.

    ✗   (C) To indicate that some of her siblings are planning on attending this university

       The student never mentions this.

    ✗   (D) To draw a contrast with other student's families

       The student does not mention other students.

3. What does the student imply about family weekend?

INFERENCE. She didn't realize the school offered a family weekend, and she's excited about the prospect of her family coming to visit her.

✗ (A) It is an event that she will likely not be able to participate in.

The student indicates the opposite.

✗ (B) It would allow her to see her family on a daily basis.

The professor indicates that this is an annual event, so there is no reason to believe it would affect her daily interactions with her family.

✗ (C) It would help take her mind off her problems about cooking.

Other than missing cooking with her family, the student has no problems with cooking.

✓ (D) It would be an opportunity to see her family sooner than expected.

CORRECT. The student seems excited when she learns about this event. She indicates that she will tell her family so that they can visit her.

4. What does the student imply about helping her sister learn to cook?

FUNCTION OF WHAT IS SAID. She had to leave for college when she was "just starting to help my sister learn how to cook her favorite meal."

✗ (A) She was embarrassed because she taught an inaccurate cooking method.

The student does not mention anything about cooking in an improper way.

✓ (B) She was upset because she didn't get a chance to finish teaching her sister.

CORRECT. Teaching her sister was abruptly ended, according to the student, because she had to leave for college. This ties into the idea of missing her family.

✗ (C) She was confused by her mother's contradictory expectations.

The student does not mention this.

✗ (D) She was disappointed that her sister was unable to learn as quickly as expected.

The student does not mention this.

5. According to the counselor, what could the student do before family weekend? *Choose 2 answers.*

DETAIL. The counselor suggests cooking with her mom and coming up with other activities that the student could do with other family members virtually.

✓ [A] Do a video call with her mother

CORRECT. The counselor suggests this exactly.

✗ [B] Write letters to her aunt

The counselor does not mention this.

✓ [C] Watch movies with her siblings

CORRECT. The counselor broadly suggests doing things over video call with her aunt and siblings, and the students specifically brings up watching movies.

✗ [D] Visit home more frequently

The counselor never mentions this.

13

Chapter 14
Conversations B

In the Listening section, conversations test your ability to comprehend everyday spoken English. You'll listen to a short conversation (about 2 to 3 minutes long) between a student and someone else—a professor or another university staff member—about a campus situation. You will be able to listen to the conversation only once. You will not be able to pause the recording or to replay any part of it (though some questions will replay a specific part of the lecture for you). You can take notes as you listen.

You will then answer five questions for that conversation. Most questions are multiple-choice with four options (select one from A, B, C, or D). Some questions may ask you to select more than one option or to fill in a table. You will have to answer the questions in order. You cannot return to a question once you have moved on to the next question.

Conversations test your understanding of main ideas, contrasts, and the speaker's tone and attitude toward the topic. They also test your ability to compare and contrast information, understand cause and effect, make connections between different parts of the conversation, and make inferences or draw conclusions.

How should you use this chapter? Here are some recommendations, according to the level you've reached in TOEFL Listening:

1. **Fundamentals.** At first, listen to the conversation once, then work on the questions untimed and check the answer after each question. Review the solutions closely, think carefully about the principles at work, and articulate what you've learned. Redo questions as necessary. As you get better, time yourself and do all of the questions for a conversation at once, without stopping.

2. **Fixes.** Do an entire conversation and its associated questions under timed conditions. Don't replay any part of the conversation while you are still answering the questions! Examine the results, learn your lessons, then test yourself with another conversation and question set.

3. **Tweaks.** Confirm your mastery by doing two conversations (plus the associated questions) in a row under timed conditions. Work your way up to doing four lectures and two conversations in one sitting. Aim to improve the speed and ease of your process.

Good luck on Listening!

14.1

 Listen to Track 142.

Now answer the questions.

1. Why does the student go to see his professor?

    (A) He wants his professor's help with his final project.

    (B) He is seeking more information about an email that his professor sent him.

    (C) He wants his professor to speak with his academic advisor.

    (D) He has a question about Appalachian English.

2. Why does the student mention that he earned poor grades during his first year of college?

    (A) He is unhappy with the grade that he earned in this professor's class.

    (B) His advisor has asked him to retake some classes during the summer.

    (C) He does not think he will earn a good grade in the research class.

    (D) Linguistics classes are especially difficult for the student.

3. What does the student need to do before deciding whether to spend the summer doing research?

    (A) Finish his linguistics final project

    (B) Complete his summer classes

    (C) Check the grades he earned on his final exams

    (D) Speak with his academic advisor about his plans

 Listen to Track 143.

Now answer the question.

4. What does the professor mean when she says this?

    (A) She believes that the student will probably earn a good grade in the summer research course.

    (B) The student's grade in the course will not be counted as part of his GPA.

    (C) The student already has a high GPA.

    (D) The student's grade will be based on the work he has already done in his linguistics course.

Listen to Track 144.

Now answer the question.

5. What does the professor mean when she says this?

    (A) The student has missed a good opportunity by not taking linguistics classes earlier.

    (B) The student has limited time to do linguistics research before he graduates.

    (C) The student should submit his final project to a linguistics conference.

    (D) The student's work is better than one might expect.

14.2

 Listen to Track 145.

Now answer the questions.

1. What are the speakers discussing?

    (A) How to complete a research project

    (B) How to send books through the mail

    (C) How to find a book using the library catalogue

    (D) How to use interlibrary loan

2. Why does the employee ask whether the student is a graduate student?

    (A) Graduate students can recall library books that are checked out to other graduate students.

    (B) The student seems unfamiliar with the university library.

    (C) Only graduate students can check out books via interlibrary loan.

    (D) The employee wants more information about the student's research project.

3. Which of the following services does interlibrary loan provide? *Choose 2 answers.*

    [A] Helping students select books to use for university research projects

    [B] Acquiring new books for the library collection

    [C] Mailing books from libraries on other campuses to the university library

    [D] Scanning parts of a book and emailing them to students

4. What will the student most likely do next?

   (A) Go to the library at the Wilmington campus.

   (B) Decide which chapters of the book he needs for his project.

   (C) Complete the online interlibrary loan form.

   (D) Find the other books he needs for his project.

 Listen to Track 146.

Now answer the question.

---

5. (A) The student does not believe that the graduate student will return the book.

   (B) The student will not be able to complete his research project.

   (C) The student wants the library employee to request that the book be returned

   (D) The student needs the book in less than two weeks.

14.3

 Listen to Track 147.

Now answer the questions.

---

1. What is the main topic of conversation?

   (A) Ways in which an interview assignment has been troublesome

   (B) Tips for how to conduct an effective interview

   (C) Techniques for persuading someone to do you a favor

   (D) Ways to make a bland life story appear more interesting

2. Why does the student switch to interviewing his grandmother?

   (A) His grandfather refused to be interviewed.

   (B) His Communications teacher requested the switch.

   (C) He could not interview his grandfather in time.

   (D) Another student also interviewed a pilot.

3. Why does the professor bring up the idea of a "consolation prize"?

   (A) To motivate the student to write the best interview in class

   (B) To explain the grandmother's reluctance to being interviewed

   (C) To suggest that a good interview is its own reward

   (D) To distract the student from worrying about the interview

4. How does the professor interpret the grandmother's refusal to do the interview?

   (A) The grandmother does not want to offer the student any life advice.

   (B) The grandmother hoped that the student would interview his grandfather.

   (C) The grandmother did actually want to be interviewed.

   (D) The grandmother is ashamed to tell her grandson about her life history.

5. Which of the student's behaviors did the professor imply have contributed to problems with his grandmother? *Choose 2 answers.*

   A   Failing to make his grandmother feel more needed or respected

   B   Asking his grandmother for advice too frequently

   C   Requesting an interview with his grandmother too unenthusiastically

   D   Insisting on having an interview with a pilot.

14.4

 Listen to Track 148.

Now answer the questions.

1. Why does the student go to see the professor?

   (A) To apply for the teaching assistant position

   (B) To ask about the teaching assistant position

   (C) To encourage her to pay him for working as her teaching assistant

   (D) To ask about his grade in her class

2. What will be the focus of the professor's upcoming class?

   (A) Issues about race

   (B) Two critical papers

   (C) Novels written by Octavia Butler

   (D) Issues about gender

3. What will the student have the opportunity to do as teaching assistant?

   (A) To recommend novels for the class to read and discuss

   (B) To grade the two critical papers

   (C) To write the class syllabus

   (D) To lead class discussion

4. What does the professor need to get approval from the department to do?

   (A) Hire a teaching assistant

   (B) Teach the class

   (C) Pay the student for working as her teaching assistant

   (D) Have more than 15 students in the class

5. What is the student concerned about?

   (A) That being teaching assistant means he will have less time to work at his job

   (B) Whether he wants to lead class discussion

   (C) That being teaching assistant will take time away from his other classes

   (D) That the professor will not offer him the teaching assistant position

14.5

 Listen to Track 149.

Now answer the questions.

1. Why does the student go to the career services office?

   (A) To confirm that he can begin an independent research project

   (B) To learn what courses are required to study biochemistry

   (C) To find out how to specialize in a certain subtopic

   (D) To get advice about how to approach a company

2. What is the student worried that a research company at the career fair might suggest?

   (A) To take a course that is not offered at this university

   (B) To transfer to a different university

   (C) To begin an independent research project

   (D) To focus on interdisciplinary aspects of biochemistry

3. What does the administrator imply about standing out when applying for jobs?

   (A) Developing a specialty in a specific topic will cause the student to stand out to employers.

   (B) It is better to look similar to other candidates then to stand out in any significant way.

   (C) The student is already standing out in relevant ways.

   (D) It is good to think about this early in the student's academic career.

4. How does the administrator suggest that the student begin his independent research project? *Choose 2 answers.*

    A By waiting until he is a senior to begin the process

    B By analyzing the research being done by professors at the university

    C By meeting with a professor

    D By talking to companies about the research projects that they are engaged in

---

 Listen to Track 150.

Now answer the question.

---

5. Why does the student say this?

    (A) To acknowledge that he cannot study insect biochemistry at this university

    (B) To acknowledge that he has significant work to do

    (C) To indicate that he has an upcoming meeting with a research company

    (D) To indicate that he needs to catch up with classwork

14.6

 Listen to Track 151.

Now answer the questions.

---

1. Why does the student go to the computer center?

    (A) To learn how to type a research paper

    (B) To find someone who will evaluate his presentation

    (C) To ask about learning how to use PowerPoint

    (D) To find out whether other students struggle in this area, too

2. How did the student probably feel when he first arrived at the computer center?

    (A) Embarrassed about his lack of knowledge with PowerPoint

    (B) Excited to be learning a new skill

    (C) Upset that only volunteer staff is available

    (D) Nervous about the amount of research that still needs to be done

3. What does the administrator imply about the student's professor?

   (A) The professor will have no opinion on the quality of the student's PowerPoint.

   (B) The professor could mistakenly believe that the student was unprepared for the project.

   (C) The professor should have taught the student the basics of PowerPoint before this assignment.

   (D) The professor did not intend for everyone to have to use PowerPoint.

4. What does the administrator imply about the student videos made a few years ago?

   (A) They were designed to help people in the same position as this student.

   (B) They are meant for only advanced PowerPoint users.

   (C) They can be used in only one of the campus's computer centers.

   (D) They will cover most, but not all, of the basics of PowerPoint.

5. What will the administrator do to help the student?

   (A) Tutor him one-on-one in PowerPoint

   (B) Contact one of the volunteers to get him started earlier

   (C) Answer the questions that the videos don't cover today

   (D) Provide a list of books that teach PowerPoint skills

14.7

 Listen to Track 152.

Now answer the questions.

1. Why does the student go to the music department office?

   (A) To begin the process of declaring a major in music

   (B) To find out how to gain access to rooms with a piano

   (C) To report that certain rooms have been left open or unlocked

   (D) To sign up for auditions for singing groups

2. Why does the student want to use the rooms downstairs?

   (A) To play music with a group of other students

   (B) To practice an instrument that he plays as a hobby

   (C) To prepare for an upcoming audition

   (D) To study in a peaceful and quiet environment

3. Has the student ever used the practice rooms before, and, if so, under what circumstances has he used them?

   (A) He has never used the rooms before.

   (B) He has used the rooms before, but only during the music department's office hours.

   (C) He has used the rooms before, when a friend has lent him the key.

   (D) He has used the rooms before, when their doors have been left unlocked or open.

4. What options does the student have to use the practice rooms outside of standard hours? *Choose 2 answers.*

   A   Borrowing the key from a student majoring in music

   B   Declaring a major in music

   C   Joining a singing group

   D   Taking a course in music theory

 Listen to Track 153.

Now answer the question.

---

5. What is the secretary's point when she says this?

   (A) Only a small number of the university's students declare a music major.

   (B) The system for assigning the rooms is extremely ineffective.

   (C) Students will probably be able to use the rooms for longer than one hour.

   (D) Very few people can use the rooms because the rules for access are so strict.

14.8

 Listen to Track 154.

Now answer the questions.

---

1. Why does the student go to see the professor?

   (A) To argue for a better grade in the class

   (B) To find out more about engineering

   (C) To borrow some coins and toothpicks from her

   (D) To discuss difficulties learning the material

2. What is the professor's concern about flashcards?

    (A) They are more expensive than candy and toothpicks.

    (B) They are not a very active form of learning.

    (C) They didn't help her to learn engineering.

    (D) They cannot be used during the student's test.

3. Why does the professor say that she set out to teach engineering?

    (A) To express dissatisfaction with her current job

    (B) To provide context for her interest in organic chemistry

    (C) To suggest that the student use an engineer's perspective

    (D) To help the student appreciate building things

4. Which tactic or tactics did the professor suggest for learning molecules? *Select all that apply.*

    [A] Appreciate them as sculptures

    [B] Model them with coins and toothpicks

    [C] Reward learning with candy

    [D] Relate them to math

 Listen to Track 155.

Now answer the question.

5. (A) To express skepticism

    (B) To request a different numerical example

    (C) To show appreciation

    (D) To utilize new understanding

Answer Key—14.1

Question	Correct Answer	Right/Wrong	Category
1	B		Gist-purpose
2	B		Detail
3	D		Detail
4	A		Function of What Is Said
5	D		Function of What Is Said

Answer Key—14.2

Question	Correct Answer	Right/Wrong	Category
1	D		Gist-content
2	A		Detail
3	C, D		Detail
4	B		Inference
5	D		Function of What Is Said

Answer Key—14.3

Question	Correct Answer	Right/Wrong	Category
1	A		Gist-content
2	D		Detail
3	B		Function of What Is Said
4	C		Detail
5	A, C		Inference

Answer Key—14.4

Question	Correct Answer	Right/Wrong	Category
1	B		Gist-purpose
2	C		Detail
3	D		Detail
4	C		Connecting Content
5	A		Detail

Answer Key—14.5

Question	Correct Answer	Right/Wrong	Category
1	C		Gist-purpose
2	A		Inference
3	D		Inference
4	B, C		Detail
5	B		Function of What Is Said

Answer Key—14.6

Question	Correct Answer	Right/Wrong	Category
1	C		Gist-purpose
2	A		Speaker's Attitude
3	B		Inference
4	D		Inference
5	C		Detail

Answer Key—14.7

Question	Correct Answer	Right/Wrong	Category
1	B		Gist-purpose
2	B		Detail
3	D		Inference
4	A, B		Detail
5	C		Function of What Is Said

Answer Key—14.8

Question	Correct Answer	Right/Wrong	Category
1	D		Gist-purpose
2	B		Detail
3	B		Function of What Is Said
4	A, B, D		Connecting Content
5	A		Function of What Is Said

Answers and Explanations—14.1

Linguistics Conference—Track 142

NARRATOR: Listen to a conversation between a student and a professor.

PROFESSOR: I'm glad you came by, Jordan. Have a seat.

STUDENT: So, Professor Zhang... I got your email... about sending my final project to a conference? I figured I'd just, you know, come in and ask you more about it. Instead of going back and forth.

PROFESSOR: Yes, well, as I said in my email, I was very impressed with your project. I actually shared it with a few other people in the department... it's very interesting work. You really went above and beyond—it would definitely fit in as a conference presentation.

STUDENT: Thanks. Um, I guess I find linguistics really interesting. I didn't even know it was a thing until this year... I wish I'd taken the intro class earlier.

PROFESSOR: Well, you've certainly made up for lost time.

STUDENT: Thanks.

PROFESSOR: So, what do you think about submitting your project to the linguistics conference?

STUDENT: Well, uh... to be honest... I was hoping you could just give me more details on, like, what it entails. You know... I don't really know much about how this kind of thing works. I was sort of surprised, when I saw your email... I've never been to a conference before.

PROFESSOR: So, here's how it works. You would work with an advisor in the linguistics department. You'd do this over the summer. You might end up deciding on some additional research to do or you might just focus on writing up what you've already done. In the end, usually what happens is, you submit your abstract to the conference in September. Then, if it's accepted, you either create a poster or you prepare a talk about your project... sometimes, both.

STUDENT: Uh, my advisor told me ... uh, I didn't get the best grades my first year. Actually, my GPA is pretty bad because of it. So my advisor suggested retaking some of those classes... anyways, I was thinking about doing that this summer. So I'm not sure.

PROFESSOR: This is really a good opportunity, though—if there's any way you can do it, you should. Your project is really promising... you have a lot of insight into Appalachian English. And going to a conference, you get to meet actual, you know, working linguists. You get to see what research is happening right now. That's a valuable experience.

STUDENT: So, uh, how does it work… over the summer? Do I just… work on the project? And then email you about it?

PROFESSOR: No, you'd need to talk to your academic advisor. You have to sign up for a particular course, to get credit for a research project. It counts for a certain number of hours, and the professor who's listed is whoever's advising you in the department—that would most likely be me.

STUDENT: It's a course… so, I'd get a grade, right?

PROFESSOR: Yes—but given the work I've seen from you already, you don't have to worry about it hurting your GPA.

STUDENT: Okay, I just need to ask my advisor… I already told him I was planning to take some summer classes, so I need to see how this all fits in. I want to make sure I can still graduate on time.

PROFESSOR: Okay. Look into it, and get back to me if you're still interested. And let me know if you need me to talk to your advisor. I'd love to have you work on this more over the summer.

1.	Why does the student go to see his professor?	**GIST-PURPOSE.** What question does the student want to talk to the professor about?
✗	(A) He wants his professor's help with his final project.	The student has already completed his final project at the time of this conversation.
✓	(B) He is seeking more information about an email that his professor sent him.	**CORRECT.** At the beginning of the conversation, the student states that he got an email from the professor (regarding his final project) and came to her office to ask more questions about it.
✗	(C) He wants his professor to speak with his academic advisor.	The professor suggests doing this at the end of the conversation, but this was not the student's original reason to visit the professor.
✗	(D) He has a question about Appalachian English.	The student's final project dealt with Appalachian English. However, the student and the professor do not discuss the content of the final project.

2.	Why does the student mention that he earned poor grades during his first year of college?	**DETAIL.** Because of poor grades, the student was planning to retake several classes during the summer. This might conflict with the professor's invitation to do a research project.
✗	(A) He is unhappy with the grade that he earned in this professor's class.	The student does not mention the grade he earned. However, based on the content of the conversation, he likely performed well in the class.
✓	(B) His advisor has asked him to retake some classes during the summer.	**CORRECT.** The student mentions his first-year grades in order to explain why he originally planned to take summer classes, rather than doing research.
✗	(C) He does not think he will earn a good grade in the research class.	The student asks whether the research class is graded later in the conversation. However, this is not why he mentions his first-year grades.
✗	(D) Linguistics classes are especially difficult for the student.	The student states that he did not take any linguistics classes until this year. So, this answer choice does not relate to his first-year grades.

3.   What does the student need to do before deciding whether to spend the summer doing research?

  ✗ (A) Finish his linguistics final project

  ✗ (B) Complete his summer classes

  ✗ (C) Check the grades he earned on his final exams

  ✓ (D) Speak with his academic advisor about his plans

DETAIL. The student indicates that he will need to speak with his academic advisor to ensure that he will graduate on time.

At the time of the conversation, the student has already finished his final project.

The student is considering whether to do research as an alternative to taking summer classes, not after finishing his summer classes.

The student is concerned about his grades, but he does not mention his final exams.

CORRECT. Before deciding whether to register for the summer research course, the student will need to speak with his academic advisor about changing his original plan to take summer classes.

Track 143

NARRATOR: Listen again to part of the conversation. Then answer the question.

PROFESSOR: No, you'd need to talk to your academic advisor. You have to sign up for a particular course, to get credit for a research project. It counts for a certain number of hours, and the professor who's listed is whoever's advising you in the department—that would most likely be me.

STUDENT: It's a course… so, I'd get a grade, right?

PROFESSOR: Yes—but given the work I've seen from you already, you won't have to worry about it hurting your GPA.

NARRATOR: What does the professor mean when she says this:

PROFESSOR: Yes—but given the work I've seen from you already, you don't have to worry about it hurting your GPA.

14

4.   What does the professor mean when she says this?

  ✓ (A) She believes that the student will probably earn a good grade in the summer research course.

  ✗ (B) The student's grade in the course will not be counted as part of his GPA.

  ✗ (C) The student already has a high GPA.

  ✗ (D) The student's grade will be based on the work he has already done in his linguistics course.

FUNCTION OF WHAT IS SAID. This segment takes place at the end of the conversation. The student has already expressed concern about his poor grades. The professor is trying to convince him to take a research course, rather than retaking other classes over the summer.

CORRECT. The student expresses concern about the course being graded, most likely because he is concerned about getting a low grade. The professor responds by reassuring him that his GPA won't decrease, which implies that he won't earn a low grade.

The professor does not suggest that this is the case.

The student mentions earlier in the conversation that his GPA is "pretty bad."

The professor's belief in the student's ability is based on the work he has done already. However, she does not state that the student's grade will be based on this.

Track 144

NARRATOR: Listen again to part of the conversation. Then answer the question.

PROFESSOR: Yes, well, as I said in my email, I was very impressed with your project. I actually shared it with a few other people in the department… it's very interesting work. You really went above and beyond—it would definitely fit in as a conference presentation.

STUDENT: Thanks. Um, I guess I find linguistics really interesting. I didn't even know it was a thing until this year… I wish I'd taken the intro class earlier.

PROFESSOR: Well, you've certainly made up for lost time.

NARRATOR: What does the professor mean when she says this:

PROFESSOR: Well, you've certainly made up for lost time.

5. What does the professor mean when she says this?

FUNCTION OF WHAT IS SAID. This exchange takes place at the beginning of the conversation. The professor is praising the student's work. The student responds by stating that he didn't know about linguistics until this year, which makes it somewhat surprising that his work is of such high quality.

✗ (A) The student has missed a good opportunity by not taking linguistics classes earlier.

The professor's comment is a positive statement, not a negative one.

✗ (B) The student has limited time to do linguistics research before he graduates.

The professor's comment refers to the quality of the student's previous work, not his future work.

✗ (C) The student should submit his final project to a linguistics conference.

This is the professor's overall opinion; however, this is not what the professor is referring to by making the statement, "Well, you've certainly made up for lost time."

✓ (D) The student's work is better than one might expect.

CORRECT. The student has only studied linguistics for a short time. However, according to the professor, his work is of very high quality. Therefore, the student has compensated for the time he didn't spend studying linguistics.

Answers and Explanations—14.2

Interlibrary Loan—Track 145

NARRATOR: Listen to a conversation between a student and a library employee.

STUDENT: Hey, so, um… can you help me with something real quick?

EMPLOYEE: Sure! What can I do for you?

STUDENT: Well, I'm trying to find this book for a research project… I pulled it up in the catalogue, but I'm sort of confused. Here—what does that mean, where it says "external resources"?

EMPLOYEE: Oh, okay. So, that book is actually at a different campus—it looks like we had a copy at this library, but somebody's already checked it out. But it says there are three copies at the Wilmington campus.

STUDENT: Oh… do you think you could recall the one that's checked out? I really, really need it.

EMPLOYEE: Let me see… oh. Are you a graduate student?

STUDENT: No, it's only my first year.

EMPLOYEE: So, it looks like it's checked out to a graduate student… they get priority. You can request a return… but they don't have to bring the book back for a couple of weeks. Unless it's another graduate student who's requesting it, or if it's a professor.

STUDENT: Yeah, that's not gonna work, then. Uh, do I just need to go to the Wilmington library?

EMPLOYEE: Oh! Okay, do you know about interlibrary loan?

STUDENT: No, I've never done that… how does it work?

EMPLOYEE: So, they can actually just send you the book from there. Here, we'll get it set up.

STUDENT: Hmm, okay. How do I get it?

EMPLOYEE: So we put in orders with them once a day, usually early in the morning. And they mail us the books… then they get here, and we'll send you an email. Or we can call you. You just come by the library office and pick it up… then when you return it, you bring it back to the same place, and we send it back.

STUDENT: Sorry, do you know how long it would be?

EMPLOYEE: It depends on how long it takes the mail to get here… today is Friday, so it might get sent out tomorrow… or they might not get it sent out before Monday. I'm not sure if their interlibrary loan office is open on Saturdays. So, probably the middle of next week, definitely before the end of the week. And then you'd have two weeks to return it.

STUDENT: Oh, man… okay. I sort of put this project off until the last minute. I was really hoping to work on it this weekend.

EMPLOYEE: Do you need the whole book? Or do you just need part of it?

STUDENT: Why?

EMPLOYEE: Well, if you only need one or two chapters, they can scan them… uh, they can just email you the scans. You'd probably get it Monday, maybe even earlier.

STUDENT: Oh, that could work. I'm not totally sure which chapters I need. But I'll see if I can figure it out.

EMPLOYEE: Yeah, the chapters should be listed in the library catalogue… yeah, here, just click on the link that says "view table of contents." And when you've figured it out, just come downstairs to the library office and we'll set it up for you. Or, there's an online form that you can fill out.

STUDENT: Okay, I'll come by the office. I want to make sure I don't mess it up.

1. What are the speakers discussing?

✗ (A) How to complete a research project

✗ (B) How to send books through the mail

✗ (C) How to find a book using the library catalogue

✓ (D) How to use interlibrary loan

GIST-CONTENT. What does the student need help with?

The student is working on a research project. However, this conversation specifically deals with checking out a book from the library.

Sending books through the mail is only mentioned as part of the interlibrary loan process. In addition, the speakers do not discuss exactly how this is done.

The student has already successfully found the book using the library catalogue. His question relates to borrowing the book, not finding it.

CORRECT. The library employee explains to the student how to use interlibrary loan to borrow a book.

2. Why does the employee ask whether the student is a graduate student?

✓ (A) Graduate students can recall library books that are checked out to other graduate students.

✗ (B) The student seems unfamiliar with the university library.

✗ (C) Only graduate students can check out books via interlibrary loan.

✗ (D) The employee wants more information about the student's research project.

DETAIL. The employee indicates that different types of book borrowers have different privileges. Graduate students and teachers can request that a book be returned early if checked out by another person.

CORRECT. The student initially wants to recall the book, so he can borrow it. The employee explains that this is only possible if he is a graduate student.

The student isn't familiar with interlibrary loan, but this isn't why the employee asks the question. Instead, she brings up a specific difference between policies for graduate students and policies for undergraduates.

The student is not a graduate student, but he is still able to use interlibrary loan.

The speakers do not discuss the research project itself.

3. Which of the following services does interlibrary loan provide? *Choose 2 answers.*

✗ [A] Helping students select books to use for university research projects

✗ [B] Acquiring new books for the library collection

✓ [C] Mailing books from libraries on other campuses to the university library

✓ [D] Scanning parts of a book and emailing them to students

DETAIL. The employee offers to use the interlibrary loan either to have an entire book sent over from a different library or to have a portion of the book scanned and emailed to the student.

The student is trying to complete a research project. However, he does not receive help in selecting book.

This is not mentioned in the conversation.

CORRECT. This is the library employee's initial suggestion to the student.

CORRECT. The student and the library employee agree on this as a solution to the student's problem.

4. What will the student most likely do next?

✗ (A) Go to the library at the Wilmington campus.

✓ (B) Decide which chapters of the book he needs for his project.

✗ (C) Complete the online interlibrary loan form.

✗ (D) Find the other books he needs for his project.

INFERENCE. What is the next step that the student will take, immediately after finishing this conversation?

The student uses interlibrary loan to avoid traveling to the other library.

CORRECT. The employee says that the other library can scan a few chapters of the book. At the end of the conversation, she shows the student how to identify these chapters.

The student says that he will go to the interlibrary loan office, rather than filling out the online form.

The speakers do not mention other books during their conversation. It is not clear whether the student needs additional books.

Track 146

NARRATOR: Listen again to part of the conversation. Then answer the question.

EMPLOYEE: So, it looks like it's checked out to a graduate student… they get priority. You can request a return… but they don't have to bring the book back for a couple of weeks. Unless it's another graduate student who's requesting it, or if it's a professor.

STUDENT: Yeah, that's not gonna work, then.

NARRATOR: What does the student mean when he says this:

STUDENT: Yeah, that's not gonna work, then.

5. **FUNCTION OF WHAT IS SAID.** The student and the employee are trying to find a way for the student to check out a book. One possible solution involves recalling the book from the student who currently has it. However, the employee mentions a problem: it may take several weeks for the book to be returned.

✗ (A) The student does not believe that the graduate student will return the book.

✗ (B) The student will not be able to complete his research project.

✗ (C) The student wants the library employee to request that the book be returned

✓ (D) The student needs the book in less than two weeks.

The issue is that the graduate student might not return the book quickly enough. The speakers don't discuss whether it will be returned eventually.

The conversation does not address whether the book is critical to the student's research project. Also, the student is eventually able to obtain the book in another way.

The student decides to look into other ways of obtaining the book, instead.

CORRECT. The employee tells the student that requesting a return might take a couple of weeks. The student responds negatively to this. The student later asks about options that might get the book to him more quickly.

Answers and Explanations—14.3

Family Interview—Track 147

NARRATOR: Listen to a conversation between a student and his professor.

PROFESSOR: Hey, Pete. Why the long face?

STUDENT: I'm just … struggling this week.

PROFESSOR: How so?

STUDENT: I've got a deadline this Friday… not your class… my Communications class… I, I need to interview someone over the age of 70.

PROFESSOR: Oh, that sounds interesting. Who are you interviewing?

STUDENT: Well, I was supposed to be interviewing my grandfather. He grew up in the country, in Kansas. He started flying crop dusting planes when he was 18 and later on worked at the state Chamber of Commerce.

PROFESSOR: It was supposed to be him? But it's not?

STUDENT: Right. I actually already did the interview a few weeks ago, but then I found out yesterday that a classmate of mine is also interviewing a grandparent who was a pilot. But his grandfather was a fighter pilot, who got captured during a combat mission and escaped. I can't compete with that. So I asked my Grandma if I could interview her instead, and she's telling me she doesn't want to do it.

PROFESSOR: Hmm, that's pretty surprising. Grandparents usually love to tell their grandchildren about their life history… it's usually a source of pride.

STUDENT: Exactly. I don't know what's going on. My Grandma actually has a pretty good story, too. She grew up on the South Side of Chicago, at the end of the Great Migration, so she saw her neighborhood really transform over the course of a couple decades. And then later when she moved to Kansas to marry my Grandpa, she was actually mayor of the city where they lived for about 10 years. I called her up yesterday and told her that I didn't want to use my interview with Grandpa, now that I knew my classmate was coming with a better pilot story. So I told her that I guess I would have to interview her instead.

PROFESSOR: Wow. I hope you didn't phrase it like that.

STUDENT: I did… I know… it sounds like I'm dreading it. I was just mad I had to do the interview again.

PROFESSOR: Well, I'm sure she feels like the "consolation prize."

STUDENT: Consolation prize?

PROFESSOR: That's a name for a prize you give to the loser of a contest. Sometimes people use it to describe someone's second choice. Your first choice was your Grandpa, but if you couldn't get him, then your consolation prize was your Grandma… basically, I'm just saying she probably feels bad that you picked him first. I mean… she was a mayor!

STUDENT: Yeah, she probably has the better story. I just enjoy talking to my Grandpa more. He doesn't lecture me as much as she does about how I should go about my life.

PROFESSOR: It sounds like overall she doesn't think that you respect her opinion or experience too much. Have you considered… making her feel more needed?

STUDENT: Yes, but I'm worried that if I make her feel more needed it will only encourage her more to tell me what to do all the time.

PROFESSOR: Well, I guess you'll have to figure out how you want to deal with it. I think… if she knew that you valued her advice, she might be more patient about waiting for you to ask for it.

STUDENT: Hmm. You might be right. Thanks for the chat.

1. What is the main topic of conversation?

   GIST-CONTENT. What issue motivated the student to come to office hours?

   ✓ (A) Ways in which an interview assignment has been troublesome

   CORRECT. The student talks about needing to change his original topic/interviewee and about how his second choice is refusing to be interviewed.

   ✗ (B) Tips for how to conduct an effective interview

   The conversation never gets into specific interviewing techniques. It centers more around getting someone to agree to be interviewed.

   ✗ (C) Techniques for persuading someone to do you a favor

   Although the professor offers the student advice about dealing with his grandmother, the general topic of persuading someone to do you a favor is not covered.

   ✗ (D) Ways to make a bland life story appear more interesting

   No one suggests or requests ways to make the grandfather's life story seem more interesting.

2. Why does the student switch to interviewing his grandmother?

   DETAIL. What prompted the student to switch from his grandfather to his grandmother?

   ✗ (A) His grandfather refused to be interviewed.

   The student had already completed the interview with his grandfather.

   ✗ (B) His Communications teacher requested the switch.

   There is no information about the teacher of the class.

   ✗ (C) He could not interview his grandfather in time.

   The student had already completed the interview with his grandfather.

   ✓ (D) Another student also interviewed a pilot.

   CORRECT. The student initially interviewed his grandfather, a pilot, but was dismayed when another student supposedly had a better pilot interview.

14

3. Why does the professor bring up the idea of a "consolation prize"?

✗ (A) To motivate the student to write the best interview in class

✓ (B) To explain the grandmother's reluctance to being interviewed

✗ (C) To suggest that a good interview is its own reward

✗ (D) To distract the student from worrying about the interview

FUNCTION OF WHAT IS SAID. What part of the conversation caused this topic to come up? To whom or what did the term refer?

The professor is not offering the student a prize for writing the best interview.

CORRECT. The professor uses "consolation prize" as a way to describe the grandmother's disappointed feelings.

"Consolation prize" does not describe a rewarding feeling the student would get.

This is close to the opposite of what is going on. The professor is identifying the current problem with conducting the interview.

4. How does the professor interpret the grandmother's refusal to do the interview?

✗ (A) The grandmother does not want to offer the student any life advice.

✗ (B) The grandmother hoped that the student would interview his grandfather.

✓ (C) The grandmother did actually want to be interviewed.

✗ (D) The grandmother is ashamed to tell her grandson about her life history.

DETAIL. What does the professor think is the real reason for her refusal?

The professor never judges the quality of life advice the student gets.

The professor suggests the opposite, that the grandmother wanted to be the first choice.

CORRECT. The professor is impressed by the grandmother's life story and believes that grandparents usually like to share their life stories. He thinks she is only refusing out of hurt feelings.

The professor suggests the opposite, saying that grandparents usually relate their life histories with pride.

5. Which of the student's behaviors did the professor imply have contributed to problems with his grandmother? *Choose 2 answers.*

✓ [A] Failing to make his grandmother feel more needed or respected

✗ [B] Asking his grandmother for advice too frequently

✓ [C] Requesting an interview with his grandmother too unenthusiastically

✗ [D] Insisting on having an interview with a pilot.

INFERENCE. The professor notes the student's lack of excitement when asking his grandmother for an interview ("consolation prize") and his reluctance to show her that he appreciates her opinions and experience.

CORRECT. Towards the end, the professor speculates that the grandmother might offer too much advice as a result of not feeling needed or respected.

This is the opposite of the student's behavior. The grandmother offers too much advice, alienating the student.

CORRECT. When the professor hears the way the student requested an interview, he tells the student that she probably feels like the "consolation prize" and might be upset at being his second choice.

Since the student is trying to interview his grandmother, he is definitely not insisting on interviewing a pilot.

Answers and Explanations—14.4

Teaching Assistant Position—Track 148

NARRATOR: Listen to a conversation between a student and his professor.

PROFESSOR: Oh, hi Gavin. Come on in.

STUDENT: Hi… thanks Professor Wolf for seeing me. I'm here… I want to talk with you about the teaching assistant position. You know I applied for it last week?

PROFESSOR: Yes, I know. I'm glad you came to see me. I was about to call you today to tell you that I would like to offer you the position; I think you will do a wonderful job.

STUDENT: Oh, wow! Thank you… wow I'm really excited. Thank you for choosing me.

PROFESSOR: You're welcome. Like I said, I think you're going to do a great job.

STUDENT: Wow, well do you mind if I, um, ask you some questions about the position?

PROFESSOR: Of course! Ask anything you like.

STUDENT: Uh, ok, thanks. The first thing is… what is the class going to be about? You mentioned that you are creating a new class, that this is the first time you will teach it?

PROFESSOR: Yes, that's right. As you know, it's an upper level seminar class and we're going to be focusing on novels. Specifically, the class is going to read several novels by Octavia Butler, which is something I haven't gotten to do before. We are going to discuss a lot of different issues about speculative fiction, race, class, and gender in her work. I'm expecting the students to be able to have in-depth discussion in class, write essays, and meet outside of class to continue those analyses. They'll also have to write and revise two critical papers.

STUDENT: Oh, wow. That will be the first speculative fiction class, right?

PROFESSOR: Right. And since I'm spending a lot of time putting together the class and making a new syllabus, I am going to need some help, which is where you come in.

STUDENT: OK, yeah. So, um, what do you think I'll be doing to help? And how many hours per week do you expect it will take?

PROFESSOR: Well, I'm still working all that out. But right now I would say it should take you about 10 hours per week. I'm going to want to you organize and keep track of discussion groups, and to grade the first round of student essays. You may also have the opportunity to lead some of the discussion in class.

STUDENT: Really? I could get to lead class discussion?

PROFESSOR: Sure, once in a while. It will be good practice for you.

STUDENT: Ok, um, that sounds great. Ten hours a week, though, that's a lot of hours. I'm worried that will take time away from my job.

PROFESSOR: It is a lot of hours. I know it's a big commitment.

STUDENT: So… do you think I could get paid for that time? I know, uh, you didn't say anything about the salary in the posting for the position, but sometimes teaching assistants get paid, right?

PROFESSOR: Uh, yes, sometimes they do.

STUDENT: So could I?

PROFESSOR: Uh, I don't know yet. Here's the issue, Gavin. I have to get approval from the department, and they only pay teaching assistants for classes if there are more than 15 students. So far I have 12 students.

STUDENT: Oh, OK. When you can let me know?

PROFESSOR: By the end of this month. I will know for sure then.

STUDENT: OK, thanks Professor. I will wait to hear from you.

1.   Why does the student go to see the professor?

GIST-PURPOSE. What does the student say he wants to talk about?

  ✗ (A) To apply for the teaching assistant position

The student asks the professor if she knows he applied for the position. He mentions that he applied the week before.

  ✓ (B) To ask about the teaching assistant position

CORRECT. The student begins the conversation by telling the professor that he is there to talk about the teaching assistant position. Then he asks her several questions about it.

  ✗ (C) To encourage her to pay him for working as her teaching assistant

The student does ask if he will be paid for the teaching assistant position. However, this is after he has asked several general questions about the position. He also does not know that he will get the position at the start of the conversation.

  ✗ (D) To ask about his grade in her class

The student and the professor do not discuss his grade. It is also not clear that the student is taking a class with the professor. They only discuss him working as a teaching assistant for a future class.

2.   What will be the focus of the professor's upcoming class?

DETAIL. The student asks about the class where he will be a teaching assistant.

  ✗ (A) Issues about race

The professor notes that the class participants will discuss issues about race as part of the analysis of the novels they will be reading. It is not the focus of the class.

  ✗ (B) Two critical papers

The professor mentions that the participants in the class will have to write two critical papers. She mentions the papers as she is talking about what she expects of the students in the class. The critical papers are not the focus of the class.

  ✓ (C) Novels written by Octavia Butler

CORRECT. The professor says that the class will be a novel seminar. She specifically says that the focus will be on novels written by Octavia Butler.

  ✗ (D) Issues about gender

The professor notes that the class participants will discuss issues about gender as part of the analysis of the novels they will be reading. It is not the focus of the class.

3.   What will the student have the opportunity to do as teaching assistant?

   ✗   Ⓐ To recommend novels for the class to read and discuss

   ✗   Ⓑ To grade the two critical papers

   ✗   Ⓒ To write the class syllabus

   ✓   Ⓓ To lead class discussion

DETAIL. The professor and the student discuss several aspects of the teaching assistant position. Both of them mention one particular opportunity.

The professor does not suggest that the student will have the opportunity to recommend novels for the class. She mentions that the class will read novels by Octavia Butler, but does not discuss which novels or any recommendations from the student.

The professor mentions that the student will grade the first round of student essays, not the two critical papers.

The professor explains that she has a lot of work to do because she is creating a new class. She mentions writing the syllabus as something she will have to do as the professor, not something the student will have to do as teaching assistant.

CORRECT. The professor mentions several things that the student will do as teaching assistant. She specifically mentions that he will have the opportunity to lead class discussion. He then asks her about it again to confirm.

4.   What does the professor need to get approval from the department to do?

   ✗   Ⓐ Hire a teaching assistant

   ✗   Ⓑ Teach the class

   ✓   Ⓒ Pay the student for working as her teaching assistant

   ✗   Ⓓ Have more than 15 students in the class

CONNECTING CONTENT. The professor tells the student she'll know about this issue by the end of the month.

The professor does not say she needs approval to hire a teaching assistant. She offers the student the teaching assistant position during the discussion.

The professor does not say she has to get approval to teach the class. In fact, she is already planning the class.

CORRECT. The student asks if he will be paid for working as a teaching assistant. The professor responds that she has to get approval from the department in order to pay him.

The professor does mention the number of students she hopes will enroll in the class. However, she does not say that she needs department approval for more than 15 students.

5. What is the student concerned about?

    ✓ (A) That being teaching assistant means he will have less time to work at his job

    ✗ (B) Whether he wants to lead class discussion

    ✗ (C) That being teaching assistant will take time away from his other classes

    ✗ (D) That the professor will not offer him the teaching assistant position

DETAIL. The student and the professor discuss the time commitment for the teaching assistant position.

CORRECT. When the student finds out the teaching assistant position will take 10 hours per week, he says that he is worried it will take time away from his job. He is expressing concern that he will have less time to work at his job.

The student responds positively to the professor's suggestion that he will have the opportunity to lead class discussion. He does not say he is worried about it.

The student does mention his concern about the time commitment. But it is not because of his other classes. In fact, he doesn't say anything about his other classes.

The professor offers him the teaching assistant position at the beginning of the conversation.

Answers and Explanations—14.5

Niche Study—Track 149

NARRATOR: Listen to a conversation between a student and an employee in the university's career services office.

STUDENT: Hello. I was wondering if I could ask you a question or two?

ADMINISTRATOR: Absolutely. What can I help you with?

STUDENT: I'm interested in studying the biochemistry of insects, but I'm not sure how to do that.

ADMINISTRATOR: What do you mean?

STUDENT: Um, well, all the courses offered are a little too general. I mean, there's biology, chemistry, biochemistry, but I'm not sure how to focus in on insects. I know this is only the first semester, but I wanna make sure that I'm taking the right courses.

ADMINISTRATOR: Oh, got it. Well, it's pretty normal for students to take general classes in their first and second years in order to get ready for the more specific classes during the junior and senior years.

STUDENT: I know, but I'm not sure how to make myself stand out to companies when I start applying for jobs after graduation.

ADMINISTRATOR: That's a great thing to think about. And it's good that you're thinking about it this early in your studies. Have you talked to any biochem companies that specialize in insects?

STUDENT: No, I wasn't sure how to approach them.

ADMINISTRATOR: It can feel a little awkward, can't it? There's a career fair coming up that will host several different companies, including some local biochem researchers. It's designed to be a place where students can ask questions and talk about potential jobs.

STUDENT: Oh, that would be great! I can go get insight into what they're looking for. Just make sure I'm on the right track.

ADMINISTRATOR: I think that's a good plan.

STUDENT: But what if what they're looking for isn't offered here? I mean, there's no class called "Biochem of Insects" or "Exoskeletons 101."

ADMINISTRATOR: That's true, the classes don't get that specific. Maybe you should consider an independent research project.

STUDENT: I thought that was just for seniors.

ADMINISTRATOR: Typically it is, but if you're this passionate about a topic, and you have the time and resources to commit to research, there's no reason why it can't begin early.

STUDENT: Huh… how do I start that?

ADMINISTRATOR: Well, in a research project you work very closely with a professor. So I'd start by looking at some of the research the professors on campus are doing to see if any are similar to the kind of work that you're interested in.

STUDENT: Okay, I can do that.

ADMINISTRATOR: Then go meet with the professor. Tell him your idea and what you specifically want to do. The more concrete your research topic, the easier it will be for the professor to guide you to the appropriate path.

STUDENT: Wow, that sounds like a lot of work, but it seems like it will pay off in the long run.

ADMINISTRATOR: I think so. This kind of initiative will really help you to focus on what you want to do and to stand out when you start applying to jobs.

STUDENT: Great, thanks. I better go get started!

1.	Why does the student go to the career services office?	**GIST-PURPOSE.** The student wants to study a specific subtopic that's not offered as a class. He's looking for guidance about how to do that.
✗	(A) To confirm that he can begin an independent research project	The administrator eventually suggests an independent research project, but that is not something that the student had considered before this meeting.
✗	(B) To learn what courses are required to study biochemistry	The student seems to have no problem understanding the available courses, but is not sure how to specialize in insect studies.
✓	(C) To find out how to specialize in a certain subtopic	**CORRECT.** The student is passionate about the study of insects, but is unsure how to pursue that in his courses.
✗	(D) To get advice about how to approach a company	This is mentioned, but was not the reason for his visit.

2.   What is the student worried that a research company at the career fair might suggest?

INFERENCE. Upon learning about the career fair, the student is excited, but also worried: "But what if what they're looking for isn't offered here?"

✓ (A) To take a course that is not offered at this university

CORRECT. The student worries that a company at the career fair may be looking for a study of more specific topics.

✗ (B) To transfer to a different university

The student does not mention this.

✗ (C) To begin an independent research project

This is something the student seems to intend to do. He is not worried that a company might suggest it.

✗ (D) To focus on interdisciplinary aspects of biochemistry

The student does not mention this issue.

3.   What does the administrator imply about standing out when applying for jobs?

INFERENCE. The administrator states that it's good that the student is starting to think about this early and she eventually suggests that an independent research project will help to achieve that goal.

✗ (A) Developing a specialty in a specific topic will cause the student to stand out to employers.

Specialization is the student's goal, not advice given to him.

✗ (B) It is better to look similar to other candidates then to stand out in any significant way.

This seems to be contradicted.

✗ (C) The student is already standing out in relevant ways.

The administrator does not mention this.

✓ (D) It is good to think about this early in the student's academic career.

CORRECT. She states that this is a valid concern, and says it is good that the student is thinking about it early.

4.   How does the administrator suggest that the student begin his independent research project? *Choose 2 answers.*

DETAIL. The student should first research what the professors at the university are studying, then meet with a professor to go over the student's proposal.

✗ [A] By waiting until he is a senior to begin the process

She says there's no reason to wait, assuming he has the time to commit this.

✓ [B] By analyzing the research being done by professors at the university

CORRECT. This will have to be done so that the student will be able to find a research project that he's interested in.

✓ [C] By meeting with a professor

CORRECT. After researching a professor, the next step will be to discuss the student's plans for a potential research project.

✗ [D] By talking to companies about the research projects that they are engaged in

The student should meet with companies for a different reason, not because of the independent research project.

Track 150

NARRATOR: Why does the student say this:

STUDENT: I better go get started!

5.   Why does the student say this?

FUNCTION OF WHAT IS SAID. The student seems to think starting an independent research project will be a big undertaking, but he believes he is up to the challenge.

✗ (A) To acknowledge that he cannot study insect biochemistry at this university

The student comes to the opposite conclusion

✓ (B) To acknowledge that he has significant work to do

CORRECT. The student seems to grasp that developing an independent research project will take a lot of work and time, but it's something that he is invested in.

✗ (C) To indicate that he has an upcoming meeting with a research company

The student has not scheduled any meetings that he referenced.

✗ (D) To indicate that he needs to catch up with classwork

There's no discussion about the classwork he has or has not completed.

Answers and Explanations—14.6

PowerPoint Problems—Track 151

NARRATOR: Listen to a conversation between a student and an employee in the campus computer center.

ADMINISTRATOR: Good afternoon! What can I do for you?

STUDENT: Hi, um, I have, I guess a strange question. I'm just, I mean, I have this presentation that I need to do for this class and, well, I've done the research and everything, but I'm not sure how to—do you offer any classes on creating PowerPoint presentations?

ADMINISTRATOR: Well, we don't offer classes, but there are several volunteers who would be happy to work with you to make your PowerPoint look more professional, or to help with templates, or things like that. What kind of help are you looking for?

STUDENT: I guess I need something a little bit more in-depth than that. To be honest, I've never actually used PowerPoint. I'm just not that comfortable with doing much other than typing papers on computers.

ADMINISTRATOR: Oh, that shouldn't be a problem. Our volunteers are great at helping students to learn new programs. And PowerPoint is pretty straightforward; there's even tutorials within the program if you decide you need some extra help.

STUDENT: That sounds good. I really want this presentation to go well, and the students who have presented already have all seemed very comfortable with the program, and I don't want to look unprepared.

ADMINISTRATOR: Sure, since you got the research done, you want to make sure that the professor is able to see the work you put into this project.

STUDENT: Right. My presentation is scheduled for next week, so I need to get started right away. Is there a volunteer available today?

ADMINISTRATOR: Actually, no. Our volunteers don't come in until the end of the week.

STUDENT: Oh no. I'm not sure I'll be able to get everything done if I have just a few days to put things together.

ADMINISTRATOR: Hmm, well, you could get started on your own. Like I said, there are some tutorials in the program. Oh, I just remembered, there are some videos one of the students made a few years back for a class project. The topic was the best ways to use PowerPoint.

STUDENT: Do the videos go through the basics?

ADMINISTRATOR: Most of them. You'll probably be able to figure out anything the video doesn't cover just by playing with the controls and tools in the program.

STUDENT: Okay, I'll try that, and then come back at the end of the week to talk to the volunteers.

ADMINISTRATOR: Tell you what, why don't you get started now, in this computer center. I'll be managing the front desk for a while, so if you have any questions, you can come talk to me.

STUDENT: That would be great, thanks so much!

ADMINISTRATOR: I'm happy to help.

1. Why does the student go to the computer center?

    GIST-PURPOSE. He wants help learning how to use PowerPoint so that he can present his research project in a professional way.

    ✗ (A) To learn how to type a research paper

    The student already knows how to do this.

    ✗ (B) To find someone who will evaluate his presentation

    He has not yet created his presentation, so there's no way that he can be asking someone for their feedback.

    ✓ (C) To ask about learning how to use PowerPoint

    CORRECT. This is his goal.

    ✗ (D) To find out whether other students struggle in this area, too

    The student does not mention this.

2. How did the student probably feel when he first arrived at the computer center?

    SPEAKER'S ATTITUDE. He stammers through asking for help and it takes him some time to finally admit that he has never used PowerPoint. He's very nervous.

    ✓ (A) Embarrassed about his lack of knowledge with PowerPoint

    CORRECT. The student's embarrassment is shown when he struggles to articulate what his problem is, and again as he slowly reveals how much help he will need.

    ✗ (B) Excited to be learning a new skill

    The student does not display any indication of excitement.

    ✗ (C) Upset that only volunteer staff is available

    First, volunteer staff is not available. Second, the student does not seem to be upset.

    ✗ (D) Nervous about the amount of research that still needs to be done

    The student indicates that he has completed his research.

3.   What does the administrator imply about the student's professor?

INFERENCE. The only reference to the professor comes when the two are talking about how the work will appear. Without a basic understanding of PowerPoint, the student might seem unprepared to the professor.

✗ (A) The professor will have no opinion on the quality of the student's PowerPoint.

If this were true, why would the student be so nervous about learning PowerPoint, and why would the administrator agree about its importance?

✓ (B) The professor could mistakenly believe that the student was unprepared for the project.

CORRECT. The administrator implies that if the presentation does not look professional, the professor might not be able to see the amount of work that was put into the project.

✗ (C) The professor should have taught the student the basics of PowerPoint before this assignment.

The conversation does not mention this.

✗ (D) The professor did not intend for everyone to have to use PowerPoint.

The conversation does not mention this.

4.   What does the administrator imply about the student videos made a few years ago?

INFERENCE. The administrator states that these videos explain how to use PowerPoint and cover most of the basic concepts.

✗ (A) They were designed to help people in the same position as this student.

The administrator does not say why they were created.

✗ (B) They are meant for only advanced PowerPoint users.

This is contradicted. The administrator mentions them because she believes they might be helpful to the man.

✗ (C) They can be used in only one of the campus's computer centers.

The administrator does not mention this.

✓ (D) They will cover most, but not all, of the basics of PowerPoint.

CORRECT. In response to the student's question, the administrator says that most of the basics will be covered, and any that aren't can be figured out independently, implying that not all of the basics are covered.

5.   What will the administrator do to help the student?

DETAIL. She offers to answer questions if the student starts his work in the computer lab she is monitoring.

✗ (A) Tutor him one-on-one in PowerPoint

The administrator does not offer this.

✗ (B) Contact one of the volunteers to get him started earlier

The administrator does not offer this.

✓ (C) Answer the questions that the videos don't cover today

CORRECT. The administrator offers to help the student get started if he works in this computer center. She specifically says she can answer any questions he has.

✗ (D) Provide a list of books that teach PowerPoint skills

The administrator does not offer this.

Answers and Explanations—14.7

Practice Rooms—Track 152

NARRATOR: Listen to a conversation between a student and an employee in the Music Department.

STUDENT: Hi, I wanted to ask about… you know, the practice rooms downstairs. With the pianos in them. Like… what's the deal with those?

MUSIC DEPARTMENT SECRETARY: What do you mean, what's the deal?

STUDENT: Well, I just wanted to practice the piano for a bit. And they've… just been open before. Like not literally open, most of the time, but… they've had the doors unlocked.

MUSIC DEPARTMENT SECRETARY: Oh, well, that's not supposed to happen. I'm guessing you're not a music major, huh.

STUDENT: No, no, I wish I were doing something that interesting. I'm actually pre-med, but I still try to… you know… put in some decent practice on the piano.

MUSIC DEPARTMENT SECRETARY: I see, OK. Well, you have a… There's two ways to get access to the practice rooms. Number one, all the music majors get keys to the rooms. So, if you declare a major in music, you'll get a key as soon as that happens, and you'll be able to use the practice rooms any time you want, 24/7. Or number two—If it's during department hours, you can come in with your student ID, and we can hold that while you have the key out.

STUDENT: When you say department hours, does that mean … like, any time there's a music class happening?

MUSIC DEPARTMENT SECRETARY: Oh, sorry, I mean during business hours here, in the department office. Monday through Friday, 8:30 to 4:30 every day, except Thursdays we're open from 10 to 6. There's theoretically a one-hour limit, but there's … I can't really remember any time when every single room was full. So it's really just, you'd have to come in during office hours.

STUDENT: OK, thanks. You haven't ever, like… No one's ever actually declared a music major, just, like, for the time being, have they? [laughs] Like just so they can get a key to the practice rooms?

MUSIC DEPARTMENT SECRETARY: Fortunately… no, we've never had to deal with that kind of situation. I mean, it's not just… There's a whole procedure involved when you declare. You'd have to pick an advisor, you'd have to… y'know, get your schedule approved and so on. I guess we… You'd have to want to use the practice rooms pretty bad, to do that.

STUDENT: Ha, yeah, I guess that'd be a bit much. But what about… what if you're in one of the groups? Like, I'm 'bout to audition for a couple a cappella groups.

MUSIC DEPARTMENT SECRETARY: Unfortunately, the rules aren't any different if you're in an ensemble. Or if you're taking any music classes just to take them or to satisfy your fine arts requirement—same thing. Although honestly, if you do get into one of the singing groups, there might be some music performance majors in there.

STUDENT: Oh, I see where you're going with this—like, I could ask to borrow their key.

MUSIC DEPARTMENT SECRETARY: Yeah. I mean, in that case your friend would be responsible if anything happens, so, I mean, just be sure to lock the door on the way out.

STUDENT: Okay, thank you very much, I appreciate your help. So, I can borrow one of the keys now, then?

MUSIC DEPARTMENT SECRETARY: Do you have your student ID?

STUDENT: Yeah, I've got it right here.

MUSIC DEPARTMENT SECRETARY: Great! I'll take that from you… Go ahead and sign the list, it's right here. There's a pen over there, if you don't have one. And then we'll give you back your ID when you bring back the key.

STUDENT: Thanks again!

MUSIC DEPARTMENT SECRETARY: No problem. Enjoy!

1.	Why does the student go to the music department office?	**GIST-PURPOSE.** What question or issue does the student want help with?
✗ (A)	To begin the process of declaring a major in music	The student only has an issue (limited access to practice rooms) because he is not a music major, and he has no intention of becoming one.
✓ (B)	To find out how to gain access to rooms with a piano	**CORRECT.** This is what the student asks about at the beginning of the conversation, and it is the basis for the entire discussion that follows.
✗ (C)	To report that certain rooms have been left open or unlocked	The student implies that this is why he's been able to get into the rooms before, but his purpose is not to "report" this. (In fact, it would be to his benefit not to report this!)
✗ (D)	To sign up for auditions for singing groups	The student has already signed up for singing auditions.

2.	Why does the student want to use the rooms downstairs?	**DETAIL.** The student gives his reasoning near the beginning of the conversation.
✗ (A)	To play music with a group of other students	The student wants to practice the piano by himself.
✓ (B)	To practice an instrument that he plays as a hobby	**CORRECT.** The student wants to "put in some decent practice on the piano." He has no plans to major in music, so he must be interested in the piano purely as a hobby.
✗ (C)	To prepare for an upcoming audition	The student does not express any interest in using the rooms to practice singing.
✗ (D)	To study in a peaceful and quiet environment	The student does not express any interest in using the rooms as a quiet study area.

3.   Has the student ever used the practice rooms before, and, if so, under what circumstances has he used them?

INFERENCE. The student reveals this information when he starts talking to the department secretary.

✗ (A) He has never used the rooms before.

When the student mentions that the rooms have been open or unlocked in the past, he is clearly implying that he used the rooms at those times.

✗ (B) He has used the rooms before, but only during the music department's office hours.

At the beginning of the conversation, the student is unaware that the rooms are available during office hours.

✗ (C) He has used the rooms before, when a friend has lent him the key.

Asking a friend to borrow the key is the department secretary's idea, not the student's.

✓ (D) He has used the rooms before, when their doors have been left unlocked or open.

CORRECT. The student mentions that the rooms have "just been open before" or "had the doors unlocked," with the clear implication that he took advantage of this to use the rooms.

4.   What options does the student have to use the practice rooms outside of standard hours? *Choose 2 answers.*

DETAIL. The department secretary indicates that music majors all have access. The student can either become a music major or borrow keys from someone who is a music major.

✓ [A] Borrowing the key from a student majoring in music

CORRECT. The department secretary mentions this possibility—with the warning that his friend (from whom he borrows the key) will be responsible for any damage that might occur.

✓ [B] Declaring a major in music

CORRECT. The department secretary informs the student that all music majors are given keys to the practice rooms.

✗ [C] Joining a singing group

The department secretary specifically says that "the rules aren't any different if you're in an ensemble."

✗ [D] Taking a course in music theory

The department secretary specifically says that "the rules aren't any different … if you're taking any music classes."

Track 153

NARRATOR: Listen again to this part of the conversation.

MUSIC DEPARTMENT SECRETARY: Oh, sorry, I mean during business hours here, in the department office. Monday through Friday, 8:30 to 4:30 every day, except Thursdays we're open from 10 to 6. There's theoretically a one-hour limit, but there's… I can't really remember any time when every single room was full. So it's really just, you'd have to come in during office hours.

NARRATOR: What is the secretary's point when she says this:

MUSIC DEPARTMENT SECRETARY: I can't really remember any time when every single room was full.

5.   What is the secretary's point when she says this?

FUNCTION OF WHAT IS SAID. Here, the secretary is discussing the limits on students' use of the practice rooms during office hours. She says this directly after mentioning a limit of one hour. Her next statement ("It's really just …") implies that the one-hour limit is not significant, so this must be the reason why.

✗ (A) Only a small number of the university's students declare a music major.

The secretary is discussing rules that apply to students who are not music majors, so music majors are irrelevant.

✗ (B) The system for assigning the rooms is extremely ineffective.

There are empty rooms not because they are assigned by a bad system, but simply because there aren't enough students who want to use them all at once.

✓ (C) Students will probably be able to use the rooms for longer than one hour.

CORRECT. The secretary says this immediately after describing the one-hour limit, and immediately before saying "It's really just" the office-hours requirement. The implication is that unless the rooms are all full, students will be allowed to continue using them.

✗ (D) Very few people can use the rooms because the rules for access are so strict.

At the times under discussion, the rooms can be used by any student at all. So the problem is not overly strict rules.

Answers and Explanations—14.8

Organic Chemistry is Hard—Track 154

NARRATOR: Listen to a conversation between a student and his professor.

PROFESSOR: Hey, Alan. How's it going?

STUDENT: Hey, Professor Haley. It's going all right, thanks. I mean… in life. For whatever reason, I feel like I'm struggling with the homework the last couple weeks.

PROFESSOR: I'm not surprised to hear that. Organic chemistry is pretty tough stuff. And since you're used to getting good grades, I bet it's a new feeling for you to feel so challenged.

STUDENT: Ha, yeah. I feel like with other subjects the content is easier for me to memorize.

PROFESSOR: Hmm, I might push back against that word: "memorize." Is your goal to learn this material or just to get a good grade in this class and then move on with your life?

STUDENT: Well… um, I definitely do want a good grade. I'm not sure how much I otherwise want to learn organic chemistry.

PROFESSOR: What do you want to learn about? What sort of field do you think you might go into?

STUDENT: I'm not sure… I get the most enjoyment out of my art classes, but I don't know if I can trust that stuff to be a career. I do like math.

PROFESSOR: Let me make a suggestion—maybe you should try to use what you like about those disciplines to help you learn organic chemistry. When you learn about new organic molecules, focus on the architecture of how they're built. Take some aesthetic enjoyment in how they're structured. Look at them

like sculptures that our universe, or some artist, has made and try to have the same sort of colorful reactions to them you might have if you were looking at an odd looking building or sculpture.

STUDENT: I see what you're saying.

PROFESSOR: Sometimes, even if we're not fascinated by a particular topic, we can try to see it through the eyes of a topic we do like. If you like math, and you see a molecule like H_2O, which, you know, has two hydrogens and one oxygen, pretend it's a composite number like 12, that has two 2's and one 3.

STUDENT: Yeah, but some of the chemical compounds are so long and complicated; it's not like remembering a simple number like 12.

PROFESSOR: True, true.

STUDENT: So what's the best way to memorize them? Just look at flashcards every day?

PROFESSOR: Flashcards definitely help, but they can also feel pretty lifeless. I'd rather you get more tactile with learning them. Most of the molecules you're memorizing are made up of carbon, oxygen, hydrogen, and nitrogen. So get some multi-colored pieces of candy or get a bunch of loose change, and assign each type of atom to a certain color of candy or type of coin. Then grab some toothpicks to represent the chemical bonds and practice actually building and arranging these molecules.

STUDENT: Oh, I kinda like that. I would probably have an easier time remembering something I made than something I read.

PROFESSOR: Exactly. I think the material gets layered more deeply in our brain that way.

STUDENT: Is that how you learned organic chemistry? Why were you so into this topic?

PROFESSOR: Good question. I actually set out to teach engineering, but the school where I was teaching already had an engineering teacher, so I volunteered to take on organic chemistry.

STUDENT: Was it hard for you to learn it?

PROFESSOR: It was. But I tried to use my love of building things in engineering to understand how molecules were put together.

STUDENT: Yeah. Okay. So you were an engineer about it… I'll try to be an artist or a mathematician.

PROFESSOR: Sounds good.

1. Why does the student go to see the professor?	**GIST-PURPOSE.** What was the central issue that motivated the student? His biggest concern?
✗ (A) To argue for a better grade in the class	He does say that getting a good grade matters. But he isn't saying that his current grade is unfair or undeserved.
✗ (B) To find out more about engineering	Although this topic comes up when the professor talks about how she got into teaching, the student's primary focus is his difficulty with organic chemistry.
✗ (C) To borrow some coins and toothpicks from her	The idea of using coins and toothpicks is something the professor offers halfway through the conversation, so it could not be the student's original purpose.
✓ (D) To discuss difficulties learning the material	**CORRECT.** The student describes his struggle learning organic chemistry and seems concerned about how to memorize such content.

2.   What is the professor's concern about flashcards?

DETAIL. What does she suggest instead? Why is that alternative better?

✗ (A) They are more expensive than candy and toothpicks.

The professor never discusses the price of any study materials.

✓ (B) They are not a very active form of learning.

CORRECT. The author calls flashcards "lifeless" and recommends instead an activity that involves building models of molecules by hand.

✗ (C) They didn't help her to learn engineering.

The professor never discusses flashcards in relation to her background in engineering.

✗ (D) They cannot be used during the student's test.

The professor never mentions any specifics about the student's test.

3.   Why does the professor say that she set out to teach engineering?

FUNCTION OF WHAT IS SAID. The professor discusses that teaching engineering was actually her first choice of career but she changed to organic chemistry for better job opportunities.

✗ (A) To express dissatisfaction with her current job

The professor gives no indication of not liking her current job, even though we know its topic was not her first choice.

✓ (B) To provide context for her interest in organic chemistry

CORRECT. The student asks the professor how she was so into organic chemistry, and the professor reveals that it was not her first choice of topic, but that she learned it for the sake of an employment opportunity.

✗ (C) To suggest that the student use an engineer's perspective

The professor explains that her own method was to relate chemistry to engineering, but she isn't trying to get the student to use engineering.

✗ (D) To help the student appreciate building things

Even though engineering is concerned with building things, the professor only brings up engineering to explain that she was not always into organic chemistry.

4.   Which tactic or tactics did the professor suggest for learning molecules? *Select all that apply.*

CONNECTING CONTENT. What were some of the ways the professor suggested for the student to better learn organic chemistry?

✓ [A] Appreciate them as sculptures

CORRECT. The professor suggests looking at a molecule's structure as one might look at an odd looking building or sculpture.

✓ [B] Model them with coins and toothpicks

CORRECT. The professor suggests building and arranging coins and toothpicks so that they mimic the structure of a given molecule.

✗ [C] Reward learning with candy

The professor suggested colored candy pieces as an alternative material for coins, but she never spoke about giving or eating the candy as a reward.

✓ [D] Relate them to math

CORRECT. The professor compared the atomic composition of water molecules to the prime composition of the number 12.

Track 155

NARRATOR: Listen again to part of the conversation. Then answer the question.

PROFESSOR: If you like math, and you see a molecule like H_2O, which, you know, has two hydrogens and one oxygen, pretend it's a composite number like 12, that has two 2's and one 3.

STUDENT: Yeah, but some of the chemical compounds are so long and complicated; it's not like remembering a simple number like 12.

NARRATOR: What does the student mean when he says this:

STUDENT: It's not like remembering a simple number like 12.

5.   **FUNCTION OF WHAT IS SAID.** This segment occurs while the professor is attempting to use the student's interest in art and math to get the student more interested in organic chemistry.

✓ (A) To express skepticism

CORRECT. The student questions whether thinking of molecules as composite numbers is realistic for more complex molecules.

✗ (B) To request a different numerical example

The student isn't asking for a bigger number, but rather pointing out that harder molecules would require thinking about much bigger numbers.

✗ (C) To show appreciation

The student may appreciate the professor's willingness to offer advice, but this claim represents the student's pushing back against the professor's last suggestion.

✗ (D) To utilize new understanding

Although the student's concern reflects that he understood the professor's idea, his purpose is to question whether the idea is viable for harder molecules.

Chapter 15

Speaking Task Type 1

Speaking questions test your ability to comprehend and respond orally to written or spoken material. You will have to speak your response aloud. There are six different speaking tasks. Speaking Task Type 1, Personal Preference, is an "independent" topic. You will be asked to provide your opinion on a specific topic. You will need to express your opinion and provide examples to support or explain that opinion.

Speaking questions test your ability to understand spoken and written information and to summarize and express opinions about that information. They also test your ability to respond orally to specific questions, including your grammar, your vocabulary, and the logical organization of your ideas.

How should you use this chapter? Here are some recommendations, according to the level you've reached in TOEFL Speaking:

0. **Everyone!** Hold yourself to the time limits whenever practicing Speaking tasks. Tape your response and listen to it afterward to analyze your performance. You can use any app on your computer or phone to tape yourself. If you don't know of a good app already, try www.vocaroo.com.

1. **Fundamentals.** Start with a type that is a "medium weakness"—not your worst Speaking question type but not your best either. Try one question and then check the sample answer. Think carefully about the principles at work. If you think you can do a better job, redo the question. Articulate what you want to do differently the next time you do this type of task.

2. **Fixes.** Do one Speaking task, examine the results, learn your lessons, then try a different type of Speaking task. Be sure to keep to the time limits. When you're ready, graduate to doing a set of six different Speaking tasks all in a row.

3. **Tweaks.** Confirm your mastery by doing a set of six different Speaking tasks all in a row under timed conditions.

Good luck on Speaking!

15.1

You will now be asked to speak about a familiar topic. Give yourself 15 seconds to prepare your response. Then record yourself speaking for 45 seconds.

 Listen to Track 156.

Talk about a game, sport, or other group activity that you played in your childhood. What did you like or dislike about it, and why?

Preparation Time: 15 seconds

Response Time: 45 seconds

15.2

You will now be asked to speak about a familiar topic. Give yourself 15 seconds to prepare your response. Then record yourself speaking for 45 seconds.

 Listen to Track 157.

How did you go to and from school when you were younger? Describe one kind of transportation and/or route you took. What did you like or dislike about it, and why?

Preparation Time: 15 seconds

Response Time: 45 seconds

15.3

You will now be asked to speak about a familiar topic. Give yourself 15 seconds to prepare your response. Then record yourself speaking for 45 seconds.

 Listen to Track 158.

Talk about a favorite author of yours. Explain why this author is one of your favorites. Give specific details and examples.

Preparation Time: 15 seconds

Response Time: 45 seconds

15.4

> You will now be asked to speak about a familiar topic. Give yourself 15 seconds to prepare your response. Then record yourself speaking for 45 seconds.

 Listen to Track 159.

Talk about a specific skill that you developed at some point in your life. What is the skill? How did you develop it? Why is it important to you?

> Preparation Time: 15 seconds
>
> Response Time: 45 seconds

15.5

> You will now be asked to speak about a familiar topic. Give yourself 15 seconds to prepare your response. Then record yourself speaking for 45 seconds.

 Listen to Track 160.

Choose a place that you like to visit when you have free time. Why do you enjoy this place? Please include specific details in your explanation.

> Preparation Time: 15 seconds
>
> Response Time: 45 seconds

15.6

> You will now be asked to speak about a familiar topic. Give yourself 15 seconds to prepare your response. Then record yourself speaking for 45 seconds.

 Listen to Track 161.

Talk about a memorable event that occurred in your life within the last few years. Describe what happened and why it was memorable for you.

> Preparation Time: 15 seconds
>
> Response Time: 45 seconds

15.7

> You will now be asked to speak about a familiar topic. Give yourself 15 seconds to prepare your response. Then record yourself speaking for 45 seconds.

> Listen to Track 162.
>
> Talk about an interesting place you have visited. Explain what you find interesting about this place. Include specific reasons and examples in your response.
>
> Preparation Time: 15 seconds
>
> Response Time: 45 seconds

15.8

> You will now be asked to speak about a familiar topic. Give yourself 15 seconds to prepare your response. Then record yourself speaking for 45 seconds.

> Listen to Track 163.
>
> Choose a public figure or important person whom you admire. Explain who this person is and why you admire him or her. Give specific reasons and examples in your answer.
>
> Preparation Time: 15 seconds
>
> Response Time: 45 seconds

Answers and Explanations—15.1

Sample Spoken Response—Track 164

A game I really liked when I was a child was tennis. I played often with my father. He won all the time… well… until I was a teenager. Uh, I really liked the sound of the ball hitting the racket and the feeling of making a really nice shot when moving through the wrist, and connecting with the ball is really satisfying. And it was also a game of strategy because you had to decide where to hit the ball. Uh… what I didn't like about it so much was, uh, it was a head game too, so once you start to get them… once your opponent has some momentum against you…

Comments

The student's response clearly addresses the question, providing several reasons why he liked playing tennis as a child. Although the response was cut off in mid-sentence at the end, the question asked only why "you like *or* dislike" the game. It isn't necessary to answer both halves of the question. The student did provide several reasons why he liked the game, so his response is sufficient to earn a good score.

Answers and Explanations—15.2

Sample Spoken Response—Track 165

OK, how I got to school… my mother drove me to school because my mother taught at the same school. We drove in a car, and I very vividly remember dodging horses and buggies 'cause we lived in the country so it was always an interesting trip… What did I dislike about it… didn't have an opportunity to meet other people or be social. I always thought riding the bus would be really cool 'cause I heard stories about the bus from classmates. But at the same time I think it was good that I didn't ride the bus because I think people would get beat up on the bus.

Comments

The student answers both parts of the question: he describes the form of transportation he took to get to school and he provides detailed reasons why he liked and disliked this method. It's okay to provide only reasons you like something (or dislike it).

Answers and Explanations—15.3

Sample Spoken Response—Track 166

So a favorite author of mine… I'd say Stephen Hawking. Uh, I'm a big fan of non-fiction books, especially ones that are, uh, related to science. Um, and there… there's something about his writing style that's incredibly down to earth for such a brilliant guy. Um, it's just… you know, it's easy to kind of make a connection to what he's talking. He does a great job of putting things, um, in… in a very understandable, uh, putting things in an understandable way. Uh, and that… that's something that I really appreciate, especially for, uh, such heavy topics like, uh, black holes, and… and time travel…

Comments

The student provides clear and detailed examples to illustrate why he likes this particular author. He could improve his response by reducing the number of "um" and "uh" interjections. A small pause (silence) to collect your thoughts is a better approach.

Answers and Explanations—15.4

Sample Spoken Response—Track 167

Um, I think learning how to drive a car. Uh, it wasn't easy for me and I didn't learn… start learning how to drive until I was a little older. Um, I didn't need to know how to drive, uh… because I was very close to my school so I walked or had a ride from someone else. Um, so, it took me a long time to figure out how to drive. I was kind of scared of it, um, I didn't like cars in general. Um, and, you know, it took me a lot of practice and a lot of time with my dad… but I learned it at some point.

Comments

The student details how she developed this skill and why it took her a long time. She could improve her response by explicitly addressing the final question: Why is it important to you? She might have said that she feels proud of herself because she kept trying even though she didn't like driving and found it scary at times.

Answers and Explanations—15.5

Sample Spoken Response—Track 168

One of my favorite places to go when I have free time is to a place near my house called Clark Park. Uh, it's a great playground. I like to go with my two-year-old son, um, and we just have a… a blast when we're there. Especially when it's… the weather's warm and it's nice out. Uh, we like to go on the swings. There's a big play area. It's maybe a hundred feet wide. Lots of oak trees. And there's… lots of dogs are there, um, just running around, and it… it's just a wonderful place to go and play when the weather's nice out.

Comments

The student provides a lot of details about the park, enough that someone could visualize going there. Note that it isn't necessary to talk about something intellectual. You will speak best about things that you know well. Go with your first instinct.

Answers and Explanations—15.6

Sample Spoken Response—Track 169

One memorable event that occurred in the last few years was my dad coming to visit me in New York City. Um, I've lived in New York for eight years and this was the first time he came to visit… and it was really special because… it was a chance for me to really have him understand my city and meet my friends… and go and do a lot of the things I like to do here. And it was really special because, uh, it was just really special to have that time with him.

Comments

The student provides concrete details to illustrate why this event was so memorable for her. At the end, she repeated herself a little bit, but this is not unusual. Even high-level responses will sometimes include a little bit of repetition.

Answers and Explanations—15.7

Sample Spoken Response—Track 170

OK… so one of my favorite places that I've ever been to is a little resort, um, out in Palos Verdes, California. Uh, it's kind of, like, the middle of nowhere. You have to really drive out there… it takes forever to get there and it's all side roads, basically, to get out there. Um, but it's beautiful. It's got the most beautiful views. Uh, it's got this really cute little restaurant called Nelson's… I think… that has this awesome little patio outside to watch the sunset. And then they also have this little par three, nine-hole course, um…

Comments

The student provides clear details that explain why she likes this place so much. She takes a little while to build up to her reasons and then runs out of time mid-sentence. But this is okay because she does fully address the question.

Answers and Explanations—15.8

Sample Spoken Response—Track 171

The person that I admire is, uh, Supreme Court Justice Ruth Bader Ginsburg. She, um, is admirable because she, uh, went to law school at a time where women were discouraged to do so, and she went to a very good law school, um… and basically made her way to the top by being both smart about how she did it. Um, I also admire her because she's not afraid to, uh, change her positions based on… on feedback, and I think that's, um, particularly admirable in a day and age where, uh, people get very, um, sort of, uh… uh, tied to their own positions.

Comments

The student provides multiple strong reasons why she admires Justice Ginsburg. Toward the end, she could improve her response by using short pauses while she's thinking about what she wants to say. It's okay to say "um" a few times, but too many in one sentence can make it hard to understand the sentence.

Chapter 16

Speaking Task Type 2

Speaking questions test your ability to comprehend and respond orally to written or spoken material. You will have to speak your response aloud. There are six different speaking tasks. Speaking Task Type 2, Choice, is an "independent" topic. You will be asked to agree or disagree with a short statement, and you will need to provide reasons to support your opinion.

Speaking questions test your ability to understand spoken and written information and to summarize and express opinions about that information. They also test your ability to respond orally to specific questions, including your grammar, your vocabulary, and the logical organization of your ideas.

How should you use this chapter? Here are some recommendations, according to the level you've reached in TOEFL Speaking:

0. **Everyone!** Hold yourself to the time limits whenever practicing Speaking tasks. Tape your response and listen to it afterward to analyze your performance. You can use any app on your computer or phone to tape yourself. If you don't know of a good app already, try www.vocaroo.com.

1. **Fundamentals.** Start with a type that is a "medium weakness"—not your worst Speaking question type but not your best either. Try one question and then check the sample answer. Think carefully about the principles at work. If you think you can do a better job, redo the question. Articulate what you want to do differently the next time you do this type of task.

2. **Fixes.** Do one Speaking task, examine the results, learn your lessons, then try a different type of Speaking task. Be sure to keep to the time limits. When you're ready, graduate to doing a set of six different Speaking tasks all in a row.

3. **Tweaks.** Confirm your mastery by doing a set of six different Speaking tasks all in a row under timed conditions.

Good luck on Speaking!

16.1

You will now be asked to give your opinion about a familiar topic. Give yourself 15 seconds to prepare your response. Then record yourself speaking for 45 seconds.

 Listen to Track 172.

Some people think that playing a team sport is the ideal way to stay fit and healthy. Others prefer to exercise alone. Which do you prefer? Explain why.

Preparation Time: 15 seconds

Response Time: 45 seconds

16.2

You will now be asked to give your opinion about a familiar topic. Give yourself 15 seconds to prepare your response. Then record yourself speaking for 45 seconds.

 Listen to Track 173.

Some people believe that universities should offer classes in life skills, such as budgeting and money management. Others think that schools should focus on academic topics. Which approach do you think is better and why?

Preparation Time: 15 seconds

Response Time: 45 seconds

16.3

You will now be asked to give your opinion about a familiar topic. Give yourself
15 seconds to prepare your response. Then record yourself speaking for 45 seconds.

 Listen to Track 174.

When researching a topic, some students prefer to rely entirely on written materials, such
as books and articles. Other students include broader sources, such as radio interviews or
television news programs. Which approach do you prefer and why?

Preparation Time: 15 seconds

Response Time: 45 seconds

16.4

You will now be asked to give your opinion about a familiar topic. Give yourself
15 seconds to prepare your response. Then record yourself speaking for 45 seconds.

 Listen to Track 175.

Some people think that having a hobby outside of work or school is essential for a good
work-life balance. Others don't believe that hobbies are important. Which view do you
agree with and why?

Preparation Time: 15 seconds

Response Time: 45 seconds

16.5

You will now be asked to give your opinion about a familiar topic. Give yourself
15 seconds to prepare your response. Then record yourself speaking for 45 seconds.

 Listen to Track 176.

Some people think that children should be allowed access to computers for only a limited
amount of time per day. Others think that children should have unlimited access to
computers. Which do you agree with? Explain why.

Preparation Time: 15 seconds

Response Time: 45 seconds

16.6

You will now be asked to give your opinion about a familiar topic. Give yourself
15 seconds to prepare your response. Then record yourself speaking for 45 seconds.

 Listen to Track 177.

Do you agree or disagree with the following statement? Why or why not? Use details and
examples to explain your answer.

All students should be required to take written communication courses, regardless of their
field of study.

Preparation Time: 15 seconds

Response Time: 45 seconds

16.7

You will now be asked to give your opinion about a familiar topic. Give yourself 15 seconds to prepare your response. Then record yourself speaking for 45 seconds.

 Listen to Track 178.

Some people think that young adults spend too much time on their cell phones. Others think that such devices are a great way to keep in touch with friends and family. Which view do you agree with? Explain why.

Preparation Time: 15 seconds

Response Time: 45 seconds

16.8

You will now be asked to give your opinion about a familiar topic. Give yourself 15 seconds to prepare your response. Then record yourself speaking for 45 seconds.

 Listen to Track 179.

Some people plan out every aspect of a trip ahead of time. Other people decide what to do only after they arrive at their destination. State which you prefer and explain why.

Preparation Time: 15 seconds

Response Time: 45 seconds

Answers and Explanations—16.1

Sample Spoken Response—Track 180

I think exercising is important to be fit and healthy. A sport can be good if you are someone who especially likes socializing… but I think a team sport can be unreliable because you have to rely on schedules for games… and other things in order to work out. If your game is canceled then you might not be able to exercise that day. So… because of that, I actually prefer to do things, um, fitness related by myself because it's… can be on a more reliable schedule, and you don't have to go to a game in order to be more active.

Comments

> The student takes a position and provides support for his opinion. His response could be improved by taking a clear position right from the start. His reply starts to say that sports are good before reversing and saying that team sports are not as good.

Answers and Explanations—16.2

Sample Spoken Response—Track 181

I agree that universities should offer classes in budgeting and money management… not just academic topics, because these are important things that were never taught to me in school. And it was only after graduating and stumbling through several years of having a job… that I… uh, gained an interest in learning how to, uh, retire… because I was maybe thinking about… about growing old and dying. And there are other goals like, uh, going to graduate school… or buying a home or… or having a family. So I read these books that were so helpful that taught me about saving money and investing. But it would have been better to learn that when I was younger… in school.

Comments

> The author chooses a side immediately and offers several concrete reasons to support his opinion. He could perhaps improve his response by speaking in a little more detail about one or two of his examples.

Answers and Explanations—16.3

Sample Spoken Response—Track 182

I… I probably prefer to rely on books or other written material as opposed to other things like, uh, radio interviews, TV shows, things like that. Uh, mostly because I think that written materials are just more easily scannable. Um, it's, you know, something… as I'm trying to, you know, process a vast amount of information, I want to able to go through something as quickly as possible, um, just to get a sense of what it's trying to tell me. Uh, and that's something that's really tough to do, um, with, you know, with… with, uh, something that you have to watch.

Comments

> The student has a firm position and solid reasons to support his opinion. He could improve his response by reducing his usage of "um" and other interjections. If you need time to think, it's okay to pause and say nothing for a moment.

Answers and Explanations—16.4

Sample Spoken Response—Track 183

I definitely think hobbies are important, um, especially for, um, a good work-life balance. And I think, you know, outside of your work hours, whatever that hobby is… If you have a family, being with your children or your significant other. Um, if you like to travel, you know, planning trips. Or if you like food, going to a new restaurant or going to, you know, a food event in your city. Um, for me, going to yoga or going to the gym after work is important. Um, and just having… consistency is extremely important, even, you know, if it's not a big hobby or if it doesn't take too much time. But having something outside of work is good for that balance.

Comments

The student states her opinion at the beginning and the end of her response, so her position is very clear to the listener. She could improve her response by offering just two or three examples and providing a little more detail for each one.

Answers and Explanations—16.5

Sample Spoken Response—Track 184

Heh, this is a pretty tough question… something I definitely have to deal with right now as a … with a two year old who loves to use his iPad and … and watch probably too much, uh, screen time. Um, I definitely… there should definitely be limits on how much screen time a kid should get. Um, you know, I… I think that it's… even as we're moving toward having, you know, more of our adult lives in… in front of screens, there's still something that… that I think kids can miss out on if they don't have that… one-on-one connection they can develop by playing and… and moving around.

Comments

The student is able to offer a very personal and universal example to support his opinion and that can help to make for a better response. Do use a personal example if one occurs to you. The student could improve his response by pausing briefly and thinking through a more complete thought before starting his next sentence.

Answers and Explanations—16.6

Sample Spoken Response—Track 185

Uh, should all students be required to take written communication courses regardless of their field of study? Um, I do think that writing is very important. Uh, it is a very applicable skill. It's… it's important for people to be able to write clearly… and have the right spelling and grammar… and make sense. However, do I think that people should be required to take a course in that? I don't think so. I feel like the, uh, course of… the field of study should already include that… that anybody who goes through it would already be… practicing how to write through their other work.

Comments

This student had a tough job. He wasn't sure what his opinion was yet—but he had to start speaking. So he bought himself some time by repeating the prompt and, later, asking the question again. If you find yourself in this situation, you can try doing what this student did to give yourself a little more time to think.

Answers and Explanations—16.7

Sample Spoken Response—Track 186

I do think that young adults spend too much time on their phones, uh, even though they are really great tools for, uh, communication. Um, they are very engaging, they're… they pull you in, and they make people… they're so wrapped up in the phone, and they… lose track of everything else that's around them. Some examples of this… When you're walking down the street, it's really common to see people unaware of traffic and other people on the sidewalk with them. Uh, or, in a restaurant, you might see a group of people, uh, there eating, but really, um, just looking at their phones.

Comments

The student immediately takes a clear position. He struggles a little bit at first to provide his reasoning. Eventually, though, he figures out how to make his point and he provides some concrete examples.

Answers and Explanations—16.8

Sample Spoken Response—Track 187

I agree with planning out your trip, um, before you go. I think that that's the best way to get a good… value for your money. I think if you look up different things to do, whether it's museums, or places to eat, or, um, beaches, you know, different things that you wanna see, different, um, cultural experiences that you wanna have, you go into your vacation prepared. That way you have all your possibilities at your fingertips. That doesn't mean that you need to… that you do every single thing that you've already looked up… but you know what's available to you, so when you're there you can…

Comments

The student offers a thorough response. First, she states a clear opinion and provides the main reason she holds that opinion. She then describes in detail why she prefers to plan in advance. She could improve her response by completing her final sentence before the tape cuts her off.

Chapter 17

Speaking Task Type 3

Speaking questions test your ability to comprehend and respond orally to written or spoken material. You will have to speak your response aloud. There are six different speaking tasks. Speaking Task Type 3, Campus Situation (Fit and Explain), is an "integrated" task. You will first read a short passage about a campus issue for 45 to 50 seconds and then listen to a short conversation between two people about that same topic. One of the people will express an opinion, including specific reasons to support that opinion. Your task will be to summarize the person's opinion and explain why she or he holds that opinion. You will be able to reread the passage while you plan your response, but you will not be able to replay any part of the conversation.

Speaking questions test your ability to understand spoken and written information and to summarize and express opinions about that information. They also test your ability to respond orally to specific questions, including your grammar, your vocabulary, and the logical organization of your ideas.

How should you use this chapter? Here are some recommendations, according to the level you've reached in TOEFL Speaking:

0. **Everyone!** Hold yourself to the time limits whenever practicing Speaking tasks. Tape your response and listen to it afterward to analyze your performance. You can use any app on your computer or phone to tape yourself. If you don't know of a good app already, try www.vocaroo.com.

1. **Fundamentals.** Start with a type that is a "medium weakness"—not your worst Speaking question type but not your best either. Try one question and then check the sample answer. Think carefully about the principles at work. If you think you can do a better job, redo the question. Articulate what you want to do differently the next time you do this type of task.

2. **Fixes.** Do one Speaking task, examine the results, learn your lessons, then try a different type of Speaking task. Be sure to keep to the time limits. When you're ready, graduate to doing a set of six different Speaking tasks all in a row.

3. **Tweaks.** Confirm your mastery by doing a set of six different Speaking tasks all in a row under timed conditions.

Good luck on Speaking!

17.1

> You will now read a short passage and listen to a conversation on the same topic. You will then be asked a question about them. After you hear the question, give yourself 30 seconds to prepare your response. Then record yourself speaking for 60 seconds.
>
> Listen to Track 188.
>
> You have 45 seconds to read the passage. Begin reading now.
>
> Reading Time: 45 seconds

New President Dr. Banerjee

The University is pleased to announce that Dr. Banerjee has accepted the position of President. Dr. Banerjee brings more than two decades of administrative experience from her work at several well-respected schools. She has an exceptional track record in the areas of budget management and fundraising, which are particularly important to the University community. In addition, the President must be a strong communicator, someone who can represent our school well on the broader public stage. Dr. Banerjee has previously served as a University spokeswoman, communicating with the media and other external parties.

> Listen to Track 189.
>
> The woman expresses her opinion about the hiring of Dr. Banerjee. State her opinion and explain the reasons she gives for holding that opinion.
>
> Preparation Time: 30 seconds
>
> Response Time: 60 seconds

17.2

> You will now read a short passage and listen to a conversation on the same topic. You will then be asked a question about them. After you hear the question, give yourself 30 seconds to prepare your response. Then record yourself speaking for 60 seconds.
>
> Listen to Track 190.
>
> You have 50 seconds to read the passage. Begin reading now.
>
> Reading Time: 50 seconds

New Requirement for First-Year Students

Effective immediately, all first-year students will be required to take an academic writing course. The course will help students to learn how to write papers appropriate for college-level courses, including how to develop a thesis statement and how to structure the paper.

The course will cover the standards for conducting research and citing that research. Students will learn when it is acceptable to paraphrase, or summarize, another author's work, and when that student should quote the author. The course will also cover how to avoid plagiarizing (or copying someone else's work without citation).

 Listen to Track 191.

The woman expresses her opinion about the new writing class requirement. State her opinion and explain the reasons she gives for holding that opinion.

Preparation Time: 30 seconds

Response Time: 60 seconds

17.3

You will now read a short passage and listen to a conversation on the same topic. You will then be asked a question about them. After you hear the question, give yourself 30 seconds to prepare your response. Then record yourself speaking for 60 seconds.

 Listen to Track 192.

You have 45 seconds to read the passage. Begin reading now.

Reading Time: 45 seconds

Proposal to Add Class Hours

Currently, students are permitted to enroll in a maximum of 16 class hours per semester. Most classes are allotted 3 or 4 class hours, so students typically enroll in 4 or 5 classes during one semester. Some science classes are allotted 5 class hours, however, so a student taking these classes would be able to enroll in a maximum of only 3 classes. In order to better accommodate science majors, it is proposed that the university allow students to enroll in a maximum of 20 class hours per semester.

Listen to Track 193.

The man expresses his opinion about the university's proposal. State his opinion and explain the reasons he gives for holding that opinion.

Preparation Time: 30 seconds

Response Time: 60 seconds

17.4

You will now read a short passage and listen to a conversation on the same topic. You will then be asked a question about them. After you hear the question, give yourself 30 seconds to prepare your response. Then record yourself speaking for 60 seconds.

 Listen to Track 194.

You have 45 seconds to read the passage. Begin reading now.

Reading Time: 45 seconds

Semesters to Trimesters

Beginning next year, the university will switch to a trimester system. Rather than two 15-week terms, the academic year will now consist of three 10-week terms. This new structure will allow students to take fewer, more intensive courses during each term. It will also be simpler for students to take transfer courses at other local campuses, most of which already use the trimester system.

 Listen to Track 195.

The man expresses his opinion of the trimester system. State his opinion and explain the reasons he gives for holding that opinion.

Preparation Time: 30 seconds

Response Time: 60 seconds

17.5

> You will now read a short passage and listen to a conversation on the same topic. You will then be asked a question about them. After you hear the question, give yourself 30 seconds to prepare your response. Then record yourself speaking for 60 seconds.
>
> Listen to Track 196.
>
> You have 50 seconds to read the passage. Begin reading now.
>
> Reading Time: 50 seconds

Drama vs. Comedy

We typically produce a comedic play during the spring term, but this year, we are instead considering a drama: Shakespeare's *Hamlet.* Since budgets have been reduced, we need to spend our funds wisely. Last fall, we produced another drama, *Romeo & Juliet,* and we would be able to reuse all of the costumes and most of the sets. In addition, this term, we have a visiting literature professor, Dr. Ludgate, who is an authority on Shakespeare and who would be able to advise us on how to develop the best possible production of this material.

> Listen to Track 197.
>
> The woman expresses her opinion about the proposed change of the play. State her opinion and explain the reasons she gives for holding that opinion.
>
> Preparation Time: 30 seconds
>
> Response Time: 60 seconds

17.6

> You will now read a short passage and listen to a conversation on the same topic. You will then be asked a question about them. After you hear the question, give yourself 30 seconds to prepare your response. Then record yourself speaking for 60 seconds.
>
> Listen to Track 198.
>
> You have 45 seconds to read the passage. Begin reading now.
>
> Reading Time: 45 seconds

Increasing Adjunct Hiring

Due to steadily increasing enrollment, it has become necessary to offer more classes in many university departments. One proposed solution is to increase hiring of adjunct professors—professors who are hired on a part-time basis to teach only a few classes—by at least 30 percent over the next five years. Many departments support this proposal because it will reduce class sizes and increase the variety of classes that can be offered.

 Listen to Track 199.

The man expresses his opinion on hiring more adjunct professors. State his opinion and explain the reasons he gives for holding that opinion.

Preparation Time: 30 seconds

Response Time: 60 seconds

17.7

You will now read a short passage and listen to a conversation on the same topic. You will then be asked a question about them. After you hear the question, give yourself 30 seconds to prepare your response. Then record yourself speaking for 60 seconds.

 Listen to Track 200.

You have 50 seconds to read the passage. Begin reading now.

Reading Time: 50 seconds

No Jobs for Ashby Scholars

The Ashby Scholarship is a prestigious, long-running university program that pays all tuition and housing costs for participating students. However, there is one downside: Ashby scholars are now strictly forbidden, under the terms of the scholarship, from performing non-volunteer work off campus. The director of the scholarship program defended this decision in a recent meeting, stating that students in the scholarship program should focus on academics and volunteer work, not on earning money. She added that since Ashby scholars do not pay for tuition or housing, it should be unnecessary for them to work for pay.

Listen to Track 201.

The woman expresses her opinion of the Ashby Scholarship job policy. State her opinion and explain the reasons she gives for holding that opinion.

Preparation Time: 30 seconds

Response Time: 60 seconds

17.8

You will now read a short passage and listen to a conversation on the same topic. You will then be asked a question about them. After you hear the question, give yourself 30 seconds to prepare your response. Then record yourself speaking for 60 seconds.

 Listen to Track 202.

You have 45 seconds to read the passage. Begin reading now.

Reading Time: 45 seconds

Graduation Moved to Stadium

In previous years, graduation has been held in the campus theater. In order to fit everyone, graduation was split into five different ceremonies by program. The first ceremony started at 8am, and the last ceremony finished after 6pm, over 10 hours later. Some students waited several hours to see a friend from another program graduate. To remedy these problems, this year's graduation ceremonies will be moved from the campus theater to the sports stadium. The sports stadium has a greater capacity, allowing students from all programs to graduate together during a single service.

 Listen to Track 203.

The man expresses his opinion about moving graduation to the stadium. State his opinion and explain the reasons he gives for holding that opinion.

Preparation Time: 30 seconds

Response Time: 60 seconds

Answers and Explanations—17.1

New President Dr. Banerjee—Track 189

NARRATOR: Now listen to two students discussing the article.

FEMALE STUDENT: Did you see the announcement?

MALE STUDENT: About Dr. Banerjee? Yes. I don't know much about her.

FEMALE STUDENT: She was at Western University before. She did a great job.

MALE STUDENT: Why do you think so?

FEMALE STUDENT: Well, they were having budget issues. The article I read said that she single-handedly fixed the problem. She helped negotiate a food services contract with a different company. They ended up getting better cafeteria food for half as much money.

MALE STUDENT: That's good. Our cafeteria food is awful.

FEMALE STUDENT: And they were enrolling more students, but they didn't have the money to hire more professors and teaching assistants. She found ways to increase alumni donations so that they were able to maintain smaller class sizes.

MALE STUDENT: How did she do that?

FEMALE STUDENT: Mostly through positive press. She started giving interviews and having other professors talk to the press about their research. So people started hearing more about the school and I guess alumni were proud to be associated with the school. And then the University started contacting alumni and asking for donations, and it was a big success.

MALE STUDENT: That's fantastic. I hope she can do that here!

FEMALE STUDENT: I think she will. I'm really optimistic that she'll have a positive impact.

NARRATOR: The woman expresses her opinion about the hiring of Dr. Banerjee. State her opinion and explain the reasons she gives for holding that opinion.

Sample Spoken Response—Track 204

The female student supports the new president of the school. Um, she says that the… Dr. Banerjee, um, single-handedly was able to fix budget issues at her previous school. Um, she did that by, um, renegotiating a food contract with a different vendor. Um, that ultimately gave the students better quality food at a much lower cost. So she was able to, you know, do something positive and also, um, save the school a lot of money. She, also, um, you know, at the previous school, they were getting a lot of new enrollments but didn't have the money to buy… hire new teachers, um, so she started to do a lot of interviews, um, and get a lot of positive press and attention on the school. Um, so through that press, you know, alumni felt proud to be associated with the school, so they wouldn't, when they reached out t… for donations, the alumni were much more likely to donate. So through those donations…

Comments

The student remembers many details from the conversation. She accurately summarizes the messages conveyed. She could improve her response by reducing the number of times she says "um" and "you know."

Answers and Explanations—17.2

New Requirement for First-Year Students—Track 191

NARRATOR: Now listen to two students discussing the announcement.

FEMALE STUDENT: I'm happy that they've added this class!

MALE STUDENT: Really? I already have such a heavy load of homework. I don't want to add even more work.

FEMALE STUDENT: Think about it. We have to write papers for nearly every class. Even if it's just a lab report, we still have to conduct research. In high school, we only learned how to write pretty straightforward papers. The expectations are a lot higher now. It's easy to get a bad grade just because of poor writing.

MALE STUDENT: That's true. I always got good grades in high school, but my first two papers haven't gotten great marks.

FEMALE STUDENT: Plus, it's taking me a long time to write papers because I don't have a good idea of exactly what I'm supposed to be doing. I'm not really sure how to develop a thesis statement.

MALE STUDENT: I know what you mean! I wrote six drafts of my last paper and I still wasn't completely satisfied with it.

FEMALE STUDENT: Well, if we learn how to write good papers now, that will save us a lot of time and effort over the next four years! We'll have to write a lot of papers—we should learn to do it efficiently.

MALE STUDENT: You're right. I'm glad that they added this course, too!

NARRATOR: The woman expresses her opinion about the new writing class requirement. State her opinion and explain the reasons she gives for holding that opinion.

Sample Spoken Response—Track 205

The female student is, uh, in support of the university's decision to require first-year students, um, to take a writing class. Um, she… she makes the point that pretty much every class that they're going to take will require them to write papers. And, uh, the expectations of papers written in high school versus papers written in college is much more high in college, so, um, many students do not have the skill set to be able to write at the college level. Um, so this writing class would be able to give them the tools that they need to… to be able to get the grades that they want. Um, right now, they are taking too… she is taking too long to write a paper because she does not know the right way to do it. Um, if she took a class she would be able to, um, write more efficiently.

Comments

> The student summarizes all of the reasons the woman supports the new writing requirement. The student could improve her response by training herself to pause briefly at the start of a new sentence to gather her thoughts. Right now, she says "um" at the start of every sentence.

Answers and Explanations—17.3

Proposal to Add Class Hours—Track 193

NARRATOR: Now listen to two students discussing the proposal.

MALE STUDENT: Have you seen the new proposal? I'm worried that it will be a disaster.

FEMALE STUDENT: Why? I'd love to take 4 science classes next semester.

MALE STUDENT: Class hours are based on the number of weekly hours that class meets and how much homework you complete outside of class. You'll have a lot more work to do if you take 20 class hours in one semester.

FEMALE STUDENT: I can handle 20 hours.

MALE STUDENT: You'll spend more than 20 hours a week. A class that's assigned 4 class hours has 4 hours of weekly lectures, but you are also expected to spend at least an equal amount of time on homework outside of class.

FEMALE STUDENT: I didn't know that… a 4-hour class is actually 8 hours of work a week?

MALE STUDENT: At *minimum*. Taking a class that has 5 class hours isn't the same as taking one that has only 4 or 3—it's considerably more work. If you take 20 class hours, then you'll have at least 40 hours a week of class or homework.

FEMALE STUDENT: I also work 15 hours a week. That would be pretty overwhelming.

MALE STUDENT: That's another problem. A lot of science students work on research projects outside of class, or work as tutors or lab assistants. It's not just about classes, we have a lot to do outside of our classwork, too. A lot of people wouldn't have time for everything.

NARRATOR: The man expresses his opinion about the university's proposal. State his opinion and explain the reasons he gives for holding that opinion.

Sample Spoken Response—Track 206

The male student does not think that it's a good idea for the, uh, university to increase the amount of maximum hours a student can take in one week. He says that, um, if the university increases the amount of hours to 20, that… some students might not realize that it's not just 20 hours of class a week… what you also have to take into account is homework. Um, so for example, a 4-hour class is going to require also at least 4 hours of homework every week. That's… and that's a minimum number… it might be more than that. You're not just adding class time, you're adding homework time as well. Um, and also he says specifically s… science students, which the program is targeting, these students also are working on top of their classroom hours as lab assistants or tutors or on research projects, so because of that, you know, their extra work…

Comments

> The student accurately conveys the man's opinion and explains his reasoning well. The student also does a good job of pausing to gather his thoughts rather than saying "um" many times. He is in mid-sentence when the timer runs out. But he has already done a good job of answering the question, so he can still earn a good score.

Answers and Explanations—17.4

Semesters to Trimesters—Track 195

NARRATOR: Now listen to two students discussing the announcement.

MALE STUDENT: I'm glad I'm graduating next year. I don't think the trimester system is going to turn out well.

FEMALE STUDENT: Well, we were the only school that was still using semesters.

MALE STUDENT: Sure, for schools around here. But how about study abroad? When I studied abroad, the program was a whole semester, not just a trimester. Students won't be able to go to that program anymore … unless they want to come back here halfway through a trimester.

FEMALE STUDENT: Yeah, I guess the schedules wouldn't line up. I didn't think of that.

MALE STUDENT: A lot of my professors have been complaining about it, too. Our classes are already designed to be 15 weeks long. What are they going to do, cut out a third of the class material so it fits into 10 weeks? It's not that simple.

FEMALE STUDENT: It'll probably take awhile to redesign all of the classes.

MALE STUDENT: Yeah, they'll have to totally change a lot of courses… or else the professors will just try to teach the same material, in two-thirds as much time. It seems like way too much trouble to be worth it.

NARRATOR: The man expresses his opinion of the trimester system. State his opinion and explain the reasons he gives for holding that opinion.

Sample Spoken Response—Track 207

The male student, uh, does not agree that the school should move from semester program to trimester program. He says that, uh, even though other local schools are using trimesters… so it might be easier on the same schedule… he, um, did a study abroad program that was also on a semester schedule. So, uh, if the program didn't have the same schedule, it would have been much more difficult to do that, um, because the schedules would not line up and students would have to, uh, they would have to… not be on the same schedule… He also said that, uh, the current classes are 15 weeks, and if they move to 10 weeks, the professors are either going to have to cut, uh, a bunch of things, which will take some time. Or… or the other thing is that they might try to teach 15 weeks worth of learning into 10 weeks, which is not ideal either.

Comments

This topic is somewhat confusing, but the student does a good job of remembering and summarizing the details. In the middle of her response, she loses track of her sentence a little bit. But she pauses for a moment and is able to get herself back on track.

Answers and Explanations—17.5

Drama vs. Comedy—Track 197

NARRATOR: Now listen to two students discussing the memo.

FEMALE STUDENT: I don't think it's a good idea to change the play to a drama this term. The drama professor hasn't considered an important factor.

MALE STUDENT: What's that?

FEMALE STUDENT: We raise a lot of our budget via ticket sales. If you look at the last couple of years, the spring comedy has always outsold the fall drama. We make almost 50 percent more from the comedy than the drama. So if we produce another drama this spring, we may not make as much money and that would make our budget problems worse.

MALE STUDENT: We can reuse the costumes and sets, though. That will save money so maybe it won't matter if we don't make as much.

FEMALE STUDENT: Why don't we produce a comedy by Shakespeare, like *A Midsummer Night's Dream*? We could still reuse everything—and we would be able to get more people to buy tickets.

MALE STUDENT: That's a good idea.

FEMALE STUDENT: We would even still be able to take advantage of Professor Ludgate's expertise. He is probably just as knowledgeable about Shakespeare's comedies.

MALE STUDENT: You're right. One of the seminars he's leading this term is based on the comedies of Shakespeare.

NARRATOR: The woman expresses her opinion about the proposed change of the play. State her opinion and explain the reasons she gives for holding that opinion.

Sample Spoken Response—Track 208

The woman does not believe that, um, the university should do a drama for the spring production instead of a comedy. Um, she says that usually, um, the comedies that the school does, uh, sells much better than the dramas that the school does. Um, she says that it… they usually… tickets sales are about 50 percent better for comedies than dramas. Um, and if they do a drama this term then the budget problems will become even worse because they won't have the opportunity to make up, um, the money with the ticket sales. She suggests that they can do a comedy if they do a Shakespeare comedy. That way they will still be able to reuse all of the, um, costumes and props and scenery that they would be reusing, um, if they did a Shakespeare drama. And the visiting professor that's working at the school also is, uh… knows about Shakespeare comedy, so then he would able to work with the…

Comments

The student addresses most of the woman's reasons for wanting to do a comedy, not a drama. The student provides very good detail, but she does run out of time while making her final point. She could improve her response by cutting down on the earlier detail just a little bit. Then she would have had time to address the woman's final point.

Answers and Explanations—17.6

Increasing Adjunct Hiring—Track 199

NARRATOR: Now listen to two students discussing the announcement.

FEMALE STUDENT: Good, they're going to offer more sections of English 240 next year… it was full last year.

MALE STUDENT: I just wish that they weren't doing it by hiring a bunch of adjuncts.

FEMALE STUDENT: Aren't they basically the same as other professors?

MALE STUDENT: Well, most of them are good teachers, but they're really hard to get in touch with outside of class. I like to go to office hours and ask questions, you know? But I had this one professor last year who was an adjunct, and he was only here one day a week. He didn't even have an office on campus. It was impossible to get in touch with him.

FEMALE STUDENT: Good point. I don't really go to office hours, but if you do…

MALE STUDENT: Plus, I feel like it's not fair to the teachers, hiring them to work part-time. They went to the trouble of getting a PhD… and now they have to teach part-time at a bunch of different schools. And they probably don't make as much money as a full professor. It doesn't seem right.

FEMALE STUDENT: Yeah, that must be tough. Maybe they should be hiring more full professors instead.

NARRATOR: The man expresses his opinion on hiring more adjunct professors. State his opinion and explain the reasons he gives for holding that opinion.

Sample Spoken Response—Track 209

The male student… um, he talks about this solution to increase the percent of adjunct professors teaching classes. The university gives some reasons for this, but the male student… his opinion is that it's not a good idea. The first reason he gives… is that they're harder to reach, these adjunct professors. Uh, they don't have an office on campus… they don't have regular office hours, um, so that students are less able to ask questions or get extra help. The second reason is that it's not fair to professors or these adjuncts, I guess, um, or maybe the whole profession… they've gone through a lot of trouble and expense to get a PhD and now they get a part-time job and they have to travel around to different schools.

Comments

> The student accurately addresses the two criticisms that the man puts forward in the conversation. The response is well-structured, with a lot of relevant detail. The student might have also briefly explained why the university wants to institute this change, but only if this addition didn't interfere with explaining the man's position.

Answers and Explanations—17.7

No Jobs for Ashby Scholars—Track 201

NARRATOR: Now listen to two students discussing the article.

MALE STUDENT: You have the Ashby scholarship, right?

FEMALE STUDENT: I do. And I understand why they've decided not to let us work… but I still think it isn't right.

MALE STUDENT: Why would you need to work, though? Don't they pay for everything?

FEMALE STUDENT: Well, I'm going to be applying for jobs next year, right? A lot of companies won't even look at your résumé if you haven't done an internship or had some kind of job. They won't even notice that you were an Ashby scholar—they'll just figure that you have no experience, so they don't want to hire you.

MALE STUDENT: Yeah, that's true. I guess experience is even more important than getting a paycheck.

FEMALE STUDENT: Their argument about the money isn't completely right, either. They pay for tuition and housing, but they don't pay for things like health insurance, or food, or even entertainment.

MALE STUDENT: Yeah, so you can afford the basics, but you don't have any spending money…

FEMALE STUDENT: Right. I can pay my tuition and pay for my housing, but I can't save any money, and there's never any extra.

NARRATOR: The woman expresses her opinion of the Ashby Scholarship job policy. State her opinion and explain the reasons she gives for holding that opinion.

Sample Spoken Response—Track 210

The woman, uh, her opinion about the Ashby Scholarship is that, uh, she disagrees with the rule, which says that she cannot have a job outside… she cannot have a job… a non-volunteer job. She can't work for pay. Her first reason is, uh, that she will need experience on her résumé in order to, uh, to get jobs after school. If she can't do an internship, it will be much harder to get a real job because most companies require some work experience. The second reason is that the scholarship does cover tuition and housing, but it isn't… it doesn't give you any money for food or health insurance, and so she needs to earn some money. Those are pretty compelling reasons to allow these students to work, I thought.

Comments

> The student fully conveys the two main reasons that the woman disagrees with the scholarship requirement. At the end, the student conveys his personal opinion about the situation. But the directions for this type of task ask the student only to explain the woman's reasoning, not his own opinion. Be careful not to give your own opinion on a question of this type.

Answers and Explanations—17.8

Graduation Moved to Stadium—Track 203

NARRATOR: Now listen to two students discussing the article.

MALE STUDENT: I'm so happy they're moving graduation to the stadium.

FEMALE STUDENT: Why? I was a little disappointed. The theater is so beautiful. And what if it rains? The stadium isn't covered.

MALE STUDENT: It rains during games sometimes, but we still go. Just take an umbrella with you. Besides, it isn't very likely. That time of year, we don't get very much rain.

FEMALE STUDENT: I suppose that's true. But the theater has a much better atmosphere.

MALE STUDENT: The theater is also very small. I think the biggest drawback is the theater's capacity. Did you know that each graduating student was allowed to invite only two guests? And only seniors can attend. My sister is in her second year and she wouldn't have been able to come, since I would have given my two tickets to my parents.

FEMALE STUDENT: I didn't realize that it was so limited.

MALE STUDENT: Many students had to make difficult choices about who to invite. Some students who didn't need both tickets were even selling their tickets to others for really inflated prices. It was terrible.

FEMALE STUDENT: You've convinced me. I agree, they should move graduation to the stadium.

NARRATOR: The man expresses his opinion about moving graduation to the stadium. State his opinion and explain the reasons he gives for holding that opinion.

Sample Spoken Response—Track 211

The male student is very happy about the decision to move, um, the graduation ceremony from the theater to the stadium. Um, he says that, you know, the main problem with the theater is that it is too small. Um, he said that past graduating students only were allowed to have two guests attend the ceremony. Um, so, because tickets were in such high demand that… that some students actually, you know, sold their graduation tickets at really inflated prices, um, which is obviously not, uh, you know, not good. Uh, he said that also only seniors are allowed to attend the ceremony and he had a… a sister who's a second-year, so you know, she wouldn't have been able to attend because his parents already had his tickets, and, uh, you know, it's j-just not enough room for everyone to be able to attend, and that's really the main problem.

Comments

The student strongly conveys the man's main complaint about moving graduation to the stadium. She includes a good amount of detail to explain his point of view. She could improve her response by varying the start of her sentences more ("Um, he says that" … "Um, he said that" … "Uh, he said that").

Chapter 18

Speaking Task Type 4

Speaking questions test your ability to comprehend and respond orally to written or spoken material. You will have to speak your response aloud. There are six different speaking tasks. Speaking Task Type 4, Academic Course (General/Specific), is an "integrated" task. You will first read a short passage about an academic subject for 45 to 50 seconds and then listen to a short lecture that provides more detail on that topic. You will respond to a specific question about something from the lecture. (Usually, you will be asked to summarize the main point and the examples given in the lecture.) You will be able to reread the passage while you plan your response, but you will not be able to replay any part of the lecture.

Speaking questions test your ability to understand spoken and written information and to summarize and express opinions about that information. They also test your ability to respond orally to specific questions, including your grammar, your vocabulary, and the logical organization of your ideas.

How should you use this chapter? Here are some recommendations, according to the level you've reached in TOEFL Speaking:

0. **Everyone!** Hold yourself to the time limits whenever practicing Speaking tasks. Tape your response and listen to it afterward to analyze your performance. You can use any app on your computer or phone to tape yourself. If you don't know of a good app already, try www.vocaroo.com.

1. **Fundamentals.** Start with a type that is a "medium weakness"—not your worst Speaking question type but not your best either. Try one question and then check the sample answer. Think carefully about the principles at work. If you think you can do a better job, redo the question. Articulate what you want to do differently the next time you do this type of task.

2. **Fixes.** Do one Speaking task, examine the results, learn your lessons, then try a different type of Speaking task. Be sure to keep to the time limits. When you're ready, graduate to doing a set of six different Speaking tasks all in a row.

3. **Tweaks.** Confirm your mastery by doing a set of six different Speaking tasks all in a row under timed conditions.

Good luck on Speaking!

18.1

You will now read a short passage and listen to a lecture on the same topic. You will then be asked a question about them. After you hear the question, give yourself 30 seconds to prepare your response. Then record yourself speaking for 60 seconds.

Listen to Track 212.

Now read a passage from a human behavior textbook. You have 45 seconds to read the passage. Begin reading now.

Reading Time: 45 seconds

The Familiarity Principle

People tend to feel more positively towards the familiar than towards the unfamiliar. Research participants who are repeatedly exposed to a stimulus, such as a picture or a word, report significantly more positive feelings towards it than do people for whom the stimulus is unfamiliar. This extends to our perception of other people. The more often someone encounters another person, the more likable they tend to find them, even if the two haven't interacted

Listen to Track 213.

Explain the familiarity principle, using the experiment described in the lecture as an example.

Preparation Time: 30 seconds

Response Time: 60 seconds

18.2

You will now read a short passage and listen to a lecture on the same topic. You will then be asked a question about them. After you hear the question, give yourself 30 seconds to prepare your response. Then record yourself speaking for 60 seconds.

Listen to Track 214.

Now read a passage from a psychology textbook. You have 50 seconds to read the passage. Begin reading now.

Reading Time: 50 seconds

Rashomon Effect

How an event is perceived by different people depends on a number of factors and can lead to greatly different interpretations of that event. This phenomenon is known as the Rashomon Effect, after the 1950 film by Japanese filmmaker Akira Kurosawa. In the film, four witnesses to a murder provide substantially different accounts of what happened. The differences are to some degree motivated by self-interest, but are also influenced by the subjectivity of the witnesses' perceptions of the event, as well as a lack of clear-cut evidence. This can lead to substantial differences even when all parties involved give their account as honestly as possible.

 Listen to Track 215.

Explain what is meant by the Rashomon Effect, using examples given in the lecture.

Preparation Time: 30 seconds

Response Time: 60 seconds

18.3

You will now read a short passage and listen to a lecture on the same topic. You will then be asked a question about them. After you hear the question, give yourself 30 seconds to prepare your response. Then record yourself speaking for 60 seconds.

 Listen to Track 216.

Now read a passage about delayed gratification. You have 45 seconds to read the passage. Begin reading now.

Reading Time: 45 seconds

Delayed Gratification

"Delayed gratification" refers to a person's ability to forgo an immediate reward for the time being, in favor of receiving a larger reward later on. The ability to delay gratification varies from person to person and depends on a number of psychological factors. Adults are usually better at delaying gratification than are children. However, after a person has reached adulthood, his or her ability to delay gratification usually stays the same throughout life.

Listen to Track 217.

Explain how performing the marshmallow experiment helped to improve the children's ability to delay gratification.

Preparation Time: 30 seconds

Response Time: 60 seconds

18.4

You will now read a short passage and listen to a lecture on the same topic. You will then be asked a question about them. After you hear the question, give yourself 30 seconds to prepare your response. Then record yourself speaking for 60 seconds.

 Listen to Track 218.

Now read the passage about Method acting. You have 50 seconds to read the passage. Begin reading now.

Reading Time: 50 seconds

Method Acting

Method acting refers to a set of techniques that actors use to prepare for roles. In Method acting, actors attempt to identify the specific roles that they portray with real or imagined experiences from their own lives. When a Method actor attempts to authentically portray a character in a certain situation, he first asks himself what would cause him to behave in that way, or how he would behave in that situation if it really happened to him. By thinking in terms of actual, lived experiences, Method actors attempt to create performances that are more true to life.

 Listen to Track 219.

Using the examples from the lecture, explain why Daniel Day-Lewis is considered a Method actor.

Preparation Time: 30 seconds

Response Time: 60 seconds

18.5

> You will now read a short passage and listen to a lecture on the same topic. You will then be asked a question about them. After you hear the question, give yourself 30 seconds to prepare your response. Then record yourself speaking for 60 seconds.
>
> Listen to Track 220.
>
> Now read a passage from a marketing textbook. You have 45 seconds to read the passage. Begin reading now.
>
> Reading Time: 45 seconds

Loyalty Marketing

An effective, well-known method of customer attraction and retention is a strategy called "loyalty marketing." This strategy includes any practice that gives customers added benefits simply for using, or continuing to use, products or services that a company sells. In recent years, loyalty marketing programs have flourished in various consumer-focused industries. Some prominent examples include airline mileage programs and reward programs for credit card users. Alternatively, a loyalty marketing program may involve price discounts that are available only to members at such places as grocery stores or gas stations.

> Listen to Track 221.
>
> Using the examples from the lecture, explain the practice of loyalty marketing.
>
> Preparation Time: 30 seconds
>
> Response Time: 60 seconds

18

18.6

> You will now read a short passage and listen to a lecture on the same topic. You will then be asked a question about them. After you hear the question, give yourself 30 seconds to prepare your response. Then record yourself speaking for 60 seconds.
>
> Listen to Track 222.
>
> Now read a passage about the field of aesthetics. You have 45 seconds to read the passage. Begin reading now.
>
> Reading Time: 45 seconds

Aesthetics

Aesthetics is the science of beauty and pleasure. Scientists in this field, known as aestheticians, seek to understand the fundamental nature of beauty, as well as how and why it affects our emotions so much. Aestheticians are also interested in how the ideals of beauty have differed across cultures and time periods. Some have even considered the idea that beauty can exist on its own, independent of human perception.

The study of aesthetics dates back over two thousand years to the ancient Greek philosopher Plato and his followers.

 Listen to Track 223.

Using the professor's examples, explain the field of aesthetics and discuss why it is not well-studied or well-understood.

Preparation Time: 30 seconds

Response Time: 60 seconds

18.7

You will now read a short passage and listen to a lecture on the same topic. You will then be asked a question about them. After you hear the question, give yourself 30 seconds to prepare your response. Then record yourself speaking for 60 seconds.

 Listen to Track 224.

Now read a passage about linguistic displacement. You have 50 seconds to read the passage. Begin reading now.

Reading Time: 50 seconds

Linguistic Displacement

Linguists have identified a number of characteristics that are common to all languages. One of these is known as displacement. All human languages let speakers communicate about things that aren't immediately present, such as an object that is in a different room. Discussing the past or the future is a type of displacement, as is discussing a person who isn't physically present. However, in some communication systems, such as certain systems of animal communication, it's only possible to communicate about things that are physically present and able to be viewed.

Listen to Track 225.

Using the concept of displacement, explain how bee communication is similar to human language.

Preparation Time: 30 seconds
Response Time: 60 seconds

18.8

You will now read a short passage and listen to a lecture on the same topic. You will then be asked a question about them. After you hear the question, give yourself 30 seconds to prepare your response. Then record yourself speaking for 60 seconds.

 Listen to Track 226.

Now read a passage about the production of insulin. You have 50 seconds to read the passage. Begin reading now.

Reading Time: 50 seconds

18

Insulin Production

In Type I diabetes, people's bodies do not make enough of a substance called insulin. Historically, people with diabetes had no chance of a healthy life—but that all changed in 1921, when Canadian scientists Frederick Banting and Charles Best first extracted insulin from the carcass of a dog and made it pure enough for human use.

Researchers gradually improved the quality of this insulin, but these improvements were very minor. For half a century, the basic production method—extracting and purifying insulin from dead animals—remained as tedious and demanding as ever.

 Listen to Track 227.

The professor describes advances in the production of human insulin. Discuss why this method of production is superior to the original method.

Preparation Time: 30 seconds
Response Time: 60 seconds

Answers and Explanations—18.1

The Familiarity Principle—Track 213

NARRATOR: Now listen to part of a lecture on this topic in a human behavior class.

PROFESSOR: There was a famous experiment in the 1960s that demonstrated the familiarity principle. It's usually referred to as the "black bag experiment." What happened was… a psychology professor paid one of his students to wear a garbage bag to class. This started on the very first day, and because he always had a bag over his head, nobody ever saw what he looked like… and he didn't talk in class or interact with anybody, he just sat there. So, on the first day, the professor polled his students, and they generally felt pretty negative towards the "black bag." They were suspicious, they were hostile, they felt uncomfortable having him there. But the guy kept coming to every class session, and the professor would ask his students what they thought. They ended up feeling significantly more positive towards the black bag guy by the time the course ended, even though none of them knew who he was, and they hadn't even talked to him. It was… enough for them to just see him a couple of times a week—the repeated exposure by itself changed their attitudes. This principle gets used a lot in advertising, actually, which is why it can seem like ads are just pushing the same thing at you, over and over again. The idea is that if you see it enough times, it doesn't matter whether you really engage with it, you'll end up feeling better about it than you did at the beginning.

NARRATOR: Explain the familiarity principle, using the experiment described in the lecture as an example.

Sample Spoken Response—Track 228

The familiarity principle, uh, basically means that, um, or explains the fact that people, uh, tend to like and feel more positively toward things that are familiar. Um, so, uh, for example, um, you know, one experiment that explored this, uh, was one where a professor, uh, had a student come to class wearing a black garbage bag, and at the first class asked how everyone felt about, you know, the guy in a garbage bag. And, uh, everyone… they felt very negative, you know, uh, had really bad feelings, um. And this person kept coming to class, still with the garbage bag. And by the end, the professor asked the class again, and just because that person, uh, in the garbage bag was there and… and coming there frequently and then being familiar with that person, uh, they actually felt much more positively towards him by the end.

Comments

> The student accurately describes the experiment and explains the familiarity principle. She could improve her response by training herself to pause briefly before expressing a complicated thought. The last sentence wanders around and is hard to follow. It would have been better for the student to express the ideas in a couple of shorter, more manageable sentences.

Answers and Explanations—18.2

Rashomon Effect—Track 215

NARRATOR: Now listen to part of a lecture on this topic in a psychology class.

PROFESSOR: OK, so why don't we look at an example from an everyday event. Let's say a friend calls you… she is distressed over problems she is having with her boyfriend. She tells you a series of detailed stories about what's happened between them, asks for advice—you know, the kind of thing a friend does when she needs help in this sort of situation.

Now, let's say that you are also friends with her boyfriend. You run into him at a coffee shop, and he doesn't know you've spoken to her. He tells you about what's going on, and from your perspective, it seems like he's talking about an entirely different situation! In both cases, most likely, the person you're speaking to is looking for solace or support over the conflict they're having. But the facts, the relative importance of the facts, the order in which these things occurred—they may vary substantially.

This is a classic example of the Rashomon Effect. It comes up a lot in relationships among people—particularly when there is conflict. Romantic relationships may be the most vulnerable to this effect, because emotion and subjectivity play such a large role in the relationship itself. But it can come up in other areas: friendships, parent–child relationships, work relationships, and so on. At times, the differing perspectives of the same circumstances can be completely astounding to an outside observer. Sometimes, the people involved may be convinced that the other person is lying! But keep in mind that each person is "witness" to the situation, and has different thoughts, emotions, perspectives, and priorities. It stands to reason that they would interpret the circumstances somewhat differently.

NARRATOR: Explain what is meant by the Rashomon Effect, using examples given in the lecture.

Sample Spoken Response—Track 229

The Rashomon Effect is when, uh, two people or multiple people experience the same event, but they… interpret it differently. Uh, a good example of this would be in relationships when a conflict happens. Um, you know, a specific example would be, say, if a boyfriend and girlfriend have a fight. Um, if those two people later describe what happened separately, they can come up with totally different versions of it. Um, and that's because, uh, they each really experienced that same thing differently, and they might have put different, uh, importance or emphasis on the things that happened and what they said. Um, you know, because one person says something but the other person thinks they meant something else and so they have totally different ideas of what happened.

Comments

The student summarizes the lecture well and provides some connection back to the passage. That connection could have been expanded a little bit (for instance, noting that the different interpretations happen even when the observers are trying to be honest). Notice that the student starts nearly every sentence with the filler word "um," even though the rest of the sentence is usually well-spoken. He could improve his response by training himself not to start every sentence with "um." It would be better just to pause silently for a moment.

Answers and Explanations—18.3

Delayed Gratification—Track 217

NARRATOR: Now listen to part of a lecture on this topic in a psychology class.

PROFESSOR: There's this famous experiment known as the Stanford Marshmallow Experiment. Researchers got a bunch of 4- or 5-year-old kids and gave them each a marshmallow. They told the kids that if they didn't eat the marshmallow now, they would get another marshmallow later, and they could eat both of them. If they did eat the marshmallow right now, they wouldn't get a second one. It turned out that some kids ate the marshmallow right away, while others were able to wait.

Then, in a second experiment, they split the kids into two groups. Before they even brought out the marshmallows, they started treating the two groups differently. In the first group, they'd promise the kids a reward, and then they'd actually give them the reward later. So they'd say that they'd give them more crayons to color with, and then they'd come back and give them the crayons. In the other group, they'd promise the kids a reward, but then they'd never give it to them, and they'd leave them disappointed.

When they did the marshmallow experiment with these two groups, they found that the kids in the first group did a much better job at not eating the marshmallow. The kids in that group learned that the researchers would actually come back and follow through on their promises, so they were more willing to wait. The other group learned that the researchers were likely to disappoint them, so they tended to eat the marshmallow right away instead of waiting for a second one.

NARRATOR: Explain how performing the marshmallow experiment helped to improve the children's ability to delay gratification.

Sample Spoken Response—Track 230

In the second phase of the marshmallow experiment, um, the researchers treated two groups of children differently. With the first group, they told them that they would bring them rewards and they did… bring them rewards. The second group, they told them they would give them rewards and they never ended up giving them to them. So then… when they tried to give the marshmallow experiment again, the first children, um, you know, *believed* the researchers and were… able to do delayed gratification. They waited for, um, the marshmallows, because they had a trust with the researchers. And the children who did not have that experience… had a harder time, um, because, you know, they thought they wouldn't have the marshmallows. So they didn't wait.

Comments

The student explains in detail how the experiment worked for both groups of children. She also explains the connection to the concept of delayed gratification. In the first part of her response, she sometimes uses the same pronouns (they, them) to refer to different groups of people or things and this can be confusing. She could improve her response by explaining a little more about what the marshmallow experiment actually was. It would also help not to use quite so many pronouns ("they" and "them" over and over), because it becomes unclear which people are being referred to (the researchers or the children).

Answers and Explanations—18.4

Method Acting—Track 219

NARRATOR: Now listen to part of a lecture on this topic in a film class.

PROFESSOR: Right now, one of the best-known Method actors is Daniel Day-Lewis. It's one thing he's really known for. You can read about how he prepares for roles; there are all kinds of stories. What you hear the most about is a movie called *My Left Foot*. The film was about a guy with cerebral palsy, who wasn't able to walk or talk. He could only communicate by writing with his left foot. So Day-Lewis played this role, and since he obviously didn't really use a wheelchair, he started using the wheelchair from the movie to get around. Even when he wasn't filming, he would use the wheelchair.

He was trying to embody... the experience, the lived experience of someone in a wheelchair because he thought this would make his performance more real. Supposedly, it might be just a myth, but supposedly, he actually hurt himself by sitting in a particular position in the wheelchair for too long.

Or, the other one is the movie *Last of the Mohicans*. He actually went out into the wilderness and hunted his own food, trying to put himself into the mindset of, basically, a hunter-gatherer. You'll read all kinds of really extreme anecdotes about Method acting, but really, any time an actor tries to link up their own experience with what their character would've been experiencing, they're doing something like that... they're using Method acting to make themselves better at the role.

NARRATOR: Using the examples from the lecture, explain why Daniel Day-Lewis is considered a Method actor.

Sample Spoken Response—Track 231

Daniel Day-Louis is a Method actor because when he is doing a part, he will put himself in situations... similar to the character so he can... understand how the character would act. Um, for example, when he played a role where he was in a wheelchair, he actually used a wheelchair all the time to, you know, know what that felt like in his body. Um, similarly, he acted another role where he was, uh, a hunter, lived in the woods ... and he went out into the woods for real and... hunted his own food. So he could understand what that was really like. Um, Method actors can either, you know, bring up their memories, um, of things they've done, or use imagined, um, situations of things they, uh, might be able to do, like... like the characters.

Comments

The student summarizes the examples well. He uses them to show that he understands how Method actors prepare to perform. In general, his wording is good, but his last sentence has many "ums" and other interjections. They make it more difficult to understand the final sentence.

Answers and Explanations—18.5

Loyalty Marketing—Track 221

NARRATOR: Now listen to part of a lecture on this topic in a marketing class.

PROFESSOR: Alright... I have some helpful examples of loyalty marketing. Whenever I buy groceries, I go to the same store... partly because it has a good selection and reasonable prices. But, I'm also a member there. I'd say about half of the groceries I regularly buy there have a discounted price for members—sometimes as much as a dollar or two. When I buy a lot of groceries at one time, umm, the savings really add up. Now, on some level I know that the store is modestly inflating the base price of its groceries to account for this. But... there is some satisfaction in seeing the total amount of money I've saved on a big grocery run. They even print it on the receipt! Plus, whenever I buy enough groceries, I get discounts on gasoline at a local gas station. So, I save money on my food, and I save money at the pump. This makes it difficult for me to rationally choose to shop at a different grocery store.

Here's another example: credit card rewards. I have several different credit cards, with roughly the same interest rate. So how do I decide which to use when I buy things? Well for me, the card that provides cash back offers the best value. Other cards offer what they call "reward points," which can be used to receive certain items for free, once enough points have been accumulated. But how do I know I'm going to want

the items they have available? No, I'd rather have the cash—because I can use cash to buy anything I want, not just the things the other companies make available.

NARRATOR: Using the examples from the lecture, explain the practice of loyalty marketing.

Sample Spoken Response—Track 232

Loyalty marketing is a way that companies, um, provide incentives for you to use their services and to… keep using their services. Um, it mi… for example, um, you know, credit cards might offer, um, reward programs, or airlines might offer frequent flier programs. Um, basically, you get rewarded for using the same company over and over. Um, if you shop at a certain store, maybe they'll give you discounts, um, to keep going at that store. But, you know, prices might be inflated to begin with, so you might look like you're getting discounts when… when really you're not getting as big of a discount as you think, but that psychology makes you feel like you're getting a good deal, and that's, um, a lot for people to, um…

Comments

The student explains the examples from the lecture and shows why they are examples of loyalty marketing. She runs out of time in the middle of a sentence. She could improve her response by training herself to have a sense of how much she can say in 60 seconds so that she is not cut off mid-sentence.

Answers and Explanations—18.6

Aesthetics—Track 223

NARRATOR: Now listen to part of a lecture on this topic in a philosophy class.

PROFESSOR: For most people, it's impossible to imagine life without beauty. And that's despite the fact that for most of us, the word 'beauty' rarely ever goes beyond what we can see with our eyes! In that most narrow sense, beauty is a property of physical things… sunsets, landscapes, cityscapes, clothes, artwork, and let's not forget people themselves. But, if we think of beauty in a broader sense… like beautiful music, beautiful feelings, beautiful sensations… it encompasses just about everything that gives meaning and enjoyment to our lives.

In reality, though, very few people ever stop to think about exactly what beauty is. And those who do think about it don't usually try to study it scientifically. So, most people would be surprised to find that there's a whole field of study dedicated to beauty. And even among the small number of people who know about aesthetics, many wonder whether it is really a genuine science or whether its goals are realistic.

In fact, the field has always had critics and doubters. Some critics have thought that pleasure and beauty simply lie beyond the realm of human understanding. Or that human language is incapable of describing how beauty works, even if we can appreciate it on another level. Either way, if those critics are right, then trying to study beauty is pointless from the beginning.

Other people have raised moral objections. They have warned that people could use their findings to manipulate people or even control their minds. And still others have feared that if we learn how beauty and pleasure work, we may lose our ability to enjoy them!

NARRATOR: Using the professor's examples, explain the field of aesthetics and discuss why it is not well-studied or well-understood.

Sample Spoken Response—Track 233

Aesthetics is the field of studying beauty. Um, you know, there are narrow views of aesthetics, whether it's, uh, beauty found in nature, flowers, sunsets, that sort of thing. Or, um, you know, as it relates to larger ideas of beauty like listening to music or having a beautiful feeling. Um, there's a lot of confusion around the field. Whether or not it's an actual science, um, is a question. Um, you know, part of that is because beauty might be beyond, um,… being quantifiable. Can you really measure it? Beauty is different to different types of people. Um, so it's hard to, have a… a, sort of, general understanding of what it is. It also… you know, if we begin to understand it, can others manipulate one another with their knowledge of beauty?

Comments

This is a challenging topic. The student does a good job of explaining what aesthetics is. He also discusses some of the questions raised by the professor. He might be able to improve his response by having a summary sentence at the end—but, overall, this is a good response to a hard question.

Answers and Explanations—18.7

Linguistic Displacement—Track 225

NARRATOR: Now listen to part of a lecture on this topic in a linguistics class.

PROFESSOR: There's an ongoing debate about whether honey bees can actually use language. Bees mostly communicate by dancing. A bee will leave the hive, and go try to find food. When it finds food, it'll come back and do a particular sort of dance to tell the other bees where the food is. If one part of the dance is longer, that means the food is further from the hive, and if it's shorter, then the food is closer. And that sort of seems like language, on the surface. You can picture the bees going out, finding food, then it seems as if they're saying to the other bees, "Look, here's where the food was." And that's actually one of the best arguments that the bees are using language.

Think about other ways that animals communicate. For instance, when a bird sees a predator, it'll call out to other birds. But it only does that if the predator is right there—so, it's just an immediate reaction. Birds don't actually have any calls that tell other birds, "I saw a predator a few miles away." On the other hand, a human could go for a walk in the jungle, see a jaguar, and then come back and warn everyone else about it later. In this sense, bee communication has more in common with human language than it does with birdsong. It has the property of displacement, where bees can sort of discuss things that happened somewhere else.

NARRATOR: Using the concept of displacement, explain how bee communication is similar to human language.

Sample Spoken Response—Track 234

Bee communication is more similar to human, uh, communication in regards to displacements. Uh, displacement means that humans are able to talk about things that are not actually in the immediate area, so either in the past, or future, um, or something about something who's not actually in… uh, really close by. And bees actually do that when they search for food and have to give directions, um, back at the hive. Not at the place where the food is found. Back at the hive to the other bees. Um, where other cxam… uh, animals such as birds can't really or have not been demonstrated to… to be able to do that. So bees seemingly are able to point to things that are outside of their immediate, um, location, uh, and share that with other bees.

Comments

The student defines displacement and explains how bees exhibit this behavior. A couple of her sentences are incomplete. She could improve her response by trying to speak in complete sentences.

Answers and Explanations—18.8

Insulin Production—Track 227

NARRATOR: Now listen to part of a lecture on this topic in a biology class.

PROFESSOR: The basic way of producing insulin didn't really change much from the 1920s all the way up to the 1980s. But when the changes finally came, they were huge—absolutely revolutionary. In fact, insulin was the first large-scale success of an entirely new branch of science… namely, genetic engineering.

In 1977, researchers pinpointed the exact location of the gene that "tells" the human body how to make insulin. Within just a few years after that, scientists had extracted that gene from human tissue, and they managed to insert it into special bacteria. Those bacteria pretty much just followed the directions given by the gene, and so that's what they kept doing… they went to work making human insulin. Not only was this technology amazing, but it was literally alive! And since there was no longer any need for animal bodies, the amount of insulin that could be made became unlimited.

Of course, messing with the genes of microscopic organisms isn't exactly cheap… so, the first genetically engineered insulin was outrageously expensive. But, just like with any other technology, the price fell as more and more was made—and given how many people have diabetes, it wasn't long before the new technology became affordable for everyone.

Just two generations ago, genetically engineered insulin would have seemed like science fiction. But today, it is so common, and so affordable, that it's even given to dogs and cats that have diabetes. A hundred years ago, we were using dogs' insulin; now, the dogs are using ours!

NARRATOR: The professor describes advances in the production of human insulin. Discuss why this method of production is superior to the original method.

Sample Spoken Response—Track 235

The methods to create insulin has become more advanced over time. Uh, initially, uh, insulin had to be extracted from animals, such as dogs, and that really limited the amount, uh, that we could use. Uh, around the 1980s a new method of production was invented where, uh, scientists actually used genetic engineering, uh, to, uh, create insulin, uh, using bacteria, um, and this allowed the supply of insulin to essentially become unlimited. Uh, when this new method was originally created, it was expensive. But over time, the technology has become cheaper and cheaper. And now it is w… very widely available, far more than it… was before with the old method.

Comments

The student does a good job of summarizing the main reasons that the new method is better than the old one. He had a little trouble in the middle of his response ("used genetic engineering, uh, to, uh, create insulin, uh, using bacteria, um"). This likely occurred because he didn't remember the exact details from the lecture. When this happens, don't try to use those details. Instead, say something simpler, such as "used genetic engineering to make insulin."

Chapter 19
Speaking Task Type 5

Speaking questions test your ability to comprehend and respond orally to written or spoken material. You will have to speak your response aloud. There are six different speaking tasks. Speaking Task Type 5, Campus Situation (Problem/Solution), is an "integrated" task. You will listen to a conversation between two people about a problem and possible solutions to that problem. Your task will be to summarize the problem and to provide your opinion as to which solution you think is best. You will not be able to replay any part of the conversation.

Speaking questions test your ability to understand spoken and written information and to summarize and express opinions about that information. They also test your ability to respond orally to specific questions, including your grammar, your vocabulary, and the logical organization of your ideas.

How should you use this chapter? Here are some recommendations, according to the level you've reached in TOEFL Speaking:

0. **Everyone!** Hold yourself to the time limits whenever practicing Speaking tasks. Tape your response and listen to it afterward to analyze your performance. You can use any app on your computer or phone to tape yourself. If you don't know of a good app already, try www.vocaroo.com.

1. **Fundamentals.** Start with a type that is a "medium weakness"—not your worst Speaking question type but not your best either. Try one question and then check the sample answer. Think carefully about the principles at work. If you think you can do a better job, redo the question. Articulate what you want to do differently the next time you do this type of task.

2. **Fixes.** Do one Speaking task, examine the results, learn your lessons, then try a different type of Speaking task. Be sure to keep to the time limits. When you're ready, graduate to doing a set of six different Speaking tasks all in a row.

3. **Tweaks.** Confirm your mastery by doing a set of six different Speaking tasks all in a row under timed conditions.

Good luck on Speaking!

19.1

You will now listen to part of a conversation. You will then be asked a question about it. After you hear the question, give yourself 20 seconds to prepare your response. Then record yourself speaking for 60 seconds.

   Listen to Track 236.

Briefly summarize the problem the speakers are discussing. Then state which of the two solutions from the conversation you would recommend. Explain the reasons for your recommendation.

Preparation Time: 20 seconds
Response Time: 60 seconds

19.2

You will now listen to part of a conversation. You will then be asked a question about it. After you hear the question, give yourself 20 seconds to prepare your response. Then record yourself speaking for 60 seconds.

   Listen to Track 237.

Briefly summarize the problem the speakers are discussing. Then state which of the two solutions from the conversation you would recommend. Explain the reasons for your recommendation.

Preparation Time: 20 seconds
Response Time: 60 seconds

19.3

> You will now listen to part of a conversation. You will then be asked a question about it. After you hear the question, give yourself 20 seconds to prepare your response. Then record yourself speaking for 60 seconds.
>
> Listen to Track 238.
>
> Briefly summarize the problem the speakers are discussing. Then state which of the two solutions from the conversation you would recommend. Explain the reasons for your recommendation.
>
> | Preparation Time: 20 seconds |
> | :---: |
> | Response Time: 60 seconds |

19.4

> You will now listen to part of a conversation. You will then be asked a question about it. After you hear the question, give yourself 20 seconds to prepare your response. Then record yourself speaking for 60 seconds.
>
> Listen to Track 239.
>
> Briefly summarize the problem the speakers are discussing. Then state which of the two solutions from the conversation you would recommend. Explain the reasons for your recommendation.
>
> | Preparation Time: 20 seconds |
> | :---: |
> | Response Time: 60 seconds |

19.5

You will now listen to part of a conversation. You will then be asked a question about it. After you hear the question, give yourself 20 seconds to prepare your response. Then record yourself speaking for 60 seconds.

 Listen to Track 240.

Briefly summarize the problem the speakers are discussing. Then state which of the two solutions from the conversation you would recommend. Explain the reasons for your recommendation.

Preparation Time: 20 seconds

Response Time: 60 seconds

19.6

You will now listen to part of a conversation. You will then be asked a question about it. After you hear the question, give yourself 20 seconds to prepare your response. Then record yourself speaking for 60 seconds.

 Listen to Track 241.

Briefly summarize the problem the speakers are discussing. Then state which of the two solutions from the conversation you would recommend. Explain the reasons for your recommendation.

Preparation Time: 20 seconds

Response Time: 60 seconds

19.7

You will now listen to part of a conversation. You will then be asked a question about it. After you hear the question, give yourself 20 seconds to prepare your response. Then record yourself speaking for 60 seconds.

 Listen to Track 242.

Briefly summarize the problem the speakers are discussing. Then state which of the two solutions from the conversation you would recommend. Explain the reasons for your recommendation.

> **Preparation Time: 20 seconds**
>
> **Response Time: 60 seconds**

19.8

You will now listen to part of a conversation. You will then be asked a question about it. After you hear the question, give yourself 20 seconds to prepare your response. Then record yourself speaking for 60 seconds.

 Listen to Track 243.

Briefly summarize the problem the speakers are discussing. Then state which of the two solutions from the conversation you would recommend. Explain the reasons for your recommendation.

> **Preparation Time: 20 seconds**
>
> **Response Time: 60 seconds**

Answers and Explanations—19.1

Museum—Track 236

NARRATOR: Listen to a conversation between two students.

MALE STUDENT: Hey, are you going on the trip to the Asian History museum?

FEMALE STUDENT: I really want to, but I can't. I have to give a presentation in my linguistics class. It counts as a third of my grade, so there's no way I can miss class that day.

MALE STUDENT: Just give the presentation on a different day, then.

FEMALE STUDENT: I don't think the professor would let me do it late, just because of a school trip.

MALE STUDENT: No, I mean you could do it early—your professor would probably be okay with that, right? If you ask to do the presentation a day earlier, that makes you look studious. You're not asking for an extension.

FEMALE STUDENT: You're right, then it wouldn't look like I was procrastinating.

MALE STUDENT: And then you can come on the trip.

FEMALE STUDENT: Although I'd have to get the work done earlier—and I have a lot of other homework to do. Also, the professor would probably rather have me present on the same day as everyone else.

MALE STUDENT: Wait, I have an idea. Do you know anybody else in the class? Maybe you could, like, record yourself giving the presentation, and then have somebody play the tape in class for you that day.

FEMALE STUDENT: That's smart. I'd just have to figure out how to make the recording, and see if they'd let me do that. But that way I'd be able to go to the history museum.

NARRATOR: Briefly summarize the problem the speakers are discussing. Then state which of the two solutions from the conversation you would recommend. Explain the reasons for your recommendation.

Sample Spoken Response—Track 244

The woman has the problem. There is a trip to a museum that, uh, she wants to go to, but… it is at the same time as a presentation she has to give for class. The two solutions are, one, um, she, uh… asks to give the presentation at different time… uh, earlier. But this solution would give her lesser time to prepare and also would be not at the same time as everyone else presenting. The second solution would be to… record the presentation and play it. I do not like the second idea because when you record something… you don't have the pressure of… public speaking. So I would choose the first one, uh, to give the presentation earlier. I think the professor would be more likely to agree because this solution still requires her to be speaking in public.

Comments

The student summarizes the problem and the two possible solutions. He states a clear preference for the first solution and explains why. He has a few small grammar errors. But these errors are infrequent enough that he can still earn a good score.

Answers and Explanations—19.2

Internet Is Down—Track 237

NARRATOR: Now listen to a conversation between two students.

MALE STUDENT: Hey, why can't I connect to the internet? Is there something wrong with my computer?

FEMALE STUDENT: No, it's not just you. It's been out all day on campus. Everybody's complaining about it. They have no idea when it'll be back up.

MALE STUDENT: I have to submit this physics assignment online in an hour! The professor uses that grading program—we have to submit our homework online by a certain time every week. I left it until the last minute, and now with the internet not working, I have a huge problem.

FEMALE STUDENT: Hmm, can you go to a coffee shop to submit it? Or anywhere off campus?

MALE STUDENT: I would, but I did the assignment on my desktop. I don't have a laptop…

FEMALE STUDENT: I'd say you could borrow mine, but I need it for class in a few minutes—I'm sorry!

MALE STUDENT: That's okay—thanks anyways.

FEMALE STUDENT: If you can't find a way to upload it, could you print it out?

MALE STUDENT: How would I turn it in, though?

FEMALE STUDENT: Put it in the professor's mailbox. I'm sure he has one.

MALE STUDENT: I do have a printer, at least. Maybe I could print out the assignment and write the time on it, or something—at least that way he'd know that I got it done on time, even if I couldn't upload it.

FEMALE STUDENT: He probably knows that the internet is out on campus. I bet he'd be okay with you submitting it on paper.

NARRATOR: Briefly summarize the problem the speakers are discussing. Then state which of the two solutions from the conversation you would recommend. Explain the reasons for your recommendation.

Sample Spoken Response—Track 245

The man is trying to decide what to do, um, because the internet is out on campus, but he has an assignment due, um… an online assignment that he has to turn in to a professor, um, that he cannot turn in because the internet is out. Um, his friend suggests maybe printing it out and putting it in the professor's mailbox, um, and maybe that… that would be okay because the whole campus is having the same problem. Um, I think that that is probably the best option. Um, if he prints it out and, you know, writes the time on it like he suggests, it will prove that he did the assignment that… when he was supposed to do. And the professor should accept that. You know, the whole campus is out, um, with internet. It is affect… affected everybody, not something unique to the…

Comments

The student chooses the solution she likes best and provides her reasoning. She takes a while, though, to state this. In the early part of her response, she might still have been debating with herself as to which solution to pick. You only have 20 seconds to prepare, so just pick one solution and state it confidently!

Answers and Explanations—19.3

Cycling Team Trip—Track 238

NARRATOR: Now listen to a conversation between two sports team coaches.

FEMALE COACH: Have you seen the weather forecast?

MALE COACH: Yes, it's calling for a lot of snow in the mountains next week.

FEMALE COACH: Does that matter? The weather is supposed to be beautiful here, sunny and warm.

MALE COACH: The problem is that the cycling team is supposed to go to a training camp in the mountains. We're planning to train the whole week of spring break. We were hoping that the weather report would get better, but the closer it gets, the more it looks like it's going to snow. I just hope we don't go all the way there and have to stay indoors instead of riding our bikes.

FEMALE COACH: I see. Is it going to be snowy all week or is it going to get better?

MALE COACH: Oh, listen to this weather report—it's going to be a lot warmer after Tuesday. Maybe we could do some weight training for the first couple of days, and then hopefully the snow will melt.

FEMALE COACH: Good, problem solved!

MALE COACH: If the snow doesn't actually melt, though… our training will be interrupted.

FEMALE COACH: Why not hold the training camp closer to home? Or did you already book a hotel?

MALE COACH: Yeah, that's the problem. We already paid for the hotel rooms and the bus. If we cancel the trip now, they definitely wouldn't refund all of our money. We'd probably only get half of the money back.

FEMALE COACH: But if you stay, you'd be sure to have good weather.

NARRATOR: Briefly summarize the problem the speakers are discussing. Then state which of the two solutions from the conversation you would recommend. Explain the reasons for your recommendation.

Sample Spoken Response—Track 246

The coach must decide whether, uh, his cycling team should travel to the mountains, um, for a, you know, a… a training week, um, as they planned, even though the weather forecast is for snow… At least for part of the week… Or they could stay home where, uh, the weather forecast is, uh, warm and sunny. Um, they have paid already, uh, for the bus and the hotel for the mountain trip, so, you know, if they do not travel, unfortunately, they will lose half of their, uh, their money. Um, the weather forecast says that it is supposed to, uh, stop snowing, so I think that it is better to keep the reservation and travel to the mountains. Um, they could do some weight training the first few days and, uh, and hopefully be able to start cycling towards the end of the week. But even if they don't… that… they could do other team building activities.

Comments

The student clearly chooses his preferred solution and offers his reasons for that solution. He could improve his response by training himself to reduce the number of times that he says "um" and "uh." It is okay to use these interjections a few times. But it is better not to use them very often.

Answers and Explanations—19.4

New Puppy—Track 239

NARRATOR: Now listen to a conversation between two students.

FEMALE STUDENT: Hey, I need help with something. Are you going to be free tomorrow?

MALE STUDENT: No, I have classes all day—why?

FEMALE STUDENT: Oh, no. I just adopted a new puppy a couple of weeks ago. He's been so good, but I have to take him outside for a walk every couple of hours… and tomorrow, I need to be on campus all morning to work on a project.

MALE STUDENT: What's the project?

FEMALE STUDENT: We're doing a group presentation in my English class. My group is getting together to rehearse.

MALE STUDENT: Wait, why do you need to meet on campus? Could you meet somewhere closer to your apartment? Then you could take your puppy outside really quickly, and it wouldn't disrupt everything.

FEMALE STUDENT: That would be easier for me. But it would probably be inconvenient for everyone else in the group—I think they all live on campus. I really want to make sure that everyone shows up for the rehearsal! This project is really important.

MALE STUDENT: That's true. But you could always ask them.

FEMALE STUDENT: The other option is, I guess I could try to take the bus home during lunch…

MALE STUDENT: Yeah, you only need to take him out for a few minutes, right? Just take the bus home, walk the dog, and then come back.

FEMALE STUDENT: Ugh, but if I did that, I wouldn't get to eat lunch. And if the bus is late, I'd be late for my afternoon class… well, I definitely need to take the puppy out, even if it's inconvenient.

NARRATOR: Briefly summarize the problem the speakers are discussing. Then state which of the two solutions from the conversation you would recommend. Explain the reasons for your recommendation.

Sample Spoken Response—Track 247

The student has a new puppy and the problem is that tomorrow she will not be able to take the puppy outside because she has to work on a group project. Um, her options are to… to arrange the group to meet somewhere close to her home. Or, to take the bus home, um, on her lunch break to… to take care of the puppy. However it is possible she, um, might be late for class. Um, it is challenging to coordinate a large group of people to meet somewhere off-campus, so I think she should take the bus home on her lunch break. If she is a little late to class, that negatively only affects her. It does not inconvenience everyone else. She made the commitment… she is responsible for the puppy.

Comments

The student provides clear reasons to support her preferred solution. She could improve her response by summarizing the conversation more concisely. This would give her more time to state her own opinion.

Answers and Explanations—19.5

Conference Presentation—Track 240

NARRATOR: Now listen to a conversation between two students.

FEMALE STUDENT: Congratulations! I heard you were invited to present your project at the zoology conference.

MALE STUDENT: Thanks, but I don't think I'll be able to go.

FEMALE STUDENT: You should go—it's a huge honor. I don't think many undergrads were invited to give presentations.

MALE STUDENT: The conference is in London. I looked at plane tickets, but it's too expensive for me to fly there.

FEMALE STUDENT: Oh—what about the train? The train is usually less expensive.

MALE STUDENT: The flight is only an hour, but the train would take most of the day. I'd have to miss an extra day of classes.

FEMALE STUDENT: This is such an important opportunity. Missing an extra day of classes is worth being able to attend the conference.

MALE STUDENT: Maybe there's another way… I wonder whether the zoology department would pay for the plane ticket… or at least part of it.

FEMALE STUDENT: That's a great idea, actually. It's an honor for them that your project was selected. They definitely want you to represent the university.

MALE STUDENT: It's a little embarrassing to have to ask for money, though. And they're already paying for my pass to go to the conference. I don't want to be too demanding.

FEMALE STUDENT: I bet they'd understand. Ask your advisor—I'm sure other people have had this issue before. They might even have special funding for students to go to conferences.

MALE STUDENT: They do have some special funding—they're paying for my pass. I don't know whether they'd be willing to allocate even more to me, though.

FEMALE STUDENT: Well, you never know until you ask.

NARRATOR: Briefly summarize the problem the speakers are discussing. Then state which of the two solutions from the conversation you would recommend. Explain the reasons for your recommendation.

Sample Spoken Response—Track 248

The man has been invited to present at a zoology conference, but the plane ticket is too expensive for him. First, the woman proposes that he takes the train instead of flying. And, uh, the problem is he would miss another day of classes, because the train takes much longer. The second proposed solution is to ask for money from the department, and, uh… which might be embarrassing. I prefer that he combines the two solutions. First ask for money and say, "If you don't… if you can't give me money, I'll take the train but that will take an additional day from classes so I prefer to fly." Uh, there's… there's no embarrassment, I don't think, uh, from not having enough money for something… you're a student. Uh, but if the school can't contribute, take the, uh, take the train to the conference instead.

Comments

The student nicely summarizes the two proposed solutions. He prefers an approach that combines both solutions. This can be a good way to answer the question, but remember that you have only 60 seconds. It's usually safer to pick one solution to make sure you have time to talk about it. (This student succeeds with the combined approach because he summarizes very concisely.)

Answers and Explanations—19.6

History Essay Deleted—Track 241

NARRATOR: Now listen to a conversation between two students.

FEMALE STUDENT: Oh, no. I can't believe this.

MALE STUDENT: What's wrong?

FEMALE STUDENT: My History essay… it's vanished from my computer! I finished it after midnight last night. I must have accidentally deleted the file instead of saving it!

MALE STUDENT: We were supposed to turn in a rough draft last week. Did you do that?

FEMALE STUDENT: Yes, I have the rough draft on my computer. Although it wasn't exactly high quality. I had two exams last week, so I wrote a quick first draft and then did most of the research and analysis this week. Now I'll have to re-create my entire paper. And it's due tomorrow.

MALE STUDENT: Start from your rough draft and write down everything that you remember right now. Then you can revise it to add more details.

FEMALE STUDENT: Doing that in one day might… my essay might not be good enough to earn a high mark. I wonder whether the professor would give me an extension so I can do a better job. I really need to get an A in this class.

MALE STUDENT: She said in the syllabus that she gives extensions. You can turn in a paper up to three days late, but she'll take some points off of your grade.

FEMALE STUDENT: Hmm. I'll have to think about whether it's better to rewrite the whole thing today… or take the extra days… if I can write a much better paper with more time.

NARRATOR: Briefly summarize the problem the speakers are discussing. Then state which of the two solutions from the conversation you would recommend. Explain the reasons for your recommendation.

Sample Spoken Response—Track 249

The woman wrote a history essay but… accidentally deleted it. The essay is due tomorrow, and she must to decide whether… she should rewrite the entire paper tonight, um, and trying to remember as much as possible what she wrote before, um, or instead maybe she should take, uh, an extension. She could take a few extra days to re-create that research and analysis… although, she would lose some points from the essay grade. Um, I think between the two options, she should take the extension so that she can thoroughly rewrite her essay. She states that she needs a good grade, so I think, um, you know, if she writes a fantastic essay and earns a perfect grade and then there would be points taken off, but she can still be in the A range.

Comments

The student states her opinion strongly and explains why she chose that solution. She has a few grammatical errors. But her response is still clear and easy to understand, so she can still earn a good score.

Answers and Explanations—19.7

Broken Air-Conditioning—Track 242

NARRATOR: Now listen to a conversation between two students.

FEMALE STUDENT: Why are you still in the library this late at night? Do you have an exam tomorrow?

MALE STUDENT: Haven't you heard about the air-conditioning? It's way too hot to sleep in my dorm.

FEMALE STUDENT: No, what happened?

MALE STUDENT: The air-conditioning in all of the dormitories on the east side of campus broke down.

FEMALE STUDENT: Wow. How long will it take to fix?

MALE STUDENT: Apparently some really old part broke… they don't even make replacement parts anymore. So the maintenance people are taking the whole thing apart. Who knows when it will be working again.

FEMALE STUDENT: This is the worst possible time that could've happened. It's been so hot and humid. If I were you, I'd go home for the weekend.

MALE STUDENT: That's an option. My mom would definitely be happy. But my home is a two-hour drive. I would miss my soccer game on Saturday.

FEMALE STUDENT: At least you'd be able to sleep. Do you know anybody who lives closer to campus who has air-conditioning?

MALE STUDENT: There is one place I can think of… although I'd have to sleep on my friend's couch, and I think he has band practice at his house every weekend. I might not get any sleep there, either.

FEMALE STUDENT: I guess there isn't a great solution.

MALE STUDENT: Either I miss the game or I don't sleep all weekend. I hope they fix the air-conditioning soon!

NARRATOR: Briefly summarize the problem the speakers are discussing. Then state which of the two solutions from the conversation you would recommend. Explain the reasons for your recommendation.

Sample Spoken Response—Track 250

The air-conditioning is broken, so the student… he is trying to find a comfortable place to sleep because he cannot sleep in his room. Um, the first solution is going home for the weekend, but that is a long drive so he will miss his soccer game… and the second solution is… sleeping at a friend who live closer to campus. Um, but that friend has, uh, band practice during the weekend, so the student will not be able to sleep well there either. Um, I believe that his best decision is to go home, um, and miss the soccer game. Sleep is very important to your health and well-being, more important than one soccer game. In addition, if he cannot sleep at his friend house, then he would play poorly probably anyway.

Comments

The student clearly states his opinion and offers good reasons to support that opinion. He also structures his sentences with well-chosen "connector words" (e.g., "so," "because," "if," "in addition"), making the logic easy to follow. He has a few small grammatical errors, but not very many.

Answers and Explanations—19.8

Covering Dr. O'Brien's Classes—Track 243

NARRATOR: Now listen to a conversation between two professors.

MALE PROFESSOR: Do you know what's going to happen with Dr. O'Brien's freshman English classes? I heard he had an emergency and needed to leave at the last minute.

FEMALE PROFESSOR: We're still figuring out how to handle it. It's actually become a big problem—there's not enough time for us to hire anybody new. We were thinking about having a few of the graduate students teach the classes, but…

MALE PROFESSOR: Why not? I'm sure the grad students can handle it.

FEMALE PROFESSOR: I'm sure they can, but if we have our graduate students teach those classes instead, then we won't have enough teaching assistants for the upper-level English classes. Plus, it's such short notice… I don't want to make them teach a whole class without time to get ready.

MALE PROFESSOR: That makes sense—it isn't fair to make the grad students teach a class without any warning. You might have to postpone the classes until next quarter. Dr. O'Brien should be back by then.

FEMALE PROFESSOR: Almost all of the first-year students have to take that class, though. There might not be enough space in those classes next quarter for everybody to take them.

MALE PROFESSOR: Maybe we could offer more sections next quarter. There'd be enough time to hire another lecturer or two, so we could offer enough English classes for all of the first-years.

NARRATOR: Briefly summarize the problem the speakers are discussing. Then state which of the two solutions from the conversation you would recommend. Explain the reasons for your recommendation.

Sample Spoken Response—Track 251

A professor, um, at the university has had to leave, um, for an emergency, and they are trying to decide who will… teach his classes. They could have, um, graduate students to teach the classes, or they could, uh, push all of the classes back until the next quarter, when the, uh, professor returns, although they would, uh, have to offer more sessions. I think that the optimal solution is, uh, to push the classes back to next quarter. Even though it's not, um, ideal, that will provide enough time to, uh, hire other instructors to share the, um, class load of students so that everyone will still, uh, be able to take the required class. I also think that, uh, asking the graduate students to teach a class with… uh, without adequate time to prepare is not the optimal solution.

Comments

The student offers a clear opinion and provides sound reasoning to support that opinion. She could improve her response by training herself to say "um" and "uh" less often.

Chapter 20
Speaking Task Type 6

Speaking questions test your ability to comprehend and respond orally to written or spoken material. You will have to speak your response aloud. There are six different speaking tasks. Speaking Task Type 6, Academic Course (Summary), is an "integrated" task. You will listen to a short lecture about an academic topic. The lecture will include specific examples. You will be asked to summarize the topic under discussion, using the same examples given in the lecture. You will not be able to replay any part of the lecture.

Speaking questions test your ability to understand spoken and written information and to summarize and express opinions about that information. They also test your ability to respond orally to specific questions, including your grammar, your vocabulary, and the logical organization of your ideas.

How should you use this chapter? Here are some recommendations, according to the level you've reached in TOEFL Speaking:

0. **Everyone!** Hold yourself to the time limits whenever practicing Speaking tasks. Tape your response and listen to it afterward to analyze your performance. You can use any app on your computer or phone to tape yourself. If you don't know of a good app already, try www.vocaroo.com.

1. **Fundamentals.** Start with a type that is a "medium weakness"—not your worst Speaking question type but not your best either. Try one question and then check the sample answer. Think carefully about the principles at work. If you think you can do a better job, redo the question. Articulate what you want to do differently the next time you do this type of task.

2. **Fixes.** Do one Speaking task, examine the results, learn your lessons, then try a different type of Speaking task. Be sure to keep to the time limits. When you're ready, graduate to doing a set of six different Speaking tasks all in a row.

3. **Tweaks.** Confirm your mastery by doing a set of six different Speaking tasks all in a row under timed conditions.

Good luck on Speaking!

20.1

You will now listen to part of a lecture. You will then be asked a question about it. After you hear the question, give yourself 20 seconds to prepare your response. Then record yourself speaking for 60 seconds.

 Listen to Track 252.

Using points and examples from the talk, explain the roles played by air resistance and gravity in bicycling.

> Preparation Time: 20 seconds
> Response Time: 60 seconds

20.2

You will now listen to part of a lecture. You will then be asked a question about it. After you hear the question, give yourself 20 seconds to prepare your response. Then record yourself speaking for 60 seconds.

 Listen to Track 253.

Using points from the lecture, explain what jury nullification is and why judges are concerned about it.

> Preparation Time: 20 seconds
> Response Time: 60 seconds

20.3

You will now listen to part of a lecture. You will then be asked a question about it. After you hear the question, give yourself 20 seconds to prepare your response. Then record yourself speaking for 60 seconds.

 Listen to Track 254.

Using the points and examples from the talk, describe the two types of mimicry used by predators and prey.

> Preparation Time: 20 seconds
> Response Time: 60 seconds

20.4

You will now listen to part of a lecture. You will then be asked a question about it. After you hear the question, give yourself 20 seconds to prepare your response. Then record yourself speaking for 60 seconds.

 Listen to Track 255.

Using the concept of planned obsolescence, explain how the printer company mentioned in the lecture increased its sales volumes.

> ### Preparation Time: 20 seconds
> ### Response Time: 60 seconds

20.5

You will now listen to part of a lecture. You will then be asked a question about it. After you hear the question, give yourself 20 seconds to prepare your response. Then record yourself speaking for 60 seconds.

 Listen to Track 256.

Using the examples from the lecture, explain why a filmmaker might deliberately include anachronisms in a film.

> ### Preparation Time: 20 seconds
> ### Response Time: 60 seconds

20.6

You will now listen to part of a lecture. You will then be asked a question about it. After you hear the question, give yourself 20 seconds to prepare your response. Then record yourself speaking for 60 seconds.

 Listen to Track 257.

Using the examples from the lecture, explain how you could determine whether a young child understood conservation.

> ### Preparation Time: 20 seconds
> ### Response Time: 60 seconds

20.7

> You will now listen to part of a lecture. You will then be asked a question about it. After you hear the question, give yourself 20 seconds to prepare your response. Then record yourself speaking for 60 seconds.
>
> Listen to Track 258.
>
> Using points from the talk, explain how the Venus flytrap and the Portuguese dewy pine capture prey.
>
> Preparation Time: 20 seconds
>
> Response Time: 60 seconds

20.8

> You will now listen to part of a lecture. You will then be asked a question about it. After you hear the question, give yourself 20 seconds to prepare your response. Then record yourself speaking for 60 seconds.
>
> Listen to Track 259.
>
> Using the examples from the lecture or similar ones, explain the difference between "showing" and "telling" when writing fiction.
>
> Preparation Time: 20 seconds
>
> Response Time: 60 seconds

Answers and Explanations—20.1

Bicycle Physics—Track 252

NARRATOR: Listen to part of a lecture in a physics class.

PROFESSOR: Bicycles… they can teach us a lot about physics, about the relationships that come into play. Think about the relationships between different physical forces, like air resistance and gravity. Maybe you have a bicycle race that's on completely flat ground. No hills at all. In that case, the cyclist only has to worry about air resistance, or the friction from moving through the air. The problem for the cyclist is that air resistance increases more quickly than speed. It's actually an exponential relationship. So if you're going slowly, increasing your speed by one mile an hour is really easy. But if you're going quickly, it takes exponentially more power to go even a little faster because the air is pushing back on you so hard. Instead of trying to work harder and harder, and get less and less speed out of it, cyclists in a flat race will focus on reducing air resistance. For example, you'll see them "drafting," where one cyclist will stay close behind another one, to avoid the wind.

On the other hand, if there's a hill in the race, cyclists won't worry about staying out of the wind. That's because there's also an exponential relationship between how steep a hill is and how hard you have to work to carry your own weight up it. On a hill, gravity becomes much more important than air resistance... you have to use a lot of energy to overcome that gravity. And the steeper the hill gets, the more important gravity is. On a very steep hill, you're using almost all of your energy just to overcome gravity. Air resistance is almost irrelevant, from a physics perspective. On the hill, all that really matters is weight. If you weigh less, gravity has less of an effect on you. So in a hilly race, you'll see racers using lighter bikes, and the smaller racers will have an advantage.

NARRATOR: Using points and examples from the talk, explain the roles played by air resistance and gravity in bicycling.

Sample Spoken Response—Track 260

When you have a bicycle race, um, there are a couple of things that, uh... related to physics, and, uh, one of them is air resistance, and this is most important when you have a flat race and, um, bikers just need to... to, sort of, go, um, in a straight line. And the issue here is to be as streamlined as possible. Imagine, you know, bikers trying to look as much like, uh, the nose of an... of an airplane and to cut through, uh, in a horizontal direction. Um, in a more hilly bicycle race, um, gravity is actually the more important consider... consideration, as that is the force that they are fighting against. So, um, things that are more important here, it's less that you are shaped like something aerodynamic, but rather that you carry as little weight as possible to pull you down against...

Comments

The topic is challenging. The student does a good job of summarizing the two examples given in the lecture. She struggles a little to explain some details, but that is to be expected when the topic is this difficult.

Answers and Explanations—20.2

Jury Nullification—Track 253

NARRATOR: Listen to part of a lecture in a legal studies class.

PROFESSOR: In most jurisdictions in the United States, judges instruct members of the jury that they should act only as "finders of facts." In other words, the job of the jury is to evaluate the truth of the evidence, to gauge how well the evidence relates to the law itself, and ultimately to reach a verdict.

What's most notable about these instructions isn't so much what they say, but rather what they don't say. The judge tells the jurors that they should not try to judge anything beyond the specific evidence of this one case. Basically, the judge is implying that the law itself is beyond question.

The biggest problem there, of course, is that the law is really *not* beyond question. The law could be a bad law for any number of reasons—everybody has read about weird laws from hundreds of years ago, some of which were still valid long after anyone would try to enforce it. For example, for a long time, Detroit—in Michigan—they had a law that it was illegal to fall asleep in the bathtub. But that's ridiculous! Nobody would convict somebody for that now. So any jury could engage in what's known as jury nullification—which is where they decide that the law itself is immoral, outdated, or simply being interpreted incorrectly.

If a jury decides that a specific law is a bad law for some reason, then it might also decide to let the defendant walk free, even if the evidence shows that the defendant really did break that law.

Jury nullification could potentially invalidate just about any specific law in force, anywhere in the country. Given the sheer level of potential power implied there, it's no wonder that judges have started reminding all their jurors to stick only to the facts and not think beyond that.

NARRATOR: Using points from the lecture, explain what jury nullification is and why judges are concerned about it.

Sample Spoken Response—Track 261

Jury nullification is where jurors think about whether, uh, the law that they are, uh, in the case is actually a good law or not, um, and if it should even be something, um, that is still set up, um, as a… as a valid law. And this is a concern for judges and to remind jurors of only thinking about the evidence and not… the law itself because you could get a situation where the jury just all decide that, you know what, that's, um, that's a bad law so we're going to say this person is not guilty and, um, could create all kinds of, uh, bad situations. They're not supposed to decide… it's a bad law. They just decide if the person is guilty.

Comments

The student does a good job of explaining a complex term. She struggles a little bit early on to state the information clearly. But she nicely summarizes the main idea at the end.

Answers and Explanations—20.3

Animal Mimicry—Track 254

NARRATOR: Listen to part of a lecture in a biology class.

PROFESSOR: So, the major idea of mimicry is that one animal mimics, or copies, some other type of animal. But biologists draw a finer distinction. What matters is, in the predator–prey relationship, which animal is doing the mimicking. Is it the predator, or is it the prey? Because mimicry… it can be useful for both.

For instance, take the snapping turtle. It's a good example of mimicry by a predator, which is called "aggressive mimicry." The snapping turtle is a carnivore… it mostly eats fish. It conceals most of its body, but it keeps its mouth open. And it has a pink tongue that looks and moves a lot like a worm does. At least, if you're a fish! So, fish that prey on worms, will basically swim into its mouth. That's a pretty typical model for aggressive mimicry: What food does the prey eat? Well, the predator will have a part of its body, that resembles that food, in order to attract the prey. Or it might mimic the prey itself, in order to lure it in. There's one genus of fireflies that are sort of cannibalistic; they prey on other types of fireflies. And they can mimic the flashing patterns of those other fireflies—but when the other fireflies approach, they get eaten.

Then, there's defensive mimicry, which is mimicry by prey. In this case, it's supposed to keep predators away. Usually, a prey animal will mimic something dangerous. Maybe even something that preys on the predator itself. For instance, there's a species of octopus that can manipulate its body shape, so it looks like a poisonous sea snake. Or… or a harmless frog might have bright patterns, like those of a poisonous frog. The predator thinks the harmless frog is poisonous and doesn't eat it.

NARRATOR: Using the points and examples from the talk, describe the two types of mimicry used by predators and prey.

Sample Spoken Response—Track 262

So the professor distinguishes between two types of mimicry: uh, mimicry done by prey and mimicry done by predators. Um, with predators, one example they used was, uh, the snapping turtle, um, that can hide most of its body and just open its mouth and stick out its tongue, and its tongue, uh, looks kind of like a worm that certain fish, uh, like to eat, so when the fish gets close to the tongue, the turtle… snaps and eats the fish. Uh, and on… on the prey side, uh, one example used is that of a… a certain type of octopus that can shift its body around to look like a poisonous snake, um, in order to scare off predators. Or, uh, they also mention the… uh, a certain type of frog that can change its color, uh, to make it look like it's a poisonous frog.

Comments

The student nicely summarizes several of the examples given in the lecture. The ideas and their relationships are clear. He could improve his response by training himself to reduce the number of times he says "um" or "uh."

Answers and Explanations—20.4

Planned Obsolescence—Track 255

NARRATOR: Listen to part of a lecture in an economics class.

PROFESSOR: You've probably noticed this yourself, if you buy a new phone once in awhile, or a new tablet, any kind of electronics. Forward compatibility, okay? You'll buy a new phone, and a year later, even though it still works fine, there's a newer model. You might keep using the same phone, but what happens is, all of the apps you use, when they update, they only work on the newer phone, and they don't work on your old phone anymore. Or your older tablet isn't compatible with the newer tablet software you're supposed to use, something like that. That's something called "planned obsolescence." There's a certain part of the market that would buy new phones anyways, just because they want the latest and greatest. But there are also other consumers who might just keep using the same old phone, as long as it works well. In order to motivate those consumers to purchase new phones, electronics companies think of ways to make their old phones obsolete. Maybe it's the issue with software that I was talking about, where the new software isn't compatible with the old hardware anymore. If you want to use the new software, you have to buy the new phone. Or maybe they'll stop repairing the older phones after a certain point, so if you break yours, you can't just get it fixed—you have to buy the new one.

In a small number of cases, it was found that electronics companies were actually programming their products to stop working after a certain "expiration date." Printers are one example. One printer company was sued pretty recently, because it was discovered that their printers would show error messages even when they weren't broken. Just, after a certain number of years, you'd get this mysterious error message—and most people wouldn't really look into it, they'd just figure that their printer was old and didn't work anymore. So they'd buy a new one. Planned obsolescence has certain benefits for companies, but when it's taken to an extreme, it's an unscrupulous way to increase sales.

NARRATOR: Using the concept of planned obsolescence, explain how the printer company mentioned in the lecture increased its sales volumes.

20

Sample Spoken Response—Track 263

The printer company used planned obsolescence in order to, uh, display error messages. It had been programmed to start displaying error messages after a certain number of years, um, in order to get, uh, the… those printer owners to… to purchase a new printer, even though there's nothing wrong with the printer. Um, so for example, um, let's say the printer company had… made an error message just pop up after two years, um, but the actual shelf-life of the printer, let's say it could have lasted for five years, seven years, eight years. Um, you know, by having that error message display after two years, it would force… well, not force, it would encourage strongly, uh, printer owners to replace their printers every two years.

Comments

The student uses the example from the lecture as a starting point to create his own hypothetical situation. This is an excellent way to demonstrate a strong understanding of the lecture. Note that it is not necessary to come up with this kind of hypothetical situation to illustrate your comprehension. The student could improve his response by trying to reduce the number of times he says "um" or "uh."

Answers and Explanations—20.5

Anachronism—Track 256

NARRATOR: Listen to part of a lecture in a film class.

PROFESSOR: "Anachronism" is what you call it when a filmmaker includes something that's actually from the wrong period in history. For instance—just to give an extreme example—you might watch a historical drama that's supposed to be set in the 1800s, but you notice there's an electrical outlet in the wall. That's presumed to be a failure on the part of the editor or the director, and sometimes it is… and that's why you'll get people, film buffs, who are really interested in trying to spot these little mistakes.

But it's more interesting when directors include anachronisms on purpose. Some of them are obvious, some are subtle. For instance, intentional anachronism can be a source of humor. If you're watching a comedy set in medieval times, with a bunch of knights, and then a cell phone rings and one of the knights pulls it out of his armor and answers it, that's funny. Some people might not even classify that as an anachronism, because it's obvious that it's done on purpose. Then there are also anachronisms that are included for convenience, to make the movie more watchable. The filmmaker might use an anachronism to improve the viewing experience of the film, even though it's known to be wrong. For example, if the dialect from that period in history would be hard for modern viewers to understand, the director won't make the actors all speak, say, Elizabethan English. She might update it a bit, so while it won't be right for the time period, it'll be watchable for current audiences.

Another reason to use anachronism might be to make the film more exciting. If the clothing of a slightly later time period was more dramatic, they might include a small anachronism in order to have more interesting costuming in the film. One example of this is the various ways Cleopatra has been depicted on film, especially before the 21st century. Her costumes are rarely technically accurate, but they're fashionable, which is sometimes the priority.

NARRATOR: Using the examples from the lecture, explain why a filmmaker might deliberately include anachronisms in a film.

Sample Spoken Response—Track 264

There are a variety of reasons why filmmakers might decide to use anachronisms in their films, um, one of which is... is to make them more watchable. Um, f... for instance, um, you know, if... if it's an action film, uh, that may use weapons, uh, in some sort of action movie, maybe weapons that were not quite invented yet but are commonly, uh, used in battles, um, that would be a perfectly good reason for a director to want to intentionally, uh, use, uh, uh, anachronism. Um, also for... for humor, the lecture describes sometimes it'll just be funny, um, even though some film buffs might think those aren't technically anachronisms because they're on purpose. Um, another reason is just for fashion, because something looks nice.

Comments

> The student provides several examples of the use of anachronisms in film. One of her examples is not from the lecture at all—she makes up the example about weapons. This is okay if you are confident about the example, but it is harder to make up your own separate example. You will probably want to stick with the examples given in the lecture—or something very close to those examples.

Answers and Explanations—20.6

Conservation—Track 257

NARRATOR: Listen to part of a lecture in a child development class.

PROFESSOR: There's something interesting about how little kids see the world. Until a certain age, they actually don't realize that if you put something in a different container, you still have the same amount of stuff. For instance, if you pour a glass of water into a bowl, adults and older kids will think it's obvious that there's the same amount of water there. But a really young kid will get confused by it. They don't really understand the difference between what something looks like and how much there is. Being able to tell the difference is called "conservation."

Here's what an experiment about conservation would look like. You could show a child two glasses of water that are exactly the same size, and they'd be filled to the same level. You ask the child whether there's the same amount of water in both glasses... they'd say "yes." Then, take one of the glasses and pour its contents into a second glass that's very tall but very thin, like a vial. So, the level of water is higher in the second glass. Then you'd ask: "Is the amount of water still the same in both glasses?" A child who's old enough to understand conservation will say that there is. A child who doesn't understand it will say, no, there's more water in the tall, thin glass, because it's filled to a higher level.

The concept of conservation applies to weight, too. You can show a very young child a round piece of clay, and then stretch it out so that it looks longer and wider. They'll think that the clay must also be heavier than it was before, since it seems as if there's more clay there. Children start to understand that things like volume and weight stay the same when they're fairly young, but they don't fully develop the understanding of conservation until they're 9, 10... maybe 11 years old.

NARRATOR: Using the examples from the lecture, explain how you could determine whether a young child understood conservation.

Sample Spoken Response—Track 265

From the lecture, it seems like there are a number of substances that you could use to illustrate whether a… a young child understands conversion. Uh, for example… you could build a snowman or a snowball, um, uh, of a certain size and then another one that's the same size, and then… take one of the snowballs and put it into a different shape or smash it on the ground… and ask them if, you know… whether it's still the same amount of snow. Um, or you could have a bowl of cereal, and put it in a different bowl to see whether… the child thinks it's still the same amount of cereal. You could use almost anything, any household product, to test this.

Comments

The student demonstrates an excellent understanding of the lecture by offering her own examples. The examples are similar to the ones in the lecture, but not exactly the same. Note: You are not required to use different examples. The instructions tell you to use the examples from the lecture, and in fact, coming up with different examples is risky, if it takes too much time or thought to do so. The student's response is not perfect (she calls the phenomenon "conversion," rather than "conservation"), but such flaws are minor.

Answers and Explanations—20.7

Carnivorous Plants—Track 258

NARRATOR: Listen to part of a lecture in a biology class.

PROFESSOR: The majority of plants… they get energy from photosynthesis. They don't "eat"—they just need sunlight, fertilized soil, minerals… then, there are the carnivorous plants. They're still plants, but they have something in common with animals. They hunt prey, usually insects. But just like animals, they've evolved different methods of hunting.

In one method, the plant uses a sort of trap. This is how the Venus flytrap got its name, actually. There's a section of the plant, a sort of specialized leaf, that has very sensitive hairs inside of it. Normally, the leaf stays open. But when anything touches the hairs—it snaps shut. A fly lands on the leaf, and it snaps shut, trapping the fly. Then digestion occurs inside of that same leaf. The really interesting thing is that the Venus flytrap can tell whether it's an insect landing on it or whether it's just a bit of dirt or something. An insect has six legs, so when it lands, it'll touch multiple hairs as it moves around, one after another. That's what causes the leaf to close. If the hairs only get touched once, it's probably not an insect.

The other method is more common, and it's simpler. Part of the plant secretes a sort of glue. One example would be the Portuguese dewy pine. Unlike the Venus flytrap, it doesn't actively trap its prey. It uses a passive method. So, the dewy pine is covered in tiny hairs, and each of these hairs has a droplet of sticky goo on it. An insect lands on it and gets stuck, and then the plant secretes chemicals that eventually digest the insect.

NARRATOR: Using points from the talk, explain how the Venus flytrap and the Portuguese dewy pine capture prey.

Sample Spoken Response—Track 266

A Venus flytrap works by, or gets food, um, probably partly through photosynthesis and soil and all… minerals and soil, similar to other plants. But it also traps animals. And it works through a mechanism where it has hairs on a leaf, and when multiple hairs are stimulated, it closes on that animal and then, um, in that, sort of, closed leaf envelope, I believe, it, uh, digests, uh, the insect. And it won't trap dirt, uh, because it can tell whether it's an insect… dirt doesn't touch multiple hairs. The other one… dewy pine has a type of sticky goo and the insects get trapped and they can't get loose. So then the plant can release chemicals to digest the insect.

Comments

> The student clearly explains how each plant works, using the examples from the lecture. He slightly mixes up one of the details, but this flaw is minor. Overall, his response is clear and accurate enough to earn a good score.

Answers and Explanations—20.8

Showing vs. Telling—Track 259

NARRATOR: Listen to part of a lecture in a creative writing class.

PROFESSOR: To write really good fiction… something that feels really immersive, where your readers will really start to trust you and engage with what's happening… to do that, you have to do more "showing" than "telling." What that means is that you can't just tell your readers what's going on, or what they should think about it. You might know what you want them to think, but you don't just tell them what to think. That makes for a boring story. Instead of that, you show them what's going on, but you don't tell them what they're supposed to think of it. You just write it in a way that, hopefully, they start thinking what you intended them to think in the first place.

For example, suppose you're writing about a character who's angry because she was just fired unfairly from a job. You could write, "She was furious! She was outraged! She felt as if her boss had treated her unfairly." But that's telling, not showing. You're telling the reader that the character is mad, and that's not very interesting. Plus, why should readers believe you? They don't know whether the character is mad, or sad, or perhaps doesn't even care.

So, to get your point across, you show them that the character is angry. You do that through her words, or through her behavior. So, instead of saying she was furious, you might say that she stormed to her boss's office, pounded on the door, and demanded to speak to her immediately. While she waited for her boss, she paced back and forth outside the door, glaring at everyone who walked by. Now, the reader knows that she was angry and frustrated, even though you didn't tell them. Plus, the reader has a picture in her head of what the anger looks like, which makes the story more descriptive, and therefore more immersive and more interesting.

NARRATOR: Using the examples from the lecture or similar ones, explain the difference between "showing" and "telling" when writing fiction.

Sample Spoken Response—Track 267

When you're writing fiction there's a big difference between showing and telling, and uh, fiction writers, um… the better ones, uh, tend to show rather than tell. Telling is with words. So if you're describing someone, you know, and you wanna show that… uh, tell that they're frustrated you just write, uh, you know, "She was feeling very frustrated." And it's almost like you're a voice inside their head and actually talking about the emotions and uh, and using those actual words. Um, if you're showing someone is frustrated it may be more through actions and behaviors, like describing how someone might be pulling out their hair or throwing things, uh, around the room, or… or, you know, kicking something, and maybe through, you know, facial, you know… describing, um, facial expressions or shouting, um, but rather than saying…

Comments

The student conveys the difference between showing and telling. She uses examples that are very similar to the examples in the lecture, but not exactly the same. Changing the examples a little bit shows that she really understood the content of the lecture. Note that there is no need to change the examples, however. In fact, doing so can be risky, if too much time or thought is involved. The student could improve her response by training herself to reduce the number of times she says "um" or "uh." In order to translate each thought to a complete sentence spoken aloud, she would be better off planning in silence for a moment or two.

Chapter 21
Writing Task Type 1

Writing questions test your ability to comprehend written or spoken material and to respond in written form. You will have to type your essay into the computer. There are two different writing tasks. Writing Task Type 1 is an "integrated" task. You will first read a short passage on an academic topic. Next, you will listen to a short lecture that adds information about the same topic. The lecture will agree or disagree with the passage in various ways (it will often disagree). Finally, you will be asked to summarize information from both the lecture and the reading passage. (Usually, you will be asked to explain how the lecturer agrees or disagrees with the passage, using the same examples given by the lecturer.) You will be able to reread the passage while you write your essay, but you will not be able to replay any part of the lecture. You will have 20 minutes to write your essay.

Writing questions test your ability to understand spoken and written information and to summarize and express opinions about that information. They also test your ability to respond in writing to specific questions, including your grammar and spelling, your vocabulary, and the logical organization of your ideas.

How should you use this chapter? Here are some recommendations, according to the level you've reached in TOEFL Writing:

0. **Everyone!** Hold yourself to the time limits whenever practicing Writing tasks. Don't write by hand. Use Microsoft Word or other word-processing software, but turn off both spell-check and grammar-check.

1. **Fundamentals.** Start with whichever essay type is a little easier for you. Try one question and then check your response against the sample answer. Fix any errors and think carefully about the principles at work. If you think you can do a better job, rewrite your essay. Articulate what you want to do differently the next time you write this type of essay.

2. **Fixes.** Do one Writing task, examine the results, learn your lessons, then try the other type of Writing task. Be sure to keep to the time limits. When you're ready, graduate to doing a set of the two different Writing tasks in a row.

3. **Tweaks.** Confirm your mastery by doing a set of the two different Writing tasks in a row under timed conditions.

Good luck on Writing!

21.1

For today's middle-aged adults, it would be difficult to imagine life without the internet. For children and younger adults, the internet has always been so universally present that not having it would simply be unimaginable. Clearly, the internet has changed the world, and the nature of knowledge, significantly. But has the internet fundamentally changed people?

According to some experts, the answer is yes—and the reality is dismal. Nicholas Carr, a sociologist who focuses on the effects of technology, says we are increasingly becoming "hunters and gatherers in an electronic forest" rather than "cultivators of personal knowledge and expertise." The main problem, according to Carr, is that the internet puts other people's ideas and experiences perpetually at our fingertips—with the result that we have become less adventurous, more cautious, and less likely to define ourselves by our own experiences.

Moreover, as studies have shown, the internet has had adverse effects on our short-term attention spans and our ability to focus on a task. When we work online, we are inundated with hyperlinks, advertisements, animations, sound, and all manner of other distractions from the information that was our original target. Many neuroscientists fear that we may lose our ability to synthesize all this diverse information and to think about its significance. In other words, our capacity for true understanding may be gradually diminishing.

Additionally, as technology journalist Steve Ciarcia points out, the internet often removes the need for critical thinking and creative problem-solving in everyday situations. As Ciarcia says, "It's only about five seconds before some guy whips out his phone and googles" the solution to an everyday conundrum. As a result, people are less motivated to experiment, less likely to enumerate all available options, and more tempted to make premature decisions.

 Listen to Track 268.

You have 20 minutes to plan and write your response. Your response will be judged on the basis of the quality of your writing and on how well your response presents the points in the lecture and their relationship to the reading passage. Typically, an effective response will be 150 to 225 words.

Response Time: 20 minutes

Summarize the points made in the lecture you just heard, explaining how they cast doubt on points made in the passage.

21.2

Give yourself 3 minutes to read the passage.

Reading Time: 3 minutes

High-Intensity Interval Training, or HIIT, has had a profound impact on the field of exercise physiology. In contrast to traditional exercise programs, which involve an hour or so of steady exercise a few times a week, HIIT workouts are brief and intense. In a HIIT workout, the participant alternates between high-effort sprinting and low-effort rest periods, for as little as 5 to 10 minutes. Although the overall exercise session is very short, and relatively few calories are burned during the session, HIIT has an unusual effect on the human body. Specifically, after exercising, people who perform a HIIT session burn fat and calories at a higher rate for up to 24 hours. This can be attributed to a phenomenon known as Excess Post-Exercise Oxygen Consumption, or EPOC. Studies have shown that HIIT participants lose more fat overall than people who perform traditional workouts; this increase in fat loss is likely due to EPOC, which causes exercisers to lose more fat even when they are not active.

This quality may also make HIIT a useful tool for athletes with limited free time, and for ordinary people who want to get in shape without making a large time commitment. The ability to perform a productive workout in only a few minutes, a few times a week, will likely make exercising more appealing. A number of surveys have revealed that limited time, or a perception that exercise is too time-consuming, is among the most common reasons for a lack of fitness. If HIIT becomes more popular and is promoted appropriately, it is likely to increase the overall level of fitness and enthusiasm towards exercise among the public.

21

 Listen to Track 269.

You have 20 minutes to plan and write your response. Your response will be judged on the basis of the quality of your writing and on how well your response presents the points in the lecture and their relationship to the reading passage. Typically, an effective response will be 150 to 225 words.

Response Time: 20 minutes

Summarize the points made in the lecture, being sure to explain how they challenge the specific points made in the reading passage.

21.3

> Give yourself 3 minutes to read the passage.
>
> **Reading Time: 3 minutes**

Consider communities that suffer from a high crime rate. Often, these communities also suffer from a high degree of general disorder. The surroundings are chaotic: buildings might be covered in graffiti, broken windows might be left unrepaired, and unoccupied houses might be left to sink into dilapidation. A high level of social chaos (including behaviors such as panhandling, public drunkenness, and petty vandalism) is also associated with high levels of crime. Given human psychology, it seems natural that living in a chaotic environment will at least correlate with crime, if not lead directly to it.

The notion that minor crime begets major crime is known as the "broken windows theory," because it was initially described in these terms. If a few windows in a building are broken and left unrepaired, over time, criminals will likely commit further crimes. Similarly, if the members of a community sense that problems will not be resolved, they have no motivation to avoid creating new problems. After all, if one broken window will never be repaired, why would it matter whether other laws were broken? This theory also applies to social issues: if people regularly fight in the street, and nothing is done about it, what does it matter if there's one more fight? The community is already in chaos, the theory goes—and thus, more chaos is inevitable. The result is an escalating wave of disorder that leads to serious crime.

To prevent crime, therefore, it's necessary to fix small issues before they turn into widespread chaos. If one broken window is fixed immediately, it's less likely that other crimes will follow. People are less likely to commit crimes in a community in which broken windows are not the norm. Likewise, if the police respond immediately to small scuffles and end them quickly, major conflicts are less likely to occur.

 Listen to Track 270.

You have 20 minutes to plan and write your response. Your response will be judged on the basis of the quality of your writing and on how well your response presents the points in the lecture and their relationship to the reading passage. Typically, an effective response will be 150 to 225 words.

Response Time: 20 minutes

Summarize the points made in the lecture, being sure to explain how they oppose the specific points made in the reading passage.

21.4

Give yourself 3 minutes to read the passage.

Reading Time: 3 minutes

The body of evidence suggests that William Shakespeare did not, in fact, author the plays for which he is known. During the period in which Shakespeare supposedly wrote, illiteracy was typical. It was common for working people to be unable to read or even write their own names, and the evidence suggests that Shakespeare's family members—his parents, as well as his children—were entirely illiterate. In addition, there is no evidence that Shakespeare ever attained a formal education. His name does not appear on the rosters of any school in the area in which he was born, and none of his teachers or classmates have mentioned him in writing. Therefore, it is likely that Shakespeare lacked formal education, and he may have been unable to write at all. Certainly, it is unlikely he would have had the knowledge to produce the plays that are credited to him.

It seems more likely that the plays of "William Shakespeare" were actually written by Sir Francis Bacon. Bacon was a well-known philosopher, scientist, and writer who was active at the same time as the supposed playwright. Contemporary writers describe the author of Shakespeare's plays as an intellectual, a description which would have fit Bacon far better than Shakespeare himself. In addition, certain parallels exist between the themes of Shakespeare's writing and those used by Bacon. For instance, Bacon was known to borrow aphorisms—brief sayings on moral and practical topics—from a number of classical authors, and Shakespeare's plays do the same. One specific aphorism used by Bacon described the world as "running on wheels" and "spinning"—Shakespeare used a nearly identical metaphor in a famous line from the play *The Two Gentlemen of Verona*.

21

 Listen to Track 271.

You have 20 minutes to plan and write your response. Your response will be judged on the basis of the quality of your writing and on how well your response presents the points in the lecture and their relationship to the reading passage. Typically, an effective response will be 150 to 225 words.

Response Time: 20 minutes

Summarize the points made in the lecture, being sure to explain how they respond to the specific arguments made in the reading passage.

21.5

Give yourself 3 minutes to read the passage.

Reading Time: 3 minutes

"Text speak," the abbreviated communication style often used in text messages or instant messages, has been largely detrimental to the normal development of language skills. In text speak, words and phrases are often shortened or intentionally misspelled. For instance, "great" might be written as "gr8," and "shaking my head" as "smh." This raises certain concerns: Is it wise for children to learn to communicate in this slipshod, lazy manner? Young people should learn to take time and care with their writing, but when most of their communication is done via text speak, they stop putting effort and thought into their writing style and develop a habit of laziness. If we hope to instill young people with good habits in other areas of life, it is critical to promote thoughtful, intelligent writing rather than to permit laziness.

Text speak is also a danger to children's language skills. A child might see a word spelled incorrectly more often than he or she sees the correct spelling. This could keep the child from ever learning the correct spelling. Or, a child might mistake a text abbreviation, such as "LOL" or "OMG," for an actual word and try to use it in formal writing. Children who mostly communicate via text speak will make more spelling errors and use more non-words, due to a lack of exposure to proper language.

The common use of text speak will likely cause levels of literacy to decline in the future. Children who do most of their reading and writing in text speak will be less able to understand literature and are less likely to become strong readers and writers. In fact, proper written language itself might fall into disuse. If texting takes the place of traditional reading and writing, there will be far fewer classic works of literature produced in the future—and fewer people who will be able to appreciate them.

 Listen to Track 272.

You have 20 minutes to plan and write your response. Your response will be judged on the basis of the quality of your writing and on how well your response presents the points in the lecture and their relationship to the reading passage. Typically, an effective response will be 150 to 225 words.

Response Time: 20 minutes

Summarize the points made in the lecture, being sure to explain how they cast doubt on the specific points made in the reading passage.

21.6

Give yourself 3 minutes to read the passage.

Reading Time: 3 minutes

Originally from Europe, western honey bees are now responsible for pollinating cultivated crops everywhere except Antarctica. Part of the reason honey bees are so popular with farmers is their tendency to transfer pollen to "conspecific" plants—plants of the same species. This is the most efficient form of pollination for any plant that cannot self-pollinate.

Therefore, it was alarming to many when western honey bee colonies began abandoning their hives for no apparent reason. This phenomenon, called colony collapse disorder, sometimes occurs naturally. But beginning around 2000, it began multiplying worldwide. First observed in North America, the trend was soon observed in many countries in Europe and parts of Asia.

The cause of colony collapse disorder remains unknown. There are two promising hypotheses, however: the pesticide theory and the multi-factor theory. At this time, it appears that the pesticide theory is the more likely explanation of colony collapse disorder globally.

First, a certain pesticide that can have adverse effects on bees began to be used in the 1990s. A 2013 report from the United States Department of Agriculture proved that these chemicals—in normal quantities—harm bees directly. This also helps explain why colony collapse disorder proliferated first in North America and only later spread to Europe and some parts of Asia. These other regions did not start using the pesticide until later than North America.

Second, fungicides can have serious impacts on bees. They can stifle their development into adult workers and can alter their behavior in some circumstances. If worker bees are underdeveloped, or if their behavior is altered, many vital functions within the colony may not be attended to properly. These fungicides do not kill bees directly. However, they may cause a colony to be inefficient or even completely nonfunctional. If this happens, honey bees have a natural tendency to abandon the colony, rather than continue to serve one that isn't working.

 Listen to Track 273.

You have 20 minutes to plan and write your response. Your response will be judged on the basis of the quality of your writing and on how well your response presents the points in the lecture and their relationship to the reading passage. Typically, an effective response will be 150 to 225 words.

Response Time: 20 minutes

Summarize the points made in the lecture, being sure to explain how they challenge the specific points made in the reading passage.

21.7

> Give yourself 3 minutes to read the passage.
>
> Reading Time: 3 minutes

Many members of the scientific community would like to defend the practice of keeping animals in zoos. However, zoos have had a detrimental effect on the welfare of wild animals. Animals would be better off, overall, if they were studied in their natural habitats rather than being kept captive.

It is almost impossible for zoos to accurately reproduce the natural habitats of animals. For instance, a single spotted hyena can claim a territory of tens of thousands of acres in the wild. It would be impossible for a zoo to provide this amount of free space. When territorial animals such as hyenas are forced to live too close to one another, they often become aggressive or depressed and may exhibit self-destructive behaviors or refuse to mate. Zoos also fail to accurately reproduce the habitats of many non-territorial animals. An animal's natural habitat is a complex, interdependent system of relationships with other species, other members of its own species, food and other resources, and conditions such as weather. Despite the zoos' best efforts, animals may not thrive in a habitat that does not reflect where they would naturally choose to live.

Zoos also raise funds by allowing members of the public to view, or sometimes even touch, wild animals. This has a serious negative effect on the welfare of these animals. Consider a situation in which zoo visitors harm an animal by deliberately taunting it or by accidentally dropping trash into its enclosure. There was even a news story recently in which a small child fell into a gorilla enclosure at a zoo. To protect the child, the gorilla was killed by its handlers. If wild animals were not forced into close proximity with humans, situations such as this one—which resulted in the untimely death of an innocent animal—would never occur.

 Listen to Track 274.

You have 20 minutes to plan and write your response. Your response will be judged on the basis of the quality of your writing and on how well your response presents the points in the lecture and their relationship to the reading passage. Typically, an effective response will be 150 to 225 words.

Response Time: 20 minutes

Summarize the points made in the lecture, being sure to explain how they oppose the specific points made in the reading passage.

21.8

> Give yourself 3 minutes to read the passage.
>
> **Reading Time: 3 minutes**

A few years ago, an inventor proposed a groundbreaking new form of transportation, called Project X, that could change the way humans travel. In this system, passengers would enter a vehicle resembling a pod. This pod would be propelled through an underground tunnel, or tube, at speeds faster than can be achieved by airplanes, using electric power and magnetic levitation. This form of transportation would be faster than air travel at a small fraction of the cost.

According to the initial designs, the first planned route for Project X would run from Los Angeles to San Francisco, in California. This route would span about 560 kilometers, and engineers believe that the trip could be completed in just over a half hour. Project X vehicles would achieve an average speed of around 970 kilometers per hour and a top speed of over 1,200 kilometers per hour. To achieve this speed, the tubes would be evacuated—in other words, most of the air would be removed from them to create a near-vacuum state, thereby reducing air friction to near zero and making such incredible speeds possible.

The benefits to society of such a travel system are obvious. First, since the system would rely on electric power only, if it were to replace even a fraction of cars and airplanes currently in use, it would reduce the total carbon emissions resulting from the burning of fossil fuels. Second, many accidents caused by those forms of transportation could be avoided, making travel safer overall. Finally, based on the initial cost projections and expected consumer demand for Project X, the system could be self-funding within the first five years, and thereafter represent a substantial source of revenue for the state of California and the companies involved in building it.

 Listen to Track 275.

You have 20 minutes to plan and write your response. Your response will be judged on the basis of the quality of your writing and on how well your response presents the points in the lecture and their relationship to the reading passage. Typically, an effective response will be 150 to 225 words.

Response Time: 20 minutes

Summarize the points made in the lecture, being sure to explain how they cast doubt on the specific points made in the reading passage.

21

Answers and Explanations—21.1

Internet: Good or Bad?—Track 268

NARRATOR: Now listen to part of a lecture on the topic you just read about.

PROFESSOR: It's more or less universal for older people to claim that people are changing for the worse. They're spoiled, pampered, rude, lazy—people have been saying the same things at least since antiquity… and probably since the Stone Age. The latest in this whole line of complaints is that "the internet is making us dumber." Honestly, that's so silly that it doesn't even merit serious discussion—but, let's discuss it anyway.

First, if we're talking about "dumber" or "smarter" in terms of IQ tests, then we absolutely aren't getting dumber, and we can prove that. In countries where most people have internet access, the average IQ score has gone up by over 10 points in just the last 20 years. That's literally the fastest improvement in history.

Hardly a surprise, since that's always what happens when there's more information available to people. They get smarter. And not only smarter, but, since there's people from all over the world on the internet, a lot of today's young people are surprisingly aware of how different cultures think about things, even if they've never traveled.

Also, school kids aren't as limited in terms of getting information. It's not like the old days anymore, where they pretty much just had to trust what their teachers told them.

Now there's some truth to these claims about shorter attention spans. But not much. And there's a flip side, which is that people are MUCH better at multitasking. Thirty years ago, parents would lose their entire train of thought if their little kid interrupted them. These days they might still get annoyed, but they're much better at jumping back into the flow of whatever they were doing. And since there's so much more information out there, I've seen plenty of kids with impressively LONG attention spans, at least for things they're actually interested in.

Sample Written Response

The lecturer argues that the internet is not making us "dumber", contrary to what the passage says. The passage states, because of the Internet Age, people have become less adventurous and more about defining their experiences through other peolpe instead. People can also now get information by looking it up, instead of figuring it out for themselves. This, the passage author thinks, has diminished our ability to think and to problem solve on our own. The lecturer argues that in areas where most people have internet access, the IQ is higher by 10 points than many years ago. This, according to the lecturer, is considered a huge jump. The lecturer also thinks that the amount of information is beneficial to people. The information gives them the ability to see things from different perspectives, and not to get information from one source only, like a teacher

The passage also states that internet has caused people to lose focus because there is too much stimulation of things around the Web. All of this information overwelms people and they lose focus, according to the passage. While the lecturer does agree that some people may have lesser attention span, she also thinks that internet has increased multi-tasking skills. She also argues that some people haven't experienced decreased attention; they have lots of attention for all the information that's out there if it's something they're interested in.

Comments

The student addresses all of the main points made by the professor. Her essay also explains how the professor's points specifically cast doubt on the points made in the passage. She is very careful to cite whether a particular piece of information came from the professor or from the passage, so her essay is easy to follow. She does have a few grammar errors, but not very many.

Answers and Explanations—21.2

High-Intensity Interval Training—Track 269

NARRATOR: Now listen to part of a lecture on the topic you just read about.

PROFESSOR: Okay, HIIT. High-intensity training. It sounds too good to be true, right? It's not necessarily that it doesn't work. But, think about the practical issues. All of the studies on HIIT, they make it clear that it's not just going for a hard run or doing a hard interval on the bike. In order for the effect on your metabolism to show up, you have to be working way harder than you'd think—you have to really be putting out maximum effort. If you do it correctly, HIIT will often make you feel sick and it's pretty painful. If you try to use HIIT to get people into exercise, you'll get some people who try it, feel terrible, and give up. Or, you'll get people who don't do it hard enough.

Plus, there's the problem of injury. Most people, their joints, ligaments, even their bones, they're not really ready for a maximum-intensity effort. It's more of a technique for people who are already in good shape, because they can go hard without hurting themselves. But how did they get in good shape to begin with? They did it by doing longer, easier workouts.

There's also the issue of the studies on HIIT. Especially back when HIIT first came about—in the 1990s—it was hard to measure changes in body fat. You'd have to use calipers to measure the fat at various points on a person's body. But studies have shown that people who try to measure with calipers, even people who are really experienced, have a very high rate of error. So if a study shows a small difference in fat loss, if they used calipers, you probably shouldn't trust it. And that's the case with most HIIT studies so far.

Sample Written Response

The lecturer disagrees with the passage that HIIT is a beneficial workout that can increase public level of exercise or fitness. The passage states that HIIT is effective because it is a high-intnsity workout that has ongoing benefits after the workout is completed. The workout only takes a few minutes to do, contrasting between high intensity exercise and then rest periods, but people continue to burn fat for hours after the workout. This phenomenon is called EPOC, which helps you lose fat even when you're not active.

While the passage says that HIIT helps people to lose more fat, the lecturer thinks that HIIT is impractical for the general public. Most people just aren't capable for that amount of intensity. Or if they are, they might get sick, feel pain, or even injured, which would deter them from wanting to continue. The lecturer thinks this would only be a beneficial exercise regimen for very fit people, but to get very fit, you'd have to do standard exrcise in the first place.

The lecturer also brings up the use of calipers to measure fat loss in the HIIT studies. According to the lecturer, calipers have been proven to be unreliable for measuring fat, and calipers were used in most of the HIIT studies that have occured this far. As a result, it may be the case that the HIIT studies are unreliable. People may not have lost as much fat as the studies claimed.

Comments

The student summarizes the passage and then explains how the lecturer refutes the points made in the passage. Note that the question asks only about the second part: how the lecturer challenges the passage. The student spent most of the first paragraph summarizing the passage. He still earned a good score because he wrote about the lecturer's opinion in the second and third paragraphs, but if he had run out of time, he might not have earned such a good score.

Answers and Explanations—21.3

Broken Windows Theory—Track 270

NARRATOR: Now listen to part of a lecture on the topic you just read about.

PROFESSOR: The broken windows theory is an interesting theory, but it's just that—merely a theory. If you actually look at what happens in real communities… it doesn't hold up. For instance, the theory says that minor issues lead to major crime. But where's the proof that broken windows actually cause bigger crimes? Maybe a community has a lot of crime for another reason that we don't know about. Or, maybe people give up on things like fixing windows in a community already besieged by serious crime.

Okay, so people are committing both small crimes and big crimes in these places. But it's not like the vandalism, the petty fights… that kind of stuff… is causing the bigger crimes. Maybe something else is causing both. To give a simple example, maybe there's a crime problem mainly because there are a lot of teenagers with nothing else to do. They're stealing cars, they're breaking windows. The solution isn't to fix the windows so they'll stop stealing cars. The solution is to give them something to keep them occupied. If you focus on fixing the broken windows, you're missing the bigger picture.

Trying to enforce a broken windows policy can backfire, too. When police departments try to enforce it, if they aren't careful, they can end up giving people citations for ridiculous things. Maybe they're ticketing people who have a broken headlight, when there are much bigger problems right down the street. It's zero tolerance policing.

And maybe that reduces chaos, which might reduce crime… but it can also hurt the public's perception of the police. People think, "Why are the cops here, arresting me for something trivial, when there are murders and robberies happening right down the street?" It doesn't even matter whether they're right… what happens is, they start thinking that the police force doesn't have the right priorities. And when people don't respect law enforcement, that in and of itself can increase crime in the long run.

Sample Written Response

The lecturer disagrees with the broken window theory, a theory that states that small crimes lead to bigger crimes. The passage uses this theory to explain why high crime rate exists in certain places. If one broken window doesn't get repaired will lead to the mentality that it doesn't matter whether other windows are broken or someone sprays graffiti on a wall. Therefore, according to the theory, it's important to stop the small crimes while they're happening.

The lecturer, on the other hand, asks for proof that small crimes lead to bigger crimes—perhaps the committing of both types of crimes might be because of other reason. For example, board teenagers with nothing better to do may breaking some windows because they are board and then eventually stealing cars. According to the lecturer, the real focus should be on finding ways to keep teenagers productive so that

they will be less likely to commit any kinds of crimes. If the community focuses on squashing the small crimes instead of the bigger picture, this will not solve the problem.

The lecturer also believes that following the broken window theory will lead the police to focus on the wrong things. They'll be too focused on minor crimes when there are more serious crimes happening at the same time. This will also lead to people distrusting the police, which will not help the lowering of crime.

Comments

The student concisely articulates the theory. She then discusses how the lecturer opposes the theory, using the specific examples cited by the lecturer. She has a few grammatical issues and some redundancy in her writing, especially in the second paragraph (perhaps … might be; board [bored] teenagers … because they are board [bored]). Her overall response, though, is still of high quality.

Answers and Explanations—21.4

Who was Shakespeare?—Track 271

NARRATOR: Now listen to part of a lecture on the topic you just read about.

PROFESSOR: People who say that somebody else actually wrote Shakespeare's plays… that's nothing more than a conspiracy theory. It's an interesting idea, but there's no evidence to back it up. Why couldn't Shakespeare have written them himself? A lot of people were illiterate during the sixteenth century, but Shakespeare probably did get a good education. The house where he grew up was only half a mile from a free public school. At the time, the curriculum taught Latin, philosophy… all sorts of things that Shakespeare wrote about. An intelligent young man, like Shakespeare supposedly was, could have picked up everything he needed just by reading widely and talking with people.

It's true that there's no proof that he went to the school, but that's just because we don't have a list of students at all, so we don't know anything about the students who went there. A lot of documents from that era either are missing or weren't created in the first place.

Besides, if Shakespeare didn't write his own plays, who did? Sir Francis Bacon is the best candidate, but it just doesn't make sense that he was the writer. Bacon was a terrible poet. There's a reason he wasn't known for his poetry! It isn't that he didn't write any, he just didn't have any talent for it, unlike his talents for philosophy or law. Whoever wrote Shakespeare's plays was one of the greatest poets to ever live. Bacon, well… he definitely wasn't that. Plus, why would Bacon want to hide his identity? You'd have to believe in some kind of complicated conspiracy theory. Of course, plenty of people have thought of these conspiracy theories, but none of them make more sense than the obvious explanation—that Shakespeare actually did write his own plays.

Sample Written Response

The lecturer disagrees with the passage's claim that Shakespeare did not write his own plays. The passage says that there is evidence that Shakespeare's family was illiterate, as was the case for many people in that time. In addition, according to the passage, there is no proof that Shakespeare received an education. The lecturer argues that there was near Shakespeare's residence a free public school where he could have received an education. The school taught subjects that Shakespeare wrote about, and the lecturer argues that Shakespeare was intelligent enough to learn what he needed by reading and talking to people. Also, there

was no records of who attended school and who did not, so there was no proof for anyone. In other words, the "no proof" argument does not serve as proof of Shakespeare's lack of formal edcuation.

The lecturer also refutes the argument that Sir Francis Bacon actually was the one that wrote Shakespeare's plays. The passage claims that Sir Francis Bacon was an intellectual and his style matched the content that was in Shakespeare's plays. However, the lecturer says Bacon actually was a terrible poet. He did write poetry under his own name, but he was not known for writign good poetry. The lecturer also doubts why Bacon would have wanted to hide his idenity. Shakespeare was very popular, so Bacon would be presumed to have wanted to claim credit.

Comments

The student clearly summarizes the main points made by the lecturer to refute the arguments in the passage. In particular, he does a good job of explaining why the "no proof of school" argument is a bad argument. He has a few grammar errors and typos, but overall, his response is still clear and easy to understand.

Answers and Explanations—21.5

Text Speak—Track 272

NARRATOR: Now listen to part of a lecture on the topic you just read about.

PROFESSOR: Text speak originated at a time when phone companies limited the length of text messages. You could only put, maybe, a few hundred characters in one message, and they'd charge you for each message sent. So users… especially children, were motivated to put as much information as possible into every message. Text speak has a bad reputation among some people, but it's not simple laziness. People aren't leaving letters out of words randomly… they're doing it to be as efficient as possible. So, don't think of text speak as a "dumbed-down" version of language. It's just a special variety of language that serves, or at least used to serve, a specific purpose.

Using text speak also gives kids more exposure to written language. Compare texting to talking on the phone. If you're talking on the phone, you aren't reading or writing at all. But when kids are on their phones now, they're reading and… writing constantly. Kids are probably getting more exposure to written language now than they used to. And the more reading you do, the better you'll be at reading. Besides, it isn't like they'll lose the ability to understand standard language, just because they can also understand text speak. Kids who learn a second language don't stop being able to understand their first language. If anything, learning a new "language" is good for the brain, not bad for it.

Besides, text speak isn't used as often as people think it is. Some messages use some text speak, but most messages aren't written that way. And most people don't use it all of the time… in every message. People who complain about text speak are picturing a language that looks totally different, but it really isn't. It's more like certain new words or phrases have been added into the language. And that happens all the time, regardless of whether you're looking at text speak or new words that just naturally develop over time.

Sample Written Response

The passage that states "text speak" is decreasing the language skills and literacy of children. The lecturer, however, disagrees with this claim and states that "text speak" is actually improving communication skills. The passage first indicates that "text speak" promotes a lazy form of communication. It increases lack of

care of time to write thoughtful and intelligent words. The lecturer explains that the shortening of words was not the result of laziness, but rather because old phones had a character limit and it was more expensive to send long texts, so those who texted used abbreviations to get more information into one text. In other words, according to the lecturer, "text speak" is not meaning that children are learning a lazy way to write. People only text that way when they have to.

The passage also claims that "text speak" will lead to poor writing style because children will not be doing enough "real" reading or writing anymore. But the lecturer argues that when the primary way of communication was speaking on the telephone, children were talking, not practice reading or writing. Texting allows children to gain more practice reading and writing, not less. The lecturer also asserts that writing texts will not cause children's language skills to deprecate. For example, when someone learns a new language, that person still remembers how to speak the first language. "Text speak" would be considered another language that children have learned, but they are not going to forget there first language.

Comments

The student explains how the lecturer refutes the main points made in the passage. She provides enough detail to understand each of the points. She could improve her response by making sure to address all of the lecturer's main points. The lecturer also asserts that "text speak" should be considered new words that have been added to the existing language. The student does not mention this point, but her response is long enough that she is still able to earn a good score.

Answers and Explanations—21.6

21

Colony Collapse Disorder—Track 273

NARRATOR: Now listen to part of a lecture on the topic you just read about.

PROFESSOR: Well, actually, very recent research has suggested that, in fact, the multi-factor theory better explains the explosion in colony collapse disorder in many parts of the world, after all.

First of all, several studies have been conducted by academic and government institutions to try to explain the causes of colony collapse disorder. All the studies concluded that no single factor—including exposure to any specific type of pesticide—was notably more correlated with colony collapse than other likely factors.

Second, even though a certain pesticide may play a large role in North American honey bee colony collapse, it can't be the reason for recent problems in Europe. After all, the European Union banned the use of these pesticides in 2013—but problems with colony collapse persist there. Also, there are some reports of a spike in colony collapse on farms that don't use any pesticides at all.

Finally, there is the fact that honey bees are known to be sensitive to a wide variety of external stressors. This includes climate change—especially in warm climates… the possibility of viruses spreading among bee populations in certain parts of the world… and a global outbreak of a parasitic mite that is known to be lethal to honey bee populations. All of these various factors add up. And… while honey bee colonies can generally survive multiple stressors in small doses, it is also known that once the combination of stressors grows too large, the bee colonies… well, they just start giving up! We need to face the fact that the sum total of stressors to bees—from deforestation, pollution, global warming, pathogens, and parasites, as well as pesticides—may have finally gotten to the point where honey bees simply cannot cope anymore.

Sample Written Response

The lecturer is arguing against the passage, which states that pesticide theory is the likely-most cause of the rise of colony collapse disorder of honey bees. The lecturer believes that multi-factor theory is the primary cause for honey bees abandoning of their colonies.

The passage claims that the chemicals in pesticides have caused direct harm to the honey bees, which supports the proof of the pesticide theory. The passage also talks about fungicides making colonies lose function. However, the lecturer weakens this argument when discussing the European ban of pesticides. Even after the ban of pesticides of Europe, colony collapse disorder continued to happen. Also, there has been reports of colony colapse disorder in places where pesticides are not used. That means that pesticides probally were not the main contributor to colony collapse disorder, according to the lecturer.

The lecturer believes that multi-factor theory makes the most sense because of bee sensitivity the many external factors they have faced, such as climate change and parasites. According to the lecturer, when honey bees are faced with too many stresses in combination, they cannot handle all of the stresses and will give up and abandon the colony. The combination of factors (multi-factor theory), the lecturer believes, is the primary cause of the rise in colony collapse. Pesticides are just one of these factors, as opposed to the main factor.

Comments

The student thoroughly addresses the second and third points made by the lecturer. His response could perhaps be improved by addressing the first point. But because he does a strong job of explaining the other points, he can still earn a good score on his response.

Answers and Explanations—21.7

The Value of Zoos—Track 274

NARRATOR: Now listen to part of a lecture on the topic you just read about.

PROFESSOR: I think, and a lot of scientists think, that conservationists criticize zoos too harshly. You have to weigh the issues against the benefits, the very significant benefits, of keeping wild animals in a zoo. For instance, people think of a zoo, and they might think of this horrible, depressing place, where animals live in cages. But in most zoos, at least in developed countries, that's just not the reality.

Take the Singapore Zoo, for instance. They have a forest habitat, a tundra habitat, and so on, and they'll have all kinds of animals from those habitats living in this massive area, similar to how they would live in the wild. People will sometimes complain that the zoo is too big, and they can't see the animals when they want to! That's a good complaint to have. And anyways, even if a zoo habitat doesn't live up to where an animal would live in the wild, don't forget, a natural habitat isn't necessarily a safe place. Some animals are kept in zoos because their natural habitat is shrinking from climate change or from... deforestation. Just because something is natural, doesn't mean that it's better for the animals' welfare.

It's true that sometimes there are negative interactions between animals and zoo visitors. It's a tragedy whenever that happens. But, it would be better to solve it with education and with technology, than to say that animals shouldn't be kept in zoos at all. Would that kid have fallen into the gorilla enclosure if there was a higher fence or if their parents knew how dangerous it was? Probably not. It's unreasonable to say that there are these negative interactions, which are totally preventable, so we should just get rid of zoos

entirely. We're not going to give up the positives, like conserving endangered species, scientific research, and so on, when instead we could focus on other solutions to prevent the negatives.

Sample Written Response

The lecturer address claims from the passage that zoos treat animals unfairly by placing them in an unatural environment. The passage also claims that interactions with humans result in harm to the animals. The lecturer argues that animals have access to natural habitats in a zoo and that negative interactions could be significantly decreased.

The passage discusses problems with placing zoo animals in an unnatural environment. For example, animals that are crammed into a smaller space than natural can cause them to become depressed and aggressive. But the lecturer points out that most good zoos take care as much as possible to match the natural habitat of the animals. The lecturer also highlights the fact that some animals are at far more less risk in a zoo than in the wild.

While the author of the passage is concerned about interactions with humans that result in harm to animals, the lecturer counters with an argument that most of these rare unhappy events could be prevented with more attention to technology. The passage mentions an example where a gorilla was killed to prevent it hurting a child who crawled into the gorilla's pen. The lecturer believes that this type of incident could be prevented with higher fences or other measures.

The lecturer is adamant that the pros associated with zoos—conservation, research, education—far outweighs the cons pointed out in the passage

Comments

> The author addresses all of the main points made by the lecturer. He shows a good grasp of the issues. The last sentence in his second paragraph contains an error that makes the meaning hard to understand ("far more less risk"). But this is the only error that creates a confusing meaning, so he can still earn a good score. Minor misspellings (e.g., "adament" for "adamant") and tiny grammatical glitches do not obscure the intended meaning.

21

Answers and Explanations—21.8

Project X—Track 275

NARRATOR: Now listen to part of a lecture on the topic you just read about.

PROFESSOR: Even if we assume that travel via the proposed Project X system worked exactly according to plan—and that's a big if—it… it's not clear that it would produce many of the advantages people expect. For one thing, it is foolish to assume that any mass transit system will be free of errors or accidents. And based on the design of the system, any such accident would almost certainly result in massive damage to the system, in addition to the loss of human life. Compare this to air travel, which overall has extremely low rates of accidents and deaths… the Project X system would have to operate almost perfectly to be deemed safer than air travel. And since the system would involve tubes built underground, safeguarding them from acts of terrorism could prove costly and difficult.

Here's another problem: The system runs on electricity. What happens if electric power is lost during operation? You know, a blackout? If power were lost suddenly while a pod was in transit, it is very hard to say exactly what would happen. Maybe everything would be fine, maybe not.

Finally, the technology described in this proposal is simply, um… unproven. Nothing in it violates any laws of physics, but there's been very little testing completed to show that it would reliably work as expected. The technology described in this system is highly advanced and very sensitive to normal wear and tear—things like dirt and cracks—and maintaining the system could prove much more expensive than predicted. When you combine that with initial cost estimates to build the planned route that are, most likely, far too low, it seems very unlikely that Project X would turn out to be as economically attractive as its inventor would predict.

Sample Written Response

The lecturer is not confident that the Project X will be as much of a transportation breakthrough that the passage describes. First, the lecturer explains that the system would have to perform almost perfectly in order to be safer and less expensive than other transportation options. Since the travel occurs in an enclosed system, there can literally be zero accidents or else it is possible the whole tunnel could be destroyed. If one plane is grounded, other planes can still fly. However, if a pod is involved in an accident, other pods couldn't travel. This would make each accident very expensive because the whole system could shut down.

The lecturer is clearly skeptical about how the system is powered, too. Because Project X would run on electricity, what would happen if the power fails? People trapped in an undergrund pod would have to be rescued. Power failures do happen and would definitely impact the safeyt and cost of Project X.

The lecturers final complaint about Project X is the unproven technology. The lecturer asserts that the technology is almost completely untested. It should work from a theoretical perspective, but nobody knows whether it actually will. Nothing exists that is similar to Project X. So the cost estimates might be completely wrong and the system might be much more expensive to build and maintain than expected. The lecturer doesn't think people will adopt a transportation system based on technology that is so untested.

Comments

> The student explains the lecturer's position very well. She details the examples from the lecture and doesn't have many errors or typos. However, the last line of her response makes a point that the lecturer does not actually say. The student assumed this herself. Be careful to reflect what the lecturer actually says, not what you might think yourself.

Chapter 22
Writing Task Type 2

Writing questions test your ability to comprehend written or spoken material and to respond in written form. You will have to type your essay into the computer. There are two different writing tasks. Writing Task Type 2 is an "independent" task. You will be asked to agree or disagree with a short statement. You will need to provide reasons and examples to support your opinion. You will have 30 minutes to write your essay.

Writing questions test your ability to understand spoken and written information and to summarize and express opinions about that information. They also test your ability to respond in writing to specific questions, including your grammar and spelling, your vocabulary, and the logical organization of your ideas.

How should you use this chapter? Here are some recommendations, according to the level you've reached in TOEFL Writing:

0. **Everyone!** Hold yourself to the time limits whenever practicing Writing tasks. Don't write by hand. Use Microsoft Word or other word-processing software, but turn off both spell-check and grammar-check.

1. **Fundamentals.** Start with whichever essay type is a little easier for you. Try one question and then check your response against the sample answer. If you think you can do a better job, redo your essay. This way, you give yourself a chance to think carefully about how to write what you are trying to convey. You also give yourself a chance to fix errors. Articulate what you want to do differently the next time you write this type of essay.

2. **Fixes.** Do one Writing task, examine the results, learn your lessons, then try the other type of Writing task. When you're ready, graduate to doing a set of the two different Writing tasks in a row.

3. **Tweaks.** Confirm your mastery by doing a set of the two different Writing tasks in a row under timed conditions.

Good luck on Writing!

22.1

> Read the question below. You have 30 minutes to plan, write, and revise your essay. Typically, an effective response will contain a minimum of 300 words.
>
> ### Response Time: 30 minutes
>
> Do you agree or disagree with the following statement?
>
> **Loyalty is the most important quality in choosing a friend.**
>
> Use specific reasons and examples to support your answer.

22.2

> Read the question below. You have 30 minutes to plan, write, and revise your essay. Typically, an effective response will contain a minimum of 300 words.
>
> ### Response Time: 30 minutes
>
> **Some people marry shortly after finishing college. Others prefer to focus on their careers first and wait until later to get married. Which of these situations do you think is better?**
>
> Use specific reasons and examples to support your answer.

22.3

> Read the question below. You have 30 minutes to plan, write, and revise your essay. Typically, an effective response will contain a minimum of 300 words.
>
> ### Response Time: 30 minutes
>
> Do you agree or disagree with the following statement?
>
> **Children are happier than adults.**
>
> Use specific reasons and examples to support your answer.

22.4

Read the question below. You have 30 minutes to plan, write, and revise your essay. Typically, an effective response will contain a minimum of 300 words.

Response Time: 30 minutes

Do you agree or disagree with the following statement?

When choosing a job, it is more important to like the job than to make a certain amount of money.

Use specific reasons and examples to support your answer.

22.5

Read the question below. You have 30 minutes to plan, write, and revise your essay. Typically, an effective response will contain a minimum of 300 words.

Response Time: 30 minutes

Do you agree or disagree with the following statement?

In the future, a majority of people will work from home.

Use specific reasons and examples to support your answer.

22.6

Read the question below. You have 30 minutes to plan, write, and revise your essay. Typically, an effective response will contain a minimum of 300 words.

Response Time: 30 minutes

Do you agree or disagree with the following statement?

People today work fewer hours and have more leisure time than previous generations did.

Use specific reasons and examples to support your answer.

22.7

> Read the question below. You have 30 minutes to plan, write, and revise your essay. Typically, an effective response will contain a minimum of 300 words.
>
> Response Time: 30 minutes
>
> Do you agree or disagree with the following statement?
>
> **Computers and the internet help to make school assignments faster and easier to complete.**
>
> Use specific reasons and examples to support your answer.

22.8

> Read the question below. You have 30 minutes to plan, write, and revise your essay. Typically, an effective response will contain a minimum of 300 words.
>
> Response Time: 30 minutes
>
> Do you agree or disagree with the following statement?
>
> **It is better to have a mentor to advise you in your career than to rely entirely on yourself.**
>
> Use specific reasons and examples to support your answer.

Answers and Explanations—22.1

Sample Written Response

I do not believe loyalty is the most important quality when it comes to choosing a friend. When I think of the single most important attribute I want a friend to have, it would be honesty.

I need to be able to trust my friends and I need to believe that they're going to be honest with me. That honesty includes telling me when I'm wrong. If I make a mistake, or if I'm making choices that my friends don't agree with, I need to know that they're going to be honest and bring it up to me. I want my friends to challenge me and make me better, and if they're too worried about appearing "disloyal" to do that, then I don't think the friendhsip is very healthy. If my friends aren't blindly loyal to me than their support is all the more meaningful. It means they critically looked at my actions and have chosen to stand behind me rather than telling me I'm right just because we're friends. It makes their support more valid.

I also believe that people need to fight their own battles. Say, for example, my best friend and I have a third friend in common who I'm not too fond of. If loyalty were the most important thing to me, I may try to sway my best friend to also start dislking the third friend or even stop associating with them. I don't think that's a fair thing to ask a friend to do, but I've certainly seen that type of control in different real life friendships. I think sometimes loyalty can lead to a sort situation where people can stop thinking for

themselves and start acting as a unit and while I think it's important to have a sense of community, you also want to keep your individuality. If everyone thought the same we would never learn from one another, and I think one of the greatest gifts of friendship is exposing each other to new things and ideas.

I don't want my friends to be loyal to me just because that's what they think friendship is. I want them to choose to be loyal when they are truly moved to do so and I want to be able to trust them enough to honestly express themselves and tell me when they think I'm wrong. I certainly would have enough respect for them and the friendship to do the same.

Comments

The author provides a clear thesis: Honesty is the most important factor. She provides multiple concrete reasons for preferring honesty over loyalty. Her hypothetical example in the second paragraph might be a little difficult to understand. If possible, use something that happened in real life. It is easier to write about something that actually happened than about something hypothetical.

Answers and Explanations—22.2

Sample Written Response

I think it's better to not rush into getting married right after college. Of course everyone is different, but I think when you graduate from college in many ways you are still growing up. The gap in maturity from high school to college is huge, and the gap from college to adulthood is even larger. When you graduate college you are not really a full adult yet. Many people start paying rent for the first time, some start cooking for themselves for the first time, or start managing their own money for the first time. You are suddenly in a new world with new responsibilities and the learning curve is quick. It takes some time to get used to being an adult.

Monogomous marriage is a deep part of our culture. Choosing the person you are going to spend the rest of your life with is a huge decision. This person will be your romantic partner, your business partner in many ways, and your co-parent if you choose to have children. When you commit to another person you should be fully capable of making adult decisions in a way I don't think most 22 year olds are capable of. Entering the work force is a huge adjustment. Living in the real world and taking care of yourself as an adult is challenging. I think you need time to learn who you are as an adult before you make any adult decisions that change the trajectory of the rest of your life.

Of course, some people who are in love and want to get married right out of college are right. They could get married on graduation day and be married for the rest of their lives because they happenned to find the right person. But why rush into things? If you've found the person you're meant to be with it doesn't matter if you marry them at 22 or at 32. You might as well wait until you've both grown into who you're meant to be to enter into a marriage. It only makes that decision more meaningful and special.

Comments

The student takes a clear stand and provides multiple reasons why she believes people should wait until they're older to marry. In the last paragraph, she acknowledges that some people may do well by marrying right away. Acknowledging that the other point of view does have merit is a good way to make your own argument more persuasive. In the middle of the essay, she uses the world "adult" so many times that it becomes repetitive. Try to find ways to vary your language. Use synonyms where you can.

Answers and Explanations—22.3

Sample Written Response

What is happiness? Is it just a life filled with playing and laughter? There are many simple pleasures in lif that children may be better able to enjoy, such as games, sweets and imagniary friends. However, there are so many profoundly happy moments that adult can enjoy that a child could not comprehend. The joy of your wedding day, graduating from university, watching your baby take his first step. These important events create such deep feelings of happiness, and can only be experienced, truly, by adults.

The kind of happiness a child experiences may be best described by the quote "Ignorance is bliss." A child lives primarily in the moment, with little regard for what may happen in the future, especially bad things that may happen. An adult can more fully understand the negative consequences that will come from a bad decision today. To understand an adults capacity for happiness, we must understand their capacity for sorrow. The human soul is like a vessel that expands as it ages. A child will feel any emotion strongly, it doesn't take much to fill him up. But that emotion is fleeting, ready to be replaced by what comes in the next minute or hour. A grown adult can wheather the daily changes between joy, sorrow, and everything between, because they have a reserve of past emtion that helps keep them centered. But in some few moments in life, an adult soul can be overwhelmed with happiness in a way not possible for a child.

In many ways, a child is infinitely happier than an adult. They are carefree, unburdened by life, and able to see the world as a giant playground. Adults must deal with problems nearly every day, they must deal with tragedy, they must deal with loss. But it is perhaps because of an adults deeper understanding of sadness, that they have a greater capacity to appreciate joy and happiness when it presents itself. A child may experience happiness more regularly and consistently than an adult, but that hapiness is a more superfical happiness. It cannot compare to the profound moments of pure joy that can be felt by an adult, an adult that has the experience and understanding to appreciate this feeling they have.

Comments

> The student provides a thoughtful discussion of happiness. Rather than simply saying that one group is definitely happier than the other, he explains that each group is happy in a different way. He uses his reasoning to conclude that adults are able to experience a deeper happiness because they also experience pain and sorrow. He does have several typos and spelling errors. His points, though, are still understandable. Typos and errors are not a big problem unless they are so numerous that the reader has difficulty understanding the essay.

Answers and Explanations—22.4

Sample Written Response

I agree with the statement, "when choosing a job, it is more important to like the job than to make a certain amount of money." This statement hints at an underlying obsession with gaining wealth in capitalist cultures that does not improve the quality of people's lives. When considering this statement, it is very important to define "liking" as it relates to job satisfaction.

Enormous pressure exists in our culture for indivdiuals to to attain high-paying jobs, but science, history, and experience clearly point out that high-paying jobs do not improve the quality of people's lives. A recent study showed that feelings of "happiness" do not increase if household income is above $70,000. Looking

  MANHATTAN PREP

into America's past, a significant number of European settlers disappeared into the woods to live with Native American tribes and assume their simpler lifestyle. Some settlers who were captured by Native Americans forcefully, assimilated into a tribe and later rescued and brought back into a European colony, would flee back into the woods to rejoin their tribe. In tribes, people worked around 20 hours a week and enjoyed immense satisfaction in their community and lifestyle. There were no divisions of wealth. Taking an extreme example, consider Warren Buffet. One of the richest men in the entire world chooses to live relatviely humbly and gives generously to charitable causes.

Considering this statement, it is important to define "liking." Sure, some people might truly "like" their job in the sense that it is "fun." An example might be Anthony Bourdain, who literally travels and eats for a living. Not all of us are so lucky, but we could more realistically stand to gain satisfaction in our workplace from achieving or working towards a goal, being involved in a community, or developing a skill. The hours for medical professionals are very long and greulling, but one would agree that they "like" restoring people to good health. In terms of community, take start-ups for example. A workplace can be incredibly hectic, but some people will put up with it because they "like" working among enterprenuers.

Comments

The student states clearly that he agrees with the question prompt. He follows up with specific examples that support his position. He also makes an interesting point: It is necessary to define what "like" means in order to address the question. This is a good way to discuss a topic when a certain word could be interpreted differently by different people. He could improve his opening paragraph by restating the prompt in his own words rather than quoting it directly.

Answers and Explanations—22.5

Sample Written Response

With advances in technology over the past decade, the number of people working from home has grown a large amount. This technology has allowed workers who were previously required to be in the office to now work from home. But the nature of available careers has changed too, creating more jobs that can be done from home. Writing of all kinds, from journalism, blogging, education writing, and reviewers has created a new category in the professional class or writing, and these workers work primarily from home.

But, the growing majority of jobs are in the service industry. Retail, restaurant, and fashion workers make up a large portion of the global economy, and it seems unlikely that many of these jobs would become remote. They'd sooner be replace by artificially intelligent software than by shifting a workforce to their homes. Likewise with manufacturing jobs, we don't see a shift of these workers to working from home, remotely controlling robots or processes from their couches. The jobs are no longer necessary, as growingly compitent robots are able to do just fine on their own, with some minimal supervision and upkeep.

Most of the jobs mentioned so far are mostly jobs considered viable in first-world countries. Millions of workers globally, in less developed nations, perform hard manual work building everything from iPhones to Yo-Yos, sneakers and jeans. These workers have very little hope of being able to work the same job, just remotely. They'll either be replaced by machines, or, the factory will move to yet another worse off country where they can pay lower wages. There are some exceptions to this, with call centers that make up so much of the "white-collar" work in parts of the world. These are jobs that could reasonably happen from home, if the workers have reliable telephones at home.

So while the types of careers that are growing, in both developed and under-developed countries, allow for remote work, there's nowhere near the number of jobs needed to offset the job lossess that will be caused by automation, or by jobs that are necessarily face-to-face. The trend is headed in the direction of more people working from home, and well paying jobs for some of them. But on the whole, it seems unlikely that we'll ever reach a majority of workers working remotely.

Comments

The student offers an impressive number of examples to support both sides of the argument. These examples illustrate the complexity of the situation. The student doesn't actually state his thesis until the end of the essay. While this is acceptable, it would be better to state the thesis in the first paragraph so that the reader is aware of the ultimate point while reading the examples.

Answers and Explanations—22.6

Sample Written Response

I agree that people generally work fewer hours now and have more leisure time than older people did. In considering this statement, it is important to clarify which "previous generations" worked more hours. We can then compare working conditions and lesirue time of these previous generations with that of our own, which for the purposes of this essay I will consider to be Industrialized nations.

When reading a text like Upton Sinclair's "The Jungle," it is clear that generations living and working during the rise of the Industrial Revolution were subjected to working very long hours. Factory workplaces requiring manual labor in some cases nearly enslaved workers, forcing young children to work Looking back into the history of the United States, laws had to be passed to limit the number of hours people could work and the age that was appropriate for people to begin working.

Nowadays, people in industrialized nations are fortunate to not work as children. They are paid a good wage and paid for vacation time, and they work only a certain number of hours. They are also allowed not to work on national holidays. These people do have more leisure time than their ancestors had.

Cultures that farmed with manual labour to provide food for themselves did not have very much leisure time. For example, the Amish in Pennsylvania still live this kind of life. Farms with animals and crops on especially small plots of land tended with manual labor, require nearly round-the clock maintenance. Most vegetables must be harvested in early hours of warm seasons. Cows are routinely milked at early hours. Ini short, it would be unheard of for someone maintaining a farm, especially with livestock, to leave their home completely for a two-week vacation. Most people in industrialized nations don't do this kind of work any more. But people in less developed nations do still have to work very hard and don't have much leisure time.

Comments

The student makes an important point in the first paragraph. Whether people work less today depends on which culture or area of the world you are discussing. The student decides to establish that the prompt is talking about industrialized nations. This is a good technique to help bound the scope of the discussion. He does go on to mention that people in less developed nations don't have much leisure time. Ultimately, though, this just serves to further support his point of view: that people in developed nations do have more leisure time.

Answers and Explanations—22.7

Sample Written Response

Computers and the internet have made some aspects of school assignments faster and easier. But school assignments have also changed in order to adjust to the speed at which students can access information. So is it really any easier now to complete these assignments?

When I was a child, completing a report on a foreign country meant heading to the library, pulling out a kid's encyclopedia and photocopying the relevant pages. First, I would just copy pieces of this onto my page and turn in my report. Eventually I started rewriting, but I relied on long quotations from my research, and finally I learned to rewrite information in my own words. All of this took a long time, especially when I had to rewrite something because I changed my mind about what I wanted to say or because I found some new information in a different book.

My first thought about the effect of the intenet on such assignments was to assume that plagiarism has only increased. It's so much easier now to just copy and paste material from some source you find online. And that would definitely make it easier to complete the assignment! However, I know that there are now tools that teachers can use to check for plagiarism and, more importantly, teachers have no doubt increased the expectations of such assignments. Or, perhaps teachers are assigning different kinds of tasks in the first place. For example, instead of asking students to develop their own ideas, the teacher might ask them to develop a website that organizes the ideas of others. In a sense, this kind of assignment is closer to what students might have to do at a real job in the real world.

As you can see above, I'm torn about this question: on the one hand, students can grab information faster, can edit faster, and can more easily apply professional formatting. But it's probably the case that the nature of such assignments have changed. Perhaps this seemingly unlimited access to information has led teachers to rethink what they assign, so that the focus is more on analysis of information, not just finding the information. After all, now it's very easy to gather a large pool of research. The challenging part is making sense of it all.

Comments

There are many valid opinions on both sides of this issue. The student provides a very thoughtful discussion of both sides. It's also very effective to use a personal example to tie to the larger question. It is more difficult, however, to try to discuss both sides than to pick one side and argue for that side. In general, it's easier to pick one side, even when you see both sides of the issue.

Answers and Explanations—22.8

Sample Written Response

I think it is better to have a mentor to advise you in your career than try and rely entirely on yourself. They can save you from greivous mistakes in what you study and how to get started in that career. For example if you were visiting a foreign country, you would buy a guide book and learn about the place you go and what you can do there. You should also do that with a career. It is also hard to rely on yourself to pursue a career. Look at the statistics for university students. Most people who have parents and grandparents who went to university will also go to university. The same is not true for people whos parents did not go to university. Without that experience to follow, it is hard to be the first.

Relying on yourself is also more difficult because of the Internet. If you don't have a mentor but use information on the computer you are also relying on someone elses expereince. This person is not writing to you but that is still advice and you do not know what you can trust of what you read. Some of the information may be wrong. A good mentor can help you decide what is correct. You may not know the things that happen in the career when you are older that you will not like. You do not know about them at the beginning but a mentor know about those things because they are having a longer career so they can tell you what to do.

In many countries, businesses are passed from father to son and daughter and this is because those families know that it is important to have that experienced advise to continue the success of that business for many generations. Even after the son is brought in, the father will stay on to advise and many family members also help governance. This is like a mentor even though it is the family giving the advise.

The best reason to have a mentor is that they can introduce you to other people who have that career and may even be someone who can be your boss. Good menrors often have successful companies and they may hire you and bring you into the company.

For these reasons it is better to have a mentor for a career than to rely on yourself.

Comments

The student states her thesis clearly and provides many good reasons to support her point of view. She does have some organizational problems. For instance, the second paragraph begins by saying that the internet is a problem, but only the first half of the paragraph is about the internet. The second half is about a different issue. It would have been better to create a new paragraph or, perhaps, to move that information into a different paragraph.

Introduction to Appendices

1. **How to Learn Vocabulary (and anything else)**
   Strengthen and expand your academic and conversational vocabulary.

2. **How English Works**
   Learn common differences between English and other languages and how these differences might affect your English performance.

3. **Consuming and Producing (Good) English**
   Find high-quality English-language resources and use them to improve your English.

4. **Achieving Things with Words**
   Explore the relationship between *how* you say (or write) something and *why* you say it.

5. **TOEFL Situations and Topics**
   Improve your knowledge of academic fields and of campus situations.

6. **Making a Sentence**
   Learn how to compose a sentence from scratch using the rules of English grammar.

7. **Combining Sentences**
   Learn about the structure of the explanations and arguments you'll be asked to read—and create—on the TOEFL.

8. **Expressing Your Thoughts in English**
   Improve your ability to turn your thoughts into English-language speech.

9. **Taking the TOEFL**

Learn good preparation habits and test-taking strategies.

10. **Other Tests and the TOEFL**

Study effectively for the TOEFL *and* other standardized exams.

App

How to Learn Vocabulary (and anything else)

Improving Written Vocabulary

The TOEFL tests not only conversational English, but also the English used in academic writing and in the classroom. This vocabulary is often at a higher academic level than spoken vocabulary. The best strategy for improving your academic vocabulary has two parts: 1) read high-quality nonfiction, and 2) make flash cards for words that you don't already know.

Part 1: Read High-Quality English Nonfiction

This is the most important thing you can do for your academic English vocabulary. Fortunately, writing that is similar to the TOEFL Reading section is widely available, often for little or no expense. Here is a list of good sources. It is by no means exhaustive (complete), but these sources will provide you with challenging, TOEFL-relevant reading material:

- *Scientific American* (Natural Sciences): scientificamerican.com
- *The Economist* (Natural Sciences, Social Sciences, Humanities): economist.com
- *The New Yorker* (Natural Sciences, Social Sciences, Humanities): newyorker.com
- *Wired* (Natural Sciences, Social Sciences): wired.com

As you read, notice words that you don't know. When you see an unfamiliar word, don't immediately look up the definition. You are more likely to remember a word if you have to think critically about its meaning. Try to figure out the word's meaning based on context clues—other information in the sentence. Once you have a guess as to what the word means, look up the definition. Were you right or wrong? Either way, make a flash card.

Part 2: Make Flash Cards

Flash cards always consist of two parts: a front and a back. On the front of the flash card, you will write the word you want to learn. On the back, you will write the definition—but you won't just copy the definition from a dictionary. Take a look at the two flash cards below. Which one would be more likely to help you remember the definition of *opulent*?

opulent	*adj.* lavishly rich or grandiose

opulent	*adj.* rich, fancy (maybe too fancy!), elaborate "Her lifestyle was so OPULENT that she even LENT her OPALS to her friends."

A flash card is supposed to help you remember the word, but a dictionary definition is not very memorable. Instead, write the definition in your own words. If you have to think about the best way to write a definition, you are more likely to remember it. Second, include one or more "memory tools" on every flash card: something catchy that will help you remember the word. Here are some examples of good memory tools:

- A sentence using the word
- Other words that sound similar and have related meanings
- A picture that helps you remember the definition of the word
- A rhyme you invent with the word to help you remember the definition
- A personal memory to associate with the word

Once you've created a lot of great flash cards, sort them into three piles:

1. GREEN: Words you usually remember, but want to study a bit more, just to be sure.
2. YELLOW: Words you sometimes remember, but sometimes forget.
3. RED: Words you usually or always forget.

The red pile contains words that you are just starting to learn. You will need to look at these words frequently in order to build strong memories. Study the yellow pile frequently as well.

The green pile does not need frequent review. When you are more familiar with a word, you don't need to study it as often in order to remember it. You will just look at it occasionally in order to make sure you have not forgotten it.

Here's a suggested study plan for your flash cards:

- Red: Review every day
- Yellow: Review every three days
- Green: Review once a week

If a word is in the red pile, but you are starting to remember it when you study, move it to the yellow pile. If a word is in the yellow pile, and you remember it every single time, move it to the green pile. And if you find yourself actually using words in the green pile in your everyday life, consider "retiring" those cards—you have learned these words for good. You might scan them once again just before the test, but you don't need to review them every week.

Note that words can also move in the *opposite* direction: If you forget a word, move it "down" to the yellow or red pile and study it more often. If you just can't seem to remember a word, try changing your flash card. You might need to create a better "memory tool" to help you recall a tricky word.

The two-part strategy described above—**reading** and **flash cards**—will help you improve your written, academic vocabulary. Next, you will learn how to improve vocabulary for speaking and listening.

Improving Spoken Vocabulary

If you speak English in exactly the same way that you write English, people will still understand you. However, there are small differences between conversational English and formal written English. An awareness of these differences will help you on the TOEFL. Here's one example:

Written: Do you have any money?

Spoken: Have you got any money?

If you are comfortable with spoken, conversational English, you are more likely to quickly understand what you hear during the TOEFL sections that involve listening to casual conversations. Also, you will be able to speak English in a more comfortable, natural-sounding way.

Now that you're studying for the TOEFL, start thinking of yourself as an *anthropologist*—somebody who studies human behavior. Your goal is to listen not just to what people say, but also to *how* they say it. When you speak with fluent English speakers, or when you watch or listen to English-language media, pay attention to words and phrases that strike you as interesting or unusual, or that you can't define easily. Normally, you might just guess the meaning from context and move on. Try to change that. Notice these interesting words and phrases, make flash cards for them, and study them until you are comfortable with them.

Some students already spend a lot of time talking to others in English or watching English-language TV shows or movies. Other students prefer to study English through "book learning"—reading and studying. Both of these approaches will help you on the TOEFL. However, the TOEFL doesn't just test academic passages and lectures, and it doesn't just test casual, spoken English. You'll need both. So, ask yourself this question: Are you more comfortable learning English from books or through speaking and listening? Whatever your preferred approach is, push yourself to practice English in the other way as well, even if it makes you uncomfortable. This will be especially valuable if you've mostly studied English via reading and writing, since for the TOEFL, you'll need to improve your ability to speak spontaneously and fluidly.

App 1

Appendix 2
How English Works

You have probably noticed that translating from one language to another is pretty complicated. If you take a sentence in French (for example) and replace every word with the equivalent English word, the new sentence in English will not make much sense. First, there often isn't an "equivalent" English word. You also need to consider the structure of sentences: Every language builds sentences from words in a slightly different way.

You don't have to become a professional linguist—someone who studies languages—to succeed on the TOEFL. However, knowing a little bit about linguistics—specifically, the ways in which some languages are different from other languages—can help you avoid mistakes or misunderstandings. Here are some common differences among languages that can help you to take the TOEFL.

Pronunciation

Your native language might use sounds that are not used in English, and vice versa. Unfortunately, unless you learned English as a very young child, you will probably always have a "foreign accent" while speaking English. That's okay! Your pronunciation does not have to be perfect. It just has to be clear and understandable.

Pronunciation is only a problem when it makes it hard for English speakers to understand you. For instance, if certain English sounds are not used in your native language, then you might have trouble producing those sounds. Working with a native English speaker can help you learn about these sounds. Ask a friend to show you how to produce certain sounds that are difficult for you.

You can also learn a bit about phonetics. Phonetics is the scientific study of how people produce different speech sounds. Studying phonetics can help you understand how to position your tongue, lips, and teeth in order to produce different sounds more effectively. MIT's OpenCourseWare website (ocw.mit.edu) has a number of free resources that you may find helpful, including a course called "Listening, Speaking, and Pronunciation." This course focuses on using pronunciation to help you speak English more clearly and to help you better comprehend rapidly-spoken English.

One specific problem occurs when English makes a distinction that your native language doesn't make. In Japanese, the English sounds "l" and "r" are considered the same sound. That makes it hard for Japanese speakers to hear the difference between these sounds in English words. If English has distinctions that your native language doesn't have, then you might need to work on pronouncing those sounds differently, in order to avoid confusing the English speakers who score your TOEFL.

Finally, if you know there are certain words that are especially hard for you to pronounce, it's okay to avoid using those words.

Vocabulary and Grammar

Sometimes, your native language makes it harder for you to learn specific English vocabulary words or grammar structures. Here are some situations to be aware of.

Distinctions: The vocabularies of different languages don't match each other perfectly. For instance, you might use the English verb *went* in this sentence:

> My mother went to the store.

In Russian, however, you couldn't translate this sentence exactly. Russian doesn't have a single verb for "to go"—you'd have to specify whether your mother walked to the store or whether she drove there, for example.

Your native language might have other situations like this. Some of them, unfortunately, can be confusing or amusing to native English speakers. For instance, if your native language uses the same word for both "like" and "love," you might accidentally use the stronger word, *love*, where *like* would be more appropriate. This can make you sound too enthusiastic. You likely already know some of these situations because of your previous English studies. Stay aware of them, and write down any new ones that you notice as you study for the TOEFL.

False friends: Be cautious with words that you are not entirely sure how to translate. There may be words in your native language that sound similar to English words but mean very different things. These types of words are called "false cognates" or "false friends." An example is the word *intoxicado*, in Spanish. The English word *intoxicated* usually describes someone who has intentionally used alcohol or drugs. The Spanish word *intoxicado*, however, can also refer to somebody who has been poisoned. That can be an important distinction! As you encounter words like these, note them down so that you don't misuse them on the TOEFL.

Connotations: Vocabulary words have both a literal meaning and a connotation. The connotation of a word is the "feeling" of that word—whether it's positive or negative, formal or casual, polite or vulgar. For instance, *thrifty* and *miserly* have the same meaning in English—they both refer to a person who avoids spending money—but *thrifty* is a positive word and *miserly* is a negative one. A good dictionary can help you to learn about the connotations of your vocabulary words, as can searching for sentences that use those words.

Nouns and verbs: English may deal with the distinction between singular and plural words differently from your native language. In this case, it's easy to mistakenly use a singular noun or verb instead of a plural one. Some languages also leave out verbs such as *is* or *are*. Leaving these verbs out in English, however, will confuse English speakers. Use flash cards to help you remember when you make mistakes with nouns or verbs.

Consuming and Producing (Good) English

The TOEFL will ask you to speak, write, read, and understand all different types of English: academic, informal, complex, simple, and so on. So, while you prepare for the TOEFL, you will want to study all different types of English. This will make you a more confident and versatile English user. In this appendix, you will learn where to find good sources for the types of English you want to study. You will also learn how best to use those sources.

Steal Good English

Appendix 1 contains a list of sources with high-quality English. When you read sentences in these sources or elsewhere, write them down. You can actually steal them. Yes, you read that correctly—steal sentences that you like. Copy them down onto flash cards. Write them from memory. Analyze how the sentence works and how the various parts fit together.

As children, we learned how to understand and speak by mimicking those around us. As adults, you can use the same technique: mimic what you read and hear. You will not, of course, write verbatim (which means word-for-word) a sentence that you swiped and memorized from an article in *Scientific American*. That would be silly (and unethical). That is not the goal when you copy sentences. Rather, you copy good English so that you can build the syntax (the structure of the sentence) into your English-speaking and English-writing brain.

Get Motivated

It is difficult to make a regular practice out of something that you don't enjoy. You do need to read some high-quality nonfiction, such as the sources listed in Appendix 1, because they cover the subject matter that you will see on the TOEFL. But—let's be honest—you will sometimes find these nonfiction materials boring. It is important to read other kinds of material too—material that you find interesting.

Try reading English materials that are useful to you in other ways—do some English-language reading related to whatever you are working on in school or at work. Alternatively, find something that you really enjoy reading. Fiction—stories and novels—can be engaging and satisfying sources of excellent English. But even for fiction, do not get so carried away that you forget your goal. Remember: Think like an anthropologist. Your job is to identify interesting, useful, or confusing words, phrases, and sentences, and write them down. When you find a great sentence in your reading, deconstruct it at every level: vocabulary, grammar, and its relationship to nearby sentences.

Listening and Speaking

Like movies? Great! Turn on English subtitles (subtitles written in English, *not* subtitles in your native language). You will simultaneously hear the English that is spoken and read it on the screen. This can be a powerful study technique to help you connect spoken English to written English.

Podcasts are another great source for English listening. Many podcasts are free and available over the internet. On the website for National Public Radio, for instance *(npr.org)*, you can listen to stories while reading the transcript at the same time.

The additional benefit to listening while reading, whether it is via subtitles on a TV show or movie or the transcript of a radio story, is that you can improve pronunciation. If you are struggling with pronunciation or speaking, try reading a radio story aloud along with the reporter.

Achieving Things with Words

English is used in different ways to fulfill different purposes. Here are some of the different ways that English might be used on the TOEFL. You can use these yourself, when responding to questions. You can also look for them when reading or listening.

Expository Use of Language

When language is expository, it is being used to *explain* or *describe*. This is the most commonly tested use of language on the TOEFL. This category includes the academic language that you find in reading passages and lectures on the TOEFL. The language may be describing or explaining facts, observations, theories, or hypotheses. This also includes asking questions to elicit facts and observations.

Questions

Asking and understanding questions is an important use of language. You might find it harder to correctly phrase questions in English than to make statements. Questions involve changes in word order, as well as the use of a specific tone or pitch. Being comfortable with asking and answering questions in English will help you on the TOEFL.

Social Use of Language

Language is sometimes used because it is conventional for social reasons. For example:

"Hi, how are you?"

"Good, and you?"

"Good, thanks."

"Okay, then, see you later!"

It's more important to understand the *social function* of these exchanges in English than to understand the literal meaning of the words. For instance, the above exchange is a conventional type of casual greeting.

Language can also cause the listener to do something. For example, to end a conversation, a professor might say, "That's it for now." Or, imagine that you are at your friend's house. It's winter and the window is open. You might say, "It's really cold in here," with the intention of getting your friend to close the window.

Both in the real world and on the TOEFL, speakers use language to convey emotions and opinions. This language is often not explicit but takes the form of proclamations, such as "Wow" or "Oh," to express surprise. "Hmm" can convey uncertainty or hesitation. "Wait a second!" can mean disagreement.

Filler Language

You will encounter filler language both on the TOEFL and in the English-speaking world. These are utterances that people make to fill gaps in speech—"um," "uh," "mm," "well," "you know," and so on. They have no meaning, other than perhaps subtly suggesting that the person is thinking. But even that will not always be true, since often, people's filler words are just a quirk of speech particular to that person.

You will hear filler speech on the sections of the TOEFL that involve listening. You can also use filler speech to buy yourself time to think during the speaking task. Don't go overboard by relying excessively on filler speech—where you can, just pause briefly to think. A short silence is okay! But the occasional "um" or "uh" is also acceptable in your spoken responses.

Implicature

Finally, there are expressions that do not mean what they appear to mean literally. This type of expression involves something called *implicature*. The speaker implies something, usually because it would be rude to say that thing outright. The TOEFL does sometimes test implicature. Here's an example:

Person 1: "Are you going to eat the rest of that sandwich?"

Person 2: "No."

Person 1 meant to *imply* that he would like to eat the rest of the sandwich himself. A typical response might be, "No, I'm not. Do you want it?" However, Person 2 either misunderstood, or ignored, the implicature. Implicature is often used to make a request politely.

Appendix 5
TOEFL Situations and Topics

The TOEFL primarily tests your ability to speak, read, write, and understand English. However, each question also deals with a type of situation or with an academic field. You don't necessarily need a lot of background to succeed on the TOEFL. However, having some basic background information on these situations and academic fields can help you better understand the questions you will see on the test.

The situations on the TOEFL revolve around things that often happen on a university campus in the United States. The academic topics come from the natural sciences, social sciences, and humanities.

Campus Situations

During the Speaking and Listening tasks, you will hear conversations that take place on a university campus. The speakers will have various roles that are associated with a campus setting—including students and professors, but also sports coaches, administrators, museum directors, bursars, and so on. If you find on practice TOEFL questions that you are coming across roles unknown to you, do some research on the Internet. A bursar, for instance, is the person (or office) who collects the tuition and fees at a university.

It is worth noting that, on the TOEFL, there are conversations in which students will make requests that challenge the rules or question the professor or another person in authority. On campuses outside of the United States, this type of interaction between a student and an authority figure might be considered rude, or it might even be prohibited. However, these situations are more common in the United States and not considered rude. Accordingly, you may see this type of conversation on the TOEFL.

TOEFL conversations may discuss campus situations or topics that are unfamiliar to you. For instance, you might not be familiar with the typical system of midterm exams and final exams, the grading systems used in the United States, the various types of assignments that students are given in classes, typical extracurricular activities, etc. You won't need in-depth knowledge of this type of information to successfully answer a TOEFL question. However, it's good to be prepared so that you are not distracted by confusing terminology while trying to listen to a question.

Where should you research to learn more about university campuses in the United States? Orientation videos—which are the videos schools make about themselves—are often available on university websites and are a reliable source. They provide more realistic representations of university life than movies and TV shows, which tend to favor drama over realism. If you search YouTube for "A Day in the Life of a First-Year Student" posted by Harvard University, you will find a Harvard orientation video.

From there, you might branch out to watch videos posted by actual students at schools you are interested in attending. And you can always contact the schools themselves and ask to get in touch with current students. If you can visit, take a tour and ask questions. This can also be an opportunity to practice English conversation.

Academic Fields

Your TOEFL *could* address a range of academic subjects in the areas of natural sciences, social sciences, and humanities. But every TOEFL is different and will not necessarily test you in a wide variety of fields. Your test could have mostly natural sciences passages and lectures, with not a single literature passage or lecture. But the possible range of fields, or topics, is representative of the various course options offered at universities in the United States.

How do you know whether you're struggling with the topic itself, or just with the English involved in the passage or lecture? If you are having trouble comprehending the core meaning of a passage, a lecture, or another academic task, even after taking extra time to review, you may need to invest time and energy in learning more about that field of study. Ask yourself—do I lack the knowledge I need to understand this topic, regardless of the language? If you don't know what a "cell" is in biology, even in your native language, that is something you want to address. You will need to possess basic knowledge in major academic areas.

Research what you don't know. You can use Wikipedia to start. Look for terms you don't understand in the field with which you are unfamiliar. From there, you might search for articles and videos on the topic in sources like *Scientific American* and *National Geographic*. Note that these sources are in English, and this is important—you will want to read up on the subject in English too, not just your native language! (You can do both if it's too hard to start in English.)

High school–level introductions to the subject are perfect. You might even skim a high school textbook, if you can get your hands on one! The method here is to expose yourself to the ideas that could come up on the exam. By the way, this isn't just conjecture—research has shown that familiarity with a topic or field of study is a major predictor of a student's ability to perform well in reading comprehension on standardized tests.

Academic Vocabulary

If you have the necessary basic knowledge of the field but are still struggling to understand a passage or lecture in English, there are two other possibilities. First, perhaps you don't know the vocabulary involved. In this case, study the basic English vocabulary commonly used in that field of study.

Alternatively, if you find that you understand the vocabulary and know the content but are still struggling, then the issue is likely grammar/sentence structure. If this is the case, continue to work on your facility with complex English sentences. Try taking a long and/or complex English sentence and breaking it down into several shorter sentences, using simple vocabulary to describe the concepts involved.

Appendix 6

Making a Sentence

Often, when you hear the word "grammar," you think of the rules listed in language textbooks. However, grammar isn't actually a set of rules that speakers consciously follow.

Most of your grammar knowledge doesn't come from books and classes. Instead, your brain builds up its "grammar sense" over time—you are not even consciously aware of it. To do this, your brain uses information from the English material that you're exposed to. That's why it's so important to spend a lot of time speaking, hearing, reading, and writing English.

In this appendix, you will learn some of the basics of English grammar—the fundamental rules that broadly describe most English sentences.

Sentence Structure and Subject–Verb Agreement

In English, a sentence generally answers a two-part question: *Who did what?* The *who* part of a sentence, the person or thing performing an action, is called the subject of the sentence. The *did what* part, the action or description, is called the predicate. Most English sentences have both a subject and a predicate (you don't have to worry about the exceptions). Take, for example, the sentence, "My friend laughed." Which parts of this sentence answer the two-part question who did what?

Subject (*who*) = "My friend"

The subject is always a noun (or pronoun—a simple stand-in for a noun).

Predicate (*did what*) = "laughed"

The predicate always contains a main verb.

If a sentence is missing either its subject or its predicate, it's called a sentence fragment. Some sentence fragments are easier to notice than others. For instance, this is a sentence fragment, because it needs a subject:

Ran to the store.

This is also a sentence fragment, although it's a little bit harder to spot:

A friend of mine who bought a nice dog last week.

This sentence is missing a main verb. The wording *who bought a nice dog last week* is called a modifier, and a modifier cannot hold the main verb of the sentence. Modifiers are discussed in the next section of this appendix.

In contrast to sentence fragments, run-on sentences do too much. They try to answer the question *who did what* more than once, without a conjunction, which is the type of word that joins sentences together. For instance, this is a run-on sentence:

> A friend of mine bought a house, she will live there with her dog.

This sentence is actually two sentences stuck together: *a friend of mine bought a house*, and *she will live there with her dog*. Because there is no conjunction (and, but, or, etc.) or semi-colon (;) between the two sentences, this sentence is a run-on. You could fix the sentence by writing this:

> A friend of mine bought a house, and she will live there with her dog.

Or you could write this:

> A friend of mine bought a house; she will live there with her dog.

One more note on subjects and predicates—in English, they must "agree" in number. If the subject of a sentence is singular (one person, one class, one car), the predicate should also have a singular verb (is, does, walks, jumps). If the subject is plural, the predicate should have a plural verb.

Modifiers

Most sentences tell you more than just *who did what*. Other than the subject and the predicate, the rest of a sentence is made up of modifiers. In the example sentence, "My friend laughed," you could add modifiers to answer more questions: Which friend? How did your friend laugh? Where did she laugh? What is her laugh like? Quickly, the sentence would become longer as it became packed with modifiers: My friend, who owns a coffee shop, laughed loudly on the train.

It is necessary to try to be very clear about what a modifier is describing—and you do that by placing a modifier near (or even right next to) what that modifier is describing. For instance, consider these two sentences:

> I put my apron, which was covered in paint, in the car.

> I put my apron in the car, which was covered in paint.

These two sentences have very different meanings. In the first example, the *apron* is covered in paint. In the second example, the *car* is covered in paint.

Why is that? Because the modifier (*which was covered in paint*) changes position. The placement of the modifier tells you what the modifier is describing.

Here are a couple of tips on modifiers:

1. Use adverbs, not adjectives, to modify verbs ("speak quickly," not "speak quick").
2. Even when modifiers are between subjects and verbs, the subject and the verb still must agree in their long-distance relationship—singular with singular and plural with plural.

Verb Tenses

English has more verb tenses than many other languages. The simple tenses—the past, present, and future—allow you to express in simple terms when an event took place. If your sentence describes a single, straightforward event, use the verb tense that matches the time frame:

Past: I went to the store yesterday.

Future: I will go to the store tomorrow.

The simple present tense, however, isn't usually used for things that are happening right now. Usually, in English, we use the simple present tense to describe things that happen often or repeatedly. For instance, "She runs on the track" doesn't mean that she's running right now. It means that she usually runs there. "He eats pizza for lunch," likewise, doesn't mean that he's eating pizza right now. It means that he usually eats pizza. If you want to talk about something that's happening right now, or something that will happen in the immediate future, use the present progressive tense:

Present progressive: I am going to the store.

The complex tenses are used to express more complicated ideas about when things happened. The most important ones to remember are the present perfect and the past perfect.

You can use the present perfect whenever something applies to both the past and the present. Whenever something started in the past, but didn't end at a particular point in the past, you can also use the present perfect. For instance, if you got to the doctor's office an hour ago and you are still waiting to see the doctor, you could say this:

Present perfect: I have waited for an hour.

There are more complicated rules related to the present perfect tense, but here's the most important one: You can't use present perfect for anything that has a particular end date in the past. For instance, this sentence is incorrect:

Present perfect (wrong): Until 2:00, I have waited for an hour.

Finally, the past perfect is a tense used to express the "past of the past." It goes back even earlier than what you're using as a past reference point—"She had already eaten dinner when he arrived to visit."

Pronouns

Pronouns take the place of nouns. *He* and *she* refer to people (or sometimes animals). Other common pronouns include *it, its, they, them, their,* and *there.*

In an English sentence, you use pronouns to avoid having to say the same noun over and over. For instance, this would be a tedious way to talk or write:

The student woke up late this morning. The student noticed that the student's alarm clock was broken. That was why the student had overslept. The student would have to get ready quickly, or the student would be late.

The role of pronouns is to help you avoid repeating phrases like *the student*. This phrase—what the pronoun replaces—is called the antecedent. The major rule of pronouns is that the pronoun and antecedent have to match. For instance, the antecedent *the student* wouldn't match the pronoun *they*, because *they* is plural and *the student* is singular. Here is how a correct paragraph might look:

> The student woke up late this morning. She noticed that her alarm clock was broken. That was why she had overslept. She would have to get ready quickly, or she would be late.

This sentence is grammatically incorrect:

> I went to the store and they were out of milk. (incorrect)

The pronoun *they* doesn't match anything in the sentence. There aren't any plural nouns. As a result, the sentence is incorrect in formal English. However, you might hear people say sentences like this in casual speech. The sentence implies that the "store owners" or maybe "the managers" were out of milk.

Improving your grammar isn't just about memorizing rules—the best way to improve your English grammar is to expose yourself to a lot of high-quality English. However, everybody makes some small grammar mistakes. Learning more about the rules of grammar can help you avoid these. Try using a grammar-checker on your own writing while you are practicing for the TOEFL. Microsoft Word has a built-in grammar-check. Grammarly.com is also an excellent resource.

App 6

Appendix 7
Combining Sentences

When it comes to putting multiple sentences together, the key is to know your purpose. What message are you trying to convey? Put the sentences together in order to make your purpose clear.

For example, are you compiling these sentences in order to explain an idea? If so, put the idea that you are explaining in the first sentence of the paragraph, to show that it's the most important part of what you're writing.

In general, you will make the purpose of your writing clear through organization. There are two elements to good organization. First, the *order* of your sentences matters. When constructing a paragraph, order your sentences to make it clear which ideas are more important. Second, *link* your sentences together to clarify the relationships between your ideas.

How to Organize an Argument or Explanation

On the TOEFL, you'll often be writing in order to make a single main point. The simplest way to organize your sentences is to put the main point first. Then, add supporting information. Finally, write a conclusion sentence that restates the main point. For example:

THESIS Sentence (your main point) _____

SUPPORTING Sentence 1 _____

SUPPORTING Sentence 2 _____

SUPPORTING Sentence 3 _____

CONCLUSION Sentence (remind the reader of your main point) _____

You can use this structure whether you are writing or speaking.

Linking Sentences Together

How do you connect sentences to one another? English has a huge number of words that serve this purpose. Choosing the correct connecting and organizing words will make your speech and writing seem more fluid.

Good organization is about linking what you *already know* to what you *don't already know*. One way to do this is via words and phrases that describe the relationship between two ideas. Let's take a simple story:

1. Henry, who was a dentist, decided to go to the beach.
2. But first, he would need a towel.
3. Also, he would have to buy sunscreen.

Using the phrase *but first* clarifies the way that sentence #1 relates to sentence #2. Sentence #2 is something that Henry needs to do first, before he can go to the beach. The word *also* tells your reader that sentence #3 is directly related to sentence #2. In this case, they both provide examples of things that Henry will need before he can go to the beach. Consider the many different connecting words and phrases that you can use to join multiple sentences together.

Let's continue the story:

4.   The dentist rarely got to go to the beach.

5.   Since he didn't have the time, this kind of vacation was a luxury for him.

6.   This fact alone made the trip all the more exciting.

Here, Henry is referred to not only as *he* but also as *the dentist*. This kind of noun substitution is quite common in English. As another example, a professor might start a lecture by talking about a "saber-toothed cat," and then later refer to it as "the predator" or even "this species." In the example above, *this kind of vacation* is another instance where *the beach*—or, more specifically, Henry going to the beach—is what's still being discussed, just using different words.

In sentence #6, the phrase *this fact alone* is called a nominalization and is common in academic writing in English. A nominalization is like a "super-pronoun." It provides a way to take a full idea expressed in a previous sentence (such as the idea that Henry doesn't usually have time for vacations) and continue to talk about it by turning it into a noun or phrase: "this fact" or "this observation" or "this idea."

In sentence #5, *since* is a connecting word. A connecting word signals the type of relationship between two ideas—in this case, cause and effect. Other common signal words include *and, then, because of, as a result, thus,* and *therefore.* Those last four signals are especially significant because they indicate causation—one thing causes another.

Transitions into opposing ideas are also common. These kinds of transitions can be accomplished through words and phrases like *but, however, on the contrary, in contrast,* and *yet.* When you see these sorts of signal words, you can trust that an opposing—or opposite or differing—view is about to be presented.

Here are some examples:

Henry wants to go on vacation, but he is rarely able to go.

Some scientists claim that the study shows that there is lead in the water, but other scientists disagree with the study's results.

Note that in these examples, you could replace *but* with *however* or *yet* and it would mean the same thing:

Some scientists claim that the study shows that there is lead in the water. However, other scientists disagree with the study's results.

Some scientists claim that the study shows that there is lead in the water, yet other scientists disagree with the study's results.

Use these signal words in your own writing and speaking to signal changes or contrasts. Doing so will make your writing more clear.

Expressing Your Thoughts in English

It is sometimes difficult to translate your thoughts into English, especially when you are under pressure. Here are some ideas that will help you with this translation process.

Identify the Issue

Think of what your brain is doing as you speak in English. You can think of the brain as including three different spaces. The first space is your "workspace." This is where you actively translate ideas into words. In order to effectively use your mental workspace, you draw on resources from two "storage areas." One storage area holds your world knowledge—the facts you know about the world and how it works. The other holds your English knowledge—everything you know about English grammar, vocabulary, and pronunciation. In order to communicate effectively in English, all three workspaces have to be working well.

Issues with world knowledge and English knowledge are discussed in the other appendices. However, you might also have trouble with the workspace itself. You might notice this issue if you do a TOEFL question poorly when you're practicing, but then understand it much better after the fact, when you review it. For some reason, even though you knew the material and you knew the meanings of the words and sentences, you had trouble turning that knowledge into a good answer.

It may be that your attention is wandering. Or perhaps it is taking you too long to understand a spoken sentence. These are symptoms of mental fatigue. Native English speakers can have these issues too while taking a standardized test. The TOEFL is a long, difficult test, and it requires a lot of attention.

If you are experiencing mental fatigue, you may need to work on improving your focus and attention span. In this case, try mindfulness techniques (widely available online) to improve your ability to focus. You may also need to work on getting faster at listening to and comprehending English. Look for sources of spoken English in which the speakers speak quickly. You might listen to English-language music or watch a news program in English. Practice understanding the English sentences quickly and fluidly.

Summarize to Practice

Summarizing what you just read or heard is a powerful exercise to help you ensure that you comprehended something. It will also help you to write or speak about that material yourself. If you're working on reading and writing, you can summarize on paper. If you're working on speaking, you can summarize aloud. Both types of summarizing force you to put what you just read or heard into your own words, boiling it down to the most important information. This challenge alone will make you better at understanding and creating. If you do nothing else, do this!

For example, if you just read a passage about the career of the artist Richard Prince (see Lecture 8.9 in Chapter 8), you could challenge yourself to boil down the passage to its main ideas from memory in just three sentences:

> Richard Prince is an artist working in the twentieth and twenty-first centuries.
>
> He is known for challenging people's understanding of what art is.
>
> He uses the *rephotograph*, which is a controversial technique for which he got sued.

Talk Around Words You Don't Know

In the example above, if you don't remember the term *rephotograph*, you could try to describe it using words you do know: "a photograph of a photograph." In English, this strategy is sometimes called "talking around an idea."

Suppose, as another example, you forgot the word for "rake." On the Speaking task on the TOEFL especially, you don't have time to try to think of entirely new ideas solely because you don't recall a single word. It's better for you to talk around the word that you don't know by describing what it is—a rake could be described as a broom to gather leaves that have fallen off of trees.

Use All-Purpose Words

App 8

Using all-purpose words—words that are general enough to capture many things—is a handy tool in English. In fact, the word *things* is a great all-purpose word! *Thing* (or *something* or *things*) and *stuff* are commonly used and perfectly acceptable, as long as it is clear what you mean. You can also use general terms, such as *tool*, *place*, or *building*.

Appendix 9
Taking the TOEFL

Strategies for approaching the TOEFL fall into two categories: 1) what you do *before* the test, and 2) what you do *during* the test.

Before the Test

Before the test, make a plan so that you are as well prepared as possible. Here are some important things to include in your plan:

- Figure out what score you want to earn on the TOEFL. Research the scores that are considered good for your target programs or schools.

- Take at least one practice test in *The Official Guide to the TOEFL Test,* and use the *Guide* and this book for further practice.

- Practice TOEFL questions both *timed* and *untimed*. You'll need both. Untimed practice is best for when you're working on learning the content and strategies. Timed practice is best later in your studies, when you want to mimic real test conditions. Timed practice is also necessary to help you assess your current ability, since the real test will always time you.

- In the last few days before the test, don't cram vocabulary. Instead, practice your Speaking openers and your Speaking tasks. (More on these below.)

During the Test

Following are some real-time techniques that will help you perform your best on test day. First, here are some general tips for the overall test.

On multiple-choice questions, start by writing down the question number. Next to it, write A, B, C, and D on your paper. As you eliminate answers, cross them off on your paper. There is **no penalty for guessing**, so if you don't know, just guess and move on!

Take a deep breath as you start each question. (This is something you can practice before you even get to the test.) It will help you release tension and anxiety, and that will help you focus.

Anxiety is physical as well as psychological. If you find yourself becoming physically tense, then stretch and shift in your chair to relax and improve blood flow. Roll your neck and shoulders around and stretch out your legs and toes.

During the break, have a snack or beverage that contains glucose (a certain kind of sugar that your brain consumes) to replenish your mental energy. Fresh fruit juice and coconut water are good sources of glucose.

Finally, orient yourself to where you are in the exam. As each new section or lecture or conversation begins, zoom out. In other words, assess from a distant, zoomed-out view. Where am I on the test? How long do I have to read? What is this passage about? What am I being asked to do on this task? From here, you will "zoom in" to do the assigned tasks. Then you'll zoom back out when you finish this task or section and start the next one.

Here are some specific recommendations for each section of the test.

Reading

First, skim the *first line* of every paragraph. *Don't read the entire passage first.* Then go to the questions and answer them as you read. The questions follow the order of the passage, and you can always access the passage while answering questions. For this reason, you can read the passage as you answer the questions.

There's always proof in the text. If you've picked the right answer, you will be able to point to the specific information in the passage that shows that your answer is correct. The "proof" for the right answer is usually pretty straightforward—it's written right there in the passage.

Listening

Lectures

On Lectures, use the pictures provided to orient yourself to what's being discussed. Ask yourself these questions to orient yourself at the beginning of Lectures:

- What's the course or class?
- What's the specific topic?

As you listen, take notes. Ask yourself these questions as you listen:

- What is the professor saying about the topic?
- What studies or research is the professor mentioning?
- What's surprising or interesting to the professor?
- What does the professor express an opinion about?

The questions on Lectures are more straightforward than they are on the Reading section, so that's the good news.

Conversations

Take notes on Conversations, too. However, keep your notes brief. Focus on these ideas:

- Who made the conversation happen? (It is usually initiated by a student, not a professor.)
- What does that person want?
- How does the other person respond—both right away and in the end?
- Are there any important side issues?

The questions won't ask you about tiny details that are only mentioned once. So, you don't need to memorize or write down everything in the conversation. But you can't go back to re-listen, so do jot down the big ideas.

Speaking

This section is often the hardest for people. You are given a very short amount of time in which to prepare and deliver your speech. Be sure to practice with a timer. Here are some key tips:

- **Don't strive for perfection.** It's even okay to be cut off mid-sentence! There is no way to give a perfect answer. You may also end with several seconds to spare. This is common and will not ruin your score. Everyone struggles with this task. It's even hard for native English speakers.

- **Simplify your decision-making by using the templates below.** Don't ponder for too long—go with your initial instinct as soon as you hear the full prompt. There is no right or wrong answer. Just pick something quickly and come up with points to support that choice, whatever it is.

- **Learn the six tasks.** Know their structure: Questions 1 and 2 ask you to speak about familiar topics. Questions 3 and 4 have you first read a short text, then listen to a talk on the same topic, then speak your answer. Questions 5 and 6 have you listen to part of a conversation or lecture, then answer aloud based on what you've heard.

Your Speaking Section Template

Certain words or phrases can help you to organize your spoken response. Plan these introductions or openers in advance. Follow this template:

App 9

- **Open your response.** How will you begin? For example, the phrase "In my opinion …" is a good opener. Come up with openers ahead of time, especially for the first two tasks. Because the first two tasks are so open-ended, it can be hard to know where to start. Plan ahead of time, so you don't get stuck on test day.

- **Introduce your main point.** "I believe that …," "It is my opinion that …," or "X is true because …" are good ways to introduce your main point.

- **Introduce your supporting examples.** "For example …," "Imagine a situation where …," and "Another reason is that …" are a few ways to introduce your supporting examples. Ideally, have a stash of 6 to 8 of these types of phrases, because you will be using them throughout all of the speaking tasks.

Final Tips for the Speaking Section

You only have a very short time to prepare, so jot down a few ideas (only one to two words for each idea—you don't have time for more) as you listen or read. Then, during your preparation time, circle the two to three ideas you want to use during your spoken response. You can number them to remind yourself to address them in a particular order. Use transition words like "First …" or "Second …" to orient the listener.

For the first two speaking tasks, use real-life examples if you can, but be ready to make something up if you can't think of a real example.

If you need a moment to think, pause and leave a brief silence—this is okay! You can use filler words such as *uh* or *um* if you need some time to think, but don't use them excessively.

Writing

Your essays will also benefit from using some templates. In general, more words are better than fewer words. So, keep writing! Use all of the allotted time to generate sentences.

Here is a commonly used essay-writing template.

Paragraph 1: Introduce the topic. Summarize the situation. State your thesis (your opinion about the situation).

Paragraph 2: Provide an example that supports your thesis. Explain why the example supports your thesis.

Paragraph 3: Provide a second example, again explaining why the example supports your thesis.

Paragraph 4: Provide a third example, again explaining why the example supports your thesis.

Paragraph 5: Conclude the essay. Summarize your opinion.

To avoid errors in both speaking and writing, err on the side of using simpler language. It's better to speak and write simply but confidently. Don't try to use overly complicated words and structures; you may end up confusing your listener or reader. However, if you feel confident, using fancier English can win you some style points. Use a difficult word you can confidently define. Ask a rhetorical question or use a more complex sentence structure.

Other Tests and the TOEFL

Most people don't take the TOEFL in isolation. The programs you're applying to may require one or more other standardized tests, such as the GRE, GMAT, LSAT, SAT, ACT, and so on. The good news is that your TOEFL studies will help you on these other tests, too. These tests all include reading comprehension using academic passages.

This is a great opportunity! You can cross-prepare—to some extent, you can prepare for both tests at once. After all, you don't have a TOEFL brain and a GRE brain—you have one brain, with one set of vocabulary, one set of grammar tools, and one ability to focus and comprehend. For example, using mindfulness techniques to improve your attention span will help you on both tests. So will reading English-language literature and making flash cards for words you don't know. Take advantage of the overlap between the tests when you decide how to study.

Interleaving is the idea that you'll learn more by studying multiple things at once. Studies have shown that learning geometry and fractions at the same time, for instance, may be more effective than studying geometry first, then moving on to fractions later. The same applies to the TOEFL. You don't need to study entirely for one test first, then switch to the other test. Studying for both at once may actually be more effective.

It is a good idea to avoid taking the two tests very close together, though. In the last few weeks before one test, you will want to focus on that test. You will need to enter the test room confident that you are ready for this specific test—the kinds of questions that will be asked, how much time you'll have to answer them, and what your strategies are for doing so.

If you are applying to graduate-level programs, take the TOEFL first. The GRE, GMAT, LSAT, and other graduate-level exams are harder, so your TOEFL studies will help you to do better on those other exams.

Citations & Acknowledgments

All questions, answers, and solutions are the original work of Manhattan Prep. All passages are the original work of Manhattan Prep, including cases in which outside sources are referred to or used for pedagogical reasons.

The U.S. government source cited below is in the public domain. Changes to the graphic were made to adapt the content for educational and pedagogical purposes. All applicable copyrights are retained by the creators of the sources.

Chapter 7, Reading Passage 3

Fox, Josh. Gasland http://one.gaslandthemovie.com/home

Chapter 14, Lecture 6, Graphic

NASA/JPL-Caltech. Topography of Gale Crater https://www.nasa.gov/mission_pages/msl/multimedia/pia15093b.html#.WOUMc_nytaR

A great number of people were involved in the creation of the book you are holding. First and foremost is Zeke Vanderhoek, the founder of Manhattan Prep. Zeke was a lone tutor in New York when he started our company in 2000. Now, well into its second decade, the company contributes to the successes of thousands of students around the globe every year.

Our Manhattan Prep resources are based on the continuing experiences of our instructors and students. As the primary editor of this book, Chris Ryan had tons of help from a fantastic team, led by Tate Shafer (on the vast Reading and Lectures sets) and Stacey Koprince (on Speaking and Writing, as well as other material). Chris is deeply indebted to Tate and Stacey for getting this book across the goal line.

A host of people contributed to the five pounds in your hands. All the academic and non-academic material for prompts, as well as the questions and commentary, was written and edited by Chris Ryan, Chris Berman, Chelsey Cooley, Laura Damone, Christine Defenbaugh, Misti Duvall, Whitney Garner, Stacey Koprince, Emily Madan, Cat Powell, Ron Purewal, Mary Richter, Tate Shafer, and Patrick Tyrrell. Example responses for Speaking and Writing tasks were provided by Rey Fernandez, Michelle Krasodomski, Dan McNaney, Nicole Spiezio, Noah Teitelbaum, Harry Tran, and Evyn Williams. Stacey Koprince wrote chapter introductions, and Mary Richter and Chelsey Cooley wrote the appendices.

Grace Trewartha conducted test-taker interviews early on and provided strategic guidance (and budget coverage!) all along the way. Mary Richter also did early scoping and design work. Derek Frankhouser created the illustrations in the book and led the production of the online audio tracks and accompanying visuals. Once the manuscript was done, Emily Sledge and Whitney Garner applied their copy-editing chops, and proofreading was provided by Cheryl Duckler. Sam Edla, Dan McNaney, and others developed the online interface. Our great colleagues at Kaplan Publishing managed the production process, making sure that all the moving pieces came together at just the right time.

Headed to grad school?

Get a head start with our free, online resources.

Whether you want to learn more about the GMAT® or GRE®, or hone skills you've already built, looking through our online resources is a great place to start.

Here's how you can get started:

- Sit in on a live online class
- Check out Interact™, our on-demand course
- Know where you stand by taking a practice te?
- Read our blog for tips and strategies

Learn more at manhattanprep.com.

Why prep with us?

ACCOMPLISHED INSTRUCTORS

When you have access to the best teachers, you'll achieve better results.

RELEVANT CURRICULUM

Curriculum based on real test questions gives you superior preparation.

REAL EDUCATION

Critical thinking — not tricks or gimmicks — will help you succeed on the test.

ENJOYABLE CLASSES

Learning can and should be fun, not something you suffer through.

Not sure what's right for you?
Give us a call and we'll help you figure out what program fits you best.
Contact us at manhattanprep.com or at 800.576.4628 | (001) 212.721.7400